MISSION COLLEGE
LEARNING RESOURCE SERVICES

FOR REFERENCE
Do Not Take
From This Room

3 1215 00022 4227

A DICTIONARY OF ENGLISH AUTHORS

A

DICTIONARY

OF

ENGLISH AUTHORS

BIOGRAPHICAL AND BIBLIOGRAPHICAL

BY

R. FARQUHARSON SHARP

BEING

A COMPENDIOUS ACCOUNT OF THE LIVES AND WRITINGS OF
UPWARDS OF 800 BRITISH AND AMERICAN WRITERS
FROM THE YEAR 1400 TO THE PRESENT TIME

NEW EDITION, REVISED
WITH AN APPENDIX BRINGING THE WHOLE UP TO DATE
AND INCLUDING A LARGE AMOUNT OF NEW MATTER

LONDON
KEGAN PAUL, TRENCH, TRUBNER & CO., LTD.
DRYDEN HOUSE, GERRARD STREET, W.
1904
Republished by Gale Research Company, Book Tower, Detroit, 1978

Library of Congress Cataloging in Publication Data

Sharp, Robert Farquharson, 1864-1945.
   A dictionary of English authors, biographical and
bibliographical, being a compendious account of the
lives and writings of upwards of 800 British and American
writers from the year 1400 to the present time.

   Reprint of the 1904 ed. published by Kegan Paul,
Trench, Trubner, London.
    1. English Literature--Bio-bibliography. 2. Ameri-
can literature--Bio-bibliography. I. A dictionary of
English authors, biographical and bibliographical. . .
Z2010.S54   1975   [PR83]   016.82'08   75-35577
ISBN 0-8103-4281-2

Z
2010
.554
1975

PREFACE TO THE NEW EDITION

In the Appendix which forms part of the present edition a large amount of new matter has been added, and numerous corrections and additions made, to the "Dictionary" as originally issued. Such articles in the main portion of the book as are marked with an asterisk are now concluded or emended by corresponding articles in the Appendix.

The scheme is throughout the same. In the case of each author the essential facts in his career are stated as briefly as is practicable, followed by as complete as possible a list of his works arranged chronologically. Departure from this rule has been made only in the case of some six or seven writers, the number of whose separate publications was so formidable as to render it impracticable to append an exhaustive catalogue of them. In these instances mention has been made of the quarter where a full list may be found.

The literary distinction of an author has been the criterion adopted by the compiler in the difficult task of selection. This will explain the omission of specialists in science, theology, law, politics, etc., who may have written much upon their own subject; their inclusion, where such has been the case, depending upon the fact of their having produced work which either is purely literary or is so widely known and read as to come within the category of general literature.

In the case of almost all the living writers dealt with in the volume, biographical or other information has been furnished by themselves. To the many who have so readily and kindly assisted him in this respect, as well as to those relatives of dead authors who have supplied valuable detail, the compiler tenders his grateful acknowledgment. In the few cases where lack of response on the part of living authors has deprived their biographies of the completeness desired by the compiler, he would prefer to attribute this to his failure to reach them with his request, rather than to any unwillingness on their part.

R. F. S.

* *The articles marked with an asterisk are continued or corrected in the Appendix.*

DICTIONARY OF ENGLISH AUTHORS.

A'BECKETT (Gilbert Abbot), 1811-1856. Born in London, 17 Feb. 1811. Educated at Westminster School, 10 Jan. 1820 to Aug. 1828. While there edited 'The Censor' and 'The Literary Beacon' with his brother William. Called to Bar at Gray's Inn, 27 Jan. 1841. Life passed in London; in legal, literary, and journalistic work. Edited 'Figaro in London,' 1832-39; contrib. to 'Punch,' 'Times,' 'Morning Herald,' 'Illustrated London News.' Married Mary Anne Glossop, 23 June 1835. Police Magistrate at Greenwich, 1849. Subsequently at Woolwich and Southwark. Died, at Boulogne, 30 Aug. 1856.

Works: 'Scenes from the Rejected Comedies by some of the Competitors for the Prize offered by B. Webster,' 1844 ; 'The Small Debts Act, with annotations, etc.,' 1845 ; 'The Quizziology of the British Drama,' 1846 ; 'The Comic Blackstone,' 1846 ; 'The Comic History of England' (2 vols.), 1847-48 ; 'The Comic History of Rome' [1852]. A'Beckett was the author of more than fifty plays, burlesques, and operettas, some of which are printed in 'Cumberland's Minor Theatre,' 'Duncombe's British Drama,' 'Lacy's Acting Edition of Plays,' and 'Webster's Acting National Drama.' He *edited:* 'The Comic Almanack,' 1835-47 ; 'Cruikshank's Table Book,' 1845 ; 'The Almanack of the Month,' 1846.

* *[His son, **Gilbert Arthur A'Beckett, 1837-1891,** was born, in London, 7 April 1837. To Westminster School, 6 June 1869 ; Queen's scholar, 1851. Matric. at Ch. Ch, Oxford, 7 June 1855 ; B.A. 1860. Mem. of Lincoln's Inn, 15 Oct. 1857. Clerkship in office of Exam. of Crim. Law Accts., June 1862. Married Elizabeth Emily Hunt, 15 Nov. 1863. Wrote various plays and extravaganzas. Died 15 Oct. 1891. He published : 'Lending a Hand' [1865 ?] ; 'Glitter' [1869] ; 'The Last of the Legends' [1873] ; 'In the Clouds' [1874] ; and *edited* 'The Tomahawk,' Nov. 1868 to June 1870.

* *[**Arthur William A'Beckett, b. 1844,** brother of preceding, was born, in Hammersmith, 25 Oct. 1844. Educated at Kensington and Felstead. Clerkship in War Office, 1861-64. Edited 'The Glow-Worm,' 1864-67 ; and other periodicals, 1864-74. Correspondent to 'Standard' and 'Globe,' 1870-71. Private Sec. to Duke of Norfolk, 1872-73. Joined staff of 'Punch,' 1874. Married Susannah Frances Winslow, 17 Feb. 1876. Student of Gray's Inn, 13 June 1877 ; called to Bar, 3 May 1882. Private Sec. to Lord Morley, 1882-83. Master of Revels, Gray's Inn, 1887 ; superintended 'Maske of Flowers.' Editor of 'Sunday Times,' April 1891-Dec. 1894. Vice-Pres. of Newspaper Soc., 1891-92; Pres., 1893-94. He has published: 'Fallen among Thieves,' 1870 ; 'The Happy Land' (with Tomline), 1873 ; 'The Doom of St. Querec' (with Burnand), 1875 ; 'Our Holiday in the Scottish Highlands' (with Sambourne), 1876 ; 'The Modern Arabian Nights' (with Sambourne), 1877 ; 'The Shadow Witness' (with Burnand), 1877 ; 'The Ghost of Greystone Grange,' 1878 ; 'The Mystery of Mostyn Manor,' 1878; 'The Maske of Flowers,' 1887 ; 'Tracked Out,' 1888 ; 'Papers from Pump-Handle Court' (from 'Punch'), [1889] ; Lyrics for 'Captain Thérèse' and 'La Cigale' (with Bur-

nand), 1890 ; 'Hard Luck,' 1890 ;
contribution to 'The Fate of Fenella,'
1892 ; 'The Member for Wrottenbo-
rough' (from 'Sunday Times'), [1892];
'Green - Room Recollections,' 1896.
He *edited* ' Britannia,' 1869.]

*ACTON (John Emerich Edward
Dalberg) Baron Acton, b. 1834.
Born, at Naples, 1834. Succeeded to
baronetcy on father's death, 31 Jan.
1837. Educated at St. Mary's Col-
lege, Oscott. Subsequently under
the tuition of Dr. Döllinger, of
Munich. M.P. for Carlow, 1859-65.
Edited ' Home and Foreign Review,'
1862-64. Returned M.P. for Bridg-
north, 1865, but unseated on scrutiny.
Married Marie, daughter of Count
Arco-Valley, of Munich, 1 Aug. 1865.
Created Baron Acton of Aldenham,
11 Dec. 1869. At Rome during Œcu-
menical Council, winter of 1869-70.
Edited 'The Chronicle'; the 'North
British Review.' Dr.Phil., Munich,
Aug. 1872. Contrib. to 'Times' on
subject of Vatican Decrees, 1874.
Contrib. to 'Quarterly Review,' 1877.
D.C.L., Oxford, 1887 ; Hon. LL.D.
Cambridge, 1888 ; Hon. Fellow, All
Souls' Coll., Oxford, 1890. Appointed
Lord-in-Waiting, 1892. Regius Prof.
of Mod. Hist., Cambridge, 1895.

Works : ' Sendschreiben an einen
deutschen Bischof,' 1870 ; 'The War
of 1870,' 1871 ; ' Zur Geschichte des
Vaticanischen Conciles,' 1871 ; 'The
Hist. of Freedom in Antiquity ; and,
The Hist. of Freedom in Christianity.
Two addresses,' 1877 ; ' Histoire de la
Liberté,' trans. by L. Borguet, 1878 ;
' George Eliot : eine biographische
Skizze,' trans. by J. Imelmann, 1886 ;
' Die neuere deutsche Geschichtswis-
senschaft,' trans. (from ' Eng. Hist.
Review '), by J. Imelmann, 1887 ; ' A
Lecture on the Study of History,' 1895.

He has *edited :* 'Les Matinées
Royales,' 1863 ; Machiavelli's ' Il
Principe ' (introduction to edn. by
L. A. Burd), 1891.

ADDISON (Joseph), 1672-1719.
Born, at Milston, Wilts, 1 May 1672.
Educated at private schools at
Amesbury and Salisbury; at Lich-

field School, 1683 ; at Charterhouse
[1685-87 ?] ; to Queen's Coll., Oxford,
1687. Demyship at Magdalen Coll.,
1689 ; B.A., 6 May 1691 ; M.A., 14
Feb. 1693 ; Fellowship, 1697-1711.
Crown Pension of £300 a year, 1699.
To France, autumn of 1699 ; lived in
Blois and Paris (1700). Tour in Italy,
winter of 1700-01. At Geneva. 1701 ;
Vienna, 1702. In Germany, Holland,
and return to England, 1703. Member
of Kitcat Club. Commissioned to
write poem to celebrate Battle of
Blenheim, 1704 ; appointed to Under-
Secretaryship of State, 1706. With
Halifax on Mission to Hanover, 1707.
M.P. for Lostwithiel, Nov. 1708 ;
election quashed, Dec. 1709. Sec. to
Lord Lieut. of Ireland, and Keeper
of Records, 1709. Contributed to
Steele's ' Tatler,' 1709-10. M.P. for
Malmesbury, 1710. Published ' Whig
Examiner,' (5 nos.) Sept.-Oct., 1710.
Bought estate of Bilton in Warwick-
shire, 1711. ' Spectator ' published
daily, 1 March 1711 to Dec. 1712.
' Cato ' produced at Drury Lane, 14
April 1713. Contrib. to ' The Guar-
dian,' May-Sept. 1713 ; to Steele's
' Lover,' and to a revived ' Spectator,'
June - Sept. 1714. Comedy 'The
Drummer' anonymously produced,
1715. Resumed political appointments,
1715-16. ' The Freeholder' (55 nos.),
published anonymously, Dec. 1715-
June 1716. Married Countess of Warwick, 3 Aug. 1716. Retired from appointments, March 1718, owing to ill-
health. Daughter born, 31 Jan. 1719.
Controversy with Steele in 'Old Whig'
(2 nos., 19 March and 2 April 1719).
Died, in London, 17 June 1719.

Works : ' Dissertatio de insignior-
ibus Romanis poetis,' 1692 ; ' A Poem
to His Majesty,' 1695 ; Latin Poem
on the Peace of Ryswick, 1697 ;
Lat. poems in 'Examen Poeticum
Duplex,' 1698, and 'Musarum Angli-
canarum Analecta,' vol. ii , 1699 ;
' Letters from Italy to the Rt. Hon.
Charles, Lord Halifax,' 1703 ;
' Remarks on several Parts of Italy,'
1705 ; 'The Campaign,' 1705 ; ' Fair
Rosamond ' (anon.), 1707 ; 'The
Present State of the War ' (anon.),

1708; Papers in 'Tatler,' 1709-10; 'Whig Examiner,' 1710; 274 nos. in 'Spectator,' 1711-12; 'The Late Tryal and Conviction of Count Tariff' (anon.), 1713; 'Cato,' 1713; Papers in 'Guardian,' 1713; in 'Lover' and new 'Spectator,' 1714; 'Essay concerning the Error in distributing modern Medals,' 1715; 'The Drummer' (anon.), 1716; [Poetical addresses to Princess of Wales and Sir G. Kneller, 1716]; 'The Freeholder' (anon.), 1715-16; Translations of Ovid's 'Metamorphoses' with Dryden and others, 1717; 'Two Poems; viz., I. On the Deluge. . . . An ode to Dr. Burnett; II. In praise of Physic and Poetry. An ode to Dr. Hannes' (Lat. and Eng.), 1718; 'The Resurrection: a poem,' 1718; 'The Old Whig' (anon.), 1719; 'The Patrician' (anon.), 1719. *Posthumous:* 'Notes upon the twelve books of Paradise Lost' (from 'Spectator'), 1719; 'Skating: a poem' (Lat. and Eng.), 1720; 'Evidences of the Christian Religion,' 1730; 'Discourse on Ancient and Modern Learning,' 1739. *Collected Works* first published by T. Tickell in 1721. *Life:* by Miss Aikin, 1843; by W. J. Courthope, 1884.

*AINSWORTH (William Harrison), 1805-1882. Born, in Manchester, 4 Feb. 1805. Educated at Manchester Grammar School, 1817-21. Articled in 1821 to Mr. Kay, solicitor, of Manchester. Contrib. to 'Arliss's Magazine,' 'Manchester Iris,' 'Edinburgh Magazine,' 'London Magazine'; and started a periodical called 'The Bœotian,' of which only six numbers appeared. In 1824 to Inner Temple. Married Anne Frances Ebers, 11 Oct. 1826. In business as a publisher for eighteen months. Life of literary activity. Visit to Switzerland and Italy, 1830. 'Rookwood' begun in 1831. Series of. novels published, 1834-81. Editor of 'Bentley's Miscellany,' March 1839 to Dec. 1841. Edited 'Ainsworth's Magazine,' 1842-54. Edited 'New Monthly Magazine,' 1845-70. Lived at Kensal Manor House. Entertained by Mayor at

Banquet in Manchester Town Hall, 15 Sept. 1881. Died, at Reigate, 3 Jan. 1882. Buried at Kensal Green.

Works: 'Considerations as to the best means of affording immediate relief to the Operative Classes in the manufacturing districts,' 1826; 'Rookwood' (anon.), 1834; 'Crichton,' 1837; 'Jack Sheppard,' 1839; 'Tower of London,' 1840; 'Guy Fawkes,' 1841; 'Old St. Paul's,' 1841; 'The Miser's Daughter,' 1842; 'Windsor Castle,' 1843; 'St. James's,' 1844; 'Lancashire Witches,' 1848; 'Star Chamber,' 1854; 'James the Second,' 1854; 'The Flitch of Bacon,' 1854; 'Ballads,' 1855; 'Spendthrift,' 1856; 'Mervyn Clitheroe' (in parts), 1857-58; 'The Combat of the Thirty,' 1859; 'Ovingdean Grange,' 1860; 'Constable of the Tower,' 1861; 'Lord Mayor of London,' 1862; 'Cardinal Pole,' 1863; 'John Law the Projector,' 1864; 'The Spanish Match,' 1865; 'Auriol,' 1865; 'Myddleton Pomfret,' 1865; 'The Constable de Bourbon,' 1866; 'Old Court,' 1867; 'South Sea Bubble,' 1868; 'Hilary St. Ives,' 1869; 'Talbot Harland,' 1870; 'Tower Hill,' 1871; 'Boscobel,' 1872; 'The Good old Times,' 1873; 'Merry England,' 1874; 'The Goldsmith's Wife,' 1875; 'Preston Fight,' 1875; 'Chetwynd Calverley,' 1876; 'The Leaguer of Lathom,' 1876; 'The Fall of Somerset,' 1877; 'Beatrice Tyldesley,' 1878; 'Beau Nash' [1879?]; 'Stanley Brereton,' 1881. The greater part of 'December Tales,' published anonymously in 1823, was Ainsworth's work; 'Sir John Chiverton' (anon.), 1826, is probably by Ainsworth and J. P. Aston. Contrib. by Ainsworth are in 'Works of Cheviot Tichburn,' 1822, and 'A Summer Evening Tale,' 1825.

AIRD (Thomas), 1802-1876. Born, at Bowden, Roxburghshire, 28 Aug. 1802. Educated at Bowden Parish School. To Edinburgh University, 1816. Intimate with Carlyle and James Hogg. Contrib. to 'Blackwood' in 1827. Editor of 'Edinburgh Weekly Journal,' 1832-33. To Dumfries, 1835. Editor of 'Dumfriesshire and Galloway Herald,' 1835-63. Took part in Burns Centenary. 1859. Presided at banquet at Dumfries for Sir Walter Scott Centenary, 1871. Unmarried. Died, at Dumfries, 25 April 1876. Buried in St. Michael's Churchyard, Dumfries.

Works : 'Murtzoufle : a tragedy in three acts ; with other Poems,' 1826 ; 'Religious Characteristics,'1827; 'The Captive of Fez,' 1830 ; 'The Old Bachelor in the Old Scottish Village,' 1845 ; 'Poetical Works,' 1848. He *edited :* D. M. Moir's 'Poetical Works,' 1852. Selections from Aird's poems are included in B. Foster's 'Summer Scenes,' 1867. *Memoir :* by Rev. J. Wallace, in 1878 edn. of 'Poetical Works.'

AKENSIDE (Mark), 1721 - 1770. Born, at Newcastle-on-Tyne, 9 Nov. 1721. Educated at Free School and private school in Newcastle. Contrib. two poems to ' Gentleman's Magazine' in 1737. In 1738 began to write 'The Pleasures of Imagination.' Sent in 1739 to Edinburgh, at Newcastle Dissenters' expense, to study for ministry. Soon abandoned theology for medicine. Member of Medical Soc. of Edinburgh, 30 Dec. 1740. In 1741 to Newcastle. To London, 1743. Sold MS. of 'Pleasures of Imagination' to Dodsley. Tour in Holland, 1744. Degree of Doctor of Physic at Leyden, 16 May 1744. Bought practice at Northampton, June 1744. To London in winter of 1745. Practice at North End, Hampstead, 1745-47 ; set up in practice in Bloomsbury, winter of 1747. Editor of 'The Museum' magazine, Jan. 1746 to 1747. M.D., Cambridge, Jan. 1753. F.R.S., 1753. Fellow of Coll. of Physicians, April 1754 ; delivered Gulstonian Lectures, Sept. 1755 ; Croonian Lectures, 1756. Principal Physician to Christ's Hospital, March 1759. Lived in Burlington St., 1760-70. Physician to Queen, 1761. Died, in London, 23 June 1770. Buried in St. James's church.

Works : 'On the Winter Solstice'

and ' Love ' (privately printed), 1740 ; 'An Epistle to the Rev. Mr. Warburton,' 1744 ; 'Dissertatio . . . de ortu et incremento Fœtus humani,' 1744 ; 'The Pleasures of Imagination' (anon.), 1744 ; 'An Epistle to Curio ' (anon.), 1744 ; 'Odes on Several Subjects ' (anon.), 1745 ; 'Ode to the Earl of Huntingdon,' 1748 ; 'The Remonstrance of Shakespeare,' 1749 ; revised version of ' The Pleasures of Imagination,' 1757 ; 'Ode to the Country Gentlemen of England,'1758 ; ' Call to Aristippus,' 1758 ; ' Notes on the Postscript to a Pamphlet, entitled, Observations Anatomical . . . by A. Monro ' (anon.), 1758 ; several poems, including ' Hymn to the Naiads,' in ' Dodsley's Miscellany,' vol. vi. 1758 ; ' Oratio anniversaria quam ex Harveii instituto in theatro Collegii Medicorum Londinensis . . . MDCCLIX., habuit Marcus Akenside,' 1760 ; ' De Dysenteria commentarius,' 1764 ; ' Ode to the late Thomas Edwards,' 1766.

Collected Poems : ed. by Dyson, 1772 ; ' Works,' with *life* by Mrs. Barbauld, 1808.

ALDRICH (Henry), 1647 - 1710. Born, in Westminster, 1647. Educated at Westminster School under Busby. Student of Ch. Ch., Oxford, 1662. B.A., May 1666 ; M.A., April 1669. Rector of Wem, Shropshire. B.D. and D.D., March, 1681. Canon of Ch. Ch., Feb. 1681 ; Dean, June 1689 to Dec. 1710. Member of Ecclesiastical Commission, 1689. Wrote ' Artis Logicæ Compendium ' (still used as text-book at Oxford), 1691. Vice-Chancellor, 1692-94. Died, at Ch. Ch., 14 Dec. 1710. Buried in Cathedral. Musician ; composed anthems and catches. Student of Chemistry. Unmarried.

Works : ' A Reply to two Discourses (by A. Woodhead) . . . concerning the Adoration of our Blessed Saviour ' (anon.), 1687 ; ' A Vindication of the Oxford Reply to two Discourses, etc.' (anon.), [1688 ?] ; ' Artis Logicæ Compendium ' (anon.), 1691 ; ' A Narrative of the Proceedings of the Lower House of Convocation . . . 10 Feb.

1700 to 5 June 1701,' 1701 ; 'Institutionis Geometricæ pars prima, etc.' (anon.). [1709].

Posthumous: 'Elementorum Architecturæ pars prima, etc.' [1750]. He *edited:* Aristeas' Histories, 1692 ; Plato's 'Symposium,' 1711 ; Josephus' Works, 1726.

ALEXANDER (William), Earl of Stirling, 1567 [?]—1640. Born, at Menstrie, near Alloa, 1567 [?]. Probably educated at Stirling Grammar School. Abroad as travelling tutor to Earl of Argyle ; afterwards tutor to Prince Henry of Scotland. Became Gentleman of the Chamber to Prince Henry. Married Janet Erskine, 1604. Appointed Collector of Crown Taxes, 1608. Knighted, 1609. At death of Prince Henry, appointed Gentleman of Chamber to Prince Charles, 1612. Working gold and silver mines in Scotland, 1613. Intimacy with Drummond of Hawthornden begun. Appointed Master of Requests, 1614. Received charter granting him jurisdiction over Nova Scotia and Canada, 1621. Secretary of State for Scotland, 1626-40. Created Lord Alexander of Tullibody and Viscount Stirling, 1630. Extraordinary Judge of Court of Session, 1631. Created Earl of Stirling and Viscount Canada, 1633 ; Earl of Devon, 1639. Died, in London, 12 Sept. 1640. Buried in High Church, Stirling.

Works : 'The Tragedie of Darius,' 1603 ; 'A Parænesis to the Prince,' 1604 ; 'The Monarchick Tragedies,' 1604 (another edn., 'newly enlarged,' 1607) ; 'Avrora,' 1604 ; 'The Alexandræan,' 1605 ; 'An Elegie on the Death of Prince Henrie,' 1612 ; Completion of pt. iii. of Sir Philip Sidney's 'Arcadia,' 1613 ; 'Doomes-day,' bks. i.-iv., 1614 ; bks. v.-xii., 1637 ; 'An Encouragement to Colonies,' 1624 ; 'Recreations with the Muses,' 1637.

Posthumous : 'Register of Royal Letters relative to . . . Scotland and Nova Scotia,' ed. by C. Rogers, 2 vols., 1884-85.

Life : by Charles Rogers, 1877.

ALFORD (Henry), 1810 - 1871. Born, in London, 10 Oct. 1810. Educated at Charmouth, 1817-21 ; at Ilminster Grammar School, 1824-27 ; pupil of Rev. J. Bickersteth at Aston, 1827-28. To Trinity Coll., Cambridge, Oct. 1828. Bell Scholarship, 1831. Eighth Classic and 34th Wrangler, Jan. 1832. B.A., 1832 ; M.A., 1835. Curate to his father at Ampton, 1833. Fellowship at Trinity Coll., 1834-35. Married Fanny Alford, 10 March 1835 Vicar of Wymeswold, 1835-53. Hulsean Lecturer at Cambridge, 1841-42. Occupied on edition of Greek Test., 1845-61. B.D., Cambridge, Nov. 1849. To Quebec Chapel, Marylebone, 1853. Dean of Canterbury, 1857-71. D.D., 1859. Contrib. to 'Sunday Mag.,' 1868-70. In last years of life lived partly at Canterbury, partly at Vine's Gate, Sevenoaks. Died, 12 Jan. 1871.

Works : 'Poems and Poetical Fragments,' 1833 ; 'Address to the Inhabitants of Bury St. Edmunds,' 1834 ; 'Faith Explained,' 1834 ; 'The School of the Heart,' 1835 ; 'Hymns,' 1836 ; 'The Clergy Watchmen,' 1840 ; 'The Abbot of Muchelnay,' 1841 ; 'Hulsean Lectures,' 1842-43 ; 'Psalms and Hymns,' 1844 ; 'Προγυμνασματα,' 1845 ; 'Poetical Works,' 1845 ; 'History and Description . . . of St. Mary's, Wymeswold,' 1846 ; 'Plain Village Sermons,' 1846 ; 'The Inspiration of Holy Scripture,' 1849 ; Vol. i. of Greek Testament, 1849 ; 'Four Lectures,' 1849 ; Sermons,' 1850 ; 'Select Poetical Works,' 1851 ; Vol. ii. of Greek Testament, 1852 ; 'Poems' (American edn.), 1853 ; 'Memoir of the Rev. H. Alford,' 1854 ; 'English Descriptive Poetry,' 1854 ; 'Quebec Chapel Sermons,' vol. i., 1854 ; vol. ii., 1855 ; vols. iii.-v., 1856 ; vols. vi., vii., 1857 ; Vol. iii. of Greek Test., 1856 ; 'Homilies on Acts of the Apostles,' 1857 ; 'Pulpit Eloquence of 17th Cent.,' 1858 ; 'Four Sermons on the Parable of the Sower,' 1858 ; Vol. iv. pt. i. of Greek Test., 1859 ; pt. ii., 1860 ; Odyssey of Homer translated, 1861 ; 'New Testament for English

Readers,' vol. i. pt. i., 1862; 'Mourning and Praise,' 1862; 'Sermons on Christian Doctrine,' 1862; 'The Queen's English '(from 'Good Words'), 1863; 'Church Movement in our Day,' 1863; 'Letters from Abroad' (from 'Good Words'), 1864; 'Meditations on Advent' (from 'Good Words'), 1865; 'The Year of Prayer,' 1866; 'Week of Prayer,' 1866 ; 'True and False Guides,' 1866 ; 'Eastertide Sermons,' 1866 ; 'How to Study the New Testament,' vol. i., 1866 ; vol. ii., 1867 ; vol. iii., 1870 ; 'The Year of Praise,' 1867 ; 'Essays and Addresses,' 1869 ; 'The State of the Blessed Dead,' 1869; 'The Coming of the Bridegroom,' 1869 ; 'Our Lord and His Twelve Disciples,' 1869 ; 'The Riviera,' 1870 ; 'The Lord's Prayer,' 1870; 'The New Testament after the Authorized Version Revised,' 1870 ; 'Biblical Revision,' 1870 ; 'The Compacted Body,' 1870. [Alford also published various minor Sermons and Addresses in pamphlet form.]

Posthumous: 'Truth and Trust,' 1871 ; 'Genesis and part of Exodus for English Readers,' 1872 ; 'The Sons of God Known and Unknown,' 1872 ; 'Life, Journal, and Letters,' ed. by his widow, 1873 ; 'Fireside Homilies' (from 'The Sunday Mag.'), 1875 [1874]. He *edited:* John Donne's 'Works,' 1839 ; 'Reminiscences by a Clergyman's Wife,' 1866.

ALISON (Sir Archibald), 1792-1867.
Born, at Kenley, Shropshire, 29 Dec. 1792. Educated by private tutor at Edinburgh, 1800-05. To Edinburgh University, Nov. 1805. Began to study Law, 1810. Called to Bar, 8 Dec. 1814. Visit to Paris, 1814 ; Switzerland, 1816 ; Ireland, 1817 ; Italy, 1818 ; Switzerland and Germany, 1821. Appointed Advocate Depute, Feb. 1823. Married Elizabeth Glencairn Tytler, 21 March 1825. Engaged on 'History of Europe,' 1829-42. Contrib. to 'Blackwood,' 1830-32, 1845-46, 1849-51. Visit to Paris, 1833. Appointed Sheriff of Lanarkshire, Oct. 1834. Left Edinburgh for Glasgow, Feb. 1835. Lived in Glasgow till death. Prominent in quelling various strikes and riots 1837-58. Lord Rector of Marischal Coll., Aberdeen, 1845. Lord Rector of Glasgow Univ., 1851. Created Baronet, 1852. Hon. D.C.L., Oxford, 1852. Engaged on second 'History of Europe,' 1853-59. Died, 23 May 1867. Buried in Glasgow.

Works: 'Travels in France' (anon. with P. F. Tytler), 1815 ; 'Principles of the Criminal Law of Scotland,' 1832 ; 'Practice of the Criminal Law of Scotland,' 1833 ; 'History of Europe during the French Revolution' (10 vols.), 1833-42 ; 'The Principles of Population,' 1840 ; 'Free Trade and Protection ' (from ' Blackwood'), 1844; 'England in 1815 and 1845,' 1845 ; 'Free Trade and a Fettered Currency,' 1847 ; 'The Military Life of John, Duke of Marlborough,' 1848 ; 'Essays,' 1850 ; 'Inaugural Address as Lord Rector of Glasgow Univ.,' 1851 ; 'History of Europe from the Fall of Napoleon in 1815 to the Accession of Louis Napoleon in 1852' (8 vols.), 1853-59 ; ' The British Empire,' 1856 ; 'Lives of Lord Castlereagh and Sir C. Stewart,' 1861.

Posthumous: 'Some Account of My Life and Writings : an Autobiography,' ed. by Lady Alison, 1883.

⁎ **ALLEN (Charles Grant Blairfindie), b. 1848.** Born, at Kingston, Canada, 24 Feb. 1848. Family removed to New Haven, Connecticut, 1857. Educated by tutor there ; at Dieppe ; and at King Edward's School, Birmingham. Postmaster, Merton Coll., Oxford, 19 Oct. 1867; B.A., 1871. Classical Lecturer, Brighton Coll., 1872 - 73. Prof. of Classics, Queen's Coll., Spanish Town, Jamaica, 1873 ; Principal, 1874-76. Returned to England, 1876 ; devoted himself to literature. Lived in London. Contrib. to 'Cornhill Magazine,' 'Daily News,' 'Globe,' 'St. James's Gazette,' ' Pall Mall Gazette.' Of late years has resided in Surrey.

Works: 'Physiological Æsthetics,' 1877 ; 'The Colour Sense,' 1879 ; ' The Evolutionist at Large' (from ' St. James's Gazette '), 1881 ; ' Early

Britain : Anglo-Saxon Britain,' 1881 ; 'Vignettes from Nature' (from 'Pall Mall Gazette '), 1881 ; 'Colin Clout's Calendar' (from 'St. James's Gazette '), 1883 ; 'The Colour of Flowers,' 1882 ; 'Flowers and their Pedigrees,' 1883 ; 'Nature Studies' (with Wilson, Foster, etc.), 1883 ; 'Biographies of Working Men,' 1884 ; 'Strange Stories' (from 'Belgravia' and 'Longman's Magazine'; there under pseud. of 'J. Arbuthnot Wilson'), 1884 ; 'Philistia' (under pseud. of 'Cecil Power '), 1884 ; 'Babylon,' 1885 ; 'Charles Darwin,' 1885 ; 'For Maimie's Sake,' 1886 ; 'Kalee's Shrine' (with M. Cotes), 1886 ; 'In All Shades,' 1886 ; 'The Beckoning Hand,' 1887 ; 'A Terrible Inheritance,' 1887 ; 'Common Sense Science,' 1887 ; 'The Devil's Die,' 1888 ; 'This Mortal Coil,' 1888 ; 'The White Man's Foot,' 1888 ; 'Force and Energy,' 1888 ; 'Dr. Palliser's Patient,' 1889 ; 'Falling in Love,' 1889 ; 'The Jaws of Death,' 1889 ; 'A Living Apparition,' 1889 ; 'The Tents of Shem,' 1889 ; 'The Sole Trustee,' 1890 ; 'The Great Taboo,' 1890 ; 'Dumaresq's Daughter,' 1891 ; 'Recalled to Life,' 1891 ; 'What's Bred in the Bone,' 1891 ; 'The Tidal Thames,' 1892 ; 'Science in Arcady,' 1892 ; 'The Duchess of Powysland,' 1892 ; 'Blood Royal,' 1893 ; 'Ivan Greet's Masterpiece,' 1893 ; 'Michael's Crag,' 1893 ; 'The Scallywag,' 1893 ; 'Post - Prandial Philosophy' (from 'Westminster Gazette '), 1894 ; 'At Market Value,' 1894 ; 'The Lower Slopes,' 1894 ; 'The British Barbarians,' 1895 ; 'In Memoriam G. P. Macdonell,' 1895 ; 'The Story of the Plants,' 1895 ; 'Under Sealed Orders,' 1895 ; 'The Woman who Did,' 1895 ; 'Moorland Idylls,' 1896 ; 'The Jaws of Death,' 1896 ; 'A Splendid Sin,' 1896. He has *translated :* Catullus' 'Attis,' 1892.

AMORY (Thomas), 1691 - 1788. Born, 1691. Very secluded life, spent partly in Ireland, partly in London. Married. Died, 25 Nov. 1788.

Works : 'Memoirs of several Ladies of Great Britain' (anon.), 1755 ; 'A

Letter to the Reviewers' (anon., referring to preceding), 1755 ; 'The Life of John Buncle, Esq.' (anon.), 2 vols., 1756-66 ; 'An Antiquarian Doctor's Sermon' (anon., attrib. to Amory), 1768 ; 'A Dialogue on Devotion' (anon.), no date.

ARBUTHNOT (John), 1667-1735. Born, at Arbuthnot, Kincardineshire, 1667 ; baptized 29 April. Educated at [Marischal Coll.?] Aberdeen. Settled in London, 1691 ; taught mathematics. At University Coll., Oxford, as Fellow-Commoner, 6 Oct. 1694-96. Took M.D. degree, St. Andrew's University, 11 Sept. 1696. Married about 1702. F.R.S., 30 Nov. 1704. Physician Extraordinary to Queen Anne, 30 Oct. 1705 ; Physician in Ordinary, Nov. 1709. Fellow of Roy. Coll. of Physicians, 27 April 1710 ; Second Censor, 30 Sept. 1723 ; 'Elect,' 5 Oct. 1727 ; Harveian Orator, 18 Oct. 1727. Physician at Chelsea Hospital, 1713. Formed 'Scriblerus Club' with Swift, Pope, Gay, and Parnell, 1714. Visits to France, 1714 and 1718. Ill health in later years. Contrib. to 'London Magazine,' 1732. To Hampstead, 1734. Died, in London, 27 Feb. 1735. Buried in St. James's Church, Piccadilly.

Works : 'Of the Laws of Chance' (anon.), 1692 ; 'Theses Medicæ de Secretione Animali,' 1696 ; 'An Examination of Dr. Woodward's Account of the Deluge' (under initials : J. A., M.D.), 1697 ; 'An Essay on the Usefulness of Mathematical Learning,' 1701 ; 'Tables of the Grecian, Roman, and Jewish Measures' [1705] ; 'A Sermon Preach'd . . . at the Mercat-Cross' (anon.), 1706 ; 'Proposals for printing a very curious discourse . . . intitled Ψευδολογια Πολιτικη' (anon.), 1712 ; 'The History of John Bull' (anon. ; in six pamphlets : (i.) 'Law is a Bottomless Pit '; (ii.) 'John Bull in his Senses '; (iii.) 'John Bull still in his Senses '; (iv.) 'An Appendix' to preceding ; (vi.) 'Lewis Baboon turned Honest '), 1712 ; 'Three Hours after Marriage' (with Gay and Pope), 1717 ; 'Reasons humbly offer'd by

the Company . . . of Upholders' (anon.), 1724 ; 'Tables of Ancient Coins' (anon.), 1727 ; 'Oratio Anniversaria Harvæiana,' 1727 ; 'Miscellanies in Prose and Verse' (3 vols.), 1727 (another ed., 4 vols., 1727-32) ; 'An Essay concerning the Nature of Ailments' (2 vols.), 1731-32 ; 'A Brief Account of Mr. John Ginglicutt's Treatise' (anon.), 1731 ; 'An Essay concerning the Effects of Air,' 1733 ; 'Γνωθι Σεαυτον,' 1734. [A further list of anonymous works attributed to Arbuthnot is given in Aitken's 'Life and Works' of Arbuthnot, 1892.]
Collected Works: In 2 vols., 1751 [1750] ; enlarged ed., with memoir, 1770.
Life: By G. A. Aitken, 1892.

* ARCHER (William), b. 1856. Born, at Perth, 23 Sept. 1856. Educated at Edinburgh University, 1872-76 ; M.A., 1876. On staff of 'Edinburgh Evening News,' 1875-78. Visit to Australia 1876-77. Student of Middle Temple, 2 Nov. 1878 ; called to Bar, 17 Nov. 1883. Dramatic critic of 'London Figaro,' 1879-81. Appointed dramatic critic of 'The World,' 1884. Instrumental in production of Ibsen's plays in London.

Works: 'The Fashionable Tragedian' (anon., with R. W. Lowe), 1877 (2nd edn., with postscript, same year) ; 'English Analyses of the French Plays represented . . . by the Comédie Française' (from 'London Figaro'), 1879 ; 'English Dramatists of To-day,' 1882 ; 'Henry Irving,' 1883 ; 'About the Theatre,' 1886 ; 'Masks or Faces?' 1888 ; 'William Charles Macready' ('Eminent Actors' series), 1890 ; 'The Theatrical "World" for 1893-97.' (criticisms reprinted yearly from 'The World'), 1894-98.
He has *translated:* Ibsen's 'Doll's House,' 1889 ; 'Ibsen's Prose Dramas,' 1890, etc., and 'Rosmersholm,' 1891 ; Kielland's 'Tales of Two Countries,' 1891 ; Ibsen's 'Peer Gynt' (with C. Archer), 1892 ; Ibsen's 'Master Builder' (with E. Gosse), 1893 ; Nansen's 'Eskimo Life,' 1893 ; Haupt-

mann's 'Hannele,' 1894 ; Ibsen's 'Little Eyolf,' 1895. Has *edited:* 'Alan's Wife,' 1893 ; Leigh Hunt's 'Dramatic Essays,' 1894 ; Hazlitt's 'Dramatic Essays,' 1895 ; and is editor of 'Eminent Actors' series, 1890, etc.

* ARNOLD (Sir Edwin), b. 1832. Born 10 June 1832. At King's School, Rochester, 1845-50. At King's Coll., London, 1850-51. Scholarship at University Coll.. Oxford, 1851 ; Newdigate Prize Poem, 1852 ; B.A., 1854 ; M.A., 1856. To King Edward's School, Birmingham, as Assistant Master, 1854. Principal of Govt. Sanscrit Coll. at Poona, and Fellow of Bombay University, 1857. Joined staff of 'Daily Telegraph,' 1861. F.R.G.S., Jan. 1875 to May 1887. C.S.I., 1 Jan. 1877. Siamese Order of White Elephant (on publication of 'The Light of Asia'), 1879. Second Class of Imperial Order of Medjidieh, 1876 ; Imperial Order of Osmanieh, 1886. K.C.I.E., 1888. Japanese Imperial Order of Rising Sun, 1892. Pres. of Birmingham and Midland Institute for 1893. Mem. Royal Asiatic Soc. Resides in London.

Works: 'The Feast of Belshazzar,' 1852 ; 'Poems, Narrative and Lyrical,' 1853 ; 'Griselda,' 1856 ; 'The Wreck of the Northern Belle,' 1857 ; 'Education in India,' 1860 ; 'The Marquis of Dalhousie's Administration,' 1862 ; 'The Poets of Greece,' 1869 ; 'Simple Transliteral Grammar of the Turkish Language,' 1877 ; 'The Light of Asia,' 1879 ; 'Indian Poetry' (in 'Trübner's Oriental Series'), 1881 ; 'Pearls of the Faith,' 1883 ; 'The Secret of Death,' 1885 ; 'India Revisited' (from 'Daily Telegraph'), 1886 ; 'Lotus and Jewel,' 1887 ; 'Poems, National and Non-Oriental' (selected), 1888 ; 'With Sa'di in the Garden,' 1888 ; 'In my Lady's Praise,' 1889 ; 'The Light of the World,' 1891 ; 'Seas and Lands' (from 'Daily Telegraph'), 1891 ; 'Japonica' (from 'Scribner's Magazine'), 1892 [1891] ; 'Potiphar's Wife,' 1892 ; 'Adzuma,' 1893 ; 'Wandering Words,' 1894 ; 'The

Tenth Muse,' 1895; 'East and West,' 1896; 'Victoria, Queen and Empress' (from 'Daily Telegraph'), 1896.

He has *translated:* 'The Book of Good Counsel,' from 'Hitopadeśa,' 1861; 'Political Poems by Victor Hugo and Garibaldi' (under initials : E. A.), 1868; 'Hero and Leander,' from Musæus [1873]; 'The Indian Song of Songs,' from 'Jayadeva,' 1875; 'Indian Idylls,' from the 'Mahâbhârata,' 1883; 'The Song Celestial,' from the 'Mahâbhârata,' 1885; 'The Chaurapanchâsika,' 1896.

*ARNOLD (Matthew), 1822-1888. Born, at Laleham, 24 Dec. 1822. Educated till 1836 at Laleham ; at Winchester, 1836-37 ; at Rugby, 1837-41. Family removed to Rugby (where his father was headmaster) in 1828. Scholarship at Balliol Coll., Oxford, Nov. 1840. To Balliol, Oct. 1841. Hertford Scholarship, 1842; Newdigate Prize, 1843 ; B.A., Dec. 1844 ; M.A., 1853 ; Fellow of Oriel Coll., 28 March 1845 to 6 April 1852. Private Sec. to Lord Lansdowne, 1847-51. Married Fanny Lucy Wightman, 10 June 1851. For a short time Assistant Master at Rugby, 1851. Appointed Lay Inspector of Schools, 1851. Prof. of Poetry at Oxford, 1857-67. Visits to France, Germany, and Holland on education business, 1859, 1865 and 1866. Hon. LL.D., Edinburgh, 1869 ; Hon. D.C.L., Oxford, 21 June 1870 ; Order of Commander of Crown of Italy (in recognition of his tutorship of the Duke of Genoa), 1871. Rede Lecturer at Cambridge, 1882. Hon. LL.D., Cambridge, 1883. Visits to America, 1883 and 1886. Died, 15 April 1888. Buried at Laleham.

Works: 'Alaric at Rome,' 1840 ; 'Cromwell,' 1843 ; 'The Strayed Reveller,' by A., 1849 ; 'Empedocles on Etna,' 1852; 'Poems' (1st series), 1853; 'Poems' (2nd series), 1855 ; 'Merope,' 1858 ; ' England and the Italian Question,' 1859 ; 'Popular Education in France,' 1861 ; 'On Translating Homer,' 1861 ; ' Last Words on Translating Homer,' 1862 ; 'A French

Eton,' 1864 ; 'Essays in Criticism' (1st series), 1865 ; 'New Poems,' 1867 ; 'On the Study of Celtic Literature,' 1867 ; 'Saint Brandan' (from 'Fraser's Magazine'), 1867 ; 'Schools and Universities on the Continent, 1868 ; 'Poems' (collected), 1869 ; 'Culture and Anarchy,' 1869 ; 'St. Paul and Protestantism,' 1870 ; 'Friendship's Garland,' 1871 ; 'A Bible Reading for Schools,' 1872 ; ' Literature and Dogma,' 1873 ; ' Higher Schools and Universities in Germany ' (part of ' Schools and Universities on the Continent,' reprinted), 1874 ; 'God and the Bible,' 1875 ; ' The Great Prophecy of Israel's Restoration,' 1875 ; 'Last Essays on Church and Religion,' 1877 ; ' Mixed Essays,' 1879 ; ' Geist's Grave ' (from ' Fortnightly Review ') 1881 ; 'Irish Essays,' 1882 ; 'Isaiah of Jerusalem,' 1883 ; 'Discourses in America,' 1885; ' Essays in Criticism ' (2nd series), 1888 ; 'Special Report on Elementary Education Abroad,' 1888 ; ' Civilization in the United States,' 1888.

Posthumous: ' Rep rts on Elementary Schools,' 1889 ; 'On Home Rule for Ireland' (two letters to the 'Times;' priv. ptd.), 1891 ; 'Letters,' ed. by G. W. E. Russell (2 vols.), 1895.

He *edited :* selections from Johnson's 'Lives of the Poets,' 1878 ; Wordsworth's Poems (in 'Golden Treasury Series '), 1879 ; Byron's Poems (in ' Golden Treasury Series '), 1881 ; 'Burke's Letters, Speeches, and Tracts on Irish Affairs,' 1881. He contributed : an introduction to 'The Hundred Greatest Men,' 1879 ; three essays to T. H. Ward's 'English Poets,' 1880 ; an introduction to J. Smith's 'Natural Truth of Christianity,' 1882 ; 'Sainte-Beuve' to ' Encyclopædia Britannica,' 1886 ; on ' Schools ' to T. H. Ward's ' Reign of Queen Victoria,' 1887.

ARNOLD (Thomas), 1795 - 1842. [Father of preceding.] Born, at East Cowes, 13 June, 1795. At school in Warminster, 1803-07 ; at Winchester, 1807-11. To Corpus Christi Coll., Oxford, as scholar, 1811 ; B.A., 27

Oct. 1814 ; M.A., 19 June 1817 ; Chancellor's Latin Essay Prize, 1815 ; Chancellor's English Essay Prize, 1817 ; Fellow of Oriel Coll., 1815-19. Ordained Deacon, Dec. 1818. Settled at Laleham-on-Thames to take pupils, 1819. Contrib. to 'British Critic,' 1819-20. Married Mary Penrose, 11 Aug. 1820. Contrib. to 'Quarterly Review,' 1825 ; to 'Edinburgh Review,' 1826 and 1836. Wrote 'History of the later Roman Commonwealth,' for 'Encyclopædia Metropolitana,' 1821-27. B.D., 29 March 1828 ; D.D., 17 Dec. 1828. Ordained Priest, June 1828 ; Head Master of Rugby, Aug. 1828 to June 1842. Contrib. to 'Sheffield Courant,' 1831-32 ; to 'Quarterly Journal of Education,' 1834-35. Purchased Fox How, Westmoreland, 1832. Contrib. to 'Hertford Reformer,' 1839-41. Regius Professor of History at Oxford, 1841. Died suddenly, at Rugby, 12 June 1842.

Works : 'The Effects of Distant Colonization on the Parent State' (privately printed), 1815 ; 'The Christian Duty of Granting the Claims of the Roman Catholics,' 1829 ; 'Sermons' (3 vols.), 1829-34 ; 'Tract on the Cholera,' 1831 ; 'Thirteen Letters on our Social Condition' (anon.), 1832 ; 'Principles of Church Reform,' 1833 (2nd and 3rd edns., same year) ; 'Postscript' to preceding, 1833 ; 'History of Rome' (3 vols.), 1838-43 ; 'On the Divisions and Mutual Relations of Knowledge,' 1839 ; 'Two Sermons on the Interpretation of Prophecy,' 1839 ; 'On the Revival of the Order of Deacons,' 1841 ; 'Christian Life,' 1841 ; 'Inaugural Lecture on the Study of Modern History,' 1841 (2nd edn. same year) ; 'Introductory Lectures on Modern History,' 1842.

Posthumous : 'Fragment on the Church,' 1844 ; 'Sermons,' 1845 ; 'Miscellaneous Works,' ed. by A. P. Stanley, 1845 ; 'History of the later Roman Commonwealth' (from 'Encyclopædia Metropolitana'), 1845 ; 'Travelling Journals,' ed. by A. P. Stanley, 1852.

He *edited :* 'Poetry of Common Life,' 1844 ; 'Thucydides,' 1830, etc. *Life :* by A. P. Stanley.

ASCHAM (Roger), **1515 - 1568.** Born, at Kirby Wiske, Yorkshire, 1515. Patronized by Sir Anthony Wingfield, and educated with his family. To St. John's Coll., Cambridge, 1530 ; B.A., 18 Feb. 1534 ; Fellowship, 23 March 1534 ; M.A., July 1537 [?] ; Appointed Greek Reader, 1538 [?]. Visit to parents in Yorkshire, 1540. Severe illness there for two years, and consequent poverty. Pension from Archbishop of York, 1540-44. Return to Cambridge, 1542. Introduced Archery there. Dissensions in University and dissatisfaction with his position there. 'Toxophilus' written, 1543-44 ; presented to Henry VIII., 1545 ; pension of £10 granted. Illness during 1545. Public Orator at Cambridge, 1546. Tutor to Princess Elizabeth, 1548-50. Return to Cambridge and visit to Yorkshire, 1550. Secretary to Sir Richard Morysin, Ambassador to Court of Emperor Charles V., 1550. To Calais 21 Sept. 1550 ; to Antwerp, 30 Sept. ; to Louvain, 6 Oct. ; to Augsburg, 28 Oct. At Augsburg, 1550-52. Visit to Italy in 1551. Recall of Embassy to England, 1553. Appointed Latin Secretary to Queen Mary, 1553. Presented by Crown with lease of Salisbury Hall, Walthamstow. Married Margaret Howe, 1 Jan. 1554 ; resigned offices at Cambridge. Position in Royal Household continued at Queen Elizabeth's accession ; reappointed Queen's tutor. Admitted Prebend of Wetwang in York Cathedral, 11 March 1560. Domestic troubles, ill health, and poverty. 'The Schoolmaster' planned, and first two books written, 1563-68. Died, 30 Dec. 1568. Buried in St. Sepulchre's Church.

Works : 'Expositiones Antiquæ in Epistolam Divi Pauli ad Titum, etc.,' 1542 ; 'Toxophilus,' 1545 ; 'Epistola J. Sturmio de Nobilitate Anglicana,' 1551 ; 'A Report and Discourse . . . of the Affaires and State of Germany, etc.' [1553 ?].

Posthumous: 'The Scholemaster' (published by Ascham's widow), 1570; Selected Letters and Latin Poems, ed. by Edward Grant as 'Familiarium Epistolarum libri tres, etc.,' 1576 (enlarged edition, ed. by William Elstob, 1703); 'Apologia pro Cœna Dominica contra Missam' (in second edn. of 'Expositiones'), 1577. Some English letters first printed in Whittaker's 'Richmondshire,' 1823.
Collected Works: ed. by Dr. Giles, 1864-65.
Life: 'Oratio de vita e obitu Rogeri Aschami,' by Edward Grant, 1576.

ASHMOLE (Elias), 1617 - 1692. Born, at Lichfield, 23 May 1617. Educated at Lichfield Grammar School, and as Cathedral Chorister. To London, 1633. Married Eleanor Mainwaring, 27 March 1638. Started as Solicitor, Oct. 1638. Wife died suddenly, 1641. Admitted to Clement's Inn, Feb. 1641. He removed to Cheshire, 1642. Commissioner of Excise at Lichfield, 1644. At Oxford on business, 1644-45. Entered Brasenose Coll. Appointed Commissioner of Excise at Worcester, 1645. Returned to Cheshire, 1646. Same year to London. Initiated as Freemason, Oct. 1646. Married the Lady Mainwaring, 16 Nov. 1649. She petitioned unsuccessfully for separation, Oct. 1657. Appointed Windsor Herald, Aug. 1660. Held various State appointments. Wife died, 1688. He married Miss Dugdale, same year. Degree of M.D. conferred on him at Oxford, 1669. Gave contents of his museum to Oxford University, 1677; Ashmolean Museum there completed, 1682. Died, 18 May 1692. Buried in South Lambeth Church.

Works: 'Theatrum Chemicum Britannicum,' 1652 [1651]; 'The Way to Bliss,' 1658; 'The Institution, Laws and Ceremonies of the most noble Order of the Garter,' 1672.
Posthumous: 'Memoirs . . . drawn up by himself by way of Diary,' 1717; 'The Antiquities of Berkshire,' 1719. He *edited* Dr. Dee's 'Fasciculus Chemicus,' 1650, under the anagrammatic pseudonym of James Hasolle.

ATHERSTONE (Edwin), 1788-1872. Born 17 April 1788. Voluminous writer in prose and verse. Died, at Bath, 29 Jan. 1872.
Works: 'The Last Days of Herculaneum,' 1821; 'A Midsummer Day's Dream,' 1824; 'The Fall of Nineveh,' bks. i.-vi., 1828; bks. vii.-xiii., 1830; complete in 30 books, 1847; 'The Sea Kings in England' (anon.), 1830; 'The Handwriting on the Wall,' 1858; 'Israel in Egypt,' 1861.
Posthumous: Dramatic Works, edited by M. E. Atherstone, 1888.

AUBREY (John), 1626-1697. Born, at Easton Pierse, Wilts, 12 March 1626. Educated at Yatton Keynel School, 1633-34; at Leigh-de-la-Mere School, 1634-38; at Blandford Grammar School, 1638-42. Matriculated Trin. Coll., Oxford, 4 June 1641. Removed from Oxford at outbreak of Civil War; went to his father at Broad Chalk, Wilts. Developed antiquarian tastes. Entered at Middle Temple, 16 April 1646. Occasional visits to Oxford. Called attention to stone monuments at Avebury, 1649. Succeeded to family estates on father's death, Oct. 1652. Chiefly resided at Broad Chalk. Visit to Ireland, 1660. Sold Herefordshire property, 1662. F.R.S., 20 May 1663. Visit to France, 1664. Sold remainder of property, 1670. Received patent from Crown permitting him to make antiquarian surveys, 1671. Occupied with topographical and antiquarian work respecting Surrey and Wiltshire, 1660-96. Unmarried. Died, at Oxford, June 1697; buried (7 June) in St. Mary Magdalene's Church.
Works: 'Miscellanies,' 1696.
Posthumous: 'The Natural History and Antiquities of the county of Surrey,' ed. by R. Rawlinson (5 vols.), 1718-19; 'Collections for Wilts,' ed. by Sir T. Phillipps (priv. ptd.). 2 pts., 1821 - 38. [MSS. in Ashmolean Museum, Oxford.]
Life: by J. Britton, 1845.

AUSTEN (Jane), 1775-1817. Born, at Steventon, Hampshire, 16 Dec. 1775. Lived there, with occasional visits to Bath, till 1801, when her family removed to Bath. Visit to Lyme, 1804. At Southampton, 1805-09. At Chawton, near Winchester, 1809-17. Occasional visits to London. To lodgings in Winchester, for medical advice, May 1817. Died, 18 July 1817. Buried in Winchester Cathedral.

Works: 'Sense and Sensibility' (anon.), 1811 ; 'Pride and Prejudice' (anon.),1813; 'Mansfield Park' (anon.), 1814 ; 'Emma' (anon.), 1816 ; 'Northanger Abbey and Persuasion,' 1818.

Posthumous: 'Lady Susan,' 'The Watsons' (unfinished), and some letters and verses, in second ed. of J. E. Austen Leigh's 'Memoir of Jane Austen,' 1871 ; 'Letters,' ed. by Lord Brabourne. 1884.

Collected Works: in 6 vols. 1882.

Life: by J. E. Austen Leigh, 1871.

* **AUSTIN (Alfred),** *Poet Laureate,* b. **1835.** Born, at Headingley, 30 May 1835. Educated at Stonyhurst Coll., 1849-52; at St. Mary's Coll., Oscott, 1852-53. B.A., London, 1853. Student of Inner Temple, 23 Jan. 1854 ; called to Bar, 17 Nov. 1857. To Italy in 1861. Joined Staff of 'Standard,' Dec. 1866. Represented 'Standard' during Œcumenical Council at Rome, winter of 1869-70 ; special correspondent during Franco-Prussian War, 1870-71. Founded 'National Review' (with W. J. Courthope) in 1883 ; ed. it till 1893. Appointed Poet Laureate, 1896. Resides in Kent.

Works: 'Randolph' (anon.), 1853; 'Five Years of It,' 1858 ; 'The Season,' 1861 ; 'My Satire and its Censors,' 1861 ; 'A Note of Admiration addressed to the Editor of the "Saturday Review,"' 1861 ; 'The Human Tragedy,' 1862 (first revision, 1876, second, 1889) ; 'An Artist's Proof,' 1864 ; 'Won by a Head,' 1866 ; 'A Vindication of Lord Byron,' 1869 ; 'Poetry of the Period' (from 'Temple Bar'), 1870 ; 'The Golden Age,' 1871 ; 'Interludes,' 1872 ;

'Rome or Death !' 1873 ; 'Madonna's Child,' 1873 ; 'The Tower of Babel,' 1874 ; 'Russia before Europe,' 1876 ; 'Tory Horrors,' 1876 ; 'England's Policy and Peril,' 1877 ; 'Leszko the Bastard,' 1877 ; 'Hibernian Horrors,' 1880 ; 'Savonarola.' 1881 ; 'Soliloquies in Song,' 1882 ; 'At the Gate of the Convent,' 1885 ; 'Prince Lucifer,' 1887 ; 'Love's Widowhood,' 1889 ; 'English Lyrics,' 1890 ; Lyrical Poems, 1891 ; Narrative Poems, 1891 ; Collected Poems (6 vols.), 1892 ; 'Fortunatus the Pessimist,' 1892 ; 'The Garden that I Love,' 1894 ; 'England's Darling,' 1895 ; 'In Veronica's Garden,' 1895.

AYTOUN (William Edmondstoune), 1813-65. Born, in Edinburgh, 21 June 1813. Educated first by private tutor. To Edinburgh Academy, 1824; at Edinburgh University, 1830-33 [?]. To London, 1833. At Aschaffenburg, Sept. 1833 to April 1834. Returned to Edinburgh. Writer to the Signet, 1835. Called to Bar. 1840. Contrib. to 'Blackwood,' 1836-40. Contrib. (with Sir T. Martin) to 'Tait's' and 'Fraser's' Mags., under pseudonym of 'Bon Gaultier.' Joined staff of 'Blackwood,' 1844. Took part in Burns Festival, 1844. Elected Prof. of Rhetoric and Belles Lettres in Edinburgh Univ., 22 Oct. 1845. M.A., Edinburgh, 26 Nov. 1849. Married Jane Emily Wilson (daughter of 'Christopher North'), April 1849. Appointed Sheriff of Orkney, 1852. Wife died, 15 April 1859. Hon. Pres. of Associated Societies of Edinburgh Univ., Dec. 1860. Visits to Germany for health, 1861 and 1862. Married Miss Kinnear, Dec. 1863. Return of bad health, 1864. Died, at Blackhills, near Elgin, 4 Aug. 1865. Buried in Edinburgh.

Works: 'Poland, Homer, and other poems' (anon.), 1832 ; 'Life and Times of Richard the First,' 1840 ; 'Our Zion' (anon.), 1840 ; 'The Drummond Schism examined and exposed' (anon.), 1842 ; 'Lays of the Cavaliers,' 1848 ; 'Bon Gaultier' Ballads (anon., with Sir T. Martin). 1849 ; 'Bothwell,'

1856 ; 'Firmilian' (under pseudonym of T. Percy Jones), 1854 ; 'Poems and Ballads of Goethe' (with Sir T. Martin), 1858 ; 'Ballads of Scotland,' 1858 ; 'Inaugural Address to the Associated Societies of the Univ. of Edinburgh,' 1861 ; 'Norman Sinclair,' 1861 ; 'Nuptial Ode to the Princess Alexandra,' 1863 ; 'The Elder's Warning' (anon., from 'Edinburgh Evening Post '), no date.

Posthumous: Fragments published in Sir Theodore Martin's *Life* of Aytoun, 1867.

BACON (Francis), Baron Verulam, 1561-1626. Born, at York House, 22 Jan. 1561. At Trinity Coll., Cambridge, April 1573 to March 1575. Admitted at Gray's Inn, 27 June 1575 ; called to Bar, 27 June 1582. With Sir Amias Paulet's embassy to France, 1576. M.P. for Melcombe Regis, 1584. M.P. for Taunton, 1586. Bencher of Gray's Inn, 1586. M.P. for Liverpool, 1589. Friendship with Earl of Essex begun, 1591. M.P. for Middlesex, 1593. Employed as Learned Counsel to Queen, 1594. M.A., Cambridge, 27 July 1594. 'Essays' published, 1597. M.P. for Southampton, 1597. Arrested for debt, Sept. 1598. Took part in trials of Earl of Essex, 5 June 1600 and 19 Feb. 1601. Knighted, 23 July 1603. Appointed on Commission to discuss Union, 1604. Pension of £60 granted as Counsel to the King, Aug. 1604. Married Alice Barnham, 10 May 1606. Speech in Parliament in favour of Union proposals, 17 Feb. 1607. Solicitor-General, 25 June 1607. Attorney-General, 27 Oct. 1613. Prosecutor in Earl of Somer-et's trial, 25 May 1616. Privy Councillor, 9 June 1616. Lord Keeper, 7 March 1617. Lord Chancellor, 7 Jan. 1618. Created Baron Verulam, 12 July 1618. Prosecution of Sir Walter Raleigh, 1618 ; of Earl of Suff.lk, 1619 ; of Sir Henry Yelverton, 1620. 'Novum Organum' published, Oct. 1620. Created Viscount St. Alban, 27 Jan. 1621. Tried for bribery, and sentenced to deprivation of office, fine of £40,000

and imprisonment in Tower, 3 May 1621. Partial mitigation of sentence by King, Sept 1621. Died, 9 April 1626. Buried at St. Michael's Church, St. Albans.

Works: 'Essays,' 1597 ; 'Declaration of the practises and treasons attempted . . . by Robert late Earle of Essex' (anon.), 1601 ; 'Apologie of the Earle of Essex. . . . Penned by himself' (or rather, by Bacon), 1603 ; 'Brief Discourse touching the happie Union of the Kingdomes of England and Scotland' (anon.), 1603 ; 'Apologie in certaine imputations concerning the late Earle of Essex,' 1604 ; 'Certaine considerations touching the better pacification . . . of the Church of England' (anon.), 1604 ; 'Of the Proficience and Advancement of Learning,' 1605 ; 'De Sapientia Veterum,' 1609; 'Charge Concerning Duels,' 1614 ; 'Instauratio Magna' ('Novum Organum '), 1620 ; 'Historie of the Raigne of King Henry the Seventh,' 1622 ; 'Historia Naturalis et Experimentalis ad condendam Philosophiam' ('Historia Ventorum '), 1622 ; 'De Dignitate et Augmentis Scientiarum,' 1623 ; 'Historia Vitæ et Mortis,' 1623 ; 'Translation of Certaine Psalmes,' 1625 ; 'Apophthegmes new and old,' 1625.

Posthumous: 'Sylva Sylvarum,' 1627 ; 'Considerations touching a warre with Spaine,' 1629 ; 'The Use of the Law' (anon.) in 'The Lawyers' Light . . . By I. D.,' 1629 ; 'Certaine Miscellany Works,' 1629 ; 'Operum Moralium et Civilium tomus,' 1638 ; 'The Elements of the Common Lawes of England,' 1640 ; 'A Wise and Moderate Discourse concerning Church Affaires' (anon.), 1641 ; 'Remaines,' 1648 ; 'The Felicity of Queen Elizabeth,' 1651 ; 'Scripta in Naturali et Universali Philosophia,' 1653 ; 'The Mirrour of State and Eloquence,' 1656 ; 'Resuscitatio,' 1657 ; 'Opuscula varia posthuma,' 1658 ; 'New Atlantis,' 1660 ; 'Opera Omnia,' 1665 ; 'Letters,' 1702 ; 'A Conference of Pleasure,' 1870 ; 'The Promus of Formularies and Elegancies,' 1883 [1882].

Collected Works, in 14 vols., ed. by Spedding, Ellis, and Heath, 1857-74. *Life*, by Spedding (2 vols.), 1878.

BAGEHOT (Walter), 1826-1877. Born, at Langport, Somersetshire, 3 Feb. 1826. At School in Bristol. To Univ. College, London, 1842 ; B.A. and Mathematical Scholarship, 1846 ; M.A. and gold medal for philosophy and political economy, 1848. In Paris, 1851. Contrib. letters to 'The Inquirer,' Dec. 1851. Called to Bar, 1852. Edited 'National Review' (with R. H. Hutton), 1855-64. Married Miss Wilson, 1858. Editor of 'The Economist,' 1860-77. Died, at Langport, 24 March 1877.

Works: 'Estimates of some Englishmen and Scotchmen' (from 'National Review'), 1858 ; 'Parliamentary Reform' (from 'Nat. Review'), 1859 ; 'The History of the Unreformed Parliament' (from 'Nat. Rev.'), 1860 ; 'Memoir of the Rt. Hon. J. Wilson' (from 'Economist'), 1861 ; 'Count your Enemies,' 1862 ; 'The English Constitution' (from 'Fortnightly Rev.'), 1867 (new ed., enlarged, 1872) ; 'A Practical Plan for Assimilating the English and American Money'(from 'Economist'), 1869 ; 'Physics and Politics,' 1872 ; 'Lombard Street,' 1873 (2nd-4th edns., same year) ; 'Some Articles on the Depreciation of Silver' (from 'Economist'), 1877.

Posthumous: 'Literary Studies,' ed. by R. H. Hutton (2 vols.), 1879 [1878]; 'Economic Studies,' ed. by Hutton,1880 ; 'Biographical Studies,' ed. by Hutton, 1881 ; 'Essays on Parliamentary Reform,' 1883 ; 'The Postulates of English Political Economy,' ed. by A. Marshall, 1885. *Collected Works:* ed. by F. Morgan, with memoir by R. H. Hutton (American ed., 5 vols.), 1889.

*****BAILEY (Philip James), b. 1816.** Born at Nottingham, 22 April 1816. Educated at schools in Nottingham. To Glasgow University, 1831. Student at Lincoln's Inn, 26 April 1834 ; called to Bar, 7 May 1840. 'Festus' written, 1836-39. Twice married.

Works: 'Festus' (anon.), 1839 ; 'The Angel World,' 1850 ; 'The Mystic,' 1855 ; 'The Age,' 1858 ; 'The Universal Hymn,' 1867 ; 'The International Policy of the Great Powers,' 1861.

BAILLIE (Joanna), 1762 - 1851. Born, at Bothwell, Lanarkshire, 11 Sept. 1762. Early youth spent at Bothwell. To school at Glasgow,1772. With family at Long Calderwood, Lanarkshire, 1778-84. In London, 1784-91. Series of 'Plays on the Passions' begun, 1798. 'De Montfort,' produced at Drury Lane, April 1800. To Hampstead on mother's death, 1806. Friendship with Sir Walter Scott. 'Constantine and Valeria' produced at Surrey Theatre, subsequently in Liverpool, Dublin and Edinburgh. 'Family Legend' produced in Edinburgh, 1810 ; at Drury Lane, 1815 and 1821. 'Separation' produced at Covent Garden. 'Henriquez,' at Drury Lane. Died, at Hampstead, 23 Feb. 1851.

Works: 'Fugitive Verses' (anon.), 1790; 'Plays on the Passions' (3 vols.), 1798 (anon.), 1802, 1812 ; 'Miscellaneous Plays,' 1804 ; 'The Family Legend,' 1810 ; 'Metrical Legends of Exalted Characters,' 1821 ; 'A Collection of Poems . . . Edited by Joanna Baillie,' 1823 ; 'The Martyr,' 1826 ; 'The Bride,' 1828 ; 'A View of the General Tenour of the New Testament regarding the Nature and Dignity of Jesus Christ,' 1831 ; 'Miscellaneous Plays' (3 vols.), 1836; 'Fugitive Verses,' 1840 ; 'Ahalya Baee,' 1849. *Posthumous:* 'Dramatic and Poetical Works,' 1851.

She *edited* anonymously: Occasional Verses,' by Sophia Baillie, 1846.

BALE (John), *Bishop of Ossory*, **1495-1563.** Born at Cove, Suffolk, 21 Nov. 1495. Educated from 1507 at Carmelite Convent, Norwich, and at Jesus Coll., Camb. Converted to Protestantism, and married. In high favour with Cromwell. Rector of Thornden, Suffolk. Wrote 'moralities.'

Retired to Germany, 1540. Returned to England, 1547 ; appointed Rector of Bishopstoke, Hampshire. Vicar of Swaffham, Norfolk, 1551. Bishop of Ossory, Aug. 1552 ; to Ireland, Dec. 1552 ; consecrated 2 Feb. 1553. Retired to Holland, 1553 ; lived there and at Basle till 1559. Returned to England, 1559 ; appointed Prebend. of Canterbury. Died, at Canterbury, 1563.

Works : 'A Tragedye or Enterlude,' 1538 ; 'Yet a Course at the Romysh Foxe' (anon. ; attrib. to Bale), 1543 ; 'A brefe Chronycle concernynge the examinacyon and death of . . . Syr J. Oldecastell,' 1544 ; 'The Epistle Exhortatorye of an Englyshe Christiane' (under signature of 'Henry Stalbrydge'; attrib. to Bale), 1544 ; 'A Mysterye of Inyquyte . . . confuted,' 1545 ; 'The Actes of Englysh Votaryes,' pt. i., 1546 ; pts. i. and ii., 1548-51 ; 'Illustrium Maioris Britanniæ Scriptorum . . . summarium,' 1548 ; 'A Comedye concernynge thre lawes,' 1550 ; 'The Apology of Johan Bale,' 1550 : 'The Ymage of both Churches,' 1550 ; 'The Vocacyon of Johan Bale,' 1553 ; 'A Soveraigne Cordial for a Christian Conscience' (anon.; attrib. to Bale), 1554 ; 'A Declaration of E. Bonner's Articles,' 1561.

Posthumous : 'Acta Romanorum Pontificum,' 1567 ; 'The Pageant of Popes' (trans. from preceding), 1574.

He *translated :* Jonas' 'The true historie of the Christen departynge of . . . Martyne Luther,' 1546 ; and *edited :* Leland's 'Laboryouse Journey,' 1549 ; Lambert's 'Treatyse . . . unto Kynge Henry VIII.,' 1555 (?).

Collected Works : 'Select Works,' 1849.

BANIM (John), **1798-1842.** Born, at Kilkenny, 3 April 1798. Educated at private schools, 1802-10 ; at Kilkenny Coll., 1810-13. In 1813 to Dublin, to study drawing in Academy of Royal Dublin Society. Returned to Kilkenny, 1815. To Dublin 1820, to adopt literary career. Contrib. to 'Limerick Evening Post' and other periodicals. 'Damon and Pythias' produced at Covent Garden, 28 May 1821. Married Ellen Ruth, 27 Feb. 1822. 'O'Hara' tales planned with brother Michael, 1822. To London, March 1822. On staff of 'Literary Register,' July 1822 to May 1823. Ill health began, 1823. Tragedy, 'The Prodigal,' accepted for Drury Lane, but not performed. Took his wife to France, and returned to London early in 1825. 'Tales by the O'Hara Family,' written in collaboration with brother, first appeared April 1825. At Eastbourne, 1827 ; at Sevenoaks, 1827-29. To Blackheath, April 1829 ; to Boulogne, Aug. 1829, owing to ill - health. Wrote for magazines and theatre. Attacked by cholera, 1832. To Paris, 1833. Lower limbs paralyzed. Moved to London, thence to Dublin, 1835. Benefit performance in Dublin Theatre, 21 July 1835. To Kilkenny in Sept. 1835. Pension of £190 per annum, 1836. Tragedy, 'Sylla' (written in 1827), produced in Dublin, June 1837. Died, 13 Aug. 1842.

Works : 'The Celt's Paradise,' 1821 ; 'Damon and Pythias,' 1821 ; 'Letter to the Committee appointed to appropriate a fund for a national testimonial, etc.,' 1822 ; 'Revelations of the Dead-Alive' (anon.), 1824 ; 'The Fetches' and collaboration in 'John Doe,' in 'Tales by the O'Hara Family' (anon.), 1825 ; 'The Nowlans' and collaboration in 'Peter of the Castle,' in 'Tales by the O'Hara Family,' 2nd series (anon.), 1826 ; 'The Boyne Water' (anon.), 1826 ; 'The Anglo-Irish of the Nineteenth Century' (anon.), 1828 ; 'The Denounced' (anon.), 1830 ; 'Chaunt of the Cholera' (with M. Banim ; anon.), 1831 ; 'The Smuggler' (anon.), 1831 ; 'The Bit o' Writin'' (with M. Banim ; anon.), 1838.

Posthumous : 'London and its Eccentricities in the year 2023' (anon.), 1845.

Life : by P. J. Murray, 1857.

BANIM (Michael), **1796 - 1874.** [Brother of preceding.] Born, at Kilkenny, 5 Aug. 1796. Educated in Kilkenny, and at Roman Catholic School. Began to study for Bar, 1812 ; but subsequently obliged to enter business. 'O'Hara' tales planned with brother, 1822. Visit to brother in London, 1826. Active part in agitation for Catholic emancipation. Return to Kilkenny, 1828. Married, 1840. Lost fortune, 1841. Appoint d Postmaster of Kilkenny, 1852 [?]. Resigned owing to ill-health, 1873. To Booterstown with family. Died there, 30 Aug. 1874.

Works : 'Crohoore of the Bill Hook' and collaboration in 'John Doe,' in 'Tales by the O'Hara Family' (anon.), 1825 ; collaboration in 'Peter of the Castle' in 'Tales by the O'Hara Family,' 2nd series (anon.). 1826 ; 'The Croppy' (anon.), 1828 ; 'Chaunt of the Cholera,' (with J. Banim ; anon.), 1831 ; 'The Ghost-Hunter and his Family' (anon.), 1833 ; 'The Mayor of Wind-Gap,' in 'Tales by the O'Hara Family,' 3rd series (anon.), 1835 ; 'The Bit o' Writin'' (with J. Banim ; anon.), 1838 ; 'Father Connell,' 1842 ; 'The Town of the Cascades,' 1864.

BARBAULD (*Mrs.* **Anna Letitia**), **1743 - 1825.** Born [Anna Letitia Aikin], at Kibworth Harcourt, Leicestershire, 20 June 1743. Early youth spent there. At Warrington, 1758-73. Married to Rev. Rochemont Barbauld, May 1774. Settled at Palgrave, Suffolk, and started boys' school with husband. No children ; adopted a nephew, Charles Rochemont Aikin, 1776. School given up, 1785. Travelled in France and Switzerland, Sept. 1785 to June 1786. In London, 1786-87. To Hampstead, April 1787. Visit to Scotland, 1794. Removed to Stoke Newington, 1802. Husband died, 1808. She died, at Stoke Newington, 9 March 1825.

Works : 'Poems,' 1773 ; 'Miscellaneous Pieces' (with J. Aikin),1773 ; 'Devotional Pieces,' 1775 ; 'Hymns in Prose : for Children' (under initials : A.L.B.), 1781 ; 'An Address to the Opposers of the Repeal of the Cor-

poration and Test Acts' (anon.), 1790 ; 'Epistle to W. Wilberforce,' 1791; 'Evenings at Home' (anon., with J. Aikin), 1792 ; 'Remarks on Mr. G. Wakefield's Enquiry, etc..' 1792 ; 'Civic Sermons' (anon.), 1792 ; 'Sins of the Government, Sins of the Nation' (anon.), 1793 ; 'The Religion of Nature' (under pseud. of 'Bob Short'), 1793 ; 'Reasons for National Penitence' (anon.), 1794 ; 'Selections from the "Spectator," etc.,' 1804 ; 'Lessons for Children' (anon.), 1808; 'The Female Speaker,' 1811 ; 'Eighteen Hundred and Eleven,' 1812.

Posthumous : 'Works, with Memoir by L. Aikin' (2 vols.), 1825 ; 'Hymns in Rhyme,' 1838 ; 'Memoir, Letters and Selection,' ed. by G. A. Ellis, 1874.

She *edited :* Akenside's 'Pleasures of Imagination,' 1794, and 'Works,' 1808 ; Samuel Richardson's 'Correspondence,' 1804 ; 'The British Novelists' (50 vols.), 1810 ; and *translated* Jauffret's 'Travels of Rolando,' 1823.

BARCLAY (**John**), **1582-1621.** Born, at Pont-à-Mousson, 28 Jan. 1582. Educated in France. To England in 1603. Returned to France, 1605. Married Louise Debonnaire, 1605. In London, 1606-16. To Rome, 1616. Argenis' completed, July 1621. Died 15 Aug. 1621.

Works : 'Satyricon' (under pseud. of Euphormio Lusininus). pt. i., second edition, 1605 (first edition said to have been published 1603, but no copy known) ; pt. ii., 1607 ; pts. i. and ii., 1610 ; 'Sylvæ,' 1606 ; 'Pietas,' 1612 ; 'Icon Animorum,' 1614 ; 'Poematum libri duo.' 1615 ; 'Parænesis ad sectarios,' 1617 ; 'Virtus Vindicata' (under pseud. of Polienus Rhodiensis), 1617 ; 'Argenis,' 1621.

He *edited :* 'De Potestate Papæ,' by his father, William Barclay, 1609.

*BARHAM (Richard Harris), 1788-1845. Born, at Canterbury, 6 Dec. 1788. Educated at St. Paul's School, London, 1800-07. Matric. Brasenose Coll., Oxford, 13 June 1807, as Pauline

Exhibitioner ; B.A., Nov. 1811. Ordained 1813 ; Curate of Ashford, 1813-14. Married Caroline Smart, 30 Sept. 1814. Curate of Westwell, 1814-17 ; Vicar of Snargate, Romney Marsh, 1817-24 ; Minor Canon, St. Paul's Cathedral, April 1821. To London, Aug. 1821. Rector of St. Mary Magdalene and St. Gregory, and Priest in Ordinary to Chapels Royal, 1824-42. Rector of St. Faith, 1824. Assisted J. G. Gorton in compilation of 'Biographical Dictionary,' 1828. Contrib. to ' Blackwood,' ' John Bull,' 'Globe,' 'Literary Gazette,' and 'London Chronicle.' Edited latter for a time. 'Ingoldsby Legends' appeared in ' Bentley's Miscellany,' 1837-43 ; in ' New Monthly Magazine,' 1843-44. Divinity Lecturer at St. Paul's, 1842. Vicar of St. Faith, 1842. Died in London, 17 June 1845. Buried in vault of St. Mary Magdalene's ; on its being burnt down his remains were removed to Kensal Green Cemetery, and memorial tablet transferred to crypt of St. Paul's.

Works : ' Look at the Clock ' [1830 ?] ; 'Ingoldsby Legends,' 1st series, 1840 ; 2nd series, 1842 ; 'Some Account of my Cousin Nicholas ' (under pseud. of Thomas Ingoldsby), 1841.

Posthumous : 3rd series of 'Ingoldsby Legends,' edited by R. H. D. Barham, 1847 ; ' Ingoldsby Lyrics ' (miscellaneous poems), 1881.

' Life and Letters,' by R. H. D. Barham, 1870.

*BARING-GOULD (Sabine), b. 1834. Born, at Exeter, 28 Jan. 1834. At King's Coll. School, London, 1345 ; at Warwick Grammar School, 1846-47. To Clare Coll., Cambridge, 1853 ; B.A., 1857 ; M.A., 1860. Ordained Deacon, 1864 ; Priest, 1865. Curate of Horbury, Yorkshire, 1864-66; Perpetual Curate of Dalton, Thirsk, 1866-71 ; Rector of East Mersea, Colchester, 1871-81. Edited 'The Sacristy,' 1871-73. Succeeded to estate of Lew Trenchard, Devon, 1872 ; Rector of Lew-Trenchard, 1881. J.P. for county of Devon, 1882.

Has taken part in excavations on prehistoric sites on Dartmoor.

Works : ' The Path of the Just,' 1857 ; ' Iceland,' 1863 ; ' Post-Mediæval Preachers,' 1865 ; ' The Book of Were - Wolves,' 1865 ; ' Curious Myths of the Middle Ages ' (2 series), 1866-68 [67] ; ' The Silver Store,' 1868 ; 'Curiosities of Olden Times,' 1869 ; ' The Golden Gate ' (3 pts.), 1869-70 ; ' The Origin and Development of Religious Belief ' (2 vols.), 1869-70 ; ' In Exitu Israel,' 1870 ; 'One Hundred Sermon-Sketches,' 1871 ; 'Legends of Old Testament Characters,' 1871 ; 'Protestant or Catholic ?' 1872 ; 'Village Conferences on the Creed,' 1873 ; ' The Lost and Hostile Gospels,' 1874 ; ' Yorkshire Oddities,' 1874 ; ' How to Save Fuel,' 1874 ; ' Some Modern Difficulties,' 1875 ; ' Village Preaching for a Year ' (2 series), 1875-84 · ' Twenty Sermon - Sketches,' 1876 ; ' The Vicar of Morwenstow,' 1876 (2nd edn. same year) ; ' The Mystery of Suffering,' 1877 ; ' Sermons to Children,' 1879 ; ' Germany, past and present,' 1879 ; 'The Preacher's Pocket,' 1880 ; ' Mehalah ' (anon.), 1880 ; 'Village Preaching for Saints' Days,' 1881 ; 'The Village Pulpit,' 1881 ; ' John Herring' (anon.), 1883 ; 'Church Songs' (with H. F. Sheppard), 1884 ; 'The Seven Last Words,' 1884 ; 'The Birth of Jesus,'1885; 'Our Parish Church,' 1885 ; ' The Passion of Jesus,' 1885 ; 'Germany ' (with A. Gilman), 1886 ; 'Nazareth and Capernaum,' 1886 ; 'The Trials of Jesus,' 1886 ; ' Golden Feather ' (anon.), 1886 ; ' Court Royal ' (anon.), 1886 ; ' Red Spider ' (anon.), 1887 ; ' The Gaverocks ' (anon.), 1887 ; ' The Way of Sorrows,' 1887 ; ' Little Tu'penny ' (anon.), 1887 ; 'Richard Cable ' (anon.), 1888 ; ' Eve' (anon.), 1888 ; 'The Death and Resurrection of Jesus,' 1888 ; ' Our Inheritance,' 1888 ; ' The Penny-comequicks,' 1889 ; ' Historic Oddities ' (2 vols.), 1889-91 ; 'Grettir the Outlaw,' 1890 [1889] ; 'My Prague Pig,' 1890 ; 'Old Country Life,' 1890 ; 'Arminell' (anon.), 1890 ; 'Conscience and Sin,' 1890 ; ' Jacquetta,' 1890 ·

2

'In Troubadours' Land,' 1891 [1890]; 'Urith,' 1891 ; 'Margery of Quether,' 1891 ; 'Songs of the West,' 1891 ; 'The Church in Germany,' 1891 ; 'Fifteen Pounds,' 1891 ; 'In the Roar of the Sea,' 1892 ; 'The Tragedy of the Cæsars,' 1892 ; 'Through all the Changing Scenes of Life,' 1892 ; 'Wagner's Parsifal at Baireuth,' 1892 ; 'Curious Survivals,' 1892 ; 'Mrs. Curgenven,' 1893 ; 'The Two John Brents,' 1893 ; 'Cheap Jack Zita,' 1893 ; 'The Icelander's Sword,' 1894 [1893] ; 'The Deserts of Southern France,' 1894 ; 'The Queen of Love,' 1894 ; 'Kitty Alone,' 1894 ; 'A Garland of Country Song,' 1894 ; 'A Book of Old Fairy Tales,' 1894 ; 'Noémi,' 1895 ; 'The Old English Fairy Tales,' 1895 ; 'A Book of Nursery Songs,' 1895 ; 'The Broom Squire,' 1896 ; 'Dartmoor Idylls,' 1896 ; 'The Golden Gate,' 1896 ; 'The Life of Napoleon Bonaparte,' 1896.

He has *translated :* W. von Hillern's 'Ernestine,' 1879 ; and *edited :* 'The Lives of the Saints' (17 vols.), 1872-89.

BARNES (William), **1801-1886.** Born, near Pentridge, Dorsetshire [22 Feb. ?] 1801 ; baptized 20 March. At school at Sturminster ; entered Solicitor's office there, 1814 or 1815 ; to another at Dorchester, 1818. Contrib. verses to 'Weekly Entertainer,' 1820. Took Mastership of School at Mere, Wiltshire, 1823 ; settled at Chantry House, Mere, 1827. Married Julia Miles [summer of 1827 ?]. Contrib. to 'Dorset County Chronicle,' 1827-35 ; to 'Gentleman's Mag.,' 1831-41. Two farces by him performed by travelling dramatic company, 1832 ; contrib. to 'Hone's Year Book,' 1832. Wrote first poems in Dorsetshire dialect, 1833. Gave up school at Mere and opened one in Dorchester, 1835. Entered name on books of St. John's Coll., Cambridge, 1837. Intimacy with Sheridan begun, 1844. Visit to London, June 1844. Sec. of Dorset County Museum at its foundation, 1845. Ordained Deacon, 28 Feb. 1847 ; Priest, 14 March

1848 ; Pastor of Whitcombe, near Dorchester, Feb. 1847 to Jan. 1852. Resided three terms at St. John's College, Cambridge, 1847, 1848, 1850 ; B.D. degree, Oct. 1850. Visit to London, 1851. Wife died, 21 June 1852. Contrib. to 'Retrospective Review,' 1853-54. Civil List Pension, April 1861 ; contrib. to 'Macmillan's Magazine,' 1861-67. Presented with Rectorship of Came, Jan. 1862. Gave up school and removed to Came, July 1862. Friendship with Tennyson and Coventry Patmore begun, 1862. Contrib. to 'Fraser's Magazine,' 1863 ; to 'Ladies' Treasury,' 1863-67. Gave readings of his poems, 1863-65. Active literary life. Severe illness, 1884. Died, at Came, 11 Oct. 1886 ; buried there.

Works : 'Orra,' 1822 ; 'The Etymological Glossary,' 1829 ; 'A Catechism of Government in General,' 1833 ; 'The Mnemonic Manual,' 1833 ; 'A Few Words on the Advantages of a more common adoption of Mathematics as a branch of Education,' 1834 ; 'A Mathematical Investigation of the principle of Hanging Doors,' 1835 ; 'An Investigation of the Laws of Case,' 1840 ; 'An Arithmetical and Commercial Dictionary,' 1841 ; 'A Pronouncing Dictionary of Geographical Names,' 1841 ; 'The Elements of Grammar,' 1842 ; 'The Elements of Linear Perspective,' 1842 ; 'Exercises in Practical Science,' 1844 ; 'Sabbath Days,' 1844 ; 'Poems of Rural Life, in the Dorset Dialect,' 1844 ; 'Poems, partly of Rural Life, in national English,' 1846 ; 'Outlines of Geography,' 1847 ; 'Se Gefylsta,' 1849 ; 'Humilis Domus,' 1849 ; 'A Philological Grammar,' 1854 ; 'Notes on Ancient Britain and the Britons,' 1858 ; 'Hwomely Rhymes : a second collection of poems in the Dorset dialect,' 1859 ; 'Views of Labour and Gold, 1859 ; 'The Song of Solomon, in the Dorset Dialect' (privately printed), 1859 ; 'Tiw,' 1862 ; 'A Grammar and Glossary of the Dorset Dialect,' 1864 ; 'Poems of Rural Life in the Dorset Dialect: third collection,' 1862 ; 'A Guide to Dorchester,' 1864 ; 'Poems of Rural Life in Common English,' 1868 ; 'Early England and the Saxon English,'1869; 'A Paper on Somerset,' 1869 ; 'An Outline of English Speechcraft,'1878; 'Poems of Rural Life in the Dorset Dialect' (collections i.-iii. together), 1879 ; 'An Outline of Redecraft,' 1880 ; 'A Glossary of the Dorset Dialect,' 1886. He *edited :* J. Poole's 'Glossary and some Pieces of Verse of the Old Dialect, etc.,' 1867. *Life :* by his daughter, Lucy Baxter, 1887.

*BARRIE (James Matthew), b. 1860.** Born, at Kirriemuir, Forfarshire, 9 May 1860. At school there, and at Dumfries Academy. At Edinburgh Univ., 1879-82. M.A., 1882. On staff of 'Nottingham Journal,' 1883. To London, 1884. Contrib. to 'St. James' Gaz.,' 'Home Chimes,' 'British Weekly,' 'Speaker,' 'National Observer.' Comedy, 'Walker, London,' produced at Toole's Theatre, 25 Feb. 1892 ; 'The Professor's Love Story,' in New York, 19 Dec. 1892 ; at Toole's Theatre, London, 25 June 1894 ; 'Jane Annie' (written with Conan Doyle) at Savoy, 13 May 1893. Married Mary Ansell, 1894.

Works : 'Better Dead,' 1887 ; 'When a Man's Single,'1888 ; 'Auld Licht Idylls,' 1888 ; 'A Window in Thrums,' 1889 ; 'An Edinburgh Eleven,' 1889 ; 'My Lady Nicotine,' 1890 ; 'The Little Minister,' 1891 (2nd edn. same year) ; 'Jane Annie' (with Conan Doyle), 1893 ; 'Sentimental Tommy,' 1896 ; 'Margaret Ogilvy,' 1896.

BARROW (*Sir* John), 1764-1848. Born, at Dragley Beck, near Ulverston, 19 June 1764. Educated at Town Bank Grammar School. Taste for mathematics. Time-keeper in an iron foundry in Liverpool, 1778-81. Voyaged to Greenland in a whaler. Subsequently mathematical master in school at Greenwich. On embassy to China with Lord Macartney, as comptroller of household, 1792-94. With him to Cape of Good Hope as private

secretary, 1796-98. Remained in S. Africa for exploration,1798-99. On military mission in Eastern S. Africa, 1799. Married Anna Maria Trüter, Aug. 1799. Returned to England, June 1803. Second secretary to Admiralty, 1804-06, 1807-45. Hon. LL.D., Edinburgh, 1821. Active part in founding of Royal Geographical Society, 1830. Contrib. to 'Quarterly Rev.,' 'Edinburgh Rev.,' 'Encyclopædia Britannica.' Created baronet, 1835. Retired from public life, 1845. Died suddenly, in London, 23 Nov. 1848. Buried in Camden Town.

Works : 'Some Account of the Public Life . . . of the Earl of Macartney,' 1807 ; 'An Account of Travels into the Interior of Southern Africa' (2 vols.), 1801-04 ; 'Travels in China,' 1804 ; 'A Voyage to Cochin China,' 1806 ; 'A Chronological History of Voyages into the Arctic Regions,' 1818 ; 'The Eventful History of the Mutiny . . . of H.M.S. Bounty' (anon.), 1831 ; 'Life of Richard, Earl Howe,' 1838 ; 'The Life of George, Lord Anson,' 1839 ; 'A Memoir of the Life of Peter the Great, 1845 ; 'Voyages of Discovery and Research within the Arctic Regions,' 1846 ; 'Autobiographical Memoir,' 1847. *Life :* by Sir G. T. Staunton, 1852.

BAXTER (Richard), 1615-1691. Born at Eaton - Constantine, near Shrewsbury, 12 [?] Nov. 1615. At Free School, Wroxeter, 1630-33 ; then for short time under tuition of Richard Wickstead at Ludlow Castle. To Court of Whitehall with introduction to Master of the Revels, 1633. Return home owing to mother's death, 1834. In charge of Wroxeter School for three months. Began theological studies. Ordained, and appointed Headmaster of new school at Dudley, 1638. Assistant minister at Bridgnorth, 1639-41. Appointed preacher at Kidderminster, 5 April 1641. Espoused cause of Parliament in Civil War. To Coventry, 1643 [?]. Chaplain to Captain Whalley's regiment, 1645. In retirement, owing to illhealth, 1647-50. 'Aphorismes of

2—2

Justification' published, 1649 ; 'The Saint's Everlasting Rest,' 1650. Returned to Kidderminster. To London, 1660. Preached before House of Commons at St. Margaret's, 30 April 1660 ; before Lord Mayor and Aldermen at St. Paul's, 10 May 1660. Appointed Chaplain to Charles II. Finally left Church of England, 16 May 1662, and retired to Acton. Married Margaret Charlton, 10 Sept. 1662. Visit to Richard Hampden in Buckinghamshire, 1665. 'A Call to the Unconverted' published, 1665. Wife died, 1681. Wrote 'Breviate' of her Life, 1681. Arrested, 28 Feb. 1685, for libel on the Church in his 'Paraphrase of the New Testament.' Trial, 30 May. Sentenced to fine of 500 marks and imprisonment till paid. Discharged from prison, 24 Nov. 1686, fine being remitted. Active in coalition of dissenters with conforming clergy, 1688. Died, 8 Dec. 1691. Buried in Christ Church, London.

Works: Between 1649 and 1691 Baxter published 148 works. Nine were published posthumously between 1692 and 1701. A complete list is given in Orme's 'Life of Baxter,' 1830, and A. B. Grosart's 'Annotated List' of Baxter's Writings, 1868. Baxter's 'Practical Works' were published in 4 vols. in 1707 ; again, in 23 vols., with life, by W. Orme, 1830. 'Reliquiæ Baxterianæ' (autobiography), edited by M. Sylvester, 1696.

BEACONSFIELD, Earl of. *See* Disraeli (Benjamin).

BEATTIE (James), 1735 - 1803. Born, at Laurencekirk, Kincardine, 25 Oct. 1735. To Marischal Coll., Aberdeen, 1749 ; M.A., 1753. Schoolmaster and parish clerk at Fordoun, 1753-58. Contrib. to 'Scots' Magazine.' Master at Aberdeen Grammar School, 1758-60. Professor of Moral Philosophy and Logic, Marischal Coll., 1760-97. Published first vol. of poems, 1761. First visit to London, 1763. Friendship with Gray begun, 1765. Married Mary Dunn, 28 June 1767. Hon. D.C.L., Oxford, 9 July 1773. Crown pension of £200, Aug.

1773. Refused Professorship of Moral Philosophy at Edinburgh, 1773. Active literary work. Failing health from 1793. Died, 18 Aug. 1803. Buried in St. Nicholas Churchyard, Aberdeen.

Works: 'Original Poems and Translations,' 1760; 'Judgment of Paris,' 1765 ; 'Verses on the Death of Churchill,' 1765 ; 'Poems on Several Subjects,' 1766 ; 'Essay on Truth,' 1770 ; 'The Minstrel,' pt. i. (anon.), 1771; pt. ii., 1774 ; 'Poems on Several Occasions,' 1776 ; 'Essays,' 1776 (2nd edn. same year) ; 'Letter to the Rev. H. Blair . . . on the Improvement of Psalmody in Scotland' (anon., privately printed), 1778 ; 'List of Two Hundred Scotticisms ' (anon.), 1779 ; 'Dissertations, Moral and Critical,' 1783 ; 'Evidences of the Christian Religion,' 1786 ; 'The Theory of Language,' 1788 ; 'Elements of Moral Science,' vol. i., 1790 ; vol. ii., 1793 ; 'Notes on Addison' (apparently not published), 1790.

Collected Poems: 1805, 1810, 1822, 1831, etc.

He *edited:* 'Essays and Fragments,' by his son, J. H. Beattie (privately printed), 1794.

Life: by Bower, 1804 ; by Sir W. Forbes, 1806.

BEAUMONT (Francis), 1584-1616. Born, at Grace-Dieu, Leicestershire, 1584. Matriculated at Broadgates Hall (now Pembroke College, Oxford), 1597. Left Univ. without degree, April 1598, on death of father. Admitted to Inner Temple, 3 Nov. 1600. First verses published, 1602. Early intimacy with John Fletcher. Wrote dramas with him, 1605-14. Lived in London, with occasional visits to Grace-Dieu. Married Ursula Isley, 1613 [?]. Had two daughters. Died, 6 March 1616. Buried in Westminster Abbey.

Works: [For plays written with John Fletcher, *see below.*] Verses prefixed to Sir John Beaumont's 'Metamorphosis of Tobacco,' 1602 ; 'Salmacis and Hermaphroditus ' (anon. ; authorship not certain), 1602 ; 'The

Masque of the Gentlemen of Grayes Inne and the Inner Temple' (anon.), [1613] ; contrib. to 'Certain Elegies, done by sundrie excellent Wits,' 1618. *Posthumous :* 'Poems,' 1640.

BEAUMONT AND FLETCHER. *Plays published in their lifetime under the joint names of Francis Beaumont and John Fletcher (q.v.), or attributed to them :* 'The Woman Hater' (anon.), 1607 ; 'The Knight of the Burning Pestle,' 1613 ; 'Cupid's Revenge' (published in Fletcher's name), 1615 ; 'The Scornful Ladie,' 1616 ; 'A King and no King,' 1619 ; 'The Maid's Tragedy' (anon.), 1619 ; 'Phylaster,' 1620 (performed 1611); 'Tragedy of Thierry, King of France' (anon., possibly by Fletcher alone), 1621.

Posthumous : 'The Elder Brother' (published in Fletcher's name), 1637 ; 'The Bloody Brother' (published under initials : B. J. F.), 1639; 'Wit Without Money' (probably by Fletcher alone), 1639 ; 'Comedies and Tragedies' (containing the following plays, some of which were subsequently published separately : 'The Mad Lover,' 'The Spanish Curate,' 'The Little French Lawyer,' 'The Custome of the Countrey,' 'The Noble Gentleman,' 'The Captaine,' 'The Beggar's Bush,' 'The Coxcombe,' 'The False One,' 'The Chances,' 'The Loyall Subject,' 'The Lawes of Candy,' 'The Lover's Progresse,' 'The Island Princesse,' 'The Humorous Lieutenant,' 'The Nice Valour,' 'The Maid in the Mill,' 'The Prophetesse,' 'Bonduca,' 'The Sea Voyage.' 'The Double Marriage,' 'The Pilgrime,' 'The Knight of Malta,' 'The Woman's Prize,' 'Love's Cure,' 'The Honest Man's Fortune,' 'The Queene of Corinth,' 'Women Pleas'd,' 'A Wife for a Moneth,' 'Wit at severall Weapons,' 'Valentinian,' 'The Fair Maide of the Inne,' 'Love's Pilgrimage,' 'The Masque of the Gentlemen of Grayes Inne, etc.,' 'Four Plays or Moral Representations in One'), 1647 ; 'The Wild-Goose Chase' (probably by Fletcher alone), 1652.

Collected Works: ed., with *memoir*, by Dyce (11 vols.), 1843-46.

BECKFORD (William), 1760-1844. Born, at Fonthill, Wilts, 1 Oct. 1760. Privately educated. At Geneva with tutor, 1777-79. Visit to Netherlands, 1780 ; to Italy, 1782. Married Lady Margaret Gordon, 5 May 1783 ; lived partly in Switzerland until her death, 26 May 1786. M.P. for Wells, 1784-90. Visit to Portugal and Spain, 1787. In Paris, 1791-92 ; at Lausanne, 1792-93. Visit to Portugal, 1794. M.P. for Hindon, 1806-20. Lived in seclusion at Fonthill Giffard, 1796-1822 ; obliged to sell estate, 1822. Removed to Bath. Died there, 2 May 1844 ; buried there. *Works :* 'Dreams, Waking Thoughts and Incidents' (anon.), 1783 ; 'Vathek,' *in English* (anon., surreptitiously published in London by S. Henley, who translated from Beckford's MS.), 1786 ; *in French* (anon.), Paris, 1787 (another edn. same year, published at Lausanne with author's name) ; 'Modern Novel Writing ; or, The Elegant Enthusiast' (under pseud. of Lady Harriet Marlow), 1796 ; 'Amezia' (under pseud. of 'Jacquetta Agneta Mariana Jenks'), 1797 ; 'Biographical Memoirs of Extraordinary Painters' (anon.), 1824 ; 'Italy, with Sketches of Spain and Portugal,' 1834 ; 'Recollections of . . . the Monasteries of Alcobaça and Batalha' (anon.), 1835. He *translated :* 'Al Raoui,' 1783. *Life :* by Cyrus Redding (anon.), 1859.

BEDDOES (Thomas Lovell), 1803-1849. Born, at Clifton, 20 July 1803. Educated at Bath Grammar School ; and at Charterhouse, June 1817-20. Contrib. sonnet to 'Morning Post,' 1819. Wrote 'The Bride's Tragedy,' 1819. To Pembroke Coll., Oxford, 1 May 1820 ; B.A., 25 May 1825 ; M.A., 16 April 1828. Assisted in publication of Shelley's Posthumous Poems, 1824. To Italy in summer of 1824. At Göttingen Univ., studying medicine, July 1825-29. To Würzburg, 1829 ; degree of M.D. there, 1832. At Zurich, June 1835 to March 1840. To Berlin, 1841. In England, 1842 ; at various towns in Germany and Switzerland, 1844-46 ; in England, 1846-47 ; settled in Frankfort, June 1847. Died, in Basle Hospital, 26 Jan. 1849. Buried in Hospital cemetery.

Works : ' The Improvisatore,' 1821; ' The Bride's Tragedy,' 1822.

Posthumous: 'Death's Jest-Book, or the Fool's Tragedy,' 1850 ; 'Poems, Posthumous and Collected,' ed. by T. F. Kelsall (2 vols.), 1851 ; 'Poetical Works,' ed. by E. Gosse (2 vols.), 1890 ; 'Letters,' ed. by E. Gosse, 1894.

BEHN (*Mrs.* **Aphra**), **1640-1689**. Born [Aphra Johnson], at Wye, Kent, 10 July 1640. Taken to West Indies early in Life. Returned to England, 1658. Married to —— Behn, 1660 [?]. In favour with Charles II. ; sent by him on secret service to Antwerp, 1665. On return to England took to playwriting. First play produced at Duke's Theatre, 1671. Various plays produced, 1671-78, 1681-87. Died, in London, 16 April, 1689. Buried in Westminster Abbey.

Works : 'The Forc'd Marriage,' 1671 ; 'The Amorous Prince,' 1671 ; 'The Dutch Lover,' 1673 ; 'Abdelazar,' 1677 ; 'The Rover,' pt. i. (anon.), 1677 ; pt. ii., 1681 ; 'The Debauchee' (anon.), 1677 ; 'The Town Fop,' 1677 ; 'Sir Patient Fancy,' 1678; 'The Feign'd Curtizans,' 1679 ; 'The Roundheads,' 1682; 'The City Heiress,' 1682 ; 'The False Count,' 1682 ; 'The Young King,' 1683 ; 'Poems upon several occasions,' 1684 ; 'The Adventures of the Black Lady,' 1684 ; two 'Pindarick Poems' and a poem to the Queen Dowager, 1685 ; 'La Montre,' 1686 ; 'Emperor of the Moon,' 1687 ; 'The Lucky Chance,' 1687 ; 'Lycidus,' 1688 ; 'A Poem to Sir Roger L'Estrange,' 1688 ; Three 'Congratulatory Poems' to the Queen, 1688 ; 'The Lucky Mistake,' 1689 ; ' Congratulatory Poem ' to the Queen, 1689.

Posthumous : 'The Widow Ranter,' ed. by "G. J.," 1690 ; 'The Younger

Brother,' ed. by Gildon, 1696 ; 'The Lady's Looking Glass,' 1697.

She *translated :* (with others) Ovid's 'Heroical Epistles,' 1683 ; Fontenelle's 'Discovery of New Worlds,' 1688; Van Dale's 'History of Oracles,' 1699 ; and *edited* 'Miscellany,' 1685.

Collected Works: 'Poetical Remains,' ed. by Gildon, 1698 ; 'Histories and Novels,' 1698 ; 'Plays,' 1702 ; 'Plays, Histories and Novels . . . with Life' (6 vols.), 1871.

BELL (Acton). *See* Brontë (Anne).

BELL (Currer). *See* Brontë (Charlotte).

BELL (Ellis). *See* Brontë (Emily Jane).

BENTHAM (Jeremy), **1748-1832**. Born, in Houndsditch, 15 Feb. 1748. Precocious ability in early years. At Westminster School, 1755-60. To Queen's Coll., Oxford, 28 June 1760 ; B.A., 1763 ; M.A., 1766. Visit to France, 1764. Called to Bar at Lincoln's Inn, 1772. Devoted himself to literary work. Visit to his brother at Zadobras, in Russia, Aug. 1785. Removed from London to Ford Abbey, near Chard, 1814. Interest in political and national affairs. Provided funds for starting the 'Westminster Review,' 1823. Abroad for health same year. Died, 6 June 1832. Left his body to be dissected. Skeleton preserved in University College.

Works: Between 70 and 80 works by Bentham were published between 1775 and 1832. His 'Collected Works' (11 vols.) were edited by Sir John Bowring, 1838-43. Some of the more important are : 'A Fragment on Government' (anon.), 1776 ; 'Introduction to the Principles of Morals and Legislation,' 1780 ; 'Panopticon,' 1791 ; 'Plan of Parliamentary Reform,' 1817 ; 'Codification and Public Instruction,' 1817. Several of Bentham's works were translated into French by Dumont, in some cases from Bentham's unpublished MSS.

Life : by Bowring, in 1838 edn. of Works.

BENTLEY (Richard), 1662-1742. Born, at Oulton, near Wakefield, 27 Jan. 1662. Educated at a day school near Oulton ; at Wakefield Grammar School, 1673-76. To St. John's Coll., Cambridge, as subsizar, 24 May 1676 ; matriculated, 6 July 1676 ; Dowman Scholar, 4 Nov. 1678 ; Constable Scholarship, 1679; B.A., 1680 ; M.A., July 1683. Master of School at Spalding for short time in 1682. Private tutor to son of Dr. Stillingfleet, 1682-89. Went to reside in Oxford, 1689. Ordained Chaplain to Dr. Stillingfleet, 16 March 1690. First Boyle Lecturer, 1692. Prebend of Worcester, 1692. Keeper of Royal Libraries, 1694. F.R.S., 1694. Chaplain in Ordinary to King, 1695. D.D., Oxford, July 1696. To official residence as Royal Librarian, in St. James's Palace, 1696. Active part in restoring Cambridge University Press. Appointed Master of Trinity Coll., Cambridge, 1 Feb. 1700. Married Joanna Bernard, 1701. Had four children. Tried before Bishop of Ely for unconstitutional practices as Master of Trinity, 1714. Bishop of Ely died before giving judgment, so trial lapsed. Deprived of degrees by University, having failed to appear in Vice-Chancellor's Court to answer suit of Conyers Middleton respecting fees, 1718. Degrees restored, 26 Mar. 1724. Again tried before Bishop of Ely for proceedings as Master of Trinity, 1733. Deprived of Mastership, 27 April 1734. Execution of sentence prevented by action of Bentley's friends. Paralytic stroke, 1739. Wife died, 1740. He died, 14 July 1742. Buried in Trinity Coll. Chapel.

Works : 'Letter to Mill' (as appendix to the 'Chronicle of Malala'), 1691 ; "The Folly and Unreasonableness of Atheism' (Boyle Lectures), 1693 ; 'Of Revelation and the Messias,' 1696 ; 'A Proposal for building a Royal Library,' 1697 ; 'Dissertation upon the Letters of Phalaris' (in second edn. of Dr. Wotton's 'Reflections upon Ancient and Modern Learning'), 1697 ; ex-

panded edition, pub. separately, with answer to C. Boyle, 1699 ; 'Emendationes in Menandri et Philemonis Reliquias' (under pseud. of 'Phileleutherus Lipsiensis'), 1710 ; 'The Present State of Trinity College,' 1710 ; 'Remarks upon a late discourse of Free-thinking' (anon.), 1713 ; 'A Sermon upon Popery,' 1715 ; 'A Sermon preached before Her Majesty,' 1717 ; 'Proposals for printing a new edition of the Greek Testament' (anon.), 1721 ; 'Emendations on the twelve books of Paradise Lost,' 1732.

Posthumous : ' 'Opuscula Philologica,' 1781 ; 'R. Bentleii et doctorum virorum Epistolæ,' 1807 ; 'Correspondence,' ed. by C. Wordsworth (2 vols.), 1842 ; 'Critica Sacra,' ed. by A. A. Ellis, 1862.

He *edited :* Malala, 1691 ; Callimachus, 1692 ; Cicero ('Tusculan Disputations '), 1709 ; Aristophanes, 1710 ; Horace, 1711 ; Terence, 1726 ; Milton ('Paradise Lost'), 1732. He also at various times annotated : Antigonus, Lucan, Lucretius, Nicander, Ovid, Phædrus, Philostratus, Plautus and Suetonius.

Collected Works : ed. by Dyce (3 vols.), 1836-38.

Life : by J. H. Monk (2nd edn.), 1833 ; by Prof. Jebb (' English Men of Letters ' series), 1882.

BERKELEY (George), *Bishop of Cloyne.* 1685-1753. Born, in County Kilkenny, 12 March 1685. To Kilkenny School, 17 July 1696. To Trinity Coll., Dublin, 21 Mar. 1700 ; Scholar, 1702 ; B.A., 1704 ; M.A., 1707 ; Fellowship, 9 June 1707 ; Tutor of College, 1707-24 ; Sub-lecturer, 1710 ; Junior Dean, 1710 and 1711 ; Junior Greek Lecturer, 1712 ; Divinity Lecturer and Senior Greek Lecturer, 1721 ; B.D. and D.D., 14 Nov. 1721 ; Hebrew Lecturer and Senior Proctor, 1722. Visit to England, 1713. Contrib. to 'The Guardian,' Mar. and Aug. 1713. Chaplain to Lord Peterborough on embassy to King of Sicily, Nov. 1713 to summer of 1714. In London, 1715-16. Abroad

1716-20 (as travelling tutor, Nov. 1716-18). To London, 1720. To Ireland, as chaplain to Lord - Lieutenant, 1721. Legacy left him by Hester Vanhomrigh, 1723. Dean of Derry, May, 1724. In London with project for Missionary College in America, 1724-28. Charter for College obtained, June 1725. Married Anne Forster, 1 Aug. 1728. To America, 4 Sept. 1728. Remained there till 1731. Scheme failed, owing to impossibility of obtaining promised grant from English Govt. In London, 1732-34. Consecrated Bishop of Cloyne, 19 May 1734. At Cloyne, 1734-52. Retired and went to England, Aug. 1752. Lived in Oxford, 1752-53 ; died there, 14 Jan. 1753 ; buried at Ch. Ch.

Works : 'Arithmetica absque Algebra aut Euclide demonstrata,' 1707 ; 'Mathematica' (anon.), 1707 ; 'Essay towards a new theory of Vision,' 1709 (2nd edn. same year) ; 'Treatise concerning the Principles of Human Knowledge,' 1710 ; 'Passive Obedience,' 1712 (2nd edn. same year) ; 'Three Dialogues between Hylas and Philonous,' 1713 ; 'De Motu,' 1721 ; 'Essay towards preventing the Ruin of Great Britain' (anon.), 1721 ; 'Proposal for the better Supplying of Churches in our Foreign Plantations' (anon.), 1725 ; 'Sermon before Soc. for Propagation of Gospel,' 1732 ; 'Alciphron' (anon.), 1732 (2nd edn. same year) ; 'Theory of Vision . . . vindicated and explained' (anon.), 1733 ; 'The Analyst' (anon.), 1734 ; 'A Defence of Free-thinking in Mathematics' (anon.), 1735 ; 'Reasons for not replying to Mr. Walton's Full Answer, etc.' (anon.), 1735 ; 'The Querist,' 1735-37 ; 'A Discourse addressed to Magistrates' (anon.), 1736 ; 'A Chain of Philosophical Reflections . . . concerning the virtues of Tar-Water, etc.,' 1744 (2nd and 3rd edns. same year ; 4th, 1746 ; 5th, 1748 ; all of these under the title of 'Siris') ; 'Letter to Thomas Prior' [on the virtues of tar-water] (anon.), 1744 ; 'Letter to the Roman Catholics of the Diocese of Cloyne,' 1745 ; Second Letter to Thomas Pryor, 1746 (the first and second letters together, as appx. to Prior's 'Authentick Narrative,' 1746) ; 'Two Letters, the one to T. Prior . . . the other to Dr. Hales' [on the virtues of tar-water], 1747 ; 'A Word to the Wise' (anon.), 1749 ; 'Maxims concerning Patriotism,' 1750 ; 'Further Thoughts on Tar-Water,' in 'Bentley's Miscellany,' 1752 ; 'A Miscellany containing several tracts on various subjects,' 1752.

Posthumous : Letter (written 1741) to Sir J. James on the Roman Catholic Controversy, 1850.

Collected Works : in 2 vols., ed. by J. Stock, 1784 ; in 2 vols., ed. by G. N. Wright, 1843 ; complete edn., with *life* by Prof. Fraser, 1871.

*BESANT (*Sir* Walter), b. 1836. Born, at Portsmouth, 14 Aug. 1836. At King's Coll., London, 1854-55. To Christ's Coll., Cambridge, 1855 ; B.A., 1859 ; M.A., 1863. Senior Professor in Royal Coll. of Mauritius, 1860-68. Sec. to Palestine Exploration Fund, 1868-86 (Hon. Sec., 1886). Collaborated with James Rice, 1871-82. Trustee to People's Palace, 1887-91. Chairman of Committee Incorporated Society of Authors, 1887-92. Editor of 'The Author' (first published 1890). Hon. Treasurer Home Arts Association, 1888-1896. Knighted, 1895. Resides in Hampstead.

Works : 'Studies in Early French Poetry,' 1868 ; 'Ready-Money Mortiboy' (with J. Rice ; anon.), 1871 ; 'Jerusalem' (with E. H. Palmer), 1871 ; 'When George the Third was King,' 1872 ; 'The French Humourists,' 1873 ; 'My Little Girl' (with Rice ; anon.), 1873 ; 'With Harp and Crown' (with Rice ; anon.), 1875 ; 'The Golden Butterfly' (with Rice ; anon.), 1876 ; 'This Son of Vulcan' (with Rice ; anon.), 1876 ; 'Our Villas' (with Rice), 1877 ; 'The Case of Mr. Lucraft' (with Rice ; anon.), 1877 ; 'Book of French,' 1877 ; 'The Monks of Thelema' (with Rice), 1878 ; 'By Celia's Arbour' (with Rice), 1878 ;

'Constantinople' (with W. J. Brod-ribb), 1879 ; ''Twas in Trafalgar Bay' (with Rice), 1879 ; 'Gaspard de Coligny,' 1879 ; 'Rabelais,' 1879 ; 'The Seamy Side' (with Rice), 1880 ; 'Sir Richard Whittington' (with Rice), 1881 ; 'The Ten Years' Tenant' (with Rice), 1881 ; 'The Chaplain of the Fleet' (with Rice), 1881 ; 'The Revolt of Man' (anon.), 1882 ; 'All Sorts and Conditions of Men,' 1882 ; 'Readings in Rabelais,' 1883 ; 'All in a Garden Fair,' 1883 ; 'Life of E. H. Palmer,' 1883 ; 'The Captain's Room,' 1883 ; 'Life in a Hospital' (from 'Gentleman's Magazine'), 1883; 'The Art of Fiction,' 1884 ; 'Dorothy Forster,' 1884 ; 'Uncle Jack,' 1885 ; Report of Palestine Exploration Fund Work, 1865 to 1866 (under initials : W. B.), 1886 ; 'Children of Gibeon,' 1886 ; 'Katherine Regina,' 1887 ; 'The World went very well then,' 1887 ; 'The Eulogy of Richard Jefferies,' 1888 ; 'Fifty Years Ago,' 1888 ; 'Herr Paulus,' 1888 ; 'The Inner House,' 1888 ; 'For Faith and Free-dom,' 1889 ; 'The Bell of St. Paul's,' 1889 ; 'To Call her Mine,' 1889 ; 'Armorel of Lyonesse,' 1890 ; 'Cap-tain Cook,' 1890 ; 'The Demoniac,' 1890 ; 'The Holy Rose,' 1890 ; 'The Literary Handmaid of the Church,' 1890 ; 'St. Katherine's by the Tower,' 1891 ; 'The Ivory Gate,' 1892 ; 'London,' 1892 ; 'Verbena Camellia Stephanotis,' 1892; 'The Rebel Queen,' 1893 ; 'The History of London,' 1893; 'Beyond the Dreams of Avarice,' 1895 ; 'In Deacon's Orders,' 1895 ; 'Westminster,' 1895 ; 'The City of Refuge,' 1896 ; 'The Charm ; and other drawing-room plays' (with W. Pollock), 1896.

He has *edited :* Drake's 'Literary Remains,' 1877 ; Stewart's 'Local Examination Series' (with R. J. Griffiths), 1877 ; Conder's 'Survey of Western Palestine,' 1881-83 ; Collins' 'Blind Love,' 1890 ; 'Hake's 'Suffering London,' 1892 ; 'Dorothy Wallis,' 1892 ; Read's 'The Cloister and the Hearth,' 1893 ; Hayne's 'Man - Hunting in the Desert,' 1894.

*BIRRELL (Augustine), b. 1850. Born, at Wavertree, near Liverpool, 19 Jan. 1850. Educated at Amer-sham Hall School. Matric., London Univ., 1866. To Trinity Hall, Cam-bridge, 1869 ; B.A., 1872. Student at Inner Temple, 17 Jan. 1873 ; called to Bar, 17 Nov. 1875 ; practises in Chancery Division. Married Mar-garet Louisa Merrielees, 21 Aug. 1878 ; she died, 1879. Married Mrs. Eleanor Tennyson, 1888. M.P. for West Fife, 1889, 1892 and 1895. Q.C., 1894.

Works : 'Obiter Dicta,' 1st series (anon.), 1884 ; 2nd series, 1887 ; 'Life of Charlotte Brontë,' 1887 ; 'Res Judicatæ,' 1892 ; 'Essays about Men, Women and Books,' 1894 ; 'The Duties and Liabilities of Trustees,' 1896.

He has *edited :* Lamb's 'Essays of Elia,' 1888 ; Locker-Lampson's 'My Confidences,' 1896 ; 'Borrow's 'La-vengro,' 1896.

*BLACK (William), b. 1841. Born, at Glasgow, 15 Nov. 1841. Educated at private schools. Studied at Glasgow School of Art. Contrib. to 'Glasgow Weekly Citizen.' First married, 1862. To London, 1864. Joined staff of 'Morning Star,' 1865. War corre-spondent during Austro-Prussian War, 1866. For a time assistant editor of 'Daily News.'

Works : 'James Merle,' 1864 ; 'Love or Marriage ?' 1868 ; 'In Silk Attire,' 1869 ; 'Kilmeny,' 1870 ; 'Mr. Pisistratus Brown, M.P., in the High-lands' (from 'Daily News '; anon.), 1871 ; 'The Monarch of Mincing Lane,' 1871 ; 'A Daughter of Heth' (anon.), 1871 ; 'Strange Adventures of a Phaeton,' 1872 ; 'Princess of Thule,' 1873 ; 'Maid of Killeena,' 1874 ; 'Three Feathers,' 1875 ; 'Mad-cap Violet,' 1876 ; 'Lady Silverdale's Sweetheart,' 1876 ; 'Green Pastures and Piccadilly,' 1877 ; 'Macleod of Dare,' 1878 ; 'Goldsmith,' 1879 ; 'White Wings,' 1880 ; 'Sunrise,' 1880 ; 'The Beautiful Wretch: The Four Macnicols : The Pupil of Aurelius,' 1881 ('The Four Mac-nicols' separately, 1882) ; 'Adven-

tures in Thule,' 1883 ; 'Yolande,'
1883 ; 'Shandon Bells,' 1883; 'Judith
Shakespeare,' 1884 ; 'White Heather,'
1885 ; 'Wise Women of Inverness,'
1885 ; 'Sabrina Zembra,' 1887 ;
'Strange Adventures of a House-
Boat,' 1888 ; 'In Far Lochaber,'
1888 ; 'Nanciebel,' 1889 ; 'The
Penance of John Logan,' 1889 ; 'The
New Prince Fortunatus,' 1890 ;
'Donald Ross of Heimra,' 1891 ;
'Stand Fast, Craig-Royston,' 1891 ;
'Wolfenberg,' 1892 ; 'The Magic
Ink,' 1892 ; 'The Handsome Humes,'
1893 ; 'Highland Cousins,' 1894 ;
'Briseis,' 1896.

**BLACKIE (John Stuart), 1809-
1895.** Born, in Glasgow, 28 July
1809. Family removed to Aberdeen
same year. Educated first at New
Academy in Aberdeen. At Marischal
College, 1821-24. Studied law for
few months, 1824. At Edinburgh
University, 1825-26. Returned home.
Student at Aberdeen University,
1826-29. At Göttingen University,
May to Oct. 1829. At Berlin, Oct.
1829 to March 1830. In Italy, April
1830 to Sept. 1831. To London, Oct.
1831 ; thence home for six months.
Began to study law in Edinburgh,
1832. Member of Faculty of Advocates, 1 July 1834. Translation of
'Faust' pub. 1834. Began to contrib. to 'Blackwood' and 'Foreign
Quarterly Review,' 1835. Appointed
first Regius Professor of Humanity at
Marischal College, May 1839. Difficulties in way of installation, owing to
action of Presbytery on his refusing
to sign unreservedly the Confession of
Faith ; in Edinburgh, mainly in connection with this, 1839-41. Contrib.
to 'Blackwood,' 'Foreign Quarterly,'
'Tait's Mag.,' etc. Installed at Aberdeen, 1 Nov. 1841. Married Eliza
Wyld, 19 April 1842. Activity respecting Test Act and Education in
Scotland. Visit to London, May
1848 ; to Oxford, June 1848 ; to
Germany, 1851. Appointed Prof. of
Greek in Edinburgh University, 2
Mar. 1852. Removed to Edinburgh
same month. Visit to Greece, 1853 ;

Contrib. to 'Edinburgh Essays,'
1856-57. To Cambridge, 1858. Visit
to Germany and Russia, 1871. Began to promote scheme of Celtic
Chair, 1874. Lecturing tour in
Wales, 1877. Visit to Egypt, 1878 ;
to Italy, 1879. Retired from Greek
Chair owing to ill-health, Oct. 1882.
Celtic Chair inaugurated by Prof.
Mackinnon's Appointment, Dec. 1882.
Presented with Silver Cup by Hellenic
Society, Mar. 1890. Visit to Turkey
and Greece, 1891. Arranged bequest
to provide Greek Travelling Scholarship at Edinburgh University, 1894.
Died 2 Mar. 1895. Buried in Edin-
burgh Cathedral.

Works: 'Intorno un Sarcofago,' 1831;
'On Subscription to Articles of Faith,'
1843 ; 'University Reform,' 1848 ;
'The Water Cure in Scotland,' 1849 ;
'The Pronunciation of Greek,' 1852 ;
'On the Studying and Teaching of Lan-
guages,' 1852 ; 'Classical Literature,'
1852 ; 'On the Living Language of
the Greeks,' 1853 ; Report on Greek
Classes in Edinburgh Univ. [1853];
'On the Advancement of Learning
in Scotland,' 1855 ; 'Lays and Legends
of Ancient Greece,' 1857 ; 'On Beauty,'
1858 ; 'Lyrical Poems,' 1860 ; 'The
Gaelic Language,' 1864 ; Translation
of Homer, 1866 ; 'On Forms of
Government,' 1867 ; 'Debate with
E. Jones on Democracy,' 1867 ;
'Political Tracts' ('On Government,'
'On Education'), 1868 ; 'Musa
Burschicosa,' 1869 ; 'War Songs of
the Germans,' 1870 ; 'Four Phases of
Morals,' 1871 ; 'Greek and English
Dialogues,' 1871 ; 'Lays of the High-
lands and Islands,' 1872 ; 'Horæ Hel-
lenicæ,' 1874 ; 'On Self-Culture,' 1874;
'The Language and Literature of
the Scottish Highlands,' 1876 ; 'Songs
of Religion and Life,' 1876 [1875];
'The Natural History of Atheism,'
1877 ; 'The Wise Men of Greece,'
1877 ; 'The Egyptian Dynasties,'
1879 ; 'Gaelic Societies, etc.,' 1880 ;
'Lay Sermons,' 1881 ; 'Altavona,'
1882; 'The Wisdom of Goethe,' 1883 ;
'The Scottish Highlanders and the
Land Laws,' 1885 ; 'What Does
History Teach ?' 1886; 'Gleanings of

Song from a Happy Life,' 1886 ;
' Messis Vitæ,' 1886 ; 'Life of Robert
Burns' (in 'Great Writers' series),
1888 ; ' Letter to the People of Scot-
land,' 1888 ; 'Scottish Song,' 1889 ;
'Essays on Subjects of Moral and
Social Interest,' 1890 ; ' A Song of
Heroes,' 1890 ; 'Greek Primer,' 1891 ;
'Christianity and the Ideal of Hu-
manity,' 1893.

He *translated:* Goethe's 'Faust,'
1834 ; Æschylus, 1850 ; and wrote
prefaces to Clyde's ' Greek Syntax,'
1856 ; C. Blackie's 'Etymological
Geography,' 1875 ; Vincent and Dickson's ' Handbook to Modern Greek,'
1879 ; the 'Còmhraidhean 'an Gaelig's
'am Beurla,' 1880 ; Locke's 'Thoughts
Concerning Education,' 1886 ; Bacon's
'Essays,' 1886 ; Crockett's 'Minstrelsy
of the Merse,' 1893.

Life: by A. M. Stoddart (2 vols.),
1895 ; biographical sketch, by H. A.
Kennedy, 1895.

*BLACKMORE (Richard Doddridge),
b. 1825.* Born, at Longworth, Berkshire, 7 June 1825. Educated at
Tiverton Grammar School. Matric.
Exeter Coll., Oxford, 7 Dec. 1843 ;
B.A., 2 Dec. 1847 ; M.A., 1852. Student of Middle Temple, 27 Jan. 1849 ;
called to Bar, 7 June 1852. Life spent
in literary pursuits.

Works: 'Poems by Melanter,'
1854 ; 'Epullia' (anon.), 1855 ; 'The
Bugle of the Black Sea ' (under pseud.
of Melanter), 1855 ; 'The Fate of
Franklin,' 1860 ; 'Clara Vaughan'
(anon.), 1864 ; 'Cradock Nowell,'
1866 ; 'Lorna Doone,' 1869 ; 'The
Maid of Sker,' 1872 ; 'Alice Lorraine,'
1875 ; ' Cripps the Carrier,' 1876 ;
' Erema,' 1877 ; 'Mary Anerley,' 1880 ;
' Christowell,' 1882 ; 'The Remarkable
History of Sir Thomas Upmore,' 1884 ;
'Springhaven,' 1887 ; 'Kit and Kitty,'
1890 [1889] ; ' Perlycross,' 1894 ;
'Tales from the Telling House,' 1896.

He has *translated:* Virgil's Georgics,
Bks. I., II., under title of 'The Farm
and Fruit of Old,' 1862 ; Georgics
(complete), 1871.

*BLACKSTONE (Sir William), 1723-
1780.* Born, in London, 10 July 1723.

To Charterhouse, 1730 ; admitted on
Foundation, 1735. To Pembroke Coll.,
Oxford, 30 Nov. 1738. Entered at
Middle Temple, 20 Nov. 1741 ; called
to Bar, 28 Nov. 1746. Fellow of All
Souls, Oxford, Nov. 1744. B.C.L., 12
June 1745. Bursar of All Souls, 1747 ;
Steward of Manors, May 1749-59. Re-
corder of Borough of Wallingford,
Berks, 30 May 1749 to 1770. D.C.L.,
Oxford, 26 April 1750 ; Assessor of
Vice - Chancellor's Court, 1753-59 ;
Delegate of Clarendon Press, July
1755 ; Member of Queen's Coll., 1757 ;
First Vinerian Prof. of English Law,
10 Oct. 1758 to 1766. Married Sarah
Clitherow, 5 May 1761. M.P. for
Hindon, Wilts, 6 May 1761. Princi-
pal of New Inn Hall, Oxford, 28 July
1761 to 1766. Divided his time be-
tween Oxford and London. Solicitor-
General to the Queen, 1763. Bencher
of Middle Temple. M.P. for West-
bury, Wilts, 1768. Judge of Common
Pleas, 9 Feb. 1770. Knighted, 1770.
Died, in London, 14 Feb. 1780. Buried
in St. Peter's Church, Wallingford.

Works: 'Essay on Collateral Con-
sanguinity' (anon.), 1750 ; ' Analysis
of the Laws of England' (anon.), 1754 ;
'Letter to the Rev. Dr. Randolph,'
1757 ; 'Considerations on Copyholders,'
1758 ; ' A Discourse on the Study of
the Law,' 1758 ; 'The Great Charter
and Charter of the Forest,' 1759 ; ' A
Treatise on the Law of Descents in
Fee-simple,' 1759 ; 'Reflections on the
Opinions of Messrs. Pratt, Morton and
Wilbraham,' 1759 ; ' A Case for the
Opinion of Counsel,' 1759 ; ' Law
Tracts (2 vols.), 1762 ; ' Commentaries
on the Laws of England ' (4 vols.),
1765-69 (2nd. and 3rd. edns. of vols. i.-
ii., 1766) ; ' A Reply to Dr. Priestly's
Remarks,' 1769 ; ' The Wilkes Case :
an answer to the Question Stated '
(anon.), 1769.

Posthumous: 'Reports of Cases
Determined in . . . Westminster Hall,
1746-79 ' (2 vols.), 1781 (2nd edn. same
year).

Life : by Clitherow, in 1813 edn. of
' Commentaries.'

BLAKE (William), 1757-1827.

Born, in London, 28 Nov. 1757. To drawing school, 1767. Began to write verse, 1768. Apprenticed to J. Basire, engraver to Soc. of Antiquaries, 1771-78. Student in Royal Academy, 1778. Engraved for magazines and books. Married Catharine Sophia Boucher, 18 Aug. 1782. Opened printseller's shop in Broad Street, 1784. Exhibited at R.A. same year. Shop given up, 1787. At Felpham, 1800-04. Returned to London. Exhibited for last time at R.A. 1808. Died, 12 Aug. 1827. Buried at Bunhill Fields, Finsbury.

Works [all engraved and coloured by hand unless otherwise stated]: 'Poetical Sketches' (printed), 1783 ; 'Songs of Innocence' (with assistance of his wife), 1789 ; 'Book of Thel,' 1789; 'Marriage of Heaven and Hell,' 1790 ; 'French Revolution' (printed), 1791 ; 'Prospectus,' 1793 ; 'Gates of Paradise,' 1793 ; 'Visions of the Daughters of Albion,' 1793 ; 'America,' 1793 ; 'Europe,' 1794 ; 'The Book of Urizen,' 1794 ; 'Songs of Experience,' 1794 ; 'The Song of Los,' 1795 ; 'The Book of Ahania,' 1795 ; 'Jerusalem,' 1804 ; 'Milton,' 1804 ; 'Descriptive Catalogue' (printed), 1809.

Collected Works : Poems, edited by R. H. Shepherd, 1868 ; by W. M. Rossetti (Aldine Series), 1874 ; Works, in facsimile of original editions, 1876.

Life : by Gilchrist, 2nd ed. 1880.

BLIND (Mathilde), 1841 - 1891. Born, 21 March 1841. Educated mainly in London and Zurich. Contrib. to 'Westminster Review,' 1870. Friendship with Mazzini. Contrib. to 'Athenæum,' 'Examiner,' 'Dark Blue,' 'Fraser's Mag.,' 'Woman's World,' 'Fortnightly Review.' Lectured on position of women ; and travelled extensively in Southern Europe and Egypt. Lived mainly in London. Died, in London, 26 Nov. 1896.

Works : 'Poems' (under pseud. of Claude Lake), 1867 ; 'Shelley,' 1870 ; 'The Prophecy of St. Oran,' 1881 ; 'George Eliot,' 1883 ; 'Tarantella,' 1885 [1884]; 'Shelley's View of Nature' (privately printed), 1886 ;

'Madame Roland,' 1886 ; 'The Heather on Fire,' 1886 ; 'The Ascent of Man,' 1888 ; 'Dramas in Miniature,' 1891 ; 'Birds of Passage,' 1895.

She *translated :* Strauss's 'The Old Faith and the New,' 1873 ; Marie Bashkirtseff's 'Journal,' 1890 ; and *edited :* Shelley's Selected Poems, 1872 ; Byron's Poems, 1886 ; Byron's 'Letters and Journals,' 1886.

*BLUNT (Wilfrid Scawen), b. 1840. Born, at Petworth House, Sussex, 17 Aug. 1840. Educated at Stonyhurst Coll. (for 8 months), 1853 ; at St. Mary's Coll., Oscott, 1855-58. Entered Diplomatic Service, 13 Dec. 1858. Attaché at the Hague, 31 Jan. 1859 ; to Athens, 10 Feb. 1859 ; to Frankfort, 13 Aug. 1860 ; to Madrid, 5 Aug. 1862 (3rd Sec., 31 Dec. 1863); to Paris, 13 July 1864 ; to Lisbon, 10 June 1865 ; to Frankfort, 30 Oct. 1865 ; to Buenos Ayres (as 2nd Sec.), 28 Jan. 1867 ; to Berne, 6 April 1869. Married Lady Anne Isabella Noel, 8 June 1869. Left Diplomatic Service, 31 Dec. 1869. Travelled in Spain, Egypt, and Palestine. Supported cause of Arabi Pasha, 1882. To Ireland, to take part in Anti-Coercion Movement, 1887. Imprisoned in Galway and Kilmainham gaols for calling public meeting in proclaimed district of Woodford, 1888. Winters since then spent in Egypt. Resides in Sussex.

Works : 'Sonnets and Songs by Proteus' (anon.), 1875 ; 'Proteus and Amadeus' (correspondence with Aubrey de Vere), 1878 ; 'The Love Sonnets of Proteus' (anon.), 1881 ; 'The Future of Islam,' 1882 ; 'The Wind and the Whirlwind,' 1883 ; 'Ideas about India,' 1885 ; 'In Vinculis,' 1889 ; 'A New Pilgrimage,' 1889 ; 'Esther,' 1892 ; 'Love-Lyrics and Songs of Proteus' (Kelmscott Press), 1892.

He *translated :* Abu Zaid's 'Romance of the Stealing of the Mare,' 1892 ; and *edited :* Lady Blunt's 'Pilgrimage to Nejd,' 1881.

BOLINGBROKE, Viscount. *See* St. John.

BORROW (George Henry), 1803-1881. Born, at East Dereham, 5 July 1803. Educated at Norwich Grammar School, 1815-18. Family changed place of residence constantly, 1803-20. Articled to Solicitor in Norwich, 1818-23. First literary publication, 1825. To London at father's death. Assisted in compilation of ' Newgate Calendar.' Tour through England ; through France, Germany, Russia and the East, as agent for British and Foreign Bible Society, 1833 - 39. Contrib. letters on his travels to ' Morning Post,' 1837-39. Married Mary Clarke, 1840. Tour in S.E. Europe, 1844. Bought estate on Oulton Broad. Lived there till about 1865. Removed to Brompton. Wife died there, 1869. Died, at Oulton, 26 July 1881.

Works : ' Romantic Ballads ' (from the Danish), 1826 ; 'Targum,' 1835 ; ' The Bible in Spain ' (3 vols.), 1843 ; 'The Zincali ' (2 vols.), 1841 ; ' Lavengro,' 1851 ; ' The Romany Rye,' 1857 ; ' Wild Wales,' 1862 ; 'Romano Lavo-Lil,' 1874.

He *translated :* F. M. von Klinger's ' Faustus,' 1825 ; Pushkin's ' The Talisman,' 1835 ; St. Luke's Gospel into Gitano dialect, ' Embéo e Majoró Lucas,'1837; 'Crixote e Majoró Lucas,' 1872; Ellis Wynn's 'Sleeping Bard,' from the Cambrian - British, 1860 ; Nasr Al-Dín's ' Turkish Jester ' (posthumous), 1884 ; Ewald's 'Death of Balder ' (posthumous), 1889.

He *edited :* ' Evangelisa San Lucusan Guissan ' (Basque translation of St. Luke's Gospel), 1838.

BOSWELL (James), 1740 - 1795. Born, at Auchinleck, 29 Oct. 1740. Educated by private tutor ; then at private school in Edinburgh ; then at Edinburgh High School and Edinburgh Univ. To Glasgow as Student of Civil Law, 8 Jan. 1759. To London, March 1760. In Edinburgh, April 1761 to Nov. 1762 ; then returned to London. Contrib. poems to ' Collections of Original Poems by Mr. Blacklock,' 1762. First met Johnson, 16 May 1763. In Berlin, July 1764. To Italy, Dec. 1764.

To Utrecht, to study Law, Aug. 1765. Tour in Italy and Corsica. Returned to Scotland, Feb. 1766. Admitted Advocate, 26 July 1766. To London on publication of ' Account of Corsica,' May 1768. Married Margaret Montgomerie, 25 Nov. 1769. Contrib. to ' London Magazine,' 1769-70, 1777-79. Frequent visits to Johnson, mostly in London, between 1772 and 1784. Elected Member of Literary Club, 30 April 1773. Voyage to Hebrides with Johnson, Aug. to Nov., 1773. Began to keep terms at Inner Temple, 1775. Auchinleck estate entailed on him, 7 Aug. 1776. Father died, 30 Aug. 1782. Called to Bar, 1786. Appointed Recorder of Carlisle, 1788. Took chambers in Temple, 1790. ' Life of Johnson ' appeared, 16 May 1791. Appointed Secretary of Foreign Correspondence to Royal Academy, July 1791. Died, in London, 19 May 1795. Buried at Auchinleck.

Works : ' Ode to Tragedy ' (anon.), 1761 ; ' Elegy upon the Death of an amiable Young Lady' (anon.), 1761 ; ' The Cub at Newmarket ' (anon.), 1762 ; Correspondence with Hon. A. Erskine, 1763 ; ' Critical Strictures on Mallet's ' Elvira ' (with Erskine and Dempster), 1763 ; ' Speeches, Arguments and Determinations ' in the Douglas case (anon.), 1767 ; ' Essence of the Douglas Cause ' (anon.), 1767 ; 'Dorando,' 1767 ; Prologue for the Opening of Edinburgh Theatre, 1767 ; ' An Account of Corsica,' 1768 ; ' British Essays in favour of the Brave Corsicans,' 1769 ; ' Decision in the Cause of Hunter *v.* Donaldson,' 1774 ; ' A Letter to the People of Scotland on the Present State of the Nation,' 1783 ; ' Ode to Samuel Johnson to Mrs. Thrale ' (by Boswell; anon.), 1784 ; 'The Journal of a Tour to the Hebrides,' 1785 (2nd ed. same year); 'Letter to the People of Scotland on the alarming Attempt to infringe the Articles of Union,' 1786 ; ' The Celebrated Letter from Samuel Johnson, LL.D., to Philip Damer Stanhope, Earl of Chesterfield, 1790 ; ' Conversation between George III. and Samuel Johnson,' 1790 ; 'No

Abolition of Slavery' (probably suppressed), 1791 ; 'Life of Johnson,' 1791 (another edn., pirated, 1792 ; 2nd authorised edn., 1793) ; 'Principal Corrections and Additions to First Edition,' 1793.

Posthumous : 'Letters to Rev. J. W. Temple,' 1857 ; 'Boswelliana : the Common-place Book of J. Boswell,' published by Grampian Club, 1874.

Life : by P. Fitzgerald, 1891.

*BOYD (Andrew Kennedy Hutchinson), b. 1825. Born, at Auchinleck, Ayrshire, 3 Nov. 1825. Educated at King's Coll. School, London, Oct. 1840 to Oct. 1841. Admitted to Middle Temple, 1842. At King's Coll., London, Oct. 1843 to July 1844. To Glasgow Univ., Nov. 1844 ; B.A., April 1846. Ordained, 1851. Incumbent of Newton-on-Ayr, 18 Sept. 1851 to Jan. 1854 ; of Kirkpatrick-Irongray, Galloway, Jan. 1854 to April 1859 ; of St. Bernard's, Edinburgh, April 1859 to Sept. 1865. D.D., Edinburgh, April 1864. Incumbent of St. Andrews, Sept. 1865. Began literary career by contributing to 'Fraser's Magazine,' under initials 'A. K. H. B.' LL.D., St. Andrews, April 1889. Moderator of General Assembly of Church of Scotland, May 1890. Fellow of King's Coll., London, 1895.

Works : 'Recreations of a Country Parson,' 1st series, 1859 ; 2nd series, 1861 ; 3rd series, 1878 ; 'Leisure Hours in Town' (anon.), 1862 ; 'The Graver Thoughts of a Country Parson' (three series), 1862, 1864, 1875 ; 'The Commonplace Philosopher' (anon.), 1862 ; 'People of whom more might have been made,' 1863 ; 'Counsel and Comfort,' (anon.), 1863 ; 'The Autumn Holidays of a Country Parson' (under initials : A. K. H. B.), (anon.), 1864 ; 'Critical Essays of a Country Parson,' 1865 ; 'Sunday Afternoons,' etc. (anon.), 1866 ; 'Lessons of Middle Age' (anon.), 1868 ; 'The Place of Ritual,' 1869 ; 'Changed Aspects of Unchanged Truths' (anon.), 1869 ; 'Present - Day Thoughts' (anon.), 1871 ; 'Seaside Musings' (anon.),

1872 ; 'A Scotch Communion Sunday' (anon.), 1873 ; 'Landscapes, Churches and Moralists' (anon.), 1874 ; 'From a Quiet Place' (anon.), 1879 ; 'Our Little Life' (anon.), 1882 ; 2nd series, 1884 ; 'A Young Man' (anon.), 1884 ; 'Towards the Sunset' (anon.), 1883 ; 'What set him Right' (anon.), 1885 ; 'Our Homely Comedy and Tragedy' (anon.), 1887 ; 'East Coast Days and Memories' (anon.), 1887 ; 'The Best Last' (anon.), 1888 ; 'Church Life in Scotland,' 1890 ; 'The Mother of us All,' 1890 ; 'Twenty-five Years of St. Andrews,' 1882 ; 'St. Andrews and Elsewhere,' 1894 ; 'Occasional and Immemorial Days,' 1895 ; 'The Last Years of St. Andrews,' 1896.

He has *edited :* 'Labourers in the Vineyard,' 1862 ; Dr. Robertson's 'Pastoral Counsels,' 1867.

*BRADDON (Mary Elizabeth) [Mrs. John Maxwell], b. 1837. Born, in London, 1837. Early contrib. to periodicals. Editor of 'Belgravia,' 1866. 'Loves of Arcadia' produced at Strand Theatre, 1860. Married to John Maxwell, 1874. 'Married Beneath Him' produced, 1882. Editor of 'The Mistletoe Bough,' 1878.

Works : 'Garibaldi,' 1861 ; 'The Trail of the Serpent,' 1861 ; 'The Lady Lisle' 1862 [1861] ; 'Ralph the Bailiff' (anon.), 1862 ; 'The Captain of the Vulture,' 1862 ; 'Lady Audley's Secret,' 1862 ; 'Aurora Floyd,' 1863 ; 'Eleanor's Victory,' 1863 ; 'John Marchmont's Legacy' (anon.), 1863 ; 'Henry Dunbar' (anon.), 1864 ; 'The Doctor's Wife' (anon.) 1864 ; 'Only a Clod' (anon.), 1865 ; 'Sir Jasper's Tenant' (anon.), 1865 ; 'The Lady's Mile' (anon.), 1866 ; 'Rupert Godwin' (anon.), 1867 ; 'Circe' (under pseud. of Babington White), 1867 ; 'Birds of Prey' (anon.), 1867 ; 'Charlotte's Inheritance' (anon.), 1868 ; 'Dead-Sea Fruit' (anon.), 1868 ; 'Run to Earth' (anon.), 1868 ; 'Fenton's Quest' (anon.), 1871 ; 'The Lovels of Arden' (anon.), 1871 ; 'The Summer Tourist,' 1871 ; 'Robert Ainsleigh' (anon.), 1872 ; 'To the Bitter End' (anon.), 1872 ; 'Milly Darrell' (anon.), 1873 ;

'Strangers and Pilgrims' (anon.), 1873 ; 'Lucius Davoren' (anon.), 1873 ; 'Taken at the Flood' (anon.), 1874 ; 'Lost for Love' (anon.), 1874 ; 'A Strange World' (anon.), 1875 ; 'Hostages to Fortune' (anon.), 1875 ; 'Dead Men's Shoes' (anon.), 1876 ; 'Joshua Haggard's Daughter' (anon.), 1876 ; 'Put to the Test' (anon.), 1876 ; 'Weavers and Weft' (anon.), 1877 ; 'An Open Verdict' (anon.), 1878 ; 'Vixen' (anon.), 1879 ; 'The Cloven Foot' (anon.), 1879 ; 'The Story of Barbara' (anon.), 1880 ; 'Just as I am' (anon.), 1880 ; 'The Missing Witness,' 1880 ; 'Asphodel' (anon.), 1881 ; 'Boscastle, Cornwall' (from 'The World'), 1881 ; 'Mount Royal' (anon.), 1882 ; 'Dross,' 1882 ; 'Marjorie Daw,' 1882 ; 'Married Beneath Him,' 1882; 'Married in Haste,' 1883 ; 'The Golden Calf' (anon.), 1883 ; 'Phantom Fortune' (anon.), 1883 ; 'Flower and Weed,' 1884 ; 'Ishmael' (anon.), 1884 ; 'Wyllard's Weird' (anon.), 1885 ; 'Under the Red Flag,' 1886 ; 'One Thing Needful' (anon.), 1886 ; 'Mohawks' (anon.), 1886 ; 'Cut by the County,' 1887 ; 'Like and Unlike' (anon.), 1887 ; 'The Fatal Three' (anon.), 1888 ; 'The Day will Come' (anon.), 1889 ; 'One Life, One Love' (anon.), 1890 ; 'Gerard' (anon.), 1891 ; 'The Venetians' (anon.), 1891 ; 'All Along the River' (anon.), 1893 ; 'Thou Art the Man' (anon.), 1894 ; 'The Christmas Hirelings,' 1894 ; 'Sons of Fire,' 1895 ; 'London Pride,' 1896.

BREWSTER (*Sir* **David**), **1781-1868.** Born, at Jedburgh, 11 Dec. 1781. Educated at Jedburgh Grammar School. To Edinburgh Univ. to study for Church, 1793. Tutor in family of Capt. Horsbrugh of Pirn, 1799-1804. Hon. M.A., Edinburgh, 12 April 1800 ; Hon. M.A., Camb., 1807. Contrib. to 'Edinburgh Magazine' ; edited it from 1802 (from 1819-26 this was called the 'Edinburgh Philosophical Journal,' edited by Brewster and Prof. Jameson, 1819-24 ; from 1824-32 Brewster continued it alone as the 'Edinburgh Journal of Science'). Ordained, March 1804. Tutor in family of Gen. Diroon of Mount Annan, 1804-07. Hon. LL.D., Aberdeen, 1807. Fellow of Royal Soc. of Edinburgh, Jan. 1808. Edited 'Edinburgh Encyclopædia,' 1808-30. Visit to London, 1809. Married Juliet Macpherson (daughter of 'Ossian' Macpherson), 31 July 1810. Contrib. first paper to Royal Soc. of London, 1813. Tour abroad for health, 1814. F.R.S., 4 May 1815 ; Copley Medal, 1815 ; Rumford Medal, 1818. Prize for scientific discoveries from French Institute, 1816. Invented Kaleidoscope, 1816. M.I.C.E., 1820. Founded Royal Scottish Soc. of Arts, and became Director, 1821. Mem. of Royal Irish Acad. of Arts and Sciences, 1822. Corresponding Member of French Institute, 1825. Assisted in organizing British Association, 1831. Hanoverian Order of Guelph, and Knighthood, 1831. One of editors of 'London and Edinburgh Philosophical Mag.,' from 1832. Hon. D.C.L., Oxford, 21 June 1832. Hon. M.A., Trinity Coll., Cambridge, 1833. Annual grant of £100 from Government. Additional annual grant of £200, 1836. Principal of St. Andrew's University, Jan. 1838 to Oct. 1859. Took part in secession of 'Free Church' from Church of Scotland, 1843. In consequence, unsuccessful attempt to eject him from position in St. Andrew's Univ., 1844. Chevalier of Order of Merit, 1847 ; Foreign Assoc. of French Institute, 1849. Pres. of Peace Congress, London, July 1851. Contrib. to 'Edinburgh Review,' 'North British Review,' and 'Quarterly Review.' Wife died, 27 Jan. 1850. Abroad with daughter, April 1850. Pres. of British Association at Edinburgh, 1851. Married Jane Kirk Purnell, 26 March 1857. Vice-Chancellor of Edinburgh Univ., 28 Oct. 1859, till death. Hon. M.D., Berlin, 1860. Pres. of Royal Soc. of Edinburgh, 1864. Died, at Allerly, 10 Feb. 1868. Buried at Melrose Abbey.

Works : 'History of Free Masonry' (anon.), 1804 ; 'Examination of the Letter addressed to Principal Hill' (anon.), 1806 ; 'Treatise on New Philosophical Instruments,' 1813 ; 'On the Optical Properties of Sulphuret of Carbon' [1814] ; 'On a new species of Coloured Fringes,' 1815 ; 'On the action of Transparent Bodies,' 1815 ; 'Description of a New Darkening Glass,' 1815 ; 'On a new . . . property of Calcareous Spar,' 1816 ; 'On the Optical Properties of Muriate of Soda,' 1816 ; 'On the Effect of Compression, etc.,' 1818 ; 'On the Laws which regulate the distribution of the Polarising Force, etc.,' 1818 ; 'Treatise on the Kaleidoscope,' 1819 ; 'Edinburgh Encyclopædia,' 1830 ; 'Life of Sir Isaac Newton,' 1831 ; 'Treatise on Optics' (in Lardner's 'Cabinet Cyclopædia), 1831 ; 'Letters on Natural Magic,' 1832 ; 'Treatise on Magnetism' (reprinted from 'Encyclopædia Britannica'), 1837 ; 'The Martyrs of Science,' 1841 ; 'More Worlds than One,' 1854 ; 'Memoirs of the Life, Writings, and Discoveries of Sir Isaac Newton,' 1855 ; Contribution to 'The British Empire,' 1856 ; 'The Stereoscope,' 1856 ; 'Memorial on the new system of Dioptric Lights,' 1859 ; 'Reply to Messrs. D. and T. Stevenson's pamphlet on Lighthouses,' 1860.

He *edited :* Ferguson's 'Lectures on Select Subjects,' 1806 ; Robinson's 'System of Mechanical Philosophy,' 1822 ; Legendre's 'Elements of Geometry,' 1824 ; Euler's 'Letters,' 1846.

Life : by his daughter, Mrs. Gordon, (3rd edn.)1881.

* **BRIDGES (Robert Seymour), b. 1844.** Born, at Walmer, Kent, 23 Oct. 1844. At Eton Coll., 1854 to July 1863. Matric. Corpus Coll., Oxford, 19 Oct. 1863 ; B.A., 1867. Travelled abroad, and subsequently studied Medicine at St. Bartholomew's Hospital. First vol. of poems pub., 1873. M.B. and M.A., Oxford, 1874. For a time on staff of St. Bartholomew's Hospital, and of Children's Hos-

pital, Great Ormonde Street. Retired from practice, 1882; settled at Yattendon, Berks. Married Mary Monica Waterhouse, 3 Sept. 1884.

Works : 'Poems,' 1873 ; 'The Growth of Love' (anon.), 1876 (revised ed., anon., 1890) ; 'Carmen Elegiacum,' 1877 ; 'Poems' (anon.), 1879 ; 'Prometheus the Firegiver,' 1884 (privately printed, 1883) ; 'Poems' (selections from previous, with additions ; priv. ptd.), 1884 ; 'Eros and Psyche,' 1885 ; 'Eight Plays' (containing 'Nero,' pts. i., ii.; 'Palicio,' 'Return of Ulysses,' 'Christian Captives,' 'Achilles in Scyros,' 'Humours of the Court,' 'Feast of Bacchus'), 1885-94 ; 'Essay on the Elements of Milton's Blank Verse,' in H. C. Beeching's edn. of 'Paradise Lost,' 1887 ; 'Feast of Bacchus' (priv. ptd.), 1889 ; 'On the Prosody of Paradise Regained and Samson Agonistes' (anon.), 1889 ; 'Shorter Poems,' 1890 ; 'Eden,' 1891 ; 'Milton's Prosody,' 1893 ; 'John Keats' (priv. ptd.), 1895. He has *edited :* Keats' Poems, 1896.

* **BRONTË (Anne), 1820 - 1849.** Born, at Thornton, 1819 ; baptized 25 March, 1820. Early life spent at Haworth, near Bradford. Educated at Miss Wooler's school at Roehead, 1835-37. Governess, April 1839 to 1845. Published poems with her sisters, 1846. To Scarborough for health, 24 May 1849. Died there, 28 May 1849.

Works : Contribution to 'Poems : by Currer, Ellis and Acton Bell,' 1846 ; 'Agnes Grey,' 1847 ; 'The Tenant of Wildfell Hall,' 1848 ; both the latter under pseud. of 'Acton Bell.'

* **BRONTË (Charlotte), 1816-1855.** Born, at Thornton, 21 April 1815. Early life spent at Haworth. At School at Cowan's Bridge, Sept. 1824 to autumn of 1825. At Miss Wooler's school at Roehead, Jan. 1831 to 1832. Returned there as teacher, 29 July 1835 to spring of 1838. Situation as governess in 1839. At home, 1840. Governess, March to Dec. 1841. To school at Brussels with her sister Emily, Feb. 1842. Returned to

Haworth, Nov. 1842. Returned to Brussels school as teacher, Jan. 1843. Returned to Haworth 2 Jan. 1844. Published poems with her sisters, 1846. 'Jane Eyre' published, 1847. Visits to London: with Emily, June 1848; Nov. 1849 (when she made acquaintance of Thackeray); 1850; 1851; 1853. Married to Arthur Nicholls, 29 June 1854. Visited Ireland with her husband, and returned with him to Haworth. Died there, 31 March 1855.

Works: Contrib. to 'Poems: by Currer, Ellis and Acton Bell,' 1846; 'Jane Eyre,' 1847; 'Shirley,' 1849; 'Villette,' 1853; all under pseudonym of Currer Bell.

Posthumous: 'The Professor: by Currer Bell,' 1857; 'Emma' (a fragment), pub. in 'Cornhill Magazine,' April 1860.

She *edited* (under pseud. of 'Currer Bell') a new edition of 'Wuthering Heights, and Agnes Grey,' with selections and prefaces, 1850.

Collected Works: with those of her sisters Anne and Emily (7 vols.), 1872-73.

Life: by Mrs. Gaskell, 4th edn., 1858; by Clement K. Shorter, 1896.

*BRONTË (Emily Jane), 1818-1848. Born, at Thornton, 1818; baptized 20 Aug. Early life spent at Haworth. At School at Cowan's Bridge, Sept. 1824 to autumn of 1825. At Miss Wooler's school at Roehead, July to October, 1835. Returned to Haworth. Teacher for six months at a school in Halifax, 1836. To school at Brussels with her sister Charlotte, Feb. 1842. Returned to Haworth at end of same year. Published poems with her sisters, 1846. Visit to London with her sister Charlotte, June 1848. Died, at Haworth, 19 Dec. 1848.

Works: Contrib. to 'Poems: by Acton, Currer and Ellis Bell,' 1846; 'Wuthering Heights' (under pseud. of Ellis Bell), 1847.

*BROUGHTON (Rhoda), b. 1840. Born at Segrwyd Hall, Derbyshire, 29 Nov. 1840. Early life spent there. First novel pubd. as serial in 'Dublin University Mag.,' 1865. Twelve years recently spent in Oxford. Resides at Richmond.

Works: 'Not Wisely, but Too Well' (anon.), 1867; 'Cometh up as a Flower' (anon.), 1867; 'Red as a Rose is She' (anon.), 1870; 'Good-Bye, Sweetheart,' 1872; 'Tales for Christmas Eve,' 1872 (another edn., entitled 'Twilight Stories,' 1876); 'Nancy,' 1873; 'Joan,' 1876; 'Second Thoughts,' 1880; 'Belinda,' 1883; 'Betty's Visions,' 1886; 'Doctor Cupid,' 1886; 'Alas!' 1890; 'A Widower Indeed' (with E. Bisland), 1891; 'Mrs. Bligh,' 1892; 'A Beginner,' 1894; 'Scylla or Charybdis,' 1895.

BROWN (John), 1810-1882. Born, at Biggar, Lanarkshire, 22 Sept. 1810. At private school in Edinburgh, 1822 - 24; at High School, 1824-26. To Edinburgh Univ., Nov. 1826. Began to study medicine, May 1827. Apprenticed to James Syme, surgeon, 1828-33. M.D., Edinburgh, 1833. Started practice in Edinburgh, where he lived till his death. Married Catharine Scott M'Kay, 4 June 1840; she died 6 Jan. 1864. F.R.C.P., 1847. Fellow of Roy. Soc. of Edinburgh, 1859. Assessor to Rector of Edinburgh Univ., 1861-62. Hon. LL.D., Edinburgh, 22 April 1874. Crown Pension, 1874. Died, in Edinburgh, 11 May 1882. Buried in New Calton cemetery.

Works: 'Horæ Subsecivæ,' ser. i., 1858; ser. ii., 1861; ser. iii., 1882; 'Rab and his Friends' (extracted from preceding), 1859; 'On the deaths of Rev. J. M'Gilchrist, J. Brown, J. Henderson,' 1860; 'With Brains, Sir!' (anon.), 1860; 'Health,' 1862; 'Marjorie Fleming' (from 'North Brit. Rev.'), 1863; 'Jeems, the Doorkeeper,' 1864; 'Minchmoor,' 1864; 'Thackeray,' 1877; 'John Leech,' 1877; 'Something about a Well,' 1882.

Life: by E. T. Maclaren, 1890; by A. Peddie (with selected letters), 1893.

BROWNE (*Sir* Thomas), 1605-1682. Born, in London, 19 Oct. 1605. Edu-

3

cated at Winchester Coll., as Scholar,
1616-23 To Broadgate Hall (now
Pembroke Coll.), Oxford, 1623 ; B.A.,
31 June 1626 ; M.A., 11 June 1629.
Practised medicine for a short time.
Tour in Ireland, France, Italy, Holland. Returned to practice near Halifax. 'Religio Medici' probably written
1635. To Norwich, 1637. M.D.,
Oxford, 10 July 1637. Married
Dorothy Mileham, 1641. 'Religio
Medici' privately published, 1642.
Sided with Royalists in Civil Wars.
Hon. Fellow of Coll. of Physicians,
6 July 1665. Knighted, on State
visit of Charles II. to Norwich, 28
Sept. 1671. Died, 19 Oct. 1682 ;
buried at Norwich.

Works : 'Religio Medici,' privately
printed, 1642 ; authorized version,
1643 ; 'Pseudodoxia Epidemica,' 1646 ;
'Hydriotaphia,' 1658.
Posthumous : 'Certain Miscellany
Tracts,' 1684 ; 'Works,' 1686 ; 'Posthumous Works,' 1712 ; 'Christian
Morals,' 1716.
Collected Works : including *Life*
and Correspondence, ed. by S. Wilkin
(4 vols.), 1835-36.

BROWNE (William), 1591-1643 [?].
Born, at Tavistock, 1591. Educated
at Tavistock Grammar School. To
Exeter Coll., Oxford ; took no degree.
Entered at Clifford's Inn ; and at
Middle Temple, Nov. 1611. Married
daughter of Sir Thomas Eversfield.
Tutor to Hon. Robert Dormer, at
Exeter Coll., 1624. Created M.A.,
Oxford, 16 Nov. 1624. Lived in
country ; for some time at Dorking.
Died, March 1643 [?].

Works : 'Two Elegies,' 1613 ;
'Britannia's Pastorals,' bk. i., 1613 ;
bk. ii., 1616 (bks. i. and ii. together,
1625) ; 'The Shepherd's Pipe,' 1614.
Posthumous : 'Britannia's Pastorals,' bk. iii., 1852 ; 'Original Poems,
never before published,' ed. by Sir
S. E. Brydges, 1815.
Collected Works : in 3 vols., ed. by
T. Davies, 1772 ; in 2 vols., ed. by
W. C. Hazlitt, 1868 ; in 2 vols., ed.
by G. Goodwin, 1894.

***BROWNING (Elizabeth Barrett),
1806-1861.** Born [Elizabeth Barrett
Moulton - Barrett], at Coxhoe, co.
Durham, 6 March 1806. [Date disputed, but this probably correct.]
Early life at Hope End, Herefordshire.
Delicate health owing to accident to
spine while at Hope End. Poem,
'Battle of Marathon,' printed for her
by her father, 1820. First publication,
1826. At Sidmouth, 1831-33. First
contrib. to 'Athenæum,' 1 July 1837.
Contrib. to 'Finden's Tableaux,' same
year. To Torquay for health, 1838 ;
brother drowned there, 11 July 1840.
Returned to London, summer of 1841.
Married to Robert Browning, 12 Sept.
1846. To Paris and Italy. Settled
in Florence, winter of 1847. Son
born, 9 March 1849. Visit to Rome,
1850 ; to England, 1851 ; winter and
spring in Paris ; to London summer
of 1852 ; return to Florence in
autumn. Winter of 1853-54 in Rome.
Visit to Normandy, July 1858. To
Rome, winter of 1859-60, and 1860-61.
Died, at Florence, 29 June 1861.

Works : 'An Essay on Mind'
(anon.), 1826 ; 'Prometheus Bound,'
1833 ; 'The Seraphim,' 1838 ; 'Poems'
(2 vols.), 1844 (reprinted at New
York as 'A Drama of Exile, etc.,'
1845) ; 'The Runaway Slave at Pilgrim's Point,' 1849 ; 'Casa Guidi
Windows,' 1851 ; 'Two Poems : by
E. Barrett and R. Browning,' 1854 ;
'Aurora Leigh,' 1857 [1856] ; 'Poems
before Congress,' 1860.
Posthumous : 'Last Poems,' 1862 ;
'The Greek Christian Poets and the
English Poets,' 1863 ; 'Selected
Poems,' ed. by Robert Browning
(2nd series), 1866, 1880 ; Letters to
R. H. Horne (2 vols.), 1877 [1876] ;
'Earlier Poems, 1826-33,' 1878 [1877] ;
'The Battle of Marathon' (in typefacsimile, privately printed), 1891.
She *edited :* Chaucer's Works (with
R. H. Horne and others), 1841.
Collected Works : (2 vols.), New
York, 1871 ; London, 1890.
Life : by J. H. Ingram ('Eminent
Women' series), 1888.

*BROWNING (Robert), 1812-1889.

Born, at Camberwell, 7 May 1812. Educated at school at Peckham, till 1826. Father printed for him volume of poems, 'Incondita,' 1824. Educated by private tutor, 1826-29; attended lectures at University Coll., London, 1829-30. Literary career decided on. Published first poem, 1833. Resided at Camberwell. Started on tour to Russia and Italy, autumn of 1833; returned to Camberwell, summer of 1834. Contrib. poems to 'Monthly Repository' (under signature 'Z.'), 1834. First met Macready, Nov. 1835. 'Strafford' produced at Covent Garden, 1 May 1837. Married Elizabeth Barrett Moulton - Barrett, 12 Sept. 1846. To Paris and Italy. Settled in Florence, winter of 1847. Son born, 9 March 1849. Visit to Rome, 1850; to England, 1851; winter and spring in Paris; to London, summer of 1852; return to Florence in autumn. In Rome, winter 1853-54. To Normandy, July 1858. In Rome, winter of 1859-60 and 1860-61. Wife died, 29 June 1861. Left Florence, July 1861. Returned to London, Sept. 1861. Settled in Warwick Crescent. Hon. M.A., Oxford, June 1867; Hon. Fellow Balliol Coll., Oct. 1867. Declined Lord Rectorship of St. Andrews Univ., 1868, 1877, and 1884; declined Lord Rectorship of Glasgow Univ., 1875. First revisited Italy, Aug. 1878. Autumns subsequently frequently spent in Venice. Hon. LL.D., Cambridge, 1879. Browning Society established, Oct. 1881. Hon. D.C.L., Oxford, 1882. Hon. LL.D., Edinburgh, 17 April 1884. Hon. Pres. Associated Societies of Edinburgh, 1885. Foreign Correspondent to Royal Academy, 1886. Son married, 4 Oct. 1887. Removed to De Vere Gardens. To Italy, Aug. 1888. In England, winter 1888-89. Return to Italy, Aug. 1889. To Asolo. Joined son at Venice, Nov. 1889; died there, 12 Dec. 1889. Buried in Poet's Corner, Westminster Abbey, 31 Dec.

Works: 'Incondita' (priv. ptd.), 1824; 'Pauline,' 1833; 'Paracelsus,' 1835; 'Strafford,' 1837; 'Sordello,' 1840; 'Bells and Pomegranates' (8 pts.:

i. 'Pippa Passes,' 1841; ii. 'King Victor and King Charles,' 1842; iii. 'Dramatic Lyrics,' 1842; iv. 'The Return of the Druses,' 1843; **v.** 'A Blot in the 'Scutcheon,' 1843; vi. 'Colombe's Birthday,' 1844; vii. 'Dramatic Romances and Lyrics,' 1845; viii. 'Luria: and a Soul's Tragedy,' 1846), 1841-46; 'Christmas Eve and Easter Day,' 1850; 'Two Poems by E. Barrett and R. Browning,' 1854; 'Men and Women' (2 vols.), 1855; 'Dramatis Personæ,' 1864 (2nd edn. same year); 'The Ring and the Book' (4 vols.), 1868-69; 'Balaustion's Adventure,' 1871; 'Prince Hohenstiel-Schwangau,' 1871; 'Fifine at the Fair,' 1872; 'Red Cotton Night - Cap Country,' 1873; 'Aristophanes' Apology,' 1875; 'The Inn Album,' 1875; 'Pacchiarotto,' 1876; 'La Saisiaz: and the Two Poets of Croisic,' 1878; 'Dramatic Idylls' (2 series), 1879-80; 'Jocoseria,' 1883; 'Ferishtah's Fancies,' 1884; 'Parleyings with Certain People,' 1887; 'Asolando,' 1890 [1889].

He *translated:* Æschylus' 'Agamemnon,' 1877; and *edited:* the forged 'Letters of Shelley,' 1852; Selections from his wife's Poems, 1866 and 1880; 'The Divine Order,' by Rev. T. Jones, 1884; his wife's Poetical Works, 1889 and 1890.

Collected Poems: in 2 vols., 1849; in 3 vols., 1863; in 6 vols., 1868; in 16 vols., 1888-89.

Life: by William Sharp ('Great Writers' series), 1890; 'Life and Letters,' by Mrs. Orr, 1891.

BRUCE (James), 1730-1794. Born, at Kinnaird, Stirlingshire, 14 Dec. 1730. At Harrow School, 21 Jan. 1742, to 8 May 1746; then with tutor till April 1747. Returned to Scotland, May 1747; to Edinburgh Univ., Nov. 1747, to study Law. Left Univ., owing to ill-health, spring of 1748. To London, July 1753. Married Adriana Allan, 3 Feb. 1754. Took share in her father's wine business. Wife died, in Paris, 9 Oct. 1754. In Spain and Portugal, Aug. to Dec. 1757; in France and Holland, 1758. Succeeded to family estates on father's

3—2

death, and returned to England, July 1758. Withdrew from wine business, Aug. 1761. Appointed Consul-General at Algiers, Feb. 1762. In Italy July 1762 to March 1763; arrived at Algiers, 20 March 1763. Resigned Consulship, Aug. 1765. Travelled in Barbary, Africa, Crete, Syria. To Egypt, July 1768. To Abyssinia, Sept. 1769; reached Goudar, 14 Feb. 1770. Lived at court of King of Abyssinia, with various expeditions of exploration, till Dec. 1771. Through Nubia to Assouan; reached there 29 Nov. 1772. Arrived at Marseilles, March 1773. Returned to England, July 1774. To Scotland, autumn of 1774. Married Mary Dundas, 20 May 1776; she died, spring of 1785. Engaged in compiling his 'Travels.' Died, at Kinnaird, from an accident, 27 April 1794; buried in Larbert churchyard.

Works: 'Travels to Discover the Source of the Nile' (5 vols.), 1790.

Life: by Alex. Murray, 1808; by Sir F. B. Head, 1830.

*BRYCE (James), b. 1838. Born, at Belfast, 10 May 1838. Educated at Glasgow High School and Univ. Matric. Trin. Coll., Oxford, as Scholar, 8 June 1857; B.A., 1862; Gaisford prizes, 1860 and 1861; Vinerian Scholar, 1861; Chancellor's Latin Essay Prize, 1862; Craven Scholar, 1862; Arnold Prize, 1863. Studied at Heidelberg, 1863. Fellow of Oriel Coll., Oxford, 1862-89. B.C.L., by decree, 9 Feb. 1865; D.C.L., by decree, 27 May 1870. Student of Lincoln's Inn, 28 Jan. 1862; called to Bar, 11 June 1867. On Schools' Inquiry Commission, 1865-66. Prof. of Jurisprudence, Owen's Coll., Manchester, 1870-75. Regius Prof. of Civil Law, Oxford, 1870-93. Prof. of Roman Law to Council of Legal Education, 1878-88. M.P. for Tower Hamlets, 1880. On Royal Commission Medical Acts, 1881. Hon. LL.D., Glasgow, Edinburgh, and Michigan. Corresponding Mem. of Institute of France. M.P. for South Aberdeen, 1885, 1886, 1892, 1895. Under-Sec. of State for Foreign Affairs, 1886. Married Elizabeth

Marion Ashton, 23 July 1889. Chancellor of Duchy of Lancaster and Member of Cabinet, 1892. F.R.S., 1894. Pres. Board of Trade, 1894. Pres. Royal Comm. Second. Education, 1894-95.

Works: 'The Plague of London' (in Greek), 1860; 'The May Queen' (Greek), 1861; 'The Holy Roman Empire,' 1864; 'The Academical Study of the Civil Law,' 1871; 'The Trade Marks Registration Acts, 1875 and 1876,' 1877; 'Transcaucasia and Ararat,' 1877; 'The Predictions of Hamilton and De Tocqueville,' 1887; 'The American Commonwealth' (3 vols.), 1888.

He has *edited:* J. Conrad's 'German Universities,' 1885; 'Handbook of Home Rule,' 1887; 'Two Centuries of Irish History,' 1888; G. Sigerson's 'Political Prisoners,' 1890; Acland and Smith's 'Studies in Secondary Education,' 1892.

BUCHANAN (George), 1506-1582. Born at Killearn, Stirlingshire, Feb. 1506. Educated at Parish School. In Paris, studying Latin, 1520-22. Served with French troops in Scotland under Albany, 1523. To St. Andrews 1524; B.A., 3 Oct. 1825. To Paris, 1526. B.A., Scottish College, Paris, 10 Oct. 1527; M.A., Mar. 1528. Elected 'Procurator of German nation,' 3 June 1529; taught in Coll. of St. Barbe, 1529-32. Tutor to Gilbert, Earl of Cassilis, 1532-36. Returned to Scotland. Tutor to a natural son of King James, 1537-38. Arrested on charge of Lutheranism, Jan. 1539; escaped from prison and fled to London, and thence to Paris and Bordeaux. Taught Latin in College of Guienne, 1539-42. Returned to Paris; taught in College of Cardinal Le Moine, 1544-47. To Portugal; to Coll. at Coimbra, 1547. Returned to England, 1552; to Paris 1553, taught in Coll. of Boncourt. Tutor to son of Count de Brissac, 1555-60. Returned to Scotland; classical tutor to Queen. Joined Reformed Church; sat in assemblies of 1563-67; Moderator, 1567; Principal of St. Andrews, 1566. To

England as secretary to Commission respecting Queen Mary, 1568. Returned to St. Andrews, Jan. 1569. Tutor to King James, Aug. 1569 to May 1578. Director of Chancery 1570; Keeper of Privy Seal, 1570-78. Died, at Edinburgh, 29 Sept. 1582. Buried there, in churchyard of Grey Friars.

Works: 'Jephthes,' 1554; 'De Caleto nuper ab Henrico II. . . . recepta Carmen,' 1558; 'Franciscanus,' 1566; 'Psalmorum Davidis paraphrasis poetica,' 1566; 'Elegiæ, Silvæ, Hendecasyllabi,' 1567; 'De Maria Scotorum Regina totaque ejus contra Regem conjuratione' (anon.), 1571; 'An Admonition direct to the Trew Lordis Mantenaris of the Kingis graces authoritie' (under initials: M. G. B.), 1571; 'Baptistes,' 1578; 'De Jure Regni apud Scotos Dialogus,' 1579; 'Rerum Scoticarum Historia,' 1582.

Posthumous: 'De Sphæra, Libri V.,' 1587; 'Satyra in Cardinalem Lotharingum,' 1590; 'De Prosodia libellus,' 1596; 'Tragœdiæ Sacræ & exteræ,' 1597; 'Vita ab ipso scripta,' 1608; 'Poemata Omnia,' 1615; 'The Chameleon,' 1710; 'Letters,' 1711.

He *translated:* Linacre's 'Rudimenta Grammatices,' 1533; Euripides' "Alcestis,' 1557; 'Medea and Alcestis,' 1567.

Collected Works: edited by T. Ruddiman (2 vols.) 1715.

Life: by David Irving, 2nd edn., 1817.

*BUCHANAN (Robert Williams), b. 1841.** Born, at Caverswall, Staffordshire, 18 Aug. 1841. At school at Merton; at Rothesay; at Glasgow High School. To Glasgow Univ., 1856. To London, 1861. Contrib. to 'Athenæum,' 'Literary Gaz.,' 'Temple Bar,' etc. Melodrama, 'The Rathboys,' written with C. Gibbon, produced at Standard Theatre, Shoreditch, 1861. Edited 'The Welcome Guest.' 'The Witchfinder' produced at Sadler's Wells Theatre, 1863. To Denmark as newspaper correspondent, 1866. Crown pension, 1871. 'A Madcap Prince' produced at Haymarket, 1874; 'A Nine Days' Queen,' 'The Queen of Connaught,' 'Paul Clifford,' 1875-82; 'Storm Beaten,' at Adelphi, 14 March 1883; 'Lady Clare,' Globe Theatre, 11 April 1883; 'A Sailor and His Lass' (with Aug. Harris), Drury Lane, 15 Oct. 1883. 'Visit to United States,' 1884-85. 'Alone in London,' written with Miss Harriett Jay, produced at Olympic, 2 Nov. 1885; 'Sophia,' Vaudeville, 12 April 1886; 'The Blue Bells of Scotland,' Novelty, 12 Sept. 1887; 'Fascination' (with Miss H. Jay), Novelty, 6 Oct. 1887; 'Partners,' Haymarket, 5 Jan. 1888; 'Joseph's Sweetheart,' Vaudeville, 8 March 1888; 'Man and the Woman,' Criterion, 19 Dec. 1889; 'Dick Sheridan,' Comedy, 3 Feb. 1894; 'The Strange Adventures of Miss Brown,' (written with 'R. Marlowe,' *i.e.*, Miss Harriett Jay), Vaudeville, 27 June 1895; 'The Romance of a Shopwalker' (written with 'R. Marlowe'), Vaudeville, 26 Feb. 1896.

Works: 'Storm-Beaten' (with C. Gibbon), 1862; 'Undertones,' 1863; 'Idylls and Legends of Inverburn,' 1865; 'London Poems,' 1866; 'Wayside Poesies' (a compilation), 1867 [1866]; 'Ballad Stories of the Affections,' 1866; 'North Coast and other Poems,' 1867; 'David Gray,' 1868; 'The Book of Orm,' 1870; 'Napoleon Fallen,' 1871; 'The Land of Lorne,' 1871; 'The Drama of Kings,' 1871; 'The Fleshly School of Poetry' (from 'Contemporary Mag.'), 1872; 'St. Abe and his Seven Wives' (anon.), 1872; 'Master Spirits,' 1873; 'White Rose and Red' (anon.), 1873; 'Poetical Works,' 1874; 'The Shadow of the Sword' (from 'Gentleman's Mag.'), 1876; 'Balder the Beautiful,' 1877; 'A Child of Nature,' 1881; 'God and the Man,' 1881; 'Ballads of Life, Love and Humour,' 1882; 'The Martyrdom of Madeline,' 1882; 'Selected Poems,' 1882; 'The Hebrid Isles,' 1883 [1882]; 'Love me for Ever,' 1883; 'A Poet's Sketch-Book,' 1883; 'Annan Water,' 1883; 'Foxglove Manor,' 1884; 'The New Abelard,' 1884; 'Poetical Works,' 1884; 'The Earthquake,' 1885; 'Matt,' 1885; 'Stormy Waters,' 1885; 'The

Master of the Mine,' 1885 ; 'That Winter Night,' 1886 ; 'A Look around Literature,' 1887 ; 'The Heir of Linne,' 1887 ; 'The City of Dream,' 1888 ; 'On Descending into Hell,' 1889 ; 'The Moment After,' 1890 ; 'Come, live with me, and be my love,' 1891 ; 'The Coming Terror,' 1891 ; 'The Outcast,' 1891 ; 'The Piper of Hamelin,' 1893 ; 'The Wandering Jew,' 1893 ; 'Woman and the Man,' 1893 ; 'Red and White Heather,' 1894 ; 'Diana's Hunting,' 1895 ; 'Lady Kilpatrick,' 1895 ; 'The Charlatan' (with H. Murray), 1895.

He has *edited :* Longfellow's 'Poems,' 1868 ; J. J. Audubon's 'Life and Adventures,' 1869 ; H. Jay's 'My Connaught Cousins,' 1883 ; Roden Noel's Poems [1892].

*BUCKLE (Henry Thomas), 1821-1862. Born, in London, 24 Nov. 1821. Educated mainly at home ; for a short time at a school in Kentish Town. Entered father's Shipowner's business, 1838. Ill-health after father's death, 1840. Travelled on Continent with mother and sister, July 1840 to 1841. On return to England gave up business and began historical study. Settled in lodgings in London, Oct. 1842. Travelled on Continent, 1843. On return lived with mother in London. Engaged on 'History of Civilization,' 1842-61. On Committee of Roy. Lit. Soc., 1852. Elected member of Athenæum Club, 1858 ; member of Polit. Econ. Club, 1858. Lectured at Royal Institution, 19 March 1858. Mother died, 1 April 1859. Contrib. to 'Fraser's Magazine,' 1858 - 59. Failing health. Started for tour in Egypt and Palestine with sons of Mr. Henry Huth, 20 Oct. 1861. Died, at Damascus, 29 May 1862 ; buried in Protestant cemetery there.

Works : 'History of Civilization in England,' vol. i., 1857 ; vol. ii., 1861 ; 'A Letter to a Gentleman respecting Pooley's Case,' 1859.

Posthumous : 'History of Civilization in France and England, Spain and Scotland' (3 vols.), 1866 ; 'Essays,' 1867 ; 'Fragment on the Reign of

Elizabeth' (in 'Fraser's Magazine,' Feb. and Aug.), 1867.

Collected Works : 'Miscellaneous and Posthumous Works,' ed. by H. Taylor (3 vols.), 1872.

Life : by A. H. Huth, 1880.

BUNYAN (John), 1628-1688. Born, at Elstow, Bedfordshire, Nov. 1628. Educated at parish school, and brought up to father's trade of tinker. Served as soldier, 1644-46. Married, 1648 [?] or 1649 [?]. Lived at Elstow. Joined Nonconformists, 1653. Removed to Bedford, 1655 [?] ; wife died there. Elected Deacon, 1655 ; Preacher, 1657. Married again, 1659. At Restoration was arrested, 12 Nov. 1660, for preaching. Imprisoned in Bedford Gaol,1660-72. Released for a few weeks in 1666. Chosen Minister to Bedford Nonconformists, Jan. 1672 ; received license to preach, 9 May 1672. Received formal pardon from Crown, 13 Sept. 1672. Perhaps imprisoned for six months in 1675, during which time 'Pilgrim's Progress' was written. Active life—preaching in neighbourhood of Bedford and in London. Chaplain to Lord Mayor of London, 1688. Died, in London, 31 Aug. 1688 ; buried in Bunhill Fields, Finsbury.

Works : 'Some Gospel Truths Opened,' 1656 ; 'Vindication' of same, 1657 ; 'A Few Sighs from Hell,' 1658 ; 'The Doctrine of the Law,' 1659 ; 'Profitable Meditations' [1661] ; 'I will pray with the Spirit,' 1663 ; 'Christian Behaviour,' 1663 ; 'The Four Last Things, etc.' [1664 ?]; 'The Holy City,' 1665 ; 'The Resurrection,' 1665 ; 'Grace Abounding,' 1666 ; 'Defence of the Doctrine of Justification,' 1672 ; 'Confession of Faith,' 1672 ; 'Difference of Judgment about Water Baptism,' 1673 ; 'Peaceable Principles,' 1674 ; 'Reprobation Asserted' [1675 ?]; 'Light for them that sit in Darkness,' 1675 ; 'Instruction for the Ignorant,' 1675 ; 'Saved by Grace,' 1675 ; 'The Strait Gate,' 1676 ; 'Pilgrim's Progress,' pt. i., 1678 (2nd edn. same year) ; pt. ii., 1684 ; 'Come, and Welcome, to Jesus Christ,' 1678 ; 'Treatise of the Fear of God,'

1679 ; 'Life and Death of Mr. Badman,' 1680 ; 'Holy War,' 1682 ; 'Barren Fig Tree,' 1682 ; 'Greatness of the Soul,' 1683 ; 'Case of Conscience Resolved,' 1683 ; 'Seasonable Counsel,' 1684 ; 'Holy Life the Beauty of Christianity,' 1684 ; 'A Caution to stir up to Watch against Sin,' 1684 ; 'Questions about the Nature . . . of the . . . Sabbath,' 1685 ; 'The Pharisee and the Publican,' 1685 ; 'Book for Boys and Girls' (in later edns. called 'Divine Emblems') 1686 ; 'Jerusalem Sinner Saved' (anon.), 1688 ; 'Advocateship of Jesus Christ,' 1688 (another edn. under title: 'Work of Jesus Christ as an Advocate,' 1688) ; 'Discourse of the . . . House of God,' 1688 ; 'Water of Life,' 1688 ; 'Solomon's Temple Spiritualized,' 1688.

Posthumous: 'Acceptable Sacrifice,' 1689 ; 'Last Sermon,' 1688 ; 'Works' (including ten posthumous works), 1692 ; 'Heavenly Footman,' ed. by C. Doe, 1698 ; 'Pilgrim's Progress,' pt. i. and ii. together, 1728 ; 'Relation of the Imprisonment of Mr. J. Bunyan' (written in Bedford Gaol), 1765.

Collected Works : ed. by S. Wilson (2 vols.), 1736 ; ed. by H. Stebbing (4 vols.), 1859.

Life : 'Life and Actions' (anon.), 1692 ; 'Life' (anon.), 1700 ; by Southey, 1830 ; by Macaulay, 1853 ; by Froude ('English Men of Letters' series), 1880 ; by Brown, 3rd edn., 1888.

BURKE (Edmund), 1729-1797. Born, in Dublin, 12 Jan. [?] 1729. Educated at a school at Ballitore, 1741-43 ; at Trinity Coll., Dublin, 1743-48 ; scholarship, 1746 ; B.A., 1748. To Middle Temple to study Law, 1750. Never called to Bar ; gave up legal studies by 1755. Took to literary work. Married Jane Nugent, 1756 [or 1757?]. Edited 'Annual Register,' 1759-88. Gradually became known by literary work. Private Sec. to William Gerard Hamilton, 1759-64. To Ireland with Hamilton, 1761. Annual pension of £300, 1763. Threw up pension, April 1764. Private Sec. to Lord Rockingham, July 1765. M.P. for Wendover,

Dec. 1765. First speech made, 27 Jan. 1766. To Ireland, summer of 1766 ; received freedom of city of Galway. Purchased estate near Beaconsfield, 1768. Appointed Agent to the Province of New York, 1771. Visit to Paris, Feb. to March, 1773. M.P. for Malton after dissolution of Parliament in Sept. 1774 ; again after dissolution in Sept. 1780 ; and again in Nov. 1790. Intimacy with Fox begun. Appointed Paymaster of the Forces, 1782. Lord Rector of Glasgow University, 1784 and 1785. Impeachment of Warren Hastings, 10 May 1787 ; trial begun, 13 Feb. 1788. Grace for conferring Hon. LL.D. degree passed, Dublin Univ., 11 Dec. 1790. Burke apparently never attended to take the degree. Again elected M.P. for Malton, Nov. 1790. Rupture with Fox, 1791. Retired from Parliament, July 1794. Two pensions of £1,200 and £2,500 granted him, Aug. 1794. Interested in foundation of Maynooth Catholic College, 1795. Established, at Beaconsfield, school for sons of French emigrants, 1796. Died, at Beaconsfield, 6 July 1797. Buried in Beaconsfield parish church.

Works : Burke's chief literary works are : 'A Vindication of Natural Society' (anon.), 1756 ; 'A Philosophical Enquiry into the Origin of our Ideas of the Sublime and the Beautiful' (anon.), 1757 ; 'An Account of the European Settlements in America' (anon., probably edited by Burke, and written by himself and his cousin, William Burke), 1757 ; 'A Short Account of a Short Administration' (anon.), 1766 ; 'Observations on a late Publication intituled "The Present State of the Nation"' (anon.), 1769 ; 'Thoughts on the Causes of the Present Discontents' (anon.), 1770 ; 'Political Tracts and Speeches,' 1777 ; 'Reflections on the Revolution in France,' 1790 (2nd edn. same year) ; 'Appeal from the New to the Old Whigs' (anon.), 1791 (2nd edn. same year) ; 'Thoughts on the Prospect of a Regicide Peace' (anon.), 1796 (11th edn. same year). [Burke published a number of his speeches, also of political pamphlets and letters, between 1774 and 1791, and many were published posthumously. A complete collection is the 'Works and Correspondence' (8 vols.), London, 1852.]

Posthumous : 'Correspondence with Dr. Laurence, 1827; 'Letters, 1744-97' (4 vols.), 1844; 'Speeches, with Memoir,' 1854; 'Letters, Speeches, and Tracts on Irish Affairs,' 1881.

Collected Works : in 8 vols., 1792-1827; in 8 vols., 1852.

Life : by MacCormick, 1798; by Bisset, 1798; by Sir James Prior, 5th edn. 1854; by MacKnight, 1858; by Morley ('English Men of Letters' series), 1879.

BURNET (Gilbert), *Bishop of Salisbury.* **1643-1715.** Born, in Edinburgh, 18 Sept. 1643. To Marischal Coll., Aberdeen, 1653; M.A., 1657. Studied theology. Probationer for Presbyterian Ministry, 1661. Visited English Universities, 1663. Travelled in Holland and France, 1664; spent some time at Court on return. F.R.S., 1664. Inducted to living of Saltoun, 29 Jan. 1665. Clerk of Presbytery of Haddington, 9 May 1667. Prof. of Divinity, Glasgow Univ., 1669; resigned living of Saltoun. To London, 1671. Returned to Glasgow and married Lady Margaret Kennedy, 1672. To London, 1673. Chaplain to King, 1673-74. Chaplain to Rolls Chapel, 1675-84. In France, Sept. to Oct., 1683. Wife died, 1684. In France, Italy, and Holland, 1685-87. In favour at Court of William of Orange. Married Mary Scott, 25 May 1687. Returned to England with William of Orange, Nov. 1687. Bishop of Salisbury, 1688. Second wife died, 1698; married Mrs. Elizabeth Berkeley same year. Appointed Governor to Duke of Gloucester, 1698. Active part in ecclesiastical politics. Died, in London, 7 March, 1715; buried in St. James's Church, Clerkenwell.

Works : [A complete list in 1823 edn. of his 'History of his Own Times.'] Chief works : 'Discourse on Sir Robert Fletcher of Saltoun,' 1665;

'Conference between a Conformist and a Nonconformist,' 1669; 'Vindication of the Authority . . . of Church and State of Scotland,' 1673; 'The Mystery of Iniquity Unveiled,' 1673; 'Rome's Glory,' 1673; 'Memories of . . . James and William, Dukes of Hamilton, 1852; 'History of the Reformation,' vol. i., 1679; vol. ii., 1681; vol. iii., 1714; 'Some Passages in the Life and Death of John Wilmot, Earl of Rochester,' 1680; 'News from France,' 1682; 'Life and Death of Sir Matthew Hale,' 1682; 'Life of Bishop Bedell,' 1685; 'Essay on the Memory of Queen Mary,' 1695; 'Exposition of the Thirty-Nine Articles,' 1699; 'A Collection of Tracts and Discourses,' 1704; 'Exposition of the Church Catechism,' 1710; 'Speech on the Impeachment of Sacheverell,' 1710.

Posthumous : 'History of his Own Times,' with *life* (2 vols.), 1723-34.

BURNEY (Charles), 1726-1814. Born, at Shrewsbury, 12 April 1726. Educated at Free School, Chester. To Shrewsbury, to study music, 1741 [?]. Articled as pupil to Dr. Arne, 1744; with him in London, 1744-47. Taken under patronage of Fulke Greville, 1747. Taught and composed music. Married Esther Sleepe, 1749. Organist of St. Dionis, Backchurch, 1749. Mem. of Roy. Soc. of Musicians, 3 Dec. 1749. Organist of Lynn Regis, 1751-60. Returned to London, 1760. Wife died, 1761. Married (privately) Mrs. Stephen Allen, 1767. Mus. Doc. degree, Oxford, June 1769. Travelled on Continent, 1770 and 1772. F.R.S., 1773. Organist of Chelsea Hospital, 1783. Mem. of Literary Club, 1784. Contrib. to 'Monthly Review,' 1790-93. Second wife died, Oct. 1796. Contrib. to Rees's 'Encyclopædia,' 1800-05. Crown pension granted, 1806. Foreign Member of Institut de France, 1810. Died, at Chelsea. 12 April 1814; buried in churchyard of Chelsea Hospital.

Works : 'Essay towards the History of the principal Comets, etc.' (anon.)

1769 ; 'The Present State of Music in France and Italy,' 1771 ; 'The Present State of Music in Germany, the Netherlands, and the United Provinces,' 1773 ; 'History of Music,' vol. i., 1776 ; vol. ii., 1782 ; vols. iii., iv., 1789 ; 'Account of an Infant Musician,' 1779 ; 'An Account of the Musical Performances . . . in 1784 in Commemoration of Handel,' 1785 ; 'Memoir of the Life and Writings of Metastasio' (3 vols.), 1796.
Life : by his daughter Frances 1832.

BURNEY (Frances), [Madame D'Arblay,] **1752-1840.** [Daughter of preceding.] Born, at King's Lynn, 13 June 1752. Family removed to London, 1760. Mother died, 1761. Father married again, 1766. No regular education. Began early to write stories, plays, poems, etc. First novel pub. anonymously, Jan. 1778. Intimacy with Mrs. Thrale, Dr. Johnson, Sheridan, Burke, etc. Appointed Second Keeper of Robes to Queen, 17 July 1786. Bad health ; retired, 7 July 1791, with pension of £100 a year. Travelled in England. Made acquaintance of Gen. D'Arblay at Mickleham, where her sister lived. Married to him, 31 July 1793. Settled at Bookham, near Norbury. Tragedy, 'Edwy and Elvina,' performed at Drury Lane, 21 March 1795 ; withdrawn after first night. Built a cottage at West Humble, near Mickleham ; removed there, 1797. Comedy, 'Love and Fashion,' accepted for Covent Garden, but withdrawn before performance, 1800. Husband went to seek employment in France, 1801. In Paris with him, 1802-05 ; at Passy, 1805-14. Visit to England with son, Aug. 1812. In Paris, 1814-15. In Belgium, March to July, 1815. Returned to England, Oct. 1815. At Bath, Feb. 1816 to June 1817 ; at Ilfracombe, June to Oct., 1817 ; at Bath, Oct. 1817 to Sept. 1818. Husband died, 3 May 1818. To London, Oct. 1818. Son died, 19 Jan. 1837. Severe illness, 1839. Died, in London, 6 Jan. 1840.

Works : 'Evelina' (anon.), 1778 ; 'Cecilia' (anon.), 1782 ; 'Brief Reflections relative to the French Emigrant Clergy' (anon.), 1793 ; 'Camilla,' 1796 ; 'The Wanderer,' 1814 ; 'Memoirs of Dr. Burney,' 1832.
Posthumous : 'Diary and Letters' (7 vols.), 1842-46.

*BURNS (Robert), **1759-1796.** Born at Alloway, 25 Jan. 1759. To school at Alloway Mill, 1764. Then to school set up by his father, under John Murdoch. At Dalrymple Parish School, 1772 ; for short time with Murdoch at Ayr, summer of 1773. Did farm-work for father at Mount Oliphant, near Alloway. Wrote first poem, 1775. To Ballochneil, to study surveying, summer of 1777. Returned to Lochlea, Tarbolton, where father had taken a farm. Became freemason, 1781. To Irvine, to enter mercantile life, 1781. Shop burnt, Jan. 1782. Returned to Lochlea. At father's death started farm at Mossgiel, near Mauchline, with brother Gilbert, 1784. Connection with Jean Armour, 1785-86. Offer of marriage rejected by her. Poems published, to raise passage money for emigration to East Indies, July 1786. Mary Campbell promised to accompany him, but died Oct. 1786. Emigration scheme abandoned. To Edinburgh, 27 Nov. 1786. Renewed intimacy with Jean Armour, June 1787. Took farm at Ellisland, near Dumfries, March 1788. Appointed Exciseman, 31 March 1788. Married Jean Armour, 3 Aug. 1788. Settled at Ellisland, 13 June 1789 ; took up his appointment as Exciseman. Left Ellisland and settled at Dumfries as Exciseman, Dec. 1791. Joined the Volunteers, 1795. To Brow, on the Solway, for health, 4 July 1796 ; returned to Dumfries, 18 July. Died there, 21 July, 1796. Buried there.

Works : 'Poems, chiefly in the Scottish Dialect,' 1786 (2nd edn., augmented, 1787) ; 'The Calf,' 1787 ; 'The Prayer of Holy Willie' (anon.), 1789 ; 'Poems' (2 vols., including new poems) 1793 ; 'An Address to the Deil,' 1795.

Posthumous: 'The Jolly Beggars' (with 'The Prayer of Holy Willie'), 1799; Works (4 vols., ed. by J. Currie), 1800; 'Poems ascribed to Robert Burns,' 1801; 'Letters addressed to Clarinda,' 1802; 'Reliques' (letters and verses), 1808. He contrib. 184 songs to 'The Scots Musical Museum,' 1787-1803; and 70 (mostly posthumous) to 'A Select Collection of Original Scottish Airs,' 1793-1805.

Collected Works (some containing new material): Allan Cunningham's edn. (8 vols.), 1834; Hogg and Motherwell's (5 vols.), 1836; Aldine edn., 1839; Whitelaw's (2 vols.), 1843-44; Chambers' 'Life and Works of Burns' (4 vols.), 1851; etc.

Life: by Chambers in 'Life and Works,' 1851; also by editors in other edns.

*BURTON (*Sir* **Richard Francis**), 1821-1890. Born, at Barham House, Herts, 19 March 1821. Taken abroad soon afterwards. To school at Tours, 1827. To school at Richmond, 1830. Returned to France, 1831. Privately educated in France and Italy, 1831-40. To Trinity Coll., Oxford, Oct. 1840; rusticated, autumn of 1841. To Bombay with commission in H.E.I.C.'s service, Oct. 1842. Joined 18th Bombay Native Infantry at Baroda. Regimental Interpreter, 1843. Journey to Medina and Mecca, 1852. To Somaliland with Speke, 1854-55. In Constantinople, 1856. Left Zanzibar, with Speke, on expedition to Central Africa, June 1857. Returned to England, 1859; Gold Medal of Royal Geographical Soc. Visit to America, 1860. Married Isabel Arundell, 22 Jan. 1861. Consul at Fernando Po, Aug. 1861. Consul at São Paulo, Brazil, 1865; travelled widely in Brazil. Consul at Damascus, Oct. 1869; exploration in Syria. Returned to England, 1871. Visit to Iceland, 1872. Consul at Trieste, 1872-90. Travelled in Land of Midian, 1876, 1877-78; in interior of Gold Coast, 1882. K.C.M.G., 1886. Died, at Trieste, 20 Oct. 1890.

Works: 'Goa and the Blue Mountains,' 1851; 'Scinde; or, the Unhappy Valley,' 1851; 'Sindh, and the Races that inhabit the Valley of the Indus,' 1851; 'Falconry in the Valley of the Indus,' 1852; 'A Complete System of Bayonet Exercise,' 1853; 'Personal Narrative of a Pilgrimage' (3 vols.), 1855-56; 'First Footsteps in East Africa,' 1856; 'The Lake Region of Central Africa,' 1860; 'The City of the Saints,' 1861; 'Wanderings in West Africa' (under initials: F.R.G.S.), 1863; 'Abeokuta,' 1863; 'The Nile Basin' (from 'Morning Advertiser'), 1864; 'A Mission to Gelele' (2 vols.), 1864; 'Stone Talk' (under pseud. of Frank Baker), 1865; 'Wit and Wisdom from West Africa,' 1865; 'Explorations of the Highlands of Brazil,' 1869; 'Letters from the Battlefields of Paraguay,' 1870; 'Zanzibar,' 1872; 'Unexplored Syria' (with C. F. T. Drake), 1872; 'Ultima Thule,' 1875; 'Two Trips to Gorilla Land,' 1876 [1875]; 'A New System of Sword Exercise,' 1876; 'Etruscan Bologna,' 1876; 'Sind Revisited,' 1877; 'The Gold Mines of Midian,' 1878; 'The Land of Midian Revisited,' 1879; 'A Glance at the "Passion-Play,"' 1881; 'Lord Beaconsfield' [1882?]; 'To the Gold Coast for Gold' (with V. L. Cameron), 1883 [1882]; 'The Book of the Sword,' 1884.

Posthumous: 'The Kasîdah of Hâjî Abdû Al Yazdi,' ed. by Lady Burton, 1894; translations of 'Il Pentamerone,' 1893; and Catullus' 'Carmina,' 1894.

He *translated:* 'Vikram and the Vampire,' 1870; Lacerda's 'Lands of Cazembe,' 1873; Camoens' Works, 1880-84; 'Arabian Nights,' 1885-86; 'Supplemental Nights,' 1886-88; Pereira da Silva's 'Manuel de Moraes' (with Lady Burton), 1886; and *edited:* 'Marcy's 'Prairie Traveller,' 1863; Stade's 'Captivity,' 1874; Leared's 'Morocco and the Moors,' 1891 [1890].

Collected Works: 'Memorial Edn.,' ed. by Lady Burton and L. Smithers, 1893, etc.

Life: by Lady Burton, 2 vols., 1893; by G. M. Stisted, 1896.

BURTON (Robert), 1577 - 1640.
Born, at Lindley, Leicestershire, 8
Feb. 1577. Educated at Nuneaton
Grammar School, and Free School at
Sutton Coldfield. To Brasenose Coll.,
Oxford, 1593. Student of Christ
Church, 1599 ; B.A., 30 June 1602 ;
M.A., 9 June 1605 ; B.D., 16 May
1614. Vicar of St. Thomas, Oxford, 29
Nov. 1616. Latin Comedy ' Philoso-
phaster ' (written in 1606), performed
at Ch. Ch., 16 Feb. 1618. Rector of
Segrave, Leicestershire, 1630 - 40.
Greater part of life spent in Oxford.
Died there, 25 Jan. 1640 ; buried in
Ch. Ch. Cathedral.

Works : ' The Anatomy of Melancholy ' (under pseud. of Democritus
Junior), 1621 (2nd edn., 1624 ; 3rd,
1628 ; 4th, 1632 ; 5th, 1638 ; latest,
1896).
Posthumous : ' Philosophaster,' ed.
by Rev. W. E. Buckley (privately
printed for Roxburghe Club), 1862.

*BUTCHER (Samuel Henry), b.
1850. Born, in Dublin, 16 April
1850. Educated at Marlborough Coll.,
Aug. 1864 to Midsummer 1869. Minor
Scholarship at Trinity Coll., Cambridge, 1869. Foundation Scholarship,
1870 ; Bell Scholarship, 1870 ; Waddington Scholarship, 1871 ; Powis
Medal, 1871 and 1872 ; Senior Classic,
and Chancellor's Medal, 1873 ; B.A.,
1873 ; M.A., 1876. Assistant-Master
at Eton, Easter to Midsummer, 1873.
Fellow of Trinity Coll., Cambridge,
1874. Assistant-Tutor there, 1874-76.
Married Rose Julia Trench, 1876.
Extraordinary Fellowship at Univ.
Coll., Oxford, 1876. Lecturer there,
1876-82. Prof. of Greek, Edinburgh
Univ., 1882. Hon. LL.D., Glasgow,
1885. Elected member of Athenæum
Club, without ballot, 2 March 1886.
Member of Scottish Universities Commission, 1889. Hon. Litt.D., Dublin,
6 July 1892. Frequent speaker and
writer on Irish questions, in Unionist
interest, since 1886. Acts on Board
of Guardians, etc., in co. Kerry, for
which county he is J.P.

Works : Translation of Homer's
' Odyssey ' (with A. Lang), 1879 ; ' De-
mosthenes ' (a biography), 1881 ;
' What we Owe to Greece,' 1882 ;
' Irish Land Acts,' 1887 ; ' Some As-
pects of the Greek Genius,' 1891 ;
Critical Text and Translation of
Aristotle's ' Poetics,' 1895.
Has *edited :* Bishop Butcher's ' Ec-
clesiastical Calendar ' (with J. G.
Butcher), 1877.

BUTLER (Joseph), *Bishop of Durham.* **1692-1752.** Born, at Wantage,
18 May 1692. Educated at Wantage
Latin School, and at Dissenting School
at Gloucester and Tewkesbury. To
Oriel Coll., Oxford, March 1715 ; B.A.,
11 Oct. 1718 ; B.C.L., 10 June 1721.
Ordained Deacon at Salisbury, Oct.
1718 ; Priest, Dec. 1718. Preacher
at Rolls Chapel, July 1719 to autumn
of 1726. Prebendary of Salisbury,
1721. Rector of Houghton-le-Skerne,
near Darlington, 1722. Rector of
Stanhope in Weardale, 1725. Lived secluded life, mainly occupied in writing
' Analogy,' published 1736. Chaplain
to Lord Talbot, 1733. D.C.L., Oxford, 8 Dec. 1733. Prebendary of
Rochester, and Clerk of Closet to
Queen Caroline, July 1736. Bishop
of Bristol, Aug. 1738. Continued to
hold Rochester prebend and Stanhope
rectorship till appointed Dean of St.
Paul's, 24 May 1740. Clerk of Closet
to King, 1746. Bishop of Durham,
July 1750. To Bristol and Bath for
health. Died, at Bath, 16 June 1752.
Buried in Bristol Cathedral.

Works : ' Several Letters to the
Rev. Dr. Clarke, from a Gentleman
in Gloucestershire ' (anon.), 1716 ;
' Letters of Thanks from a Young
Clergyman to the Rev. Dr. Hare '
(anon.), 1719 ; ' Fifteen Sermons,'
1726 ; ' The Analogy of Religion,'
1736 ; ' Sermon preached before the
Society for Propagating the Gospel,'
1739 ; ' Sermon preached before the
Lord Mayor,' 1740 ; ' Sermon preached
before the House of Lords,' 1741 ;
' Sermon preached at the annual
meeting of the Charity Children,'
1745 ; ' Sermon preached before the
House of Lords,' 1747 ; ' Sermon
preached before the Governors of the

London Infirmary,' 1748 ; Visitation Charge at Durham, 1751.

Posthumous : 'Some Remains, hitherto unpublished,' ed. by E. Steere, 1853.

Collected Works : ed. by Dr. Kippis, 1804 ; ed. by Rt. Hon. W. E. Gladstone (2 vols.), 1896.

Life : by T. Bartlett, 1839 ; by Samuel Butler, 1896.

BUTLER (Samuel), 1612 - 1680. Born, at Strensham, Worcestershire, 1612. Educated at Worcester Free School. Possibly to Cambridge, about 1627 [?]. Probably attendant to Countess of Kent, at Wrest, for some years from 1628. Acted as secretary to various people ; including Jeffereys (a J.P.), Sir Samuel Luke, and Sir Henry Rosewell. Visited France and Holland. Secretary to Lord Carbury and Steward of Ludlow Castle, 1660. Married about this time. Uneventful life of poverty. Confined to house with gout, Oct. 1679 to Easter 1680. Died in Rose Street, Covent Garden, 25 Sept. 1680. Buried in churchyard of St. Paul's, Covent Garden.

Works : 'Hudibras,' pt. i. (anon.), 1663 (pirated and unauthorized ed., 1662) ; pt. ii. (anon.), 1664 ; pt. iii. (anon.), 1678 ; ' Ode to the Memory of Du Val,' 1671 ; ' Two Letters' (anon.), 1672 ; ' Geneva Ballad' (anon.), 1674.

Posthumous : 'Hudibras,' pts. i.-iii. together, 1710 ; ' Genuine Remains, in Verse and Prose' (2 vols.), 1759. ['Posthumous Works,' ed. by Sir Roger L'Estrange, 1715, probably spurious.]

Works attributed to Butler : 'Letter from Mercurius Civicus to Mercurius Rusticus,' 1643 ; ' Acts and Monuments of our Late Parliament' (under pseud. of 'John Canne'), 1659 ; continuation of same, 1659 ; 'Proposals for farming out Liberty of Conscience,' 1663 ; 'A New Ballad of King Edward and Jane Shore,' 1671 ; 'Mercurius Menippeus,' 1682 ; 'The Plagiary Expos'd,' 1691 ; 'The Secret History of the Calves' Head Club,' 1703.

Collected Works : ed. by G. Gilfillan, with *life*, 1854 ; 'Aldine' edn., 1893.

*BUTLER (Samuel), b. 1835. Born, at Langar Rectory, Notts, 4 Dec. 1835. At Shrewsbury School, Aug. 1848 to Oct. 1854. To St. John's Coll., Cambridge, Oct. 1854 ; B.A., 1858. To Canterbury Settlement, New Zealand, 29 Sept. 1859. Left New Zealand, 1864. Returned to England same year ; settled in Clifford's Inn, where he now resides. Studied painting for several years and exhibited at Royal Academy. Abandoned painting for literary career, 1875. Published musical compositions (in collab. with H. Festing Jones), 1885 ; cantata 'Narcissus' (with H. Festing Jones), 1888.

Works : ' A First Year in Canterbury Settlement,' 1863 ; 'Erewhon' (anon.), 1872 ; 'The Fair Haven' (under pseudonym ' John Pickard Owen '), 1873 (2nd ed., bearing author's name, same year) ; ' Life and Habit,' 1877 ; ' Evolution, Old and New,' 1879 ; ' Unconscious Memory,' 1880 ; ' Alps and Sanctuaries of Piedmont and the Canton Ticino,' 1881 ; ' Luck, or Cunning, as the Main Means of Organic Modification?' 1886 ; ' Ex Voto,' 1888 ; ' Life of Bishop Butler ' (2 vols.), 1896.

BYROM (John), 1692-1763. Born, at Kersall Cell, Broughton, near Manchester, 29 Feb. 1692. At Merchant Taylors' School [1707-08 ?]. Entered at Trin. Coll., Camb., 6 July 1708 ; Scholar, May 1709 ; B.A. 1712 ; Fellow of Trin. Coll., 1714 ; M.A., 1715. Contrib. to 'Spectator,' 1714. Went abroad, 1716. Studied medicine at Montpelier. Returned to London, 1718. Married Elizabeth Byrom, 14 Feb. 1721. Began to teach new system of Shorthand which he had invented, 1723. F.R.S., 17 March 1724. Succeeded to property from uncle, 1733 ; to family estates, 1740. Act of Parliament giving him sole right for twenty-one years of publishing and teaching his Shorthand system, May 1742. Died, 26 Sept. 1763.

Works : 'Tunbridgialia' (anon.), 1726 ; 'An Epistle to a Gentleman of the Temple,' 1749 ; 'Enthusiasm ' (anon.), 1751 ; 'The Universal English Shorthand,' 1767.

Posthumous: 'Miscellaneous Poems' (2 vols.), 1773 ; 'Private Journal and Literary Remains' (published by Chetham Society), 1854 ; 'Poems,' ed. by A. W. Ward (Chetham Soc.), 1894, etc.

BYRON (George Gordon Noel), *Lord Byron.* **1788-1824.** Born, in London, 22 Jan. 1788. Lame from birth. Early years spent with mother in Aberdeen. Educated at private schools there, and at Grammar School, 1794-98. Succeeded to title on death of grand-uncle, May 1798. To Newstead with his mother, autumn of 1799. Made ward in Chancery under guardianship of Lord Carlisle. To school at Nottingham. To London for treatment for lameness, 1799. To Dr. Glennie's school at Dulwich, 1799. At Harrow, summer of 1801 to 1805. To Trinity Coll., Cambridge, Oct. 1805 ; M.A., 4 July 1808. On leaving Cambridge, settled at Newstead. Took seat in House of Lords, 13 March 1809. Started on 'grand tour,' 2 July 1809, to Spain, Malta, Turkey, Greece. Returned to England, July 1811. Settled in St. James's Street, London, Oct. 1811. Spoke for first time in House of Lords, 27 Feb. 1812. Married Anne Isabella Milbanke, 2 Jan. 1815. Settled in Piccadilly Terrace, London, March 1815. Daughter born, 10 Dec. 1815. Separation from wife, Feb. 1816. Left England, 24 April 1816. To Belgium, Germany, Switzerland, Italy. Amour with Miss Clairmont, 1816-17. Daughter born by her, Jan. 1817 (died April 1822). Settled in Venice, 1817. Amour with Countess Guiccioli, April to Oct., 1819. To Ravenna, Christmas 1819. Prolific literary production. 'Marino Faliero' performed at Drury Lane, spring of 1821. To Pisa, Oct. 1821. 'The Liberal' published (4 nos. only), with Leigh Hunt and Shelley, 1823. Elected member of Greek Committee in London, 1823. Sailed from Genoa for Greece, 15 July 1823. Raising Suliote troops on behalf

of Greeks against Turks at Missolonghi, Dec. 1823. Serious illness, Feb. 1824. Died, 19 April 1824. Buried in England, at Hucknall Torkard.

Works: 'Fugitive Pieces' (privately printed, all destroyed except two copies), 1806 (a facsimile privately reprinted, 1886) ; 'Poems on Various Occasions' (anon., same as preceding, with omissions), 1807 ; 'Hours of Idleness,' 1807 ; 'English Bards and Scotch Reviewers' (anon.), 1809 (2nd edn. same year) ; Poems contrib. to J. C. Hobhouse's 'Imitations and Translations,' 1809 ; 'Childe Harold,' cantos 1 and 2, 1812 (2nd-5th edns., same year) ; 'The Curse of Minerva' (anon.), 1812 ; 'The Waltz' (under pseud. of 'Horace Hornem'), 1813 ; 'The Giaour,' 1813 ; 'The Bride of Abydos,' 1813 (2nd-5th edns., same year) ; 'The Corsair,' 1814 ; 'Ode to Napoleon Buonaparte' (anon.), 1814 ; 'Lara' (anon., with Rogers's 'Jacqueline'), 1814 ; 'Hebrew Melodies,' 1815 ; 'Siege of Corinth' (anon.), 1816 ; 'Parisina,' 1816 (second edn., with preceding work, same year) ; 'Poems,' 1816 ; 'Poems on his Domestic Circumstances,' 1816 ; 'Prisoner of Chillon,' 1816 ; 'Childe Harold,' canto 3, 1816 ; 'Monody on the Death of Sheridan' (anon.), 1816 ; 'Fare Thee Well!' 1816 ; 'Manfred,' 1817 (2nd edn., same year) ; 'The Lament of Tasso,' 1817 ; 'Poems Written by Somebody' (anon.), 1818 ; 'Childe Harold,' canto 4, 1818 ; 'Beppo' (anon.), 1818 ; 'Suppressed Poems,' 1818 ; 'Three Poems not included in the Works of Lord Byron,' 1818 ; 'Don Juan,' cantos 1 and 2 (anon.), 1819 ; 'Mazeppa,' 1819 ; 'Marino Faliero,' 1820 ; 'Don Juan,' cantos 3-5 (anon.), 1821 ; 'Prophecy of Dante' (with 2nd edn. of 'Marino Faliero'), 1821 ; 'Sardanapalus, The Two Foscari, and Cain,' 1821 ; 'Letter . . . on the Rev. W. L. Bowles's Strictures on Pope,' 1821 ; 'Werner,' 1822 ; 'Don Juan,' cantos 6-14 (anon.), 1823 ; 'The Liberal,' with Leigh Hunt and Shelley (anon., 4 nos.), 1823 ; 'The Age of Bronze' (anon.), 1823 ;

'The Island,' 1823 (2nd edn., same year) ; 'The Deformed Transformed,' 1823 ; 'Heaven and Earth' (anon.), 1824 ; 'Don Juan,' cantos 15, 16 (anon.), 1824 (canto 17 of 'Don Juan,' 1829, and 'Twenty Suppressed Stanzas,' 1838, are spurious) ; 'Parliamentary Speeches,' 1824 ; 'The Vision of Judgment' (anon., reprinted from pt. i. of 'The Liberal '), 1824.

Posthumous: 'Correspondence with a Friend' (3 vols.), 1825 ; 'Letters and Journals,' edited by T. Moore (2 vols.), 1830.

Collected Works: in 8 vols., 1815-17 ; in 5 vols., 1817 ; in 8 vols., 1818-20 ; in 4 vols., 1828 ; 'Life and Works' (17 vols.), 1832-35, etc.

Life: 'Lord Byron and his Contemporaries,' by Leigh Hunt, 1826 ; life by Moore, 1830 ; by Galt, 1830 ; by Jeaffreson, 1883 ; by Roden Noel ('Great Writers' series), 1890.

CAINE (Thomas Henry Hall), b. 1853. Born, at Runcorn, Cheshire, 14 May 1853. At school in Isle of Man and at Liverpool. Educated as an architect ; never practised. Contrib. to 'Builder' and 'Building News.' Was for short time Schoolmaster at Maughold, Isle of Man. Became journalist, 1880. To London, 1881. On staff of 'Liverpool Mercury,' 1881-88. Lived with D. G. Rossetti, 1881-82. First novel published, 1885. Has contrib. to 'Athenæum,' 'Academy,' 'Times,' etc. Play, 'Ben-my-Chree' (dramatized, with Wilson Barrett, from 'The Deemster') produced at Princess's Theatre, 17 May 1888 ; 'The Good Old Times' (with Wilson Barrett) produced, at Princess's Theatre, 12 Feb. 1889 ; play, 'The Manxman,' dramatized, by Wilson Barrett, from novel, produced at Leeds, 20 Aug. 1894 ; second version, Shaftesbury Theatre, London, 18 Nov. 1895. Travelled in Iceland, 1889 ; in Morocco, 1891. To Poland and Russia on behalf of Russo-Jewish Committee, 1892. Opened Philosophical Institution, Edinburgh, and Arts Club, Edinburgh, 1894. Visit to U.S.A., 1895 ; to Canada on behalf of Authors' Society, with reference to Copyright Question, 1896. Has resided in and near London, 1881-90 ; at Keswick, 1890-93 ; in Isle of Man, since 1 May 1893.

Works: 'Richard III. and Macbeth,' 1877 ; 'Recollections of Dante Gabriel Rossetti,' 1882 ; 'Sonnets of Three Centuries,' 1882 ; 'Cobwebs of Criticism,' 1883 ; 'The Shadow of a Crime,' 1885 ; 'A Son of Hagar,' 1886 ; 'Life of S. T. Coleridge,' 1887 ; 'The Deemster,' 1887 ; 'The Bondman,' 1890; 'The Prophet,' 1890; 'The Scapegoat,' 1891 ; 'The Little Manx Nation,' 1891; 'Capt'n Davy's Honeymoon,' 1893 [1892] ; 'The Little Man Island.' 1894 ; 'The Manxman,' 1894; 'The Christian,' 1897 ; 'The Eternal City,' 1901.

He has *edited:* Maeterlinck's 'Princess Maleine, etc.,' 1892.

CALVERLEY (Charles Stuart), 1831-1884. Born [Charles Stuart Blayds], at Martley, Worcestershire, 22 Dec. 1831. Father assumed name of Calverley, 1852. Educated by private tutors ; then at Marlborough. At Harrow, Sept. 1846 to July 1850. To Balliol Coll., Oxford, as scholar, Nov. 1850 ; Chancellor's Prize, 1851. Resumed family name of Calverley, 1852. Removed to Christ's Coll., Camb., Oct. 1852 ; Craven Scholarship, 1854 ; Camden Medal, 1853 and 1855; Browne Medal, 1855; Latin Essay Prize, 1856 ; B.A., 1856 ; M.A., 1859 ; Fellow of Christ's Coll., 14 Dec. 1857 to 24 June 1863. Married Ellen Calverley, 1863. Called to Bar at Inner Temple, 1 May 1865. Severe accident, winter of 1866 ; obliged to relinquish profession. Died, at Folkestone, 17 Feb. 1884 ; buried there.

Works: 'Verses and Translations' (under initials: C. S. C.), 1862; 'Translations into English and Latin,' 1866 ; 'Theocritus, translated into English Verse,' 1869 ; 'Fly Leaves' (under initials: C. S. C.), 1872.

Collected Works: 'Literary Remains,' with *memoir* by W. J. Sendall, 1885.

CAMDEN (William), 1551-1623.
Born, in London, 2 May 1551. Educated at Christ's Hospital and St. Paul's School. To Magdalen Coll., Oxford, 1566, probably as chorister; thence to Broadgates Hall (afterwards Pembroke Coll.) and Christ Church. Supplicated for B.A. degree, 12 June 1570, and 5 March 1574; admitted, 6 March 1574; supplicated for M.A., 3 June 1588. Left Oxford and returned to London, 1571. In Oxford for short time in 1573. Pursued antiquarian researches. Appointed Second Master at Westminster School, 1575. 'Britannia' published, May 1586. Lay Prebend of Ilfracombe, 1589-1623. Headmaster of Westminster School, March 1593 [to 1599 ?]. Appointed Clarencieux King-of-Arms, Oct. 1597. Controversy with Ralph Brooke *re* 'Britannia,' 1599 - 1600. Appointed 'historian' to projected Anti-Romish College at Chelsea, 1610; scheme fell through. 'Annals' published, 1615. Latter years of life passed at Chislehurst. Endowed History Lectureship at Oxford, 1622. Died, at Chislehurst, 9 Nov. 1623. Buried in Westminster Abbey.

Works: 'Britannia,' 1586; 'Institutio Græcæ Grammatices Compendiaria,' 1597; 'Reges, Reginæ, nobiles, &c., in Ecclesia Collegiata B. Petri Westmonasterij sepulti' (anon.), 1600; 'Anglica, Hibernica, Normanica, Cambrica e veteribus scripta,' 1602; 'Remaines of a greater Worke, concerning Britaine' (under initials: M. N.), 1605; 'Actio in Henricum Garnetum,' 1607; 'Annales,' pt. i., 1615; pts. i. and ii., 1625; pt. ii. separately (uniform with 1615 edn. of pt. i.), 1627.

Posthumous: 'Historie of Princesse Elizabeth' (anon.), 1630; 'V. Cl. G. Cambdeni Elogia Anglorum,' 1653; 'V. Cl. Gulielmi Camdeni et illustrium Virorum ad G. Camdenum Epistolæ' (with *life* by Thomas Smith), 1691.

*CAMPBELL (Thomas) 1777-1844.
Born, in Glasgow, 27 July, 1777. Educated at Glasgow Grammar School, 1784-91; at Glasgow University, Oct. 1791 to Spring, 1796. As private tutor at Downie, 1796-97. Returned to Glasgow. Removed to Edinburgh to study Law. A few weeks later undertook literary work for Messrs. Mundell and Co., publishers. Also gave private tuition. First poems published, April 1799. To Germany, 1800; studied and wrote poems. Returned to London, April 1801. Married Matilda Sinclair, 10 Oct. 1803. Devoted himself to literary work, and lived in London for rest of life. Crown pension of £200 granted him, 1805. Lectured on poetry at Royal Institution, 1810. Visit to Paris, 1814. Royal Institution lectures repeated at Liverpool and Birmingham, 1819. In Germany and Austria, May to Nov. 1820. Edited 'New Monthly Magazine,' Nov. 1820 to 1830. Scheme of London University conceived, 1824. Visit to Berlin Univ., Sept. 1825. Lord Rector of Glasgow Univ., 1826-29. Wife died, 1828. Edited 'Metropolitan Magazine,' 1831-32. Founded Polish Association, 1832. Visit to Paris and Algiers, 1834. Returned to London, 1835. Settled in Victoria Square, Pimlico, with niece (Mary Campbell) as companion. Edited 'The Scenic Annual' for 1838. To Boulogne for health, June 1843. Died there, 15 June 1844. Buried in Westminster Abbey.

Works: 'The Pleasures of Hope,' 1799; 'Annals of Great Britain' (anon.), 1807; 'Gertrude of Wyoming,' 1809; 'Essay on English Poetry,' 1819; 'Specimens of the British Poets' (7 vols.), 1819; 'Miscellaneous Poems,' 1824; 'Theodric,' 1824 [?] (2nd edn., 1824); 'Rectorial Address,' 1827; 'Poland,' 1831 [?] (2nd edn., 1831); 'Life of Mrs. Siddons' (2 vols.), 1834; 'Letters from the South' (2 vols.), 1837; 'Life of Petrarch' (2 vols.), 1841; 'The Pilgrim of Glencoe,' 1842; 'History of Our Own Times' (anon.), 1843.

Posthumous: 'Life and Letters,' ed. by W. Beattie, 1849.

He *edited:* Byron's Works (with Moore, Scott, etc.), 1835; Shakespeare's Plays, 1838 ; ' Frederick the Great; his Court and Times,' 1842-43. *Collected Poems:* in 2 vols., 1810, 1815 ; in 2 vols., 1828 ; in 2 vols., 1833, 1837, 1839, 1851 (ed. by W. A. Hill, illustrated by Turner), etc.

* **CARLETON (William), 1794-1869.** Born, at Prillisk, co. Tyrone, 20 Feb. 1794 (according to his autobiography; 4 March according to his tombstone). Educated at various small schools in neighbourhood. Intended for Church, but idea soon abandoned. Apprenticed to stone-cutter, 1814. Private tutor in farmer's family, co. Louth, 1814. To Dublin, 1818 ; engaged in tuition. Clerk to Sunday School Society. Married Jane Anderson, [1820?]. Began to contribute to various periodicals ; to ' Christian Examiner,' 1828-30 ; to ' National Magazine,' 1830-31. Granted Crown pension of £200, 14 July 1848. Visit to London, Oct. to Nov., 1850. Died, at Sandford, co. Dublin, 30 Jan. 1869.

Works: 'Traits and Stories of the Irish Peasantry' (anon.), 2 series, 1830-33 ; 'Tales of Ireland' (anon.), 1834; 'Fardorougha the Miser,' 1839; 'Father Butler,' 1839 ; 'The Fawn of Springvale, etc.,' 1841 (2nd ed., entitled 'Jane Sinclair,' 1849); 'Valentine McClutchy,' 1845 ; 'Rody the Rover,' 1845 ; 'Parra Sastha,' 1845 ; 'Art Maguire,' 1847 ; 'The Black Prophet,' 1847 ; 'The Emigrants of Ahadarra,' 1847 ; 'The Tithe Proctor,' 1849 ; 'The Clarionet, etc.,' 1850 ; 'Red Hall,' 1852 (2nd edn., entitled 'The Black Baronet,' 1857) ; 'The Squanders of Castle Squander,' 1852 ; 'Willy Reilly,' 1855 (2nd edn., same year) ; 'The Emigrants,' 1857 ; 'The Evil Eye,' 1860 ; 'The Double Prophecy,' 1862 ; 'Redmond, Count O'Hanlon,' 1862 ; 'The Silver Acre, etc.,' 1862.

Posthumous: 'The Fair of Emyvale, etc.,' 1870 ; 'Farm Ballads,' 1873 ; 'Farm Festivals,' 1881 ; 'Farm Legends,' 1882 ; 'The Red Haired Man's Wife,' 1889.

Life: (including Autobiography and Letters) by D. J. O'Donoghue, 1896.

CARLYLE (Thomas), 1795 - 1881. Born, at Ecclefechan, 4 Dec. 1795. First educated at village school. To Annan Grammar School, 1805. To Edinburgh Univ., Nov. 1809, to study for Church. Mathematical tutorship at Annan, 1814-16. Schoolmastership, 1816 - 19, at Kirkcaldy, where intimacy with Edward Irving was begun. Idea of ministry given up. To Edinburgh with Irving, to study for Bar, Dec. 1819. Four years of struggle. Worked for 'Edinburgh Encyclopædia,' 1820-23. Contrib. to 'New Edinburgh Review,' 1821-22 ; 'Edinburgh Review,' 1827-29, 1831-32 ; 'Foreign Review,' 1828-30 ; 'Foreign Quarterly Review,' 1831-33, 1843 ; 'Fraser's Magazine,' 1830-33, 1835, 1837, 1839, 1841, 1844, 1847, 1849, 1875 ; 'Westminster Review,' 1831 ; 'New Monthly Magazine,' 1832 ; 'London and Westminster Review,' 1837-38, 1842, 1855 ; 'Examiner,' 1839 ; 'Leigh Hunt's Journal,' 1850 : 'Keepsake,' 1852 ; 'Proceedings of Soc. of Scotch Antiquaries,' 1854 ; 'Macmillan,' 1863, 1867. Tutor to sons of Mrs. Buller, Jan. 1822 to June 1824. Contrib. a life of Schiller to 'London Magazine,' 1823-24. 'Wilhelm Meister' translation accepted for publication. Returned to Scotland, March 1825. Married Jane Baillie Welsh, 17 Oct. 1826. Increasing literary reputation in Edinburgh. Contrib. to various reviews, chiefly articles on German literature. Settled at Craigen-puttock, May 1828. To London, Aug. 1831 ; joined there by his wife, Oct. 1831. Return to Craigenputtock, April 1832. In Edinburgh, Jan. to May, 1833. 'Sartor Resartus' appeared in 'Fraser's Magazine,' Nov. 1833 to Aug. 1834. Pecuniary difficulties. To London, May 1834 ; settled in Cheyne Row, 10 June 1834. Engaged on 'French Revolution,' Feb. 1835 to Jan. 1837 ; MS. of first vol. accidentally destroyed, March 1835. Lectured at Willis's Rooms, on German literature, May 1837 ; on Spiritual History of Man, May 1838 ; on French Revolution, May 1839 ; on Hero Worship, May 1840. Agitated for institution of London Library, 1839 (it was started the next year). Engaged on 'Cromwell,' 1840-45. Visits to Ireland, 1846 and 1849. 'Latter Day Pamphlets' written, 1850. At work on 'Frederick the Great,' 1851-65. Ill health of wife, 1860-65. Elected Lord Rector of Edinburgh Univ., Nov. 1865. Wife died, 21 April 1866. Winter at Mentone, 1866-67. Pres. of Edin. Philos. Inst., 1868 and 1877. President of London Library, 1870-81. Prussian Order of Merit, Feb. 1874. Failing health and inability to write. Died 4 Feb. 1881. Buried at Ecclefechan.

Works : ' Life of Friedrich Schiller ' (anon.), 1825 ; 'German Romance' (translations ; anon.), 1827 ; 'French Revolution,' 1837 ; 'Sartor Resartus' (anon. ; from 'Fraser's Mag.'), 1838 ; 'Critical and Miscellaneous Essays,' 1839 ; 'Chartism,' 1840 (2nd edn. same year) ; 'On Heroes,' 1841 ; 'Past and Present,' 1843 ; 'Life and Letters of Oliver Cromwell,' 1845 ; 'Latter-Day Pamphlets,' 1850 ; 'Life of John Sterling,' 1851 ; ' Occasional Discourse on the Nigger Question' (from 'Fraser's Mag.'), 1853 ; 'History of Friedrich II.,' vol. i., ii., 1858 ; vol. iii., 1862 ; vol. iv., 1864 ; vol. v., vi., 1865 ; 'Inaugural Address at Edinburgh,' 1866 ; ' Shooting Niagara' (from 'Macmillan's Mag.'), 1867 ; 'Mr. Carlyle on the War' (from the 'Times '), 1871 ; 'The Early Kings of Norway' (from 'Fraser's Mag.'), 1875.

Posthumous : ' Reminiscences,' ed. by Froude, 1881 ; 'Letters to Mrs. Basil Montagu and B. W. Proctor' (privately printed), 1881 ; 'Reminiscences of My Irish Journey in 1849,' ed. by Froude, 1882 ; 'Last Words,' 1882 ; Correspondence with Emerson, 1883 ; 'Early Letters,' 1886 ; Correspondence with Goethe, 1887.

He *translated :* Legendre's 'Geometry,' 1824 ; Goethe's 'Wilhelm Meister' (anon.), 1824 ; Musæus' 'Dumb Love,' 1827.

Collected Works : in 16 vols., 1856-58 ; in 34 vols., 1869-71 ; in 37 vols., 1871-74 ; etc.

Life : by Froude (two lives), 1882

and 1884 ; by Dr. Garnett ('Great Writers' series), 1887.

CARROLL (Lewis). *See* Dodgson (C. L.).

CARY (Henry Francis), 1772-1844. Born, at Gibraltar, 6 Dec. 1772. Father settled in Staffordshire. Educated first at Rugby, 1783-85 ; at Sutton Coldfield Grammar School, 1785-87 ; at Birmingham Grammar School, 1787-90. Contrib. to 'Gentleman's Magazine,' from 1788. To Ch. Ch., Oxford, 29 April 1790 ; B.A., 14 Jan. 1794 ; M.A., 23 Nov. 1796. Ordained, Spring of 1796 ; Vicar of Abbott's Bromley, Staffordshire. Married Jane Ormsby, 19 Sept. 1796. Instituted in living of Kingsbury, Warwickshire, 27 June 1800 ; removed thither, 12 Nov. 1800. Occupied on Dante translation, 1797-1812. To London, 1807. Reader at Berkeley Chapel, 1810-13. To Chiswick, as Curate and Lecturer, 1814. Curate of Savoy, June 1816. Contrib. to 'London Magazine,' 1821-24. Assistant-Keeper of printed books in British Museum, June 1826 to July 1837. Crown pension, 23 Aug. 1841. Died, at Willesden, 14 Aug. 1844. Buried in Westminster Abbey.

Works : ' Sonnets and Odes,' 1788 ; ' Ode to General Kosciusko,' 1797.

Posthumous : 'Lives of English Poets,' 1846 ; 'The Early French Poets,' 1846.

He *translated :* Dante's ' Divina Commedia,' 1814 (' Inferno,' 1805) ; Aristophanes' 'Birds,' 1824 ; Pindar, 1833 ; and *edited :* Cowper's Poems, 1839 ; Milton, Thomson, and Young's Poems, 1841.

Life : by his son, H. Cary, 1847.

CAXTON (William), 1422[?]-1491. Born, in Kent, 1422 [?]. Apprenticed to a mercer in London, 24 June 1438. To Bruges, *c.* 1441. Set up in business there at expiration of apprenticeship, 1446. Visit to London 1453. Appointed Governor of Merchant Adventurers at Bruges, 1465. Married, 1469 [?]. Gave up business and

4

took service in household of Duchess of Burgundy, 1471. Engaged on translation of 'Le Recueil des Histoires de Troye,' 1469-71. Printed it, 1474 [?]. Returned to England, 1476. Practised art of printing, and translated a large number of works, 1476-91. At court of Edward IV. and Richard III. Audited parochial accounts of St. Margaret's, Westminster, 1478-84. Died, 1491. Buried at St. Margaret's, Westminster.

Translations by Caxton : ' Recueyll of the histories of Troye, 1474 [?] ; 'The Game and Play of the Chess,' 1474-75 ; 'The History of Jason,' 1477 ; 'Description of Britain,' 1480 ; 'The Mirrour of the World,' 1480 ; 'The History of Reynard the Fox,' 1481 ; 'The History of Godfrey of Boulogne,' 1481 ; Polychronicon,' 1482 ; 'Caton,' 1483 ; 'The Golden Legend,' 1483 ; 'The Knight of the Tower's Book,' 1484 ; 'The Fables of Æsop,' 1484 ; 'The Order of Chivalry,' 1484 [?] ; 'The Curial,' 1484 [?] ; 'The Life of Saint Winifred,' 1485 [?] ; 'The Life of Charles the Great,' 1485 ; 'The Knight Paris,' 1485 ; 'The Book of Good Manners,' 1487 ; 'The Royal Book,' 1488 [?] ; 'The Doctrinal of Sapience,' 1489 ; 'Fayts of Arms,' 1489 ; 'The Historie of Blanchardin and Eglantine,' 1489 [?] ; 'Four Sons of Aymon,' 1489 [?] ; ' Eneydos,' 1490 ; ' Art and Craft to know well how to die,' 1490.

He *edited :* Earl Rivers' 'Dictes . . . of the Philosophres,' 1477 ; Chaucer's 'Canterbury Tales,' 1478 ; Earl Rivers' 'Cordial,' 1479 ; 'The Cronycles of England,' 1480 ; Cicero's 'De Senectute,' 1481 ; 'The Pylgremage of the Sowle,' 1483 ; 'Four Sermons,' 1483 ; Gower's 'Confessio Amantis,' 1483.

He *printed* in all upwards of seventy works (including all the above), 1474-91.

CENTLIVRE (*Mrs.* **Susannah**), 1667 [?]-1723. Born [Susannah Freeman ? or Rawkins ?], in Ireland [?], 1667 [?]. Is said to have run away from home on father's second marriage, and lived in Cambridge with Anthony Hammond ; in London, for about a year, with a nephew of Sir Stephen Fox ; and subsequently with a Capt. Carroll, for about eighteen months. Plays produced at Drury Lane, 1700-22 ; others occasionally at Lincoln's Inn Fields and Haymarket. First appeared as an actress at Bath, in her 'Love at a Venture,' 1706. Joined company of strolling players. Married to Joseph Centlivre, head cook to Queen Anne and George I., 1706 [?]. Died in London, 1 Dec. 1723. Buried in St. Martin's-in-the-Fields, and afterwards transferred to St. Paul's, Covent Garden.

Works : 'The Perjur'd Husband,' 1700 (produced at Drury Lane, 1700) ; 'Love at a Venture,' 1706 (prod. at Bath, 1706 [?]) ; 'The Beau's Duel,' 1702 (prod. Lincoln's Inn Fields, 1702) ; 'The Stolen Heiress' (anon.), [1703] (prod. Lincoln's Inn Fields, 1702) ; 'Love's Contrivance' (anon.), 1703 (prod. Drury Lane, 1703) ; 'The Gamester' (anon.), 1705 (prod. Lincoln's Inn Fields, 1705 [?]) ; 'The Bassett Table' (anon.), 1706 (prod. Drury Lane, 1705) ; 'The Platonick Lady' (anon.), 1707 (prod. Drury Lane, 1706) ; 'The Busy Body,' 1709 (prod. Drury Lane, 1709) ; 'The Man's Bewitched,' [1710] (prod. Haymarket, 1709) ; 'A Bickerstaff's Burial,' [1710?] (prod. Drury Lane, 1710) ; ' Marplot,' 1711 (prod. Drury Lane, 1710) ; 'The Perplex'd Lovers,' 1712 (prod. Drury Lane, 1712) ; 'The Wonder !' 1714 (prod. Drury Lane, 1714) ; 'A Gotham Election,' 1715 (not acted ; 2nd edn., called 'Humours of Elections,' 1737) ; 'A Wife Well Managed,' 1715 (prod. Drury Lane, 1715 [?]) ; 'A Poem, humbly presented to . . . George, King of Great Britain, upon his Accession to the Throne,' 1715 ; 'The Cruel Gift' (with Rowe), 1717 (prod. Drury Lane, 1716) ; 'A Bold Stroke for a Wife' (with Mottley), 1718 (prod. Drury Lane, 1718) ; 'The Artifice,' 1721 (prod. Drury Lane, 1722).

Collected Works : in 3 vols., with *life*, 1761 (2nd edn., 1872).

CHAMBERS (Robert), 1802-1871. Born, in Peebles, 10 July 1802. Educated at Burgh and Grammar schools there. Family removed to Edinburgh, Dec. 1813. He followed and went to school there, 1814-15. Taught in Portobello for a time, 1816. Two clerkships for short periods, 1817. Started book-shop in Leith Walk, 1818. Moved to India Place, 1823. Started 'The Kaleidoscope' with his brother, 6 Oct. 1821. Edited it till 12 Jan. 1822. Made acquaintance of Scott, and engaged in literary work. Published various works. Married Anne Kirkwood, 7 Dec. 1829. Established 'Chambers's Journal,' with his brother William, 4 Feb. 1832. Started with him publishing firm of W. and R. Chambers, 1833. Fellow of Royal Soc. of Edinburgh, 1840. Received freedom of Peebles, 1841. Moved to St. Andrews, 1841. F.G.S., 1844. Returned to Edinburgh, 1844. Visit to Switzerland, 1848 ; to Norway, 1849 ; to Iceland, 1855 ; to U.S.A., 1860. Settled in London, March 1861. LL.D., St. Andrews, 1861. Elected member of Athenæum Club, 1860. Visit to France and Belgium, 1862. Wife and daughter died, Sept. 1863. Married Mrs. Frith, Jan. 1867 ; she died, 18 Jan. 1870. Hon. LL.D., St. Andrews, 1868. Died, at St. Andrews, 17 March 1871.

Works : ' Illustrations of the Author of Waverley,' 1822 ; 'Traditions of Edinburgh' (2 vols.), 1823 ; ' Fires which have occurred in Edinburgh,' 1824 ; ' Walks in Edinburgh,' 1825 ; ' Popular Rhymes of Scotland,' 1826 ; ' Picture of Scotland ' (2 vols.), 1827 ; ' History of the Rebellion in Scotland ... 1638 till 1660' (2 vols.), 1828 ; 'History of the Rebellion in Scotland in 1745-46 ' (2 vols.), 1828 ; 'The Scottish Ballads,' 1829 ; ' The Scottish Songs,' 1829 ; ' History of the Rebellions in Scotland . . . in 1689 and 1715,' 1829 ; 'Scottish Jests and Anecdotes ' [1830 ?] ; ' The Life of King James I.' (2 vols.), 1830 ; ' Biographical Dict. of Eminent Scotsmen ' (4 vols.), 1832-35 ; ' Gazetteer of Scotland ' (with W. Chambers), 1832 ;

' Poems ' (privately printed), 1835 ; ' Life of Sir Walter Scott' [1835 ?] 'History of the English Language and Literature,' 1836 ; 'The Land of Burns ' (with Prof. Wilson), 1840 ; 'Popular Rhymes ... of Scotland ' (anon.), 1842 ; ' Vestiges of the Natural History of Creation ' (anon.), 1844 ; ' Cyclopædia of English Literature ' (with R. Carruthers ; 2 vols.), 1844 ; 'Romantic Scotch Ballads,' 1844 ; ' Explanation ; a sequel to " Vestiges, etc.," ' 1845 ; ' Select Writings ' (7 vols.), 1847 ; ' Ancient Sea Margins,' 1848 ; 'The History of Scotland, 1849 ; ' Life and Works of Robert Burns,' 1851 ; ' Tracings of the North of Europe,' 1851 ; ' Tracings in Iceland and the Faröe Islands,' 1856 ; ' Domestic Annals of Scotland from the Reformation to the Revolution ' (2 vols.), 1858 ; ' Domestic Annals of Scotland from the Revolution to the Rebellion of 1745,' 1861 ; ' Edinburgh Papers,' pt. i.-v., 1859-61 ; ' Songs of Scotland prior to Burns,' 1862 ; ' Book of Days ' (2 vols.), 1862, 64 ; ' Essays, Familiar and Humorous' (from ' Chambers's Journal '), 1866 ; ' Life of Smollett,' 1867.

Posthumous : ' The Threiplands of Fingask,' 1880.

He *edited :* Bishop Forbes' ' Jacobite Memoirs of the Rebellion of 1745,' 1834 ; J. Currie's ' Life of Burns,' 1838 ; Burns' ' Poetical Works,' 1838, and ' Prose Works,' 1839 ; Sir William Forbes' ' Memoirs of a Banking House,' 1860 ; and published, with his brother, ' Chambers's Information for the People,' 1835 ; ' Chambers's Miscellany,' 1869, etc. ; ' Chambers's Encyclopædia ' (10 vols.), 1859-68 ; and started ' Chambers's Educational Course,' 1835.

Life : ' Memoir,' by W. Chambers, 13th edn. 1884.

CHAMBERS (William), 1800-1883. Born, at Peebles, 16 April 1800. At Burgh and Grammar schools there. With family to Edinburgh, Dec. 1813. Apprenticed to bookseller, 8 May 1814 to May 1819. Settled as bookseller in Leith Walk, close to his brother's late shop, May 1819. Bought printing press. Printed 'The Kaleidoscope,' which his brother Robert edited 6 Oct. 1821 to 12 Jan. 1822. Removed to Broughton Street, 1823. Established 'Chambers's Journal' with his brother Robert, Feb. 1832. Started with him publishing firm of W. and R. Chambers, 1833. Married Harriet Beddon Clark, 4 June 1833. Edited 'Chambers's Historical Newspaper,' 1836. Visit to Holland, 1838 ; to Germany, 1848 ; to U.S.A., 1853. Received freedom of Peebles, 1841. Presented Peebles with the Chambers Institution, opened 9 Aug. 1859. Lord Provost of Edinburgh, 1865-69. Hon. LL.D., Edin., 1872. Active promoter of Edinburgh improvements ; and of scheme for restoration of St. Giles's Church (reopened 23 May 1883). Attended levée at St. James's Palace, 2 May 1866. Declined offer of Knighthood, 1881. Accepted offer of Baronetcy, May 1883 ; but died, at St. Andrews, before title could be bestowed, 20 May 1883. Buried in St. Andrew's Churchyard.

Works : 'The Life and Anecdotes of David Ritchie' (privately printed), 1820 ; 'A History of the Gipsies' (printed by himself), 1821 ; 'The Book of Scotland,' 1830 ; 'Gazetteer of Scotland' (with R. Chambers), 1832 ; 'Tour in Holland,' 1839 ; 'Truth and Trust' (anon.), 1848 ; 'Glenormiston,' 1849 ; 'Fiddy,' 1851 ; 'Things as they are in America,' 1854 ; 'Peebles and its Neighbourhood,' 1856 ; 'American Slavery and Colour,' 1857 ; 'Youths' Companion,' 1858 [1857] ; 'Something of Italy,' 1862 ; 'History of Peeblesshire,' 1864 ; 'Chambers's Historical Questions,' 1865 ; 'France,' 1866 ; 'About Railways,' 1866 ; 'Chambers's Miscellaneous Questions,' 1866 ; 'Sketches, light and descriptive,' 1866 ; 'Wintering at Mentone,' 1870 ; 'Ailie Gilroy,' 1872 ; 'Memoir of Robert Chambers,' 1872 ; 'Biography Exemplary and Instructive,' 1873 ; 'A Week at Welwyn,' 1873 ; 'Kindness to Animals,' 1877 ; 'Stories of Old Families' (2 vols.), 1878 ; 'Stories of Remarkable Persons,' 1878 ; 'Story of a Long and Busy Life,' 1882.

He *edited :* 'Poems for Young People,' 1851 ; 'Chambers's Social Science Tracts,' nos. 1-6, 1860 ; new edn. of Robert Chambers's 'Life of Sir Walter Scott,' 1871 ; and *with his brother,* 'Chambers's Information for the People,' 1833 ; 'Chambers's Miscellany,' 1869, etc. ; 'Chambers's Encyclopædia' (10 vols.), 1859-68 ; and started 'Chambers's Educational Course,' 1835.

Life : in 'Memoir of R. Chambers, by himself, 13th edn., 1884.

CHAPMAN (George), 1559 [?]-1634. Born, near Hitchin, 1559 [?]. Educated at Trinity Coll., Oxford [?]. First poems printed, 1594. First part of Homer translation pub., 1598. Prolific writer for stage. Died, in London, 12 May 1634. Buried in churchyard of St. Giles-in-the-Fields.

Works : 'Σκια Νυκτος' (under initials : G.W. Gent.), 1594 ; 'Ovid's Banquet of Sence' (anon.), 1595 ; Completion of Marlowe's 'Hero and Leander,' 1598 ; 'The Blind Beggar of Alexandria,' 1598 ; 'Seaven Bookes of the Iliades of Homere,' translated, 1598 ; 'Achilles' Shield' translated, 1598 ; 'An Humorous Dayes Mirth' (under initials : G.C.), 1599 ; 'Eastward Hoe' (with Jonson and Marston), 1605 ; 'All Fools,' 1605 ; 'The Gentleman Usher,' 1606 ; 'Monsieurd'Olive,' 1606 ; 'Sir Gyles Goosecappe' (anon.), 1606 (performed 1601) ; 'Bussy d'Ambois' (anon.), 1607 ; 'The Tragedie of Cæsar and Pompey' (anon.), 1607 ; 'The Conspiracie and Tragedie of Charles, Duke of Byron,'1608 (performed 1605); 'Euthymiæ Raptus,' 1609 ; 'The Iliades of Homer' (complete), [1611]; 'May Day,' 1611 ; 'The Widowes Teares' ("by Geor. Chap."), 1612 ; Translation of Petrarch's 'Seven Penitentiall Psalms,' 1612 ; 'An Epicede' (anon.), 1612 ; 'The Revenge of Bussy d'Ambois,'1613 ; 'Memorable Masque,' 1614 ; 'Eugenia,' 1614 ; 'Andromeda Liberata,' 1614 ; 'Twenty Four Bookes of Homere's Odisses translated,' 1614 ; Iliad and Odyssey translations together, 1616 ; 'Divine Poem' of Musæus translated. 1617 ; Hesiod's

'Georgicks' translated, 1618 ; 'Two Wise Men' (anon.), 1619 ; 'Pro Vere Autumni Lachrymæ,' 1622 ; 'A Justification of a Strange Action of Nero,' 1629 ; Homer's 'Batrachomyomachia' translated, 1624 ; 'The Warres of Pompey and Cæsar' (anon.), 1631.

Posthumous: 'The Ball' (with Shirley). 1639 (acted 1632); 'The Tragedy of Chabot' (with Shirley), 1639 (acted 1635) ; 'The Tragedy of Alphonsus, Emperor of Germany,' 1654 ; 'Revenge for Honour,' 1654.

He contributed verses to : Jones's 'Nennio,' 1595 ; Jonson's 'Sejanus,' 1605, and 'Volpone,' 1606; Fletcher's 'Faithful Shepherdesse,' 1610 [?] ; 'Parthenia,' 1611 ; Field's 'A Woman is a Weathercock,' 1612.

Collected Works: in 3 vols., 1874-75.

CHATTERTON (Thomas), 1752-1770. Born, at Bristol, 20 Nov. 1752. Educated at Colston's Hospital, Bristol, Aug. 1760 to July 1767. First poems printed in 'Farley's Bristol Journal,' 1763 and 1764. Apprenticed to a Bristol attorney, July 1767. First of 'Rowley' poems written, 1768. Success with pseudo-antique poems. Apprentice indentures cancelled, April 1770. Left Bristol for London, 24 April 1770. Contributed to various periodicals, but resources gradually failed. Only one poem separately printed in lifetime. Committed suicide, 25 Aug. 1770. Buried in Shoe Lane Workhouse Churchyard. Afterwards transferred to graveyard in Gray's Inn Road.

Works: 'An Elegy on the much lamented death of William Beckford, Esq.' (anon.), 1770.

Posthumous: 'The Execution of Sir Charles Baldwin' (ed. by T. Eagles), 1772 ; 'Poems supposed to have been written at Bristol, by Thomas Rowley and others' (ed. by T. Tyrwhitt), 1777 (2nd edn., same year) ; 'Miscellanies in Prose and Verse' (ed. by J. Broughton), 1778 ; 'Rowley' poems, ed. by Dean Milles, 1782 ; Supplement to 'Miscellanies,' 1784 ; 'Rowley' poems, ed. by L. Sharpe, 1794 ; 'The Revenge,' 1795.

Poetical Works: in 1 vol., 1795 ; in 3 vols., 1803 ; in 2 vols., 1875 ; in 1 vol., 1885.

Life: by Gregory, 1789 ; by Davis (with letters), 1806 ; by Dix, 1837 ; by Wilson, 1869, and memoirs in edns. of works.

CHAUCER (Geoffrey), 1340[?]-1400. Born, in London [?], 1340 [?]. Page in household of Duke of Clarence, 1357. Took part in King's expedition into France, 1359 ; taken prisoner in Brittany. Was 'Valettus' to the King in 1361. Pension of 20 marks granted him by King, June 1367 ; Yeoman of King's Chamber at that time. Abroad again, 1369 and 1370. To Italy on Commission respecting commercial treaty, Dec. 1372 to autumn of 1373. Married, 1374 [?]. Grant of daily pitcher of wine (afterwards commuted to second pension of 20 marks), 23 April 1374. Comptroller of Customs, 8 June 1374. Pension of £10 granted him by Duke of Lancaster, 13 June 1374. Two custodianships, 1375. On secret service with Sir John Burley, 1376 ; with Sir Thomas Percy in Flanders, 1377 ; in France and Italy, 1378 and 1379. Second Comptrollership of Customs, 1382. Knight of the Shire for Kent, 1386. Deprived of Comptrollerships, 1386. 'Canterbury Tales' probably written, 1387 to 1393. Financial difficulties ; sold pensions, May 1388. Appointed Clerk of King's Works, 1389 ; superseded, 1391. Probably Forester of North Petherton Park, Somersetshire, 1391-98. Grant of £20 a year for life from King Richard II., 1394 ; of 40 marks from King Henry IV., 1399. Took lease of house in Westminster, Christmas Eve, 1399. Died, 25 Oct. 1400. Buried in Westminster Abbey.

Works: 'Assembly of Fowls,' first printed, 1478 ; 'Canterbury Tales,' first printed by Caxton, 1478 [?], by Pynson, 1493 [?], by Wynken de Worde, 1498 ; 'Troilus and Cressida,' first printed (anon.), 1482 [?] ; 'The House [or 'Book'] of Fame,' first printed by Caxton, 1486 [?]; Chaucer's translation of Boethius' 'De Consolatione Philosophiæ,' first printed, 1490 (?).

Collected Works. earliest, 1532, 1542, etc. ; latest (Kelmscott Press), 1896.

Life : by Godwin, 2nd edn., 1804 ; memoirs in various edns. of works.

CHESTERFIELD [Philip Dormer Stanhope], 4th Earl of, 1694-1773. Born, in London, 22 Sept. 1694. Early education at home. To Trinity Hall, Cambridge, 1712 ; M.A., 1714. Visit to the Hague and Paris, 1714. Appointed Gentleman of the Bedchamber to the Prince of Wales, 1715. M.P. for St. Germains, Cornwall, 1715 ; entered House of Commons as Lord Stanhope of Shelford, while still a minor. First speech, 5 Aug. 1715. To avoid consequence of discovery of his having been elected during his minority, returned to Paris. Returned to England and to Parliament early in 1716. Appointed Captain of Gentlemen Pensioners, 1723 ; resigned, or was dismissed from post, 1725. Refused Order of Bath, 1725. Succeeded to earldom on his father's death, 1726. Appointed Ambassador at the Hague, April 1728 ; arrived there, 5 May. Visit to England on leave, Oct. 1729. Knight of the Garter, May 1730 ; Lord Steward, June 1730. Returned to the Hague, Aug. 1730. Signed second Treaty of Vienna, 16 March 1731. Recalled from Embassy, 1732. Dismissed from post of Lord Steward in consequence of opposition to Walpole's Excise Bill, April 1733. Married Melosina' de Schoulenbourg, Baroness of Aldborough and Countess of Walsingham, 5 Sept. 1733. Contrib. to ' Fog's Journal,' 1736. Contrib. to ' Common Sense,' 1737-39. 'Letters to his Son' written, 1738-68. Visit to France, 1741. Contrib. to ' Old England,' 1743. On special mission as Ambassador to the Hague, Jan. to May, 1745. To Dublin as Lord Lieutenant of Ireland, June 1745. Returned to England, April 1746. Exchanged Lord Lieutenancy for Secretaryship of State, Nov. 1746 ; resigned the latter,

Feb. 1748. Life of retirement begun. Declined Presidentship of Council, Dec. 1750. Brought about reformation of Calendar, 1751. Contrib. to 'The World,' 1753-54. Refused to resume Lord Lieutenancy of Ireland, 1754. Member of Académie des Belles Lettres of Paris, Aug. 1755. Last appearance in House of Lords, 10 Dec. 1755. Effected combination between Duke of Newcastle and Pitt, 1757. Letters to his godson and heir, Philip Stanhope, written 1761-70. Son died, 16 Nov. 1768. Died, at Blackheath, 24 March 1773.

Works : ' The Case of the Hanover Forces in the Pay of Great Britain . . . examined ' (with E. Waller ; anon.), 1743 ; ' A Vindication of a late pamphlet intituled, "The Case of the Hanover Troops," etc.' (anon.), 1743 ; ' A Farther Vindication of the Case of the Hanover Troops ' (anon.), 1743 ; ' An Apology for a late Resignation ' [anon., 1748] ; ' The Œconomy of Human Life' (anon. ; by Chesterfield [?], or R. Dodsley [?]), 1751.

Posthumous : ' Letters to his Son ' (2 vols.), 1774 ; ' Miscellaneous Works ' (with memoir by Maty, 2 vols.), 1777 ; ' Characters of Eminent Personages of his own Time,' 1777 ; ' Supplement ' to his Letters, 1777 ; ' The World ' (under pseud. of ' Adam FitzAdam,' by Chesterfield and others), 1782 ; ' The Art of Pleasing,' 1783 ; ' Letters to his Heir,' 1783 ; ' Genuine Memoirs of Asiaticus,' 1784.

Life : by W. Ernst, 1893.

CHURCHILL (Charles), 1731-1764. Born, in Westminster, Feb. 1731. Educated at Westminster School, 1739-49 [?]. Made a 'Fleet marriage' with Miss Scot, 1748. Entered at Trinity Coll., Cambridge, 1749, but did not take up residence. Ordained Curate to South Cadbury, Somersetshire, 1753. Ordained Priest, 1756 ; took curacy under his father at Rainham. Succeeded father at his death to curacy and lectureship of St. John's, Westminster. Added to small income by tuition. Separation from his wife, Feb. 1761. Contrib. to 'The Library,'

1761. Resigned lectureship in consequence of protests of parishioners, Jan. 1763. Assisted Wilkes in editing 'The North Briton,' 1762-63. Copious publication of satires and poems. At Oxford during Commemoration, 1763. Died, at Boulogne, 4 Nov. 1764. Buried in St. Martin's Churchyard, Dover.

Works: 'The Rosciad' (anon.), 1761; 'The Apology, addressed to the Critical Reviewers,' 1761; 'Night' (anon.), 1761; 'The Ghost,' bks. i., ii. (anon.), 1762; bk. iii., 1762; bk. iv., 1763; 'The Prophecy of Famine,' 1763; 'The Conference,' 1763; 'An Epistle to W. Hogarth,' 1763; 'The Author,' 1763; 'Poems,' 1763; 'Gotham,' 1764; 'The Duellist,' 1764 (2nd edn. same year); 'The Candidate,'1764; 'The Times'(anon.),1764; 'Independence' (anon.), 1764; 'The Farewell' (anon.), 1764.

Posthumous: 'Sermons' (possibly by his father), 1765.

Collected Works: in 4 vols., 1765; in 4 vols., 1774; in 2 vols., with *life*, 1804.

CIBBER (Colley), *Poet Laureate.* **1671-1757.** Born, in London, 6 Nov. 1671. Educated at Grantham Free School, 1682-87. Not long after enlisting in forces of Earl of Devonshire he abandoned army, and in 1690 went to London and joined company of Theatre Royal. First appeared as an actor, 1691; at Theatre Royal, 1691-95. Married Miss Shore, 1692. Followed Betterton to new theatre in Little Lincoln's Inn Fields, 1695. Wrote prologue for opening of theatre. His first play 'Love's Last Shift' produced there, Jan. 1696. At Haymarket, 1706-08. At Drury Lane, 1708-32. Share in patent of Drury Lane, March 1708. Concerned with management of Haymarket, 1709-10; of Drury Lane, 1710-33. Appointed Poet Laureate, 3 Dec. 1730. Retired from stage, 1733. Reappeared on one or two occasions afterwards; last appearance, 15 Feb. 1745. Died, 12 Dec. 1757. Buried in vault of Danish Church (now British and Foreign Sailors' Church), Whitechapel.

Works: 'Love's Last Shift,' 1694; 'A Poem on the Death of Queen Mary,' 1695; 'Woman's Wit,' 1697 (another edn., under title of 'The Schoolboy,' anon., 1707); 'Xerxes,' 1699; acting version of Shakespeare's 'King Richard III.,' 1700; 'Love makes a Man,' 1701; 'She Would and she Would not,' 1703; 'The Careless Husband,' 1705; 'Perolla and Izadora,' 1706; 'The Comical Lovers' (anon), 1707; 'The Double Gallant.' 1707; 'The Lady's Last Stake,' [1708]; 'The Rival Fools,' [1709]; 'Cinna's Conspiracy' (anon.; attributed to Cibber), 1713; 'Myrtillo,' 1715; 'Hob; or the Country Wake,' 1715; 'Venus and Adonis,' 1716; 'The Non-Juror,' 1718; 'Ximena,' 1718; 'Plays' (2 vols.), 1721; 'The Refusal,' 1721; 'Cæsar in Ægypt,'1725; 'The Provoked Husband' (with Vanbrugh), 1728; 'The Rival Queans,' 1729; 'Love in a Riddle,' 1719 [1729]; 'Damon and Phillida' (anon., founded on preceding), 1729; 'A Journey to London' (adapted from Vanbrugh), 1730; 'An Ode for His Majesty's Birth-Day,' 1731; 'An Ode to His Majesty for the New Year,' 1731; 'Chuck,' 1736; 'Apology,' 1740; 'A Letter . . . to Mr. Pope,' 1742; 'The Egotist; or, Colley upon Cibber,' 1743; 'Another Occasional Letter to Mr. Pope,' 1744; 'Papal Tyranny in the Reign of King John' (founded on Shakespeare's 'King John'), 1745; 'The Temple of Dulness' (anon. attributed to Cibber), 1745; 'The Character and the Conduct of Cicero,' 1747; 'The Lady's Lecture,' 1748.

Dramatic Works: in 4 vols., 1760.

CLARENDON [Edward Hyde], Earl of, 1609-1674. Born, at Dinton, Wilts, 18 Feb. 1609. Early education at home. Matric. Magdalen Hall, Oxford, 31 Jan. 1623; B.A., 14 Feb. 1626. Entered at Middle Temple, 1625; called to Bar, 22 Nov. 1633. Married Anne Ayliffe, 1629; she died 1630. Concerned in production of Masque by Inns of Court, Feb. 1634. Married Frances Aylesbury, 10 July 1634. Keeper of Writs and Rolls of

Common Pleas, Dec. 1634. M.P. for Wootton Bassett in Short Parliament, April to May, 1640 ; for Saltash in Long Parliament, 1640. Active political life, till expelled from House of Commons, 11 Aug. 1642. Lived in All Souls' Coll., Oxford, Oct. 1642 to March 1645. Knighted and appointed Privy Councillor, 22 Feb. 1643 ; Chancellor of Exchequer, 3 March 1643 to 1660. Brought about the summoning of the Oxford Parliament, Dec. 1643. To Jersey with Prince of Wales, April 1646. Occupied himself writing his 'History of the Rebellion.' After death of Charles I. went on embassy to Spain, Nov. 1694 to March 1651. Joined Charles II. at Paris, Nov. 1651. Sec. of State, Nov. 1651 to Aug. 1654 ; Lord Chancellor, Jan. 1658 to 1667. Entered London with King at Restoration, 1 June 1660. High Steward of Cambridge Univ., 1660. Chancellor of Oxford Univ., Oct. 1660 to Dec. 1667. Raised to Peerage as Baron Hyde of Hindon, 3 Nov. 1660 ; created Viscount Cornbury and Earl of Clarendon, 20 April 1661. Unsuccessfully charged with high treason, 10 July 1663. Deprived of Great Seal, 30 Aug. 1667. To avoid impeachment for high treason, was allowed to retire to Calais, 29 Nov. 1667. To Rouen, 25 Dec. 1667 ; returned to Calais, 21 Jan. 1668. To Bourbon, April 1668 ; to Avignon, June1668 ; at Montpelier, July 1668 to June 1671 ; at Moulins, June 1671 to May 1674 ; to Rouen, May 1674. Active literary work during his exile. Died, at Rouen, 9 Dec. 1674. Buried in Westminster Abbey.

Works : 'Speech at a Conference between both Houses,' 1641 ; 'Argument before the Lords,' 1641 ; 'Transcendent and Multiplied Rebellion ... discovered' (anon.), 1645 ; 'A Full Answer to an infamous and trayterous Pamphlet' (anon.), 1648 ; 'A Letter from a true and lawful Member of Parliament' (anon.), 1656 ; 'Narrative of the Settlement of Ireland,' 1668 ; 'Animadversions upon a book intituled, Fanaticism fanatically imputed to the Catholick Church'

(anon.), 1674 ; 'Second Thoughts' (anon.), *n.d.*

Posthumous : 'A Brief View and Survey of . . . Mr. Hobbes's Book, entitled Leviathan,' 1676 ; 'History of the Rebellion and Civil Wars in England' (3 vols.), 1702-04 ; Supplement to preceding, 1717 ; 'History of the Rebellion and Civil Wars in Ireland,' 1720 ; 'A Collection of Several Tracts,' 1727 ; 'An Essay on an Active and Contemplative Life,' 1765 ; 'Religion and Policy,' 1811 ; 'Essays, Moral and Entertaining,' 1815,

'Life and Letters,' by T. H. Lister, 3 vols., 1838.

CLARKE (Charles Cowden), **1787-1877.** Born, 15 Dec. 1787, at Enfield, where his father kept a school. Educated there ; early acquaintance with Keats. Parents removed to Ramsgate [1810 ?]. Several visits to London early in life. Made acquaintance of Leigh Hunt, Shelley, Hazlitt, Charles and Mary Lamb. Contrib. to Leigh Hunt's 'Pocket Book,' 1820. At father's death, settled in London as bookseller and publisher, 1820. Entered partnership with Alfred Novello. Married Mary Victoria Novello, 5 July 1828. Contrib. to 'Atlas,' 'Temple Bar,' 'Examiner,' 'Gentleman's Magazine,' 'Tatler,' 'London Journal,' etc., and published various works. Lectured on Shakespeare at various times, 1834 - 56. Wrote several works with wife. At Nice, 1856-61. Settled in Genoa, 1861. Died there, 13 March 1877. Buried in Staglieno Cemetery.

Works : 'Readings in Natural Philosophy,' 1828 ; 'Tales from Chaucer,' 1833 ; 'Adam the Gardener,' 1834 ; 'The Princess Narina,' 1844 ; 'Perseverance,' 1844 ; 'Carmina Minima,' 1859 ; 'Many Happy Returns of the Day' (with his wife), 1860 ; 'Shakespeare Characters,' 1863 ; 'Molière's Characters,' 1865 ; 'Idyl of London Streets' (with his wife), 1875 ; 'Recollections of Writers' (with his wife), 1878 ; 'The Shakespeare Key' (with his wife), 1879.

He *edited :* 'The Riches of Chaucer,'

1835 ; Nichol's Library Edition of British Poets, 1860 ; a number of separate edns. of poets' works ; Chaucer's 'Canterbury Tales,' 1875 ; and (with his wife) Shakespeare's Plays, 1864 and 1869.

*CLARKE (Mary Victoria Cowden), b. 1809. [Wife of preceding.] Born [Mary Victoria Novello], 22 June 1809, in London. Spent some years at Boulogne. Governess in private family, 1819-20. Married to Charles Cowden Clarke, 5 July 1828. Lived in London, engaged in literary work, 1828-56. At Nice, 1856-61. Settled in Genoa, 1861. Husband died there, 1877. Since his death has lived with her sister in Genoa. Various visits to England, Germany, Austria, and Switzerland, 1877-91. Has contributed to 'Athenæum,' 'All the Year Round,' 'National Magazine,' 'Atlantic Monthly,' 'Ladies' Companion,' 'Sharpe's London Magazine,' 'British Journal,' 'Monthly Chronicle,' 'People's Journal,' 'Hone's Table Book,' 'Manchester Examiner,' 'Temple Bar,' 'Musical Times,' 'Century Magazine,' 'St. Nicholas Magazine,' 'Merry England,' 'Girl's Own Paper.'

Works : 'Complete Concordance to Shakespeare,' 1845 ; 'Shakespeare Proverbs,' 1848 ; 'Kit Barn's Adventures,' 1849 ; 'The Girlhood of Shakespeare's Heroines' (3 vols.), 1851-52 (abridged edn., 1879) ; 'The Iron Cousin,' 1854 ; 'The Song of Drop o' Wather,' 1856 ; 'World - Noted Women,' 1858 ; 'Many Happy Returns of the Day' (with her husband), 1860 ; 'The Life and Labours of Vincent Novello,' 1864 ; 'The Trust,' 1873 ; 'A Rambling Story,' 1874 ; 'Idyl of London Streets' (with her husband), 1875 ; 'Recollections of Writers' (with her husband), 1878 ; 'The Shakespeare Key' (with her husband), 1879 ; 'Honey from the Weed,' 1881 ; 'Verse-Waifs,' 1883 ; 'A Score of Sonnets to one Object,' 1884 ; 'Shakespeare's Self,' 1885 ; 'Uncle, Peep, and I,' 1886 ; 'Centennial Biographic Sketch of Charles Cowden Clarke,'

1887 ; 'Memorial Sonnets,' 1888 ; 'My Long Life' (autobiography), 1896.

She has *edited :* Shakespeare's Plays, 1860 (with her husband, 1864 and 1869).

CLEMENS (Samuel Langhorne). *See* Twain (Mark).

CLOUGH (Arthur Hugh), 1819-1861. Born, at Liverpool, 1 Jan. 1819. Educated at a school at Chester, Nov. 1828 to summer 1829 ; at Rugby, 1829-37. Scholarship at Balliol Coll., Oxford, Nov. 1836 ; took up residence, Oct. 1837 ; B.A., 21 May 1841 ; M.A., 26 Oct. 1843. Fellowship at Oriel Coll., 1842-48 ; Tutor, 1843 to Oct. 1848. Visit to Paris with Emerson, May 1848. In Rome, winter of 1848 to July 1849. Principal of University Hall, London, Oct. 1849 to 1851. Friendship with Carlyle. Prof. of English Literature, Univ. Coll., London, 1850. To Boston, Mass., Oct. 1852. Took pupils in America. Returned to England, July 1853. Examinership in Education Dept. of Privy Council Office, 1853. Married Blanche Smith, June 1854. To France and Vienna as Sec. to Commission of Report on Military Education, 1856. Health began to fail, 1860. To Greece, Pyrenees, and Italy, 1861. Died, at Florence, 13 Nov. 1861. Buried in Protestant Cemetery there.

Works : 'The Bothie of Tober-na-Vuolich,' 1848 ; 'Ambarvalia' (with T. Burbidge), 1849 (Clough's share of the work separately issued, same year) ; 'Greek History in a Series of Lives from Plutarch,' 1860.

He *edited :* Dryden's 'Plutarch's Lives,' 1859.

Posthumous: 'Poems, with Memoir,' ed. by F. T. Palgrave, 1862 ; 'Letters and Remains' (privately printed), 1865 ; 'Poems and Prose Remains,' with selected Letters and Memoir, edited by his wife (2 vols.), 1869.

Life : by S. Waddington, 1883.

COBBETT (William), 1762-1835. Born, at Farnham, 9 March 1762.

Early life spent in agricultural work. To London, May 1783, as attorney's clerk. Enlisted in 54th Regt., 1784. Joined regiment in Nova Scotia, 1785. Discharge, 1791. Married Ann Reid, 5 Feb. 1792. To St. Omer, March 1792. To Philadelphia, Oct. 1792 ; engaged in teaching. Edited 'The Censor,' Jan. 1796 to Jan. 1797 ; 'Porcupine's Gazette,' March 1797 to Dec. 1799. Took Federal side in politics. Started business as bookseller, July 1796. To New York, 1797. Edited 'The Rushlight' there, Feb. to April, 1800. To England, June 1800. Ed. 'The Porcupine in London,' Oct. 1800 to Nov. 1801. Kept bookshop in Piccadilly, 1801-03. Edited 'Cobbett's Weekly Political Register,' Jan. 1802 to June 1835. Active in cause of Reform. Started 'Parliamentary Debates,'1803 (taken over by Hansard, 1812). Edited 'Cobbett's Spirit of the London Journals,' 1804. Settled at Botley, Hampshire, 1805. Started 'Cobbett's Complete Collection of State Trials,' 1809. Imprisoned for libel, 1810-12. In America, 1817-19. Returned to London ; edited 'Cobbett's Evening Post,' Jan. to March, 1820. Opened seed-farm at Kensington,- 1821. Silver medal from Soc. of Arts, 1823. Unsuccessfully prosecuted for incitement to sedition, July 1831. M.P. for Oldham 1832. Died, at Normandy Farm, Guildford, 19 June 1835.

Works : 'The Soldier's Friend' (anon.) 1792 ; 'Observations on the Emigration of Dr. J. Priestley' (anon.), 1794 ; 'Le Tuteur Anglais,' 1795 ; 'A Bone to Gnaw for the Democrats' (under pseud. of 'Peter Porcupine'), 1795 ; 'A Kick for a Bite' (by 'Peter Porcupine '), 1795 ; 'A Little Plain English' (by 'Peter Porcupine '), 1795 ; 'Life of Thomas Paine '[1796 ?]; 'A New Year's Gift to the Democrats' (by 'Peter Porcupine '), 1796 ; 'A Prospect from the Congress Gallery' (by 'Peter Porcupine '), 1796 ; 'The Bloody Buoy,' 1796 ; 'The Scare-Crow,' 1796 ; 'The Life and Adventures of Peter Porcupine,'1796 ; 'The Guillotina' (anon.), [1796 ?] ; 'The Democratiad' (anon.), 1796 ; 'The

Gros Mousqueton Diplomatique,'1796 ; 'The Censor' (8 pts.), 1796-97 ; 'The Republican Judge,' 1797 ; 'Detection of a Conspiracy,' 1798 ; 'Democratic Principles Illustrated' (by 'Peter Porcupine '), 2 pts., 1798 ; 'Remarks on the Explanation lately Published by Dr. Priestley' (by 'Peter Porcupine'),1799 ; 'The Trial of Republicanism,' 1799 ; 'A Concise and Comprehensive History of Prince Suworow's Campaign,' 1800 ; 'The Rushlight' (by 'Peter Porcupine '), 1800 ; 'Porcupine's Works' (12 vols.), 1801 ; 'A Collection of Facts and Observations,' 1801 ; 'Letters to the Rt. Hon. H. Addington,' 1802 (2nd edn. same year) ; 'Important Considerations,' 1803 ; 'Cobbett's Weekly Political Register,' 1803-35 ; 'Cobbett's Parliamentary Debates,' 1803-12 ; 'The Political Proteus' (from 'Political Register'), 1804; 'Parliamentary History of England,' 1806 ; 'Elements of Reform,' 1809 ; 'Cobbett's Complete Collection of State Trials,' 1809, etc. ; 'Porcupine Revived,' 1813 ; 'The Pride of Britannia Humbled,' 1815 ; 'Letters on the late War,' 1815 ; 'Paper against Gold,' 1815 ; 'Address to the Clergy of Massachusetts,' 1815 ; 'A Year's Residence in the United States' (3 pts.), 1818-19 ; 'A Grammar of the English Language,' 1818 ; 'An Answer to the Speech of the Attorney-General,' 1820 ; 'The American Gardener,' 1821 ; 'Cobbett's Monthly Religious Tracts' (also called 'Cobbett's Sermons,' 12 pts.), 1821-22; 'Cottage Economy,' 1821 ; 'Links of the Lower House' (anon.), 1821 ; 'Cobbett's Collective Commentaries,' 1822 ; 'Cobbett's Gridiron,' 1822 ; 'Reduction no Robbery,' 1822 ; 'Cobbett's French Grammar,' 1823 ; 'Surplus Population,' 1823 ; 'A History of the Protestant Reformation in England and Ireland,'(2 pts.), 1824-27; 'Gold for Ever,' 1825 ; 'The Woodlands,' 1825 ; 'Big O and Sir Glory,' 1825 ; 'Cobbett's Poor Man's Friend,' 1826 ; 'The English Gardener,' 1827 ; 'A Treatise on Cobbett's Corn,' 1828 ; 'Facts for the Men of Kent,' 1828 ; 'A Letter to the Pope,' 1828 ; 'Noble

Nonsense,' 1828 ; 'The Emigrant's Guide,' 1829 ; 'Advice to Young Men,' 1829 ; 'Good Friday,' 1830 ; 'Rural Rides' (from 'Polit. Reg.'), 1830 ; 'Eleven Lectures,' 1830 ; 'Cobbett's Plan of Parliamentary Reform,' 1830 ; 'History of the Regency and Reign of King George IV.' (2 vols.), 1830-34 ; 'A Spelling-Book,' 1831 ; 'Cobbett's Penny Trash' (3 nos.), 1831 ; 'Cobbett's Twopenny Trash' (2 vols.), 1831-32 ; 'Cobbett's Manchester Lectures,' 1832 ; 'A Geographical Dictionary of England and Wales,' 1832 ; 'Cobbett's Tour in Scotland' (from 'Polit. Reg.'), 1833 ; 'A New French and English Dictionary,' 1833 ; 'Life of Andrew Jackson,' 1834 ; 'Surplus Population, and Poor-Law Bill,' 1835 ; 'Cobbett's Legacy to Labourers,' 1834 ; 'Cobbett's Legacy to Peel,' 1835 ; 'Cobbett's Legacy to Parsons,' 1835 ; 'Cobbett's Opinion of the Whig Ministry,' 1835.

Posthumous : 'Selections' from his Political Works, ed. by J. M. and J. P. Cobbett (6 vols.), 1835.

Cobbett *translated :* Von Martens' 'The Law of Nations,' 1794 ; Moreau de Saint Méry's 'Topographical . . . description of . . . Saint Domingo,' 1796 ; 'The Empire of Germany divided into departments,' 1803 ; Sievrac's 'Elements of the Roman History,' 1828.

He *abridged :* Aufrere's 'Cannibal's Progress,' 1798 ; wrote appendix to Playfair's 'History of Jacobinism,' 1796 ; and introduction to Tull's 'Horsehoeing Husbandry,' 1822.

Life : by R. Huish, 1835 ; by Edward Smith, 1878.

COLERIDGE (Hartley), 1796-1849. [Eldest son of Samuel Taylor Coleridge (q.v.)], born, at Clevedon, Somersetshire, 19 Sept. 1796. Educated at Ambleside School. Visit to London, 1807. Matric., New Inn Hall, Oxford, 6 May 1815 ; B.A., Merton Coll., 11 Feb. 1819. Fellow of Oriel Coll., 1819-20. Deprived of fellowship on ground of intemperance. In London, 1821-23. Returned to Ambleside to engage in tuition. Contrib. occasion-

ally to 'Blackwood's Mag.,' 1826-31. Tuition abandoned, 1830. Lived in house of Mr. Bingley, a publisher, at Leeds, engaged in literary work, 1831-33. Took up residence at Grasmere. Assistant master at Sedbergh Grammar School for two short periods in 1837 and 1838. Returned to Grasmere. Died there, 6 Jan. 1849.

Works : 'Biographia Borealis,' 1833 (another edn. entitled 'Lives of Northern Worthies,' edited by Derwent Coleridge, 1852 ; an extract, published separately as 'Lives of Illustrious Worthies of Yorkshire,' 1835); 'Poems,' 1833.

Posthumous : 'Essays and Marginalia' (ed. by Derwent Coleridge), 1851.

He *edited :* Massinger and Ford's Dramatic Works, 1840.

Life : by Derwent Coleridge, in 1851 edn. of Hartley Coleridge's 'Poems.'

COLERIDGE (Samuel Taylor), 1772-1834. Born, at Ottery St. Mary, 21 Oct. 1772. Educated at Christ's Hospital, July 1782 to Sept. 1790. Fell in love with Mary Evans, sister of schoolfellow. Sizarship at Jesus Coll., Cambridge, Feb. 1791; matric., March 1792; Browne medal for Greek ode, 1792; foundation scholarship, June 1793. To London in winter of 1793. Enlisted in 15th Dragoons, 4 Dec. 1793, under name of Silas Tomkyn Comberback ; sent to Reading. Discharged, 10th April 1794 ; returned to Cambridge. In June 1794 visited Oxford and met Southey. During same year became engaged to Sara Fricker, sister-in-law of Robert Lovell. Scheme for 'Pantisocracy' (ideal community in America) formed with Southey, Lovell and George Burnett. Left Cambridge at end of 1794, without degree. Friendship with Charles Lamb begun in London. Contributed verses to 'Morning Chronicle,' 1794-95. Returned with Southey to Bristol ; end of acquaintance with Mary Evans. In 1795 delivered political lectures in Bristol, and prepared book of poems for Joseph Cottle, bookseller. Married Sara Fricker, 4 Oct. 1795; settled at

Clevedon. Later in 1795 returned to Bristol. Tour to northern towns in Jan. 1796, to collect subscribers to periodical 'The Watchman.' Only ten numbers of this published. In winter of 1796 settled with Charles Lloyd at Nether Stowey. In 1797 received visit from Charles and Mary Lamb, and visited Wordsworth in Dorsetshire. Invitation to become Unitarian Minister at Shrewsbury refused, 1798. Contributed 'Ancient Mariner' to Lyrical Ballads in 1798. Accepted annuity from Josiah and Thomas Wedgwood, 1798. Son Berkeley born, 30 May 1798. Tour in Germany with Wordsworth, 1798-99. Son Berkeley died 16 Feb. 1799. Return to London, Sept. 1799. Contrib. to 'Morning Post,' 1799 to 1800. Removed to Keswick, July 1800. Use of laudanum begun; failing health. Son Derwent born 14 Sept. 1800. Tours in Scotland and Wales, 1802. Daughter Sara born, 22 Dec. 1802. To Malta in April 1804, as secretary to Governor. To Naples and Rome, Dec. 1805. Return to England, Aug. 1806. With his family in Bristol, 1807. Acquaintance with De Quincey begun. Lectured at Royal Institution, 1808. To Grasmere with Wordsworth. 'The Friend' published, Aug. 1809 to March 1810. To London, 1810. Estrangement with his wife. Lectured and contributed to 'Courier,' 1810-13. Drama, 'Remorse,' produced at Drury Lane, 23 Jan. 1813. Lectured at Bristol, 1813. Chiefly employed play-writing, and on 'Biographia Literaria,' 1814-15. To house of Mr. Gillman at Highgate (where he spent remainder of life), 15 April 1816. Last lectures, early in 1818. Rhine tour with Wordsworths, 1828. Visit to Cambridge, 1833. Died, 25 July 1834.

Works: 'Fall of Robespierre' (act i. by Coleridge; acts ii., iii. by Southey), 1794; 'Moral and Political Lecture delivered at Bristol,' 1795; 'Conciones ad Populum,' 1795; 'The Plot Discovered,' 1795; 'The Watchman,' 1796; 'Ode on the Departing Year,' 1796; 'Poems on various subjects,' 1796; 'Fears in Solitude,' 1798;

'France,' 1798; 'Frost at Midnight,' 1798; 'Ancient Mariner' contributed to Lyrical Ballads,' 1798; Poems contributed to 'Annual Anthology,' 1800; 'The Friend,' 1809-10; contributions to Southey's 'Omniana,' 1812; 'Remorse,' 1813; 'Christabel, Kubla Khan and Pains of Sleep,' 1816; 'The Statesman's Manual,' 1816; 'Blessed are ye that sow beside all waters: a lay Sermon,' 1817; 'Biographia Literaria,' 1817; 'Sibylline Leaves,' 1817; 'Zapolya,' 1817; 'Aids to Reflection in the formation of a Manly Character,' 1825; 'Poetical Works, including Dramas,' 1829; 'On the Constitution of Church and State,' 1830.

Posthumous: 'Table Talk,' 1835; 'Literary Remains,' 1836-38; 'Letters,' ed. by T. Allsop, 1836; 'Confessions of an Enquiring Spirit,' 1840; 'Treatise on Method' (from 'Encyclopædia Metropolitana'), 1845; 'Hints towards a formation of a more comprehensive Theory of Life,' 1848; 'Notes and Lectures upon Shakespeare,' 1849; 'Essays on his Own Times, forming a second series of "The Friend,"' 1850; 'The Relation of Philosophy to Theology,' 1851; 'Lay Sermons,' 1852; 'Notes upon English Divines,' 1853; 'Notes, theological, political and miscellaneous,' 1853; 'Anima Poetæ; from the unpublished note-books of S. T. Coleridge. Ed. by E. H. Coleridge,' 1895; 'Letters; edited by E H. Coleridge,' 1895.

He *translated:* Schiller's 'Wallenstein,' 1800.

Collected Works: in 7 vols., ed. by W. G. T. Stedd, 1884; 'Poems,' ed. by W. Bell Scott, 1894.

Life: by H. D. Traill, 1884.

COLLIER (Jeremy), 1650 - 1726. Born, at Stow Qui (or Quire), Cambridgeshire, 23 Sept. 1650. Educated at his father's school at Ipswich. To Caius Coll., Cambridge, as 'poor scholar,' 10 April 1669; B.A., 1672; M.A., 1676. Ordained Deacon, 24 Sept. 1676; Priest, 24 Feb. 1677. Chaplain to Dowager Countess of Dorset at Knowle, 1677-79. Rector of Ampton, Suffolk, 25 Sept. 1679 to

1685. Lecturer at Gray's Inn, 1685 [or 1686 ?]. Took up definite position as non-juror. Imprisoned for three months in Newgate owing to political pamphlet, 1688. Another short imprisonment, Nov. 1692. Much controversial writing on political and religious topics, Attack on stage begun, 1698. Consecrated as nonjuring bishop, 1713. Religious controversy; and abortive attempt to form union with Eastern Church. Died, in London, 26 April 1726. Buried in churchyard of St. Pancras.

Works : 'The Difference between the Present and Future State of our Bodies,' 1686 ; 'The Comparison between Giving and Receiving,' 1687 ; 'The Office of a Chaplain' (anon.), 1688 ; 'The Desertion discuss'd' (anon.), 1688 ; 'Vindiciæ Juris Regni' (anon.), 1689 ; 'Animadversions upon the Modern Explanation of . . . a king *de facto*' (anon.), 1689 ; 'A Caution against Inconstancy' (anon.), 1690 ; 'A Dialogue concerning the Times,' 1690 ; 'To the Right Hon. the Lords and the Gentlemen,' 1690 ; 'Dr. Sherlock's Case' (anon), 1691 ; 'A Brief Essay concerning the Independency of Church Power' (anon.), 1692 ; 'The Case of giving Bail,' 1692 ; 'A Reply' (to remarks on preceding), 1693 ; 'A Persuasive to Consideration tendered to the Royalists' (anon.), 1693 ; 'Remarks upon the "London Gazette,"' 1693 ; 'Miscellanies' (afterwards pt. i. of 'Essays upon several Moral Subjects'), 1694 ; 'A Defence of the Absolution,' 1696 ; 'A further Vindication of the Absolution,' 1696 ; 'A Reply to the Absolution of a Penitent,' 1696 ; 'An Answer to the Animadversions' (on preceding ; anon.), 1696 ; 'The Case of the two Absolvers,' 1696 ; 'Essays upon several Moral Subjects,' 1697 ; 'A short View of the Immorality and Profaneness of the English Stage,' 1698 ; (2nd and 3rd edns. same year) ; 'A Defence of the Short View,' 1699 ; 'A Second Defence,' 1700 ; 'The Great Historical, Geographical, Genealogical, and Poetical Dictionary,' vol. i., 1701 ; vols. ii., iii., 1705 ; vol. iv., 1721 ; 'A Letter to a Lady concerning the New Playhouse' (anon.), 1706 ; 'A Further Vindication of the Short View,' 1708 ; 'An Ecclesiastical History of Great Britain,' vol. i., 1708 ; vol. ii., 1714 ; 'An Answer to some Exceptions' (to preceding), 1715 ; 'Some Remarks on Dr. Kennet's . . . Letters,' 1717 ; 'Reasons for restoring some Prayers' (anon.), *1717 ; 'A Defence of the Reasons' (anon.), 1718 ; 'A Vindication of the Reasons and Defence' (anon.), pt. i., 1718 ; pt. ii., 1719 ; 'A Further Defence' (anon.), 1720 ; 'Essays' (collected), 1722 ; 'Several Discourses upon Practical Subjects,' 1725 ; 'God not the Author of Evil,' 1726.

Collier *translated :* 'Sleidan's Commentaries,' bks. ix.-xii., 1689 ; Marcus Aurelius' 'Meditations,' 1701 ; Gregory of Nazianzus 'Upon the Maccabees,' 1716 ; and wrote prefaces to : translation of Cicero 'De Finibus' by S. Parker, 1702 ; and 'Human Souls naturally Immortal,' 1707.

Life : by T. Lathbury, in 1852 edn. of 'Ecclesiastical History.'

COLLINS (Edward James Mortimer), 1827-1876. Born, at Plymouth, 29 June 1827. Educated at various private schools. In situations in London, 1838. Assistant master at school at Westbury, Wilts, 1843-45. Contrib. poem to 'Bath and Cheltenham Gazette,' 1844. Contrib. to 'Felix Farley's Journal,' 1847-49. Private Tutor at Windermere, 1847-48. In Paris, 1848. Schoolmaster at Lechlade and Rothwell, 1849. Edited 'Lancaster Gazette,' 1850. Married Mrs. Susan Crump, 9 May 1850. Schoolmaster at Launceston, 1851. Mathematical Master at Queen Elizabeth's Coll., Guernsey, 1852-55. Kept private school in Guernsey, 1855-56. Private Tutor at Carlisle, 1858. Literary activity ; edited several provincial newspapers, and wrote constantly for London press, 1851-66. Contributor to 'Owl,' 'Church and State Review,' 'Realm,' 'Press,' 'Globe,' 'Punch,' 'British Quarterly,' 'Temple Bar' 'Tinsley's Magazine,' 'World,' etc. Took cottage at Knowl

Hill, Berks, 1862. Wife died, 5 Aug.
1867. Married Frances Cotton, 4
May 1868 ; settled at Knowl Hill.
Died there, 28 July 1876.

Works: 'Idyls and Rhymes,' 1855 ;
'Summer Songs,' 1860 ; ' Who is the
Heir?', 1865 ; 'Sweet Anne Page,'
1868 ; ' The Ivory Gate,' 1869 ;
' Letter to the Rt. Hon. B. Disraeli '
(anon., in verse), 1869 ; ' The Vivian
Romance,' 1870 ; 'The Inn of Strange
Meetings,' 1871 ; ' The Secret of Long
Life ' (anon.), 1871 ; ' The Marquis
and Merchant,' 1871 ; ' The British
Birds,' 1872 ; ' Two Plunges for a
Pearl,' 1872 ; 'Princess Clarice,' 1872 ;
' Squire Sylvester's Whim,' 1873 ;
' Miranda,' 1873 ; ' Mr. Carington '
(under pseudonym of Robert Turner
Cotton), 1873 ; 'Transmigration,' 1874 ;
' Frances ' (with his wife), 1874 ;
' Sweet and Twenty ' (with his wife),
1875 ; ' Blacksmith and Scholar ' and
' From Midnight to Midnight,' 1876
[1875] ; 'A Fight with Fortune,' 1876 ;
'The Village Comedy ' (with his wife),
1878 [1877].

Posthumous: ' Letters and Friend-
ships,' edited by his wife, 1877 ; ' You
Play Me False ' (with his wife), 1878 ;
' Pen Sketches by a Vanished Hand,'
ed. by Tom Taylor, 1879 ; 'Thoughts
in my Garden ' ed. by E. Yates, 1880.
Life: by his wife, in ' Letters and
Friendships,' 1877.

COLLINS (William) 1721-1759.
Born, at Chichester, 25 Dec. 1721.
Probably educated first at Chichester.
Scholar of Winchester Coll., 19 Jan.
1733. Contrib. verses to 'Gentleman's
Magazine ' (Jan. and Oct. 1739), while
still at school. Matriculated at
Queen's Coll., Oxford, 22 March 1740 ;
Demyship at Magdalen Coll., 29 July
1741 ; B.A., 18 Nov. 1743. Visit to
uncle in Flanders. Thought of entering Army or Church, but eventually
devoted himself to literature in London. Failing health ; visit to France.
Lived with sister at Chichester on his
return. For a time in a madhouse at
Chelsea. Visit to Oxford, 1754. Died,
at Chichester, 12 June 1759. Buried,
at St. Andrew's Church, Chichester.

Works: 'Persian Eclogues ' (anon.),
1742 (another edn. anon., entitled
' Oriental Eclogues,' 1757) ; ' Odes,'
1747 [1746] ; ' Verses humbly addressed to Sir Thomas Hanmer '
(anon.), 1743.
Posthumous: ' An Ode on the
Popular Superstitions of the Highlands,' 1788.
Collected Works: ed. by Langhorne, with *life,* 1765, etc. ; ed. by
Mrs. Barbauld, 1797 ; ed. by A. Dyce,
1827 ; ed. by Moy Thomas, with *life,*
1858.

**COLLINS (William Wilkie), 1824-
1889.** Born, in London, Jan. 1824.
Educated at private school. Tour
with his parents in Italy, 1837-38.
Articled to a firm of tea merchants
[1838 ?]. Student at Lincoln's Inn,
18 May 1846 ; called to Bar, 21 Nov.
1851. Began to devote himself to
literature, 1848. Contrib. to ' Household Words,' 1856 ; and to ' All the
Year Round.' ' The Lighthouse,' produced at the Olympic theatre, Aug.
1857 ; ' The Red Vial,' at Olympic,
Oct. 1858 ; ' The Frozen Deep,' at
Olympic, 27 Oct. 1866 ; 'No Thoroughfare ' (dramatized from novel), at
Adelphi, Dec. 1867 ; ' Black and
White ' (written with Fechter), at
Adelphi, March, 1868 ; ' The Woman
in White ' (dramatized from novel), 9
Oct. 1871 ; ' Man and Wife,' at Prince
of Wales's, 22 Feb. 1873. Visit to
United States, 1873-74. 'The Moon-
stone ' (dramatized from novel), pro-
duced at Olympic, Sept. 1877 ; ' The
New Magdalen,' at Olympic ; ' Rank
and Riches,' at Adelphi, 9 June 1883.
Died, in London, 23 Sept. 1889.
Buried at Kensal Green.

Works: ' Memoir of the Life of
William Collins,' 1848 ; ' Antonina,'
1850 ; ' Rambles beyond Railways,'
1851 ; ' Basil,' 1852 ; ' Mr. Wray's
Cash Box,' 1852 ; ' Hide and Seek,'
1854 ; ' After Dark,' 1856 ; ' Dead
Secret,' 1857 ; ' The Queen of Hearts,'
1859 ; ' The Woman in White,' 1860 ;
' A Message from the Sea ' (with
Dickens), 1861 [1860] ; ' No Name,'
1862 ; ' My Miscellanies,' 1862 ; 'The

Frozen Deep' (with Dickens ; privately printed), 1866 ; ' Armadale,' 1866 ; ' No Thoroughfare ' (with Dickens), 1867 ; 'The Moonstone,' 1868 ; ' Man and Wife,' 1870 ; 'No Name,' dramatized (privately printed), 1870 ; 'The Woman in White,' dramatized (privately printed), 1871 ; 'Poor Miss Finch,' 1872 ; 'The New Magdalen,' 1873 ; ' Miss or Mrs. ?', 1873 ; 'The New Magdalen,' dramatized (privately printed), 1873 ; 'Readings and Writings in America,' 1874 ; ' Miss Gwilt,' drama adapted from ' Armadale' (privately printed), 1875 ; 'The Law and the Lady,' 1875 ; 'Alicia Warlock,' 1875 ; 'The Two Destinies,' 1876 ; 'The Moonstone,' dramatized (privately printed), 1877 ; 'The Haunted Hotel,' 1879 [1878] ; 'The Fallen Leaves,' 1879 ; 'A Rogue's Life,' 1879 ; 'Jezebel's Daughter,' 1880 ; ' Considerations on the Copyright Question,' 1880 ; 'The Black Robe,'1881; 'Heart and Science,' 1883 ; 'I say No,' 1884 ; 'The Evil Genius,'1886; 'The Guilty River,'1886; 'Little Novels,' 1887 ; 'The Legacy of Cain,' 1888.

Posthumous : ' Blind Love,' ed. by W. Besant, 1890.

COLMAN (George), the Elder, 1732-1794. Born, in Florence, March [or April?], 1732. At Westminster School, 1746-51. To Ch. Ch., Oxford, 5 June 1751 ; B.A., 18 April 1755 ; M.A., 18 March 1758. Contributed to 'The Student,' 1751 ; to Hawkesworth's 'The Adventurer,' Sept. 1753 ; ed. 'The Connoisseur,' with Bonnell Thornton, Jan. 1754 to Sept. 1756. Called to Bar at Lincoln's Inn, 1755. On Oxford Circuit, 1759. Farce, 'Polly Honeycombe,' produced at Drury Lane, 5 Dec. 1760 ; 'The Jealous Wife' produced, 12 Feb. 1761. Started 'St. James's Chronicle,' with Bonnell Thornton and Garrick, 1761. The following plays produced at Drury Lane : 'The Musical Lady,' 6 M .ch 1762 ; a version of ' Philaster,' 8 Oct. 1763 ; 'The Deuce is in Him,' 4 Nov. 1763 ; 'The Clandestine Marriage' (written with Gar-

rick), 20 Feb. 1766 ; 'The English Merchant,' 21 Feb. 1767. Purchased Covent Garden Theatre (with Powell, Harris, and Rutherford), and opened it, 14 Sept. 1767. Married Miss Ford, 1767 [?]; she died, 29 March 1771. The following plays produced at Covent Garden : 'The Oxonian in Town,' 7 Nov. 1767; 'Man and Wife,' 7 Oct. 1769 ; 'The Portrait,' 22 Nov. 1770 ; 'The Fairy Prince,' 12 Nov. 1771 ; ' Achilles in Petticoats,' 16 Dec. 1773 ; a version of ' Comus,' 16 Oct. 1773 ; 'The Man of Business,' 31 Jan. 1774. Resigned management, 26 May 1774, and retired to Bath. Contrib. a series of papers called 'The Gentleman ' to 'The London Packet,' July to Dec., 1775. A version of Ben Jonson's ' Epicœne,' produced at Drury Lane, 13 Jan. 1776 ; 'The Spleen,' 7 March 1776 ; 'New Brooms,' 21 Sept. 1776. Manager of Haymarket, 1777-85. 'The English Merchant' produced there, 15 May 1777; 'Polly,' 19 June 1777 ; 'A Fairy Tale' (written with Garrick), 18 July 1777 ; 'The Spanish Barber,' 30 Aug. 1777 ; 'The Female Chevalier,' 18 May 1778; 'The Suicide,' 11 July 1778; 'The Separate Maintenance,' 31 Aug. 1779; 'The Manager in Distress,' 30 May 1780 ; 'The Genius of Nonsense,' 2 Sept. 1780 ; 'Harlequin Teague,' 1782 ; 'Tit for Tat,' 29 Dec. 1786 ; 'Ut Pictura Poesis,' 18 May 1789. Pall-bearer at Dr. Johnson's funeral, 20 Dec. 1784. Paralytic stroke, 1785. Mind gradually gave way. Died, in Paddington, 14 Aug. 1794. Buried in vaults of Kensington Church.

Works : 'Polly Honeycombe' (anon.), 1760 ; ' Ode to Obscurity ' (anon.), 1760 ; 'The Jealous Wife,' 1761 ; 'Critical Reflections on the Old English Dramatick Writers' (anon.),1761 ; 'The Clandestine Marriage' (with Garrick), 1761 ; 'The Musical Lady' (anon.), 1762 ; 'The Deuce is in Him' (anon.), 1763 ; 'Terræ Filius' (4 nos., anon.), 1764 ; 'The English Merchant,' 1767 ; 'T. Harris Dissected,' 1768 ; 'True State of the Differences, etc.,' 1768 (2nd edn. same year); ' Occasional Prelude,' 1768 ; 'The

Portrait' (anon.; date misprinted MCCCLXX.), 1770 ; 'Man and Wife' (anon.), 1770 ; 'The Oxonian in Town' (anon.), 1769 ; 'The Fairy Prince' (anon.), 1771 ; 'The Man of Business,' 1774 ; 'The Spleen,' 1776 ; 'Occasional Prelude,' 1776 ; 'New Brooms,' 1776 ; 'Dramatic Works,' 1777 ; 'A Fairy Tale' (adapted, with Garrick, from 'A Midsummer Night's Dream'), 1777 ; 'The Sheep-shearing' (adapted from 'Winter's Tale'), 1777 ; 'The Manager in Distress,' 1780 ; 'Prose on Several Occasions,' 1787 ; 'Tit for Tat' (anon.), 1788 ; 'Ut Pictura Poesis,' 1789.

Posthumous : 'Some Particulars of the Life of the late George Colman, written by himself' (ed. by R. Jackson, 1795 ; 'Miscellaneous Works,' 1797.

He *translated :* Terence's 'Comedies,' 1765 ; Horace's 'Art of Poetry,' 1783 ; and *edited :* 'Poems by Eminent Ladies' (with Bonnell Thornton), 1755 ; Beaumont and Fletcher's 'Philaster,' with alterations, 1763 ; 'Comus,' altered from Milton, 1772 ; Jonson's 'Epicœne,' with alterations, 1776 ; Beaumont and Fletcher's 'Dramatic Works,' 1778 ; Foote's 'Devil upon Two Sticks,'1778 ; Foote's 'Maid of Bath,' 1778 ; Foote's 'The Nabob,' 1778 ; Foote's 'A Trip to Calais,' 1778 ; Lillo's 'Fatal Curiosity,' with alterations, 1783.

Life : in Peake's 'Memoirs of the Colman Family,' 1841.

COLMAN (George), the Younger, 1762-1836. Born, in London, 21 Oct. 1762. Educated at Marylebone School, Christmas 1770 to March 1771; at Westminster School, 30 June 1772 to 1778. To Christ Church, Oxford, 28 Jan. 1779 ; removed from Oxford, autumn of 1781. At King's Coll., Aberdeen, 1781-83. Farce 'The Female Dramatist' anonymously produced at Haymarket, 16 Aug. 1782. Admitted Mem. of Lincoln's Inn, 1784. 'Two to One,' produced at Haymarket, 19 June 1784 ; 'Turk and no Turk,' 9 July 1785 ; 'Inkle and Yarico,' 4 Aug. 1787 ; 'Ways

and Means,' 10 July 1788 ; 'Battle of Hexham,' 11 Aug. 1789 ; 'Surrender of Calais,' 30 July 1791 ; 'Poor old Haymarket,' 15 June 1792 ; 'Mountaineers,' 3 Aug. 1793 ; 'New Hay at the Old Market' (afterwards known as 'Sylvester Daggerwood '), 9 June 1795 ; 'The Heir at Law,' 15 July 1797. Married Clara Morris, 3 Oct. 1784, at Gretna Green ; remarried publicly, at Chelsea Church, 10 Nov. 1788. Manager of Haymarket, 1789. Purchased patent of Haymarket, 1794. 'The Iron Chest' produced at Drury Lane, 12 March 1796 ; 'Blue Beard,' 23 Jan. 1798 ; 'Feudal Times,' 19 Jan. 1799. 'Blue Devils' produced at Covent Garden, 24 April 1798 ; 'Poor Gentleman,' 11 Feb. 1801 ; 'John Bull,' 5 March 1803 ; 'Who wants a Guinea ?' 18 April 1805 ; 'We Fly by Night,' 28 Jan. 1806 ; 'X. Y. Z.,' 11 Dec. 1810 ; 'The Law of Java,' 11 May 1822. 'Review' produced at Haymarket, 2 Sept. 1800 ; 'Gay Deceivers,' 22 Aug. 1804 ; 'Love Laughs at Locksmiths,' 25 July 1803 ; 'The Africans,' 29 July 1808. Reckless management of Haymarket, and constant financial difficulties. Lieutenant of Yeomen of the Guard, 13 May 1820 to 1831. Examiner of Plays, 19 Jan. 1824 till death. Possibly a second time married, to Mrs. Gibbs, with whom he had lived [since 1795 ?]. Died, in Brompton Square, 17 Oct. 1836. Buried in vaults of Kensington Church.

Works : 'The Man of the People' (anon.), 1782 ; 'Two to One,' 1785 ; 'Inkle and Yarico,' [1787] ; 'Ways and Means,'1788 (2nd edn. same year); 'The Battle of Hexham' (anon.), 1790 ; 'The Surrender of Calais,' 1792 ; 'The Mountaineers' (anon.), 1794 ; 'New Hay at the Old Market,' 1795 (2nd edn. under title 'Sylvester Daggerwood,' 1808) ; 'The Iron Chest,' 1796 (2nd edn. same year) ; 'My Night-Gown and Slippers,' 1797 (other edns. under title 'Broad Grins,' 1802, etc.) ; 'Blue-Beard,' 1798 (2nd, 3rd, 4th edns. same year) ; 'Feudal Times,' 1709 (2nd edn. same year) ; 'The Heir

at Law,' 1800 ; 'The Poor Gentleman,' [1801] ; 'Epilogue to the . . .
Maid of Bristol,' [1803] ; 'John Bull,'
1805 ; 'Who Wants a Guinea?' 1805 ;
'The Africans,' 1808 ; 'Blue Devils,'
1808 ; 'The Gay Deceivers,' 1808 ;
'Love Laughs at Locksmiths,' 1808 ;
'The Review,' 1808 ; 'Poetical Vagaries,' 1812 ; 'The Maskers of Moorfields,' 1815 ; 'Eccentricities for Edinburgh,' 1816 ; 'The Gnome King'
(anon.), 1819 ; 'X. Y. Z.' (anon.),
1820 ; 'The Law of Java,' 1822 ; 'The
Circle of Anecdote and Wit,' 1823 ;
'Dramatic Works,' ed. with life, by
J. W. Lake, 1827 ; 'Random Records,'
1830 ; 'Sermon for a General Fast . . .
By a Layman' [no date].

He *edited :* Gay's 'Achilles in
Petticoats,' with alterations, 1774 ;
Palmer's 'Like Master, like Man,'
1811 ; 'Posthumous Letters . . . addressed to F. Colman and G. Colman
the elder,' 1820.

Life : in Peake's 'Memoirs of the
Colman Family,' 1841.

* **CONGREVE (William), 1670-1729.**
Born, at Bardsey, near Leeds, 10 Feb.
1670. Soon after his birth, family
removed to Lismore. Educated at
Kilkenny School. To Trinity Coll.,
Dublin, 5 April 1685 ; M.A., 1696.
Entered Middle Temple, but soon
abandoned law. Play, 'The Old
Batchelor,' produced, Jan. 1693 ;
'The Double Dealer,' Nov. 1693 ;
'Love for Love,' 30 April 1695 ; 'The
Mourning Bride,' 1697 ; 'The Way of
the World,' 1700. Commissioner for
Licensing Hackney Coaches, July
1695 to Oct. 1707. Abandoned play-
writing. Joined Vanbrugh in theatrical management for short time in
1705. Commissioner of Wine Li-
censes, Dec. 1705 to Dec. 1714. Appointed Secretary for Jamaica, Dec.
1714. Member of Kit-Cat Club.
Intimacy with Duchess of Marlborough
in later years of life. Died, in London,
19 Jan. 1729. Buried in Westminster
Abbey.

Works : 'The Mourning Muse of
Alexis,' 1659 ; 'The Old Batchelor,'
[1693] ; 'The Double Dealer,' [1694] ;

'A Pindarique Ode, humbly offer'd ...
the King,' 1695 ; 'Love for Love.'
[1695] ; 'Amendments upon Mr.
Collier's false and imperfect Citations'
(anon.), 1698 ; 'The Birth of the
Muse,' 1698 ; 'The Mourning Bride.'
1697 (2nd edn. same year) ; 'Incognita'
(anon.), 1700 ; 'The Way of the
World,' 1700 ; 'The Judgment of Paris,'
1701 ; 'A Pindarique Ode, humbly
offer'd to the Queen,' 1706 ; 'Works'
(3 vol.), 1710 ; 'A Letter to . . . Viscount Cobham,' 1729.

He *translated :* Book III. of Ovid's
'Art of Love,' 1709 ; Ovid's 'Metamorphoses' (with Dryden, Addison,
etc.), 1717 ; La Fontaine's 'Tales and
Novels' (with other translators), 1762;
and assisted Dryden in revision of
translation of Virgil, 1697.

He *edited :* Dryden's 'Dramatick
Works,' 1717.

Collected Works : 1731, etc.

CONINGTON (John), 1825-1869.
Born, at Boston, Lincolnshire, 10 Aug.
1825. At Beverley Grammar School,
1836-38 ; at Rugby, 1838-43. Matric.
at University Coll., Oxford, 30 June
1843 ; Demyship at Magdalen Coll.,
Oct. 1843. Hertford and Ireland
scholarships, 1844. Returned to University Coll. as scholar, 1846. B.A.,
22 April 1847 ; M.A., 1850 ; Chancellor's Latin Verse Prize, 1847 ;
English Essay Prize, 1848 ; Latin
Essay Prize, 1849. Visit to Germany,
1847. Student at Lincoln's Inn, 1849;
not called to Bar. Fellow of Univ.
Coll., Oxford, 19 Feb. 1847 to 14
June 1855. Eldon Law Scholarship,
1849. Contrib. to 'Morning Chronicle,'
1849-50. Returned to Oxford, 1850.
Prof. of Latin Language and Literature, Oxford, 1855-69. Hon. Fellow
of Corpus Christi Coll., Oxford, 30
Oct. 1856. Died, at Boston, Lincolnshire, 23 Oct. 1869.

Works : Edition of Æschylus' 'Agamemnon,' 1848 ; 'Epistola Critica,'
1852 ; Edition of Æschylus' 'Choë-
phoroe,' 1857 ; Edition of Virgil (part
of vol. i. in collab. with Goldwin
Smith), 3 vols., 1858, 1863, 1871 ;
'The Poetry of Pope' (in 'Oxford

Essays '), 1858 ; Translation of 'Odes and Carmen Sæculare' of Horace, 1863 ; 'The University of Oxford and the Greek Chair,' 1863 ; Translation of Virgil's 'Æneid,' 1866 : 'The Style of Lucretius and Catullus,' 1867 ; Translation of Homer's 'Iliad,' 1868 ; Translation of 'Satires, Epistles and Ars Poetica' of Horace, 1870.

Posthumous : 'Translation of Persius,' 1872 ; 'Miscellaneous Writings,' ed. by J. A. Symonds, with *memoir* by H. J. S. Smith, 1872.

COOK (Eliza), 1812-1889. Born, in Southwark, 12 Dec. 1812. Contrib. to 'New Monthly,' 'Metropolitan,' 'Literary Gazette,' and other periodicals. Edited 'Eliza Cook's Journal,' 1849-54. Wrote various songs as well as poems. Civil List Pension, 1864. Died, 24 Sept. 1889.

Works: 'Lays of a Wild Harp,' 1835 ; 'Melaia and other Poems,' 1838 ; 'Poems . . . Second Series,' 1845 ; 'Jottings from my Journal,' 1860 ; 'Poems, selected and ed. by the author,' 1861 ; New Echoes, and other Poems,' 1864 ; 'Diamond Dust,' 1865.

Collected Poems: in 4 vols., 1851-53 ; in one vol., 1860 ; etc.

COOPER (James Fenimore), 1789-1851. Born [James Cooper], in Burlington, New Jersey, 15 Sept. 1789. Educated at village school, Otsego, and by private tutor ; to Yale, Jan. 1803 ; expelled for breach of regulations, 1805. Entered Merchant Marine, autumn 1806. Midshipman, 1 Jan. 1808. Married Miss De Lancey, 1 Jan. 1811. Resigned commission in Navy, 6 May, 1811. First novel published anonymously, 1820. Surname changed by Act of Legislature to Fenimore Cooper, April 1826. Resided mainly at Cooperstown, N.Y., occupied in literary pursuits, till his death there, 14 Sept. 1851. Buried in Episcopal Churchyard.

Works : 'Precaution' (anon.), 1820 ; 'The Spy' (anon.), 1821 ; 'The Pioneers' (anon.), 1823 ; 'The Pilot' (anon.), 1824; 'Lionel Lincoln' (anon.),

1825 ; 'The Last of the Mohicans (anon.), 1826 ; 'The Prairie' (anon.), 1827; 'The Red Rover' (anon.), 1828; 'Notions of the Americans' (anon.), 1828 ; 'The Wept of Wish-ton-Wish' (anon.), 1829 (republished as 'The Borderers,' and 'The Heathcotes') ; 'The Water - Witch' (anon.), 1830 ; 'The Bravo' (anon.), 1831 ; 'Letter to Gen. Lafayette,' 1831; 'The Heidenmauer' (anon.), 1832 ; 'The Headsman' (anon.), 1833 ; 'Letter to his Countrymen,' 1834 ; 'The Monikins' (anon.), 1835 ; 'Sketches of Switzerland' 2 pts. (anon.), 1836 (republished as 'A Residence in France'); 'Gleanings in Europe' (anon.), 1837 ; 'England' (anon.), 1837 ; 'Italy' (anon.), 1838 ; 'The American Democrat,' 1838 ; 'The Chronicles of Cooperstown' (anon.), 1838 ; 'Homeward Bound' (anon.), 1838 ; 'Home as Found' (anon.), 1838 (republished as 'Eve Effingham') ; 'History of the Navy of the U.S.A.,' 1839 ; 'The Pathfinder' (anon.), 1840 ; 'Mercedes of Castile'. (anon.), 1840 ; 'The Deerslayer' (anon.), 1841 ; 'The Two Admirals' (anon.), 1842 ; 'The Wing-and-Wing' (anon.), 1842 (republished as 'The Jack o' Lantern') ; 'The French Governess,' 1843 ; 'The Battle of Lake Erie,' 1843 ; 'Wyandotte' (anon.), 1843 ; 'Ned Myers,' 1843 ; 'Afloat and Ashore,' vols. i., ii. (anon.), 1844 ; 'Proceedings . . . in the case of A. S. Mackenzie,' 1844 ; 'Afloat and Ashore' vols. iii., iv., 1844 (republished as 'Lucy Hardinge') ; 'Satanstoe,' 1845 ; 'The Chainbearer' (anon.), 1846 ; 'Lives of Distinguished American Naval Officers,' 1846 ; 'The Redskins' (anon.), 1846 (republished as 'Ravensnest') ; 'The Crater' (anon.), 1847 (republished as 'Mark's Reef ') ; 'Jack Tier,' 1848 (republished as 'Captain Spike') ; 'The Oak Openings' (anon.), 1848 (republished as 'The Bee Hunter') ; 'The Sea Lions' (anon.), 1849 ; 'The Ways of the Hour' (anon.), 1850.

Life: by T. R. Lounsbury, 1883.

*COURTHOPE (William John), b. 1842. Born, at South Malling, Sussex, 17 July 1842. At Harrow, Sept.

1856 to July 1861. To New Coll., Oxford, 1861 ; B.A., 1865 ; Newdigate Prize Poem, 1864 ; Chancellor's English Essay Prize, 1868. Examiner in Education Dept., 1870. Civil Service Commissioner, 1887 ; Chief Commissioner, 1892. Mem. of Athenæum Club, 1892. C.B., 1895. Registrar of Roy. Lit. Fund, 1893. Prof. of Poetry, Oxford, 1895. Hon. D.L., Durham, 1895. Hon. Fellow New Coll., Oxford, 1896. For some time part-editor of 'National Review.'

Works : 'The Three - hundredth Anniversary of Shakespeare's Birth,' 1864 ; 'The Genius of Spenser,' 1868 ; 'Ludibria Lunæ,' 1869 ; 'The Paradise of Birds,' 1870 ; 'Addison,' 1884 ; 'The Liberal Movement in English Literature,' 1885 ; 'History of English Poetry,' 1895, etc.

He has *edited :* Pope's Works (with W. Elwin), 1871.

COWLEY (Abraham), 1618-1667.
Born, in London, 1618. King's Scholar at Westminster School, 1628 [?]-1636, First poems published, 1633. Scholar of Trinity Coll., Cambridge, 14 June 1637 ; B.A., 1639 ; Minor Fellow, 30 Oct. 1640 ; M.A., 1642 ; Major Fellow, 1642. Latin Comedy, 'Naufragium Joculare' performed before University, 2 Feb. 1638. 'The Guardian' performed, 12 March 1641 ; rewritten and produced at Lincoln's Inn Fields as 'The Cutter of Coleman Street,' 16 Dec. 1661. Ejected from Cambridge as a Royalist, and removed to St. John's Coll., Oxford, 1664. Afterwards in household of Earl of St. Alban's, and in Court of exiled Queen in France. Engaged on diplomatic services. Returned to England, 1656. Studied Medicine. M.D., Oxford, 2 Dec. 1657. Removed to Chertsey, April 1665. Died there, 28 July 1667. Buried in Westminster Abbey.

Works : 'Poetical Blossoms' (anon.), 1633 ; 'Love's Riddle,' 1638 ; 'Naufragium Joculare,' 1638 ; 'A Satyre : the Puritan and the Papist,' 1643 [?] ; 'Ad Populum' (anon.), 1644 ; 'The Mistress,' 1647 ; 'The Foure Ages of England' (anon.), 1648 ; 'The Guar-

dian,' 1650 (second version, entitled : 'The Cutter of Coleman Street,' 1663) ; 'Poems,' 1656 ; ' Ode upon the Blessed Restoration,' 1660 ; 'Vision concerning ... Cromwell the Wicked,' 1661 ; 'A Proposal for the Advancement of Experimental Philosophy,' 1661 ; 'A. Couleii Plantarum libri duo,' 1662 ; 'Verses upon several Occasions,' 1663 ; 'Verses lately written,' 1663.

Posthumous : 'A Poem on the late Civil War,' 1679 ; 'Love's Chronicle' (anon.), [1730 ?].

He *translated :* 'Anacreon' (anon., with Willis, Wood and Oldham), 1683.

Collected Works : ed., with *life*, by T. Sprat, 1668 (subsequent edns., some enlarged, 1689-1721) ; ed., with *life*, by Grosart, 1880-81.

COWPER (William), 1731 - 1800.
Born, at Great Berkhampstead Rectory, 15 Nov. 1731. At a school in Market Street, Herts, 1737-39. Under the care of an oculist, 1739-41. At Westminster School, 1741-49. Student at Middle Temple, 29 April 1748. Articled to a solicitor for three years, 1850. Called to Bar, 14 June 1754. Depression of mind began. Commissioner of Bankrupts, 1759-65. Contrib. nos. 111, 115, 134, 139 to 'The Connoisseur,' 1756 ; to Duncombe's 'Translations from Horace,' 1756-57 ; to 'The St. James's Chronicle,' 1761. Symptoms of insanity began to appear ; taken to a private asylum at St. Albans, Dec. 1763. Left there and settled in Huntingdon, June 1765. Began to board in house of Mr. and Mrs. Unwin there, Nov. 1765. Removed with Mrs. Unwin and family to Olney, Bucks, autumn of 1767. Assisted John Newton, curate of Olney, in parochial duties. Fresh attack of insanity, 1773-74. On recovery, showed more activity in literary work. Friendship with Lady Austen, 1781-83. Contrib. to 'Gentleman's Mag.,' June 1784 and Aug. 1785. Removed from Olney to Weston, Nov. 1786. Attack of insanity, 1787. Contrib. to 'Analytical Review,' Feb. 1789. Crown pension of £300 a year granted, 1794. Visited various places in Norfolk with Mrs. Unwin, summer of

1795. Settled at Dereham Lodge, Oct. 1795. Died there, 25 April 1800. Buried in Dereham Church.

Works: 'Olney Hymns' (anon., with J. Newton),1799; 'Anti-Thelyph-thora' (anon.), 1781 ; 'Poems,' 1782 ; 'John Gilpin' (anon.),1783; 'The Task,' 1785 (the fly-leaf bears the words: 'Poems . . . Vol. II.') ; Translation of 'Iliad and Odyssey,' 1791 ; 'Poems' ('On the receipt of my mother's picture'—'The Dog and the Water Lily'), 1798.

Posthumous: 'Adelphi,' 1802 ; 'Life and Posthumous Writings,' ed. by Hayley, 1803 (2nd ed., 1804 ; 3rd , entitled 'Life and Letters,' 1809) ; 'Memoir of the early life of William Cowper' (autobiographical), 1816 ; 'Table Talk,' 1817 ; 'Hymns,' 1822 ; 'Private Correspondence' (2 vols.), 1824 ; 'Poems, the early productions of W. Cowper,' ed. by J. Croft, 1825 ; 'Minor Poems,' 1825 ; 'The Negro's Complaint,' 1826.

He *translated:* 'Homer,' 1791; 'The Power of Grace,' by Van Lier, 1792 ; 'Poems by Mme. De la Motte Guion' (posth.), 1801 ; Milton's Latin and Italian Poems (posth.), 1808.

Collected Works: ed. by Newton (10 vols.), 1817 ; ed. by Mewes (3 vols.),1834 ; ed. by Grimshawe (8 vols.), 1835 ; ed. by Southey (15 vols.), 1836-37.

Life: by Hayley, 1803 ; by Bruce, in Aldine edn. of Works, 1865 ; by Benham, in Globe edn. of Works, 1870.

CRABBE (George), 1754 - 1832. Born, at Aldeborough, 24 Dec. 1754. Educated at private schools at Bungay and Stowmarket. After leaving school, worked in warehouse at Slaughden ; apprenticed as errand-boy to a doctor at Wickham Brook, near Bury St. Edmunds, 1768 ; to a surgeon at Woodbridge, 1771. Contrib. to 'Wheble's Mag.,' 1772. Returned to Aldeborough, 1775, to work in ware-house. Studied medicine. After a visit to London, became assistant to surgeon in Aldeborough, and after-wards set up in practice there. To London to make living by literature,

April 1780. Ultimate success, mainly through assistance of Burke. Ordained Deacon, 21 Dec. 1781, as curate to Rector of Aldeborough. Ordained Priest, Aug. 1782. To Belvoir, as Chaplain to Duke of Rutland, 1782. Given degree of LL.B. by Archbishop of Canterbury, and presented (by Thurlow) with livings of Frome, St. Quentin and Ever-shot, Dorsetshire. Married Sarah Elmy, Dec. 1783. Accepted curacy of Stathern, 1785. Contrib. to 'Annual Register,' 1784. Voluminous writer, but published little. Exchanged Dorsetshire livings for Rectorship of Muston and Alling-ton, and settled at Muston 25 Feb. 1789. Removed to Parham as curate of Sweffling and Great Glemham, 1792. Took Great Glemham Hall, 1796. Returned to Muston, Oct. 1805. Wife died, 31 Oct. 1813. Rector of Trow-bridge, Wiltshire, and Croxton, near Belvoir, June 1814. Visited London, 1817 and 1822. Visited Scott in Edinburgh, autumn 1822. Died, at Trowbridge, 3 Feb. 1832. Buried there.

Works: 'Inebriety' (anon.), 1775 ; 'The Candidate,' 1780 ; 'The Library' (anon.), 1781 ; 'The Village,' 1783 ; 'The Newspaper,' 1785 ; 'A Discourse . . . after the funeral of the Duke of Rutland,' 1788 ; 'Poems,' 1807 ; 'The Parish Register,' 1807 ; 'The Borough,' 1810 ; 'Tales,' 1812 ; 'The Variation of public opinion and feelings con-sidered,' 1817 ; 'Tales of the Hall,' 1819.

Posthumous: 'Posthumous Ser-mons,' ed. by J. D. Hastings, 1850.

Collected Works: with letters, and *life* by his son George, 1834.

*CRAIK (Dinah Maria), 1826-1887. Born [Dinah Maria Mulock], at Stoke-upon-Trent, 20 April 1826. To London, 1846 [?]. First novel produced, 1849. Settled at North End, Hampstead, 1855 [?]. Civil List Pension, 1864. Married George Lillie Craik, 29 April 1865. Settled soon afterwards at Shortlands, Kent, where she lived till her death. Died suddenly, 12 Oct. 1887.

Works: [all anon.], 'Cola Monti,'

1849 ; 'The Ogilvies,' 1849 ; 'Olive,' 1850 ; 'The Head of a Family,' 1851 ; 'Alice Learmont,' 1852 ; 'Agatha's Husband,' 1852 ; 'Bread upon the Waters,' 1852 ; 'A Hero,' 1853 ; 'Avillon,' 1853 ; 'John Halifax, Gentleman,' 1856 ; 'Nothing New,' 1857 ; 'A Woman's Thoughts about Women,' 1858 ; 'Poems,' 1859 ; 'Romantic Tales,' 1859 ; 'A Life for a Life,' 1859 ; 'Domestic Stories,' 1860 ; 'Our Year,' 1860 ; 'Studies from Life,' 1861 ; 'Mistress and Maid,' 1862 ; 'The Fairy-Book,' 1863 ; 'A New Year's Gift to Sick Children,' 1865 ; 'Home Thoughts and Home Scenes,' 1865 ; 'A Noble Life,' 1866 ; 'Christian's Mistake,' 1866 ; 'The Marriages,' 1867 ; 'Woman's Kingdom,' 1868 ; 'The Unkind Word,' 1869 ; 'A Brave Lady,' 1870 ; 'Fair France,' 1871 ; 'Hannah,' 1871 ; 'Little Sunshine's Holiday,' 1871 ; 'Twenty Years Ago,' 1871 ; 'Adventures of a Brownie,' 1872 ; 'Songs of our Youth,' 1874 ; 'My Mother and I,' 1874 ; 'Sermons out of Church,' 1875 ; 'The Little Lame Prince,' 1875 ; 'The Laurel Bush,' 1877 ; 'Will Denbigh,' 1877 ; 'A Legacy,' 1878 ; 'Young Mrs. Jardine,' 1879 ; 'Thirty Years,' 1880 ; 'Children's Poetry,' 1881 ; 'His Little Mother,' 1881 ; 'Plain Speaking,' 1882 ; 'An Unsentimental Journey,' 1884 ; 'Miss Tommy,' 1884 ; 'About Money,' 1886 ; 'King Arthur,' 1886 ; 'Fifty Golden Years,' 1887 ; 'An Unknown Country,' 1887.

Posthumous : 'Concerning Man,' 1888.

She *translated :* Guizot's 'M. de Barante,' 1867 ; Mme. de Wit's 'A French Country Family,' 1867, 'A Parisian Family,' 1870, and 'An Only Sister,' 1873 ; and *edited :* 'Is it True ?' 1872.

CRASHAW (Richard), 1613 [?]-1649. Born, in London, 1613 [?]. Educated at Charterhouse. Admitted at Pembroke Hall, Cambridge, 6 July 1631 ; matriculated, 26 March 1632. B.A., 1634. First vol. of poems published, 1634. Removed to Peterhouse,

1636 ; elected Fellow, 1637 ; M.A., 1638. Perhaps incorporated at Oxford, 1641. During Civil War, expelled from Peterhouse for refusing to take Oath, Dec. 1643. To Oxford ; London ; and Paris, where he entered Roman Church. To Rome, with introductions from Queen Henrietta Maria, 1648 [?]. Appointed attendant to Card. Palotta. Sub - Canon of Church of Our Lady of Loreto, 24 April 1649. Died, at Loreto, 25 Aug. 1649 ; buried there.

Works : 'Epigrammatum Sacrorum Liber' (anon.), 1634 ; 'Steps to the Temple . . . With other Delights of the Muses' (2 pts.), 1646 (2nd edn., enlarged, 1648 ; 3rd, called 'Sacred Poems,' with engravings after drawings by Crashaw, 1652).

Posthumous : 'Carmen Deo nostro' (anon.), 1652 ; 'A Letter . . . to the Countess of Denbigh' (in verse), 1653 ; 'Poemata et Epigrammata,' 1670.

Collected Works : ed. by W. D. Turnbull, 1858 ; ed. by Dr. Grosart, 1872.

*CRAWFORD (Francis Marion), b. 1854. Born, at Bagni di Lucca, Italy, 2 Aug. 1854. Educated at Paul's School, Concord, U.S.A., Sep. 1866 to June 1869 ; subsequently with tutor in England. At Trinity Coll., Cambridge, 1873-74. At Carlsruhe, 1874-75. At Heidelberg, 1875-76. At University of Rome, 1876-78. To India, 1879; editor of 'Indian Herald,' at Allahabad, 1879-80. To Italy, 1880 ; to America, 1881. Studied at Harvard Univ., 1881-82. To Italy, May 1883. Settled near Sorrento, and has principally lived there since 1883. Visit to Constantinople, 1884. Married Miss Berdan, 1884. Awarded 'Moubinne' Prize and Gold Medal by French Academy, 1889. Visits to America, 1893 and 1894.

Works : 'Mr. Isaacs,' 1882 ; 'Dr. Claudius,' 1883 ; 'To Leeward,' 1883 ; 'An American Politician,' 1884 ; 'A Roman Singer,' 1884 ; 'Zoroaster,' 1885 ; 'A Tale of a Lonely Parish,' 1886 ; 'Saracinesca,' 1887 ; 'Marzio's Crucifix,' 1887 ; 'Paul Patoff,' 1887 ;

'With the Immortals,' 1888 ; 'Greifenstein,' 1889 ; 'Sant' Ilario,' 1889 ; 'A Cigarette Maker's Romance,' 1890; 'Khaled,' 1891 ; 'The Witch of Prague,' 1891 ; 'The Three Fates,' 1892 ; 'The Children of the King,' 1893 ; 'Don Orsino,' 1893 ; 'Marion Darche,' 1893 ; 'The Novel,' 1893 ; 'Pietro Ghisleri,' 1893 ; 'The Upper Berth,' 1894 ; 'Love in Idleness,' 1894; 'Katharine Lauderdale,' 1894 ; 'Casa Braccio,' 1895 ; 'Constantinople,' 1895; 'The Ralstons,' 1895 ; 'Adam Johnstone's Son,' 1896 ; 'Taquisara,' 1896.

* **CREIGHTON (Mandell)**, *Bishop of London*, **b. 1843**. Born, at Carlisle, 5 July 1843. At Carlisle Grammar School, 1851-57. At Durham Grammar School, Sep. 1857 to July 1862. Postmastership at Merton Coll., Oxford, Oct. 1862; B.A., 1867; M.A., 1870. Fellow and Tutor of Merton Coll., 1866-75. Ordained Deacon, 1870 ; Priest, 1873. Public Examiner at Oxford, 1871-72, 1875-76, 1883-84. Married Louise Hume Von Glehn, 1872. Vicar of Embleton, Northumberland, 1874-84. Select Preacher at Oxford, 1875-77, 1883, 1886-88. Rural Dean of Alnwick, 1882-84. Hon. Canon, Newcastle-on-Tyne, 1882-85. Fellow of Emanuel Coll., Cambridge, and Dixie Prof. of Eccles. Hist., 1884-91. Ed. 'English Historical Review,' 1886-91. Incorp. M.A., Camb., 1885 ; D.D., 1891. Hon. D.C.L., Durham, 1885; LL.D., Glasgow, 1883 ; Hon. LL.D., Harvard, 1886. Select Preacher, Camb., 1887 ; Public Examiner, 1888-89. Canon of Worcester, 1885-90 ; Exam. Chaplain to Bishop of Worcester, 1886-90. Hon. Fellow Merton Coll., Oxford. 1889 ; of Emanuel Coll., Camb., 1891. D.D., Oxford, 1891. Bishop of Peterborough, April 1891. Hon. D. Litt., T.C.D., 1892. Hulsean Lect., Camb., 1893 ; Rede Lect., 1895. Hon. D.C.L., Oxford, 1894. Romanes Lect., 1896. Represented Anglican Church at Coronation of Czar at Moscow, May 1896. Bishop of London, Nov. 1896.

Works : 'History of Rome,' 1875 ;

'The Age of Elizabeth,' 1876 ; 'The Tudors and the Reformation,' 1876 ; 'Life of Simon de Montfort,' 1876 ; 'The Shilling History of England,' 1879 ; 'A History of the Papacy during the period of the Reformation,' vols. i., ii., 1882 ; 'Memoir of Sir George Grey' (priv. printed), 1884 ; 'Cardinal Wolsey,' 1888 ; 'The Hope of Youth,' 1888 ; 'Carlisle,' 1889 ; 'Persecution and Tolerance' (Hulsean Lectures), 1895 ; 'The Early Renaissance in England' (Rede Lecture), 1895 ; 'The English National Character' (Romanes Lecture), 1896 ; 'Queen Elizabeth,' 1896.

He has *translated :* Ranke's 'History of England' (with others), 1881 ; and *edited :* 'Epochs of English History,' 1876-78 ; 'Historical Biographies,' 1876-79 ; Lang's 'Geography for Beginners,' 1881 ; 'Epochs of Church History,' 1886, etc.

CROKER (John Wilson), 1780-1857. Born, in Galway. 20 Dec. 1780. Educated at schools in Cork and Portarlington. To Trinity Coll., Dublin, Nov. 1796 ; B.A., 1800 ; LL.B. and LL.D., 1809. Entered at Lincoln's Inn, 1800. Studied law for two years. Contrib. letters on French Revolution to 'The Times' ; and assisted in starting 'The Cabinet' and 'The Picnic.' Returned to Dublin, 1802. Called to Irish Bar, 1802. Married Rosamond Pennell, 1806. M.P. for Downpatrick, May 1807 to 1812. Acting Chief Secretary for Ireland, 1808. Assisted in starting 'Quarterly Review,' Feb. 1809 ; contrib. frequently to it, 1809-64. LL.B. and LL.D., Dublin, 1809. Secretary of the Admiralty, 9 Oct. 1809 to Nov. 1830. F.R.S., 5 July 1810. M.P. for Athlone, 1812-18 ; for Yarmouth, I. of W., 1819-20 ; for Bodmin, 1820-26 ; for Aldeburgh, 1826-27 ; for Dublin Univ., 1827-30 ; for Aldeburgh, 1830-32. Appointed Privy Councillor, 16 June 1828. First to make use of term 'Conservatives,' in 'Quarterly Review' for Jan. 1830. Retired from public life, Aug. 1832. Chiefly occupied in literary pursuits till his death. Died, at Hampton, 10 Aug. 1857. Buried at West Moulsey.

Works : 'Theatrical Tears' (anon.), 1804 ; 'Familiar Epistles to Frederick Jones, Esq.' (anon.), 1804 ; 'An Intercepted Letter' (anon.), 1804 ; 'Songs of Trafalgar,' 1804 ; 'The History of Cutchacutchoo' (anon.), 1805 ; 'The Amazoniad' (anon.), 1806 ; 'A Sketch of the State of Ireland' (anon.), 1808 ; 'The Battle of Talavera' (anon.), 1809 ; 'Key to the Orders in Council,' 1812 ; 'A Letter on the fittest style . . . for the Wellington Testimonial,' 1815 ; 'Monarchy according to the Charter' (anon.), 1816 ; 'Stories for Children from the History of England,' 1817 ; 'A Second Letter from the King to his People,' 1821 ; 'Two Letters on Scottish Affairs' (under pseud. of Edward Bradwardine Waverley), 1826; 'Progressive Geography for Children,' 1828 ; 'Military Events of the French Revolution of 1830,' 1831 ; 'History of the Guillotine' (from 'Quarterly Review'), 1853 ; 'Correspondence with Lord John Russell on . . . Moore's Diary,' 1854 ; 'E-says on the Early Period of the French Revolution' (from 'Quarterly Review '), 1857.

Posthumous : 'The Croker Papers'; correspondence and diaries, ed. with *life,* by L. J. Jennings (3 vols.), 1884.

He *translated :* Chateaubriand's 'Monarchy according to the Charter,' 1816 ; 'Royal Memoirs on the French Revolution,' 1823 ; and *edited :* 'Memoirs of the Embassy of the Marshal de Bassompierre,' 1819 ; Lady Hervey's 'Letters,' 1821-22 ; 'The Suffolk Papers,' 1823 ; Horace Walpole's 'Letters to Lord Hertford,' 1824 ; Countess of Suffolk's 'Letters,' 1824 ; Boswell's 'Life of Johnson,' 1831 ; 'John, Lord Hervey's Memories of the Court of George II.,' 1848.

CROSS (Marian). *See* Eliot (George).

CUMBERLAND (Richard), 1732-1811. Born, at Trinity Coll., Dublin, 19 Feb. 1732. Educated at a school at Bury St. Edmunds, 1738-44 ; at

Westminster School, 1744-46. To Trinity Coll., Cambridge, 1747 ; B.A., 1750 ; Fellowship, 1752 ; M.A., 1754. Private Secretary to Lord Halifax in Board of Trade; and afterwards Crown Agent to Nova Scotia. Married Elizabeth Ridge, 19 Feb. 1759. Ulster Secretary to Lord-Lieutenant of Ireland, 1761. Clerk of Reports in Board of Trade, 1762. Began to write plays. 'The Summer's Tale' produced, 1765 ; 'The Brothers' at Covent Garden, 1769 ; 'The West Indian,' 1771 ; 'The Fashionable Lover,' Jan. 1772 ; 'The Choleric Man,' 1774 ; 'The Battle of Hastings,' 1778. Secretary to Board of Trade, 1776. On secret mission to Spain, 1780-81. On abolition of Board of Trade, he retired to Tunbridge Wells. Great literary activity; many plays produced, including : 'The Walloons,' 20 April 1782; 'The Jew,' 1794 ; 'The Wheel of Fortune,' 1795, etc. Edited 'The London Review' 1809. Died, at Tunbridge Wells, 7 May 1811. Buried in Westminster Abbey.

Works : 'An Elegy, written on St. Mark's Eve' (anon.), 1754 ; 'The Banishment of Cicero,' 1761 ; 'The Summer's Tale' (anon.), 1765 ; 'A Letter to the Bishop of O—d' (anon.), 1767 ; 'Amelia' (anon.), 1768 ; 'The Brothers' (anon.), 1770 ; 'The West Indian' (anon.), 1771 ; 'Timon of Athens, altered from Shakespeare,' 1771 ; 'The Fashionable Lover' (anon.), 1772 ; 'The Note of Hand' (anon.), 1774 ; 'The Choleric Man,' 1775 ; 'The Widow of Delphi' (anon.), 1775 ; 'Odes,' 1776 ; 'The Battle of Hastings,' 1778 ; 'Calypso,' 1779 ; 'Anecdotes of Eminent Painters in Spain,' 1782 ; 'A Letter to Richard, Lord Bishop of Landaff,' 1783 ; 'The Mysterious Husband,' 1783 ; 'The Carmelite,' 1784 ; 'Character of the late Lord Viscount Sackville,' 1785 ; 'The Natural Son,' 1785 ; 'The Observer' (anon.), 1785 ; 'An accurate . . . Catalogue of the several Paintings in the King of Spain's Palace at Madrid,' 1787 ; 'Arundel' (anon.), 1789 ; 'The Impostors,' 1789 ; 'A Volume of Comedies,' 1791 ; 'Curtius

rescued from the Gulph' (anon.),
1792 ; 'Calvary,' 1792 ; 'The Armourer' (anon.), 1793 ; 'The Box-
Lobby Challenge,' 1794 ; 'The Jew,'
1794 ; 'First Love,' 1795 ; 'Henry'
(anon.), 1795 ; 'The Wheel of Fortune,' 1795 ; 'False Impressions,'
1797 ; 'The Days of Yore,' 1798 ;
'Joanna of Montfaucon' (adapted
from Von Kotzebue), 1800 ; 'A Poetical Version of certain Psalms of David,'
1801 ; 'A Few Plain Reasons why
we should believe in Christ,' 1801 ;
'The Tailor's Daughter,' 1804 ; 'A
Melo-Dramatic Piece' [1805] ; 'A
Hint to Husbands,' 1806 ; 'Memoirs,'
1806 ; 'The Jew of Mogadore,' 1808 ;
'John de Lancaster,' 1809 ; 'Retrospection,' 1811.

Posthumous : 'Posthumous Dramatic Works' (2 vols.), 1813.

He *translated :* Lucan's 'Pharsalia,'
1760 ; Aristophanes' 'Clouds,' 1797.

CUNNINGHAM (Allan), 1784-1842.
Born, at Keir, Dumfriesshire, 7 Dec.
1784. Educated at village school.
Apprenticed to his brother James,
stonemason, 1795. Wrote songs and
verses. To London, April 1810. Obtained employment from sculptor. Employed on staff of 'The Day' to write
poetry and political reports. Married
Jean Walker, 1 July 1811. Acted as
secretary to Francis Chantrey, 1814-
41. Worked at literature in spare
time. Contributed to 'Blackwood,'
1819-21 ; to 'London Magazine' ; to
'The Popular Encyclopædia,' 1841.
Edited 'The Anniversary,' 1829-30.
Presented with Freedom of Dumfries,
1831. Died, in London, 30 Oct. 1842.
Buried at Kensal Green.

Works : 'Songs,' 1813 ; 'Sir Mar-
maduke Maxwell, etc.,' 1822 ; 'Tra-
ditional Tales of the English and
Scottish Peasantry,' 1822 ; 'The Songs
of Scotland,' 1825 ; 'Paul Jones,'
1826 ; 'Sir Michael Scott,' 1828 ;
'The Lives of the most eminent
British Painters, etc.' 1829 ; 'The
Maid of Elvar,' 1833 ; 'Biographical
and Critical History of the British
Literature of the last Fifty Years'
(from 'The Athenæum'), 1834 ; 'The

Cabinet Gallery of Pictures,' 1834 ;
'Lord Roldan,' 1836.

Posthumous : 'The Life of Sir David
Wilkie' (ed. by P. Cunningham), 1843 ;
'Poems and Songs' (ed. by P. Cun-
ningham), 1847.

He *edited :* Burns' Works, 1834 ;
Pilkington's 'General Dictionary of
Painters,' 1840 ; Thomson's 'The
Seasons,' 1841.

Life : by David Hogg, 1875.

DANIEL (Samuel), 1562-1619. Born,
near Taunton [?], 1562. At Magdalen
Hall, Oxford, [1579-82 ?]. Possibly
with Lord Stafford on an embassy to
France, 1586. Visit to Italy, about
1588 or 1589. Tutor to William
Herbert, son of Earl of Pembroke ;
lived at Wilton, Salisbury. Some
sonnets of his first printed in 1591
edn. of Sidney's 'Astrophel and
Stella.' This being done without his
knowledge, he published fifty sonnets,
under title 'Delia,' in 1592. Tutor
to Anne Clifford, daughter of Countess
of Cumberland, about 1598 [?], at
Skipton, Yorkshire. Possibly succeeded Spenser as poet laureate, 1599.
Considerable literary activity and reputation. Masques by Daniel performed
before royalty at Hampton Court, 1604 ;
at Oxford, 1605 ; at Whitehall, 1610 ;
in London, 1614. Controller of the
Children of the Revels to the Queen,
1604-18. Groom of the Queen's Privy
Chamber, 1607-19. Removed from
London to a farm near Beckington,
Wilts, about 1603 [?]. Died there,
Oct. 1619. Probably married.

Works : 'Delia,' 1592 (2nd edition
same year) ; 'Cleopatra,' 1594 ; 'First
Fowre Bookes of the Civile Wars,'
1595 ; 5th, 1595 ; 6th, 1601 ; 7th and
8th, 1609 ; 'Musophilus,' 1599 ; 'A
Letter from Octavia,' 1599 ; 'Poeticall
Essayes,' 1599 ; 'Works . . . augmented,' 1601 (with new title-page,
1602) ; 'The Defence of Rhyme,'
1602 ; 'A Panegyricke Congratula-
torie,' 1603 ; 'The Vision of the
Twelve Goddesses,' 1604 ; 'The
Queenes Arcadia' (anon.), 1605 ;
'Philotas' 1605 ; 'Ulisses and the
Syren,' 1605 ; 'Certaine Small Poems,'

1605 ; 'Certaine Small Workes,' 1607 ; 'Tethys Festival,' 1610 (also issued with 'The Order and Solemnitie of the Creation,' 1610) ; 'The Collection of the Historie of England,' pt. i., 1612 ; pt. ii., 1617 ; 'Hymen's Triumph, 1615.

He *translated :* P. Giovio's 'Imprese,' 1585 ; and contrib. verses to the 1611 and 1613 editions of Florio's 'Montaigne.'

Collected Works : ed. by his brother, John Daniel, 1623.

D'ARBLAY (Madame). *See* Burney (Frances).

*DARLEY (George), 1795-1846. Born, in Dublin, 1795. To Trinity Coll., Dublin, 1815 ; B.A., 1820. To London, 1822. Contrib. to 'London Mag.,' under pseud. of 'John Lacy.' Joined staff of 'Athenæum.' Travelled in Italy. Died, in London, 23 Nov. 1846.

Works : 'The Errors of Ecstacie,' 1822 ; 'The Labours of Idleness' (under pseud. 'Guy Penseval '), 1826; 'A System of Popular Geometry,' 1826 ; 'Sylvia,' 1827 ; 'A System of Popular Algebra,' 1827 ; 'A System of Popular Trigonometry,' 1827 ; 'The Geometrical Companion,' 1828 ; 'The New Sketch-Book' (under pseud. of 'G. Crayon, Jun.'), 1829 ; 'Familiar Astronomy,' 1830 ; 'Nepenthe' (anon., privately printed) [1839 ?] ; 'Thomas à Becket,' 1840 ; 'Ethelstan,' 1841.

He *edited :* Beaumont and Fletcher's Works, 1840.

Collected Poems : privately printed, 1890.

*DARWIN (Charles Robert), 1809-1882. Born, 12 Feb. 1809, at Shrewsbury. Educated at Mr. Case's day-school at Shrewsbury, 1817 ; at Shrewbury School, 1818-25. To Edinburgh University, 1825. Medical career given up in favour of clerical. Matriculated at Christ's Coll., Cambridge, Oct. 1827 ; entered upon residence, Lent term 1828 ; B.A., 1832 ; M.A., 1837. Sailed as 'naturalist' on the 'Beagle,' 27 Dec. 1831. Return to England, 6 Oct. 1836. Idea of clerical career abandoned. To Cambridge, Dec.

1836. In London, 1837-42. F.R.S., 24 Jan. 1839 ; Royal medal, 1853 ; Copley medal, 1864. Married Emma Wedgwood, 29 Jan. 1839. Secretary to Geological Society, 1838-41. In consequence of ill-health, removed to Down, Kent, 1842. Lived there, engaged in scientific work, till his death. Occasional visits to friends ; and to meetings of British Association, Southampton, 1846 ; Oxford, 1847 ; Birmingham, 1849 ; Glasgow, 1855. County Magistrate, 1857. Hon. LL.D., Cambridge, 1877. Died, 19 April 1882. Buried in Westminster Abbey.

Works : 'Letters to Prof. Henslow' (privately printed for Cambridge Philosophical Society), 1835 ; 'Journal and Remarks, 1832-36 ' [being vol. iii. of 'Narrative of the Surveying Voyages of H.M. Ships 'Adventure' and 'Beagle'], 1839 (2nd edn. published separately, 1845); 'Zoology of the Voyage of H.M.S. "Beagle "' (edited by Darwin, with contributions to pts. i. and ii.), 1840-43 ; 'The Structure and Distribution of Coral Reefs : being the first part of the Geology of the Voyage of the "Beagle," ' 1842 (2nd edn. published separately, 1874) ; 'Geological Observations on the Volcanic Islands visited during the Voyage of H.M.S. "Beagle": being the second part of the Geology of the Voyage, etc.,' 1844 ; 'Geological Observations on South America : being the third part of the Geology of the Voyage of the "Beagle,"' 1846 (2nd edn. of the two preceding published together as 'Geological Observations on the Volcanic Islands and parts of South America visited, etc.,' 1876); 'Monograph of the Fossil Lepadidæ,' 1851 ; 'Monograph of the Sub-class Cirrepedia,' 1851 ; 'Monograph of the Balanidæ,' 1854 ; 'Monograph of the Fossil Balanidæ and Verrucidæ of Great Britain,' 1854 ; 'On the Origin of Species by Means of Natural Selection,' 1859 ; 'On the Various Contrivances by which Orchids are fertilized by Insects,' 1862 ; 'The Movements and Habits of Climbing Plants,' 1868 ; 'The Variations of Animals and Plants under Domestication,' 1868 ; 'The Descent of Man,'

1871 ; 'The Expression of the Emotions in Man and Animals,' 1872 ; 'The Effect of Cross and Self Fertilization in the Vegetable Kingdom,' 1876 ; 'The Different Forms of Flowers on Plants of the same Species,' 1877 ; 'The Power of Movement in Plants' (with F. Darwin), 1880 ; 'The Formation of Vegetable Mould, through the Action of Worms,' 1881 ; Various papers communicated to scientific journals, 1835-82.

Posthumous : 'Essay on Instinct' (published in Romanes' 'Mental Evolution in Animals'), 1883 ; 'The Life and Letters of Charles Darwin, including an Autobiographical Chapter,' ed. by F. Darwin, 1887.

DARWIN (Erasmus), 1731-1802. Born, at Elston Hall, Notts, 12 Dec. 1731. At Chesterfield School, 1741-50. To St. John's Coll., Camb., 1750 ; Exeter Scholar ; B.A., 1754. To Edinburgh to study medicine, 1754. M.B., Cambridge, 1755. Settled in practice in Nottingham, Sept. 1756 ; removed to Lichfield, Nov. 1756. Married Mary Howard, Dec. 1757 ; she died, 1770. Married Mrs. Chandos-Pole, 1781 ; lived, first at her estate, Radbourne Hall ; subsequently at Derby, and Breadsall Priory, near Derby. Died suddenly, at Breadsall Priory, 18 April 1802. Buried in Breadsall Church.

Works : 'Loves of the Plants' (anon., pt. ii. of 'Botanic Garden'), 1789 ; 'Economy of Vegetation' (anon., pt. i. of 'Botanic Garden'), 1792 ; 'Zoonomia,' 1794-96 ; 'A Plan for the Conduct of Female Education in Boarding Schools,' 1797 ; 'Phytologia,' 1800.

Posthumous : 'The Temple of Nature,' 1803 ; 'Collected Poems,' 1807.

He *edited :* C. Darwin's 'Experiments establishing a Criterion, etc.,' 1780.

Life : by A. Seward, 1804 ; by E. Krause, trans. by W. S. Dallas, 1879.

DASENT (Sir George Webbe), 1817-1896. Born, at St. Vincent, West Indies, 22 May 1817. To Westmin-ster School, 14 April 1831 ; Minor Candidate, 1832. At King's Coll., London, 1836. To Magdalen Hall, Oxford, 28 April 1836. B.A., 6 June 1840 ; M.A., 8 July 1843 ; D.C.L., 1852. Secretary to Sir Thomas Cartwright, at Stockholm, 1836. Admitted to Middle Temple, 30 May 1844 ; called to Bar, 30 Jan. 1852. Married Frances Louisa Delane, 4 April 1846. Advocate of Doctors' Commons, 2 Nov. 1852. Assistant-editor of the 'Times,' 1845-70. Frequent contributor to 'Quarterly Review,' 'Edinburgh Review,' and other periodicals. Civil Service Commissioner, 5 Feb. 1870 to 1892. Knighted, 27 June 1876. Member of Royal Commission on Historical Manuscripts. Died, at Ascott, 11 June 1896.

Works : 'Annals of an Eventful Life' (anon.), 1870 ; 'Three to One,' 1872 ; 'Jest and Earnest,' 1873 ; 'Half a Life,' 1874 ; 'The Vikings of the Baltic,' 1875.

He *translated :* 'The Prose, or Younger Edda,' 1842 ; Rask's 'Icelandic Grammar,' 1843 ; Asbjörnsen and Moe's 'Popular Tales from the Norse,' 1859 ; Thorgeirrson's 'Story of Burnt Njal,' 1861 ; 'The Story of Gisli the Outlaw,' 1866 ; Asbjörnsen's 'Tales from the Fjeld,' 1874 ; the 'Orkneyinga Saga,' 1887 ; Hacon's 'Saga,' 1894 ; and *edited :* 'Eutychianus's Theophylus in Icelandic, etc.,' 1865 ; Cleasby's 'Icelandic-English Dictionary,' 1874.

DAVENANT (Sir William), Poet Laureate. 1606-1668. Born, at Oxford, Feb. 1606. Educated at Magdalen Coll. School, Oxford ; and at Lincoln Coll., 1620[?]-22 [?]. Page to Duchess of Richmond ; afterwards to Fulke Greville, Lord Brooke. Play, 'The Cruel Brother,' performed, 1630. Appointed Poet Laureate, 13 Dec. 1638. Governor of King and Queen's Company of Players, 27 June 1639. Active part in Civil War ; escaped imprisonment and took refuge in France. Knighted after Siege of Gloucester, Sept. 1643. Returned to France after King's defeat. Became Roman Cathollc. Sent on private mission from Queen to King, 1646. Returned to Paris. Sent by Queen on mission to Virginia, 1650. Captured by Parliament ship soon after start, and imprisoned in Cowes Castle ; thence to London for trial. Imprisoned in the Tower, 1651-53. First wife, Anne, died, 1655. Was twice married. Licensed to give dramatic entertainments at Rutland House, 1656 ('The Siege of Rhodes' produced there, 1656), and at Cockpit, in Drury Lane, 1658. Imprisoned for short time in 1659 on account of implication in Sir George Booth's insurrection. At Restoration, license granted him to maintain a company of players, 1660. These acted at Salisbury Court Theatre, or at the Cockpit, Nov. 1660 to Spring of 1662. Under patronage of Duke of York, the company was installed in new Lincoln's Inn Fields Theatre, March or April 1662. Successful production of plays. Died, in Lincoln's Inn Fields, 7 April 1668. Buried in Westminster Abbey.

Works: 'The Tragedy of Albovine,' 1629 ; 'The Cruel Brother,' 1630 ; 'The Just Italian,' 1630 ; 'The Temple of Love' (with Inigo Jones), 1634; 'The Triumphs· of the Prince d'Amour' (anon.), 1635 ; 'The Platonick Lovers,' 1636 ; 'The Witts,' 1636; 'Britannia Triumphans' (with Inigo Jones), 1637 ; 'Madagascar,' 1638 ; 'Ode in Remembrance of Master Shakespeare,' 1638 ; 'Salmacida Spolia,' 1639 ; 'To the honorable . . . House of Commons,' [1641] ; 'The Unfortunate Lovers,' 1643 ; 'London,' 1648 ; 'Love and Honour,' 1649 ; 'Gondibert,' 1651 ; 'The Siege of Rhodes,' 1656 (revised and altered edn., 1663); 'The First Dayes Entertainement at Rutland House' (anon.), 1657 ; 'The Cruelty of the Spaniards in Peru' (anon.), 1658; 'The History of Sir Francis Drake' (anon.), 1659 ; 'Poem to the King's most sacred Majesty,' 1660 ; 'Poem upon his sacred Majestie's most happy return,' 1660 ; 'The Rivals' (anon.; altered from 'The Two Noble Kinsmen'), 1668.

Posthumous: 'The Man's the

Master,' 1669 ; 'The Tempest' (with Dryden), 1670 ; 'New Academy of Complements' (anon., with Lord Buckhurst and Sir Chas. Sedley), 1671 ; 'Macbeth . . . with all the Alterations, etc.,' 1673.

Collected Works: in 3 pts., ed. by his widow, 1673 ; in 5 vols., ed. by Laing and Maidment ('Dramatists of the Restoration' series), with *life*, 1872-74.

DAVIDSON (John), b. 1857. Born, at Barrhead, Renfrewshire, 11 April 1857. Family removed to Greenock, 1862 ; educated at Highlanders' Academy there. Entered chemical laboratory of a sugar refinery, 1869. In Public Analysts' Office, 1870-71. Engaged in tuition until 1889. At Edinburgh Univ. for one session. Married 1885. To London, 1890.

Works: 'Bruce: a drama,' 1886 ; 'Smith : a Tragedy,' 1888 ; 'Plays,' 1889 ; 'Perfervid,' 1890 ; 'In a Music-Hall,' 1891 ; 'The Great Men and a Practical Novelist,' 1891 ; 'Laura Ruthven's Widowhood ' (with C. J. Wills), 1892 ; 'Fleet Street Eclogues,' 1893 ; 'Sentences and Paragraphs,' 1893 ; 'A Random Itinerary,' 1894 [1893] ; 'Ballads and Songs,' 1894 ; 'Baptist Lake,' 1894 ; 'A Full and True Account of the Wonderful Mission of Earl Lavender,' 1895 ; 'Fleet Street Eclogues : second series,' 1896 [1895] ; 'Miss Armstrong's and other Circumstances,' 1896 ; 'New Ballads,' 1896.

He has *translated:* Montesquieu's 'Persian Letters,' 1892 ; Coppée's 'For the Crown,' 1896.

DAY (Thomas), 1748-1789. Born, in London, 22 June 1748. Succeeded to family estate of Bear Hill, Berkshire, July 1749. Mother removed with him to Stoke Newington ; soon afterwards married again, and settled at Bear Hill, 1755. At school at Stoke Newington, and at Charterhouse, 1755-63. Matric. Corpus Christi Coll., Oxford, 1 June 1764 ; left, without degree, 1766. Admitted to Middle Temple, 12 Feb. 1765; called to Bar,

14 May 1775; never practised. After disappointments in love, endeavoured to train two orphan girls on his own principles, in order that he might marry one of them. Scheme failed. Visit to France. On return, after other love disappointments, settled in London; engaged in literary work, with occasional travelling. Married Esther Milnes, 7 Aug. 1778; spent the winter in Hampstead. Bought house at Abridge, Essex, 1779. Removed to Anningsley, Surrey, 1781. Life of great seclusion and asceticism. Killed by accident on horseback, 28 Sept. 1789. Buried at Wargrave.

Works : 'The Dying Negro' (anon., with J. Bicknell), 1773 ; 'Ode for the New Year' (anon.), 1776 ; 'The Devoted Legions,' 1776 ; 'The Desolation of America' (anon.) 1777 ; 'Two Speeches,' 1780 ; 'Reflexions on the Present State of England,' 1782 (2nd edn. same year) ; 'Letters of Marius,' 1784 ; 'Fragments of Original Letters on the Slavery of Negroes,' 1784 ; 'Dialogue between a Justice of the Peace and a Farmer,' 1785 ; 'Four Tracts,' 1785 ; 'Letter to Arthur Young,' 1788 ; 'History of Little Jack,' 1788 ; 'History of Sandford and Merton '(anon.), vol. i., 1783 ; vol. ii., 1787 ; vol. iii., 1789.

Life : by J. Keir, 1791 ; by Blackman, 1862.

DEFOE (Daniel), 1661[?]-1731.
Born [Daniel Foe, name changed to Defoe in 1703], in Cripplegate, 1660 or 1661. To school at Newington Green, 1674 or 1675. Went into business about 1685 [?]. Sided with Monmouth in Rebellion, 1685. Liveryman of City of London, 26 Jan. 1688. With William's army, 1688. Bankrupt, about 1692[?]. Accountant to the Commissioners of the Glass Duty, 1695-99. Vigorous partisan of King William. Prosecuted for libelling the Church, 1703. Sentenced to fine, pillory, and imprisonment during Queen's pleasure, July 1703. Stood in pillory, which populace guarded and wreathed with flowers, July 1703. Imprisoned in Newgate. Released from prison, Aug. 1704. Wrote ' The Review,' Feb. 1704 to June 1713. Sent to Edinburgh as secret agent in favour of Union, autumn 1706. Returned to England, spring 1708. On another mission to Scotland, 1708 ; again in 1712. Active political controversialist and pamphleteer. Prosecuted for libel and imprisoned, 22 April 1713, but pardoned immediately. Found guilty of libelling Lord Annesley, 12 July 1715, but escaped sentence. Wrote periodical 'Mercurius Politicus,' 1716-20 ; edited 'Mist's Journal,' Aug. 1717 to Oct. 1724. Started 'Whitehall Evening Post,' 1718, and 'Daily Post,' 1719 ; wrote in 'Whitehall Evening Post,' 1718-20 ; in 'Daily Post,' 1719-25 ; in 'Applebee's Journal,' 1720-26. Died, in Moorfields, 26 April 1731. Buried in Bunhill Fields.

Works : A complete list of Defoe's works, numbering upwards of 250, is given in William Lee's ' Life of Defoe.' 1869. His political, religious, and social Controversial Tracts date from 1694 to 1731. In fiction, some of his best-known works are ; ' The Life and Strange Surprising Adventures of Robinson Crusoe,' 1719 ; 'The Further Adventures of Robinson Crusoe,' 1719 ; 'Life of Captain Singleton,' 1720 ; 'Moll Flanders,' 1722 ; 'Journal of the Plague Year,' 1722; 'Life of John Sheppard,' 1724.

Collected Works : ' A True Collection of the Writings of the Author of The True Born Englishman, Corrected by Himself' (anon.), 1703 ; 'Novels,' 1810 ; 'Novels and Miscellaneous Works,' 20 vols., 1840-41 ; 'Works,' with memoir by Hazlitt, 1840-43.

Life, by W. Lee, 1869.

DEKKER (Thomas), 1570[?]-1641.
Born, in London, 1570[?]. Practically nothing known of life except constant literary activity. Wrote a number of plays from 1598 onwards. Died, 1641 [?].

Works: 'Canaans Calamitie,' 1578 ; 'The Shoemaker's Holiday ' (anon.), 1600 ; 'The Pleasant Comedie of Old Fortunatus' (anon.), 1600 ; 'Satiromastix,' 1602; 'The Wonderfull Yeare 1603' (anon.), 1602; 'The Batchelar's Banquet' (anon.), 1603; 'Patient Grissil' (with Haughton and Chettle), 1603; 'Magnificent Entertainment given to King James,' 1604; 'The Honest Whore,' 1604; 'The Seven Deadly Sinnes of London,' 1606; 'Newes from Hell,' 1606; 'The Double P.P.' (anon.), 1606; 'A Knight's Conjuring,' 1607; 'Westward Ho' (with Webster), 1607; 'Northward Ho' (with Webster), 1607; 'The Whore of Babylon,' 1607; 'The Famous History of Sir Thomas Wyat' (with Webster), 1607; 'The Dead Tearme,' 1608; 'The Belman of London' (anon.), 1608; 'Lanthorne and Candlelight,' 1608 (2nd and 3rd edns., 1609; 4th, anon.. entitled 'O per se O,' 1612); 'The Ravevens [Raven's] Almanacke,' 1609; 'The Guls Horne-booke,' 1609; 'Work for Armourers,' 1609; 'Fowre Birds of Noah's Arke,' 1609; 'The Roaring Girle' (with Middleton), 1611; 'If it be not good, etc.,' 1612; 'Troia-Nova Triumphans,' 1612; 'A Strange Horse Race,' 1613; 'Villanies Discovered' (anon.), 1616; 'Dekker, his Dreame,' 1620; 'Greevous Grones for the Poore' (anon.), 1621; 'The Virgin Martyr' (with Massinger), 1622; 'A Rod for Run-Awayes,' 1625; 'Warres, Warres, Warres,' 1628; 'Britannia's Honour,' 1628; 'London's Tempe,' 1629; 'Second part of The Honest Whore,' 1630; 'Match Mee in London,' 1631; 'The Wonder of a Kingdome,' 1636.

Posthumous: 'The Sun's Darling' (with Ford), 1656; 'The Witch of Edmonton' (with Ford and Rowley), 1658.

Collected works: Dramatic Works, with memoir, in 4 vols., 1873; Non-Dramatic Works, ed. by A. B. Grosart (5 vols.), 1884-86.

DENHAM (*Sir* John), **1615-1669.** Born, in Dublin, 1615. At school in London. Entered at Lincoln's Inn, 28 April 1631; called to Bar, 1638. Matriculated Trinity Coll., Oxford, 18 Nov. 1631. Married Ann Cotton,

25 June 1634. Inherited family estates on father's death, 1638. Took King's side in Civil War, being High Sheriff of Surrey. Governor of Farnham Castle, 1642. Taken prisoner and sent to London. Lived at Oxford, 1643-47. In attendance on Charles I., Henrietta Maria, and Charles II., respectively, till 1651. Returned to England, winter of 1651. Forbidden to live in London, 1655; settled at Bury, Suffolk, 1658. Abroad with Earl of Pembroke, 1659. Surveyor General of Works, June 1660. Arranged Coronation Ceremony for Charles II., 1661; created Knight of the Bath. Married Margaret Brooke, 25 May 1665. She died, 6 Jan. 1667. He died, in London, March 1669. Buried in Westminster Abbey.

Works: 'The Sophy' (anon.), 1642; 'Cooper's Hill' (anon.), 1642; a verse adaptation of Cicero's 'Cato Major,' 1648; 'Anatomy of Play' (anon.), 1651; 'The Destruction of Troy' (anon.; trans. from 'Virgil's Æneid,' Book II.), 1656; 'Panegyrick on ... Gen. George Monck' (anon.; attrib. to Denham), 1659; 'A Relation of a Quaker' (anon., attrib. to Denham), 1659; 'Second and Third Advices to a Painter,' 1667 (another edn. same year); 'The Famous Battel of the Catts' (anon.), 1668; 'Poems and Translations,' 1668.

Posthumous: 'The Gaming Humour considered' (anon.), 1684; 'A Version of the Psalms of David,' 1714.

DE QUINCEY (THOMAS), 1785-1859. Born, in Manchester, 15 Aug. 1785. Educated privately at Salford; at Bath Grammar School, 1797 [?]-99; at school at Winkfield, Wilts, 1799-1800. To Manchester Grammar School, winter of 1800. Ran away from latter, July 1802. Lived a roving life in Wales, July to Nov., 1802. To London, Nov. 1802; after great distress there reconciled with family. Matric. Worcester Coll., Oxford, 17 Dec. 1803; left, without degree, 1807. Friendship with Coleridge begun, 1807. Visit to Oxford, and in London, 1808. Student of

Middle Temple, 1808 [?] With Wordsworth at Grasmere, Dec. 1808 to Feb. 1809. Settled in cottage at Townend, Westmoreland, Nov. 1809. In Edinburgh with Professor Wilson, winters of 1814-15 and 1815-16. Habitual taking of opium began, 1813. Married Margaret Simpson, winter of 1816. Contrib. to 'Blackwood' and 'Quarterly Review.' Edited 'Westmoreland Gazette,' 1819-20. To London, 1821. Through Lamb's introduction, became contributor to 'London Magazine,' in which the 'Confessions of an Opium-Eater' appeared, Oct. to Nov., 1821. Contrib. to 'London Magazine,' 1821-24 ; to Knight's 'Quarterly Magazine,' 1824. In Westmoreland, 1825. Contributed to 'Blackwood,' 1826-49. Settled in Edinburgh, 1828 ; wife and children joined him there, 1830. Contrib. to 'Edinburgh Literary Gazette,' 1828-30 ; to 'Tait's Magazine,' 1834-51. Relapse into opium habit after wife's death in 1837 ; improvement in 1844. In Glasgow, March 1841 to June 1847. To Edinburgh, 1847. Died there, 8 Dec. 1859. Buried in West Churchyard, Edinburgh.

Works : 'Confessions of an English Opium-Eater' (anon.), 1822 ; 'Klosterheim' (anon.), 1832 ; 'The Logic of Political Economy,' 1844 ; 'Selections, grave and gay, from his writings,' edited by himself (4 vols.), 1853-60.

Collected Works : in 20 vols., 1853-55.

Life : by H. A. Page, 1877 ; by Prof. Masson, 1881.

DE TABLEY, *Baron* [John Byrne Leicester-Warren], **1835-1895.** Born, at Tabley House, Knutford, Cheshire, 26 April 1835. Educated at Eton till 1852. Matric., Ch. Ch., Oxford, 20 Oct. 1852 ; B.A., 1856 ; M.A., 1860. Student of Lincoln's Inn, 4 May 1857; called to Bar, 17 Nov. 1860. F.S.A., 25 Jan. 1883. Succeeded to title, 1887. Unmarried. Died, 22 Nov. 1895.

Works : 'Essay on Greek Federal Coinage,' 1863 ; 'On Some Coins of Lycia,' 1863 ; 'Eclogues and Mono-

dramas' (under pseud. 'William P. Lancaster '), 1864 ; 'Studies in Verse ' (under pseud. 'William P. Lancaster '), 1865 ; 'Philoctetes' (anon.), 1866 ; 'Orestes' (under pseud. 'William P. Lancaster '), 1867 ; 'A Screw Loose,' (under pseud. 'William P. Lancaster '), 1868 ; 'Ropes of Sand' (under pseud. 'William P. Lancaster '), 1869 ; 'Rehearsals,' 1870; 'Searching the Net,' 1873 ; 'The Soldier of Fortune,' 1876 ; 'A Guide to the Study of Bookplates,' 1880 ; 'Poems, dramatic and lyrical,' 2 series, 1893-95.

*DE VERE (Aubrey Thomas), b. 1814. Born, at Curragh Chase, co. Limerick, 10 Jan. 1814. Educated Trinity Coll., Dublin. Has lived mainly in Ireland.

Works : 'The Waldenses,' 1842 ; 'The Search after Proserpine,' 1843 ; 'English Misrule and Irish Misdeeds, 1848 ; 'Picturesque Sketches of Greece and Turkey,' 1850 ; 'Poems,' 1855 [1854] ; 'Heroines of Charity,' 1854 ; 'May Carols,' 1857 ; 'Select Specimens of the English Poets,' 1858 ; 'The Sisters,' 1861 ; 'Inisfail,' 1862 ; 'The Infant Bridal,' 1864 ; 'The Church Settlement of Ireland,' 1866 ; 'Ireland's Church Property,' 1867 ; 'Pleas for Secularization,' 1867 ; 'St. Thomas of Canterbury,' 1867 ; 'Irish Odes,' 1869 ; 'The Legends of St. Patrick,' 1872; 'Alexander the Great,' 1874 ; 'St. Thomas of Canterbury,' 1876 ; 'Antar and Zara,' 1877 ; 'The Fall of Rora . . . and other poems,' 1877 ; 'Legends of the Saxon Saints,' 1879 ; 'Constitutional and Unconstitutional Political Action.' 1881 ; 'The Foray of Queen Meane,' 1882 ; 'Ireland and Proportional Representation,' 1885 ; 'Legends and Records of the Church and the Empire,' 1887 ; 'Essays, chiefly on Poetry,' 1887 ; 'St. Peter's Chains,' 1888 ; 'Essays, chiefly literary and ethical,' 1889 ; 'The Household Poetry Book,' 1893 ; 'Mediæval Records and Sonnets,' 1893 ; 'Religious Problems of the Nineteenth Century,' ed. by J. G. Wenham, 1893.

Collected Works : Poetical Works,

1884 ; Selected Poems, ed. by J. Dennis, 1890 ; ed. by G. E. Woodberry, 1894.

*DICKENS (Charles), 1812-1870. Born, at Landport, Portsea, 7 Feb. 1812. (Christened 'Charles John Huffam,' but never used last two names.) Family moved to Chatham, 1816. To school under Mr. Giles, Baptist minister. Family moved to Camden Town. Neglected education. Father arrested for debt, 1822 [?]. Dickens obtained situation as packer in a blacking warehouse. At Mr. Jones's school in Hampstead Road, 1824-26. Employed as solicitor's clerk, May 1827 to Nov. 1828. Taught himself shorthand. Parliamentary reporter to 'The True Sun,' 1831-32 ; for 'The Mirror of Parliament' ; for 'The Morning Chronicle,' from 1835. Contributed papers, afterwards pub. as 'Sketches by "Boz,"' to 'Monthly Mag.,' 'Morning Chronicle,' 'Evening Chronicle,' 'Bell's Life,' and 'Library of Fiction,' 1833-35. Married Catherine Hogarth, 2 April 1836. 'The Strange Gentleman' produced at St. James's Theatre, 29 Sept. 1836 ; 'Is she his Wife?' same theatre, 6 March 1837. Edited 'Bentley's Miscellany,' 1837-39. Growing popularity. Freedom of City of Edinburgh, summer of 1841. Severe illness, autumn of same year. Visit to America and Canada, Jan. to June, 1842. Visits to Italy. July to Nov., 1844, and Jan. to June, 1845. First editor of 'Daily News,' 21 Jan. to 9 Feb., 1846; subsequently an occasional contributor. Started General Theatrical Fund. Visit to Switzerland, June to Nov., 1846; in Paris, Nov. 1846 to Feb., 1847 (with visit to London, Dec. 1846). Active part in various amateur theatrical performances for charities, 1847-52. 'Household Words' started, 30 March 1849 ; edited it till 1859. Testimonial at Birmingham, 1853. At Boulogne, summers of 1853, 54, 56. In Switzerland and Italy, autumn of 1853; in Paris, Nov. 1855 to May 1856. Bought Gadshill Place, 1856 ; settled there, 1860. First public 'Reading'

from his works, 29 April 1858. Separation from his wife, May 1858. On cessation of 'Household Words,' started 'All the Year Round,' 30 April 1859. Four series of public Readings, 1858-59, 1861-63, 1866-67, 1868-70, in London, provinces and Scotland. Readings in Paris, 1863. Severe illness in 1865. Readings in America, Dec. 1867 to April 1868. Breakdown of health. Last Reading, in London, 1 March 1869. Died, at Gadshill, 9 June 1870. Buried in Westminster Abbey.

Works: 'Sketches by Boz,' 1st series, 1835 ; 2nd, 1836 ; 'Sunday under Three Heads . . . By Timothy Sparks,' 1836 ; 'The Strange Gentleman . . . By "Boz,"' 1837 ; 'The Village Coquettes,' 1836 ; 'Posthumous Papers of the Pickwick Club,' 1837 (in monthly nos., April 1836 to Nov. 1837) ; 'Memoirs of Joseph Grimaldi, edited by "Boz,"' 1838 ; 'Oliver Twist . . . By "Boz"' (from 'Bentley's Miscellany'; 2 vols.), 1838 ; 'Sketches of Young Gentlemen' (anon.), 1838 ; 'Life and Adventures of Nicholas Nickleby,' 1839 (in monthly nos., April 1838 to Oct. 1839) ; 'Sketches of Young Couples' (anon.), 1840 ; 'Master Humphrey's Clock,' vol. i., 1840 ; vols. ii. and iii., 1841 (in weekly nos., April 1840 to Nov. 1841) ; 'Barnaby Rudge,' 1841 ; 'The Old Curiosity Shop,' 1841 ; 'American Notes,' 1842 ; 'A Christmas Carol,' 1843 ; 'The Life and Adventures of Martin Chuzzlewit,' 1844 (in monthly nos., Jan. 1843 to July 1844) ; 'The Chimes,' 1844 ; 'The Cricket on the Hearth,' 1845 ; 'Pictures from Italy' (from 'Daily News'), 1846 ; 'The Battle of Life,' 1846 ; 'Dealings with the firm of Dombey and Son,' 1848 (in monthly nos., Oct. 1846 to April 1848) ; 'The Haunted Man,' 1848 ; 'The Personal History of David Copperfield,' 1850 (in monthly nos., May 1849 to Nov. 1850); 'Bleak House,' 1853 (in monthly nos., March 1852 to Sept. 1853) ; 'A Child's History of England' (from 'Household Words'), 1854 ; 'Hard Times for these Times' (from 'House-

hold Words'), 1854; 'Little Dorrit,'
1857 (in monthly nos., Dec. 1855 to June
1857) ; 'A Tale of Two Cities' (from
'All the Year Round'), 1859 ; 'The
Uncommercial Traveller,' 1861 [1860]
(originally in weekly parts, Jan. to
Oct., 1860 ; 2nd edn. enlarged, 1868 ;
3rd edn. enlarged, 1869) ; 'Great Ex-
pectations' (from 'All the Year
Round'), 1861 ; 'Our Mutual Friend,'
1865 (in monthly nos., May 1864 to
Nov. 1865) ; 'The Mystery of Edwin
Drood' (unfinished) six nos., April to
Sept., 1870.

Posthumous: 'Speeches,' 1870 ;
'Mr. Nightingale's Diary,' 1877 ; 'Is
she his Wife?' 1877 ; 'The Lamp-
lighter,' 1879 ; 'The Mudfog Papers'
(from 'Bentley's Miscellany'), 1880 ;
'Letters' (3 vols.), 1880-82.

He *edited:* 'The Pic-Nic Papers,'
1841 ; J. Overs' 'Evenings of a
Working Man,' 1844 ; 'Method of
Employment,' 1852 ; A. A. Procter's
'Legends and Lyrics,' 1866 ; 'Re-
ligious Opinions of the late C. H.
Townshend,' 1869.

Collected Works: in 22 vols., 1858-
69 ; in 21 vols., 1867-74.

Life: by Forster, 1872 ; by Marzials
1887.

DIGBY (*Sir* **Kenelm**), 1603-1665.
Born, at Gayhurst, Bucks, 11 July
1603. Early youth spent at Gayhurst.
In Spain, Aug. 1617 to April 1618.
At Gloucester Hall (now Worcester
Coll.), Oxford, autumn of 1618 to
1620. In Paris, Angers, and Florence,
1620-22. To Madrid, March 1623 ;
attached to household of Prince
Charles ; returned to England with
him, Oct. 1623. Knighted by James I.,
23 Oct. 1623. Appointed Gentleman
of Privy Chamber to Prince Charles.
Secretly married Venetia Stanley,
Jan. [?] 1625. Friendship with Ben
Jonson and Earl of Clarendon. On
privateering expedition, Dec. 1627 to
Feb. 1629. Inherited library from
former tutor, Allen, 1632 ; presented
it to Bodleian Library, Oxford. Wife
died suddenly, 1 May 1633. He
retired to Gresham Coll., 1633-35.
Abjured Romanism for Protestantism,
1630 ; returned to Roman Church,
1635. To France, 1636 ; returned to
England, 1639. Summoned to Bar of
Parliament on suspicion of treason, 27
Jan. 1641 ; imprisoned, Jan. [?] 1642
to July 1643. Released at request of
Queen-Dowager of France, on condi-
tion of leaving for France and not re-
turning without Parliament's permis-
sion. Property confiscated, Nov. 1643.
In Paris, 1643-49. Chancellor to
Queen of France. Returned to
England, Aug. 1649 ; banished again.
Returned, by permission, early in 1654
Engaged in diplomatic service by
Cromwell. Went abroad again, and
returned to England after Restoration.
Lectured at Gresham Coll., 23 Jan.
1661. On first Council of Royal Soc.,
1663. Forbidden the Court, 1664.
Died, in London, 11 June 1665.
Buried in Christ Church, Newgate.

Works: 'A Conference with a
Lady,' 1638 ; 'Sir Kenelm Digby's
Honour maintained,' 1641 ; 'Observations upon Religio Medici,' 1643 ;
'Observations on Bk. II., canto IX.,
stanza 22 of Spenser's "Faery
Queene,"' 1643 ; 'A Treatise of the
Nature of Bodies,' 1644 ; 'A Treatise
declaring the Operations and Nature
of Man's Soul,' 1644 ; 'The Royall
Apologie' (anon.), 1648 ; 'Institu-
tionum Peripateticorum libri quinque'
(probably written with Thomas White),
1651 ; 'Letters [with Lord G. Digby]
. . . concerning Religion,' 1651 ; 'A
Discourse concerning Infallibility in
Religion' (anon.), 1652 ; 'A Late
Discourse . . . touching the Cure of
Wounds by the Powder of Sympathy,'
1658 ; 'A Discourse concerning the
Vegetation of Plants,' 1661.

Posthumous: 'Choice and Experi-
mented Receipts in Physick and Chi-
rurgery,' 1668 ; 'The Closet of . . .
Sir Kenelm Digby Opened,' 1669 ;
'Private Memoirs,' ed. by Sir H. N.
Nicholas (2 pts.), 1827-28 ; 'Journal
of a Voyage into the Mediterranean,'
ed. by J. Bruce, 1868 ; 'Poems,' ed.
by G. F. Warner, 1877.

He *translated:* Bishop of Ratisbon's 'Treatise of Adhering to God,'
1653-54.

*DISRAELI (Benjamin) 1st *Earl of Beaconsfield*, **1804-1881**. Born, in London, 21 Dec. 1804. Educated at school at Blackheath. Articled to solicitor, 18 Nov. 1821. Entered at Lincoln's Inn, 1824. Visit to Spain, Italy, and Levant, 1828-31. Worked at literature for five years. M.P. for Maidstone, July 1837. Married Mrs. Wyndham Lewis, 23 Aug. 1839. M.P. for Shrewsbury, 1841. Visit to Germany and France, autumn of 1845. Leader of Opposition in House of Commons, Sept. 1848. Chancellor of Exchequer, Feb. 1852. Contrib. to 'The Press' newspaper, 1853-58. Chancellor of Exchequer second time, 1865; Prime Minister, March to Nov., 1868. Active political life. Wife died, 15 Dec. 1872. Prime Minister second time, Jan. 1874 to March 1880. Last speech in House of Commons, 11 Aug. 1876. Created Earl of Beaconsfield, 12 Aug. 1876. Died, 19 April 1881. Buried at Hughenden.

Works: 'Vivian Grey' (anon.) pt. i., 1826 ; pt. ii., 1827 ; 'The Star Chamber' (anon. ; suppressed), 1826 ; 'The Voyage of Captain Popanilla' (anon.), 1828 ; 'The Young Duke' (anon.), 1831 ; 'Contarini Fleming' (anon.), 1832 ; 'England and France' (anon.), 1832 ; 'What is he?' (anon.), 1833 ; 'The Wondrous Tale of Alroy' (anon.), 1833 ; 'The Present Crisis Examined,' 1834 ; 'The Rise of Iskander,' 1834 ; 'The Revolutionary Epic,' 1834 ; 'Vindication of the British Constitution,' 1835 ; 'Letters of Runnymede' (anon.), 1836 ; 'The Spirit of Whiggism,' 1836 ; 'Venetia' (anon.), 1837 ; 'Henrietta Temple' (anon.), 1837 ; 'The Tragedy of Count Alarcos' (anon.), 1839 ; 'Coningsby,' 1844 ; 'Sybil,' 1845 ; 'Tancred,' 1847 ; 'Mr. Gladstone's Finance,' 1862 : 'Lothair,' 1870 ; 'Novels and Tales' (collected), 1870-71 ; 'Endymion,' 1880.

Posthumous: 'Home Letters,' 1885 ; 'Correspondence with his Sister,' 1886.

He *edited* the following editions of works by his father : 'Curiosities of Literature,' 1849 ; 'Charles I.,' 1851 ; 'Works,' 1858-59 ; 'Amenities of Literature,' 1881; 'Literary Character,' 1881 ; 'Calamities of Authors,' 1881.

Life: by Kebbel, 1888 ; by Froude, 1890.

DISRAELI (Isaac), **1766 - 1848.** [Father of preceding.] Born, at Enfield, May 1766. Educated at a school near Enfield. At Amsterdam, 1780-82. Contrib. to 'Gentleman's Magazine,' Dec. 1786 and July 1789; to 'St. James's Chronicle,' Nov. 1787. In France, 1787 - 89. In Devonshire, owing to ill-health, 1795-98. Married Maria Basevi, 10 Feb. 1802. Elected Warden of London Synagogue of Spanish and Portuguese Jews, 3 Oct. 1813, but declined the office. Active literary life. Removed from London to Bradenham House, Bucks, 1829. Hon. D.C.L., Oxford, 4 July 1832. Became blind, 1839. Died, at Bradenham, 19 Jan. 1848. Buried there.

Works: 'A Defence of Poetry,' 1790; 'Narrative Poems,' 1803 ; 'Curiosities of Literature' (anon.) vol. i., 1791; vol. ii., 1793 ; vol. iii., 1817 ; vols. iv. and v., 1823 ; vol. vi., 1834 (various edns. of whole, 1793-1841); 2nd series, 1823 ; 'A Dissertation on Anecdotes' (anon.), 1793 ; 'Domestic Anecdotes of the French Nation' (anon.), 1794 ; 'Essay on the Manners and Genius of the Literary Character,' 1795 (enlarged edn. under title of 'The Literary Character' anon., 1818) ; 'Miscellanies,' 1796; 'Vaurien' (anon.), 1797; 'Flim-Flams' (anon.); 1797; 'Mejnoun and Leila,' 1797; 'Romances,' 1799; 'Despotism' (anon.), 1811; 'Calamities of Authors' (anon.),1812-13 ; 'Quarrels of Authors' (anon.), 1814; 'Inquiry into the Literary and Political Character of James I.,' 1816 ; 'Commentaries on the Life and Reign of Charles I.,' 1828 - 31 ; 'Eliot, Hampden, and Pym' (anon.), 1832 ; 'The Genius of Judaism' (anon.), 1833 ; 'The Illustrator Illustrated' (anon.), 1838 ; 'Amenities of Literature,' 1840.

Collected Works: ed. by Benjamin Disraeli, 1858-59.

Life: by Benjamin Disraeli, in 1849 edn. of 'Curiosities of Literature.'

6

DIXON (William Hepworth), 1821-1879. Born, at Great Ancoats, Manchester, 30 June 1821. Lived as a boy with grand-uncle, who educated him. Started life as clerk to a merchant in Manchester. Contrib. to 'North of England Mag.,' 1842-43 ; to Jerrold's 'Illuminated Mag.,' 1843. For short time editor of 'Cheltenham Journal,' 1846. To London, summer of 1846. Entered at Middle Temple. Called to Bar, 1 May 1854. Contrib. regularly to 'Daily News' and 'Athenæum.' Deputy Commissioner of Exhibition of 1850. F.S.A., 8 June 1852 ; F.R.G.S., 27 Nov. 1854. Editor of 'Athenæum,' Jan. 1853 to Aug. 1869. Contrib. to 'Gentleman's Mag.,' 1860. Travelled in Spain, Portugal and Morocco, 1861 ; in East, 1863. Founded Palestine Exploration Fund, 1863. To United States, 1866. To Russia, 1867. J.P. for Middlesex and Westminster, 1869. Member of London School Board, 1870. To Spain, 1872. Created Knight Commander of Crown by Emperor Wilhelm of Germany, 4 Oct. 1872. Procured free opening of Tower of London, 1872. Libel action against 'Pall Mall Gaz.,' Nov. 1872. In Canada and U.S.A., autumn of 1874. In Italy and Germany, 1875. In Cyprus, 1878. Died, in London, 27 Dec. 1879. Buried in Highgate Cemetery.

Works : 'Azamoglan' (privately printed), [1840 ?] ; 'John Howard and the Prison World of Europe,' 1849 ; 'The London Prisons,' 1850 ; 'William Penn,' 1851 ; 'The French in England' (anon.), 1852 ; 'Robert Blake,' 1852 ; 'Personal History of Lord Bacon,' 1861 ; 'Proof-Private : Lord Bacon's Confession,' 1861 ; 'The Story of Lord Bacon's Life,' 1862 ; 'The Holy Land,' 1865 ; 'New America,' 1867 ; 'Free Voting,' 1868 ; 'Our Representative System,' 1868 ; 'Spiritual Wives,' 1868 ; 'Her Majesty's Tower,' vols. i., ii., 1869 ; vols. iii., iv., 1871 ; 'Free Russia,' 1870 ; 'Secret History of "The International" Working Men's Association' (under pseud. 'Onslow Yorke'), 1872 [1871]; 'The Switzers,' 1872 ; 'The History of Two Queens,'

2 vols., 1873-74 ; 'The White Conquest,' 1876 [1875]; 'Diana, Lady Lyle,' 1877 ; 'Ruby Gray,' 1878 ; 'Royal Windsor,' vols. i., ii., 1879 [1878] ; 'British Cyprus,' 1879.

Posthumous : 'Royal Windsor,' vols. iii., iv., 1880.

He *edited :* 'Lady Morgan's Memoirs,' 1862 ; F. W. Evans's 'Religious Communism ' [1871].

DOBELL (Sydney Thompson), 1824-1874. Born, at Cranbrook, Kent, 5 April 1824. Family removed to Cheltenham, 1836. Educated privately. Married Emily Fordham, 18 July 1844. Literary activity, and enthusiasm in patriotic causes of various countries. Visit to Switzerland, Aug. 1850. Lived in Edinburgh, 1854-57. Wintered in Isle of Wight, 1858-61. Increasing ill-health. Wintered near Cannes, 1862 ; in Spain, 1863 ; in Italy, 1864. Lived in Gloucestershire from 1866 till death. Died, at Barton-End House, Gloucestershire, 22 Aug. 1874. Buried in Painswick Cemetery.

Works : 'The Roman' (under pseud. 'Sydney Yendys'), 1850 ; 'Balder' (anon.), 1854 [1853] ; 'Sonnets on the War ' (with A. Smith ; anon.), 1855 ; 'England in Time of War,' 1856 ; 'The Nature of Poetry,' 1857 ; 'Of Parliamentary Reform,' 1865.

Collected Works : Poems (2 vols.), 1875 ; Prose, 1876 ; 'Thoughts on Art, Philosophy and Religion,' ed. by G. Nichol, 1876 ; 'Life and Letters' (2 vols.), 1878.

*DOBSON (Henry Austin), b. 1840.** Born, at Plymouth, 18 Jan. 1840. Educated at schools at Beaumaris, Coventry and Strasburg. Returned from Strasburg, 1856. Intended at first to become Civil Engineer ; but was appointed Clerk in Board of Trade, Dec. 1856. Frequent contributor to periodicals. Elected Member of Athenæum Club, 1891.

Works : 'Vignettes in Rhyme,' 1873 ; 'Civil Service Handbook of English Literature,' 1874 ; 'Proverbs in Porcelain,' 1877 ; 'Hogarth,' 1880 (enlarged edn., 1891); 'Eighteenth Century Essays,' 1882; 'Fielding,' 1883; 'Old-World Idylls,' 1883; 'Thomas Bewick and his pupils,' 1884; 'At the Sign of the Lyre,' 1885; 'Richard Steele,' 1886; 'Life of Oliver Goldsmith,' 1888 [1887]; 'Poems on several occasions,' 1889; 'Horace Walpole,' 1890; 'Four Frenchwomen,' 1890; 'The Ballad of Beau Brocade,' 1892; 'Eighteenth Century Vignettes,' first series, 1892; second series, 1894; third series, 1896; 'Coridon's Song,' 1894; 'The Story of Rosina,' 1895.

He has *edited*: White's 'Civil Service History of England,' 1870; Gay's 'Fables,' 1882; Goldsmith's 'Vicar of Wakefield,' 1883, 1885, and 1890; Defoe's 'Robinson Crusoe,' 1883; Selections from Herrick, 1883; Beaumarchais' 'Le Barbier de Seville,' 1884; Lang's 'Ballades and Verses Vain,' 1884; Selections from Steele, 1885; Selections from Goldsmith, 1887; Selections from Prior, 1889; Goldsmith's 'Poems and Plays,' 1889; 'The Quiet Life,' 1890; Goldsmith's 'Citizen of the World,' 1891; Fielding's 'Journal of a Voyage to Lisbon,' 1892; Holbein's 'Dance of Death,' 1892; Chelidonius' 'Little Passion' of Dürer, 1894; Marteilhe's 'Memoirs of a Protestant,' 1895; Jane Austen's 'Works,' 1895, etc.

* **DODGSON** (Charles Lutwidge), b. **1832**. Born, 1832. Matric., Ch. Ch., Oxford, 23 May 1850; Student, 1852-70; B.A., 1854; M.A.. 1857. Ordained Deacon, 1861. Mathematical Lecturer, Ch. Ch., 1855-81.

Works:* 'A Syllabus of Plane Algebraical Geometry,' 1860; 'The Formulæ of Plane Trigonometry,' 1861; 'A Guide to the Mathematical Student,' 1864; 'Alice's Adventures in Wonderland' (under pseud. 'Lewis Carroll'), 1866 [1865]; 'An Elementary Treatise on Determinants,' 1867; 'The Fifth Book of Euclid treated

* It should be noted that Mr. Dodgson states, with reference to this list, that he 'neither claims nor acknowledges any connection with the books not published under this name.'

Algebraically,' 1868; 'Phantasmagoria' (by 'Lewis Carroll'), 1869; 'Songs from "Alice's Adventures in Wonderland,"' 1870; 'Through the Looking-Glass' (by 'Lewis Carroll'), 1871; 'Facts, Figures and Fancies,' (reprint of part of Phantasmagoria), 1871; 'Euclid, Bk. V., proved Algebraically,' 1874; 'The Hunting of the Snark' (by 'Lewis Carroll'), 1876; 'Euclid and his Modern Rivals,' 1879; 'Doublets' (by 'Lewis Carroll'), 1879; 'Rhyme and Reason' (by 'Lewis Carroll'), 1883; 'Lawn Tennis Tournaments,' 1883; 'The Principles of Parliamentary Representation,' 1884; 'A Tangled Tale' (by 'Lewis Carroll'), 1885; 'Alice's Adventures Underground: a facsimile of the original MS.,' 1886; 'The Game of Logic' (by 'Lewis Carroll'), 1887; 'Curiosa Mathematica,' pt. i., 1888; 'Sylvie and Bruno' (by 'Lewis Carroll'), 1889; 'The Nursery "Alice,"' 1890; 'Sylvie and Bruno concluded' (by 'Lewis Carroll'), 1893; 'Symbolic Logic,' pt. i., 1896.

He has *edited*: Euclid, Bks. i. ii., 1882.

DODSLEY (Robert), **1703-1764.** Born, near Mansfield [?], Notts, 1703. Apprenticed to a stocking-weaver; ran away, and entered domestic service. Contrib. a poem to 'Country Journal,' Sept. 1729. In domestic service till 1735. 'The Toy-Shop' produced at Covent Garden, 3 Feb. 1735. Opened a bookseller's shop in Pall Mall, 1735. 'The King and the Miller of Mansfield' produced at Drury Lane, 1 Feb. 1737; 'Sir John Cockle at Court,' 23 Feb. 1738; 'The Blind Beggar of Bethnal Green,' 3 April 1741. Published for Pope, Young, Akenside and Dr. Johnson. Imprisoned for libel, 1739. Published 'The Publick Register,' Jan. to June, 1741. Published 'The Museum,' March 1746 to Sept. 1747. 'The Triumph of Peace' produced at Drury Lane, 21 Feb. 1749. Published 'The World,' 1753 57. 'Cleone' produced at Covent Garden, 2 Dec. 1758. Founded 'The Annual Register,'

1758. Retired from business, 1759. Died, at Durham, 25 Dec. 1764. Buried in churchyard of Durham Abbey.

Works: 'Servitude . . . by a Footman' (anon.), [1729] (republished as 'The Footman's Friendly Advice to his Brethren of the Livery . . . By R. D., Footman'[1731]); 'An Entertainment designed for Her Majesty's Birthday,' 1732; 'An Entertainment designed for the Wedding of Governor Lowther,' 1732; 'A Muse in Livery,' 1732 (2nd edn., same year); 'The Toy-Shop,' 1735; 'The Art of Preaching' (anon.), [1735 ?]; 'The King and the Miller of Mansfield,' [1737]; 'Sir John Cockle at Court' (anon.), 1738; 'The Chronicle of the Kings of England' (under pseud. of 'Nathan Ben Saddi'), bk. i., 1740; bk. ii., 1741; 'The Blind Beggar of Bethnal Green,' 1741; 'Pain and Patience,' 1742; 'Colin's Kisses,' 1742; 'The Book of the Chronicle of James the Nephew' (anon.), 1743; 'A Select Collection of Old Plays' (anon.; 12 vols.), 1744; 'Rex et Pontifex,' 1745; 'The Preception' (anon.), 1748; 'A Collection of Poems by Several Hands' (anon.), vols. i.-iii., 1748; vol. iv., 1749; vols. v., vi., 1758; 'Trifles,' 1748; 'The Triumph of Peace,' 1749; 'The Economy of Human Life' (anon.; possibly by Lord Chesterfield), [1751] (2nd edn., same year); 'Public Virtue,' 1753; 'Theatrical Records' (anon.), 1756; 'Melpomene' (anon.), 1757; 'Cleone,' 1758; 'Select Fables,' 1761; 'Fugitive Pieces,' 1761.

Posthumous: 'Miscellanies,' 1777. He *edited:* Shenstone's Works, 1764.

*DONNE (John), 1573-1631. Born, in London, 1573. Privately educated. Matric. Hart Hall, Oxford, 23 Oct. 1584. Took no degree. Probably travelled abroad, 1588-91. Admitted to Lincoln's Inn, 6 May 1592. With Earl of Essex to Cadiz, June 1596. Secretary to Sir Thomas Egerton, Aug. 1596 to 1601. Wrote many poems and satires. Married secretly

Anne More, niece of Lady Egerton, Dec. [?] 1600. Dismissed from secretaryship when marriage was discovered. Lived at a friend's house at Pyrford till 1604; then with brother-in-law, Sir Thomas Grymes, at Peckham; and subsequently lived at Mitcham. Gradually obtained favour at Court of James I. Degree of M.A., Oxford, conferred, 10 Oct. 1610. To Germany, France and Belgium with Sir Robert Drury, Nov. 1611 to Aug. 1612. Studied theology. Ordained, Jan. 1615, and appointed Chaplain to King. Degree of D.D., Cambridge, granted at King's request, March 1615. Rector of Keyston, Hants, Jan. 1616; of Sevenoaks, July 1616. Divinity Reader to Lincoln's Inn, Oct. 1616 to Feb. 1622. Wife died, 15 Aug. 1617. To Germany with Lord Doncaster, as Chaplain, April 1619. Dean of St. Paul's, 27 Nov. 1621. Prolocutor to Convocation, 1623 and 1624. Rector of Blunham, Beds, 1622; Vicar of St. Dunstan's-in-the-West, 1623. Died, in London, 31 March 1631. Buried in St. Paul's Cathedral.

Works: 'Pseudo-Martyr,' 1610; 'Conclave Ignatii,' 1610 [?] (only two copies known); an English version of preceding, 'Ignatius his Conclave' (anon.), 1611; 'An Anatomy of the World' (anon.), 1611; 'The Progress of the Soule' (anon.), 1621; 'A Sermon' [on Judges xx. 15], 1622; 'A Sermon' [on Acts i. 8], 1622; 'Encænia,' 1623; 'Devotions upon Urgent Occasions,' 1624 (2nd edn. same year); 'The First Sermon preached to King Charles,' 1625; 'A Sermon preached to the King's M^{tie},' 1626; 'Four Sermons,' 1625; 'A Sermon of Commemoration of the Lady Dåvers,' 1627; 'Death's Duell,' 1630.

Posthumous: 'Poems by J. D.,' 1633; 'Juvenilia,' 1633; 'Six Sermons,' 1634; 'LXXX Sermons,' 1640; 'Βιαθανατος,' 1644; 'Poems,' 1649; 'Fifty Sermons,' 1649; 'Essays in Divinity,' 1651; 'Letters to Several Persons of Honour,' 1651; 'Paradoxes, Problemes, Essayes, etc.,' 1652; 'Fasciculus Poematum' (mostly spurious), 1652; 'Six and twenty Sermons,' 1660; 'A Collection of Letters,' 1660.

Collected Works: 'Poetical Works,' life, by Izaak Walton (3 vols.), 1779; ' Poems,' ed. by Hannah, 1843; Unpublished Poems,' ed. by Sir John Simeon, 1858; ' Poems,' ed. by Sir John Simeon, 1858; ' Works,' ed. by Alford, 1839; ' Poems,' ed. by Grosart (2 vols.), 1872-73.

Life: by Walton, ed. by Causton, 1855.

DORAN (John), 1807-1878. Born, in London, 11 March 1807. Educated at Matheson's Academy, Margaret Street; gained medal presented by Duke of Kent, 1819. Travelling tutor to George Murray, eldest son of Lord Glenlyon, 1823-28; contributed during same time to ' Literary Chronicle.' A melodrama, ' Justice, or the Venetian Jew,' produced at Surrey Theatre, 8 April, 1824. Other tutorships, 1828-37. Contributed translations of foreign lyrics to 'Bath Journal.' Married Emma Gilbert, 3 July 1834. Lived for a time at Knaresborough. Travelled abroad, 1837-40. Doctor's degree at Marburg University. Editor of ' Church and State Gazette,' 1841-52. First contributed to ' Athenæum,' 1854; acted as editor, 1869-70. Editor of ' Notes and Queries,' Oct. 1872 till his death. Died, at Notting Hill, 25 Jan. 1878; buried at Kensal Green.

Works: 'Sketches and Reminiscences,' 1828; 'History of Reading,' 1835; ' Filia Dolorosa' (expanded from a fragment written by Mrs. Romer), 1852; 'Table Traits,' 1854; ' Habits and Men,' 1854; ' Lives of the Queens of the House of Hanover,' 1855; 'Knights and their Days,' 1856; 'Monarchs Retired from Business,' 1857; 'History of Court Fools,' 1858; 'New Pictures and Old Panels,' 1859; 'Book of the Princes of Wales,' 1860; 'Memoir of Queen Adelaide,' 1861; 'Their Majesties' Servants,' 1864 [1863]; 'Saints and Sinners,' 1868; 'A Souvenir of the War of 1870-1,' 1871; 'A Lady of the Last Century,' 1873; ' " Mann " and Manners at the Court of Florence,' 1876; 'London in the Jacobite Times,' 1877; 'Memories of our Great Towns,' 1878.

Posthumous: ' In and about Drury Lane' (from ' Temple Bar '), 1881.

He *edited:* Xenophon's ''Αναβασις,' 1852; Young's ' Night Thoughts,' 1853, and 'Works,' 1854; 'The Bentley Ballads,' 1858; Horace Walpole's 'Journal of the Reign of King George the Third,' 1859; Tuckerman's 'The Collector,' 1868.

*DOUDNEY (Sarah), b. 1843. Born, at Portsmouth, 1843. Childhood spent in village of Lovedean, Hampshire. At school at Southsea. Two poems pub, in ' All the Year Round,' 1861. Contrib. to 'Churchman's Family Mag.,' 1861-64. Resides in Hampshire.

Works: 'The Angels of Christmas,' 1870; ' Faith Harrowby,' 1871; 'Psalms of Life,' 1871; 'Under Gray Walls,' 1871; 'Monksbury College,' 1872; 'The Beautiful Island' (with others), 1872; 'Wave upon Wave,' 1873; 'Janet Darney,' 1873; ' Nothing but Leaves,' 1875; 'Brave Seth,' 1877; 'Stories of Girlhood,' 1877; 'Strangers Yet,' 1880; 'When We Two Parted,' 1880; 'Stepping Stones,' 1880; 'Michaelmas Daisy,' 1882; 'Stories of Girlhood,' 1882; 'Anna Cavaye,' 1882; ' Nelly Channell,' 1883; 'What's in a Name?' 1883; 'Miss Stepney's Fortune' (anon.), 1883; 'A Woman's Story,' 1883; 'A Long Lane with a Turning,' 1884; 'The Strength of her Youth,' 1884; 'Prudence Winterburn,' 1886 [1885]; 'When we were Girls Together,' 1886; 'A Son of the Morning,' 1887; 'The Missing Rubies,' 1887; 'Miss Willowburn's Offer,' 1888 [1887]; 'The Vicar of Redcross,' 1888; 'Thy Heart's Desire,' 1888; ' Under False Colours,' 1889 [1888]; 'Where the Dew Falls in London,' 1889; 'Gatty Fenning,' 1890; 'Thistle Down,' 1890; 'The Family Difficulty,' 1891; 'Where Two Ways Meet,' 1891; 'Godiva Durleigh,'

1891 ; 'Through Pain to Peace,' 1892 ;
'A Child of the Precinct,' 1892 ;
'Voices in the Starlight,' 1892 ;
'Drifting Leaves,' 1892 ; 'My Mes-
sage,' 1892 ; 'Violets for Faithfulness,'
1893 ; 'A Romance of Lincoln's Inn,'
1893 ; 'Louie's Married Life,' 1894 ;
'A Vanished Hand,' 1896 [1895];
'Bitter and Sweet,' 1896 [1895];
'Katharine's Keys,' 1896 [1895].
She has *edited :* H. White's 'Echoes
from a Sanctuary,' 1891.

DOUGLAS (Gavin), *Bishop of Dunkeld,* **1474** [?]-**1522.** Born, in Scotland,
1474 [or 1475 ?]. To St. Andrew's
University, 1489; B.A., 1492 ; M.A.,
1494. Subsequently possibly at
University of Paris. Ordained Rector
of Monymusk, Aberdeenshire, 1496 ;
subsequently Parson of Lynton, and
Rector of Prestonkirk. Provost of
St. Giles, Edinburgh, 1501 [?]. Freedom of City of Edinburgh, 30 Sept.
1513. Abbot of Aberbrothock, 1514.
Bishop of Dunkeld, Jan. 1515 ; imprisoned by Duke of Albany in connection with the appointment, 1515-16 ;
released and appointment definitely
made, 1516. Visit to France on Political Matters, 1517. Went to Court
of Henry VIII., 1521 ; was removed
from bishopric, 1522. Died, in London, Sept. 1522 ; buried in the Savoy
Hospital Church.

Works [all posthumous]: 'The Palis
of Honoure' [1553 ?] ; Translation of
Virgil's 'Æneid,' 1553 ; 'A Description of May,' 1752 ; 'A Description of
Winter,' 1754 ; 'Select Works' (with
memoir), 1787 ; 'Political Works . . .
with Memoir by **J.** Small' (4 vols.),
1874.

*****DOWDEN (Edward),** b. **1843.** Born,
in Cork, 3 May 1843. Student at
Queen's Coll., Cork, 1858-59. Matric.
Trinity Coll., Dublin, 1859 ; B.A.,
1863 ; M.A., 1867 ; Vice-Chancellor's
Prizes for English verse and English
prose ; First Senior Moderator in
Logic and Ethics, 1863. Contrib. to
'Temple Bar' and 'Fraser's Mag.'
while at college. Studied Theology,
1863-65. Married Mary Clerke, 1866.
Professor of English Literature, Trin.

Coll., Dublin, 1867 ; LL.D., 1872.
Hon. LL.D., Edinburgh, 1887. Cun-
ningham Gold Medal of Royal Irish
Academy. Pres. of English Goethe
Soc., 1888. First 'Taylorian' Lecturer
at Oxford, 1889; Hon. D.C.L., Oxford,
1892. Hon. D.Litt., Dublin, 1892.
Wife died, 1892. 'Clark' Lecturer,
Trinity Coll., Cambridge, 1893-96.
Political as well as literary activity.
Married Elizabeth Dickinson West,
Dec. 1895. Commissioner on Board
of National Education in Ireland,
1896. LL.D., Princeton, New Jersey,
Oct. 1896. Contributor to 'Saturday
Review,' 'Academy,' 'Chambers'
Encyclopædia,' etc.

Works : 'Shakspere ; a critical
study,' 1875 ; 'Poems,' 1876 ; 'Studies
in Literature,' 1878 ; 'Shakspere' (in
'Green's Literature Primers'), 1877 ;
'Southey' (in 'English Men of Letters'
series), 1879 : Life of Shelley, 1886 ;
'Transcripts and Studies,' 1888 ; 'Introduction to Shakespeare,' 1893 ;
'New Studies in Literature,' 1895.

He has *edited :* 'Shakespeare Scenes
and Characters,' 1876 ; 'The Correspondence of Robert Southey with
Caroline Bowles,' 1881 ; Shakespeare's 'Sonnets,' 1881 ; Spenser's
Poems, 1882 ; 'The Passionate Pilgrim,' 1883 ; Shakespeare's 'Romeo
and Juliet,' 1884 ; 'The International
Shakspere,' 1887, etc. ; 'Sir H. Taylor's Correspondence,' 1888 ; Goethe's
'Wilhelm Meister,' 1890 ; 'Lyrical
Ballads.' 1890 ; Shelley's Poems,
1890 ; Wordsworth's Poems, 1892 ;
Sir E. K. Sullivan's 'Tales from Scott,'
1894.

**DOYLE (*Sir* Francis Hastings
Charles).** *Bart.* **1810-1888.** Born, at
Nunappleton, Yorkshire, 22 Aug. 1810.
Educated at Eton till 1828. Matric.,
Ch Ch., Oxford, 6 June 1828 ; B.A.,
1832 ; B.C.L., 1843 ; M.A., 1847 ;
Fellow of All Souls Coll., 1835-45.
Student of Inner Temple, 11 Oct.
1832 ; called to Bar, 17 Nov. 1837.
Succeeded to Baronetcy on his father's
death, 6 Nov. 1839. Married Sidney
Will ams-Wynn, 12 Dec. 1844. Prof.
of Poetry, Oxford, and Fellowship

(for second time) at All Souls' Coll., 1867-77 ; created D.C.L., 11 Dec. 1877. Receiver-General of Customs, 1846-69; Commissioner of Customs, 1869-83. Died, 8 June 1888.

Works: 'Miscellaneous Verses,' 1834 ; 'The Two Destinies,' 1844 ; 'The Duke's Funeral' [1852] ; 'The Return of the Guards, and other Poems,' 1866 ; 'Lectures delivered before the University of Oxford, 1868,' 1869 ; 'Lectures on Poetry. . . Second series,' 1877 ; 'Robin Hood's Bay,' 1878 ; 'Reminiscences and Opinions,' 1886.

He *translated :* Sophocles' 'Œdipus Tyrannus,' 1849.

DRAYTON (Michael), 1563 - 1631. Born, at Hartshill, Warwickshire, 1563. Probably page in household of Sir Henry Goodere of Powlesworth. First work published (and suppressed), 1591. Wrote many poetical works. Wrote for stage, 1597-1602. Esquire to Sir Walter Aston, 1603. Probably not married. Died, 1631. Buried in Westminster Abbey.

Works: 'The Harmonie of the Church,' 1591 (suppressed ; reissued as 'A Heavenly Harmonie,' 1610); 'Idea,' 1593 ; 'The Legend of Piers Gaveston,' 1593 ; 'Matilda,' 1594 ; 'Endymion and Phœbe' [1594] ; 'Ideas Mirrour,' 1594 ; 'Mortimeriados,' 1596 (reissued as 'The Barrons' Wars,' 1603); 'Poemes Lyrick and Pastorall' [1605?]; 'England's Heroicall Epistles,' 1597 ; 'The First Part of the . . . Life of Sir John Oldcastle' (probably by Munday, Drayton, and others), 1600 ; 'To the Majestie of King James,' 1603 ; 'A Pæan Triumphall,' 1604 ; 'The Owle,' 1604 ; 'Moyses in a Map of his Miracles,' 1604 ; 'Poems,' 1605; 'Poems Lyrick and Pastorall : Odes, Eglogs, etc.' [1606?] ; 'The Historie of the Life and Death of the Lord Cromwell,' 1609; 'Poly-Olbion, pt. i. [1612] ; pt. ii., 1622 ; 'Poems,' 1619; 'Certain Elegies' (anon., with Beaumont and others), 1620 ; 'The Battaile of Agincourt, etc.,' 1627 ; 'The Muses Elizium,' 1630 ;'Noah's Floud' (anon.), 1630.

He contrib. verses to Morley's 'First Book of Ballets,' 1595 ; Middleton's 'Legend of Duke Humphrey,' 1600 ; De Serres 'Perfect Use of Silk-wormes,' 1607 ; Davies' 'Holy Rood,' 1609 ; Murray's 'Sophonisba,' 1611 ; Tuke's 'Discourse against Painting . . . of Women,' 1616 ; Chapman's ' Hesiod,' 1618 : Munday's 'Primaleon of Greece,' 1619 ; Vicars' 'Manuductio' [1620 ?] ; Holland's 'Naumachia,' 1622 ; Sir J. Beaumont's 'Bosworth Field,' 1629.

Collected Works : in 1 vol., 1748 ; in 4 vols., 1753 ; ed. by J. P. Collier, 1856.

DRUMMOND (William), 1585-1649. Born, at Hawthornden, 13 Dec. 1585. Educated at Edinburgh High School till 1601 ; at Edinburgh University, 1601-05 ; M.A., 27 July 1605. To London, 1606. In France, studying law at Bourges and Paris, 1607-08. In Scotland, 1609. In London, 1610. Returned to Hawthornden as laird, same year, at father's death. Betrothed to Miss Cunningham of Barns, 1614[?] ; she died, 1615. Severe illness, 1620. Took out a patent for mechanical appliances, mostly military, Dec. 1627. Presented library to Edinburgh University, 1627. Married Elizabeth Logan, 1632. Political activity 1638-48. Died, 4 Dec. 1649, at Hawthornden. Buried in Lasswade Church.

Works : 'Tears on the Death of Meliades,' 1613 ; 'Mausoleum' (a collection of elegies by various writers), 1613 ; 'Poems' (anon.), 1616 ; 'Forth Feasting' (anon.), 1617 ; 'Flowers of Zion,' 1623 ; 'The Cypresse Grove,' 1625 ; Sonnet on the Death of King James, 1625 ; 'A Pastorall Elegie,' 1638 ; 'A Speech to the Noblemen, etc.,' 1639 ; 'Considerations to the Parliament,' 1639 ; 'Speech for Edinburgh to the King,' 1641 ; 'Σκιαμαχια,' 1642 ; 'Remoras for the National League,' 1643 ; 'Objections against the Scots answered,' 1646 ; 'Vindication of the Hamiltons,' 1648.

Posthumous : 'The History of Scotland,' 1655 ; 'Poems,' 1656 ; 'Polemo-Middenia' (anon. ; attrib. to

Drummond), 1683; Extracts from MSS. (ed. by Laing in 'Archæologica Scotica'), 1827. 'Conversations with Jonson,' 1842.

Collected Works : 'Poems,' 1711 ; 'Poems,' ed. by W. S. Ward (4 vols.), 1894.

Life : by Prof. Masson, 1873.

DRYDEN (John), 1631 - 1700. Born, at Aldwinkle All Saints, Northamptonshire, 9 Aug.[?] 1631. Educated first at a school at Tichmarsh ; at Westminster School, as scholar, 1640[?] - 1650. Scholarship at Trinity Coll., Cambridge, 11 May 1650 ; matriculated, 6 July 1650 ; 'discommuned' in July 1652, but allowed to continue residence on apology ; B.A., Jan. 1654. To London, possibly as clerk to Judge Sir Gilbert Pickering ; afterwards made living by literature. Married Lady Elizabeth Howard, 1 Dec. 1663. Member of Royal Soc., 26 Nov. 1662. Play, 'The Wild Gallant,' performed at King's Theatre, Feb. 1663 ; 'Rival Ladies,' 1663 ; 'The Indian Queen' (with Sir Robert Howard), Jan. 1664 ; 'The Indian Emperor,' 1665. At Charlton, Wilts, during plague and fire of London. 'Secret Love,' King's Theatre, March 1667 ; 'Sir Martin Mar-all' (adapted from Molière), 1667. Position as dramatist established ; contract with King's Theatre to provide three plays a year. Degree of M.A. conferred at King's request by Archbp. of Canterbury, 1668. Poet Laureate and Historiographer Royal, 1670-88. Lived in Fetter Lane, 1673-82; in Long-Acre, 1682-86. Collector of Customs in Port of London, 17 Dec. 1683. Religious controversies, 1686-88. Dramatic writing, 1690-92. Poems and translations from classics, 1693-97. Died in Gerrard St., Soho, 1 May 1700. Buried in Westminster Abbey.

Works : 'A Poem upon the Death of his late Highness Oliver' (also known as 'Heroic Stanzas '), 1659 (2nd edn., same year) ; 'Astræa Redux,' 1660 ; 'To His Sacred Majesty, a Panegyrick on his Coronation,' 1661 ; 'The Rival Ladies,' 1664 ; 'Annus Mirabilis,' 1667 ; 'The Indian Emperor,' 1667 ; 'Of Dramatick Poesie,' 1668 ; 'Secret Love' 1668 ; 'Sir Martin Mar-all' (anon.), 1668 ; 'The Wild Gallant,', 1669; 'The Tempest' (with Davenant), 1670 ; 'Tyrannic Love,' 1670 ; 'An Evening's Love,' 1671 ; 'Conquest of Granada' (2 pt.), 1672 ; 'Marriage à la Mode,' 1673 ; 'The Assignation,' 1673 ; 'Amboyna,' 1673 ; 'Notes and Observations on the Empress of Morocco' (anon.), 1674 ; 'The State of Innocence,' 1674 ; 'The Mall' (anon. ; attributed to Dryden), 1674 ; 'Aurungzebe,' 1676 ; 'All for Love,' 1678 ; 'The Kind Keeper,' 1678 ; 'Œdipus' (with Lee), 1679 ; 'Troilus and Cressida,' 1679 ; 'The Spanish Friar,' 1681 ; 'Absalom and Achitophel' (anon.), pt. i., 1681 ; pt. ii. (with Tate ; anon.), 1682 ; 'His Majesty's Declaration Defended' (anon.), 1681 ; 'The Medal' (anon.), 1682 ; 'Mac Flecknoe' (anon.), 1682; 'Religio Laici,' 1682 ; 'The Duke of Guise' (with Lee), 1683 ; 'Vindication' of same, 1683 ; 'Albion and Albanius,' 1685 ; 'Threnodia Augustalis,' 1685 ; 'Defence of Papers written by the late King' (anon.), 1686 ; 'The Hind and the Panther' (anon.), 1687 ; A Song for St. Cecilia's Day,' 1687 ; 'Britannia Rediviva,' 1688 ; 'Don Sebastian,' 1690 ; 'Amphitryon,' 1690 ; 'King Arthur,' 1691; 'Cleomenes,' 1692 ; 'Eleonora,' 1692; 'Love Triumphant,' 1694 ; 'Alexander's Feast,' 1697 ; 'Fables, Ancient and Modern, translated . . . With Original Poems,' 1700.

He *translated :* Maimbourg's 'History of the League,' 1684 ; Bohour's 'Life of Xavier,' 1688 ; 'Juvenal and Persius,' 1693 ; Dufresnoy's 'Art of Painting,' 1695 ; 'Virgil,' 1697 ; preface and two epistles in trans. of Ovid's 'Epistles,' 1680 ; most of trans. in vols. i., ii. of 'Miscellany Poems,' 1684-85 ; some in vols. iii. iv., 1685-94.

He wrote nearly 100 prologues and epilogues ; and contrib. verses or prefaces to 'Lachrymæ Musarum,' 1649; Hoddesdon's 'Sion and Parnassus,'

1650 ; Sir R. Howard's Poems, 1660 ; Charleton's ' Chorea Gigantum,' 1663 ; [possibly to ' Covent Garden Drollery,' 1672 ; and ' New Court Songs and Poems,' 1672] ; Lee's ' Alexander,' 1677 ; Roscommon's ' Essay on Translated Verse,' 1680 ; a translation of Plutarch, 1683 ; Anne Killigrew's 'Poems,' 1686 ; Walsh's ' Dialogue concerning Women,' 1691 ; St. Evremond's 'Miscellaneous Essays,' 1692 ; Sir H. Sheere's trans. of Polybius, 1693 ; Congreve's ' Double Dealer,' 1694.

Collected Works: ' Poems on Various Occasions,' ed. by Tonson, 1701 ; ' Dramatic Works,' ed. by Tonson, 1701 ; ed. by Congreve (6 vols.), 1717 ; Original Poems and Translations, ed. by Tonson (2 vols.), 1742 ; ' Poems and Fables,' 1753 ; Poems, ed. by Derrick (4 vols.), 1760 ; ' Critical and Miscellaneous Prose Works,' ed. by Malone (4 vols.), 1800 ; by Scott (18 vols.), 1808 ; ' Aldine ' edn., 1854 ; ' Globe ' edn., 1870, etc.

Life: by Johnson (in ' Lives of Poets ') ; by Malone, 1800 ; by Scott in 1808 edn. of ' Works ' ; by Bell in ' Aldine ' edn. of Works, 1854 ; by Christie in ' Globe ' edn., 1870 ; by Saintsbury (' English Men of Letters ' series), 1881.

DUGDALE (*Sir* **William**), **1605-1686.** Born, at Shustoke, near Coleshill, Warwickshire, 12 Sept. 1605. Educated by the curate of Nether-Whitacre, near Shustoke; afterwards at Coventry Free School, 1615-20. Married Margery Huntbache, 17 March 1622; lived with wife's father till July 1624 ; at Fillongley, Warwickshire, 1624-25. Bought Blythe Hall, near Coleshill, 1625 ; went to live there, 1626. Antiquarian and historical tastes. ' Blanch Lyon ' Pursuivant Extraordinary, 24 Sept. 1638 ; ' Rouge Croix' Pursuivant, 18 March 1639. Attended the King, as Pursuivant, at York, June 1642 ; at Oxford, Oct. 1642. M.A., Oxford, Nov. 1642. Chester Herald, 16 April 1644. Visit to Paris, summer of 1648. Working upon antiquarian research, 1649-60.

Resumed herald's position at Restoration. Appointed ' Norroy,' 14 June 1660. Visitations to his province as Norroy, 1662-70. Garter King-of-Arms, and Knighthood, 24 May 1677. Died, at Blythe Hall, 10 Feb. 1686.

Works: ' A Full Relation of the passages concerning the late treaty . . . at Uxbridge ' (anon.), 1645 ; ' Monasticon Anglicanum ' (with Dodsworth), vol. i., 1655 ; vol. ii., 1661 ; vol. iii., 1673 (English version, by J. Wright, 1693) ; ' Antiquities of Warwickshire,' 1656 ; ' The History of St. Paul's Cathedral,' 1658 ; ' History of Imbanking and Drayning of divers Fenns and Marshes,' 1662 ; ' Origines Juridiciales,' 1666 ; ' The Baronage of England ' (2 vols.), 1675-76 ; ' A Short View of the late Troubles in England ' (anon.), 1681 ; ' The Ancient Usage in bearing . . . Arms,' 1682 ; ' A perfect copy of all Summons of the Nobility to the Great Councils and Parliaments,' 1685.

Posthumous: ' Life ' (autobiography), 1713 ; ' Life, Diary, and Correspondence,' ed. by W. Hamper, 1827.

He *edited* Sir H. Spelman's ' Glossarium Archæologicum,' 1666, and ' Concilia,' vol. ii., 1666.

DUNBAR (**William**), **1460**[?]**-1520**[?] Born, 1460 [?]. [Possibly to St. Andrew's University, 1475 ; B.A., 1477 ; M.A., 1479.] For some time a begging friar of Franciscan order ; travelled so in France. [Possibly on various Crown missions abroad, 1490-1500.] Granted Crown pension of £10 a year, 15 Aug. 1500 ; eventually increased to £80 a year for life. Took full orders as Priest; performed Mass at court, 1504. Visited London, probably with ambassadors to arrange marriage of James IV., 1503. Possibly killed at Flodden, 8 Sept. 1513 ; more probably died later, unless his poem, ' The Orisone,' 1517, be spurious.

Works: Dunbar's Poems, with the exception of ' The Thistle and the Rose' (printed with ' Vertue and Vyce,' by J. Bellentyne, in 1750), were first printed by Pinkerton, in vol. i. of ' Ancient Scotish Poems,' 1786 ; and by J. Sibbald in vols. i., ii. of 'Chronicle of Scottish Poetry,' 1802. Later editions are by D. Laing (2 vols.), 1834 ; by J. Small (for Scottish Text Society),1884; by J. Schipper (Vienna), 1892. *Life:* by Laing, in 1834 edn. of **Works.**

D'URFEY (Thomas), 1653 - 1723.
Born, at Exeter, 1653. First play, 'The Siege of Memphis,' produced at King's Theatre, 1676. Prolific writer of comedies, songs, odes, prologues,epilogues, satires, etc. Popular favourite for many years, but fell into distressed circumstances about 1710. Benefit performances for him at Drury Lane, 15 June 1713 and 3 June 1714. Died, in London, 26 Feb. 1723. buried at St. James's, Piccadilly.

Works: 'The Siege of Memphis,' 1676 ; 'Archerie Revived' (with Shotterel), 1676 ; 'The Fond Husband,' 1676 ; 'Madam Fickle.' 1677 ; 'The Fool turn'd Critic' (anon.), 1678 ; 'Trick for Trick,' 1678 ; 'Squire Oldsapp,'1679; 'The Virtuous Wife,' 1680; 'The Happy Lover' (anon.), [1680 ?] ; 'Sir Barnaby Whig,' 1681 ; 'The Progress of Honesty' (anon.), 1681 ; 'The Royalist,' 1682 ; 'Butler's Ghost' (anon.), 1682 ; 'The Whig Rampant' (anon.), 1682 ; 'The Injured Princess' (adapted from 'Cymbeline'), 1682 ; 'The Whig's Exaltation' (anon.), 1682; 'New Collection of Songs and Poems,' 1683 ; 'A Carrouse to the Emperor' (anon.), 1683 ; 'The Malcontent,' 1684 ; 'A Fond Husband,' 1685; 'An Elegy upon . . . Charles II.,' 1685 ; 'Advice to the Ladies of London' (anon.), 1685 ; 'The Discontented Lady,' 1685 ; 'A Commonwealth of Women,' 1686 ; 'Banditti,' 1686 ; 'The Conquering Virgin,' [1687 ?]; 'A Fool's Preferment,' 1688 ; 'Collin's Walk through London and Westminster' (anon.), 1690 ; 'New Poems,' 1690 ; 'Bussy d'Amboise' (adapted from Chapman), 1691; 'Love for Money,' 1691 ; 'Wit for Money' (anon.), 1691 ; 'A Pindarick Poem on the Royal Navy,' 1691 ; 'The Marriage Hater Matched,' 1692 ; 'The

Northern Ditty' (anon.), [1692 ?] ; 'The Richmond Heiress,' 1693 ; 'Comical History of Don Quixote,' pts. i., ii., 1694 ; pt. iii., 1696 ; 'Gloriana,' 1695 ; 'Cinthia and Endimion,' 1697 ; 'The Intrigues at Versailles,' 1697 ; 'The Campaigners,' 1698 ; 'The Famous History of the Rise and Fall of Massaniello,' (2 pts.), 1699-1700 ; 'The Bath,' 1701 ; 'Tales, Tragical and Comical,' 1704 ; 'Wonders in the Sun,' 1706; 'A New Ode,' 1706 ; 'Stories, Moral and Comical,' 1706 ; 'The French Pride abated,'1708 ; 'The Modern Prophets,' [1709] ; 'The Old Mode and the New, [1709] ; 'Court Gallantry,' 1714 ; 'Vive le Roy,' 1714 ; 'Songs Compleat' (2 vols.), 1719 ; 'Wit and Mirth,' 1719 ; 'New Operas, with Comical Stories and Poems on Several Occasions,' 1721.

Posthumous: 'Miscellaneous Poems,' 1726 ; 'The English Stage Italianized,' 1727.

EDGEWORTH (Maria), 1767-1849.
Born, at Black Bourton, Oxfordshire, 1 Jan. 1767. In Ireland with father, 1773-75. To School in Derby, 1775 ; in London, 1780. Home to Edgeworthstown, 1782. Began to write stories. To Clifton with parents, Dec. 1791 ; returned to Edgeworthstown, winter of 1793. Visit to France with father, Oct. 1802 to March 1803. Visit to London, spring of 1803 ; to Bowood, autumn of 1818 ; to London, 1819 ; to Paris and Switzerland, 1820 to March 1821. Returned to Edgeworthstown and lived there for rest of life. Occasional visits to London. Visit to Scotland, spring of 1823. Friendship with Sir Walter Scott ; he visited her at Edgeworthstown, 1825. Active philanthropy during famine of 1846. Died, at Edgeworthstown, 22 May 1849.

Works: 'Letters to Literary Ladies,' 1795 ; 'Parent's Assistant' (anon.), pt. i., 1796 ; in 6 vols., 1800 ; 'Practical Education,' 1798 ; 'Castle Rackrent' (anon.), 1800 ; 'Early Lessons,' 1801 ; 'Belinda,' 1801 ; 'Moral Tales,' 1801 ; 'Irish Bulls,' 1802 ; 'Popular

Tales,' 1804; 'Modern Griselda,' 1804;
'Leonora,' 1806 ; 'Tales from Fashionable Life,' 1809 ; 2nd series, 1812 ;
'Patronage,' 1814 ; 'Continuation of
Early Lessons,' 1815 ; 'Harrington,'
1817 ; 'Ormond,' 1817 ; 'Comic
Dramas,' 1817 ; vol. ii. of R. L.
Edgeworth's 'Memoirs,' 1820; 'Frank,'
1822 ; 'Harry and Lucy, concluded,'
1825 ; 'Garry Owen,' 1832 ; 'Helen,'
1834.

Collected Works : in 14 vols.,
1825; in 18 vols., 1832-33 ; in 12
vols., 1893.

Life : by H. Zimmern, 1883 ('Eminent Women' series) ; 'Life and
Letters,' ed. by Aug. Hare, 1894.

**EDGEWORTH (Richard Lovell),
1744-1817.** [Father of preceding.]
Born, in Bath, 31 May 1744. At
schools at Warwick, Drogheda, and
Longford, 1752-61. At Trinity Coll.,
Dublin, 26 April to Oct. 1761. Matric.
Corpus Coll., Oxford, 10 Oct. 1761.
Eloped to Scotland with, and married,
Anna Maria Elers, 1763. At Edg-
worthstown, 1764-65 ; returned to
England and settled at Hare Hatch,
near Maidenhead, 1765. Interested in
mechanical experiments; devised tele-
graph. Medal from Soc. of Arts for
invention, 1768. Friendship with
Erasmus Darwin and Thomas Day.
Succeeded to family estates, 1769.
Visit to France, with Day, 1771-73.
Wife joined him for a short time in
1772 and returned to England. He
returned on her death, March 1773.
Married Honora Sneyd, 17 July 1773.
At Edgeworthstown, 1773-76. Returned to England, and settled at
Northchurch, Herts. Second wife
died, 30 April 1780. He married her
sister Elizabeth, 25 Dec. 1780. To
Edgeworthstown, 1782. Aide-de-
camp to Lord Charlemont, 1783. Contrib. to 'Philosophical Transactions,'
1783-84 ; to 'Transactions of Irish
Academy,' 1788-95. At Clifton, 1791-
92. Returned to Ireland. Third
wife died, Nov. 1797. M.P. in Irish
Parliament for St. John's Town, co.
Longford, 1798. Married Miss Beau-
fort, 31 May 1798. Contrib. to

'Monthly Mag.,' 1801 ; to 'Nicholson's
Journal,' 1801-17. In Paris with
daughter Maria, Oct. 1802 to March
1803. Member of Board on Irish
Education, 1806-11 ; on Reclamation
of Bogs, 1810. Died, at Edgeworthstown, 13 June 1817.

Works : 'Letter to the Earl of
Charlemont on the Telegraph,' 1797 ;
'Practical Education' (with Maria
Edgeworth), 2 vols., 1798 ; 'Poetry
explained for . . . Young People,'
1802 ; 'Essay on Irish Bulls' (with
Maria Edgeworth), 1802 ; 'Essays on
Professional Education,' 1809 ; 'Read-
ings in Poetry,' 1816 ; 'Essay on the
Construction of Roads,' 1817 (2nd edn.
same year).

Posthumous : 'Memoirs . . . begun
by himself, and concluded by his
daughter, Maria Edgeworth' (2 vols.),
1820.

He *edited :* Maria Edgeworth's
'Popular Tales,' 1805 ; 'Comic
Dramas,' 1817 ; 'Harrington,' 1817.

**EDWARDS (Amelia Blandford),
1831-1892.** Born, 1831. Began to
contribute to periodicals, 1853. Hon.
Sec. and Vice-Pres. of Egypt Exploration Fund. Hon. L.H.D.
Degree, Columbia Coll., New York,
1887. Lectured in United States,
1889-90. Died, 15 April 1892.

Works : 'My Brother's Wife,' 1855 ;
'A Summary of English History,'
1856 ; 'The Ladder of Life,' 1857 ;
'The Young Marquis' [1857] ; 'Hand
and Glove,' 1858 ; 'The History of
France,' 1858 ; Letterpress to 'The
Photographic Historical Portrait
Gallery,' 1860 ; 'Sights and Stories,'
1862 ; 'The Story of Cervantes,' 1863
[1862] ; 'Barbara's History,' 1864
[1863] ; 'Ballads,' 1865 ; 'Miss Carew,'
1865 ; 'Half a Million of Money,'
1865 ; Poems in 'Home Thoughts and
Home Scenes,' 1865 ; 'Debenham's
Vow,' 1870 ; 'Untrodden Peaks,'
1873 ; 'In the Days of my Youth,'
1873 ; 'Monsieur Maurice,' 1873 ; 'A
Thousand Miles up the Nile,' 1877
[1876] ; 'A Poetry-Book of Elder
Poets,' 1879 ; 'A Poetry-Book of
Modern Poets,' 1879 ; 'Lord Bracken-

bury,' 1880 ; 'Pharaohs, Fellahs and Explorers,' 1891.

She *translated :* Loviot's 'A Lady's Captivity among the Chinese Pirates,' [1853] ; Maspero's ' Egyptian Archæology,' 1887.

EGAN (Pierce), 1772-1849. Born, probably in London, 1772. At early age reported sporting events for newspapers. Married, 1813. Wrote, set up, and printed ' The Mistress of Royalty,' 1814. First no. of 'Life in London' published, 15 July 1821. Various imitations, dramatized versions and piracies followed its success. He prepared dramatic version produced at Sadler's Wells, 8 April 1822. Varied literary work. Started 'Pierce Egan's Life in London and Sporting Guide' (afterwards incorporated in ' Bell's Life in London ') as editor, 1 Feb. 1824. Last ten years of life spent in retirement. Died, at his house in Pentonville, 3 Aug. 1849.

Works : 'The Mistress of Royalty' (anon.), 1814 ; ' Boxiana' (4 vols.), 1818-24 ; ' Walks through Bath,' 1819 ; 'Life in London,' 1821 ; 'The Fancy Tog's Man *v.* Young Sadboy the Milling Quaker,' 1821 ; 'Real Life in London' (2 vols.), 1821-22 ; 'The Life and Extraordinary Adventures of S. D. Hayward,' 1822 ; ' Account of the trial of Mr. Fauntleroy' [1824] ; ' Account of the trial of John Thurtell and Joseph Hunt,' 1824 ; 'The Life of an Actor,' 1825 ; ' Anecdotes, original and selected, of the Turf,' 1827 ; 'Finish to the Adventures of Tom, Jerry and Logic,' 1828 ; 'Trip to Ascot Races,' 1828 ; 'The Show Folks,' 1831 ; ' Matthews's Comic Annual,' 1831 ; 'Pierce Egan's Book of Sports and Mirror of Life,' 1832 ; 'The Pilgrims of the Thames,' 1838.

He *edited :* Grose's 'Classical Dict. of the Vulgar Tongue,' 1823.

[His son, **Pierce Egan (1814-80)**, began life as an illustrator, but took to fiction. Wrote a large number of stories of a ' popular' description, chiefly in ' London Journal.']

* **ELIOT (George)** [*pseud.*, i.e. Marian Evans, afterwards Cross], **1819-1880.**

Born [Marian Evans], at Arbury farm, near Chilvers Coton, Warwickshire, 22 Nov. 1819. To boarding school at Attleborough, 1824 ; at school at Nuneaton, 1827 [or 1828] to 1832 ; at school at Coventry, 1832-35. Contrib. a religious poem to 'Christian Observer,' Jan. 1840. Went with father to live at Coventry, March, 1841. Friendship with Mr. and Mrs. Bray begun, 1841. Occupied completing translation of Strauss's 'Life of Jesus' (originally undertaken by Miss Brabant), 1844-46. Visit to continent after father's death, summer of 1849. Lived at Geneva, Oct. 1849 to March 1850. Lived with the Brays, at Rosehill, Coventry, May 1850 to Sept. 1851. Contrib. to ' Westminster Review,' Jan. 1851 ; acted as assistant editor, Sept. 1851 to Oct. 1853. Met George Henry Lewes, 1851; lived with him from July 1854. With him in Germany, July 1854 to March 1855. First novel, ' Amos Barton,' appeared in ' Blackwood's Mag.,' 1857. Lived at Richmond, Sept. 1855 to 1858. To Munich and Dresden, 1858. Lived at Wandsworth, Feb. 1859 to 1860. Visits to Italy, summer of 1860 and 1861. Lived in Blandford Square, London, Dec. 1860 to Nov. 1863 ; settled at North Bank, Regent's Park, Nov. 1863. Visit to Spain, 1867. Friendship with Mrs. Cross and her son begun, in Rome, 1869. Bought house at Witley, near Godalming, 1876 ; G. H. Lewes died there, 28 Nov. 1878. Married to John Walter Cross, 6 May 1880. Lived at Witley till Dec. 1880 ; then settled in Cheyne Walk, Chelsea. Died 22 Dec. 1880.

Works : ' Amos Barton ' in ' Cornhill Mag.,' 1857 ; 'Scenes of Clerical Life ' (anon.), 1858 ; ' Adam Bede,' 1859 ; 'The Mill on the Floss,' 1860 ; ' Silas Marner,' 1861 ; 'Romola' (from 'Cornhill Mag.'), 1863 ; ' Felix Holt,' 1866 ; 'The Spanish Gypsy,' 1868 ; 'Agatha,' 1869 ; ' Middlemarch,' in 8 pts., 1871-72 (complete edn., 1872) · 'The Legend of Jubal, and other Poems,' 1874 ; 'Daniel Deronda,' 1876 ; 'Impressions of Theophrastus Such,' 1879.

Posthumous : 'Essays,' ed. by C. L. Lewes, 1884.

She *translated :* Strauss's ' Life of Jesus ' (anon.), 1846 ; Feuerbach's 'Essence of Christianity,' 1854.

Collected Works : 'Novels ' (6 vols.), 1867-78 ; ' Works ' (20 vols.), 1878-80.

Life : by J. W. Cross, 1884.

ELLIOTT (Ebenezer), 1781-1849. Born, at New Foundry, Masborough, Yorkshire, 17 March 1781. Educated at various small schools. Worked for his father, in iron trade, 1797-1804. Diligent student ; wrote poetry from age of seventeen. Married [about 1805 ?]. His wife predeceased him. Lost all his money and was for some time supported by wife's sisters. With some capital raised by them he started iron business in Sheffield, 1821. Lost heavily again in 1837. Literary and political activity at Sheffield. 'Corn-Law Rhymes' produced, 1831. Chartist delegate from Sheffield at meeting in Palace Yard, Westminster, 1838. Left Chartist ranks at time of O'Connor's Anti-Corn Law Repeal Movement. Retired from business, 1841 ; settled at Great Houghton, near Barnsley. Died there, 1 Dec. 1849. Buried in Darfield Church.

Works : 'The Vernal Walk' (anon.), 1801 ; 'Night' (anon.), 1818 ; ' Peter Faultless' (anon.), 1820 ; 'Love : a poem,' 1823 ; 'The Village Patriarch' (anon.), 1829 ; 'Corn-Law Rhymes' (anon.), 1831 ; 'The Splendid Village,' etc. (3 vols.), 1833-35 ; 'More Verse and Prose' (anon.), 1850.

Collected Works : ' Poetical Works,' 1840 ; ed. by E. Elliott (2 vols.), 1876.

Life : 'Life,' by Watkin, 1850 ; 'Memoirs,' by Searle, 1850.

ELYOT (Sir Thomas), 1488 [?]-1546. Born, probably in Wiltshire, 1488 [?]. Educated at home. Studied medicine for some time. Clerk of Assize on Western Circuit, 1511-28. At father's death settled at Combe, near Woodstock. On Commission of Peace for Oxfordshire, July 1522. Clerk of Privy Council, 1523 - 30. Married Margaret Abarrow, 1525 [?]. Sheriff of Oxfordshire and Berkshire, 1527.

Knighted, 1530. On Commission to inquire into Wolsey's estates, 1530. First literary work, 1531. Ambassador to Court of Charles V. of Spain, chiefly with regard to Henry VIII.'s divorce from Catharine of Aragon, Oct. 1531 to spring of 1532 ; and again in 1535. Sheriff of Cambridgeshire, 1532 ; of Cambridgeshire and Huntingdonshire, 1544. M.P. for Cambridge, 1542. Died, 20 March 1546 ; buried in Carleton Church.

Works : 'The Boke named the Gouernour,' 1531 ; 'Pasquil the Playne,' 1533 ; 'Of the Knowledge which maketh a Wise Man,' 1533 ; 'The Castel of Helth ' [1534 ?] (no copy known of 1st edn. ; 2nd edn., 1539) ; 'The Bankette of Science,' 1539 ; ' Dictionary' (Latin and English), 1538 (called ' Bibliotheca Eliotæ ' in 1550 and succeeding edns.) ; 'The Defence of Good Women,' 1545 ; 'A Preservative agaynste Deth,' 1545.

He *translated :* ' A Swete and Devoute Sermon of Holy Saynt Ciprian,' 1534 ; Pico della Mirandola's 'Rules of a Christian Lyfe,' 1534 ; Isocrates' Oration to Nicocles (under title of 'The Doctrinal of Princes '), 1534 ; Plutarch's ' The Education or Bringinge up of Children ' [1535 ?], and ' Howe one may take Profyte of his Enemyes ' [1545 ?] ; 'The Image of Governance,' 1541.

* EMERSON (Ralph Waldo), 1803-1882. Born, in Boston, Mass., 25 May 1803. Educated at Boston Grammar School, 1811-15 ; Latin School, 1815-17. To Harvard University, 1817 ; graduated, 1821. Engaged in tuition. Kept school at Boston, 1822-25. Studied Theology in Cambridge Divinity School, 1825-28. Approbated to preach, 1826. Ordained, 11 March 1829 as joint pastor, with Rev. H. Ware, of Second Church, Boston; succeeded to Ware's position, 1830. Married Ellen Louisa Tucker, Sept. 1829. Resigned pastorate, 1832. Wife died, Feb. 1832. Tour in Europe, 1833 ; friendship with Carlyle begun. Returned to U.S.A., 1834 ; preached in New Bedford ;

and settled in Concord. Lectured on various subjects, 1835, 1836, 1837. Married Lidian Jackson, Sept. 1835. Finally adopted literary life. Frequently lectured. Symposium, or Transcendental Club, formed, 1836. Edited 'The Dial,' 1842 to April 1844. Lecturing tour in England, 1847 - 49. Edited 'Massachusetts Quarterly Review' (3 vols.), 1847-50. Contrib. to 'Atlantic Monthly' from its beginning in Nov. 1857. LL.D., Harvard, 1866 ; elected on Board of Overseers, 1867. Mental shock owing to partial destruction of house by fire, July 1872. To England and Egypt with daughter. Returned to Concord, 1873. Suffered from aphasia in later years. Died, at Concord, 27 April 1882.

Works: 'Right Hand of Fellowship to Rev. H. B. Goodwin,' 1830; 'Historical Discourse,' 1835; 'Nature' (anon.), 1836 (another edn., with 'Lectures on the Times,' 1844) ; 'An Oration' (Dartmouth Coll.), 1838 ; 'An Oration' (Phi Beta Kappa Soc.), 1838 ; (new edn. called 'Man Thinking,' 1844); 'An Address' (Divinity Coll.), 1838; 'The Method of Nature,' 1841 ; 'Essays, first series,' 1841 ; 'The Young American,' 1844 ; 'Essays, second series,' 1844 ; 'Man the Reformer,' 1844; 'Orations, Lectures and Addresses,' 1844 ; 'An Address' (on Negro Emancipation), 1844; 'Poems,' 1847; 'Essays, Lectures and Orations,' 1848 ; 'Miscellanies,' 1849 ; 'Representative Men,' 1850 ; 'Essays and Orations.' 1853 ; 'English Traits,' 1856 ; 'The Conduct of Life,' 1860 ; 'Orations, Lectures and Essays,' 1866; 'May-Day,' 1867 ; 'Society and Solitude,' 1870 ; 'Poetry and Criticism,' 1874 ; 'Parnassus,' 1875 ; 'Power, Wealth, Illusions' (from 'The Conduct of Life'), 1876 ; 'Letters and Social Aims,' 1876 ; 'Culture, Behavior, Beauty' (from 'The Conduct of Life'), 1876 ; 'Books, Art, Eloquence' (from 'Society and Solitude'), 1877 ; 'Success, Greatness, Immortality' (from 'Society and Solitude,' and 'Letters and Social Aims'), 1877; 'Love, Friendship, Domestic Life'

(from 'Essays' and 'Society and Solitude'), 1877 ; 'Fortune of the Republic,' 1878 ; 'The Preacher' (from 'Unitarian Review'), 1880.

Collected Works: 'Complete Works' (2 vols.), 1866 ; 'Prose Works' (2 vols.), 1870 ; Correspondence with Carlyle (2 vols.), 1883 ; 'Complete Works' (Riverside edn., 11 vols.), 1883-84.

He *edited :* Marchioness Ossoli's 'Memoirs,' 1852 ; Gladwin's translation of Sadi's 'Gulistan,' 1865 ; 'Plutarch's 'Morals,' 1870 ; Channing's 'The Wanderer,' 1871 ; 'The Hundred Greatest Men,' 1879.

Life : by Searle, 1855 ; by O. W. Holmes ('American Men of Letters' series), 1885; by Dr. Garnett ('Great Writers' series), 1887.

ETHEREGE (*Sir George*), 1635 [?]- 1691. Born, 1635 [?]. Perhaps educated at Cambridge, and subsequently at one of the Inns of Court. Comedy, 'The Comical Revenge,' produced at Lincoln's Inn Fields Theatre, 1664 ; other plays, 1667 - 76. Knighted, about 1680 [?]. Married about same time. To Hague on diplomatic mission, 1684 [?]; at Ratisbon, 1685-88. To Paris ; died there, 1691.

Works : 'The Comical Revenge,' 1664 ; 'She Wou'd if She Cou'd,' 1667 ; 'The Man of Mode,' 1676.

Collected Works : 1704 ; ed. by A. W. Verity, 1888.

EUSDEN (Laurence), *Poet Laureate,* 1688-1730. Born, Aug. [?] 1688. Educated at St. Peter's School, York. To Trinity Coll., Cambridge, as 'pensioner,' 24 March 1705 ; scholar, 2 April 1706 ; B.A., 1708 ; M.A., 1712 ; Minor Fellow, 2 Oct. 1711 ; Fellow, 2 July 1712 ; Third Sublector, 2 Oct. 1712 ; Second Sublector, 1713, Contrib. to 'Spectator' and 'Guardian.' Contrib. to Steele's 'Poetical Miscellanies,' 1714. Poet Laureate, 24 Dec. 1718. Ordained Chaplain to Lord Willoughby de Broke, 1724 [?]. Rector of Coningsby, Lincolnshire, 1729-30. Died, at Coningsby, 27 Sept. 1730. Buried there.

Works : 'A Letter to Mr. Addison,

1714 (another edn., same year, entitled 'The Royal Family'); 'Original Poems and Translations by Mr. Hill, Mr. Eusden, etc.,' 1714; 'Verses at the Last Publick Commencement at Cambridge,' 1714 (2nd edn. same year); 'Poem on the Marriage of the Duke of Newcastle,' 1717; 'Poem to Her Royal Highness on the Birth of the Prince,' 1718; 'Ode for the New Year,' 1720; 'An Ode for the Birthday,' 1721; 'Three Poems to Lord Chancellor Macclesfield,' 1722; 'The Origin of the Knights of the Bath,' 1725; 'Three Poems' to the King and Queen, 1727.

He *translated :* Ovid's 'Metamorphoses,' with Dryden, etc., 1717; Musæus' 'Hero and Leander,' 1750.

EVANS (Marian). *See* Eliot (George).

EVELYN (John), 1620-1706. Born, at Wotton, 31 Oct. 1620. From age of five lived in household of his grandmother, at Lewes. Educated at Southover Free School. Admitted to Middle Temple as student, 13 Feb. 1637. Fellow Commoner of Balliol Coll., Oxford, 10 May, 1638. Took no degree. Took chambers in Temple, 1640. In Holland, July to Oct., 1641. In Civil War joined King's army, Nov. 1642, but was not received, and returned to Wotton. In France, Nov. 1643 to Oct. 1644; in Italy, Oct. 1644 to April 1646; returned through Switzerland to Paris; married Mary Browne there, 27 June, 1647. Returned to England, Sept. 1647, without his wife. Returned to Paris, 1 Aug. 1649. Visit to England, 1650. Returned to England to live, Feb. 1652; his wife returned, June 1652; they settled at Sayes Court, Deptford. Inaugurated scheme of Royal Society; first meeting held, Jan. 1661; elected fellow and member of Council. On various Metropolitan Commissions, 1662. On commission for care of prisoners and wounded in Dutch War, 1644. Hon. D.C.L, Oxford, 1669. Member of Council of foreign plantations, 28 Feb. 1671. Commissioner for Privy Seal, Dec. 1685 to March 1687.

Sec. to Royal Soc., Dec. 1772 to Dec. 1773. Left Sayes Court and settled with brother at Wotton, May 1694. Treasurer of Greenwich Hospital, 1695 to Aug. 1703. Inherited Wotton estate from his brother, Oct. 1699. Died there, 27 Feb. 1706; buried in Wotton Church.

Works : 'Of Liberty and Servitude,' 1649; 'The State of France . . . in the ninth year of . . . Lewis XIII.,' (under initials : J. E.), 1652; 'A Character of England' (anon.), 1659; 'Apology for the Royal Party' (anon.), 1659; 'The late Newes from Brussels Unmasked' (anon.), 1660; 'A Poem upon His Majesty's Coronation,' 1661; 'Encounter between the French and Spanish Ambassadors,' 1661; 'Fumifugium,' 1661; 'Tyrannus' (anon.), 1661; 'Sculptura,' 1662; 'Sylva,' 1664; 'Kalendarium Hortense,' 1664; 'Public Employment, and an Active Life, preferred to Solitude,' 1667; 'The three late famous Impostors' (under initials : J. E.), 1669; 'Navigation and Commerce,' 1674; 'A Philosophical Discourse of Earth,' 1676; 'The Whole Body of Antient and Modern Architecture,' 1680; 'Mundus Muliebris' (anon.), 1690; 'Mundus Foppensis' (anon.), 1691; 'Numismata,' 1697; 'Acetaria' (anon.), 1699.

Posthumous : 'Diary,' ed. by W. Bray as 'Memoirs . . . of John Evelyn,' 2 vols., 1818; 'Life of Mrs. Godolphin,' ed. by Bp. Wilberforce, 1847; 'History of Religion,' ed. by R. M. Evanson, 1850.

He *translated :* Lucretius, Bk. I., 1656; 'The French Gardener,' 1658; 'The Golden Book' of St. Chrysostom, 1659; Naudé's 'Instructions concerning the erection of a Library,' 1661; Pt. II. of 'The Mystery of Jesuitism,' 1658; Fréart de Chambray's 'Parallel of Ancient Architecture with the Modern,' 1664, and 'Idea of the Perfection of Painting,' 1668; La Quintinie's 'The Compleat Gardener,' 1698.

He *edited :* translation, by his son John, of René Rapin's 'Of Gardens,' 1673.

Life : by H. B. Wheatley, in 1879 edn. of 'Diary.'

FALCONER (William), 1732-1769.
Born, in Edinburgh, 11 Feb. 1732.
At sea on merchant vessels in youth.
Exchanged into Navy, 1749. On
merchant vessel again, 1750. Contrib.
poems to 'Gentleman's Magazine.'
Re-entered Navy, 1760 [?]. Midshipman on 'Royal George,' 1762. Purser
of frigate 'Glory,' 176£. Married
Miss Hicks, 1763 [?]. Purser to 'Swift-
sure,' 1767. Declined offer of partnership with John Murray, publisher, Oct.
1768. Purser of 'Aurora' frigate,
bound for India, with promise of secretaryship to Commissioners of H.E.I.C.
Sailed, 2 Oct. 1869 ; ship was lost.

Works : 'A Poem, Sacred to the
Memory of His Royal Highness,
Frederick, Prince of Wales,' 1751 ;
'Ode on the Duke of York's Second
Departure from England,' 1762 ; 'The
Shipwreck,' 1762 ; 'An Universal Dic-
tionary of the Marine,' 1769.
Collected Poems : first published in
Johnson's 'English Poets,' 1790.
Life : by J. S. Clarke, in 1804 edn.
of 'The Shipwreck'; by R. Carruthers,
in 1858 edn.

FARQUHAR (George), 1678-1707.
Born, in Londonderry, 1678. Edu-
cated at Londonderry. To Trinity
Coll., Dublin, as sizar, 17 July 1694.
Left college, 1695 [?] ; appeared soon
after on Dublin stage. To London,
1697 [?]. First play, 'Love and a
Bottle,' produced at Drury Lane, 1699;
'The Constant Couple,' in 1700 ; 'Sir
Harry Wildair,' in 1701. Presented
by Earl of Orrery with lieutenant's
commission, 1700 [?]. In Holland,
1700. Married, 1703 [?]. Visit to
Dublin, 1704 ; continued to produce
plays. Sold commission to pay debts.
Died, April 1707.

Works : 'Love and a Bottle,' 1699 ;
'Sir Harry Wildair,' 1701 ; 'The In-
constant,' 1702 ; 'The Twin Rivals,'
1702 ; 'The Stage-coach' (with Motteux ; anon.), 1705 ; 'The Recruiting
Officer' [1706] ; 'The Beaux Strata-
gem' [1707] ; 'Love's Catechism'
(anon.; compiled by Farquhar from
preceding), 1707.

Posthumous : 'The Constant Couple,'
1710.
Collected Works : 'Comedies,' 1710 ;
'Works' (in 2 vols.), 1718-36 ; in 2
vols., 1892.
Life : by Wilkes, in 1775 edn. of
'Works'; by A. C. Ewald, in 1892
edn.

*FARRAR (Frederick William),
Dean of Canterbury,* b. 1831. Born,
in Bombay, 7 Aug. 1831. To King
William's Coll., Isle of Man, 1839 ;
afterwards at King's Coll., London.
Classical Exhbn., London Univ., 1850 ;
B.A., 1852 ; University Scholar, 1852.
Scholar of Trinity Coll., Cambridge,
1852 ; B.A., 1854 ; M.A., 1857.
Chancellor's English Verse Prize, 1852;
Le Bas Prize, 1856 ; Norris Prize,
1857. Ordained Deacon, 1854 ; Priest,
1857. Assistant-master at Marlborough, 1854-56 ; at Harrow, 1856-
71. Head Master of Marlborough,
Jan. 1871 to April 1876. B.D.,
Cambridge, 1872 ; D.D., 1873. University Preacher, Cambridge, 1868,
1869, 1872, 1874 ; Hulsean Lecturer,
1870. Hon. Chaplain to Queen, 1869;
Chaplain in Ordinary, 1873. Canon
of Westminster Abbey and Rector of
St. Margaret's, Westminster, April
1876 to 1895. Archdeacon of Westminster, 24 April 1883 to 1895.
Bampton Lecturer, Oxford, 1885.
Visit to America, 1885. Lady Margaret Preacher, Cambridge, 1890.
Chaplain to House of Commons, 1890-
95. Deputy Clerk of Closet to Queen,
1894-95. Dean of Canterbury, 1895.

Works : 'The Arctic Region,' 1852 ;
'The Influence of the Revival of
Classical Studies,' 1858 (2nd edn. same
year) ; 'Lyrics of Life,' 1859 ; 'Julian
Home,' 1859 ; 'An Essay on the Origin
of Language,' 1860 ; 'St. Winifred's'
(anon.), 1863 ; 'Chapters on Language,'
1865 ; 'Greek Grammar Rules,' 1866 ;
'On Some Defects in Public School
Education,' 1867 ; 'The Fall of Man,'
1868 ; 'Seekers after God,' 1868 ;
'Families of Speech,' 1870 ; 'The
Witness of Christ to History' (Hulsean Lectures), 1871 ; 'The Silence
and the Voices of God,' 1874 ; 'Life

of Christ,' 1874 (2nd to 12th edns. same year) ; 'The English Clergy,' 1875 ; 'In the Days of thy Youth,' 1876 ; 'Saintly Workers,' 1878 ; 'Eternal Hope,' 1878 ; 'The Life and Work of St. Paul,' 1879 ; 'Ephphatha,' 1880 ; 'Mercy and Judgment,' 1881 ; 'The Early Days of Christianity,' 1882 ; 'My Object in Life,' 1883 ; 'General Aims of the Teacher,' 1883 ; 'The Messages of the Books,' 1884 ; 'The History of Interpretation' (Bampton Lectures), 1886 ; 'Sermons and Addresses delivered in America,' 1886 ; 'Every-Day Christian Life,' 1887 ; 'Solomon,' 1887 ; 'Africa and the Drink Trade,' 1888 ; 'Lives of the Fathers,' 1889 ; 'Sermons,' 1889, etc.; 'The Minor Prophets,' 1890 ; 'The Passion Play at Oberammergau,' 1890 ; 'Truths to Live by,' 1890 ; 'Social and Present-Day Questions,' 1891 ; 'Darkness and Dawn,' 1891 ; 'The Voice from Sinai,' 1892 ; 'William Holman Hunt' (with Mrs. Meynell), 1893 ; 'Our English Ministers' (with others), 1893 ; 'The Lord's Prayer : Sermons,' 1893 ; 'The Life of Christ, as represented in Art,' 1894 ; 'Gathering Clouds,' 1895 ; 'Westminster Abbey,' 1897. [Also a variety of separate sermons and pamphlets.]

He has *edited* : 'Essays on a Liberal Education,' 1867 ; Scott's 'Tales of a Grandfather,' 1888 ; Lane's 'Life and Writings of A. Vinet,' 1890 ; 'The Imitation of Christ,' 1894 ; Lessing's 'Nathan the Wise,' 1894 ; Père Hyacinth's 'Last Will and Testament,' 1895 ; and several books of the Bible in the Cambridge Bible, Expositor's Bible, etc.

FAWCETT (Henry) 1833-1884. Born, at Salisbury, 26 Aug. 1833. Educated at school at Alderbury, 1841 [?]-47; at Queenwood Agricultural Coll., 3 Aug. 1847-49 ; at King's Coll. School, London, 1849-52. To Peterhouse, Cambridge, Oct. 1852 ; migrated to Trinity Hall, Oct. 1853. B.A., 1856 ; M.A., 1859. Fellowship at Trinity Hall, Dec. 1856. Entered at Lincoln's Inn, 26 Oct. 1854 ; settled there as student, Nov. 1856. Visit to Paris,

1857. Accidentally blinded while shooting, 17 Sept. 1858. Returned to Trinity Hall. Read papers on Political Economy at British Assoc., Sept. 1859. Member of Polit. Econ. Club, 1861. Prof. of Polit. Econ., Cambridge, 27 Nov. 1863 to 1884. Resigned Fellowship, 1866, to be re-elected same year under new statutes permitting marriage. Married Millicent Garrett, 23 April 1867. Life spent in London, except during lectures at Cambridge. Read paper on 'Proportional Representation' at Social Science Assoc., 1859. M.P. for Brighton, 12 July 1865 ; re-elected Nov. 1868. M.P. for Hackney, 24 April 1874 ; re-elected, 31 March 1880. as Postmaster-General. Contrib. at various times to 'Macmillan's Magazine' and 'Fortnightly Review' (List of articles is given in Leslie Stephen's 'Life' of Fawcett). Severe illness in Nov. 1882. Doctor of Polit. Econ., Wurzburg, 1882. F.R.S., 1882. Lord Rector of Glasgow Univ., and Hon. LL.D. degree, 1883. Corresponding member of Institute of France, 1884. Died, at Cambridge, 6 Nov. 1884 ; buried at Trumpington.

Works : 'Mr. Hare's Reform Bill, simplified and explained,' 1860 ; 'The Leading Clauses of a new Reform Bill,' 1860 ; 'Manual of Political Economy,' 1863 ; 'The Economic Position of the British Labourer,' 1865 ; 'Pauperism,' 1871 ; 'Essays and Lectures' (with Mrs. Fawcett), 1872 ; 'The Present Position of the Government' (from 'Fortnightly Review'), 1872 ; 'Speeches on Some Current Political Questions,' 1873 ; 'Free Trade and Protection,' 1878 ; 'Indian Finance' (from 'Nineteenth Century'), 1880 ; 'State Socialism' (from his 'Manual of Polit. Econ.'), 1883 ; 'Labour and Wages' (from 'Manual of Polit. Econ.'), 1884.

Life : by Leslie Stephen, 1885.

FENTON (Elijah), 1683-1730. Born, at Shelton, Staffordshire, 20 May 1683. To Jesus Coll., Cambridge [1700 ?] ; B.A., 1704 ; removed to Trinity Hall, 1726. Secretary to Earl of Orrery.

7

Afterwards Assistant Scoolmaster at Headley, Surrey, and Headmaster of Sevenoaks Grammar School; resigned in 1710. First volume of poems published, 1707. Tutor to Earl of Orrery's son [1714?-1720?]. Tutor to Craggs (Sec. of State), [1720?-1721]. Tragedy, 'Mariamne,' produced, 1723. Tutor to son of Lady Trumbull [1725?]; spent remainder of life as her auditor of accounts. Died, at Easthampstead, Berkshire, Aug. 1730.

Works: 'Ode to the Sun' (anon.), 1707; 'Oxford and Cambridge Miscellany Poems,' 1709; 'Ode addressed to the Savoir Vivre Club' (anon.), [1710?]; 'An Epistle to Mr. Southerne,' 1711: 'Poems on Several Occasions,' 1717; 'Life of Milton' (prefixed to 'Paradise Lost'), 1725.

He *edited:* Edmund Waller's Works, 1729; and *translated:* Homer's 'Odyssey' (with Pope and Broome), 1725; Secundus' 'Basia,' 1731.

Collected Works: 'Poetical Works,' with life, 1802; ed. by Dr. Johnson, 1822.

Life: in Johnson's edn. of 'Works,' 1822.

FERRIER (Susan Edmonstone), 1782-1854. Born, in Edinburgh, 7 Sept. 1782. After mother's death and marriage of sisters, kept house for father till his death in 1829. Visits to Sir Walter Scott, 1811, 1829, 1831. Visit to London, 1830. Eyesight failed. Died, in Edinburgh, 5 Nov. 1854.

Works: 'Marriage' (anon.; with Miss Clavering), 1818; 'The Inheritance' (anon.), 1824; 'Destiny' (anon.), 1831.

Collected Works: in 6 vols., 1882; in 1 vol., ed. by R. B. Johnson, 1894.

FIELD (Nathaniel), 1587-1633. Born, in Cripplegate, 1587; baptized, 17 Oct. 1587. One of the children of the Queen's Revels. First play, 'A Woman is a Weathercocke,' performed before King at Whitehall [1610?]. Joined King's Players, about 1615. Various plays produced at Black-

friars Theatre. Married Anne ———, [1618?]. Retired from stage about 1623. Died, Feb. 1633; buried, 20 Feb.

Works: 'A Woman is a Weathercocke,' 1612; 'Amends for Ladies,' 1618; 'The Fatal Dowry' (with Massinger; under initials: 'P. M. and N. F.'), 1632.

Posthumous: 'The Remonstrance of Nathaniel Field,' 1865.

FIELDING (Henry) 1707-1754. Born, at Sharpham Park, Somersetshire. 22 April 1707. Family moved to East Stour, Dorsetshire, 1710. Educated at Eton [1719?-1725?]. At Leyden, studying Law [1725-27?]. Returned to London. First play, 'Love in several Masques,' produced at Drury Lane, Feb. 1728. Probably returned to Leyden for a short time in 1728. Prolific writer of plays, 1727-37. Married Charlotte Cradock, 1735 [?]. Manager of Haymarket Theatre, 1736-37. Entered Middle Temple, 1 Nov. 1737; called to Bar, 20 June 1740. Edited 'The Champion,' with J. Ralph; contrib. articles, 27 Nov. 1739 to 12 June 1740. Revised his play, 'The Wedding Day,' for Garrick; produced 17 Feb. 1743. Wife died, 1743 [?]. Ed. 'The True Patriot,' 5 Nov. 1745 to 10 June 1746. Edited 'The Jacobite's Journal,' Dec. 1747 to Nov. 1748. Married Mary Daniel, 27 Nov. 1747. Lived at Twickenham. Moved to house in Bow Street, when appointed J.P. for Westminster, Dec. 1748. Chairman of Quarter Sessions, Hick's Hall, May 1749. Ed. 'Covent Garden Journal,' Jan. to Nov. 1752. Severe illness, winter of 1749, and spring of 1754. Moved to Ealing, May 1754. To Lisbon for health, July 1754. Died there, 8 Oct. 1754; buried in English cemetery there.

Works: 'Love in Several Masques,' 1728; 'Rape upon Rape' (anon.), 1730 (another edition, called: 'The Coffee-house Politicians,' 1730); 'The Temple Beau,' 1730; 'The Author's Farce' (under pseud. 'H. Scriblerus Secundus'), 1730; 'Tom Thumb' (by 'Scriblerus Secundus '), 1730 (with additional act, 1731) ; ' The Welsh Opera' (by 'Scriblerus Secundus'), 1731 (2nd edn. same year, called : 'The Grub Street Opera') ; 'The Letter-Writers' (by 'H. Scriblerus Secundus '), 1731 ; ' The Lottery ' (anon.), 1732 ; ' The Modern Husband,' 1732 ; ' The Covent Garden Tragedy ' (anon.), 1732 ; ' The Debauchees ' (or ' The Old Debauchees'; anon.), 1732 ; ' The Mock Doctor' (anon. ; from Molière), 1732 ; 'The Miser,' 1733 ; 'The Intriguing Chambermaid,' 1734 (from Regnard) ; ' Don Quixote in England,' 1734 ; ' An Old Man taught Wisdom,' 1735 ; ' The Universal Gallant,' 1735 ; ' Pasquin,' 1736 ; ' The Historical Register for the Year 1736' (anon.), 1737 ; ' Eurydice,' 1737 ; ' Tumble-down Dick,' 1737 ; 'The Vernon-iad' (anon.), 1741 ; 'The Crisis' (anon.), 1741 ; ' Miss Lucy in Town' (anon.), 1742 ; ' Letter to a Noble Lord ' (respecting preceding ; anon.), 1742 ; ' The History of the Adventures of Joseph Andrews ' (2 vols. ; anon.), 1742 (2nd edn. same year) ; ' A Full Vindication of the Duchess Dowager of Marlborough ' (anon.), 1742 ; ' Plutus ' (from Aristophanes, with W. Young), 1742 ; ' The Wedding Day,' 1743 ; ' Miscellanies ' (including ' Jonathan Wild,' 3 vols.), 1743 (2nd edn. same year) ; ' Proper Answer to a Scurrilous Libel,' 1747 ; 'The History of Tom Jones ' (6 vols.), 1749 ; ' A Charge delivered to the Grand Jury,' 1749 ; ' A True State of the Case of Bosavern Penlez,' 1749 ; 'An Enquiry into the Causes of the late Increase of Robbers, etc.,' 1751 ; ' Amelia,' 1751 ; ' Examples of the Interposition of Providence,' 1752 ; ' Proposals for Making an effectual Provision for the Poor,' 1753 ; ' A Clear State of the Case of Elizabeth Canning,' 1753.

Posthumous : ' Journal of a Voyage to Lisbon,' 1755 ; 'The Fathers,' 1778.

He *translated :* Ovid's ' Art of Love,' under title of ' The Lover's Assistant,' 1859 ; and *edited :* the 2nd edn. of Sarah Fielding's ' Adventures of David Simple,' 1744, and ' Familiar Letters,' 1747.

Collected Works : ed. by Murphy, in 4 vols., 1762 ; ed. by Chalmers, in 10 vols., 1806 ; ed. by Roscoe, 1840 ; ed. by Herbert, 1872 ; ed. by Leslie Stephen, 10 vols. 1882 ; ed. by G. Saintsbury, 12 vols. 1893.

Life : by F. Lawrence, 1855 ; by Austin Dobson, 1883.

FIELDING (Sarah), 1710 - 1768. [Sister of preceding.] Born, at East Stour, Dorsetshire, 8 Nov. 1710. First novel published, 1744. Died, at Bath, 1768.

Works : ' The Adventures of David Simple,' vols. i., ii. (anon.), 1744 (2nd edn. same year) ; vol. iii., 1752 ; ' Familiar Letters between the principal characters in David Simple ' (anon.), 1747 ; ' The Governess' (from ' Gentleman's Mag.' ; anon.), 1749 ; 'The Cry' (anon. ; with Jane Collier), 1754 ; ' Lives of Cleopatra and Octavia ' (anon. ; privately printed), 1757 ; ' The Countess of Dellwyn' (anon.), 1759.

Posthumous : ' History of Ophelia,' 1785.

She *translated :* Xenophon's ' Memoirs of Socrates,' 1762.

FINLAY (George), 1799 - 1875. Born, at Faversham, Kent, 21 Dec. 1799. Educated privately. Studied Law in Glasgow ; subsequently went to Göttingen University, 1821. Visit to Greece, Nov. 1823 to Dec. 1824 ; met Byron there. Returned to Scotland, 1825. To Greece again, 1827 ; remained there, active on behalf of Greek people, till his death. Contrib. to ' Blackwood's Mag.,' ' Athenæum,' ' Saturday Review ' ; and a series of letters to the ' Times,' 1864-70. Died, at Athens, 26 Jan. 1875.

Works : ' The Hellenic Kingdom,' 1836 ; ' Remarks on the Topography of Oropia,' 1838 ; ''Επιστολη προς τους Αθηναιους,' 1844 ; 'Greece under the Romans,' 1844 ; ' On the Site of the Holy Sepulchre,' 1847 ; ' The History of Greece . . . 1204 to 1461,' 1851 ; ' History of the Byzantine and Greek Empires ' (2 vols.), 1853-54 ; 'The History of Greece under the Otto-

7—2

man and Venetian Domination,' 1856; 'History of the Greek Revolution,' 1861 ; 'Παρατηρησεις επι της εν Ελβετια και Ελλαδι προϊστορικης αρχαιολογιας,' 1869 ; 'A History of Greece. ... B.C. 146 to A.D. 1864' (collected from preceding works, and ed. by H. F. Tozer), 1877.

Life : 'Autobiography' in vol. i. of 1877 edn. of 'History of Greece.'

FITZGERALD (Edward), 1809 - 1883. Born, at Bredfield House, Woodbridge, Suffolk, 31 March 1809. At King Edward VI.'s Grammar School, Bury St. Edmunds, 1821-26. To Trinity Coll., Camb., Oct. 1826 ; B.A., 1830. Visit to Paris, 1830. Family removed to Ipswich, 1825 ; to Boulge Hall, near Bredfield, 1835. Intimate friendship with Thackeray and Carlyle. Married Lucy Barton, 1856 [?]. Lived at Farlingay Hall, near Woodbridge, 1853-60; in Woodbridge, 1860-74 ; at Little Grange, 1874-83. Died, suddenly, at Merton Rectory, Norfolk, 14 June 1883. Buried at Boulge.

Works: 'Euphranor' (anon.), 1851; 'Polonius' (anon.), 1852 ; Trans. of 'Six Dramas' of Calderon, 1853 ; Trans. of the 'Salámán and Absál' of Jánú (anon.), 1856 ; Trans. of the 'Rubáiyát' of Omar Khayyám (anon.), 1859 ; Trans. of Æschylus' 'Agamemnon' (anon.), 1876 ; Trans. of Calderon's 'Mighty Magician' (anon.), 1877.

Posthumous : 'Works' (2 vols.), 1887; 'Letters and Literary Remains,' ed. by W. Aldis Wright (3 vols.), 1889 ; 'Letters,' ed. by W. A. Wright (2 vols.), 1894 ; 'Letters to Fanny Kemble, 1871-1883,' ed. by W. A. Wright, 1895.

He *edited :* 'Selections from the Poems and Letters of Bernard Barton,' 1842 ; 'Readings in Crabbe,' 1882.

FLETCHER (Giles), 1588 [?]—1623. [Brother of Phineas Fletcher, *q. v.*] Born, probably in London, about 1588. Probably educated at Westminster School. To Cambridge, 1602 [?]. Scholar of Trin. Coll., Camb., 12 April 1605 ; B.A., 1606 ; Minor

Fellow of Trin. Coll., 17 Sept. 1608. Reader in Greek Grammar, 1615 ; Reader in Greek Language, 1618. Ordained, 1618. Rector of Alderton, Suffolk. Died, 1623.

Works : 'Christ's Victorie and Triumph,' 1610 ; 'The Reward of the Faithfull,' 1623 ; 'Licia' (anon.), [1593].

Collected Poems : ed. by A. B. Grosart, 1868.

FLETCHER (John), 1579 - 1625. Born, at Rye, Dec. 1579. Possibly 'pensioner' of Corpus Coll., Camb., 1591 ; Bible - Clerk, 1593. Early intimacy with Francis Beaumont. Collaborated with him, 1605 - 14. Died, in London, Aug. 1625 ; buried at St. Saviour's, Southwark, 29 Aug.

Works : [For plays published under the joint names of Francis Beaumont and John Fletcher, *see supra :* Beaumont and Fletcher.] 'The Faithful Shepherdess' [1609 ?] ; 'The Tragedy of Thierry, King of France' (anon. ; possibly by Fletcher), 1621.

Posthumous : 'The Two Noble Kinsmen' (published in names of Fletcher and Shakespeare ; probably by Fletcher [and Massinger ?]), 1634; 'The Elder Brother' (published in Fletcher's name ; probably written with Beaumont), 1637 ; 'Monsieur Thomas,' 1639 ; 'Wit Without Money' (published in Beaumont and Fletcher's names ; probably by Fletcher), 1639 ; 'Rule a Wife and Have a Wife,' 1640 ; 'The Coronation' (anon.), 1640; 'The Night Walker' (with Shirley ?), 1640.

FLETCHER (Phineas), 1582-1650. [Brother of Giles Fletcher, *q. v.*] Born, at Cranbrook, Kent, 8 April 1582. Educated at Eton. Scholar of King's Coll., Cambridge, 24 Aug. 1600 ; B.A., 1604 ; M.A., 1608 ; Fellow of King's Coll., 1611 [?] ; B.D. Left Cambridge, 1616. Chaplain to Sir H. Willoughby, 1616-21. Rector of Hilgay, Norfolk, 1621-50. Married Elizabeth Vincent, 1622 [?]. Died, at Hilgay, winter of 1650.

Works : 'Locustæ,' 1627 ; 'Sicelides' (anon.), 1631; 'The Way to Blessedness,' 1632; 'Joy in Tribulation,' 1632; 'The Purple Island' (anon.), 1633 ; 'Elisa' (anon.), 1633 ; 'Piscatorie Eclogs' (anon.), 1633 ; 'Sylva Poetica,' 1633.

Posthumous: 'A Father's Testament,' 1670.

He *edited:* 'De Literis Antiquæ Britanniæ,' by his father, Giles Fletcher, 1633.

FONBLANQUE (Albany William), 1793-1872. Born, in London, 1793. To Woolwich, to study for Engineers, 1897, but compelled to give up studies for two years through illness. Studied law, 1810 - 12. Adopted journalism as profession,' 1812. On staff of 'Times' and 'Morning Chronicle,' and contrib. to 'Examiner,' 'London Mag.,' and 'Westminster Review,' 1820 - 30. Married Miss Keane, 1829. On staff of 'The Atlas.' Principal leader-writer to 'The Examiner,' 1826 ; editor, Sept. 1830-47 ; proprietor, 1835 [?]-65. Appointment on Board of Trade, 1847. Represented Great Britain in International Statistical Congress, 1854. Retired from public during last ten years of life. Died, 13 Oct. 1872.

Works: 'England under Seven Administrations,' 1837.

Life: 'Life and Labours of Albany Fonblanque,' ed. by E. B. de Fonblanque, 1874.

FOOTE (Samuel), 1720-1777. Born, in Truro, Jan. 1720 [?]; baptized 27 Jan. 1720. At school at Worcester. Matric. at Worcester Coll., Oxford, 1 July 1737 ; took no degree. Became an actor; first appeared at Haymarket Theatre, 6 Feb. 1744. Acted in Dublin same year. Acted in London, 1745-49. Lived in Paris, 1750-52. Acted in London, 1753-57 ; in Dublin, winter of 1757-58 ; in Edinburgh, spring of 1759 ; in Dublin, winter of 1759-60. Manager of Haymarket, 1760 ; of Drury Lane, 1761. Acted till 1766 ; in that year lost leg through accident. Granted patent to build a theatre. Opened new theatre

in Haymarket, May 1767. Visited Dublin, 1768. Manager of Edinburgh theatre, 1770. Sold patent of London theatre, 16 Jan. 1777. Died, at Dover, 21 Oct. 1777. Buried in West Cloister of Westminster Abbey.

Works: 'The Genuine Memoirs ... of Sir J. D. Goodere' [1741 ?]; 'A Treatise on the Passions' [1747]; 'The Roman and English Comedy Consider'd.' 1747 ; 'Taste,' 1752 ; 'The Englishman in Paris,' 1753 ; 'The Knights,' 1754 ; 'The Englishman Returned from Paris,' 1756 ; 'The Author,' 1757 ; 'The Minor,' 1760 ; 'A Letter . . . to the Reverend Author of the " Remarks . . . on The Minor," ' 1760 ; 'The Orators,' 1762 ; 'The Comic Theatre ; being a free Translation of all the best French Comedies, by S. Foote and others' (5 vols.), 1762 ; 'The Lyar' (adapted from Corneille), 1764 ; 'The Mayor of Garratt,' 1764 ; 'The Patron,' 1764 ; 'The Commissary,' 1765 ; 'The Lame Lover,' 1770 ; 'Apology for "The Minor," ' 1771 ; 'A Trip to Calais' (under pseud.: 'Timothy Timbertoe '), 1775 ; 'The Bankrupt,' 1776.

Posthumous: 'The Maid of Bath' (anon.), 1778 ; 'The Devil upon Two Sticks,' 1778 ; 'The Nabob,' 1778 ; 'The Cozeners' (anon.), 1778 ; 'The Capuchin,' 1778.

Collected Works: in 4 vols., 1763-78 ; in 3 vols., 1880.

Life: 'Memoirs' (anon.), [1788]; by W. Cooke, 1805 ; by J. Bee, in 1830 edn. of 'Works.'

FORD (John), 1586-1650 [?]. Born, at Ilsington, Devonshire, 1586. Baptized 17 April. Probably matric. at Exeter Coll., Oxford, 26 March 1601. Admitted to Middle Temple, 16 Nov. 1602. Wrote plays, 1628-39. Probably spent later years of life in Devonshire ; and died there, about 1650 [?].

Works: 'Fames Memoriall,' 1606 ; 'Honor Triumphant,' 1606 ; 'A Line of Life,' 1620 ; 'The Lovers' Melancholy,' 1629 ; ''Tis Pitty She's a Whore,' 1633 ; 'The Broken Heart,' 1633 ; 'Love's Sacrifice,' 1633 ; 'The

Chronicle Historie of Perkin Warbeck,' 1634; 'The Fancies Chast and Noble,' 1638; 'The Ladies' Triall,' 1639.

Posthumous: 'The Sun's Darling' (with Dekker), 1656 (another edn. same year); 'The Witch of Edmonton' (with Rowley, Dekker, and others), 1658.

Collected Works: ed. by Weber (2 vols.), 1811; ed. by Gifford (2 vols.), 1827; ed. by Dyce (3 vols.), 1869.

Life: by Gifford, revised in 1869 edn. of 'Works.'

FORSTER (John), 1812-1876. Born, at Newcastle, 2 April 1812. At school at Newcastle. Play, 'Charles at Tunbridge,' performed at Newcastle theatre, 2 May 1828. To Cambridge, Oct. 1828. Removed to University Coll., London, Nov. 1828. Student at Inner Temple, 10 Nov. 1828; called to Bar, 27 Jan. 1843. Contrib. to 'Newcastle Magazine,' 1829. Dramatic critic of 'True Sun,' 1832. Editor of 'The Reflector' series of essays, 1832-33. Contrib. to 'Courier' and 'Athenæum.' Literary and dramatic critic to 'Examiner,' 1833. Edited 'Foreign Quarterly Review,' 1842-43. Contrib. to 'Shilling Magazine' and 'Edinburgh Review,' 1845, 1856. Editor of 'Daily News,' Feb. to Oct., 1846. Editor of 'Examiner,' 1847 to Dec. 1855. Contrib. to 'Quarterly Review,' Sept. 1854 to 1855. Secretary to Commissioners of Lunacy, Dec. 1855 to Feb. 1861. Married Mrs. Eliza Ann Colburn, 24 Sept. 1856. Commissioner of Lunacy, Feb. 1861 to 1872. Died, 2 Feb. 1876. Buried at Kensal Green.

Works: 'Rhyme and Reason' (anon.), 1832; 'Lives of the Statesmen of the Commonwealth' (5 vols., in 'Lardner's Cyclopædia'), 1836-39; 'The Life and Adventures of Oliver Goldsmith,' 1848(enlarged edn. called 'Life and Times' of Goldsmith, 1854); 'Historical and Biographical Essays,' 1858; 'The Arrest of the Five Members by Charles I.,' 1860; 'The Debates on the Grand Remonstrance,' 1860; 'Life of Landor' (2 vols.), 1869; 'Life of Dickens' (3 vols.),

1872-74; 'Life of Jonathan Swift,' vol. i., 1876.

He *edited:* Evelyn's 'Diary,' 1850-52.

FOSTER (John), 1770-1843. Born, at Wadsworth Lane, near Halifax, 17 Sept. 1770. At Baptist Coll., Bristol, Sept. 1791 to May 1792. Baptist preacher at Newcastle, 1792. In Dublin, 1793-94. Returned to England, 1794. To Dublin again, 1795. Returned to Wadsworth Lane, Feb. 1796. Baptist minister at Chichester, 1797. To Battersea, 1799. Minister at Downend, Bristol, 1800-04; at Sheppard's Barton, near Frome, 1804-06. Contrib. to 'Eclectic Review,' 1806-39. Married Maria Snooke, May 1808; settled at Bourton, Gloucestershire. Minister at Downend again, 1817-21. Removed to Stapylton, Gloucestershire, 1821. Lectured in Broadmead Chapel, Bristol, 1822-23. Wife died, 1832. Contrib. to 'Morning Chronicle,' 1834-35. Died, 15 Oct. 1843. Buried in Downend Baptist Chapel burial-ground.

Works: 'Essays,' 1805 (2nd edn. same year); 'Discourse on Missions,' 1818; 'On the Evils of Popular Ignorance,' 1820; 'Introductory Observations on Dr. Marshman's Statement,' 1828.

Posthumous: 'Contributions . . . to the "Eclectic Review"' (2 vols.), 1844.

He *edited:* Doddridge's 'Rise and Progress of Religion,' 1825; Hall's 'Works,' 1832.

Life: 'Life and Correspondence,' by J. E. Ryland, 1846.

＊FOWLER (Thomas), b. 1832. Born, at Burton-Stather, Lincs., 1 Sept. 1832. Early education by private tutors. At King William's Coll., Isle of Man, Jan. 1848 to Dec. 1849. Matric. at Merton Coll., Oxford, as Postmaster, 31 May 1850; B.A., 1854; M.A., 1857. Ordained Deacon, 1855; Priest, 1857. Denyer Theol. Prize Essay, 1858. Fellow of Lincoln Coll., 1855-81; Tutor, 1855-73. Memb. of Hebdomadal Council, 1869. Select Preacher, 1872-73. Prof. of Logic,

1873-88. President of Corpus Christi Coll., 23 Dec. 1881. Hon. LL.D., Edinburgh, 1882. B.D. and D.D., Oxford, 1886. Has contributed to 'Saturday Review,' 'Spectator,' 'Academy,' 'Macmillan's Magazine,' 'Fortnightly Review,' 'Dictionary of National Biography,' 'Encyclopædia Britannica,' etc.

Works : ' The Elements of Deductive Logic,' 1867 ; ' The Elements of Inductive Logic,' 1870 ; ·Locke,' 1880 ; ' Bacon,' 1881 ; 'Shaftesbury and Hutcheson,' 1882 ; ' Progressive Morality,' 1884 ; ' The Principles of Morals,' pt. i. (with J. M. Wilson), 1886 ; pt. ii. (by T. Fowler alone), 1887 ; pts. i. and ii. together, 1894 ; ' The History of Corpus Christi Coll.,' 1893.

He has *edited :* Bacon's ' Novum Organum,' 1878 ; Locke's ' Conduct of the Understanding,' 1881.

FOX (John), 1516-1587. Born, at Boston, Lincolnshire, 1516. To Oxford, 1532 ; probably to Magdalen Coll. School, and afterwards to Magdalen Coll. B.A., 17 July 1537 ; M.A., 6 June 1543. Probationary Fellow of Magdalen Coll., July 1538 ; Fellow, 25 July 1539. Resigned Fellowship, July 1545. Tutor to son of William Lucy, 1545-46. Married Agnes Randall, 3 Feb. 1547. Tutor to children of **Earl** of Surrey, at Reigate, 1548-53. Ordained Deacon, 24 June 1550. With Protestant Refugees in Germany and Switzerland, 1554-58. Returned to England, Oct. 1559. Ordained Priest, 25 Jan. 1560. Under Duke of Norfolk's patronage, 1559-64. Prebendary of Salisbury Cathedral and Vicar of Shipton, 1563. At Waltham, 1565-66. Lived in Grub Street, London, 1570-87. Canon of Durham, 14 Oct. 1572 ; resigned same year. Died, in London, 18 April 1587. Buried in St. Giles's Church, Cripplegate.

Works : ' De non plectendis morte adulteris Consultatio,' 1548 (another edn., called ' De lapsis in Ecclesiam recipiendis,' 1549) ; ' De Censura,' 1551 ; ' Tables of Grammar,' 1552 ;

' Commentarii rerum in Ecclesia gestarum,' 1554 (another edn., called ' Chronicon Ecclesiæ,' 1564) ; ' Christus Triumphans,' 1556 ; ' Ad inclytos . . . Angliæ proceres . . . Supplicatio,' 1557 ; ' Locorum Communium Logicalium Tituli,' 1557 ; ' Rerum in Ecclesia gestarum . . . maximarumque per Europam Persecutionum ac Sanctorum Dei Martyrum . . . Commentarii ' (2 pts.), 1559, 1563 (English trans., called ' Actes and Monuments.' 1563) ; ' Syllogisticon,' 1563 ; ' A Sermon of Christ Crucified,' 1570 (Latin trans., called ' De Christo Crucifixio Concio,' 1571) ; ' Reformatio Legum,' 1571 ; ' De Oliva Evangelica,' 1577 (English trans., by James Bell, 1578) ; ' A Sermon at the Christening of a certaine Jew,' 1578 ; ' A New Year's Gift ' [1579 ?] ; ' Contra Hieron. Osorium Responsio Apologetica,' 1577 (English trans., 1581) ; ' The Pope Confuted ' (anon.), 1580 ; ' De Christo gratis justificante,' 1583 (English trans., 1598).

Posthumous : ' Eicasmi,' 1587.

He *translated :* Œcolampadius' ' Sermon . . . to Yong Men and Maydens ' [1550 ?] ; Regius' ' Instruccyon of Christen fayth ' (anon.), [1550 ?] ; Luther's ' Fruitfull Sermon . . . made of the Angelles ' (anon.) [1554 ?] ; and ed. : Ridley's ' Friendly Farewel,' 1559.

FREEMAN (Edward Augustus), 1823-1892. Born, at Harborne, Staffordshire, 2 Aug. 1823. Educated at school at Northampton, 1831-37 ; at Cheam, 1837-39 ; with private tutor, 1840-41. Verses pubd. in ' Cromer Telegraph,' 1834. Matric. Trinity Coll., Oxford, as scholar, 7 June 1841 ; B.A., 10 May 1845 ; M.A., 14 Jan 1848 ; Fellow, May 1845 to April 1847 ; Reader in Rhetoric, 1846. Married Eleanor Gutch, 13 April 1847. Settled at Oaklands, Gloucestershire, 1849 ; removed to Lanrumney, Cardiff, 1855. Contrib. to ' British Quarterly Rev.,' 1851-81 ; to ' North Brit. Rev.,' 1854-66 ; to ' Edin. Rev.,' 1856-65 ; to ' National Rev.,' 1858-64 ; to ' Fortnightly Rev.,' 1865-89 ; to ' Mac·

millan's Mag.,' 1870-92 ; **to** 'Contemp. Rev.,' 1877-91, etc., etc. Hon. D.C.L., Oxford, 22 June 1870. Rede Lecturer, Camb., 1872. Hon. Mem. Hist. Soc. of Massachusetts, 1873. Hon. LL.D., Camb., 1874. Knight Commander of Greek Order of Redeemer, 1875. Corresp. Mem. of Imp. Acad. of Science, St. Petersburg, 1876. Hon. Fellow Trin. Coll., Oxford, 1880. Mem. of Royal Commission on Ecclesiastical Courts, 1881. Regius Prof. of Modern Hist., and Fellow of Oriel Coll., Oxford, 1884. Hon. LL.D., Edinburgh, 17 April 1884. Ill health from 1886. Died, at Alicante, 16 March 1892. Buried in Protestant Cemetery there.

Works: ' Principles of Church Restoration,' 1846 ; 'Thoughts on the Study of History,' 1849 ; 'History of Architecture,' 1849 ; 'Notes on the Architectural Antiquities of . . . Gower,' 1850 ; 'An Essay on . . . Window Tracery in England,' 1850 ; 'Remarks on the Architecture of Llandaff Cathedral,' 1850 ; 'Poems' (with G. W. Cox), 1850 ; 'The preservation and restoration of Ancient Monuments,' 1852 ; 'Suggestions with regard to certain proposed alterations in the Universities' (with F. H. Dickinson), 1854 ; 'The History and Conquest of the Saracens,' 1856 ; 'The History and Antiquities of St. David's' (with W. B. Jones), 1856 ; 'Ancient Greece and Mediæval Italy,' 1857 ; 'History of Federal Government,' vol. i. (no more pubd.), 1863 ; 'Leominster Priory Church' (with G. F. Townsend), [1863]; 'The History of the Norman Conquest of England' (6 vols.), 1867-79 ; 'Old English History for Children,' 1869 ; 'History of the Cathedral Church of Wells,' 1870 ; 'Historical Essays' (4 series), 1871-92 ; 'General Sketch of European History,' 1872 ; 'The Growth of the English Constitution,' 1872 ; 'The Unity of History,' 1872 ; 'Comparative Politics,' 1874 ; Disestablishment and Disendowment,' 1874 ; 'History of Europe,' 1876 ; Historical and Architectural Sketches,' 1876 ; 'The Turks in Europe,' 1877 ;

'The Ottoman Power in Europe,' 1877 ; 'How the Study of History is let and hindered,' 1879 ; 'A Short History of the Norman Conquest,' 1880 ; 'The Historical Geography of Europe,' 1881 ; 'Sketches from the Subject and Neighbour Lands of Venice,' 1881 ; 'An Introduction to American International History,' 1882 ; 'The Reign of William Rufus,' 1882 ; 'Lectures to American Audiences,' 1882 ; 'English Towns and Districts,' 1883 ; Letterpress to 'Cathedral Cities: Ely and Norwich,' 1883 ; 'Some Impressions of the United States,' 1883 ; 'The Office of the Historical Professor,' 1884 ; 'Greater Greece and Greater Britain,' 1886 ; 'The Methods of Historical Study,' 1886 ; 'The Chief Periods of European History,' 1886 ; 'Exeter,' 1887 ; 'Four Oxford Lectures,' 1888 ; 'William the Conqueror,' 1888 ; 'Sketches from French Travel,' 1891 ; 'The History of Sicily' (4 vols.), 1891-94 ; 'Sicily: Phœnician, Greek and Roman,' 1892.

Posthumous: 'Studies of Travel' (papers from 'Sat. Rev.,' 'Pall Mall Gaz.,' and 'Guardian,' ed. by F. Freeman), 1893.

He *edited:* 'Historical Course for Schools,' 1872, etc. ; 'Historic Towns' (with W. Hunt), 1887 [1886], etc.

Life: 'Life and Letters,' by W. R. W. Stephens, 1895.

FROUDE (James Anthony), 1818-1894. Born, at Dartington, Devon, 23 April 1818. At Westminster School, 1830-33. Matric. Oriel Coll., Oxford, 10 Dec. 1835. B.A., 28 April 1842 ; Chancellor's Eng. Essay Prize, 1842; Fellow of Exeter Coll., 1842-49 ; M.A., 2 March 1843. Ordained Deacon, 1844. Contrib. to 'Westminster Rev.' Rector of St. Andrew's Univ., and Hon. LL.D., 23 March 1869. For some time editor of 'Fraser's Mag.' Resigned Deaconship, under Clerical Disabilities Act, 21 Sept. 1872. Lectured in U.S.A., 1872. On political mission to Cape of Good Hope, Dec. 1874 to March 1875. Travelled in Australia, 1885 ; and in West Indies. Regius Prof. of

Modern Hist. Oxford, 1892. Died 20 Oct. 1894.

Works: 'Shadows of the Clouds' (under pseud : 'Zeta'), 1847 ; 'A Sermon . . . on the death of the Rev. G. M. Coleridge,' 1847 ; 'The Nemesis of Faith,' 1849 (2nd edn. same year) ; 'The Book of Job' (from 'West. Rev.'), 1854 ; 'Suggestions on the best means of teaching English History,' 1855 ; 'History of England' (12 vols.), 1856-70 ; 'Short Studies on Great Subjects' (2 vols.), 1867 ; second ser., 1871 ; third ser., 1877 ; fourth ser., 1883 ; 'Inaugural Address' at St. Andrew's, 1869 ; 'The Cat's Pilgrimage,' 1870 ; 'Calvinism,' 1871 ; 'The English in Ireland in the Eighteenth Century' (3 vols.), 1872-74 ; 'Cæsar,' 1879 ; 'Bunyan,' 1880 ; 'Two Lectures on South Africa,' 1880 ; 'Thomas Carlyle : history of the first forty years of his life' (2 vols.), 1882 ; 'Luther,' 1883 ; 'Thomas Carlyle : history of his life in London' (2 vols.), 1884 ; 'Oceana,' 1886 ; 'The English in the West Indies,' 1888 (2nd edn. same year) ; 'Liberty and Property' [1888] ; 'The Two Chiefs of Dunboy,' 1889 ; 'Lord Beaconsfield,' 1890 ; 'The Divorce of Catharine of Arragon,' 1891 ; 'The Spanish Story of the Armada,' 1892 (2nd edn. same year) ; 'Life and Letters of Erasmus,' 1894 (2nd edn. same year).

Posthumous: 'English Seamen in the Sixteenth Century,' 1895 ; 'Lectures on the Council of Trent,' 1896 (2nd edn. same year).

He *edited:* 'The Pilgrim,' by W. Thomas, 1861 ; Carlyle's 'Reminiscences,' 1881-82 ; J. W. Carlyle's 'Letters and Memorials,' 1883

FULLER (Thomas), 1606 - 1661. Born, at Aldwinkle, Northamptonshire, June 1606. Educated at village school and by his father. To Queen's Coll., Cambridge, 29 June 1621; B.A., 1625 ; M.A., 1628 ; B.D., 11 June 1635. Ordained, 1630 ; Perpetual Curate to St. Benet's, Cambridge, 1630-33. Prebend of Netherbury, 18 June 1631 to 1641. Rector of Broadwindsor, Dorsetshire, 1634-41. Married, 1637 [?]. Proctor for Diocese of Bristol, 1640. Settled in London after wife's death, 1641. Curate of Savoy, 1641-43. Removed to Oxford, 1643. Chaplain to Sir Ralph Hopton, 1643-1644. Entered Princess Henrietta's household at Exeter, 1644. Bodley Lecturer at Exeter, 21 March 1646. To London, April 1646. Perpetual Curate of Waltham Abbey, 1648 [or 1649 ?]. Married Hon. Mary Roper, 1651. Rector of Cranford, March 1658. Created D.D. by Royal Letters Patent, Aug. 1660. Died, in London, 16 Aug. 1661. Buried at Cranford.

Works: [besides a number of separate sermons] 'David's Hainous Sinne,' 1631 ; 'The History of the Holy Warre,' 1639 ; 'Joseph's Party-coloured Coat' (under initials T. F.), 1640 ; 'The Holy State' and 'The Profane State,' 1642 ; 'Truth Maintained,' 1643 ; 'Good Thoughts in Bad Times,' 1645 ; 'Andronicus,' 1646 (2nd and 3rd edns. same year) ; 'The Cause and Cure of a Wounded Conscience,' 1647 ; 'Good Thoughts in Worse Times,' 1647 ; 'A Pisgah-sight of Palestine,' 1650 ; contrib. to 'Abel Redivivus,' 1651 ; 'A Comment on Matt. iv. 1-11,' 1652 ; 'The Infant's Advocate,' 1652 ; 'A Comment on Ruth' (anon.), 1654 ; 'Ephemeris Parliamentaria' (anon.), 1654 ; 'A Triple Reconciler,' 1654 ; 'The Church History of Britain,' 1655 ; 'History of the University of Cambridge,' 1655 ; 'History of Waltham Abbey,' 1655 ; 'A Collection of Sermons' (5 pts.), 1656-57 ; 'The Best Name on Earth,' 1657 ; 'The Appeal of Injured Innocence,' 1659 ; 'An Alarum to the Counties of England and Wales' (anon.), 1660 (2nd and 3rd edns. same year) ; 'Mixt Contemplations in Better Times,' 1660 ; 'A Panegyrick to His Majesty,' 1660.

Posthumous: 'The History of the Worthies of England' (ed. by J. Fuller), 1662 ; 'Collected Sermons' (ed. by J. E. Bailey and W. E. A. Axon), 1891.

He *edited:* Rev. H. Smith's 'Sermons,' 1657 ; **J.** Spencer's ' Καινα και Παλαια,' 1658.

Life: ' Life ' (anon.), 1661 ; ' Life,' by J. E. Bailey, 1874 ; by Rev. M. J. Fuller, 1884.

FULLERTON (*Lady* Georgiana Charlotte), 1812-1885. Born [Georgiana Charlotte Leveson - Gower], at Tixall Hall, Staffordshire, 23 Sept. 1812. Early life spent in Paris. Married there to Alexander George Fullerton, 13 July 1833. Lived in Paris till 1841 ; afterwards in Cannes and in Rome. Joined Roman Catholic Church, 29 March 1846. Enrolled in Third Order of St. Francis, 1856. Lived at Slindon, Sussex, 1857-75 ; afterwards at Bournemouth. Died there, 19 Jan. 1885. Buried in cemetery of Convent of Sacred Heart, Roehampton.

Works: ' Ellen Middleton,' 1844 ; ' Grantley Manor,' 1847 ; ' The Old Highlander' (anon.; privately printed), 1849 ; ' Lady-Bird,' 1852 ; ' The Life of St. Frances of Rome,' 1855 ; ' La Comtesse de Bonneval ' (in French ; from ' Le Correspondant '), 1857 (English translation, 1858) ; ' Rose Leblanc' (in French), 1861 ; ' Laurentia,' 1861 ; ' Too Strange not to be True,' 1864 ; ' Constance Sherwood,' 1865 ; ' A Stormy Life,' 1867 ; ' The Convent Prize Book ' (anon.), 1868 ; ' The Helpers of the Holy Souls,' 1868 ; ' Mrs. Gerald's Niece,' 1869 ; ' The Gold Digger,' 1872 ; ' Dramas from the Lives of the Saints : Germaine Cousin,' 1872 ; ' Life of Louisa de Carvajal,' 1873 ; ' Seven Stories,' 1873 ; ' Sketch of the Life of . . . Father H. Young,' 1874 ; ' Life of Mère Marie de la Providence,' 1875 ; ' The Miraculous Medal,' 1880 ; ' A Will and Way,' 1881 ; ' The Fire of London ' [1882]; ' Life of Elizabeth, Lady Falkland,' 1883.

She *translated :* Deynordt's ' Life . . . of . . . J. Berchmans,' 1866 ; Verdenal's ' Miracle at Metz ' [1866]; Silvio Pellico's ' Life of the Marchesa G. Falletti di Barolo,' 1866 ; ' Anne Severin,' 1869 ; Mrs. Craven's ' Natalie Narischkin,' 1877 ; D'Aulney's

' The Notary's Daughter,' 1878 ; Baunard's ' Life of Mère Duchesne,' 1879, and ' Life of . . . Madeleine Berat,' 1880 ; Mrs. Craven's ' Eliane,' 1882; Mme. de Navery's ' The Strawcutter's Daughter ' [1896]; and *edited :* ' Our Lady's Little Books,' 1860-61. *Life:* by Mrs. Craven, 1888.

✻**FURNIVALL** (Frederick James), b. 1825. Born, at Egham, Surrey, 4 Feb. 1825. At schools at Englefield Green, Turnham Green, and Hanwell. At Univ. Coll., London, 1841-42. To Trinity Hall, Camb., 1842 ; B.A., 1847 ; M.A., 1850. Student of Lincoln's Inn, 26 Jan. 1846 ; called to Bar, 30 Jan. 1849. Hon. Sec. Philological Soc., 1852-96 ; for a time editor of its ' New Engl. Dict.' Founded Early English Text Society, 1864 ; Chaucer Society, 1868 ; Ballad Society, 1868 ; New Shakspere Society, 1873 ; Browning Society, 1881 ; Wyclif Society, 1882 ; Shelley Society, 1885. Hon. Ph.D., Berlin, 4 Feb. 1885. Resides in London.

Works: Ed. works for Philological Soc., 1854 ; for Roxburghe Club, 1861-65 ; ed. ' Le Morte Arthur,' 1864 ; ed. works for Early English Text Society, 1864-96 ; ed. Bishop Percy's MS., 1867 ; ed. works for Ballad Soc., 1868-74 ; ed. works for Chaucer Soc., 1868-96 ; ' The Succession of Shakspere's Works,' 1874 ; ed. works for New Shakspere Soc., 1876-84 ; ed. collected works and separate quartos of Shakspere, 1877-91 ; ' Mr. Swinburne's "Flat Burglary" on Shakspere,' 1879 ; ' To the Trinity, and other Withdrawers from the New Shak. Soc.,' 1881 ; ' The "Co." of Pigsbrook & Co,' [1881] ; ' How the Browning Society came into being,' 1884 ; ed. Manning's ' Story of England,' 1887 ; ed. ' The Troublesome Raigne of John, King of England,' 1888 ; ' Robert Browning's Ancestors' [1890] ; ' Early History of the Working Men's College,' 1891 ; ' On Shakspere's Signatures' [1895].

GALT (John), 1779-1839. Born, at Irvine, Ayrshire, 2 May 1779.

Family removed to Greenock 1789. Educated at local schools. Held posts in Greenock Custom House, and in merchant's office in Greenock till 1803. Contrib. to local newspapers. To London, June 1804. In commercial partnership, 1803-06. Entered at Lincoln's Inn, 1806; never called to Bar. Travelled in Europe and Asia Minor, 1809 - 11. Married Miss Tilloch, 1811 [?]. Ed. 'Political Rev.,' 1812. Wrote various plays and contributed to periodicals. At Finnart, near Greenock, 1818-20. First novel published, in 'Blackwood's Mag.,' 1820. Removed from London to Esk Grove, near Musselburgh, 1823. Secretary to Canada Company, 1823; accompanied Commission to Upper Canada. In Canada again, 1826-29; superintendent of Canada Co., 1827-29. Arrested for debt on return to England, 1829. Ed. 'The Courier,' 1830. Settled in Old Brompton, 1831. Contrib. to 'Frazer's Mag.' To Greenock, to live with his sister, 1834. Died, at Greenock, 11 April 1839; buried there.

Works : 'The Battle of Largs' (suppressed), 1803; 'Voyages and Travels in the years 1809, 1810 and 1811,' 1812; 'The Life and Administration of Cardinal Wolsey,' 1812; 'The Tragedies of Maddalon Agamemnon,' etc.,' 1812; 'Letters from the Levant,' 1813; 'The New British Theatre' (ed. by Galt, containing several plays by him), 4 vols., 1814-15; 'The Majolo,' 1816; 'Life and Studies of Benjamin West' (2 pts.), 1816-20; 'The Crusade,' 1816; 'The Appeal' (anon.), 1818; 'All the Voyages round the World,' (under pseud. 'Samuel Prior'), 1820; 'A Tour of Asia' (under pseud. 'Rev. T. Clark'), [1820 ?]; 'The Wandering Jew' (under pseud. 'T. Clark'), 1820; 'The Earthquake' (anon.), 1820; 'Pictures, historical and biographical,' 1821; 'The Annals of the Parish' (anon.), 1821; 'The Ayrshire Legatees' (anon.), 1821; 'The Steamboat' (under pseud. 'Thomas Duffle'), 1822; 'The Provost' (anon.), 1822; 'Sir Andrew Wylie' (anon.), 1822; 'The Gathering of the West' (anon.),

1823; 'The Entail' (anon.), 1823; 'Ringham Gilhaize' (anon.), 1823; 'The Spaewife' (anon.), 1823; 'Rothelan' (anon.), 1824; 'The Bachelor's Wife,' 1824; 'The Omen' (anon.), 1825; 'The Last of the Lairds' (under pseud. 'Malachi Mailings'), 1826; 'Lawrie Todd,' 1830; 'Southennan,' 1830; 'Life of Lord Byron,' 1830 (2nd edn. same year); 'The Lives of the Players,' 1831; 'Bogle Corbet,' 1831; 'The Member' (under pseud., 'A. Jobbry'), 1832; 'The Radical' (anon.), 1832; 'Stanley Buxton' (anon.), 1832; 'Poems,' 1833; 'Stories of the Study,' 1833; 'Eben Erskine,' 1833; 'The Ouranologos,' pt. i. (no more published), 1833; 'Autobiography,' 1833; 'Literary Life and Miscellanies,' 1834.

Posthumous : 'The Demon of Destiny,' ed. by H. Pigott (privately printed), 1839; 'The Painter,' 1841.

He *edited :* A. Graydon's 'Memoirs.' 1822; G. Thorburn's 'Forty Years' Residence in America,' 1834; Lady Charlotte Bury's 'Diary,' vols. iii., iv., 1839; Pigott's 'Records of Real Life,' 1839.

Collected Works : ed. by D. S. Meldrum, 1895, etc.

Life : by D. M. Moir in 1841 edn. of 'Annals of the Parish.'

*GARDINER (Samuel Rawson), b. **1829.** Born, at Ropley, Hants, 4 March 1829. At Winchester Coll., Sept. 1841 to Dec. 1847. Matric. Christ Ch., Oxford, 20 Oct. 1847; Student, 1850-51; B.A., 1851; Hon. Student, 1878. Married (i.) Isabella Irving, 8 Jan. 1856. Prof. of Mod. Hist., King's Coll., London, 1876-85. Hon. LL.D., Edinburgh, 1881. Civil List Pension, Aug. 1882. Married (ii.) Bertha Meriton Cordery, 15 July 1882. Fellow of All Souls' Coll., Oxford, 1884-91; M.A., 1884. Editor of 'English Historical Rev.,' since 1886. Fellow of Merton Coll., Oxford, July 1892.

Works : 'History of England. 1603-1616' (2 vols.), 1863; 'Prince Charles and the Spanish Marriage' (2 vols.), 1869; 'The Thirty Years' War,'

1874 ; 'History of England . . . 1624-1628 ' (2 vols.), 1875 ; 'The First Two Stuarts and the Puritan Revolution,' 1876 ; 'The Personal Government of Charles I.' (2 vols.), 1877 ; ' Outline of English History.' 1881 ; ' Introduction to the Study of English History ' (with J. B. Mullinger), 1881 ; ' The Fall of the Monarchy of Charles I.,' vols. i., ii., 1882 ; ' Illustrated English History,' 1883 ; ' History of England ... 1603-1642 ' (collected from among preceding, 10 vols.), 1883-84 ; ' Historical Biographies,' 1884 ; ' The History of the Great Civil War ' (3 vols.), 1886-91 ; ' A Student's History of England from the earliest times to 1885 ' (3 vols.), 1890-91 ; ' History of the Commonwealth and Protectorate ' (2 vols.), 1896-97 ; Cromwell's Place in History,' 1897.

He has *edited :* ' Parliamentary Debates in 1610,' 1862 ; ' Letters and other Documents illustrating the relations between England and Germany at the commencement of the Thirty Years' War ' (2 vols.), 1865-68 ; ' Narrative of the Spanish Marriage Treaty' (translated by himself), 1869 ; ' Notes of the Debates in the House of Lords . . . 1621, 1624, 1626,' 1870-79 ; 'The Fortescue Papers,' 1871 ; ' Debates in the House of Commons in 1625,' 1873 ; ' Documents relating to the Proceedings against W. Prynne,' 1877 ; 'The Hamilton Papers,' 1880 (' Addenda,' 1893) ; Browning's ' Strafford,' 1884 ; ' Reports of Cases in the Courts of Star Chamber and High Commission,' 1886 ; ' The Constitutional Documents of the Puritan Revolution,' 1889.

GARNETT (Richard), b. 1835. Born, at Lichfield, 27 Feb. 1835. Educated in London, 1844-50. Assistant in Library, British Museum, 1851; Assistant Keeper of Printed Books, 1875 ; Superintendent of Reading-Room, 1875-84 ; Keeper of Printed Books, 1890. Married Olivia Narney Singleton, 13 June 1863. Hon. LL.D., Edinburgh, April 1883. Contributor to ' Encycl. Brit.,' and ' Dict. of Nat. Biog.' President of Library Association, 1892-93. President of Biblio-graphical Soc., since 1895. C. B., 1895. Corresp. Memb. of Historical Soc. of Massachusetts, 1896.

Works: 'Primula' (anon.), 1858 ; ' Io in Egypt,' 1859 ; ' Poems from the German,' 1862 ; ' Idylls and Epigrams,' 1869 (the ' Epigrams ' republished as : ' A Chaplet from the Greek Anthology,' 1892) ; ' On the System of classifying books . . . at the British Museum,' 1878 ; ' On the Printing of the British Museum Catalogue ' [1882] ; 'The Late J. Winter Jones,' 1884 ; ' Photography in Public Libraries,' 1886 ; ' Changes at the British Museum since 1877,' 1887 ; ' Shelley and Lord Beaconsfield ' (priv. ptd.), 1887 ; ' Life of Thomas Carlyle,' 1887 ; ' Life of Emerson,' 1888 ; 'The Twilight of the Gods,' 1888 ; ' Life of John Milton,' 1890 [1889] ; ' Iphigenia in Delphi,' 1890 ; ' Poems,' 1893 ; 'The Age of Dryden,' 1895 ; ' William Blake,' 1895 ; ' Richmond,' 1896 ; ' Dante, Petrarch, Camoens : cxxiv Sonnets translated by R. Garnett,' 1896.

He has *edited :* R. Garnett (the elder)'s ' Philological Essays,' 1859 ; ' Relics of Shelley,' 1862 ; Coleridge's ' Notes on Stillingfleet,' 1875 ; ' Florilegium Amantis' (selection from Coventry Patmore's poems), 1879 ; Selected Poems of Shelley, 1880 ; 'Select Letters of Shelley,' 1882 ; T. Garnett's 'Essays in Natural History,' 1883 ; De Quincey's ' Confessions of an English Opium-Eater,' 1885 ; Pérès' ' Historic and other doubts,' 1885 ; Warter's ' An Old Shropshire Oak,' 1886-91 ; Lowell's ' My Study Windows,' 1887 ; Peacock's Works, 1891 ; Mary Shelley's ' Tales and Stories,' 1891 ; De Guaras' ' Accession of Queen Mary,' 1892 ; Beckford's ' Vathek,' 1893 ; Drayton's ' Battaile of Agincourt,' 1893 ; Milton's Prose selected, 1894 ; Miss Zimmern's trans. of Porphyry ' To his wife Marcella,' 1896.

GARRICK (David), 1717-1779. Born, in Hereford, 19 Feb. 1717. Educated at Lichfield Grammar School, 1727. At Lisbon for short time to learn wine trade, 1727. Pupil of Samuel Johnson, at Edial, 1736. To London with Johnson, March 1737. ☞ Entered at Lincoln's Inn, 9 March 1737. Set up wine business with his brother, 1738. Play 'Lethe' produced at Drury Lane, April 1740. Became an actor, 1741. Wrote plays, 1741-75. Played at Goodman's Fields Theatre, 1741-42; in Dublin, 1742; at Drury Lane, 1742-45; in Dublin in 1745 and 1746; at Covent Garden, 1745-47. Joint manager of Drury Lane with Lacy, 1747. Played at Drury Lane, 1747-63, 1765-76. Married Eva Marie Violetti, 22 June 1749. Visited Paris, 1752. Tour in France and Italy, 1763-65. Retired from stage, 1776. Died, in London, 20 Jan. 1779. Buried in Westminster Abbey.

Works: 'The Lying Valet,' 1741; 'Lethe,' 1741; 'Lilliput' (anon.), 1747; 'Miss in her Teens' (anon.), 1747; 'To Mr. Gray on his Odes' (anon.), [1757 ?]; 'The Guardian' (anon.), 1759; 'The Enchanter' (anon.), 1760; 'The Fribbleraid' (anon.), 1761; 'The Farmer's Return from London' (anon.), 1762; 'The Sick Monkey' (anon.), 1765; 'The Clandestine Marriage' (with G. Colman), 1766; 'Neck or Nothing' (anon.), 1766; 'Cymon' (anon.), 1767; 'A Peep behind the Curtain' (anon.), 1767; 'Ode upon dedicating a Building . . . to Shakespeare' (anon.), 1769; 'The Theatres' (anon.), 1772; 'Love in the Suds' (anon.), 1772; 'The Irish Widow' (anon.), 1772; 'Albumazar' (anon.), 1773; 'A Christmas Tale' (anon.), 1774; 'The Theatrical Candidates' (anon.), 1775; 'May Day' (anon.), 1775; 'Bon Ton' (anon.), 1775; 'The Fairies,' 1775.

He *adapted* plays by Shakespeare, Beaumont and Fletcher, Wycherley, Jonson, Fagan, Southern, etc.

Collected Works: 'Poetical Works' (2 vols.), 1785; 'Dramatic Works' (3 vols.), 1798; 'Private Correspondence' (2 vols.), 1831-32.

Life: by T. Davies, 1780; by Murphy, 1801; by P. Fitzgerald, 1868; by Jos. Knight, 1894.

GARTH (*Sir* **Samuel**), **1661-1719.** Born, in Yorkshire, 1661. At School at Ingleton. To Peterhouse, Camb., 1676; B.A., 1679; M.A., 1684. To Leyden to study medicine, 1687. M.D., Camb., 7 July 1691. Fellow of Coll. of Physicians, 26 June 1693; Gulstonian Lecturer, 1694; Harvey Orator, 1697. Censor, Oct. 1702. Mem. of Kit-Cat Club, 1703. Married Martha Beaufoy. Knighted, 1714. Physician in Ordinary to King, and Physician General to army. Died, in London, 18 Jan. 1719. Buried at Harrow.

Works: 'Oratio Laudatoria' (Harveian Oration), 1697; 'The Dispensary: a poem' (anon.), 1699 (2nd and 3rd edns. same year); 'A Prologue for the 4th of November,' 1711; 'A Complete Key to the seventh edition of "The Dispensary,"' 1714; 'Claremont' (anon.), 1715.

He *translated:* Demosthenes' 'First Philippick,' 1702; Ovid's 'Metamorphoses,' 1717.

Collected Works: 'Works,' 1769; 'Poetical Works,' 1771; ed. by Dr. Johnson, 1822.

Life: in 1769 edn. of Works; by Dr. Johnson, in 1822 edn. of Poems.

GASCOIGNE (**George**), **1530[?]-1577.** Born, at Cardington, Beds., 1530[?]. Educated, probably in Westmoreland, and at Trinity Coll., Camb. Took no degree. Entered at Middle Temple, 1547 [?]. Student of Gray's Inn, 1555. M.P. for Bedford, 1557-59. Married Mrs. Elizabeth Breton, 1566 [?]. Lived at Walthamstow from about 1566 till death. M.P. for Midhurst, 1572. Unseated on petition. To Holland, March 1572. Served for short time under Prince of Orange. Returned to England, 1575. Devoted himself to literature. Died, at Stamford, Lincolnshire, 7 Oct. 1577.

Works: 'A Hundred Sundrie Flowres,' unauthorized publication, 1572; authorized version, called 'The Posies of George Gascoigne,' 1575; 'The Glasse of Government,' 1575; 'The Princelye Pleasures at the Courte of Kenelworthe,' 1576; 'The Steele

Glas,' 1576 ; 'The Droomme of Doomesday,' 1576 ; 'A Delicate Diet,' 1576; 'The Spoyle of Antwerp' (anon.; attrib. to Gascoigne), [1577 ?].

He *edited :* Sir H. Gilbert's 'Discourse of a new Passage, etc.,' 1576 ; and contrib. commendatory verses to : Holiband's 'French Littleton,' 1566 ; 'The Noble Art of Venerie,' 1575 ; 'Cardanus Comfort,' 1576.

Collected Works : ed. by A. Jeffes, 1587 ; ed. by W. C. Hazlitt (2 vols.), 1868-70.

Life : by F. E. Schelling, 1894.

GASKELL (*Mrs.* **Elizabeth Cleghorn**), **1810-1865.** Born [Elizabeth Cleghorn Stevenson], in Chelsea, 29 Sept. 1810. Mother died Oct. 1810. Lived with her aunt in youth. At school at Stratford-on-Avon, 1825-27. Married to Rev. William Gaskell, 30 Aug. 1832. Lived in Manchester. Intimacy with William and Mary Howitt, and Dickens. Contrib. to 'Household Words' from first no., March 1850. Friendship with Charlotte Brontë begun, 1850. Active literary life. Died suddenly, at Holybourne, Hampshire, 12 Nov. 1865. Buried at Knutsford.

Works : 'Clopton Hall,' in Howitt's 'Visits to Remarkable Places,' 1840 ; 'Mary Barton' (anon.), 1848 ; 'The Moorland Cottage' (anon.), 1850 ; 'Ruth' (anon.), 1853 ; 'Cranford' (anon.), 1853 ; 'North and South' (anon.), 1855 ; 'Lizzie Leigh' (anon.), 1855 ; 'Life of Charlotte Brontë,' 1857 (2nd and 3rd edns. same year) ; 'Round the Sofa,' 1859 ; 'My Lady Ludlow,' 1859 ; 'Right at Last' (anon.), 1860 ; 'Lois the Witch,' 1861 ; 'A Dark Night's Work,' 1863 ; 'Sylvia's Lovers,' 1863 (2nd and 3rd edns. same year) ; 'The Grey Woman,' 1865 ; 'Hand and Heart,' 1865 ; 'Cousin Phyllis,' 1865.

Posthumous : 'Wives and Daughters,' 1866.

She *edited :* 'Mabel Vaughan,' 1857 ; C. A. Vecchi's 'Garibaldi at Caprera,' 1862.

Collected Works : in 7 vols., 1873.

GATTY (*Mrs.* **Margaret**), **1809-1873.** Born [Margaret Scott], at Burnham Rectory, Essex, 3 June 1809. Early taste for literature and art. Married to Rev. Alfred Gatty, 8 July 1839. Lived at Ecclesfield, Yorkshire. Ed. 'Aunt Judy's Mag.,' 1866-73. Died, at Ecclesfield, 4 Oct. 1873 ; buried there.

Works : 'Recollections of the Rev. A. J. Scott' (with her husband), 1842 ; 'The Family Godmothers,' 1851 ; 'Parables from Nature' (5 series), 1855-71 ; 'Worlds not Realized,' 1856 ; 'Proverbs Illustrated,' 1857 ; 'The Poor Incumbent,' 1858 ; 'Legendary Tales,' 1858 ; 'Aunt Judy's Tales,' 1859 [1858] ; 'The Human Face Divine,' 1860 ; 'The Old Folks from Home,' 1862 ; 'Aunt Judy's Letters,' 1862 ; 'British Seaweeds,' 1863 ; 'Aunt Sally's Life' (reprinted from 'Aunt Judy's Letters'), 1865 ; 'Domestic Pictures,' 1866 ; 'The Children's Mission Army' (from 'Mission Life'), 1869 ; 'Mission Shillings,' 1869 ; 'Waifs and Strays of Natural History,' 1871 ; 'Select Parables from Nature,' 1872 ; 'A Book of Emblems,' 1872 ; 'The Mother's Book of Poetry,' 1872 ; 'The Book of Sun Dials,' 1872.

She *translated :* Macé's 'History of a Bit of Bread,' 1864 ; and *edited :* Mrs. J. H. Gatty's 'Melchior's Dream,' 1862.

Life : in 1885 edn. of 'Parables from Nature.'

*****GAY** (**John**), **1685-1732.** Born, at Barnstaple, 1685 ; baptized 16 Sept. 1685. Educated at Barnstaple Grammar School. For short time apprentice in a London shop ; returned to Barnstaple ; thence again to London, probably as secretary to Aaron Hill. Sec. to Duchess of Monmouth, 1712-14. Contrib. to 'Guardian,' 1713. 'The Wife of Bath' produced at Drury Lane, 12 May 1713. In Hanover as sec. to Lord Clarendon, 8 June to Sept., 1714. 'What-d'ye-Call-it' produced at Drury Lane, 23 Feb. 1715. 'Three Hours after Marriage' (written with Pope and Arbuthnot), Drury Lane, 16 Jan. 1717. To Aix with

William Pulteney (afterwards Earl of Bath), 1717. At Cockthorpe with Lord Harcourt, 1718. Severe losses in South Sea Bubble. Under patronage of Duchess of Queensberry from 1720. 'The Captives' produced at Drury Lane, 15 Jan. 1724; 'The Beggar's Opera,' Lincoln's Inn Fields, 29 Jan. 1728; sequel, 'Polly,' forbidden by Lord Chamberlain, 1729; 'Acis and Galatea,' Haymarket, May 1732; 'Achilles' (posthumous), Covent Garden, 10 Feb. 1733. Died, in London, 4 Dec. 1732. Buried in Westminster Abbey.

Works : 'Wine,' 1708; 'The Present State of Wit' (anon.), 1711; 'The Mohocks' (anon.), 1713; 'Rural Sports,' 1713; 'The Wife of Bath,' 1713; 'The Fan,' 1714; 'The Shepherd's Week,' 1714; 'A Letter to a Lady' (anon.), 1714; 'What-d'ye-Call-it,' 1715; 'A Journey to Exeter,' 1715; 'Court Poems,' 1716; 'God's Revenge against Punning' (under pseud. of 'Sir James Baker'), 1716; 'Trivia,' 1716; 'An Admonition . . . to the famous Mr. Frapp' (under pseud. of Sir James Baker), 1717; 'Letter to W— L—, Esq.,' 1717; 'Epistle to Pulteney,' 1717; 'Three Hours after Marriage' (with Pope and Arbuthnot), 1717; 'Two Epistles,' [1720 ?]; 'Poems' (2 vols.), 1720; 'A Panegyrical Epistle' (anon.; attrib. to Gay), 1721; ' An Epistle to . . . Henrietta, Duchess of Marlborough,' 1722; 'The Captives,' 1724 (2nd edn. same year); 'Fables,' first series, 1727; second ser., 1738; 'The Beggar's Opera,' 1728 (2nd and 3rd edns. same year); 'Polly,' 1729 (another edn. same year); 'Acis and Galatea' (anon.), 1732.

Posthumous : 'Achilles,' 1733; 'The Distress'd Wife,' 1743; 'The Rehearsal at Goatham,' 1754; 'Gay's Chair : poems never before printed,' 1820.

Collected Works : 'Plays,' 1760; 'Works' (4 vols.), 1770; ed. by Dr. Johnson (2 vols.), 1779; ed. by J. Underhill (2 vols.), 1893.

Life : by Coxe, 1797; by W. H. K. Wright, in 1889 edn. of ' Fables';

by J. Underhill in 1893 edn. of Poems.

GENEST (John), 1764-1839. Born, at Dunker's Hill, Devonshire, 1764. To Westminster School, 15 June 1774. To Trin. Coll., Camb., as Pensioner, 9 May 1780; B.A., 1784; M.A., 1787. Ordained, 1785[?]. Private Chaplain to Duke of Ancaster. At Bath for health, 1830-39. Died there, 15 Dec. 1539; buried in St. James's Church, Bath.

Works : 'Some Account of the English Stage' (anon.; 10 vols.), 1832.

GIBBON (Edward), 1737-1794. Born, at Putney, 27 April 1737. To school in Putney; afterwards at school at Kingston-on-Thames, Jan. 1746 to 1748 [?]. At Westminster School, Jan. 1748 to 1750. To Bath for health, 1750. To school at Esher, Jan. 1752. At Magdalen Coll., Oxford, 3 April 1752 to June 1753. To Lausanne, as pupil of M. Pavillard, June 1753. Returned to England, Aug. 1758. Held commission in Hampshire militia, 12 June 1759 to 1770. In Paris, 28 Jan. to 9 May, 1763; at Lausanne, May 1763 to April 1764; in Italy, April 1764 to May 1765. Returned to England; lived with father at Buriton. After father's death settled in London, 1772. Prof. of Ancient History at Royal Academy, 1774. M.P. for Liskeard, 11 Oct. 1774 to Sept. 1780. Lord Commissioner of Trade and Plantations, 1779. M.P. for Lymington, June 1781 to March 1784. Settled at Lausanne, Sept. 1783. Visit to England, 1788 and 1793. Died, in London, 16 Jan. 1794. Buried at Fletching, Sussex.

Works : 'Essai sur l'étude de la Littérature' (in French), 1761 (Eng. trans., 1764); 'Mémoires Littéraires de la Grande-Bretagne' (with Deyverdun), 2 vols., 1767-68; 'Critical Observations on the Sixth Book of the Æneid' (anon.), 1770; ' History of the Decline and Fall·of the Roman Empire' (6 vols.), 1776-88 (2nd and 3rd edns. in same period).

Posthumous: 'An Historical View of Christianity' (with Bolingbroke, Voltaire, and others), 1806 ; 'Antiquities of the House of Brunswick,' ed. by Lord Sheffield, 1814 ; 'Memoirs,' ed. by Lord Sheffield, 1827 ; 'Life' (autobiog.), ed. by H. H. Milman, 1839 ; 'The Autobiographies of Edward Gibbon,' ed. by J. Murray, 1896 ; 'Private Letters,' ed. by R. E. Prothero, 1896.

Collected Works: 'Miscellaneous Works,' in 2 vols., 1796 ; in 5 vols., 1814.

Life: by J. C. Morrison ('English Men of Letters' series), 1878.

GIFFORD (William), **1756 - 1826.** Born, at Ashburton, April 1756. Educated at Ashburton Free School. Afterwards at work on a farm. At sea, 1767-70. To school again at Ashburton, 1770. Apprenticed to shoemaker, 1 Jan. 1772. To school again, 1776. Matric. at Exeter Coll., Oxford, as Bible Clerk, 16 Feb. 1779 ; B.A., 10 Oct. 1782. Travelling tutor to son of Lord Grosvenor, 1781. Unsuccessfully prosecuted for libel in 'The Baviad,' 1797. Edited 'Anti-Jacobin,' Nov. 1797 to July 1798. Editor of 'Quarterly Review,' Feb. 1809 to Sept. 1824. Held posts of Commissioner of Lottery and Paymaster of Gentlemen - Pensioners. Died, in London, 31 Dec. 1826 ; buried in Westminster Abbey.

Works: 'Easton Chronicle' (anon.), 1789 ; 'The Baviad' (anon.), 1791 ; 'The Mæviad' (anon.), 1795 (two preceding pubd. together, 1797); 'Epistle to Peter Pindar' (anon.), 1800 ; 'An Examination of the strictures . . . on the translation of Juvenal,' 1803.

He *translated:* 'Juvenal' (with *autobiography*), 1802 ; 'Persius,'1821 ; and *edited:* Massinger's 'Works,' 1805 ; Ben Jonson's 'Works,' 1816 ; Ford's 'Dramatic Works,' 1827 ; Shirley's 'Dramatic Works,' 1833.

* **GILBERT** (William Schwenck), b. **1836.** Born, in London, 18 Nov. 1836. At Great Ealing School, Michaelmas 1850 to Michaelmas 1852. To London University, 1852 ; B.A.,

1857. Intended to enter Royal Artillery, but postponement of exam. rendered him ineligible on score of age. Student of Inner Temple, 11 Oct. 1855 ; called to Bar, 17 Nov. 1863. Clerk in Privy Council Office, 1857-62. Joined Northern Circuit and practised for four years ; after which devoted himself to literary work. Married Lucy Agnes Turner, 6 Aug. 1867. 'Dulcamara' produced at St. James's Theatre, Jan. 1866 ; 'Happy Arcadia' at Gallery of Illustration ; 'The Palace of Truth,' Haymarket, 20 Nov. 1870 ; 'Sensation Novel,' Gallery of Illustration, Dec. 1871 ; 'Pygmalion and Galatea,' Haymarket, 9 Dec. 1871 ; 'Thespis,' Gaiety, 20 Dec. 1871 ; 'The Wicked World,' Haymarket, 4 Jan. 1873 ; 'Charity,' Haymarket, 3 Jan. 1874 ; 'Sweethearts,' Prince of Wales's, 7 Nov. 1874 ; 'Trial By Jury,' Royalty, 25 March 1875 ; 'Broken Hearts,' Court, 9 Dec. 1875 ; 'Tom Cobb,' St. James's, 1876 ; 'Dan'l Druce,' Haymarket, Sept. 1876 ; 'Engaged,' Haymarket, 3 Oct. 1877 ; 'The Sorcerer,' Opera Comique, 17 Nov. 1877 ; 'The Ne'er-do-Weel,' Olympic, 1878 ; 'Gretchen,' Olympic, March 1879 ; 'Foggerty's Fairy,' Criterion, 15 Dec. 1881 ; 'H.M.S. Pinafore,' Opera Comique, 28 May 1878 ; 'The Pirates of Penzance,' Opera Comique, 3 April 1880 ; 'Patience,' Savoy, 23 April 1881 ; 'Iolanthe,' Savoy, 25 Nov. 1882 ; 'Princess Ida,' Savoy, 5 Jan. 1884 ; 'Comedy and Tragedy,' Lyceum, 26 Jan. 1884 ; 'The Mikado,' Savoy, 14 March 1885 ; 'Ruddigore,' Savoy, 22 Jan. 1887 ; 'The Yeomen of the Guard,' Savoy, 3 Oct. 1888 ; 'Brantinghame Hall,' St. James's, 29 Nov. 1888 ; 'The Gondoliers,' Savoy, 7 Dec. 1889 ; 'The Mountebanks,' Lyric, 4 Jan. 1892 ; 'Utopia,' Savoy, 7 Oct. 1893 ; 'His Excellency,' Lyric, 27 Oct. 1894 ; 'The Grand Duke,' Savoy, 7 March 1896. . Appointed J.P. for Middlesex, June 1891.

Works: 'La Vivandière, 1868 ; 'Robert the Devil,' 1868 ; '"Bab" Ballads,' 1869 [1868]; 'More "Bab" Ballads,' [1873]; 'The Wicked World (privately printed), 1873 ; 'Trial By Jury,' 1875 ; ' Original Plays ' (2 series), 1876 - 81 (reissue, with 3rd series, 1886-95) ; ' The Sorcerer,' 1877 ; ' H.M.S. Pinafore,' 1878 ; 'Gretchen,' 1879 ; 'The Pirates of Penzance,' 1880 ; ' Patience,' 1881 ; ' Iolanthe,' 1882 ; ' Princess Ida,' 1884 ; ' Original Comic Operas ' (coll.), 1885 ; 'The Mikado,' 1885 ; ' Ruddigore,' 1887 ; 'The Yeomen of the Guard,' 1888 ; 'The Gondoliers,' 1889 ; ' Foggerty's Fairy, and other tales,' 1890 [1889] ; ' Original Comic Operas ' (collected), 1890 ; 'The Mountebanks,' 1892 ; ' Utopia,' 1893 ; · 'His Excellency' [1894] ; 'The Grand Duke,' 1896.

[Editions of his plays not mentioned above have, for the most part, appeared in ' Lacy's Acting Edition of Plays.']

*GLADSTONE (William Ewart), b. 1809. Born, in Liverpool, 29 Dec. 1809. At Eton, 1821-27. Matric. Ch. Ch., Oxford, 23 Jan. 1828. Student, 1829-39 ; B.A., 1832 ; M.A., 1834 ; Hon. Student, 1867 ; Hon. D.C.L., 5 July 1848 ; Hon. Fellow All Souls' Coll., 1858. M.P. for Newark, 1832-45. Student at Lincoln's Inn, 25 Jan. 1833. Junior Lord of Treasury, Dec. 1834 ; Under Sec. for Colonies, Jan. to April, 1835. Married Catherine Glynne, 25 July 1839. Privy Councillor, 1841. Vice-President of Board of Trade, Sept. 1841 to May 1843 ; President, May 1843 to Feb. 1845. Master of Mint, Sept. 1841 to Feb. 1845. Sec. of State for Colonies, Dec. 1845 to July 1846. M.P. for Oxford Univ., 1847 ; re-elected, 1852 - 65. Chancellor of Exchequer, Dec. 1852 to Feb. 1855. Lord High Commissioner to Ionian Islands, winter 1858-59. Chancellor of Exchequer, June 1859 to July 1866. Lord Rector Edinburgh Univ., 1859-65. M.P. for South Lancashire, 1865-68 ; for Greenwich, 1868-74 ; re-elected 1874-80. Premier and First Lord of Treasury, Dec. 1868 to Feb. 1874 ; Chancellor of Exchequer, Aug. 1873 to Feb. 1874.

Resigned Leadership of Liberal Party. Jan. 1875. Visit to Ireland, Oct. to Nov., 1877; received Freedom of City of Dublin. Lord Rector of Glasgow Univ., Nov. 1877. M.P. for Midlothian, 1880. Premier and Chancellor of Exchequer, April 1880 to Dec. 1882 ; Premier and First Lord of Treasury, Dec. 1882 to June 1885. Premier and Lord Privy Seal, Feb. to July, 1886. Premier, First Lord of Treasury and Lord Privy Seal, Aug. 1892 to March 1894. Romanes Lecturer, Oxford, Oct. 1892. Freedom of City of Liverpool, 3 Dec. 1892. Retired from public life, March 1894.

Works [exclusive of political speeches, addresses, and pamphlets] : 'The State in its relations with the Church,' 1838 ; 'Church Principles considered in their results,' 1840 ; ' Manual of Prayers from the Liturgy,' 1845 ; ' On the place of Homer in Classical Education,' 1857 ; ' Studies on Homer and the Homeric Age' (3 vols.), 1858 ; ' " Ecce Homo," ' 1868 ; ' A Chapter of Autobiography,' 1868 ; ' Juventus Mundi,' 1869 ; ' The Vatican Decrees,' 1874 ; ' Vaticanism,' 1875 ; ' Rome and the Newest Fashions in Religion ' (a reprint of the two preceding, with 'Speeches of the Pope '), 1875 ; 'The Church of England and Ritualism ' (from ' Contemporary Rev.'), 1876 ; ' Homeric Synchronism,' 1876 ; ' Homer,' 1878 ; ' Gleanings of Past Years ' (7 vols.), 1879 ; ' Landmarks of Homeric Study,' 1890 ; 'The Impregnable Rock of Holy Scripture ' (from ' Good Words '), 1890 ; ' An Introduction to the People's Bible History,' 1895 ; ' Studies Subsidiary to the Works of Bishop Butler,' 1896 ; ' On the Condition of Man in a Future Life,' pt. i., 1896.

He has *translated* : Farini's 'The Roman State from 1815 to 1850,' 1851 ; the 'Odes ' of Horace, 1894 ; and *edited* : Bishop Butler's 'Works,' 1896.

GODWIN (William), 1756-1836. Born, at Wisbeach, Cambs., 3 March 1756. Family removed to Deben-

8

ham, Suffolk, 1758 ; to Guestwick, Norfolk, 1760. At school at Guestwick, 1760-64 ; at Hindolveston, 1764-67 ; with tutor, 1767-71. Master at Hindolveston School, 1771-73. To Hoxton Academy, London, 1773. Minister at Ware, Herts, 1778. In London, 1779. Minister at Stowmarket, Suffolk, 1780-82 ; returned to London, 1782. Minister at Beaconsfield in 1783 ; gave up ministry that year and took to literature. Intimacy with Mary Wollstonecraft begun, 1796 ; married her, 29 March 1797. Daughter Mary (afterwards Mrs. Shelley) born 30 Aug. 1797 ; wife died, 10 Sept. 1797. Married Mrs. Mary Jane Clairmont, Dec. 1801. Friendship with Coleridge, Lamb, Wordsworth. 'Tragedy of Antonio' produced at Drury Lane, 13 Dec. 1800 ; 'Faulkener' produced, Dec. 1807. Financial troubles. Wife started publishing business. Friendship with Shelley begun, 1812. Bankrupt, 1822. Yeoman Usher of Exchequer, 1833 - 36. Died, in London, 7 April 1836. Buried in Old St. Pancras Churchyard.

Works : 'Life of Chatham' (anon.), 1783 ; 'Sketches of History' 1784 ; 'Enquiry concerning Political Justice,' 1793 ; 'Things as they are ; or, the Adventures of Caleb Williams,' 1794 ; 'Cursory Strictures on the Charge of Chief-Justice Eyre,' 1794 ; 'The Enquirer,' 1797 ; 'Memoirs of the Author of a Vindication of the Rights of Women,' 1798 (2nd edn. same year) ; 'St. Leon,' 1799 ; 'Antonio,' 1800 ; 'Thoughts occasioned by . . . Dr. Parr's Spital Sermon,' 1801 ; 'Life of Geoffrey Chaucer,' 1803 ; 'Fleetwood,' 1805 (French trans. same year) ; 'Fables' (under pseud. 'Edward Baldwin'), 1805 ; 'The Looking-Glass' (under pseud. 'Theophilus Marcliffe,' attrib. to Godwin), 1805 ; 'Faulkener,' 1807 ; 'Essay on Sepulchres,' 1809 ; 'Dramas for Children' (anon.), 1809 ; 'History of Rome' (by 'E. Baldwin'), 1809 ; 'New and improved Grammar of the English Language' (anon.), 1812 ; 'Lives of Edward and John Philips,'

1815 ; 'Mandeville,' 1817 ; 'Of Population,' 1820 ; 'Life of Lady Jane Grey' (by 'E. Baldwin '), 1824 ; 'History of the Commonwealth of England' (4 vols.), 1824-28 ; 'The History of England for the use of Schools' (by 'E. Baldwin '), 1827 ; 'History of Greece' (by 'E. Baldwin ' 1828 ; 'Cloudesley' (anon.), 1830 ; 'Thoughts on Man,' 1831 ; 'Deloraine,' 1833 ; 'Lives of the Necromancers,' 1834.

Posthumous : 'Essays,' 1873.

He *translated :* Lord Lovat's 'Memoirs,' 1797 ; and *edited :* Mary Godwin's 'Posthumous Works,' 1798 ; his son (W. Godwin)'s 'Transfusion,' 1835.

Life : by C. Kegan Paul, 1876.

• [His first wife, **Mary Wollstonecraft**, was born 27 April 1759. Companion to a lady, 1778-80. Kept school at Newington Green with her sister, 1783-85. Acquaintance with Dr. Johnson. Governess in Lord Kingsborough's family, 1787-88. To London ; worked as reader and translator for Dr. Johnson, 1788-92. Met William Godwin, Nov. 1791. To Paris, 1792. Lived with Gilbert Imlay, 1793-96. Attempted suicide, 1796. Intimacy with William Godwin begun, 1796 ; married to him, 29 March 1797. Died, in London, 10 Sept. 1797.

Works : 'Thoughts on the Education of Daughters,' 1787: 'Original Stories' (anon.), 1788 ; 'Vindication of the Rights of Men,' 1790 ; 'Vindication of the Rights of Women,' vol. i., 1792 (no more pub.) ; 'Historical and Moral View of . . . the French Revolution,' vol. i., 1794 (no more pub.) ; 'Letters written in Norway,' 1796. *Posthumous :* 'Posthumous Works,' ed. by W. Godwin (4 vols.), 1798 ; 'Letters to Imlay,' ed. by C. Kegan Paul, 1879. She *translated :* Salzmann's 'Elements of Morality,' 1790.]

* GOLDSMITH (Oliver). 1728-1774. Born, at Pallas, Co. Longford, 10 Nov. 1728. Family removed to Lissoy, 1730. At village school, 1734-35 ;

at school at Elphin, 1736-39 ; at Athlone, 1739-41 ; at Edgeworthstown, 1741-44. To Trin. Coll., Dublin, as Sizar, 11 June 1744 ; Smyth Exhibition, 1747 ; B.A., 27 Feb. 1749 With his mother at Ballymahon, 1749 - 51. Rejected as a clergyman, 1751. Private tutorship, 1751-52. To Edinburgh to study medicine, autumn of 1752. To Leyden, 1754. Travelled on the Continent, 1755-56. Possibly took M.B. degree at Louvain or Padua. Returned to London, Feb. 1756. Set up in practice as physician. Master at school at Peckham, winter of 1756 to 1757. Contrib. to 'Monthly Review,' April to Sept., 1757, Dec. 1758 ; to 'Literary Mag.,' Jan. 1757, Jan. to May, 1758 ; to 'Critical Review,' Nov. 1757, Jan. to Aug., 1759, March 1760 ; to 'The Busybody,' Oct. 1759. Ed. 'Lady's Mag.,' 1759-60. Friendship with Johnson begun, 1761. Contrib. to 'The Public Ledger,' Jan. to Feb., 1760 ; to the 'British Mag.,' Feb. 1760 to Jan. 1763. Visit to Bath for health, 1762. Removed to Islington, winter of 1762. Tried again to set up as physician, 1765. Settled in Temple, 1767 ; lived there till death. 'The Good-natured Man' produced at Covent Garden, 29 Jan. 1768 ; 'She Stoops to Conquer,' Covent Garden, 15 March 1773 ; 'The Grumbler' (adapted from S₁d-ley), Covent Garden, 8 May 1773. Contrib. to 'Westminster Mag.,' Jan. to Feb., 1773 ; to 'Universal Mag.,' April 1774. Died, in London, 4 April 1774. Buried in the Temple.

Works : 'Memoirs of a Protestant' (anon.), 1758 ; 'Enquiry into the Present State of Polite Learning' (anon.), 1759 ; 'The Bee' (anon. ; 8 nos.), 1759 ; 'A History of the Seven Years' War,' 1761 ; 'A Poetical Dictionary' (anon.), 1761 ; 'History of Mecklenburgh,' 1762 ; 'The Mystery Revealed,' 1742 [1762] ; 'The Citizen of the World' (anon.), 1762 ; 'Life of Richard Nash' (anon.), 1762 ; 'The Art of Poetry on a New Plan' (anon. ; attrib. to Goldsmith), 1762 ; 'The Martial Review' (anon.), 1763 ;

'An History of England' (anon.), 1764 ; 'The Traveller,' 1765 ; 'Essays,' 1765 ; 'The Vicar of Wakefield' (2 vols.), 1766 ; 'History of Little Goody Two-Shoes' (anon. ; attrib. to Goldsmith), 1766 ; 'The Good-natured Man,' 1768 ; 'The Roman History' (2 vols.), 1769 (abridged by Goldsmith, 1772) ; 'The Deserted Village,' 1770 ; 'The Life of Thomas Parnell,' 1770 ; 'Life of . . . Viscount Bolingbroke' (anon.), 1770 ; 'The History of England' (4 vols.), 1771 (abridged, 1774) ; 'Threnodia Augustalis,' 1772 ; 'She Stoops to Conquer,' 1773 ; 'Retaliation,' 1774 (2nd to 5th edns. same year) ; 'The Grecian History' (2 vols.), 1774 ; 'A History of the Earth' (8 vols.), 1774.

Posthumous : 'Miscellaneous Works,' 1775 ; 'The Haunch of Venison,' 1776 ; 'A Survey of Experimental Philosophy' (2 vols.), 1776 ; 'Poems and Plays,' 1777 ; 'Poetical and Dramatic Works,' 1780 ; 'The Captivity,' 1836 ; 'Asem, the Man-Hater,' 1877.

He *translated :* (under pseud. of 'James Willington') Bergerac's 'Memoirs of a Protestant,' 1758 ; Plutarch's 'Lives' (with J. Collyer), 1762 ; Formey's 'Concise History of Philosophy,' 1766 ; Scarron's 'Comic Romance,' 1776 ; and *edited :* Newbery's 'Art of Poetry,' 1762 ; 'Poems for Young Ladies' (anon.), 1767 ; 'Beauties of English Poesy,' 1767 ; T. Parnell's 'Poems,' 1770.

Collected Works : in 5 vols., ed. by J. W. M. Gibbs, 1884-86.

Life : by J. Forster, 6th edn., 1877 ; by Austin Dobson, 1888.

GORE (*Mrs.* **Catherine Grace Frances**), **1799-1861.** Born [Catherine Grace Frances Moody], at East Retford, 1799. Early literary precocity. Married to Capt. Charles Arthur Gore, 15 Feb. 1823. 'The School for Coquettes' produced at Haymarket Theatre, 1831 ; 'Lords and Commons' at Drury Lane; 'The King's Seal,' 1835 ; 'King O'Neil,' 1835 ; 'The Queen's Champion,' 1835; 'The Maid of Croissy,' 1835. Actively

8—2

employed in novel-writing, also composed music. Lived in France for some years from 1832. Comedy, 'Quid pro Quo,' won £500 prize offered by Webster at Haymarket Theatre; produced there, 18 June 1844. Died, at Lyndhurst, Hampshire, 29 Jan. 1861; buried in Kensal Green cemetery.

Works: 'Theresa Marchmont,'1824; 'The Bond,' 1824; 'The Lettre de Cachet' (anon.), 1827; 'The Reign of Terror' (anon.), 1827; 'Hungarian Tales' (anon.), 1829; 'Romance of Real Life' (anon.), 1829; 'Women as they are; or, the Manners of the Day' (anon.), 1830 (2nd edn. same year); 'Pin Money' (anon.), 1831; 'The Tuileries' (anon.), 1831; 'Mothers and Daughters' (anon.), 1831; 'The Historical Traveller,' 1831; 'The Fair of May Fair' (anon.), 1832; 'The Opera' (anon.), 1832; 'The Sketch-Book of Fashion' (anon.), 1833; 'Polish Tales' (anon.), 1833; 'The Hamiltons' (anon.), 1834; 'The Maid of Croissy,' 1835; 'King O'Neil,' 1835; 'The Diary of a Désennuyée' (anon.), 1836; 'Mrs. Armytage' (anon.), 1836; 'Memoirs of a Peeress' (anon.), 1837; 'Stokeshill Place' (anon.), 1837; 'The Heir of Selwood' (anon.), 1838; 'Mary Raymond,' 1838; 'The Rose Fancier's Manual,' 1838; 'The Woman of the World' (anon.), 1838; 'The Cabinet Minister' (anon.) 1839; 'The Courtier of the Days of Charles II.,' 1839; 'Dacre of the South,' 1840; 'The Dowager,' 1840; 'Preferment,' 1840; 'Cecil' (anon.), 1841; 'Cecil a Peer' (sequel to preceding), 1841; 'Greville,' 1841; 'The Soldier of Lyons,' 1841; 'The Ambassador's Wife,' 1842; 'The Man of Fortune,' 1842; 'Ormington' (anon.), 1842; 'The Banker's Wife,' 1843; 'The Inundation,' 1843; 'Modern Chivalry' (under initials: C. F. G.), 1843; 'The Money-Lender,' 1843; 'Quid pro Quo' (under initials: C. F. G.), 1844; 'Agathonia' (anon.), 1844; 'The Birthright,' 1844; 'The Popular Member,' 1844; 'Self' (anon.). 1845; 'The Snow Storm,' 1845; 'The Story of a Royal Favourite,' 1845; 'The Débutante,' 1846; 'New Year's Day,' 1846 (2nd edn. same year); 'Men of Capital' 1846; 'Peers and Parvenus,' 1846; 'Sketches of English Character,' 1846; 'The Queen of Denmark,' 1846; 'Castles in the Air,' 1847; 'Temptation and Atonement,' 1847; 'The Diamond and the Pearl,' 1848; 'The Inundation,' [1848]; 'A Good Night's Rest,' 1852; 'The Dean's Daughter,' 1853; 'The Lost Son,' 1854; 'Progress and Prejudice,' 1854; 'Mammon,' 1855; 'A Life's Lessons,' 1856; 'The Two Aristocracies,' 1857; 'Heckington,' 1857.

She *contributed* to: 'The Tales of all Nations,' 1827; 'Heath's Picturesque Annual,' 1832; The Edinburgh Tales' (vols. i.-iii.), 1845; 'The Tale Book,' 1859.

Posthumous: 'The Royal Favourite,' 1863.

She *edited:* 'The Lover and the Husband,' 1841; 'The Woman of a Certain Age,' 1841; 'Fascination,' 1842; 'Modern French Life,' 1842; 'The Queen of Denmark,' 1846; and probably was the translator of Saintine's 'Picciola,' 1837.

*GOSSE (Edmund William), b. 1849. Born, in London, 21 Sept. 1849. Educated privately. Assistant in Library, British Museum, 1867 - 75. Appointed Translator to Board of Trade, 1875. Married Ellen Epps, 13 Aug. 1875. Clark Lecturer on Eng. Lit., Trin. Coll., Camb., 1884-86, and 1886-89. Hon. M.A., Camb., 1885. Visit to U.S.A., winter of 1884-85; lectured before various Universities. Presided at inauguration of Shelley memorial at Horsham, 1892; of Keats memorial, Hamps ead, 1894. Resides in London.

Works: 'Madrigals, Songs, and Sonnets' (with J. A. Blaikie), 1870; 'On Viol and Flute,' 1873; 'The Ethical Condition of the Early Scandinavian People' [1874]; 'King Erik,' 1876; 'The Unknown Lover,' 1878; 'Studies in the Literature of Northern Europe,' 1879; 'New Poems,' 1879; 'Gray' ('Eng. Men of

Letters' series), 1882 ; 'Memoir of Thomas Lodge' (priv. ptd.), 1832 ; 'Seventeenth Century Studies,' 1883 ; 'Cecil Lawson,' 1883 ; 'A Critical Essay on . . . George Tinworth,' 1883 ; 'An Epistle to Dr. O. W. Holmes' (in verse), 1884 ; 'The Masque of Painters' (priv. ptd.), 1885 ; 'From Shakespeare to Pope,' 1885 ; 'Firdausi in Exile, and other poems,' 1885 ; 'Raleigh,' 1886 ; Life of William Congreve,' 1888 ; 'A History of Eighteenth Century Literature, 1660-1780,' 1889 ; 'The Life of P. H. Gosse,' 1890; 'Robert Browning : personalia,' 1890 ; 'Gossip in a Library,' 1891; 'The Secret of Narcisse,' 1892 ; 'Wolcott Balestier' (priv. ptd.), 1892 ; 'Questions at Issue,' 1893; 'In Russet and Silver,' 1894 ; 'The Jacobean Poets,' 1894 ; 'Critical Kit - Kats,' 1896.

He has *translated :* Ibsen's 'Hedda Gabler,' 1891 ; Ibsen's 'Master Builder' (with W. Archer), 1893 ; La Motte Fouqué's 'Undine,' 1897 ; and *edited :* Works of Samuel Rowlands, 1880 ; 'English Odes,' 1881 ; Works of Thomas Lodge, 1882 ; Gray's Works, 1884 ; Sir Joshua Reynolds' 'Discourses,' 1884 ; 'Selected Poems of Gray,' 1885 ; Shirley's Plays, 1888 ; Beddoes' 'Poetical Works,' 1890 ; E. Marx-Aveling's translation of Ibsen's 'Lady from the Sea,' 1890 ; 'Heinemann's International Library,' 1890, etc. ; Nash's 'Unfortunate Traveller,' 1892 ; Zola's 'Attack on the Mill,' 1892 ; Beddoes' Letters, 1894 ; Björnson's Novels, 1894, etc. ; 'Conversations of James Northcote,' 1894 ; Smith's 'Nollekens and his Times,' 1894 ; 'The Tavern of the Three Virtues,' 1896 ; La Motte Fouqué's 'Undine,' 1896 ; Carlyle's 'On Heroes,' 1896 ; 'Literatures of the World ' series, 1897, etc.

GOWER (John), 1325[?]-1408. Born about 1325 [?]. Probably travelled abroad in his youth, and lived subsequently mainly in Kent. Married Agnes Groundolf, 25 Jan. 1397. Resided at Southwark. Became blind, 1400. Died Sept.[?]

1408 ; buried in St. Saviour's, Southwark.

Works : 'Confessio Amantis,' ed. by Caxton, 1493 [1483].

Posthumous: 'Balades and other poems' (pubd. by Roxburghe Club), 1818 ; 'Poema quod docitur Vox Clamantis ' (Roxburghe Club), 1850.

GRATTAN (Thomas Colley), 1792-1864. Born, in Dublin, 1792. At school at Athy. Studied law in Dublin for short time, then took commission in militia. To Bordeaux (intending to go thence to Venezuela), 1818 ; married Eliza O'Donnel and settled near Bordeaux, 1818. Afterwards lived in Paris. Contrib. to 'Westminster Rev.,' Edinburgh Rev., 'New Monthly Mag.,' etc. Started and ed. 'The Paris Monthly Review of British and Continental Literature ' (15 nos.), Jan. 1822 to April 1823. Play, 'Ben Nazir,' produced at Drury Lane, 21 May 1827. In Brussels, 1828-30. In Holland and Germany, 1830-32. Gentleman of Privy Chamber to William IV., 1832. Returned to Brussels. Contrib. to 'The Times' letters on the Brussels Riots, 1834. At Boston, U.S.A., as British Consul to State of Massachusetts, 1839-46. Assisted in proceedings for delimitation of N.E. boundary, 1842. Returned to England, 1846. Consulship transferred from him to his eldest son. Died, in London, 4 July 1864.

Works : 'Philibert,' 1819 ; 'Highways and Byways,' 1st ser. (2 vols., anon.), 1823 ; 2nd ser. (3 vols., anon.), 1825 ; 3rd ser. (3 vols., anon.), 1827 ; 'The History of Switzerland ' (anon.), 1825 ; 'Ben Nazir,' 1827 ; 'Traits of Travel' (3 vols., anon.), 1829 ; 'The History of the Netherlands' (in vol. x. of 'Lardner's Cyclopædia'), 1830 ; 'The Heiress of Bruges,' 1831 ; 'Jacqueline of Holland,' 1831 ; 'Legends of the Rhine' (anon.), 1832 ; 'Agnes de Mansfeldt,' 1836 ; 'The Boundary Question,' 1843 ; 'The Master Passion,' 1845 ; 'Chance Medley of Matter,' 1845 ; 'The Cagot's Hut,' 1852 ; 'The Forfeit Hand,' 1857 ; 'The Curse of the

Black Lady,' 1857 ; 'Civilized America' (2 vols.). 1859 ; 'England and the Disrupted States of America,' 1861 ; 'Beaten Paths,' 1862.

GRAY (Thomas), 1716-1771. Born, in London, 26 Dec. 1716. Early education at Burnham. To Eton, 1727[?]. To Pembroke Hall, Camb., as Pensioner, summer of 1734 ; transferred to Peterhouse, 9 Oct. 1734. Took no degree ; left University, Sept. 1738. Travelled abroad with Horace Walpole, March 1739 to Sept. 1740. Returned to Peterhouse, Camb., as Fellow-Commoner, Oct. 1742 ; LL.B., 1743. Lived chiefly at Cambridge for remainder of life. Removed to Pembroke Coll., 6 March 1756. In London, Jan. 1759 to June 1761. Prof. of History and Mod. Languages, Cambridge, 28 July 1768. Increasing ill-health. Died, at Cambridge, 30 July 1771. Buried at Stoke Pogis.

Works : 'Ode on a distant prospect of Eton College' (anon.), 1747 ; 'An Elegy wrote in a Country Churchyard' (anon.), 1751 (2nd-4th edns. same year) ; 'Six Poems,' 1753 ; 'The Progress of Poesy ; and, The Bard,' 1758 ; 'Poems' (collected ; two independent edns.), 1768 ; 'Ode, performed . . . at the installation of . . . A. H. Fitzroy, Duke of Grafton' (anon.), 1769.

Posthumous : '**A** Catalogue of the Antiquities . . . in England and Wales' (anon. ; priv. ptd.), [1773] ; 'Life and Letters,' ed. by W. Mason, 1774 ; 'The Bard,' ed. by J. Martin, 1837 ; 'Correspondence with W. Mason,' ed. by J. Mitford, 1853. *Collected Works :* 'Poems,' ed. by W. Mason, 1775 ; 'Poems and Letters' (priv. ptd.), 1879 ; 'Works,' ed. by E. Gosse (4 vols.), 1884. *Life :* by E. Gosse, 1882.

* **GREEN (John Richard), 1837-1883.** Born, at Oxford, 12 Dec. 1837. At Magdalen Coll., School, 1845-51 ; with private tutors, 1851 - 53. Matric. Jesus Coll., Oxford, 7 Dec. 1855 ; Scholar, 1855-60 ; B.A., 1860 ; M.A.,

1862. Ordained Deacon, 1860. Curate of St. Barnabas, King Square, London, 1860-63. Curate of Holy Trinity, Hoxton, 1863-66 ; perpetual curate of St. Philip's, Stepney, 1866-69. Contrib. to 'Saturday Rev.,' 1862. Prosecuted historical studies. Librarian of Lambeth Palace, 1869-83. Gave up clerical life, 1869. Married Alice Stopford, June 1877. Hon. Fellow Jesus Coll., Oxford, 1877-83. Hon. LL.D., Edinburgh, 1878. Visit to Egypt, 1881. Increasing ill-health. Died, at Mentone, 7 March 1883.

Works : 'Short History of the English People,' 1874 ; 'Stray Studies from England and Italy,' 1876 ; 'A History of the English People' (4 vols., expanded from preceding), 1877-80 ; 'Readings from English History,' 1879 ; 'A Short Geography of the British Islands' (with his wife), 1880 ; 'The Making of England,' 1881. *Posthumous :* 'The Conquest of England' (completed by his wife), 1883.

He *edited :* 'Literature Primers,' 1875-79 ; 'History Primers,' 1875-84 ; 'Classical Writers,' 1879-82 ; Addison's 'Essays,' 1880.

GREEN (Thomas Hill), 1836-1882. Born, at Birkin, Yorkshire, 7 April 1836. At Rugby, 1848-55. Matric. Balliol Coll., Oxford, 30 May 1855 ; B.A., 1859 ; M.A., 1862. Chancellor's Prize Essay, 1862. Historical lecturer at Balliol Coll., 1860 ; Fellow, Nov. 1860 to 1882 ; Librarian, 1864 ; Senior Dean, 1865 ; Lecturer and Tutor, 1869 ; Dean, 1871-72 ; Classical Tutor, 1875. Assistant Commissioner to Royal Commission on Middle-Class Schools, Dec. 1864. Married Charlotte Symonds, 1 July 1871. Whyte Prof. of Moral Philosophy, Oxford, 1878-82. Died, at Oxford, 26 March 1882.

Work : 'Liberal Legislation and Freedom of Contract,' 1881. *Posthumous :* 'Prolegomena to Ethics,' ed. by A. C. Bradley, 1883 ; 'The Witness of God ; and, Faith,' ed. by A. Toynbee, 1883 ; translation (with others) of Lotze's 'Logik' and

'Metaphysik,' 1884; 'Lectures on the Principles of Political Obligation,' 1895.

He *edited :* Hume's 'Philosophical Works' (with T. H. Grose, etc.), 1874, etc.

Collected Works : ed. by R. L. Nettleship, with *life* (3 vols.), 1885-88.

GREENE (Robert), 1560[?] - 1592. Born, at Norwich, 1560 [?]. To St. John's Coll., Cambridge, as Sizar, 26 Nov. 1575; B.A., 1579; removed to Clare Hall; M.A., 1583. Travelled abroad, 1579-80. Married, 1585 [or 1586?]; lived at Norwich. Deserted his wife, 1586; settled in London. Incorporated M.A., Oxford, July 1588. Died, in London, 3 Sept. 1592; buried in New Churchyard, near Bethlehem Hospital.

Works : 'Mamillia,' 1583; 'The Myrrour of Modestie' (under initials: R. G.) 1584; 'Gwydonius,' 1584 (later edns., called 'Greene's Carde of Fancie,' 1587, etc.); 'Arbasto,' 1584; 'Morando,' 1584 (another edn., with addition of second part, 1587); 'Planetomachia,' 1585; 'Penelope's Web,' 1587; 'Euphues his Censure,' 1587; 'Perimedes the Blacke-Smith,' 1588; 'Pandosto,' 1588; 'Alcida,' probably published 1589 (earliest edn. known, 1617); 'The Spanish Masquerado,' 1589 (2nd edn. same year); 'Menaphon,' 1589 (later edns. called, 'Greene's Arcadia; or, Menaphon,' 1599, etc.); 'Ciceronis Amor,' 1589; 'Greenes Orpharion,' probably pubd. 1590 (earliest edn. known, 1599); 'The Royal Exchange,' 1590; 'Greenes Mourning Garment,' probably pubd. 1590 (earliest edn. known, 1616); 'Greenes Never too Late,' 1590; 'Greenes Farewell to Folly,' 1591; 'A Maiden's Dreame,' 1591; 'A Notable Discovery of Coosnage,' 1591; 'The Second part of Conny-catching,' 1591; 'The Thirde and last part of Conny-catching,' 1592; 'A Disputation betweene a Hee Conny-catcher and a Shee Conny-catcher' (under initials: R. G.), 1592 (another edn., called, 'Theeves Falling Out,' 1617);

'The Black Bookes Messenger' (under initials: R. G.), 1592; 'The Defence of Conny-catching' (anon.; attrib. to Greene), 1592; 'Philomela,' 1592; 'A Quip for an Upstart Courtier,' 1592 (2nd and 3rd edns. same year).

Posthumous : 'The Repentance of Robert Greene,' 1592; 'Greenes Vision,' (1592 ?); 'The Historie of Orlando Furioso,' 1594; 'A Looking Glass for London and England' (with T. Lodge), 1594; 'The Honorable Historie of frier Bacon and frier Bongay,' 1594; 'The First Part of the Tragicall Raigne of Selimus' (anon.; attrib. to Greene), 1594; 'Greens Groatsworth of Wit,' 1596; 'The Scottish Historie of James the fourth,' 1598; 'The Comicall Historie of Alphonsus, King of Aragon,' 1599; 'A pleasant conceyted Comedie of George a Greene' (anon.; attrib. to Greene), 1599; 'A Paire of Turtle Doves' (anon.; attrib. to Greene), 1606.

He *edited :* (anon.), 'Euphues Shadow, by T. L.' 1592.

Collected Works : ed. by Dyce (2 vols.), 1831; ed. by Grosart (15 vols.), 1881-86.

Life : Memoirs by Dyce and Grosart in edns. of Greene's works.

GREVILLE *(Sir* **Fulke), Lord Brooke, 1554-1628.** Born, at Beauchamp Court, Warwickshire, 1554. To Shrewsbury School, 17 Oct. 1564. Friendship with Philip Sidney begun. Matric. at Jesus Coll., Cambridge, 20 May 1568. Held post in Court of Marches, 1576-77. In favour at Elizabeth's court. To Heidelberg with Sidney, Feb. 1577. Accompanied diplomatic mission to Flanders, 1578. To Germany again, 1579. Secretary for Principality of Wales, 20 April 1583; held office till death. Served in Normandy under Henry of Navarre, 1591. M.P. for Warwickshire, 1592-93, 1597, 1601, 1620. Estate of Wedgnock Park granted him by Queen, 1597. Knight of the Bath, Oct. 1597. Treasurer of the Wars, March 1598; Treasurer of the Navy,

Sept. 1598. Castle of Warwick granted him, 1605. Chancellor of the Exchequer, Oct. 1614 to Jan. 1621. Created Baron Brooke, 29 Jan. 1621. Took seat in House of Lords, 15 Nov. 1621. On Council of War, 1624 ; on Council of Foreign Affairs, 1625. Died, from wound inflicted by a servant, 30 Sept. 1628. Buried in St. Mary's Church, Warwick.

Works: Contributions to 'The Phœnix Nest,' 1593 ; to Bodenham's 'Belvedere,' 1600; to 'Englands Helicon,' 1600 ; 'The Tragedy of Mustapha' (anon.), 1609.

Posthumous: 'Certaine Learned and Elegant Workes of the Rt. Hon. Fulke, Lord Brooke,' 1633 ; 'The Life of the renowned Sir Philip Sidney,' 1625 ; 'The Remains of Sir Fulk Grevill,' 1670.

Collected Works: ed. by Grosart, with *memoir* (4 vols.), 1870.

GRIFFIN (Gerald), 1803 - 1840. Born, in Limerick, 12 Dec. 1803. Educated there. Contrib. to local periodicals. To Adare. to live with his brother, 1820. To London, autumn of 1823. Contrib. to 'Literary Gazette.' Opera, 'The Noyades,' produced at English Opera House, 1826. Returned to Limerick, Feb. 1827. Published various novels. To London Univ., to study law, 1828. Returned to Ireland, spring of 1829. To London, autumn 1829. Returned to Ireland, 1830. Visit to Scotland, 1838. Joined Catholic Society of Christian Brothers, Aug. 1838. Died, at Cork, 12 June 1840. Play, 'Gisippus,' posthumously performed at Drury Lane, 1842.

Works: 'Holland - Tide' (anon.), 1827 ; 'Tales of the Munster Festivals' (anon.), 1827 ; 'The Collegians' (anon.), 1829 ; 'The Christian Physiologist' (anon.), 1830 (another edn., called 'The Offering of Friendship,' 1854) ; 'The Rivals ; and, Tracy's Ambition' (anon.), 1830 ; 'The Invasion' (anon.), 1832 ; 'Tales of My Neighbourhood' (anon.), 1835 ; 'The Duke of Monmouth' (anon.), 1836.

Posthumous: 'Gisippus,' 1842 ;

'Talis Qualis,' 1842 ; 'The Day of Trial,' 1854 [1853]; 'The Kelp-Gatherer,' 1854 [1853] ; 'A Story of Psyche,' 1854 [1853] ; 'The Voluptuary Cured,' 1854 [1853] ; 'The Young Milesian,' 1854 [1853] ; 'Card Drawing,' 1857.

Collected Works: in 8 vols., 1842-43.

Life: by D. Griffin, 1843.

GROTE (George), 1794-1871. Born, at Clay Hill, Kent, 17 Nov. 1794. At school at Sevenoaks, June 1800 to 1804 ; At Charterhouse, 1804 - 10. Lived at home, 1810-20. Clerk in his father's Bank, 1810-16 ; partner, 1816-43. Married Harriet Lewin, 5 March 1820. Active part in promotion of London University, opened 1828 ; Mem. of Council, 1828 - 71. Contrib. to 'Westminster Rev.,' 1826, 1843 and 1866 ; to 'Spectator,' 1839 and 1847 ; to 'Classical Museum,' 1844 ; to 'Edinburgh Rev.,' 1856. Travelled on Continent, 1830. M.P. for City of London, Dec. 1831, Jan. 1835, and July 1837. Travelled in Italy, Oct. 1841 to spring of 1842. Retired from banking, 1843. F.G.S., 1843. Resided partly in London, partly at Burnham Beeches. Visit to Paris, 1844 ; to Switzerland, 1847. Mem. of Council of University Coll., 1850 ; Treasurer, 1860 ; President, 1868-71. Elected on Governing body of new University of London, 1850 ; Vice-Chancellor, 1862. Trustee of British Museum, 1859. D.C.L., Oxford, 1853. F.R.S., 1857. Correspondent of French Acad. of Moral and Political Sciences, 1857 ; Foreign Associate, 1864. Prof. of Ancient History to Royal Academy, 1859. Foreign Mem. of Institute of France, Feb. 1864. Refused Peerage, Nov. 1869. Died, in London, 18 June 1871 ; buried in Westminster Abbey.

Works: 'Statement of the Question of Parliamentary Reform,' 1821 ; 'Analysis of the Influence of Natural Religion' (under pseud. of Philip Beauchamp), 1822 ; 'Essentials of Parliamentary Reform,' 1831 ; 'History of Greece,' vols. i. ii., 1846; vols.

iii. iv., 1847 ; vols. v. vi., 1848 ; vols. vii. viii., 1850; vols. ix. x., 1852; vol. xi., 1853 ; vol. xii., 1856 ; 'Seven Letters on the Recent Politics of Switzerland' (from 'Spectator'), 1847 ; 'Plato's Doctrine respecting the Rotation of the Earth,' 1860 ; 'Plato and the other Companions of Sokrates,' 1865 ; Review of J. S. Mill's 'Examination of Hamilton' (from 'Westminster Rev.'), 1868 [1867].

Posthumous : 'Aristotle,' ed. by A. Bain and G. C. Robertson (2 vols.), 1872 ; 'Poems' (priv. ptd.), 1872 ; 'Minor Works,' ed. by A. Bain, 1873; 'Posthumous Papers' (priv. ptd.), 1874 ; 'Fragments on Ethical Subjects,' ed. by A. Bain, 1876.

He *edited :* G. Waddington's 'History of the Reformation,' 1841 ; J. Mill's 'Analysis of the Phenomena of the Human Mind,' 1869.

Life : by Mrs. Grote, 1873.

HAKLUYT (Richard), 1552[?]-1616. Born, in Herefordshire, 1552 [?]. Educated at Westminster School. To Ch. Ch., Oxford, as Student, 1570 ; B.A., 19 Feb. 1574 ; M.A., 27 Jan. 1577. Ordained, 1575 [?]. To France, with Sir Edward Stafford, as Chaplain, 1583. Appointed Prebendary of Bristol, 1586. Returned to England, 1588. Rector of Wetheringselt, Suffolk, April 1590. Married, 1594 [?]. Wife died, 1597 [?]. Prebendary of Westminster, May 1602. Archdeacon, 1603. Chaplain of Savoy, 1604. Second marriage, March 1604. Interested in colony of Virginia, 1606. Died, in London, 23 Nov. 1616 ; buried in Westminster Abbey.

Works : 'Divers Voyages touching the Discovery of America' (under initials : R. H.), 1582 ; 'The Principall Navigations, Voiages, and Discoveries of the English Nation,' 1589 (enlarged edn., 3 vols., 1598-1600).

Posthumous : 'A Discourse concerning Western Planting,' 1877 (written 1584).

He *translated :* Laudonnière's 'A Notable History,' 1587 ; Ferdinand Soto's 'Virginia richly Valued,' 1609;

and *edited :* Anglerius' 'De Orbe Novo decades octo,' 1587 ; Galvano's 'Discoveries of the World,' 1601.

HALES (John), 1584-1656. Born, in Bath, 19 April 1584. Educated at Bath Grammar School. To Corpus Christi Coll., Oxford, as scholar, 16 April 1597 ; B.A., 9 July 1603 ; Fellow of Merton Coll., 1605 ; M.A., 20 June 1609 ; Lecturer in Greek to University, 1612. Fellow of Eton Coll., 24 May 1613 to April 1649. To Holland with Sir Dudley Carleton, as Chaplain, 1616. To Eton, 1619. Canon of Windsor, 23 May 1639 ; installed, 27 June ; deprived of canonry by Parliamentary Committee, 1642. Tutor to William Salter, in Buckinghamshire, 1649. Returned to Eton. Died there, 19 May 1656. Buried there.

Works : 'Oratio Funebris' (on Sir Thomas Bodley), 1613 ; 'A Sermon,' 1617 ; 'Anonymi dissertatio de pace et concordia Ecclesiæ,' 1630 ; 'The Way towards the finding of a Decision of the Chief Controversie, etc.,' (anon.), 1641 ; 'A Tract concerning Schisme,' 1642 (anon. ; 2nd edn. same year) ; 'Of the Blasphemie againste the Holy Ghost' (anon. ; attrib. to Hales), 1646.

Posthumous : 'Golden Remains,' 1659 ; 'Sermons preached at Eton,' 1660 ; 'Several Tracts,' 1677.

Collected Works : ed. by Lord Hailes (3 vols.), 1765.

HALIBURTON (Thomas Chandler), 1796-1865. Born, at Windsor, Nova Scotia, 17 Dec. 1796. Educated at Windsor Grammar School. To King's Coll., Windsor, 1810 ; B.A., 1815. Married Louisa Neville, 1816. Called to Bar, 1820. Mem. for County of Annapolis in Legislative Assembly, 1826-29. Chief Justice of Nova Scotia Inferior Court of Common Pleas, 1829-41 ; of Supreme Court, Jan. 1841 to Feb. 1856. Wife died, 1840. Contrib. to 'Nova Scotian' (under pseud. of 'Sam Slick'), 1835-36. Visit to England, 1842. Contrib. to 'Fraser's Mag.,' 1846-47. Pension of £300 per annum, 1856. To England,

1856 ; settled in London. Married Mrs. Sarah Harriet Williams, 1856. Mem. of Athenæum Club. Hon. M.A., King's Coll., Windsor, N.S., 1858 ; Hon. D.C.L., Oxford, 1858. M.P. for Launceston, 29 April 1859 to 6 July 1865. Contrib. to 'Dublin University Mag.,' 1858-59. Died, at Isleworth, 27 Aug. 1865.

Works : 'A General Description of Nova Scotia,' 1825 ; 'An Historical and Statistical Account of Nova Scotia' (2 vols.), 1829 ; 'The Clock-maker' (3 series, under pseud. of 'Sam Slick'), 1837-40 ; 'The Bubbles of Canada' (anon.), 1839 ; 'A Reply to the Report of the Earl of Durham' (anon.), 1839 ; 'The Letter Bag of the Great Western' (anon.), 1840 ; 'Traits of American Humour,' 1843 ; 'Sam Slick's Wise Saws and Modern Instances' (2 vols.), 1843 ; 'The Old Judge' (2 vols.), 1843 ; 'The Ameri-cans at Home' (3 vols.), 1843 ; 'The Attaché' (by 'Sam Slick,' 2 series), 1843-44 ; 'Rule and Misrule of the English in America' (anon. ; 2 vols.), 1851 (another edn., called : 'The English in America,' anon., same year) ; 'Nature and Human Nature' (anon.), 1855 ; 'Address on the present condition . . . of British N. America,' 1857 ; 'Speech in House of Commons,' 1860 ; 'The Season Ticket' (anon., from 'The Dublin University Mag.'), 1860.

Life : by F. Blake Crofton, 1889.

HALIFAX, Marquis of. *See* Savile (G.).

HALLAM (Arthur Henry), 1811-1833. [Son of Henry Hallam (*q.v.*).] Born, in London, 1 Feb. 1811. Visit to Germany and Switzerland, 1818. At first privately educated ; after-wards at Eton, till 1827. Contrib. to 'Eton Miscellany,' 1827. In Italy, winter 1827-28. Returned to England, June 1828. To Trin. Coll., Camb., Oct. 1828. Friendship with Tennyson formed there. B.A., 1832. Contrib. to 'Englishman's Mag.,'1831. Student of Inner Temple, 1832. With father in Germany, 1833. Died suddenly, at Vienna, 15 Sept. 1833.

Works : 'Remarks on Prof. Ros-setti's "Disquisizioni sullo Spirito Antipapale"' (under initials : T. H. E. A.), 1832.

Posthumous : 'Remains, in prose and verse,' ed. by his father (priv. ptd.), 1834.

HALLAM (Henry), 1777 - 1859. Born, at Windsor, 9 July 1777. At Eton, 1790-94. Contrib. to 'Musæ Etonenses,' 1795. Matric. Ch. Ch., Oxford, 20 April 1795 ; B.A., 1799. F.S.A., 12 March 1801. Student at Inner Temple ; called to Bar, 2 July 1802. Commissioner of Records ; afterwards Commissioner of Stamps, 1806-26. Married Julia Elton, 1807. Withdrew from legal practice and en-gaged in historical studies. Vice-Pres. of Soc. of Antiquaries, 1824-59. Royal Medal for historical achieve-ments, 1830. Lived mainly in London. M.A., Oxford, 1832 ; Hon. D.C.L., 5 July 1848. Founder and Treasurer of Statistical Soc., 1834. Bencher of Inner Temple, 1841. Hon. Prof. of History to Royal Society. Foreign As-sociate of Institute of France. Hon. LL.D., Harvard Univ., 1848. Died, at Penshurst, Kent, 21 Jan. 1859.

Works : 'A View of the State of Europe during the Middle Ages,' 1818 (supplementary vol. of 'Notes,' 1848) ; 'The Constitutional History of England,' 1827 ; 'The Introduction to the Literature of Europe' (4 vols.), 1837-39 ; 'Letters addressed to Lord Ashley, etc.,' [1844].

He *edited :* A. H. Hallam's 'Re-mains,' 1834.

HALLIWELL, afterwards HALLI-WELL-PHILLIPPS (James Orchard), 1820-1889. Born, in Chelsea, 21 June 1820. Educated at private schools. Contrib. to 'The Parthenon,' Nov. 1836 to Jan. 1837. To Trin. Coll., Camb., 13 Nov. 1837 ; removed to Jesus Coll., April 1838, as scholar. Took no degree. F.S.A., 14 Feb. 1839. F.R.S., 30 May 1839. Mem. of Astronomical Soc. Started Cam-bridge Antiquarian Soc., acting as Secretary, 1840. Left Cambridge, 1840 ; settled in London with his father. Edited 'The Archæologist' (with T. Wright), Sept. 1841 to June 1842. Married Henrietta Elizabeth Molyneux Phillipps, 9 Aug. 1842. Lived first in London, in his father's house ; afterwards at Islip. Accused of selling to British Museum manuscripts abstracted from Trin. Coll., Camb., 1844. Removed to Brixton Hill, 1852. Enthusiastic Shakespearian student and collector. Instrumental in purchase of Shakespeare's house, Stratford-on-Avon, 1863. Wife inherited her father's estates in Worcestershire, 1867. She developed softening of brain as result of accident, 1872 ; he adopted additional name of Phillipps, and management of Worcestershire property. Wife died, 1879. He married Mary Rice Hobbs, 1879. Settled at Hollingbury, near Brighton, 1880. Hon. LL.D., Edinburgh, 1883. Died, at Hollingbury, 3 Jan. 1889. Buried in Patcham churchyard.

Works : Halliwell-Phillipps's publications (including both original works and cases of editorship), dating from 1838 to 1881, number upwards of 270. Of these the greater proportion are on Shakespearian topics. A complete bibliography, compiled by Justin Winsor, is published as No. 10 of 'Bibliographical Contributions to the Library of Harvard University.' A fairly representative list is given in Allibone's 'Dictionary of English Literature.'

*HARDY (Thomas), b. 1840. Born, near Dorchester, 2 June 1840. Articled as pupil to architect, 1856. To London, 1862. Student at King's Coll., 1865-66. Medal of Inst. of Brit. Architects for Essay, 1863 ; Tite Prize, 1863. Contrib. story to 'Chambers's Journal,' 1865 ; frequent contributor to periodicals since then. Married Emma Lavinia Gifford, 17 Sept. 1874. Unsettled residence in England, France and Germany, 1874-82. Settled in Dorsetshire, 1883. Visited Italy, 1887. J.P. for Dorsetshire, 1894. Dramatized version (written with J. Comyns Carr) of 'Far from the Madding Crowd,' produced at Prince of Wales's Theatre, Liverpool, 27 Feb. 1882 ; at Globe Theatre, London, May 1882 ; 'The Three Wayfarers,' produced at Terry's Theatre, 3 June 1893. ͛ Dramatized version (by L. Stoddard) of 'Tess of the D'Urbervilles,' produced at Fifth Avenue Theatre, New York, March 1897.

Works : 'Desperate Remedies' (anon.), 1871 ; 'Under the Greenwood Tree' (anon.), 1872 ; 'A Pair of Blue Eyes,' 1873 ; 'Far from the Madding Crowd,' 1874 ; 'The Hand of Ethelberta,' 1876 ; 'The Return of the Native,' 1878 ; 'The Trumpet Major,' 1880 ; 'A Laodicean,' 1881 ; 'Two on a Tower,' 1882 ; 'The Romantic Adventures of a Milkmaid' (reprinted, in New York, from 'The Graphic'), 1884 ; 'The Mayor of Casterbridge,' 1886 ; 'The Woodlanders,' 1887 ; 'Wessex Tales,' 1888 ; 'The Melancholy Hussar' (in 'Three Notable Stories'), 1890 ; 'A Group of Noble Dames,' 1891 ; 'Tess of the D'Urbervilles,' 1892 ; 'Life's Little Ironies,' 1894 ; 'Note' on William Barnes (from 'Athenæum'), and ballad 'The Fire at Tranter Sweatley's' (from 'Gentleman's Mag.'), in L. Johnson's 'Art of Thomas Hardy,' 1894 ; 'The Spectre of the Real' (with F. Henniker, in the latter's 'In Scarlet and Grey'), 1896 ; 'Jude the Obscure,' 1896 ; 'The Well-Beloved,' 1897.

Collected Works : 1895, etc.

*HARE (Augustus John Cuthbert), b. 1834. Born, in Rome, 13 March 1834. Adopted by the widow of his uncle Augustus [*q.v.*], Aug. 1835. At private schools, spring 1841 to Christmas 1846. At Harrow, Jan. 1847 to Easter 1848. Privately educated, Aug. 1848 to 1853. Matric. Univ. Coll., Oxford, 16 March 1853 ; B.A., 1856 ; M.A., 1859. Active literary life. Has travelled much on Continent and in England. Winters usually spent abroad. Lectured in Rome, winter 1869-70. Knight of St. Olaf of Sweden, 27 Feb. 1879. Frequent contributor to periodicals. Since 1880 has chiefly resided at Holmhurst, near Hastings.

Works : 'Epitaphs from Country Churchyards,' 1856 ; 'Murray's Handbook for Berks, Bucks and Oxfordshire,' 1860 ; 'A Winter at Mentone' [1862] ; ✍'Murray's Handbook for Durham and Northumberland,' 1863 ; 'Walks in Rome,' 1871 ; 'Wanderings in Spain,' 1873 ; 'Memorials of a Quiet Life' (3 vols.), 1872-76 ; 'Days Near Rome,' 1875 ; 'Cities of Northern and Central Italy,' 1876 ; 'Walks in London,' 1878 ; 'Life and Letters of Frances, Baroness Bunsen,' 1879 [1878]; 'Cities of Southern Italy and Sicily,' 1883 ; 'Cities of Central Italy,' 1884 ; 'Cities of Northern Italy,' 1884 ; 'Florence,' 1884 ; 'Venice,' 1884 ; 'Sketches of Holland and Scandinavia,' 1885 ; 'Studies in Russia,' 1885 ; 'Paris,' 1887 ; 'Days near Paris,' 1887 ; 'South-Eastern France,' 1890 ; 'South-Western France,' 1890; 'North-Eastern France,' 1890 ; 'The Story of Two Noble Lives,' 1893 ; 'Sussex,' 1894 ; 'Life and Letters of Maria Edgeworth,' 1894 ; 'Westminster' (from 'Walks in London '), 1894 ; 'North-Western France,' 1895 ; 'Biographical Sketches,' 1895 ; 'The Gurneys of Earlham,' 1895 ; 'The Rivieras,' 1896 ; 'The Story of My Life' (autobiog.), vols. i.-iii., 1896.

HARE (Angustus William), 1792-1834. [Uncle of preceding.] Born, in Rome, 17 Nov. 1792. To England, 1797; brought up by his aunt, Lady Jones, at Worting, near Basingstoke. To Winchester as 'commoner,' 1804 ; elected into College, 1806. Matric., New Coll., Oxford, 3 July 1810 ; Fellow, 1812-29 ; B.A., 1814 ; M.A., 1818. Travelled in Italy, 1817-18. Returned to New Coll., as Tutor, 1822. Ordained, 1825. Rector of Alton-Barnes, Wilts, 1829-34. Married Maria Leycester, 2 June 1829. To Italy for health, winter of 1833. Died, in Rome, 18 Feb. 1834 ; buried in old Protestant Cemetery there.

Works : 'A Layman's Letter' (with J. C. Hare, anon.), 1824 ; 'Guesses at Truth' (with J. C. Hare, anon.), first series, 1827 ; 'Offences in the Ministry,' 1832.

Posthumous : 'Sermons to a Country Congregation,' 1836 ; 'Guesses at Truth' (with J. C. Hare), 2nd series, 1847-48 ; 'The Alton Sermons,' 1874.

HARE (Julius Charles), 1795-1855. [Brother of preceding.] Born, at Valdagno, Italy, 13 Sept. 1795. To England, 1799. At Tunbridge School, 1804. Removed owing to ill-health. In Germany with parents, 1804-05. At Charterhouse, 1806-12. To Trin. Coll., Camb., 1812 ; B.A., 1816 ; Fellow, Oct. 1818 ; M.A., 1819. In Italy, winter 1818-19. Settled in Temple to study law, 1819. Classical Lecturer, Trin. Coll., Camb., 1822 ; gave up law. Ordained, 1826. In Italy 1831. Rector of Hurstmonceaux, June 1832 to 1855. Edited 'The Philological Museum,' 1832-33. Select Preacher, Cambridge, 1839. Archdeacon of Lewes, April 1840 to 1855. Married Esther Maurice, 1844. Preb. of Chichester, Jan. 1851 to 1855. Chaplain to Queen, June 1853 to 1855. Died, at Hurstmonceaux, 23 Jan. 1855 ; buried there.

Works : 'A Layman's Letter' (with A. W. Hare ; anon.), 1824 ; 'The Children of Light,' 1828 ; 'A Vindication of Niebuhr's History of Rome,' 1829 ; 'A Funeral Sermon,' 1835 ; 'The Better Prospects of the Church,' 1840 ; 'The Victory of Faith,' 1840 ; 'Sermons preacht in Hurstmonceaux Church ' (2 vols.), 1841-49 ; 'Privileges imply Duties,' 1842 ; 'The Unity of the Church,' 1845 ; 'The Mission of the Comforter,' 1846 ; 'Vindication of the Chevalier Bunsen' [1846] ; 'Guesses at Truth' (anon.; with A. W. Hare; 2 series), 1827-48 ; 'A Letter to the Dean of Chichester,' 1848 ; 'Thou shalt not bear false witness,' 1849 ; 'The True Remedy for the Evils of the Age,' 1850 ; 'A few words on the rejection of the Episcopal Bill, etc.,' 1850 ; 'A Letter to the Hon. R. Cavendish,' 1850 (2nd edn. same year) ; 'The Life of Luther,' 1855 ; 'Miscellaneous Pamphlets,' 1855.

Posthumous : 'Charges to the Clergy of the Archdeaconry of Lewes,'

1856 ; 'Sermons preacht on particular occasions,' 1858 ; 'Fragments of two Essays in English Philology,' 1873.

He *translated :* La Motte Fouqué's 'Sintram,' 1820 ; Niebuhr's 'History of Rome ' (with C. Thirlwall), 1828-42 ; 'English Hexameter Translations from Schiller, Göthe, etc.,' 1847 ; and *edited :* 'Portions of the Psalms,' 1839 ; J. Sterling's 'Essays and Tales,' 1848.

HARRINGTON (James), 1611-1677.
Born, at Upton, Northamptonshire, 7 Jan. 1611. To Trin. Coll., Oxford, 1629. Took no degree. Travelled in Holland, France and Italy ; at Court of Elector Palatine in Holland. Groom of Bedchamber to Charles I. Married Miss Dorrel [or Dayrell ?]. Formed Rota Club, to discuss theories of his 'Oceana'; club existed, Nov. 1659 to Feb. 1660. Imprisoned in Tower on political charge, 26 Nov. 1661. Sent to St. Nicholas Island, 1662 ; afterwards to Plymouth. After his release, settled in Westminster. Died there, 11 Sept. 1677 ; buried in St. Margaret's Church.

Works : 'Noah's Dove,' 1645 ; 'The Commonwealth of Oceana,' 1656 ; 'The Prerogative of Popular Government ' (2 pts.), 1657-58 ; 'The Stumbling Block of Disobedience' (anon.), 1658 ; 'Brief Directions of Popular Government ' (anon.), 1659 ; 'A Discourse upon this saying : The Spirit of the Nation is not yet to be trusted with Liberty' [1659] ; 'Aphorisms Political,' 1659 ; 'The Art of Law-Giving,' 1659 ; 'A Discourse shewing, that the Spirit of Parliaments . . . is not to be trusted for a settlement, etc.,' 1659 ; 'A Parallel of the Spirit of the People,' 1659 ; 'Politicaster,' 1659 ; 'Pour enclouer le Canon,' 1659 ; 'Valerius and Publicola,' 1659 ; 'The Wayes and Meanes, whereby an equal and lasting commonwealth may be . . . introduced, etc.,' 1660 ; 'The Rota'(anon.), 1659 ; 'The Censure of the Rota upon Mr. Milton's book,' 1660 ; 'A Holy Oyl' (under initials : J. H.), 1669.

He *translated :* 'Two of Virgil's Eclogues and two books of his Æneis,' 1658 ; 'Virgil's Æneis,' bks. iii.-vi., 1659.

Collected Works : ed., with *life,* by J. Toland, 1700.

*HARRISON (Frederic), b. 1831.
Born, in London, 18 Oct. 1831. At private school, 1841-44 ; at King's Coll. School, Easter 1844 to July 1849. Scholarship at Wadham Coll., Oxford, June 1848 ; Matric., 26 April 1849 ; B.A., 1853 ; Fellow, 1854-70 ; Tutor, 1854-56; M A., 1859. Student of Lincoln's Inn, 14 Jan. 1854 ; called to Bar, 26 Jan. 1858. On Royal Commission on Trade Unions, 1867-69. Sec. to Royal Commission for Digest of Law, 1869-70. Married Ethel Bertha Harrison, 17 Aug. 1870. Joint-founder of Positivist School, 1870. Prof. of Jurisprudence and Int. Law to Council of Legal Education, 1877-89. Has contrib. to 'Westminster Rev.,' 1860-64 ; to 'Fortnightly Rev.,' from 1865 ; to 'Contemporary Rev.,' from 1875 ; to 'Nineteenth Century,' from 1877 ; to 'New York Forum,' 1890-97 ; to 'Positivist Rev.,' from 1893 ; to 'Cosmopolis,' 1896. Pres. of English Positivist Committee, from 1880. Alderman of London County Council, Feb. 1889 to Oct. 1894.

Works : 'The Meaning of History,' 1862 ; 'Sunday Evenings for the People,' 1867 ; 'Martial Law' (from 'Daily News'), 1867 ; 'The Political Function of the Working Classes,' 1868 ; 'Order and Progress,' 1875 ; 'Science and Humanity' [1879] ; 'The Present and the Future,' 1880 ; 'Martial Law in Kabul ' (from 'Fortnightly Rev.'), 1880 ; 'Destination,' 1881 ; 'The Crisis in Egypt,' 1882 ; 'Sutton Place, Guildford' [1882] ; 'Politics and a Human Religion,' 1885 ; 'The Choice of Books,' 1886 ; 'Mr. Gladstone!—or Anarchy !'[1886] ; 'A New Year's Address,' 1886 ; 'The Positivist Library of Aug. Comte,' 1886 ; 'A New Year's Address,' 1887 ; 'Marriage,' 1887 ; 'Oliver Cromwell,' 1888 ; 'A New Year's Address,' 1888 ; 'In Memoriam J. Cotter Morison,

1888 ; 'The Centenary of the French Revolution,'1889 ; 'A New Era,' 1889 ; 'In Memoriam Omnium Animarum,' 1890 ; 'The Industrial Republic,'1890; 'Moral and Religious Socialism,' 1891; 'The Presentation of Infants,' 1891 ; 'Annals of an Old Manor House,' 1893 ; 'The Meaning of History,' 1894 ; 'Early Victorian Literature' (2 series), 1895-97.

He has *translated :* Comte's 'Social Statics,' 1875 ; and *edited :* F. G. Fleay's 'Three Lectures on Education,' 1883 ; 'The New Calendar of Great Men,' 1892 [1891]; Carlyle's 'Past and Present,' 1897.

* HARTE (Francis Bret), b. 1839. Born, at Albany, N. Y., 25 Aug. 1839. To California, 1854. Worked successively as miner, school-teacher, express messenger, printer, newspaper editor. Major and Staff Officer of Volunteers, Northern Californian Indian War, 1862 - 63. Assistant-Keeper of Archives, U.S. Surveyor General Office, 1863. U.S. Deputy Marshal for California, 1863. Sec. of San Francisco branch of U.S.A. Mint, 1864-70. Edited 'Overland Monthly,' July 1868-70. Prof. of Literature, Univ. of California 1870-71. To New York, 1871. Subsequently lived at Boston and Newport, R.I. On staff of 'Atlantic Monthly,' 1872-73. U.S. Consul at Crefeld, 1878-80 ; at Glasgow, March 1880 to July 1885. Of late years has resided in England.

Works : 'The Lost Galleon, 1869 ; 'Condensed Novels,' 1870 ; 'That Heathen Chinee' (from 'Overland Monthly'), 1871 ; 'The Luck of Roaring Camp,' 1870 ; 'Poems,' 1871 ; 'East and West Poems,' 1871 ; 'Lothaw' [1871] ; 'Stories of the Sierras,' 1872 ; 'Mrs. Skaggs's Husbands,' 1872 ; 'M'liss,' 1872 ; 'Truthful James and other poems' [1872] ; 'Poetical Works' [1872] ; 'Complete Works,' 1873 ; 'The Little Drummer' [1873] ; 'An Episode of Fiddletown' [1873] ; 'Echoes of the Foot-Hills,' 1874 ; 'The Fool of Five-Forks' [1875] ; 'Tales of the Argonauts,' 1875 ; 'The Pagan Child,' 1876 ;

'Wan Lee' [1876]; 'Gabriel Conroy' [1876] ; 'Two Men of Sandy Bar,' 1876 ; 'Thankful Blossom,' 1877 ; 'The Hoodlum Band,' 1878 ; 'The Story of a Mine' [1877] ; 'My Friend the Tramp' [1878]; 'Drift from Two Shores,' 1878 ; 'Jinny' [1878] ; 'The Man on the Beach' [1878] ; 'The Twins of Table Mountain,' 1879 ; 'An Heiress of Red Dog,' 1879 ; 'Jeff Briggs's Love-Story,' 1880 ; 'Complete Works,' 1880, etc. ; 'Works,' 1882, etc. ; 'Flip,' 1882 ; 'In the Carquinez Woods,' 1883 ; 'On the Frontier,' 1884 ; 'Californian Stories,' 1884 ; 'Maruja,' 1885 ; 'By Shore and Sedge,' 1885 ; 'The Queen of the Pirate Isle,' 1886 : 'Snow-Bound at Eagle's,' 1886 ; 'Devil's Ford,' 1887 ; 'A Millionaire of Rough and Ready,' 1887 ; 'The Crusade of the "Excelsior,"' 1887 ; 'The Argonauts of North Liberty,' 1888 ; 'A Phyllis of the Sierras, and a Drift from Redwood Camp,' 1888 ; 'Cressy,' 1889 ; 'The Heritage of Dead'ow Marsh,' 1889 ; 'A Ward of the Golden Gate,' 1890 ; 'A Waif of the Plains,' 1890 ; 'A First Family of Tasajara,' 1891 ; 'A Sappho of Green Springs,' 1891 ; 'Tales, Poems, and Sketches,' 1892 ; 'Colonel Starbottle's Client,' 1892 ; 'Sally Dows,' 1893 ; 'Susy,' 1893 ; 'A Protégée of Jack Hamlin's,' 1894 ; 'The Bell-Ringer of Angel's,' 1894 ; 'Clarence,' 1895 ; 'In a Hollow of the Hills,' 1895 ; 'Barker's Luck,' 1896.

He has *edited :* J. H. Mason's 'Life of J. A. Garfield,' 1881.

HARTLEY (David), 1705 - 1757. Born, at Luddenden, Halifax, June [?] 1705 ; baptized, 21 June. At Bradford Grammar School. To Jesus Coll., Camb., as 'ordinary sizar,' 21 April 1722; B.A., 14 Jan. 1726 ; Fellow, 13 Nov. 1727 to 8 June 1730 ; M.A., 17 Jan. 1729. Married, June 1730. Married second time, Nov. 1735 ; settled in London. Removed to Bath, May 1742. Died there, 23 Aug. 1757.

Works : 'Some Reasons why the Practice of Inoculation ought to be

introduced into the town of Bury,'
1733 ; ' Ten Cases of Persons who
have taken Mrs. Stephens's Medicines,'
1738 ; ' A View of the present Evidence for and against Mrs. Stephens's
Medicines,' 1739 ; ' De Lithotriptico a
Joanna Stephens nuper invento,' 1741;
' Observations on Man,' 1749 ; 'Ad . . .
R. Mead, Epistola,' 1751.

Posthumous: ' Prayers, and Religious Meditations,' 1809.

Life : by his son, in 1791 edn. of
' Observations on Man.'

HAWES (Stephen), d. 1523 [?].
Probably born in Suffolk. Educated
at Oxford. Groom of Chamber to
Henry VII. Died, about 1523 [?].

Works: 'The Passetyme of Pleasure,'
1506 ; ' The Conversyon of Swerers,'
1509; 'A Joyfull Medytacyon '[1509];
' A Compendyous story . . . called the
Example of Vertu ' [1512 ?] ; ' The
Comfort of Lovers,' *n. d.*

* **HAWKINS** (*Sir* John), **1719-1789.**
Born, in London, 30 March 1719.
Articled to an attorney. Contrib. to
'Gentleman's Mag.,' from 1739. Mem.
of Madrigal Soc., 1741 [?]. Perhaps
contrib. anonymously to ' Universal
Spectator,' 1747. Mem. of Academy
of Ancient Music. Married Sidney
Storer, 1753. Gave up business as
attorney, 1769. J.P. for Middlesex,
1761 ; Chairman of Quarter Sessions,
19 Sept. 1765. Knighted, 23 Oct.
1772. Died, in Westminster, 21
May 1789 ; buried in cloisters of
Westminster Abbey.

Works : ' Observations on the
State of the Highways,' 1763 ; ' The
Principles and Power of Harmony '
(anon.), 1771 ; ' The General History
of the Science and Practice of Music'
(5 vols.), 1776 ; ' Dissertation on the
Armorial Ensigns of the County of
Middlesex,' 1780 ; ' The Life of
Samuel Johnson,' 1787.

Posthumous: Contribution to 'Poetical Miscellanies ' (anon.), 1790.

He *edited :* Walton's ' Compleat
Angler,' 1760 ; Johnson's Works,
1787-89.

*HAWTHORNE (Julian), b. 1846.
Born, in Boston, Mass., 22 June
1846. At school at Concord. In
Europe with parents, 1853-60. At
Harvard Coll., 1863-67 ; took no
degree. Studied Civil Engineering
at Cambridge, Mass., for a short
time in 1868. In Dresden, Oct.
1868 to 1870. Hydrographic Engineer in Docks Dept., New York,
1870-72. In Dresden, 1872-74 ; in
London, Sept. 1874 to Oct. 1881. On
staff of ' Spectator.' Contrib. to
various magazines. In Ireland, winter
1881-82. To New York, March 1882.
Has resided there since. Literary
Editor of New York ' World,' 1885.
Visit to Europe on Industrial Commission, 1889.

Works: 'Bressant,' 1873 ; 'Idolatry,'
1874 ; ' Garth,' 1875 ; 'Saxon Studies,'
1876 ; ' The Laughing Mill,' 1879 ;
' Archibald Malmaison,' 1879 ; ' Ellice
Quentin,' 1880 ; ' Prince Saroni's
Wife,' 1880 ; ' The Yellow Cap,' 1880 ;
' Sebastian Strome,' 1879 ; ' Fortune's
Fool,' 1883 ; ' Dust,' 1883 ; ' Beatrix
Randolph,' 1884 ; ' Noble Blood,'
1884 ; ' Nathaniel Hawthorne and his
Wife,' 1885[1884]; 'Love—or a Name?'
1885 ; ' Miss Cadogna,' 1885 ; ' John
Parmelee's Curse,' 1886 ; ' The Trial
of Gideon,' 1886 ; ' The Great Bank
Robbery,' 1887 ; 'Confessions and
Criticism,' 1887 ; 'An American Pen-
man,' 1888 ; ' David Poindexter's Disappearance,' 1888 ; ' A Dream and
a Forgetting,' 1888 ; ' Section 558,'
1888 ; ' The Spectre of the Camera,'
1888 ; ' A Tragic Mystery,' 1888 ;
' Constance,' 1889 ; ' Another's Crime,'
1889 ; ' Pauline,' 1890 ; ' An American
Monte Cristo,' 1893 [1892] ; ' Humours of the Fair,' 1893 ; ' The Confessions of a Convict,' 1893 ; ' A Fool
of Nature,' 1896.

He *edited :* his father's ' Dr.
Grimshawe's Secret,' 1882.

**HAWTHORNE (Nathaniel), 1804-
1864.** [Father of preceding.] Born,
in Salem, Mass., 4 July 1804. At
school there. At Raymond, Maine,
1818-19. At Salem, 1819-21. Issued weekly paper, ' The Spectator,'

Aug. to Sept., 1820. To Bowdoin Coll., Brunswick, 1821 ; B.A., 1825. At Salem, engaged in literary pursuits, 1825-37. Contrib. to 'The Token,' 1831-38 ; 'New England Mag.,' 1834-35 ; 'Knickerbocker,' 1837. Editor of 'The American Mag. of Useful and Entertaining Knowledge,' 1836. Contrib. to the 'Democratic Review,' 1838-46. Weigher and Gauger of Customs at Boston, 1839-41. Joined the 'Arcadia' settlement at Brook Farm, April 1841. Married Sophia Amelia Peabody, 9 July 1842. Lived at the Old Manse, Concord, Mass., 1842-46. At Salem, as Surveyor of Customs, 1846 - 49. Removed to Lennox, Mass., 1850 ; to West Newton, near Boston, 1851 ; to Concord, 1852. American Consul at Liverpool, 1853 - 57 ; travelled on Continent, 1857-59 ; returned to America, 1860. Contrib. to 'Atlantic Monthly,' 1860-64. Died, at Plymouth, N. H., 18 May 1864. Buried at Concord.

Works : 'Fanshawe' (anon.), 1828 ; 'Twice-Told Tales,' 1st series, 1837 ; 2nd series, 1842 ; 'Grandfather's Chair' (pt. i.), 1841 ('Famous Old People,' 1841, and 'Liberty Tree,' 1842, extracted from preceding) ; 'Biographical Stories for Children,' 1842 ; 'Mosses from an Old Manse' (2 vols.), 1846 ; 'The Scarlet Letter,' 1850 ; 'The House of the Seven Gables,' 1851 ; 'True Stories from History and Biography,' 1851 ; 'The Wonder Book,' 1851 ; 'The Snow Image, etc.,' 1851 ; 'The Blithedale Romance,' 1852 ; 'Life of Franklin Pierce,' 1852 ; 'The Tanglewood Tales,' 1853 ; 'A Rill from the Town Pump,' 1857 ; 'The Marble Faun' (English edn. called 'Transformation'), 1860 ; 'Our Old Home,' 1863 ; 'Pansie' [1864].

Posthumous : 'Tales' (2 vols.), 1866 ; 'Passages from the American Note-books of Hawthorne,' 1868 ; 'Passages from the English Note-books of Hawthorne,' 1870 ; 'Passages from the French and Italian Note-books of Hawthorne, 1871; 'Septimius Felton,' 1872 ; 'The Dolliver Romance,' 1876 ;

'Tales of the White Hills,' 1877 ; 'A Virtuoso's Collection, etc.,' 1877 ; 'Legends of New England,' 1877 ; 'Legends of the Province House,' 1877 ; 'Dr. Grimshawe's Secret,' 1883 ; 'Sketches and Studies,' 1883.

He *edited :* H. Bridge's 'Journal of an African Cruiser,' 1865.

Collected Works : in 12 vols., 1883.

Life : by Henry James, 1880 ; by Julian Hawthorne, 1885.

HAYWOOD (Mrs. Eliza) 1693 [?]-1756. Born [Eliza Fowler], in London, 1693 [?]. Married to —— Haywood early in life. First appeared as an actress in Dublin, about 1715. Settled in London. Play, 'The Fair Captive,' produced at Lincoln's Inn Fields, 4 March 1721 ; 'A Wife to be Lett,' at Drury Lane, 12 Aug. 1723 ; 'Frederick Duke of Brunswick - Lunenburgh,' at Lincoln's Inn Fields, 4 March 1729 ; 'Opera of Operas' (written with W. Hatchett), Haymarket, 1733. Voluminous writer of fiction. Died, in London, 25 Feb. 1756.

Works : 'The Fair Captive,' 1721 ; 'The British Recluse,' 1722 ; 'Idalia,' 1723 ; 'Lassellia,' 1724 ; 'The Rash Resolve,' 1724 (2nd. edn. same year) ; 'Letters of a Lady of Quality,' 1724 ; 'The Injur'd Husband,' 1724 ; 'Poems on several occasions,' 1724 ; 'Love in Excess,' 1724 (2nd-5th edns. same year) ; 'A Wife to be Lett,' 1724 ; 'Works' (4 vols.), 1724 ; 'The Surprise,' 1725 ; 'The Fatal Secret, 1725 ; 'The Disguis'd Prince' (anon.), 1725 ; 'Fantomima,' 1725 ; 'The Tea Table,' 1725 ; 'Memoirs of a certain island adjacent to Utopia' (anon.), 1725 ; 'Secret Histories, Novels and Poems,' 1725 (2nd edn. same year) ; 'The Mercenary Lover' (anon.), 1726 ; 'The Secret History of the Present Intrigues of the Court of Caramania' (anon.), 1727 ; 'The Life of Madam de Villesache,' 1727 ; 'The Fair Hebrew' (anon.), 1729 ; 'Persecuted Virtue' (anon.), 1729 ; 'Frederick, Duke of Brunswick-Lunenburgh, 1729 ; 'Love Letters on all occasions,' 1730 ; 'The Unfortunate Princess,' 1741 ; 'A Present for a Servant Maid' (anon.), 1743; 'The Virtuous Villager,' 1742 ; 'The Fortunate Foundlings' (anon.), 1744 ; 'The Female Spectator' (24 pts.), 1744-46 ; 'The Parrot' (9 pts.), 1746 ; 'The Fruitless Enquiry,' 1747 ; 'Epistles for the Ladies' (2 vols., anon.), 1749 ; 'The History of Miss Betsy Thoughtless,' 1751 ; 'The History of Jemmy and Jenny Jessamy ' (anon.), 1753 ; 'The Invisible Spy' (under pseud. of 'Exploralibus '), 1755 ; 'The Wife' (anon.), 1756 ; 'The Husband, in Answer to the Wife ' (anon.), 1756.

Posthumous : 'History of Leonora Meadowson' (2 vols.), 1788.

She *translated :* 'Mary Stuart,' 1725 ; Mme. de Gomez's 'La Belle Assemblée' [1732 ?], and L'Entretien des Beaux Esprits,' 1734 ; Chev. Mouki's 'The Virtuous Villager' (anon.), 1742.

*HAZLITT (William), 1778 - 1830. Born, at Maidstone, 10 April 1778. In Ireland with parents, 1780-83 ; in America, 1783-87. Privately educated for some years. At Hackney Unitarian Coll., 1793-97. Visit to Coleridge, 1798. Began to study painting. In Paris, winter 1802-03. Painted various portraits on his return. Married Sarah Stoddart, 1 May 1808. Settled at Winterslow. Removed to London, 1812. Lectured at Russell Institution, Jan. 1812. Parliamentary Reporter to 'Morning Chronicle,' 1812-14 ; dramatic critic to same, 1814-16. Friendship with Lamb and Leigh Hunt. Contrib. to 'The Champion,' 1814-16 ; to 'The Examiner,' 1814-27 ; to 'Edinburgh Review,' 1814-30 ; to 'The Yellow Dwarf,' Jan. to May 1818 ; to 'Scots Mag.' 1819 ; to 'Atlas,' 1829-30 ; to 'London Mag.,' 1821 ; to 'New Monthly Mag.,' 1822-30 ; to 'The Liberal,' 1822-23. Lectured at Surrey Institution, 1818, 1819-20. Separated from his wife, 1819. In Scotland, arranging for a divorce from her under Scotch law, spring of 1822 ; matter settled, June 1822. Married Mrs. Bridgewater, 1824. Travelled on Continent,

Sept. 1824 to Oct. 1825. Parted from second wife, Nov. 1825. Died, in London, 18 Sept. 1830.

Works : 'An Essay on the Principles of Human Actions' (anon.), 1805 ; 'Free Thoughts on Public Affairs' (anon.), 1806 ; 'Reply to the Essay on Population by . . . Malthus' (anon.), 1807 ; 'A New and Improved Grammar of the English Tongue,' 1810 ; 'The Round Table' (with Leigh Hunt ; from 'Examiner'; 2 vols.), 1817 ; 'Characters of Shakespeare's plays,' 1817 ; 'A View of the English Stage' (from 'Morning Chronicle'), 1818 (another edn. enlarged, called 'Criticisms and Dramatic Essays,' 1851) ; 'Lectures on the English Poets,' 1818 ; 'Lectures on the English Comic Writers,' 1819 ; 'Letter to W. Gifford,' 1819 ; 'Political Essays,' 1819 ; 'Lectures chiefly on the Dramatic Literature of the reign of Queen Elizabeth,' 1820 ; 'Table Talk' (2 vols.), 1821-22 ; 'Liber Amoris' (anon.), 1823 ; 'Characteristics ' (anon.), 1823 ; 'Select British Poets,' 1824 (suppressed ; another edn. called 'Select Poets of Great Britain,' 1825) ; 'Sketches of the Principal Picture Galleries in England' (anon.), 1824 (enlarged edn., called 'Criticisms on Art,' 1843-44) ; 'The Spirit of the Age' (anon.), 1825 ; 'The Plain Speaker' (anon), 1826 ; 'Notes of a Journey through France and Italy ' (anon., from 'Morning Chronicle'), 1826 (another edn., with author's name, same year) ; 'The Life of Napoleon Buonaparte,' vols. i., ii., 1828 ; vols. iii., iv., 1830.

Posthumous : 'Literary Remains' (2 vols.), 1836 ; 'Painting and the Fine Arts' (from 'Encycl. Brit.'), 1838 ; 'Sketches and Essays,' 1839 (another edn., called 'Men and Manners,' 1852) ; 'Winterslow: essays and characters,' 1850 ; 'Dramatic Essays,' ed. by W. Archer and R. W. Lowe, 1895 [1894].

He *edited :* an abridgement of A. Tucker's 'Light of Nature' (anon.), 1807 ; 'Eloquence of the British Senate ' (anon.), 1807 ; 'Memoir of T. Holcroft' (anon.), 1816 ; 'Conver-

sations of J. Northcote,' 1830 ; North-
cote's ' Life of Titian,' 1830.

Life : by W. Carew Hazlitt, 1867.

HEBER (Reginald), *Bishop of Calcutta.* **1783-1826.** Born, at Malpas,
Cheshire, 21 April 1783. First education at Whitchurch Grammar School ;
with private tutor, 1796-1800. Matric., Brasenose Coll., Oxford, 8 Nov.
1800; Latin verse prize, 1800; Newdigate, 1803 ; B.A., 1804 ; Fellow of
All Souls, 1804 ; English Essay, 1805 ;
M.A., 1808. Travelled in Germany,
Russia and Crimea, 1805-07. Ordained, 1807 ; Vicar of Hodnet, 1807-
23. Married Amelia Shipley, April
1809. Contrib. to ' Christian Observer' and 'Quarterly Rev.' Prebendary of St. Asaph, 1812. Bampton Lecturer, Oxford, 1815. Preacher
at Lincoln's Inn, 1822. D.D., Oxford,
by diploma, 10 Feb. 1823. Bishop of
Calcutta, 1823. Died, at Trichinopoly,
3 April 1826. Buried there.

Works : ' A Sense of Honour '
(prize essay), 1805 ; ' Palestine '
(Newdigate poem), 1807 ; ' Europe,'
1809 (2nd edn. same year) ; ' Poems,'
1812 ; 'The Personality and Office of
the Christian Comforter' (Bampton
lectures), 1816.

Posthumous: 'Hymns,' edited by
his wife, 1827 ; ' Narrative of a
Journey through the upper Provinces
of India' (2 vols.), 1828 ; ' Sermons
preached in England,' ed. by Mrs.
Heber, 1829 ; ' Sermons preached in
India,' ed. by Mrs. Heber, 1830;
' Sermons,' ed. by Sir R. H. Inglis
(3 vols.), 1837 ; ' Poetical Works,'
1841.

He *edited:* Jeremy Taylor's works,
1822.

Life : by Mrs. Heber (including
correspondence and some unpublished
works), 1830 ; by G. Smith, 1895.

HELPS (*Sir* Arthur), 1813-1875.
Born, at Balham Hill, Streatham, 10
July 1813. At Eton, 1829-32. Matric. Trin. Coll., Camb., 1832 ; B.A.,
1835 ; M.A., 1839. Priv. Sec. to
Chancellor of Exchequer, 1836[?]-39 ;
to Sec. for Ireland, 1839. Commissioner of French, Danish and Spanish

Claims. Married Bissel Fuller.
Clerk of Privy Council, June 1860
to March 1875. Hon. D.C.L., Oxford, 8 June 1864. C.B., June 1871;
K.C.B., July 1872. Died, in London,
7 March 1875.

Works : ' Thoughts in the Cloister
and the Crowd ' (anon.), 1835 ; 'Essays
written in the intervals of Business'
(anon.), 1841 ; ' Catherine Douglas '
(anon.), 1843 ; ' King Henry II.'
(anon.), 1843 ; ' The Claims of Labour '
(anon.), 1844 ; 'Friends in Council,'
ser. i. (2 pts.), 1847-49; ser. ii., 1859 ;
'A Letter from one of the Special Con-
stables in London ' (anon.), 1848 ;
' The Conquerors of the New World '
(anon.), 1848 ; ' Companions of my
Solitude ' (anon.), 1851 ; ' A Letter on
" Uncle Tom's Cabin " ' (anon.), 1852 ;
' The Spanish Conquest in America '
(4 vols.), 1855-61 ; ' Oulita the Serf '
(anon.), 1858 ; ' Organization in Daily
Life ' (anon.), 1862 ; ' Life of Las
Casas,' 1868 [1867] ; ' Realmah '
(anon.), 1868 ; ' Life of Columbus '
(with H. P. Thomas), 1869 ; ' Life of
Pizarro,' 1869 ; ' Casimir Maremma '
(anon.), 1870 ; ' Brevia ' (anon.), 1871 ;
' Conversations on War ' (anon.), 1871;
' Life of Hernando Cortes,' 1871 ;
' Life and Labours of Mr. Brassey,'
1872 (3rd edn. same year) ; 'Thoughts
upon Government,' 1872 ; ' Some Talk
about Animals ' (anon.), 1873 ; ' Ivan
de Biron ' (anon.), 1874 ; ' Social Pres-
sure ' (anon.), 1875.

He *edited:* the Prince Consort's
' Speeches,' 1862 ; the Queen's ' Leaves
from the Journal of our Life in the
Highlands,' 1868 ; the Queen's 'Moun-
tain, Loch and Glen.' 1869 ; T.
Brassey's ' Work and Wages,' 1872.

**HEMANS (*Mrs.* Felicia Dorothea),
1793-1835.** Born [Felicia Dorothea
Browne], in Liverpool, 25 Sept. 1793.
Family removed to Gwrych, North
Wales, 1800. Educated there. Early
precocity ; a volume of poems pub.,
1808. Married to Capt. Hemans,
1812 ; separated from him, 1818.
Contrib. to ' Edinburgh Monthly
Mag.,' 1820. Prize Poem, Royal Soc.
of Literature, 1821. Tragedy, 'The

Vespers of Palermo,' produced at Covent Garden, 12 Dec. 1823. Contrib. to 'Blackwood's Mag.,' and 'Colburn's Mag.' Life mainly spent in Wales till 1828; removed to Liverpool, 1828; to Dublin, 1831. Died, in Dublin, 16 May 1835 ; buried in St. Anne's Church.

Works : 'Poems,' 1808 ; 'England and Spain,' 1808 ; 'The Domestic Affections,' 1812 ; 'The Restoration of the Works of Art to Italy,' 1816 ; 'Modern Greece' (anon.), 1817 ; 'Translations from Camoens and other poets' (anon.), 1818 ; 'Tales and Historic Scenes,' 1819 ; 'The Meeting of Bruce and Wallace,' 1819 ; 'The Sceptic,' 1820 ; 'Superstition and Error,' 1820 ; 'Stanzas on the Death of the late King,' 1820 ; 'Dartmoor,' 1821 ; 'Welsh Melodies,' 1822 ; 'The Vespers of Palermo' (anon.), 1823 ; 'The Siege of Valencia,' 1823; 'Lays of Many Lands,' 1825 ; 'The Forest Sanctuary,' 1825 ; 'Poems' (American edn.), 1825 ; 'Records of Women,' 1828 (2nd edn. same year) ; 'Songs of the Affections,' 1830 ; 'Hymns on the Works of Nature,' 1833 ; 'Hymns for Childhood,' 1834 ; 'National Lyrics and Songs for Music,' 1834 ; 'Scenes and Hymns of Life,' 1834.

Collected Works: ed. by Mrs. Hughes (7 vols.), 1839.

Life : by Mrs. Hughes, 1839 ; by W. M. Rossetti, in 1873 edn. of 'Works.'

* HENLEY (William Ernest), b. 1849. Born, at Gloucester, 1849. Educated at Crypt Grammar School (intermittently, on account of ill-health), 1861-67. Contrib. to London periodicals from 1869. Married Anna Boyle, 1878. Editor of 'London,' 1877-78 ; of 'Mag. of Art,' 1882-86 ; of 'Scots Observer' (afterwards 'National Observer'), 1888-94. Play, 'Beau Austin' (written with R. L. Stevenson), produced at Haymarket Theatre, 3 Nov. 1890. LL.D., St. Andrews, 1893. Editor of 'New Review' since Jan. 1895.

Works : 'Memorial Cat. of French and Dutch Loan Collections, Edin-

burgh Internat. Exhbn. of 1886,' 1887 ; 'A Book of Verses,' 1888 ; 'The Graphic Gallery of Shakespeare's Heroines,' 1888 ; 'Pictures at Play' (anon. ; attrib. to A. Lang and W. E. Henley), 1888 ; 'A Century of Artists,' 1889 ; 'Views and Reviews,' 1890 ; 'Lyra Heroica,' 1892 [1891] ; 'Three Plays' (with R. L. Stevenson), 1892 ; 'The Song of the Sword,' 1892 (2nd edn., called : 'London Voluntaries, etc.,' 1893) ; 'A Book of English Prose' (with C. Whibley), 1894 ; 'A London Garland,' 1895 ; 'Macaire' (with R. L. Stevenson), 1895.

He has *edited :* 'The Tudor Translations,' 1892-96 ; 'English Classics,' 1894-96 ; 'The Poetry of Robert Burns' (with T. F. Henderson), 1896-97 ; Byron's Works, 1897, etc.

HERBERT (Edward), *Lord Herbert of Cherbury,* **1583-1648.** Born, at Eyton-on-Severn, 3 March 1583. At school in Shropshire, 1594-96. Matric. Univ. Coll., Oxford, June 1596. Married Mary Herbert, 28 Feb. 1599. To London, 1600. Knight of the Bath, 24 July 1603. M.P. for Merionethshire, 1604-11. Sheriff of Montgomeryshire, 1605. Travelled abroad, 1608-09 and 1610. Served in army of Prince of Orange, 1614 ; abroad, 1614-17. English Ambassador at Paris, 1619-24. Created Lord Castleisland of Kerry, 1624 ; Lord Herbert of Cherbury, 7 May 1629. Mem. of Council of War, 27 June 1632. Retired to Montgomery Castle, 1642. Obliged to cede it to Parliamentary army, Sept. 1644. To London, Oct. 1644 ; obtained pension from Parliament. Steward of Duchy of Cornwall and Warden of Stannaries, 26 Oct. 1646. Died, in London, 20 Aug. 1648. Buried in St. Giles-in-the-Fields.

Works : 'De Veritate' (Paris), 1624 (London, 1633) ; 'De Causis Errorum, etc.,' 1645.

Posthumous : 'The Life and Reigne of King Henry the Eighth,' 1649 ; 'Expeditio in Ream insulam,' 1656 ; 'De Religione Gentilium,' 1663 ;

9 —2

'Occasional Verses,' 1665 ; 'The Life of Edward, Lord Herbert of Cherbury, written by himself' (ed. by Horace Walpole), 1764 ; 'A Dialogue between a Tutor and a Pupil,' 1768.

HERBERT (George), 1593-1633.
[Brother of preceding.] Born, at Montgomery Castle, 3 April 1593. At Westminster School, 1605 [?]-09 ; King's Scholar, 5 May 1609. Matric., Trin. Coll., Camb., 18 Dec. 1609 ; B.A., 1613 ; M.A., 1616 ; Minor Fellow, 3 Oct. 1614 ; Major Fellow, 15 March 1616 ; Prelector in School of Rhetoric, 1618 ; Deputy Public Orator, 21 Oct. 1619 ; Public Orator, 18 Jan. 1619 to 1627. Contrib. to 'Cambridge Elegies,' 1612, 1619. Prebend. of Layton Ecclesia, 1625. Married Jane Danvers, 5 March 1629. Rector of Fugglestone-with-Bemerton, Wilts, April 1630. Died, at Bemerton, 3 March 1633. Buried in Bemerton church.

Works : 'Parentalia,' 1627 ; 'Oratio, qua . . . Principis Caroli Reditum ex Hispaniis celebravit Georgius Herbert,' 1623.
Posthumous : 'The Temple' (priv. ptd. ; only one copy known), 1633 (two other edns., publicly ptd., same year) ; 'Jacula Prudentum,' 1651 (originally pubd. in 'Witt's Recreation,' 1640, as 'Outlandish Proverbs') ; 'Herbert's Remains,' 1652 ; 'Musæ Responsoriæ ad Andreæ Melvini Scoti Anti-Tami-Cami-Categoriam' (pubd. as appendix to Vivian's 'Ecclesiastes Solomonis'), 1662.
He *translated :* Cornaro's 'Treatise of Temperance,' 1634 ; J. de Valdes' 'Hundred and Ten Considerations,' 1638.
Collected Works: ed. by Grosart (3 vols.), 1874 ; ed. by R. A. Wilmott, 1893.
Life : by Izaak Walton, 1670.

HERRICK (Robert), 1591-1674.
Born, in London, July [?] 1591 ; baptized, 24 Aug. Probably educated at Westminster School ; and at St. John's Coll., Camb. Removed to Trinity Hall, 1616 ; B.A., 1617 ; M.A., 1620. Rector of Dean Prior,

Devonshire, 2 Oct. 1629 to 1647. Deprived of living, 1647 ; returned to London. Restored to living, 24 Aug. 1662. Died, at Dean Prior, Oct. 1674 ; buried in Dean Prior church, 15 Oct.
Works : 'King Obron's Feast' (anon. ; in 'A Description of the King and Queene of Fayries'), 1635 ; 'His Mistris Shade' (anon. ; in Shakespeare's 'Poems'), 1640 ; 'Hesperides' (with 'Noble Numbers'), 1648 ; Poems in 'Lacrymæ Musarum,' 1649 ; Poems in 'Witt's Recreations,' 1650.
Collected Works : ed. by Lord Dundrennan (2 vols.), 1823 ; by Grosart (3 vols.), 1876 ; by A. W. Pollard, 1891 ; by Saintsbury (2 vols.), 1893.

HEYWOOD (John), 1497 [?]-1580[?].
Born, in London [?], 1497 [?]. Chorister at Chapel Royal. Possibly at Broadgates Hall (afterwards Pembroke Coll.), Oxford. Musician and provider of Court entertainments. Married. Later life probably spent at Malines. Died, about 1580 [?].
Works : 'A Mery Play between the Pardoner and the Frere,' 1533 (anon. ; only one copy known) ; 'A Mery Play between Johan the Husband, Tyb the Wife, and Sir Jhan the Priest,' 1533 (anon. ; only one copy known) ; 'The Play of the Wether,' 1533 ; 'The Play of Love,' [1533] ; 'Of Gentylnes and Nobylyte' (anon. ; attrib. to Heywood) [1535] ; 'The Four P.P.' [1545 ?] ; 'A dialogue conteining the number in effect of all the proverbes in the Englishe tongue' [1549] ; 'The Spider and the Flie,' 1556.
Posthumous : 'A Dialogue on Wit and Folly,' ed. F. W. Fairholt, 1846.

HEYWOOD (Thomas), 1575 [?]-1650 [?]. Born, in Lincolnshire, 1575 [?]. Probably educated at Peterhouse, Camb. A member of Henslowe's company of players ; of Earl of Southampton's company ; and of Earl of Worcester's (afterwards the Queen's) company. Voluminous writer of plays. Translated several Latin classical works. Died, 1650 [?].

Works : 'If you know not me, you know nobody' (2 pts.), 1606 ; 'A Woman kilde with Kindnesse,' 1607 ; 'The Fair Maid of the Exchange' (anon.), 1607 ; 'The Rape of Lucrece,' 1608 ; 'Troia Britannica,' 1609 ; 'The Golden Age,' 1611 ; 'An Apology for Actors,' 1612 ; 'A Funeral Elegy on the Death of Prince Henry,' 1613 ; 'The first and second parts of King Edward the Fourth' (anon.), 1613 ; 'A Marriage Triumph' on the Nuptials of the Prince Palatine, 1612 ; 'The Silver Age,' 1613 ; 'The Brazen Age,' 1613 ; 'The Four Prentices of London,' 1615; 'The Captives,' 1624 ; 'Γυναικειον,' 1624 ; 'England's Elizabeth,' 1631 ; 'The Fair Maid of the West,' 1631 ; 'Eromena,' 1632 ; 'The Iron Age,' 1632 ; 'The English Traveller,' 1633 ; 'A Maidenhead Well Lost,' 1634 ; 'The Late Lancashire Witches' (with R. Brome), 1634 ; 'The Hierarchy of the Blessed Angels,' 1635 ; 'Philocothonista,'1635; 'Love's Maistresse,' 1636 ; 'A Challenge for Beauty,' 1636 ; 'The Royall King,' 1637 ; 'A True Description of His Majesty's Royal Ship,' 1637 ; 'A Curtain Lecture' (under initials: T. H.), 1637 ; 'Pleasant Dialogues and Dramas,' 1637 ; 'The Royal King and the Loyal King,' 1637 ; 'Porta Pietatis,' 1638 ; 'The Wise Woman of Hogsdon,' 1638 ; 'Londini Status Placatus,' 1639 ; 'The Exemplary Lives . . . of Nine of the most worthy Women of the World,' 1640 ; 'The Life of Merlin,' 1641 ; 'Machiavel' (anon.), 1641 ; 'Fortune by Land and Sea' (with Rowley), 1655.

He *translated :* 'Two . . . notable Histories' of Sallust, 1608 ; and *edited :* Lydgate's 'Life and Death of Hector,' 1614 ; Cooke's 'Greene's Tu Quoque,' 1622 ; Sir R. Barckley's 'Felicitie of Man,' 1631 ; Marlowe's 'Jew of Malta,' 1633.

Collected Works : in 6 vols,, with memoir, 1874.

HOBBES (Thomas), 1588 - 1679. Born, at Westport, Wilts, 5 April 1588. At school at Westport, 1592-96 ; thence to Malmesbury, 1596, and afterwards at another school at Westport. To Magdalen Hall, Oxford, 1603 ; B.A.. 5 Feb. 1608. Tutor and secretary to William Cavendish, son of first Earl of Devonshire, 1608-28 ; travelled abroad with him, 1610. Travelling tutor to son of Sir Gervase Clifton, 1629-31. Tutor to third Earl of Devonshire, 1631-40. Travelled abroad with him, 1634-37. Fled to Paris at meeting of Long Parliament, Nov. 1640. Remained there till 1651, when he retreated to England in consequence of complications caused by publication of 'Leviathan.' Resumed post of secretary to Earl of Devonshire, 1663. Pension of £100 from Charles II. at Restoration. Lived in London till 1675 ; remainder of life spent at country seats of Earl of Devonshire. Died, at Hardwick, Derbyshire, 4 Dec. 1679. Buried in Hault Hucknall Church.

Works : 'De Mirabilibus Pecci' [1636 ?] ; 'Elementorum Philosophiæ sectio tertia de Cive' (under initials : T.H.), 1642 ; 'Tractatus Opticus' (in Mersenne's 'Cogitata Physico-Mathematica'), 1644 ; 'Humane Nature,' 1650 ; 'De Corpore Politico,' 1650 ; 'Epistle to Davenant,' 1651 ; 'Leviathan,' 1651 ; 'Of Liberty and Necessity,'1654 ; 'Elementorum Philosophiæ sectio prima de Corpore,' 1655 ; 'A Briefe of the Art of Rhetorique' (anon.), [1655 ?] ; 'Questions concerning Liberty, Necessity and Chance,' 1656 ; 'Στιγμαι Ἀγεωμετριας,' 1657 ; 'Elementorum Philosophiæ sectio secunda de Homine,' 1658 ; 'Examinatio et Emendatio Mathematicæ Hodiernæ,' 1660 ; 'Dialogus Physicus,' 1661; 'Problemata Physica,'1662; 'Mr. Hobbes considered,' 1662 ; 'De Principiis et Ratiocinatione Geometrarum,' 1666 ; 'Quadratura Circuli,' 1669 ; 'Rosetum Geometricum,' 1671 ; Three Papers presented to the Royal Society attacking Dr. Wallis, 1671 ; 'Lux Mathematica' (under initials : R. R.), 1672 ; 'Principia et Problemata aliquot Geometrica' (under initials ; T. H.), 1674 ; 'Decameron Physiologicum,'

1678 ; 'Behemoth' (written, and suppressed, 1668), privately published, 1679; publicly (under initials : T. H.), 1680 ; 'Vita, authore seipso,' 1679. *Posthumous :* 'An Historical Narration concerning Heresie,' 1680 ; 'T. H. Malmesb. Vita' (in 'Vitæ Hobbianæ Auctarium'), 1681; 'Dialogue between a Philosopher and a Student of the Common Law,' 1681 ; 'An Answer to . . . The Catching of the Leviathan,' 1682 ; 'Hobbes's Tripos,' 1684 ; 'Historia Ecclesiastica,' 1688.

He *translated :* 'Thucydides,' 1629 ; Homer's 'Iliad and Odyssey,' 1675.

Collected Works : 'Opera Philosophica,' 1668 ; 'Moral and Political Works,' ed. by J. Campbell, 1750 ; Complete Works, ed. by Sir W. Molesworth (16 vols.), 1839-45.

Life : by G. C. Robertson, 1886.

HOGG (James), 1770-1835. Born, at Ettrick, Selkirkshire, 1770 ; baptized, 9 Dec. 1770. Employed as shepherd in various quarters till 1800. Managed his father's farm at Ettrick, 1801-03. Made unsuccessful attempts at sheep-farming on his own account. Having by this time published some poems, settled in Edinburgh, 1810, to take up literary career. Ed. 'The Spy,' Sept. 1810 to 1811. Presented by Duke of Buccleuch with the farm of Eltrive Lake, Yarrow, 1816. Settled there. Helped to start 'Blackwood's Mag.,' 1817 ; became frequent contributor. Married Margaret Phillips, 1820. Visit to London, 1832. Entertained at a public dinner there ; also at Peebles in 1833. Died, 21 Nov. 1835. Buried in Ettrick churchyard.

Works : 'Scottish Pastorals,' 1801 ; 'The Shepherd's Guide,' 1807 ; 'The Mountain Bard,' 1807 ; 'The Forest Minstrel' (mainly by Hogg), 1810 ; 'The Queen's Wake,' 1813 ; 'The Hunting of Badlewe' (under pseud. of 'J. H. Craig'), 1814 ; 'The Pilgrims of the Sun,' 1815 ; 'Mador of the Moor,' 1816 ; 'The Poetic Mirror' (anon.), 1816 ; 'Dramatic Tales' (anon.), 1817 ; 'The Long Pack' (anon.), 1817; 'The Brownie of Bodsbeck' (2 vols.), 1818 ; 'Jacobite Relics

of Scotland' (2 vols.), 1819-20 ; 'Winter Evening Tales,' 1820 ; 'The Royal Jubilee' (anon.), 1822 ; 'The Three Perils of Man' (3 vols.), 1822 ; 'The Three Perils of Women' (3 vols.), 1823 ; 'The Private Memoirs and Confessions of a Justified Sinner' (anon.), 1824 ; 'Queen Hynde,' 1825 ; 'The Shepherd's Calendar,' 1829 ; 'Songs' (anon.), 1831 ; 'Altrive Tales,' 1832 ; 'A Queer Book' (anon.), 1832; 'A Series of Lay Sermons,' 1834 ; 'The Domestic Manners and Private Life of Sir Walter Scott,' 1834 ; 'Tales of the Wars of Montrose,' 1835.

Collected Works : in 2 vols., ed. by Blackie, with *life* by Rev. T. Thomson, 1865-66.

HOLINSHED (Raphael), 1520 [?]-1580 [?]. Born, probably in Cheshire, about 1520 [?]. Worked in printing office of Reginald Wolfe. 'Chronicle' begun about 1574. Died, 1580 [?].

Works : 'The . . . Chronicles of England, Scotlande, and Irelande' (3 vols.), 1577.

HOLMES (Oliver Wendell), 1809-1894. Born, at Cambridge, Mass., 29 Aug. 1809. At schools at Cambridge and Andover, 1819-25. To Harvard University, summer of 1825 ; B.A., 1829. First poems appeared in the Harvard 'Collegian,' 1830. Studied medicine in Paris, 1833-35. M.D., Cambridge, Mass., 1836. Prof. of Anatomy and Physiology, Dartmouth Coll., 1838-40. Married Amelia Lee Jackson, 15 June 1840. Prof. of Anatomy, Harvard Univ., 1847-82; Professor Emeritus, 1882. Gave up medical practice, 1849. Contributor to 'Atlantic Monthly' from 1857. Edited 'The Atlantic Almanack' with D. G. Mitchell, 1867. Hon. LL.D., Harvard, 1886. Visit to Europe, 1886. Hon. LL.D. Cambridge, 1886 ; Hon. D.C.L., Oxford, 1886 ; Hon. LL.D., Edinburgh, 1886. Died, in Boston, Mass., 7 Oct. 1894. Buried there.

Works : 'Poems,' 1836 ; 'Boyston Prize Dissertations,' 1838 ; 'Lectures on Homœopathy, 1842 ; 'Terpsichore,'

1843 ; 'Urania,' 1846 ; 'An Introductory Lecture,' 1847 ; 'Astræa,'
1850 ; 'The Benefactors of the Medical School of Harvard,' 1850 ; 'Oration' [before New England Soc.], 1855 ;
'The Autocrat of the Breakfast Table,'
1858 ; 'The Professor at the Breakfast Table,' 1860 ; 'Currents and
Counter-Currents in Medical Science,'
1861 ; 'Songs in Many Keys,' 1861 ;
'Elsie Venner,' 1861 ; 'Border Lines
in some provinces of Medical Science,'
1862 ; 'Oration' [on Independence
Day], 1863; 'Soundings from the "Atlantic," ' 1866 ; 'The Guardian Angel'
1867 ; 'Wit and Humour,' 1867 ;
'Mechanism in Thought and Morals,'
1870 (2nd edn., 'with Notes and After-
thoughts,' same year) ; 'The Poet at
the Breakfast Table,' 1872 ; 'The
Claims of Dentistry,' 1872 ; 'Songs of
Many Seasons,' 1875 ; 'The Story of
Iris,' 1877 ; 'John Lothrop Motley,'
1878 ; 'The School-Boy,' 1879 ; 'The
Iron Gate,' 1881 ; 'Pages from an
Old Volume of Life,' 1883 ; 'Medical
Essays,' 1883 ; 'Grandmother's Story,
and other poems,' 1883 ; 'Ralph Waldo
Emerson,' 1885 ; 'A Mortal An-
tipathy,' 1885 ; 'The Last Leaf,' 1886 ;
'Our Hundred Days in Europe,' 1887 ;
'Before the Curfew,' 1888 ; 'Over
the Teacups,' 1891 [1890].
Collected Works : in 13 vols., 1891.
Life : by J. T. Morse, 1896.

HOME (John), 1722-1808. Born,
at Leith, 22 Sept. 1722. Educated at
Leith Grammar School, and at Edinburgh Univ. Licensed Probationer
of Presbyterian Church, 4 April 1745.
Enlisted as Volunteer during Rebellion of 1745-46. Minister of Athel-
staneford, 11 Feb. 1747. Tragedy
'Agis' refused by Garrick, 1747.
Tragedy 'Douglas' refused by Garrick,' 1755 ; performed in Edinburgh,
14 Dec. 1756 ; produced at Covent
Garden, 14 March 1757. Pension of
£100 from Princess of Wales, 1757.
Returned to Scotland. Indicted by
Presbytery; resigned ministry, 7 June
1757. Tutor to Prince of Wales,
1757. Sec. to Lord Bute, 1757.
'Agis' produced by Garrick at Drury

Lane, 21 Feb. 1758. 'The Siege of
Aquileia' produced at Drury Lane,
21 Feb. 1760. Pension of £300 from
George III., 1760. Conservator of
Scots Privileges at Campvere, Hol-
land (sinecure), 1763-70. 'The Fatal
Discovery' produced at Drury Lane,
23 Feb. 1769. Married Mary Home,
1770. 'Alonzo' produced at Drury
Lane, 27 Jan. 1773. To Bath with
Hume, April 1776 ; to Edinburgh
with him, July 1776. 'Alfred,' pro-
duced, at Drury Lane, 21 Jan. 1778.
Enlisted in South Fusiliers,' 1778.
Died, at Murchiston, 5 Sept. 1808.

Works : 'Douglas' (anon.), 1757 ;
'Agis' (anon.), 1758 ; 'The Siege of
Aquileia' (anon.), 1760 ; 'Dramatick
Works,' 1760 ; 'The Fatal Discovery'
(anon.), 1769 ; 'Alonzo' (anon.), 1773 ;
'Alfred' (anon.), 1778 ; 'The History
of the Rebellion in . . . 1745,' 1802.
Collected Works : ed. by H. Mac-
kenzie (3 vols.), 1822.
Life : by H. Mackenzie, 1822.

HOOD (Thomas), 1799-1845. Born,
in London, 23 May 1799. At school
in London. In mercantile house,
1813-15. Health failed. At Dundee,
1815-18 ; contrib. to local Press from
1814. Articled to firm of engravers
in London, 1818 ; but owing to ill-
health devoted himself to literature.
On staff of 'London Mag.,' 1821-23.
Married Jane Reynolds, 5 May 1824.
Edited 'The Gem,' 1829; edited 'The
Comic Annual,' 1830-42. Financial
losses, 1834. Lived at Coblentz,
1835-37 ; at Ostend, 1837-40. Re-
turned to England, April 1840.
Joined staff of 'New Monthly Mag.,'
1840; editor, Aug. 1841 to Jan. 1844 ;
'The Song of the Shirt,' published in
'Punch,' Christmas 1843. Started
'Hood's Mag.,' Jan. 1844. Crown
Pension of £100 granted to his wife,
Nov. 1844. Died, at Hampstead, 3
May 1845. Buried in Kensal Green
Cemetery.

Works : 'Odes and Addresses to
Great People' (anon.), 1825 ; 'Whims
and Oddities' (2 ser.), 1826-27 ;
'National Tales' (2 vols.), 1827 ; 'The
Plea of the Midsummer Fairies,'

1827 ; 'The Epping Hunt,' 1829 ; 'The Dream of Eugene Aram,' 1831 ; 'Tylney Hall' (3 vols.), 1834 ; 'Hood's Own,' 1839 ; 'Up the Rhine,' 1840 (2nd edition same year) · 'Whimsicalities' (2 vols.), 1844.

Posthumous : 'Fairy Land' (with his daughter, Mrs. Broderip), 1861 [1860]; 'Hood's Own,' 2nd series, ed. by his son, 1861. *Collected Works:* 'Poems' (2 vols.), 1846 ; 'Works,' ed. by his son and daughter (10 vols.), 1869-73. *Life:* 'Memorials,' by Mrs. Broderip, 1860.

HOOK (Theodore Edward), 1788-1841. Born, in London, 22 Sept. 1788. Early education at private schools. At Harrow, June 1804 to 1810. Wrote opera libretti, farces and melodramas during school days. Matric. St. Mary Hall, Oxford, 2 July 1810. Accountant-General and Treasurer at Mauritius, Oct. 1813. Deprived of office owing to deficit in treasury, and sent back to England, 1818. Imprisoned, 1823-25. Edited 'The Arcadian,' 1820 ; edited 'John Bull,' 1820-41 ; edited 'New Monthly Mag.,' 1837-38. F.S.A., 27 Feb. 1840. Died, at Fulham, 24 Aug. 1841.

Works: 'The Soldier's Return' (anon.), 1805 ; 'Catch Him Who Can,' 1806 ; 'The Invisible Girl,' 1806 ; 'Tekeli,' 1806 ; 'The Fortress,' 1807 ; 'Siege of St. Quintin,' 1807 ; 'Music Mad,' 1808 ; 'Killing No Murder,' 1809 ; 'Safe and Sound,' 1809 ; 'The Man of Sorrow' (3 vols.), 1809 ; 'The Trial by Jury,' 1811 ; 'Darkness Visible,' 1811 (2nd edition same year); 'Pigeons and Crows,' 1819 ; 'Facts illustrative of the treatment of Napoleon Buonaparte in St. Helena' (anon.), 1819 ; 'Exchange No Robbery,' (anon.), 1820 ; 'Tentamen' (under pseud. of 'Vicesimus Blenkinsop'), 1820 ; 'Peter and Paul,' 1821 ; 'Sayings and Doings,' 1st series (3 vols.; anon.), 1824 ; 2nd series (3 vols ; anon.), 1825 ; 3rd series (3 vols.), 1828 ; 'Reminiscences of Michael Kelly,' 1826 ; 'Maxwell' (anon.), 1830 ; 'The Life of Sir David Baird' (2 vols.;

anon.),1832 ; 'The Parson's Daughter' (anon.), 1833 ; 'Love and Pride ' (anon.), 1833 ; 'Gilbert Gurney' (anon.), 1836; 'Jack Brag' (anon.), 1837 ; 'Pascal Bruno,' 1837 ; 'Births, Deaths, and Marriages' (anon.), 1839; 'Gurney Married' (anon.), 1839 ; 'Cousin Geoffrey,' 1840 ; 'Precept and Practice,' 1840.

Posthumous: 'Fathers and Sons,' 1842 ; 'Peregrine Bunce' (perhaps spurious), 1842 ; 'The Widow and the Marquess,' 1842 ; 'The Ramsbottom Letters,' 1872 ; 'The Ramsbottom Papers' [1874].

He *edited :* 'Peter Priggins, 1841 ; 'The Parish Clerk,' 1840. *Collected Works:* 'Choice Humourous Works' [1873]. *Life:* 'Life and Remains,' by R. H. D. Barham, 1877.

HOOK (Walter Farquhar), *Dean of Chichester.* **1798-1875.** [Nephew of preceding.] Born, in London, 13 March, 1798. At school at Hertford, 1807-09 ; at Tiverton, 1809-12 ; at Winchester, 1812-17. Matric., Ch. Ch., Oxford, 17 Dec. 1817 ; Student, 1817-27 ; B.A., 1821 ; M.A., 1824 ; B.D. and D.D., 1837. Student of Lincoln's Inn, 1819. Ordained Deacon, 30 Sept. 1821 ; Curate to his father at Whippingham, I. of W., 1821-25. Perpetual Curate of Molesey, near Birmingham, 1826-31. Lecturer at St. Philip's, Birmingham, 1827. Chaplain in Ordinary to King, 1827. Vicar of Holy Trinity, Coventry, 1828-37. Prebendary of Lincoln, 1832-59. Select Preacher, Oxford, 1833-34 and 1858-59. Married Anna Delicia Johnstone, 4 June 1829. Vicar of Leeds, 1837-59. Chaplain in Ordinary to Queen, 1839-75. Dean of Chichester, 1859-75. F.R.S., 5 June 1862. (Refused Deanery of Rochester, 1870 ; of Canterbury and St. Paul's, 1871; of Winchester, 1872.) Died, at Chichester, 20 Oct. 1875. Buried in Mid-Lavant churchyard, near Chichester.

Works [besides a number of sermons, addresses and religious tracts published between 1828 and 1868]:

'The Peculiar Character of the Church of England,' 1822 ; 'The Last Days of Our Lord's Ministry,' 1832 ; 'The Catholic Clergy of Ireland,' 1836 ; 'Private Prayers,' 1836 ; 'A Book of Common Prayer,' 1836 ; 'Five Sermons preached before the Univ. of Oxford,' 1837 ; 'A Letter to his Parishioners on the use of the Athanasian Creed' (anon.), 1838 ; 'Hear the Church,' 1838 ; 'The Gospel . . . the Basis of Education,' 1839 ; 'Presbyterian Rights asserted' (anon.), 1839 ; 'A Call to Union,' 1839 ; 'Prayers for Young Christians,' 1841 ; 'Sermons on various subjects,' 1841 ; 'Letter to the Bishop of Ripon,' 1841 ; 'Reasons for Contributing towards the support of an English Bishop at Jerusalem,' 1842 ; 'A Church Dictionary,' 1842 (2nd edn. same year) ; 'Mutual Forbearance in Things Indifferent,' 1843 ; '"Take Heed what ye hear,"' 1844 ; 'The Cross of Christ,' 1844 ; 'A Dictionary of Ecclesiastical Biography' (8 vols.), 1845-52 ; 'On the means of rendering more efficient the education of the People,' 1846 (9th edn. same year) ; 'The Three Reformations,' 1847 ; 'Sermons suggested by the Miracles' (2 vols.), 1847-48 ; 'Sermons on the Ordinances of the Church,' 1847 ; 'The Nonentity of Romish Saints,' 1849 ; 'A Companion to the Altar,' 1849 ; 'Letter to Sir W. Farquhar,' 1850 ; 'A Church School Hymn Book,' 1850 ; 'Duty of English Churchmen,' 1851 ; 'Discourses,' 1853 ; 'Lives of the Archbishops of Canterbury,' vol. i., 1860 ; vol. ii., 1862 ; vols. iii., iv., 1865 ; vol. v., 1867 ; vols. vi., vii., 1868 ; vol. viii., 1869 ; vol. ix., 1872 ; vols. x., xi., 1875 ; vol. xii., 1876 ; Disestablished Church in . . . America,' 1869.

Posthumous : 'The Church and its Ordinances,' ed. by his son, W. Hook (2 vols.), 1876.

Life: 'Life and Letters,' by W. R. W. Stephens, 1878.

HOOKER (Richard), 1554 [?]-1600. Born, at Heavitree, Exeter, March 1554 [?]. Educated at Exeter Grammar School. To Corpus Christi Coll., Oxford, as Clerk, 1567 ; Scholar, 24 Dec. 1573 ; B.A., 14 Jan. 1574 ; M.A., 29 March 1577 ; Fellow of C.C.C., 1577-81 ; Deputy to Prof. of Hebrew, July 1579. Rusticated, Oct. to Nov., 1579. Ordained, 1581 [?]. Married Joan Churchman, 1581. Rector of Drayton-Beauchamp, Bucks, Dec. 1584 to March 1585. Master of the Temple, 17 March 1585 to 1591. Rector of Boscombe, Wilts, 1591-95. Sub-dean and Canon of Salisbury. 1591. Rector of Bishopsbourne, Canterbury, July 1595 till his death. Died, at Bishopsbourne, 2 Nov. 1600. Buried in Bishopsbourne church.

Works : 'Of the Lawes of Ecclesiastical Politie,' Bks. i.-iv. [1594 ?] ; Bk. v., 1597.

Posthumous [the first six of the following edited by H. Jackson] : 'Answer to the Supplication that Mr. Travers made to the Council,' 1612 ; 'A Learned Discourse of Justification,' 1612 ; 'A Learned Sermon of the Nature of Pride,' 1612 ; 'A Remedie against Sorrow and Fear,' 1612 ; 'A Learned and Comfortable Sermon of the Certainty . . . of Faith,' 1612 ; 'Two Sermons upon part of St. Jude's Epistle,' 1614 ; 'Of the Lawes of Ecclesiastical Politie,' Bks. vi., viii., 1648 ; Bk. vii. [previously reported lost], in 1662 edn. of Hooker's 'Works.'

Collected Works: ed. by Gauden, 1662 ; ed. by Keble, 7th edn., ed. by Dean Church and Canon Paget, 1888.

Life : by Izaak Walton, 1665 ; by Keble in his edn. of Hooker's 'Works.'

HORNE (Richard Henry), 1803-1884. Born, in London, 1 Jan. 1803. Educated at Sandhurst. Mid-hipman in Mexican Navy. Served in War against Spain, 1829. At conclusion of War went to U.S.A. Returned to England. Contrib. to 'Monthly Repository,' under initials : M.I.D. Contrib. poem to 'Athenæum,' 1828. Edited 'Monthly Re-

pository,' July 1836 to June 1837.
Sub-commissioner to report on Employment of Children in Mines, 1843.
Contrib. to 'Howitt's Journal'; to
'Household Words,' June 1851. Married Miss Foggs, 1847. To Australia
with W. Howitt, 1852 ; Commander
of Gold Escort, Victoria, 1852 ; Commissioner of Crown Lands for Gold
Fields, 1853-54 ; Territorial Magistrate, 1855. Returned to England,
1869. Substituted Christian name
'Hengist' for 'Henry.' Civil List Pension, 1874. Contrib. to 'Harper's
Mag.,'   'New   Quarterly   Mag.,'
'Fraser's Mag.,' 'Longman's Mag.';
and other periodicals. Died, at Margate, 13 March 1884. Buried there.

Works : 'Exposition of the . . .
Barriers excluding Men of Genius
from the Public' (anon.), 1833 ;
'Spirit of Peers and People,' 1834 ;
'Cosmo de Medici,' 1837 ; 'The
Death of Marlowe,' 1837 ; 'The Russian
Catechism' [1837 ?] ; 'Life of Van Am-
burgh' (under pseud. 'Ephraim Watts'),
[1838] ; 'Gregory VII.,' 1840 ; 'The
History of Napoleon' (2 vols.), 1841 ;
'Orion,' 1843 (6th edn. same year) ;
'A New Spirit of the Age' (with
Mrs. Browning and R. Bell), 1844
(2nd edn. same year) ; 'The Good-
natured Bear,' 1846 ; 'Memoirs of a
London Doll,' 1846 ; 'Ballad Ro-
mances,' 1846 ; 'Judas Iscariot,'
1848 ; 'The Poor Artist' (anon.),
1850 ; 'The Dreamer and the
Worker' (2 vols.), 1851 ; 'Australian
Facts and Prospects,' 1859 ; 'Prome-
theus the Fire-bringer,' 1864 ; 'The
South - Sea Sisters,' [1866] ; 'The
"Lady Jocelyn's" Weekly Mail,'
1869 ; 'The Great Peace-maker' (from
'Household Words'), 1872 ; 'The
Countess Von Labanoff' (from 'New
Quarterly Mag.'), 1877 ; 'Laura Di-
balzo,' 1880 ; 'King Nihil's Round
Table,' 1881 ; 'Bible Tragedies'
[1881] ; 'Soliloquium Fratris Rogeri
Baconis' (from 'Fraser's Mag.'),
1882 ; 'The Last Words of Cleanthes'
(from 'Longman's Mag.'), [1883] ;
'Sithron' (anon.), 1883.

He - *edited :* Black's trans. of
Schlegel's 'Lectures,' 1840 ; 'Poems

of Geoffrey Chaucer Modernised,'
1841 ; 'Shakespeare's Works,' 1857 ;
L. Marie's 'Notes . . . on . . . Prize
Essays on the Vine,' 1860.

HOUGHTON, *Baron* [**Richard
Monckton Milnes**], 1809-1885. Born,
in London, 19 June, 1809. Educated
at Hundhill Hall School, and privately.
Matric. Trin. Coll., Camb., Oct. 1827 ;
M.A., 1831. Travelled on Continent,
1832-35. M.P. for Pontefract, 1837-
63. Married Hon. Annabel Crewe,
30 July 1851. One of founders of
Philobiblon Soc., 1853. Hon. D.C.L.,
Oxford, 20 June 1855. Created Baron
Houghton, July 1863. F.R.S., 1868.
Visit to Canada and U.S.A., 1875.
Hon. Fellow, Trin. Coll., Camb., 1875-
85. Secretary for Foreign Corre-
spondence, Royal Acad., 1878. Hon.
LL.D., Edinburgh, 1878. Trustee
of British Museum, 6 May 1881.
Pres. London Library, 1882. Died,
at Vichy, 11 Aug. 1885. Buried at
Fryston.

Works : 'Memorials of a Tour in
some parts of Greece,' 1834 ; 'Poems
of Many Years,' 1838 ; 'Memorials
of a Residence on the Continent, and
Historical Poems,' 1838 (another edn.
called : 'Memorials of Many Scenes,'
1844) ; 'A Speech on the Ballot,'
1839 ; 'Poetry for the People,' 1840 ;
'One Tract More' (anon.), 1841 ;
'Thoughts on Purity of Election,'
1842 ; 'Palm-Leaves,' 1844 ; 'Poems,
legendary and historical,' 1844 ;
'Real Union of England and Ireland,'
1845 ; 'Life, Letters, and Literary
Remains of John Keats' (2 vols.),
1848 ; The 'Events of 1848,' 1849 ;
'Answer to R. Baxter,' 1852 ; 'On
the Apologies for the Massacre of
St. Bartholomew' [1856] ; 'A Discourse of Witchcraft,' 1858 ; 'Good
Night and Good Morning,' 1859 ;
'Address on Social Economy,' 1862 ;
'Monographs,' 1873 ; 'Poetical Works'
(collected ; 2 vols.), 1876.

He *edited :* 'The Tribute' (with
Lord Northampton), 1836 ; Keats'
'Poetical Works,' 1854 ; 'Boswelliana,'
1856 and 1874 ; 'Another Version of Keats' "Hyperion"' [1856] ;

D. Gray's 'The Luggie,' 1862 ; Peacock's Works, 1875 ; Bishop Cranmer's ' Recantacyons' (with J. Gairdner), 1885.

Life : by Sir T. Wemyss Reid, 1890.

HOWELL (James), 1594[?]-1666. Born, in Wales, 1594 [?]. Matric., Jesus Coll., Oxford, 16 June 1610 ; B.A., 17 Dec. 1613. Manager of a glass-works in London, 1614-16 ; travelled abroad on same business, 1616-22. Tutor to sons of Lord Savage for short time in 1622. Travelled in France, same year. In Spain on political mission, 1622-24. Fellow of Jesus Coll., Oxford, 1623. Sec. to Lord Scrope, at York, 1626-30. M.P. for Richmond, Yorks, 1627. Lord President of the North, 1628. On embassy to Denmark, with Earl of Leicester, 1632. Clerk of Council at Nottingham, Aug. 1642. Arrested, in London, during Civil War, 1643 ; imprisoned in the Fleet, possibly also for debt, 1643-51. Gift of £200 from Charles II., Feb. 1661. Appointed Historiographer Royal, 1661. Unmarried. Died, in London, 1666 ; buried, in precincts of Temple Church, 3 Nov. 1666.

Works [exclusive of a large number of political and controversial pamphlets, pubd. between 1643 and 1664] : ' Δενδρολογια,' pt. i., 1640 (French version, 1640 ; Latin version, 1646) ; pt. ii., 1650 ; 'The Vote,' 1642 ; 'Instructions for Forreine Travel,' 1642 ; ' Mercurius Hibernicus,' 1643 ; 'Epistolæ Ho-elianæ,' vol. i., 1645 ; vol. ii., 1647 ; vols. i., ii., iii., 1650 ; vols. i., ii., iii., iv., 1655 ; 'A Perfect Description of the People and Country of Scotland,' 1649 ; 'A Winter Dream,' 1649 ; 'A Trance,' 1649 ; 'A Vision,' 1651 ; 'S.P.Q.V.,' 1651 ; 'Ah! Ha! Tumulus, Thalamus,' 1653 ; 'Londinopolis,' 1657 ; 'Lexicon Tetraglotton,' 1660 [1659-60] ; 'Θηρολογια,' 1660 ; 'Twelve Treatises of the Later Revolutions,' 1661 ; 'A Brief Account of the Royal Matche' (under initials : J. H.), 1662 ; 'New English Grammar' (Eng. and Span.), 1662 ;

'Another Grammar of the Spanish . . . toung' (Eng. and Span.), 1662 ; 'Poems,' 1664.

Posthumous: 'A French Grammar,' 1673.

He *translated :* 'St. Paul's late Progress upon Earth,' 1644 ; 'A Venetian Looking-glass,' 1648 ; Giraffi's 'Exact History of the late Revolutions,' 1650 ; 'The Process and Pleadings in the Court of Spain upon the death of A. Ascham,' 1651 ; 'History of the . . . Jews,' 1652 ; 'The Nuptials of Peleus and Thetis,' 1654 ; Paracelsus' 'Aurora,' 1659 ; Valentine's 'Triumphant Chariot of Antimony,' 1661 ; Paracelsus' 'Archidoxis,' 1661 ; and *edited :* Cotgrave's 'French and English Dictionary,' 1650 ; ' Parthenopœia,' 1654 ; Sir R. B. Cotton's 'Posthuma,' 1651 ; Sir J. Finet's ' Philoxenis,' 1656.

* **HOWELLS (William Dean), b. 1837.** Born, at Martin's Ferry, Ohio, 1 March 1837. Family removed to Hamilton, Ohio, 1840 ; to Dayton, Ohio, 1849. Worked with his father as printer. Contrib. to 'Cincinnati Gaz.,' 1858. News Editor of 'Ohio State Journal,' 1859. U.S. Consul at Venice, 1861-65. Married Elinor G. Mead, 24 Dec. 1862. Returned to America. Assistant-Editor of ' Atlantic Monthly,' 1866 ; Editor, 1872-81. Play, 'A Counterfeit Presentment,' produced at Boston Museum, 1878 ; ' Yorick's Love,' 1880 ; 'A Foregone Conclusion,' Madison Square Theatre, N.Y., 1886 ; 'A Terrible Ruffian,' Avenue Theatre, London, Dec. 1895. Also author of farces 'The Mouse-Trap' and 'Evening Dress.' Visit to Europe, 1882-83. Contributed 'Editor's Study' to 'Harper's Mag.,' 1886-91. Part-Editor of ' The Cosmopolitan,' 1892.

Works : 'Poems of two Friends' (with J. Piatt), 1860 ; 'Life of Abraham Lincoln,' 1860 ; 'Venetian Life,' 1866 ; ' Italian Journeys,' 1867 ; 'Suburban Sketches,' 1868 ; 'No Love Lost,' 1869 ; 'Their Wedding Journey,' 1871 ; 'Poems,' 1873 ; 'A Chance Acquaintance,' 1874 ; 'A

Foregone Conclusion,' 1875 ; 'A Day's Pleasure,' 1876 ; 'Life of R. B. Hayes,' 1876 ; 'Out of the Question,' 1877 ; 'The Parlor-Car,' 1877 ; 'A Counterfeit Presentment,' 1877 ; 'The Lady of the Aroostook,' 1879 ; 'The Undiscovered Country,' 1880 ; 'A Fearful Responsibility,' 1881 ; 'Dr. Breen's Practice,' 1881 ; 'A Modern Instance,' 1882 ; 'The Sleeping-Car,' 1883 ; 'A Woman's Reason,' 1883 ; 'The Register,' 1884 ; 'Three Villages,' 1884 ; 'Indian Summer,' 1885 ; 'The Rise of Silas Lapham,' 1885 ; 'The Elevator,' 1885 ; 'Tuscan Cities,' 1886 [1885] ; 'A Little Girl among the Old Masters,' 1886 ; 'The Minister's Charge,' 1886 ; 'Modern Italian Poets,' 1887 ; 'April Hopes,' 1887 ; 'Library of Universal Adventure' (with T. S. Perry), 1887 ; 'Annie Kilburn,' 1888 ; 'A Sea Change,' 1888 ; 'A Hazard of New Fortunes,' 1889 ; 'The Shadow of a Dream,' 1890 ; 'A Boy's Town,' 1890 ; 'Criticism and Fiction,' 1891 ; 'An Imperative Duty,' 1891 ; 'Mercy,' 1892 [1891] ; 'A Letter of Introduction,' 1892 ; 'The World of Chance,' 1893 ; 'The Coast of Bohemia,' 1893 ; 'A Traveller from Altruria,' 1894 ; 'Impressions and Experiences,' 1896 ; 'Idylls in Drab,' 1896 ; 'The Landlord at Lion's Head,' 1897.

He has *edited*: 'Choice Autobiographies' (8 vols.), 1877-78.

HOWITT (William), **1792-1879**. Born, at Heanor, Derbyshire, 18 Dec. 1792. At Friends' Public School, Ackworth, Yorks., 1802-06 ; to school at Tamworth, 1806. Contributed to 'Monthly Mag.,' 1805. Married Mary Botham, 16 April 1821. Lived in Staffordshire, 1821-22. Kept druggist's shop at Nottingham, 1823-36 ; Alderman of Nottingham, 1833. Lived at Esher, 1836-39 ; at Heidelberg, 1840-43 ; at Clapton, 1843-48 ; in London, 1848-52. On staff of 'People's Journal,' April 1846 to Jan. 1847. Edited 'Howitt's Journal of Lit.' (with his wife), 1847-49. In Australia, N.S. Wales and Tasmania, 1852-54. After his return to Eng-

land became much interested in spiritualism. Contrib. to 'Spiritual Mag.' Lived at Highgate, 1854-66 ; at Esher, 1866-70 ; Tyrol in summer and Rome in winter, 1870-79. Civil List pension of £140, 19 June 1865. Died, in Rome, 3 March 1879 ; buried in Protestant cemetery there.

Works : 'Commemorative Verses' (anon.), 1818 ; 'The Forest Minstrel' (with his wife), 1823 ; 'The Desolation of Eyam' (with his wife), 1827 ; 'The Book of the Seasons,' 1831 ; 'A Popular History of Priestcraft,' 1833 ; 'Pantilla' (2 vols.), 1835 ; 'Three Death Cries' (anon.), 1835 ; 'The Rural Life of England,' 1838 ; 'Colonization and Christianity,' 1838 ; 'The Boy's Country - Book,' 1839 ; 'Visits to Remarkable Places,' 1840 ; 'The Rural and Domestic Life of Germany,' 1842 ; 'A Serious Address,' 1843 ; 'German Experiences,' 1844 ; 'The Life and Adventures of Jack of the Mill' (2 vols.), 1844 ; 'Johnny Darbishire,' 1845 ; 'Homes and Haunts of the most eminent British Poets' (2 vols.), 1847 ; 'The Hall and the Hamlet' (2 vols.), 1848 ; 'The Year-Book of the Country,' 1850 ; 'Madam Dorrington,' 1851 ; 'The Literature and Romance of Northern Europe' (with his wife), 1852 ; 'Stories of English and Foreign Life' (with his wife), 1853 ; 'A Boy's Adventures,' 1854 ; 'Land, Labour and Gold,' 1855 ; 'Tallangetta,' 1857 ; 'The Man of the People,' 1860 ; 'Ruined Abbeys and Castles of Great Britain' (with his wife ; 2 ser.), 1862-64 ; 'Letters on Transportation,' 1863 ; 'The History of the Supernatural' (2 vols.), 1863 ; 'The History of Discovery in Australia' (2 vols.), 1865 ; 'Nicodemians and Thomasians,' 1865 ; 'Woodburn Grange,' 1867 ; 'The Northern Heights of London,' 1869 ; 'The Mad War-Planet,' 1871.

He *translated :* Dr. Cornelius' 'Student Life of Germany,' 1841 ; 'Peter Schlemihl,' 1843 ; Holthaus' 'Wanderings of a Journeyman Tailor,' 1844 ; Bremer's 'Life in Dalecarlia,' 1845 ; Nicander's 'Renounced Treasure,' 1845 ; Ennemoser's 'History of

Magic,' 1854 ; 'The Religion of Rome,' 1873 ; and *edited :* E. Sargent's 'Peculiar,' 1864.

[His wife, **Mary Howitt**, was born [Mary Botham], at Coleford, Gloucestershire, 12 March 1799. Educated at home. Married, 16 April 1821. Collaborated with her husband, 1827-64, and wrote and edited a number of books alone. After her husband's death, she was granted a Civil List pension of £100, April 1879. Silver Medallist of Lit. Acad. of Stockholm. Joined Church of Rome, Jan. 1888. Died, in Rome, 30 Jan. 1888. Her *Works* consisted of upwards of 110 publications. For those written in collaboration with her husband, see above. Those written alone were mainly books for young people. Her 'Autobiography' was published posthumously in 1889.]

HUGHES (Thomas), 1823 - 1896. Born, at Uffington, Berks, 20 Oct. 1823. At school at Twyford, 1830-33 ; at Rugby, 1833-41. Matric., Oriel Coll., Oxford, 2 Dec. 1841 ; B.A., 1845. Student of Lincoln's Inn, 21 Jan. 1845 ; removed to Inner Temple, 18 Jan. 1848 ; called to Bar there, 28 Jan. 1848. Married Anne Frances Ford, 17 Aug. 1847. F.S.A., 22 March 1849 ; resigned 1854. M.P. for Lambeth, 1865-68 ; for Frome, 1868-74. Q.C., 23 June 1869. Bencher of Lincoln's Inn, 31 May 1870. Visit to U.S.A., 1870. Founded Colony of Rugby, Tennessee, 1880. Judge of County Court Circuit No. 9, July 1882. Died, at Brighton, 22 March 1896.

Works : 'History of the Working Tailors' Association, 34, Great Castle Street' (under initial: H.), [1850] ; 'A Lecture on the Slop System,' 1852 ; 'Tom Brown's School Days' (anon.), 1857 ; 'The Scouring of the White Horse' (anon.), 1859 [1858] ; 'Account of the Lock-out of Engineers,' 1860 ; 'Tom Brown at Oxford,' 1861 ; 'Religio Laici,' 1861 (another edn., called 'A Layman's Faith,' 1868) ; 'The Cause of Freedom,' 1863 ; 'Alfred the Great,'

1869 ; 'Memoir of a Brother,' 2nd edn., 1873 ; 'Lecture on the History and Objects of Co-operation,' 1878 ; 'The Old Church : What shall we do with it ?' 1878 ; 'The Manliness of Christ,' 1879 ; 'Rugby, Tennessee,' 1881 ; 'A Memoir of Daniel Macmillan,' 1882 ; 'Address . . . on the occasion of . . . a testimonial, etc.,' 1885 ; 'James Fraser, second Bishop of Manchester,' 1887 ; 'Co-operative Production' [1887] ; 'David Livingstone,' 1889 ; 'Vacation Rambles' (from 'Spectator'), 1895.

He *edited :* Whitmore's 'Gilbert Marlowe,' 1859 ; Lowell's 'Biglow Papers,' 1859 ; the Comte de Paris' 'Trade Unions of England,' 1869 ; Philpot's 'Guide Book to the Canadian Dominion,' 1871 ; Maurice's 'The Friendship of Books,' 1874 ; Kingsley's 'Alton Locke,' 1876 ; 'A Manual for Co-operators' (with E. V. Neale), 1881 ; 'Gone to Texas,' 1884 ; Lowell's 'Poetical Works,' 1891 ; Marriott's 'Charles Kingsley,' 1892.

HUME (David), 1711-1776. Born, in Edinburgh, 26 April 1711. Probably educated at Edinburgh University. Lived in France, 1734-37. Settled at home, at Ninewells, Berwickshire, 1737. Tutor in household of Marquis of Annandale, April 1745 to April 1746. Sec. to Gen. St. Clair in expedition against Canada, 1746-47. With Gen. St. Clair on embassy to Austria and Italy, 1748. Returned to Ninewells, 1749. Removed with his sister to Edinburgh, 1751. Keeper of Advocates' Library, 28 Jan. 1752 to 1757. Prosecuted historical studies. To Paris, as Sec. to Ambassador, Earl of Hertford, Oct. 1763. Pension of £400, 1765. To England, bringing Rousseau with him, Jan. 1766. Returned to Edinburgh, same year. In London, as Under Secretary of State, 1767-68. Settled in Edinburgh, 1769. Died there, 25 Aug. 1776. Buried in Calton Hill Cemetery.

Works : 'A Treatise of Human Nature' (anon.), vols. i., ii., 1739 ; vol. iii., 1740 ; 'Essays, moral and political' (2 vols., anon.), 1741-42 ;

'Philosophical Essays concerning Human Understanding' (anon.), 1748; 'A True Account of the behaviour . . . of Archibald Stewart' (anon.), 1748; 'An Enquiry concerning the Principles of Morals,' 1751; 'Political Discourses' 1752 (2nd edn. same year); 'Essays and Treatises on Several Subjects' (4 vols.), 1753-54; 'The History of England'[under the House of Stuart] (2 vols.), 1754-57; 'Four Dissertations,' 1757; 'The History of England under the House of Tudor' (2 vols.), 1759; 'The History of England from the Invasion of Julius Cæsar to the accession of Henry VII.' (2 vols.), 1762; 'A Concise Account of the dispute between Mr. Hume and Mr. Rousseau' (anon.), 1766; 'Scotticisms' (anon.), 1770.

Posthumous : 'Autobiography,' 1777; 'Two Essays,' 1777; 'Dialogues concerning Natural Religion,' 1779.

Collected Works : 'Philosophical Works,' ed. by T. H. Green and T. H. Grose (4 vols.), 1878 [1875-78].

Life : by J. H. Burton, 1846.

HUNT (James Henry Leigh), 1784-1859. Born, at Southgate, 19 Oct. 1784. At Christ's Hospital School, 1792 - 99. Contrib. to 'Juvenile Library,' 1801; to 'European Mag.,' 1801; to 'Poetical Register,' 1801-11; to 'The Traveller,' 1804-05. Clerk to his brother Stephen, 1803 [?]-05. Dramatic critic to 'The News' (started by his brother John), 1805. Clerkship in War Office, 1806 [?]-08. Edited 'The Examiner,' 1808-21; frequently contributed afterwards. Married Marianne Kent, 3 July 1809. Edited 'The Reflector,' 1810; 'Imprisoned in Surrey gaol, for remarks in 'Examiner' on Prince Regent, 3 Feb. 1813 to 3 Feb. 1815. Settled at Hampstead, 1816. Friendship with Shelley and Keats. Edited 'The Indicator,' Oct. 1819 to March 1821. Edited, and wrote, 'The Literary Pocket-Book,' 1819-22. Sailed for Italy, 15 Nov. 1821, but driven by storm to land at Dartmouth. Sailed again, May 1822; arrived at Leghorn, June. Contrib. to 'New Monthly Mag.,' 1821-50. Edited 'The Liberal' (with Shelley and Byron), 1822-23. To Genoa with Byron, Sept. 1822. In Florence, 1823-25. Edited 'The Literary Examiner,' 1823. Returned to England, Sept. 1825. Lived at Highgate, 1825-28. Edited 'The Companion,' Jan. to July, 1828. Contrib. to 'The Keepsake,' 1828. Lived at Epsom, 1828-30 [?]. Edited 'The Chat of the Week,' June to Aug., 1830. Edited (and wrote) 'The Tatler' 4 Sept. 1830 to 13 Feb. 1832. Lived in Chelsea, 1833-40. Contrib. to 'Tait's Mag.,' 1833; to 'Monthly Chronicle,' Oct. 1838 to Feb. 1839. Edited 'Leigh Hunt's London Journal,' 1834 to Dec. 1835; 'The Monthly Repository,' July 1837 to April 1838. Contrib. to 'Musical World,' Jan. to March, 1839. Lived in Kensington, 1840-53. Play, 'A Legend of Florence,' produced at Covent Garden, 7 Feb. 1840. Contrib. to 'Westminster Rev.,' 1837; to 'Edinburgh Rev.,' 1841-44; to 'Ainsworth's Mag.,' 1845, to 'Atlas,' 1846; etc. Crown Pension of £200, Oct. 1847. Edited 'Leigh Hunt's Journal,' 1850-51. Lived in Hammersmith, 1853-59. Contrib. to 'Musical Times,' 1853-54; to 'Household Words,' 1853-54; to 'Fraser's Mag.,' 1858-59; to 'Spectator,' Jan. to Aug. 1859. Died, at Putney, 28 Aug. 1859. Buried in Kensal Green Cemetery.

Works : 'Juvenilia,' 1801; 'Classic Tales' (5 vols.), 1806-07; 'Critical Essays on the Performers of the London Theatres' (from 'The News'), 1807; 'An Attempt to show the Folly . . . of Methodism' (anon., from 'Examiner'), 1809; 'Reformist's Reply to the Edinburgh Review,' 1810; 'The Feast of the Poets' (anon.), 1814; 'The Descent of Liberty,' 1815; 'The Story of Rimini,' 1816; 'The Round Table' (with Hazlitt, from 'Examiner,' 2 vols.), 1817; 'Foliage,' 1818; 'Hero and Leander,' 1819; 'Bacchus and Ariadne,' 1819; 'Poetical Works,' 1819; 'The Literary Pocket-Book' (4 vols.), 1819-22; ('The Months' (selected from vol. i. of preceding), 1821; 'Ultra-Crepidarius,'

1823 ; 'Lord Byron and some of his Contemporaries,' 1828 ; 'The Companion,' 1828 ; 'The Tatler,' 1830-32 ; 'Christianism' (anon. ; priv. ptd.), 1832 (enlarged edn., called : 'The Religion of the Head,' 1853) ; 'Poetical Works,' 1832 ; 'Sir Ralph Esher,' 1832 ; 'The Indicator and the Companion' (2 vols.), 1834 ; 'Captain Sword and Captain Pen,' 1835 ; 'The Seer,' 1840-41 ; 'The Palfrey,' 1842 ; 'One Hundred Romances of Real Life' (from 'Leigh Hunt's London Journal'), 1843 ; 'Poetical Works,' 1844 ; 'Imagination and Fancy,' 1844 ; 'Wit and Humour, selected from the English Poets,' 1846 ; 'Stories from the Italian Poets' (2 vols.), 1846 ; 'A Saunter through the West-End' (from 'Atlas'), 1847 ; 'Men, Women, and Books' (2 vols.), 1847 ; 'A Jar of Honey from Mount Hybla,' 1848 ; 'The Town' (2 vols.), 1848 ; 'A Book for a Corner,' 1849 ; 'Readings for Railways,' 1849 ; 'Autobiography' (3 vols.), 1850 (later edns., expanded, 1859 and 1860) ; 'Table-Talk,' 1851 ; 'The Religion of the Heart,' 1853 ; 'The Old Court Suburb,' 1855 ; 'Stories in Verse,' 1855 ; 'Poetical Works' (Boston, 2 vols.), 1857.

Posthumous : 'Poetical Works,' ed. by his son, 1860 ; 'Correspondence,' 1862 ; 'Tale for a Chimney Corner,' 1869 ; 'Day by the Fire,' 1870 ; 'Wishing Cap Papers' (from 'Examiner'), 1873.

He *translated :* Tasso's 'Amyntas,' 1820 ; F. Redi's 'Bacchus in Tuscany,' 1825 ; and *edited :* Shelley's 'Masque of Anarchy,' 1832 ; Sheridan's Dramatic Works, 1840 ; The Dramatic Works of Wycherley, Congreve, Vanbrugh and Farquhar, 1840 ; Chaucer's Poems Modernized (with Horne and others), 1841 ; T. Hunt's 'Foster Brother,' 1845 ; 'Finest Scenes' from Beaumont and Fletcher, 1855 ; 'The Book of the Sonnet' (with S. A. Lee, *posthumous*), 1867.

Life : 'Autobiography,' 1850, etc. ; 'Life,' by Cosmo Monkhouse, 1893.

HUTCHESON (Francis), 1694-1746. Born, at Drumalig, co. Down, 8 Aug.

1694. To school at Saintfield, 1702 ; afterwards at Killelagh. To Glasgow, 1710. Returned to Ireland, 1716 ; took holy orders. Kept a school in Dublin for some years. Prof. of Moral Philosophy, Glasgow Univ., 1729-46. Died, in Glasgow, 1746.

Works : 'An Inquiry into the Original of our Ideas of Beauty and Virtue' (anon.), 1725 ; 'Essay on the Nature and Conduct of the Passions and Affections' (anon.), 1728 ; 'De Naturali Hominum Socialitate,' 1730 ; 'Considerations on Patronages,' 1735 ; 'Philosophiæ Moralis Institutio Compendiaria,' 1742 ; 'Metaphysicæ Synopsis' (anon.), 1742.

Posthumous : 'Reflections upon Laughter,' 1750 ; 'System of Moral Philosophy,' ed. by his son (2 vols.), 1755 ; 'Logic,' 1764.

Life : by Leechman, in 1755 edn. of 'System of Moral Philosophy.'

*HUXLEY (Thomas Henry), 1825-1896.** Born, at Ealing, 4 May 1825. At school there. Studied medicine at Charing Cross Hospital. M.B., London, 1845. Assistant-surgeon to H.M.S. 'Victory,' 1846 ; to H.M.S. 'Rattlesnake,' 1847-50. F.R.S., 1851 ; Medal, 1852. Prof. of Nat. Hist. at Royal School of Mines, 1854 ; Fullerian Prof. to Royal Institution, 1854 ; Examiner to London Univ., 1854. Croonian Lecturer to Royal Soc., 1858. Prof. of Comparative Anatom to Royal Coll. of Surgeons, 1863-70. Hon. LL.D., Edinburgh, 1866. Pres. Geological Soc., 1869. Edited 'Journal of the Ethnological Soc.' (with G. Busk and Sir J. Lubbock), 1869-70. Pres. Ethnological Soc., 1870. Pres. British Association, 1870. Memb. of London School Board, 1870-72. Lord Rector of Aberdeen Univ., 1872-74. Sec. of Royal Soc., 1873. Wollaston Medal, Geol. Soc., 1876. Hon. LL.D., Dublin, 1878 ; Hon. LL.D., Cambridge, 1879 ; Hon. Ph.D., Breslau ; Hon. M.D., Würzburg. Corresponding member of many foreign scientific bodies. Member of various scientific and educational commissions. Knight of Pole Star of Sweden. Fellow of

Eton Coll., 13 May 1879 ; afterwards Governor. Memb. of Senate of London Univ., 29 Aug. 1883. Inspector of Salmon Fisheries, 1881-1885. Rede Lecturer, Camb., June 1883. Pres. Royal Soc., July 1883-1885. F.R.C.S., 1884. Hon. D.C.L., Oxford, 17 June 1885. Trustee of British Museum, 29 Feb. 1888. Privy Councillor, Aug. 1892. Romanes Lecturer, Oxford, May 1893. Frequent contributor to periodicals. Died, 29 June 1895.

Works : ' On the Educational Value of the Natural History Sciences,' 1854; ' The Oceanic Hydrozoa,' 1859 ; 'Evidence as to Man's Place in Nature,' 1863 ; ' On our Knowledge of the Causes of the Phenomena of Organic Nature,' 1863 ; ' Lectures on the Elements of Comparative Anatomy,' 1864; ' An Elementary Atlas of Comparative Osteology,' 1864 ; ' Catalogue of the . . . Fossils in the Museum of Practical Geology (with R. Etheridge), 1865 ; ' Palæontologia Indica : Vertebrate Fossils,' 1866 ; ' Lessons in Elementary Physiology,' 1866 ; ' An Introduction to the Classification of Animals,' 1869 ; ' Protoplasm : the Physical Basis of Life,' 1869 ; ' Lay Sermons, Addresses, and Reviews,' 1870 (' Essays,' selected from preceding, 1871) ; ' A Manual of the Anatomy of Vertebrated Animals,' 1871 ; ' On Yeast,' 1872 ; ' Critiques and Addresses,' 1873 ; ' A Course of Practical Instruction in Elementary Biology ' (with H. N. Martin), 1875 ; ' A Manual of the Anatomy of Invertebrated Animals,' 1877 ; ' American Addresses,' 1877; ' Physiography,' 1877 ; ' Hume,' 1879 ; ' Science Primers : Introductory,' 1880 ; 'The Crayfish,' 1880 ; 'Science and Culture,' 1881 ; ' Inaugural Address to Fishery Congress,' 1883 ; ' Essays upon some Controverted Questions,' 1892 ; ' Evolution and Ethics,' 1893 ; ' Collected Essays ' (9 vols.), 1893-94.

He *translated :* Koelliber's 'Manual of Human Histology ' (with G. Busk), 1853-54; Von Siebold's ' On Tape and Cystic Worms,' 1857 ; *edited :* Prescott's ' Strong Drink and Tobacco Smoke,' 1869 ; 'Science Primers ' (with

Prof. Roscoe and B. Stewart), 1872, etc.; and contributed prefatory notes to various scientific publications.

INCHBALD (Elizabeth), 1753-1821. Born [Elizabeth Simpson], at Stanningfield, Suffolk, 15 Oct. 1753. Left home in April 1772, with intention of going on the London stage. Married to Joseph Inchbald, 9 June 1772. First appeared on the stage at Bristol, 4 Sept. 1772. Acting with her husband in Scotland, 1772-76. In Paris, July to Sept. 1776. Acting with her husband in England, 1776-79 ; he died, suddenly, 6 June 1779. Friendship with Mrs. Siddons and J. P. Kemble. Continued to act at York till 1780. At Covent Garden, Oct. 1780 to July 1782 ; at Haymarket, July to Sept., 1782 ; in Dublin, Nov. 1782 to spring of 1783 ; returned to Covent Garden, 1783. Play, ' The Mogul Tale,' produced at Haymarket, 1784. Plays produced at Haymarket, Covent Garden, and Drury Lane, 1784-1805. Contrib. to ' Edinburgh Review.' Retired from stage, 1789. Died, at Kensington House, 1 Aug. 1821. Buried in Kensington Churchyard.

Works : ' Appearance is against them ' (anon.), 1785 ; ' I'll Tell you What,' 1786 ; ' The Widow's Vow ' (anon.), 1786 ; ' The Mogul Tale ' (anon.), 1788 ; ' Such Things Are,' 1788 (2nd edn. same year) ; ' The Midnight Hour ' (from the French of Damaniant), 1787 ; ' The Child of Nature ' (from the French of Countess de Genlis), 1788 ; ' Animal Magnetism ' (anon.), 1788 ; ' The Married Man ' (from the French of Néricault-Destouches), 1789 ; ' Next Door Neighbours,' 1791 ; ' A Simple Story ' (4 vols.), 1791 ; ' Everyone has his Fault,' 1793 ; ' The Wedding Day,' 1794 ; ' Nature and Art ' (2 vols.), 1796 ; ' Wives as they Were, and Maids as they Are,' 1797 ; ' Lovers' Vows ' (from the German of Kotzebue), 1798 ; ' The Wise Men of the East ' (from the German of Kotzebue), 1799 ; ' To Marry or Not to Marry,' 1805. She *edited :* ' The British Theatre '

(25 vols.), 1808 ; 'The Modern Theatre' (10 vols.), 1811 ; 'A Collection of Farces' (7 vols.), 1815 ; and contributed 'remarks' to plays by Addison, Cibber, Colman, Lillo, Machlin, Norton, Otway, Rowe, Shakespeare, Southerne, Thomson.

Life : 'Memoirs,' by J. Boaden (2 vols.), 1833.

INGELOW (Jean), 1820-1897. Born, at Boston, Lincs., 1820. Active literary life. Died, in Kensington, 20 July 1897.

Works : 'A Rhyming Chronicle' (anon.), 1850 ; 'Allerton and Dreux' (anon., 2 vols.), 1851 ; 'Tales of Orris' [1860] ; 'Poems,' 1863 (4th edn. same year); 'Studies for Stories, from Girls' Lives' (anon.), 1864 ; 'Stories told to a Child' (anon.), 1865 ; 'Home Thoughts and Home Scenes' (anon.), 1865 ; 'Little Rie and the Rosebuds' (anon.), 1867 ; 'The Suspicious Jackdaw' (anon.), 1867 ; 'The Grandmother's Shoe' (anon.), 1867 ; 'The Golden Opportunity' (anon.), 1867 ; 'Deborah's Book' (anon.), 1867 ; 'A Story of Doom,' 1867 ; 'The Moorish Gold' (anon.), 1867 ; 'The Minnows with Silver Tails' (anon.), 1867 ; 'The Wild-Duck Shooter' (anon.), 1867 ; 'A Sister's Bye-Hours' (anon.), 1868 ; 'Mopsa the Fairy,' 1869 ; 'The Little Wonder-Horn,' 1872 ; 'Off the Skelligs' (4 vols.), 1872 ; 'Fated to be Free,' 1875 ; 'Poems,' second series, 1876 ; 'Poems' (collected ; 2 vols.), 1879 ; 'Sarah de Berenger,' 1879 ; 'Don John,' 1881 ; 'The High Tide on the Coast of Lincolnshire, 1571,' 1883 ; 'Poems,' third series, 1885 ; 'John Jerome,' 1886 ; 'Lyrical and other poems' (selected), 1886 ; 'The Little Wonder-Box,' 1887 ; 'Very Young ; and, Quite Another Story,' 1890.

INGOLDSBY. *See* **Barham.**

IRVING (Washington), 1783-1859. Born, in New York, 3 April 1783. Educated at private schools, 1787-99. In a lawyer's office, 1801-04. Contrib. to 'Morning Chronicle,' under pseud. of 'Jonathan Oldstyle,' 1802. Tra-

velled in Europe, 1804-06. Edited 'Salmagundi,' with his brother, William, and J. K. Paulding, Jan. to Oct., 1807. Partner with his brothers in a mercantile house, 1810-17. Assistant Editor of 'Analectic Mag.,' 1813-14. In England, 1815-20. Travelled on Continent, 1820-25. Attaché to the U.S.A. Legation at Madrid, 1826-29. Sec. to U.S.A. Legation in London, 1829-32. Medal of Roy. Soc. of Lit., 1830. Hon. LL.D., Oxford, 1831. Returned to New York, 1832 ; settled at Sunnyside. Contrib. to 'Knickerbocker Mag.,' 1839-40. U.S.A. Ambassador to Spain, 1842-46. Returned to America, April 1846. Unmarried. Died, at Sunnyside, 28 Nov. 1859.

Works : 'A History of New York' (under pseud. of 'Diedrich Knickerbocker') 1809 ; 'The Sketch-Book of Geoffrey Crayon,' 1819 ; 'Bracebridge Hall' (by 'Geoffrey Crayon,' 2 vols.), 1822 ; 'Letters of Jonathan Oldstyle' 1824 (3rd edn. same year) ; 'Tales of a Traveller' (by 'Geoffrey Crayon'), 1824 ; 'A History of . . . Christopher Columbus' (3 vols.), 1828; 'A Chronicle of the Conquest of Granada,' 1829 ; 'Voyages . . . of the Companions of Columbus,' 1831; 'The Alhambra' (by 'Geoffrey Crayon'), 1832 ; 'Complete Works' (pubd. in Paris), 1834 ; 'Abbotsford and Newstead Abbey' (anon.), 1835 ; 'Tour on the Prairies,' 1835 ; 'Legends of the Conquest of Spain' (anon.), 1835; 'The Crayon Miscellany' (anon.), 1835 ; 'Astoria' (3 vols.), 1836 ; 'The Adventures of Captain Bonneville,' 1837 ; 'Biography and Poetical Remains of M. M. Davidson,' 1841 ; 'The Life of Oliver Goldsmith,' 1844 ; 'A Book of the Hudson' (edited by 'Geoffrey Crayon'), 1849 ; 'The Life of Mahomet,' 1850 ; 'The Lives of Mahomet and his Successors,' 1850 ; 'Chronicles of Wolfert's Roost,' 1855 ; 'Life of Washington,' vols. i., ii., 1855 ; vol. iii., 1856 ; vol. iv., 1857 ; vol. v., 1859 ; 'Wolfert Webber,' 1856 ; 'Works' (15 vols.), 1857.

Posthumous : 'Spanish Papers,' ed. by P. M. Irving, 1866 ; 'Biographies

10

and Miscellaneous Papers,' ed. by P. M. Irving, 1867.

He *translated :* Navarette's 'Coleccion de los Viages, etc.,' 1825 ; and *edited :* Campbell's ' Poems,' 1810 ; Bonneville's ' Rocky Mountains,' 1843. *Collected Works :* in 1 vol., 1834 ; in 27 vols., 1880-83. *Life :* ' Life and Letters,' by P. M. Irving, 1862-63.

JAMES (George Payne Rainsford), 1801-1860. Born, in London, 9 Aug. 1801. Educated at school at Putney. Travelled on Continent in youth. Contributed to periodicals, and eventually adopted literary career. Historiographer · Royal, 1839. British Consul at Massachusetts, 1850[?]-52 ; at Norfolk, Virginia, 1852-56 ; at Venice, 1856-60. Died, at Venice, 9 May 1860. Buried in the Lido Cemetery.

Works : ' Life of Edward the Black Prince,' 1822 ; 'The Ruined City,' 1828 ; ' Adra,' 1829 ; ' Richelieu ' (anon.), 1829 ; ' Darnley ' (anon.), 1830 ; ' De L'Orme ' (anon.), 1830 ; ' Philip Augustus ' (anon.), 1831 ; ' Henry Masterton ' (anon.), 1832 ; ' History of Charlemagne,' 1832 ; ' Memoirs of Great Commanders,' 1832 ; ' The String of Pearls ' (anon.), 1832 ; ' Mary of Burgundy ' (anon.), 1833 ; ' Delaware ' (anon.), 1833 ; ' Life . . . of John Marston Hall,' 1834 ; ' One in a Thousand,' 1835 ; ' On the Educational Institutions of Germany,' 1835 ; ' My Aunt Pontypool ' (anon.), 1835 ; ' Gipsey,' 1835 ; The Desultory Man,' 1836 ; ' Attila,' 1837 ; 'Life . . . of Louis XIV.,' 1838 ; ' The Huguenot,' 1838 ; 'The Robber ' (anon.), 1838 ; ' Brief Hist. of the U.S. Boundary Question,' 1839 ; ' Henry of Guise,' 1839 ; ' Charles Tyrrell,' 1839 ; ' Blanche of Navarre,' 1839 ; 'The Gentleman of the Old School,' 1839 ; ' A Book of the Passions,' 1839 ; ' The King's Highway,' 1840 ; ' Man-at-Arms,' 1840 ; ' The Jacquerie,' 1841 ; 'The Ancient Regime,' 1841 ; ' Corse de Leon,' 1841 ; 'Some Remarks on the Corn Laws,' 1841 ; ' Morley Ernstein,' 1842 ; ' The Woodman,' 1842 ; ' Hist. of . . . Richard Cœur - de - Lion ' (4 vols.), 1842-49 ; ' Hist. of Chivalry,' 1843 ; ' The Commissioner ' (anon.), 1843 ; ' Forest Days,' 1843 ; ' The False Heir,' 1843 ; ' Eva St. Clair,' 1843 ; ' Arabella Stuart,' 1844 ; 'Rose D'Albret,' 1844 ; 'Agincourt,' 1844 ; 'Works' (collected ; 21 vols.), 1844-49 ; ' The Smuggler,' 1845 ; ' Arrah Neil,' 1845 ; ' The Stepmother,' 1845 ; 'Heidelberg,' 1846 ; ' Russell,' 1847 ; ' Life of Henry IV. of France,' 1847 ; 'A Whim' (anon.), 1847 ; ' The Convict,' 1847 ; 'The Castle of Ehrenstein,' 1847 ; 'The Last of the Fairies ' [1848] ; 'Beauchamp,' 1848 ; ' Margaret Graham,' 1848 ; ' Cameralzaman,' 1848 ; ' Sir Theodore Broughton,' 1848 ; ' Delaware,' 1848 ; ' The Forgery,' 1849 ; ' The Fight of the Fiddlers,' 1849 ; ' An Investigation of the . . . Murder of John, Earl of Gowrie, and Alexander Ruthven, etc.,' 1849 ; ' John Jones's Tales for Little John Jones's,' 1849 ; ' Dark Scenes of History,' 1849 ; 'The Old Oak Chest,' 1850 ; 'Gowrie,' 1851 ; 'The Fate,' 1851 ; ' Henry Smeaton,' 1851 ; 'Pequinillo,' 1852 ; ' A Story Without a Name,' 1852 ; 'Revenge,' 1852 ; 'Adrian' (with M. B. Field), 1852 ; ' Agnes Sorrel,' 1853 ; 'The Vicissitudes of a Life,' 1853; ' Arabella Stuart,' 1853 ; ' An Oration on the . . . Duke of Wellington,' 1853 ; ' Ticonderoga,' 1854 ; ' Prince Life,' 1856 ; ' The Old Dominion,' 1856 ; ' Leonora d'Orco,' 1857 ; ' Lord Montagu's Page,' 1858.

Posthumous : ' Bernard Marsh,' 1864.

He *edited :* ' Memoirs of Celebrated Women,' 1837 ; the ' Vernon Letters,' 1841 ; Ireland's ' David Rizzio,' 1849.

JAMES (Henry), b. 1843. Born, in New York City, 15 April 1843. Travelled in Europe with parents, 1854-60. Educated in New York, Geneva, Paris, and Boulogne. Lived at Newport, Rhode Island, 1860-66. To Harvard Law-school, 1862. First contrib. to periodicals, 1865. Lived at Cambridge, Mass., 1866-69. To Europe, 1869. Since then has re-

sided mainly in London. Play ' Guy
Domville,' produced at St. James's
Theatre, London, 5 Jan. 1895.

Works: 'Transatlantic Sketches,'
1875 ; ' A Passionate Pilgrim,' 1875 ;
'Roderick Hudson,' 1876 ; 'The
American,' 1877 ; ' Watch and Ward,'
1878 ; ' French Poets and Novelists,'
1878 ; 'The Europeans,' 1878 ; 'Daisy
Miller,' 1878 ; ' An International
Episode,' 1879 ; ' Hawthorne ' (' Eng.
Men of Letters ' series), 1879 ; 'The
Madonna of the Future,' 1879 ; 'Con-
fidence,' 1880 [1879] ; ' Diary of a
Man of Fifty,' 1880 ; 'A Bundle of
Letters ' (from ' The Parisian '), 1880 ;
'Washington Square,' 1881 ; ' The
Portrait of a Lady,' 1881 ; ' The
Siege of London,' 1883 ; 'Daisy Miller'
(dramatised from novel), 1883 ; ' Por-
traits of Places,' 1883 ; ' A Little
Tour in France,' 1884 ; ' Tales of
Three Cities,' 1884 ; 'Stories Revived,'
1885 ; 'The Author of Beltraffio, etc.,'
1885 ; ' The Bostonians,' 1886 ; 'The
Princess Casamassima' ; ' Partial Por-
traits,' 1888 ; ' The Aspern Papers,'
1888 ; ' The Reverberator,' 1888 ; 'A
London Life,' 1889 ; ' The Tragic
Muse,' 1890 ; ' The Lesson of the
Master,' 1892 ; ' The Private Life,'
1893 ; ' The Real Thing,' 1893 ;
' Essays in London and Elsewhere,'
1893; 'Theatricals' (2 series), 1894 ;
'Terminations,' 1895 ; ' Embarrass-
ments,' 1896 ; ' The Other House.'
1896 ; ' The Spoils of Poynton,' 1897.

He has *translated :* Daudet's ' Port
Tarascon,' 1891 ; and *edited:* Balestier's ' The Average Woman ' ; ' The
Odd Number,' from De Maupassant,
1891.

**JAMESON (Anna Brownell), 1794-
1860.** Born [Anna Brownell Murphy],
in Dublin, 17 May 1794. Family removed to England, 1798. Governess
in Marquis of Winchester's family,
1810-14. Travelled with a pupil in
France and Italy, summer of 1821
to 1822. Governess in family of Mr.
Littleton, 1822-25. Married to Robert
Jameson, 1825. Obtained legal appointment in Canada for her husband,
1833. To Germany same year ;

friendship with Major Noel, Ottilie
Van Goethe, Tieck, Schlegel, etc.
Joined her husband in Canada, 1836 ;
returned without him, 1838. Friend-
ship with Lady Byron. Active
literary life. Visit to Germany, 1845.
To Italy, with her niece (afterwards
Mrs. Macpherson), 1847. Crown
Pension, 1851. Quarrel with Lady
Byron, about 1853. Died, at Ealing,
17 March 1860.

Works : ' A Lady's Diary ' (anon.),
1826 (another edn., anon., called
'The Diary of an Ennuyée,' same
year) ; ' The Loves of the Poets'
(anon.), 1829 ; ' Memoirs of Celebrated Female Sovereigns ' (2 vols.),
1831 ; ' Characteristics of Women ' (2
vols.), 1832 ; Letterpress to ' Beauties
of the Court of King Charles II.'
(illustrated by her father), 1833 ;
Letterpress to ' Fantasien,' 1834 ;
' Visits and Sketches ' (4 vols.), 1834 ;
' The Romance of Biography,' 1837 ;
' Sketches of Germany,' 1837 ; 'Winter
Studies and Summer Rambles in
Canada,' 1838 ; 'Handbook to the
Public Galleries of Art in and near
London,' 1842 ; 'Companion to the
most celebrated Private Galleries in
London,' 1844 ; ' Memoirs of the
Early Italian Painters ' (2 vols.), 1845;
'Memoirs and Essays,' 1846 ; Letter-
press to 'The Decorations of the
Garden Pavilion, etc.,' 1846 ; 'Sacred
and Legendary Art ' (2 vols.), 1848 ;
'Legends of the Monastic Orders,'
1850 ; ' Legends of the Madonna,'
1852 ; ' Handbook to the Court of
Modern Sculpture in the Crystal
Palace,' 1854 ; ' A Commonplace
Book,' 1854 ; ' Sisters of Charity,'
1855 ; ' The Communion of Labour,'
1856.

Posthumous : ' The History of Our
Lord,' completed by Lady Eastlake
(2 vols.), 1864.

She *translated :* Princess Amelia of
Saxony's 'Social Life in Germany,'
1840 ; G. F. Waagen's ' Peter Paul
Rubens,' 1840.

Life : by Mrs. Macpherson, 1878.

* **JEBB (Richard Claverhouse), b.
1841.** Born, at Dundee, 27 Aug.

10—2

1841. At St. Columba's School, Co. Dublin, Aug. 1853 to Dec. 1854 ; at Charterhouse School, Jan. 1855 to May 1858. Matric. Trin. Coll., Camb., Oct. 1859 ; B.A., 1862 ; M.A. 1865 ; Fellow of Trin. Coll., 1863 ; Tutor, 1872-75 ; Public Orator, 1869. Sec. of (and helped to found) Cambridge Philological Soc. Governor of Charterhouse School, 1871 - 75 ; re-elected, 1893. Classical Examiner, London Univ., 1872. Married Mrs. Caroline Lane Reynolds, 17 Aug. 1874. Prof. of Greek, Glasgow Univ., 1875-89. Greek Order of the Saviour, 1878. Hon. LL.D., Edinburgh, 1878. Visit to U.S.A., 1884. Hon. LL.D., Harvard Univ., 1884. Corresp. Mem. of German Archæological Institute, 1884. D.Litt., Cambridge, 1886. LL.D., Dublin, 1888. Ph.D., Bologna, 1888. Regius Prof. of Greek, Cambridge, 1889. Pres. of Hellenic Soc. of London, 23 June 1890. F.S.A., 1890. Hon. LL.D., Glasgow, 1891. Hon. D.C.L., Oxford, 1891. M.P. for Cambridge Univ., 1891 ; re-elected, 1892 and 1895. Lecturer at Johns Hopkins Univ., Baltimore, 1892. On Royal Commission on Secondary Education, 1894. Pres. of Teachers' Guild of Great Britain and Ireland, 1896. Chairman of Joint Committee on Secondary Education, 1897. Fellow of Univ. of London, 1897.

Works : Milton's 'Areopagitica' (priv. ptd.), 1872 ; 'Translations into Greek and Latin Verse,' 1873 ; 'An Address to the Students of the Cambridge School of Art,' 1875 ; 'The Attic Orators' (2 vols.), 1876 ; 'Some Remarks' on an article by Prof. Mahaffy on preceding, 1876 ; 'A Rejoinder' to Prof. Mahaffy's 'Reply,' 1876 ; 'Greek Literature,' 1877 ; 'Translation' (with H. Jackson and W. E. Currey), 1878 ; 'Modern Greece,' 1880 ; 'Bentley,' 1882 ; 'Homer,' 1887 ; 'Erasmus,' 1890 ; 'The Growth and Influence of Classical Greek Poetry,'1893 ; 'The Work of the Universities for the Nation,' 1893.

He has *translated :* the 'Characters' of Theophrastus, 1870 ; and *edited :* 'Selections from the Attic Orators,'

1880 ; the Plays of Sophocles, with translation and commentary, 1883-96.

JEFFERIES (Richard), 1848-1887. Born, at Coate Farm, Wilts, 6 Nov. 1848. Educated at schools at Sydenham and Swindon. Ran away from home, 11 Nov. 1864, but was soon afterwards sent back. Contrib. to 'North Wilts Advertiser' and 'Wilts and Gloucester Herald.' On staff of 'North Wilts Herald' as reporter, March 1866 to 1867. Ill-health 1867-68. Visit to Belgium, 1870. Contrib. to 'Fraser's Mag.,' and other periodicals, from 1873. Married Miss Baden, July 1874. Lived first at Coate ; afterwards at Swindon till Feb. 1877. Removed to Surbiton, 1877. Contrib. to 'Pall Mall Gaz.,' 'Graphic,' 'St. James's Gaz.,' 'Standard,' 'World,' etc. Severe ill-health began, 1881. Removed to West Brighton, 1882 ; to Eltham, 1884 ; afterwards lived at Crowborough ; and at Goring, Sussex. Died, at Goring, 14 Aug. 1887. Buried at Broadwater, Sussex.

Works : 'Reporting, Editing, and Authorship' [1873] ; 'A Memoir of the Goddards of North Wilts '[1873]; 'Jack Brass, Emperor of England,' 1873 ; 'The Scarlet Shawl,' 1874 ; 'Restless Human Hearts' (3 vols.), 1875 ; 'Suez-cide,' 1876 ; 'World's End' (3 vols.), 1877 ; 'The Gamekeeper at Home ' (under initials, R. J.; from 'Pall Mall Gaz.'), 1878 ; 'Wild Life in a Southern County' (under initials, R. J.; from 'Pall Mall Gaz.'), 1879 ; 'The Amateur Poacher' (under initials: R. J.), 1879 ; 'Greene Ferne Farm,' 1880 ; 'Round about a Great Estate,' 1880 ; 'Hodge and his Masters' (2 vols.), 1880 ; 'Wood Magic,' 1881 ; 'The Story of My Heart,' 1883 ; 'Nature Near London' (from 'Standard '), 1883 ; 'The Dewy Morn' (2 vols.), 1884 ; 'Red Deer,' 1884 ; 'The Life of the Fields,' 1884; 'After London,' 1885 ; 'The Open Air,' 1885 ; 'Amaryllis at the Fair,' 1887.

Posthumous : 'Field and Hedgerow,' ed. by his wife, 1889 ; 'History of Swindon,' ed. by G. Toplis, 1897 ; 'Early Fiction,' ed. by G. Toplis, 1897.

He *edited :* Gilbert White's 'Natural History of Selborne,' 1887.

Life : 'The Eulogy of Richard Jefferies,' by Sir W. Besant, 1888.

JEFFREY (Francis) *Lord Jeffrey,* **1773-1850.** Born, in Edinburgh, 23 Oct. 1773. At Edinburgh High School, Oct. 1781 to 1787 ; at Glasgow Univ., 1787-89. Studied Law in Edinburgh, 1789-91. Matric. Queen's Coll., Oxford, 17 Oct. 1791. Left Oxford, 5 July 1792. Studied Law in Edinburgh, 1792-93. Called to Scotch Bar, 16 Dec. 1794. Visit to London, 1798. Married Catherine Wilson, 1 Nov. 1801 ; settled in Edinburgh. Contrib. to 'Monthly Rev.,' 1802. Started 'Edinburgh Review,' with Sydney Smith and others ; first number appeared, 10 Oct. 1802 ; he edited it till June 1829 ; contrib. to it, Oct. 1802 to Jan. 1848. Joined Volunteer regiment, 1803. One of founders of 'Friday Club,' 1803. Visit to London, 1804. Wife died, 8 Aug. 1805. Visit to London, 1806. Duel with Moore (followed by reconciliation), at Chalk Farm, 11 Aug. 1806. Legal practice in Scotland increasing. Fell in love with Charlotte Wilkes, 1810 ; followed her to America, 1813 ; married her in New York, Nov. 1813. Tour with her in America. Returned to England, Feb. 1814. Settled at Craigcrook, near Edinburgh, 1815. Visit to Continent same year. Joined Bannatyne Club, 1826. Dean of Faculty of Advocates, Edinburgh, 2 July 1829 ; Lord Advocate, 1830. M.P. for Forfarshire Burghs, 1830 ; unseated owing to irregularity in election. M.P. for Malton, April and June 1831. Ill-health, in London, 1831. M.P. for Edinburgh, Dec. 1832 to 1834. Judge of Court of Sessions, as Lord Jeffrey, June 1834. Ill-health, 1841. Died, in Edinburgh, 26 Jan. 1850. Buried in Dean Cemetery.

Works : 'A Summary View of the rights and claims of the Roman Catholics of Ireland' (anon.), 1808 ; 'A Short Vindication of the late Major A. Campbell' (anon.), 1810 ; 'Contributions to the Edinburgh Review' (4 vols.), 1844.

He *edited :* J. Playfair's Works, 1822 ; Byron's Poems, 1845.

Life : (with selected Correspondence) by Lord Cockburn, 1852.

JERROLD (Douglas William), 1803-1857. Born, in London, 3 Jan. 1803. Early years spent at Wilby, Kent. Family removed to Sheerness, 1807, where his father leased a theatre. Acted juvenile parts occasionally. At school in Sheerness. Midshipman in Navy, Dec. 1813 to Oct. 1815. Father having lost money, family removed to London. Apprenticed to printer. Contrib. to 'Arliss's Mag.' Play, 'More Frightened than Hurt,' produced at Sadler's Wells Theatre, 30 April 1821. Contrib. to 'Sunday Monitor,' 'Weekly Times,' 'Ballot,' and other periodicals, from 1819. Married Mary Swann, 1824, but continued at first to live at home. 'Dramatic writer' to Coburg Theatre. 'Black-Eyed Susan' produced at Surrey Theatre, 8 June 1829 ; engaged by Elliston as 'dramatic writer' there. 'The Devil's Ducat,' Adelphi, 16 Dec. 1830 ; 'The Bride of Ludgate,' Drury Lane, 8 Dec. 1831. Wrote plays till 1835. Contrib. during same period to 'Athenæum,' 'Morning Herald,' 'Monthly Mag.' Owing to money losses, retired to Paris, 1835. Contrib. to 'Blackwood's Mag.,' 'Freemas n's Quarterly,' etc. Part-manager of Strand Theatre, 1836. Contrib. to 'Punch' (over signature : 'Q.'), Sept. 1841 to 1857. 'Time Works Wonders' produced at Haymarket, 26 April 1845. Edited 'Illuminated Mag.,' 1843-45 ; 'Douglas Jerrold's Shilling Mag.,' Jan. 1845 to 1848 ; 'Douglas Jerrold's Weekly Newspaper,' 1846 ; 'Lloyd's Weekly Newspaper,' 1852-57. Died, at Kilburn Priory, 8 June 1857. Buried, in Norwood Cemetery.

Works : 'The Smoked Miser' [1823] ; 'The Witch of Durncleugh,' 1823 ; 'Beau Nash,' 1825 ; 'Ambrose

Gwinett,' 1828 ; 'Fifteen Years of a Drunkard's Life' [1828 ?] ; 'Law and Lions' [1828 ?] ; 'John Overy,' 1828 ; 'Martha Willis,' 1828 ; 'The Flying Dutchman,' 1829 ; 'Thomas à Becket,' 1829 ; 'Vidocq,' 1829 ; 'Black-Eyed Susan,' 1829 ; 'The Rent Day,' 1832 ; 'The Housekeeper,' 1833 ; 'Nell Gwynne,' 1833 ; 'The Wedding-Gown,' 1834 ; 'Doves in a Cage,' 1835 ; 'The Hazard of the Die,' 1835 ; 'The School-fellows,' 1835 ; 'The Perils of Pippins,' 1836 ; 'Men of Character' (3 vols.), 1838 ; 'The Hand-Book of Swindling' (under pseud. of 'Capt. Barabbas White-feather'), [1839] ; 'The White Mil-liner,' 1841 ; 'Bubbles of the Day,' 1842 ; 'Time Works Wonders,' 1842 ; 'Gertrude's Cherries,' 1842 ; 'The Prisoner of War,' 1842 ; 'Punch's Letters to his Son' (from 'Punch'), 1843 ; 'The Story of a Feather,' 1844 ; 'Punch's Complete Letter-Writer' (from 'Punch'), 1845 ; 'Mrs. Caudle's Curtain Lectures' (from 'Punch,' anon.), 1846 ; 'The Chronicles of Clovernook,' 1846 ; 'A Man Made of Money,' 1849 ; 'The Catspaw,' 1850 ; 'Retired from Business' [1851] ; 'Works' (8 vols.), 1851-54 ; 'Heads of the People' [1852] ; 'Cakes and Ale,' 1852 ; 'St. Cupid,' 1853 ; 'A Heart of Gold,' 1854.

Posthumous : 'Wit and Opinions,' ed. by B. Jerrold, 1859 ; 'The Brown-rigg Papers,' 1860 ; 'Other Times' (from 'Lloyd's'), 1868 ; 'The Bar-ber's Chair and Hedgehog Letters' (from 'Douglas Jerrold's Weekly Newspaper'), 1874 ; 'Tales,' ed. by J. L. Robertson, 1891.

Collected Works : ed. by B. Jerrold (4 vols.), 1863-64.

Life : by W. B. Jerrold, 1859.

[His son, **William Blanchard Jer-rold** (1826-1884), born, 23 Dec. 1826 ; married Lillie Blanchard, 1849 ; en-gaged in journalism ; edited 'Lloyd's,' 1857-84 ; spent much time in Paris ; wrote a number of plays and miscel-laneous works, including : 'Life and Remains of Douglas Jerrold,' 1859 ; 'Life of Napoleon III.' (4 vols.), 1874-82 ; 'Life of George Cruikshank' (2 vols.), 1882 ; etc., etc.]

JOHNSON (Richard), 1573-1659 [?]. Born, in London, 1573 ; baptized, 24 May. Worked as an appren-tice. Afterwards obtained Freedom of the City of London. Perhaps held a post at Court. Died, about 1659 [?].

Works : 'The Nine Worthies of London,' 1592 ; 'Famous Historie of the Seaven Champions of Christendom,' pt. i., 1596 (no copy known ; 1597 edn. is probably the second) ; pt. ii., 1608 ; pt. iii., 1616 ; 'Anglorum La-chrimæ,' 1603 ; The Pleasant Walks of Moorefields,' 1607 ; 'The Pleasant Conceites of Old Hobson,' 1607 ; 'The Most Pleasant History of Tom a Lin-colne,' 1607 ; 'The Crowne Garland of Golden Rose,' 1612 ; 'A Remem-brance of the Honors due to . . . Robert, Earle of Salisbury' (anon.), 1612 ; 'Looke on me, London' (anon.), 1613 ; 'The Golden Garland of Princely Pleasures,' 1620 ; 'The His-tory of Tom Thumbe,' 1621 ; 'Dainty Conceits,' 1630.

*** JOHNSON (Samuel), 1709-1784.** Born, at Lichfield, 18 Sept. 1709. At Lichfield School, 1719-24 ; at school at Stourbridge, 1724-26. Matric., Pembroke Coll., Oxford, 16 Dec. 1728 ; resided till Dec. 1729 ; removed name from books, 1731. Usher at Market Bosworth School, 1732 [?]. At Bir-mingham, working for publisher of 'Birmingham Journal,' 1732-34. Re-turned to Lichfield, 1734. Married Mrs. Porter, 9 July 1735. Lived at Edial, near Lichfield, taking pupils (one of whom was David Garrick), 1735-37. To London, with Garrick, March 1737. Brought his wife to London, winter of 1737. Contrib. to 'Gentleman's Mag.,' 1738-48 ; wrote 'Parliamentary Debates' for it, 1738-43. Began to work upon his 'Dic-tionary,' 1747. Wrote prologue for opening of Drury Lane under Garrick's management, 1747 ; tragedy 'Irene' produced there, 6 Feb. 1749. Edited (and wrote greater part of) 'The Rambler,' March 1750 to March 1752. Wife died, 17 March 1752. Contrib. to 'The Adventurer,' 1753-54. Visit to Oxford, 1754 ; degree of M.A., by diploma, 10 Feb. 1755. Contrib. to 'Universal Visitor,' 1756 ; to 'Literary Mag.,' 1756 ; edited 'Literary Mag.,' 1756-58. Edited (and wrote greater part of) 'The Idler,' April 1758 to April 1760. Crown Pension of £300, July 1762. First meeting with Boswell, 16 May 1763. Founded 'The Literary Club' with Sir Joshua Reynolds, Burke, Goldsmith, and others, 1763. Friendship with the Thrales begun, 1764. Hon. LL.D., Dublin, 1765. Tour in Scotland with Boswell, in 1773. In Wales with the Thrales, 1774 ; to Paris with them, 1775. Engaged on 'Lives of the Poets,' 1777-81. Hon. D.C.L., Oxford, 30 March 1775. Paralytic stroke, 17 June 1783. Visit to Oxford with Boswell, June 1784. Died, in London, 13 Dec. 1784. Buried in Westminster Abbey.

Works : 'London' (anon.), 1738 ; 'Marmor Norfolciense' (anon.), 1739 ; 'A compleat vindication of the licensees of the Stage' (anon.), 1739 ; 'Proposals for publishing "Bibliotheca Harleiana,"' 1742 ; 'Catalogus Bibliothecæ Harleianæ' (with others; anon.), 1743-45; 'An Account of the life of Mr. Richard Savage' (anon.), 1744 ; 'An Account of the life of J. P. Barretier' (anon.), 1744 ; 'Miscellaneous Observations on the Tragedy of Macbeth,' 1745 ; 'Plan for a Dictionary of the English Language,' 1747 ; 'The Vanity of Human Wishes,' 1749 ; 'Irene,' 1749 ; 'A New Prologue' (anon.), 1750 ; 'The Rambler' (4 vols.), 1750-52 ; 'A Dictionary of the English Language,' 1755 ; 'Account of an attempt to ascertain the Longitude at Sea' (anon.), 1755 ; 'The Idler' (103 nos.), 1758-60 ; 'The Review of a Free Inquiry' (anon.), 1759 ; 'The Prince of Abyssinia' (afterwards pub. as 'Rasselas'), 1759 (2nd edn. same year) ; 'The False Alarm' (anon.), 1770 ; 'Thoughts on the late Transactions respecting Falkland's Islands' (anon.), 1771 ; 'The Patriot' (anon.), 1774 ; 'A Journey to the Western Isles of Scotland' (anon.), 1775 ; 'The Convict's Address' (anon.),

1777 ; 'Prefaces Biographical and Critical to the Works of the most eminent English Poets,' 1779.

Posthumous : 'Poetical Works,' 1785 (2nd edn. same year) ; 'Prayers and Meditations,' ed. by G. Strahan, 1785 ; 'Memoirs of Charles Frederick, King of Prussia,' ed. by Harrison, 1786; 'Debates in Parliament' (anon.), 1787 ; 'Correspondence with Mrs. Thrale,' 1788 ; 'Sermons left for Publication' (attrib. to Johnson), 1788 ; 'A Sermon . . . for the Funeral of his Wife,' 1788 ; 'Letter to the Earl of Chesterfield,' ed. by Boswell, 1790 ; 'An Account of the Life of Dr. Samuel Johnson from his Birth to his Eleventh Year, written by himself,' 1805 ; 'A Diary of a Journey into North Wales,' ed. by R. Duppa, 1816 ; 'Letters,' ed. by G. P. Hill (2 vols.), 1892.

He *translated :* Lobo's 'Voyage to Abyssinia,' 1735 ; and *edited :* Sir T. Browne's 'Christian Morals,' with life of the author, 1756 ; Shakespeare's Plays (8 vols.), 1765 ; 'The Works of the English Poets' (68 vols.), 1779-81. He contributed a 'Life of Ascham' to Bennet's edn. of Ascham's 'English Works,' 1763, as well as a number of prefaces and dedications to works by his friends.

Collected Works : ed. by Hawkins and Stockdale (13 vols.), 1787 ; ed. by F. P. Walesby (11 vols.), 1825.

Life : by Boswell, 1791.

JONES (*Sir* **William**), 1746-1794. Born, in Westminster, 28 Sept. 1746. At Harrow School, 1753-64. Matric., Univ. Coll., Oxford, 15 March 1764 ; Scholar, 31 Oct. 1764 ; Fellow, 1766 ; B.A., 1768 ; M.A., 1773. Private tutor to Lord Althorp, 1765-70. F.R.S., 1772. Mem. of Literary Club, 1773. Called to Bar at Middle Temple, 1774. Commissioner of Bankruptcy, 1776. Judge of High Court at Calcutta, 1783-94. Knighted, 19 March 1783. Married Anna Maria Shipley, April 1783. Arrived at Calcutta, Dec. 1783. Founded Bengal Asiatic Soc., Jan. 1784. Edited 'The Asiatic Miscellany,' 1787. Wife returned to Europe, owing to ill-health,

Dec. 1793. He died, at Calcutta, 27 April 1794. Buried there.

Works: 'Traité sur la Poésie Orientale,' 1770 ; 'Dissertation sur la littérature Orientale ' (anon.), 1771 ; 'Grammar of the Persian Language,' 1771 ; 'Lettre à Monsieur A*** du P***' (anon.), 1771 ; 'Poems, consisting chiefly of translations from the Asiatick Languages' (anon.), 1772 ; 'Poeseos Asiaticæ Commentariorum libri sex,' 1774 ; 'A Dialogue between a Country Farmer and a Gentleman' (anon.), 1778 ; 'A Speech,' 1780 ; 'An Inquiry into the Legal Mode of Suppressing Riots' (anon.), 1780 ; 'An Essay on the Law of Bailments,' 1781 ; 'The Muse Recalled,' 1781 ; 'An Ode in imitation of Alcæus' (anon.), [1782] ; ' The Principles of Government' (anon.), 1782 ; 'A Letter to a Patriot Senator' (anon.), 1783 ; 'On the Orthography of Asiatick Words,' 1784 ; ' On the Gods of Greece, Italy and India,' 1875 ; ' On the Hindus,' 1786 ; 'On the Arabs,' 1787 ; ' On the Tartars,' 1788 ; 'On the Persians,' 1789 ; 'On the Chinese,' 1790 ; ' On the Borderers, Mountaineers and Islanders of Asia,' 1791 ; 'On the Origin and Families of Nations,' 1792 ; ' On Asiatick History,' 1793 ; 'On the Philosophy of the Asiaticks,' 1794.

He *translated:* 'Life of Nader Shah' (into French), 1770 (English version, 1773) ; 'The Moallakat,' 1782 ; ' The Mahomedan Law of Succession,' 1782 ; ' Sacontalá,' 1789 ; 'Al-Sirájiyyah, or Mahomedan Law of Inheritance,' 1792 ; Mann's ' Institutes,' 1796.

Collected Works: 'Works,' ed. by A. M. Jones (6 vols.), 1799 ; two supplemental vols., 1801 ; 'Poetical Works,' 1810 ; ' Discourses, etc.,' 1821.

Life: 'Memoirs,' by Lord Teignmouth, 1804.

JONSON (Ben), 1573[?]-1637. Born, in Westminster [?], 1573 [?]. Educated at St.-Martin's-in-the-Fields Parish School ; and at Westminster School. Worked as a bricklayer for a short time ; afterwards served with English troops in Flanders. Returned to England about 1592 ; married soon afterwards. First acted, and wrote for stage, about 1595. Imprisoned for killing a fellow-actor in a duel, 1598. Became a Roman Catholic, same year. ' Every Man in His Humour,' produced at Globe Theatre, 1598. Wrote plays for Henslowe's company, 1599-1602. 'Sejanus,' produced at Globe Theatre, 1603. Prolific writer of plays ; and of Masques, for Court performance, 1605-30. Imprisoned for a short time in connection with political allusions in play 'Eastward Ho,' 1605. In France, as tutor to son of Sir W. Raleigh, 1613. Journey to Scotland, on foot, 1618. Elected Burgess of Edinburgh, Sept. 1618. Visited Drummond of Hawthornden. Returned to England, spring of 1619. Visit to Oxford, 1620 ; received Hon. M.A. degree. Ill-health began, 1626. Chronologer to City of London, Sept. 1628 ; deprived of salary, 1631 ; restored to post, Sept. 1634. Died, in London, 6 Aug. 1637. Buried in Westminster Abbey.

Works: ' Every Man Out of His Humour,' 1600 (2nd edn. same year) ; 'Cynthia's Revels,' 1600 ; ' Every Man in his Humour,' 1601 ; 'Poëtaster,' 1602 ; Additions to 'Jeronymo,' 1602 ; 'A Particular Entertainment,' 1603 ; ' Part of King James his . . . Entertainment,' 1604 ; ' Sejanus,' 1605 ; ' Eastward Ho ' (with Chapman and Marston), 1605 (3rd edn. same year) ; ' Hymenæi,' 1606 ; ' Volpone,' 1607 ; ' Description of the . . . Masque ' at Viscount Hadington's Marriage [1608] ; ' Epicœne,' 1609 ; 'The Character of two royall Masques,' 1609 ; ' Ben Jonson, his Case is Altered,' 1609 ; 'The Masque of Queenes,' 1609 ; 'Cateline his Conspiracy,' 1611 ; 'The Alchemist,' 1612 ; 'Certayne Masques,' 1615 ; ' Works ' (2 vols.), 1616-40 ; 'Lovers Made Men ' (known as 'The Masque of Lethe ' ; anon.), 1617 ; ' The Masque of Augures,' 1621 ; 'Neptune's Triumph ' (anon.), [1623] ; 'The Fortunate Isles ' [1624] ; ' Love's Triumph through Callipolis,' 1630 ; 'Chloridia ' [1630 ?] ; 'The New Inne,' 1631.

Posthumous : 'The Bloody Brother, by B. J. F.' (mainly by Fletcher; perhaps part by Jonson), 1639; ' Underwoods,' 1640; 'Execration against Vulcan,' 1640 ; 'The English Grammar,' 1640 ; 'The Widow' (with Fletcher and Middleton), 1652 ; 'The Fall of Mortimer' (anon.; completed by another hand), 1771 ; 'The Sad Shepherd,' ed. by F. G. Waldron, 1783.

He *translated :* 'Horace his Art of Poetrie,' 1640.

Collected Works : in one vol., 1692; in 7 vols., ed. by Whalley, 1756 ; ed. by Gifford, 1816.

Life : by J. A. Symonds, 1886.

*****JOWETT (Benjamin), 1817-1893.** Born, at Camberwell, 15 April 1817. At St. Paul's School, 16 June 1829 to 1836. Scholar, Balliol Coll., Oxford, Dec. 1835 to 1839 ; matric., 30 Nov., 1836 ; Hertford Scholar, 1837 ; Fellow, Balliol Coll., 1838-70 ; Tutor, 1843-70. B.A., 1839 ; Latin Essay Prize, 1841 ; M.A., 1842. M.A., Durham, 1842. Ordained Deacon, 1842 ; Priest, 1845 ; Mem. of Commission on I.C.S. Exams., 1853. Regius Prof. of Greek, Oxford, 1855-93. Master of Balliol Coll., 1870-93. Hon. Doc., Leyden Univ., Feb. 1875. Vice - Chancellor of Oxford Univ., 1882-86. Hon. LL.D., Edinburgh, 1884 ; Hon. LL.D., Dublin, 1886 ; Hon. LL.D., Cambridge, 1890. Died, at Oxford, 1 Oct. 1893.

Works : 'De Etruscorum Cultu,' 1841 ; Edition of 'Epistles to Galatians, Thessalonians and Romans' (2 vols.), 1855 ; 'On the Interpretation of Scripture,' in 'Essays and Reviews,' 1860 ; Translation of Plato's Dialogues (4 vols.) 1871 ; 'Lord Lytton,' 1873 ; Translation of Thucydides (2 vols.) 1881 ; Translation of the 'Politics' of Aristotle (2 vols.), 1885.

Posthumous : 'College Sermons,' ed. by Hon. W. H. Fremantle, 1895.

Life : by E. Abbott and L. Campbell, 1897.

KAVANAGH (Julia), 1824-1877. Born, at Thurles, 1824. With her parents in France, during child-hood. To London 1844. Adopted literary life. Contrib. to 'Argosy,' 1877. Later years spent at Nice. Died there, 28 Oct. 1877.

Works : 'The Montyon Prizes' (anon.), 1846 ; 'Madeleine,' 1848 ; 'The Three Paths,' 1848 ; 'Women in France during the Eighteenth Century,' 1850 ; 'Nathalie,' 1850 ; 'Women of Christianity,' 1852 ; 'Daisy Burns,' 1853 ; 'Grace Lee,' 1855 ; 'Rachel Gray,' 1856 ; 'A Summer and Winter in the Two Sicilies' (2 vols.), 1858 ; 'Adèle,' 1858 ; 'Seven Years,' 1859 ; 'French Women of Letters' (2 vols.), 1862 [1861] ; 'English Women of Letters,' 1862 ; 'Queen Mab,' 1863 ; 'Beatrice,' 1864 ; 'Sybil's Second Love,' 1867 ; 'Dora,' 1868 ; 'Silvia,' 1870 ; 'Bessie,' 1872 ; 'John Dorrien,' 1875 ; 'Pearl Fountain' (with B. Kavanagh), 1876 ; 'Two Lilies,' 1877.

Posthumous : 'Forget - me - Nots,' ed. by C. W. Wood, 1878.

KAYE (*Sir* John William), 1814-1876. Born, at Acton, 1814. Educated at Eton, and at Royal Mil. Coll., Addiscombe. To India, as Cadet in Bengal Artillery, 1832. Married Mary Catherine Puckle, 1839. Left army, 1841. Started 'Calcutta Review,' 1846. Returned to England, 1845. Frequent contributor to periodicals. Post in Home service of H.E.I.C., 1856. Sec. to Political Department, Home Office, 1858-74. F.R.S., 1866. K.C.S.I., May 1871. Died, at Forest Hill, 24 July 1876.

Works : 'The Story of Basil Bouverie' (anon.), 1842 ; 'Peregrine Pultuney' (anon.), 1844 ; 'History of the War in Afghanistan' (2 vols.), 1851 ; 'The Administration of the East India Company,' 1853 ; 'The Life and Correspondence of Charles, Lord Metcalfe' (2 vols.), 1854 (2nd edn. same year); 'The Life and Correspondence of Henry St. George Tucker,' 1854 ; 'The Life and Correspondence of Sir John Malcolm' (2 vols.), 1856 ; 'Christianity in India,' 1859 ; 'The History of the Sepoy War' (3 vols.), 1864-76 (another edn..

continued by Col. Malleson, pub. as 'Kaye and Malleson's History of the Indian Mutiny,' 1888-89) ; 'Lives of Indian Officers' (from 'Good Words'), 1867 ; Letterpress to 'India, Ancient and Modern,' 1867 ; 'The Essays of an Optimist' (from 'Cornhill Mag.'), 1870.

He *edited:* Buckle's 'Memoirs . . . of the Bengal Artillery,' 1852 ; Tucker's 'Memorials of Indian Government,' 1853 ; 'Selections from the papers of Baron Metcalfe,' 1855 ; 'The Autobiography of Miss Cornelia Knight,' 1861 ; Taylor's 'People of India' (with J. F. Watson), 1868.

KEATS (John), 1795-1821. Born, in London, 31 Oct. 1795. At school at Enfield, at irregular periods between 1801 and 1810. His mother removed to Edmonton, 1806. Apprenticed to Surgeon at Edmonton, 1810. To London, 1814. Studied medicine at St. Thomas's and Guy's Hospitals. Appointed Dresser at Guy's, March 1816. Licentiate of Apothecaries' Hall, 25 July 1816. Contrib. to 'The Examiner,' 1816-17. Friendship with Leigh Hunt and Haydon begun about this time. Abandoned medical career, 1817. Visit to Oxford, Sept. to Oct. 1817 ; Contrib. poems to 'The Champion,' 1817 ; wrote dramatic criticism for it, Dec. 1817 to Jan. 1818. At this period resided mainly with his brothers at Hampstead. Walking tour with Charles Armitage Brown in Northern England and Scotland, June to Aug. 1818. Engaged to Fanny Brawne, Dec. 1818. One brother married and went to America, June 1818 ; the other died, Dec. 1818. Lived at Shanklin and Winchester successively during early part of 1819 ; settled in Westminster, Oct. 1819. Contrib. 'Ode to a Nightingale' to 'Annals of the Fine Arts,' 1819 ; 'La Belle Dame Sans Merci' to 'The Indicator,' 1820. Consumption set in, Feb. 1820. Sailed with Joseph Severn to Italy, Sept. 1820 ; arrived at Naples in Oct. ; at Rome in Nov. Died, in Rome, 23 Feb. 1821. Buried in Old Protestant Cemetery there.

Works: 'Poems,' 1817 ; 'Endymion,' 1818 ; 'Lamia ; Isabella ; the Eve of St. Agnes,' 1820.

Posthumous: 'Life, Letters and Literary Remains,' ed. by R. Monckton Milnes, 1848 ; 'Letters to Fanny Brawne,' ed. by H. Buxton Forman, 1878 ; 'Letters,' ed. by H. Buxton Forman, 1895.

Collected Works: ed. by H. Buxton Forman (4 vols.), 1883.

Life: by Lord Houghton, revised edn. 1867 ; by W. M. Rossetti, 1887 ; by Sidney Colvin, 1887.

KEBLE (John), 1792-1866. Born, at Fairford, Gloucestershire, 25 April 1792. Early education by his father. Matric. Corpus Christi Coll., Oxford, 12 Dec. 1806 ; Scholar, 1806 - 12 ; B.A., 1810 ; Fellow of Oriel Coll., 1812-35 ; M.A., 1813 ; English Essay and Latin Essay Prizes, 1812 ; Public Examiner, 1813 and 1821-23 ; Tutor of Oriel Coll., 1818-23. Ordained Deacon, 1815 ; Priest, 1816. Curate of East Leach and Burthorpe, 1815. Resided at Oxford till May 1823 ; then returned to Fairford. Curate of Southrop, 1823-25 ; of Hursley, Winchester, 1825-26. Returned to Fairford, 1826, to assist his father (who was Vicar of Coln St. Aldwins). Oxford Examiner for India House exams., 1830-32. Professor of Poetry, Oxford, 1831-42. Married Charlotte Clarke, 10 Oct. 1835. Vicar of Hursley, March 1836 to 1866. Contrib. to 'British Mag.' Died, at Bournemouth, 29 March 1866. Buried in Hursley Churchyard.

Works: 'On Translation from Dead Languages' (anon. ; priv. ptd.), 1812 ; 'The Christian Year' (2 vols. ; anon.), 1827 ; Tracts nos. 4, 13, 40, 52, 54, 57, 60, 89 of 'Tracts for the Times,' 1833 - 34 ; Contributions to 'Lyra Apostolica,' 1836 ; 'The Psalter . . . in English Verse' (anon.), 1839 ; 'The Case of Catholic Subscription to the 39 Articles' (priv. ptd.), 1841 ; 'An Horology' (under initials : J. K.), [1842] ; 'De Poeticæ Vi Medicæ' (2 vols.), 1844 ; 'Heads of Consideration on the Case of Mr. Ward,' 1845 ;

'Lyra Innocentium' (anon.), 1846;
'Sermons Academical and Occasional,'
1847 ; ' Against Profane Dealing with
Holy Matrimony in regard of a man
and his wife's sister,' 1849 ; ' Pastoral
Tracts on the Gorham Question,' 1850;
'Church Matters in 1850' [1850];
' On the Representation of the Univer -
sity of Oxford,' 1852 ; 'A very few
plain thoughts on the proposed addition of Dissenters to the University
of Oxford,' 1854 ; 'An Argument for
not proceeding immediately to repeal
the laws which treat the Nuptial
Bond as Indissoluble,' 1857 ; 'Sequel '
to preceding, 1857 ; ' On Eucharistical
Adoration,' 1857 ; 'The Life of
Thomas Wilson, Bishop of Sodor and
Man,' 1863 ; 'A Litany of Our
Lord's Warnings,' 1864 ; and a few
separate sermons.

Posthumous : 'Letter to a Member
of Convocation ' (from ' Lit. Churchman '), 1867 ; 'Sermons Occasional
and Parochial,' 1867 ; ' Village Sermons on the Baptismal Service,' 1869
[1868] ; 'The State in its relations
with the Church' (from 'British Critic '),
1869 ; ' Miscellaneous Poems,' ed. by
Canon Moberly, 1869 ; ' Letters of
Spiritual Counsel,' ed. by R. F. Wilson, 1870 ; ' Sermons for the Christian
Year,' ed. by Pusey (11 vols.), 1875-
80 ; ' Studia Sacra,' ed. by Canon
Norris, 1877 ; 'Occasional Papers and
Reviews,' ed. by Pusey, 1877 ; 'Outlines of Instructions . . . for the
Church Seasons,' ed. by R. F. Wilson,
1880.

He *translated :* Irenæus, for Pusey's
' Library of the Fathers,' 1838 ; and
edited : Hooker's Works, 1836 ; R. H.
Froude's 'Remains' (with Newman),
1838-39 ; Bishop Wilson's 'Works,'
1863; 'Hymns for Little Children,'
1848.

Life : by Sir J. T. Coleridge, 1870.

KEIGHTLEY (Thomas), 1789-1872.
Born, in Dublin, 17 Oct. 1789. To
Trin. Coll., Dublin, 4 July 1803. B.A.,
1808. To London, 1824. Active
literary life. Civil List Pension, 1855.
Died, at Erith, Kent, 4 Nov. 1872.

Works : 'The Fairy Mythology'

(2 vols. ; anon.), 1828 ; 'History of
the War of Independence in Greece'
(2 vols.), 1830 ; 'The Mythology
of Ancient Greece and Italy,' 1831
(abridged version, 1832) ; 'Outlines
of History' (anon.), 1831 ; 'Tales and
Popular Fictions,' 1834 ; 'The Crusaders,' 1834 ; 'History of Greece,'
1835 ; 'The History of Rome to the
end of the Republic,' 1836 ; 'Secret
Societies of the Middle Ages ' (anon.),
1837 ; 'History of England ' (2 vols.),
1837 - 39 ; 'History of the Roman
Empire,' 1840 ; ' An Elementary History of England,' 1841 ; 'An Elementary History of Greece,' 1841 ;
' Notes on the Bucolics and Georgics
of Virgil,' 1846 ; 'A History of India,'
[1846-47] ; 'Additional illustrations
of the Bucolics, etc.,' 1850 ; 'Account
of the Life . . . of John Milton,'
1855 ; 'The Shakespeare Expositor,'
1867.

He *translated :* Van Koetsveld's
'The Manse of Mastland,' 1860 ; and
edited : Virgil's 'Bucolics and Georgics,' 1847 ; Horace's 'Satires and
Epistles,' 1848 ; Ovid's 'Fasti,' Bk.
vi., 1839 ; Ovid's 'Fasti' complete,
1848 ; Sallust's 'Catalina and Jugurtha,' 1849 ; Milton's Poems, 1859 ;
Shakespeare's 'Plays,' 1864 ; 'Shakespeare's ' Plays and Poems,' 1865.

**KEMBLE (Frances Anna), 1809-
1893.** Born, in London, 27 Nov.
1809. First appearance at Covent
Garden Theatre, 5 Oct. 1829 ; acted
there till 1832. Tragedy, 'Francis I.,'
produced at Covent Garden, 15
March 1832. Acted with her father
in America, 1832-34. Married Pierce
Butler, 7 Jan. 1834. Separated from
him, 1846. Visit to England, 1847 ;
acted in Manchester and London.
Acted in America, autumn 1847 to
spring 1848. Obtained divorce from
husband, 1848. First Public Reading
in London, April 1848 ; in Philadelphia, Oct. 1849. Resumed maiden
name. Lived at Lenox, Mass., 1849-
68 ; lived near New York, 1868-69.
Gave public Readings in America,
1856-60, 1866-68. In Europe, 1869-73.
In America, 1873-77. Returned to

London, 1877. Died there, 15 Jan. 1893.

Works : ' Francis the First,' 1832 ; 'Journal of F. A. Butler,' 1835 ; 'The Star of Seville,' 1837 ; ' Poems,' 1844 ; ' A Year of Consolation,' 1847; 'Plays,' 1863 ; ' Journal of a Residence on a Georgian Plantation,' 1863 ; ' Poems,' 1866 [1865]; ' Record of a Girlhood,' 1878 ; ' Record of Later Life ' (3 vols.), 1882 ; ' Notes upon some of Shakespeare's Plays,' 1882 ; ' Poems,' 1883 ; ' Far Away and Long Ago,' 1889 ; ' Further Records ' (2 vols.), 1890.

KEN (Thomas), *Bishop of Bath and Wells,* 1637 - 1711. Born, at Berkhampstead, Hertfordshire, July 1637. Scholar of Winchester Coll., Sept. 1651 ; admitted, Jan. 1652. Fellow of New Coll., Oxford, 1656-66. To Hart Hall, Oxford, 1656 ; to New Coll., 1657 ; B.A., 3 May 1661; M.A., 21 Jan. 1665 ; Tutor of New Coll., 1661. Ordained 1661 [or 1662]. Rector of Little Easton, Essex, 1663-65. Domestic Chaplain to Bishop of Winchester, and Rector of St. John-in-the-Soke, 1665. Fellow of Winchester Coll., 8 Dec. 1666. Rector of Brightstone (or Brixton), I. of W., 1667-69. Prebendary of Winchester, 1669. Rector of East Woodhay, Hampshire, 1669-72. Lived at Winchester, 1672-79. Travelled on Continent, 1675. D.D., Oxford, 1679. To the Hague, as Chaplain to Mary Princess of Orange, 1679-80. Returned to Winchester, 1680 ; appointed Chaplain to King. With Lord Dartmouth to Tangier, as Chaplain, Aug. 1683. Returned to England, April 1684. Bishop of Bath and Wells, Nov. 1684 ; compelled to resign, as a Non-juror, April 1691. For rest of life under patronage of Lord Weymouth. Crown pension, 1704. Died, at Longleat, 19 March 1711. Buried at Frome Selwood.

Works : ' Manual of Prayers' (anon.), 1674 (another edn., with ' Hymns,' 1695) ; Funeral Sermon for Lady Margaret Mainard, 1682 ; ' Sermon preached at Whitehall,' 1685 ; ' An Exposition on the Church Catechism ; or, Practice of Divine Love ' (anon.), 1685 (another edn., with ' Directions for Prayer,' 1686) ; ' Pastoral Letter,' 1688 ; ' Prayers for the use of all persons who come to Bath for cure ' (anon.), 1692 ; ' A Letter to the Author of a " Sermon preached at the Funeral of her late Majesty " ' (anon.), 1695 (another edn., called ' A Dutifull Letter,' 1703) ; ' The Royal Sufferer ' (under initials : T. K.; attributed to Ken), 1699; ' Expostulatoria,' 1711.

Collected Works : ed. by Hawkins (4 vols.), 1721.

Life : by Dean Plumptre, revised edn., 1890.

KILLIGREW (Thomas), 1612-1683. Born, in Lothbury, London, 7 Feb. 1612. Page to Charles I., 1633. Married Cecilia Crofts, 29 June 1636. In France, 1635-40 [?] ; plays ' The Prisoners,' ' Claracilla,' ' The Parson's Wedding,' produced at Drury Lane about same period. Imprisoned on charge of treason, 1642-44. To Oxford, 1644. With Prince Charles in France, 1647. Ambassador at Venice, 1651-52. Remained abroad till 1660. After wife's death, married Charlotte de Hesse, 28 Jan. 1655. Groom of Bedchamber to Charles II., 1660. Afterwards Chamberlain to the Queen. Granted Royal Patent to erect a theatre, Aug. 1660 ; second patent, Jan. 1663. First Drury Lane Theatre opened by him, 8 April 1663 ; theatre burnt down, Jan. 1672. Master of Revels, 1673. New Drury Lane Theatre opened, 26 March 1674. Died, at Whitehall, 19 March 1683. Buried in Westminster Abbey.

Works : ' The Prisoners, and Claracilla,' 1641 ; ' Comedies and Tragedies' (containing : ' The Princess,' ' The Parson's Wedding,' ' The Pilgrim,' ' Cecilia and Clorinda,' ' Thomaso,' ' Bellamira her Dream,' ' Claracilla,' ' The Prisoners '), 1664.

KINGLAKE (Alexander William), 1809-1891. Born, at Taunton, 5 Aug. 1809. Early education at Eton. Matric. Trin. Coll., Camb., 1828 ; B.A., 1832 ;

M.A., 1836. Student of Lincoln's Inn, 14 April 1832 ; called to Bar, 5 May 1837. Travelled in East, 1835. Contrib. to 'Quarterly Rev.,' Dec. 1844 and March 1845. To Algiers, 1845 ; accompanied St. Arnaud's forces. With English forces during Crimean War, 1854. M.P. for Bridgewater, 1857-69. Contrib. to 'Blackwood's Mag.,' Sept. 1872. Died, in London, 2 Jan. 1891.

Works : 'Eothen' (anon.), 1844 ; 'Invasion of the Crimea,' vols. i., ii., 1863 ; vols. iii., iv., 1868 ; vol. v., 1875 ; vol. vi., 1880 ; vols. vii., viii. 1887.

KINGSLEY (Charles), 1819-1875. Born, at Holne Vicarage, Devonshire, 12 June 1819. At school at Clifton, 1831-32 ; at Helston, Cornwall, 1832-36. Family removed to London, 1836. Student at King's Coll., London 1836-38. Matric. Magdalene Coll., Camb., Oct. 1838 ; Scholar, 1839 ; B.A., 1842 ; M.A., 1860. Ordained Curate of Eversley, Hampshire, July 1842. Married Fanny Grenfell, 10 Jan. 1844 ; Rector of Eversley, same year. Clerk in Orders, St. Luke's, Chelsea, 1844-49. Canon of Middleham, 1845. Prof. of English Lit., Queen's Coll., London, 1848. Contrib. (under pseud. of 'Parson Lot') to 'Politics for the People,' 1848 ; and to 'The Christian Socialist,' 1850-51. Contrib. to 'Fraser's Mag.,' 1848, etc. Ill-health, winter 1848-49. First visit to Continent, 1851. At Torquay, winter 1853-54. Chaplain in Ordinary to the Queen, 1859. Prof. of Modern History, Cambridge, 1860-69. Increasing ill-health from 1864. Pres. of Social Science Congress, 1869. Canon of Chester, 1869. Visit to West Indies, winter 1869-70. Resided at Chester, May 1870 to 1873. Pres. of Midland Institute, 1872. Canon of Westminster, 1873. Visit to America, 1874. Died, at Eversley, 23 Jan. 1875. Buried there.

Works : 'The Saint's Tragedy,' 1848 ; 'Twenty-five Village Sermons,' 1849 ; 'Alton Locke' (anon.), 1850 ;

'Cheap Clothes and Nasty' (under pseud. 'Parson Lot'), 1850 ; 'The Application of Associative...Principles to Agriculture,' 1851 ; 'Yeast' (anon.), (from 'Fraser's Mag.'), 1851 ; 'The Message of the Church to Labouring Men,' 1851 ; 'Phaethon,' 1852 ; 'Sermons on National Subjects' (2 ser.), 1852-54 ; 'Hypatia' (from 'Fraser's Mag.'), 1853 ; 'Alexandria and her Schools,' 1854 ; 'Who causes Pestilence?' 1854 ; 'Sermons for the Times,' 1855 ; 'Westward Ho !' 1855 ; 'Glaucus,' 1855 ; 'The Heroes,' 1856 [1855] ; 'Two Years Ago,' 1857 ; 'Andromeda,' 1858 ; 'The Good News of God,' 1859 ; 'Miscellanies,' 1859 ; 'The Limits of Exact Sciences as applied to History,' 1860 ; 'Why should we pray for Fair Weather?' 1860 ; 'Town and Country Sermons,' 1861 ; 'A Sermon on the death of ... the Prince Consort,' 1862 [1861] ; 'Speech of Lord Dundreary ... on the great Hippocampus question' (anon.), 1862 ; 'The Gospel of the Pentateuch,' 1863 ; 'The Water Babies,' 1863 ; 'What, then, does Dr. Newman mean?' 1864 ; 'The Roman and the Teuton,' 1864 ; 'Hints to Stammerers' (anon.), 1864 ; 'David,' 1865 ; 'Hereward the Wake,' 1866 ; 'The Temple of Wisdom,' 1866 ; 'Three Lectures on the "Ancien Régime,"' 1867 ; 'The Water of Life,' 1867 ; 'The Hermits,' 1868 ; 'Discipline,' 1868 ; 'God's Feast,' 1869 ; 'Madame How and Lady Why,' 1870 [1869] ; 'At Last,' 1871 ; 'Poems,' 1872 [1871] ; 'Town Geology,' 1872 ; 'Prose Idylls,' 1873 ; 'Plays and Puritans,' 1873 ; 'Health and Education,' 1874 ; 'Westminster Sermons,' 1874 ; 'Lectures delivered in America,' 1875.

Posthumous : 'Letters to Young Men,' 1877 ; 'True Words for Brave Men,' ed. by his wife, 1878 ; 'All Saints' Day, and other Sermons,' ed. by W. Harrison, 1878 ; 'From Death to Life,' ed. by his wife, 1887.

He *edited :* Mansfield's 'Paraguay,' 1856 ; Tauler's 'History and Life,' 1857 ; Brooke's 'The Fool of Quality,' 1859 ; Bunyan's 'Pilgrim's Progress,' 1860 [1859] ; 'South by West,' 1874.

Collected Works : in 28 vols., 1880-85.

Life : 'Letters and Memories,' by his wife, 1877.

KINGSLEY (Henry), 1830-1876. [Brother of preceding.] Born, at Barnach, Northamptonshire, 2 Jan. 1830. At King's Coll. School, London, 30 April 1844 to Jan. 1847 ; at King's Coll., Jan. 1847 to 1848. Matric. Worcester Coll., Oxford, 6 March 1850. Took no degree. In Australia, 1853-58. Student of Inner Temple, 1862. Married Sarah Maria Kingsley Haselwood, 17 July 1864. Lived at Wargrave. Edited 'Edinburgh Daily Review,' 1869-72 ; war-correspondent for same during Franco-Prussian War 1870-72. Died, at Cuckfield, Sussex, 24 May 1876.

Works : 'The Recollections of Geoffrey Hamlyn,' 1859 ; 'Ravenshoe,' 1862 ; 'Austin Elliot,' 1863 ; 'The Hillyars and Burtons,' 1865 ; 'Leighton Court,' 1866 ; 'Silcote of Silcotes,' 1867 ; 'Mademoiselle Mathilde,' 1868 ; 'Stretton,' 1869 ; 'Tales of Old Travels,' 1869 ; 'Old Margaret,' 1871 ; 'The Lost Child,' 1871 ; 'The Boy in Gray,' 1871 ; 'Hetty,' 1871 ; 'The Harveys,' 1872 ; 'Hornby Mills,' 1872 ; 'Valentin,' 1872 ; 'Oakshott Castle' (under pseud. of 'Granby Dixon'), 1873 ; 'Reginald Hetherege,' 1874 ; 'Number Seventeen,' 1875 ; 'The Grange Garden,' 1876 ; 'Fireside Studies,' 1876.

Posthumous : 'The Mystery of the Island,' 1877.

He *edited :* Defoe's 'Robinson Crusoe,' 1868.

Collected Works : 'Novels,' ed. by C. K. Shorter, 1894, etc.

*KIPLING (Rudyard), b. 1865. Born, in Bombay, 30 Dec. 1865. At United Service Coll., Westward Ho, 18 Jan. 1878 to July 1882. To Lahore, as sub-editor of 'Lahore Civil and Military Gaz.,' 1882. Contrib. to Allahabad 'Pioneer.' Left India, 1889. Travelled in China, Japan, and America ; returned to England, Sept. 1889. Travelled in America, South Africa, Australia, and New Zealand,

June 1891 to 1896. Married Caroline Starr Balestier, 18 Jan. 1892. Returned to England, 1896. Elected memb. of Athenæum Club, 2 April 1897.

Works : 'Departmental Ditties,' 1888 ; 'Plain Tales from the Hills,' 1888 ; 'Soldiers Three,' 1888 ; 'The Story of the Gadsbys' [1888] ; 'In Black and White' [1888] ; 'Under the Deodars' [1888] ; 'Wee Willie Winkie' [1888] ; 'The Phantom 'Rickshaw' [1888] ; 'The Light that Failed,' 1890 ; 'Letters of Marque' (unauthorized collection),1891 ; 'Life's Handicap,' 1891 ; ' The City of Dreadful Night ' (unauthorized collection), 1891 ; 'Barrack-room Ballads,' 1892 ; 'The Naulahka' (with W. Balestier), 1892 ; 'Many Inventions,' 1893 ; 'The Jungle Book,' 1894 ; 'The Second Jungle Book,' 1895 ; 'Soldier Tales' (selected from previous publications), 1896 ; 'The Seven Seas,' 1896.

KNIGHT (Charles), 1791 - 1873. Born, at Windsor, 15 March 1791. At school at Ealing, 1803-05. Apprenticed to his father (a bookseller), 1805. Parliamentary reporter for 'Globe' and 'British Press,' 1812. Edited 'The Windsor and Eton Express,' 1812-26. Married Miss Vinicombe, 1815. Wrote Masque for Princess Charlotte's marriage, 1816. Overseer of parish, Windsor, 1818. Ed. 'The Plain Englishman,' with E. H. Locker, Feb. 1820 to Dec. 1822. Editor of 'The Guardian,' June 1820 to Dec. 1822 ; of 'The Etonian,' Oct. 1820 to July 1821. Started as publisher in London, 1823. Edited 'Knight's Quarterly Magazine,' 1823-25 ; 'The Brazen Head' (with others), 1826. Publishing business collapsed, 1827. Contrib. to 'Sphinx,' 'London Mag.,' etc. Edited pubns. of Soc. for Diffusion of Useful Knowledge, 1827-46. Ed. 'The British Almanack and Companion,' 1828. Started again as publisher, 1829. Publisher to Soc. for Diffusion of Useful Knowledge, 1829-46. Publisher to Commission on Poor Law, 1835. Edited 'The Voice of the People,' 1848. Retired from publishing, 1851. Died, at Addlestone, Surrey, 9 March 1873.

Works: 'Arminius,' 1814 ; 'The Bridal of the Isles, etc.,' 1817 ; 'The Menageries,' 1828 ; 'The Elephant,' 1830 ; 'The Results of Machinery' (anon.), 1831 ; 'Capital and Labour' (anon.), 1831 ; 'Trades Unions and Strikes,' 1834 ; 'The Newspaper Stamp' (anon.), 1836 ; 'Shakespere's Biography,' 1843 ; 'A Volume of Varieties,' 1844 ; 'William Caxton,' 1844 ; 'Capital and Labour,' 1845 ; 'Old England,' 1845 ; 'Half-hours with the Best Authors' (4 vols.), [1847-48] ; 'Studies of Shakespere,' 1849 ; 'The Struggles of a Book against Excessive Taxation,' 1850 ; 'The Case of the Authors as Regards the Paper Duty,' 1851 ; 'Half-hours of English History' [1851]; 'Old Lamps or New,' 1853 ; 'The Old Printer and the Modern Press,' 1854; 'Once upon a Time' (2 vols.), 1854 ; 'Knowledge is Power,' 1855 ; 'The Popular History of England' (8 vols.), 1856-62 ; 'Passages of a Working Life' (3 vols.), 1864[1863]-65 ; 'Shadows of the Old Booksellers,' 1865 ; Begg'd at Court,' 1867 ; 'Half-hours with the Best Letter Writers,' 1867.

He *edited :* Fairfax's translation of Tasso's 'Godfrey of Bulloigne,' 1817 ; Shakespeare's Works, 1839 (and many subsequent editions) ; 'London' (4 vols.), 1841-44 ; 'Mind among the Spindles,' 1844 ; 'Memoirs of a Working Man,' 1845 ; 'Pictorial Half-hours of London Topography' [1851].

KNOLLES (Richard), 1550[?]-1610. Born [at Cold Ashby, Northamptonshire ?], about 1550. Educated at Lincoln Coll., Oxford ; B.A., 26 Jan. 1565 ; M.A., July 1570. Fellow of Lincoln Coll. [1565 ?]. Master of Sandwich Grammar School. Died, at Sandwich, June 1610 ; buried there, 2 July.

Works: 'A Generall Historie of the Turkes from the first beginning of that Nation,' 1603 (2nd edn., enlarged, 1610) ; 'The Six Bookes of a Common Weale written by J. Bodin . . . done into English,' 1606.

KNOWLES (James Sheridan), 1784-1862. Born, at Cork, 12 May 1784. At his father's school there, 1790-93. Family removed to London, 1793. Left home on his father's second marriage, 1800. Served as ensign in Wilts Militia, 1804 ; in Tower Hamlets Militia, 1805-06. Studied medicine. M.D., Aberdeen, 1808. Resident Vaccinator to Jennerian Soc., 1808. First appeared on the stage, at Bath, 1809. Married Maria Charteris, 25 Oct. 1809. Play, 'Leo,' produced by Edmund Kean at Waterford, 1810. 'Brian Boroihme' produced at Belfast, 1811 (at Covent Garden, 20 April 1837); 'Caius Gracchus,' at Belfast, 13 Feb. 1815 ; at Covent Garden, 18 Nov. 1823. Kept a school at Belfast, 1812-16 ; at Glasgow, 1816-28. 'Virginius' produced at Glasgow, 1820 ; at Covent Garden, 17 May 1820 ; 'William Tell,' Covent Garden, 1825. On staff of Glasgow 'Free Press,' Jan. 1823 to Dec. 1824. 'The Beggar's Daughter of Bethnal Green' produced at Drury Lane, 28 May 1828. Removed from Glasgow to Newhaven, near Edinburgh, 1830. Contrib. to 'Literary Souvenir,' 'Keepsake,' and other periodicals. 'Alfred the Great' produced at Drury Lane, 28 April 1831 ; 'The Hunchback,' Covent Garden, 5 April 1832 ; 'The Wife,' Covent Garden, 24 April 1833. Acted in America, 1834. 'The Daughter,' Drury Lane, 29 Nov. 1836 ; 'The Bridal,' Haymarket, 26 June 1837 ; 'The Love Chase,' Haymarket, 10 Oct. 1837 ; 'Woman's Wit,' Covent Garden, 23 May 1838 ; 'Maid of Mariendorpt,' Haymarket, 9 Oct. 1838 ; 'Love,' Covent Garden, 4 Nov. 1839 ; 'John of Procida,' Covent Garden, 19 Sept. 1840 ; 'Old Maids,' Covent Garden, 2 Oct. 1841. Wife died, Feb. 1841. Married Miss Elphinstone, 1842. 'The Rose of Arragon,' Haymarket, 4 June 1842 ; 'The Secretary,' Drury Lane, 24 April 1843. Retired from stage, 1843. Contrib. to various periodicals. Civil List Pension, 1848. One of committee for purchase of Shakespeare's Birthplace, 1848. Joined the Baptists about this time. Entertained at banquet in Cork, May 1862. Died, at Torquay, 30 Nov. 1862. Buried in Glasgow Necropolis.

Works : 'The Welch Harper' [1796]; 'Fugitive Pieces,' 1810 ; 'The Senate' (under pseud. 'Selim'), 1817 ; 'Virginius,' 1820 (third edn. same year) ; 'Caius Gracchus,' 1823 ; 'The Elocutionist,' 1823 ; 'William Tell,' 1825 ; 'The Beggar's Daughter of Bethnal Green,' 1828 (second edn., called 'The Beggar of Bethnal Green,' 1834) ; 'Alfred the Great,' 1831 ; 'The Hunchback,' 1832 ; 'The Magdalen,' 1832 ; 'A Masque' [on the death of Sir Walter Scott], 1832 ; 'The Wife,' 1833 ; 'The Daughter,' 1837 (second edn. same year) ; 'The Love Chase,' 1837 ; 'The Bridal' (from Beaumont and Fletcher), [1837] ; 'Woman's Wit,' 1838 ; 'Dramatic Works,' 1838 ; 'The Maid of Mariendorpt,' 1838 ; 'Love,' 1840 ; 'John of Procida,' 1840 ; 'Old Maids,' 1841 ; 'The Rose of Arragon,' 1842 ; 'The Secretary,' 1843 ; 'Dramatic Works' (3 vols.), 1843 ; 'George Lovell,' 1847 ; 'Fortescue' (from 'Sunday Times') 1847 (priv. ptd., 1846) ; 'The Rock of Rome,' 1849 ; 'The Idol demolished by its own Priest,' 1851 ; 'The Gospel attributed to Matthew is the Record of the whole original Apostlehood,' 1855 ; 'Dramatic Works,' 1856.

Posthumous : 'True unto Death,' 1866 (another edn., called 'Alexina,' same year) ; 'Brian Boroihme,' 1872 (priv. ptd., 1871) ; 'Lectures on Dramatic Literature' (2 vols.), 1873 ; 'Various Dramatic Works' (priv. ptd.) 1874.

He *edited :* J. A. Mason's 'Treatise on the Climate,' 1850.

Life : by R. B. Knowles, revised edn. 1872.

KNOX (John), 1505-1572. Born, at Haddington, 1505. Educated at Haddington School. To Glasgow Univ., 25 Oct. 1522. Practised as a notary in Haddington. Probably ordained Deacon. Private tutor, 1544 [?]-47. Received 'call' as

preacher at St. Andrews, 1547 ; preached Reformed doctrine. Prisoner in French galleys, July 1547 to Feb. 1549. Returned to England, 1549. Preached at Berwick, 1549-51. Prosecuted by Catholics, 1550 ; but prosecution abandoned. Preached at Newcastle, 1550-51. Chaplain to King, 1551-53. Preached in Buckinghamshire and Kent, June to Oct. 1553. Married Marjory Bowes, July[?] 1553. To Newcastle, Dec. 1553. At Dieppe, Jan. to Feb., 1554. Travelled in France and Switzerland, March to Nov. 1554. Intimacy with Calvin begun. English Pastor at Frankfort-on-Maine, Nov. 1554 to March 1555. At Geneva, March to Aug. 1555. Returned to Berwick, Aug. 1555. Returned to Geneva, July 1556. Received Freedom of City of Geneva, 1559. Left Geneva, Jan. 1559. Returned to Scotland, April 1559. His preaching at Perth resulted in insurrection. Formal establishment of Reformed Church in Scotland, Aug. 1560. Active in spread of Reformation doctrine. Prosecuted for treason, and acquitted, Dec. 1563. Visit to England, Dec. 1566 to June 1567. Died, in Edinburgh, 24 Nov. 1572. Buried in St. Giles's Churchyard.

Works : Tract on the Sacrament [1549 ?] ; 'A Declaration what true Prayer is,' 1554 ; 'A Confession and Declaration of Prayer,' 1554 ; 'An Exposition of the Sixth Psalm,' 1554 ; 'A Godly Letter,' 1554 ; 'A Faythfull Admonition,' 1554 ; 'The Order of Geneva' (liturgy ; compiled by Knox, Whittingham, and others), 1556 ; Letter to the Queen Dowager, 1556 (enlarged edn., 1558) ; 'Apology for the Protestants in Prison in Paris,' 1557 ; 'The First Blast of the Trumpet' (anon.), 1558 ; 'The Appellation of John Knox . . . from the cruell Sentence pronounced by the Bishops and Clergy,' 1558 ; 'A Letter addressed to the Commonalty of Scotland,' 1558 ; 'The First Book of Discipline' (compiled by Knox and others), 1560 ; 'An Answer to a great number of Blasphemous Cavillations written by an . . . Adversarie to God's Eternal Predestination,' 1560 ; 'The Ordoure and Doctrine of the General Faste' (compiled by Knox and John Craig), 1560 ; 'A Sermon preached . . . in the Publique audience, etc.,' 1566.

Posthumous : 'A Fort for the Afflicted,' 1580 ; 'History of the Reformation,' bks. i.-iii., 1584 ; bks. iv., v., 1644.

Collected Works : ed. by D. Laing (6 vols.), 1846-64.

Life : by T. M'Crie, 1812 (and many subsequent edns.).

KYD (Thomas), 1557[?] - 1595[?]. Born, 1557 [?]. Probably educated at Merchant Taylors' School. Prolific writer of plays. Died, 1595 [?].

Works : 'The Rare Triumphs of Love and Fortune' (anon. ; attrib. to Kyd), 1589 ; 'The Truethe of the . . . Murthering of John Brewen' (anon.), 1592 (only one copy extant) ; 'True Reporte of the Poisoning of Thomas Elliot' (anon.; attrib. to Kyd), 1592 ; 'The Spanish Tragedy,' 1592 (anon.; no copy known ; 2nd edn. 1594 [?]) ; 'The Tragedye of Solyman and Perseda' (anon.; attrib. to Kyd), 1592 (no copy known ; later edn., 1599).

Posthumous : 'The First Part of Jeronimo' (anon.), 1605.

He *translated :* Tasso's ' The Householder's Philosophie' (under initials : T. K.), 1588 ; Garnier's 'Cornelia,' 1594 ; Garnier's 'Pompey the Great,' 1595.

LAMB (Charles), 1775-1834. Born, in London, 10 Feb. 1775. At Christ's Hospital, 1782-89. Clerk in South Sea House, 1789-92. Clerk in India House, 1792-1825. Appointed guardian to his sister Mary Ann, 1796. Intimacy with Coleridge, who had been his schoolfellow. Contrib. four sonnets to 'Poems' by Coleridge, 1796. Contrib. to 'Morning Post,' 'Morning Chronicle,' and 'The Albion,' 1800-03. Farce, 'Mr. H.,' produced at Drury Lane, 10 Dec. 1805. Contrib. to 'The Reflector,' 1811 ; to 'Gentleman's Mag.,' 1813 ; to 'London Mag.,' 1820-33. Visit to Continent with his

sister, 1822. He and his sister adopted Emma Isola, 1823. Retired from India House, March 1825. Removed to Enfield, Herts. Contrib. to 'New Monthly Mag.,' 1826. Removed to Edmonton, 1833. Died, at Edmonton, 27 Dec. 1834. Buried there.

Works : 'Original Letters, etc., of Sir John Falstaff and his friends' (with J. White ; anon.), 1796 ; 'Blank Verse' (with C. Lloyd), 1797 ; 'A Tale of Rosamund Gray and Old Blind Margaret,' 1798 ; 'John Woodvil,' 1802 ; 'Mrs. Leicester's School' (anon. ; with Mary Lamb), 1807 ; 'Tales from Shakespeare' (with Mary Lamb), 1807 ; 'The Adventures of Ulysses,' 1808 ; 'Specimens of English Dramatic Poets,' 1808 ; 'Poetry for Children' (anon. ; with Mary Lamb), 1809 ; 'Prince Dorus,' 1811 ; 'Works' (2 vols.), 1818 ; 'Essays of Elia' (anon. ; from 'London Mag.'), 1823 ; 'Album Verses,' 1830 ; 'Satan in Search of a Wife' (anon.), 1831 ; 'The Last Essays of Elia,' 1833.

Posthumous : 'Letters' (with life by Talfourd), 1837.

Life : by Barry Cornwall, 1866 ; by Ainger, revised edn., 1888.

[His sister, **Mary Ann Lamb, 1764-1847** [*see above*], was born in London, 3 Dec. 1764 ; first appearance of occasional insanity, Sept. 1796 ; having stabbed her mother in a fit of insanity, was put under her brother's guardianship, 1796. Died, in London, 20 May 1847. For her works, in collaboration with her brother, see above. *Life :* by Mrs. Gilchrist, 1889.]

LANDON (Letitia Elizabeth), 1802-1838. Born, in Chelsea, 14 Aug. 1802. Educated at a school in Chelsea, and privately. Contrib. to 'Literary Gaz.,' from 1820. Edited 'The Drawing-Room Scrap-Book,' 1832-38. Married to George Maclean, 7 June 1838. Died, suddenly, at Cape Coast Castle, 15 Oct. 1838.

Works : 'The Fate of Adelaide,' 1821 ; 'The Improvisatrice' (under initials : L.E.L.), 1824 ; 'The Trou-

11

badour' (under initials : L.E.L.), 1825 ;
'The Golden Violet' (under initials :
L.E.L.), *1827 ; 'The Venetian
Bracelet' (under initials : L.E.L.),
1829 ; 'Romance and Reality' (under
initials : L.E.L.), 1831 ; 'The Easter
Gift' (anon.), 1832 ; 'Francesca Car-
rara' (under initials : L.E.L.), 1834 ;
'The Vow of the Peacock' (anon.),
1835 ; 'Traits and Trials of Early
Life' (under initials : L.E.L.), 1836 ;
'Ethel Churchill' (under initials .
L.E.L.), 1837 ; 'A Birthday Tribute
. . . to . . . Princess Alexandrina
Victoria' (under initials : L.E.L.),
[1837] ; 'Duty and Inclination,' 1838 ;
'Flowers of Loveliness' (under initials : L.E.L.), 1838.

Posthumous : 'The Zenana,' ed. by
E. Roberts, 1839 ; 'Life and Literary
Remains,' by L. Blanchard (2 vols.),
1841 ; 'Lady Anne Granard,' 1842.
She *translated :* the 'Odes' in
Isabel Hill's translation of Mme. de
Staël's 'Corinne,' 1833.

Collected Works : in 2 vols., 1838.
Life : by L. Blanchard, 1841.

*LANDOR (Walter Savage), 1775-
1864. Born, at Warwick, 30 Jan.
1775. At school at Knowle, 1779-85 ;
at Rugby, 1785-91. With private
tutor, 1791-93. Matric. Trin. Coll.,
Oxford, 13 Nov. 1792 ; rusticated,
1794 ; did not return to Oxford.
Visit to Paris, 1802. Settled at
Bath, 1805 ; intimacy with Southey
begun, 1808. In Spain, Aug. to Nov.,
1808. Settled at Llanthony Abbey,
Monmouthshire, 1809. Married Julia
Thuillier, May 1811. Removed to
Jersey, and thence to Tours, 1814.
To Italy, Sept. 1815. Lived at Como,
1815-18. At Pisa, 1818-21 ; at Florence, 1821-35. Visit to England,
1832. Quarrelled with his wife and
went to England, 1835. Returned to
Florence, 1858. Died there, 17 Sept.
1864.

Works : 'Poems,' 1795 ; 'Moral
Epistle respectfully dedicated to Earl
Stanhope,' 1795 ; 'Gebir' (anon.), 1798
(Latin version, by Landor, 1803) ;
'Poems from the Arabic and Persian'
(anon.), 1800 ; 'Poetry' (anon.), 1802 ;

'Simonidea' (anon.), 1806 ; 'Three
Letters . . . to D. Francisco Riqueline,'
1809 ; 'Count Julian' (anon.), 1812 ;
'Commentary on the Memoirs of Mr.
Fox' (anon.), 1812 ; 'Idyllia Heroica,'
1814 (enlarged edn., 1820) ; 'Poche Os-
servazioni sullo stato attuale di que'
popoli che vogliono governarsi per
mezzo delle Rappresentanze,' 1821 ;
'Imaginary Conversations,' vols. i., ii.,
1824 ; vols. iii., iv., 1828 ; vol. v.,
1829 ; 'Gebir, Count Julian, and other
Poems,' 1831 ; 'Citation and Examination of William Shakespeare' (anon.),
1834 ; 'The Letters of a Conservative,' 1836 ; 'Terry Hogan' (anon.,
attrib. to Landor), 1836 ; 'Pericles
and Aspasia,' 1836 ; 'A Satire on
Satirists,' 1836 ; 'The Pentameron and
Pentalogia' (anon.), 1837 ; 'Andrea of
Hungary and Giovanna of Naples,'
1839 ; 'Fra Rupert,' 1840 ; 'Works'
(collected, 2 vols.), 1846 ; 'Hellenics,'
1847 ; 'Poemata et Inscriptiones,'
1847 ; 'Imaginary Conversation of
King Carlo Alberto and the Duchess
Belgoioiso,' 1848 ; 'Italics,' 1848 ;
'Popery, British and Foreign,' 1851 ;
'Imaginary Conversations of Greeks
and Romans,' 1853 ; 'The Last Fruit
off an Old Tree,' 1853 ; 'Letters of an
American,' 1854 ; 'Letter . . . to R.
W. Emerson,' [1856] ; 'Antony and
Octavius,' 1856 ; 'Dry Sticks,' 1858 ;
'Hebrew Lyrics' (anon.), 1859 ;
'Savonarola e il Priore di San Marco,'
1860 ; 'Heroic Idyls, with additional
poems,' 1863.

Collected Works : in 8 vols., 1876.
Life : by J. Forster, 1869 ; by
Sidney Colvin, 1881.

*LANG (Andrew), b. 1844. Born, at
Selkirk, 31 March 1844. At Edin-
burgh Academy, 1854-60. At St.
Andrew's Univ., 1860-61. Matric.
Balliol Coll., Oxford, 28 Jan. 1865 ;
Exhibitioner, 1865-68 ; Fellow, Merton
Coll., 1868-76 ; B.A., 1869 ; M.A.,
1875. Gifford Lecturer on Natural
Religion, St. Andrew's Univ., 1888.

Works : 'Ballads and Lyrics of Old
France,' 1872 ; 'Oxford,' 1880 ;
'XXII Ballades in Blue China,' 1880
(enlarged edn., 'XXXII Ballades,'

1881) ; 'The Library,' 1881 ; 'Notes . . . on a collection of pictures by Mr. **J. E.** Millais,' 1881 ; 'Helen of Troy,' 1882 ; 'Ballades and Verses Vain' (selected by Austin Dobson), 1884 ; 'The Princess Nobody' [1884]; 'Much Darker Days' (under pseud. 'A. Huge Longway'), 1884; 'Custom and Myth,' 1884 ; 'Rhymes à la Mode,' 1885 [1884]; 'That Very Mab' (anon. ; with May Kendall), 1885 ; 'The Mark of Cain,' 1886 ; 'Letters to Dead Authors,' 1886 ; 'Books and Book-men,' 1886 ; 'In the Wrong Paradise,' 1886 ; 'The Politics of Aristotle : introductory essays,' 1886 ; 'Lines on the inaugural meeting of the Shelley Society' (from 'Sat. Rev.' ; priv. ptd. for Shelley Society), 1886 ; 'Myth, Ritual, and Religion' (2 vols.), 1887 : 'He' (with W. H. Pollock, anon.), 1887 ; 'The Gold of Fairnilee' [1888] ; 'Grass of Parnassus,' 1888 ; 'Pictures at Play' (anon. ; with W. E. Henley), 1888 ; 'Ballads of Books' (edited), 1888 ; 'Letters on Literature,' 1889 ; 'Lost Leaders' (from 'Daily News'), 1889 ; 'Prince Prigio,' 1889 ; 'Old Friends,' 1890 ; 'How to Fail in Literature,' 1890 ; 'Life . . . of Sir Stafford North-cote,' 1890 ; 'Essays in Little,' 1891 ; 'Angling Sketches,' 1891 ; 'A Batch of Golfing Papers by Andrew Lang and others' (ed. by R. Barclay), [1892]; 'The Tercentenary of Izaak Walton' (priv. ptd.), 1893 ; 'St. Andrews,' 1893; 'Homer and the Epic,' 1893 ; 'The World's Desire' (with Rider Haggard), 1894 ; 'Ban and Arrière Ban,' 1894 ; 'Cock Lane and Commonsense,' 1894 ; 'A Monk of Fife,' 1896 ; 'The Life . . . of John Gibson Lockhart,' 1897 [1896]; 'Pickle, the Spy,' 1897 ; 'Modern Mythology,' 1897.

He has *translated* Homer's 'Odyssey' (with S. H. Butcher), 1879 ; 'Theocritus, Bion and Moschus,' 1880 ; Homer's 'Iliad' (with Leaf and Myers), 1883 ; 'Aucassin and Nicolette,' 1887 ; Deulin's 'Johnny Nut,' 1887 ; 'The Dead Leman, and other tales from the French' (with P. Sylvester), 1889.

Has *edited :* Poe's 'Poems,' 1881 ; Molière's 'Les Précieuses Ridicules,'

1884 ; 'English Worthies' (8 vols.), 1885-87 ; trans. of Herodotus' 'Eu-terpe,' 1888 ; Perrault's 'Popular Tales,' 1888 ; 'The Blue Fairy Book,' 1889 ; 'The Red Fairy Book,' 1890 ; Colonna's 'Hypnerotomachia,' 1890 ; Burns' 'Selected Poems,' 1891 ; 'The Blue Poetry Book,' 1891 ; 'The Green Fairy Book,' 1892 ; Waverley Novels, 1892, etc. ; Kirk's 'Secret Commonwealth of Elves,' 1893 ; 'The True Story Book,' 1893 ; 'The Yellow Fairy Book,' 1894 ; Scott's 'Lyrics and Ballads,' 1894 ; Scott's 'Selected Poems,' 1895 ; 'The Red True Story Book,' 1895 ; 'Border Ballads,' 1895 ; 'The Animal Story Book,' 1896 ; Burns' 'Poems and Songs,' 1896 ; Walton's 'Compleat Angler,' 1896 ; 'A Collection of Ballads,' 1897.

Has *contributed introductions* to : Grimm's 'Household Tales,' 1884 ; Lamb's 'Beauty and the Beast' [1887]; Lamb's 'Adventures of Ulysses,' 1890 ; Longinus 'On the Sublime,' 1890 ; R. F. Murray's 'Poems,' 1894.

LA RAMÉE (Louise de). *See* **Ouida.**

LAW (William), 1686-1761. Born, at King's Cliffe, Northamptonshire, 1686. Matric. Emmanuel Coll., Camb., as Sizar, 7 June 1705 ; B.A., 1708 ; Fellow, 1711 ; M.A., 1712. Ordained, 1711. Suspended from degrees for a political offence, April 1713. Non-juror, 1714. Perhaps held curacies in London and Fotheringay. Founded a girls' school at King's Cliffe, 1727. Tutor to Edward Gibbon (father of historian), 1720 [?], and to Gibbon's sisters from 1730 [?]. Removed to King's Cliffe, 1740. Literary activity, and extensive charitable work. Died, at King's Cliffe, 9 April 1761. Buried there.

Works : 'A Sermon preached . . . July 7, 1713,' 1713 ; 'The Bishop of Bangor's late Sermon . . . answer'd,' 1717 ; 'A Second Letter to the Bishop of Bangor,' 1717 ; 'A Reply to the Bishop of Bangor's Answer,' 1719 ; 'Remarks upon . . . the Fable of the Bees,' 1724 ; 'The Absolute Unlawful-ness of the Stage Entertainment fully demonstrated,' 1726 ; 'A Practical

11—2

Treatise upon Christian Perfection,' 1726 ; ' A Serious Call to a Devout and Holy Life,' 1729 ; ' The Case of Reason,' 1731 ; ' A Demonstration of the . . . Errors of a late book called " A Plain Account, etc.," ' 1737 ; ' The Grounds and Reasons of the Christian Regeneration,' 1738 [?], , (3rd edn., 1750) ; ' An Earnest . . . Answer to Dr. Trapp's Discourse,' 1740 ; ' An Appeal to all that doubt . . . the truths of the Gospel,' 1740 ; ' The Spirit of Prayer,' 1750 ; ' Extract of a letter . . . to one requesting a conversation on the Spiritual Life' [1750 ?] ; ' Answer to a question, Where shall I go . . . to be in the Truth ?' [1750 ?] ; ' The Way to Divine Knowledge,' 1752 ; ' The Spirit of Love ' (2 pts.), 1752-54 ; ' The Christian Sacrament and Sacrifice ' (anon.), 1754 ; ' Reflections on a favourite Amusement ' (anon.), 1756 ; ' A Short . . . Confutation of the Rev. Dr. Warburton's projected Defence . . . of Christianity,' 1757 ; ' The Religion of Reason ; an extract' (anon.), 1757 ; ' Of Justification by Faith and Works,' 1760 ; ' A Collection of Letters,' 1760.

Posthumous : ' An Humble . . . Address to the Clergy,' 1761 ; ' Letters to a Lady inclined to join the Church of Rome,' 1779.

Collected Works : in 9 vols., 1762 ; in 9 vols. (priv. ptd.; ed. by G. B. Morgan), 1892-93.

Life : by Canon Overton, 1881.

*LECKY (William Edward Hartpole), b. 1838. Born, at Newtown Park, near Dublin, 26 March 1838. Educated at Trin. Coll., Dublin ; B.A., 1859 ; M.A., 1863. Married Elizabeth, Baroness de Dedem, 14 June 1871. Hon. LL.D., Dublin, 1879. Hon. LL.D., St. Andrews, 1885. Hon. D.C.L., Oxford, 1888. Hon. Litt.D., Cambridge., 1891. Corresponding Mem. of Institute of France, 1894. Hon. LL.D., Glasgow, 1895. Hon. Mem. Royal Academy, March 1895. Trustee, National Portrait Gallery, 1895. M.P. for Dublin University, Dec. 1895. Privy Councillor, 22 June 1897.

Works : ' The Religious Tendencies of the Age ' (anon.), 1860 ; ' The Leaders of Public Opinion in Ireland ' (anon.), 1861 ; ' History of the Rise and Influence of the Spirit of Rationalism in Europe' (2 vols.), 1865 ; ' History of European Morals ' (2 vols.), 1869 ; ' A History of England in the Eighteenth Century,' vols. i., ii., 1878 ; vols. iii., iv., 1882 ; vols. v., vi., 1887 ; vols. vii., viii., 1890 ; ' Poems,' 1891 ; ' The Political Value of History,' 1892 ; ' The Empire, its value and its growth,' 1893 ; ' Democracy and Liberty ' (2 vols.), 1896.

He has *contributed :* A ' prefatory memoir ' to the Earl of Derby's ' Speeches and Addresses,' 1894 ; a ' prefatory letter ' to Daunt's ' Life spent for Ireland,' 1896 ; and a ' prefatory memoir ' to Swift's ' Prose Works,' 1897.

LEE (Nathaniel), 1653 [?] - 1692. Born, probably at Hatfield, 1653 [?]. Educated at Westminster School. To Trin. Coll., Camb., 7 July 1665 ; B.A., Jan. 1668. Acted in London, 1672. Devoted himself to dramatic writing. 1675. ' Nero ' performed at Drury Lane, 1675 ; ' Gloriana,' Drury Lane, 1676 ; ' Sophonisba,' Drury Lane, 1676 ; ' The Rival Queens,' 1677 ; ' Mithridates,' Drury Lane, March 1678 ; ' Œdipus ' (written with Dryden), Duke's Theatre, 1679 ; ' Cæsar Borgia,' Duke's Theatre, 1680 ; ' Theodosius,' Duke's Theatre, 1680 ; ' Lucius Junius Brutus,' Duke's Theatre, 1681 ; ' The Princess of Cleve,' Duke's Theatre, Nov. 1681 ; ' The Duke of Guise ' (written with Dryden), Drury Lane, 4 Dec. 1682 ; ' Constantine the Great,' Drury Lane, 1684. Went mad, 1684 ; confined in Bethlehem Hospital, 11 Nov. 1684. Discharged, recovered, 1689. ' The Massacre of Paris ' produced at Drury Lane, 1690. Died, in London, May [?] 1692 ; buried in St. Clement Dane's Church, 6 May.

Works : ' Nero,' 1675 ; ' Gloriana,' 1676 ; ' Sophonisba,' 1676 ; ' The Rival Queens,' 1677 ; ' Mithridates,' 1678 ; Adaptation (with Dryden) of

Sophocles' 'Œdipus,' 1679 ; 'Cæsar Borgia,' 1680 ; 'Theodosius,' 1680 ; 'Lucius Junius Brutus,' 1681 ; 'The Duke of Guise' (with Dryden), 1683 ; 'Constantine the Great,' 1684 ; 'Lucius Junius Brutus,' 1689 ; 'The Princess of Cleve,' 1689 ; 'The Massacre of Paris,' 1690. *Collected Works:* in 2 vols., 1713.

* **LEE (Vernon)** [pseud., *i.e.* Miss Violet Paget], **b. 1856.** Born, in France, 1856. Has resided for many years in and near Florence.

Works: 'Studies of the Eighteenth Century in Italy,' 1880 ; 'Belcaro,' 1882 ; 'The Prince of a Hundred Soups,' 1883 ; 'Ottilie,' 1884 ; 'Euphorion,' 1884 ; 'The Countess of Albany,' 1884 ; 'Miss Brown,' 1884 ; 'A Phantom Lover,' 1886 ; 'Baldwin,' 1886 ; 'Juvenilia,' 1887 ; 'Hauntings,' 1890 ; 'Vanitas,' 1892 ; 'Althea,' 1894 ; 'Renaissance Fancies and Studies,' 1895 ; 'Limbo, and other Essays,' 1897.

LEFANU (Joseph Sheridan), 1814-1873. Born, in Dublin, 28 Aug. 1814. Early education private. To Trin. Coll., Dublin, 1833. Joined staff of 'Dublin Univ. Mag.,' 1837 ; editor, 1869-72. Called to Irish Bar, 1839. Purchased 'The Warder,' 'Evening Packet,' and 'Evening Mail'; combined them as 'Evening Mail.' Married Susan Bennett, 1844. After her death in 1858, retired from society. Novels mostly written after 1858. Died, in Dublin, 7 Feb. 1873.

Works: 'The Cock and Anchor' (anon.), 1845 ; 'The Fortunes of Colonel Torlogh O'Brien' (anon.), 1847 ; 'The House by the Churchyard,' 1863 ; 'Uncle Silas,' 1864 ; 'Wylder's Hand,' 1864 ; 'Guy Deverall,' 1865 ; 'All in the Dark,' 1866 ; 'The Tenants of Malory,' 1867 ; 'A Lost Name,' 1868 ; 'Haunted Lives,' 1868 ; 'The Wyvern Mystery,' 1869 ; 'Checkmate,' 1871 ; 'The Rose and the Key,' 1871 ; 'Chronicles of Golden Friars,' 1871 ; 'In a Glass Darkly,' 1872 ; 'Morley Court' (anon.), 1873 ; 'Willing to Die,' 1873.

Posthumous: 'The Purcell Papers,' ed. by A. P. Graves, 1880 ; 'The Watcher, and other weird stories,' 1894 ; 'Poems,' ed. by A. P. Graves, 1896.

Life: by A. P. Graves, in 1880 edn. of 'The Purcell Papers.'

* **LELAND (Charles Godfrey), b. 1824.** Born, at Philadelphia, 15 Aug. 1824. At Princeton Coll., 1842-45 ; B.A., 1845. To Europe, autumn of 1845. At Heidelberg Univ., 1846-47. At Munich, and travelling in Germany, March to Oct. 1847. In Paris, Oct. 1847 to June 1848. Returned to Philadelphia, Oct. 1848. Called to Bar, 1851. Frequent contributor to periodicals. In New York, 1851-55. Edited 'Illustrated News,' 1851-53. Joined staff of Philadelphia 'Evening Bulletin.' Edited 'Continental Monthly,' 1862. Edited 'Philadelphia Press,' May 1867 to 1869. Married, 1856. In Europe, mainly in London, May 1869 to 1879. In America, 1879-83. Hon. M.A., Harvard, 1882, Since 1883 has lived in Europe, mainly in London and Florence. Enthusiastic philologist and antiquary. F.R.L.S., 1884. Mem. of American Philosophical Soc., and of Massachusetts Genealogical Soc. Pres. of first European Folk-Lore Congress, Paris, 1889 ; organized second Congress, London, 1891.

Works: 'Meister Karl's Sketch-Book,' 1855 ; 'The Poetry and Mystery of Dreams,' 1855 ; 'Sunshine in Thought,' 1863 ; 'Centralization' [1863] ; 'Legends of Birds,' 1864 ; 'To Kansas and back,' 1866 ; 'The "Union Pacific," Eastern Division,' 1867 ; 'Hans Breitmann's Party' (anon.), [1868] ; 'Hans Breitmann and his Philosopede,' 1869 ; 'The Art of Conversation' (anon.), 1869 ; 'Hans Breitmann as a Politician,' 1869 ; 'Hans Breitmann in Church' [1870] ; 'Breitmann as a Uhlan' [1871] ; 'Hans Breitmann in Europe' [1871] ; 'The Breitmann Ballads' (collected), 1871 ; 'The Music-Lesson of Confucius,' 1872 ; 'The Egyptian Sketch-Book,' 1873 ; 'The English Gipsies,' 1873 ; 'Fusang,'

1875 ; 'English Gipsy Songs' (with
E. H. Palmer and J. Tuckey), 1875 ;
'Johnnykin and the Goblins,' 1877
[1876] ; 'Pidgin-English Sing-Song,'
1876 ; 'Abraham Lincoln,' 1879 ;
'The Minor Arts,'1880 ; 'The Gipsies,'
1882 ; 'The Algonquin Legends of
New England,' 1884 ; 'Brand New
Ballads,' 1885 ; 'Snooping' [1886] ;
'Practical Education,' 1888 ; 'Draw-
ing and Designing,' 1888 ; 'A Dictionary of Slang' (with A. Barrère),
1889-90 ; 'Manual of Wood-Carving,'
1890 ; 'Quickness of Perception'
[1891] ; 'Gypsy Sorcery,' 1891 ;
'Etruscan Roman Remains in Popular
Tradition,' 1892 ; 'The Hundred
Riddles of the Fairy Bellaria,' 1892 ;
'Leather Work,' 1892 ; 'Memoir' (2
vols.),1823 ; 'Elementary Metal Work,'
1894 ; 'Hans Breitmann in Germany—
Tyrol' [1895] ; 'Legends of Florence,'
1895, etc. ; 'Songs of the Sea, '1895 ;
'Manual of Mending and Repairing,'
1896 ; 'Slang, Jargon, and Cant'
(with A. Barrère), 1897.

He has *translated :* Heine's 'Pic-
tures of Travel,'1856 ; Heine's 'Book of
Songs,' 1864 ; Humboldt's 'Letters to
a Lady,' 1864 ; Eichendorff's 'Me-
moirs of a Good-for-Nothing,' 1866 ;
'Gaudeamus,' by Scheffel and others,
1872 ; Heine's 'Works,' 1892 ; Heine's
'Letters,' 1893 ; and *edited :* 'Art
Work Manuals,' 1881, etc. ; 'Life of
J. P. Beckwourth,' 1892.

LELAND (John), 1506 [?] - 1552.
Born, in London, Sept. 1506 [?]. Educated at St. Paul's School, London ;
and at Christ's Coll., Camb. B.A.,
1522. Afterwards studied at All
Souls' Coll., Oxford, and in Paris.
Ordained. Tutor to son of Duke of
Norfolk, about 1525. Librarian and
chaplain to King Henry VIII. Rector
of Pepeling, near Calais, 1530. King's
Antiquary, 1533. Dispensed from
residence at Pepeling, 1536. Antiquarian tour in England, 1536-42.
Rector of Hasely, Oxfordshire, April
1542. Canon of King's Coll. (afterwards Christ Church), Oxford, 1542-
45. Prebendary of Salisbury. Later
years spent in London. Became in-

sane through over-work. In custody
of his brother, 21 March 1550 till his
death. Died, in London, 18 April.
1552. Buried in church of St.
Michael le Querne (destroyed in Fire
of London).

Works : 'Næniæ in mortem Thomæ
Viati,' 1542 ; 'Genethliacon illustris-
simi Eaduardi Principis Cambriæ,'
1543 ; 'Assertio inclytissimi Arturij,
regis Britanniæ,' 1544 ; 'Κυκνειον
'Ασμα,' 1545 ; 'Nænia in mortem
Henrici Duddelegi,'1545 ; 'Bonnonia
Gallo-mastrix,' 1545 ; ''Εγκωμιον της
Ειρηνης,' 1546 ; 'The Laboryouse
Journey and Serche of J. Leylande
for Englandes Antiquitees,' 1549.

Posthumous : 'A Record of Ancient
Hystoryes in Latin,' 1577 ; 'Principum ac illustrium . . . in Anglia
virorum Encomia, etc.,' 1589 ; 'Commentarii de Scriptoribus Britannicis,'
ed. by A. Hall, 1709 ; 'Itinerary' (9
vols.), 1710-12 ; 'Collectanea,' ed. by
T. Hearne, 1715.

Life : by Huddesford, 1772.

LEMON (Mark), 1809-1870. Born,
in London, 30 Nov. 1809. At school
at Cheam till 1824. To a brewery at
Boston, Lincs., 1824. Subsequently
manager of a brewery in Kentish
Town ; and dealer in beer, 1837-41.
First play, 'P. L.,' produced at Strand
Theatre, 25 April 1835. A number of
plays produced at Adelphi, Surrey,
Strand, Olympic, and other theatres,
1835-60. Contrib. to 'Household
Words,' 'Once a Week,' 'Illustrated
London News,' 'Illuminated Mag.'
Successively editor of 'London Journal,'
1858-59, 'Family Herald,' 'Once a
Week.' Founded 'The Field,' 1 Jan.
1853, and edited it for some years ;
founded 'Punch,' with H. Mayhew,
17 July 1841 ; sole editor from 1843
till his death. Lectures, 'About London,' delivered at Gallery of Illustration, Jan. 1862 to 1863. Died, at
Crawley, Sussex, 23 May 1870. Buried
at Ifield Church.

Works : 'What will the World
Say ?' 1841 ; 'The Turf,' 1842 ;
'The House of Ladies' [1845] ; 'The
Enchanted Doll,' 1849 ; 'Prose and

Verse,' 1852 ; 'Betty Morrison's Pocket-Book,' 1856 ; 'The Heir of Applebite' (from 'Punch'), 1856; 'A Christmas Hamper' [1860] ; 'Hearts are Trumps' [1863] ; 'Wait for the End,' 1863 ; 'Tom Moody's Tales,' 1864 [1863] ; 'The Jest-Book,' 1864 ; 'Legends of Number Nip,' 1864 ; 'Loved at Last,' 1864 ; 'Falkner Lyle,' 1866 ; 'Leyton Hall,' 1867 ; 'Golden Fetters,' 1867 ; 'Up and Down the London Streets,' 1867 ; 'Fairy-Tales,' 1868 ; 'Tinykin's Transformations,' 1869 ; and a number of plays printed in 'Lacy's Acting Edition,' 'Duncombe's British Theatre,' 'Dicks's Standard Plays,' etc.

Posthumous : 'The Small House over the Water, etc.,' 1888.

LENNOX (*Mrs.* **Charlotte**) **1720-1804.** Born [Charlotte Ramsay], in New York, 1720. To England, 1735[?]. Being unprovided for at her father's death, went on the stage for a short time. Married to —— Lennox, 1748 [?]. Friendship with Dr. Johnson and Richardson. Edited 'The Ladies' Museum,' 1760-61. Play, 'The Sister' (dramatized from her novel 'Henrietta '), produced at Covent Garden, 18 Feb. 1769 ; 'Old City Manners' (adapted from Jonson, Chapman and Marston's 'Eastward Hoe !'), Drury Lane, 9 Nov. 1775. Ill-health and distress in later years. Pension from Royal Literary Fund, 1803. Died, in London, 4 Jan. 1804.

Works : 'Poems on Several Occasions' (anon.), 1747 ; 'The Life of Harriot Stuart' (anon.), 1751 [1750] ; 'The Female Quixote' (anon), 1752 ; 'Shakespear Illustrated' (3 vols., anon.), 1753-54 ; 'Philander' (anon.), 1758 ; 'Henrietta' (anon.), 1758 ; 'Sophia,' 1762 ; 'The Sisters,' 1769 ; 'Old City Manners,' 1775 ; 'Euphemia,' 1790 ; 'Memoirs of Henry Lennox,' 1804.

She *translated :* 'Memoirs of the Countess of Berci,' 1756 ; 'Memoirs of the Duke of Sully,' 1756 ; 'Memoirs for the History of Madame de Maintenon,' 1757 ; Brumoy's 'Greek Theatre' (with Johnson and others), 1759 ; the Duchesse de la Vallière's 'Meditations,' 1774.

L'ESTRANGE (*Sir* **Roger**). **1616-1704.** Born, at Hunstanton, 17 Dec. 1616. Probably educated at Cambridge. To Scotland with army of Charles I., 1639. Sentenced, by House of Commons, to death for share in Royalist plot, 28 Dec. 1644. Imprisoned till spring of 1648, when he escaped from Newgate with connivance of Governor. At first went to Kent, carrying on Royalist propaganda ; but soon withdrew to Holland. Returned to England, Aug. 1653. Active political pamphleteer. Appointed Surveyor of the Imprimery, 15 Aug. 1663. Married Mary Doleman. Edited 'The Kingdom's Intelligencer,' and 'The News,' each weekly, Aug. 1663 to Jan. 1666. Edited (and wrote) 'The Observator,' April 1681 to March 1687. M.P. for Winchester, March 1685. Arrested on political charge, 3 March 1696. Imprisoned till May 1696. Died, in London, 11 Dec. 1704. Buried in the church of St. Giles-in-the-Fields.

Works : His literary works (exclusive of a large number of controversial pamphlets and such works as 'The Gentleman Pothecary,' 1678, and 'Love Letters between a Nobleman and his Sister,' posth., 1734) consist of the following *translations :* F. de Quevedo Villegas' 'Visions,' 1667 ; Cardinal Bona's 'Guide to Eternity,' 1672 ; M. d'Alcoforado's 'Five Love Letters from a Nun to a Cavalier,' 1678 ; 'Tully's Offices,' 1680 ; 'Twenty Select Colloquies of Erasmus,' 1680 ; 'The Spanish Decameron,' 1687 ; 'The Fables of Æsop,' 1692 ; Seneca's 'Morals,' 1693 ; Terence's 'Comedies,' 1698 ; 'Tacitus,' 1698 ; Flavius Josephus' Works, 1702.

LEVER (Charles James), 1806-1872. Born, in Dublin, 31 Aug. 1806. Educated at private schools. To Trin. Coll., Dublin, 14 Oct. 1822 ; B.A., 1827.

Visit to Holland and Germany, 1828;
to Canada, 1829. Returned to Dublin,
1830 ; studied medicine. M.B., Trin.
Coll., Dublin, 1831. Held various
Board of Health appointments, 1831-
33. Married Catherine Baker, 1832 or
1833. Contrib. fiction to 'Dublin Univ.
Mag.,' from May 1836. In Brussels,
1840-42 ; returned to Dublin, 1842.
Editor of 'Dublin Univ. Mag.,' 1842-
45. In Belgium and Germany, 1845-
47. In Florence, 1847-57. British
Consul at Spezzia, 1857 - 67 ; at
Trieste, 1867-72. Visit to Ireland,
1871. LL.D., Dublin, 1871. Died
suddenly, at Trieste, 1 June 1872.

Works : 'The Confessions of Harry
Lorrequer' (anon.), 1839 ; 'Horace
Templeton,' 1840 [?] ; 'Charles
O'Malley' (anon.), 1841 ; 'Our Mess'
(vol. i., 'Jack Hinton, the Guards
man' ; vols. ii., iii., 'Tom Burke of
Ours'), 1843 ; 'Arthur O'Leary'
(anon.), 1844 ; 'St. Patrick's Eve,'
1845 ; 'Tales of the Trains' (under
pseud. : 'Tilbury Tramp'), 1845 ; 'The
O'Donoghue,' 1845 ; 'The Knight of
Gwynne,' 1847 ; 'Diary and Notes of
Horace Templeton' (anon.), 1848 ;
'Confessions of Con Cregan' (anon.),
1849-50 ; 'Roland Cashel,' 1850 ; 'The
Daltons,' 1852 ; 'The Dodd Family
Abroad,' 1854 ; 'Sir Jasper Carew'
(anon.), [1855] ; 'The Fortunes of
Glencore,' 1857 ; 'The Martins of
Cro' Martin,' 1856 ; 'Davenport
Dunn' [1857-59]; 'One of Them,'
1860 ; 'Maurice Tiernay' (anon.),
1861 ; 'Barrington' [1862] ; 'A Day's
Ride,' 1864 ; 'Cornelius O'Dowd
upon Men and Women' (anon.),
1864-65 ; 'Luttrell of Arran,' 1865 ;
'Tony Butler' (anon.), 1865 ; 'Sir
Brook Fossbrooke,' 1866 ; 'The
Bramleighs of Bishop's Folly,' 1868 ;
'Paul Gosslett's Confessions,' 1868 ;
'That Boy of Norcott's,' 1869 ; 'A
Rent in a Cloud, and St. Patrick's
Eve,' 1871 ; 'Lord Kilgobbin,' 1872.
Collected Novels : ed. by his
daughter, 1897, etc.
Life : by W. F. Fitzpatrick, 1879.

LEWES (George Henry), 1817-1878.
Born, in London, 18 April 1817. At
schools in London, Jersey, Brittany,
and Greenwich. For a time worked in
a lawyer's office ; afterwards studied
medicine. After some years spent in
France and Germany, became an actor.
Acted in London at various times,
1841-50. Play, 'The Noble Heart,'
produced in Manchester, 16 April
1849 ; at Olympic, London, Feb.
1850. Married Agnes Jervis, 18
Feb. 1841. Adopted literary career.
Contributed to various periodicals.
Wrote various plays and farces.
Editor of 'The Leader,' 1850. Met
Mary Anne Evans ('George Eliot'),
1851 ; lived with her, July 1854 till
his death. To Germany with her,
July 1854. Returned to England,
March 1855. Editor of 'Fortnightly
Rev.,' May 1865 to Dec. 1866. Died,
in London, 30 Nov. 1878.

Works : 'Biographical History of
Philosophy' (4 vols.), 1845-46 ; 'The
Spanish Drama,' 1847 ; 'Ranthorpe'
(anon.), 1847 ; 'Rose, Blanche and
Violet,' 1848 ; 'Life of Maximilien
Robespierre,' 1849 ; 'The Noble
Heart,' 1850 ; 'A Chain of Events'
(under pseud. 'Slingsby Lawrence' ;
with Charles J. Mathews, 1852) ·
Comte's 'Philosophy of the Sciences,'
1853 ; 'Life and Works of Goethe,'
1855 ; 'Seaside Studies,' 1858 ; 'Physiology of Common Life' (2 vols.),
1859-60 ; 'Studies in Animal Life,'
1862 ; 'Aristotle,' 1864 ; 'Problems
of Life and Mind' (5 vols.), 1874
[1873] - 79 ; Selections from the
'Modern British Dramatists' (2 vols.),
1867 ; text to 'Female Characters of
Goethe' [1874] ; 'On Actors and the
Art of Acting,' 1875. [Also several
plays and farces, publ. in Lacy's
Acting Edition, written under pseud.
of 'Slingsby Lawrence.']
Posthumous : 'The Study of Psychology,' 1879.
He *edited :* J. F. W. Johnston's
'Chemistry of Common Life,' 1859.

**LEWIS (Matthew Gregory), 1775-
1818.** Born, in London, 9 July 1775.
At Westminster School, June 1783 to
1790. Matric., Ch. Ch., Oxford, 27
April 1790 ; B.A., 1794 ; M.A., 1797.

Visit to Paris, 1791 ; to Weimar, autumn 1792-93. Attaché to British Embassy at the Hague, 1794. M.P. for Hindon, 1796-1802. Play, 'The Castle Spectre,' produced at Drury Lane, 14 Dec. 1797 ; 'The East Indian' (afterwards called : 'Rich and Poor'), Drury Lane, 24 April 1799 ; 'Adelmorn,' Drury Lane, 4 May 1801 ; 'Alphonso,' Covent Garden, 15 Jan. 1802 ; 'The Captive,' Covent Garden, 1803 ; 'The Harper's Daughter,' Covent Garden, 4 May 1803 ; 'Rugantino,' Covent Garden, 1805 ; 'Adelgitha,' Drury Lane, 1807 ; 'The Wood Demon' (afterwards called 'One o'clock'), Covent Garden, 1807 ; 'Venoni,' Drury Lane, 1 Dec. 1808 ; 'Timour the Tartar,' Covent Garden, 29 April 1811. In West Indies, Jan. to March 1816. In Italy, May 1816 to Dec. 1817. In West Indies, Feb. to May 1818. Sailed for England, 4 May ; died at sea, 14 May 1818.

Works : 'The Monk' (anon.), 1796 : 'Village Virtues' (anon.), 1796 ; 'The Castle Spectre,' 1798 ; 'Tales of Terror,' 1799 [?] ; 'The Love of Gain' (from Juvenal), 1799 ; 'The East Indian,' 1799 ; 'Adelmorn,' 1801 (2nd edn. same year) ; 'Alfonso, King of Castile,' 1801 ; 'Tales of Wonder' (with Scott and Southey). 1801 ; 'Adelgitha,' 1806 ; 'Feudal Tyrants,' 1806 ; 'Romantic Tales,' 1808 ; 'Venoni,' 1809 ; 'One o'clock,' 1811 ; 'Timour the Tartar,' 1812 ; 'Poems,' 1812 ; 'Koenigsmark the Robber' [1815?].

Posthumous: 'Raymond and Agnes' [1820 ?] ; 'The Isle of Devils,' 1827 ; 'Journal of a West Indian Proprietor,' 1834 ; 'My Uncle's Garret Window,' 1841.

He *translated :* Schiller's 'The Minister' ('Kabale and Liebe'), 1798 ; Kotzebue's 'Rolla,' 1799 ; Zschokke's 'The Bravo of Venice' ('Abellino'), 1805.

Life : 'Life and Correspondence' (2 vols.), 1839.

LILLO (George), 1693-1739. Born, in London, 4 Feb. 1693. Assisted his father in jewellery business. Play

'Silvia' produced at Drury Lane, 10 Nov. 1730 ; 'The Merchant' (afterwards called : 'The London Merchant, or the History of George Barnwell'), Drury Lane, 22 June 1731 ; 'Britannia, or the Royal Lovers,' Covent Garden, 11 Feb. 1734 ; 'The Christian Hero,' Drury Lane, 13 Jan. 1735 ; 'Fatal Curiosity,' Haymarket, 1736 ; 'Marina' (adapted from 'Pericles '), Covent Garden, 1 Aug. 1738 ; 'Elmerick,' posthumously produced, Drury Lane, 23 Feb. 1740 ; adaptation of 'Arden of Faversham,' posthumously produced, Drury Lane, 19 July 1759. Died, in London, 3 Sept. 1739. Buried in St. Leonard's, Shoreditch.

Works : 'Silvia' (anon.), 1731 ; 'The London Merchant,' 1731 (2nd edn. same year) ; 'The Christian Hero,' 1735 ; 'Fatal Curiosity,' 1737 ; 'Marina,' 1738.

Posthumous : 'Britannia and Batavia,' 1740 ; 'Elmerick,' 1740 ; 'Arden of Faversham' (adapted), 1762.

Collected Works : ed. by T. Davies, with *memoir* (2 vols.), 1775.

LILLY (William Samuel), b. 1840. Born, at Fifehead, Dorsetshire, 10 July 1840. To St. Peter's Coll., Camb., Oct. 1858 ; senior scholar, 1859 ; LL.B., 1862 ; LL.M., 1870. Indian Civil Servant, 1861 ; to Madras, same year. Under-Sec. to Govt. of Madras, 1869. Left India, owing to ill-health, 1870. Student of Inner Temple, 27 April 1869 ; called to Bar, 17 Nov. 1873. Sec. to Catholic Union of Great Britain, since 1874. Married Susannah Louisa Hall, 16 Dec. 1878. J.P. for Middlesex and London, 1886. Mem. of Athenæum Club, under Rule II., 1887. Hon. Fellow, St. Peter's Coll., 1893. Frequent contributor to 'Quarterly Rev.,' 'Nineteenth Century,' 'Fortnightly Rev.,' etc.

Works : 'Ancient Religion and Modern Thought,' 1884 ; 'Chapters in European History' (2 vols.), 1886 ; 'A Century of Revolution,' 1889 ; 'On Right and Wrong,' 1890 ; 'On Shibboleths,' 1892 ; 'The Great

Enigma,' 1892 ; 'Manual of the Law specially affecting Catholics' (with J. E. P. Wallis), 1893 ; 'The Claims of Christianity,' 1894 ; 'Four English Humourists of the Nineteenth Century.' 1895 ; 'Essays and Speeches,' 1897.

He has *edited :* 'Characteristics from the Writings of J. H. Newman,' 1875 ; 'Characteristics . . . from the Writings of Henry Edward, Cardinal Archbishop of Westminster ' [1885].

* **LINTON** (*Mrs.* **Elizabeth Lynn**), b. 1822. Born [Elizabeth Lynn], at Keswick, 10 Feb. 1822. To London, 1845. Adopted literary career. On staff of 'Morning Chronicle,' 'Daily News,' 'Morning Star,' etc. Married to William James Linton, 26 March 1858. Removed to Malvern, 1895.

Works : ' Azeth, the Egyptian' (anon.), 1847 ; 'Amymone,' 1848 ; 'Realities,' 1851 ; 'Witch Stories,' 1861 ; 'The Lake Country,' 1864 ; 'Grasp your Nettle,' 1865 ; 'Lizzie Lorton of Greyrigg,' 1866 ; 'Sowing the Wind,' 1867 ; 'Ourselves,' 1869 ; 'The True History of Joshua Davidson' (anon.), 1872; 'Patricia Kemball,' 1875 ; 'The Mad Willoughbys ' [1876]; 'The Atonement of Leam Dundas,' 1876 ; 'The World Well Lost,' 1877 ; 'Under Which Lord ?' 1879 ; 'At Night in a Hospital' (from 'Belgravia'), [1879] ; 'With a Silken Thread,' 1880 ; 'The Rebel of the Family,' 1880 ; 'My Love,' 1881 ; 'The Girl of the Period' (from 'Sat. Rev.'), 1883 ; 'Ione,' 1883 ; 'The Rift in the Lute' [1885]; 'Stabbed in the Dark' [1885]; 'The Autobiography of Christopher Kirkland,' 1885 ; 'Paston Carew,' 1886 ; 'Through the Long Night,' 1889 ; 'About Ireland,' 1890 ; 'An Octave of Friends,' 1891 ; 'About Ulster,' 1892 ; 'The One Too Many,' 1894 ; 'In Haste and at Leisure,' 1895 ; 'Dulcie Everton,' 1896.

LIVINGSTONE (David), 1813-1873. Born, at Blantyre, 19 March 1813. Worked in cotton factory in Glasgow, 1823-38. Attended classes at Anderson Coll., and Glasgow University,

1836-38. Training for Missionary, under auspices of London Missionary Soc., Sept. 1838 to Nov. 1840. Licentiate of Faculty of Physicians, Glasgow Univ., Nov. 1840. Ordained Missionary, 20 Nov. 1840. Sailed for Cape of Good Hope, 8 Dec. 1840. Missionary and Exploring labours in South and Central Africa, 1841-56. Married Mary Moffat, 1844. Hon. LL.D., Glasgow, Dec. 1854. In England, 1856 - 57. Gold Medal, Royal Geog. Soc., 15 Dec. 1856. Freedom of City of London, 21 May 1857 ; of Cities of Glasgow, Edinburgh, and Dundee, 1857. Hon. D.C.L., Oxford, 1857. F.R.S., 1857. Exploring in Africa, 1858-64. In England, July 1864 to Aug. 1865. In India, Sept. 1865 to Jan. 1866. Resumed exploration in Africa, April 1866. Relieved by H. M. Stanley, Oct. 1871. Died, in Africa, 1 May 1873. Buried in Westminster Abbey, 18 April 1874.

Works : 'Missionary Travels and Researches in South Africa,' 1857 ; 'Cambridge Lectures,' 1858 ; 'Narrative of an Expedition to the Zambesi' (with C. Livingstone), 1865.

Posthumous : 'Last Journals,' ed. by H. Waller (2 vols.), 1874.

Life : by J. Marrat, 1877 ; by W. G. B. Blaikie, 1888 ; by Thomas Hughes, 1891.

LOCKE (John), 1632-1704. Born, at Wrington, Somerset, 29 Aug. 1632. At Westminster School, 1646[?] - 52. Matric. Ch.Ch., Oxford, as Junior Student, 27 Nov. 1652 ; B.A., 14 Feb. 1656 ; M.A., 29 June 1658 ; Greek Lecturer, 1661 ; Reader in Rhetoric, 1662 ; Censor of Moral Philosophy, 1663. Student at Gray's Inn, 1656. Incorporated at Cambridge, 1663. Sec. to Sir Walter Vane on embassy to Brandenburg, Dec. 1665 to Feb. 1666. Settled again at Oxford on his return to England. F.R.S., 23 Nov. 1668. Studied medicine, and practised as physician. B.Med., Oxford, 6 Feb. 1675. Resided in house of first Earl of Shaftesbury, as physician, from 1667. Visit to France, Sept. 1672. Sec. of

Presentations to Earl of Shaftesbury, when latter became Lord Chancellor, Nov. 1672. Sec. to Council of Trade, Oct. 1673-75. At Montpellier, for health, Dec. 1675 to March 1677. In Paris, as tutor to a son of Sir John Banks, May 1677 to June 1678 ; at Montpellier, Oct. to Nov. 1678 ; in Paris, Nov. 1678 to April 1679. Returned to England. Resided chiefly with Earl of Shaftesbury, 1679-81 ; at Oxford, 1681-83. Being suspected of treason, retired to Holland, autumn of 1683. Expelled from studentship at Ch. Ch., Oxford, Nov. 1684. In Holland, 1683-89. Returned to England, Feb. 1689. Commissioner of Appeals, 1689-1704. Lived at Westminster, 1689-91 ; removed to Oates, High Laver, Essex, 1691. Mem. of Council of Trade, May 1696 to 1700. Lived at Oates, boarding in household of Sir Francis Masham, 1700-04. Died, at Oates, 28 Oct. 1704. Buried in High Laver Churchyard.

Works : ' Methode nouvelle de dresser les Recueils,' 1686 (English trans., called : ' A New Method of Making Commonplace Books,' 1697) ; 'Epistola de Tolerantia,' 1689 (English trans. by W. Popple, same year) ; ' A Second Letter concerning Toleration ' (signed : ' Philanthropus '), 1690 ; ' A Third Letter ' (signed : ' Philanthropus '). 1690 ; ' An Essay concerning Humane Understanding,' 1690 ; ' Two Treatises of Government ' (anon.), 1690 ; ' Five Letters concerning the Inspiration of the Holy Scriptures ' (anon. ; attrib. to Locke), 1690 ; 'Some Considerations of the consequences of the Lowering of Interest ' (anon.), 1692 ; ' Some Thoughts concerning Education ' (anon.), 1693 ; ' The Reasonableness of Christianity'(anon.), 1695 ; 'Short Observations on a printed paper intituled, For encouraging the Coining of Silver Money in England "' (anon.), 1695 ; ' Further Considerations concerning Raising the Value of Money,' 1695 ; ' Letter to the . . . Lord Bishop of Worcester,' 1697 ; 'Reply to the Bishop of Worcester's Answer to his Letter,' 1697 ; ' Reply to the Bishop's Answer to his Second

Letter,' 1697 ; 'A Commonplace Book in reference to the Holy Bible' (anon. ; attrib. to Locke), 1697.

Posthumous : ' A Paraphrase and Notes on the Epistle of St. Paul to the Galatians ' (6 pts.), 1705-1707 ; ' The History of Our Saviour ' (anon. ; attrib. to Locke), 1705 ; 'Select Moral Books of the Old Testament. . . paraphrased' (anon. ; attrib. to Locke), 1706 ; ' A Paraphrase and Notes on the First Epistle . . . to the Corinthians' (anon.), 1706 ; 'Posthumous Works,' 1706 ; ' Some Familiar Letters,' 1708 ; 'Remains,' 1714 ; ' A Collection of several Pieces,' 1720 ; ' Elements of Natural Philosophy ' [1750?] ; 'Some thoughts on the conduct of the Understanding,' 1762 ; ' Observations upon the Growth and Culture of Vines and Olives,' 1766 ; ' Discourses translated from Nicole's "Essays,"' ed. by T. Hancock, 1828 ; ' Original Letters of Locke, A. Sidney and Lord Shaftesbury,' ed. by T. Forster, 1830.

He *edited :* Æsop's ' Fables,' 1703.

Collected Works : in 3 vols , 1714 ; in 10 vols., 1823.

Life : by H. R. Fox Bourne, 1876 ; by T. Fowler, 1880.

LOCKER - LAMPSON (Frederick) 1821-1895. Born [Frederick Locker], at Greenwich Hospital, 1821. Educated at various private schools, 1829-36. Clerk in colonial broker's in London, Sept. 1837 to Dec. 1838. Visit to Continent, 1840. Clerk at Somerset House, March 1841. Transferred to Admiralty, Nov. 1842. Married (i.) Lady Charlotte Bruce, 4 July 1849. Contrib. to 'Cornhill Mag.' from 1860. Wife died, 26 April 1872. Married (ii.) Hannah Jane Lampson, 6 July 1874. Took additional surname of Lampson on death of wife's father, 1890. Died, at Rowfant, 30 May 1895.

Works : ' London Lyrics,' 1857 ; ' Lyra Elegantiarum,' 1867 (first edn. suppressed ; revised edn. same year).

Posthumous : ' My Confidences,' ed. by A. Birrell, 1896.

LOCKHART (John Gibson) 1794-1854. Born, at Cambusnethan, Lan-

arkshire, 14 July 1794. At school in
Glasgow. At Glasgow Univ., 1805-
09. Matric. Balliol Coll., Oxford, as
Exhibitioner, 16 Oct. 1809 ; B C.L.,
1817. Studied law in Edinburgh,
1813-16 ; Advocate, 1816. Travelled
in Germany, 1816-17 ; visited Goethe
at Weimar. Contrib. to ' Blackwood's
Mag.' from Oct. 1817. Friendship with
Sir Walter Scott begun, May 1818.
Married Sophia Scott, 29 April 1820.
Lived at Chiefswood, near Abbotsford.
Active literary life. Removed to
London, 1825. Edited ' Quarterly
Review,' 1825-53. Called to Bar at
Lincoln's-Inn, 22 Nov. 1831. D.C.L.,
Oxford, 13 June 1834. Auditor of the
Duchy of Lancaster, 1843. Withdrew
from society in later years. In Italy,
winter 1853-54. Died, at Abbots-
ford, 25 Nov. 1854. Buried in Dry-
burgh Abbey.

Works : ' Peter's Letters to his
Kinsfolk' (under pseud.' Peter Morris'),
1819 ; ' Valerius ' (anon.), 1821 ;
' Some passages in the life of Mr.
Adam Blair ' (anon.), 1822 ; ' Regin-
ald Dalton ' (anon.), 1823 ; ' The
History of Matthew Wald ' (anon.),
1824 ; ' Life of Robert Burns,' 1828 ;
' History of Napoleon Buonaparte '
(anon.), 1829 ; ' History of the late
War,' 1832 ; ' Memoirs of the Life
of Sir Walter Scott ' (7 vols.), 1836-
38 ; ' Songs of the Edinburgh Squad-
ron ' (anon.), 1839 ; ' The Ballantyne
Humbug Handled,' 1839 ; ' Theodore
Hook ' (anon.), 1852.

He *edited :* Motteux's translation
of ' Don Quixote,' 1822 ; Sir W.
Scott's ' Poetical Works ' (under
initials J. G. L.), 1833-34 ; Byron's
Works (with Sir W. Scott), 1835 ;
and *translated :* ' Ancient Spanish
Ballads,' 1823.

Life : ' Life and Letters,' by A.
Lang, 1897.

LODGE (Thomas), 1558 [?]-1625.
Born, in London, 1558 [?]. At Merchant Taylors' School, March, 1570 to
1573 [?]. To Trin. Coll., Oxford, as
Servitor, 1573 [?] ; B.A., 8 July 1577 ;
M.A., 3 Feb. 1581. Student of Lincoln's Inn, 26 April 1578. Devoted

himself to literature. Married (i.) Joan
——, 1583. Tragedy, ' The Wounds of
Civill War,' produced, 1587 [?] ; ' A
Looking Glasse for London and England ' (written with Greene), produced
8 March 1592. Possibly wrote other
plays with Greene. Visited Ca-
naries, 1588-89 [?] ; South America,
1591-93. Moved from London to
Low Leyton, Essex, 1596 ; began
to study medicine. M.D., Avignon,
1600. M.D., Oxford, 25 Oct. 1602.
Licentiate, Coll. of Physicians, 1610.
Practised in London. Travelled frequently on Continent. Married (ii.)
Jane Aldred. Died, in London, Sept.
[?] 1625.

Works : ' Defence of Plays,' 1580 [?] ;
' An Alarum against Usurers,' 1584 ;
' Scillaes Metamorphysis,' 1589 (later
edn., called : ' A most pleasant historie
of Glaucus and Scilla,' 1610) ; ' Rosa-
lynde' (anon.), 1590 ; ' Robert, second
Duke of Normandy.' 1591 ; ' Catha-
ros ' (anon.), 1591 ; ' Euphues Shadow'
(anon.), 1592 ; ' Phillis,' 1593 ; ' Life
and death of William Longbeard'
(anon.), 1593 ; ' The Wounds of Civill
War,' 1594 ; ' A Looking Glasse for
London ' (with Greene), 1594 ; ' A
Fig for Momus ' (anon.), 1595 ; ' The
Divel Conjured ' (anon.), 1596 ; ' A
Margarite of America,' 1596 ; ' Wits
Miserie,' 1596 ; ' Prosopopeia,' 1596 ;
' Paradoxes ' (anon.), 1602 ; ' A Trea-
tise of the Plague,' 1603.

He *translated :* Josephus' Works,
1602 ; Seneca's Works, 1614 ; ' A
Learned Summary of Du Bartas,'
1625.

Collected Works : ed. by E. Gosse,
with *memoir,* 1878-82.

***LONGFELLOW (Henry Wads-
worth), 1807-1882.** Born, at Portland, Maine, 27 Feb. 1807. At school
there. To Bowdoin Coll., 1822 ; B.A.,
1825. Contrib. to various periodicals
while at college. Elected Prof. of
Mod. Languages, Bowdoin, 1825.
Travelled in Europe, June 1826 to
Aug. 1829. Began professional
duties at Bowdoin, Sept. 1829. Contrib. to ' North American Rev.,' April
1831 to Oct. 1840. Married (i.) Mary

Storer Potter, Sept. 1831. Smith Prof. of Mod. Lan., Harvard Univ., Dec. 1834. Travelled in Europe, April 1835 to Dec. 1836 ; wife died, at Rotterdam, 29 Nov. 1835. Began professional duties at Harvard, Dec. 1836. Contrib. ' The Psalm of Life ' to ' Knickerbocker Mag.,' June 1838. In Europe, for health, autumn of 1842. Married (ii.) Frances Elizabeth Appleton, 13 July 1843. Resigned Professorship, 1854. Active literary life. Contrib. to ' Atlantic Monthly,' 1857-76 Wife burnt to death, 9 July 1861 Visit to Europe, May 1868 to 1869. Hon. LL.D., Camb., 16 June 1868. Received by Queen at Windsor, July 1868. Hon. D.C.L., Oxford, 27 July 1869. Died, at Cambridge, Mass., 24 March 1882. Buried at Mount Auburn Cemetery, Cambridge.

Works : ' Syllabus de la Grammaire Italienne ' (in French), 1832 ; ' Outre-Mer ' (2 vols.), 1835 ; ' Hyperion ' (2 vols.), 1839 ; ' Voices of the Night,' 1839 ; ' Ballads and other Poems,' 1841 ; ' Poems on Slavery,' 1842 ; ' The Spanish Student,' 1843 ; ' The Belfry of Bruges,' 1846 ; ' Evangeline,' 1847 ; ' Kavanagh,' 1849 ; ' The Seaside and the Fireside,' 1850 ; ' The Golden Legend,' 1851 ; ' The Song of Hiawatha,' 1855 ; ' The Courtship of Miles Standish,' 1858 ; ' Tales of a Wayside Inn,' 1863 ; ' Flower - de - Luce,' 1867 ; ' The New England Tragedies,' 1868 ; ' The Divine Tragedy,' 1871 ; ' Christus ' (consisting of : ' Divine Tragedy,' ' Golden Legend,' and ' New England Tragedies '), 1872 ; ' Three Books of Song,' 1872; ' Aftermath,' 1873 ; ' The Hanging of the Crane,' 1874 ; ' The Masque of Pandora,' 1875 ; ' Poems of the " Old South "' (with Holmes, Whittier, and others), 1877 ; ' The Skeleton in Armour,' 1877; ' Kéramos,' 1878 ; ' Ultima Thule,' 1880.

Posthumous : ' In the Harbour,' 1882 ; ' Michael Angelo,' 1884.

He *translated :* L'Homond's ' Elements of French Grammar,' 1830 ; J. Manrique's ' Coplas,' 1833 ; Dante's Divine Comedy ' (3 vols.), 1867-70 ; and *edited :* ' Manuel de Proverbes

Dramatiques,' 1830 ; ' Novelas Españolas,' 1830 ; ' Cours de Langue Française,' 1832; ' Saggi de' Novellieri Italiani d'ogni Secola,' 1832 ; ' The Waif,' 1845 ; ' The Poets and Poetry of Europe,' 1845 ; ' The Estray,' 1847 ; ' Poems of Places ' (31 vols.), 1876-79.

Collected Works : in 11 vols., 1866.

Life : ' Life,' by his brother, Samuel Longfellow, 1886 ; ' Final Memorials,' by same, 1887.

LOVELACE (Richard),. 1618-1658. Born, at Woolwich, 1618. Early education at Charterhouse. Matric.,Gloucester Hall, Oxford, 27 June 1634 ; created M.A., 31 Aug. 1836. Incorp. at Camb.,1637. Comedy, 'The Scholar,' played at Oxford, 1636. In Royalist Army, as Ensign under Lord Goring, 1638-39. Succeeded to family property in Kent, 1639. Imprisoned in Gatehouse, Westminster, on political charge, April to June, 1642. Left England, 1646 ; Colonel of French regiment, 1646-48. Returned to England, 1648 ; on return was again imprisoned, in Petre House, Aldersgate, till Dec. 1849. Died, in London, 1658. Buried in St. Bride's Church.

Works : ' Lucasta,' 1649.

Posthumous : ' Posthume Poems,' ed. by his brother, 1659.

LOVER (Samuel), 1797-1868. Born, in Dublin, 24 Feb. 1797. Privately educated there. Early aptitude for music. In office of his father (a stockbroker), 1812-14. Began to study painting,1814. Married (i.) Miss Berrel, 1827. Memb. of Royal Hibernian Acad., 1828 ; Secretary, 1830. Contrib. to ' Dublin Literary Gaz.' Exhibited at Royal Acad., London, 1833. One of founders of ' Dublin Univ. Mag.,' 1833. To London, 1835 ; engaged in miniature painting. Play, ' The Olympic Picnic,' produced at Olympic Theatre, 1835 ; ' The Beau Ideal,' 1836 ; ' Rory O'More ' (dramatized from his novel), Adelphi Theatre, 1837 ; ' The White Horse of the Peppards,' Adelphi ; ' The Happy Man,' Haymarket; ' The Greek Boy,' Covent Garden ; ' Il Paddy Whack in Italia,' Lyceum. Helped to form ' Bentley's

Miscellany,' 1837. Gave up painting owing to failing eyesight, 1844. Produced entertainment, 'Irish Evenings,' performed by himself at Princess's Concert Rooms, March 1844 ; performed it in America, 1846-48 ; ' Paddy's Portfolio,' 1848. Wife died, 1847. Play ' Sentinels of the Alma,' produced, Haymarket ; 'Macarthy More,' Lyceum. Married (ii.) Mary Wandby, Jan. 1852. Ill-health from 1864. Removed to St. Heliers, Jersey ; died there, 6 July 1868. Buried at Kensal Green.

Works [exclusive of various farces printed in Lacy's, Webster's, and Duncombe's ' Acting Editions '] : ' Rory O'More ' (ballad), 1826 ; ' Legends and Stories of Ireland ' (2 series), 1831-34 ; ' Rory O'More ' (novel), 1837 ; ' Songs and Ballads,' 1839 ; ' Handy Andy,' 1842 ; ' Treasure Trove,' 1844 ; ' Lyrics of Ireland,' 1858 ; ' Rival Rhymes in Honour of Burns ' (under pseud. ' Ben Trovato '), 1859 ; ' Volunteer Songs,' 1859 ; ' Metrical Tales, and Other Poems,' 1860 [1859].

Life : by W. Bayle Bernard, 1874. *Collected Works :* ' Poetical Works ' [1880].

LOWELL (James Russell), 1819- 1891. Born, at Cambridge, Mass., 22 Feb. 1819. Early education with tutor. To Harvard Univ., 1834 ; B.A., 1838 ; LL.B., 1840. Called to Bar, 1840. Soon devoted himself to literature. Married (i.) Maria White, 26 Dec. 1844. Active in support of Abolition of Slavery. Contrib. ' Biglow Papers' to 'Boston Courier,' 1846- 48. Part editor of ' The Pioneer,' 1843. Corresponding editor of ' National Anti-Slavery Standard,' 1848. Contrib. to ' Dial,' ' Democratic Rev.,' ' Mass. Quarterly Rev. '; to ' Putnam's Monthly ' from 1853. Visit to Europe, 1851-52. Wife died, 1853. Prof. of Mod. Languages, Harvard, Jan. 1855. Married (ii.) Frances Dunlap, Sept. 1857. Edited 'Atlantic Monthly' from 1857-62 ; part editor of ' North American Rev.,' 1863-72. Visit to Europe, 1872-75. Hon. D.C.L., Oxford, 18

June 1873. Hon. LL.D., Camb., 1874. U.S.A. Ambassador in Madrid, 1877- 80 ; in London, 1880-85. Hon. LL.D., Edinburgh, 1884. Hon. LL.D., Harvard, St. Andrew's, and Bologna. Returned to America, 1885. Died, 12 Aug. 1891.

Works : ' Class Poem,' 1838 ; ' A Year's Life,' 1841 ; ' Poems,' 1844 (3rd edn. same year) ; ' The Vision of Sir Launfal,' 1645 ; ' Conversations on Some of the Old Poets,' 1845 ; ' Reader ! Walk up at Once ! . . . A Fable for Critics ' (anon.), 1848 (2nd edn. same year) ; ' Poems,' 1848 ; ' The Biglow Papers ' (anon.), 1st series, 1848 ; 2nd series, 1867 ; ' Poems ' (2 vols.), 1849 ; ' Poetical Works ' (2 vols.), 1858 ; ' Mason and Slidell,' 1862 ; ' Fireside Travels,' 1864 ; 'The President's Policy,' 1864 ; ' Ode recited at the Commemoration of the Living and Dead Soldiers of Harvard University,' 1865 ; ' Under the Willows,' 1869 [1868] ; ' My Study Windows,' 1870 ; ' The Cathedral,' 1870 ; ' Among my Books,' 1st series, 1870 ; 2nd series, 1876 ; ' The Courtier,' 1874 ; ' Three Memorial Poems,' 1876 ; ' Favourite Poems,' 1877 ; ' A Moosehead Journal,' 1877 ; ' Works ' (5 vols.), 1881 ; ' Democracy, and Other Addresses,' 1887 ; ' Richard III. and the Primrose Criticism,' 1887 ; ' Heartsease and Rue,' 1888 ; ' Political Essays,' 1888 ; ' Address ' [to American Mod. Language Soc.], 1890.

Posthumous : ' Last Literary Essays and Addresses,' ed. by E. Norton, 1891 ; ' The Old English Dramatists,' 1892 ; ' Letters,' ed. by C. E. Norton, 1895 [1894] ; ' Last Poems,' ed. by C. E. Norton, 1895.

He *edited :* Keats' Poems, 1854 ; Shelley's Poems, 1875.

Collected Works : in 10 vols., 1890- 91.

LUBBOCK (Sir John), Bart., b. 1834. Born, in London, 30 April 1834. At Eton, 1845-48. To post in his father's bank, 1848 ; partner, 1856. Married (i.) Ellen Frances Hordern, 10 April 1856. F.R.S., 1858. Pres. Ethnological Soc., 1863. Succeeded to

Baronetcy, 1865. Pres, Entomological Soc., 1866. Mem. of International Coinage Commission, 1868 ; of Public Schools Commission, 1868 ; of Advancement of Science Commission, 1870. Pres. Anthropological Institute, 1870. M.P. for Maidstone, 1870 and 1874. Vice-Pres. Royal Soc., 1871. Vice-Chancellor, London Univ., 1872-80. Hon. D.C.L., Oxford, 9 June 1875. Hon. LL.D., Dublin, 1878. Trustee of British Museum, 13 March 1878. Pres. Inst. of Bankers, 1879. Wife died, 1879. M.P. for London Univ., 1880. Pres. British Association, 1881. Pres. Linnæan Soc., 1881-86. Hon. LL.D., Camb., 1883. Pres. Working Men's Coll., 1883. Hon. LL.D., Edinburgh, 1884. Hon. M.D., Würzburg, 1884. Married (ii.) Alice Augusta Laurentia Lane-Fox-Pitt-Rivers, 17 May 1884. Rede Lecturer, Camb., 1886. Mem. of Education Commission, 1888 ; of Gold and Silver Commission, 1888. Vice-Chairman London County Council, 1888-89; Chairman, 1890-92. Pres. London Chamber of Commerce, 1888-92. Privy Councillor, 1890. Chairman of Committee of Design on New Coinage, 1891. Pres. International Library Conference, 1897.

Works [exclusive of over 100 Memoirs in the Transactions of various scientific societies] : ' Prehistoric Times,' 1865 ; ' A Proposal to Extend the System Pursued by H.M.C.S. Commissioners, etc.,' 1869 ; 'The Origin of Civilization,' 1870 ; ' On the Origin and Metamorphoses of Insects,' 1873 ; ' On the Bank Act of 1844,' 1873 ; ' Monograph of the Thysanura and Collembola,' 1873 ; ' On British Wild Flowers,' 1875 ; ' On Certain Relations between Plants and Insects,' 1878 ; ' Scientific Lectures,' 1879 ; ' Addresses,' 1879 ; ' Ants, Bees, and Wasps,' 1882 ; ' Fifty Years of Science,' 1881 ; ' Chapters in Popular Natural History ' [1883] ; ' Proportional Representation ' (from ' Nineteenth Century '), 1884 ; ' Representation,' 1885 ; ' Flowers, Fruits, and Leaves,' 1886 ; 'The Pleasures of

Life,' 1887 ; 'Mr. Gladstone and the Nationalities of the United Kingdom ' (from the ' Times '), 1887 ; ' On the Senses, Instincts, and Intelligence of Animals,' 1888 ; ' The Beauties of Nature,' 1892 ; 'A Contribution to our Knowledge of Seedlings,' 1892 ; ' The Uses of Life,' 1894 ; ' The Scenery of Switzerland,' 1896.
He has *edited:* S. Nilsson's ' Primitive Inhabitants of Scandinavia,' 1868 ; ' Modern Science,' 1891, etc.; and *contributed prefaces* to : C. P. K. Jackson's ' Our Ancient Monuments,' 1880 ; H. C. MacCook's ' Tenants of an Old Farm,' 1888 ; H. Hall's ' Antiquities and Curiosities of the Exchequer,'1891 ; G. Lubbock's ' Some Poor Relief Questions,' 1895.

LYDGATE (John), 1370[?]-1450 [?]. Born, at Lydgate, near Newmarket, about 1370. Perhaps educated at Benedictine School at Bury St. Edmunds. Joined Benedictine Order at Bury St. Edmunds. Ordained Deacon, 1393 ; Priest, 1397. Prolific writer of poetry. Court poet from 1412. Prior of Hatfield, Essex, 1423-34. Crown pension, 1440. Died about 1450. Buried at Bury St. Edmunds' Monastery.

Works: 'The Temple of Glas, [1479.?] ; ' The Fable of the Horse, the Sheep, and the Goose ' [1479 ?] ; ' Chorl and Bird ' [1479 ?] ; ' Stans Puer ad Mensam ' (anon.; attrib. to Lydgate), [1479 ?] ; ' Curia Sapientiæ ' [1481 ?] ; ' The Life of Our Lady,' 1484 ; ' Falls of Princes ' (trans. from Boccaccio), 1494 ; ' The Assembly of Gods,' 1498 ; ' Our Lady's Lamentacion ' [1500 ?] ; ' The Vertue of ye Masse ' [1500 ?] ; ' On the Procession at the Feast of Corpus Christi ' [1500 ?] ; ' A Godly Narrative how St. Augustine . . . Raised two Dead Bodies ' [1500 ? ; no copy known] ; 'The Story of Thebes ' [1500 ?] ; ' Troy Book,' 1513 ; 'A Treatyse called Galand ' [1520 ?] ; 'The Damage and Destruccyon in Realmes ' [1520 ?] ; ' Verses on the Kings of England,' 1530 ; ' Life of Albon and Amphabel,' 1533 ; ' Secreta Secretorum' {printed for E. E. Text Soc.), 1893.

*LYLY (John), 1554-1606. Born, in Kent, 1554. Student of Magdalen Hall, Oxford, 1569; matric., 8 Oct. 1571; B.A., 27 April 1573; M.A., 1 June 1575. Incorp. M.A., Cambridge, 1579. Settled in London, and engaged in literary work. Wrote plays for Children of the Revels. M.P. for Hindon, Feb. to March 1589; for Aylesbury, Feb. to April 1593; for Appleby, Sept. 1597 to Feb. 1598; for Aylesbury, Oct. to Dec. 1601. Married, 1595[?]. Died, in London, Nov. 1606; buried in Church of St. Bartholomew-the-Less, 30 Nov.

Works: 'Euphues,' pt. i., 1579 (2nd edn. same year); pt. ii., 1580 (2nd edn. same year); 'Alexander and Campaspe,' 1584 (another edn., called 'Campaspe,' same year); 'Sapho and Phao' (anon.), 1584; 'Pappe with a Hatchet' (anon.), [1589]; 'Endimion,' 1591; 'Gallathea' (anon.), 1592; 'Midas' (anon.), 1592; 'Mother Bombie' (anon.), 1594; 'The Woman in the Moone,' 1597; 'Love's Metamorphosis,' 1601. Collected Works: 'Six Court Comedies,' 1632; 'Dramatic Works,' ed. by F. W. Fairholt (2 vols.), 1858.

LYNDSAY (Sir David), 1490-1555. Born, near Haddington [?], 1490. Probably educated at Haddington School and St. Salvator's Coll. Attached to Court of James IV. and James V., till 1522. Married Janet Douglas, 1522. Lyon King-of-Arms, and Knight, 1529[?] On Embassy to Court of Emperor Charles V., June to Aug., 1531. In France with Duke of Albany, on embassy concerning marriage of James V., 1536. To Court of Henry VIII. to restore insignia of Garter on death of James V., 1544. During last years of life espoused Protestant cause. On Embassy to King of Denmark, 1548. Died, 1555.

Works: 'The Complaynte and testament of a Popinjay,' 1538; 'The Tragical death of David Beatō,' 1546;

'The Complaynt of Scotland' (anon.; attrib. to Lyndsay), [1549 ?]; 'Ane Dialog betuix Experience and ane Courteour' [1554 ?]. Posthumous: 'Ane Dialog and other poems,' 1558; 'The History of the Squyer William Meldrum' [1582?]; 'Ane Satyre of the Thrie Estaits,' 1602; 'A Supplement . . . in contemplation of Side Tailes and Muzzled Faces' [1690 ?]. Collected Works: ed. by Chalmers (3 vols.), 1806; ed. for Early English Text Soc., 1863-71; ed. by Laing (3 vols.), 1879.

LYTTON (Edward George Earle Lytton Bulwer-), Baron Lytton, 1803-1873. Born [Edward George Earle Lytton Bulwer], in London, 25 May 1803. Educated privately. Matric. Trin. Coll., Camb., Easter, 1822; removed to Trin. Hall, Oct. 1822; Chancellor's Medal for Prize Poem, 1825; B.A., 1826; M.A., 1835. First visit to Paris, autumn of 1825. Married Rosina Doyle Wheeler, 29 Aug. 1827. Settled near Pangbourne. Prolific contributor to periodicals. Removed to London, Sept. 1829. Active literary life. Edited 'New Monthly Mag.,' Nov. 1831 to Aug. 1833. M.P. for St. Ives, 1831-32. Legal separation from his wife, April 1836. Play, 'The Duchess de la Vallière,' produced at Drury Lane, 1836; 'The Lady of Lyons,' Drury Lane, 1838; 'Richelieu,' Drury Lane, 1839; 'The Sea-Captain' (afterwards called 'The Rightful Heir'), Haymarket, 1839; 'Money,' Haymarket, 1840. M.P. for Lincoln, 1833-41. Baronet, July 1838. Joint editor (with Brewster and Lardner) of 'Monthly Chronicle,' 1841. Play, 'Not so Bad as we Seem,' acted at Devonshire House, 1851. Succeeded to estate of Knebworth at his mother's death, Dec. 1843; assumed surname of Lytton, Feb. 1844. M.P. for Hertfordshire, 1852-66. Hon. D.C.L., Oxford, 9 June 1853. Lord Rector of Glasgow Univ., 1856 and 1858. Sec. of State for Colonies, 1858-59. Privy Councillor, June 1858. Hon. LL.D.,

Cambridge 1864. Created Baron Lytton of Knebworth, 14 July 1866. G.C.M.G. 15 Jan. 1870. Died, at Torquay, 18 Jan. 1873. Buried in Westminster Abbey.

Works : 'Ismael,' 1820 ; 'Delmour' (anon.), 1823 ; 'A Letter to a late Cabinet Minister,' 1824 ; 'Sculpture' [1825] ; 'Weeds and Wild Flowers' (anon.; priv. ptd.), 1825 ; 'O'Neill' (anon.), 1827 ; 'Falkland' (anon.) 1827 ; 'Pelham' (anon.), 1828 ; 'The Disowned' (anon.), 1829 ; 'Devereux' (anon.), 1829 ; 'Paul Clifford' (under initials : E. B. L.), 1830 ; 'The Siamese Twins,' 1831 ; 'Eugene Aram' (anon.), 1832 ; 'Asmodeus at large' (anon.), 1833 ; 'Godolphin' (anon.), 1833 ; 'England and the English,' 1833 (2nd edn. same year) ; 'Pilgrims of the Rhine' (anon.), 1834 ; 'The Last Days of Pompeii' (anon.), 1834 ; 'Letter to a Cabinet Minister,' 1834 ; 'The Student' (from 'New Monthly Mag.'), 1835 ; 'Rienzi,' 1835 ; 'The Duchesse de la Vallière' (under initials : E. B. L.), 1836 ; 'Athens, its rise and fall' (2 vols.), 1837 ; 'Ernest Maltravers' (anon.), 1837 ; 'Alice' (anon.), 1838 ; 'Leila,' 1838 ; 'Calderon the Courtier' (anon.), 1838 ; 'The Lady of Lyons' (under initials : E. B. L.), 1838 ; 'Richelieu' (anon.), 1838 ; 'The Sea - Captain' (anon.), 1839 ; 'Money' (anon.), 1840 ; 'Works' (10 vols.), 1840 ; 'Night and Morning' (anon.), 1841 ; 'Dramatic Works,' 1841 ; 'Zanoni' (anon.), 1842 ; 'Eva,' 1842 (2nd edn. same year) ; 'The Last of the Barons' (under initials : E. L. B.), 1843 ; 'Confession of a Water Patient,' 1845 ; 'The Crisis' (anon.), 1845 ; 'The New Timon' (anon.), 1846 ; 'Lucretia' (anon.), 1846 ; 'A Word to the Public' (anon.), 1847 ; 'Harold' (anon.), 1848 ; 'King Arthur,' 1848-49 (2nd edn., 1849) ; 'The Caxtons' (from 'Blackwood's Mag.'), 1849 ; 'Night and Morning,' 1851 ; 'Letter to John Bull. Esq.,' 1851 (11th edn. same year) ; 'Not so Bad as we Seem,' 1851 ; 'Outlines of the early history of the East,' 1852 ; 'Poetical and Dramatic Works' (5 vols.), 1852-54 ; 'My Novel' (from 'Blackwood' ;

under pseud.: 'Pisistratus Caxton') 1853 ; 'Address to the Associated Societies of the University of Edinburgh,' 1854 ; 'Clytemnestra' (anon.), 1855 ; 'Speech at the Leeds Mechanics' Institution,' 1854 ; 'What will he do with it?' (under pseud. : Pisistratus Caxton), 1859 ; 'Novels' (43 vols.), 1859-63 ; 'St. Stephen's' (anon.), 1860 ; 'A Strange Story' (anon. ; from 'All the Year Round'), 1862 ; 'Caxtoniana,' 1863 ; 'The Boatman' (from 'Blackwood' ; under pseud. : Pisistratus Caxton), 1864 ; 'The Lost Tales of Miletus,' 1866 ; 'The Rightful Heir' (anon.), 1868 ; 'Miscellaneous Prose Works,' 1868 ; 'Walpole,' 1869 ; 'The Coming Race' (from 'Blackwood' ; anon.), 1871 ; 'Kenelm Chillingly' (anon.), 1873 ; 'The Parisians' (from 'Blackwood'), 1873.

Posthumous : 'Speeches,' and other political writings, ed. by his son, 1874 ; 'Pausanias the Spartan,' ed. by his son, 1876 ; 'Life, Letters, and Literary Remains' (autobiog.), ed. by his son, 1883.

He *translated :* 'Poems and Ballads' from Schiller, **1844** ; Horace's 'Odes and Epodes,' 1869.

Collected Works: in 37 vols., 1873-75.

Life : by T. Cooper, 1873.

LYTTON (Edward Robert Bulwer), *Earl of Lytton,* **1831-1891.** [Son of preceding.] Born, in London, 8 Nov. 1831. To Harrow, June 1846. Removed after a short time ; afterwards educated at Bonn. To Washington, as Sec. to Lord Dalling, Oct. 1849 ; Attaché to Embassy at Florence. Feb. 1852 ; at Paris, Aug. 1854 ; at the Hague, 1856 ; at St. Petersburg. April 1858 ; at Constantinople, June 1858 ; at Vienna, Jan. 1859 ; Second Sec., Vienna. Oct. 1862 ; Sec. of Legation at Copenhagen, Jan. 1863 ; at Athens, May 1864. Married Edith Villiers, 4 Oct. 1864. Sec. of Legation at Lisbon, April 1865 ; at Madrid, Feb. 1868 ; at Vienna, Sept. 1868 ; Sec. to Embassy at Paris, Oct. 1872. Succeeded to title of Baron Lytton at his father's death, Jan. 1873. British

12

Ambassador at Lisbon, Dec. 1874. Viceroy of India, 1876-80. G.C.B., 1 Jan. 1876 ; G.C.S.I., 12 April 1876. Created Earl of Lytton, April 1880. British Ambassador at Paris, 1887-91. Privy Councillor, 29 June 1888. Died suddenly in Paris, 24 Nov. 1891. Buried at Knebworth.

Works : ‘Clytemnestra’ (under pseud.: ‘Owen Meredith’), 1855 ; ‘The Wanderer’ (by ‘Owen Meredith’), 1859 ; ‘Lucile’ (by ‘Owen Meredith’), 1860 ; ‘Tannhäuser’ (with Julian Fane ; under pseud. of ‘Neville Temple and Edward Trevor’), 1861 ; ‘Serbski Pesme’ (by ‘Owen Meredith’), 1861 ; ‘The Ring of Amasis’ (by ‘Owen Meredith’), 1863 ; ‘The Poetical Works of Owen Meredith’ (2 vols.), 1867 ; ‘Chronicles and Characters,’ 1868 [1867] ; ‘Orval,’ 1869 ; ‘Julian Fane,’ 1871 ; ‘Fables in Song,’ 1874 ; ‘Life, Letters, and Literary Remains of his father,’ 1883 ; ‘Glenaveril,’ 1885 ; ‘After Paradise,’ 1887.

Posthumous : ‘Marah,’ ed. by Lady Lytton, 1892 ; ‘King Poppy,’ 1892 (priv. ptd., 1875).

He *translated :* Edler’s ‘Baldine,’ 1886.

MACAULAY (Thomas Babington) *Baron Macaulay,* **1800-1859.** Born, at Rothley Temple, Leicestershire, 25 Oct. 1800. Early education at a day-school at Clapham ; at school at Little Shelford, near Cambridge, and afterwards at Aspenden Hall, Herts., 1812-18. Matric., Trin. Coll., Camb., Oct. 1818 ; English Prize Poem, 1819 and 1821 ; Craven Scholarship, 1821 ; B.A., 1822 ; Fellow of Trin. Coll., Oct. 1824 to 1831 ; M.A., 1825. Student of Lincoln’s Inn ; called to Bar, 1826. Contrib. to periodicals from 1823. Commissioner in Bankruptcy, Jan. 1828. M.P. for Calne, Feb. 1830. Commissioner of Board of Control, June 1832 ; Sec. to Board, Dec. 1832. M.P. for Leeds, Dec. 1832. In India, as Mem. of Supreme Council, 1834-38. M.P. for Edinburgh, 1839 ; re-elected, 1841 and 1846. Sec. for War, 1839-41. Paymaster-General,

1846-48. Defeated at Edinburgh 1847 ; withdrew from political life. Lord Rector, Glasgow Univ., Nov. 1849. F.R.S., Nov. 1849. Prof. of Ancient Hist., Royal Acad., 1850. Fellow of Univ. of London, 1850-59. Trustee of British Museum, 1847. Re-elected M.P. for Edinburgh, July 1852. Mem. of Institute of France, 1853. Knight of Prussian Order of Merit, 1853. Hon. D.C.L., Oxford, June 1854. Pres. of Philosophical Inst., Edinburgh, 1854. Member of Academies of Utrecht, Munich, and Turin. Created Baron Macaulay, 10 Sept. 1857. High Steward of Borough of Cambridge, 1857. Died, in London, 28 Dec. 1859. Buried in Westminster Abbey.

Works : ‘Pompeii’ [1819] ; ‘Evening’ [1821] ; ‘Critical and Miscellaneous Essays’ (Philadelphia, 5 vols.), 1841-44 ; ‘Lays of Ancient Rome,’ 1842 ; ‘Critical and Historical Essays’ (from ‘Edinburgh Rev.’), 1843 ; ‘History of England,’ vols. i., ii., 1849 ; vols. iii., iv., 1855 ; vol. v. (*posthumous*), ed. by Lady Trevelyan, 1861 ; ‘Inaugural Address’ [at Glasgow], 1849 ; ‘Speeches’ (2 vols.), 1853 (edn. ‘corrected by himself,’ 1854).

Posthumous : ‘Biographies contributed to the Encyclopædia Britannica,’ 1860 ; ‘Miscellaneous Writings,’ ed. by T. F. Ellis, 1860 ; vol. v. of ‘History of England’ (*see* above), 1861.

Collected Works : ed. by Lady Trevelyan (8 vols.), 1866.

Life : by Sir G. O. Trevelyan, 1876.

*McCARTHY (Justin), b. 1830. Born, in Cork, 22 Nov. 1830. Educated at a school in Cork. Journalist in Cork, 1848-52. On staff of ‘Northern Daily Times,’ 1853-59. Married Charlotte Allman, 27 March 1855. Parliamentary Reporter to ‘Morning Star,’ 1860 ; Foreign Editor, 1861 ; Editor, 1864-68. Travelled in U. S. A., 1868-71. Frequent contributor to periodicals. M.P., Co. Longford, April 1879 to Nov. 1885 ; for N. Longford, 1885-86. Defeated at Londonderry, 1886, but gained seat on petition ; retained seat till

1892. Re-elected M.P. for N. Longford, July, 1892. Lectured in America, 1869-70, 1870-71, 1886-87. On staff of 'Daily News' since 1870. Chairman of Irish Parliamentary Party, Nov. 1890 to Jan. 1896.

Works: 'Paul Massie' (anon.), 1866 ; 'The Waterdale Neighbours' (anon.), 1867 ; 'Con Amore,' 1868 ; 'My Enemy's Daughter,' 1869 ; 'Lady Judith,' 1871 ; 'Modern Leaders,' 1872 ; 'Prohibitory Legislation in the United States' (from 'Fortnightly Rev.'), 1872 ; 'A Fair Saxon,' 1873 ; 'Linley Rochford,' 1874 ; 'Dear Lady Disdain.' 1875 ; 'Miss Misanthrope,' 1878 ; 'History of Our Own Times' vols. i.-iv., 1879-80 (expanded edn., 1882) ; vol. v., 1897 ; 'Donna Quixote,' 1879 ; 'The Comet of a Season,' 1881 ; 'The Epoch of Reform,' 1882 ; 'Maid of Athens,' 1883 ; 'History of the Four Georges,' 1884, etc. ; 'The Right Honourable' (with Mrs. Campbell-Praed), 1886 ; 'The Rebel Rose' (anon. ; with Mrs. Campbell-Praed), 1887 (second edn., called the 'Rival Princess,' 1890); 'The Ladies' Gallery' (with Mrs. Campbell-Praed), 1888 ; 'Ireland's Cause in England's Parliament,' 1888 ; 'Roland Oliver' [1889] ; 'The Grey River' (with Mrs. Campbell-Praed and M. Mempes), 1889 ; 'Charing Cross to St. Paul's,' 1891 [1890]; 'Sir Robert Peel,' 1891 ; 'The Dictator,' 1893; 'Pope Leo XIII.,' 1896 ; 'The Riddle Ring,' 1896 ; 'The "Daily News" Jubilee' (with Sir J. R. Robinson), 1896.

He has *edited:* W. White's 'Inner Life of the House of Commons,' 1897.

*MACDONALD (George), b. 1824. Born, at Huntley, Aberdeenshire, 1824. Educated at King's Coll., Aberdeen ; and Aberdeen University. Studied for ministry, at Independent Coll., Highbury ; and acted for a time as Independent Minister. Removed to London and adopted literary career. Edited 'Good Words for the Young.' 1870-72. Civil List Pension, 1877. Of late years has resided chiefly in Italy.

Works: 'Poems and Essays' (anon.),

1851 ; 'Within and Without,' 1856 ; 'Poems,' 1857 ; 'Phantastes,' 1858 ; 'David Elginbrod,' 1863 ; 'Adela Cathcart,' 1864 ; 'The Portent,' 1864; 'Alex Forbes of Howglen,' 1865 ; ''Επεα 'Απτερα : Unspoken Sermons' (3 series), 1867-89 ; 'Annals of a Quiet Neighbourhood,' 1867 [1866] ; 'Dealings with the Fairies,' 1867 ; 'The Disciple '[1867] ; 'Guild Court,' 1868 [1867] ; 'England's Antiphon,' 1868 ; 'The Seaboard Parish,' 1868 ; 'Robert Falconer,' 1868 ; 'The Miracles of Our Lord,' 1870 ; 'Ranald Bannerman's Boyhood,' 1871 ; 'At the Back of the North Wind,' 1871 ; 'The Princess and the Goblin,' 1872 [1871] ; 'Works of Fancy and Imagination' (10 vols.), 1871 ; 'Wilfrid Cumbermede,' 1872 [1871] ; 'The Vicar's Daughter,' 1872 ; 'Gutta Percha Willie,' 1873 ; 'Malcolm,' 1875 ; 'The Wise Woman,' 1875 ; 'St. George and St. Michael,' 1876 [1875] ; 'Thomas Wingfield, Curate,' 1876 ; 'The Marquis of Lossie,' 1877; 'Paul Faber, Surgeon,' 1879 [1878] ; 'Sir Gibbie,' 1879 ; 'A Book of Strife,' 1880 ; 'Mary Marston,' 1881; 'The Gifts of the Child Christ' (2 vols.), 1882 ; 'Castle Warlock,' 1882; 'Orts,' 1882 ; 'Weighed and Wanting,' 1882 ; 'The Princess and Curdie,' 1883 [1882] ; 'Donal Grant,' 1883 ; 'The Imagination, and other essays' (Boston), 1883 ; 'What's Mine's Mine,' 1886 ; 'Home Again,' 1887 ; 'The Elect Lady,' 1888 ; 'Cross Purposes' [1890] ; 'The Light Princess' [1890] ; 'A Rough Shaking,' 1891 [1890] ; 'There and Back,' 1891; 'The Flight of the Shadow,' 1891 ; 'The Hope of the Gospel,' 1892 ; 'Heather and Snow,' 1893 ; 'Poetical Works' (2 vols.), 1893 ; 'Lilith,' 1895; 'The Lost Princess,' 1895 ; 'Salted with Fire,' 1897.

He has *edited:* Shakespeare's 'Hamlet,' 1885 ; Sir Philip Sidney's 'Cabinet of Gems,' 1892.

MACKENZIE (Henry), 1745-1831. Born. in Edinburgh, Aug. 1745. Educated at Edinburgh High School, and at Edinburgh Univ. Articled to

Solicitor in Edinburgh. To London, 1765. Returned to Edinburgh. Appointed Attorney for the Crown. Play, 'The Prince of Tunis,' produced at Edinburgh Theatre, 1773 ; 'The Shipwreck' (adapted from Lillo's 'Fatal Curiosity'), Covent Garden, 10 Feb. 1783 ; 'The Force of Fashion,' 1789 ; 'The White Hypocrite,' 1789. Married Penuel Grant, 1776. Edited 'The Mirror,' Jan. 1779 to May 1780. Edited 'The Lounger,' Feb. 1785 to Jan. 1787. Contrib. to 'Edinburgh Herald,' 1790-93. Comptroller of Taxes for Scotland, 1804-31. Died, in Edinburgh, 14 Jan. 1831.

Works: 'The Man of Feeling' (anon.), 1771 ; 'The Pursuits of Happiness' (anon.), 1771 ; 'The Man of the World' (anon.), 1773 ; 'The Prince of Tunis' (anon.), 1773 ; 'Julia de Roubigné' (anon.), 1777 ; 'The Shipwreck' (altered from Lillo), 1784 ; 'Review of the Principal Proceedings of the Parliament of 1784' (anon.), 1785 [?] ; 'The Lounger' (anon.), 1787 ; 'Letters of Brutus' (anon.), 1791 ; 'Additional Letters of Brutus' [1793] ; 'Life of Thomas Paine' (anon. ; abridged from Chalmers), 1793 ; 'Works' (collected, 3 vols. ; probably surreptitiously published), 1807 ; 'Works' (8 vols.), 1808 ; 'Miscellaneous Works' (3 vols.), 1819 ; 'Virginia' (anon.), [1820] ; 'Account of the Life and Writings of John Home,' 1822.

MACKINTOSH (*Sir* James), 1765-1832. Born, at Aldourie, Loch Ness, 24 Oct. 1765. At school at Fortrose, 1775-80 ; at King's Coll., Aberdeen, Oct. 1780 to Oct. 1784. To Edinburgh, to study Medicine. To London, 1788. Married Catherine Stuart, 18 Feb. 1789. Visit to Brussels, 1790. Contrib. to 'The Oracle,' 1790; to 'Monthly Review,' 1795-96. Called to Bar at Lincoln's Inn, 1795. Wife died, 8 April 1797. Married Catherine Allen, 10 April 1798. Lectured on Philosophy at Lincoln's Inn, 1799 and 1800. Appointed Recorder of Bombay, 1803. Knighted, same year. Arrived in Bombay, May 1804.

Founded Literary Society of Bombay, 1805. Judge in Vice-Admiralty Court, Bombay, 1806. Returned to England, owing to ill-health, April 1812. M.P. for Nairn, 1813-19. Lived near Aylesbury, 1813-18. Prof. of Law and General Politics at Haileybury College, Feb. 1818 to 1824. Settled at Mardocks, near Ware. M.P. for Knaresborough, 1819 - 32. Contrib. 'History of England,' vols. i.-iii., and 'Life of Sir Thomas More' to 'Cabinet Cyclopædia,' 1830 ; 'Ethical Philosophy' to 'Encyclopædia Britannica,' 1830. Commissioner of Board of Control, Nov. 1831. Died, in London, 30 May 1832. Buried at Hampstead.

Works: 'Disputatio . . . de Actione Musculari,' 1787 ; 'Vindiciæ Gallicæ,' 1791 ; 'Discourse on the Study of the Law of Nature and Nations,' 1799 ; 'Speech in defence of Peltier,' 1803 ; 'Plan of a Comparative Vocabulary of Indian Languages,' 1806 ; 'Speech . . . on the Bill for disfranchising the Borough of East Retford,' 1828 ; 'Dissertation on the Progress of Ethical Philosophy' (priv. ptd.), 1830 ; 'Speech . . . on the . . . Bill to amend the Representation of the People,' 1831.

Posthumous: 'History of the Revolution in England in 1688,' 1834 ; 'Tracts and Speeches' (priv. ptd.), 1840.

He *edited:* Rev. R. Hall's 'Works,' 1832, etc.

Collected Works: in 3 vols., 1846.

Life: by R. J. Mackintosh, 1836.

MACKLIN (Charles), 1699 [?]-1797. Born, in Ireland, 1699 [?]. Name originally McLaughlin, but form 'Macklin' eventually adopted. At school near Dublin. Ran away from home. Perhaps served in a publichouse in London, and at Trin. Coll., Dublin, as servant. Joined strolling company of actors in Bristol. Acted in London, 1725-48. Married (i.) Grace Purvor [or, Mrs. Ann Grace ?], 1735 [?]. Play, 'King Henry VII.,' produced at Drury Lane, 18 Jan. 1746 ; 'A Will and no Will,' 23 April 1746 ;

'The Suspicious Husband Criticised,' Drury Lane, 24 March 1747 ; 'The Fortune Hunters,' 1748. Acted in Dublin, 1748-50 ; in London, 1750-53. Play, 'Covent Garden Theatre,' produced at Covent Garden, 8 April 1752. Retired from stage, 1753. Kept a tavern in Covent Garden, March 1754 to Jan. 1758. Wife died, 1758 [?]. Reappeared on stage, at Drury Lane, 12 Dec. 1759, in his 'Love à la Mode.' Acted in London, 1759-63. Married (ii.) Elizabeth Jones, 10 Sept. 1759. 'The Married Libertine' produced, Covent Garden, 28 Jan. 1761. In Dublin, 1761 - 63. 'The True-Born Irishman' produced at Smock Alley Theatre, Dublin, 1763 (at Covent Garden, as 'The Irish Fine Lady,' 28 Nov. 1767) ; 'The True-Born Scotchman,' Crow Street Theatre, Dublin, 7 Feb. 1766 (at Covent Garden, as 'The Man of the World,' 10 May 1781). Acted in London, 1772-89. Died in London, 11 July 1797. Buried in St. Paul's, Covent Garden.

Works : 'Mr. Macklin's Reply to Mr. Garrick's Answer,' 1743 ; 'The Genuine Arguments of the Council,' etc. (anon. ; attrib. to Macklin), 1774; 'Love à la Mode,' 1784 ; 'The Man of the World' (under initials : C. M.), 1786.

Life : by E. A. Parry, 1891.

MACPHERSON (James), 1736-1796. Born, at Kingussie, Invernesshire, 27 Oct. 1736. Early education at parish school. Matric., King's Coll., Aberdeen, Feb. 1753. To Marischal Coll., 1755. Probably studied at Edinburgh Univ., winter of 1755 - 56. After leaving Edinburgh, was master in school at Ruthven ; and afterwards private tutor. Contrib. to 'Scots Mag.,' 1758. Friendship with Home and Dr. Carlyle, who encouraged him in publication of translations of Gaelic poems. Travelled in Highlands, 1760. collecting material. To London, 1761. Sec. to Governor of Pensacola, West Florida, 1764. Returned to England 1766. Employed by Government to write on political questions. Agent

to Nabob of Arcot, 1780. M.P. for Camelford, 1780-96. Died, at Badenoch, Invernesshire, 17 Feb. 1796. Buried in Westminster Abbey.

Works : 'The Highlander' (anon.), 1758; 'Fragments of Ancient Poetry, collected in the Highlands' (anon.), 1760 ; Ossian's 'Fingal,' translated from the Gaelic, 1762 ; Ossian's 'Temora,' translated, 1763 ; 'Introduction to the History of Great Britain and Ireland,' 1771 ; translation of Homer's 'Iliad,' 1773 ; 'A History of Great Britain, from the Restoration to the Accession of the House of Hanover' (2 vols.), 1775; 'Original Papers, containing the Secret History of Great Britain' (2 vols.), 1775 ; 'The Rights of Great Britain asserted against the claims of America' (anon.), 1776 ; 'A Short History of the Opposition during the last Session' (anon.), 1779; 'The History and Management of the East India Company' (anon.), 1779.

He *edited :* 'Letters from Mahommed Ali Chang, Nabob of Arcot, to the Court of Directors,' 1779.

Collected Works: 'Poetical Works,' 1802.

Life : by T. B. Saunders, 1894.

*MAHAFFY (John Pentland), b. **1839.** Born, at Chapponnaire, Lake of Geneva, 26 Feb. 1839. In Germany till 1850. Matric., Trin. Coll., Dublin, June 1857 ; Scholar, 1858 ; B.A., 1860 ; M.A., 1863 ; Fellow, 1864 ; Precentor of Chapel, 1867 ; Lecturer in Ancient History, 1869 ; Prof. of Ancient History, 1871 ; Donnellan Lecturer, 1873 ; B.D. and D.D., 1886 ; Hon. Mus. Doc., 1891. Ordained Deacon, 1864 ; Priest, 1866. Gold Cross of Greek Order of Saviour, 1877. Chaplain to Lord-Lieut. of Ireland, 1880. Hon. Fellow Queen's Coll., Oxford, 1882. J.P. for Co. Dublin, 1889. Governor of Irish National Gallery, 1889. Hon. D.C.L., Oxford, 1892. Hon. Mem. of Parnassus of Athens, 1895. Corresp. Mem. of Academy of Vienna, 1896.

Works: 'Twelve Lectures on Primitive Civilization,' 1868 ; 'Prolego-

mena to Ancient History,' 1871 ;
'Kant's Critical Philosophy for English Readers,' vols. i.-iii., 1872-74 ;
complete edn. (with J. H. Bernard ;
2 vols.), 1889 ; 'Social Life in Greece,'
1874 ; 'Old Greek Life,' 1876 ;
'Rambles and Studies in Greece,'
1876 ; 'The Attic Orators . . . Reply
to the "Remarks" of R. C. Jebb,'
1876 ; 'Euripides,' 1879 ; 'History of
Classical Greek Literature' (2 vols.),
1880 ; 'Descartes,' 1880 ; 'Old Greek
Education,' 1881 ; 'The Decay of
Modern Preaching,' 1882 ; 'Alexander's Empire' (with A. Gilman),
1887 ; 'Greek Life and Thought,'
1887 ; 'The Principles of the Art
of Conversation,' 1887 ; 'Sketches
from a Tour through Holland and
Germany,' 1889 [1888]; 'Greek
Pictures,' 1890 ; 'The Greek World
under Roman Sway,' 1890 ; 'On
the Flinders Petrie Papyri' (2 vols.),
1891 ; 'Problems in Greek History,'
1892 ; 'The Empire of the Ptolemies,'
1895 ; 'Survey of Greek Civilization,'
1897.

He has *translated :* Fischer's 'Commentary on Kant's Critick,' 1866 ;
and *edited :* 'Euripides' Hippolytus,'
1881 ; translation of Duruy's 'History
of Rome,' 1883-86 ; trans. of Duruy's
'Hist. of Greece,' 1892; 'Revenue
Laws of Ptolemy Philadelphus' (with
B. Grenfell), 1896.

MAINE (*Sir* **Henry James Sumner**),
1822 - 1888. Born, at Caversham
Grove, Oxon., 15 Aug. 1822. Early
Education•at a school at Henley-on-
Thames. To Christ's Hospital, 1829.
To Pembroke Coll., Camb., as Exhi-
bitioner, 1840 ; Foundation Scholar,
1841 ; Chancellor's Medallist, 1842
and 1844 ; Browne Medallist, 1842
and 1843 ; Craven Scholar, 1843 ;
B.A., 1844 ; Tutor, Trinity Hall,
1844-47 ; M.A. and LL.D., 1847;
Regius Prof. of Civil Law, 1847-54.
Married Jane Maine, 21 Dec. 1847.
Student, Lincoln's Inn, 4 June, 1847 ;
called to Bar, 11 June, 1850. Con-
trib. to 'Morning Chronicle,' 1851.
Reader of Jurisprudence and Civil
Law to Inns of Court, 1852-62. Con-

trib. to 'Sat. Rev.,' 1855-61. Bar-
rister of Middle Temple, 4 Oct. 1862;
Bencher, 21 Nov. 1873. Legal Mem.
of Athenæum Club, 1862. Mem. of
Council, Calcutta, 1862-69. Vice-
Chancellor of Calcutta Univ., 1863.
Hon. D.C.L., Oxford, 21 June 1865.
Mem. of American Academy, 1866.
Corpus Prof. of Jurisprudence, Oxford,
1869-78; incorporated Fellow of Corpus
Christi Coll., 26 Feb. 1870. K.C.S.I.,
20 May 1871. Mem. of Council of
Sec. of State for India, Nov. 1871 to
1888. Fellow of London Univ., and
Mem. of Senate, 1871-88. Lectured
at Manchester, 1873. F.R.S., 4 June
1874. Rede Lecturer, Camb., Jan.
1875. Mem. of Dutch Institute,
1876 ; of Accad. dei Lincei, 1877.
Master of Trinity Hall, Camb.,
1877-88. Mem. of Madrid Academy,
1878. Corresp. Mem. of Acad. des
Sciences Morales, Dec. 1881 ; Foreign
Member, 1883. Hon. Fellow Corpus
Christi Coll., Oxford, 1882. Mem. of
Royal Irish Academy, 1882 ; of Washington Anthropological Soc., 1883 ;
of Moscow Juridical Soc., 1884.
Whewell Prof. of International Law,
Camb., 1887-88. Hon. Fellow Pembroke Coll., Camb., 1887-88. Died,
at Cannes, 3 Feb. 1888.

Works : 'Memoir of H. F. Hallam'
(under initials : H. S. M.), [1851] ;
'Ancient Law,' 1861 ; 'Village Com-
munities,' 1871 (3rd edn., with large
additions), 1876 ; 'The Early History
of the Property of Married Women,'
1873 ; 'The Effects of Observation of
India on modern European thought,'
1875 ; 'Lectures on the Early
History of Institutions,' 1875 ; 'Dissertations on Early Law and Custom,' 1883; 'Popular Government,'
1885 ; 'The Whewell Lectures: International Law,' 1888.

Life : 'Life and Speeches,' by Sir
M. E. Grant Duff, 1892.

MAITLAND (**Samuel Roffey**), 1792-
1866. Born, in London, 7 Jan. 1792.
Educated at private schools till 1807 ;
afterwards privately. To St. John's
Coll., Camb., Oct. 1809 ; migrated to
Trinity Coll., 1810. Left Cambridge,

1811 ; took no degree. At home, 1811-15. Returned to Cambridge, to keep terms necessary for Bar, 1815. Called to Bar, at Inner Temple, 1816. Married Selina Stephenson, 19 Nov. 1816. Removed to Taunton, 1817. Ordained Curate of St. Edmund's, Norwich, 27 June 1821. Perpetual Curate of Christ Church, Gloucester, May 1823 to 1827. Travelled on Continent, investigating missionary work among Jews, 1828. Contrib. to 'British Mag.' from 1835 ; Editor, 1839-49. Librarian and Keeper of MSS., Lambeth Palace, 1838-48. F.R.S., 18 April 1839. D.D., 1 Feb. 1848. Remainder of life, from 1849, spent in retirement at Gloucester. Died there, 19 Jan. 1866.

Works: 'A Dissertation on the Primary Objects of Idolatrous Worship' (anon.), 1817 ; 'An Enquiry into the Grounds on which the Prophetic Period of Daniel and St. John has been supposed to consist of 1260 years,' 1826 ; 'Letter to the Rev. C. Simeon,' 1828 (2nd edn. same year) ; 'A Second Enquiry, etc.,' 1829 ; 'The 1260 Days, in reply to a Review, etc.,' 1830 ; 'An Attempt to elucidate the Prophecies concerning Antichrist,' 1830 ; 'Letter to the Rev. W. Digby,' 1831 ; 'Eruvin' (anon.), 1831 ; 'Facts and Documents Illustrative of . . . the Ancient Albigenses and Waldenses,' 1832 ; 'The Voluntary System' (anon. ; from 'Gloucestershire Chronicle'), 1834 ; 'The 1260 Days, in reply to . . . W. Cunningham,' 1834 ; 'The Translation of Bishops,' 1834 ; 'Letter to the Rev. H. J. Rose,' 1834 ; 'A Second Letter' [to the same], 1835 ; 'Letter to the Rev. J. King,' 1835 ; 'Remarks on . . . Rev. J. King's Pamphlet,' 1836 ; 'A Review of Fox the Martyrologist's "History of the Waldenses,"' 1837 ; 'Six Letters on Fox's "Acts and Monuments"' (from 'British Mag.'), 1837 ; 'Remarks on the . . . Committee of the Gloucester and Bristol Diocesan Church Building Association,' 1837 ; 'Letter to the Rev. W. H. Mill,' 1839 ; 'A Letter to a Friend on the "Tract for the Times,

No. 89,"' 1841 ; 'Notes on the Contributions of Rev. E. Townsend to the new edn. of Fox's "Martyrology"' (3 pts.), 1841-42 ; 'The Owl' (priv. ptd.), 1842 ; 'A List of some of the Early Printed Books . . . at Lambeth' (priv. ptd.), 1843 ; 'The Dark Ages' (from 'British Mag.'), 1844 ; An Index of English Books printed before 1600 in Lambeth Library, 1845 ; 'Remarks on the first vol. of Strype's "Life of Archbishop Cranmer"' (from 'British Mag.'), 1848 ; 'Ecclesiastical History Society' (from 'British Mag.'), 1849 ; 'Essays on Subjects connected with the Reformation in England' (from 'British Mag.'), 1849 ; 'Illustrations and Enquiries relating to Mesmerism,' 1849 ; 'A Plan of a Church History Society,' 1850 ; 'Eight Essays,' 1852 ; 'Remarks' [on Bishop of Oxford's Convocation Charge], 1855 ; 'Superstition and Science,' 1855 ; 'False Worship,' 1856 ; 'Chatterton,' 1857 ; 'Notes on Strype' [1858].

He *translated :* Saint Bernard's 'Holy War,' 1827 ; and *edited :* 'A Supplication for Toleration addressed to King James I.,' 1859.

***MALLOCK** (William Hurrell), b. 1849. Born, in Devonshire, 1849. Privately educated. Matric. Balliol Coll., Oxford, 25 April 1870. Newdigate Prize, 1871. Left Oxford, 1875. Has spent many years abroad.

Works: 'The Isthmus of Suez,' 1871 ; 'Every Man his Own Poet' (anon.), 1872 ; 'The New Republic' (anon.), 1877 ; 'The New Paul and Virginia,' 1878 ; 'Lucretius,' 1878 ; 'Is Life Worth Living?',1879 ; 'Poems,' 1880 ; 'A Romance of the Nineteenth Century,' 1881 ; 'Social Equality,' 1882 ; 'Property and Progress' (from 'Quarterly Rev.'), 1884 ; 'The Landlords and the National Income,' 1884 ; 'Atheism and the Value of Life,' 1884 ; 'The Old Order Changes' (from 'Nat. Rev.'), 1886 ; 'In an Enchanted Island,' 1889 ; 'A Human Document,' 1892 ; 'Labour and the Popular Welfare,' 1893 ; 'Verses,' 1893 ; 'Studies of Contemporary

Superstition,' 1895 ; 'The Heart of Life,' 1895 ; 'Classes and Masses,' 1896.

He has *edited :* 'Letters and Remains' of the 12th Duke of Somerset, 1893.

MALONE (Edmund), 1741-1812. Born, in Dublin, 4 Oct. 1741. Early education at private school in Dublin. To Trin. Coll., Dublin, 1756 ; scholar, 1760 ; B.A., 1762. To England, 1759. Student of Inner Temple, 1763. Friendship with Dr. Johnson begun, 1765. Travelled in France, 1766-67. Called to Irish Bar at King's Inns, 1767. Contrib. to Irish periodicals. Settled in London, May 1777. Resided there till his death. Mem. of Literary Club, 1782. Friendship with Boswell begun, 1785 ; assisted him in preparing 'Life of Johnson' for press. Engaged in Shakespearean criticism. Hon. D.C.L., Oxford, 5 July 1793. Hon. LL.D., Dublin, 1801. Unmarried. Died, in London, 25 May 1812. Buried in Kilbixy Churchyard.

Works : 'Attempt to ascertain the order in which the Plays of Shakespeare were written,' 1778 ; 'Supplement to Johnson's edn. of Shakespeare' (anon.), 1780 ; 'Cursory Observations on the Poems attributed to Thomas Rowley' (anon.), 1782 ; 'A Second Appendix to Mr. Malone's Supplement,' 1783 ; 'A Dissertation on the three parts of "King Henry VI.,"' 1787. 'Letter to the Rev. R. Farmer,' 1792 ; 'An Enquiry into the Authenticity of certain papers' [the Ireland Forgeries], 1796 ; 'An Account of the incidents from which the title and part of the story of Shakespeare's Tempest were derived' (priv. ptd.), 1808. 'Biographical Memoir of W. Windham' (anon.), 1810.

Posthumous : 'Correspondence . . . with the Rev. J. Davenport,' ed. by J. O. Halliwell, 1864 ; 'Original Letters . . . to J. Jordan,' ed. by J. O. Halliwell, 1864.

He *edited :* 'The Tragicall Hystory of Romeus and Juliet,' 1780 ; Gold-

smith's Works, 1780 ; Shakespeare's Works (11 vols.), 1790 ; Sir Joshua Reynolds' 'Writings,' 1797 ; Dryden's Works (4 vols.), 1800 ; the 1807 edn. of Boswell's 'Life of Johnson'; Hamilton's 'Parliamentary Logick,' 1808.

Life : by Sir James Prior, 1864.

MALORY (*Sir* Thomas) *fl.* **1470.** Perhaps born in Wales. No details of life known.

Works : 'Le Morte Arthur'; printed by Caxton, 1485 (only two copies known) ; reprinted by Wynkyn de Worde, 1498 (only one copy known) and 1529 (only one copy known) ; ed. by O. Sommer, 1889.

MALTHUS (Thomas Robert), 1766-1834. Born, near Guildford, 17 Feb. 1766. Educated privately. To Jesus Coll., Camb., as Pensioner, 8 June 1784 ; B.A., 1788 ; M.A., 1791 ; Fellow, 10 June 1793 to March 1804. Ordained Curate of Albury, Surrey, 1795 [?]. Travelled in Northern Europe, 1799 ; in France and Switzerland, 1802. Married Harriet Eckersall, 13 March 1804. Prof. of Hist. and Polit. Econ. at Haileybury Coll., 1805 ; lived there till his death. Visit to Ireland, 1817. F.R.S., 1819. Associate of Royal Soc. of Literature, 1824. Travelled on Continent, 1825. Foreign Associate of Académie des Sciences morales et politiques, 1833. Mem. of Royal Acad. of Berlin, 1833. Mem. of Statistical Soc., 1834. Mem. of French Institute. Died, suddenly, at St. Catherine's, near Bath, 23 Dec. 1834. Buried in Bath Abbey Church.

Works : 'Essay on the Principle of Population' (anon.), 1798 ; 'An Investigation of the cause of the present High Price of Provisions' (anon.), 1800 (2nd edn. same year) ; 'Letter to Samuel Whitbread, Esq., M.P.,' 1807 ; 'Letter to . . . Lord Granville,' 1813 ; 'Observations on the Effects of the Corn Laws,' 1814 (2nd edn. same year) ; 'Grounds of an Opinion on the Policy of Rest.icting the Importation of Foreign Corn,' 1815 ; 'An Inquiry into the Nature and Progress of Rent,'

1815 ; 'Statements respecting the East India College,' 1817 ; 'Principles of Political Economy,' 1820 ; 'The Measure of Value,' 1823; 'On the Measure of the Conditions necessary to the supply of Commodities,' 1825 ; 'On the meaning . . . attached to the term Value of Commodities,' 1827 ; 'Definitions in Political Economy,' 1827 ; 'Summary View of the Principle of Population,' 1830.
Life : 'Malthus and his Work,' by J. Bonar, 1885.

MANDEVILLE (Bernard de), 1670 [?]-1733. Born, at Dordrecht, 1670 (?). Educated at Erasmus School at Rotterdam ; and at Rotterdam Univ. M.D., Leyden, 1691. Settled in London. Practised as physician there. Died there, 21 Jan. 1733.

Works : 'De Medicina Oratio Scholastica,' 1685 ; 'De Brutorum Operationibus,' 1689 ; 'De Chylosi Vitiata,' 1691 ; 'Some Fables' (anon.), 1703 ; 'Æsop Dressed,' 1704 ; 'Typhon in Verse,' 1704 ; 'The Grumbling Hive' (anon.), 1705 ; 'The Virgin Unmasked,' 1709 ; 'Treatise of hypochondriack and hysterick Passions,' 1711 ; 'The Fable of the Bees' (anon.), 1714 ; 'The Mischiefs that ought justly to be apprehended from a Whig Government' (anon.), 1714 ; 'Free Thoughts on Religion' (anon.), 1723 ; 'A Conference about Whoring' (anon.), 1725; 'A Modest Defence of Publick Stews' (under pseud. 'Phil-Porney'), 1725 ; 'An Enquiry into the Causes of the frequent Executions at Tyburn, 1725; 'An Enquiry into the Origin of Honour' (anon.), 1732 ; 'A Letter to Dion' (anon.), 1732.
Posthumous : 'Zoologia Medicinalis Hibernica,' published under Mandeville's name, really written by J. Keogh, 1744 (a previous edn. in Keogh's name was published in 1739).
He *translated :* B. L. de Muralt's 'Divine Instinct,' 1751.

MANDEVILLE (*Sir* John), *fl.* 1350[?]. The name under which the famous book of travels, composed about 1350, was written. The author is pos-

sibly identical with Jean de Bourgogne, who died at Liège, Nov. 1372. Earliest known MS. in French, 1371. First printed : in Dutch, 1470[?]; in German, 1475[?] ; in French, 1480 ; in Italian, 1480 ; in Latin, 1485[?] ; in English, 1499.

MANSEL (Henry Longueville), 1820-1871. Born, at Cosgrove, Northamptonshire, 6 Oct. 1820. At school at East Farndon, 1828-30 ; at Merchant Taylors' School, Sept. 1830 to 1839. Matric., St. John's Coll., Oxford, as Scholar, 1 July 1839 ; Fellow, 1839-55 ; B.A., 1843 ; M.A., 1847 ; Dean of Arts, 1847 ; Tutor, 1850-64 ; B.D., 1852. Took private pupils at Oxford. Ordained Deacon, Xmas 1844 ; Priest, Xmas 1845. Member of Hebdomadal Council, Oxford, Oct. 1854. Prelector of Moral Philos., 1855-59. Married Charlotte Augusta Taylor, 16 Aug. 1855. Contrib. article 'Metaphysics' to 'Encycl. Brit.,' 1857. Bampton Lecturer, 1858. Waynflete Prof. of Moral and Metaphysical Philosophy, 1859-67 ; Select Preacher, 1860-62, 1869-71. Professor Fellow of S John's Coll., 8 April 1864 to 1867 : Hon. Fellow, 1868-71. Examining Chaplain to Bp. of Peterborough, 1864 68. Visit to Italy, 1865. D.D., Oxford. 1867. Prof. of Ecclesiastical Hist., and Canon of Christ Church, 1867-68. Dean of St. Paul's, 1868-71. Hon. Canon of Peterborough. Died, suddenly, at Cosgrove, 31 July 1871.

Works : 'The Demons of the Wind,' 1838 ; 'On the Heads of Predicables,' 1847 ; 'Scenes from an unfinished Drama entitled Phrontisterion' (anon.), 1850 ; 'Prolegomena Logica.' 1851 ; 'The Limits of Demonstrative Science,' 1853 ; 'Man's Conception of Eternity,' 1854 ; 'Psychology the Test of Moral and Metaphysical Philosophy,' 1855 ; 'A Lecture on the Philosophy of Kant,' 1856 ; 'The Limit of Religious Thought' (Bampton Lectures), 1858 (2nd edn. same year) ; 'Examination of the Rev. F. D. Maurice's Strictures' [on the preceding], 1859 ; 'Metaphysics' (from 'Encycl. Brit.'), 1860 ; 'Letter to Prof. Goldwin Smith,' 1861 ;

'A Second Letter' [to the same],
1862 ; 'The Spirit a Divine Person,'
1863 ; 'The Witness of the Church,'
1864 ; 'The Philosophy of the Con-
ditioned' (from 'Contemp. Rev.'),1866 ;
'Two Sermons preached in Peterborough Cathedral' (by Mansel and
S. Gedge), 1868.

Posthumous: 'Letters, Lectures and
Reviews,' ed. by H. W. Chandler,
1873 ; 'The Gnostic Heresies of the
First and Second Centuries,' ed. by
J. B. Lightfoot, 1875.

He *edited :* Aldrich's 'Artis Logicæ
Rudimenta,' 1852 ; Hamilton's Lectures (with J. Veitch), 1859.

Life : by Lord Carnarvon, in edn.
of ' The Gnostic Heresies,' 1875.

**MARLOWE (Christopher), 1564-
1593.** Born, at Canterbury, Feb.[?]
1564 ; baptized, 26 Feb. Educated at
King's School, Canterbury. Matric.
Corpus Christi Coll., Camb., 17 March
1581 ; B.A., 1583 ; M.A., 1587.
Probably settled in London soon afterwards. Warrant for his arrest, on
ground of heretical views expressed in
his writings, issued 18 May 1593.
Killed, in a tavern quarrel at Deptford,
1 June 1593.

Works : 'Tamburlaine the Great'
(anon.), 1590.

Posthumous : ' Edward II.,' Cassel,
1594 (only one copy known ; another
edn., London, 1598) ; 'The Tragedy
of Dido' (with T. Nash), 1594 ; 'Hero
and Leander,' 1598 ; 'The Tragical
History of . . . Dr. Faustus,' 1601[?],
(earliest copy extant, 1604) ; 'The
Massacre at Paris' [1600] ; 'The
Famous Tragedy of the Rich Jew of
Malta,' 1633 ; 'Lust's Dominion,'
1657 ; 'A Most Excellent Ditty of the
Lover's promises to his beloved'
[1650 ?].

He *translated :* Ovid's 'Amores,'
1590[?] and 1598[?] ; 'Lucan's First
Booke,' 1600.

Collected Works: ed. by G. Robinson, 3 vols., 1826 ; ed. by A. Dyce,
3 vols., 1850 ; ed. by A. H. Bullen,
3 vols., 1885.

MARRYAT (Frederick), 1792-1848.
Born, in Westminster, 10 July 1792.

Educated at private schools. Entered
Navy, Sept. 1806. At sea, 1806-15 ;
Lieut., Dec. 1812 ; Commander, June
1815. Royal Humane Society's Medal
for saving life, 1818. Married Catherine Shairp, Jan. 1819. F.R.S.,
1819. At sea, 1820-26. Post-Captain,
1826. C.B., 26 Dec. 1826. At sea,
1828-30. Resigned command, 1830.
Equerry to Duke of Sussex, 1830.
Edited 'Metropolitan Mag.,' 1832-35.
French Legion of Honour, 1833. On
Continent, mainly at Brussels, 1836.
In America, 1837-38. In London,
1839-43. At Langham, Norfolk, 1843-
48. Died there, 9 Aug. 1848.

Works : 'Suggestions for the Aboli-
tion of . . . Impressment,' 1822 ; 'The
Naval Officer' (anon.), 1829 ; 'The
King's Own' (anon.), 1830 ; 'Newton
Forster' (anon. ; from 'Met. Mag.'),
1832 ; 'Peter Simple' (anon. ; from
'Met. Mag.'), 1834 ; 'Jacob Faithful'
(anon. ; from 'Met. Mag.'), 1834 ;
'The Pacha of Many Tales' (anon.),
1835 ; 'Mr. Midshipman Easy' (from
'Met. Mag.'), 1836 ; 'Japhet in Search
of a Father' (anon. ; from 'Met. Mag.'),
1836 ; 'The Pirate and the Three
Cutters,' 1836 ; 'Snarleyyow,' 1837 ;
'The Phantom Ship,' 1839 ; 'A Diary
in America' (2 series), 1839 ; 'Olla
Podrida,' 1840 ; 'Poor Jack,' 1840 ;
'Joseph Rushbrook,' 1841 ; 'Master-
man Ready,' 1841 ; 'Percival Keene,'
1842 ; 'Narrative of the Travels and
Adventures of Monsieur Violet,' 1843 ;
'The Settlers in Canada,' 1844 ; 'The
Mission,' 1845 ; 'The Privateer's Man.'
1846 ; 'The Children of the New
Forest,' 1847.

Posthumous : 'The Little Savage'
(2 pts.), 1848-49 ; 'Valerie,' 1849 ;
'The Floral Telegraph' [1850 ?].

He *edited :* 'Rattlin the Reefer' [b
Hon. E. G. C. Howard]. 1836.

Collected Novels : 1896, etc.

Life: 'Life and Letters,' by Florence
Marryat, 1872 ; life by D. Hannay,
1889.

MARSTON (John), 1575[?]-1634.
Born, at Coventry[?], 1575 [?]. Matric.
Brasenose Coll., Oxford, 4 Feb. 1592 ;
B.A., 6 Feb. 1594. Wrote plays,

1599-1607.' Ordained Rector of Christ-
church, Hampshire, Oct. 1616 to Sept.
1631. Married Mary Wilkes. Died,
in London, 25 June 1634 ; buried in
Temple Church.

Works : 'The Metamorphosis of
Pygmalion's Image' (under initials :
W.K.), 1598 ; 'The Scourge of Vilanie'
(under pseud : W. Kinsayder), 1598 ;
'The History of Antonio and Mellida'
(under initials : J. M.), 1602 ; 'Antonio's Revenge,' 1602 ; 'The Malcontent,' 1604 ; 'Eastward Hoe' (with
Jonson and Chapman), 1605 ; 'The
Dutch Courtezan,' 1605 ; 'Para-
sitaster,' 1606 ; 'The Wonder of
Women,' 1606 ; 'What You Will,'
1607 ; 'Histriomastix' (anon. ; probably partly by Marston), 1610 ; 'The
Insatiate Countess,' 1613 ; 'Jack
Drum's Entertainment' (anon. ; probably by Marston), 1616 ; 'Tragedies
and Comedies' (anon.), 1633 (another
edn., with his name, same year).

Collected Works : ed. by J. O.
Halliwell (3 vols.), 1856 ; by A. H.
Bullen (3 vols.), 1887.

**MARSTON (John Westland), 1819-
1890.** Born, at Boston, Lincs., 30 Jan.
1819. Articled to a solicitor in
London, 1834. Contrib. to 'The
Sunbeam.' Strong literary and dra-
matic tastes. Edited 'National Mag.,'
1837-56. Editor of 'The Psyche,'
1839. Married Eleanor Jane Potts,
May 1840. Play, 'The Patrician's
Daughter,' produced, Dec. 1842 ; 'The
Heart and the World,' 1847 ; 'Strath-
more,' 1849 ; 'Philip of France and
Marie de Méranie,' 1850 ; 'Anne
Blake,' 1852 ; 'A Life's Ransom,'
1857 ; 'A Hard Struggle,' 1858 ; 'The
Wife's Portrait,' 1862 ; 'Pure Gold,'
Sadler's Wells, 10 Nov. 1863 ; 'Donna
Diana,' 1863 ; 'The Favourite of For-
tune,' Haymarket, 2 April 1866 ; 'A
Hero of Romance,' Haymarket, 14
March 1868 ; 'Life for Life,' Lyceum,
6 March 1869 ; 'Lamed for Life,'
Royalty, 12 June 1871 ; 'Broken
Spells' (with W. G. Wills), Court,
27 March 1872 ; 'Put to the Test,'
Olympic, 24 Feb. 1873 ; 'Under Fire,'
1885. Hon. LL.D., Glasgow, 1863.

Frequent contributor to 'Athenæum.'
Died, in London, 5 Jan. 1890.

Works : 'Poetry as an Universal
Nature,' 1838 ; 'Poetic Culture,' 1839 ;
'The Patrician's Daughter,' 1841 ;
'Gerald,' 1842 ; 'The Heart and the
World,' 1847 ; 'Trevanion' (with
W. B. Bernard),' 1849 ; 'Strathmore,'
1849 ; 'Philip of France and Marie
de Méranie,' 1850 ; 'Anne Blake,'
1852 ; 'The Death Ride,' 1855 ; 'A
Lady in her Own Right,' 1860 ; 'The
Family Credit,' 1862 ; 'The Wife's
Portrait' [1870] ; 'Dramatic and
Poetical Works' (2 vols.), 1876 ; 'Our
Recent Actors' (2 vols.), 1888.

**MARSTON (Philip Bourke), 1850-
1887.** [Son of preceding.] Born, in
London, 13 Aug. 1850. Almost total
loss of sight, 1853 ; developing later in
life into total blindness. Died, in
London, 13 Feb. 1887.

Works : 'Song-Tide, and other
poems,' 1871 ; 'All in All,' 1875 ;
'Wind Voices,' 1883.

Posthumous : 'For a Song's Sake,
and other Stories,' ed. by William
Sharp, 1887 ; 'Garden Secrets,' ed. by
Mrs. Moulton, 1887 ; 'A Last Harvest,'
ed. by Mrs. Moulton, 1891 ; 'Collected
Poems,' ed. by Mrs. Moulton, 1892.

*MARTIN (*Sir* Theodore), b. 1816.
Born, in Edinburgh, 16 Sept. 1816.
At Edinburgh High School, 1824-
30 ; at Edinburgh Univ., 1830-34.
Practised as solicitor in Edinburgh,
1840-45. To London, 1846. Settled
in business as Parliamentary agent.
Contrib. to 'Fraser's Mag.,' 'Tait's
Mag.,' 'Blackwood's Mag.,' 'West-
minster Rev.,' 'Quarterly Rev.,'
Married Helena Faucit, 25 Aug.
1851. Hon. LL.D., Edinburgh, 1873.
C.B., 1875. J.P. for Denbighshire.
K.C.B., March 1880. Rector of St.
Andrew's Univ., Nov. 1880 to 1884.
K.C.V.O., 1896.

Works : 'Disputation between the
Body and the Soul' (under initials :
T. M.), 1838 ; 'Dante and Beatrice'
(anon.), [1844] ; 'Bon Gaultier Ballads' (with W. E. Aytoun ; anon.),
1845 ; 'Madonna Pia' (anon. ; priv.

ptd.), 1855 ; 'Poems, original and translated' (priv. ptd.), 1862 ; 'Memoir of W. E. Aytoun,' 1867 ; 'Horace,' 1870 ; 'Essays on the Drama' (2 vols., priv. ptd.), 1874-89 ; 'The Life of H.R.H. the Prince Consort' (5 vols.), 1875-80 ; 'Inaugural Address' [at St. Andrew's], 1881; 'Life of Lord Lyndhurst,' 1883 ; 'Shakespeare or Bacon?' (from 'Blackwood's Mag.'), 1888.

He has *translated:* Hertz's 'King René's Daughter,' 1850 ; Oehlenschläger's 'Coreggio,' 1854 ; Oehlenschläger's 'Aladdin,' 1857 ; Goethe's 'Poems and Ballads' (with W. E. Aytoun), 1859 ; The 'Odes' of Horace, 1860 ; 'Catullus,' 1861 ; Dante's 'Vita Nuova,' 1862 ; Goethe's 'Faust,' pt. i., 1865 ; pt. ii. 1886 ; 'Odes, Epodes, and Satires of Horace,' 1870 ; Schiller's 'William Tell,' 1870 ; Heine's 'Poems and Ballads,' 1878 ; Horace's 'Works,' 1881 ; Schiller's 'Song of the Bell,' 1889 ; Virgil's 'Æneid,' Bks. i.-vi., 1896 ; and *edited:* Urquhart's translation of Rabelais' 'Gargantua,' 1838.

[Lady Martin was born, in London, 11 Oct. 1820. First appearances on stage, at Richmond, 1833 ; at Covent Garden, 5 Jan. 1836 ; last appearance, in Manchester, Oct. 1879. She has published : 'On Some of Shakespeare's Female Characters,' 1885 (enlarged edn., 1893)].

MARTINEAU (Harriet), 1802-1876.

Born, at Norwich, 12 June 1802. Early education at home. At a school at Norwich, 1813-15. At Bristol, 1818-19. Returned to Norwich, April 1819. Contrib. to 'Monthly Repository,' from 1821. Severe illness, 1827, followed by financial difficulties. Wrote three prize essays for Central Unitarian Association, 1830-31. Visit to her brother James at Dublin, 1831. Engaged on 'Illustrations of Political Economy,' Feb. 1832 to Feb. 1834. Settled in London. Visit to America, Aug. 1834 to Aug. 1836. Travelled on Continent, 1839. Refused Crown Pensions, 1834, 1841, and 1873. Testimonial raised to her by her friends, 1843. Lived at Tynemouth, 1839-45 ; at Ambleside, Westmorland, 1845 till her death. Friendship with Wordsworth. Visit to Egypt and Palestine, Aug. 1846 to July 1847. Contrib. to 'Daily News,' 1852-66 ; to 'Edinburgh Review,' from 1859. Died, at Ambleside, 27 June 1876.

Works: 'Devotional Exercises' (anon.), 1823 ; 'Addresses, with Prayers' (anon.), 1826 ; 'Traditions of Palestine,' 1830 ; 'Five Years of Youth,' 1831 ; 'Essential Faith of the Universal Church,' 1831 ; 'The Faith as unfolded by many Prophets,' 1832 ; 'Providence as manifested through Israel,' 1832 ; 'Illustrations of Political Economy' (9 vols.), 1832-34 ; 'Poor Laws and Paupers Illustrated,' 1833-34 ; 'Illustrations of Taxation,' 1834 ; 'Miscellanies' (2 vols., Boston), 1836 ; 'Society in America,' 1837 ; 'Retrospect of Western Travel,' 1838 ; 'How to Observe,' 1838 ; 'Addresses,' 1838 ; 'Deerbrook,' 1839 ; 'The Martyr Age of the United States' (under initials : H. M.), 1840 ; 'The Playfellow' (4 pts. : 'The Settlers at Home' ; 'The Peasant and the Prince' ; 'Feats on the Fiord' ; 'The Crofton Boys'), 1841 ; 'The Hour and the Man,' 1841 ; 'Life in the Sick Room' (anon.), 1844 ; 'Letters on Mesmerism,' 1845 (2nd edn. same year) ; 'Forest and Game-Law Tales' (3 vols.), 1845-46 ; 'Dawn Island,' 1845 ; 'The Billow and the Rock,' 1846 ; contribution to 'The Land we Live In' (with C. Knight and others), 1847, etc. ; 'Eastern Life,' 1848 ; 'History of England during the Thirty Years' Peace' (with C. Knight), 1849 ; 'Household Education,' 1849 ; 'Introduction to the History of the Peace,' 1851 ; 'Letters on the Laws of Man's Nature' (with H. G. Atkinson), 1851 ; 'Half a Century of the British Empire' (only 1 pt. pubd.), [1851] ; 'Sickness and health of the people of Bleaburn' (anon.), 1853 ; 'Letters from Ireland' (from 'Daily News '), 1853 ; 'Guide to Windermere' [1854] ; 'A Complete Guide to the English Lakes' [1855] ; 'The Factory Controversy,' 1855 ; 'History of the American Compromises' (from 'Daily News') 1856 ; 'Sketches from Life' [1856] ; 'Corporate Traditions and National Rights' [1857] ; 'British Rule in India,' 1857 ; 'Guide to Keswick' [1857] ; 'Suggestions towards the Future Government of India,' 1858 ; 'England and her Soldiers,' 1859 ; 'Endowed Schools of Ireland' (from 'Daily News '), 1859; 'Health, Husbandry, and Handicraft,' 1861 ; 'Biographical Sketches' (from 'Daily News '), 1869 [1868].

Posthumous: 'Autobiography,' ed. by M. W. Chapman, 1877 (3rd edn. same year) ; 'The Hampdens,' 1880 [1879].

She *translated:* Comte's 'Positive Philosophy,' 1853.

Life: by Mrs. Fenwick Miller, 1884.

*MARTINEAU (James), b. 1805. [Brother of preceding.] Born, at Norwich, 21 April 1805. At Norwich Grammar School till 1819 ; at Dr. Lant Carpenter's school at Bristol, 1819 - 21. Studied civil engineering, 1821-22. At Manchester New Coll., York, 1822 - 27. Temporary schoolmastership at Bristol, 1827-28. Presbyterian minister in Dublin, 1828-32 ; in Liverpool, 1832-57. Married Helen Higginson, 18 Dec. 1828. Prof. of Mental and Moral Philosophy, Manchester New Coll., 1840. Edited 'The Prospective Review,' 1845. To London, 1857. Minister of Little Portland Street Chapel, 1859-72. Principal of Manchester New Coll., London, 1869 - 85. Hon. LL.D., Harvard, 1872 ; Doc. Theol., Leyden Univ., 1875 ; Hon. D.D., Edinburgh Univ., 1884 ; Hon. D.C.L., Oxford, 20 June, 1888 ; Hon. Litt. D., Dublin, 1892.

Works [exclusive of a number of sermons and addresses dating from 1834 to 1881] : 'The Rationale of Religious Inquiry,' 1836 ; 'The Bible,' 1839 ; 'Lectures in the Liverpool Controversy,' 1839 ; 'Hymns for the Christian Church and Home,' 1840 ; 'Endeavours after the Christian Life' (2 vols.), 1843-47 ; 'Miscellanies,' [Boston] 1852 ; 'Studies of Christianity,' 1858 ; 'Essays, Philosophical and Theological' (2 vols.), [New York] 1868 ; 'The New Affinities of Faith,' 1869 ; 'The Place of Mind in Nature,' 1872 ; 'Hymns of Praise and Prayer,' 1874 ; 'Religion as affected by Modern Materialism,' 1874 ; 'Modern Materialism' (from 'Contemp. Rev.'), 1876; 'Hours of Thought on Sacred Things' (2 vols.), 1876-79 ; 'Ideal Substitutes for God,' 1878 ; 'In Memoriam John Kenrick' (from 'Theolog. Rev.'; priv. ptd.), 1878 ; 'The Relations between Ethics and Religion,' 1881 ; 'A Study of Spinoza,' 1882 ; 'Types of Ethical Theory' (2 vols.), 1885 ; 'A Study of Religion' (2 vols.), 1888 ; 'The Seat of Authority in Religion,' 1890 ; 'Essays, Reviews, and Addresses' (4 vols.), 1890-91 ; 'Home Prayers,' 1891 ; 'The Three Stages of Unitarian Theology' [1894].

MARVELL (Andrew), 1621-1678. Born, at Winestead - in - Holderness, Yorks, 31 March 1621. Educated at Hull Grammar School, of which his father was master. Matric. Trin. Coll., Camb., as Sizar, 14 Dec. 1633 ; Scholar, 13 April 1638 ; B.A., 1638. Left Cambridge, 1641. Travelled abroad. Tutor to daughter of Lord Fairfax, 1650[?]-53. Tutor to William Dutton (a ward of Oliver Cromwell), 1653-57 ; lived at Eton. Assistant to Milton (as Sec. of Foreign Tongues), 1657. M.P. for Hull, in Cromwell's Parliament. 1660 ; re-elected, Dec. 1660 and April 1661. On Embassy to Russia, Sweden, and Denmark with Earl of Carlisle, July 1663 to Jan. 1665. Prolific political and ecclesiastical controversial writer. Died, suddenly, in London, 18 Aug. 1678 ; buried in the church of St. Giles-in-the-Fields. Probably married.

Works: 'The First Anniversary of the Government,' 1655 ; 'The Character of Holland,' 1665 ; 'Clarendon's House-Warning,' 1667 ; 'The Rehearsal Transpos'd,' pt. i. (anon.), 1672 ; pt. ii., 1673 ; 'An Apology and Advice for some of the Clergy,' 1674 ; 'Dialogue between two Horses,' 1675 ; 'Plain Dealing' (under initials : A. M.), 1675 ; 'A Letter from a

Parliament Man to his Friend '(anon.; attrib. to Marvell), 1675 ; ' Mr. Smirke' (under pseud. : 'Andreas Rivetus, Junior '), 1686 ; 'A Seasonable Question and a Useful Answer' (anon. ; attrib. to Marvell), 1676 ; 'An Account of the Growth of Popery . . . in England' (anon.), 1677 ; 'A Seasonable Argument to persuade all the Grand Juries in England to petition for a new Parliament' (anon. ; attrib. to Marvell), 1677 ; 'Advice to a Painter' (anon.), 1678 ; 'Remarks upon a disengenuous Discourse writ by one T. D.' (anon.), 1678.

Posthumous : 'A Short Historical Essay touching General Councils,' 1680 ; 'Miscellaneous Poems,' 1681 ; 'Characters of Popery,' 1689 ; 'Poems on Affairs of State,' 1689 ; 'The Royal Manual,' 1751.

He contributed poems to 'Musa Cantabrigiensis,' 1637 ; 'Lacrymæ Musarum,' 1639 ; Lovelace's 'Poems,' 1649 ; Primerose's 'Popular Errors,' 1651 ; 'Paradise Lost,' 2nd edn., 1674 ; and probably *translated :* Suetonius, 1672.

Collected Works : ed. by T. Cooke (2 vols.), 1726 ; ed. by E. Thompson (3 vols.), 1776 ; ed. by Grosart, 1872-75 ; 'Poems and Satires,' ed. by G. A. Aitken (2 vols.), 1892.

Life : by J. Dove, 1832.

MASSEY (Gerald), b. 1828. Born, near Tring, Herts, 29 May 1828. Educated at National Schools Worked in silk factory, 1836-43. To London, as errand-boy, 1843. Editor of 'Spirit of Freedom,' April 1849-1851. On staff of 'Athenæum,' 1853-69 ; of 'Quarterly Rev.,' 1859-66.

Works : ' Poems and Chansons' (priv. ptd.), 1846 ; 'Voices of Freedom and Lyrics of Love,' 1851 ; 'The Ballad of Babe Christabel,' 1854 (2nd-4th edns. same year) ; 'War Waits,' 1855 (2nd edn. same year) ; 'Craigcrook Castle,' 1856 (2nd edn. same year) ; 'Robert Burns,' 1859 ; 'Poetical Works,' 1861 [1860]; 'Havelock's March,' 1861 ; 'Shakespeare's Sonnets never before Interpreted,' 1866 ; 'A Tale of Eternity,' 1870 ; 'Concerning Spirit-

ualism' [1871] ; 'The Secret Drama of Shakespeare's Sonnets,' 1872 (re-written, 1890) ; 'A Book of the Beginnings' (2 vols.), 1881 ; 'The Natural Genesis' (2 vols.), 1883 ; 'The Devil of Darkness in the Light of Evolution' (priv. ptd.), [1887]; 'Gnostic and Historic Christianity' (priv. ptd.), [1887]; 'The Hebrew and other Creations fundamentally explained' (priv. ptd.), [1887]; 'The Historical Jesus and Mythical Christ' (priv. ptd.), [1887]; 'The Logia of the Lord' (priv. ptd.), [1887]; 'Luniolatry' (priv. ptd.), [1887]; 'Man in Search of his Soul' (priv. ptd.), [1887]; 'Paul the Gnostic Opponent of Peter' (priv. ptd.), [1887]; 'The Seven Souls of Man' (priv. ptd.), [1887]; 'The Coming Religion' (priv. ptd.), [1889]; 'My Lyrical Life' (2 vols.), 1889.

MASSINGER (Philip), 1583-1640. Born, at Salisbury, 1583 ; baptised 24 Nov. Possibly page to Earl of Pembroke in boyhood. Matric., St. Alban Hall, Oxford, 14 May 1602. Left Oxford, 1606 ; took no degree. To London ; took to writing plays. Collaborated with Nathaniel Field, Cyril Tourneur, Daborne and others ; with Fletcher, 1613-25. Wrote plays for King's Company of Players, 1616-23, 1625-40 ; for Queen's Company, 1623-25. Married. Died, suddenly, in London, March 1640 ; buried, in St. Saviour's, Southwark, 18 March.

Works : 'The Virgin Martir' (with T. Dekker), 1622 ; 'The Duke of Millaine,' 1623 ; 'The Bondman,' 1624 ; 'The Roman Actor,' 1629 ; 'The Picture,' 1630 ; 'The Renegado,' 1630 ; 'The Emperor of the East,' 1632 ; 'The Maid of Honour,' 1632 ; 'The Fatal Dowry' (with N. Field ; anon.), 1632 ; 'A New Way to pay Old Debts,' 1633 ; 'The Great Duke of Florence,' 1636 ; 'The Unnaturall Combat,' 1639. [Several plays known to have been printed are lost.]

Posthumous : 'Three new Playes ; viz., The Bashful Lover, Guardian, Very Woman,' 1655 ; 'The Old Law' (with Middleton and Rowley), 1656 ; 'The City Madam,' 1658 ; 'The Par-

liament of Love,' ed. by Gifford, 1805 ;
'Believe as You List,' ed. for Percy
Soc., 1849.

Collected Works : ed. by Coxeter
(4 vols.), 1759 ; ed. by Monck Mason
(4 vols.), 1779 ; ed. by Gifford (4
vols.}, 1805.

MASSON (David), b. 1822. Born,
in Aberdeen, 2 Dec. 1822. Educated
at Marischal Coll., and Univ., Aberdeen, 1835-39 ; at Edinburgh Univ.,
1839-42. Journalist in Aberdeen,
1842-44. In London, 1844-45 ; contributed to periodicals. In Edinburgh,
1845-47. In London, 1847-65. Edited
'Macmillan's Mag.,' 1859-65 ; 'The
Reader,' 1863 ; Prof. of English Language and Literature, Univ. Coll.,
London, 1853 to Oct. 1865. Prof. of
Rhetoric and English Lit., Edinburgh
Univ., 1865-95. Lectured at Royal
Institution, 1865. Editor of Register
of Privy Council of Scotland, 1879.
Historiographer Royal for Scotland,
since 1893. Married Rosaline Orme.

Works : 'History of Rome,' 1848 ;
'The British Museum' (anon.), 1850 ;
'College Education and Self-Educa-
tion' [1854] ; 'Essays,' 1856 ; 'Life
of John Milton' (6 vols.), 1859 [1858]-
80 ; 'British Novelists and their
Styles,' 1859 ; 'Recent British Philosophy,' 1865 ; 'The State of Learning
in Scotland,' 1866 ; 'Drummond of
Hawthornden,' 1873 ; 'Wordsworth,
Shelley, Keats and other Essays,'
1874 ; 'The Three Devils,' 1874 ;
'Chatterton,' 1874 ; 'De Quincey,'
1881 ; 'Carlyle, personally and in his
writings,' 1885 ; 'Edinburgh Sketches
and Memories,' 1892 ; contribution to
In the Footsteps of the Poets' [1893];
'James Melvin,' 1895.

He has *edited :* Goldsmith's 'Works,'
1869 ; Milton's 'Poetical Works,'
1874 ; J. Bruce's 'The Quarrel between the Earl of Manchester and
Oliver Cromwell,' 1875 ; 'Register of
Privy Council of Scotland,' 1880-87 ;
De Quincey's 'Selected Essays,' 1888 ;
De Quincey's 'Collected Writings,'
1889, etc.

**MATURIN (Charles Robert), 1782-
1824.** Born, in Dublin, 1782. To
Trin. Coll., Dublin, as scholar, 1798 ;
B.A., 1800. Married Henrietta Kingsbury, 1802. Ordained Curate of
Loughrea ; afterwards of St. Peter's,
Dublin. Kept a school, and also
engaged in literature. Tragedy 'Bertram' produced at Drury Lane, 9 May
1816 ; 'Manuel,' Drury Lane, 8 March
1817 ; 'Fredolfo,' Covent Garden,
12 May 1817. Lived for some time
in London. Died, in Dublin, 30 Oct.
1824 ; buried in St. Peter's, Dublin.

Works : 'The Fatal *r* Revenge'
(under pseudonym : 'Dennis Jasper
Murphy'), 1807 ; 'The Wild Irish
Boy' (anon.), 1808 ; 'The Milesian
Chief' (anon.), 1812 ; 'Bertram,' 1816
7th edn. same year) ; 'Manuel'
(anon.), 1817 ; 'Women' (anon.),
1818 ; 'Sermons,' 1819 ; 'Fredolfo,'
1819 ; 'Melmoth the Wanderer'
(anon.), 1820 ; 'The Universe' (probably written by J. Wills), 1821 ;
'Six Sermons on the Errors of the
Roman Catholic Church,' 1824 ; 'The
Albigenses' (anon.), 1824.

Life : in 1892 edn. of 'Melmoth.'

⁂ MAX-MULLER (Friedrich), b. 1823.
Born, at Dessau, 6 Dec. 1823.
[Adopted one of his Christian names
(Max) as part surname in 1850.] At
school in Dessau and Leipzig. At
Leipzig Univ., 1840-42 ; at Berlin
Univ., spring 1842 to Sept. 1843 ;
M.A. and Ph.D., Leipzig, Sept.
1843. In Paris, 1845-46. To Eng-
land, June 1846. Settled in Oxford,
1848 ; Deputy Taylorian Prof., 1850 ;
Hon. M.A., Ch. Ch., 4 Dec. 1851 ;
Taylorian Prof., 1854-68 ; M.A., 13
Dec. 1855 ; Curator of Bodleian
Library, 1856 ; Fellow of All Souls'
Coll., 1858 ; Oriental Librarian, Bod-
leian, 1865-67 ; Corpus Prof. of Com-
parative Philology, 1868. Married
Georgina Adelaide Grenfell, 3 Aug.
1859. Lectured at Royal Institution
1861-64, 1870, 73, 87, etc. Rede
Lecturer, Camb., 1868. Hon. LL.D.,
Camb., 1868. Foreign Mem. of Institute of France, 1869. Hon. LL.D.,
Edinburgh, 1870. Lectured at Stras-
burg Univ., 1872. Lectured on 'Re-
ligions of the World' in Westminster

Abbey, 3 Dec. 1873. Ordre pour le Merite, 1874. Delegate of Univ. Press, Oxford, 13 Nov. 1877. Hibbert Lecturer, Chapter House, Westminster, 1878. Order of Corona d'Italia, 1880. Lectured on India at Cambridge, 1882. Gifford Lecturer in Natural Religion, Glasgow Univ., 1888-92. Pres. of Aryan Section, Internat. Congress of Orientalists, Stockholm, 1889 ; Order Northern Star of Sweden, 1889. Hon. LL.D., Bologna, 1890. Order of Albrecht der Bär, 1891. Pres., Internat. Congress of Orientalists, London, 1892. Hon. LL.D., Dublin, 1892. Visit to Constantinople, 1893 ; Star of Medjidieh, 1893. Jubilee Degree, Leipzig, Sept. 1893. Commander of Légion d'Honneur, 1895. Hon. Ph.D., Buda-Pesth, 1895. Privy Councillor, 1896. Hon. Mem., Imperial Acad. of Vienna, 1897.

Works: ' Proposals for a Missionary Alphabet,' 1854 ; ' Suggestions for the assistance of Officers,' 1854 ; ' The Languages of the Seat of War in the East,' 1855 ; ' Deutsche Liebe' (anon.), 1857 ; ' Buddhism and the Buddhist Pilgrims,' 1857 ; ' The German Classics,' 1858 ; ' Correspondence [with Sir G. Trevelyan] relating to the Establishment of an Oriental College in London' (from ' The Times,' anon.), 1858 ; ' A History of Ancient Sanskrit Literature,' 1859 ; ' Lectures on the Science of Language' (2 ser.), 1861, 64 ; ' On Ancient Hindu Astronomy and Chronology,' 1862 ; ' A Sanskrit Grammar for Beginners,' 1866 ; ' Chips from a German Workshop' (4 vols.), 1867-75 ; ' On the Stratification of Language,' 1868 ; ' Ueber den Buddhistischen Nihilismus.' 1869 ; ' A Sanskrit Grammar for Beginners,' 1870 ; ' Speech at the German Peace Festival' (in Germ. and Eng.), 1871 ; ' Ueber die Resultate der Sprachwissenschaft,' 1872 ; ' Introduction to the Science of Religion,' 1873 ; ' On Missions,' 1873 ; ' Lectures on the Origin and Growth of Religion,' 1878 ; ' Selected Essays,' 1881 ; ' India,' 1883 ; ' Biographical Essays,' 1884 ; ' The Science of

Thought,' 1887 ; ' Three Introductory Lectures on the Science of Thought,' 1887 ; ' Biographies of Words,' 1888 ; ' Natural Religion,' 1888 ; ' Physical Religion,' 1891 ; ' Anthropological Religion,' 1892 [1891] ; ' Theosophy,' 1893 ; ' Three Lectures on the Vedânta Philosophy,' 1894 ; ' Contributions to the Science of Mythology,' 1897.

He has translated : ' Hitopadesa, 1844 ; ' Kalidâsa,' 1847 ; ' Rig-Veda-Pratisakhya,' 1869 ; 'The Upanishads,' (2 pts.), 1879, 84 ; ' The Dhammapada,' 1881 ; Kant's 'Critique of Pure Reason,' 1881 ; ' Vedic Hymns,' 1891, etc. ; ' Buddhist Mahayana Texts,' 1894 ; and edited : ' Handbooks for the Study of Sanskrit,' 1864-66 ; ' Memoirs of Baron Stockmar,' 1872 ; ' The Hymns of the Rig-Veda,' 1849, 56, 69, 73 ; ' Schiller's Letters,' 1875 ; ' The Sacred Books of the East,' 1879, etc. ; ' Buddhist Texts from Japan,' 1881, etc. ; ' The Ancient Palm Leaves, etc.' (with Bunyiu Nanjio), 1884 ; 'The Dharma-Samgraha' (with H. Wenzel), 1885 ; W. Scherer's ' Hist. of German Literature,' 1886 ; ' Sacred Books of the Buddhists,' 1895, etc.

MAXWELL (Mrs. John). See Braddon.

MAY (Thomas), 1595-1650. Born [at Mayfield, Sussex ?], 1595. Matric. Sidney Sussex Coll., Camb., as Fellow-Commoner, 7 Sept. 1609 ; B.A., 1612. Student at Gray's Inn, 6 Aug. 1615. Devoted himself to drama and general literature. Joined Parliamentary side in Civil War. Secretary for the Parliament, 1646-50. Died, in London, 13 Nov. 1650. Buried in Westminster Abbey.

Works: 'The Heir,' 1622 ; ' A Continuation of Lucan's Historicall Poem,' 1630 (Latin version, 1640) ; ' The Tragedy of Antigone' (under initials : T. M.), 1631 ; ' The Reigne of King Henry the Second,' 1633 ; ' The Victorious Reigne of King Edward the Third,' 1635 ; ' The Tragedie of Cleopatra' (under initials : T. M.), 1639 ; 'The Tragedy of Julia Aggripina'

(under initials : T. M.), 1639 ; 'A
Discourse concerning the Success of
former Parliaments' (anon.), 1642 ;
'A True Relation from Hull,' 1643 ;
'The Character of a Right Malignant'
(anon.; attrib. to May), 1644 ; 'The
Lord George Digby's Cabinet and Dr.
Goff's Negotiations,' 1646 ; 'The History of the Parliament of England
which began Nov. the Third, 1640,'
1647 ; 'Historiæ Parliamenti Angliæ
Breviarium' (under initials : T. M.),
1650 (English version same year) ;
'The Changeable Covenant' (anon.;
attrib. to May), 1650.

Posthumous : 'The Life of a Sa-
tirical Puppy called Nim' (under
initials : T. M.; possibly by May),
1657 ; 'Julius Cæsar,' 1658 ; 'The
Old Couple,' 1658.

He *translated :* Lucan's ' Pharsalia,'
Bks. i.-iii., 1626 ; complete, 1627 ;
Virgil's 'Georgics,' 1628 ; 'Selected
Epigrams of Martial,' 1629 ; Barclay's
'Argenis,' 1629 ; Barclay's 'Icon Ani-
morum,' 1631.

MAYHEW (Henry), 1812 - 1887.
Born, in London, 25 Nov. 1812. To
Westminster School, 14 Jan. 1822.
Ran away to sea ; sailed to Calcutta.
On his return, articled to his father
(a solicitor). Edited 'Figaro in London' (with Gilbert à Beckett), 1832-
39 ; 'The Thief,' 1832. Farce, 'The
Wandering Minstrel,' produced, Fitzroy Theatre, 16 Jan. 1834 ; 'But
however——' (written with H. Baylis),
Haymarket, 30 Oct. 1838 ; 'Mont
Blanc' (from Labiche ; written with
Athol Mayhew), [1874]. One of the
projectors of 'Punch,' 1841 ; for some
time joint editor with Mark Lemon
and E. S. Coyne. Edited 'The Comic
Almanack,' 1848. Contrib. to ' Morning Chronicle.' Visited Germany
several times. Edited 'Only Once
a Year,' 1870. Died, in London,
25 July 1887. Buried at Kensal
Green.

Works : 'But however——' (with
H. Baylis), [1838] ; 'What to Teach,
and How to Teach It,' 1842 ; 'The
Prince of Wales's Library: the
Primer' [1844] ; 'The Good Genius'

(with Aug. Mayhew), 1847 ; 'The
Greatest Plague of Life' (with Aug.
Mayhew), 1847 ; 'The Image of his
Father' (with Aug. Mayhew), 1848 ;
'Whom to Marry' (with Aug. Mayhew), 1848 ; 'The Magic of Kindness,'
(with Aug. Mayhew), 1849 ; 'The
Image of his Father,' 1850 ; 'Acting
Charades ' (with Aug. Mayhew), 1850;
'1851 ; or, the Adventures of Mr.
and Mrs. Sandboys' (with G. Cruik-
shank), 1851 ; 'London Labour and
London Poor,' 1851 ; 'The Mormons,'
1852 ; 'The Story of a Peasant Boy
Philosopher,' 1854 ; 'Living for Ap-
pearances' (with Aug. Mayhew),
1855 ; 'The Wonders of Science,'
1855 ; 'The Great World of London,'
1856 ; 'The Rhine,' 1856 ; 'The
Upper Rhine,' 1858 ; 'The Criminal
Prisons of London' (with J. Binny),
1862 ; 'The Boyhood of Martin
Luther,' 1863 ; 'German Life and
Manners in Saxony,' 1864 ; 'The Shops
and Companies of London,' 1865 ;
'Young Benjamin Franklin' [1870] ;
'Report concerning . . . Working
Men's Clubs' [1871] ; 'London Char-
acters' (with others), 1874 ; 'Mont
Blanc' (with Athol Mayhew ; priv.
ptd.), 1874.

MELVILLE (George John Whyte-).
See Whyte-Melville.

MELVILLE (Herman), 1819-1891.
Born, in New York City, 1 Aug. 1819.
Went to sea, 1836. Schoolmaster,
1837-40. To sea again, Jan. 1841.
Ran away from ship on Marquesas
Islands, 1842. Rescued after four
months' captivity among the Typees.
For short time clerk at Honolulu.
Returned to Boston, 1844. Married
Elizabeth Shaw, 4 Aug. 1847. Lived
in New York, 1847-50 ; at Pittsville,
Mass., 1850-63. Visits to Europe,
1849 and 1856. Frequently lectured
in America, 1857-60. Returned to
New York, 1863. District Officer,
New York Custom House, Dec. 1866-
86. Died, in New York, 28 Sept.
1891.

Works : 'Typee,' 1846 ; 'Omoo,'
1847 ; 'Mardi,' 1849 ; 'Redburn,'
1849 ; 'White-Jacket' 1850 ; 'Moby

13

Dick,' 1851 (English edn., called 'The Whale,' same year) ; 'Pierre,' 1852; 'Israel Potter,' 1855 (in 1865 edn. called : 'The Refugee') ; 'Piazza Tales,' 1856 ; 'The Confidence Man,' 1857 ; 'Battle-Pieces,' 1866 ; 'Clarel,' 1876 ; 'John Marr and Other Sailors' (priv. ptd.), 1888 ; 'Timoleon' (priv. ptd.), 1891.

*MEREDITH (George), b. 1828. Born, in Hampshire, 12 Feb. 1828. First publication was a poem, 'Chillianwallah,' in 'Chambers' Journal,' 7 July 1849. Active literary life. Lectured on 'Comedy' at London Institution, 1 Feb. 1877. Pres. of Soc. of Authors, 1892. Widower.

Works : 'Poems' [1851]; 'The Shaving of Shagpat,' 1856 [1855]; 'Farina,' 1857 ; 'The Ordeal of Richard Feverel,' 1859 ; 'Evan Harrington' (from 'Once a Week'), 1861 ; 'Modern Love,' 1862 ; 'Mary Bertrand,' 1862 ; 'Emilia in England,' 1864 (in later edns. called 'Sandra Belloni') ; 'Rhoda Fleming,' 1865 ; 'Vittoria' (from 'Fortnightly Rev.'), 1867 ; 'The Adventures of Harry Richmond (from 'Cornhill Mag.'), 1871 ; 'Beauchamp's Career' (from 'Fortnightly Rev.'), 1876 ; 'The House on the Beach' (from 'New Quarterly Rev.'), unauthorized edn., New York, 1877 ; 'The Egoist,' 1879; 'Tne Tragic Comedians' (from 'Fortnightly Mag.'), 1881 ; 'Poems and Lyrics of the Joy of Earth,' 1883 ; 'Diana of the Crossways' (enlarged from 'Fortnightly Rev.'), 1885 ; 'Ballads and Poems of Tragic Life,' 1887 ; 'A Reading of Earth,' 1888 ; 'The Case of General Ople and Lady Camper' (from 'New Quarterly Mag.'), [New York, 1890]; 'The Tale of Chloe' [New York, 1890] ; 'One of our Conquerors' (from 'Fortnightly Rev.'), 1891 ; 'Jump-to-Glory Jane' (from 'Universal Rev.'), 1892 ; 'The Empty Purse, etc.,' 1892 ; 'Lord Ormont and his Aminta' (from 'Pall Mall Mag.'), 1894 ; 'The Tale of Chloe : The House on the Beach : The Case of General Ople and Lady Camper,' 1894 ; 'The Amazing Marriage' (from 'Scribner's

Mag.'), 1895 ; 'An Essay on Comedy,' 1897 ; 'Selected Poems,' 1897.
Collected Works : 1896, etc.

MEREDITH (Owen), pseud. See Lytton (E. R. B.), Earl of Lytton.

MERIVALE (Charles), Dean of Ely 1808-1893. Born, in London, 8 March 1808. At Harrow, Jan. 1818 to Dec. 1824 ; at Haileybury College, 1825-26. Intention of entering H.E.I.C.'s service given up. Scholar, St. John's Coll., Camb., 1826 ; Browne Medalist, 1829 ; B.A., 1830 ; M.A., 1833 ; B.D., 1840 ; D.D., 1870. Fellow, St. John's Coll., 1833-48 ; Hon. Fellow, 1874. Ordained Deacon, 1833 ; Priest, 1834. Select Preacher, Camb., 1838. Whitehall Preacher, 1840. Rector of Lawford, 1848-70. Married Judith Mary Sophia Frere, 2 July 1850. Hulsean Lecturer, Camb., 1862. Chaplain to Speaker, 1863-69. Boyle Lecturer, 1864-65. Hon. D.C.L., Oxford, 13 June 1866. Dean of Ely, 1869. D.D., Durham, 1883. Hon. LL.D., Edinburgh, 1884. Died, at Ely, 27 Dec. 1893.

Works : 'The Church of England a Faithful Witness,' 1839 ; 'Sermons Preached in the Chapel Royal, Whitehall,' 1841 ; 'History of the Romans under the Empire' (7 vols.), 1850-62; 'The Fall of the Roman Republic,' 1853 ; 'Open Fellowships,' 1858 ; 'The Conversion of the Roman Empire,' 1864 ; 'The Conversion of the Northern Nations,' 1866 [1865]; 'The Contrast between Pagan and Christian Society,' 1872 ; 'General History of Rome,' 1875 ; 'Four Lectures on Some Epochs of Early Church History,' 1879 ; 'Herman Merivale, C.B,' [1884]. [Also several separate sermons.]

He translated : Keats' 'Hyperion' (into Latin), 1863 ; Homer's 'Iliad,' 1869 ; and edited : Sallust's 'Catilina et Jugurtha,' 1852 ; translation of Abeken's 'Account of the Life and Letters of Cicero,' 1854.

*MERIVALE (Herman Charles), b. 1839. Born, in London, 27 Jan. 1839. At Harrow, May 1851 to July

1856. Matric. Balliol Coll., Oxford, 26 Jan. 1857 ; B.A., 1861. Student of Inner Temple, 21 March 1860 ; called to Bar, 26 Jan. 1864. Edited 'Time and the Hour,' 1864 ; 'Annual Register,' 1870-80. Gave up legal profession, 1874. Married Elizabeth Pittman, 13 May 1878. Play, 'Son of the Soil,' produced at Court Theatre, 1865 ; 'All for Her' (written with Palgrave Simpson) Mirror [afterwards Holborn] Theatre, 1875 ; 'Forget-me-not' (with F. C. Grove), Lyceum, 21 Aug. 1879 ; 'The Cynic,' Theatre Royal, Manchester, 19 Nov. 1881, Globe Theatre, London, 14 Jan. 1882; 'Fédora' (adapted from Sardou), Hay-market, 5 May 1883; 'Our Joan' (with his wife), 1883 ; 'The White Pilgrim,' Wallack's Theatre, New York, 1883 ; 'The Whip Hand' (with his wife), Cambridge, 1884 ; 'The Butler' (with his wife), Toole's Theatre, 6 Dec. 1886 ; 'Civil War' (adaptation), Gaiety, 27 June 1887 ; 'The Don' (with his wife), Toole's Theatre, 7 March 1888 ; 'Ravenswood,' Lyceum, 20 Sept. 1890 ; 'The Queen's Proctor' (adaptation), Royalty, 2 June 1896.

Works: 'The White Pilgrim' (priv. ptd.), 1874 ; 'Faucit of Balliol,' 1882 ; 'The White Pilgrim, and Other Poems,' 1883 ; 'Binko's Blues,' 1884 ; 'Florien,' 1884 ; 'Life of W. M. Thackeray (with F. T. Marzials), 1891. [Also various plays printed in 'Lacy's Acting Edition of Plays,' vols. 97, 100, 103, 113, 115.]

*MEYNELL (*Mrs.* **Alice Christiana**). Born in London. Youngest daughter of the late Mr. T. J. Thompson. Youth spent in Italy. Educated by her father. Married Wilfrid Meynell, 1877. Has resided chiefly in London.

Works: 'Preludes,' 1875 ; 'The Poor Sisters of Nazareth' [1889] ; 'Poems,' 1893 ; 'The Rhythm of Life,' 1893 ; 'The Colour of Life,' 1896 ; 'The Children,' 1897 [1896] ; 'The Flower of the Mind,' 1897.

She has *translated :* Barbé's 'Lourdes' [1894] ; and *edited :* Selected Poems of T. G. Hake, 1894 ;

'Poetry of Pathos and Delight,' from Coventry Patmore's works, 1896.

MIDDLETON (Conyers), 1683-1750. Born, in Yorkshire, 27 Dec. 1683. Matric., Trin. Coll., Camb., 19 Jan. 1700 ; B.A., 1703 ; Fellow, 1706-10 ; M.A., 1707 ; D.D., 1717. Ordained Curate of Trumpington. Married (i.) Mrs. Sarah Drake, 1710. Rector of Coveney. Tried for libel on Bentley, 1721 and 1723. 'Protobibliothecarius' of University Library, Dec. 1721. In Italy, 1724-25. Wife died, 19 Feb. 1731. Woodwardian Professor, Cambridge, 1731-34. Married (ii.) Mary Conyers Place, 1734. She died, 26 April 1745. Rector of Hascombe, Surrey, March 1747. Married (iii.) Anne Powell. Died, at Hildersham, 28 July 1750.

Works : 'A Full and Impartial Account of all the late Proceedings . . . against Dr. Bentley' (anon.), 1719 ; 'Second Part' of same (anon.), 1719 ; 'Some Remarks upon a Pamphlet entitled "The Case of Dr. Bentley Further Stated"' (anon.), 1719 ; 'A True Account of the Present State of Trinity College' (anon.), 1719 ; 'Remarks . . . upon the Proposals lately published by Richard Bentley for a New Edition of the Greek Testament' (anon.), 1721 (3rd edn. same year) ; 'Some Further Remarks' on the same. 1721 ; 'Bibliothecæ Cantabrigiensis Ordinandæ Methodus,' 1723 ; 'De Medicorum apud Veteres Romanos degentium Conditione,' 1726 ; 'Dissertationis . . . contra anonymos quosdam . . . auctores Defensio,' 1727 ; 'A Letter from Rome,' 1729 ; 'A Letter to Dr. Waterland' (anon.), 1731 ; 'A Defence' of same (anon.), 1731 ; 'Some Further Remarks on a Reply to the Defence of the Letter to Dr. Waterland' (anon.), 1732 ; 'Oratio de novo Physiologiæ explicandæ munere,' 1732 ; 'Remarks on some Observations addressed to the Author of the Letter to Dr. Waterland' (anon.), 1733 ; 'A Dissertation concerning the Origin of Printing in England,' 1735 ; 'The History of the Life of Marcus Tullius Cicero' (2 vols.), 1741 (3rd

13—2

edn. same year) ; 'Germana quædam _ antiquitatis eruditæ Monu-
menta,' 1745 ; 'A Treatise on the
Roman Senate,' 1747 ; 'An Introductory Discourse to a larger work . . .
concerning the Miraculous Powers
which are supposed to have subsisted
in the Christian Church' (anon.),
1747 (2nd edn. same year) ; 'Remarks
on two Pamphlets' concerning same
(anon.), 1748 ; 'A Free Inquiry into
the Miraculous Powers, etc.,' 1749 ;
'An Examination of the Lord Bishop
of London's Discourses concerning
the Use and Intent of Prophecy,'
1750.

Posthumous: 'A Vindication of the
Free Inquiry,' 1751 ; 'Dissertationis
de servili medicorum conditione,' ed.
by W. Heberden, 1761.

He *translated:* 'The Epistles of
M. T. Cicero to M. Brutus,' etc.,
1743.

Collected Works: 'Miscellaneous
Works' (4 vols.), 1752.

**MIDDLETON (Thomas), 1570[?]-
1627.** Born, in London, 1570 [?].
Student at Gray's Inn, 1593 [?].
Began to write plays about 1600.
Wrote a number of plays and masques.
Married (i.) Mary Morbeck, 1603 [?].
After her death he married (ii.) Mag-
dalen ——, 1627 [?]. Appointed City
Chronologer, 6 Sept. 1620. Died, at
Newington Butts, July 1627 ; buried
in parish church, 4 July.

Works: 'The Wisdom of Solomon
Paraphrased,' 1597 ; 'Microcynion'
(under initials : T. M. ; attrib. to
Middleton), 1559 ; 'Master Constable
Blurt' (anon.), 1602 ; 'The Blacke
Booke' (under initials : T. M. ; attrib.
to Midd'eton), 1604 ; 'Father Hub-
burd's Tales' (under pseud. ; 'Oliver
Hubburd'),1604; 'Michaelmas Terme'
(anon.) 1607 ; 'The Phœnix' (anon.),
1607 ; 'A Trick to Catch the Old-
One' (under initials : T. M.), 1608 ;
'The Famelie of Love' (anon.), 1608 ;
'Your Five Gallants' [1608] ; 'A
Mad World, my Masters' (under
initials : T. M.), 1608 ; 'Sir Robert
Sherley,' 1609 ; 'The Roaring Girle'
(with Dekker), 1611 ; 'The Triumphs

of Truth,' 1613 ; 'Civitatis Amor'
(anon.), 1616 ; 'The Tryumphs of
Honor and Industry' (under initials :
T. M.), 1617 ; 'A Faire Quarrell'
(with Rowley), 1617 ; 'The Peace-
maker' (anon. ; attrib. to Middleton),
1618 ; 'The Inner Temple Masque,'
1619 ; 'The Triumphs of Love and
Antiquity,' 1619 ; 'The World Tost
at Tennis' (with Rowley), 1620 ;
'The Sunne in Aries,' 1621 ; 'The
Triumphs of Honor and Virtue,' 1622 ;
'The Triumphs of Integrity,' 1623 ;
'A Game at Chess' (anon. [1624],
3rd. edn. same year) ; 'The Triumphs
of Health and Prosperity,' 1626.

Posthumous : 'A Chast Mayd in
Cheape-side,' 1630 ; 'The Widdow'
(with Jonson and Fletcher), 1652 ;
'The Changeling' (with Rowley),
1653 ; 'The Spanish Gipsie' (with
Rowley), 1653 ; 'The Old Law' (with
Massinger and Rowley), 1656 ; 'No
Wit, No Help like a Woman's,' 1657 ;
'Two new playes ; viz., More Dissem-
blers besides Women'; 'Women Be-
ware Women,' 1657 ; 'The Mayor of
Quinborough,' 1661 ; 'Anything for
a Quiet Life,' 1662 ; 'The Witch,'
1778.

Collected Works : ed. by Dyce,
1840 ; by A. H. Bullen, 1885-86.

MILL (James), 1773-1836. Born,
at Northwater Bridge, Forfarshire, 6
April 1773. Educated at Parish
School ; and at Montrose Academy.
Friendship with Hume begun at
latter. Tutor for some time to the
daughter of Sir James Stuart. To
Edinburgh Univ., 1790. Licensed to
preach, 4 Oct. 1798. To London,
1802. Contrib. to 'Anti-Jacobin Review,' 1802 ; and other periodicals.
Edited 'The Literary Journal,' 1802-
06 ; edited 'St. James's Chronicle,'
1805-08[?]. Married Harriet Burrow,
5 June 1805. Contrib. to 'British
Rev.,' 'Monthly Rev.,' 'Eclectic Rev.';
to 'Edinburgh Rev.,' 1808-13 ; to
'The Philanthropist,' 1811-17. Friendship with Bentham begun, 1808 ; with
Ricardo, 1811. Assistant to Examiner
of India Correspondence, India House,
May 1819 ; Second Assistant, April

1821 ; Assistant Examiner, April 1823 ; Examiner, Dec. 1830. Contrib. to 'Encycl. Brit.,' 1816-23. Political Economy Club founded, 1820. Helped to found 'Westminster Rev.,' 1824 ; frequent contributor, 1824-29. One of founders of London University ; member of original Council, 1825. Contrib. to 'London Rev.,' 1835-36. Died, in London, 23 June 1836. Buried in Kensington Church.

Works : ' Essay on the Impolicy of a Bounty on the Exportation of Grain' (anon.), 1804 ; 'Commerce Defended,' 1808 ; 'History of British India' (3 vols.), 1817 ; ' Elements of Political Economy,' 1821 ; 'Essays' (priv. ptd.), [1825?] ; ' Analysis of the Phenomena of the Human Mind,' 1829 ; 'On the Ballot' (anon.), [1830] ; 'Fragment on Mackintosh' (anon.), 1835.

Posthumous : 'The Principles of Toleration,' 1837.

He *translated :* C. F. D. De Villiers' ' Essay on the Spirit and influence of the Reformation,' 1805.

Life : by Prof. Bain, 1882.

MILL (John Stuart), 1806-1873.
[Eldest son of preceding.] Born, in London, 20 May 1806. Educated by his father. In France, May 1820 to July 1821. On return studied for Bar for short time, till appointment as Junior Clerk in Examiner's Office, India House, May 1823 ; Assistant Examiner, 1828 ; First Assistant, 1836 ; Head of Office, 1856. Founded Utilitarian Soc., winter of 1822. Contrib. to ' Traveller,' 1822 ; to 'Morning Chronicle,' 1823 ; to ' Westminster Rev.,' 1824-28, 1835-38, 1864 ; to 'Parliamentary Hist. and Rev.,' 1826-28. Founded Speculative Soc., 1825. In Paris, 1830. Contrib. to ' Examiner ' and ' Monthly Rev.,' 1831-34 ; to 'Tait's Mag.,' 1832 ; to ' Monthly Repository,' 1834 ; and to ' Jurist.' Editor 'London Rev.,' afterwards 'Westminster Rev.,' 1834-40. Friendship with Mrs. Taylor begun, 1850 ; married her, April 1851. Proprietor of ' Westminster Rev.,' 1837-40. Severe illness, 1839. Correspondence with Comte, 1841-46. Con-

trib. to ' Edinburgh Rev.,' 1845-46, 1863. Severe illness, 1854. Retired from India House, 1858. In South of France, winter of 1858-59 ; wife died, at Avignon. For remainder of life spent half the year at Blackheath, half at Avignon. Contrib. articles on ' Utilitarianism ' to ' Fraser's Mag.,' 1861. M.P. for Westminster, 1865-68. Lord Rector of St. Andrew's Univ., 1866. Died, at Avignon, 8 May 1873 ; buried there.

Works : ' A System of Logic ' (2 vols.), 1843 ; ' Essays on some Unsettled Questions of Political Economy,' 1844 ; 'Principles of Political Economy ' (2 vols.), 1848 ; 'Memorandum on the Improvements in the Administration of India during the last Thirty Years ' (anon.), 1858 ; 'On Liberty,' 1859 ; 'Thoughts on Parliamentary Reform,' 1859 (2nd edn. same year); 'Dissertations and Discussions ' (4 vols.), 1859-75 ; 'Considerations on Representative Government,' 1861 (2nd edn. same year); 'Utilitarianism' (from ' Fraser's Mag.'), 1863 ; ' Examination of Sir William Hamilton's Philosophy,'1865 (2nd edn. same year); ' Auguste Comte and Positivism ' (from ' Westminster Rev.'), 1865 ; ' Inaugural Address ' at Univ. of St. Andrew's, 1867 ; 'Speech on the Admission of Women to the Electoral Franchise,' 1867 ; ' England and Ireland,' 1868 ; 'The Subjection of Women,' 1869 (2nd edn. same year); ' Chapters and Speeches on the Irish Land Question,' 1870 ; ' Speech in favour of Woman's Suffrage,' 1871.

Posthumous : 'Autobiography,' ed. by Miss Taylor, 1873-74 ; ' Nature ; the Utility of Religion ; and Theism,' ed. by Miss Taylor, 1874 (2nd edn. same year); 'Views . . . on England's Danger through the Suppression of her Maritime Power,' 1874 ; ' Early Essays,' ed. by J. W. M. Gibbs, 1897.

He *edited :* Bentham's 'Rationale of Judicial Evidence,' 1827 ; and the 1869 edn. of James Mill's ' Analysis of the Phenomena of the Human Mind.'

Life : 'Autobiography,' 1873 ; 'Criticism, with Personal Recollections,' by Prof. Bain, 1882 ; 'Life,' by W. L. Courtney, 1889.

MILLER (Hugh), 1802-1856. Born, at Cromarty, 10 Oct. 1802. At school at Cromarty. Apprenticed to stonemason, 1819-22. Journeyman mason, 1822-34. Contrib. to 'Inverness Courier,' 1829. Accountant in Commercial Bank, Cromarty, 1834 to Dec. 1839. Married Lydia Falconer Fraser, 7 Jan. 1837. To Edinburgh, Dec. 1839. Editor of 'The Witness,' Jan. 1840 ; part proprietor, 1845. Visit to England, 1845. Brain gave way suddenly under severe illness ; committed suicide, at Shrub Mount, near Edinburgh, 23 Dec. 1856. Buried in Grange Cemetery.

Works : 'Poems written in the Leisure Hours of a Journeyman Mason' (anon.), 1829 ; 'Letters on the Herring Fishery' (anon. ; from 'Inverness Courier'), 1829 ; 'Words of Warning to the People of Scotland,' 1834 [?] ; 'Scenes and Legends of the North of Scotland,' 1835 ; 'Letter... to Lord Brougham,' 1839 ; 'Memoir of William Forsyth,' 1839 ; 'The Whiggism of the Old School,' 1839 ; 'The Old Red Sandstone' (from 'The Witness'), 1841 ; 'The Two Parties in the Church of Scotland,' 1841 ; 'The Two Mr. Clarks' (anon.), 1843 ; 'Sutherland as it was and is' (anon.), 1843 ; 'The Riots in Ross' (anon.), 1843 ; 'Sutherland and the Sutherlanders' (anon.), 1844 ; 'First Impressions of England and its People,' 1847 ; 'Footprints of the Creator,' 1849 ; 'Thoughts on the Educational Question,' 1850 ; 'My Schools and Schoolmasters,' 1852 ; 'The Fossiliferous Deposits of Scotland,' 1854 ; 'Geology versus Astronomy' [1855] ; 'Strange but True' [1856].

Posthumous : 'The Testimony of the Rocks,' 1857 ; 'The Cruise of the Betsy,' ed. by W. S. Symonds, 1858 ; 'Sketchbook of Popular Geology,' ed. by his wife, 1859 ; 'The Headship of Christ,' 1861 ; 'Essays,' ed. by P. Bayne, 1862 ; 'Tales and Sketches,' ed. by his wife, 1863 ; 'Edinburgh and its Neighbourhood,' ed. by his wife, 1864 ; 'Leading Articles on Various Subjects,' ed. by J. Davidson, 1870.

He *edited :* 'Sermons for Sabbath Evenings,' 1848.

Life : 'Life and Letters,' by P. Bayne, 1871.

MILMAN (Henry Hart), *Dean of St. Paul's,* **1791-1868.** Born, in London, 10 Feb. 1791. At school at Greenwich and Eton. Matric. Brasenose Coll., Oxford, 25 May 1810 ; Newdigate Prize Poem, 1812 ; Chancellor's Latin Verse Prize, 1813 ; B.A., 1814 ; Fellow of B.N.C., 1814-19 ; M.A., 1816 ; Chancellor's English Essay Prize, 1816 ; Chancellor's Latin Essay Prize, 1816. Ordained Deacon, 1816 ; Priest, 1816. Vicar of St. Mary's, Reading, 1817-35. Play 'Fazio' (originally produced at Surrey Theatre under title of 'The Italian Wife') performed at Covent Garden, 5 Feb. 1818. Frequent contributor to 'Quarterly Rev.' Prof. of Poetry, Oxford, 1821-31. Married Mary Ann Cockell, 11 March 1824. Bampton Lecturer, 1827. Canon of Westminster and Rector of St. Margaret's, Westminster, 1835-49. Dean of St. Paul's, 1849. B.D. and D.D., Oxford, 1849. Died, near Ascot, 24 Sept. 1868. Buried in St. Paul's Cathedral.

Works : 'The Belvidere Apollo,' 1812 ; 'Alexander tumulum Achillis invisens,' 1813 ; 'Fazio,' 1815 ; 'A Comparative Estimate of Sculpture and Painting' (priv. ptd.), 1816 ; 'In historia scribenda quænam præcipua inter auctores veteres et novos sit differentia ?' (priv. ptd.), 1816 ; 'Samor.' 1818 (2nd edn. same year) ; 'The Fall of Jerusalem,' 1820 (2nd edn. same year) ; 'The Martyr of Antioch,' 1822 ; 'Belshazzar,' 1822 ; 'Anne Boleyn,' 1826 ; 'The Character and Conduct of the Apostles' (Bampton Lectures), 1827 ; 'History of the Jews' (anon.), 1829 ; 'Life of Edward Gibbon,' 1839 ; 'Poetical Works,' 1839 ; 'History of Christianity from the Birth of Christ to the Abolition of Paganism in the Roman Empire'

(3 vols.), 1840; 'History of Latin Christianity . . . to the Pontificate of Pope Nicholas V.' (6 vols.), 1855; 'A Memoir of Lord Macaulay,' 1862 (2nd 'edn. same year); 'Hebrew Prophecy,' 1865.

Posthumous: 'Annals of St. Paul's Cathedral,' ed. by A. Milman, 1868; 'Savonarola, Erasmus, and other essays,' ed. by A. Milman, 1870.

He *translated:* 'Nala and Damayanti' (with H. H. Wilson), 1835; Horace's 'Works,' 1849; Sophocles' 'Agamemnon,' 1865; Euripides' 'Bacchæ,' 1865; and *edited:* Gibbons' 'Hist. of Decline and Fall of Roman Empire,' 1838-39.

MILNES (R. Monckton). *See* Houghton.

*MILTON (John), 1608-1674. Born, in London, 9 Dec. 1608. At St. Paul's School, 1620 [?]-25. Pensioner of Christ's Coll., Camb., 12 Feb. 1625; matric. 9 April 1625; B.A., 26 March 1629; M.A., 3 July 1632. Lived with his father at Horton, Bucks., July 1632 to April 1638. Travelled on continent, April 1638 to July 1639. On his return, settled in London and took pupils. Took active part in ecclesiastical controversy, 1641-42. Married (i.) Mary Powell, May [?] 1643; separated from her shortly afterwards; reconciled, 1645. Latin Secretary to Council of State, March 1649. Became blind, 1650. Wife died, 1652. Married (ii.) Catharine Woodcock, 12 Nov. 1656; she died, Feb. 1658. At Restoration, was arrested for treasonable publications, summer of 1660; released soon afterwards. Married (iii.) Elizabeth Minshull, 24 Feb. 1663. Died, in London, 8 Nov. 1674. Buried in St. Giles's, Cripplegate.

Works: 'A Masque ['Comus'] presented at Ludlow Castle' (anon.), 1637; 'Lycidas' in 'Justa Edouardo King Naufrago,' 1638; 'Of Reformation touching Church Discipline in England' (anon.), 1641; 'Of Prelatical Episcopacy' (anon.), 1641; 'Animadversions upon the Remonstrant's Defence against Smectymnuus' (anon.), 1641; 'The Archbishop of Canterburie's Dream' (anon.), 1641; 'The Reason of Church Government urged against Prelaty,' 1641; 'Tyrannicall Government anatomized' (anon.), 1642; 'An Apology against . . . "A Modest Confutation of the Animadversions"' (anon.), 1642; 'News from Hell' (anon.), 1642; 'The Doctrine and Discipline of Divorce' (anon.), 1643; 'Of Education' (anon.), [1644]; 'Areopagitica,' 1644; 'Tetrachordon,' 1645; 'Colasterion' (anon.), 1645; 'Poems,' 1645; 'The Tenure of Kings and Magistrates' (under initials: J. M.), 1649; 'Observations on the Articles of Peace,' 1649; 'Εικονοκλαστης' (anon.), 1649; 'The Grand Case of Conscience . . . stated' (anon.), 1650; 'Pro Populo Anglicano Defensio,' 1650; 'The Life and Reign of King Charles' (anon.), 1651; 'A Letter written to a Gentleman in the Country,' 1653; 'Pro Populo Anglicano Defensio Secunda,' 1654; 'Pro se Defensio contra Alexandrum Morum,' 1655; 'Scriptum Domini Protectoris . . . contra Hispanos,' 1655; 'A Treatise of Civil Power in Ecclesiastical Causes,' 1659; 'Considerations touching the likeliest means to remove Hirelings out of the Church,' 1659; 'The Ready and Easy Way to Establish a Free Commonwealth' (anon.), 1659; 'Brief Notes upon a late Sermon . . . by Matthew Griffith,' 1660; 'Paradise Lost,' 1667; 'Accidence commenc't Grammar' (anon.), 1669; 'The History of Britain,' 1670; 'Artis Logicæ Plenior Institutio,' 1670; 'Paradise Regained. . . To which is added "Samson Agonistes,"' 1671; 'Poems, etc., upon several Occasions,' 1673; 'Of True Religion, etc.' (under initials: J. M.), 1673; 'Epistolarum Familiarum liber unus,' 1674.

Posthumous: 'Literæ Pseudo-Senatus Anglicani,' 1676; 'Character of the Long Parliament' (possibly spurious), 1681; 'A Brief History of Moscovia,' 1682; 'De Doctrina Christiana libri duo posthumi,' 1825.

He *translated:* Martin Bucer's 'Judgment concerning Divorce,' 1644;

'A Declaration or Letters Patent of the Election of this present King of Poland' (anon.), 1674 ; and *edited*. Raleigh's 'Cabinet Council,' 1658.

Collected Works : in 8 vols., ed. by J. Mitford, 1851.

Life : by Prof. Masson (6 vols.), 1859-80.

MINTO (William), 1845 - 1893. Born, at Nether Auchintoul, Aberdeenshire, 10 Oct. 1845. At schools at Gallowhill, Tough, Bruckhills, Fisherford, and Huntly. To Aberdeen University, 1861 ; M.A., 1865. Attended Divinity Hall, 1865 - 66. Matric. Merton Coll., Oxford, 18 Oct. 1866 ; left, without degree, 1867. Returned to Aberdeen. Assisted Prof. of Nat. Philosophy, Nov. to Dec., 1867. Afterwards assisted Prof. of Logic and Eng. Lit. Examiner in Mental Philosophy, Aberdeen, 1872. Engaged in literary work. To London, 1873. Joined staff of 'Examiner,' 1873 ; Editor, 1874-78. Afterwards on staff of 'Daily News' (from 1880) and 'Pall Mall Gaz.' Contrib. to 'Encycl. Brit.,' and various periodicals. Married Cornelia Griffiths, 8 Jan. 1880. Edited 'London Opinion,' 1880. Prof. of Logic and Eng. Lit., Aberdeen, 1880. Ill - health from 1891. Died, 1 March 1893.

Works : 'Manual of English Prose Literature,' 1872 ; 'Characteristics of English Poets from Chaucer to Shirley,' 1874 ; 'Daniel Defoe,' 1879 ; 'The Crack of Doom,' 1886 ; 'The Mediation of Ralph Hardelot,' 1888 ; 'Was she good or bad ?' 1889.

Posthumous : 'Logic, Inductive and Deductive,' 1893 ; 'Plain Principles of Prose Composition,' 1893 ; 'The Literature of the Georgian Era,' ed. by W. Knight, 1894.

He *edited :* Scott's 'Lay of the Last Minstrel,' 1882 ; Scott's 'Poetical Works,' 1888, and 'Lady of the Lake,' 1891 ; W. Bell Scott's 'Autobiographical Notes,' 1892.

MITFORD (Mary Russell), 1787-1855. Born, at Alresford, Hampshire, 16 Dec. 1787. At school in London,

1798-1802. Precocious literary ability. Lived with her parents at Reading, 1802-20. They removed to Three Mile Cross, near Reading, April 1820 ; she lived there till 1851. Contrib. 'Our Village' to 'Lady's Mag.' from 1819. Play 'Julian' produced at Covent Garden, 15 March 1823 ; 'Foscari,' Covent Garden, 4 Nov. 1826 ; 'Rienzi,' Drury Lane, 9 Oct. 1828 ; 'Charles I.,' Victoria Theatre, July 1834 ; libretto of opera 'Sadak and Kalascade,' Lyceum Theatre, 20 April 1835. Contributed to various periodicals. Friendship with Mrs. Browning begun, 1836. Civil List Pension, 1837. Edited 'Finden's Tableaux,' 1838 - 41. Removed to Swallowfield, near Reading, 1851. Died there, 10 Jan. 1855. Buried in village churchyard.

Works : 'Miscellaneous Poems,' 1810 ; 'Christina,' 1811 ; 'Watlington Hill,' 1812 ; 'Blanche of Castile,' 1812 ; 'Narrative Poems on the Female Character,' 1813 ; 'Julian,' 1823 (3rd edn. same year) ; 'Our Village,' vol. i., 1824 ; vol. ii., 1826 ; vol. iii., 1828 ; vol. iv., 1830 ; vol. v., 1832 (complete, 1843) ; 'Foscari,' 1826 ; 'Dramatic Scenes, Sonnets and other Poems,' 1827 ; 'Rienzi,' 1828 (4th edn. same year) ; 'Stories of American Life,' 1830 ; 'The Sister's Budget' (anon.), 1831 ; 'American Stories for Children,' 1832 ; 'Charles the First,' 1834 ; 'Belford Regis,' 1835 ; 'Sadak and Kalascade' [1835] ; 'Country Stories,' 1837 ; 'Works' (Philadelphia), 1841 ; 'Recollections of a Literary Life' (3 vols.), 1852 ; 'Atherton,' 1854 ; 'Dramatic Works' (2 vols.), 1854.

Posthumous : 'Life . . . in a selection from her Letters,' ed. by A. G. L'Estrange (3 vols.), 1870 [1869] ; 'Letters . . . Second series,' ed. by H. Chorley (2 vols.), 1872.

She *edited :* 'Stories of American Life,' 1830 ; 'Lights and Shadows of American Life,' 1832 ; 'Tales for Young People . . . selected from American Writers,' 1835 ; 'Fragments des Œuvres d' A. Dumas,' 1846.

MONTAGU (*Lady* **Mary Wortley**), **1689-1762.** Born [Mary Pierrepont; Lady Mary in 1690, when her father became Earl of Kingston], in London, 1689 ; baptized, 26 May. Early taste for literature. Married to Edward Wortley Montagu, 12 Aug. 1712. In favour at Court. Friendship with Pope begun. In Vienna with her husband (appointed Ambassador to the Porte), Sept. 1716 to Jan. 1717 ; in Constantinople, May 1717 to June 1718. Returned to England, Oct. 1718. Estrangement from Pope, 1722. Lived abroad, apart from husband, July 1739-1762. Died, in England, 21 Aug. 1762.

Works : 'Court Poems' (anon. ; surreptitiously published), 1716 (misdated 1706 on title-page) ; authorised edn., as 'Six Town Eclogues' (under initials : Rt. Hon. L. M. W. M.), 1747.

Posthumous : 'Letters of Lady M——y W——y M——e' (3 vols.), 1763 ; 'Poetical Works of the Right Hon. Lady M——y W——y M——e,' 1781.

Collected works : 'Works,' ed. by J. Dallaway (5 vols.), 1803 ; 'Letters and Works,' third edn., ed. by W. Moy Thomas, with *memoir* (2 vols.), 1861.

MONTGOMERY (**James**), **1771-1854**. Born, at Irvine, Ayrshire, 4 Nov. 1771. To Moravian school at Fulneck, near Leeds, 1777-87. Worked as shop-assistant, 1787-92. Clerk in office of 'Sheffield Register' (afterwards 'Sheffield Iris'), April 1792 ; editor, 1794 ; proprietor, 1795-1825. Imprisoned in York Castle for libel, Jan. to April 1795, and Jan. to July 1796. Contrib. to 'Eclectic Rev.,' and other periodicals. Prolific writer of poetry. Lectured on Poetry at Royal Institution, 1830 and 1831. Crown Pension, 1835. Unmarried. Died, in Sheffield, 30 April 1854. Buried in Sheffield Cemetery.

Works : 'Prison Amusements' (under initials : J. M.), 1797 ; 'The Whisperer' (under pseud. 'Gabriel Silvertongue'), 1798 ; 'The Ocean,' 1805 ; 'The Wanderer of Switzer-land,' 1806 ; 'Poems on the abolition of the Slave Trade' (with J. Grahame and E. Benger), 1809 ; 'The West Indies,' 1810 ; 'The World before the Flood,' 1813 ; 'Verses to the Memory of the late Richard Reynolds,' 1817 ; 'Greenland,' 1819 ; 'Songs of Zion,' 1822 ; 'The Chimney - Sweeper's Friend,' 1824 ; 'Prose by a Poet' (anon.), 1824 ; 'The Christian Psalmist,' 1825 ; 'The Pelican Island,' 1826 ; 'The Christian Poet,' 1827 (2nd edn. same year) ; 'An African Valley,' 1828 ; 'An Essay on the Phrenology of the Hindoos and Negroes,' 1829 ; 'Verses in commemoration of . . . J. Hervey,' 1833 ; 'Lectures on Poetry,' 1833 ; 'A Poet's Portfolio,' 1835 ; 'Hymns for the opening of Christ Church, Newark on Trent,' 1837 ; 'Our Saviour's Miracles,' 1840 ; 'Poetical Works,' 1841 ; 'Original Hymns,' 1853.

He *edited :* Cowper's 'Poems,' 1824 ; 'Journal of Voyages and Travels, by the Rev. D. Tyerman and G. Bennet,' 1831 ; 'The Christian Correspondent,' 1837 ; Milton's 'Poetical Works,' 1843 ; 'Gleanings from Pious Authors,' 1850.

Life : 'Memoirs,' by J. Holland and J. Everett (7 vols.), 1854-56.

* **MOORE** (**Thomas**), **1779-1852.** Born, in Dublin, 28 May 1779. At school in Dublin. Contrib. verses to 'Anthologia Hibernica,' 1793. To Trin. Coll., Dublin, 1794 ; B.A., 1798 [or 1799?]. Student at Middle Temple, 1799. Admiralty Registrar at Bermuda, Aug. 1803. Left deputy in office and removed to New York, 1804 ; travelled in U.S.A. Returned to London, Nov. 1804. Contrib. to 'Edinburgh Rev.' from 1806. Married Bessie Dyke, 25 March 1811. Settled near Ashbourne. Friendship with Byron begun, 1811. Visit to Paris, 1817. His deputy at Bermuda proved defaulter for £6,000, 1818. In Paris and Italy, 1819-22. Returned to England, April 1822 ; debt to Admiralty reduced to £1,000, and paid by Lord Lansdowne's help. Settled in Wiltshire again, Nov. 1822. Literary

Fund Pension, 1835 ; Civil List Pension, 1850. Died, 25 Feb. 1852. Buried at Bromham.

Works : 'The Poetical Works of the late Thomas Little' (pseud.), 1801 ; 'Epistles, Odes, and other poems,' 1806 ; 'Irish Melodies' (10 nos.), 1807-34; 'Corruption and Intolerance' (anon.), 1808 ; 'The Sceptic' (anon.), 1809 ; 'Letter to the Roman Catholics of Dublin,' 1810 (2nd edn. same year); 'M.P.,' 1811 ; 'Intercepted Letters ; or, the Twopenny Post-Bag' (under pseud. 'Thomas Brown the Younger'), 1813 (11th edn. same year); 'National Airs,' 1815 ; 'Lines on the Death of ——[*i.e.,* Sheridan'], (anon.), 1816 ; 'The World at Westminster' (anon.), 1816 ; 'Sacred Song,' 1816 ; 'Lalla Rookh,' 1817 (6th edn. same year) ; 'The Fudge Family in Paris' (by 'Thomas Brown the Younger'), 1818 (8th edn. same year) ; 'Tom Crib's Memorial' (anon.), 1819 (4th edn. same year) ; 'Rhymes on the Road' (by 'Thomas Brown the Younger'), 1823 ; 'The Loves of the Angels,' 1823 (5th edn. same year) ; 'Fables for the Holy Alliance' (by 'Thomas Brown the Younger'), 1823 ; 'Evenings in Greece' [1825 ?] ; 'The Fudges in England' (by 'Thomas Brown the Younger'), 1825 ; 'Memoirs of Captain Rock' (anon.), 1824 ; 'Memoirs of the Life of Sheridan,' 1825 (3rd edn. same year) ; 'The Epicurean,' 1827 (with addition of 'Alciphron,' 1839); 'Rhymes of the Times' (anon.), 1827 ; 'Odes upon Cash, Corn, Catholics and other matters' (anon.), 1828 ; 'Legendary Ballads' [1830 ?]; 'The Life and Death of Lord Edward Fitzgerald' (2 vols.), 1831 ; 'The Summer Fête' [1831] ; 'Travels of an Irish Gentleman in search of a Religion' (anon.), 1833 ; 'History of Ireland' (in Lardner's 'Cabinet Cyclopædia,' 4 vols.), 1835-46 ; 'Poetical Works,' 1840 ; 'Songs, Ballads and Sacred Songs,' 1849.

Posthumous: 'Memoirs, Journals and Correspondence,' ed. by Earl Russell (8 vols.), 1853-56.

He *translated :* 'Odes of Anacreon,' 1800 ; and *edited :* Byron's 'Letters and Journals,' 1830 ; Sheridan's Works, 1833 ; Byron's Works, 1835.

Life : by H. R. Montgomery, 1860.

MORE (Hannah), 1745-1833. Born, at Stapleton, Gloucestershire, 2 Feb. 1745. Precocious abilities in childhood. Adopted literary career. Visit to London, 1774 ; friendship with Garrick begun. Play, 'The Inflexible Captive,' translated from Metastasio, performed at Exeter and Bath, 1775. Tragedy, 'Percy,' produced at Covent Garden, 10 Dec. 1777 ; 'The Fatal Falsehood,' Covent Garden, 6 May 1779. Gave up connection with stage after Garrick's death. Settled at Cowslip Green, near Bristol, 1785. Started Sunday-schools, with her sisters' help, in her parish of Blagdon, 1789. Took part in 'Blagdon Controversy,' 1800-02. Removed to Barley Wood, 1802; to Clifton, 1828. Died, at Clifton, 7 Sept. 1833. Buried at Wrington, Gloucestershire.

Works : 'The Search after Happiness,' 1773 (2nd edn. same year) ; 'The Inflexible Captive,' 1774 (3rd edn. same year) ; 'Sir Eldred of the Bower and the Bleeding Rock,' 1776 ; 'Ode to Dragon' (anon.), 1777 ; 'Essays on Various Subjects,' 1777 ; 'Percy' (anon.), 1778 ; 'Works . . . in prose and verse,' 1778 ; 'The Fatal Falsehood,' 1779 ; 'Sacred Dramas,' 1782 ; 'Florio' ; . . . and, The Bas Bleu,'1786; 'Slavery,'1788; 'Thoughts on the Importance of the Manners of the Great' (anon.), 1788 ; 'Bishop Bonnor's Ghost' (anon.), 1789 ; 'An Estimate of the Religion of the Fashionable World' (anon.), 1791 ; 'Remarks on the Speech of M. Dupont,' 1793 (3rd edn. same year) ; 'Village Politics' (under pseud. 'Will Chip'), 1793 ; 'Hints to all Ranks of People' (anon.), [1795] ; Tracts signed 'Z,' in 'Cheap Repository Tracts,' 1795-98; 'A Hymn of Praise' (anon.), [1796] ; 'Strictures on the Modern System of Female Education' (2 vols.), 1799 (3rd edn. same year) ; 'Works' (8 vols.), 1801 ; 'Hints towards forming the character of a Young Princess' (anon. ; 2 vols.), 1805 ; 'Cœlebs in search of a Wife' (anon.), 1808; 'Practical Piety' (2 vols.) 1811 (4th edn. same year); 'Christian Morals' (2 vols.), 1813 (5th edn. same year); 'Essay on the Character and Practical Writings of St. Paul,' 1815 (3rd edn. same year); 'Poems' (collected), 1816; 'Works' (19 vols.), 1818-19; 'Stories for the Middle Ranks of Society,' 1819; 'Moral Sketches of prevailing Opinions of Manners,' 1819 (5th edn. same year); 'Bible Rhymes on the Names of all the Books of the Old and New Testaments,' 1821; 'The Spirit of Prayer,' 1825 (3rd edn. same year); 'The Feast of Freedom,' 1827; 'Poems' (collected), 1829; 'Works' (11 vols.), 1830.

She *edited:* 'Poems' by Ann Yearsley, 1785.

Collected Works: 'Miscellaneous Works' (2 vols.), 1840.

Life: by H. Thompson, 1838.

Posthumous: 'Letters . . . to Zackary Macaulay,' ed. by A. Roberts, 1860.

MORE (*Sir* Thomas), **1478-1535.** Born, in London, 7 Feb. 1478. Early education at a school in London. Entered household of Archbishop of Canterbury, 1491. At Canterbury Hall, Oxford, 1492-94. Student of Law at New Inn, 1494; removed to Lincoln's Inn, 1496; called to Bar, 1501; Reader in Law, Furnivall's Inn, 1501. Friendship with Erasmus begun, 1497. Lived near the Charterhouse, and devoted himself much to religious meditation, 1499-1503. Mem. of Parliament, 1504. Married (i.) Jane Colte, 1505; lived in Bucklersbury. Travelled on Continent, 1508. Wife died, 1511 [?]; he married (ii.) Mrs. Alice Middleton within a month afterwards. Bencher of Lincoln's Inn, 1509; 'Reader,' 1511 and 1516. Under-Sheriff of London, 1510-19. On Embassy to Flanders, May to Nov. 1515. On Commission of Peace for Hampshire, 1515 and 1528. On Embassy to Calais, autumn of 1516. Master of Requests, and Privy Councillor, 1518. With King at 'Field of Cloth of Gold,' June 1520.

Knighted, and appointed Sub-Treasurer to King, 1521. With Wolsey on Embassy to Calais and Bruges, 1521. Removed to Chelsea, 1523. M.P. [for Middlesex ?], 1523. Speaker of House of Commons, April 1523. High Steward of Oxford Univ., 1524; of Cambridge Univ., 1525. Chancellor of Duchy of Lancaster, July 1525. On Embassy to Amiens, Aug. 1527; to Cambrai, July 1528. Lord High Chancellor, Oct. 1529 to May 1532. Lived in retirement, 1532-34. Imprisoned in Tower for refusing oath to Act of Succession, 17 April 1534. Indicted of High Treason, 1 July 1535. Beheaded, 6 July 1535. Buried in Church of St.-Peter-in-the-Tower.

Works: 'Libellus vere aureus nec minus salutaris quam festivus de optimo reip. statu deque nova insula Utopia' [1516], (earliest Eng. trans., by R. Robinson, 1551); 'Epigrammata,' 1518; 'Epistola ad Germanŭ Brixiŭ,' 1520; 'Eruditissimi viri G. Rossei [pseud.] opus . . . quo refellet . . . Lutheri calumnias,' 1523; 'A Dyaloge . . . of the Veneration and worshyp of Ymages, etc.,' 1529; 'Supplycacyon of Soulys' [1529?]; 'The Cōfutacyon of Tyndale's Answere' (to More's 'Dyaloge'), 1532; 'The Second parte of the Cōfutacyon,' 1533; 'The Apologye of Syr Thomas More,' 1533; 'The Debellacyon of Salem and Bizance,' 1533; 'A Letter impugnynge the erronyouse wrytyng of John Fryth against the blessed Sacrament,' 1533; 'The Answere to the fyrste parte of . . . The Souper of the Lorde,' 1534; 'The Boke of the fayre Gentylwoman,' *n.d.* (only one copy known).

Posthumous: 'A Dyaloge of Comfort against Tribulation,' 1553; 'Workes . . . wrytten . . . in the Englysh tonge,' 1557; 'Omnia Latina Opera,' 1565; 'Epistola in qua . . . respondet literis Joannis Pomerani,' 1568; 'Dissertatio Epistolica de aliquot . . . Theologastrorum ineptiis,' 1625; 'Epistola . . . ad Academiam Oxon.,' 1633.

He *translated:* Lucian's 'Dialogues' (with Erasmus), 1506 ; F. Pico's 'Lyfe of John Picus, Earl of Mirandola' [1510].

Collected Works: 1629.

Life: by T. E. Bridgett, 1891.

*MORIER (James Justinian), 1780 [?]-1849. Born, at Smyrna, 1780 [?]. Educated at Harrow. Entered Diplomatic Service, 1807. Priv. Sec. to Sir Harford Jones on Mission to Persian Court, Oct. 1807. Returned to England, Nov. 1809. To Teheran as Sec. of Embassy to Sir Gore Ouseley, July 1810. Recalled, Oct. 1815. Retired from Diplomatic Service, 1817. Married Harriet Greville. Special Commissioner in Mexico, 1824-26. Latter years of life chiefly spent at Brighton ; occupied in literature. Died there, 19 March 1849.

Works: 'A Journey through Persia, Armenia and Asia Minor,' 1812 ; 'A Second Journey through Persia, etc.,' 1818 ; 'The Adventures of Hajji Baba of Ispahan' (anon.), 1824 ; 'Zohrab the Hostage' (anon.), 1832 ; 'Ayesha' (anon.), 1834 ; 'Abel Allnutt' (anon.), 1837 ; 'An Oriental Tale' (anon.), [1839] ; 'The Adventures of Tom Spicer' (anon.), 1840 ; 'The Mirza,' 1841 ; 'Misselmah' (anon.), 1847 ; 'Martin Toutrond' (in French), 1849 (English version by the author, 1852).

He *edited:* W. Hauff's 'The Banished,' 1839 ; 'St. Roche,' 1847.

MORLEY (Henry), 1822 - 1894. Born, in London, 15 Sept. 1822. At school at Neuwied, on the Rhine. At King's Coll., London, 1838-43. Qualified as medical doctor, 1843 ; practised in Somerset, and afterwards in Shropshire, 1844-48. Kept school near Liverpool, 1848-49. Contrib. to 'Journal of Public Health,' 1849. Returned to London, 1849. Part editor of 'Household Words,' and 'All the Year Round,' 1850-65 ; Sub-editor, and subsequently editor, of 'Examiner,' same date. Married Miss Sayer, 1852. English Lecturer at King's Coll., 1857-65. Prof. of Eng. Language and Lit., University Coll., London, 1865-89. Prof. of Eng. Language and Lit., Queen's Coll., London, 1878-89. Hon. LL.D., Edinburgh, 1879. Principal of University Hall, 1882-89. Removed to Carisbrooke, Isle of Wight, 1890. Died there, 14 May 1894.

Works: 'The Dream of the Lilybell,' 1845 ; 'A Tract upon Health,' 1847 ; 'Sunrise in Italy,' 1848 ; 'How to make Home Unhealthy' (anon., from 'Journal of Public Health'), 1850 ; 'A Defence of Ignorance' (anon.), 1851 ; 'Palissy the Potter,' 1852 ; 'Jerome Cardan,' 1854 ; 'Cornelius Agrippa,' 1856 ; 'Gossip' (from 'Household Words'), 1857 ; 'Memoirs of Bartholomew Fair,' 1859 [1858]; 'Fables and Fairy Tales.' 1860 [1859] ; 'Oberon's Horn,' 1861 [1860] ; 'English Writers,' 1864-67, 1887-95 ; 'Sketches of Russian Life' (anon.), 1866 ; 'The King and the Commons,' 1868 ; 'Tables of English Literature,' 1870 ; 'First Sketch of English Literature' [1873] ; 'The Chicken Market,' 1877 ; 'Illustrations of English Religion,' 1877 ; 'Of English Literature in the Reign of Victoria,' 1881 ; 'Early Papers and some Memories,' 1891.

He *edited:* Reprint of 'The Spectator,' 1868 ; 'Cassell's Library of English Literature,' 1875-81 ; 'Morley's Universal Library,' 1883-88 ; Boswell's 'Life of Johnson,' 1885 ; 'Montaigne's Essays,' 1886 ; 'The Tales of the Sixty Mandarins' [1886]; 'Cassell's National Library,' 1886-90; Marlow's 'Faustus,' 1887 ; Rabelais' 'Gargantua,' 1888 ; Schiller's 'Poems and Plays,' 1889 ; 'Carisbrooke Library,' 1889-91 ; 'Don Quixote,' 1890 ; Bacon's 'Essays,' 1891 ; 'Companion Poets,' 1891-92 ; Aristotle's 'Politics,' Butler's 'Analogy,' 'Faust,' 'Imitation of Christ,' Molière, Æschylus, Sheridan, in 'Best Hundred Books,' 1892-93 ; Defoe's 'Journal of the Plague Year,' 1893 ; Stow's 'Survey of London,' 1893.

*MORLEY (John), b. 1838. Born, at Blackburn, Lancs., 24 Dec. 1838. At Cheltenham Coll., Feb. 1855 to 1856. Matric. Lincoln Coll., Oxford,

5 Nov. 1856 ; Scholar, 1856-60 ; B.A.,
1859 ; M.A., 1874.   Student at Lincoln's Inn, 5 April 1862; called to
Bar, 17 Nov. 1873.   For a short time
editor of 'Literary Gazette.'   Edited
'Fortnightly Rev.,' 1867 to Oct. 1882 ;
'Pall Mall Gaz.,' May 1880 to Aug.
1883 ; 'Macmillan's Mag.,' 1883-85.
Hon. LL.D., Glasgow, 1879.   M.P.
for Newcastle-on-Tyne, Feb. 1883 to
1895.   Chief Sec. for Ireland, Feb.
1886 ; and Aug. 1892 to 1895.   Privy
Councillor, 1886. Bencher of Lincoln's
Inn, 1891. Hon. LL.D., Camb., 1892.
Trustee of British Museum, 25 May
1894.   F.R.S., 1894.   M.P. Montrose,
1896.   Hon. D.C.L., Oxford, 1896.

Works : 'Modern Characteristics'
(anon.), 1865 ; 'Edmund Burke,' 1867 ;
'Critical Miscellanies,' 1st ser., 1871 ;
2nd ser., 1877 ; 'Voltaire,' 1872 (2nd
edn. same year) ; 'Rousseau' (2 vols.),
1873 ; 'The Struggle for National
Education,' 1873 ; 'Our Compromise'
(from 'Fortnightly Rev.'), 1874 ;
'Diderot and the Encyclopædists' (2
vols.), 1878 ; 'Burke '(' Eng. Men of
Letters ' ser.), 1879 ; 'Life of Richard
Cobden,' 1881 ; 'Aphorisms,' 1887 ;
'On the Study of Literature,' 1887 ;
'Walpole,' 1889 ; 'Studies in Literature,' 1891 ; 'Machiavelli ' (Romanes
lecture), 1897.

He has *edited:* 'English Men of
Letters ' series, 1878, etc. ; 'Twelve
English Statesmen,' 1888, etc.

MORRIS (*Sir* Lewis), b. 1833.
Born, at Carmarthen, 23 Jan. 1833.
At school at Carmarthen Grammar
School, 1842-48 ; at Cowbridge, 1848-
50 ; at Sherborne, 1850-52.   Matric.
Jesus Coll., Oxford, 26 June 1851 ;
Scholar, 1855 ; B.A., 1856 ; M.A.,
1858 ; Chancellor's Prize, 1858.
Student of Lincoln's Inn, 21 Nov.
1856 ; called to Bar, 18 Nov. 1861.
Practised, 1861-80.   Married Mrs.
Florence Pollard, 1868.   Hon. Fellow,
Jesus Coll., Oxford, 1877.   Greek
Order of Saviour, 1879.   Hon. Sec.
Univ. Coll. of Wales, 1879.   Mem.
of Departmental Committee on Welsh
Education, 1880.   J.P. for Carmar-
thenshire, 1880. Jubilee Medal, 1887.

Knighted, 1895.   Hon. Fellow, Trin.
College, London, 1895.   Member of
Athenæum Club.

Works : 'Songs of Two Worlds,' 1st
series (anon.), 1871 ; 2nd series, 1874 ;
3rd series, 1875 (ser. 1-3, 1878) ; 'The
Epic of Hades ' (anon.), 1876 - 77 ;
'Gwen ' (anon.), 1879 ; 'The Ode of
Life' (anon.), 1880 ; 'Poetical Works'
(3 vols.), 1882 ; 'Songs Unsung,' 1883 ;
'Gycia,' 1886 ; 'Songs of Britain,'
1887 ; Works, 1890 ; 'A Vision of
Saints,' 1890 ; 'Ode on the Marriage
of H.R.H. the Duke of York '[1893] ;
'Songs without Notes,' 1894 ; 'Idylls
and Lyrics,' 1896 ; 'Selected Poems,'
1897.

MORRIS (William), 1834 - 1896.
Born, at Walthamstow, 24 March
1834.   At Marlborough Coll., Feb.
1848 to Dec. 1851.   Matric. Exeter
Coll., Oxford, 2 June 1852 ; B.A.,
1856 ; M.A., 1875 ; Hon. Fellow,
1882.   Founded 'Oxford and Cambridge Mag.,' 1856.   For some time
after leaving Oxford studied painting
and architecture.   Married Jane
Burden, 26 April 1859.   Started
manufactory of artistic house decorations and implements, 1863. Lectured
on art in Birmingham, London and
Nottingham, 1878-81.   Contrib. to
various periodicals.   In later years,
active in support of Socialist doctrines.
Started Kelmscott Press, 1891. Died,
in London, 3 Oct. 1896.

Works [exclusive of various broad-
sides and single sheets printed for
distribution] : 'Sir Galahad,' 1858 ;
'The Defence of Guenevere,' 1858 ;
'The Life and Death of Jason,' 1867 ;
'The Earthly Paradise ' (3 vols.),
1868 [1868-70];'Love is Enough,' 1873
[1872] ; 'The Two Sides of the River,
etc.' (priv. ptd.), 1876 ; 'The Story of
Sigurd the Volsung,' 1877 [1876] ;
'The Decorative Arts' [1878]; 'Hopes
and Fears for Art,' 1882 ; 'Art and
Socialism,' 1884 ; 'Textile Fabrics,'
1884 ; 'A Summary of the Principles
of Socialism ' (with H. M. Hyndman),
1884 ; 'For Whom shall we Vote ?'
(anon.), [1884] ; 'Chants for Social-
ists,' 1885 ; 'Useful Work *v.* Useless

Toil,' 1885 ; 'The Manifesto of the Socialist League,' 1885 ; 'A Short Account of the Commune of Paris' (with E. B. Bax), 1886 ; 'The God of the Poor' [1886]; 'The Labour Question from the Socialist Standpoint,' 1886 ; 'The Aims of Art,' 1887 ; 'Alfred Linnell,' 1887 ; 'The Tables Turned,' 1887 ; 'A Dream of John Ball,' 1888 ; 'True and False Society,' 1888 ; 'Signs of Change,' 1888 ; 'A Tale of the House of the Wolfings,' 1889 ; 'The Roots of the Mountains,' 1890 [1889]; 'Monopoly,' 1890 ; 'News from Nowhere,' 1891 [1890] ; 'Poems by the Way,' 1891 ; 'The Story of the Glittering Plain,' 1891 ; 'A King's Lesson,' 1891 ; 'Under an Elm Tree,' 1891 ; 'The Socialist Ideal of Art,' 1891 ; 'Addresses' [at Birmingham Art Gallery], 1891 ; 'The Reward of Labour' [1892] ; 'Gothic Architecture,' 1893 ; 'Socialism (with E. B. Bax), 1893 ; 'The Wood beyond the World,' 1894 ; 'Letters on Socialism' (priv. ptd.), 1894 ; 'Concerning Westminster Abbey' (anon.), [1894]; 'Child Christopher,' 1895 ; 'The Well at the World's End,' 1896 ; 'The Water of the Wondrous Isles,' 1897.

He *translated :* 'Grettis Saga' (with M. E. Magnusson), 1869 ; 'Völsunga Saga' (with M. E. Magnusson), 1870 ; 'Three Northern Love-Stories' (with M. E. Magnusson), 1875 ; Virgil's 'Æneid,' 1876 [1875] ; Homer's 'Odyssey,' 1887 ; 'The Saga Library' (with M. E. Magnusson ; 5 vols.), 1891-95 ; 'The Order of Chivalry,' 1892-93 ; 'Of the Friendship of Amis and Amile,' 1894 ; 'The Tale of Beowulf' (with A. J. Wyatt), 1895 ; 'Old French Romances,' 1896; and *edited :* 'Arts and Crafts Essays,' 1893.

Collected Works : 'Poetical Works,' 1896.

MOTHERWELL (William), 1797-1835. Born, in Glasgow, 13 Oct. 1797. At school in Edinburgh, 1805-08 ; in Paisley, 1809-14. At Glasgow Univ., 1818-19. Contrib. verses to the Greenock 'Visitor,' 1818. In Sheriff-

Clerk's office, Paisley, 1819. Sheriff-Clerk Depute of Renfrewshire, May 1819 to Nov. 1829. Edited 'Paisley Mag.,' 1828 ; 'Paisley Advertiser.' 1828-30 ; 'Glasgow Courier,' 1830-35. Contrib. to 'The Day,' 1832-35. To London, to give evidence before a Committee of House of Commons, Aug. 1835. Died, in Glasgow, 1 Nov. 1835. Buried in Necropolis, Glasgow.

Works : 'Renfrewshire Characters and Scenery' (under pseud. : 'Isaac Brown '), 1824 ; 'Minstrelsy, Ancient and Modern,' 1827 ; 'Jeannie Morrison' [1832]; 'Poems, Narrative and Lyrical,' 1832.

He *edited :* 'The Harp of Renfrewshire,' 1819 ; A. Henderson's 'Scottish Proverbs,' 1832 ; Burns' 'Poems' (with Hogg), 1835.

Collected Works : ed. by J. M'Conechy, with *life,* 1846.

MOTLEY (John Lothrop), 1814-1877. Born, at Dorchester, Mass., 15 April 1814. To Harvard Univ., 1827 ; B.A., 1831. Studied at Berlin and Göttingen Universities, 1832-33. Married Mary Benjamin, 2 March 1837. Advocate, 1837. Sec. of American Legation, St. Petersburg, winter of 1841-42. Contrib. to 'North American Rev.' from 1845. Mem. of Massachusetts House of Representatives, 1849. In Europe, 1851-56. In Boston, 1856-57. Contrib. to first no. of 'Atlantic Monthly,' Nov. 1857. Returned to England, 1858. Hon. LL.D., Harvard, 1860 ; Hon. D.C.L., Oxford, 1860. To America, 1861. U. S. A. Ambassador at Vienna, 1861-67. Returned to Boston, June 1868. To England, 1868 ; resided there till his death. Ambassador to England, 1869-70. Foreign Assoc. of French Academy, 1876 ; Dr.Phil., Gröningen ; Corresp. Mem. Institute of France ; F.S.A. ; Hon. LL.D., Cambridge ; Hon. LL.D., New York ; Hon. LL.D., Leyden ; Mem. of numerous American and foreign historical societies. Last visit to America, 1875. Died, near Dorchester, Devonshire, 29 May 1877. Buried at Kensal Green.

Works: 'Morton's Hope,' 1839 ; 'Merry Mount,' 1849 ; 'History of the Rise of the Dutch Republic,' 1856 ; 'History of the United Netherlands,' vols. i., ii., 1860 ; vols. iii., iv., 1868 ; 'Causes of the Civil War in America,' 1861 ; 'Historic Progress and American Democracy,' 1869 ; 'The Life and Death of John Barneveld,' 1874.

Posthumous : 'Correspondence,' ed. by G. W. Curtis, 1889.

Life : by O. W. Holmes, 1878.

MOZLEY (James Bowling), 1813-1878. Born, at Gainsborough, Lincolnshire, 15 Sept. 1813. Family removed to Derby, 1815. At Grantham Grammar School, 1822-28. Matric. Oriel Coll., Oxford, 1 July 1830 ; B.A., 1834 ; English Essay Prize, 1835 ; M.A., 1838 ; Fellow of Magdalen Coll., 1840-56 ; B.D., 1846 ; D.D., 1871. Intimacy with Pusey at Oxford. Contrib. to 'British Critic' and 'Guardian.' Part editor of 'Christian Remembrancer,' 1845-55. Rector of Old Shoreham, Sussex, 1856-78. Married Amelia Ogle, July 1856. Bampton Lecturer, Oxford, 1865 ; Select Preacher, 1869. Canon of Worcester, 1869-71. Regius Prof. of Divinity, Oxford, and Canon of Ch. Ch., 1871-78. Died, at Shoreham, 4 Jan. 1878.

Works : 'The Influence of Ancient Oracles,' 1836 ; 'Observations on the Propositions to be submitted to Convocation' (anon.), 1845 ; 'A Treatise on the Augustinian Doctrine of Predestination,' 1855 ; 'The Primitive Doctrine of Baptismal Regeneration,' 1856 ; 'A Review of the Baptismal Controversy,' 1862 ; 'Subscription to the Articles,' 1863 ; 'Eight Lectures on Miracles,' 1865 ; 'Observations on the Colonial Church Question,' 1867 ; 'The Roman Council,' 1870 [1869] ; 'The Principle of Causation,' 1872 ; 'Sermons preached before the University of Oxford,' 1876 ; 'Ruling Ideas in Early Ages,' 1877.

Posthumous : 'Essays, Historical and Theological,' ed. by his sister, 1878 ; 'The Theory of Development' (from 'Christian Remembrancer'),

1878 ; 'Sermons, Parochial and Occasional,' 1879 ; 'Lectures, and other Theological Papers,' 1883 ; 'Letters,' ed. by his sister, with *life*, 1885 [1884].

MÜLLER (F. Max). *See* Max-Müller.

MULOCK (Dinah Maria). *See* Craik.

MUNDAY (Anthony), 1553-1633. Born, in London, 1553. Perhaps an actor in early youth. Apprenticed to a stationer, Oct. 1576. Visit to Rome, 1578. Active opponent of Catholics. Probably resumed acting soon after return to England. Married, 1583[?]. Wrote plays, pageants, and romances, 1584 - 1602. Abroad with Earl of Pembroke's company of players, 1598-99. Died, in London, 10 Aug. 1633. Buried in St. Stephen's, Coleman Street.

Works [several lost] : 'The Mirrour of Mutabilitie,' 1579 ; 'The Paine of Pleasure,' 1580 ; 'Zelavto,' 1580 ; 'A View of Sundry Examples' [1580] ; 'An Advertisement and Detence for Trueth' [1581] ; 'A Breefe Discourse of the Taking of Edm. Campion,' 1581 ; 'A Courtly Controversie betweene Love and Learning,' 1581 ; 'A Breefe and True Reporte of the Execution of Certaine Traytours' (anon.), 1582 ; 'A Discoverie of Edmund Campion and his Confederates' (anon.), 1582 ; 'A Breefe Aunswer made unto two seditious Pamphlets,' 1582 ; 'The English Romayne Lyfe,' 1582 ; 'A Watch-Woorde to England' (under initials : A. M.), 1584 ; 'Fidele and Fortunio,' 1584 ; 'A Banquet of Daintie Conceyts,' 1588 ; 'The Masque of the League and the Spanyard discovered,' 1592 ; 'The Defence of Contraries' (anon.), 1593 ; 'John a Kent and John a Cumber,' 1595 ; 'Sir John Oldcastle' (pubd. as Shakespeare's ; probably by Munday, Drayton, Hathway, and Wilson), 1600 ; 'The Downfall of Robert Earl of Huntingdon' (anon. ; with H. Chettle), 1601 ; 'The Death of Robert Earl of Huntingdon' (anon. ; with H. Chettle).

1601 ; 'The Strangest Adventure that ever happened,' 1601 ; 'The Triumphs of reunited Britannia' [1605] ; 'Campbell,' 1609 ; 'Chryso-Thriambos,' 1611 ; 'A Briefe Chronicle of the Successe of the Times,' 1611 ; 'Himatia-Poleos,' 1614 ; 'Metropolis Coronata' (anon.), 1615 ; 'Chrysanaleia,' 1616 ; 'Siderothriambos' (under initials: A. M.), 1618 ; 'The Triumphs of the Golden Fleece,' 1623.

He *translated :* 'The famous . . . Historie of Palladino,' 1588 ; 'Palmerin d'Oliva,' 1588 ; 'The Famous History of Palmendos,' 1589; 'Gerileon of England,' 1592 ; G. Telin's 'Archaioplutus,' 1592 ; 'Amadis de Gaule' (under pseud : 'Lazarus Piot'), 1595 ; 'The Second Booke of Amadis de Gaule,' 1595 ; Van den Busche's 'The Orator' (under pseud.: 'Lazarus Piot'), 1596 ; 'The Second Part of the honourable Historie of Palmerin d'Oliva,' 1597 ; Gabelhouer's 'Boock of Physicke,' 1599 ; J. Texeira's 'Strangest Adventure that ever happened,' 1601; 'Palmerin of England,' 1602 ; 'A True and admirable Historie of a Mayden of Confolens' (under initials: A. M.), 1603 ; 'The famous . . . Historie of Primaleon' (anon.), 1619 (originally pubd. 1595, but no copy known) ; and *edited :* 'Two godly . . . Sermons of Calvin,' 1584 ; Stow's 'Survey of London,' 1618.

*MURRAY (David Christie), b. 1847. Born, at West Bromwich, Staffordshire, 13 April 1847. Educated at private school at West Bromwich. On staff of 'Birmingham Morning News' as reporter, 1871-72. To London, 1873. On staff of 'Daily News' and 'World,' 1873-74. Special correspondent of 'Times' and 'Scotsman' in Russo-Turkish War, 1875. Gave up journalism soon afterwards. Lived in Belgium for some years ; afterwards travelled extensively on Continent and in Australia and New Zealand. Acted in his play, 'Ned's Chum,' produced at Globe Theatre, 16 Oct. 1891. Visit to U.S.A., 1896 ; lectured there.

Works : 'A Life's Atonement,' 1880 ; 'Joseph's Coat,' 1881 ; 'Coals of Fire,' 1882 ; 'Val Strange,' 1883 ; 'Hearts,' 1883 ; 'A Model Father' [1883] ; 'By the Gate of the Sea,' 1883 ; 'The Silver Lever,' 1884 ; 'The Way of the World,' 1884 ; 'A Bit of Human Nature,' 1885 ; 'Rainbow Gold,' 1885 ; 'First Person Singular,' 1886 ; 'Aunt Rachel,' 1886 ; 'Cynic Fortune,' 1886 ; 'A Novelist's Note-Book,' 1887 ; 'Old Blazer's Hero,' 1887 ; 'One Traveller Returns' (with H. Herman), 1887 ; 'The Weaker Vessel,' 1888 ; 'Schwartz,' 1889 ; 'The Queen's Scarf,' 1889 ; 'A Dangerous Catspaw' (with H. Murray), 1889 ; 'Wild Darrie' (with H. Herman), 1889 ; 'Paul Jones's Alias' (with H. Herman), 1890 ; 'John Vale's Guardian,' 1890 ; 'Bob Martin's Little Girl,' 1892 ; 'The Great War of 189—' (with P. H. Colomb), 1893 ; 'Time's Revenges,' 1893 ; 'A Wasted Crime,' 1893 ; 'The Making of a Novelist,' 1894 [1893] ; 'A Rising Star,' 1894 ; 'In Direst Peril,' 1894 ; 'The Investigations of John Pym,' 1895 ; 'The Martyred Fool,' 1895 ; 'Mount Despair,' 1895 ; 'A Capful o' Nails,' 1896 ; 'The Bishop's Amazement,' 1896 ; 'A Rogue's Conscience,' 1897.

MURRAY (John), 1778-1843. Born, in London, 27 Nov. 1778. Educated at various private schools. Succeeded to partnership in his father's publishing business, 1795. Dissolved partnership and started on his own account, 1802. London publisher of 'Edinburgh Rev.,' 1806. Married Anne Elliot, 6 March 1807. Started 'Quarterly Rev.,' Feb. 1809. Connection with Byron as publisher, 1811-21. Publisher for Napier, Croker, Borrow, etc. Joint publisher of 'Blackwood's Mag.,' Aug. 1818 to Jan. 1819. Published 'The Representative,' Jan. to July 1826. Died, in London, 27 June 1843.

Life : Smiles' 'A Publisher and his Friends,' 1891.

MURRAY (John), 1808 - 1892. [Eldest son of preceding.] Born, in

London, 16 April 1808. At Charter-house, July 1819 to May 1826. To Edinburgh Univ., Dec. 1826 ; B.A., 5 Jan. 1828. Travelled on Continent, 1829-30. Assisted his father in pub-lishing business from 1830. Started series of 'Murray's Hand Books,' 1836. After his father's death con-tinued publishing business. Married Marion Smith, 6 July 1847. Pub-lished 'Murray's Mag.,' 1887 - 91. Died, in London, 2 April 1892.

Works : ' Holland, Belgium, and the Rhine,' 1836 ; 'South Germany,' 1837 ; 'Switzerland,' 1838 ; ' France,' 1843 ; 'Scepticism in Geology' (anon.), 1877.

He *edited:* 'Unpublished Letters of Lawrence Sterne ' [1856].

MURRAY (Lindley), 1745-1826. Born, at Swatara, Pennsylvania, 22 April 1745. To school at Philadelphia, 1751. Soon afterwards removed with his parents to North Carolina. To New York, 1753. Assisted his father (a merchant) in business, from 1759 ; but, owing to literary tastes, ran away to a school at Burlington, New Jersey. Brought back to New York ; placed under a tutor, and studied law. Called to Bar, 1765. Married Hannah Dobson, 22 June 1767. Practised as lawyer in New York. In England, 1770-71. To England again, owing to failing health, 1784 ; settled at Holdgate, near York. De-voted remainder of life to literary and scientific pursuits. Died, at Holdgate, 16 Jan. 1826.

Works : ' The Power of Religion on the Mind' (anon.), 1787 (6th edn. same year) ; ' Some Account of the Life . . . of Sarah Grubb ' (anon.), 1792 ; 'English Grammar,' 1795 (abridged edn., by author, 1797) ; ' English Exercises,' 1797 ; ' Key ' to preceding, 1797 ; 'English Reader,' 1799 ; ' Sequel to the English Reader,' 1800 ; ' Introduction to the English Reader,' 1801 ; ' Lecteur Français,' 1802 ; ' First Book for Children,' 1804 ; ' English Spelling Book,' 1804 ; ' Introduction au Lecteur Français,' 1807 ; ' Biographical Sketch of Henry

Tuke,' 1815 ; ' Compendium of Re-ligious Truth and Practice,' 1815 ; ' The Duty and Benefit of a Daily Perusal of the Holy Scriptures in Families,' 1817.

Posthumous : ' Memoirs,' ed. by E. Frank, 1826.

He *edited :* 'Selection from Bishop Home's Commentary on the Psalms,' 1812 ; 'Extracts from the Writings of divers eminent Authors . . . re-presenting the evils . . . of Stage Plays,' 1799.

Life : by W. H. Egle, 1885.

NAIRNE (Carolina), *Baroness Nairne,* **1766-1845.** Born [Carolina Oliphant), at Gask, Perthshire, 16 Aug. 1766. Early interest in Scottish ballads. Married to Major William Murray Nairne, 2 June 1806. Lived in Edinburgh. Contributed anony-mously to the 'Scottish Minstrel,' 1821-24. Husband became Baron Nairne, the peerage being revived by Act of Parliament, June 1824. Re-moved to Clifton with her son, after her husband's death, 1829 ; to Ire-land, 1831. On Continent, autumn of 1834 to 1843. Returned to Gask, 1843. Died there, 26 Oct. 1845 ; buried there.

Works [posthumous] : ' Lays from Strathearn,' 1846 ; ' Life and Songs,' ed. by C. Rogers, 1869 (2nd edn. same year).

NAPIER (*Sir* **William Francis Patrick), 1785-1860.** Born, at Cel-bridge, Co. Kildare, 17 Dec. 1785. Educated at Celbridge Grammar School. Ensign in Royal Irish Ar-tillery, June 1800 ; Lieutenant, April 1801 ; Captain in 43rd Regt., 1804. Took part in expedition against Copenhagen, 1807 ; in Sir John Moore's campaign in Spain, winter of 1808-09. With his regiment in Portu-gal, spring of 1809 to autumn of 1811. Married Caroline Amelia Fox, Feb. 1812. In Peninsula with regiment, March 1812 to Jan. 1813 ; Major, May 1812. In England, Jan. to Aug., 1813. In Peninsula, Aug. 1813 to 1814 ; Brevet Lieut.-Colonel, Nov. 1813. Retired from active service,

14

1819. C.B., 1819. Settled in London;
took great interest in fine arts, and
contributed to various periodicals.
Removed to Bromham, Cornwall,
1826 ; to Freshford, near Bath, 1831.
Colonel, July 1830. Annual Grant
for Distinguished Services, from May
1841. Major-General, Nov. 1841.
Lieut.-Governor of Guernsey, Feb.
1842 ; removed thither, April 1842 ;
resigned, 1847. K.C.B., 27 April
1848. Lieut.-General, Nov. 1851 ;
General, Dec. 1859. Died, at Clapham Park, 10 Feb. 1860. Buried at
Norwood.

Works : 'History of the War in the
Peninsula' (6 vols.), 1828-40 (followed by five pamphlets in answer to
objections to the History, viz., 'A
Reply to Lord Strangford's "Obser-
vations,"' 1828 ; 'A Reply to various
Opponents,' 1833 ; 'Colonel Napier's
Justification of his third volume,'
1833 ; 'A Letter to Gen. Lord Vis-
count Beresford,' 1834 ; 'Counter-
Remarks to Mr. D. M. Perceval's
Remarks,' 1835) ; 'Observations Illus-
trating Sir John Moore's Campaign,'
1832 ; 'Observations on the Corn
Laws,' 1841 ; 'The Conquest of
Scinde' (2 vols.), 1845 ; 'Notes on
the State of Europe,' 1848 ; 'Six
Letters in vindication of the British
Army,' 1849 ; 'History of Sir Charles
Napier's Administration of Scinde,'
1851 ; 'Comments upon a Memor-
andum of the Duke of Wellington,'
1854 ; 'Life and Opinions of Gen.
Sir C. J. Napier' (4 vols.), 1857 ;
'Gen. Sir Charles Napier and the
Directors of the East India Company,'
1857.

He *edited :* Admiral Sir C. Napier's
'The Navy,' 1851 ; General Sir C. J.
Napier's 'Defects, Civil and Military,
of the Indian Government,' 1853, and
'William the Conqueror,' 1858.

Life : by Lord Aberdare, 1864.

NASH (Thomas), 1567-1601. Born,
at Lowestoft [?], 1567 ; baptized, Nov.
1567. Matric., St. John's Coll.,
Camb., as Sizar, Oct. 1582 ; B.A.,
1586. Settled in London, 1588 ;
adopted literary career. Took active

part in 'Martin Mar-Prelate' controversy, under pseud. of 'Pasquil.'
Play, 'The Terrors of the Night,'
produced, 1593 ; 'Summer's Last
Will and Testament,' privately performed, 1593 ; 'The Isle of Dogs,'
performed by the Lord Admiral's
Company, June 1597. In Fleet
Prison, autumn of 1597. Died,
1601.

Works : 'The Anatomie of Ab-
surditie,' 1589 ; 'A Countercuffe
given to Martin Junior' (under
pseud. : 'Pasquil'), 1589 ; 'The Re-
turne of the Renowned Cavalier Pas-
quill of England' (anon.), 1589 ;
'Martin's Month's Minde' (under
pseud. : 'Marphoreus'), 1589 ; 'The
First Parte of Pasquil's Apologie'
(anon.), 1590 ; 'A Wonderful . . .
Astrologicall Prognostication' (under
pseud. : 'Thomas Scarlet'), 1591 ;
'Pierce Pennilesse his Supplication to
the Devill,' 1592 (another edn. same
year); 'Strange Newes of the Intercept-
ing certaine Letters,' 1592; 'Christ's
Teares over Jerusalem,' 1593 ; 'The
Terrors of the Night,' 1594 ; 'The
Unfortunate Traveller, 1594 ; 'The
Tragedie of Dido' (with Mar-
lowe), 1594 ; 'Have with you to
Saffron - Walden,' 1596 ; 'Nashe's
Lenten Stuffe,' 1599 ; 'A Pleasant
Comedie called Summer's Last Will
and Testament,' 1600.

He *translated :* Evenkellius' 'Γυμ-
νασιαρχον,' 1648 ; and *edited :* Sir
Philip Sidney's 'Astrophel and Stella,'
1591.

Collected Works : ed. by Grosart (6
vols.), 1883-85.

NETTLESHIP (Henry), 1839-1893.
Born, at Kettering, Northamptonshire, 5 May 1839. At Lancing Coll.,
1849-52 ; at Durham Coll., 1852-54 ;
at Charterhouse, 1854-57. Matric.,
Corpus Christi Coll., Oxford, as
Scholar, 3 April 1857 ; Hertford
Scholarship and Gaisford Greek Prose
Prize, 1859 ; Craven Scholarship,
1861 ; B.A., 1861 ; Fellow of Lincoln
Coll., 1861-71; Tutor, 1862-68; M.A.,
1863 ; Chancellor's Latin Essay Prize,
1863. At Berlin Univ., for some

months in 1865. Assistant Master at Harrow, 1868 - 73. Married Matilda Steel, 1870. Fellow of Corpus Christi Coll., Oxford, 1873-93 ; Tutor, 1875 ; Corpus Prof. of Latin, 1878-93. Died, at Oxford, 10 July 1893.

Works: 'Suggestions introductory to a study of the Æneid,' 1875 ; 'The Roman Satura,' 1878 ; 'Ancient Lives of Vergil,' 1879 ; 'Vergil,' 1879 ; 'Moritz Haupt,' 1879 ; 'Lectures and Essays on Subjects connected with Latin Literature,' 1st series, 1885 ; 2nd series, ed. by F. Haverfield, 1885 ; 'The Study of Modern European Languages and Literatures in the University of Oxford, 1887 ; 'Passages for translation into Latin Prose,' 1887 ; 'Key' to preceding, 1887 ; 'Contributions to Latin Lexicography,' 1889 ; 'The Moral Influence of Literature : Classical Education in the Past and at Present. Two Addresses,' 1890.

He *edited:* Virgil's Works (with Prof. Conington), 1858 ; Persius' 'Satires,' 1872 ; T. H. Steel's 'Sermons,' 1882 ; Pattison's 'Essays,' 1889 ; Seyffert's 'Dict. of Classical Antiquities' (with J. E. Sandys), 1891 ; Pattison's 'Isaac Casaubon,' 2nd edn., 1892.

NEWCASTLE, Margaret Cavendish, *Duchess of.* 1624 [?]-1674. Born [Margaret Lucas], at St. John's, Essex, 1624 [?]. Maid of Honour to Queen, 1643-45 ; to Paris with her, 1645. Married there to William Cavendish, Marquis (afterwards Duke) of Newcastle, April 1645. Returned to England, 1660. Died, in London, Jan. 1674 ; buried, in Westminster Abbey, 7 Jan.

Works: 'Philosophical Fancies,' 1653 ; 'Poems and Fancies,' 1653 ; 'Philosophical and Physical Opinions,' 1655 (2nd edn., called : 'Grounds of Natural Philosophy,' 1668) ; 'The World's Olio,' 1655 ; 'Nature's Pictures,' 1656 ; 'Plays,' 1662 ; 'Orations of Divers Sorts,' 1662 ; 'Philosophical Letters,' 1664 ; 'CCXI. Sociable Letters,' 1664 ; 'Observations upon Experimental Philosophy,' 1666 ; 'The Life of . . .

William Cavendish, 1667 ; 'Plays never before printed,' 1668 ; 'The Description of a new World,' 1668. *Posthumous:* Autobiography, ed. by Sir E. Brydges, 1814.

NEWMAN (John Henry), 1801-1890. Born, in London, 21 Feb. 1801. At School at Ealing, 1808-16. Matric., Trin. Coll., Oxford, 14 Dec. 1816 ; Scholar, 1819-22 ; B.A., 1820. Student of Lincoln's Inn, 1819. Fellow of Oriel Coll., Oxford, April 1822 to 1845 ; Tutor, 1826-31. Friendship with Pusey begun, 1823. Ordained, 13 June 1824 ; Curate of St. Clement's, Oxford. Contrib. to 'Encycl. Met.,' 1824-29. Vice-Principal of Alban Hall, March 1825 to 1826. Preacher at Whitehall, 1827. Vicar of St. Mary's, Oxford, 1828 to Sept. 1843. Select Preacher, 1831-32. Travelled on Continent, winter 1832-33. Contrib. to 'Brit. Mag.,' 1833-36 ; to 'British Critic,' 1837-42. One of the promoters of the 'Oxford Movement,' 1833. Editor of 'British Critic,' 1838-41. Retired from Oxford, 1842 ; lived life of seclusion at Littlemore till 1845. Received into Roman Catholic Church, at Littlemore, 9 Oct. 1845. To Rome, Oct. 1846 ; ordained Priest there, and received degree of D.D. Returned to England, Dec. 1847. Founded Oratory at Birmingham, 1848 ; founded Oratory in London, 1850. Lost libel action brought against him by Dr. Achilli, 1853. Rector of Catholic Univ., Dublin, 1854-58. Returned to Birmingham, 1858 ; contrib. to 'Atlantis,' 1858-70 ; to 'Rambler,' 1859-60 ; to 'The Month,' 1864-66. Founded Catholic school at Edgbaston, 1859. Hon. Fellow, Trin. Coll., Oxford, 1877. Created Cardinal, 12 May 1879. Returned to Edgbaston, July 1879. Resided there till his death, 11 Aug. 1890. Buried at Rednall.

Works: 'St. Bartholomew's Eve' (anon.; with J. W. Bowden), 1821 ; 'Suggestions on behalf of the Church Missionary Society,' 1830 ; 'The Arians of the Fourth Century,' 1833 ;

14—2

'Five Letters on Church Reform' (from 'The Record'), 1833; Tracts nos. 1-3, 6-8, 10, 11, 15, 19-21, 31, 33, 34, 38, 41, 45, 47, 71, 73-75, 79, 82, 83, 85, 88, 90 in 'Tracts for the Times,' 1834-41; 'Parochial Sermons' (6 vols.), 1834-42; 'The Restoration of Suffragan Bishops,' 1835; 'Letter to Parishioners,' 1835; 'Elucidations of Dr. Hampden's Theological Statements' (anon.), 1836; 'Lyra Apostolica' (anon.), 1836; 'Letter to the Margaret Professor of Divinity,' 1836; 'Make Ventures for Christ's Sake,' 1836; 'Lectures on the Prophetical Office of the Church,' 1837; 'Letter to the Rev. G. Fausett,' 1838; 'Lectures on Justification,' 1838; 'Plain Sermons' (with others), 1839, etc.; 'The Church of the Fathers' (anon.), 1840; 'The Tamworth Reading Room' (under pseud. : 'Catholicus,' from 'The Times'), 1841; 'Letter . . . to the Rev. K. W. Jelf' (with initials : J. H. N.), 1841; 'Letter to Richard, Bishop of Oxford,' 1841; 'Sermons bearing on Subjects of the Day,' 1843; 'Sermons . . . preached before the University of Oxford,' 1843; 'Essay on the Development of Christian Doctrine,' 1845; 'The proposed Decree on the subject of No. XC.' (anon.), 1845; 'Dissertatiunculæ quædam critico - tueologicæ,' 1847; 'Loss and Gain' (anon.), 1848; 'Discourses addressed to Mixed Congregations,' 1849; 'Lectures on certain difficulties felt by Anglicans in submitting to the Catholic Church,' 1850; 'Christ upon the Waters' [1850]; 'Lectures on the present position of Catholics in England,' 1851; 'Discourses on the Scope and Nature of University Education,' 1852; 'The Second Spring,' 1852; 'Verses on Religious Subjects' (under initials : J. H. N.), 1853; 'Hymns,' 1854; 'Lectures on the History of the Turks' (anon.), 1854; 'Who's to Blame?' (from 'Catholic Standard'), 1855; 'Remarks on the Oratorian Vocation' (priv. ptd.), 1856; 'Callista' (anon.), [1856]; 'The Office and Work of the Universities,' 1856; 'Sermons preached on Various Occa-

sions,' 1857; 'Lectures and Essays on University Subjects,' 1858; 'Hymn Tunes of the Oratory' (anon. ; priv. ptd.), 1860; 'The Tree beside the Waters' [1860]; 'Verses for Penitents' (anon. ; priv. ptd.), 1860; 'Mr. Kingsley and Dr. Newman : a correspondence,' 1864; 'Apologia pro Vitâ Suâ,' 1864; 'Letter to the Rev. E. B. Pusey,' 1866 (2nd edn. same year); 'The Pope and the Revolution,' 1866; 'The Dream of Gerontius' (under initials : J. H. N.), 1866; 'Verses on Various Occasions,' 1868; 'Works' (36 vols.), 1868-81; 'Essay in Aid of a Grammar of Assent,' 1870; 'Essays, critical and historical' (2 vols.), 1872; 'The Trials of Theodoret,' 1873; 'Causes of the Rise and Success of Arianism,' 1872; 'The Heresy of Apollinaris,' 1874; 'Tracts, theological and ecclesiastical,' 1874; 'Letter . . . to . . . the Duke of Norfolk,' 1875; 'The Via Media of the English Church,' 1877; 'Two Sermons' (priv. ptd.), 1880; 'Prologue to the Andria of Terence' (priv. ptd.), 1882; 'What is of obligation for a Catholic to believe concerning the Inspiration of the Canonical Scriptures' [1884]; 'Meditations and Devotions,' 1893.

Posthumous : 'Letters and Correspondence' (2 vols.), ed. by Miss Mozley, 1891 [1890].

He *translated* Fleury's 'Ecclesiastical History,' 1842; 'Select Treatises of St. Athanasius,' 1842-44; and *edited :* R. H. Froude's 'Remains' (with Keble), 1838; Sutton's 'Godly Meditations,' 1838; 'Hymni Ecclesiæ,' 1838; 'Bibliotheca Patrum' (with Pusey and others), 1838, etc. ; Bishop Sparrow's 'Rationale upon the Book of Common Prayer,' 1839; Dr. Wells' 'The Rich Man's Duty,' 1840; 'Catena Aurea,' 1841; 'The Cistercian Saints,' pts. i., ii., 1844; 'Maxims of the Kingdom of Heaven,' 1860; Terence's 'Phormio,' 1864, and 'Eunuchus,' 1866; W. Palmer's 'Notes of a Visit to the Russian Church,' 1882; Plautus' 'Aulularia,' 1883; Terence's 'Andria,' 1883. [He also contributed prefaces to a number of theological publications, 1838-82.]

Life : by Wilfrid Meynell, 1890.

NEWTON (*Sir* **Isaac**), **1642-1727.** Born, at Woolsthorpe, Lincolnshire, 25 Dec. 1642. At Grantham Grammar School, 1654-56, 1660-61. Matric., Trin. Coll., Camb., as Subsizar, 5 June 1661 ; Scholar 28 April 1664 ; B.A., Jan. 1665. Occupied in mathematical investigations. First idea of law of Universal Gravitation, 1665. At Woolsthorpe, 1665-67. Returned to Cambridge, 1667 ; Fellow of Trin. Coll., 1 Oct. 1667 ; Lucasian Professor, 1669-1701. F.R.S., 11 Jan. 1672 ; Member of Council, 1699. M.P. for Cambridge Univ., 1689. Warden of the Mint, March 1696 ; Master, 1699. Foreign Associate of French Academy, 1699. M.P. for Cambridge Univ., Nov. 1701 to July 1702. Pres. of Royal Soc., 1703-27. Knighted, 15 April 1705. Died, at Kensington, 20 March, 1727. Buried in Westminster Abbey.

Works : Newton's published works number upwards of 230. A full list is given in G. J. Gray's 'Bibliography of the Works of Sir Isaac Newton,' 1888. The 'Principia' was published in 1687.

Collected Works : ed. by S. Horsley, (incomplete), in 5 vols., 1779-85.

Life : by Sir David Brewster, 2nd edn. 1860.

NICHOL (**John**), **1833-1894.** Born, at Montrose, 8 Sept. 1833. At school in Glasgow, 1839 - 42 ; at Western Academy, 1842-46 ; at Kelso Grammar School, 1847-48. At Glasgow Univ., Nov. 1848 to April 1855. Matric. Balliol Coll., Oxford, 24 April, 1855 ; B.A., 1859 ; Exhibitioner, 1859-61 ; M.A., 1874. Student of Gray's Inn, 12 Nov. 1859. Married Jane Stewart Bell, 10 April 1861. Prof. of Eng. Lit., Glasgow Univ., April 1862 to 1889. Lived in Glasgow. Contrib. to 'Encycl. Britannica,' 'Dict. of Nat. Biog.,' and various reviews, magazines and other periodicals. Visit to America, autumn of 1865. Hon. LL.D., St. Andrew's,

25 Feb. 1873. Removed to London, autumn of 1890. Died, at Brighton, 11 Oct. 1894. Cremated, at Woking ; ashes buried in Grange Cemetery. Edinburgh.

Works : 'Leaves' (priv. ptd.), 1854; 'Fragments of Criticism' (priv. ptd.), 1860 ; 'Inaugural Address' at Glasgow Univ., 1862 ; 'Address on National Education,' 1869 ; 'Sketch of the Early History of Scottish Poetry,' 1871 ; 'Hannibal,' 1873 ; 'Tables of European Literature and History,' 1877 [1876] ; 'Tables of Ancient Literature and History,'1877 ; 'Primer of English Composition,' 1879 ; 'Byron,' 1880 ; 'The Death of Themistocles,' 1881 ; 'Robert Burns,' 1882 ; 'American Literature,' 1882 ; 'Scotch University Reform,' 1888. 'Francis Bacon' (2 vols.), 1888-89 ; 'Questions and Exercises on English Composition' (with W. S. McCormick), 1890 ; 'Reminiscences of Ober-Ammergau,' 1890 ; 'The Teaching of English Literature in our Universities,' 1891 ; 'Thomas Carlyle,' 1892.

He *edited :* George Herbert's 'Poems,' 1863 ; Sydney Dobell's 'Poems,' 1875, and 'Thoughts on Art, etc.,' 1876.

Life : by Prof. Knight, 1896.

*NOEL (**Roden Berkeley Wriothesley**), **1834-1894.** Born, 27 Aug. 1834. Matric., Trin. Coll., Camb., 1855 ; B.A., 1858. Married Alice De Broë, 21 March 1863. Groom of Privy Chamber to Queen, 1867-71. Died suddenly, at Mainz, 26 May 1894.

Works : 'Behind the Veil,' 1863 ; 'Beatrice,' 1868 ; 'The Red Flag,' 1872 ; 'Livingstone in Africa,' 1874 ; 'The House of Ravensburg,' 1877 ; 'A Little Child's Monument,' 1881 ; 'A Philosophy of Immortality,' 1882 ; 'Songs of the Heights and Deeps,' 1885 [1884] ; 'Essays on Poetry and Poets,' 1886 ; 'A Modern Faust,' 1888 ; 'Life of Lord Byron,' 1890 ; 'Poor People's Christmas,' 1890 ; 'Selected Poems' ('Canterbury Poets' series), 1892.

Posthumous: 'My Sea, and other poems,' ed. by S. Addleshaw, 1896.

He *edited :* Selection from Spenser's poems, 1887 ; Otway's 'Plays,' 1888.

*NORRIS (William Edward), b. 1847. Born, in London, 18 Nov. 1847. At Eton, 1860-64. Student of Inner Temple, 13 Nov. 1871 ; called to Bar, 17 Nov. 1874. Married Frances Isobel Ballenden, 22 April 1871 ; she died, 1881. Resides at Torquay.

Works : 'Heaps of Money,' 1877 ; 'Mademoiselle de Mersac,' 1880 ; 'Matrimony,' 1881 [1880] ; 'No New Thing,' 1883 ; 'Thirlby Hall,' 1883 ; 'A Man of his Word,' 1885 ; 'Adrian Vidal,' 1885 ; 'My Friend Jim,' 1886 ; 'A Bachelor's Blunder,' 1886 ; 'Major and Minor,' 1887 ; 'Chris,' 1888 ; 'The Rogue,' 1888 ; 'Miss Shafto,' 1889 ; 'Mrs. Fenton,' 1889 ; 'The Baffled Conspirators,' 1890 ; 'Marcia,' 1890 ; 'Misadventure,' 1890 ; 'Jack's Father,' 1891 ; 'Miss Wentworth's Idea,' 1891 ; 'Mr. Chaine's Sons,' 1891 ; 'A Deplorable Affair,' 1893 ; 'Matthew Austin,' 1894 ; 'Saint Ann's,' 1894 ; 'A Victim of Good Luck,' 1894 ; 'The Spectre of Strathannan,' 1895 ; 'The Despotic Lady,' 1895 ; 'Billy Bellew,' 1895 ; 'The Dancer in Yellow,' 1896 ; 'Clarissa Furiosa,' 1897.

NORTH (Christopher), *pseud. See* Wilson (J.)

NORTH (Roger), 1653-1734. Born, at Tostock, Suffolk, 3 Sept. 1653. At school at Thetford, till 1666. Matric. Jesus Coll., Camb., 30 Oct. 1667. Left Cambridge, 1669 ; took no degree. Student of Middle Temple, 21 April 1669 ; called to Bar, 1675. Resided in Temple. Steward to see of Canterbury, 1678. King's Counsel, 1682. Bencher of Middle Temple. Solicitor-General to Duke of York, 1684. M.P. for Dunwich, 1685. Attorney-General to Queen, 1686. Married Mary Gayer, 1696. Last forty years of life spent at Rougham, Norfolk. Died there, 1 March 1734.

Works : 'A Discourse on Fish and Fish Ponds' (anon.), 1683.

Posthumous: 'Examen,' 1740 ; 'Life of the Rt. Hon. Francis North,' 1742; 'Lives of . . . Sir Dudley North . . . and Dr. John North,' 1744 ; 'A Discourse of the Poor,' 1753 ; 'Discourse on the Study of the Laws,' 1824 ; 'Memoires of Musick,' ed. by Dr. Rimbault, 1846 ; 'Autobiography,' ed. by A. Jessopp, 1877 ; 'Lives of the Norths, with a selection from the North correspondence . . . and Roger North's Autobiography,' ed. by Dr. Jessopp, 1890.

NORTH (*Sir* Thomas), 1535 [?]-1601[?]. Born, about 1535[?]. Probably educated at Peterhouse, Camb. Student of Lincoln's Inn, 1557. Adopted literary career. Freedom of City of Cambridge, 1568. With his brother, Lord North, on Embassy to French Court, 1574. Knighted, 1591. J.P. for Cambridge, 1592. Married (i.) Mrs. Elizabeth Rich, (ii.) Mrs. Judith Bridgewater. Pension from Queen, 1601. Died, about 1601[?].

Works : 'The Diall of Princes' (trans. from Guevara's 'Libro Aureo'), 1557 ; Translation of 'The Morall Philosophie of Doni,' 1570 ; Translation of Plutarch's 'Lives,' 1579.

NORTON (*Mrs.* Caroline Elizabeth Sarah), 1808-1877. Born [Caroline Elizabeth Sarah Sheridan], in London, 1808. Precocious literary ability. Married (i.) to Hon. George Chapple Norton, 30 June 1827 ; rupture with him, 1836. Edited 'La Belle Assemblée,' 1832-36 ; 'The English Annual,' 1834. Prolific writer of poems and novels ; contributed frequently to periodicals. Husband died, 24 Feb. 1875. Married (ii.) to Sir William Stirling-Maxwell, 1 March 1877. Died, 15 June 1877.

Works : 'The Sorrows of Rosalie' (anon.), 1829 ; 'The Undying One,' 1830 (2nd edn. same year) ; 'Poems' (Boston), 1833 ; 'The Wife and Woman's Reward' (anon.), 1835 ; 'The Dream,' 1840 ; 'Lines' [on the Queen], [1840] ; 'A Voice from the Factories' (anon.), 1836 ; 'The Child of the Islands,' 1845 ; 'Aunt Carry's

Ballads for Children,' 1847 ; 'Stuart of Dunleath,' 1851 ; 'English Laws for Women in the Nineteenth Century' (priv. ptd.), 1854 ; 'A Letter to the Queen on Lord Chancellor Cranworth's Marriage and Divorce Bill,' 1855 ; 'The Centenary Festival' (from 'Daily Scotsman'), [1859] ; 'The Lady of La Garaye,' 1862 [1861] ; 'Lost and Saved,' 1863 ; 'Old Sir Douglas' (from 'Macmillan's Mag.'), 1868 [1867].

She *edited* : 'A Residence at Sierra Leone,' 1849 ; Miss Stapleton's 'The Pastor of Silverdale,' 1867 ; 'The Rose of Jericho,' 1870.

NORTON (Thomas), **1532 - 1584.** Born, in London, 1532. Probably educated at Cambridge. Sec. to Protector. Student of Inner Temple, 1555. Married (i.) Margery Cranmer, 1556[?]. M.P. for Gatton, 1558. Called to Bar, 1560[?]. Play, 'Gorboduc' (written with T. Sackville), performed in Inner Temple Hall, 6 Jan. 1561. M.P. for Berwick, 1562. Counsel to Stationers' Company, 1562. Married (ii.) Alice Cranmer, 1567[?]. Remembrancer of City of London, Feb. 1571. M.P. for City of London, April 1571 ; re-elected, 1572 and 1580. In Rome, 1579-80. Licenser of Press, Jan. 1581. Solicitor to Merchant Taylors' Company, June 1581. Confined to his house for opinions on English Episcopacy, spring of 1582. Imprisoned in Tower on a charge of treason, Jan. 1584 ; released soon afterwards. Died, at Sharpenhoe, 10 March 1584.

Works : 'The Institution of Christian Religion' (anon.), 1562 ; 'The Tragedie of Gorboduc' (with T. Sackville, unauthorized edn., 1565 ; authorized edn., called : 'The Tragedie of Feerex and Porrex,' 1570) ; 'A Bull granted by the Pope to Dr. Harding' (anon.), [1567] ; 'A Disclosing of the Great Bull' (anon.), [1567] ; 'An Addition Declaratorie to the Bulles' (anon.), [1567] ; 'The Queenes Majestes poore deceyved Subjects,' 1569 ; 'A Warning against the dangerous Practices of Papistes' (anon.), [1569] ; 'Orations of Arsanes' (anon.; attrib. to Norton), [1570].

He *translated :* Peter Martyr's 'Epistle to the Duke of Somerset,' 1550 ; Calvin's 'Institutions of the Christian Religion,' 1561 ; Nowell's 'A Catechisme . . . of Christian Religion,' 1570.

OCCLEVE (Thomas), **1370[?]-1450** [?]. Born, about 1370[?]. Held post in Office of Privy Seal, 1406[?]-1430[?]. Died, about 1450[?].

Works : 'Poems,' ed. by G. Mason, 1796 ; 'De Regimine Principum,' ed. by T. Wright, 1860 ; Collected Works, pubd. by Early Eng. Text Soc., 1892.

O'KEEFFE (John),**1747-1833.** Born, in Dublin, 24 June 1747. At school in Dublin. Afterwards studied art there for a short time, but before long became an actor. Married Mary Heaphy, 1 Oct. 1774. First play, 'Tony Lumpkin in Town,' produced at Haymarket Theatre, 2 July 1778. To London, 1780. Plays produced at Haymarket Theatre, 1778-96 ; at Covent Garden, 1782-1813 ; at Drury Lane, 1798. [Became totally blind, 1797. Crown pension, 1820. Died, at Southampton, 4 Feb. 1833.

Works : 'The She-Gallant' (anon.), 1767 ; 'The Son - in - law,' 1779 ; 'Tony Lumpkin in Town,' 1780 ; 'The Banditti' (anon.), 1781 ; 'The Dead Alive,' 1783 ; 'The Birthday,' 1783 ; 'The Agreeable Surprise' (anon.), 1784 ; 'The Young Quaker' (anon.), 1784 ; 'The Beggar on Horseback,' 1785 ; 'Patrick in Prussia,' 1786 ; 'Peeping Tom of Coventry,' 1786 ; 'The Poor Soldier' (anon.), 1786 ; 'The Prisoner at Large,' 1788 ; 'The Farmer,' 1788 ; 'The Castle of Andalusia' (anon.), 1788 ; 'The Little Hunchback,' 1789; 'Fontainbleau,' 1790 ; 'The Basket-Maker,' 1790 ; 'Wild Oats,' 1791 ; 'Modern Antiques,' 1792 ; 'The London Hermit,' 1793 ; 'Sprigs of Laurel,' 1793 ; 'The World in a Village,' 1793 ; 'The Irish Mimic,' 1795 ; 'Life's Vagaries,' 1795 ; 'Sherwood' (anon.), 1795 ; 'Oat-

lands,' 1795; 'The Lad of the
Hills' (anon.), 1796; 'Dramatic
Works' (4 vols.), 1798; 'The High-
land Reel,' 1800; 'The Lie of a Day,'
1800; 'The Positive Man,' 1800;
'Recollections' (2 vols.), 1826.

OLDHAM (John), 1653-1683. Born,
at Shipton-Moyne, Gloucestershire,
9 Aug. 1653. Early education at
Tetbury Grammar School. Matric.,
St. Edmund Hall, Oxford, 17 June
1670; B.A., May 1674. Schoolmaster at Croydon, 1675-78. Private
tutorship at Reigate, 1678-81; afterwards in London. Died at Holme-
Pierrepoint, Nottingham (the seat of
Lord Kingston, who had been a
patron of his), 9 Dec. 1683.

Works: 'Satires upon the Jesuits'
(anon.), 1681; 'Poems and Translations,' 1683.

Posthumous: 'Remains in Prose
and Verse,' 1684.

He *translated:* 'Anacreon' (with
others), 1683.

Collected Works: in 3 vols., ed. by
E. Thompson, 1770.

OLDMIXON (John), 1673 - 1742.
Born, at Oldmixon, near Bridgwater,
1673. Early ability in verse writing.
Opera, 'The Grove,' produced at
Drury Lane, 1700; 'The Governor
of Cyprus,' Lincoln's Inn Fields, 1703.
Married Elizabeth Parry, March 1703.
Edited 'The Muses Mercury,' Jan.
1707 to Jan. 1708; 'The Medley,' Oct.
1710 to Aug. 1711. Political agent at
Bridgwater, 1718. Died, in London,
9 July 1742.

Works: 'Poems on Several Occa-
sions,' 1696; 'Thyrsis' (in Motteux's
'The Novelty'), 1697; 'A Poem
humbly addrest to the . . . Earl of
Portland,' 1698; 'The Grove,' 1700;
'The Governour of Cyprus,' 1703;
'Amores Britannici,' 1703; 'A Pas-
toral Poem on the Victories at
Schellenburgh and Blenheim,' 1704;
'The British Empire in America'
(2 vols.), 1708; 'The History of
Addresses' (anon.), 1709-10; 'Letter
to the Seven Lords, etc.' (anon.),
1711; 'Reflections on Dr. Swift's

Letter to the Earl of Oxford' (anon.),
[1712]; 'The Dutch Barrier Ours,'
1712; 'The Secret History of Eu-
rope,' pts. i., ii., 1712; pt. iii., 1713;
pt. iv., 1715; 'Life and History of
Belisarius' (anon.), 1713; 'Arcana
Gallica' (anon.), 1714; 'Memoirs of
North Britain' (anon.), 1715; 'Me-
moirs of Ireland,' 1716; 'Court
Tales' (anon.), 1717; 'Defence of
Mr. Maccartney' (anon.), 1719;
'Critical History of England' (anon.;
2 vols.), 1724-26; 'Review of Dr.
Zachary Grey's Defence' (anon.),
1725; 'Clarendon and Whitlock
Compared' (anon.), 1727; 'An Essay
on Criticism' (anon.), 1728; 'The
History of England during the Reigns
of the Royal House of Stuart' (anon.),
1730; 'Reply to Bishop Atterbury's
Vindication,' 1732; 'A Reply to the
. . . Reflections upon him in three
Weekly Miscellanies,' 1733; 'The
History of England during the Reigns
of King William and Queen Mary,
Queen Anne, King George I.,' 1735;
'The History of England during the
Reigns of Henry VIII., Edward VI.,
Queen Mary, Queen Elizabeth,' 1739;
'History and Life of Robert Blake'
(anon.; attrib. to Oldmixon), [1740?];
'The British Empire in America'
(anon.), 1741.

Posthumous: 'Memoirs of the
Press,' 1742.

He *translated:* Tasso's 'Amintas,'
1698; 'Mr. Le Clerc's Account of
the Earl of Clarendon's History of
the Civil Wars,' 1710; Bonhours'
'Arts of Logick and Rhetorick,' 1728;
and *edited:* 'The Life and Posthumous Works of A. Maynwaring,'
1715; Nixon's 'Cheshire Prophecy,'
1745.

**OLIPHANT (Carolina), afterwards
BARONESS NAIRNE,** *see* Nairne.

OLIPHANT (Laurence), 1829-1888.
Born, at Capetown, 1829. At school
near Salisbury till 1841. In Ceylon
(where his father was Chief Justice)
with private tutor, 1841-46. Travelled
on Continent with his parents, 1846-
48. Returned with them to Ceylon
and became private sec. to his father.

To England with his mother, 1851. Student at Lincoln's Inn, 1851. Began to study law at Edinburgh, 1852. Tour in Russia, winter of 1852-53. On staff of 'Daily News,' 1853. In Canada, as Sec. to Lord Elgin, 1853-54. In Crimea during the War, 1855, as correspondent to the 'Times.' In America, 1856. Sec. to Lord Elgin on the latter's mission to China and Japan, 1857-59. Visit to Italy, 1860. First Sec. to Lega- tion at Yeddo, June 1861 ; returned to England, wounded, same year. Started 'The Owl,' with Sir A. Borth- wick and others, 1864 ; contrib. to nos. 1-10. Frequent contributor to 'Blackwood's Mag.,' from 1865. M.P. for Stirling Burghs, 1865 ; resigned, 1867. To America, to join Thomas Lake Harris's community at Brocton, 1867. His mother joined him there, 1868. Returned to England, 1870. Corre- spondent for 'The Times' during Franco-Prussian War, 1870-72. Mar- ried (i.) Alice Le Strange, June 1872. Returned to Brocton with wife and mother, 1873. Employed by Harris in commercial and financial business ; his wife sent to California. In Palestine in connection with Jewish colonization there, 1879-80. Joined by his wife in England, 1880. Visit to Egypt with her, winter of 1880-81. To Brocton on account of illness of his mother, May 1881 ; she died soon afterwards. Rupture of rela- tions with Harris. To Palestine with his wife, 1882 ; settled at Haifa. Wife died, 2 Jan. 1887. Visit to America, 1888. Married (ii.) Rosamund Dale Owen, 16 Aug. 1888. Died, at Twick- enham, 23 Dec. 1888.

Works: 'A Journey to Katmandu,' 1852 ; 'The Russian Shores of the Black Sea,' 1853 (2nd edn. same year) ; 'Minnesota and the Far West,' 1855 ; 'The Transcaucasian Provinces the proper field of operation for a Christian Army,' 1855 ; 'The Trans- caucasian Campaign,' 1856 ; 'Narra- tive of the Earl of Elgin's Mission to China and Japan ' (2 vols.), 1859 ; 'Patriots and Filibusters,' 1860 ; 'Universal Suffrage and Napoleon

the Third,' 1860 ; 'On the Present State of Political Parties in America,' 1866 ; 'Piccadilly,' 1870 (2nd edn. same year) ; 'The Land of Gilead,' 1880 ; 'The Land of Khemi,' 1882 ; 'Traits and Travesties,' 1882 ; 'Altiora Peto,' 1883 ; 'Sympneumata, 1885 ; 'Massollam,' 1886 ; 'Episodes in a Life of Adventure,' 1887 ; 'Haifa,' 1887 ; 'Fashionable Philo- sophy,' 1887 ; 'The Star in the East,' 1887 ; 'Scientific Religion,' 1888.

Life : by Mrs. Oliphant, 1891.

OLIPHANT (Mrs. Margaret Oli- phant), 1828-1897. Born [Margaret Oliphant Wilson], at Wallyford, Mid- lothian, 4 April 1828. Active literary career since 1849. Married to Francis Wilson Oliphant, 4 May 1852 ; he died, 1859. Of late years resided at Wimbledon. Died there, 25 June 1897. Buried at Eton.

Works : 'Passages in the Life of Mrs. Margaret Maitland' (anon.), 1849 ; 'Merkland' (anon.), 1851 ; 'Caleb Field' (anon.), 1851 ; 'Memoirs and Resolutions of Adam Graeme' (anon.), 1852 ; 'Harry Muir' (anon.), 1853 ; 'Katie Stewart' (anon.), 1853 ; 'The Quiet Heart' (anon.), 1854 ; 'Magdalen Hepburn' (anon.), 1854 ; 'Lilliesleaf' (anon.), 1855 ; 'Zaidee,' 1856 ; 'The Three Gifts,' 1857 ; 'The Athelings,' 1857 ; 'Adam Graeme,' 1857 ; 'The Days of my Life' (anon.), 1857 ; 'Sundays,' 1858 ; 'Orphans' (anon.), 1858 ; 'The Laird of Norlaw' (anon.), 1858 ; 'Agnes Hopetoun's Schools,' 1859 ; 'Lucy Crofton' (anon.), 1860 ; 'The House on the Moor' (anon.), 1861 ; 'The Last of the Mortimers' (anon.), 1862 ; 'Life of Edward Irving' (2 vols.), 1862 (2nd edn. same year) ; 'Chronicles of Car- lingford : Salem Chapel' (anon.), 1863 ; 'Chronicles of Carlingford : The Rector and the Doctor's Family' (anon.), 1863 ; 'Heart and Cross' (anon.), 1863 ; 'Chronicles of Carlingford : The Per- petual Curate' (anon.), 1864 ; 'Agnes,' 1866 [1865] ; 'A Son of the Soil' (anon.), 1866 : 'Chronicles of Carling- ford : Miss Marjoribanks' (anon.), 1866 ; 'Madonna Mary,' 1867 ; 'Brown-

lows,' 1868 ; 'The Minister's Wife,'
1869 ; 'Historical Sketches of the
Reign of George II.' (2 vols.), 1869 ;
'The Three Brothers,' 1870 ; 'John,'
1870 ; Francis of Assisi' [1870] ;
'Squiré Arden,' 1871 ; 'Ombra,' 1872 ;
'Memoir of Count de Montalembert'
(2 vols.), 1872 ; 'At His Gates,' 1872 ;
'May,' 1873 ; 'Innocent,' 1873 ; 'A
Rose in June,' 1874 ; 'For Love and
Life,' 1874 ; 'The Story of Valentine,'
1875 ; 'Whiteladies,' 1875 ; 'The
Makers of Florence,' 1876 ; 'The
Curate in Charge' (5th edn. same
year), 1876 ; 'Phœbe, Junior,' 1876 ;
'Mrs. Arthur,' 1877 ; 'Young Musgrave,' 1877 ; 'Carita,' 1877 ; 'Dante,'
1877 ; 'Dress,' 1878 ; 'The Primrose
Path,' 1878 ; 'Within the Precincts,'
1879 ; 'The Greatest Heiress in
England,' 1880 [1879] ; 'Molière'
(with F. B. C. Tarver), 1879 ; 'He
that Will not when he May,' 1880 ;
'A Beleaguered City,' 1880 ; 'Cervantes,' 1880 ; 'Harry Joscelyn,'
1881 ; 'The Literary History of England' (3 vols.), 1882 ; 'In Trust,'
1882 ; 'A Little Pilgrim in the Unseen' (anon.), 1882 ; 'It was a Lover
and his Lass,' 1883 ; 'The Ladies
Lindores,' 1883 ; 'Sheridan,' 1883 ;
'Hester,' 1883 ; 'The Wizard's Son,'
1884 ; 'Sir Tom,' 1884 ; 'Two Stories
of the Seen and the Unseen' (anon.),
1885 ; 'Madam,' 1885 [1884]; 'Oliver's
Bride,' 1886 ; 'A Country Gentleman,'
1886 ; 'Effie Ogilvie,' 1886 ; 'A House
divided against itself,' 1886 ; 'The
Son of his Father,' 1887 ; 'The Makers
of Venice,' 1887 ; 'Joyce,' 1888 ; 'The
Second Son,' 1888 ; 'Memoir of the
Life of John Tulloch,' 1888 ; 'The
Land of Darkness' (anon.), 1888 ;
'Cousin Mary,' 1888 ; 'Lady Car,'
1889 ; 'Neighbours on the Green,'
1889 ; 'A Poor Gentleman,' 1889 ;
'Sons and Daughters,' 1890 ; 'Royal
Edinburgh,' 1890 ; 'The Mystery of
Mrs. Blencarrow' [1890] ; 'Kirsteen,'
1890 ; 'The Duke's Daughter,' 1890 ;
'Janet,' 1891 ; 'Jerusalem,' 1891 ;
'Memoir of the Life of Laurence
Oliphant,' 1891 ; 'The Railway Man
and his Children,' 1891 ; 'The Vic-
torian Age of English Literature'

(with F. R. Oliphant), 1892 ; 'The
Marriage of Elinor,' 1892 ; 'The
Cuckoo in the Nest,' 1892 ; 'Diana
Trelawny,' 1892 ; 'The Heir Pre-
sumptive and the Heir Apparent,'
1892 ; 'Thomas Chalmers,' 1893 ;
'The Sorceress,' 1893 ; 'Lady William,'
1893 ; 'Historical Characters from the
Reign of Queen Anne,' 1894 ; 'A
House in Bloomsbury,' 1894 ; 'The
'Prodigals and their Inheritance,'
1894 ; 'Two Strangers,' 1894 ; 'Who
was Lost and is Found,' 1894 ; 'Sir
Robert's Fortune,' 1895 ; 'The Makers
of Modern Rome,' 1895 ; 'A Child's
History of Scotland,' 1895 ; 'Jeanne
D'Arc,' 1896 ; 'Old Mr. Tredgold,'
1896 ; 'The Two Marys,' 1896 ; 'The
Unjust Steward,' 1896 ; 'The Ways
of Life,' 1897.

She has *edited :* 'Foreign Classics
for English Readers,' 1877, etc.

**O'SHAUGHNESSY (Arthur Wil-
liam Edgar), 1844-1881.** Born, in
London, 14 March 1844. Educated
privately. Junr. Assistant, British
Museum Library, June 1861 ; Assistant in Zoology Dept., Aug. 1863.
Married Eleanor Marston, 1873. Died
30 Jan. 1881.

Works : 'An Epic of Women,'
1870 ; 'Lays of France,' 1872 ; 'Music
and Moonlight,' 1874 ; 'Toyland'
(with his wife), 1875.

Posthumous : 'Songs of a Worker,'
ed. by A. W. N. Deacon, 1881.

Life : by L. C. Moulton, with selections from his poems, 1894.

OTWAY (Thomas), 1652-1685. Born,
at Trotton, Sussex, 3 March 1652.
Educated at Winchester Coll., till
1669. Matric., Ch. Ch., Oxford, 27
May 1669 ; left in 1672, without
degree. To London ; devoted himself
to writing plays. Produced. at Dorset
Gardens Theatre, 'Alcibiades,' 1675 ;
'Don Carlos,' 1676 ; 'Titus and
Berenice,' 1677 ; 'The Cheats of
Scapin,' 1677; 'Friendship in Fashion,'
1678. Enlisted, to serve in army in
Holland, 1678. Ensign in Duke of
Monmouth's regiment, Feb. 1678 ;
Lieutenant, Nov. 1678. Returned to
England, 1679. Produced, at Dorset

Gardens Theatre, 'The Orphan,' Feb. 1680, History and Fall of Caius Marius,' 1680 ; 'The Souldier's Fortune,' 1681 ; 'Venice Preserved,' Feb. 1682 ; 'The Atheist,' 1684. Died, in London, April 1685. Buried in St. Clement Danes Churchyard.

Works : 'Alcibiades,' 1675 ; 'Don Carlos,' 1676 ; 'Titus and Berenice ... With a farce called The Cheats of Scapin ' (adapted from Racine and Molière), 1677 ; 'Friendship in Fashion,' 1678 ; 'The Orphan,' 1680 ; ' History and Fall of Caius Marius,' 1680 ; 'The Poet's Complaint of his Muse,' 1680 ; 'The Souldier's Fortune,' 1681 ; 'Venice Preserv'd,' 1682 ; 'The Atheist,' 1684.
Posthumous : ' Windsor Castle,' 1685 ; 'The History of the Triumvirates' (trans. from the French), 1686.
Collected Works : in 2 vols., 1713 ; in 3 vols., ed. by W. T. Thornton, 1813.

*OUIDA [*pseud.*, *i.e.* **Louise de La Ramée**], b. **1840.** Born, at Bury St. Edmunds, 1840. Has resided for many years in Italy.

Works : 'Held in Bondage,' 1863 ; 'Strathmore,' 1865 ; 'Chandos,' 1866 ; 'Cecil Castlemaine's Gage,' 1867 ; 'Idalia,' 1867 ; 'Under Two Flags,' 1867 ; 'Tricotrin,' 1869 ; ' Puck ' (anon.), 1870 ; 'Folle-Farine,' 1871 ; ' A Dog of Flanders,' 1872 ; 'Pascarel,' 1873 ; 'Two Little Wooden Shoes,' 1874 ; 'Signa,' 1875 ; 'In a Winter City,' 1876 ; 'Ariadne,'1877 ; 'Friendship,' 1878 ; 'Moths,'1880 ; 'A Village Commune,' 1881 ; 'In Maremma,' 1882 ; ' Bimbi,' 1882 ; ' Frescoes,' 1883 ; 'Wanda,' 1883 ; ' Princess Napraxine,' 1884 ; 'Pipistrello,' 1884 ; 'Othmar,' 1885 ; 'A Rainy June,' 1885 ; ' Don Gesualdo,' 1886 ; ' A House Party,' 1887 ; 'Guilderoy,' 1889 ; ' Ruffino,' 1890 ; 'Syrlin,' 1890 ; 'The Tower of Taddeo,' 1890 ; 'Santa Barbara,' 1891 ; 'The New Priesthood,' 1893 ; 'The Silver Christ,' 1894 ; 'Two Offenders,' 1895 ; 'Views and Opinions,' 1895 ; 'Toxin,' 1895 ; ' Le

Selve,' 1896 ; 'The Massarenes,' 1897 ; 'Dogs,' 1897 ; 'The Altruist,' 1897.

OVERBURY (*Sir* **Thomas**), **1581-1613.** Born, at Compton-Scorpion, Warwickshire, 1581 ; baptized, 18 June. Commoner of Queen's Coll., Oxford, 1595 ; matric., 27 Feb. 1596 ; B.A., 15 Nov. 1598. Student of Middle Temple, 1597. Visit to Scotland, 1601 ; friendship with Robert Carr (afterwards Viscount Rochester) begun. In favour at Court ; appointed Server to the King. Knighted, 19 June 1608. Visit to Holland, 1609. In consequence of an intrigue imprisoned in the Tower, 26 April 1613. Died there, of slow poisoning, 15 Sept. 1613. Buried in Tower church.

Works [all posthumous] : ' A Wife now the Widow of Sir Thomas Overbury,' 1614 (4th edn. same year) ; ' The first and second parts of the Remedy of Love ' (translated from Ovid), 1620 ; 'Sir Thomas Overbury his Observations in his Travailes,' 1626.
Collected Works : ' Miscellaneous Works,' 1756 ; ' Works,' ed. by E. F. Rimbault, 1856.

PAGET (**Violet**). *See* Lee (Vernon).

PAINE (**Thomas**), **1737-1809.** Born, at Thetford, Norfolk, 29 Jan. 1737. Educated at Thetford Grammar School. At sea, 1755-56. In London, working as staymaker, 1756-58. Removed to Dover, 1758 ; to Sandwich, 1759. Married (i.) Mary Lambert, 17 Sept. 1759. She died, at Margate, 1760. Returned to Thetford, as Excise Officer, July 1761 ; to Grantham, Dec. 1762 ; to Alford, Aug. 1764. Dismissed from Office, Aug. 1765 ; restored, Feb. 1768 ; sent to Lewes ; dismissed again, April 1774. Married (ii.) Elizabeth Ollive, 26 March 1771 ; separated from her, June 1774. To Philadelphia, Nov. 1774, with introduction to Franklin. Contrib. to 'Pennsylvania Journal,' 1775-76. Editor of 'Pennsylvania Mag.,' Jan. 1775 to Aug. 1776. Took part in American War of Independence. Sec. to Committee of Foreign Affairs,

April 1777 to Jan. 1779. Clerk to Pennsylvania Assembly, Nov. 1779 to Dec. 1780. M.A., Pennsylvania Univ., 4 July 1780. Sec. to Col. Laurens on Mission to France, Feb. to Aug., 1781. Presented with estate of New Rochelle, 1784. Visit to England in connection with his invention of an iron bridge, 1787-90. To Paris, 1790. French citizen, Aug. 1793 ; Mem. of Convention, Sept. 1793. On Committee to form Republican Constitution, Oct. 1793. Imprisoned in Paris, Dec. 1793 to Nov. 1794. Returned to America, Oct. 1802. Contrib. to 'The Prospect,' 1804-05. Died, in New York, 8 July 1809.

Works : ' The Case of the Officers of Excise' (anon.), [1772] ; ' Common Sense' (anon.), 1776 ; 'Large Additions to Common Sense' (anon.), 1776 ; ' Epistle to the People called Quakers,' 1776 ; 'Dialogue between Gen. Montgomery and an American Delegate,' 1776 ; ' The American Crisis ' (13 nos. ; anon.), 1776-83 ; 'The Public Good,' 1780 ; ' Letter addressed to the Abbé Raynal,' 1782 ; ' Thoughts on the Peace,' 1783 ; ' Letter to the Earl of Shelburne,' 1783 ; ' Dissertation on Government,' 1786 ; 'Prospects on the Rubicon ' (anon.), 1787 ; (another edn., called : ' Prospects on the War,' 1793) ; 'Letter to Sir G. Staunton,' 1788 ; 'The Rights of Man ' (2 pts.), 1791-92 ; ' Address and Declaration of the Friends of Universal Peace and Liberty' [1791] ; 'Letter to the Abbé Siêyes,' 1792 ; ' Four Letters on Government,' 1792 ; ' Address to the Republic of France ' [1792] ; 'Letter addressed to the Addressers,' 1792 ; 'Speech in Convention on bringing Louis Capet to trial,' 1792 ; ' Lettre . . . au Peuple françois ' [1792] ; 'Opinion . . . concernant le judgment de Louis XVI.,' 1792 ; · Works,' 1792 ; 'Miscellaneous Articles,' 1792 ; ' Reasons for wishing to preserve the life of Louis Capet' [1793] ; 'Prospects on the War and Paper Currency,' 1793 ; ' Rational and Revealed Religion ' (anon.), 1794 ; 'The Age of Reason,' pt. i., 1794 ; pt. ii., 1795 ; pt. iii., 1811 ; ' Letter to the French Con-

vention,' 1794 ; ' Dissertations on First Principles of Government,' 1795 ; 'The Decline and Fall of the English System of Finance,' 1796 ; ' Letter to George Washington,' 1796 ; 'Agrarian Justice opposed to Agrarian Law,' 1797 ; 'Lettre . . . sur les Cultes,' 1797 ; 'Letter to the Hon. T. Erskine,' 1797 ; 'Letter to Camille Jourdan,' 1797 ; ' Atheism Refuted,' 1798 ; ' Maritime Compact,' 1801 ; ' Letter to Samuel Adams,' 1802 ; ' Letters to Citizens of the United States,' 1802 ; 'Letter to the People of England,' 1804 ; 'To the French Inhabitants of Louisiana,' 1804 ; 'To the Citizens of Pennsylvania,' 1805 ; 'On the Causes of Yellow Fever,' 1805 ; 'On Constitutions, Governments and Charters,' 1805 ; ' Observations on Gunboats,' 1806 ; 'Letter to A. A. Dean,' 1806 ; ' On the Political and Military Affairs of Europe,' 1806 ; ' To the People of New York,' 1807 ; ' On Governor Lewis's Speech,' 1807 ; 'On Mr. Hale's Resolutions,' 1807 ; ' Three Letters to Morgan Lewis,' 1807 ; ' On the question, Will there be War ?' 1807 ; ' Essay on Dreams,' 1807.

Posthumous : ' Reply to the Bishop of Llandaff,' 1810 ; ' The Origin of Freemasonry,' 1811 ; ' Miscellaneous Letters and Essays,' 1819 ; ' Miscellaneous Poems,' 1819.

Collected Works : ed. by M. D. Conway, 1894.

Life : by M. D. Conway, 3rd edn., 1893.

PALEY (William), **1743 - 1805.** Born, at Peterborough, July 1743. Educated at Giggleswick Grammar School (of which his father was headmaster). To Christ's Coll., Camb., as Sizar, Oct. 1759 ; Scholar and Exhibitioner, Dec. 1759 ; B.A., 1763 ; M.A., 1766. Schoolmaster at Greenwich, 1763-66. ·, Ordained Deacon, 1766 ; Priest, 21 Dec. 1767. Fellow of Christ's Coll., Camb., June 1766 ; Prælector, 1767-69 ; Hebrew Lecturer, 1768-70 ; Tutor, March 1771. Preacher at Whitehall, 1771-76. Rector of Musgrave, Cumberland, May 1775 to 1777. Married (i.) Jane Hewitt, 6 June 1776.

Vicar of Dalston, Cumberland, 1776-93. Vicar of Appleby, 1777 to Aug. 1782. Prebendary of Carlisle, 1780 to Jan. 1795. Archdeacon, and Rector of Great Salkeld, Aug. 1782 to May 1805 ; Chancellor of the Diocese, 1785 to Jan. 1795. Wife died, May 1791. Vicar of Aldingham, May 1792 to March 1795 ; Vicar of Stanwix, 1793 to March 1795. Prebendary of St. Pancras, St. Paul's Cathedral, Aug. 1794. Sub-dean of Lincoln, Jan. 1795. D.D., Camb., 1795. Rector of Bishop-Wearmouth, March 1795. Resided there till his death. Married (ii.) Miss Dobinson, 14 Dec. 1795. Died, at Lincoln, 25 May 1805. Buried in Carlisle Cathedral.

Works: 'A Defence on the "Considerations on the propriety of requiring a subscription to Articles of Faith '" (anon.), 1774 ; 'Caution recommended in the use . . . of Scripture Language,' 1777 ; 'Advice addressed to the Young Clergy of the Diocese of Carlisle,' 1781 ; 'A Distinction of Orders in the Church defended,' 1782 ; 'Principles of Moral and Political Philosophy,' 1785 ; 'The young Christian instructed,' 1790 ; 'Horæ Paulinæ,' 1790 (2nd edn. same year) ; 'The Use and propriety of local and occasional preaching,' 1790 ; 'Reasons for Contentment,' 1792 ; 'View of the Evidences of Christianity,' 1794 (2nd edn. same year) ; 'Dangers incidental to the Clerical Character,' 1795 ; 'A Sermon preached at the Assizes at Durham,' 1795 ; 'A Short Memoir of the Life of Edward Law, D.D.,' 1800; 'Natural Theology,' 1802.

Posthumous: 'Sermons on Several Subjects,' 1808 ; 'Sermons and Tracts,' 1808 ; 'Sermons on Various Subjects' (2 vols.), 1825.

Collected Works: in 8 vols., 1805-08 ; in 5 vols., 1819 ; etc., etc.

Life · by G. W. Meadley, 2nd edn., 1810.

PALGRAVE (*Sir* **Francis**), **1788-1861.** Born (Francis Cohen), in London, 8 July 1788. Privately educated. Articled to a firm of solicitors,

1803. Called to Bar at Middle Temple, 1827. Frequent contributor to 'Edinburgh Rev.' and 'Quarterly Rev.' Assumed surname of Palgrave, and married Elizabeth Turner, 13 Oct. 1823. Knighted, 1832. On Municipal Corporations Commission, 1832. Deputy-Keeper of the Public Records, 1836-61. F.R.S. Died, at Hampstead, 6 July 1861.

Works: 'History of England,' 1831 ; Conciliatory Reform ' [1831] ; 'The Rise and Progress of the English Commonwealth,' 1832 ; 'Reply to . . . the Statement drawn up by C. P. Cooper' (anon.), 1832 ; 'Observation on . . . the Establishment of New Municipal Corporations' (priv. ptd.), 1832 ; 'Essay on the original authority of the King's Council,' 1834 ; 'Documents and Records illustrating the History of Scotland,' 1837 ; 'Truths and Fictions of the Middle Ages,' 1837 ; 'Annual Reports' as Deputy-keeper of the Public Records, 1840-61 ; 'Handbook for Travellers in Northern Italy,' 1842 ; 'The Lord and the Vassal' (anon.), 1844 ; 'The History of Normandy and England' (4 vols.), 1851-64.

He *translated:* Homer's 'Βατραχομυομαχια,' 1797 ; and *edited:* 'Une Chanson . . . des grievouses oppressions,' 1818 ; 'Parliamentary Writs,' 1827-34 ; Wace's 'Romant des ducs de Normandie ' [1828] ; 'Rotuli Curiæ Regis,' 1835 ; 'The Antient Kalendars and Inventories of the Treasury,' 1836 ; 'Les noms et armes de Chivalers et Bachelers qe feurent en la bataylle à Borchbrigge' [1840 ?].

*PALGRAVE (**Francis Turner**), b. **1824.** [Son of preceding.] Born, at Great Yarmouth, Norfolk, 28 Sept. 1824. At Charterhouse, 1838-43. Matric., Balliol Coll., Oxford, 1 Dec. 1842 ; Scholar, 1842-47 ; Fellow of Exeter Coll., 1847-62 ; B.A., 1851 ; M.A., 1856. Vice-Principal of Training Coll. for Schoolmasters, Kneller Hall, 1850-55. Assistant-Sec., Education Dept., Privy Council, 1855.

Private Sec. to Earl Granville, 1858-64. Hon. LL.D., Edinburgh, 23 April, 1878. Prof. of Poetry at Oxford, 1885-95.

Works: 'Preciosa' (anon.), 1852; 'Idyls and Songs,' 1854; 'The Works of Alfred de Musset' [a review], 1855; 'The Passionate Pilgrim' (under pseud. 'Henry J. Thurstan'), 1858; 'The Golden Treasury,' 1861; 'Descriptive Hand-Book to the Fine Art Collection of the International Exhibition,' 1862; 'Essays on Art,' 1866; 'Hymns,' 1867; 'The Five Days' Entertainments at Wentworth Grange,' 1868; Text to 'Gems of English Art,' 1869; 'Lyrical Poems,' 1871; 'A Lyme Garland' [1874]; 'The Children's Treasury of English Song,' 1875; 'The Visions of England (2 parts), 1880-81; 'The Life of . . . Jesus Christ, illustrated from the Italian Painters,' 1885; 'Ode for the 21st of June,' 1887; 'The Treasury of Sacred Song,' 1889; 'Amenophis, and other Poems,' 1892; 'Prothalamion,' 1893; 'Golden Treasury: book second,' 1896; 'Landscape in Poetry,' 1897.

He has *edited:* Clough's 'Poems,' 1862; Vols. 3, 4, of Sir F. Palgrave's 'History of Normandy,' 1864; 'Selected Poems of Wordsworth,' 1865; 'Songs and Sonnets of Shakespeare,' 1865; 'Scott's Poems'(with memoir), 1866; 'Chrysomela, from Herrick,' 1877; Keats' 'Poems,' 1884; Tennyson's 'Lyrical Poems,' selected, 1885; J. C. Sharp's 'Glen Desseray,' 1888.

PARNELL (Thomas), 1679-1718. Born, in Dublin, 1679. To Trin. Coll., Dublin, 1693; B.A., 1697; M.A., 1700. Ordained Deacon, 1700; Priest, 1703. Minor Canon of St. Patrick's, Dublin, 16 Aug. 1704. Archdeacon of Clogher and Vicar of Clontibret, 9 Feb. 1706 to May 1716. Married Anne Minchin, 1706 [?]; she died, Aug. 1711. B.D. and D.D., Dublin, 1712. Contrib. to 'Spectator' and 'Guardian,' 1712-13. Prebendary of Dunlavin, May 1713. Mem. of 'Scriblerus Club,' 1713. Vicar of Finglas, May 1716. Died, at Chester,

Oct. 1718; buried in Holy Trinity churchyard, 24 Oct.

Works: 'An Essay on the Different Stiles of Poetry' (anon.), 1713; 'Poems,' 1717.

Posthumous: 'Poems on Several Occasions,' ed. by Pope, 1722; 'Posthumous Works,' 1758.

He *translated:* Homer's 'Battle of the Frogs and Mice,' 1717.

Collected Works: ed. by G. A. Aitken, 1894.

PARR (Samuel), 1747-1825. Born, at Harrow, 26 Jan. 1747. At Harrow School, Easter 1752 to 1761. Assisted his father in business of apothecary and surgeon, 1761-64. Began to study Divinity, 1764. To Emmanuel Coll., Camb., as Sizar, Oct. 1765; left Cambridge, 1766. Assistant-master at Harrow, Feb. 1767 to 1771. Ordained Deacon, Dec. 1769; Priest, 1778. M.A., Camb., 14 Dec. 1771. Failed in candidature for Head-mastership of Harrow, and started a school at Stanmore, Oct. 1771. Married (i.) Jane Morsingale, Nov. 1771. Head-master of Colchester Grammar School, 1777-79; of Norwich Grammar School, 1779-85. Rector of Asterby, Lincs., 1780-83. LL.D., Camb., 1781. Perpetual Curate of Hatton, Warwickshire, 1783-89. Prebendary of Wenlock Barnes, in St. Paul's Cathedral, March 1783. Removed to Hatton, 1785; took pupils there; resided there till his death. Rector of Wadenhoe, Northamptonshire, 1789. Rector of Graffham, Hunts, 1802. Wife died, 9 April 1810. Married (ii.) Mary Eyre, 17 Dec. 1816. Died, at Hatton, 6 March 1825. Buried in Hatton Church.

Works: 'Two Sermons preached at Norwich,' 1780; 'Discourse on the late Fast' (under pseud.: 'Phileleutherus Norfoliciensis'), 1781; 'Discourse on Education,' 1786; 'Præfatio ad Bellendenum de Statu,' 1787; 'Letter from Irenopolis to the Inhabitants of Eleutheropolis' (anon.), 1792 (2nd edn. same year); 'Sequel to the Printed Paper late circulated in Warwickshire,' 1792 ; 'Remarks on the Statement of Dr. C. Combe' (anon.), 1795 ; 'Spital Sermon,' 1801 ; 'A Sermon preached on the late Fast Day,' 1804 ; 'Fast Day Sermon,' 1808 ; 'Characters of the late Charles James Fox' (under pseud. ; 'Philopatris Varvicensis'; 2 vols.), 1809.

Posthumous: 'Letter to . . . Dr. Milner,' ed. by J. Lynes, 1825 ; 'Sermons preached on Several Occasions' (4 vols.), 1831.

He *edited:* G. Bellendenus's 'De Statu,' 1787 ; 'Tracts by Warburton and a Warburtonian,' 1789 ; 'Four Sermons,' 1822 ; 'Metaphysical Tracts,' 1837.

Collected Works: in 8 vols., 1828.

Life: 'Memoirs,' by W. Field, 1828.

*PATER (Walter Horatio), 1839-1894.** Born, in London, 4 Aug. 1839. Early education at a school at Enfield. At King's School, Canterbury, 1853-58. Matric. Queen's Coll., Oxford, 11 June 1858 ; B.A., 1862 ; Fellow of Brasenose Coll., 1864 ; M.A., 1865 ; Junior Dean, 1866 ; Tutor, 1867-83 ; Dean, 1871 ; Lecturer, 1873. Contrib. to 'Westminster Rev.,' 'Fortnightly Rev.,' etc., from 1866. Died, at Oxford, 30 July 1894. Buried in St. Giles's Cemetery, Oxford.

• *Works:* 'Studies in the History of the Renaissance,' 1873 ; 'Marius the Epicurean,' 1885 ; 'Imaginary Portraits,' 1887 ; 'Appreciations,' 1889 ; 'Plato and Platonism,' 1893 ; 'The Child in the House,' 1894.

Posthumous: 'Greek Studies,' ed. by C. L. Shadwell, 1895 ; 'Miscellaneous Studies,' ed. by C. L. Shadwell, 1895 ; 'Gaston de Latour,' ed. by C. L. Shadwell, 1896 ; 'Essays from the "Guardian"' (priv. ptd.), 1897.

PATMORE (Coventry Kearsey Deighton), 1823-1896. Born, at Woodford, Essex, 23 July 1823. Educated privately. First poems written about 1839. For some time engaged in scientific studies. Assistant Librarian, British Museum, 1846-65. Married (i.) Emily Augusta Andrews, 11 Sept. 1847 ; settled in Hampstead. Wife

died, 5 July 1862. Married (ii.) Mary Byles, 1865 ; settled in Sussex. After death of second wife, removed to Hastings. Removed to Lymington, 1891. Died there, 26 Nov. 1896. Buried there.

Works: 'Poems,' 1844 ; 'Tamerton Church Tower,' 1853 ; 'The Angel in the House' (anon. ; 2 pts.: 'The Betrothal,' 'The Espousals'), 1854-56 ; 'Faithful for Ever,' 1860 ; 'The Victories of Love,' 1863 ; 'Odes' (anon.; priv. ptd.), [1868] ; 'The Unknown Eros' (anon.), 1877 ; 'Florilegium Amantis' (selected poems), ed. by R. Garnett [1879] ; 'Poems' (4 vols.), [1879] ; 'How I Managed and Improved my Estate' (anon.) 1886 ; 'Poems' (2 vols.), 1887 ; 'Principle in Art,' 1889 ; 'Religio Poetæ,' 1893 ; 'The Rod, the Root, and the Flower,' 1895.

He *translated:* St. Bernard 'On the Love of God' (with M. C. Patmore), 1891 ; and *edited:* 'The Children's Garland from the Best Poets,' 1862 [1861] ; 'Bryan Waller Procter: an autobiographical fragment,' 1877.

PATTISON (Mark), 1813 - 1884. Born, at Hornby, Yorks, 10 Oct. 1813. Educated by his father. Matric. Oriel Coll., Oxford, 5 April 1832 ; B.A., 1836 ; M.A., 1840 ; Fellow of Lincoln Coll., 8 Nov. 1839 to 1860 ; Tutor, 1842-55. Ordained Deacon, 1841 ; Priest, 1843. Denyer Theological Prize, Oxford, 1841 and 1842 ; B.D., 1851. Frequent contributor to periodicals, 1842-83. Rector of Lincoln Coll., Oxford, 1861-84. Married Emilia Frances Strong, 10 Sept. 1861. Mem. of Athenæum Club, 1862. Died, at Harrogate, 30 July 1884. Buried in Harlow Hill Churchyard.

Works: 'Casauboniana' (anon.), 1840 ; 'Tendencies of Religious Thought in England, 1688-1750,' in 'Essays and Reviews,' 1860 ; 'Suggestions on Academical Organization,' 1868 [1867] ; 'Isaac Casaubon,' 1875 ; 'Milton,' 1879.

Posthumous: 'Memoirs,' ed. by his wife, 1885 ; 'Sermons,' 1885 ; 'Essays,' ed. by H. Nettleship (2 vols.), 1889.

He *edited :* Pope's 'Essay on Man,' 1869 ; Pope's 'Satires and Epistles,' 1872 ; Milton's 'Sonnets,' 1883.

*PAYN (James), b. 1830. Born, at Cheltenham, 28 Feb. 1830. Educated at Eton and at Woolwich Academy. To Trin. Coll., Camb., 1850 ; B.A., 1853. Contrib. to 'Westminster Rev.,' 'Times,' 'Nineteenth Century,' and other periodicals from 1854. Editor of 'Chambers' Journal,' 1858-74 ; of 'Cornhill Mag.,' 1882 to July 1896. Contrib. 'Notebook' to 'Illustrated London News' from 1888.

Works : 'Stories from Boccaccio,' 1852 ; 'Poems,' 1853 ; 'Stories and Sketches,' 1857 ; 'Furness Abbey' [1858]; 'Leaves from Lakeland' [1858]; 'The Foster-Brothers' (anon.), 1859 ; 'A Handbook to the English Lakes' [1859] ; 'The Bateman Household,' 1860 ; 'Richard Arbour,' 1861 (another edn., called 'A Family Scapegrace,' 1869) ; 'Melibæus in London,' 1862 ; 'Furness Abbey,' 1863; 'Lost Sir Massingberd' (anon.), 1864 ; 'Married Beneath Him' (anon.), 1865; 'People, Places, and Things' (anon.), 1865 ; 'The Clyffards of Clyffe' (anon.), 1866 ; 'Mirk Abbey' (anon.), 1866 ; 'Lights and Shadows of London Life' (anon.), 1867 ; 'The Lakes in Sunshine' (2 vols.), 1867-70 ; 'Carlyon's Year' (anon.), 1868 ; 'Blondel Parva' (anon.), 1868 ; 'Bentinck's Tutor' (anon.), 1868 ; 'Found Dead' (anon.), 1869 ; 'A County Family' (anon.), 1869 ; 'Maxims, by a Man of the World' (anon.), 1869 ; 'A Perfect Treasure' (anon.), 1869 ; 'Gwendoline's Harvest' (anon.), 1870; 'Like Father, like Son' (anon.), 1871 ; 'Not Wooed, but Won,' 1871 ; 'Cecil's Tryst' (anon.), 1872; 'A Woman's Vengeance' (anon.), 1872 ; 'Murphy's Master', (anon.), 1873 ; 'The Best of Husbands,' 1874 ; 'At her Mercy' (anon.), 1874 ; 'Walter's Word,' 1875 ; 'Halves,' 1876 ; 'Fallen Fortunes,' 1876 ; 'What he Cost Her,' 1877 ; 'By Proxy,' 1878 ; 'Less Black than we're Painted,' 1878 ; 'High Spirits,' 1879 ; 'Two Hundred Pounds Reward,' 1879 ; 'Under One Roof,' 1879 ; 'A Marine Residence,' 1879 ; 'A Confidential Agent,' 1880 ; 'From Exile,' 1881 ; 'A Grape from a Thorn,' 1881 ; 'Some Private Views,' 1881 ; 'For Cash Only' [1882] ; 'Kit,' 1883 ; 'Thicker than Water,' 1883 ; 'Some Literary Recollections,' 1884 ; 'The Canon's Ward,' 1884 ; 'In Peril and Privation,' 1885 ; 'The Talk of the Town,' 1885 ; 'The Luck of the Darrells,' 1885 ; 'The Heir of the Ages,' 1886 ; 'Glow-worm Tales,' 1887 ; 'Holiday Tasks,' 1887 ; 'A Prince of the Blood,' 1887 ; 'The Eavesdropper,' 1888 ; 'The Mystery of Mirbridge,' 1888 ; 'The Burnt Million,' 1890 ; 'Notes from the "News,"' 1890 ; 'The Word and the Will,' 1890 ; 'Sunny Stories,' 1891 ; 'A Stumble on the Threshold,' 1892 ; 'A Modern Dick Whittington,' 1892 ; 'A Trying Patient,' 1893 ; 'Gleams of Memory,' 1894 ; 'In Market Overt,' 1895 ; 'The Disappearance of George Driffeld,' 1896.

PEACOCK (Thomas Love), 1785-1836. Born, at Weymouth, 18 Oct. 1785. At a school at Englefield Green, 1793-98. To London, 1801. Sec. to Sir Home Riggs Popham, winter of 1808-09. Friendship with Shelley begun, 1812 ; visit to Edinburgh with him, 1813. Appointed to post in East India House, 1819; Chief Examiner, 1836. Married Jane Gryffydh, 20 March 1820. Settled at Lower Halliford, 1823. Retired from East India House, March 1856. Died, at Halliford, 23 Jan. 1866. Buried in Shepperton Cemetery.

Works : 'The Monks of St. Mark,' 1804 ; 'Palmyra,' 1806 ; 'The Genius of the Thames,' 1810 ; 'The Philosophy of Melancholy,' 1812 ; 'Sir Proteus' (under pseudonym : 'P. M. O'Donovan, Esq.'), 1814 ; 'Headlong Hall' (anon.), 1816 ; 'Melincourt' (anon.), 1817 ; 'Nightmare Abbey' (anon.), 1818 ; 'Sir Hornbook' (anon.) 1818 ; 'Rhododaphne' (anon.), 1818 ; 'Maid Marian' (anon.), 1822 ; 'The Misfortunes of Elphin' (anon.), 1829; 'Crotchet Castle' (anon.), 1831 ;

'Paper Money Lyrics,' 1837 ; 'Gryll Grange' (anon.), 1861.

He *translated :* 'Gli Ingannati ; and Ælia Lælia Crispis,' 1862.

Collected Works : ed., with *memoirs,* by Sir H. Cole (3 vols.), 1873 ; by R. Garnett (10 vols.), 1891.

PEARSON (John), *Bishop of Chester,* 1613-1686. Born, at Great Snoring, Norfolk, 28 Feb. 1613. At Eton, 1623 - 31. Matric., Queen's Coll., Camb., 10 June 1631 ; Scholar of King's Coll., April 1632 ; Fellow, 1634-40 ; B.A., 1635 ; M.A., 1639. Ordained, 1639. Prebendary of Salisbury Cathedral, 1640-61. Chaplain to Lord-Keeper Finch, for short time in 1640. Rector of Thorington, Suffolk, Oct. 1640 to 1846. Rector of St. Christopher-le-Stocks, London, Aug. 1660 to June 1661. Prebendary of Ely, Aug. 1660. Archdeacon of Surrey, Sept. 1660 to 1686. D.D., 1660. Chaplain to King, 1660. Master of Jesus Coll., Camb., Nov. 1660 to April 1662. Margaret Prof. of Theology, Cambridge, June 1661. Master of Trin. Coll., Camb., April 1662 to Feb. 1673. F.R.S., 1667. Bishop of Chester, Feb. 1673. Died, at Chester, 16 July 1686. Buried in Chester Cathedral.

Works : ' Anthologia Cantabrigiensis in Exanthemata Regia,' 1632 ; 'Justa Edovardo King,' 1638; 'Christ's Birth not mistimed, 1649 ; 'The Patriarchal Funeral,' 1658 ; ' An Exposition of the Creed,' 1659 ; 'No Necessity of Reformation of the Publick Doctrine of the Church of England,' 1660 ; ' An Answer to Dr. Burges his Word,' 1660 ; ' Præfatio Parænetica ad Vetus Testamentum Græcum,' 1665 ; ' Promiscuous Ordinations are destructive to the honour and safety of the Church of England ' (anon.), 1668 ; ' Vindiciæ Epistolarum S. Ignatii,' 1672 ; 'A Sermon preached . . . at the Abbey Church in Westminster,' 1673.

Posthumous. ' Opera Posthuma Chronologica ' (3 pts.), 1687-88 ; 'The Excellency of Forms of Prayer,' 1711; 'Twelve Sermons,' 1803 ; 'Adver-

saria Hesychiana,' ed. by Dean Gaisford (2 vols.), 1844 ; 'Minor Theological Works,' ed., with *memoir,* by Archdeacon Churton, 1844.

He *edited :* 'Sir L. Cary . . . his Discourse of Infallibility,' 1651 ; "Ιερο-κλεους . . . 'υπομνημα,' 1655 ; Canon Hales' ' Golden Remains,' 1659 ; 'Critici Sacri' (with others), 1660 ; 'Vetus Testamentum Græcum,' 1665.

PEELE (George), 1558[?]-1597 [?]. Born, in London, 1558 [?]. At Christ's Hospital, 1565-70 [?]. Matriculated, Broadgates Hall, Oxford, March 1571; removed to Christ Church, 1574 ; Student, 1574-79 ; B.A., 12 June 1577 ; M.A., 6 July 1579. Married, 1580 [?]. Became actor and dramatist. Notorious for dissipated life. Died, 1597 [?].

Works : 'The Aravgnement of Paris ' (anon.), 1584 ; 'The Device of the Pageant borne before Woolston Dixie, Mayor' (anon.), 1585 ; ' A Farewell . . . to Sir John Norris & Syr Francis Drake,' 1589 ; ' An Eclogue Gratulatory,' 1589 ; ' Polyhymnia,' 1590 ; ' Descensus Astreæ,' 1591 ; 'The Famous Chronicle of King Edward the first,' 1593 ; 'The Honour of the Garter ' [1593] ; ' The Battell of Alcazar ' (anon.), 1594 ; 'The Old Wives' Tale ' (under initials : G. P.), 1595.

Posthumous : ' The Love of King David and Fair Bethsabe,' 1599 ; ' Anglorum Feriæ ' (priv. ptd.), 1830. *Collected Works :* ed. by A. Dyce (3 vols.), 1829-39 ; ed. by A. H. Bullen (2 vols.), 1888.

PEPYS (Samuel), 1633-1703. Born, in London [?], 23 Feb. 1633. Early education at a school at Huntingdon. At St. Paul's School, London, as Scholar. Matric., Trin. Hall, Camb., 21 June 1650 ; removed to Magdalene Coll., as Sizar, 5 March 1651 ; B.A., 1653 ; M.A., 1660. Married Elizabeth St. Michel, 1 Dec. 1655. Sec. to Sir Edward Montagu, 1656-60. Clerk of the Acts, July 1660. Clerk of Privy Seal, July 1660. Justice of the Peace, Aug. 1660. Younger Brother of the Trinity

15

House, Feb. 1662. Mem. of Tangier Commission, Aug. 1662; Treasurer, March 1665. F.R.S., 15 Feb. 1665. Surveyor - General of Victualling Office, Oct. 1665. Visit to France and Holland, 1669. Sec. for the Affairs of the Navy, 1673. M.P. for Castle Rising, Nov. 1673. Master of Trinity House, 1676 and 1685. Governor of Christ's Hospital, 1676 ; Treasurer, 1698 ; Vice-Pres., 1699. Master of Clothworkers' Co., 1677. M.P. for Harwich, 1679. Committed to Tower, on charge of Treason, 22 May, 1679 ; released March 1680. To Tangier with Lord Dartmouth, 1683. Pres., Royal Soc., Nov. 1684. M.P. for Harwich, 1685. Sec. of Admiralty, June 1686. Resigned office, March 1689. Imprisoned in Gate-house on charge of Treason, 28 June to July, 1689. Retired to Clapham, 1690. Died there, 26 May 1703. Buried in St. Olave's, Hart Street.

Works : 'The Portugal History' (under initials : S. P., Esq.), 1677 ; 'Memoirs relating to the State of the Royal Navy' (anon.), 1690.

Posthumous : 'Diary,' ed. by Lord Braybrooke, 1825 ; ed. by H. B. Wheatley (9 vols.), 1893, etc.

PERCY (Thomas), *Bishop of Dromore,* **1729-1811.** Born, at Bridgnorth, Shropshire, 13 April, 1729. Early education at Bridgnorth Grammar School. Matric., Christ Church, Oxford, 7 July 1746 ; B.A., 1750 ; M.A., 1753. Vicar of Easton-Maudit, Northamptonshire, 1753-82. Rector of Wilby, 1756-82. Married Anne Gutteridge, 1759. Active literary life. Chaplain to George II., 1769. D.D., Camb., 1770. Dean of Carlisle, 1778-82. Bishop of Dromore, 1782. Suffered from blindness in last years of life. Died at Dromore, 30 Sept. 1811, Buried in Dromore Cathedral.

Works : 'Hau Kiou Choaun ; or, the Pleasing History' (from the Chinese ; 4 vols., anon.), 1761 ; 'Miscellaneous Pieces relating to the Chinese' (2 vols., anon.), 1762 ; 'Five Pieces of Runic Poetry, from the Islandic Language' (anon.), 1763 ;

'The Song of Solomon, newly translated' (anon.), 1764 ; 'Reliques of Ancient English Poetry' (3 vols.), 1765 ; 'A Letter describing the ride to Hulme Abbey from Alnwich' (anon.), [1765] ; 'Four Essays' (anon.), 1767 ; 'A Key to the New Testament,' 1769 ; 'A Sermon' [on John xiii. 35], 1769; 'Northern Antiquities' (anon.), 1770 ; 'The Hermit of Warkworth' (anon.), 1771 ; 'The Matrons' (anon.), 1772 ; 'Life of Dr. Oliver Goldsmith' (anon.), 1774 ; 'A Sermon' [on Prov. xxii. 6], 1790 ; 'An Essay on the Origin of the English Stage,' 1793.

He *translated :* P. H. Mallet's 'Northern Antiquities,' 1770 ; and *edited :* Surrey's 'Poems,' 1763 ; the 'Household Book of the Earl of Northumberland,' 1768.

PHILIPS (Ambrose), 1675 [?]-1749. Born, in Shropshire [?], 1675 [?]. Early education at Shrewsbury School. To St. John's Coll., Camb., as Sizar, 15 June 1693 ; B.A., 1696 ; Fellow of St. John's Coll., 28 March 1699 to 24 March 1708 ; M.A., 1700. Visits to Continent, 1703 and 1710. J.P. for Westminster, 1714. Commissioner for Lottery, 1717. Founded and edited 'The Freethinker,' 1718-19. To Ireland, as Sec. to Bishop of Armagh, 1724. M.P. for Co. Armagh in Irish Parliament, 1725. Sec. to Lord Chancellor, Dec. 1726. Judge of Prerogative Court, Aug. 1733. Returned to London, 1748. Died there, 18 June 1749.

Works : 'The Life of John Williams,' 1700 ; 'Pastorals' (from Tonson's 'Miscellany'), 1710 ; 'The Distrest Mother,' 1712 ; 'An Epistle to Charles, Lord Halifax,' 1714 ; 'Epistle to the Hon. James Craggs,' 1717 ; 'Papers from "The Freethinker"' (3 vols.), 1718-19 ; 'The Briton,' 1722; 'Humphrey, Duke of Gloucester,' 1723 ; 'A Collection of Old Ballads,' 1723 ; 'An Ode on the Death of William, Earl Cowper,' 1728 ; 'The Tea-Pot' [1725?] ; 'To the Hon. Miss Carteret,' 1725 ; 'To . . . Lord Carteret,' 1726 ; 'Codrus,' 1728 ; 'Pastorals, Epistles, Odes, etc.,' 1748.

He *translated:* 'The Odes of Sappho,' 1713 ; P. de La Croix's 'Persian Tales,' 1709.

PHILIPS (Katherine), 1631-1664. Born [Katherine Fowler], in London, 1 Jan. 1631. Educated in London. Married to James Philips, 1647. After her marriage, formed society of persons known by fanciful names ; herself adopting that of Orinda. Tragedy, 'Pompey' (from Corneille), produced at Smock-Alley Theatre, Dublin, Feb. 1663. Died, in London, 22 June 1664. Buried in church of St. Benet Sherehog.

Works: 'Pompey' (anon.), 1663 (3rd edn., same year) ; 'Poems' (unauthorized edition), 1664.
Posthumous: 'Poems,' ed. by Sir C. Cotterel, 1667 ; 'Letters of Orinda to Poliarchus,' 1705.

PINERO (Arthur Wing), b. 1855. Born, in London, 24 May 1855. Educated for the legal profession. First appearance as an actor, Theatre Royal, Edinburgh, 22 June 1874 ; acted there till Feb. 1875. At Alexandra Theatre, Liverpool, 1875-76. First appearance in London, Globe Theatre, 15 April 1876. At Lyceum Theatre, Sept. 1876 to Aug. 1880. Married Mrs. Myra Emily Moore Hamilton ('Miss Myra Holme'), 19 April 1883. Play, 'Two Can Play at That Game,' produced at Lyceum Theatre, 1877 ; '£200 a Year,' Globe, Oct. 1877 ; 'Daisy's Escape,' Lyceum, Sept. 1879 ; 'Hester's Mystery,' Folly (afterwards Toole's), June 1880 ; 'Bygones,' Lyceum, Sept. 1880 ; 'The Money-Spinner,' Prince's Theatre, Manchester, 5 Nov. 1880, St. James's, London, 8 Jan. 1881 ; 'The Squire,' St. James's, 29 Dec. 1881 ; 'The Rector,' Court, 24 March 1883 ; 'Lords and Commons,' Haymarket, 24 Nov. 1883 ; 'The Rocket,' Prince of Wales's Theatre, Liverpool, 30 July 1883, 'Low Water,' Globe, 12 Jan. 1884 ; 'The Ironmaster' (adapt.), St. James's, 17 April, 1884 : 'In Chancery,' Lyceum Theatre, Edinburgh, 19 Sept. 1884 ; 'Mayfair,' St. James's, 31 Oct. 1885 ; 'The Magistrate,'

Court, 21 March 1885 ; 'The Schoolmistress,' Court, 27 March 1886 ; 'The Hobby Horse,' St. James's, 23 Oct. 1886 ; 'Dandy Dick,' Court, 27 Jan. 1887 ; 'Sweet Lavender,' Terry's, 21 March 1888 ; 'The Weaker Sex,' Theatre Royal, Manchester, 20 Sept. 1888, Court Theatre, London, 16 March 1889 ; 'The Profligate,' Garrick, 24 April 1889 ; 'The Cabinet Minister,' Court, 23 April 1890 ; 'Lady Bountiful,' Garrick, 7 March 1891 ; 'The Times,' Terry's, 24 Oct. 1891 ; 'The Amazons,' Court, 7 March 1893 ; 'The Second Mrs. Tanqueray,' St. James's, 27 May 1893 ; 'The Notorious Mrs. Ebbsmith,' Garrick, 13 March 1895 ; 'The Benefit of the Doubt,' Comedy, 16 Oct. 1895 ; 'The Princess and the Butterfly,' St. James's, 29 March 1897.

Works: 'Plays' (including : 'The Profligate,' 'Lady Bountiful,' 'The Times,' 'The Magistrate,' 'The Hobby Horse,' 'The Cabinet Minister,' 'Dandy Dick,' 'Sweet Lavender,' 'The Schoolmistress,' 'The Weaker Sex,' 'The Amazons '), with prefaces by M. C. Salaman (11 vols.), 1891-95 ; 'The Second Mrs. Tanqueray,' 1895 ; 'The Notorious Mrs. Ebbsmith,' 1895 ; 'The Benefit of the Doubt,' 1896.

PINKERTON (John), 1758-1826. Born, in Edinburgh, 17 Feb. 1758. Educated at a school in Edinburgh, and at Lanark Grammar School. Articled to a lawyer, 1775-80. To London, 1781. Active literary life. Contrib. to 'Gentleman's Mag.,' 1788. Married Miss Burgess, 1793. For some time editor of 'Critical Rev.' During later years of life resided in Paris. Died there, 10 March 1826.

Works: 'Craigmillar Castle' (anon.), 1776 ; 'Walpoliana' (anon.), 1779 ; 'Rimes' (anon.), 1781 ; 'Two Dithyrambic Odes' (anon.), 1782 ; 'Select Scottish Tragic Ballads' (anon., 2 vols.), 1781-83 ; 'Essay on Medals' (anon.), 1784 ; 'Letters of Literature' (anon.), 1785 ; 'Ancient Scottish Poems never before in print,' 1786 ; 'The Treasury of Wit' (under pseud. 'H. Bennet, M.A.'), 1787 ; 'Disserta-

15—2

tion on the Origin and Progress of the Scythians,' 1787 ; 'Vitæ Antiquæ Sanctorum qui habitaverunt in . . . Scotia,' 1789 ; 'Enquiry into the History of Scotland preceding the Reign of Malcolm III.,' 1789 ; 'Medallic History of England' (anon.), 1790 ; 'Scottish Poems reprinted from scarce editions,' 1792 ; 'The History of Scotland from the Accession of the House of Stuart to that of Mary,' 1797 ; 'Iconographia Scotica,' 1797 ; 'The Scottish Gallery,' 1799 ; 'Modern Geography' (2 vols.), 1802 ; 'Recollections of Paris' (2 vols.), 1806 ; 'General Collection of . . . Voyages and Travels' (17 vols..), 1808-14 ; 'New Modern Atlas,' 1808-09 ; 'Petralogy' (2 vols.), 1811.

He *edited :* Barbour's 'The Bruce,' 1790.

Posthumous : 'Literary Correspondence' (2 vols.), 1830.

PIOZZI (*Mrs.* **Hester Lynch**), 1741-1821. Born [Hester Lynch Salusbury], at Bodvel, Carnarvonshire, 16 Jan. 1741. Contrib. to 'St. James's Chronicle' while still a young girl. Married to Henry Thrale, 11 Oct. 1763. Friendship with Johnson begun, 1764. Husband died, 4 April 1781. Intimacy with Gabriel Piozzi begun, 1780 ; married to him, in London (at Roman Catholic Church), 23 July, in Bath (at Anglican Church), 25 July 1784. In Italy, 1784-87. Lived at Streatham, 1787-95 ; in Wales, 1795 to 1809. Husband died, March 1809 ; after that she resided mainly in Bath. Died, 2 May 1821.

Works : 'Anecdotes of the late Samuel Johnson,' 1786 ; 'Letters to and from the late Samuel Johnson,' 1788 ; 'Observations and Reflections made in the course of a Journey through France, Italy, and Germany' (2 vols.), 1789 (another edn. same year) ; 'British Synonymy,' 1794 ; 'Retrospection' (2 vols.), 1801.

`  ` *Posthumous :* 'Two Letters . . . to W. A. Conway,' 1843 ; 'Autobiography, Letters, and Literary Remains,' ed. by A. Hayward (2 vols.), 1861 (2nd edn. same year).

She *edited :* 'The Arno Miscellany,' 1784.

Life : by L. B. Seeley, 1891.

PLANCHÉ (**James Robinson**), **1796-1880.** Born, in London, 27 Feb. 1796. Articled to a bookseller, 1810. Upwards of seventy dramatic pieces produced, 1818-71. Married Elizabeth St. George, 26 April 1821. F.S.A., 24 Dec. 1829 to 1852. Rouge Croix Pursuivant at Arms, Heralds' Coll., 13 Feb. 1854 ; Somerset Herald, 7 June 1866. Civil List Pension, June 1871. Died, in Chelsea, 30 May 1880.

Works [exclusive of a number of dramas, burlesques, and extravaganzas, mostly printed in 'Lacy's Acting Edition of Plays,' or in Cumberland's' or Duncombe's ' British Theatre '] : 'Costumes of Shakespeare's King John ' (5 pts.), 1823-25 ; 'Shere Afkun,' 1823 ; 'Descent of the Danube,' 1828 ; 'History of British Costumes,' 1834 ; 'A Catalogue of the collection of Ancient Arms . . . the property of Bernard Brocas,' 1834 ; 'Continental Gleanings' [1836 ?] ; 'Regal Records,' 1838 ; 'Souvenir of the Bal Costumé . . . at Buckingham Palace,' 1843 ; 'The Pursuivant of Arms,' 1852 ; 'A Corner of Kent,' 1864 ; 'Pieces of Pleasantry for Private Performance' [1868] ; 'Recollections and Reflections' (2 vols.), 1872 ; 'William with the Ring,' 1873 ; 'The Conqueror and his Companions' (2 vols.), 1874 ; 'A Cyclopædia of Costume' (2 vols.), 1876-79 ; 'Suggestions for establishing an English Art Theatre,' 1879 ; 'Extravaganzas,' ed. by T. F. D. Croker and S. Tucker (5 vols.), 1879 ; 'Songs and Poems,' 1881.

He *translated :* Hoffmann's 'King Nutcracker,' 1853 ; Countess d'Aulnoy's 'Fairy Tales,' 1885 ; 'Four-and-twenty Fairy Tales selected from those of Perrault, etc.,' 1858 ; and *edited :* H. Clark's 'Introduction to Heraldry,' 1866.

POE (**Edgar Allan**), **1809-1849.** Born, in Boston, Mass., 19 Jan. 1809. Left an orphan while very young. Adopted by John Allan, of Richmond,

Va. To England, 1815. At school at Stoke Newington, 1815-20. Returned to America. At school at Richmond, Va., 1820-25. Matric. Univ. of Virginia, 14 Feb. 1826; left university, Dec. 1826. In Boston, 1827-28. Enlisted as private in U.S. Army under name of Edgar A. Perry, 26 May 1828 ; Sergeant-Major, 1 Jan. 1829 ; obtained discharge, April 1829. To Military Academy, West Point, July 1830 ; cashiered, March 1831. In Baltimore, 1831-35. To Richmond, June 1835. Editor of 'Southern Literary Messenger,' Nov. 1835 to Jan. 1837. Married Virginia Clemm, 16 May 1836. To New York, 1837. Removed to Philadelphia, June 1838. Assistant-editor of Philadelphia 'Gentleman's Mag.,' July 1839 to June 1840. Editor of 'Graham's Mag.,' April 1841 to spring of 1842. To New York, April 1844. On staff of 'Evening Mirror,' Oct. 1844 to April 1845. Lectured before New York Historical Soc., 28 Feb. 1845. Assistant-editor of 'Broadway Journal,' March to Dec., 1845. Removed to Fordham, spring of 1846. Wife died, 30 Jan. 1847. Engaged to be married to Mrs. Sarah Elmira Shelton. Started to Philadelphia for the marriage, 30 Sept. 1849 ; died, at Baltimore, 3 Oct. 1849.

Works : 'Tamerlane, and other Poems' (anon.), 1827 ; 'Al-Aaraaf, Tamerlane, and Minor Poems,' 1829 ; 'Poems,' 1831 ; 'Narrative of Arthur Gordon Pym' (anon.), 1838 ; 'The Conchologist's First Book,' 1839 ; 'Tales of the Grotesque and the Arabesque' (2 vols.), 1840 ; 'The Raven, and other Poems,' 1845 ; 'Tales,' 1845 ; 'Eureka,' 1848. *Collected Works :* ed. by R. W. Griswold (3 vols.), 1850. *Life :* by G. E. Woodberry, 1885.

*POLLOCK (*Sir* **Frederick**), *Bart.*, b. **1845.** Born, in London, 10 Dec. 1845. At Eton, 1858-63. To Trin. Coll., Camb., 1863 ; Browne's Medallist, 1866 ; B.A., 1867 ; Chancellor's Medallist, 1867 ; Fellow, 1868 ; M.A., 1870. Student at Lincoln's Inn, 9 Jan. 1868 ; called to Bar, 1 May 1871. Married Georgina Harriet Deffel, 13 Aug. 1873. Hon. LL.D., Edinburgh, 1880. Prof. of Jurisprudence, Univ. College, London, 1882-83. Corpus Prof. of Jurisprudence, Oxford, and Fellow of Corpus Christi Coll., 1883 ; re-elected, 1888 and 1893. M.A., Oxford, by decree, 27 Feb. 1883. Prof. of Common Law, Inns of Court, 1884-90. Editor of 'Law Quarterly Rev.,' since 1885. Sometime Hon. Librarian Alpine Club. Succeeded to Baronetcy, 1888. Hon. Mem., Juridical Soc. of Berlin, 1890. To Trinidad, as Mem. of Judicial Inquiry Commission, 1892. Hon. LL.D., Dublin, 1892. Corresp. Mem. of Institute of France, 1893. Tagore Law Lecturer, Calcutta, winter of 1893-94. Hon. LL.D., Harvard, 1895. Editor of 'Law Reports' since 1895.

Works : 'A Tabular View of the Supreme Court of Judicature Bill' [1873] ; 'Principles of Contract,' 1876 [1875] ; 'Leading Cases done into English' (anon.), 1876 (enlarged edn., 1892) ; 'A Digest of the Law of Partnership,' 1877 ; 'Spinoza,' 1880 ; 'Essays in Jurisprudence and Ethics,' 1882 ; 'The Fishery Laws,' 1883 ; 'The Land Laws,' 1883 ; 'English Opportunities and Duties in the Historical and Comparative Study of the Law,' 1883 ; 'The Law of Torts,' 1887 ; 'An Essay on Possession in the Common Law' (with R. S. Wright), 1888 ; 'An Introduction to the History of the Science of Politics,' 1890 ; 'Oxford Lectures,' 1890 ; 'The Early History of Mountaineering' (chapter in Badminton Series volume), 1892 ; 'The History of English Law before the time of Edward I.' (with F. W. Maitland ; 2 vols.), 1895 ; 'A First Book of Jurisprudence,' 1896.

He has *edited :* W. K. Clifford's 'Lectures and Essays' (with Leslie Stephen), 1879 ; 'The Revised Reports,' 1891, etc.

POPE (**Alexander**), **1688 - 1744.** Born, in London, 21 May 1688. Educated at schools at Twyford (near Winchester) and in London. Precocious literary ability. Contrib. to Tonson's 'Poetical Miscellanies,' 1709; to 'Lintot's Miscellany,' 1712; to 'Spectator,' 1712; to 'Guardian,' 1713. Friendship with Addison begun, 1711. Rupture with Addison, and formation of friendship with Swift, 1713. Friendship with Lady Mary Wortley Montagu [q.v.], 1715-22; with Martha Blount, 1712-44. Contrib. to Steele's 'Poetical Miscellanies,' 1714. Active literary and social career. Removed to Twickenham, 1719; resided there till his death. Edited 'Grub Street Journal,' Jan. 1730 to Dec. 1737. Friendship with Arbuthnot, Gay, Bolingbroke, Warburton, etc. Events in life mainly literary or controversial. Died, at Twickenham, 30 May 1744. Buried in Twickenham Church.

Works: 'Essay on Criticism' (anon.), 1711; 'Miscellanies' (with Swift; anon.), 1711; 'Ode for Music,' 1713; 'Windsor Forest,' 1713; 'Narrative of Dr. Robert Norris' (anon.), 1713; 'The Rape of the Lock' (from 'Lintot's Miscellany'), 1714; 'A Key to the Lock' (under (pseud., 'Esdras Barnivelt), 1715; 'The Temple of Fame,' 1715; 'To the Ingenious Mr. Moore,' 1716; 'A full and true Account of a horrid . . . Revenge by Poison on the body of Mr. Edmund Curll' (anon), 1716; 'The Worms,' 1716; 'A Roman Catholic version of the First Psalm,' 1716; 'Works,' 1717; 'Three Hours after Marriage' (with Gay and Arbuthnot). 1717; 'A Complete Key to the Non-Juror' (anon.), 1718; 'Eloisa to Abelard,' 1720; 'Miscellanea,' 1727 [1726]; 'Several Copies of Verses on occasion of Mr. Gulliver's Travels' (anon.), 1727; 'Miscellanies' (with Swift), vols. i., ii., 1727; vol. iii., 1728; vol. iv., 1732; 'The Dunciad,' 1728 (4th edn. same year); 'Of False Taste,' 1731; 'Of the Use of Riches,' 1732; 'Esther' (oratorio libretto; written with Arbuthnot), [1732?]; 'An Essay on Man' (anon.), pt. i.-iii., 1733; pt. iv., 1734; 'Of the Knowledge and Characters of Men,' 1733; 'Sober Advice from Horace to the Young Gentlemen about Town' (anon.), [1734]; 'Epistle . . . to Dr. Arbuthnot,' 1735; 'Of the Characters of Women,' 1735; 'Ethic Epistles, Satires, etc.,' 1735; 'Letters of Mr. Pope and several Eminent Persons' (2 vols.), 1735; 'The Impertinent,' 1737; 'One Thousand Seven Hundred and Thirty-Eight,' 1738; 'The Universal Prayer' (anon.), 1738; 'Poems, and Imitations of Horace,' 1738; 'The Trial of Mr. Whiston' (anon.), 1740; 'Memoirs of . . . Martinus Scriblerus' (with Arbuthnot), 1741.

Posthumous: 'The Character of Katharine, late Duchess of Buckinghamshire,' 1746; 'Verses upon the late D——ss of M——' (anon.), 1746; 'Supplement to the Works of Alexander Pope,' 1757; 'Additions,' 1776; 'Supplemental Volume,' 1825.

He *translated:* Statius' 'Thebais,' bk. i., 1712; Homer's 'Iliad' (6 vols.), 1715-20; Homer's 'Odyssey' (5 vols.), 1725-26; various Satires and Epistles of Horace, 1733, 34, 37, 38; and *edited:* T. Parnell's 'Poems on Several Occasions,' 1722; Shakespeare's 'Dramatic Works,' 1725; Chaucer's 'Canterbury Tales . . . turn'd into modern Language,' 1737; 'Selecta Poemata Italorum qui Latine scripserunt,' 1740.

Collected Works: in 10 vols. (with *life*), ed. by Rev. W. Elwin and W. J. Courthope, 1871-89.

PORSON (Richard), **1759 - 1808.** Born, at East Ruston, Norfolk, 25 Dec. 1759. Early education at village schools, and by the curate of the parish. At Eton, Aug. 1774 to 1778. To Trin. Coll., Camb., Oct. 1778; Scholar, 1780; Craven Scholar, 1781; B.A., 1782; Chancellor's Prize Medal, 1782; Fellow of Trin. Coll., 1782; M.A., 1785. Obliged to give up Fellowship, owing to his not having taken holy orders, July 1792. Annuity purchased for him by his friends. Settled in rooms in the Temple, 1792. Regius Prof. of Greek, Cambridge, Nov. 1792. Continued to reside in London. Pursued classical studies.

Contrib. to 'Maty's Review,' 'Gentleman's Mag.,' 'Monthly Review,' 'Morning Chronicle,' etc. Married Mrs. Lunan, Nov. 1796 ; she died, 12 April 1797. Principal Librarian of newly-founded London Institution, April 1806. Died, in London, 25 Sept. 1808. Buried in chapel of Trin. Coll., Cambridge.

Works: 'Letters to Mr. Archdeacon Travis' (from 'Gentleman's Mag.'), 1790 ; Edition of Toup's 'Emendationes in Suidam,' 1790 ; Edition (anon.) of Æschylus, 1794 ; Editions of Euripides' 'Hecuba,' 1797, 'Orestes,' 1798, 'Phœnissæ,' 1799, and 'Medea,' 1801 ; Edition of Homer's 'Iliad' and 'Odyssey' (with Grenville and others), 1800.

Posthumous: 'Ricardi Porsoni Adversaria,' ed. by J. H. Monk and C. J. Blomfield, 1812 ; 'Tracts and Miscellaneous Criticisms,' ed. by T. Kidd, 1815 ; 'Aristophanica,' ed. by P. P. Dobree, 1820 ; Edition of the 'Lexicon of Photius,' ed. by P. P. Dobree (2 vols.), 1822 ; 'The Devil's Walk,' ed. by H. W. Montagu [1830]; 'Correspondence,' ed. by H. R. Luard, 1867.

PORTER (Anna Maria), 1780-1832. Born, at Durham, 1780. Educated at Edinburgh. Commenced literary career at early age. Part editor (with her sister Jane [q.v.] and T. F. Dibdin) of 'The Quiz,' 1797. To London, with her mother and sister, 1802. Play, 'The Fair Fugitives,' produced at Covent Garden, May 1803. Lived for some time with her mother and sister at Esher. Returned with her sister to London on their mother's death, 1831. Visit to her brother at Bristol, May 1832. Died, at Montpellier, near Bristol, 21 Sept. 1832. Buried in St. Paul's Churchyard, Bristol.

Works: 'Artless Tales' (2 vols. ; anon.), 1795 ; 'Tales of Pity' [1795?]; 'Walsh Colville' (anon.), 1797 ; 'Original Poems' (anon.) [1798 ?] ; 'Octavia' (anon.), 1798 ; 'The Lake of Killarney,' 1804 (later edn. called : 'Rose de Blaquière,' 1856) ; 'A Sol-

dier's Friendship and a Soldier's Love,' 1805 ; 'The Hungarian Brothers,' 1807 ; 'Don Sebastian,' 1809 ; 'Ballad Romances, and other Poems,' 1811 ; 'The Recluse of Norway,' 1814 ; 'The Knight of St. John,' 1817 ; 'The Fast of St. Magdalen,' 1818 ; 'The Village of Mariendorpt,' 1821 ; 'Roche-Blanche,' 1822 ; 'Honor O'Hara,' 1826 ; 'Tales Round a Winter Hearth' (with Jane Porter), 1826 ; 'Coming Out' (with 'The Field of the Forty Footsteps' by Jane Porter), 1828 ; 'The Barony,' 1830.

PORTER (Jane), 1776-1850. [Sister of preceding.] Born, at Durham, 1776. Educated at Edinburgh. Part editor (with her sister and T. F. Dibdin) of 'The Quiz,' 1797. Created 'Lady of Chapter of St. Joachim' by the King of Würtemberg after the success of her novel, 'Thaddeus of Warsaw.' Tragedy 'Switzerland' performed at Drury Lane, 5 Feb. 1819 ; 'Owen, Prince of Powys,' Drury Lane, 28 Jan. 1822. Lived for some time with her mother and sister at Esher. Returned to London with her sister, 1831. Visit to her brother at St. Petersburg, 1842. Grant from Literary Fund, Nov. 1842. Contrib. to 'Gentleman's Mag.,' 'Amulet,' and other periodicals. Died, at Bristol, 24 May 1850.

Works: 'Thaddeus of Warsaw,' 1803 ; 'A Sketch of the Campaigns of Count A. Suwarrow Rymnikski' (anon.), 1804 ; 'The Scottish Chiefs,' 1810 ; 'The Pastor's Fireside,' 1815 ; 'Duke Christian of Luneburg,' 1824 ; 'Tales Round a Winter Hearth' (with A. M. Porter), 1826; 'The Field of the Forty Footsteps' (with A. M. Porter's 'Coming Out'), 1828 ; 'Sir Edward Seaward's Narrative of his Shipwreck,' 1831.

She *edited:* 'Young Hearts. By a Recluse,' 1834.

PRAED (Winthrop Mackworth), 1802-1839. Born, in London, 26 July 1802. At school at Langley Broom, 1810-14 ; at Eton, March 1814 to 1821. Edited 'The Etonian,' with

W. Blunt, 1821. To Trin. Coll., Camb., Oct. 1821 ; Browne Medallist for Greek Ode, 1822 and 1823 ; for Greek Epigrams, 1822 and 1824 ; Chancellor's Medal for English Poem, 1823 and 1824 ; B.A., 1825. Contrib. to Knight's 'Quarterly Mag,' 1822. Part editor of 'The Brazen Head,' 1826. At Eton, as private tutor to Lord Ernest Bruce, 1825-27. Fellow, Trin. Coll., Camb., 1827 ; Seatonian prize poem, 1830. Called to Bar at Middle Temple, 29 May 1829. Contrib. to 'Times,' 'Morning Post,' 'Albion,' etc. M.P. for St. Germans, by purchasing seat, Dec. 1832; constituency disfranchised same year by Reform Bill. M.P. for Great Yarmouth, 1834-37. Sec. to Board of Control, Dec. 1834 to April 1835. Married Helen Bogle, 1835. M.P. for Aylesbury, 1837. Deputy High Steward to Univ. of Cambridge. Died, in London, 15 July 1839. Buried at Kensal Green.

Works : 'Carmen Græcum : Pyramides Ægyptiacæ' [1822] ; 'Epigrammata' [1822] ; 'Australasia' [1823]; 'Carmen Græcum : In Obitum T. F. Middleton' [1823] ; 'Lillian,' 1823 ; 'Athens' [1824] ; 'Epigrammata' [1824] ; 'Speech in Committee on the Reform Bill,' 1832 ; 'Trash' (anon.), 1833.

Collected Works : 'Poetical Works,' ed. by R. W. Griswold (New York), 1844 ; ed. by Derwent Coleridge, revised edn. (2 vols.), 1885 ; 'Essays,' ed. by Sir G. Young, 1887 ; 'Political and Occasional Poems,' ed. by Sir G. Young, 1888.

PRESCOTT (William Hickling), 1796-1859. Born, at Salem, Mass., 4 May 1796. Early education at Salem. At school in New York, Jan. 1803 to June 1808. Parents removed to Boston, 1808. To Harvard Coll., Aug. 1811 ; B.A., 1814. While at Harvard lost the sight of one eye through an accident ; the other soon afterwards became seriously and permanently affected. At St. Michael's, Azores, for health, Oct. 1815 to April 1816 Travelled in Europe, 1816-17.

In Boston, winter 1817-1818. Married Susan Amory, 4 May 1820. Adopted literary career. Corresponding Mem. of French Academy, Feb. 1845. Corresponding Mem., Royal Soc. of Berlin, Feb. 1845. Visit to England, 1850. Died, in Boston, 28 Jan. 1859. Buried in St. Paul's Church, Boston.

Works : 'Life of Charles Brockden Brown,' 1834 ; 'History of the Reign of Ferdinand and Isabella' (3 vols.), 1838 ; 'History of the Conquest of Mexico' (3 vols.), 1843 ; 'Critical and Historical Essays,' 1845 ; 'History of the Conquest of Peru' (2 vols.), 1847 ; 'Memoir of . . . J. Pickering,' 1848 ; 'The History of the Reign of Philip II.,' vols. i., ii., 1855 ; vol. iii., 1858 ; 'Memoir of the Hon. A. Lawrence' (priv. ptd.), 1856 ; 'The Life of Charles V. after his Abdication' (vol. iii. of Robertson's 'Hist. of the Reign of Charles V.'), 1857.

He *edited :* Mme. Calderon de la Bara's 'Life in Mexico,' 1843.

Life : by G. Ticknor, 1863.

PRIOR (Matthew), 1664 - 1721. Born, probably in Dorsetshire, 21 July 1664. Educated at Westminster School ; King's Scholar, 1681. To St. John's Coll., Camb., as Scholar, 1682 ; B.A., 1686 ; Fellow, April 1688. For a short time tutor to sons of Lord Exeter. Gentleman of Bedchamber to the King. In Holland, as Sec. to Lord Dursley, 1690[?]-97. Sec. of State in Ireland, 1697. Sec. to English Embassy in Paris, 1698. Returned to England, Nov. 1699 ; appointed Under-Sec. of State. Hon. M.A., Camb., 1700. Commissioner of Trade, 1700-07. M.P. for East Grinstead, Feb. to June, 1701. Commissioner of Customs, 1711-14. In Paris, 1711, and 1712-14. Imprisoned on political charge, March 1715 to 1717. Presented by Lord Harley with property of Down Hall, Essex, 1720[?]. Died, at Wimpole, 18 Sept. 1721.

Works : 'The Hind and the Panther transversed' (anon.), 1687 ; 'Hymn to the Sun,' 1694 ; 'To the King : an Ode,' 1695 ; 'An English

Ballad' (anon.), 1695 ; 'Verses on the death of Queen Mary,' 1695 ; 'Carmen Seculare for the year 1700 ' (anon.), 1700 ; 'Letter to Monsieur Boileau Despréaux ' (anon.), 1704 ; 'An Ode . . . to the Queen' (anon.), 1706 ; 'Pallas and Venus' (anon.), 1706 ; 'Poems,' 1707 (unauthorised) ; 'Poems,' 1709 ; 'A Fable of the Widow and her Cat' (with Swift), 1711 ; 'Poems,' 1716 (unauthorised) ; 'The Dove' (anon.), 1717 ; 'Poems,' 1718 ; 'The Conversation' (anon.), 1720 ; 'The Curious Maid' (anon.), 1720.

Posthumous : 'Down Hall,' 1723 ; 'The Turtle and the Sparrow,' 1723 ; 'The Unequal Match' (anon.), 1737 ; 'History of his Own Time,' 1740 ; 'Miscellaneous Works' (2 vols.), 1740. *Collected Works :* ed. by R. B. Johnson (2 vols.), 1892.

PROCTER (Adelaide Ann), 1825-1864. Born, in London, 30 Oct. 1825. Early literary ability. Contrib. poems to 'Book of Beauty,' 1843. Contrib. to 'Household Words' (under pseud. 'Mary Bernick ') from 1853 ; also to 'Cornhill,' 'Good Words,' 'All the Year Round.' Visit to Italy, 1853. Active interest in social position of women. To Malvern, for health, 1862. Died there, 2 Feb. 1864. Buried at Kensal Green. *Works :* 'Legends and Lyrics,' vol. i., 1858 (2nd edn. same year) ; vol. ii., 1861 ; 'A Chaplet of Verse,' 1862 (2nd edn. same year). She *edited :* 'The Victoria Regia,' 1861.

PROCTER (Bryan Waller). 1787-1874. [Father of preceding.] Born, at Leeds, 21 Nov. 1787. At Harrow, Feb. 1801 to 1804 [?]. Articled to a Solicitor at Calne, 1804 [?]-07. To London, 1807. Practised as solicitor. Contrib. to 'Literary Gaz.,' from 1815 ; to 'London Mag.,' from 1820. Friendship with Leigh Hunt and Charles Lamb. Tragedy 'Mirandola ' produced at Covent Garden, Jan. 1821. Married Anne Skepper, 1824. Commissioner in Lunacy, 1832-61. Died, in London, 5 Oct. 1874.

Works : 'Dramatic Scenes, and other poems' (under pseud. 'Barry Cornwall '), 1819 ; 'Marcian Colonna ' (by 'Barry Cornwall '), 1820 ; 'A Sicilian Story' (by 'Barry Cornwall '), 1820 (2nd edn. same year) ; 'Mirandola' (by 'Barry Cornwall '), 1821 (2nd edn. same year) ; 'Poetical Works of Barry Cornwall ' (3 vols.), 1822 ; 'The Flood of Thessaly' (by 'Barry Cornwall '), 1823 ; 'Effigies Poeticæ ' (anon.), 1824 ; 'English Songs' (by 'Barry Cornwall '), 1832 ; 'The Sea, The Sea' (anon.), 1834 ; 'Life of Edmund Kean ' (anon.), 1835 ; 'Essays and Tales in Prose ' (2 vols., Boston), 1853 ; 'Charles Lamb' (by 'Barry Cornwall '), 1866. *Posthumous :* ' Autobiographical Fragment,' ed. by Coventry Patmore, 1877.

He *edited :* Ben Jonson's Works, 1838 ; Shakespeare's Works, 1843 ; 'Selections from Browning' (with J. Foster), 1863 ; Lamb's 'Essays of Elia,' 1879.

PRYNNE (William), 1600-1669. Born, at Swanswick, Somersetshire, 1600. Early education at Bath Grammar School. Matric. Oriel Coll., Oxford, 24 April 1618 ; B.A., 22 Jan. 1621. Student of Lincoln's Inn, 1621 ; called to Bar, 1628. Consigned to Tower on a charge of treason, 1 Feb. 1633 ; sentenced, 17 Feb. 1634, to fine and imprisonment for life. Expelled from Lincoln's Inn ; deprived of Oxford degree, 29 April 1634 ; pilloried, 7 May and 10 May 1634. Sentenced again to increased fine, 14 June 1637. Pilloried, 30 June 1637. Imprisoned in Carnarvon Castle, July 1637 ; afterwards in Mount Orgueil Castle, Jersey. Released, restored to degree and legal position, and pecuniarily compensated, Nov. 1640. Espoused Parliamentary cause in Civil War. Prolific pamphleteer on political and theological subjects. Mem. of Committee of Accounts, Feb. 1644. Commissioner for visitation of city of Oxford, May 1647. M.P. for Newport, Nov. 1648. Arrested on political charge, Dec. 1648 ; released, Jan. 1649. Im-

prisoned again, 30 June 1650 to 18
Feb. 1653. Took his seat in Long
Parliament, 1659-60. M.P. for Bath,
1660 and 1661. Keeper of the Tower
Records, 1660. Unmarried. Died,
in Lincoln's Inn, 24 Oct. 1669. Buried
there.

Works : [A full list of Prynne's
Works, which number upwards of 200,
are given by J. Bruce in the Camden
Society's 'Documents relating to the
Proceedings against William Prynne,'
1877. The most important are :]
'Histrio-Mastix,' 1633 ; 'The Sovereign Power of Parliaments,' 1643 ;
'The Opening of the Great Seal of
England,' 1643 ; 'Hidden Works of
Darkness brought to Public Light,'
1645 ; 'Canterbury's Doom,' 1646 ;
'A Plea for the House of Lords,'
1648 ; 'The First Part of an Historical
Collection of the Ancient Councils
and Parliaments of England,' 1649 ;
'A Short Demurrer to the Jews' long-
discontinued Remitter into England,'
1656 ; 'A Brief Register of the several
kinds of Parliamentary Writs' (4 pts.),
1659-64 ; 'The Signal Loyalty and
Devotion of God's true Saints towards
their Kings,' 1660 ; 'An Exact Chronological Vindication . . . of our . . .
King's Supreme Ecclesiastical Jurisdiction' (3 vols.), 1665-70 ; 'Aurum
Reginæ,' 1668 ; 'Brief Animadversions
on the Fourth Part of the Institutes
of the Laws of England compiled by
Sir Edward Coke,' 1669.

Posthumous : 'An Exact Abridg-
ment of the Records in the Tower of
London,' 1689.

PURCHAS (Samuel), 1575[?]-1626.
Born, in Essex, 1575 [?]. Educated
at St. John's Coll., Camb. Ordained
Curate of Purleigh, Essex, 1600 [?].
Married Jane Lease, Dec. 1601.
Vicar of Eastwood, Essex, 1604-13.
Chaplain to Archbishop of Canterbury,
1614. Rector of St. Martin's, Lud-
gate, 1614-26. Died, Sept. [?] 1626.

Works : 'Purchas his Pilgrimage,'
1613 ; 'Purchas his Pilgrim : Micro-
cosmus, etc.,' 1619 ; 'Hakluytus
Posthumus, or Purchas his Pilgrimes,'
1625.

PYE (Henry James), 1745-1813.
Born, in London, 20 Feb. 1745.
Early education at home. Matric.
Magdalen Coll., Oxford, 12 July
1762 ; created -M.A., 3 July 1766.
Married (i.) Mary Hook, 1766.
Created D.C.L., Oxford, 9 July 1773.
M.P. for Berkshire, 1784-90. Ap-
pointed Poet Laureate, 1790. Police
Magistrate for Westminster, 1792.
Play 'The Siege of Meaux' produced
at Covent Garden, 19 May 1794 ;
'Adelaide,' Drury Lane, 25 Jan. 1800 ;
'A Prior Claim' (written with S. J.
Arnold), Drury Lane, 29 Oct. 1805.
Wife died, 1796. Married (ii.) Martha
Corbett, Nov. 1801. Died, at Pinner,
11 Aug. 1813.

Works : 'The Rosciad of Covent
Garden' (anon. ; attrib. to Pye), 1762 ;
'Beauty' (anon.), 1766 ; 'Elegies'
(anon.), 1768 ; 'The Triumph of
Fashion' (anon.), 1771 ; 'Farringdon
Hill' (anon.), 1774 ; 'The Progress of
Refinement,' 1783 ; 'Shooting' (anon.),
1784 ; 'Aeriphorion,' 1784 ; 'Poems'
(collected), 1787 ; 'Amusement,' 1790 ;
'The Siege of Meaux,' 1794 ; 'The
Democrat' (anon.), 1795 ; 'War
Elegies of Tyrtæus imitated,' 1795 ;
'Sketches on Various Subjects'
(anon.), 1796 ; 'Naucratia,' 1798 ;
'The Inquisitor' (with J. P. Andrews),
1798 ; 'The Aristocrat' (anon.), 1799 ;
'Carmen Seculare,' 1800 ; 'Adelaide,'
1800 ; 'Alfred,' 1801 ; 'Verses on
Several Subjects,' 1802 ; 'A Prior
Claim' (with S. J. Arnold), 1805 ;
'Comments on the Commentators of
Shakespeare,' 1807 ; 'Summary of the
Duties of a Justice of the Peace out
of Sessions,' 1808.

He *translated :* 'Six Olympic Odes
of Pindar,' 1775 ; Aristotle's 'Poetics,'
1788 ; Bürger's 'Lenore,' 1796 ;
Homer's 'Hymns and Epigrams,'
1810 ; and *edited :* Francis's translation of the Odes of Horace, 1812.

QUARLES (Francis), 1592-1644.
Born, at Romford, Essex, 1592 ; baptized, 8 May. Educated at a school
in Essex, and at Christ's Coll., Camb.
B.A., 1608. Studied law for a short
time at Lincoln's Inn. To Germany,

in suite of Princess Elizabeth, 1613. Married Ursula Woodgate, 28 May 1618. In Dublin, as private Secretary to Archbishop of Armagh, 1628 [?]-32[?]. Chronologer of City of London, Feb. 1639 to Sept. 1644. Supported Royalist cause in Civil War. Died, in London, 8 Sept. 1664. Buried in church of St. Olave, Silver Street.

Works: 'A Feast of Wormes,' 1620; 'Hadessa,' 1621; 'Job Militant,' 1624; 'Sions Elegies,' 1624; 'Sions Sonnets,' 1624; 'Alphabet of Elegies upon the . . . death of Doctor Aylmer,' 1625; 'Argalus and Parthenia,' 1629; 'The Historie of Samson,' 1631; 'Divine Fancies,' 1632; 'Divine Poems,' 1633; 'Emblemes,' 1634-35; 'Elegy upon Sir Julius Cæsar.' 1636; 'Elegie upon . . . Mr. John Wheeler,' 1637; 'Elegy on Dr. Wilson,' 1638; 'Elegy on Lady Luckyn,' 1638; 'Hieroglyphikes of the Life of Man,' 1638; 'Memorials upon the Death of Robert Quarles,' 1639; 'Sighs at the Contemporary Deaths of the Countesse of Cleaveland and Mistresse Cecily Killegrue,' 1640; 'Enchyridion,' 1640; 'Observations Concerning Princes and States,' 1642; 'Barnabas and Boanerges' (2 pts.), 1644-66; 'The Loyall Convert' (anon.), 1643; 'The Whipper Whipt' (anon.), 1644; 'The New Distemper' (anon.), 1645.

Posthumous: 'Solomons Recantation,' 1645; 'Midnights Meditations of Death,' 1646; 'The Shepheard's Oracles,' 1646; 'A Direfull Anathema against Peace-Haters,' 1647; 'The Virgin Widow,' 1649.

Collected Works: ed. by A. B. Grosart (3 vols.), 1880-81.

✱QUILLER-COUCH (Arthur Thomas), b. 1863. Born, at Bodmin, 21 Nov. 1863. At Newton Abbot Coll., Jan. 1874-79; at Clifton Coll., 1879-81. Matric. Trin. Coll., Oxford, 14 Oct. 1882; Scholar, 1882; B.A., 1886; Classical Lecturer, Trin. Coll., 1886-7. To London, spring of 1888. Married Louisa Amelia Hicks, 22 Aug. 1889. On staff of 'Speaker' since Jan. 1890.

Removed from London to Fowey, Cornwall, 1892.

Works: 'Athens' (priv. printed), 1881; 'Dead Man's Rock' (under initial : 'Q.'), 1887; 'The Astonishing History of Troy Town' (by 'Q.'), 1888; 'The Splendid Spur' (by 'Q.'), 1889; 'The Blue Pavilions' (by 'Q.'), 1891; 'Noughts and Crosses' (by 'Q.'), 1891; 'The Warwickshire Avon,' 1892 [1891]; '"I saw Three Ships"' (by 'Q.'), 1892; 'The Delectable Duchy' (by 'Q.'), 1893; 'Green Bays,' 1893; 'Wandering Heath' (by 'Q.'), 1895; 'Fairy Tales. . . retold by Q.,' 1895; 'Adventures in Criticism,' 1896; 'Ia' (by 'Q.'), 1896; 'Poems and Ballads' (by 'Q.'), 1896.

He has *translated:* Bazin's 'A Blot of Ink' (with P. M. Franche), 1892; and *edited:* 'The Golden Pomp: a Procession of English Lyrics,' 1895; 'English Sonnets,' 1897.

RADCLIFFE (*Mrs.* Ann), 1764-1823. Born [Ann Ward], in London, 9 July 1764. Married William Radcliffe, 1787. Occupied with literature, 1789-1802. Spent last twenty years of her life practically in retirement. Died, 7 Feb. 1823. Buried in St. George's Burial Ground, Bayswater Road.

Works: 'The Castles of Athlin and Dunbayne,' 1789; 'A Sicilian Romance,' 1790; 'The Romance of the Forest' (anon.), 1791; 'The Mysteries of Udolpho,' 1794; 'A Journey . . . through Holland,' 1795; 'The Italian,' 1797; 'Poems,' 1816.

Posthumous: 'Gaston de Blondeville,' 1826.

RAMSAY (Allan), 1686-1758. Born, at Leadhills, near Crawford, Lanarkshire, 15 Oct. 1686. Educated at village school at Crawford. Apprenticed to a wig-maker in Edinburgh, 1701. At conclusion of apprenticeship, set up in business. Married Christian Ross, 1712. Mem. of Jacobite 'Easy Club,' 1712-15. Prolific writer of occasional poetry. Started business as a bookseller, 1716 [?]. Drama, 'The Gentle Shepherd,' performed in Edinburgh, 1729. Built a theatre in Edinburgh, 1736 ; closed it, 1737. Retired from business, 1755. Died, in Edinburgh, 7 Jan. 1758. Buried in Old Greyfriars Churchyard.

Works : 'The Battel' (anon.), 1716 ; 'Tartana' [1717 ?] ; 'Scots Songs,' 1718 ; 'The Scriblers Lash'd,' 1718 ; ' Christ's Kirk on the Green,' 1718 ; 'Elegies on Maggie Johnson, John Cowper and Lucky Wood,' 1718 ; 'Content,' 1720 ; 'The Prospect of Plenty,' 1720 ; 'Robert, Richy and Sandy,' 1721 ; ' Poems ' (2 vols.), 1721-28 ; 'Fables and Tales,' 1722 ; 'A Tale of Three Bonnets ' (anon.), 1722 ; 'The Fair Assembly,' 1723 ; 'Health,' 1724 ; 'The Tea - Table Miscellany ' (3 vols.), 1724-27 ; ' The Ever Green ' (2 vols.), 1724 ; 'The Gentle Shepherd,' 1725 ; 'A Scots Ode to the British Antiquarians' [1726] ; 'New Miscellany of Scots Songs,' 1727 ; 'A Collection of Thirty Fables,' 1730 ; 'The Morning Interview,' 1731 ; 'An Address of Thanks from the Society of Rakes ' (anon.), 1734 ; 'Collection of Scots Proverbs,' 1737 ; 'Hardyknute,' by Lady Wardlaw, completed by Ramsay, 1745 ; 'The Vision ' (anon.), 1748.

Collected Works : in 3 vols., 1851.

Life : by O. Smeaton, 1896.

RANDOLPH (Thomas), 1605-1635. Born, at Newnham - cum - Badby, Northamptonshire, 1605 ; baptized 15 June 1605. Educated at Westminster School as King's Scholar. Matric., Trin. Coll., Camb., 8 July 1624 ; B.A., Jan. 1628 ; Minor Fellow, Sept. 1629 ; Major Fellow, March 1632 ; M.A., 1632. Incorporated M.A. at Oxford, 1632. Settled in London, 1632. Intimacy with Ben Jonson. Died, at Blatherwick, March 1635 ; buried, in the parish church, 17 March.

Works : 'Aristippus' (anon.), 1630 ; 'The Jealous Lovers,' 1632.

Posthumous : ' Poems, with the Muses Looking-Glasse, and Amyntas,' 1638.

Collected Works : ed. by W. C. Hazlitt (2 vols.), 1875.

*RAWLINSON** (George), *Canon of Canterbury,* b. 1812. Born, at Chadlington, Oxfordshire, 23 Nov. 1812. At Swansea Grammar School, Feb. to June, 1824 ; at Ealing School, Feb. 1825 to June 1830. Matric. Trin. Coll., Oxford, 7 Nov. 1834 ; B.A., 1838 ; Fellow, Exeter Coll., 1840-46 ; M.A., 1841 ; Tutor, 1841 ; Denyer Theolog. Prize Essay, 1842 and 1843 ; Sub-Rector and Divinity Reader, 1844 ; Bampton Lecturer, 1859 ; Camden Prof. of Ancient History, 1861-89. Ordained Deacon, 1841 ; Priest, 1842. Married Louisa Wildman Chermside, July 1846. Curate of Merton, Oxfordshire, 1846-47. Classical Examiner to Council of Military Education, 1859-70. Corresp. Mem. of Royal Acad. of Turin, 1860. Mem. of Athenæum Club, 1870. Canon of Canterbury, Sept. 1872 ; Proctor for Dean and Chapter of Canterbury, 1873 ; Rector of All Hallows, Lombard St., 1888. Contrib. to ' Contemp. Rev.,' ' Leisure Hour,' 'Sunday at Home,' 'Princeton Rev.,' 'Clergyman's Mag.,' ' Isis,' ' Oxford and Cambridge Mag.,' etc. F.R.G.S., 1890.

Works : 'The Historical Evidences of the Truth of the Scripture Records,' 1859 ; 'The Contrasts of Christianity with the Heathen and Jewish Systems,' 1861 ; 'The Five Great Monarchies of the Ancient Eastern World ' (4 vols.), 1862-67 ; 'A Manual of Ancient History,' 1869 ; ' Historical Illustrations of the Old Testament ' [1871] ; 'The Sixth Great Oriental Monarchy,' 1873 ; 'The Seventh Great Oriental Monarchy,' 1876 ; 'The Origin of Nations' [1877] ; 'St. Paul in Damascus and Arabia,' 1877 ; 'Ezra, Nehemiah, and Esther ' (' Pulpit Commentary '), 1880 ; ' History of Ancient Egypt,' 1881 ; 'Exodus ' (' Pulpit Commentary '), 1882 ; 'The Religions of the Ancient World ' [1882] ; 'The Antiquity of Man ' [1883] ; 'The Early Prevalence of Monotheistic

Beliefs' [1883] ; 'Religious Teachings of the Sublime and Beautiful in Nature' [1883] ; 'Egypt and Babylon,' 1885 [1884] ; 'Biblical Topography,' 1886 ; 'Ancient History,' 1887 ; 'Ancient Egypt,' 1887 ; 'Moses' [1887] : 'History of Phœnicia,' 1889 ; 'The Kings of Israel and Judah' [1889] ; 'Phœnicia' ('Story of Nations' series), 1889 ; 'Isaac and Jacob' [1890] ; 'Ezra and Nehemiah : their Lives and Times' [1891] ; 'History of Parthia' [1893].

He has contributed to : 'The Speaker's Commentary,' Smith's 'Dict. of the Bible,' 'The Bible Educator,' 'Encycl. Brit.,' 'Present-Day Tracts,' 'Old Testament Commentary for English Readers.'

He has *translated :* 'Herodotus' (annotated ; with Sir H. C. Rawlinson and Sir J. Wilkinson), 4 vols., 1858-60 ; and *edited :* R. S. C. Chermside's 'Sermons,' 1868.

READE (Charles), 1814-1884. Born, at Ipsden, Oxfordshire, 8 June 1814. Privately educated, 1822-27 ; at school at Staines, 1827-29. At home, 1829-31. Matric., Magdalen Coll., Oxford, 26 July 1831 ; Demy, 1831-35 ; B.A., 18 June 1835 ; Vinerian Scholar, 1835 ; Fellow of Magdalen Coll., July 1835 ; M.A., 1838 ; Vinerian Fellow, 1842 ; D.C.L., 1 July 1847 ; Vice-Pres., Magdalen Coll., 1851. Student of Lincoln's Inn, Nov. 1836 ; called to Bar. 16 Jan. 1843. Friendship with Mrs. Seymour begun, 1852. Play 'The Ladies' Battle' (adapted from Scribe and Legouvé), produced at Olympic Theatre, 7 May 1851 ; 'Angelo,' Olympic, 11 Aug. 1851 ; 'A Village Tale,' Strand, 12 April 1852 ; 'The Lost Husband,' Strand, 26 April 1852 ; 'Masks and Faces,' Haymarket, 20 Nov. 1852 ; 'Gold,' Drury Lane, 10 Jan. 1853 ; 'Two Loves and a Life' (with Tom Taylor), Adelphi, 20 March 1854 ; 'The Courier of Lyons' (afterwards called 'The Lyons Mail'), Princess's, 26 June 1854 ; 'The King's Rival' (with Tom Taylor), St. James's, 1 Oct. 1854 ;

'Honour before Titles,' St. James's, 3 Oct. 1854 ; 'Peregrine Pickle,' St. James's, Nov. 1854 ; 'Art' (afterwards called 'Nance Oldfield'), St. James's, 17 April 1855 ; 'The First Printer' (with Tom Taylor), Princess's, 3 March 1856 ; 'Never Too Late to Mend' (dramatized from his novel), Princess's, 4 Oct. 1865 ; 'The Double Marriage' (dramatized from novel 'White Lies'), Queen's Theatre, 24 Oct. 1867 ; adaptation of Tennyson's 'Dora,' Adelphi, 1 June 1867 ; 'Foul Play' (with Dion Boucicault ; dramatized from novel), Holborn Theatre, 1868 (revised version, called 'The Scuttled Ship,' by Reade alone, Olympic, 1877) ; 'Free Labour' (dramatized from novel 'Put Yourself in his Place'), 28 May 1870 ; 'The Robust Invalid' (adapted from Molière), Adelphi, 15 June 1870 ; 'Shilly Shally,' Gaiety, 1 April 1872 ; 'Kate Peyton's Lovers' (dramatized from novel 'Griffith Gaunt'), Queen's Theatre, 1 Oct. 1875 ; 'Drink' (dramatized from Zola), Princess's, 2 June 1879 ; 'Love and Money' (with H. Pettitt), 18 Nov. 1882 ; 'Single Heart and Double Face,' Edinburgh, Nov. 1883. Died, in London, 11 April 1884. Buried in Willesden Churchyard.

Works : 'Peg Woffington,' 1853 ; 'Christie Johnstone,' 1853 ; 'Two Loves and a Life' (with Tom Taylor), 1854 ; 'The King's Rival' (with Tom Taylor), 1854 ; 'Masks and Faces' (with Tom Taylor), 1854 ; 'It is Never Too Late to Mend,' 1856 ; 'White Lies,' 1857 ; 'The Course of True Love never did run Smooth,' 1857 ; 'Jack of all Trades,' 1858 ; 'Autobiography of a Thief,' 1858 ; 'Love me Little, Love me Long,' 1859 ; 'The Eighth Commandment,' 1860 ; 'The Cloister and the Hearth,' 1861 ; 'Hard Cash,' 1863 ; 'Griffith Gaunt,' 1866 ; 'Foul Play' (with Dion Boucicault), 1868 ; 'Put Yourself in his Place,' 1870 ; 'A Terrible Temptation,' 1871 ; 'The Wandering Heir,' 1872 ; 'A Simpleton,' 1873 ; 'A Lost Art Revived,' 1873 ; 'A Hero and a Martyr,' 1874 ; 'Trade

Malice,' 1875 ; 'A Woman Hater,' 1877 ; 'Readiana.' 1883.

Posthumous : 'The Perilous Secret,' 1884 ; 'Singleheart and Doubleface,' 1884 ; 'The Jilt, and other Tales,' 1884 ; 'Good Stories of Man and other Animals,' 1884 ; 'Bible Characters,' 1888.

Life : by C. L. and C. Reade, 1887.

REID (Thomas), 1710-1796. Born, at Strachan, Kincardineshire, 26 April 1710. Early education at Kincardine parish school. To Marischal College, Aberdeen, 1722 ; B.A., 1726. Studied for Presbyterian ministry. Licensed preacher, Sept. 1731. Librarian of Marischal Coll., 1733-36. Minister of New Machar, Aberdeen, 1737. Married Elizabeth Reid, 1740. 'Regent' (afterwards Prof. of Philosophy) at King's Coll., Aberdeen, Oct. 1751 to May 1764. Founded Philosophical Society, 1758 ; it existed till 1773. Hon. D.D., Marischal Coll., 18 Jan. 1762. Prof. of Moral Philosophy, Glasgow Univ., May 1764 to Oct 1796 ; deputed active duties of professorship to an assistant, 1780. Died, in Glasgow, 7 Oct. 1796.

Works : 'An Inquiry into the Human Mind on the Principles of Common Sense,' 1764 ; 'Essays on the Intellectual Powers of Man,' 1785; 'Essays on the Active Powers of Man,' 1788. [He contributed : 'An Essay on Quantity' to the 'Philosophical Transactions' for 1748 ; 'A Brief Account of Aristotle's Logic' to Kame's 'Sketches of the History of Man,' vol. ii., 1774 ; 'A Statistical Account of the University of Glasgow' to Sinclair's 'Statistical Account of Scotland,' 1799.]

Collected Works : ed. by Sir W. Hamilton (2 vols.), 1846-63.

Life : by Dugald Stewart, 1803.

REID (Thomas Mayne), 1818-1883. Born, at Ballyroney, co. Down, 4 April 1818. Educated for Presbyterian ministry ; but emigrated to America, 1840. Varied occupations, 1840-43. In Philadelphia, as journalist, 1843-46. On staff of 'New York

Herald' and 'Spirit of the Times,' 1846. Served in Mexican War as second lieutenant in New York Volunteers, Dec. 1846 to 1848. To Europe, 1849. Married Elizabeth Hyde, 1853. Edited 'The Little Times,' 1867. In New York, 1867 - 70. Edited 'Mayne Reid's Mag.,' 1869-70. Returned to England, 1870. Died, at Ross, Herefordshire, 22 Oct. 1883. Buried at Kensal Green.

Works : 'The Rifle Rangers,' 1850; 'The Scalp-Hunters,' 1851 ; 'The English Family Robinson,' 1851 ; 'The Desert Home,' 1852 ; 'The Boy Hunters,' 1853 ; 'The Young Voyageurs,' 1854 [1853]; 'The Forest Exiles,' 1855 [1854] ; 'The Hunter's Feast' [1855]; 'The White Chief,' 1855 ; 'The Quadroon,' 1856 ; 'The Bush Boys,' 1856 ; 'The Young Yägers,' 1857 ; 'The War Trail,' 1857 ; 'Ran away to Sea,' 1858 ; 'The Plant Hunters,' 1858 ; 'Oceola,' 1859 ; 'The Boy Tar,' 1860 [1859] ; 'The Wood Rangers,' 1860 ; 'Odd People,' 1860 ; 'Quadrupeds' [1860]; 'Bruin,' 1861 ; 'The Wild Huntress,' 1861 ; 'The Maroon,' 1862 ; 'Croquet,' 1863 ; 'The Cliff - Climbers,' 1864 ; 'Garibaldi Rebuked,' 1864 ; 'The Ocean Waifs,' 1864; 'The White Gauntlet,' 1865 [1864] ; 'The Boy Slaves,' 1865 ; 'The Headless Horseman,' 1866 ; 'Afloat in the Forest,' 1866 ; 'The Bandolero,' 1866 ; 'The Giraffe Hunters,' 1867 ; 'The Guerilla Chief,' 1867 ; 'The Child Wife,' 1868; 'Works' (15 vols.), 1868 ; 'The Fatal Cord,' 1869 ; 'The Yellow Chief' [1870] ; 'The White Squaw' [1870]; 'The Castaways,' 1870 ; 'The Lone Ranche,' 1871 ; 'The Finger of Fate,' 1872; 'The Death-Shot,' 1873 ; 'Half-Blood,' 1875 ; 'The Mountain Marriage,' 1875 ; 'The Flag of Distress,' 1876 ; 'Gwen Wynn,' 1877 ; 'The Queen of the Lakes,' 1879 ; 'Gaspar the Gaucho,' 1880 [1879] ; 'The Free Lances,' 1881.

Posthumous : 'Love's Martyr' [1884] ; 'The Land of Fire' [1884]; 'The Chase of Leviathan,' 1885 [1884]; 'The Lost Mountain,' 1885 ; 'The Pierced Heart,' 1885 ; 'The Vee-

Boers' [1885]; 'The Star of Empire'
[1888]; 'No Quarter,' 1888 ; 'The
Naturalist in Siluria,' 1889.
He *translated:* L. de Bellamare's
'The Wood Rangers,' 1860 ; 'A Hero
in Spite of Himself,' 1861, and 'The
Tiger-Hunter,' 1862 ; and *edited:*
Charles Beach's 'Lost Lenore,' 1864 ;
F. Whitlaker's 'The Cadet Button,'
1878.
Life: by his Wife, 1890.

RICARDO (David), **1772 - 1823.**
Born, in England, 19 April 1772.
Early education in England ; in
Holland, 1783-85. Began to assist
his father in business on Stock Ex-
change, 1786. Married Priscilla Anne
Wilkinson, 20 Dec. 1793. Mem. of
newly founded Geological Soc., 1807.
Bought the estate of Gatcombe Park,
Gloucestershire, 1813. Retired from
business, 1814. Sheriff, 1818. M.P.
for Portarlington, Ireland, 1819-23.
Visit to Continent, 1822. Died, at
Gatcombe Park, 11 Sept. 1823.

Works : 'The High Price of Bullion
a proof of the depreciation of Bank
Notes,' 1810 (3rd edn., same year) ;
'Observations on some passages in . . .
the Edinburgh Review,' 1811 ; 'Reply
to Mr. Bosanquet's Practical Observations,' 1811 ; 'Essay on the Influence
of a Low Price of Corn on the Profits
of Stock,' 1815 (2nd edn., same year);
'Proposals for an Economical and
Secure Currency,' 1816 (2nd edn.,
same year) ; 'On the Principles of
Political Economy and Taxation,'
1817 ; 'On Protection to Agriculture'
1822 (4th edn. same year); 'Plan
for the Establishment of a National
Bank,' 1824.
Posthumous: Letters to T. R. Malthus, 1887.
Collected Works: ed. by McCul-
loch, 2nd edn., 1852.

*RICHARDSON (Samuel), 1689-
1761. Born, in Derbyshire, 1689.
Apprenticed to a stationer, 1706.
Afterwards employed as compositor
at a printing works. Set up as printer
on his own account, 1719. Married
(i.) Martha Wilde. She died, 25

Jan. 1731. Married (ii.) Elizabeth
Leake. Began novel writing, 1739.
Master of Stationers' Company, 1754.
Died, in London, 4 July 1761. Buried
in St. Bride's Church.
Works : 'Pamela' (anon.), 1741-
42 ; 'Clarissa' (anon.), 1748 ; 'The
History of Sir Charles Grandison'
(anon.), 1754 (2nd edn. same year).
Posthumous: 'Correspondence,' ed.
by A. L. Barbould (6 vols.), 1804.
He *edited:* 'A Tour thro' . . .
Great Britain,' 1742 ; Sir T. Roe's
'Negotiations in his Embassy to the
Ottoman Porte,' 1746 ; 'The Life . . .
of Balbe Berton ' [1760 ?].
Collected Works: ed. by E. Man-
gin (19 vols.), 1811 ; ed. by Leslie
Stephen (12 vols.), 1883.

*RITCHIE (Mrs. Anne Isabella), b.
1837. [Daughter of W. M. Thackeray (q.v.).] Born in London, 9 June
1837. Some years in early life spent
in Paris. Contrib. to 'Cornhill Mag.'
and other periodicals, from 1860. Resided for many years in Kensington.
Married Richmond Thackeray Ritchie,
2 Aug. 1877. Has latterly resided at
Wimbledon.
Works : 'The Story of Elizabeth'
(anon.), 1863 ; 'The Village on the
Cliff' (anon.), 1867; 'Five old Friends'
(anon.), 1868 ; 'To Esther,' 1869 ;
'Old Kensington,' 1873 (4th edn.
same year) ; 'Toilers and Spinsters,'
1874 ; 'Bluebeard's Keys,' 1874 ;
'Miss Angel,' 1875 ; 'Madame de
Sévigné,' 1881 ; 'Miss Williamson's
Divagations,' 1881 ; 'A Book of
Sybils,' 1883 ; 'Mrs. Dymond,' 1885;
'Records of Tennyson, Ruskin and
Browning,' 1892 ; Letterpress to
'Alfred, Lord Tennyson and his
friends,' 1893 ; 'Chapters from some
Memoirs,' 1894 ; 'Lord Amherst'
(with R. Evans), 1894.
She has *edited:* W. M. Thackeray's
'The Orphan of Pimlico. etc.,' 1876 ;
A. Evans' 'Poems and Music,' 1880 ;
Mrs. Gaskell's 'Cranford,' 1891 ;
Countess d'Aulnoy's 'Fairy Tales,'
1892 ; Miss Mitford's 'Our Village,'
1893 ; Miss Edgeworth's 'Castle
Rackrent,' 1895, 'Ormond,' 1895,

'Popular Tales,' 1895, and 'Helen,' 1896.

ROBERTSON (William). 1721-1793. Born, at Borthwick, Midlothian, 19 Sept. 1721. Early education at Borthwick parish school and at Dalkeith Grammar School. To Edinburgh Univ., 1733. Licensed by Presbytery as preacher, June 1741. Minister of Gladsmuir, 1743. Served in volunteers against Pretender's army, 1745. Mem. of General Assembly, 1746. Married Mary Nisbet, 1751. Part ed. of 'Edinburgh Rev.,' 1755. Visit to London, 1758. Minister of Lady Yester's Chapel. Edinburgh, June 1758 to April 1761. Created D.D., Edinburgh, 1758. Chaplain of Stirling Castle, 1759. Minister of Old Greyfriars, Edinburgh, April 1761. Chaplain to the King, Aug. 1761. Principal of Edinburgh Univ., 1762-92. Moderator of General Assembly, 1763-80. Mem. of Royal Acad. of History, Madrid, Aug. 1777. Mem. of Acad. of Sciences, Padua, 1781. Mem. of Imperial Acad., St. Petersburg, 1783. Historiographer for Scotland, 6 Aug. 1783. Died, at Grange House, near Edinburgh, 11 June 1793.

Works : 'The Situation of the World at the time of Christ's Appearance,' 1755 ; 'History of Scotland' (2 vols.), 1759 ; 'History of the Reign of the Emperor Charles V.' (3 vols.), 1769 ; 'History of America' (2 vols.), 1777 ; 'Historical Disquisition concerning the Knowledge which the Ancients had of India,' 1791. *Collected Works :* in 12 vols., ed. by Dugald Stuart, with *memoir*, 1817 ; in 11 vols., ed. by R. A. Davenport, with *memoir*, 1824.

ROGERS (Samuel), 1763-1855. Born, at Stoke Newington, 30 July 1763. Educated at schools at Stoke Newington and Hackney. Entered his father's bank about 1775. Contrib. to 'Gentleman's Mag.,' 1781. Visit to Scotland, 1789 ; to Paris, 1802. Gained prominent position as poet ; also as collector and patron of fine

arts. Visits to Italy, 1815 and 1822. Offered Laureateship, but declined it, 1850. Died, in London, 18 Dec. 1855. Buried in Hornsey Churchyard. Unmarried.

Works : 'An Ode to Superstition' (anon.), 1786 ; 'The Pleasures of Memory' (anon.), 1792 ; 'Epistle to a Friend' (anon.), 1798 ; 'Verses written in Westminster Abbey after the funeral of the Rt. Hon. C. J. Fox' (anon.), [1806] ; 'The Voyage of Columbus' (anon.), 1810 (priv. ptd.,1808) ; 'Poems,' 1812 ; 'Miscellaneous Poems' (with E. C. Knight and others ; anon.), 1812 ; 'Jacqueline' (anon.), 1814 ; 'Human Life,' 1819 ; 'Italy,' pt. i. (anon.), 1822 ; pt. ii., 1828 ; revised edn. of the whole, 1830 ; 'Poems' (2 vols.), 1834. *Posthumous :* 'Poetical Works,' 1856 ; 'Table Talk,' ed. by A. Dyce, 1856 ; 'Recollections,' ed. by W. Sharpe, 1859 (2nd edn. same year). *Life :* 'Early Life,' by P. W. Clayden, 1887 ; 'Rogers and his Contemporaries,' by P. W. Clayden, 1889.

*ROSSETTI (Christina Georgina),** **1830-1894.** Born, in London, 5 Dec. 1830. Contrib. to 'The Germ' (under pseud. 'Ellen Alleyne'), 1850. Active literary life ; also intimately interested in religious work. Ill health for many years in later life. Died, in London, 29 Dec. 1894. Buried in Highgate Cemetery.

Works : 'To my Mother on the Anniversary of her Birth' (priv. ptd.), 1842 ; 'Verses' (priv. ptd.), 1847 ; 'Goblin Market,' 1862 ; 'The Prince's Progress,' 1866 ; 'Commonplace,' 1870 ; 'Sing Song,' 1872 ; 'Speaking Likenesses,' 1874 ; 'Annus Domini,' 1874 ; 'Seek and Find' [1879] ; 'Called to be Saints' [1881] ; 'A Pageant,' 1881 ; 'Letter and Spirit' [1883] ; 'Time Flies,' 1885 ; 'Poems . . . Enlarged edition,' 1891 ; 'The Face of the Deep,' 1892 ; 'Verses,' 1893. *Posthumous :* 'New Poems,' ed. by W. M. Rossetti, 1896 ; 'Maude,' 1897. *Life :* 'Brief Memoir,' by E. A. Proctor, 1895.

ROSSETTI (Dante Gabriel), 1828-1882. [Brother of preceding.] Born, in London, 12 May 1828. [Christened Gabriel Charles Dante, but always used above form of Christian name.] Educated at private school in London, 1836-37 ; at King's Coll., 1837-41. Studied drawing at F. S. Cary's Art School, 1842-46 ; at Royal Academy, 1846-48. Member of 'Pre-Raphaelite Brotherhood,' with Holman Hunt, Woolner, and Millais. Contrib. to 'The Germ,' 1850. Contrib. poems to 'Oxford and Cambridge Mag.,' 1856 ; 'Fortnightly Rev.,' 1869 ; 'Athenæum,' 1873-74. Active artistic and literary life. Married Elizabeth Eleanor Siddal, 23 May 1860. She died, 11 Feb. 1862. Buried his MS. poems in her coffin ; they were disinterred, Oct. 1869. Failing health from 1872. Died, at Birchington, 9 April 1882. Buried there.

Works : 'Sir Hugh the Heron' (priv. ptd.), 1843 ; 'Poems,' 1870 (2nd edn. same year ; new edn., with alterations, 1881) ; 'Ballads and Sonnets,' 1881 ; 'Verses' (priv. ptd.), 1881.

Posthumous : 'Family Letters,' ed. by W. M. Rossetti, 1895 ; 'Hand and Soul' (from 'The Germ') ; ptd. at Kelmscott Press), 1895.

He *translated :* 'The Early Italian Poets,' 1861 (another edn., called 'Dante and his Circle,' 1874 [1873]).

Collected Works: in 2 vols., ed. by W. M. Rossetti, 1886.

Life : by William Sharp, 1882 ; 'D. G. Rossetti as Designer and Writer,' by W. M. Rossetti, 1889 ; Memoir by W. M. Rossetti in edn. of 'Family Letters,' 1895.

ROSSETTI (William Michael), b. 1829. [Brother of preceding.] Born, in London, 25 Sept. 1829. At King's Coll. School, Sept. 1837 to Feb. 1845. Clerk in Inland Revenue Office (Excise), Feb. 1845 ; Assistant Sec., July 1869. Took active part in 'Pre-Raphaelite' movement, from 1848. Edited 'The Germ,' 1850. Married Emma Lucy Madox Brown, 31 March 1874 ; she died, 12 April 1894. Retired from Civil Service, 31 Aug. 1894.

Works : 'Swinburne's Poems and Ballads,' 1866 ; 'Fine Art,' 1867 ; 'Notes on the Royal Academy Exhibition' (with A. C. Swinburne), 1868 ; 'Memoir of Shelley' [1870] ; 'Lives of Famous Poets,' 1878 ; 'Shelley's Prometheus Unbound,' 1886 ; 'Life of John Keats,' 1887 ; 'Dante Gabriel Rossetti as Designer and Writer,' 1889.

He has *translated :* Dante's 'Inferno,' 1865 ; and *edited :* Whitman's Poems, 1868 ; 'Italian Courtesy-Books, etc.' (for E. E. Text Soc.), 1869, etc. ; Shelley's Poems, 1870 ; 'Moxon's Popular Poets,' 1870-80 ; 'Chaucer's Troylus and Cryseyde compared with Boccaccio's Filostrato,' 1873-83 ; Blake's Poems, 1874 ; O. Madox Brown's 'The Dwale Bluth' (with F. Hueffer), 1876 ; D. G. Rossetti's 'Collected Works,' 1886 ; H. H. Gilchrist's 'Anne Gilchrist,' 1887 ; Shelley's 'Adonais,' 1891 ; F. W. L. Adams 'Tiberius,' 1894 ; D. G. Rossetti's 'Family Letters,' with memoir, 1895 ; Augusta Webster's 'Mother and Daughter,' 1895 ; C. G. Rossetti's 'New Poems,' 1896.

ROWE (Nicholas), 1674-1718. Born, at Little Barford, Bedfordshire, 1674 ; baptized, 30 June. Early education at a school at Highgate. To Westminster School as King's Scholar, 1688. Called to Bar at Middle Temple. Abandoned legal profession after death of his father in 1692. Married (i.) Antonia Parsons, 1700 [?]. Play, 'The Ambitious Stepmother,' produced at Lincoln's Inn Fields, 1700 ; 'Tamerlane,' 1702 ; 'The Fair Penitent,' 1703 ; 'The Biter,' 1704 ; 'Ulysses,' 1706. 'The Royal Convert,' Haymarket, 25 Nov. 1707 ; 'Jane Shore,' Drury Lane, 2 Feb. 1714 ; 'Lady Jane Grey,' Drury Lane, 20 April 1715. Wife died, 1706. Under-Secretary to Sec. of State for Scotland, 1709-11. Poet Laureate, Aug. 1715. Surveyor of Customs, Oct. 1715. Married (ii.) Anne Devenish, 1717. Clerk of Council

16

to Prince of Wales. Clerk of Pre-
sentations, 1718. Died, in London, 6
Dec. 1718. Buried in Westminster
Abbey.

Works : ' The Ambitious Step-
mother,' 1701 ; ' Tamerlane,' 1702 ;
'The Fair Penitent,' 1703 ; 'Britannia's
Charge to the Sons of Freedom,' 1703 ;
'The Biter,' 1705 ; ' Ulysses,' 1706 ;
' Ode on the late Glorious successes of
Her Majesty's Arms,' 1707 ; 'The
Royal Convert,' 1708 ; ' The Tragedy
of Jane Shore ' [1714] ; 'Poems on
Several Occasions,' 1714 ; ' Mæcenas,'
1714 ; 'The Tragedy of Lady Jane
Grey,' 1715 ; ' Ode for the New Year
1716,' 1716.

He *translated :* Boileau's ' Lutrin,'
1708 ; De La Bruyère's ' Characters,'
1708 ; Quillet's ' Callipædiæ,' 1710 ;
Lucan's ' Pharsalia,' 1718 ; and *edited :*
Shakespeare's Works, 1709.

Collected Works : in 3 vols., 1727 ;
in 2 vols., ed. by Dr. Johnson, 1792.

ROWLEY (William), 1585[?]-1642[?].
Born, 1585[?]. For many years an
actor and dramatist. Collaborated
frequently with Middleton. Probably
retired from stage about 1630. Married Isabel Tooley, 1637. Died 1642[?].

Works : 'The Travailes of the Three
English Brothers' (with Wilkins and
Day), 1607 ; 'A Search for Money,'
1609 ; ' A Fair Quarrel' (with Mid-
dleton), 1617 ; ' A Courtly Masque :
the device called, The World Tost at
Tennis' (with Middleton), [1620];
' A Farewell Elegie on the Death of
Hugh Atwell,' 1621 ; ' A New Wonder:
a Woman Never Vext,' 1632 ; ' All's
Lost by Lust,' 1633 ; 'A Match at
Midnight,' 1633 ; 'A Shoomaker a
Gentleman,' 1638 ; 'The Changeling'
(with Middleton), 1653 ; 'The Spanish
Gipsy' (with Middleton), 1653 ; 'Fortune by Land and Sea' (with Heywood), 1655 ; 'The Excellent Comedy
called the Old Law ' (with Massinger
and Middleton), 1656 ; 'The Witch
of Edmonton ' (with Dekker, Ford,
and others), 1658 ; 'A Cure for a
Cuckold' (with Webster), 1661 ; 'The
Thracian Wonder,' 1661 ; 'The Birth
of Merlin ' (pubd. as by Shakspeare

and Rowley, but written by Rowley
alone), 1662.

*RUSKIN (John), b. 1819 Born, in
London, 8 Feb. 1819. Privately edu-
cated. Matric. Ch. Ch., Oxford, 20
Oct. 1836 ; went into residence, 14
Jan. 1837 ; Newdigate Prize Poem,
1839 ; B.A., May 1842 ; M.A., 28
Oct. 1843 ; Hon. Student, Ch. Ch.,
1867 ; Hon. Fellow, Corpus Christi
Coll., 1871 ; Slade Prof. of Fine Art,
1869-79 and 1883-85. Contrib. to
various periodicals, from 1834. Rede
Lecturer, Camb., 1867 ; Hon. LL.D.,
Camb., 15 May 1867. Endowed
School of Drawing in Taylorian Mu-
seum, Oxford, 1871.

Works : ' Salsette and Elephanta '
(Newdigate Prize Poem), 1839 ;
' Modern Painters,' vol. i. (anon.)
1843 ; vol. ii. (anon.), 1846 ; vols. iii.,
iv., 1856 ; vol. v., 1860 ; 'The Seven
Lamps of Architecture,' 1849 ; 'Poems'
(under initials : J. R.), 1850 ; 'The
King of the Golden River ' (anon.),
1851 ; ' The Stones of Venice,' vol. i.,
1851 ; vols. ii., iii., 1853 ; abridged
edn. of whole, 1879 ; 'Examples of
the Architecture of Venice,' 1851 ;
' Notes on the Construction of Sheep-
folds,' 1851 ; ' Pre-Raphaelitism,'
1851 ; 'The National Gallery' (from
the ' Times,' anon.), 1852 ; ' Giotto
and his Works in Padua ' (3 pts.),
1854-60 ; ' Lectures on Architecture
and Painting,' 1854 ; ' Letters to the
"Times" on the principal Pre-Raphaelite Pictures in the Exhibition,'
1854 ; ' The Opening of the Crystal
Palace,' 1854 ; ' Notes on . . . the
Royal Academy,' no. i., 1855 ; no. ii.,
1856 ; no. iii., 1857 ; no. iv., 1858 ;
no. v., 1859 ; ' The Harbours of England,' 1856 ; ' Notes on the Turner
Gallery at Marlborough House,' 1857 ;
' Catalogue of the Turner Sketches in
the National Gallery,' pt. i., 1857 (enlarged edn. same year) ; ' Catalogue
of the Sketches and Drawings by J.
M. W. Turner . . . at Marlborough
House,' 1857 (enlarged edn., 1858) ;
' The Elements of Drawing,' 1857 ;
' The Political Economy of Art,' 1857 ;
' Inaugural Address at the Cambridge

School of Art,' 1858 ; 'The Oxford Museum' (with H. W. Acland), 1859; 'The Two Paths,' 1859 ; 'The Unity of Art' (priv. ptd.), 1859 ; 'The Elements of Perspective,' 1859 ; 'Selections' from his works, 1861 ; '"Unto this Last,"' 1862 ; 'Sesame and Lilies,' 1865 ; 'An Enquiry into some of the Conditions at present affecting the Study of Architecture in our Schools,' 1865 ; 'The Ethics of the Dust,' 1866 : 'The Crown of ᵦWild Olive,' 1866 ; 'Time and Tide by Weare and Tyne,' 1867 ; 'First Notes on the General Principles of Employment for the Destitute and Criminal Classes' (priv. ptd.), 1868 ; 'Leoni' (under initials : J. R.), 1868 ; 'The Queen of the Air,' 1869 ; 'Samuel Prout' (priv. ptd.), 1870 ; 'The Future of England' [1870]; 'Verona and its Rivers,' 1870 ; 'Lectures on Art,' 1870 ; 'Catalogue of Examples . . . in the University Galleries, 1870 ; 'Works' (11 vols.), 1871-83 ; 'Fors Clavigera' (8 vols.), 1871-84 ; ['Index' to preceding, 1887 ;] 'Munera Pulveris,' 1872 ; 'Aratra Pentelici,' 1872 ; 'The Relation between Michael Angelo and Tintoret,' 1872 ; 'The Eagle's Nest,' 1872 ; 'The Sepulchral Monuments of Italy,' 1872 ; 'Instructions in Elementary Drawing' (priv. ptd.), 1872 ; 'Instructions in the Preliminary Exercises,' 1873 ; 'Love's Meinie,' 1873 ; 'The Nature and Authority of Miracle' (priv. ptd.), 1873 ; 'Val d'Arno,' 1874 ; 'Frondes Agrestes' (selected from 'Modern Painters'), 1875 ; 'Notes on Some of the Principal Pictures in the . . . Royal Academy,' 1875 ; 'Proserpina' (10 pts.), 1875-86 ; 'Deucalion' (8 pts.), 1875-83 ; 'Mornings in Florence' (8 pts.), 1875-77 ; 'Ariadne Florentina,' 1876 ; 'Letters to the "Times,"' (anon.), 1876 ; 'Letter to Young Girls' [1876]; 'St. Mark's Rest,' 1877-84 ; 'Guide to the Principal Pictures in the Academy of Fine Arts at Venice,' 1877 ; 'Yewdale and its Streamlets,' 1877 ; 'The Laws of Fésole' (4 pts.), 1877-79 ; 'Abstract of the Objects . . . of St. George's Guild' [1878]; 'Notes by Mr. Ruskin on his Collection of Drawings by the late J. M. W. Turner,' 1878 ; 'Letters to the Clergy' (priv. ptd.), 1879 ; 'Circular respecting . . . St. Mark's,' 1879-80 ; 'Elements of English Prosody,' 1880 ; 'Notes . . . on S. Prout and W. Hunt,' 1880 ; 'Arrows of the Chace' (2 vols.). 1880 ; 'The Lord's Prayer and the Church,' 1880 ; '"Our Fathers have told us,"' 1880-85 ; 'General Statement explaining the . . . St. George's Guild,' 1882 ; 'The Art of England,' 1883-84 ; 'Cœli Enarrant' (selected from 'Modern Painters'), 1884 ; 'Catalogue of Selected Examples of Native Silica in the British Museum,' 1884 ; 'The Pleasures of England,' 1884 ; 'In Montibus Sanctis' (selected from 'Modern Painters'), 1884 ; 'The Storm-cloud of the Nineteenth Century,' 1884 ; 'On the Old Road' (2 vols.), 1885 ; 'Præterita' (3 vols.), 1885-88 ; 'Notes on the Principal Pictures of Sir J. E. Millais,' 1886 ; 'Dilecta' (2 pts.), 1886-87 ; 'Hortus Inclusus,' 1887 ; 'Poems,' 1891 ; 'Gold' (priv. ptd.), 1891 ; 'Letters . . . to various Correspondents' (priv. ptd.), 1892 ; 'Stray Letters to a London Bibliophile' (priv. ptd.), 1892 ; 'The Poetry of Architecture,' 1893 [1892] ; 'Three Letters and an Essay on Literature,' 1893 ; 'Letters to W. Ward' (priv. ptd.), 1893 ; 'Letters addressed to a College Friend,' 1894 ; 'Letters . . . to Ernest Chesneau' (priv. ptd.), 1894 ; 'Letters on Art and Literature' (ed. by T. J. Wise ; priv. ptd.), 1894 ; 'Verona, and other Lectures,' 1894 ; 'Letters to . . . Rev. J. P. Faunthorpe' (ed. by T. J. Wise ; priv. ptd.), 1895, etc.; 'Studies in Both Arts,' 1895.

He has *edited :* A. C. Owen's 'The Art Schools of Mediæval Christendom,' 1876 ; 'Bibliotheca Pastorum,' vols. i., ii., 1876-77 ; vol. iv., 1885 ; F. Alexander's 'The Story of Ida,' 1883 ; F. Alexander's 'Roadside Songs of Tuscany,' 1884-85 ; 'Dame Wiggins of Lee,' 1885 ; 'Ulric the Farm Servant,' 1886 ; F. Alexander's 'Christ's Folk in the Apennine'; and has contributed prefatory letters or introductions to various works.

*RUSSELL (William Clark), b. 1844.
Born, in New York, 24 Feb. 1844.
Educated at private schools at Winchester and Boulogne, 1853-56. In British Merchant Service, 1857-64. Adopted literary career. Married Alexandrina Henry, 27 June 1868. On staff of 'Newcastle Daily Chronicle,' and of 'Daily Telegraph' respectively. Gave up journalism, 1887. Of late years has resided at Bath.

Works: 'John Holdsworth' (anon.), 1875 ; 'The Wreck of the "Grosvenor"' (anon.), 1877 ; 'The Little Loo,' 1878 ; 'A Sailor's Sweetheart,' 1880 ; 'An Ocean Free-Lance,' 1881 ; 'The "Lady Maud" Schooner Yacht,' 1882; 'My Watch Below' (anon.), 1882 ; 'A Sea Queen,' 1883 ; 'Round the Galley-Fire,' 1883 ; 'Sailors' Language,' 1883 ; 'Jack's Courtship,' 1884 ; 'English Channel Ports, etc.,' 1884 ; 'On the Fo'k'sle Head,' 1884 ; 'A Forecastle View of the Shipping Commission,' 1885 ; 'A Strange Voyage,' 1885 ; 'In the Middle Watch,' 1885 ; 'A Voyage to the Cape,' 1886 ; 'A Book for the Hammock,' 1887 ; 'The Frozen Pirate,' 1887 ; 'The Golden Hope,' 1887 ; 'The Death-Ship,' 1888 ; 'The Mystery of the "Ocean Star,"' 1888 ; 'Betwixt the Forelands,' 1889 ; 'Marooned,' 1889 ; 'The Romance of Jenny Harlowe,' 1889 ; 'William Dampier,' 1889 ; 'An Ocean Tragedy,' 1890 ; 'The Romance of a Wreck,' 1890 ; 'Horatio Nelson,' 1890 ; 'Collingwood,' 1891 ; 'A Marriage at Sea,' 1891 ; 'Master Rockafellar's Voyage,' 1891 ; 'My Danish Sweetheart,' 1891 ; 'A Strange Elopement,' 1892 ; 'Mrs. Dines' Jewels,' 1892 ; 'The British Seas' (with others), 1892; 'Alone on a Wide, Wide Sea,' 1892 ; 'The Emigrant Ship,' 1893 ; 'List, ye Landsmen!' 1893 ; 'The Tragedy of Ida Noble,' 1893 ; 'Miss Parson's Adventure,' 1894 [1893] ; 'The Good Ship "Mohock,"' 1894 ; 'The Phantom Death,' 1895 ; 'The Convict Ship,' 1895 ; 'Heart of Oak,' 1895 ; 'What Cheer?' 1896 ; 'The Tale of the Ten,' 1896 ; 'The Honour of the Flag,' 1896 ; 'A Noble Haul,' 1897 ;

'A Tale of Two Tunnels,' 1897 ; 'The Last Entry,' 1897.
He has *edited:* 'Nelson's Words and Deeds : a Selection,' 1890.

*RUSSELL (*Sir* William Howard), b. 1820. Born, at Lilyvale, co. Dublin, 28 March 1820. Educated at Rev. Dr. Geoghegan's School, Dublin ; afterwards at Trin. Coll., Dublin, 1838-40. Joined staff of the 'Times,' 1843. Married (i.) Mary Burrowes, 26 Sept 1846. Student at Middle Temple, 2 May 1846 ; called to Bar, 7 June 1850. Special Correspondent of the 'Times' during Crimean War (present at Alma, Inkerman, Balaclava, etc.), 1854-56 ; at Coronation of Czar in Moscow, 1856 ; during Indian Mutiny (Siege of Lucknow, Battle of Bareilly Oude campaign), 1857-58 ; during Italian campaign, 1859 ; during Civil War in United States (Battle of Bull Run), 1861-62 ; during war between Prussia and Austria (Battle of Sadowa), 1866 ; during Franco-German War (Battles of Wörth, Sedan, Siege of Paris), 1870. LL.D., Trin. Coll., Dublin, 1856. Has edited 'Army and Navy Gazette' since 1858. Wife died, 1867. With suite of Prince of Wales in Egypt, 1868. Hon. Private Sec. to Prince of Wales on his visit to India, 1875-76. Accompanied Lord Wolseley's forces in S. Africa, 1879-80 ; war in Egypt, 1883-84. War medals and decorations : Turkish War Medal, Osmanieh Medjidieh, Indian Mutiny (clasp for Lucknow), Crimean, Officer of Legion of Honour, Austrian Order Franz Josef, Portuguese and Greek orders St. Sauveur, South African War Medal, etc. Married (ii.) Countess Antonietta Matilda Alexandrina Pia Malvezzi, 18 Feb. 1884. Knighted, 1895. Is an F.Z.S. and F.R.G.S.

Works : 'The War' (2 vols.), 1855-56 ; 'Rifle Clubs and Volunteer Corps,' 1859 ; 'My Diary in India' (2 vols.), 1860 ; 'The Battle of Bull Run,' 1861 ; 'My Diary North and South' (3 vols.), 1863-65 ; 'A Memorial of the Marriage of . . . Albert Edward, Prince of Wales,' 1864 ; 'Gen. Todleben's History of the Defence of Sebastopol,' 1865 ; 'The Atlantic Telegraph' [1866] ; 'The Adventures of Doctor Brady' (from 'Tinsley's Mag.'), 1868 ; 'A Diary in the East during the Tour of the Prince and Princess of Wales,' 1869 ; 'My Diary during the last Great War,' 1874 ; 'The Prince of Wales's Tour: a Diary in India,' 1877 ; 'The Crimea,' 1881 ; 'Hesperothen,' 1882 ; 'A Visit to Chile,' 1890 ; 'The Great War with Russia,' 1895.

He has *edited :* 'The Crimean Diary of Sir C. A. Windham,' 1897.

RYMER (Thomas), 1641 - 1713. Born, at Yafforth, Yorkshire, 1641. Early education at a school at Danby-Wiske. Matric. Sidney Sussex Coll., Camb., as Minor Pensioner, 29 April 1658. Took no degree. Student of Gray's Inn, 2 May 1666 ; called to Bar, 16 June 1673. Devoted himself mainly to literature. Historiographer Royal, 1692. Appointed to edit publication of the treaties between Great Britain and the Foreign Powers, 1693. Engaged on this till his death. Died, in London, 14 Dec. 1713. Buried in St. Clement Danes Church.

Works : 'Edgar,' 1678 ; 'The Tragedies of the Last Age considered' [1678] ; 'A General Draught . . . of Government in Europe' (anon.), 1681 ; 'Of the Antiquity, Power, and Decay of Parliaments,' 1684 ; 'A Poem on the arrival of Queen Mary,' 1689 ; 'A Short View of Tragedy,' 1693 [1692] ; 'Three Letters to the Bishop of Carlisle' (anon.), 1702-06.

He *translated :* 'Cicero's Prince,' 1668 ; Rapin's 'Reflections on Aristotle's Treatise of Poesie,' 1674 ; and *edited :* 'Foedera,' vols. i.-xv., 1704-13.

SACKVILLE (Thomas), *Earl of Dorset*, 1536-1608. Born, at Buckhurst, Sussex, 1536. Probably educated at Sullington Grammar School. Incumbent of the Chantry at Sullington Church, 1546. Called to Bar at Inner Temple. Married Cicely Baker, 1554. M.P. for Westmoreland, 1558 ; for East Grinstead, 1559 ; for Aylesbury, 1563. Tragedy 'Gorboduc' (written with Norton), performed in Inner Temple Hall, 1561. Grand Master of Freemasons, 1561-67. Travelled on Continent, 1563 - 66. Knighted, and created Baron Buckhurst, 8 June 1567. Privy Councillor. Lord Lieutenant of Sussex, 1569. On political missions to France, 1568 and 1571. To Holland, 1587 and 1589 ; to France, 1591 and 1598. Created M.A., Camb., Aug. 1571. Commissioner for Ecclesiastical Causes, 1588. K.G., 24 April 1589. Chancellor of Oxford University, Dec. 1591 ; incorporated M.A., 6 Jan. 1592. Commissioner of Writs, 1592[?]. Lord Treasurer, 1599. Lord High Steward, 1601. Created Earl of Dorset, 13 March 1604. Died suddenly, at Whitehall, 19 April 1608. Buried in Westminster Abbey.

Works : Contribution to 'A Myrroure for Magistrates,' 1559-63 ; 'The Tragedy of Gorboduc' (with Norton), 1565 ; Verses contributed to Sir T. Hoby's 'Courtier,' 1561 ; and possibly to 'A Paradise of Dainty Devices,' 1576.

Collected Works : ed. by Rev. R. W. Sackville West, 1859.

ST. JOHN (Henry), *Viscount Bolingbroke*, 1678-1751. Born, in London, 1678 ; baptized 10 Oct. Educated at Eton. Married (i.) Francis Winchcombe, 1700. M.P. for Wootton-Bassett, Dec. 1701. Hon. D.D., Oxford, 1702. Sec. for War, 1704. Re-elected M.P. for Wootton-Bassett, 1705. Sec. of State, 1710-14. M.P. for Berkshire, Oct. 1710. Created Viscount Bolingbroke and Baron St. John of Lydiard Tregoze, 7 July 1712. Sec. of State to Pretender, July 1714 to 1716. Abandoned Jacobite Cause, 1716. Wife died, Nov. 1718. Married (ii.) Mme. Marie Claire de Villette, May 1720. Restored to favour at English Court, 1723. Resumed political life. Contrib. to 'The Craftsman,' 1727-34. In later years spent much time in France. Political career ended, 1740. Died, in London, 12 Dec. 1751. Buried at Battersea.

Works : 'Letter to the "Examiner"'

(anon.), 1710 ; 'Considerations upon the Secret History of the White Staff' (anon. ; attrib. to Bolingbroke), 1714 ; 'The Public Spirit of the Whigs' (anon. ; with Swift), 1714 ; 'The Representation of the Lord Viscount Bolingbroke' (anon. ; attrib. to Bolingbroke), 1715 ; 'Letter . . . to the Dean of St. Patrick's' (anon.), 1715 ; 'The Occasional Writer' (anon.), 1727 ; 'Observations on the Public Affairs of Great Britain' (under pseud. : 'W. Raleigh'), 1729 ; 'The Craftsman Extraordinary' (3 pts. ; anon.), 1729 ; 'Letter to Caleb Danvers' (under pseud. : 'John Trott'), 1730 ; 'A Final Answer to the Remarks on the Craftsman's Vindication' (anon.), 1731 ; 'The Freeholder's Political Catechism' (from 'The Craftsman'), 1733 ; 'The Idea of a Patriot King' (anon.), [1735 ?] ; 'A Dissertation upon Parties' (from 'The Craftsman,' 1735 (2nd edn. same year) ; 'Good Queen Anne Vindicated' (anon.), 1748 ; 'A Collection of Political Tracts' (anon.), 1748 ; 'Letters on the Spirit of Patriotism' (anon.), 1749 ; 'A Familiar Letter to the most impudent man living' (anon.), 1749.

Posthumous : 'Letters on the Study and Use of History' (2 vols.), 1752 ; 'Reflections concerning Innate Moral Principles,' 1752 ; 'Letters to Dr. Jonathan Swift,' 1752 ; 'Letter to Sir W. Wyndham,' 1753 ; 'Reflections on the State of the Nation,' 1753 ; 'Introductory Letter to Pope,' 1753 ; 'Letters and Correspondence,' ed. by G. Parke (4 vols.), 1798.

Collected Works : ed. by D. Mallet (5 vols.), 1754.

Life : by T. Macknight, 1863.

*SAINTSBURY (George Edward Bateman), b. 1845. Born, at Southampton, 23 Oct. 1845. At King's Coll. School, London, autumn 1858 to summer 1863. Matric. Merton Coll., Oxford, 17 Oct. 1863 ; Postmaster, 1863-68 ; B.A., 1867 ; M.A., 1873. Student of Inner Temple, 1866. Assistant-Master, Manchester Grammar School, 1868. Married Emily Fenn King, 2 June 1868. Senior Classical Master, Elizabeth Coll., Guernsey, 1868-74. Headmaster of Elgin Educational Institute, 1874-76. Removed to London, 1876. Frequent contributor to periodicals since 1876. Prof. of Rhetoric and English Literature, Edinburgh Univ., 1895. Removed to Edinburgh, Oct. 1895.

Works : 'Primer of French Literature,' 1880 ; 'Dryden,' 1881 ; 'Short History of the Life and Writings of A. R. Le Sage' (priv. ptd.), [1881] ; 'Short History of French Literature,' 1882 ; 'Marlborough,' 1885 ; 'History of Elizabethan Literature,' 1887 ; 'Manchester,' 1887 ; 'Essays in English Literature,' 1st series, 1890 ; 2nd series, 1895 ; 'Essays on French Novelists,' 1891 ; 'Miscellaneous Essays,' 1892 ; 'The Earl of Derby,' 1892 ; 'Corrected Impressions,' 1895 ; 'Inaugural Address delivered at Edinburgh,' 1895 ; 'History of Nineteenth Century Literature,' 1896 ; 'Sir Walter Scott,' 1897 ; 'The Flourishing of Romance and the Rise of Allegory,' 1897.

He has *translated :* Balzac's 'The Chouans,' 1890 ; Merimée's 'Chronicle of the Reign of Charles IX.,' 1890 ; Scherer's 'Essays on English Literature,' 1891.

He has *edited :* Corneille's 'Horace,' 1882 ; Dryden's Works, 1882, etc. ; 'French Lyrics,' 1882 ; 'Specimens of French Literature,' 1883 ; 'Specimens of English Prose Style,' 1885 ; Voltaire's 'Merope,' 1885 ; Quinet's 'Lettres à sa Mère,' 1885 ; Sainte-Beuve's 'Causeries du Lundi,' 1885 ; Gautier's 'Scenes of Travel,' 1886 ; 'Gulliver's Travels,' 1886 ; Racine's 'Esther,' 1886 ; 'The Vicar of Wakefield,' 1886 ; Molière's 'L'École des Femmes,' 1888 ; 'The Pocket Library of English Literature,' 1891 - 92 ; Swift's 'Polite Conversation,' 1892 ; Florio's 'Montaigne,' 1892, etc.; Fielding's Works, 1893, etc. ; Herrick's Works, 1893 ; Madame de Staël's 'Corinne,' 1894 ; Sterne's Works, 1894 ; Jane Austen's 'Pride and Prejudice,' 1894 ; Marmontel's 'Moral Tales,' selected, 1895 ; Peacock's Novels, 1895, etc. ; Richardson's 'Letters from Sir Charles Grandison,' 1895 ;

Smollett's Works, 1895, etc.; Balzac's 'Comédie Humaine' (trans. by various writers), 1895, etc.

*SALA (George Augustus Henry), 1828-1895. Born, in London, 24 Nov. 1828. Educated at a school in Paris, 1839-41 ; at Turnham Green, 1842. Studied drawing, 1842-43. Worked as scene-painter and book-illustrator, 1845-48. Contributed to 'Family Herald,' 1845 ; to 'Chat' (which he afterwards edited), 1848. Started 'Conservative Mag.' (only one number pubd.), 1850. Contrib. to 'Household Words,'from 1851 ; to 'Illustrated Times,' 1855 ; to 'Comic Times,' 1855. Edited weekly paper, 'London,' 1853-54. To St. Petersburg, on commission for 'Household Words,' 1856. First wrote for 'Daily Telegraph,' 1857 ; remained on its staff for greater part of life. One of founders of Savage Club, 1857. On staff of 'All the Year Round,' 1858-70. Married (i.) Mrs. Harriet Sala, 1859. Contrib. to 'The Welcome Guest,' 1859 ; to 'Cornhill Mag.,' 1860. Started 'Temple Bar,' Dec. 1860 ; edited it till 1866. Contrib. 'Echoes of the Week' to 'Illustrated London News,' 1860-86 ; to 'Sunday Times,' 1886-94. Mem. of Reform Club, 13 March 1862. Special Correspondent to 'Daily Telegraph,' in United States, Nov. 1863 to Dec. 1864 ; in Algeria, 1865 ; during Austro-Italian War, Nov. 1865 to 1867 ; in Paris, 1867 and 1870 ; in Rome, 1870 ; in Spain, 1875 ; in Russia and Turkey, 1876-77 ; in Paris, 1878 ; in America, Dec. 1879 to spring of 1880 ; in St. Petersburg, 1881 and 1883 ; in America, Australia and India (also lecturing), Dec. 1884 to 1885. Wife died, Dec. 1885. Married (ii.) Bessie Stannard, 1891. Started 'Sala's Journal' with her, May 1892 ; it ceased to be published, 1894. Civil List Pension, 1895. Died, at Brighton, 8 Dec. 1895.

Works: 'Ye Belle Alliance' [1856]; 'A Journey Due North,' 1858 ; 'How I tamed Mrs. Cruiser,' 1858 ; 'Twice Round the Clock' [1859] ; 'Gaslight and Daylight,' 1859; 'The Baddington Peerage,' 1860 ; 'Lady Chesterfield's Letters to her Daughter,' 1860 ; 'Looking at Life,' 1860 ; 'Narrative of the Grand Volunteer Review,' 1860 (2nd edn. same year) ; 'Target Shooting,' 1860 ; 'Make your Game,' 1860 ; 'Dutch Pictures,' 1861 ; 'The Seven Sons of Mammon,' 1862 ; 'The Two Prima Donnas,' 1862 ; 'The Ship Chandler,'1862; 'Accepted Addresses,' 1862 ; 'The Strange Adventures of Captain Dangerous,' 1863 ; 'Breakfast in Bed,' 1863 ; 'The Perfidy of Captain Sly-Boots,' 1863 ; 'Robson,' 1864 ; 'After Breakfast,' 1864 ; 'Quite Alone,' 1864 ; 'My Diary in America,' 1865 ; 'A Trip to Barbary,' 1866 ; 'William Hogarth,' 1866 ; 'From Waterloo to the Peninsula,' 1867 [1866] ; 'Notes and Sketches of the Paris Exhibition,' 1868 ; 'The Battle of the Safes,' 1868 ; 'Rome and Venice,' 1869 ; 'Wat Tyler, M.P ,' 1869 ; 'The Late M. D——.' [1870] ; 'Charles Dickens' [1870] ; 'Papers, humorous and pathetic,' 1872; 'Under the Sun,' 1872 ; 'The Story of the Comte de Chambord,' 1873 ; 'India and the Prince of Wales' [1875] ; 'Paris Herself Again,' 1880 [1879]; 'The Hats of Humanity' [1880] ; 'America Revisited,' 1882 ; 'Living London,' 1883 ; 'Stories with a Vengeance' (with others), 1883 ; 'Dead Men tell no Tales' [1884] ; 'Echoes of the Year 1883,' 1884 ; 'A Journey Due South,' 1885 ; 'Mrs. General Mucklestrap's Four Tall Daughters' [1887] ; 'Right Round the World' [1887] ; 'Dublin Whiskey' [1888] ; 'Not a Friend in the World' [1890] ; 'Things I have Seen and People I have Known,' 1894 ; 'London Up to Date,' 1894 ; 'Life and Adventures' (autobiog.), 1895 (3rd edn. same year); 'The Thorough Good Cook,' 1895 ; 'Brighton as I have known it,' 1895.

He *edited :* Lamb's 'Complete Correspondence and Works,' 1869 ; 'Yankee Drolleries' [1870] ; and contributed introductions to various publications.

SANDYS (George), 1578 - 1644. Born, at Bishopsthorpe, 2 March 1578. Matric., St. Mary Hall, Oxford, 5 Dec. 1589. Took no degree. Travelled

in Europe and the East, 1610-15. To
America, as Treasurer of Virginian
Company, April 1621. Returned,
1631[?]. Appointed Gentleman of
Privy Chamber to Charles I. Agent
in England to Legislative Assembly
of Virginia, 1638. Died, at Boxley,
Kent, 1644. Buried in Boxley Church.

Works : ' A Relation of a Journey,'
1615 ; ' Ovid's Metamorphoses translated into English Verse,' bks. i.-v.,
1621 ; complete, 1626 ; ' Sacræ Hep-
tades ' (under initials 'S.G.' ; attrib. to
Sandys), 1626 ; ' Paraphrase upon the
Psalmes of David,' 1636 ; ' A Paraphrase upon the Divine Poems,' 1638 ;
Translation of De Groot's ' Christ's
Passion,' 1640 ; ' A Paraphrase upon
the Song of Solomon,' 1641.

Collected Works : ' Poetical Works,'
ed. by Rev. R. Hooper, 1872.

SAVAGE (Richard), 1690 [?]-1743.
Born, about 1690 [?]. Play, ' Woman's a Riddle,' produced at Lincoln's
Inn Fields, 4 Dec. 1716 ; ' Love in a
Veil,' Drury Lane, 17 June 1718 ;
' Sir Thomas Overbury,' Drury Lane,
12 June 1723. Condemned to death,
for murder in a tavern brawl, Nov.
1727 ; pardoned, March 1728. Member of Lord Tyrconnel's household,
1728-34. Pension from Queen Caroline, 1732-37. Arrested for debt in
Bristol, 10 Jan. 1743. Died in
prison there, 1 Aug. 1743. Buried in
St. Peter's Churchyard, Bristol.

Works : ' The Convocation,' 1717 ;
' Memoirs of Theophilus Keene '
(anon.; attrib. to Savage), 1718 ;
' Love in a Veil,' 1719 ; ' Sir Thomas
Overbury,' 1724 ; ' A Poem, sacred to
the glorious memory of . . . King
George,' 1727 ; ' Nature in Perfection,'
1728 ; ' The Bastard,' 1728 ; ' The
Author to be Let ' [1728 ?] ; ' The
Wanderer,' 1729 ; 'Verses occasioned
by Lady Tyrconnel's Recovery,' 1730 ;
' Poem to the Memory of Mrs. Oldfield ' (anon.; attrib. to Savage),
1730 ; ' A Collection of Pieces . . .
publish'd on occasion of the Dunciad,'
1732 ; ' The Volunteer Laureat ' (6
nos.), 1732-37 ; ' On the Departure of
the Prince and Princess of Orange,'

1734 ; ' The Progress of a Divine,'
1735 ; ' Poem on the Birthday of the
Prince of Wales,' 1735 ; ' Of Public
Spirit in regard to Public Works,' 1737.

Posthumous : ' London and Bristol
Compared,' 1744 ; ' Various Poems,'
1761.

He *edited :* ' Miscellaneous Poems
and Translations, by several hands,'
1726.

Collected Works : in 2 vols., 1775.

SAVILE (George), *Marquis of
Halifax,* **1633-1695.** Born, at Thorn-
hill, Yorkshire, 11 Nov. 1633. Part
of his education perhaps conducted
abroad. Married (i.) Dorothy Spencer,
29 Dec. 1656. M.P. for Pontefract,
April 1660. Created Baron Savile of
Eland and Viscount Halifax, Jan.
1668. Commissioner of Trade, 1669.
Wife died, 16 Dec. 1670. Privy
Councillor, 1672. Married (ii.) Gertrude Pierrepoint, Nov. 1672. In
great favour at Court, from 1680-83.
Created Marquis of Halifax, Aug.
1682. Excluded from Privy Council
by James II., 1685; afterwards appointed President of Council. Prime
Mover in proclamation of William
and Mary as King and Queen, 1689.
Lord Privy Seal, Feb. 1689 to Feb.
1690. Excluded from Privy Council,
1692. Died, in London, 5 April 1695.
Buried in Westminster Abbey.

Works : ' Letter to a Dissenter '
(under initials T. W.), 1687 ; ' The
Character of a Trimmer ' (under
initials : Sir W. C.), 1688 ; ' The
Anatomy of an Equivalent ' (anon.),
1688 ; ' The Ladies-New-Years-Gift,
or Advice to a Daughter ' (anon.),
1688 ; ' Historical Observations upon
the Reigns of Edwards I., II., III.,
and Richard III.' (anon.), 1689 ; ' A
Letter from a Nobleman in London '
(anon.), [1689] ; ' The Character of
the Protestants in Ireland ' (anon. ;
attrib. to Halifax), 1689 ; ' Essay
upon Taxes,' 1693 ; ' Maxims,' 1693 ;
' Rough Draught of a New Model at
Sea,' 1694 ; ' Institutions, Essays and
Maxims ' (anon.), 1695.

Posthumous : ' Miscellanies by the
most noble George Lord Savile,'

1700; 'Character of King Charles II.,' 1750; 'Political, Moral, and Miscellaneous Thoughts and Reflections,' 175C

*SAYCE (Archibald Henry), b. 1846. Born at Shirehampton, near Bristol, 25 Sept. 1846. At Grosvenor Coll., Bath, 1860-64. Matric. Queen's Coll., Oxford, 9 March, 1865; scholar, 1865-69; B.A., 1869; M.A., 1871; Fellow of Queen's Coll., 1869; Tutor, 1870-79; Deputy Prof. of Comparative Philology, 1876-90; Hibbert Lecturer, 1887; Prof. of Assyriology, 1891. Ordained Deacon, 1870; Priest, 1871. Mem. of Old Test. Revision Committee, 1874-84. Hon. LL.D., Dublin, 1881; Hon. D.D., Edinburgh, 1889. Hon. Mem. of Royal Acad. of Madrid, 1883; of Asiatic Soc. of Bengal, 1884; of Anthropological Soc. of Washington, 1886; of Pekin Oriental Soc., 1890; of Polynesian Soc., 1891; of Royal Irish Academy, 1891; of American Oriental Society, 1893; of Imperial Archæological Soc. of Moscow, 1894.

Works : 'An Assyrian Grammar,' 1872; 'The Astronomy and Astrology of the Babylonians,' 1874; 'The Principles of Comparative Philology,' 1874; 'An Elementary Grammar ... of the Assyrian Language in the Cuneiform Type' [1875]; 'A Lecture on the Study of Comparative Philology,' 1876; 'Lectures upon the Assyrian Syllabary and Grammar,' 1877; 'Babylonian Literature' [1877]; 'Introduction to the Science of Language' (2 vols.), 1880; 'The Ancient Hebrew Inscription discovered at the Pool of Siloam,' 1881; 'Dr. Appleton' (with J. H. Appleton), 1881; 'Fresh Light from the Ancient Monuments,' 1884; 'The Witness of Ancient Monuments to the Old Testament Scriptures' [1884]; 'The Ancient Empires of the East,' 1884; 'Assyria,' 1885; 'Introduction to the books of Ezra, Nehemiah, and Esther,' 1885; 'Lectures on the Origin and Growth of Religion,' 1887; 'The Hittites,' 1888; 'The Life and Times of Isaiah,' 1889; 'The Races

of the Old Testament,' 1891; 'Social Life among the Assyrians and Babylonians,' 1893; 'The "Higher Criticism" and the Verdict of the Monuments,' 1894 [1893]; 'A Primer of Assyriology' [1894]; 'The Egypt of the Hebrews and Herodotus,' 1895; 'Patriarchal Palestine,' 1895.

He has *edited :* G. Smith's 'History of Babylonia,' 1877; G. Smith's translation of the 'History of Sennacherib,' 1878; G. Smith's 'Chaldean Account of Genesis,' 1880; 'Herodotus,' bks. i.-iii., 1883; H. S. Palmer's 'Sinai,' 1892; W. S. W. Vaux's 'Persia,' 1893; Maspero's 'Dawn of Civilization : Egypt and Chaldea,' 1894; Maspero's 'Struggle of the Nations— Egypt, Syria, and Assyria,' 1896.

*SCOTT (Michael), 1789-1835. Born, in Glasgow, 1789. Educated at Glasgow High School, and at Glasgow Univ. In Jamaica, as Estate Manager, 1806-10; in mercantile house, 1810-17. Returned to Scotland, 1817. Married, 1818. In Jamaica, 1818-22. Returned to Scotland, 1822. Remained there till his death. Contrib. to 'Blackwood's Mag.' from 1829. Died, 1835.

Works : 'Tom Cringle's Log' (anon.), 1833; 'The Cruise of the Midge' (anon.), 1834.

*SCOTT (*Sir* Walter), *Bart.*, 1771- 1832. Born, in Edinburgh, 15 Aug. 1771. At Edinburgh High School, 1778-82; at Kelso Grammar School, 1782-83. At Edinburgh Univ., Nov. 1783 to 1786. Apprenticed to his father (Writer to the Signet), May 1786. Began to study for Bar, 1789. Mem. of Speculative Soc., Jan. 1791. Called to Scotch Bar, 11 July 1792. Married Charlotte Margaret Carpenter, 24 Dec. 1797; settled in Edinburgh. Removed to Lasswade, 1798. First visit to London, 1799. Sheriff of Selkirkshire, 16 Dec. 1799. Contrib. to 'Edinburgh Rev.' from 1803. Friendship with Wordsworth begun, 1803. Removed to Ashestiel, near Selkirk, 1804. Partnership in printing firm of James Ballantyne,

1805. Clerk of Session, March 1806 to Aug. 1830. Sec. to Commission on Scotch Jurisprudence, 1807. Promoter of 'Quarterly Review,' first pubd. 1809. Started 'Edinburgh Annual Register,' 1810. Purchased Abbotsford, 1811 ; removed thither, May 1812. Refused Laureateship, Sep. 1813. Freedom of City of Edinburgh, 1813. Visit to Continent, 1815. Mem. of Scotch Regalia Commission, 1818. Created Baronet, 30 March 1820. Degrees of Hon. D.C.L., Oxford, and Hon. LL.D., Camb., offered him, May 1820 ; but he was prevented on this and other occasions from attending to receive them. Pres. of Royal Soc. of Edinburgh, Nov. 1820. Founder and Pres. of Bannatyne Club, 1823 ; Mem. of Roxburghe Club, 1823. Visit to Ireland, 1825. Bankrupt through failure of firm of Ballantyne and Co., 1826. Wife died, 15 May, 1826. To Italy, for health, 1831. Returned to Abbotsford, July 1832. Died there, 21 Sept. 1832. Buried at Dryburgh Abbey.

Works : 'The Eve of Saint John,' 1800 ; 'The Lay of the Last Minstrel,' 1805 ; 'Ballads and Lyrical Pieces,' 1806 (2nd edn. same year) ; 'Marmion,' 1808 ; 'Life of Dryden' (from his edn. of Dryden's Works), 1808 ; 'The Lady of the Lake,' 1810 ; 'The Vision of Don Roderick,' 1811 ; 'Glenfinlas,' 1812 ; 'Rokeby,' 1813 ; 'The Bridal of Triermain' (anon.), 1813 (2nd edn. same year) ; 'Waverley' (anon.), 1814 ; 'The Border Antiquities of England and Scotland' (2 vols.), 1814-17 ; 'The Lord of the Isles,' 1815 ; 'Guy Mannering' (anon.), 1815 ; 'The Field of Waterloo,' 1815 ; 'Paul's Letters to his Kinsfolk' (anon.),1816 ; 'The Antiquary' (anon.), 1816 ; 'Tales of my Landlord' (under pseud. : 'Jedediah Cleisbotham '), 1st series ('The Black Dwarf,' 'Old Mortality '), 1816 ; 2nd ser. ('The Heart of Midlothian '), 1818 ; 3rd ser. ('The Bride of Lammermoor'; 'The Legend of Montrose'), 1819 ; 4th ser. ('Count Robert of Paris,' 'Castle Dangerous '), 1832 ; 'Harold the Dauntless ' (anon.), 1817 ; 'Rob

Roy ' (anon.), 1818 ; 'The Visionary' (under pseud. : 'Sonambulus '), 1819 ; 'Novels and Tales of the author of "Waverley "' (41 vols.), 1819-33 ; 'Description of the Regalia of Scotland' (anon.),1819 ; 'Ivanhoe' (anon.), 1819 ; 'Memorials of the Haliburtons,' 1820 ; 'Miscellaneous Poems,' 1820 ; 'The Monastery' (anon.), 1820 ; 'Poetical Works' (12 vols.), 1820 ; 'The Abbot' (anon.), 1820 ; 'Kenilworth' (anon.), 1821 ; 'The Pirate' (anon.), 1821 ; 'Poetical Works' (11 vols.), 1821-30 ; 'Halidon Hill,' 1822 ; 'The Fortunes of Nigel' (anon), 1822 ; 'Peveril of the Peak' (anon.), 1822 ; 'Quentin Durward' (anon.), 1823 ; 'A Bannatyne Garland' (anon.) [1823 ?] ; 'St. Ronan's Well' (anon.), 1824 ; 'Redgauntlet' (anon.), 1824 ; 'Tales of the Crusaders' (anon. ; 'The Betrothed,' 'The Talisman '), 1825 ; 'Provincial Antiquities and Picturesque Scenery of Scotland,' 1826 ; 'Letter to the Editor of the "Edinburgh Weekly Journal "' (anon.), 1826 ; 'A Second Letter ' [to the same] (anon.), 1826 ; 'A Third Letter' [to the same] (anon.), 1826 ; 'Thoughts on the proposed change of Currency' (under pseud. 'Malachi Malagrowther '), 1826 ; 'Woodstock' (anon.), 1826 ; 'Life of Napoleon Buonaparte' (anon.), 1827 ; 'Chronicles of the Canongate' ('Highland Widow,' 'The Two Drovers,' 'The Surgeon's Daughter ;' 2 vols.), 1827 ; 2nd ser. ('Saint Valentine's Day ; or, the Fair Maid of Perth '), 1828 ; 'Miscellaneous Prose Works' (6 vols.), 1827 ; 'Tales of a Grandfather,' 1st series, 1828 ; 2nd ser., 1829 ; 3rd ser., 1830 ; 4th ser., 1831 ; 'Religious Discourses' (anon), 1828 ; 'Anne of Geierstein' (anon.), 1829 ; 'The Doom of Devorgoil,' 1830 ; 'Poetical Works' (11 vols.), 1830 ; 'Lectures on Demonology,' 1830 ; 'The History of Scotland' (2 vols.), 1830.

Posthumous : 'Letters to R. Polwhele, etc.,' 1832 ; 'Essays on Chivalry, Romance and the Drama' [1888] ; 'Journal,' 1890 ; 'Familiar Letters,' 1894 [1893].

He *translated :* Bürger's 'The Chase,' and 'William and Helen,' 1796 ; Goethe's 'Goetz von Ber- lichingen,' 1799 ; 'Memoirs of the Marchioness de la Rochejaquelin,' 1827 ; and *edited :* 'Minstrelsy of the Scottish Border' (3 vols.), 1802-03 ; Thomas of Ercildoune's 'Sir Tristrem,' 1804 ; Sir H. Slingsby's 'Original Memoirs written during the Great Civil War,' 1806 ; 'Memoirs of Cap- tain George Carleton,' 1808 ; 'Dry- den's Works,' 1808 ; Robert Carey's 'Memoirs,' 1808 ; J. Strutt's 'Queen- hoo Hall,' 1808 ; Sir R. Sadler's 'State Papers and Letters,' 1809 ; Lord Somers' 'Collection of Scarce and Valuable Tracts,' 1809-15 ; A. Seward's 'Poetical Works,' 1810 ; 'English Minstrelsy,' 1810 ; 'Secret History of the Court of James the First, 1811 ; Sir P. Warwick's 'Me- moirs of the Reign of King Charles I.,' 1813 ; Swift's 'Works,' 1814 ; S. Rowland's 'The Letting of Hu- morous Blood,' 1814 ; Lord Somer- ville's 'Memorie of the Somervilles,' 1815 ; P. Carey's 'Trivial Poems and Triolets,' 1820 ; 'The Novelists' Library,' 1821 - 24 ; R. Franck's 'Northern Memoirs,' 1821 ; Lord Fountainhall's 'Chronological Notes of Scottish Affairs,'1822 ; J. Gwynne's 'Military Memoirs of the Great Civil War,' 1822 ; 'The Bannatyne Mis- cellany,' 1827 ; 'Proceedings in the Court Martial held upon John, Master of Sinclair,' 1828 ; 'Memorials of George Bannatyne,' 1829 ; 'Trial cf Duncan Terig,' 1832.
Collected Works : 'Miscellaneous Prose Works' (30 vols.), 1834-71 ; 'Poetical Works' (12 vols.), 1833-34.
Life: by J. G. Lockhart (7 vols.), 1837-38.

*SEDLEY (*Sir* Charles), *Bart.* 1639-1701.* Born, at Aylesford, Kent, 1639. Matric., Wadham Coll., Ox- ford, 22 March 1656. Succeeded to Baronetcy. 1656. M.P. for New Romney, 1668-81, 1690-95, 1696-1701. Married. Died, 20 Aug. 1701.
Works : 'The Earle of Pembroke's Speech in the House of Peeres'

(anon.), 1648 ; 'The Last Will and Testament of the Earl of Pembroke' [1650] ; 'The Mulberry Garden,' 1668 ; 'Antony and Cleopatra,' 1677 ; 'Bellamira,' 1687.
Posthumous : 'Beauty the Con- queror,' 1702 ; 'The Grumbler' (anon.), 1702 ; 'The Tyrant King of Crete,' 1702 ; 'The Happy Pair,' 1702.
Collected Works : 1707.

*SEELEY (*Sir* John Robert), 1834- 1895.* Born, in London, 10 Sept. 1834. Early education at a school at Stanmore, and at City of London School. Matric., Christ's Coll., Camb., as Scholar, 1852 ; B.A., 1857 ; M.A., 1860. Fellow of Christ's Coll., July 1858 to 1869. Assistant Master, City of London School, 1860-63. Prof. of Latin, University Coll., London, 1863- 69. Prof. of Modern Hist., Camb., Oct. 1869. Married Mary Agnes Phillott, 1869. Professorial Fellow, Caius Coll., Camb., Oct. 1882. K.C.M.G., 1894. Died, at Cam- bridge, 13 Jan. 1895.
Works : 'Three Essays on . . . King Lear' (by Seeley, W. Young, and E. A. Hart), 1851 ; 'David and Samuel' (under pseud. 'John Robertson'), 1859 ; 'The Greatest of all the Plantagenets' (anon.), 1860 (new edn., called : 'The Life and Reign of Edward I.,' 1872) ; 'Classical Studies as an introduction to the Moral Sciences,' 1864 [1863] ; 'Ecce Homo' (anon.), 1866 (5th edn. same year) ; 'An English Primer' (with E. A. Abbott), 1869 ; 'Roman Im- perialism,' 1869 ; 'Lectures and Essays,' 1870 ; 'English Lessons for English People' (with E. A. Abbott), 1871 ; 'Life and Times of Stein,' (3 vols.), 1878 ; 'Natural Religion,' 1882 (anon. ; 2nd edn. same year) ; 'The Expansion of England,' 1883 ; 'Short History of Napoleon the First,' 1886 ; 'Greater Greece and Greater Britain,' 1887 ; 'Goethe : reviewed after sixty years,' 1894.
Posthumous : 'The Growth of British Policy,' ed. by G. W. Pro- thero (2 vols.), 1895 ; 'Introduction to

Political Science,' ed. by H. Sidgwick, 1896.

He *edited :* 'The Student's Guide to the University of Cambridge,' 1863 ; Livy, bk. i., 1871.

SELDEN (John), 1584-1654. Born, at Salvington, Sussex, 16 Dec. 1584. Early education at Chichester Free School. Matric., Hart Hall, Oxford, 24 Oct. 1600. Took no degree. Student of Clifford's Inn, 1602 ; removed to Inner Temple, May 1604 ; called to Bar, 14 June 1612. Imprisoned for five weeks on political charge, 1621. M.P. for Borough of Lancaster, 1623 ; for Great Bedwin, 1626 ; for Ludgershall, 1628-29. Imprisoned on political charge, June 1629 to May 1631. Bencher of Inner Temple, 1633. M.P. for Oxford University, 1640-53. Lay Member of Assembly of Divines, 1643. Keeper of Rolls and Records in the Tower, 1643. Commissioner of Admiralty, 1645. Grant of £5,000 from Parliament, 1646. Latter years of life spent at White Fryers, as manager of estates of Countess Dowager of Kent, whom he is said to have married. Died there, 30 Nov. 1654. Buried in Temple Church.

Works : 'Jani Anglorum Facies Altera,' 1610 ; 'England's Epinomis,' 1610 ; 'The Duello' (anon.), 1610 ; 'Titles of Honour,' 1614 ; 'Analecton,' 1615 ; 'De Dis Syris,' 1617 ; 'Historie of Tithes,' 1618 ; 'Marmora Arundelliana,' 1628 ; 'De Successionibus,' 1631 ; 'Antiduello' (anon.), 1632 ; 'Mare Clausum,' 1635 ; 'De Successione in Pontificatum,' 1638 ; 'De Jure Naturali,' 1640 ; 'Judicature in Parliament,' 1640 ; 'A Brief Discourse concerning the Powers of Peers and Commons' (anon. ; attrib. to Selden), 1640 ; 'Privileges of Baronage,' 1642 ; 'De Anno Civili,' 1644 ; 'Uxor Ebraica,' 1646 ; 'De Synedriis,' 1650-55 ; 'Metamorphosis Anglorum' (anon. ; attrib. to Selden), 1653 ; 'Decem Scriptores,' 1653 ; 'Vindiciæ,' 1653.

Posthumous : 'On the Nativity of Christ,' 1661 ; 'Of the Office of Lord Chancellor' (ed. by W. Dugdale), 1671 ; 'Table Talk,' 1689.

He *edited :* Eadmer's 'Historiæ,' 1623 ; Eutychius's 'Ecclesiæ Origines,' 1642.

Collected Works: ed. by D. Wilkins (3 vols.), 1725.

SHADWELL (Thomas), 1640-1692. Born, at Broomhill House, Norfolk, 1640. At school at Bury St. Edmunds, 1645-46. Matric., Caius Coll., Cambridge, as Pensioner, 17 Dec. 1656 ; took no degree. Studied Law at Middle Temple. First play, 'The Sullen Lovers,' produced at Lincoln's Inn Fields, 5 May 1668. Devoted himself mainly to drama, 1668-82. Poet-Laureate and Historiographer Royal, 1688. Died suddenly, in London, 19 Nov. 1692.

Works : 'The Sullen Lovers,' 1668 ; 'The Royal Shepherdess,' 1669 ; 'The Humourists,' 1671 ; 'The Miser,' 1672 ; 'Epsom Wells,' 1673 ; 'Notes and Observations on the Empress of Morocco' (anon. ; with Dryden and John Crown), 1674 ; 'Psyche,' 1675 ; 'The Libertine,' 1676 ; 'The Virtuoso,' 1676 ; 'The History of Timon of Athens,' 1678 ; 'A True Widow,' 1679 ; 'The Woman-Captain,' 1680 ; 'The Medal of John Bayes' (anon.), 1682 ; 'Satyr to his Muse' (anon. ; attrib. to Shadwell), 1682 ; 'The Lancashire Witches, and Teague O'Divelly,' 1682 ; 'A Lenten Prologue' [1683 ?] ; 'The Squire of Alsatia,' 1688 ; 'Bury Fair,' 1689 ; 'A Congratulatory Poem on his Highness the Prince of Orange' (under initials : T. S.), 1689 ; 'A Congratulatory Poem to . . . Queen Mary,' 1689 ; 'The Amorous Bigotte,' 1690 ; 'Ode on the Anniversary of the King's Birth,' 1690 ; 'Ode to the King on his Return from Ireland,' [1690] ; 'The Scowrers,' 1691 ; 'Votum Perenne,' 1692.

Posthumous : 'The Volunteers,' 1693.

He *translated :* Juvenal's Tenth Satire, 1687.

Collected Works: 'Dramatic Works' (4 vols.), 1720.

SHAFTESBURY, Anthony Ashley Cooper, *3rd Earl of,* **1671 - 1713.** Born, in London, 26 Feb. 1671. Early education under tutorship of John Locke [*q.v.*]. At a private school, 1682-83 ; at Winchester, Nov. 1683 to 1686. Travelled on Continent, 1686-89. M.P. for Poole, May 1695 ; re-elected, Nov. 1695. Retired from Parliament, owing to ill-health, July 1698. Visit to Holland, 1698-99. Succeeded to Earldom, on death of his father, 10 Nov. 1699. Took his seat in House of Lords, 19 Jan. 1700. In Holland, Aug. 1703 to Aug. 1704. Married Jane Ewer, Aug. 1709. To Italy, for health, autumn of 1711. Died, in Naples, 15 Feb. 1713. Buried at St. Giles's.

Works : 'An Inquiry concerning Virtue' (anon.), 1699 ; 'A Letter concerning Enthusiasm' (anon.), 1708 ; 'Sensus Communis' (anon.), 1709 ; 'The Moralists' (anon.), 1709 ; 'Soliloquy, or Advice to an Author' (anon.), 1710 ; 'Characteristics of Men, Manners, Opinions, Times' (3 vols.), 1711 ; 'A Notion of the Historical Draught . . . of the Judgment of Hercules' (anon.), 1713 ; 'Several Letters written by a Noble Lord to a Young Man at the University' (anon.), 1716.

Posthumous : 'Letters . . . to R. Molesworth,' 1721 ; 'Letters, collected,' 1746 ; 'Original Letters by Locke, Sidney, and Shaftesbury,' ed. by T. Foster, enlarged edn. 1847.

He *edited :* B. Whichcot's 'Select Sermons,' 1689.

SHAIRP (John Campbell), 1819-1885. Born, at Houstoun, Linlithgowshire, 30 July 1819. Early education at Houston. At Edinburgh Academy, Oct. 1829 to 1834. At Glasgow Univ., autumn of 1836 to 1839 ; Snell Exhibitioner, April 1840. Matric., Balliol Coll., Oxford, 3 June 1840 ; Newdigate Prize Poem, 1842 ; B.A., 1844 ; M.A., 1877. Assistant Master at Rugby, 1846-57. Married Eliza Douglas, 23 June 1853. Assistant to Prof. of Latin at St. Andrews Univ., Oct. 1857 ; Professor, 1861-72.

Contrib. to 'Good Words,' and 'North British Review.' Principal of United Coll. of St. Salvator and St. Leonard, 1868-85. Pres. of Educational Institute of Scotland. Prof. of Poetry, Oxford, June 1877 to 1885. Died, at Ormsary, Argyll, 18 Sept. 1885. Buried in Houstoun Church.

Works : 'Charles the Twelfth,' 1842 ; 'The Wants of the Scottish Universities,' 1856 ; 'The Uses of the Study of Latin Literature,' 1858 ; 'Kilmahoe,' 1864 ; 'John Keble,' 1866 ; 'Studies in Poetry and Philosophy,' 1868 ; 'Culture and Religion,' 1870 ; 'Life and Letters of J. D. Forbes' (with P. G. Tait and A. A. Reilly), 1873 ; 'Address' [on Missions], 1874 ; 'On Poetic Interpretation of Nature,' 1877 (2nd edn. same year) ; 'Robert Burns,' 1879 ; 'Aspects of Poetry,' 1881.

Posthumous : 'Sketches in History and Poetry,' ed. by G. J. Veitch, 1887 ; 'Glen Desseray, and other Poems,' ed. by F. T. Palgrave, 1888 ; 'Portraits of Friends,' 1889.

He *edited :* Dorothy Wordsworth's 'Recollections of a Tour Made in Scotland,' 1874.

Life : by Prof. W. Knight, 1888.

SHAKESPEARE (William), 1564-1616. Born, at Stratford-on-Avon, 22 or 23 April 1564. Educated at Stratford Grammar School, 1571-77[?]. Perhaps apprenticed to his father (a butcher), 1577. Married Ann Hathaway, 1582. To London, 1586 ; acted, and wrote for stage. Plays probably written between 1591 and 1611. Bought New Place, Stratford, May 1597. Bought a house in Blackfriars, 1613. Died, at Stratford-on-Avon, 23 April 1616. Buried in Stratford Church.

Works : The following are known to have been printed in Shakespeare's lifetime : 'Venus and Adonis,' 1593 ; 'Lucrece,' 1594 ; 'Richard III.,' 1597 ; 'Richard II.,' 1597 ; 'Romeo and Juliet,' 1597 ; 'Henry IV., Pt. I.,' 1598 ; 'Love's Labour's Lost,' 1598 ; 'Henry V.,' 1600 ; 'Midsummer Night's Dream,' 1600 ; 'Merchant of Venice,'

1600; 'Henry IV., Pt. II.,' 1600; 'Much Ado about Nothing,' 1600 ; 'Titus Andronicus,' 1600 ; 'Merry Wives of Windsor,' 1602 ; 'Hamlet,' 1603 ; 'King Lear,' 1608 ; 'Sonnets,' 1609 ; 'Troilus and Cressida,' 1609.

His 'Comedies, Histories, and Tragedies,' ed. by J. Heminge and H. Condell, were first published in 1623 ; his 'Works,' ed. by N. Rowe (7 vols.), 1709-10.

*SHARP (William), b. 1856. Born, at Garthland Place, Paisley, 12 Sept. 1856. Educated at Blair Lodge, Glasgow Academy, and Glasgow Univ. B.Sc., Glasgow, 1871. Early youth spent in West of Scotland. Travelled in Australia, 1877-78. In Scotland, 1877-78. Held Secretarial post in a Bank in London, autumn 1878 to 1881. During that time contrib. to 'Pall Mall Gazette,' ' Examiner,' etc. Has devoted himself to literature since 1881. Art Critic to 'Glasgow Herald' since 1885. Married Elizabeth Amelia Sharp, 31 Oct. 1884. Visits to America, 1892, 1894, 1897. Frequent contributor to periodicals.

Works : ' The Human Inheritance,' 1882 ; ' Dante Gabriel Rossetti,' 1882; ' Earth's Voices,' 1884 ; ' Life of Shelley,' 1887 ; ' The Sport of Chance,' 1888 [1887] ; ' Romantic Ballads,' 1889 (priv. ptd., 1888) ; ' Life of Heine,' 1888 ; ' Children of To-Morrow,' 1889 ; 'Life of Robert Browning,' 1890 ; ' Sospiri di Roma ' (priv. ptd.), 1891 ; ' Flower o' the Vine : Romantic Ballads and Sospiri di Roma ' (New York), 1892 ; ' Life and Letters of Joseph Severn,' 1892 ; ' A Fellowe and his Wife' (with Blanche Willis Howard), 1892 ; ' Vistas,' 1894 (enlarged American edition, 1895) ; ' Fair Women in Painting and Poetry,' 1894 ; ' The Gipsy Christ, and other tales,' 1895 ; ' Ecce Puella,' 1896 ; ' Madge o' the Pool,' 1896 ; ' Wives in Exile ' (Boston), 1896.

He has *edited :* ' Canterbury Poets' series, since 1885 ; Shakespeare's ' Songs, Poems, and Sonnets,' 1885 ; Scott's Poems, 1885-86 ; De Quincey's ' Confessions of an Opium-Eater,'

1886 ; 'Great English Painters,' 1886; ' Sonnets of this Century,' 1886 ; P. B. Marston's ' For a Song's Sake ' [1887], and 'Song-Tide,' 1888 ; 'American Sonnets,' 1889 ; 'Great Odes' [1890] ; translation of Sainte-Beuve's ' Essays on Men and Women,' 1890 ; ' Ossian,' 1896 ; 'Selected Poems of Matthew Arnold,' 1896 ; ' Mrs. William Sharp's ' Lyra Celtica,' 1896.

SHELLEY (*Mrs.* Mary Wollstonecraft), 1797-1851. [Daughter of William Godwin, *q.v.*] Born, in London, 30 Aug. 1797. Met Shelley, 1814. Eloped to Continent with him, 28 July 1814 ; returned, Sept. 1814. Married to Shelley, after his wife's suicide, 30 Dec. 1816. Lived at Marlow, 1817-18. To Italy, on account of Shelley's health, March 1818 ; he was drowned there, 8 July 1822. She returned to London, 1823 ; devoted herself to literature. Travelled on Continent, 1840, 1842-43. Died, in London, 21 Feb. 1851. Buried in Bournemouth Churchyard.

Works : ' History of a Six Weeks' Tour through a Part of France, etc.' (with her husband ; anon.), 1817 ; ' Frankenstein ' (anon.), 1818 ; 'Valperga ' (anon.), 1823 ; 'The Last Man ' (anon.), 1826 ; ' The Fortunes of Perkin Warbeck ' (anon.), 1830 ; ' Lodore ' (anon.), 1835 ; ' Falkner ' (anon.), 1837 ; ' Lives of the most Eminent, Literary, and Scientific Men of France ' (anon. ; 2 vols.), 1838-39 ; ' Rambles in Germany and Italy ' (2 vols.), 1844.

Posthumous : ' The Choice,' ed. by H. B. Forman (priv. ptd.), 1876.

She *edited :* Shelley's ' Posthumous Poems ' [1824] ; ' Poetical Works,' 1839 ; ' Essays, etc.,' 1840.

Collected Works : 'Tales and Stories,' ed. by R. Garnett, 1891.

Life : ' Life and Letters,' by F. A. Marshall, 1889.

SHELLEY (Percy Bysshe), 1792-1822. Born, at Field Place, near Horsham, Sussex, 4 Aug. 1792. Educated privately, 1798-1802 ; at a school at Brentford, 1802-04 ; at Eton, July 1804 to 1809. Wrote poetry while at

Eton. Matric., University Coll., Oxford, 10 April 1810. Expelled (with Hogg) from Oxford for publication of 'The Necessity of Atheism,' 25 March 1811. Married (i.) Harriet Westbrook, 28 Aug. 1811. Lived for a few weeks with Hogg in Edinburgh; thence to Keswick, Nov. 1811. Friendship formed there with Southey. Friendship with Godwin begun, Jan. 1812. In Dublin, spring of 1812; at Lynmouth, June to Sept. 1812; in Carnarvonshire, Sept. 1812 to Feb. 1813; in Ireland, Feb. to April 1813; to London, April 1813. Removed to Bracknell, July 1813; in Edinburgh, winter 1813-14; returned to Bracknell, spring of 1814. On account of his having been married in Scotland as a minor, he remarried his wife in London, 24 March 1814. Estrangement from his wife, and meeting with Mary Godwin, 1814. To Continent with Mary Godwin, 28 July 1814; returned with her to England, Sept. 1814. Friendship with Byron begun, 1816. At Geneva with him, summer of 1816. Mrs. Shelley committed suicide, Dec. 1816. He married (ii.) Mary Godwin, 30 Dec. 1816; settled with her at Marlow, spring of 1817. Friendship with Keats begun, 1817. Removed to Italy, March 1818. Drowned, 8 July 1822. His body cremated on the shore near Via Reggio, 6 Aug. 1822. His ashes buried in old Protestant Cemetery, Rome, Dec. 1822.

Works : 'Zastrozzi' (under initials: P. B. S.), 1810; 'Original Poetry: by Victor and Cazire,' 1810 (reprinted 1898); 'Posthumous Fragments of Margaret Nicholson, 1810 (priv. ptd., ed. by H. B. Forman, 1877); 'St. Irvyne' (anon.), 1811; 'Poetical Essay on the Existing State of Things,' 1811; 'The Necessity of Atheism,' 1811; 'An Address to the Irish People,' 1812; 'Proposals for an Association,' 1812; 'Declaration of Right,' 1812; 'Letters to Lord Ellenborough' [1812]; 'The Devil's Walk,' 1812; 'Queen Mab,' 1813; 'A Vindication of Natural Diet' (anon.), 1813; 'A Refutation of Deism' (anon.), 1814; 'Alastor,' 1816; 'Proposal for putting Reform to the Vote' (anon.), 1817, 'History of a Six Weeks' Tour through a Part of France' (with his wife; anon.), 1817; 'Laon and Cythna,' 1818 [1817] (recalled; and reissued as 'The Revolt of Islam,' 1817); 'Address to the People on the Death of Princess Charlotte' [1818]; 'Rosalind and Helen,' 1819; 'The Cenci,' 1819; 'Prometheus Unbound,' 1820; 'Œdipus Tyrannus' (anon.), 1820; 'Epipsychidion' (anon.), 1821; 'Adonais,' 1821; 'Hellas,' 1822.

Posthumous : 'Posthumous Poems,' ed. by Mrs. Shelley [1824]; 'The Masque of Anarchy,' ed. by Leigh Hunt, 1832; 'The Shelley Papers' (from 'Athenæum') 1833; 'Essays, etc.,' ed. by Mrs. Shelley, 1840; 'The Dæmon of the World,' ed. by H. B. Forman (priv. ptd.), 1876; 'Notes on Sculptures in Rome and Florence' (ed. by H. B. Forman; priv. ptd.), 1879.

Collected Works : ed. by H. Buxton Forman (8 vols.), 1880 [1876-80].

Life : by Prof. Dowden, 1886.

SHENSTONE (William), 1714-1763. Born, at Leasowes, Hales Owen, Shropshire, 18 Nov. 1714. Early education at schools there; and at Solihul, near Birmingham. Matric., Pembroke Coll., Oxford, 25 May 1732. Took no degree. Unmarried. Lived retired life at Leasowes. Died there, 11 Feb. 1763. Buried in Hales Owen Churchyard.

Works : 'Poems upon Various Occasions' (anon.; priv. ptd.), 1737; 'The Judgment of Hercules' (anon.), 1741; 'The School-Mistress' (anon.), 1742.

Collected Works : 'Works in Prose and Verse' (3 vols.), 1764-69.

SHERIDAN (Richard Brinsley), 1751-1816. Born, in Dublin, 30 Oct. 1751. Parents removed to London, 1758. Educated at Harrow, 1762-68. Parents removed to Bath, 1771. Eloped with Elizabeth Linley, 1772; secretly married to her at Calais. Formally married, in London, 13 April 1773. Settled in London, spring of 1774. 'The Rivals' pro-

duced at Covent Garden, 17 Jan.
1775 ; 'St. Patrick's Day ; or, The
Scheming Lieutenant,' Covent Gar-
den, May 1775 ; 'The Duenna,'
Covent Garden, 21 Nov. 1775. Pur-
chased a share in Drury Lane Theatre,
June 1776 ; Manager, Sept. 1776 to
Feb. 1809. 'A Trip to Scarborough'
(adapted from Vanbrugh's 'The Re-
lapse') produced at Drury Lane, 24
Feb. 1777 ; 'The School for Scandal,'
Drury Lane, 8 May 1777 ; 'The
Critic,' Drury Lane, 30 Oct. 1779.
M.P. for Stafford, 1780. Under-
Secretary of State, 1782. Concerned
in impeachment of Warren Hastings,
1787-88. Intimacy with Prince of
Wales begun, 1787. Wife died, 1792.
Drury Lane Theatre rebuilt, 1792-94 ;
new house opened, 21 April 1794.
Married (ii.) Esther Ogle, 27 April
1795. 'Pizarro' (adapted from
Kotzebue's 'Spaniards in Peru') pro-
duced at Drury Lane, 24 May 1799.
Privy Councillor and Treasurer of
Navy, 1799. Receiver of Duchy of
Cornwall, 1804. Drury Lane Theatre
burnt down, 24 Feb. 1809. Died, in
London, 7 July 1816. Buried in
Westminster Abbey.

Works : 'Clio's Protest' (under
pseud. : 'Asmodeo') [1771] ; 'The
Rivals,' 1775 ; 'St. Patrick's Day ;
or, The Scheming Lieutenant,' 1775 ;
'The General Fast' (anon.) [1775 ?] ;
'The Duenna,' 1775 ; 'A Trip to
Scarborough,' 1777 ; 'The School for
Scandal' (anon.), 1777 ; 'Verses to
the Memory of Garrick,' 1779 ; 'The
Critic,' 1781 ; 'The Legislative Independence of Ireland' (a speech), 1785;
'Speech . . . against Warren Hastings,' 1788 ; 'A Comparative Statement of the two Bills for the better
Government of the British Possessions
in India,' 1788 ; 'Dramatic Works'
[1795 ?] ; 'Pizarro,' 1799 ; 'Speech
. . . on the Motion to address His
Majesty' [1798] ; 'Speech . . . on
the Union with Ireland,' 1799 ;
'Speech . . . on the Army Estimates,'
1802.

Posthumous : 'Speeches' (5 vols.),
1816 ; 'An Ode to Scandal,' 2nd edn.
1819 ; 'Speeches in the Trial of

Warren Hastings,' ed. by E. A. Bond
(4 vols.), 1859-61.

He *translated :* 'The Love Epistles
of Aristænetus' (with N. B. Halhed),
1771.

Collected Works : ed. by F. Stain-
forth, 1874.

Life : by T. Moore, 1825 ; by Mrs.
Oliphant 1883 ; by W. F. Rae,
1896.

SHIRLEY, *pseud.* See Skelton
(*Sir J.*).

SHIRLEY (James), 1596 - 1666.
Born. in London, 18 Sept. 1596. At
Merchant Taylors' School, Oct. 1608
to June 1612. Matric., St. John's
Coll., Oxford, 1612. Removed to
Catherine Hall, Cambridge. B.A.,
1617. Ordained Curate of parish
near St. Albans. Resigned Curacy
on becoming a Roman Catholic. Kept
a Grammar school at St. Albans,
1623-24. This failing, he removed
to London ; devoted himself to literature. Mem. of Gray's Inn, 1634.
Wrote many plays till 1640. Valet
of Chamber to Queen Henrietta
Maria. Kept a school in Whit-
Friars, 1640-46. Resumed career of
dramatist, 1646. Died, in London,
Oct. 1666. Buried in church of St.
Giles'-in-the-Fields, 29 Oct.

Works : 'Eccho' (no copy known),
1618 (another edn., called : 'Nar-
cissus, or the Self-Lover,' 1646) ; 'The
Wedding,' 1629 ; 'The Grateful Ser-
vant,' 1630 ; 'The School of Comple-
ment' (also known as 'Love Tricks '),
1631 ; 'Changes,' 1632 ; 'The Wittie
Fair One,' 1633 ; 'A Contention for
Honour and Riches,' 1633 ; 'The
Bird in a Cage,' 1633 ; 'The Triumph
of Peace,' 1633 ; 'The Traytor,' 1635;
'Hide Park,' 1637 ; 'The Young
Admirall,' 1637 ; 'The Gamester,'
1637 ; 'The Example,' 1637 ; 'The
Lady of Pleasure,' 1637 ; 'The Royall
Master,' 1638 ; 'The Duke's Mistris,'
1638 ; 'The Maide's Revenge,' 1639 ;
'The Ball' (with Chapman), 1639 ;
'Chabot, Admiral of France' (with
Chapman), 1639 ; 'The Opportunitie,'
1640 ; 'The Coronation' (pubd. under
Fletcher's name), 1640 ; 'St. Patrick

for Ireland,' 1640 ; 'The Constant Maid,' 1640 (another edn., called : 'Love will finde out the Way,' 1661) ; 'The Humorous Courtier,' 1640 ; 'The Arcadia,' 1640 ; 'Poems,' 1646 ; 'The Triumph of Beautie,' 1646 ; 'The Way made Plain to the Latin Tongue,' 1649 ; 'Grammatica Anglo-Latina,' 1651 ; 'The Cardinal,' 1652 ; 'Six New Playes,' 1653 [1652]; 'Cupid and Death' (under initials : J. S.), 1653 ; 'The Gentleman of Venise,' 1655 ; 'The Polititian,' 1655; 'The Rudiments of Grammar,' 1656 ; ''Εισαγωγη,' 1656 ; ' Honour and Mammon ; and, the Contention of Ajax and Ulysses,' 1659 ; 'Andromana' (under initials : J. S.), 1660.

Posthumous : ' An Essay towards an Universal and Rational Grammar,' ed. by J. T. Philipps, 1726 ; 'Double Falsehood' (pubd. under Shakespeare's name ; probably by Shirley), 1728 ; 'Jenkin of Wales,' ed. by J. O. Halliwell, 1861.

Collected Works : ' Dramatic Works and Poems,' ed., with memoir, by A. Dyce (6 vols.), 1833.

*SHORTHOUSE (Joseph Henry), b. 1834. Born, in Birmingham, 9 Sept. 1834. Educated at schools at Tottenham and elsewhere. For many years actively engaged in business as manufacturer of Chemicals. Married Sarah Scott, 19 Aug. 1857. Resides at Edgbaston. Has contributed to 'Macmillan's Mag.,' 'Nineteenth Century,' etc.

Works : 'John Inglesant' (priv. ptd.), 1880 ; published, 1881 ; 'On the Platonism of Wordsworth ' [1882]; 'The Little Schoolmaster Mark,' 1883-84 ; 'Sir Percival,' 1886 ; 'A Teacher of the Violin,' 1888 ; 'The Countess Eve,' 1888 ; 'Blanche, Lady Falaise,' 1891.

He has *edited :* G. Herbert's 'The Temple,' 1882 ; M. Molinos' 'Golden Thoughts,' 1883 ; F. Morse's 'Peace' [1888].

*SIDGWICK (Henry), b. 1838. Born, at Skipton, Yorkshire, 31 May 1838. At Rugby, Midsummer 1852 to Michaelmas 1855. Matric., Trin.

Coll., Camb., 1855 ; B.A., 1859 ; M.A., 1862 ; Fellow of Trin. Coll., 1859-69 ; Lecturer, 1859-75 ; Prælector of Moral and Political Philosophy, 1875 ; Hon. Fellow Trin. Coll., 16 April 1881 ; Knightbridge Prof. of Moral Philosophy, 1883 ; Litt.D., 1884. Married Eleanor Mildred Balfour, 4 April 1876. Took active part in founding of Newnham Coll., Camb., 1870-80. Hon. LL.D., Glasgow, 1881 ; Hon. LL.D., Edinburgh, 1884 ; Hon. LL.D., St. Andrew's, 1884 ; Hon. D.C.L., Oxford, 1890 ; Dr. in Polit. Science, Buda-Pest Univ., 1896 ; Mem Danish Royal Soc. of Sciences, 1897.

Works : ' The Ethics of Conformity and Subscription,' 1870 ; 'The Methods of Ethics,' 1874 ; Supplement to first edition of preceding, 1878 ; Supplement to second edition, 1884 ; ' The Principles of Political Economy,' 1883 ; 'The Scope and Method of Economic Science,' 1885 ; 'Outlines of the History of Ethics,' 1886 ; 'The Elements of Politics,' 1891.

He has *edited :* Sir J. R. Seeley's 'Introduction to Political Science,' 1896.

*SIDNEY (Algernon). 1622-1683. Born, at Penshurst, Kent, 1622. Travelled on Continent with his father in his youth. Espoused Parliamentary cause, 1643. Commission in army, 1644. Governor of Chichester, May 1645. M.P. for Cardiff, Dec. 1645. Governor of Dublin, July 1646. Lieutenant of Dover Castle, Oct. 1648 to March 1651. Mem. of Council of State, Nov. 1651. Executed for alleged complicity in Rye House Plot 7 Dec. 1683.

Works : 'Discourses concerning Government,' 1698 ; 'Letters to the Hon. Henry Saville,'1742 ; 'A General View of Government in Europe,' 1744. *Collected Works :* ed. by J. Robertson, 1772.

SIDNEY (Sir Philip), 1554-1586. Born, at Penshurst, Kent, 30 Nov. 1554. Lay Rector of Whitford, Flintshire, May 1564. Educated at Shrewsbury School, Nov. 1564 to 1568.

Matric. Ch. Ch., Oxford, 1568. Probably took no degree. Mem. of Gray's Inn, 1568. To Paris, in suite of Earl of Lincoln, May 1572. Appointed Gentleman of Bedchamber to Charles I., with title of Baron, Aug. 1572. Studying in Lorraine, and at Strasburg, Heidelberg, Frankfort, and Vienna, Sept. 1572 to autumn 1573 ; in Italy, Oct. 1573 to July 1574 ; at Vienna, July 1574 to Feb. 1575 ; visited Prague and Dresden ; returned to London, May 1575. Attached to Court of Queen Elizabeth. On Embassy to Germany, Feb. to June, 1577. His masque, ' The Lady of May,' performed before the Queen at Wanstead, May 1578. Friendship with Spenser begun, 1578. President of ' The Areopagus,' 1578. Being temporarily out of favour at Court, spent some months in retirement at Wilton (seat of his sister, Countess of Pembroke) in 1580 ; returned to Court, Oct. 1580. Steward to Bishopric of Winchester, 1580. M.P. for Kent, Jan. 1581 to Sept. 1585. With Duke of Anjou in Antwerp, Feb. to March 1582. Knighted, 8 Jan. 1583. General of the Horse, 1583. Grant of land in colony of Virginia, 1583. Married Frances Walsingham, 20 Sept. 1583. Joint Master of Ordnance with Earl of Warwick, July 1585. Governor of Flushing and Rammekins, Nov. 1585. Died, at Arnhem, 17 Oct. 1586. Buried, in St. Paul's Cathedral, 16 Feb. 1587.

Works : ' The Countesse of Pembroke's Arcadia,' 1590 (later edns., 'with sundry new additions of the same author,' 1598, etc.) ; ' Syr P. S., his Astrophel and Stella,' 1591 ; ' An Apologie for Poetry,' 1595.

Posthumous : ' Correspondence of Sir Philip Sidney and H. Languet,' ed. by S. A. Pears, 1845.

Collected Poems : ed. by A. B. Grosart (2 vols.), 1873.

Life : by H. R. F. Bourne, 1891.

*SKEAT (Walter William), b. 1835. Born in London, 21 Nov. 1835. At King's Coll. School, 1845-46. At school at Highgate, 1851-53. Studied at Cambridge before entering college, 1854. Matric. Christ's Coll., Camb., 1855 ; scholar, 1855-60 ; B.A., 1858; M.A., 1861 ; Fellow of Christ's Coll., 1860-61 ; Litt.D., 1886. Ordained Deacon, 1860 ; Priest, 1861 ; Curate of East Dereham, Norfolk, 1861-62 ; Curate of Godalming, 1863. One of founders of English Dialect Soc., 1873 ; Pres. 1873-96. Incorporated M.A. at Oxford, Exeter Coll., 12 June 1875. Prof. of Anglo-Saxon, Camb., May 1878 ; re-elected Fellow of Christ's Coll., Jan. 1883. Hon. LL.D., Edinburgh, 1884. Hon. D.Litt., Dublin, 1892. Ph.D., Halle, 1894. Hon. D.C.L., Oxford, 1896.

Works : ' A Tale of Ludlow Castle,' 1866 ; ' A Mœso-Gothic Glossary,' 1868 ; ' A Hand List of Some Cognate Words in English, Latin, and Greek,' 1871 ; ' Questions for Examination in English Literature,' 1873 ; ' A List of English Words, the Etymology of which is illustrated by Comparison with the Icelandic,' 1876 ; ' An Etymological Dictionary of the English Language, arranged on an Historical Basis,' 1882 ; 'Supplement ' to preceding, 1884 ; ' A Concise Etymological Dictionary,' 1882 ; ' Principles of English Etymology' (2 series), 1887-91 ; ' A Concise Dictionary of Middle English ' (with A. L. Mayhew), 1888; ' A Primer of English Etymology,' 1892 ; ' A Student's Pastime ' (from ' Notes and Queries '), 1896.

He has *translated :* Uhland's 'Songs and Ballads,' 1864 ; and *edited* [besides various works edited for the Early English Text Society, 1865-97 ; for the English Dialect Society, 1868-96 ; for the Chaucer Society, 1872-92 ; for the Clarendon Press, 1874-96]: 'Specimens of Early English . . . 1250-1400 ' (with R. Morris), 1867 (enlarged edn., '1150-1393,' 2 pts., 1882-94) ; ' Passio Sancti Vincentii,' 1868 ; ' Piers the Plowman,' 1869 ; ' The Holy Gospels in Anglo-Saxon, Northumbrian, and old Mercian,' 1871-87 ; Chatterton's Poems, 1871 ; ' Specimens of English Literature, from A.D. 1394 to A.D. 1579,' 1871 ; ' Shakespeare's Plutarch,' 1875 ; ' The Two

Noble Kinsmen,' 1875 ; Wycliffe's 'New Testament,' 1879 ; Wycliffe's 'Job, Psalms, etc.,' 1881 ; E. Guest's 'History of English Rhythms,' 1882 ; 'The Tale of Gamelyn,' 1884 ; 'The Kingis Quair,' 1884 ; 'Piers the Plowman . . . in three parallel texts,' 1886 ; Chaucer's 'To Rosamounde,' 1891 ; 'Twelve Facsimiles of Old English Manuscripts,' 1892 ; Chaucer's 'House of Fame,' 1893 ; 'Chaucer's Works' (6 vols.), 1894 ; 'The Student's Chaucer,' 1895 ; 'Chaucerian and Other Pieces,' 1897.

SKELTON (*Sir* John), **1831-1897.** Born, in Edinburgh, 18 July 1831. At school at St. Andrew's, 1843-46. To Edinburgh Univ., 1846. Called to Scotch Bar, 1854. Frequent contributor (under pseud.: 'Shirley ') to periodicals since 1854. Married Anne Adair Lawrie, 30 July 1867. Sec. of Local Govt. Board, Scotland, 1868-92 ; Chairman, 1892 ; Vice-Pres. and Chairman, 1894-97. Hôn. LL.D., Edinburgh, 1878. Commissioner of Supply for county of Aberdeen. C.B., 1887 ; K.C.B., 22 June 1897. Died, in Edinburgh, 20 July 1897.

Works : 'Nugæ Criticæ' (under pseud.: 'Shirley '), 1862 ; 'Thalatta,' 1862 ; 'John Dryden' (from 'Fraser's Mag.'), 1865 ; 'A Campaigner at Home' (under pseud.: 'Shirley '), 1865 ; 'Benjamin Disraeli ' (anon.), 1868 ; 'The Great Lord Bolingbroke,' 1868 ; 'Boarding Out of Pauper Children in Scotland,' 1876 ; 'The Impeachment of Mary Stuart,' 1876 ; 'Essays in Romance,' 1878 ; 'The Crookit Meg,' 1880 ; 'Essays in History and Biography,' 1883 ; 'Maitland of Lethington' (2 vols.), 1887-88 ; 'The Handbook of Public Health,' 1890 ; 'The Local Government (Scotland) Act in relation to Public Health,' 1890 (2nd edn. same year) ; 'Mary Stuart,' 1893 ; 'The Table-Talk of Shirley,' 1895 ; 'Summers and Winters at Balmawhapple : a second series of the Table-Talk of Shirley,' 1896.

He *edited :* W. G. Dickson's 'Treatise on the Law of Evidence in Scotland,' 1864 ; 'The Comedy of the

Noctes Ambrosianæ,' 1876 ; 'The Royal House of Stuart,' 1890.

*SMART (Christopher), 1722-1770. Born, at Shipbourne, Kent, 11 April 1722. Early education at Maidstone and at Durham, 1733-39. Matric. Pembroke Coll., Camb., 30 Oct. 1739 ; B.A., 1743 ; Fellow, 1745-53 ; M.A., 1747. Edited 'The Student,' 1750-51. Married Anna Maria Carnan, 1753. Contrib. to 'The Universal Visitor,' 'The Midwife,' 'The Old Woman's Mag.,' etc. Confined in a lunatic asylum for two years. Died, in King's Bench Prison, 18 May 1770.

Works : 'On the Eternity of the Supreme Being,' 1750 ; 'A Solemn Dirge, sacred to the Memory of . . . Frederic, Prince of Wales,' 1751 ; 'An Occasional Prologue and Epilogue to Othello' [1751] ; 'On the Immensity of the Supreme Being,' 1751 ; 'On the Omniscience of the Supreme Being,' 1752 ; 'Poems on Several Occasions,' 1752 ; second series [1763] ; 'The Hilliad,' 1753 ; 'On the Power of the Supreme Being,' 1754 ; 'Hymn to the Supreme Being,' 1756 ; 'On the Goodness of the Supreme Being,' 1756 ; 'A Song to David,' 1763 ; 'Poems' (priv. ptd.) [1763 ?] ; 'Hannah' [oratorio libretto] [1764 ?] ; 'Ode to . . . the Earl of Northumberland,' 1764 ; 'Abimelech ' [oratorio libretto], [1768 ?].

He *translated :* ' Carmen Alexandri Pope in S. Cæciliam latine redditum,' 1743 ; Horace's Works (2 vols.), 1756 ; ' The Poems of Phædrus,' 1765 ; 'The Psalms of David,' 1765 ; 'The Parables of our Lord,' 1768.

Collected Poems : in 2 vols., with memoir, 1791.

SMILES (Samuel), b. **1812.** Born, at Haddington, 23 Dec. 1812. Educated at schools at Haddington and Edinburgh Univ. Studied medicine; practised as surgeon at Haddington, 1832-38. Gave up practice, 1838. Editor of 'Leeds Times,' 1838-44. Sec. of Leeds and Thirsk Railway, 1845-54 ; to South-Eastern Railway, 1854-66. Hon. LL.D., Edinburgh, 1878. Frequent contributor to periodicals. Italian Order of SS. Maurice and Lazare, 1887 ; Servian Order of St. Sava, 6 May 1897.

Works: 'Physical Education,' 1838; ' History of Ireland,' 1844 ; ' Railway Property' [1849] ; 'The Life of George Stephenson,' 1857 (3rd edn., same year); ' Self-Help,' 1859 ; ' Brief Biographies,' 1860 ; ' Workmen's Earnings, Strikes, and Savings,' 1861 ; 'Lives of the Engineers' (3 vols.), 1861-62 ; ' James Brindley and the Early Engineers' (abridged from preceding), 1864 ; ' Industrial Biography,' 1863 ; 'Lives of Boulton and Watt,' 1865 ; ' The Huguenots . . . in England and Ireland,' 1867 ; ' Character,' 1871 ; ' The Huguenots in France,' 1873 ; 'Thrift,' 1875 ; ' The Life of a Scotch Naturalist,' 1876 ; ' George Moore,' 1878 (2nd edn. same year) ; ' Robert Dick, Baker,' 1878 ; ' Duty,' 1880 ; ' Men of Invention and Industry,' 1884 ; ' Life and Labour,' 1887 ; ' A Publisher and his Friends' (2 vols.), 1891 ; ' Jasmin,' 1891 ; ' Josiah Wedgwood,' 1894.

He has *edited:* ' A Boy's Voyage Round the World,' 1871 ; J. Nasmyth's ' Autobiography,' 1883.

SMITH (Adam), 1723-1790. Born, at Kirkcaldy, Fifeshire, 5 June 1723. Early education at village school there. To Glasgow Univ., 1737 ; Snell Exhibitioner, 1740. Matric. Balliol Coll., Oxford, 7 July 1740. Returned to Kirkcaldy, 1746. Removed to Edinburgh, 1748 ; lectured at Edinburgh Univ., 1751. Friendship with Hume begun, 1751. Prof. of Logic, Glasgow Univ., 1751-55 ; of Moral Philosophy, 1755-63. Contrib. to ' Edinburgh Rev.,' 1755. Travelled in France with Duke of Buccleugh, 1763-66. At Kirkcaldy, 1766-76. In London, 1776-78. Returned to Edinburgh, on appointment as Commissioner of Customs. 1773. Lord Rector, Glasgow Univ., and LL.D., 1787. Died, in Edinburgh, 8 July 1790. Buried there.

Works: ' The Theory of Moral Sentiments,' 1759 ; 'An Inquiry into the Nature and Causes of the Wealth of Nations ' (2 vols.), 1776.

Posthumous: ' Essays on Philosophical Subjects,' ed. by J. Black and J. Hutton, 1795 ; 'Lectures on Justice, Police, Revenue, and Arms, delivered in the University of Glasgow,' ed. by E. Cannan, 1896.

Collected Works: in 5 vols., ed. by J. Steward, 1811-12.

Life: by R. B. Haldane, 1887.

SMITH (Alexander), 1830-1867. Born, at Kilmarnock, Ayrshire, 31 Dec. 1830. Worked for some years in a lace factory in Glasgow. Contrib. verses to the ' Glasgow Citizen,' 1850. Sec. to Edinburgh Univ., 1854-67. Married Flora MacDonald, 1857. Contributor to ' Encyclopædia Brit.,' ' National Mag.,' ' Macmillan's Mag.,' ' The Quiver,' and other periodicals. Died, at Wardie, near Edinburgh, 5 Jan. 1867.

Works : ' The Life-Drama,' 1852 ; ' Poems,' 1853 (2nd edn. same year) ; ' Sonnets on the War' (with Sydney Dobell), 1855 ; 'City of Poems,' 1857 ; ' Edwin of Deira,' 1861 ; ' Dreamthorp,' 1863 ; ' A Summer in Skye ' (2 vols.), 1865 ; ' Alfred Hagart's Household,' 1866 ; ' Miss Oona McQuarrie,' 1866.

Posthumous : ' Last Leaves,' ed. by P. P. Alexander, with *memoir,* 1868.

He *edited:* Burns' Poetical Works, 1865 ; J. W. S. Hows' 'Golden Leaves from the American Poets,' 1866.

＊SMITH (Goldwin), b. 1823. Born, at Reading, 13 Aug. 1823. At Eton, 1836-41. Matric., Ch. Ch., Oxford, 26 May 1841 ; Demy of Magdalen Coll., 1842-46 ; Hertford Scholar, 1842 ; Ireland Scholar, 1845 ; B.A., 1845 ; Chancellor's Latin Verse Prize, 1845 ; Chancellor's Latin Essay and English Essay Prizes, 1846 ; M.A., 1848 ; Stowell Civil Law Fellow, Univ. Coll., 1846-50 ; Fellow, 1850-68 ; Tutor, 1851-54 ; Hon. Fellow, 1868. Student of Lincoln's Inn, 2 Nov. 1842 ; called to Bar, 11 June 1850. Assistant-Sec.

to Commission on Oxford Univ., 1850. Regius Prof. of Modern Hist., Oxford, 1858-66. Lecturer in Modern Hist. and Hon. Fellow, Oriel Coll., 1867. Member of Education Commission, 1859. Lectured in U.S.A., 1864; LL.D., Brown Univ., 7 Sept. 1864. Prof. of English and Constitutional Hist., Cornell Univ., 1868-71. To Canada, 1871. Mem. of Senate of Toronto Univ., 1873-75. Edited 'Canadian Monthly,' 1872 74. Hon. D.C.L., Oxford, 14 June 1882. Chief contributor to 'The Bystander,' 1880-83 and 1889-90 ; to 'The Week,' 1883-87.

Works: 'Inaugural Lecture' at Oxford [1859] ; 'Concerning Doubt' (anon.), 1861 ; 'The Foundation of the American Colonies,' 1861 ; 'The Study of History,' 1861 ; 'On Some Supposed Consequences of the Doctrine of Historical Progress,' 1861 ; 'Lectures on Modern History delivered at Oxford,' 1861 ; 'Rational Religion,' 1861 ; 'Irish History and Irish Character,' 1861 ; 'The Suppression of Doubt is not Faith' (anon.), 1861 ; 'An Oxford Professor on Church Endowments,' 1862 ; 'The Empire' (from 'Daily News'), 1863 ; 'Does the Bible sanction American Slavery?' 1863 ; 'A Letter to a Whig Member of the Southern Independence Association,' 1864 ; 'A Plea for the Abolition of Tests in the University of Oxford,' 1864 ; 'England and America,' 1865 ; 'Speeches and Letters . . . on the Rebellion' (2 vols.), 1865 ; 'The Elections to the Hebdomadal Council,' 1866 ; 'The Civil War in America,' 1866 ; 'Three English Statesmen,' 1867 ; 'The Reorganization of the University of Oxford,' 1868 ; 'The Irish Question,' 1868 ; 'A Short History of England down to the Reformation,' 1869 ; 'The Relations between America and England,' 1869 ; 'The Political Destiny of Canada,' 1879 ; 'Cowper,' 1880 ; 'Lectures and Essays,' 1881 ; 'The Conduct of England to Ireland,' 1882 ; 'False Hopes,' 1883 ; 'The Wrongs of Ireland' [1886] ; Dismemberment no Remedy' [1886] ; 'A Trip to England,' 1888 ;

'Prohibitionism in Canada and the United States' (from 'Macmillan's Mag.'), 1889 ; 'Life of Jane Austen,' 1890 ; 'Loyalty, Aristocracy, and Jingoism,' 1891 ; 'Canada and the Canadian Question,' 1891 ; 'The Moral Crusader, W. L. Garrison,' 1892 ; 'Bay Leaves : translations from the Latin Poets,' 1893 ; 'Specimens of Greek Tragedy, translated,' 1893 ; 'Essays on Questions of the Day,' 1893 ; 'Oxford and her Colleges,' 1894 ; 'Guesses at the Riddle of Existence,' 1897.

He has *edited:* J. B. Greene's 'Notes on Ireland,' 1886.

SMITH (Horatio), 1779-1849. Born, in London, 1779. Stockbroker by profession. Contrib., with his brother James, to 'The Pic-nic,' 1802 ; 'The Monthly Mirror,' 1807-10 ; 'New Monthly Mag.,' etc. Married. In later years of life resided at Brighton. Died, at Tunbridge Wells, 12 July 1849.

Works: 'The Runaway,' 1800 ; 'Trevanion,' 1801 ; 'Rejected Addresses' (anon. ; with his brother James), 1812 (8th edn. same year) ; 'First Impressions,' 1813 (2nd edn. same year) ; 'Horace in London,' 1813 (4th edn. same year) ; 'Amaranthus the Nympholept' (anon.), 1821 ; 'Gaieties and Gravities' (anon. ; 3 vols.), 1825 ; 'Brambletye House' (anon.), 1826 ; 'The Tor Hill' (anon.), 1826 ; 'Reuben Apsley' (anon.), 1827 ; 'Tales of the Great St. Bernard,' 1828 ; 'Zillah' (anon.), 1828 ; 'The New Forest' (anon.), 1829 ; 'Walter Colyton' (anon.), 1830 ; 'Midsummer Medley for 1830,' 1830 ; 'Festivals, Games, and Amusements,' 1831 ; 'Tales of the Early Ages' (anon.), 1832 ; 'Gale Middleton' (anon.), 1833 ; 'The Involuntary Prophet' (anon.), 1835 ; 'The Tin Trumpet' (under pseud.: 'Paul Chatfield, M.D.'), 1836 ; 'Jane Lomax' (anon.), 1838 ; 'The Moneyed Man,' 1841 ; 'Adam Brown' (anon.), 1843 ; 'Arthur Arundel' (anon.), 1844 ; 'Love and Mesmerism,' 1845 ; 'Poetical Works' (2 vols.) 1846.

He *edited :* James Smith's 'Memoirs,' 1840 ; 'Oliver Cromwell,' 1840 ; J. Smith's 'Comic Miscellanies,' 1841 ; Dr. Macarthy's 'Massaniello,' 1842.

SMITH (Sydney), 1771-1845. Born, at Woodford, Essex, 3 June 1771. At school at Southampton, 1777-82. At Winchester School, July 1782 to 1789. Matric., New Coll., Oxford, 7 Feb. 1789 ; Fellow, 1790-1800 ; B.A., 1792 ; M.A., 1796. Ordained, 1794. Curate of Nether-Avon, Wilts., 1794-97. To Edinburgh, as private tutor to Michael Beach, 1798. Married Catherine Amelia Pybus, 2 July 1800. Founder of 'Edinburgh Review,' 1803 ; contributor till March 1827. Removed to London, 1803. Lectured at Royal Institution, 1804, 1805, 1806. Preacher at Foundling Hospital, March 1805 to Oct. 1808. Rector of Foston-le-Clay, Yorkshire, 1806-29. Rector of Londesborough, 1825-32. Visit to Paris, 1826. Canon of Bristol, 1828. Rector of Combe-Florey, Somersetshire, 1829-31. Canon Residentiary of St. Paul's Cathedral, 1831. Visit to Paris, 1835. Died, in London, 22 Feb. 1845. Buried at Kensal Green.

Works [exclusive of separate sermons] : 'Six Sermons,' 1800 ; 'Sermons' (2 vols.), 1801 (2nd edn. same year) ; 'Letters on the Subject of the Catholics' (under pseud. : 'Peter Plymley'), 1807-08 ; 'Sermons' (2 vols.), 1809 ; 'The Judge that smites contrary to the Law' (priv. ptd.), 1824 ; 'Catholic Claims,' 1825 ; 'Letter to the Electors on the Catholic Question,' 1826 (2nd edn. same year) ; 'Mr. Dyson's Speech to the 'Freeholders on Reform,' 1831; Three 'Letters to Archdeacon Singleton,' 1837, 1838, 1839 ; 'Letter to Lord John Russell,' 1838 ; 'Ballot,' 1839 (3rd edn. same year) ; 'Works' (4 vols.), 1839-40 ; 'Letters on American Debts,' 1844 (2nd edn. same year).

Posthumous : 'A Fragment on the Irish Roman Catholic Church,' 1845 (7th edn. same year) ; 'Sermons preached at St. Paul's Cathedral,'

1846 ; 'Elementary Sketches of Moral Philosophy,' ed. by Lord Jeffrey, 1850 (2nd edn. same year ; priv. ptd., 1849) ; 'Essays' (from 'Edinburgh Rev.') [1874].

Collected Works : in 3 vols., 1854.

Life : 'Life and Letters,' by Lady Holland, 1855 ; 'Life,' by S. J. Reid, 1884.

SMITH (William Robertson), 1846-1894. Born, at Keig, Aberdeenshire, 8 Nov. 1846. Educated at Aberdeen Univ. ; New Coll., Edinburgh ; Bonn Univ. ; and Göttingen Univ. Assistant to Prof. of Physics, Edinburgh Univ., 1868-70. Prof. of Hebrew, Free Church Coll., Aberdeen, 1870-81 ; removed from chair on account of alleged 'heretical' views on Old Testament ; re-elected, 1888. Mem. of Old Testament Revision Committee, 1872. Travelled in Arabia, 1879-80. Lord Almoner's Prof. of Arabic, Cambridge Univ., Jan. 1883 to 1886. M.A., Camb., 1883. Librarian to Cambridge Univ., Feb. 1886 to 1889. Sir Thomas Adams's Prof. of Arabic, Cambridge Univ.,1889. Hon. LL.D., Aberdeen. Hon. D.D., Strasburg. Hon. Litt.D., Trin. Coll., Dublin. Died, at Cambridge, 31 March 1894. Buried at Keig.

Works : 'What History teaches us to seek in the Bible,' 1870 ; 'Sermon' [on Luke xix. 5], 1877 ; 'Answer to the Form of Libel now before the Free Church Presbytery,' 1878 ; 'Additional Answer,' 1878 ; 'Answer to the Amended Libel,' 1879 ; 'An Open Letter to Principal Rainy,' 1880 (2nd edn. same year) ; 'Letter . . . to Rev. Sir H. W. Moncrieff' (priv. ptd.) [1880] ; 'The Old Testament in the Jewish Church,' 1881 ; 'The Prophets of Israel,' 1882 ; 'Kinship and Marriage in Early Arabia,' 1885 ; 'Lectures on the Religion of the Semites' (2 series), 1889-94.

He *edited :* Ninth edn. of 'Encycl. Brit.' (with Prof. Baynes), 1875, etc ; J. Wellhausen's 'Prolegomena to the History of Israel,' 1885 ; W. Wright's 'Lectures on the Comparative Grammar of the Semitic Languages,' 1890.

SMOLLETT (Tobias George), 1721-
1771. Born, in the 'Lennox,' Dum-
bartonshire, 1721 ; baptized, 19 March
1721. Early education at school at
Dumbarton. Apprenticed to a doctor.
To London, 1739. Entered Navy as
Surgeon's Mate, Oct. 1740. After
Carthagena expedition, retired from
Navy ; settled in Jamaica. Married
there Anne Lascelles, 1747. Returned to London, and devoted
himself to literature. Visit to Paris,
1749 [?]. M.D., Marischal Coll., Aberdeen, 1750. Edited 'Critical Review,' 1756-60. Imprisoned three
months for libel, 1759. Edited
' British Mag.,' 1760-67 ; 'The Briton,'
May 1762 to Feb. 1763. Travelled
abroad, June 1763 to spring 1765.
To Italy, 1768 ; settled at Monte
Nuovo, near Leghorn. Died there,
17 Sept. 1771. Buried at Leghorn.

Works : ' Advice ' (anon.), 1746 ;
' Reproof ' (anon.), 1747 ; 'Adven-
tures of Roderick Random ' (anon.),
1748 ; ' The Regicide ' (anon.), 1749 ;
' The History and Adventures of an
Atom ' (anon.), 1749 ; ' Adventures of
Peregrine Pickle ' (anon.), 1751 ;
' Essay on the External Use of Water,'
1752 ; 'Adventures of Ferdinand,
Count Fathom ' (anon.), 1753 ; ' The
Reprisal ' (anon.), 1757 ; ' Compleat
History of England . . . to the
Treaty of Aix-la-Chapelle ' (4 vols.),
1757-58 ; ' Continuation ' of preceding
(5 vols.), 1763-65 ; ' Adventures of
Sir Launcelot Greaves ' (anon.), 1762 ;
' Travels Through France and Italy '
(2 vols.), 1766 ; ' The Present State
of All Nations ' (8 vols.), 1768-69 ;
' The Expedition of Humphrey
Clinker ' (anon.), 1771 (misprinted
1671 on title-page of 1st edn.).
Posthumous : ' Ode to Independ-
ence,' 1773.
He *translated :* ' Gil Blas ' (anon.),
1749 ; ' Don Quixote,' 1755 ; ' Vol-
taire's Works (with others), 1761-74 ;
' The Adventures of Telemachus,'
1776 ; and *edited :* ' A Compendium of
Authentic and Entertaining Voyages,'
1756.
Collected Works : in 6 vols., 1790.
Life : by R. Anderson, 1796.

SOMERVILE (William), 1675-1742.
Born, at Wolseley, Staffordshire, 2 Sept.
1675. Early education at Stratford-
on-Avon. Scholar of Winchester
Coll., 1690. Matric., New Coll., Oxford, 24 Aug. 1694 ; Fellow, 1694-1705.
Student of Middle Temple, 1696. Life,
after leaving Oxford, spent at Edstone,
Warwickshire. Married Mary Bethel,
1 Feb. 1708. Died, at Edstone, 17
July 1742. Buried at Wootton.

Works : ' Occasional Poems,' 1727 ;
' The Chase,' 1735 (3rd edn. same
year) ; ' Hobbinol,' 1740 (3rd edn.
same year) ; 'Field Sports,' 1742.
Collected Works : in 2 vols., 1766.

SOUTHERN (Thomas), 1660-1746.
Born, at Oxmanton, co. Dublin, 1660.
To Trin. Coll., Dublin, 1676. Student of Middle Temple, 1678. Matric., Pembroke Coll., Oxford, 28 Nov.
1679 ; B.A., 1683. Prolific writer of
plays ; first play performed, 1682.
Served in the Army ; reached rank of
Captain. Later years of life spent at
Westminster. Died there, 26 May
1746.

Works : ' The Loyal Brother,' 1682 ;
' The Disappointment,' 1684 ; ' Sir
Anthony Love,' 1691 ; ' The Wives'
Excuse,' 1692 ; ' The Maid's Last
Prayer,' 1693 ; ' The Fatal Marriage,'
1694 ; ' Oroonoko,' 1696 ; ' The Fate
of Capua,' 1700 ; ' The Spartan Dame,'
1719 (3rd edn. same year) ; ' Works '
(2 vols.), 1721 ; ' Money the Mistress,'
1726.
He *edited :* ' Pausanias,' 1696.
Collected Works : in 3 vols., with
memoir, 1774.

*SOUTHEY (Robert), 1774 - 1843.
Born, in Bristol, 12 Aug. 1774.
Early education at schools at Bristol
and Corston. To Westminster School,
2 April 1788 ; expelled for an article
in ' The Flagellant,' 1792. Matric.
Balliol Coll., Oxford, 3 Nov. 1792 ;
went into residence, Jan. 1793 ; left
Oxford, 1794. Friendship with Coleridge begun, June 1794. Married (i.)
Edith Fricker, 14 Nov. 1795. Travelled in Spain with his uncle, 1795-96.
Returned to Bristol, 1796. Removed

to London, Feb. 1797. Student of Gray's Inn, 7 Feb. 1797. Second visit to Spain, 1800-01. Private Sec. to Irish Chancellor of Exchequer, 1801. Settled at Greta Hall, near Keswick, 1803; lived there till his death. Crown Pension, 1807. Poet Laureate, 1813. Hon. D.C.L., Oxford, 14 June 1820. Civil List Pension, 1835. Declined a Baronetcy. Also declined to sit as M.P. for Downton Borough, for which he was returned, 1826. Frequent contributor to 'Quarterly Rev.' Wife confined in a lunatic asylum, Oct. 1834; died, 16 Nov. 1837. Married (ii.) Caroline Anne Bowles, 4 June 1839. Lost mental powers in last years of life. Died, at Keswick, 21 March 1843. Buried in Crosthwaite Churchyard.

Works : 'The Fall of Robespierre' (Act I., by Coleridge ; Acts II., III., by Southey), 1794 ; 'Poems . . . by R. Lovell and R. Southey,' 1795 ; 'Joan of Arc,' 1796 ; 'Letters written during a Short Residence in Spain and Portugal,' 1797 ; 'Minor Poems' (2 vols.), 1797-99 ; 'Thalaba the Destroyer,' 1801 ; 'Metrical Tales, and Other Poems,' 1805 ; 'Madoc,' 1805 ; 'Letters from England' (under pseud.: 'Don Manuel Alvarez Espriella'; 3 vols.), 1807 ; 'The Curse of Kehama,' 1810 ; 'The History of Brazil' (3 vols.), 1810-19 ; 'Omniana' (2 vols.; anon.), 1812 ; 'Life of Nelson' (2 vols.), 1813 ; 'Carmen Triumphale,' 1814 ; 'Odes to the Prince Regent, etc.,' 1814 ; 'Roderick,' 1814 ; 'Minor Poems' (3 vols.), 1815 ; 'The Lay of the Laureate : Carmen Nuptiale,' 1816 ; 'The Poet's Pilgrimage to Waterloo,' 1816 ; 'Summary of the Life of Arthur, Duke of Wellington' (anon.; from 'Quarterly Rev.'), 1816 ; 'Wat Tyler,' 1817 (another edn., with additional Preface, same year) ; 'Letter to W. Smith, Esq., 1817 (4th edn. same year) ; 'Life of John Wesley' (2 vols.), 1820 ; 'A Vision of Judgment,' 1821 ; 'History of the Expedition of Orsua,' 1821 ; 'History of the Peninsular War' (3 vols.), 1823-32 ; 'The Book of the Church' (2 vols.), 1824 ; 'A Tale of Paraguay,' 1825 ;

'Vindiciæ Ecclesiæ Anglicanæ,' 1826 ; 'Sir Thomas More' (2 vols.), 1829 ; 'All for Love, etc.,' 1829 ; 'Lives of Uneducated Poets,' 1829 ; 'Selections' from his Poems, 1831 ; 'Essays, Moral and Political' (2 vols.), 1832 ; 'Selections' from his Prose, 1832 ; 'Letter to John Murray, Esq.' (anon.), 1833 ; 'Lives of the British Admirals' (with R. Bell ; 5 vols.), 1833-40 ; 'The Doctor,' vols. i.-v. (anon.), 1834-37 ; vols. vi., vii., ed. by J. W. Warter, 1847 ; 'Poetical Works' (collected ; 10 vols.), 1837-38.

Posthumous : 'Life of the Rev. Andrew Bell' (3 vols.), 1844 (vol. i., by R. Southey ; vols. ii., iii., by C. C. Southey) ; 'Oliver Newman,' ed. by H. Hill, 1845 ; 'Robin Hood' (poems by Southey and his wife), 1847 ; vols. vi., vii. of 'The Doctor' [*see above*], 1847 ; 'Life and Correspondence, ed. by his son, C. C. Southey,' (6 vols.), 1849-50 ; 'Common-Place Book' (4 vols.), 1849-51 ; Selections from his 'Letters,' ed. by J. W. Warter (4 vols.), 1856.

He *translated :* 'Amadis of Gaul,' 1803 ; 'Palmerin of England,' 1807 ; 'Chronicle of the Cid,' 1808 ; and *edited :* 'Annual Anthology' (2 vols.), 1799-1800; Chatterton's Works(with J. Cottle), 1803 ; 'Specimens of the later English Poets,' 1807 ; 'Remains of H. Kirke White, with an Account of his Life,' 1808-22 ; 'The Byrth, Lyf, and Actes of Kyng Arthur,' 1817 ; 'Pilgrim's Progress,' 1830 ; J. Jones' 'Attempts in Verse,' 1831 ; 'Select Works of the British Poets,' 1831 ; Dr. Watts' 'Horæ Lyricæ,' 1834 ; Cowper's Works, 1836-37.

Collected Works : in 10 vols., 1837-38.

Life : by C. T. Browne, 1854 ; by Prof. Dowden, 1876.

SOUTHWELL (Robert), 1561[?]-1595. Born, probably in Nottinghamshire, 1561 [?]. Educated at Douai and Paris. Enrolled in Society of Jesus, at Rome, 1578. Prefect of English Jesuits Coll., Rome, 1583 [?]. Ordained Priest, 1584. Sent to England as Missionary, 1586. Domestic

Chaplain to Countess of Arundel. Imprisoned in Tower, 1592-95. Executed, at Tyburn, 21 Feb. 1595.

Works : ' An Epistle of Comfort to the Reverend Preistes ' [Paris, 1592 ?]; ' A Short Rule of Good Life ' [1592 ?] ; ' Saint Peter's Complaynt ' (anon.), 1595 (2nd edn. same year) ; ' Mœoniæ ' (under initials : R. S.), 1595 ; ' An Humble Supplication to her Maiestie ' (anon.; attrib. to Southwell), 1595 ; ' The Triumphs ouer Death,' 1596.

Posthumous : ' Marie Magdalen's Funerall Teares,' 1602 ; ' A Fourefould Meditation, of the Foure Last Things ' (under initials : R. S.), 1606. *Collected Works:* ' Complete Poems,' ed. by A. B. Grosart, with *memoir*, 1872.

*SPENCER (Herbert), b. 1820. Born, at Derby, 27 April 1820. Privately educated. Civil Engineer, 1837-46. Sub-editor of ' The Economist,' 1848-53. Contrib. to various reviews. Life mainly devoted to philosophical studies since 1855 ; occupied on his ' Synthetic Philosophy ' since 1860. Visit to U.S.A., 1882. Has declined all academical distinctions. Resides in London.

Works : ' Social Statics,'1851[1850]; ' A Theory of Population ' (from ' Westminster Rev.'), 1852 ; ' Over-Legislation,' 1854 ; ' Railway Morals and Railway Policy,' 1855 ; ' The Principles of Psychology,' 1855 (enlarged edn., 2 vols., 1870-72) ; ' Essays . . . from the Quarterly Reviews,' series i., 1858 ; series ii., 1863 ; series iii., 1874 ; library edn. (3 vols.), 1891 ; ' Education,' 1861 ; ' First Principles,' 1862 ; ' The Principles of Biology,' (2 vols.), 1864-67 ; ' The Classification of the Sciences,' 1864 ; ' The Study of Sociology,' 1873 ; ' The Principles of Sociology ' (3 vols.), 1876-96 ; ' The Man versus the State,' 1884 ; ' The Factors of Organic Evolution,' 1887 ; ' The Principles of Ethics ' [including ' The Data of Ethics,' 1879, and ' Justice,' 1891] (2 vols), 1892-93 ; ' The Inadequacy of Natural Selection ' (from ' Contemp. Rev.') [1893] ; ' A Rejoinder to Prof. Weismann ' (from

' Contemporary Rev.') [1893] ; ' Weismannism Once More ' (from ' Contemp. Rev.'), 1894 ; ' Against the Metric System ' (from the ' Times '), 1896 ; ' Various Fragments [1852 - 1896],' 1897.

He has *edited:* ' Descriptive Sociology ' (8 pts.), 1873-81.

SPENCER (Edmund), 1552-1599. Born, in London, 1552 [?]. Early education at Merchant Taylors' School. To Pembroke Hall, Camb., as Sizar, 20 May 1569 ; B.A., 16 Jan. 1573 ; M.A., 26 June 1576. Settled in London, 1578. Sec. to Lord-Lieut. of Ireland, 1580. Received grant of land in co. Cork, 1586. Clerk of Council of Munster, 1588. Visited by Sir Walter Raleigh, 1589 ; to England with him, to be presented at Court. Lived in Ireland, 1591-95. Married [Elizabeth Boyle ?], 11 June 1594. Sheriff of co. Cork, 1598. Died, in London, 16 Jan. 1599. Buried in Westminster Abbey.

Works : ' The Shepheardes Calendar,' 1579 ; ' Three Proper, and Wittie, Familiar Letters: lately passed between Two Universitie Men' (anon.), 1580 ; ' The Faerie Queene,' bks. i.-iii., 1590 ; bks. iv.-vi., 1596 ; ' Muiopotmos,' 1590 ; ' Complaints,' 1591 ; ' Prosopopoia,' 1591 ; ' Teares of the Muses,' 1591 ; ' Daphnaida,' 1591 ; ' Amoretti and Epithalamion,' 1595 ; ' Colin Clout's Come Home Againe,' 1595 ; ' Prothalamion,' 1596 ; ' Foure Hymnes, etc.,' 1596 ; ' A View of the State of Ireland,' 1596.

Collected Works: ed. by J. Aikin (5 vols.), 1842 ; ed. by A. B. Grosart (9 vols.), 1882-84.

Life : by Dean Church, 1888.

STANHOPE (Philip Henry), 5th Earl Stanhope, 1805-1875. Born, at Walmer, 30 Jan. 1805. Matric., Ch. Ch., Oxford, 19 April 1823 ; B.A., 1827 ; Created D.C.L., 11 June 1834 ; M.A., 18 Dec. 1854 ; Hon. Student, Ch. Ch., 1858-75. M.P. for Wootton-Bassett, 1830-31 ; for Hertford, 1832-52. Under-Sec. of State for Foreign Affairs, 1834-35 ; Sec. to Board of Control, 1845-46. F.R.S.,

1827. Married Emily Hariett Kerrison, 10 July 1834. F.S.A., 1841 ; Pres., 1846. Succeeded to Earldom, 1855. Founded Stanhope Modern History Prize at Oxford, 1855. Chairman of National Portrait Gallery, 1857. Lord Rector of Marischal Coll., Aberdeen, 1858. Hon. LL.D., Camb., 1864. Foreign Member of French Acad., 1872. Hon. Antiquary to Royal Academy. Governor of Wellington Coll. Trustee of British Museum. Died, at Bournemouth, 24 Dec. 1875.

Works: 'Life of Belisarius,' 1829 ; 'History of the War of the Succession in Spain' (2 pts), 1832-33 ; 'Lord John Russell and Mr. Macaulay on the French Revolution' (anon.), 1833 ; 'Letters from Switzerland' (anon. ; priv. ptd.), 1834 ; 'History of England from the Peace of Utrecht to the Peace of Versailles' (7 vols.), 1836-54 ; 'Speech . . . on the Law of Copyright,' 1842 ; 'Essai sur la Vie du Grand Condé' (priv. ptd.), 1842 (English version, 1845) ; 'Historical Essays' (from 'Quarterly Rev.'), 1849 ; 'The Forty-five,' 1851 ; 'Letter to Jared Sparks,' 1852 ; 'Secret Correspondence connected with Mr. Pitt's return to Office in 1804' (priv. ptd.), 1852 ; 'Lord Chetham at Chevening' (priv. ptd.), 1855 ; 'Addresses delivered at Manchester, Leeds, and Birmingham,' 1856 ; 'Address delivered . . . as Lord Rector of Marischal Coll.,' 1858 ; 'Life of the Rt. Hon. William Pitt' (4 vols.), 1861-62 ; 'Miscellanies,' 1863 ; 'History of England during the Reign of Queen Anne, until the Peace of Utrecht, 1870 (2nd edn. same year) ; 'Miscellanies : second series,' 1872.

Posthumous : 'The French Retreat from Moscow, etc.' (from 'Quarterly Rev.'), 1876 ; 'Notes of Conversations with the Duke of Wellington,' 1888.

He *edited :* Earl of Peterborough's 'Letters to General Stanhope,' 1834 ; Hon. A. Stanhope's 'Spain under Charles the Second,' 1840 ; 'Extracts from Dispatches of the British Envoy at Florence' (priv. ptd. for Roxburghe Club), 1843 ; 'Correspond-ence between . . . William Pitt and Charles Duke of Rutland,' 1842 ; Earl of Chesterfield's Letters,' 1845 ; 'Memoirs of Sir Robert Peel' (with E. Cardwell), 1856-57.

STANLEY (Arthur Penrhyn), *Dean of Westminster,* **1815-1881.** Born, at Alderley, Cheshire, 13 Dec. 1815. Educated at Rugby, 1829-34. Matric., Balliol Coll., Oxford, 30 Nov. 1833 : Scholar, 1833-38 ; Ireland Scholar, 1837 ; Newdigate Prize, 1837 ; B.A., 1837 ; Fellow of Univ. Coll., 1838-51 ; Latin Essay Prize, 1839 ; Ellerton Theol. Prize, 1840 ; M.A., 1840. Ordained Deacon, 1839 ; Priest, 1841. Select Preacher, Oxford Univ., 1845-46, 1872-73. Sec., Oxford Univ. Commission, 1850-52. Canon of Canterbury Cathedral, 1851-58. Travelled widely on Continent and in Palestine. Contrib. to 'Quarterly Rev.,' 1850-73 ; to 'Edinburgh Rev.,' 1850-81 ; to 'Fraser's Mag.,' 1865-80 ; to 'Macmillan's Mag.,' 1860-81 ; to 'Good Words,' 1861-81 ; to 'Contemporary Rev.,' 1866-75 ; to 'Nineteenth Century,' 1878-80. Chaplain to Prince Consort, 1854-61. Exam. Chaplain to Bishop of London, 1854-64. Regius Prof. of Eccles. Hist., Oxford, 1856-64. B.D. and D.D., Oxford, 1858. Canon of Ch. Ch., Oxford, 1858-64. Mem. of Hebdomadal Council, Oxford, 1860-64. Deputy Clerk of Closet, and Hon. Chaplain in Ordinary to Queen and Prince of Wales, 1863. Married Lady Augusta Bruce, 23 Dec. 1863. Dean of Westminster, 1864. Hon. LL.D., Camb., 1864. Hon. Fellow of Univ. Coll., Oxford, 1864-81. To Moscow, for marriage of Duke of Edinburgh. 1874. Lord Rector St. Andrew's Univ., 1875. Visited U.S.A., 1878. Died, at Westminster, 18 July 1881. Buried in Westminster Abbey.

Works [exclusive of separate sermons]: 'The Gypsies,' 1837 ; 'Do States, like Individuals, inevitably tend . . . to decay ?' 1840 ; 'Life and Correspondence of T. Arnold' (2 vols.), 1844 (3rd edn. same year) ; 'Sermons and Essays on the Apostolical Age,'

1847 ; 'The Study of Modern History,' 1854 ; 'Historical Memorials of Canterbury,' 1855 (2nd edn. same year) ; The Re˜ormation,' 1856 ; 'Sinai and Palestine,' 1856 (3rd edn. same year) ; 'Three Introductory Lectures on the Study of Ecclesiastical History,' 1857 ; 'The Unity of Evangelical and Apostolical Teaching,' 1859 ; 'Freedom and Labour,' 1860 ; 'Lectures on the History of the Eastern Church,' 1861 ; 'Sermons preached before. . . the Prince of Wales during his tour in the East,' 1863 ; 'The Bible, its Form and its Substance,' 1863 ; 'Lectures on the History of the Jewish Church' (3 pts.). 1863-76 ; 'A Letter to the Lord Bishop of London,' 1863 ; 'The South African Controversy,' 1867 ; 'An Address on the Connection of Church and State,' 1868 (2nd edn. same year) : 'Historical Memorials of Westminster Abbey,' 1868 (2nd edn. same year) ; 'The Three Irish Churches,' 1869 ; 'Essays,' 1870 ; 'The Athanasian Creed' (from 'Contemp. Rev.'), 1871 ; 'The National Thanksgiving,' 1872 ; 'Lectures on the History of the Church of Scotland,' 1872 ; 'The Early Christianity of Northumbria' (from 'Good Words'), 1875 ; 'Inaugural Address at St. Andrew's,' 1875 ; 'Addresses and Sermons delivered at St. Andrew's, 1877 ; Addresses and Sermons delivered during a visit to the United States,' 1879 ; 'Memoirs of Edward and Catherine Stanley,' 1879 ; 'Christian Institutions,' 1881.

Posthumous : 'Sermons on Special Occasions,' 1882 ; 'Sermons for Children, 1887 ; 'Letters and Verses,' ed. by R. E. Prothero, 1895.

He *edited :* T. Arnold's 'Miscellaneous Works,' 1845 ; 'Addresses and Charges of E. Stanley, Bishop of Norwich,' 1851 ; T. Arnold's 'Travelling Journals,' 1852 ; 'The Epistle of St. Paul to the Corinthians' (2 vols.), 1855 ; 'The Utrecht Psalter : Reports,' 1874 ; S. Greg's 'A Layman's Legacy,' 1877 ; Bishop Thirlwall's 'Letters to a Friend,' 1881.

Life : by R. E. Prothero and Dean Bradley, 1893.

*STANLEY (Henry Morton), b. 1841. Born [John Rowlands], near Denbigh, 28 Jan. 1841. Educated at parish school, St. Asaph. Pupil teacher, 1854-56. Sailed to New Orleans as cabin-boy, 1856. Was adopted there by a merchant of name of Stanley ; assumed name of Henry Morton Stanley in place of his own. Served in Confederate Army, 1861-62. In Asia Minor as newspaper correspondent, 1866. Foreign correspondent for 'New York Herald' from 1867. In Africa (rescue of Livingstone), 1871-72. Gold Medal, Geographical Soc., 1873. Second exploration in Africa (Descent of the Congo), 1874-78. Palm of Officer of Public Instruction, Paris, 28 June 1878. Third exploration in Africa, 1879-84. Hon. Freedom of City of London, 13 Jan. 1887. Fourth exploration in Africa (Emin Pasha relief expedition), 1887-89. Hon. D.C.L., Oxford, 1890 ; Hon. LL.D., Camb., 1890 ; Hon. LL.D., Edinburgh, 1890 ; Hon. D.C.L., Durham, 1890. Married Dorothy Tennant, 12 July 1890. Lectured in U.S.A., 1890-91 ; in England, 1891 ; in Australia and New Zealand, 1892. M.P. for North Lambeth, 1895.

Works : 'How I found Livingstone,' 1872 (2nd edn. same year) ; 'My Kalulu,' 1873 ; 'Coomassie and Magdala,' 1874 ; 'Through the Dark Continent' (2 vols.), 1878 ; 'The Congo' (2 vols.), 1885 ; 'My African Travels' (a lecture ; priv. ptd.), 1886 ; 'The Rescue of Emin Pasha' (a lecture ; priv. ptd.), 1890 ; 'In Darkest Africa' (2 vols.), 1890 ; 'Across Africa' (a lecture ; priv. ptd.), 1890 ; 'The Great Forest of Central Africa' (a lecture ; priv. ptd.), 1890 ; 'My Dark Companions and their Strange Stories,' 1893 ; 'My Early Travels and Adventures,' 1895.

STEELE (*Sir* Richard), 1672-1729. Born, in Dublin, March 1672. Early education at Charterhouse, Nov. 1684 to Nov. 1689. Matric., Ch. Ch., Oxford, 13 March 1690 ; Postmaster Merton Coll., 1691. Left Oxford,

1694. Took no degree. Entered the army, 1695. Priv. Sec. to Lord Cutts, 1696-97. Commission in the Guards, 1697. Play, 'The Funeral,' produced at Drury Lane, Dec. 1701 ; 'The Lying Lover,' Dec. 1703 ; 'The Tender Husband,' April 1705. Married (i.) Mrs. Margaret Stretch, 1705. Gentleman-Waiter to Prince George of Denmark, Aug. 1706 to Oct. 1708. Wife died, Dec. 1706. Gazetteer, May 1707 to Oct. 1710. Married (ii.) Mary Scurlock, Sept. 1707. Contrib. to 'The Muses Mercury,' 1707 ; to 'Spectator,' March 1711 to Dec. 1714 ; to 'Guardian,' March to Oct. 1713 ; to 'The Englishman,' Oct. 1713 to Nov. 1715. Commissioner of Stamp Office, Jan. 1710 to June 1713. M.P. for Stockbridge, 1713 ; expelled from House of Commons on account of passages in writings, 1714. Surveyor of Royal Stables at Hampton Court, 1714. Lieutenant for County of Middlesex, and J.P., 1714. Governor of Royal Company of Comedians, 1715-20. Knighted, 1715. M.P. for Boroughbridge, 1715. Commissioner of Forfeited Estates in Scotland, 1715. Edited 'The Theatre' (under pseud. 'Sir John Edgar'), Jan. to April 1720. M.P. for Wendover, March 1722. Comedy, 'The Conscious Lovers,' produced at Drury Lane, Nov. 1722. Later years spent in retirement, mainly in Wales. Died at Carmarthen, 1 Sept. 1729.

Works: 'The Procession' (anon.), 1695 ; 'The Christian Hero,' 1701 ; 'The Funeral,' 1702 ; 'The Lying Lover,' 1704 ; 'The Tender Husband,' 1705 ; 'Letter to Dr. Sacheverell' (under pseud. 'Isaac Bickerstaff'), 1709 ; 'The Tatler' (under pseud. 'Isaac Bickerstaff,' 4 vols.), 1709-11 ; Contributions to 'The Spectator,' 1711-14 ; to 'The Guardian,' 1713 ; to 'The Englishman,' 1713-15 ; 'The Importance of Dunkirk Considered,' 1713 ; 'The Englishman's Thanks to the Duke of Marlborough' (anon.), 1712 ; 'The Crisis,' 1713 ; 'Letter to the Tongue-loosed Doctor' (under pseud. 'Isaac Bickerstaff') 1713 ; 'Speech on the proposal of Sir T.

Hanmer for Speaker,' 1714 ; 'Letter to a Member of Parliament,' 1714 ; 'Apology for Himself and his Writings,' 1714 ; 'A Defence of drinking to the pious memory of K. Charles I.,' 1714 ; 'Romish Ecclesiastical History of Late Years,' 1714 ; 'Letter from the Earl of Mar to the King,' 1715 ; 'The Lover ; to which is added, the Reader,' 1715 ; 'Political Writings,' 1715 ; 'Town-Talk' (9 nos.), 1715-16 ; 'Chit - Chat' (under pseud. 'Humphrey Philroye'), 1716 ; 'The British Subjects' Answer to the Pretender's Declaration,' 1716 ; 'Speech for Repealing of the Triennial Act,' 1716 ; 'The Tea Table,' 1716 ; 'An Account of the Fish-Pool' (with J. Gilmore), 1718 ; 'Letter to the Earl of O—d,' 1719 ; 'The Spinster,' 1719 ; 'The Antidote' (2 nos. ; anon.), 1719 ; 'Inquiry into the Manner of Creating Peers' (anon.), 1719 ; 'The Plebeian' (anon.), 1719 ; 'The Theatre' (under pseud. 'Sir John Edgar'), 1720 ; 'The Crisis of Poverty,' 1720 ; 'A Nation a Family,' 1720 ; 'The D—n of W—r still the same' (anon.), 1720 ; 'State of the Case between the Lord Chamberlain, etc.,' 1720 ; 'The Conscious Lovers,' 1723 ; 'Dramatick Works,' 1723 ; 'Woods' Melancholly Complaint' (anon.), 1725.

Posthumous: 'Epistolary Correspondence,' ed. by J. Nichols, 1787.

He *translated:* Cerri's 'Account of the State of the Roman Catholic Religion,' 1715 ; and *edited:* 'Poetical Miscellanies,' 1714 ; 'The Ladies' Library,' 1714.

Life: by G. A. Aitken, 1889.

STEPHEN (James Kenneth), 1859-1892. Born, in London, 25 Feb. 1859. At schools at Southborough and Thorpe Mandeville, 1868-71 ; at Eton, 1871-78. Matric., King's Coll., Camb., as Scholar, 1878 ; B.A., 1882. Student of Inner Temple, 13 Nov. 1880 ; called to Bar, 25 June 1884. Private historical tutor to Duke of Clarence for three months in 1883. Fellow of King's Coll., Camb., 1885. Contrib. to 'St. James's Gaz.,' 'Sat. Rev.,' 'Pall Mall Gaz.,' and other periodiçals, from 1886. Started 'The Reflector,' 1888. Clerk of Assize for South Wales Circuit, 1888-90. Resided at Cambridge, 1891. Died, 3 Feb. 1892.

Works: 'International Law and International Relations,' 1884 ; 'The Living Languages,' 1891 ; 'Lapsus Calami' (under initials : 'J. K. S.'), 1891 (4th edn. same year) ; 'Quo Musa Tendis ?' 1891.

Collected Works : 'Lapsus Calami, and other verses,' ed. by Sir H. Stephen, 1896.

*STEPHEN (Leslie), b. 1832. Born, in Kensington, 28 Nov. 1832. Early education at Eton and at King's Coll., London. Matric.,Trin. Hall, Camb., 1851 ; B.A., 1854 ; M.A., 1857 ; Fellow Trin. Hall, 1855. Left Cambridge and settled in London, 1864. Married (i.) Harriet Marion Thackeray, 1864 ; she died, 1875. Editor of 'Cornhill Mag.,' 1871-82. Married (ii.) Julia Prinsep Duckworth, 1878. Editor of 'Dict. of Nat. Biog.,' 1882-91. Clark Lecturer in English Literature, Camb., 1883-84. LL.D., Camb. Hon. Fellow Trin. Hall, Camb. Pres. of Ethical Society.

Works: 'Sketches from Cambridge' (anon.), 1865 ; 'The "Times" on the American War' (under initials : 'L. S.'), 1865 ; 'The Play-Ground of Europe,' 1871 ; 'Essays on Freethinking,' 1873 ; 'Hours in a Library' (3 vols.), 1874-79 ; 'History of English Thought in the Eighteenth Century' (2 vols.), 1876 ; 'Samuel Johnson,' 1878 ; 'Alexander Pope,' 1880 ; 'The Science of Ethics,' 1882 ; 'Swift,' 1882 ; 'Life of Henry Fawcett,' 1885 ; 'What is Materialism ?' 1886 ; 'An Agnostic's Apology,' 1893 ; 'The Life of Sir James Fitz-James Stephen,' 1895 ; 'Social Rights and Duties' (2 vols.), 1896.

He has *translated :* Berlepsch's 'The Alps,' 1861 ; and *edited :* W. K. Clifford's 'Lectures and Essays' (with Sir F. Pollock), 1879 ; Fielding's Works, 1882 ; Richardson's Works, 1883 ; 'Dictionary of National Biography,' vols. i.-xxvi., 1885-91.

STERNE (Laurence), 1713-1768. Born, at Clonmel, 24 Nov. 1713. At school at Halifax, 1723-31. Matric., Jesus Coll., Camb., 1732 : Sizarship, July 1733 ; Scholar, July 1734 ; B.A., Jan. 1736 ; M.A., 1740. Ordained Deacon, March 1736 ; Priest, Aug. 1738. Vicar of Sutton-on-the-Forest, Yorks., 1738. Prebendary of York Cathedral, Jan. 1741. Married Elizabeth Lumley, 30 March 1741. Vicar of Stillington, 1741. Curate of Coxwold, Yorks., 1760. Lived mainly in France, 1762-67. Died, in London, 18 March 1768. Buried in Burial Ground of St. George's, Hanover Square.

Works : 'The Case of Elijah and the Widow of Zarephath considered,' 1747 ; 'The Abuses of Conscience,' 1750 ; 'The Life and Opinions of Tristram Shandy' (9 vols.), 1759-67 ; 'The Sermons of Mr. Yorick' (7 vols.), 1760-69 ; 'A Sentimental Journey through France and Italy, by Mr. Yorick' (2 vols.), 1768.

Posthumous : 'The History of a Good Warm Watch-Coat,' 1769 ; 'Letters . . . to his Most Intimate Friends,' ed. by his daughter (3 vols.), 1775 ; 'Letters from Yorick to Eliza,' 1775 ; 'Letters to his Friends on various occasions,' 1775 ; 'Original Letters, never before published,' 1788 ; 'Seven Letters written by Sterne and his Friends, hitherto unpublished' (priv. ptd.), 1844.

Collected Works : ed. by G. Saintsbury (6 vols.), 1894.

Life : by P. H. Fitzgerald, 1864.

*STEVENSON (Robert Louis Balfour) 1850-1894.** Born, in Edinburgh, 13 Nov. 1850. Educated at private schools, and at Edinburgh University. Originally intended for profession of Engineer. Gave it up, and studied Law ; was called to Scottish Bar. Owing to ill-health, did not practise. Travelled on Continent, and in America. Married Mrs. Fanny Van de Grift Osbourne, 1880. Settled in Samoa, Oct. 1890. Died there, 8 Dec. 1894. Buried there.

Works : 'The Pentland Rising

(anon.), 1866 ; 'The Charity Bazaar' (anon,) [1868]; 'An Inland Voyage,' 1878 ; 'Edinburgh,' 1879 [1878] ; 'Travels with a Donkey in the Cevennes,' 1879 ; 'Virginibus Puerisque,' 1881 ; 'Not I, and other poems' (priv. ptd.), 1881 ; 'Familiar Studies of Men and Books,' 1882 ; 'New Arabian Nights,' 1882 ; 'Treasure Island,' 1883 ; 'The Silverado Squatters,' 1883 ; 'A Child's Garden of Verses,' 1885 (2nd edn. same year) ; 'Prince Otto,' 1885 ; 'The Dynamiter' (with his wife), 1885 ; 'The Strange Case of Dr. Jekyll and Mr. Hyde,' 1886 ; 'Kidnapped,' 1886 ; 'Ticonderoga' (priv. ptd.), 1887 ; 'The Merry Men,' 1887 ; 'Underwood's,' 1887 ; 'Memories and Portraits,' 1887 ; 'The Black Arrow,' 1888 ; 'The Wrong Box' (with L. Osbourne),1889 ; 'The Master of Ballantrae,' 1889 ; 'Ballads,' 1890 ; 'Father Damien,' 1890 ; 'The Wrecker' (with L. Osbourne) [1892] ; 'Three Plays' (with W. E. Henley), 1892 ; 'Across the Plains,' 1892 ; 'A Footnote to History,' 1892 ; 'Catriona,' 1893 ; 'Island Nights' Entertainments,' 1893 ; 'The Ebb-Tide' (with L. Osbourne), 1894; 'Macaire' (with W. E. Henley), 1895.

Posthumous : 'Vailima Letters,' ed. by Sidney Colvin, 1895 ; 'Songs of Travel, and other verses,' ed. by Sidney Colvin, 1896 ; 'Weir of Hermiston,' ed. by Sidney Colvin, 1896 ; 'St Ives' (unfinished ; completed by A. T. Quiller-Couch), 1897.

Collected Works : ed. by Sidney Colvin, 1894, etc.

STILL (John), *Bishop of Bath and Wells,* **1543(?)-1608.** Born, at Grantham, 1543[?]. Educated at Christ Coll., Camb. Lady Margaret's Prof. of Divinity, Camb., 1750. Prebendary of Westminster,1573. Master of St. John's Coll., Camb., 1574 ; of Trin. Coll., Camb., 1577. Archdeacon of Sudbury, March 1577. Bishop of Bath and Wells, Feb. 1593. Died, 26 Feb. 1608.

Works : 'A ryght pithy, pleasant, and merie Comedy, intytuled Gammer Gurton's Needle . . . Made by Mr. S., Master of Art,' 1575.

STOWE (Mrs. Harriet Elizabeth Beecher), 1812-1896. Born [Harriet Elizabeth Beecher Beecher], at Litchfield, Conn., 14 June 1812. At school kept by her sister at Hartford, as scholar and teacher, 1824-32. Removed, with her father, to Cincinnati, 1832. Married to Rev. Calvin Ellis Stowe, Jan. 1836. Contrib. 'Uncle Tom's Cabin,' as serial, to 'National Era,' 1851-52. Removed to Andover, where her husband was Prof. of Sacred Lit., 1852. Visits to Europe, 1853, 56, 59. Removed to Hartford, 1864. Part-editor of 'Hearth and Home,' 1868. Contrib. paper on 'Lady Byron' to 'Atlantic Monthly,' Sept. 1869. Husband died there, 22 Aug. 1886. Failing health in later years. Died, at Hartford, Conn., 1 July 1896.

Works : 'Uncle Tom's Cabin' (from 'National Era'), 1852 ; 'A Key to Uncle Tom's Cabin,' 1853 ; 'A Peep into Uncle Tom's Cabin ; for Children,' 1853 ; 'Sunny Memories of Foreign Lands' (2 vols.), 1854 ; 'Geography for My Children,' 1855 ; 'The Christian Slave : a drama' (dramatized from 'Uncle Tom's Cabin '), 1855 ; 'Dred,' 1856 (another edn., called 'Nina Gordon,' 1866) ; 'Our Charley,' 1858 ; 'The Minister's Wooing,' 1859 ; 'The Pearl of Orr's Island,' 1862 ; 'Reply on Behalf of the Women of America,' 1863 ; 'The Ravages of a Carpet,' 1864 ; 'House and Home Papers' (under pseud. 'Christopher Crowfield'), 1864 ; 'Religious Poems,' 1865 ; 'Stories about our Dogs,' 1865 ; 'Little Foxes,' 1865 ; 'Queer Little People,' 1867 ; 'Daisy's First Winter,' 1867 ; 'The Chimney Corner' (under pseud. 'Christopher Crowfield'), 1868 ; 'Men of Our Times,' 1868 ; 'The American Woman's Home' (with C. E. Beecher), 1869 ; 'Old-Town Folks,' 1869 ; 'Lady Byron vindicated,' 1869 ; 'Little Pussy Willow,' 1870 ; 'Pink and White Tyranny,' 1871 ; 'Sam Lawson's Fireside Stories,' 1871 ; 'My Wife and I,' 1872 ; 'Palmetto Leaves,' 1873 ; 'Betty's Bright Idea,' 1875 ; 'We and our Neighbours,' 1875 ; 'Footsteps of the Master,' 1876 ; 'Bible Heroines,' 1878 ; 'Poganuc People,' 1878 ; 'A Dog's Mission,' 1881. *Life :* [to the year 1888] by her son, C. E. Stowe, 1889.

*STUBBS (William), *Bishop of Oxford,* **b. 1825.** Born, at Knaresborough, 21 June 1825. At Ripon Grammar School, Sept. 1839 to Dec. 1843. Matric., Ch. Ch., Oxford, 23 April 1844 ; Servitor, 1844-48 ; B.A., 1848 ; Fellow of Trin. Coll., 1848-51 ; M.A., 1851. Ordained Deacon, 1848 ; Priest, 1850 ; Vicar of Navestock, Essex, 1850-67. Married Catherine Dellar, 20 June 1859. Diocesan Inspector of Schools, Rochester, 1860-66. Librarian and Keeper of MSS., Lambeth, 1862-67. Regius Prof. of Modern Hist., Oxford, 1866 - 84 ; Fellow of Oriel Coll., 1867-84 ; Curator of Bodleian Lib., 1868 ; Select Preacher, 1870 ; Mem. of Hebdomadal Council, 1872. Rector of Cholderton, Wilts., 1875-79. Hon. Fellow, Balliol Coll., Oxford, 1876 ; Hon. Student, Ch. Ch., 1878 ; D.D. (by decree), 10 June 1879. Hon. LL.D., Camb., 1879. Canon of St. Paul's, 1879-84. Hon. LL.D., Edinburgh, 1880. Mem. of Royal Commission on Ecclesiastical Courts, 1881. Bishop of Chester, 1884-88. Pres. of Surtees Soc., 1884. Mem. of Royal Commission on Historical MSS., 1886. Hon. Doc., Heidelberg, 1886. Bishop of Oxford, 1888. Hon. Fellow, Oriel Coll., Oxford, 1888. Hon. LL.D., Dublin, 1890. Hon. D.C.L., Oxford, 1893. Hon. Mem. Royal Soc. of Science, Göttingen, 1872 ; of Historical Soc. of Massachusetts, 1876 ; Foreign Mem. of Royal Bavarian Acad., 1880 ; of American Acad. of Arts, 1881 ; Corresp. Mem. of Royal Prussian Acad., 1882 ; Hon. Mem. Imp. Univ., Kieff, 1884 ; of Royal Danish Acad., 1885 ; Corresp. Mem. of Institute of France, 1887 ; of American Philosophical Soc., 1891 ; Fellow of Royal S. c. of Edinburgh, 1892.

Works [exclusive of separate sermons]*:* 'Registrum Sacrum Anglicanum,' 1858 ; ' Chronicles and Memorials of the Reign of Richard I.,' 1865 ; ' An Address delivered by way of Inaugural Lecture,' 1867 ; 'The Constitutional History of England' (3 vols.), 1874-78 ; 'The Early Plantagenets,' 1876 ; 'Seventeen Lectures on the study of Mediæval and Modern History,' 1886. He has *edited :* ' The Foundation of Waltham Abbey,' 1861 ; J. L. von Mosheim's 'Institutes of Ecclesiastical History,' 1863 ; ' Chronicles and Memorials of the Reign of Richard I.' (2 vols.), 1864-65 ; 'Gesta Regis Henrici Secundi,' 1867 ; 'Chronica Magistri Rogeri de Hovendene,' 1868 ; 'Councils and Ecclesiastical Documents relating to Great Britain and Ireland ' (with A. W. Haddan), 1869 ; 'Select Charters and other illustrations of English Constitutional History,' 1870 ; C. Hardwick's ' History of the Christian Church,' 1872 ; 'Memoriale Fratris Walteri de Coventria,' 1872, etc. ; ' Memorials of St. Dunstan,' 1874 ; ' Radulfi de Diceto . . . Opera Historica,' 1876, etc. ; ' The Historical Works of Gervase of Canterbury,' 1879, etc. ; ' Chronicles of the Reigns of Edward I. and Edward II.' (2 vols.), 1882-83 ; E. Guest's ' Origines Calticæ' (with C. Deedes), 1883 ; 'Willelmi Malmesbiriensis de Regum gestis Anglorum, etc.,' 1887, etc.

SUCKLING *(Sir* John), 1609-40[?] Born, at Whitton, Middlesex, 1609 ; baptized, 10 Feb. 1609. Matric., Trin. Coll., Camb., 1623. Went abroad, 1628. Fought in the army of Gustavus Adolphus, 1631. Knighted, about 1635[?]. Raised a troop of horse for Charles I., 1639. Retired to Con tinent, to escape impeachment for High Treason, 1641. Died, in France, about 1640[?].

Works : 'Sessions of the Poets,' 1637 ; 'Aglaura,' 1637 ; 'The Discontented Colonell,' 1639.

Posthumous : ' A Coppy of a Letter found in the privy lodgeings at Whitehall' (anon.), 1641 ; ' The Coppy of a Letter written to the lower house of Parliament ' (anon.), 1641 ; ' Fragmenta Aurea,' 1646 ; ' The Goblins,'

1646 ; 'Letters to Several Persons of Honour,' 1659 ; 'The Sad One,' 1659 ; 'Last Remains,' 1659.
Collected Works : ed. with *memoir,* by W. C. Hazlitt (2 vols.), 1874.

SURREY, Henry Howard, *Earl of*, 1516[?]-1547. Born, probably at Kenninghall, Norfolk, 1516[?]. Possibly educated at Ch. Ch., Oxford. Married Lady Francis Vere, 1535. Knighted, Oct. 1536. K.G., April 1542. With the army in Scotland, 1542. Field-Marshal of English army on the Continent, 1544. Summoned back to England, 1546. Executed, on a charge of high treason, 19 Jan. 1547.

Works [posthumous] *:* 'Poems' in 'Tottel's Miscellany,' 1557 ; 'Songes and Sonettes,' 1567 ; 'Works,' ed. by G. F. Nott, 1815.
He *translated :* Virgil's 'Æneid,' bks. ii. and iv., 1557.

*SWIFT (Jonathan), 1667 - 1745. Born, in Dublin, 30 Nov. 1667. At school at Kilkenny, 1673-82. Matric., Trin. Coll., Dublin, as Pensioner, 24 April 1682 ; B.A. 1686. Emigrated to England, and joined his mother at Leicester, 1688. Lived in house of Sir W. Temple, at Moor Park, as his Secretary, and Tutor to Esther Johnson, 1689-92. Entered at Hart Hall, Oxford, 14 June 1692 ; M.A., 5 July 1692. Ordained Deacon, 18 Oct. 1694 ; Priest, 13 Jan. 1695. Prebend of Kilroot, Ireland, 1695. Returned to Moor Park, 1696-98. To Dublin, as Chaplain to Earl of Berkeley, 1699 ; Rector of Agher, and Vicar of Laracor and Rathbeggan, March 1699. Prebend of Dunlavin, 1700. Returned to England with Earl of Berkeley, 1701. B.D. and D.D., Dublin, 1702. Subsequent life spent partly in Ireland, partly in England. Edited 'The Examiner,' Nov. 1710 to June 1711. Founded the Brothers' Club, 1711 ; the Scriblerus Club, 1712. Dean of St. Patrick's, 23 Feb. 1713. Friendship with Esther Johnson ["Stella"] begun, 1700. Friendship with Esther Vanhomrigh ["Vanessa"] begun, 1710 ; she died, 1723. Contributed

to 'London,' 1734. Mind began to give way, 1737. Died, in Dublin, 19 Oct. 1745. Buried in St. Patrick's Cathedral.

Works : 'A Discourse of the Contests . . . between the Nobles and the Commons, etc.' (anon.), 1701 ; 'A Tale of a Tub' (anon.), 1704 ; 'Predictions' (under pseud. : 'Isaac Bickerstaff'), 1707 ; 'Vindication' of preceding, 1709 ; 'Meditation upon a Broomstick' (anon.), 1710 ; 'A New Journey to Paris' (under pseud. 'Sieur Du Baudrier'), 1711 ; 'Miscellanies,' 1711 ; 'The Conduct of the Allies' (anon.), 1711 ; 'Some advice . . . to the Members of the October Club' (anon.), 1712 ; 'Letter to the Lord High Treasurer,' 1712 ; 'A Proposal for Correcting . . . the English Tongue,' 1721 ; 'Some Reasons to prove that no person is obliged, by his principles as a Whig, to oppose Her Majesty' (anon.), 1712 ; 'The Publick Spirit of the Whigs' (anon.), 1714 ; 'A Preface to the B——p of S——r—m's Introduction' (under pseud. 'Gregory Misosarum'), 1713 ; 'The Conduct of the Purse of Ireland,' 1714 ; 'Essays,' 1714 ; 'The Art of Punning,' 1719 ; 'Proposal for the Universal Use of Irish Manufactures' (anon.), 1720 ; 'Defence of English Commodities,' 1720 ; 'Right of Precedence' (anon.), 1720 ; 'The Wonderful Wonder of Wonders' (anon.) [1720 ?] ; 'Letter of Advice to a Young Poet,' 1721 ; 'Letter to a Gentleman lately entered into Holy Orders,' 1721 ; 'The Journal' (anon.), 1722 ; 'Letter from a Lady of Quality' (anon.), 1724 ; Two Letters under pseud. 'M. B. Drapier,' 1724 ; 'Gulliver's Travels' (anon.), 1726 ; 'Cadenus and Vanessa' (anon.), 1726 ; 'The Intelligencer' (with Sheridan), 1729 ; 'The Journal of a Modern Lady' (anon.), 1729 ; 'Proposal for Preventing the Children of the Poor from being a Burthen, etc.' (anon.), 1730 ; 'The Presbyterians' plea . . . examined' (anon.), 1731 ; 'The Advantages proposed by repealing the Sacramental Test, etc.,' 1732 ; 'On Poetry' (anon.), 1733 ; 'Scheme for

a Hospital for Incurables' (anon.).
1733 ; 'Poems on Several Occasions,'
1734 ; 'Proposals for erecting a Pro
testant Nunnery in the City of Dub
lin' (anon.), 1736 ; 'The Beast's Con
fession to the Priest,' 1738 ; 'Complet·
Collection of Genteel and Ingeniou-
Conversation' (under pseud. 'Simon
Wagstaff'), 1738 ; 'An Imitation of
the Sixth Satire of the Second Book
of Horace,' 1738 ; 'Verses on the
Death of Dr. Swift, written by himself,' 1739 ; 'Some Free Thoughts
upon the Present State of Affairs'
(anon.), 1741 ; 'Literary Correspondence,' 1741 ; 'Three Sermons,'
1744 ; 'The Difficulty of Knowing
One's Self,' 1745. [Also a number of
small controversial tracts, anonymous
ballads printed on single sheets, etc.]
  Posthumous : ' Brotherly Love,'
1754 ; 'History of the Four Last
Years of the Queen,' 1758 ; 'Letters'
(3 vols.), 1767 ; 'Letters' (6 vols.),
1761-69 ; 'Sermons' [1790 ?].
  He *edited :* Sir W. Temple's Letters,
1700 ; Sir W. Temple's Works, 1720 ;
Arbuthnot and Pope's 'Miscellaneous
Works,' 1742.
  Collected Works : ed. by Sir Walter
Scott (19 vols.), 1814.
  Life : by H. Craik, 1882 ; by **J.**
Churton Collins, 1895.

*SWINBURNE (Algernon Charles),
b. 1837. Born, in London, 5 April
1837. Early education in France.
At Eton, 1849-53. Matric., Balliol
Coll., Oxford, 24 Jan. 1856. Contrib. to 'Undergraduate Papers,'
1857-58. Took no degree. Left Oxford, 1860 ; afterwards spent some
time in Italy. Contrib. to 'Once-a-
Week,' Feb. to Sept. 1862 ; to 'Fortnightly Rev.,' from 1870 ; to 'The
Dark Blue,' 1871 ; to 'Nineteenth
Century,' 'Athenæum,' 'Gentleman's
Mag.,' 'Encycl. Brit.,' etc. Of late
has resided near London.
  Works : 'The Queen - Mother ;
Rosamond,' 1860 ; 'Dead Love,' 1864 ;
'Atalanta in Calydon,' 1865 ; 'Chaste-
lard,' 1865 ; 'Cleopatra,' 1866 ; 'Un
published Verses' (priv. ptd.) [1866] ;
'Poems and Ballads,' 1st series, 1866;

2nd series, 1878 ; 3rd series, 1889 ;
'Notes on Poems and Reviews,' 1866;
'A Song of Italy,' 1867 ; 'Appeal to
England against the Execution of the
Condemned Fenians' (from 'Morning
Star'), 1867 ; 'Siena,' 1868; 'William
Blake,' 1868 (2nd edn., same year) ;
'Ode on the Proclamation of the
French Republic,' 1870 ; 'Songs be-
fore Sunrise,' 1871 ; 'Under the Mi-
croscope,' 1872 ; 'Bothwell,' 1874 ;
'Essays and Studies,' 1875 ; 'George
Chapman,' 1875 ; 'Songs of Two
Nations,' 1875 ; 'Note of an English
Republican on the Muscovite Crusade,'
1876 ; 'Erectheus,' 1876 ; 'Note on
Charlotte Brontë,' 1877 ; 'A Study
of Shakespeare,' 1880 [1879] ; 'The
Heptalogia' (anon.), 1880 ; 'Studies
in Song,' 1880 ; 'Songs of the Spring-
tides,' 1880 ; 'Dolorida' (in French ;
priv. ptd.) [1880 ?]; 'Mary Stuart,'
1881 ; 'Tristram of Lyonesse,' 1882 ;
'A Century of Roundels,' 1883 ; 'A
Midsummer Holiday,' 1884 ; 'Marino
Faliero,' 1885 ; 'A Word for the
Navy,' 1886 ; 'A Study of Victor
Hugo,' 1886 ; 'Miscellanies,' 1886 ;
'The Jubilee, 1887,' 1887 ; 'Locrine,'
1887 : 'The Ballad of Dead Man's
Bay' (priv. ptd.), 1889 ; 'The Brothers,' 1889 ; 'A Study of Ben Jonson,' 1889 ; 'A Sequence of Sonnets
on the Death of Robert Browning'
(priv. ptd.), 1890 ; 'The Sisters,'
1892 ; 'Grace Darling' (priv. ptd.),
1893 ; 'The Ballad of Bulgarie'
(priv. ptd.), 1893 ; 'Studies in Prose
and Poetry,' 1894 ; 'Robert Burns'
(priv. ptd.), 1896 ; 'The Tale of
Balen,' 1896.
  He has *edited :* Byron's Poems, selected, 1866 ; Coleridge's 'Christabel,'
1869 ; C. J. Wells' 'Joseph and his
Brethren,' 1876 ; Herrick's Poems,
1891.

**SYMONDS (John Addington), 1840-
1893.** Born, at Bristol, 5 Oct. 1840.
At Harrow School, May 1854 to 1858.
Matric., Balliol Coll., Oxford, 28 May
1858 ; Exhibitioner, 1859-62 ; New-
digate Prize, 1860 ; B.A., 1862 ;
Fellow of Magdalen Coll., 1862-64 ;
English Essay Prize, 1863 : M.A.,

18

1865. Student of Lincoln's Inn, 1862. Married Janet Catherine North, 10 Nov. 1864. Settled in London. Frequent visits to Continent. Removed to Clifton, Nov. 1868. Removed to Davos Platz, Switzerland, for health, 1876. Resided there for greater part of each year, till his death. Died, in Rome, 19 April 1893.

Works: 'The Escorial,' 1860; 'The Renaissance,' 1863; 'An Introduction to the Study of Dante,' 1872; 'The Renaissance of Modern Europe,' 1872; 'Studies of the Greek Poets,' 1st series, 1873; 2nd series, 1876; 'Sketches in Italy and Greece,' 1874; 'The Renaissance in Italy' (5 pts.), 1875-86 ('The Age of the Despots,' 1875; 'The Revival of Learning,' 1877; 'The Fine Arts,' 1877; 'Italian Literature,' 2 vols., 1881; 'The Catholic Reaction,' 2 vols., 1886); 'Many Moods,' 1878; 'Shelley: a Biography,' 1878; 'Sir Philip Sidney,' 1878; 'Sketches and Studies in Italy,' 1879; 'New and Old,' 1880; 'Animi Figura,' 1882; 'Italian Byways,' 1883; 'Shakspere's Predecessors in the English Drama,' 1884; 'Vagabunduli Libellus,' 1884; 'Ben Jonson,' 1886; 'Essays' (2 vols.), 1890; 'Our Life in the Swiss Highlands' (with his daughter Margaret), 1892; 'Life of Michelangelo Buonarroti' (2 vols.), 1893 [1892]; 'In the Key of Blue,' 1893; 'Walt Whitman,' 1893.

Posthumous: 'Blank Verse,' 1894; 'Giovanni Boccaccio as Man and Author,' 1895 [1894].

He *translated:* 'The Sonnets of Michelangelo Buonarroti and Tommaso Campanella,' 1878; 'Wine, Women and Song,' 1884; 'Life of Benvenuto Cellini,' 1887; 'Memoirs of Count Carlo Gozzi,' 1890.

He *edited:* J. A. Symonds (the eider)'s 'Miscellanies,' 1871; J. Conington's 'Miscellaneous Writings,' 1872; 'Selected Works of Ben Jonson,' 1886; and *contributed introductions* to: Sir T. Browne's 'Religio Medici,' 1886; 'The Best Plays of Christopher Marlowe,' 1887; 'The Best Plays of Thomas Heywood,' 1888; 'The Best Plays of Webster

and Tourneur,' 1888; J. Van der Straet's 'Dante' 1892.

Life: by Horatio F. Brown, 1895.

TALFOURD (*Sir* **Thomas Noon**), **1795-1854.** Born, at Doxey, near Stafford, 26 May 1795. Educated at a school at Mill Hill, and at Reading Grammar School. To London, to study Law, 1813. On staff of 'London Mag.' Contrib. to 'Edinburgh Review,' 'Quarterly Review,' 'New Monthly Mag.,' etc. Called to Bar at Middle Temple, Feb. 1821. Married Miss Rutt, 1821. Sergeant-at-Law, 1835. M.P. for Reading, 1835-41, 1847-49. Play, 'Ion,' produced at Covent Garden, 26 May 1836; 'The Athenian Captive,' Haymarket, 1838; 'Glencoe,' Haymarket, 23 May 1840. Hon. D.C.L., Oxford, 20 June 1844. Recorder of Banbury, Queen's Sergeant, 1846. Judge of Court of Common Pleas, 1849-54. Knighted, 30 Jan. 1850. Died, suddenly, at Stafford, 13 March 1854.

Works: 'Poems on Various Subjects' (anon.), 1811; 'An Attempt to estimate the Poetical Talent of the Present Age,' 1815; 'Ion' (priv. ptd.), 1835; 'The Athenian Captive,' 1838; 'Observations on the Law of Copyright,' 1838; 'Glencoe' (priv. ptd.), 1839; 'Three Speeches . . . in favour of an Extension of Copyright,' 1840; 'Speech for the Defendant in the Prosecution, the Queen v. Moxon,' 1841; 'Recollections of a first visit to the Alps' (priv. ptd.), 1841; 'Dramatic Works,' 1843; 'Vacation Rambles and Thoughts' (2 vols.), 1845; 'The Castilian' (anon.; priv. ptd.), 1853; 'Supplement to "Vacation Rambles,"' 1854.

Posthumous: 'Memoirs of Charles Lamb,' edited (from memoirs by Talfourd in his edns. of Lamb's 'Letters' and 'Final Memorials') by P. Fitzgerald, 1892.

He *edited:* W. D. Dickinson's 'Practical Guide to the Quarter Sessions,' 3rd edn., 1829; Charles Lamb's 'Letters,' 1837; and 'Final Memorials,' 1848; W. F. Deacon's 'Annette,' 1852.

TANNAHILL (Robert), 1774-1810. Born, in Paisley, 3 June 1774. Apprenticed to his father (a weaver), 1785-90. In England, working as weaver, 1800-02. Returned to Scotland, 1802. Contrib. verses to local periodicals from 1805. Gained popularity as song writer. Committed suicide, 17 May 1810.

Work: 'The Soldier's Return,' 1807.

Posthumous: 'Poems and Songs,' 1815 ; 'Works,' 1838.

TATE (Nahum), 1652-1715. Born, in Dublin, 1652. Matric., Trin. Coll., Dublin, 1668. Removed to London a few years later ; devoted himself to literature. Poet Laureate, 1692. Edited 'The Monitor,' 1713. Died, at Southwark, 12 Aug. 1715.

Works: 'Poems,' 1677 ; 'Brutus of Alba,' 1678 ; 'The Loyal General,' 1680 ; 'King Lear' (altered from Shakespeare), 1681 ; 'The Sicilian Usurper' (altered from Shakespeare), 1681 ; 'The Ingratitude of a Commonwealth' (altered from Shakespeare), 1682 ; 'The Second Part of Absolom and Achitophel' (anon.; with Dryden), 1682 ; 'Cuckolds-Haven,' 1685 ; 'A Duke and no Duke,' 1685 ; 'On the Sacred Memory of Our Late Sovereign,' 1685 ; 'A Poem occasioned by the late Discontents,' 1691 ; 'Characters of Virtue and Vice Described,' 1691 ; 'A Present for the Ladies,' 1693; 'Poem on the Late Promotion of several eminent Persons,'1694; 'Elegy on the Death of Archbishop Tillotson,' 1695 ; 'Elegy on the Death of Queen Mary,' 1695; 'Anniversary Ode,' 1698 ; 'Miscellanea Sacra,' 1698 ; 'Elegies,' 1699 ; 'Funeral Poems,' 1700 ; 'Panacea, 1700 ; 'A Congratulatory Poem on the New Parliament,' 1701 ; 'Portrait-Royal,' 1703 ; 'The Song for New Year's Day,' 1703 ; 'The Triumph,' 1705 ; 'Britannia's Prayer for the Queen,' 1706 ; 'The Triumph of Union,' 1707 ; 'A Congratulatory Poem to . . . Prince George of Denmark,' 1708 ; 'An Essay for Promoting of Psalmody,' 1710 ; 'The

Muse's Memorial,' 1712 ; 'The Muse's Bower,' 1713.

He *translated :* Ovid's 'Epistles,' 1683 ; Fracastoro's 'Syphilis,' 1686 ; Bishop Heliodorus' 'Triumphs of Love,' 1687 ; Cowley's 'History of Plants,' 1693 ; 'The Life of Louis of Bourbon,' 1693 ; Juvenal's Satires (with others), 1693 ; 'The Four Epistles of A. G. Busbequius,' 1694 ; 'The Psalms of David' (with N. Brady), 1696 ; Lucian's Works (with others), 1711 ; and *edited :* 'Poems by Several Hands,' 1685 ; 'A Memorial for the Learned,' 1686 ; Sir W. Petty's 'Political Anatomy of Ireland,' 1691 ; Sir J. Davies' 'The Original Nature . . . of the Soul,' 1697.

TAYLOR (*Sir* **Henry), 1800-1886.** Born, at Bishop Middleham, Durham, 1800. Served in Navy as Midshipman, 1814. To London, 1816. In Civil employment for some years, in London ; at Barbados for few months in 1820. Settled in London, 1823. Held post in Colonial Office, 1824-72. Married the Hon. Theodosia Alicia Ellen Frances Charlotte Spring-Rice, 1839. Hon. D.C.L., Oxford, 2 July 1862. K.C.M.G., 30 June 1869. Died, at Bournemouth, 27 March 1886.

Works: 'Isaac Comnenus' (anon.), 1827 ; 'Philip Van Artevelde,' 1834; 'The Statesman,' 1836 ; 'Edwin the Fair,' 1842 ; 'The Eve of the Conquest,' 1847 ; 'Notes from Life,' 1847; 'Notes from Books,' 1849 ; 'The Virgin Widow,' 1850 ; 'St. Clement's Eve,' 1862 ; 'Poetical Works' (3 vols.), 1864 [1863] ; 'A Sicilian Summer,' 1868 ; 'Crime considered, in a letter to the Rt. Hon. W. E. Gladstone,' 1868 ; 'Autobiography . . . 1800-1875' (2 vols.), 1885 (priv. ptd., 1874-77); 'Works' (5 vols.), 1877-78.

Posthumous: 'Correspondence,' ed. E. Dowden, 1888.

TAYLOR (Jeremy), *Bishop of Down, Connor and Dromore,* **1613-1667.** Born, at Cambridge, 15 Aug. 1613. At Cambridge Free School, 1616-26. Sizar, Gonville and Caius

Coll, Camb., 18 Aug. 1626 ; matric., 17 March 1627 ; B.A., 1631 ; M.A., 1634 ; Incorp. Fellow of All Souls Coll., Oxford, 20 Oct. 1635. Ordained chaplain to Archbishop Laud. Chaplain to Charles I., 1638. Rector of Uppingham, 1638-42. Married Phœbe Landisdale, 27 May 1639. Created D.D. from Brasenose Coll., Oxford, 1 Nov. 1642. With the King, as Chaplain, during Civil War. Kept a school in Wales, with W. Nicholson and W. Wyatt, 1646-47. Chaplain to Earl of Carbery, at Golden Grove, Carmarthenshire, 1647-57. Settled in Ireland, as Rector of Lisburn and Portmore, 1658. Bishop of Down and Connor, Jan. 1661. Privy Councillor, Ireland, Feb. 1661. Bishop of Dromore, June 1661. Vice-Chancellor, Dublin Univ., 1661. Died, at Lisburn, 13 Aug. 1667. Buried in Dromore Cathedral.

Works : 'A Sermon preached . . . in Oxford, upon the Anniversary of the Gunpowder Treason,' 1638 ; 'Of the Sacred Order and Offices of Episcopacy,' 1642 ; 'A Discourse concerning Prayer Extempore' (anon.), 1646 ; 'A New and Easie Institution of Grammar,' 1647 ; 'Θεολογια Ἐκλεκτικη,' 1647 ; 'Treatises' (4 pts.), 1648 ; 'An Apology for . . . set forms of Liturgie,' 1649 ; 'The Great Exemplar,' 1649 ; 'The Martyrdom of King Charles I.,' 1649 ; 'Sermon at the Funeral of Frances, Countess of Carbery,' 1650 ; 'The Rule and Exercises of Holy Living,' 1650 ; 'The Rule and Exercises of Holy Dying,' 1651 ; 'Twenty-eight Sermons,' 1651 ; 'A Short Catechism' (anon.), 1652 ; 'A Discourse of Baptism,' 1652 ; 'The Real Presence,' 1654 ; 'Ενιαυτος,' (3 pts.), 1653-55 ; 'The Golden Grove' (anon.), 1655 ; 'Unum Necessarium,' 1655 ; 'Deus Justificatus,' 1656 ; 'An Answer to a Letter written by the Bishop of Rochester,' 1656 ; 'A Discourse of Auxiliary Beauty' (anon.), 1656 ; 'A Discourse of . . . Friendship' (under initials : J.T., D.D.), 1657 (2nd edn., called : 'The Measure and Offices of Friendship,' same year) ; 'Συμβολον Ηθικη-Πολεμικον,' 1657 ; 'The Ephesian Matron' (anon.), 1659 ; 'Ductor Dubi-

tantium,' 1660 ; 'The Worthy Communicant,' 1660 ; 'Sermon preached at the Consecration of two Archbishops, etc.,' 1661 ; 'Rules and Advices to the Clergy of Down and Connor.' 1661 ; 'A Sermon preached at the Opening of Parliament,' 1661 ; 'Via Intelligentiæ,' 1662 ; 'Sermon preached at the Funeral of the Archbishop of Armagh,' 1663 ; 'Ἑβδομας Ἐμβολιμαιος' (6 pts.), 1661-63 ; 'A Dissuasive from Popery,' 1664 (3rd edn. same year) ; 'Second Part' of preceding, 1667.

Posthumous : 'Συμβολον Θεολογικον,' 1673-74 ; 'Christ's Yoke an Easy Yoke,' 1675 ; 'Contemplations of the State of Man,' 1684 ; 'A Discourse on the Lord's Supper,' 1792.

He *edited :* 'The Psalter of David, 1644.

Collected Works : in 15 vols., ed. by Bishop Heber, 1822.

Life : by H. K. Bonney, 1815.

TAYLOR (John), 1580-1654. Born, at Gloucester, Aug. 1580. In youth apprenticed to a waterman. Served in fleet under Earl of Essex. On return to England, took up trade of waterman. Collector of Tower Dues on Wine. Retired to Oxford at Civil War. Returned to London, 1646. Kept a public-house in Long Acre. Known as the 'Water-Poet.' Died there, Dec. 1654. Buried in Churchyard of St. Martin's-in-the-Fields.

Works : Taylor's separate publications number upwards of 120, dating from 1614 to 1654. The more important of these have been collected and edited by the Spenser Society in 8 vols., 1869-78. A fairly representative list is presented by the entries in the British Museum Catalogue.

TAYLOR (Tom), 1817-1880. Born, at Sunderland, 1817. Early education at school there. Studied at Glasgow Univ., 1831-32, 1835-36. Matric., Trin. Coll., Camb., 1837 ; B.A., 1840 ; Fellow, 1842 ; M.A., 1843. Prof. of English Literature, Univ. Coll., London. Called to Bar at Middle Temple, Nov. 1845. Assistant Sec. to Board of Health, 1850 ; Sec., 1854.

Married **Laura W.** Barker, 19 June 1855. Sec. to Local Government Act Office, 1858-72. Wrote over 100 dramatic pieces, 1845-80. Editor of Punch, 1874-80. For some time Art Critic to 'The Times' and 'The Graphic.' Died, at Wandsworth, 12 July 1880.

Works : 'The King's Rival' (with Charles Reade), 1854 ; 'Masks and Faces' (with Charles Reade), 1854 ; Two Loves and a Life' (with Charles Reade), 1854 ; 'Barefaced Impostors' (anon. ; with F. G. B. Ponsonby and G. C. Bentinck) [1854] ; 'The Local Government Act, 1858, etc.,' 1858 ; 'The Railway Station, painted by W. P. Frith, described,' 1862 ; 'Handbook of the Pictures in the International Exhibition of 1862,' 1862 ; Text to Birket Foster's 'Pictures of English Landscape,' 1863 [1862] ; 'A Marriage Memorial' [1863] ; 'The King's Rival' (with C. Reade), 1864 ; 'Masks and Faces' (with C. Reade), 1864 ; 'Two Loves and a Life' (with C. Reade), 1864 ; 'Catalogue of the Works of Sir Joshua Reynolds' (with C. W. Franks), 1869 ; 'The Theatre in England' (from 'The Dark Blue'), 1871 ; 'Leicester Square,' 1874 ; 'Historical Dramas,' 1877. [Also a number of separate dramatic pieces, published in Lacy's Acting Edition of Plays.]

He *translated :* Vicomte Hersart de la Villemarque's 'Ballads and Songs of Brittany,' 1865 ; and *edited :* 'The Life of B. R. Haydon,' 1853 ; C. R. Leslie's 'Autobiographical Recollections,' 1860 ; Mortimer Collins' 'Pen Sketches by a Vanished Hand,' 1879.

TAYLOR (William), **1765 - 1836.** Born, at Norwich, 7 Nov. 1765. At school at Norwich and at Palgrave. Travelled on Continent, Aug. 1779 to Jan. 1781 ; and May 1781 to Nov. 1782. Settled in his father's house, and engaged in business. Retired from business, 1791 ; devoted himself to literature. Contrib. to 'Monthly Rev.,' 1793-1824 ; to 'Monthly Mag.,' 1796-1824 ; to 'Annual Rev.,' 1802-07 ; to 'Critical Rev.,' 1803-09 ; to

'Athenæum,' 1807-08. Edited 'The Iris,' 1825-26. Died, at Norwich, 5 March 1836. Buried there.

Works : Translation of Lessing's 'Nathan the Wise,' 1805 (priv. ptd., 1791) ; Translation of Goethe's 'Iphigenia in Tauris' (anon.), 1793 ; Translation of Wieland's 'Dialogues of the Gods,' 1795 ; Translation of Bürger's 'Ellenore' (anon.), 1796 : 'Tales of Yore, translated from different foreign languages,' 1810 ; 'A Letter concerning the first two chapters of Luke' (anon.), 1810 ; 'English Synonyms Discriminated,' 1813 ; 'Historic Survey of German Poetry' (3 vols.), 1828-30 ; 'A Memoir of the late P. M. Martineau' (anon. ; with F. Elwin), 1831.

Life : by J. W. Robberds, 1843.

TEMPLE (*Sir* **William**), **1628-1699.** Born, in Blackfriars, 1628. At schools at Penshurst and Bishop's Stortford, till 1643. Lived at home, 1643-45. Matric., Emmanuel Coll., Camb. 1645[?]. Travelled on Continent 1647-53[?]. Married Dorothy Osborn 1654. Member of Irish Convention at Restoration, 1660. M.P. for Carlow, 1661. Abroad on business of State, 1665-69. In retirement at Sheen, 1669-73. In Holland on State business, 1673-76, 1678-79. Retired from public life, 1685. Died, at Moor Park, Surrey, 27 Jan. 1699.

Works : 'Poems' (under initials : Sir W. T.) [1670?] ; 'Observations upon the United Provinces of the Netherlands,' 1672 ; 'Miscellanea' (anon.), 1680 ; 'Memoirs of what past in Christendom from . . . 1672 . . . to . . . 1679,' 1692 ; 'An Answer to a scurrilous pamphlet' (anon. ; attrib. to Temple), 1693 ; 'An Essay upon Taxes' (anon.), 1693 ; 'An Introduction to the History of England,' 1695.

Posthumous : 'Letters written by Sir W. Temple during his being Ambassador at the Hague,' ed. by D. Jones, 1699 ; 'Letters written . . both at home and abroad,' ed. by J. Swift (3 vols.), 1700-03 ; 'Miscellanea (2nd ser.), ed. by J. Swift, 1701.

Collected Works : ed. by J. Swift (2 vols.), 1720.

*TENNYSON (Alfred), *Baron Tennyson,* **1809-1892.** Born, at Somersby, Lincs., 6 Aug. 1809. Educated at Louth Grammar School, till 1820 ; at home, 1820-28. Matric, Trin. Coll., Camb., 1828 ; Chancellor's English Prize Poem, 1829 ; left Cambridge, owing to death of his father, Feb. 1831. Lived at Somersby till 1835. Married Emily Sellwood, 13 June 1850. Poet Laureate, Nov. 1850. Settled at Farringford, I. of W., 1853. Hon. D.C.L., Oxford, 20 June 1855. Hon. Fellow Trin. Coll., Camb., May 1869. F.R.S. Play ' Queen Mary,' produced at Lyceum Theatre, 18 April 1876 ; ' The Falcon,' St. James's ; ' The Cup,' Lyceum, 3 Jan. 1881 ; 'The Promise of May,' Globe, 11 Nov. 1882; 'The Foresters,' Daly's Theatre, New York, 17 March 1892 ; ' Becket,' Lyceum, 6 Feb. 1893. Created Baron Tennyson of Aldworth, Jan. 1884. Died, at Aldworth, 6 Oct. 1892. Buried in Westminster Abbey.

Works : ' Poems by Two Brothers ' (anon. ; with Charles and Frederick Tennyson), 1827 ; ' Timbuctoo,' 1829 ; ' Poems, chiefly lyrical,' 1830 ; 'Poems,' 1833 [1832] ; ' The Lover's Tale ' (priv. ptd.), 1833 ; ' Poems ' (2 vols.), 1842 ; ' The Princess,' 1847 ; 'In Memoriam' (anon.), 1850 (2nd edn. same year) ; ' Poems ' (6th edn.), 1850 ; ' Poems ' (7th edn.), 1851 ; ' Ode on the Death of the Duke of Wellington,' 1852 ; Poems ' (8th edn.), 1853 ; 'The Charge of the Light Brigade' (priv. ptd.) [1855] ; ' Maud,' 1855 ; ' Enid and Nimuë' (priv. ptd.), 1857 ; ' Idylls of the King ' (4 pts.), 1859 ; 'A Welcome' [to Princess of Wales], 1863 ; ' Idylls of the Hearth,' 1864 (another edn., same year, called : ' Enoch Arden, etc.') ; ' The Victim ' (priv. ptd.), 1867 ; 'Idylls of the King ' (8 pts.), 1869 ; ' The Holy Grail,' 1870 [1869] ; 'The Windows,' 1871 [1870] (priv. ptd., 1867) ; ' Gareth and Lynette,' 1872 ; ' A Welcome ' [to Duchess of Edinburgh], 1874 ; ' **The Lover's** Tale ' (priv. ptd.), 1875 ; ' Queen Mary,' 1875 ; ' Harold,' 1877 [1876] ; ' Ballads and other Poems,' 1880 ; ' The Promise of May,' 1882 ; ' Becket,' 1884 ; 'The Cup and The Falcon,' 1884 ; ' Tiresias,' 1885 ; ' To H.R.H. Princess Beatrice ' (priv. ptd.), 1885 ; ' Poetical Works,' 1886 ; 'Locksley Hall Sixty Years After,' 1887 ; ' To Edward Lear,' 1889 ; 'Demeter,' 1889 ; ' The Foresters,' 1892 ; ' Idylls of the King ' (12 pts.), 1892.

Posthumous : 'The Death of Œnone,' 1892.

Collected Works : 1894.

TENNYSON (Charles), 1808-1879. [Eldest brother of preceding.] Born, at Somersby, Lincs., 1808. Educated at Louth Grammar School till 1820 ; at home, 1820-28. Matric., Trin Coll., Camb., 1828 ; Bell Scholarship, 1828 ; B.A., 1832. Ordained Deacon, 1835 ; Priest, 1835. Curate of Tealby, 1835. Vicar of Grasby, Lincs., 1835-79. Married Louisa Sellwood, 1837. Took additional surname of Turner, on succeeding to estate of his great-uncle, 1838. Contrib. poems to 'Macmillan's Mag.,' 1860. Died, at Cheltenham, 25 April 1879.

Works : 'Poems by Two Brothers ' (with Alfred and Frederick Tennyson), 1829 ; ' Songs and Fugitive Pieces,' 1830 ; ' Sonnets,' 1864 ; ' Sonnets, Lyrics, and Translations,' 1873.

Posthumous : ' Collected Sonnets, old and new,' 1880.

*TENNYSON (Frederick), b. 1807. [Brother of preceding.] Born, at Louth, 5 June 1807. Early education at Louth Grammar School. At Eton, 1820-27. Matric., Trin. Coll., Camb., 1829 ; B.A., 1832. Browne Medallist (for Greek Ode), Camb. After leaving Cambridge lived abroad for some years. Married Maria Giuliotti, 1839. Settled in Florence. Removed to Jersey, 1859.

Works : ' Poems by Two Brothers ' (anon. ; with Alfred and Charles Tennyson), 1827 ; ' The Isles of

Greece.' 1890 ; 'Daphne,' 1891 ; 'Poems of the Day and Year,' 1895. He has *edited :* H. Melville's 'Veritas,' 1874.

*THACKERAY (William Makepeace), 1811-1863. Born, at Calcutta, 18 July 1811. Brought to England at his father's death, 1816. At Charterhouse School, 1822-28. Matric., Trin. Coll., Camb., Feb. 1829. Left Cambridge, 1830 ; took no degree. Travelled on Continent, 1830-31. Lived in Hare Court, Temple, and studied Law, 1831-32. Edited 'National Standard,' May to Dec. 1833. After severe monetary losses, removed to Paris, Dec. 1833. Contrib. to 'Fraser's Mag.' from about 1836. Married Isabella Gethin Creagh Shawe, 20 Aug. 1836. Settled in London. Contrib. to 'Fraser's Mag.,' 'New Monthly Mag.,' 'Ainsworth's Mag.,' 'Times,' 'Westminster Rev.,' etc. Separation from his wife, 1840. Travelled in East, Aug. to Oct. 1844. Contrib. to 'Punch,' 1842-50. Called to Bar at Middle Temple, 26 May 1848. First lectured in London, 1851. In America lecturing, Dec. 1852 to spring of 1853 ; again, Dec. 1855 to April 1856. Lectured in England and Scotland, 1856. Stood as M.P. for City of Oxford, 1857 ; was defeated. Edited 'Cornhill Mag.,' Nov. 1859 to March 1862. Died, in London, 24 Dec. 1863. Buried at Kensal Green.

Works : 'The Yellowplush Correspondence' (anon.), 1838 ; 'The Paris Sketch-book' (under pseud. 'Mr. Titmarsh'), 1840 ; 'An Essay on the Genius of George Cruikshank' (anon.), 1840 ; 'Comic Tales and Sketches' (under pseud. 'Michael Angelo Titmarsh'), 1841 ; 'The Second Funeral of Napoleon' (under pseud. 'M. A. Titmarsh'), 1841 ; 'The Irish Sketch-Book' (2 vols.), 1843 ; 'The Luck of Barry Lyndon,' 1844 ; 'Notes of a Journey from Cornhill to Cairo,' 1846 ; 'Mrs. Perkins's Ball' (under pseud. 'M. A. Titmarsh') [1847] ; 'The Book of Snobs,' 1848 ; 'Vanity Fair.' 1848 ; 'Our Street' (under pseud.

'M. A. Titmarsh), 1848 ; 'Dr. Birch and his Young Friends' (under pseud. 'M. A. Titmarsh '), 1849 ; 'The History of Samuel Titmarsh ; and the Great Hoggarty Diamond,' 1849 ; 'An Interesting Event' (under pseud. 'M. A. Titmarsh '), 1849 ; 'The History of Pendennis' (2 vols.), 1849-50 ; 'Rebecca and Rowena' (under pseud. 'M. A. Titmarsh '), 1850 ; Text to 'Sketches after English Landscape Painters,' 1850 ; 'The Kickleburys on the Rhine' (under pseud. 'M. A. Titmarsh '), 1851 ; 'The History of Henry Esmond,' 1852 ; 'The English Humourists of the Eighteenth Century,' 1853 ; 'Men's Wives,' 1853 ; 'The Newcomes' (2 vols.), 1854-55 ; 'Miscellanies' (4 vols.), 1854-57 ; 'Ballads,' 1855 ; 'The Rose and the Ring' (under pseud. 'M. A. Titmarsh '), 1855 ; 'The Virginians' (2 vols.), 1858-59 ; 'Lovel the Widower,' 1861 ; 'The Four Georges,' 1861 ; 'The Adventures of Philip,' 1862 ; 'Roundabout Papers,' 1863 [1862].

Posthumous : 'Dennis Duval,' 1867 ; 'Ballads and Tales,' 1869 ; 'The Orphan of Pimlico,' 1876 ; 'Etchings while at Cambridge,' 1878 : 'The Chronicle of the Drum,' 1886 ; 'A Collection of Letters . . . 1847-1855,' 1887 ; 'Sultan Stork, etc.,' 1887.

Collected Works : in 26 vols., 1869-86.

Life : by A. Trollope, 1879 ; by H. C. Merivale and E. T. Marzials, 1891.

THIRLWALL (Connop), *Bishop of St. David's,* 1797-1875. Born, at Stepney, 11 Feb. 1797. Early education at Charterhouse School. Matric., Trin. Coll., Camb., 1814 ; Craven Scholar, 1815 ; Bell's Scholar, 1815 ; Chancellor's Medallist, 1818 ; B.A., 1818 ; Minor Fellow, Trin. Coll., 1818 ; M.A., 1821. Student of Lincoln's Inn, Feb. 1820. Called to Bar, 1825. Ordained Deacon, 1827 ; Priest, 1828. Rector of Kirby-under-Dale, Yorks., 1834-40. B.D. and D.D., 1840. Bishop of St. David's, July 1840 to May 1874. Died, at Bath, 27 July 1875.

Works [exclusive of separate sermons and episcopal charges, etc.] : 'Primitiæ' (priv. ptd.), 1809 ; 'History of Greece' (8 vols.), 1835-47 ; 'The Advantages of Literary and Scientific Institutions,' 1850 ; 'Inaugural Address' [at the Edinburgh Philosophical Institution], 1861 ; 'The Present State of Relations between Science and Literature,' 1867.

Posthumous : 'Remains, literary and theological,' ed. by J. J. S. Perowne (3 vols.), 1877-78 ; 'Letters, literary and theological,' ed. by J. J. S. Perowne and L. Stokes, 1881 ; 'Letters to a Friend,' ed. by Dean Stanley, 1881.

He *translated :* Schleiermacher's 'Critical Essay on the Gospel of St. Luke,' 1825 ; Niebuhr's 'History of Rome' (with J. C. Hare), 1828.

THOMPSON (Alice). *See* Meynell.

THOMSON (James), **1700 - 1748.** Born, at Ednam, Roxburghshire, 11 Sept. 1700. Early education at Jedburgh Grammar School. To Edinburgh Univ., 1715. For some time studied theology ; but eventually abandoned idea of clerical career. Settled in London, 1725. Devoted himself to literature. Play 'Sophonisba' produced at Drury Lane, 28 Feb. 1730. Travelled on Continent, Dec. 1730 to Dec. 1731. Secretary of Briefs, 1736-37. Surveyor - General of Leeward Islands, 1737. 'Agamemnon' produced at Drury Lane, 6 April 1738. Died, at Richmond, 27 Aug. 1748. Buried there. (Play 'Coriolanus' posthumously produced at Covent Garden, 13 Jan. 1749.)

Works : 'Winter,' 1726 (3rd edn. same year) ; 'Summer,' 1727 ; 'A Poem sacred to the memory of Sir Isaac Newton,' 1727 (3rd edn. same year) ; 'Spring,' 1728 ; 'Britannia' (anon.), 1729 ; 'Poem on the Death of Congreve,' 1729 ; 'Sophonisba,' 1730 ; 'The Seasons,' 1730 ; 'Works' (2 vols.), 1730-36 ; 'Liberty' (5 pts.), 1735-36 ; 'A Poem to the Memory of . . . Lord Talbot,' 1737 ; 'Works' (2 vols.), 1738 ; 'Agamemnon,' 1738 ; 'Edward and Elenora,' 1739 ; 'The

Masque of Alfred' (anon. ; with D. Mallet), 1740 ; 'Tancred and Sigismunda,' 1745 ; 'The Castle of Indolence,' 1748 (2nd edn. same year).

Posthumous : 'Coriolanus,' 1749 ; 'Poems on Several Occasions,' 1750 ; 'Unpublished Letters to Mallet' [1857].

Collected Works : 1757, 1762, etc.

Life : by L. Morel, 1895.

THOMSON (James), **1834 - 1882.** Born, at Port Glasgow, 23 Nov. 1834. Educated at Caledonian Orphan Asylum, 1843-50. At Ballincollig, near Cork, as assistant regimental schoolmaster, 1850-52 ; at Military Training College, Chelsea, 1852-54. Contrib. to Tait's 'Edinburgh Mag.,' 1858 ; to 'National Reformer,' 1860-75. Served as regimental schoolmaster till 1862. After leaving army, held various secretaryships. Visit to America, 1872 ; to Spain as correspondent to 'New York World,' 1873. Contrib. to 'Cope's Tobacco Plant,' 1875-81. Contrib. at various times to 'Daily Telegraph,' 'Athenæum,' 'Weekly Dispatch,' 'Fortnightly Rev.,' 'Fraser's Mag.,' 'Cornhill Mag.' Died, in London, 3 June 1882. Buried in Highgate Cemetery.

Works : 'The City of Dreadful Night,' 1880 ; 'Vane's Story,' 1880 ; 'Essays and Phantasies,' 1881.

Posthumous : 'The Story of a Famous Old Jewish Firm, etc.,' 1883 ; 'A Voice from the Nile,' ed. by B. Dobell, 1884 [1883] ; 'Shelley' (priv. ptd.), 1884 ; 'Selections from Original Contributions by J. Thomson to "Cope's Tobacco Plant,"' 1889 ; 'Poetical Works,' ed. by B. Dobell (2 vols.), 1895 ; 'Biographical and Critical Studies,' ed. by B. Dobell, 1896.

Life : by H. S. Salt, 1889.

THOREAU (Henry David), **1817-1862.** Born, at Concord, U.S.A., 12 July 1817. [Christened 'David Henry,' but generally used form 'Henry David.'] Early education at Boston, 1818-23, and at Concord, 1823-33. To Harvard Univ., 1833 ; B.A., 1837. Schoolmaster, at Con-

cord, 1837-39. For short time took
up his father's trade of pencil-making.
Fri-ndship with Emerson begun,
about 1837. Contrib. to 'The Dial,'
1840-44. Lived with Emerson at
Concord, 1841-43. Held post of
private tutor, at Staten Island, 1843-
44. Lived in hut at Walden Pond,
July 1845 to Sept. 1847. Lived in
Emerson's house at Concord, autumn
1847 to 1849. Returned to his
father's house, 1849 ; lived there for
remainder of his life. Made expeditions to Cape Cod, Canada, Maine
Forests, etc., 1846-60. Ill-health
began, 1855. Died, at Concord,
6 May 1862. Buried there.

Works: ' A Week on the Concord
and Merrimack Rivers,' 1849 ;
' Walden,' 1854.

Posthumous: 'Excursions,' 1863 ;
' The Maine Woods,' 1864 ; ' Cape
Cod,' 1864 ; ' Letters to Various
Persons,' 1865 ; ' A Yankee in
Canada,' 1866 ; ' Early Spring in
Massachusetts' (from his journal),
1881 ; 'Summer' (from his journal),
1884 ; ' Winter' (from his journal),
1888 ; ' Anti-Slavery and Reform
Papers,' 1890 ; ' Autumn ' (from his
journal), 1892 ; 'Miscellanies,' 1894 ;
'Familiar Letters,' 1894.

Life: by H. S. Salt, 1890.

THRALE (*Mrs.*). *See* Piozzi.

TICKELL (Thomas), 1686 - 1740.
Born, at Bridekirk, Cumberland,
1686. Matric., Queens' Coll., Ox-
ford, 16 May 1701 ; B.A., 1705 ;
M.A., 22 Feb. 1709. Friendship
with Addison. Appointed by him
Under - Secretary of State, 1717.
Married, 1726. Secretary to Lords
Justices of Ireland, 1724-40. Died,
at Bath, 21 April 1740.

Works: ' A Poem to . . . the
Lord Privy Seal on the Prospect of
Peace,' 1713 ; Translation of Homer's
' Iliad,' Bk. I. (pubd. under Tickell's
name, but possibly by Addison), 1715 ;
' An Epistle from a Lady in England
to a Gentleman at Avignon ' (anon.),
1717 ; ' An Ode occasioned by Earl
Stanhope's Voyage to France,' 1718 ;

' An Ode to the Earl of Sutherland '
(anon.), 1720 ; ' Kensington Gardens '
(anon.), 1722 ; 'To Sir G. Kneller '
(anon.), 1722 ; ' On Her Majesty's
rebuilding the Lodgings of the Black
Prince and Henry V. at Queen's
College, Oxford,' 1733.
He *edited:* Addison's Works, 1722,
etc.
Collected Works: ed. by T. Park,
1807.

TOOKE (John Horne), 1736-1812.
Born [John Horne ; adopted additional name of Tooke in 1782 as a
compliment to a patron] at West-
minster, 25 June 1736. Early educa-
tion at schools in Soho and in Kent.
At Westminster School, 1744-46 ; at
Eton, 1746-53. Matric. St. John's
Coll., Camb., 1755 ; B.A., 1758 ;
M.A., 1771. Ordained Vicar of New
Brentford in 1760 ; but gave up orders
in 1773, and took up pursuit of law.
Imprisoned for libel, 1777-78. Tried
on charge of high treason, but ac-
quitted, 1794. M.P. for Old Sarum,
Feb. 1801 to 1802. Died, at Wimbledon, 18 March 1812. Buried at
Ealing.

Works: 'The Petition of an En-
glishman ' (anon.). 1765 ; ' A Sermon,'
1769 ; ' An Oration delivered at a
. . . Meeting of the Freeholders of
Middlesex ' [1770] ; ' Letter to John
Dunning, Esq.,' 1778 ; ' Letter to
Lord Ashburton,' 1782 ; 'Ἔπεα
Πτεροεντα,' 1786 ; ' Letter to a Friend
on the Reported Marriage of the
Prince of Wales,' 1787 ; ' Two Pair
of Portraits,' 1788 ; ' Letter on the
Meeting at the Crown and Anchor
Tavern,' 1791 ; ' Proceedings in an
Action for Debt,' 1792 ; ' Letter
on Parliamentary Reform.' 1794 ;
' Speeches . . . during the West-
minster Election, 1796 ' [1796] ;
' Letter to the Editor of "The
Times,"' 1807.
Life: by J. A. Grabaeu, 1828.

TOURNEUR (Cyril), *fl.* 1610. No
details of life known.

Works: ' The Transformed Metamorphosis,' 1600 ; ' The Revenger's

Tragædie,' 1607; 'A Funerall Poeme
upon the death of Sir Francis Vere,'
1609; 'The Atheist's Tragedie,' 1611;
'Three Elegies on the . . . death of
Prince Henrie,' 1613.
Collected Works: 'Plays and
Poems,' ed. by J. C. Collins (2 vols.),
1878 [1877].

*TRAILL (Henry Duff), b. 1842.
Born, at Blackheath, 14 Aug. 1842.
At Merchant Taylors' School, 1853-
61. Matric. St. John's Coll., Oxford,
1 July 1861; B.A., 1865; B.C.L.,
1868; D.C.L., 1873. Student of
Inner Temple, 17 Nov. 1866; called
to Bar, 7 June 1869. Inspector of
Returns under Education Act, 1870-
71. Gave up legal profession, and
devoted himself to journalism and
literature, 1871. Frequent contributor to periodicals. On staff of
'Pall Mall Gaz.,' 1873-80; of 'St.
James's Gaz.,' 1880-82; of 'Daily
Telegraph,' 1882-96; of 'Saturday
Rev.,' 1883-94. Editor of 'Observer,'
1889-91.

Works: 'Central Government,'
1881; 'Sterne,' 1882; 'Recaptured
Rhymes,' 1882; 'The New Lucian,'
1884; 'Coleridge,' 1884; 'Shaftesbury,' 1886; 'William the Third,'
1888; 'Strafford,' 1889; 'Saturday
Songs' [1890]; 'Number Twenty'
[1892]; 'The Marquis of Salisbury,'
1892; 'The Barbarous Britishers'
[1896]; 'The Life of Sir John Franklin,' 1896; 'From Cairo to the Soudan
Frontier,' 1896; 'Lord Cromer,' 1897;
'The New Fiction, and other Essays,'
1897.
He has *edited:* 'The Capitals of
the World,' 1892; 'Social England,'
(6 vols.), 1893-97; Disraeli's 'Sybil,'
1895; Carlyle's Works (Centenary
edn.), 1896, etc.

**TRELAWNY (Edward John), 1793-
1881.** Born, in London, 2 [or 3] Nov.
1793. At school for a short time.
Served in Navy for some years from
1814, but eventually deserted, and
led a roving life till 1821. Acquaintance with the Shelleys begun, 1822.
Buried Shelley's ashes in Rome, 1823.
With Byron in Greece, 1823-24.

Afterwards travelled in America.
Settled at Sompting, near Worthing,
1870. Died there, 13 Aug. 1881.
Buried in Protestant cemetery, Rome.
Works: 'Adventures of a Younger
Son' (anon.), 1831; 'Recollections of
the last days of Shelley and Byron,'
1858.

TRENCH (Richard Chenevix),
Archbishop of Dublin, **1807-1886.**
Born, in Dublin, 9 Sept. 1807. Early
education at Twyford; at Harrow,
1819-25. Matric. Trin. Coll., Camb.
1825; B.A., 1829; M.A., 1833;
B.D., 1850; D.D., 1856. Travelled
on Continent, 1829. Married Hon.
Frances Mary Trench, 31 May 1832.
Ordained Deacon, 1832; Priest, 1833.
Curate of Curdridge, 1835-40; of
Alverstoke, 1840 - 45. Rector of
Itchinstoke, 1845-46. Hulsean Lec-
turer, Camb., 1845-46. Chaplain to
Bp. of Oxford, 1847-64. Professor of
Divinity, King's Coll., London, 1847-
58. Dean of Westminster, Oct. 1856
to 1863. Dean of Order of Bath,
1856-64. Archbishop of Dublin and
Bishop of Glendalough and Kildare,
Jan. 1864; resigned, Nov. 1884.
Chancellor of Order of St. Patrick,
1864-84. D.D., Dublin, 1864. Died,
in London, 28 March 1886. Buried
in Westminster Abbey.

Works [exclusive of separate ser-
mons, ecclesiastical charges, etc.]:
'The Story of Justin Martyr,' 1835;
'Sabbation,' 1838; 'Notes on the
Parables of Our Lord,' 1841; 'Poems
from Eastern Sources,' 1842; 'Geno-
veva,' 1842; 'Five Sermons,' 1843;
'Exposition of the Sermon on the
Mount,' 1844; 'Hulsean Lectures
for 1845,' 1845; 'Hulsean Lectures
for 1846,' 1846; 'Sacred Poems for
Mourners,' 1846; 'Notes on the
Miracles of Our Lord,' 1846; 'The
Star of the Wise Men,' 1850; 'On
the Study of Words,' 1851; 'On the
Lessons in Proverbs,' 1853; 'Sy-
nonyms of the New Testament,' 1854
(2nd edn. same year); 'Alma,' 1855;
'English, Past and Present,' 1855;
'Five Sermons,' 1856; 'On some
Deficiencies in our English Diction-

aries,' 1857 ; 'On the Authorized Version of the New Testament,' 1858 ; 'A Select Glossary of English Words used formerly in Senses different from their Present,' 1859 ; 'Sermons Preached in Westminster Abbey,' 1860 ; 'Commentary on the Epistles to the Seven Churches in Asia,' 1861 ; 'The Subjection of the Creature to Vanity,' 1863 ; 'The Salt of the Earth, etc.,' 1864 ; 'Gustavus Adolphus, etc.,' 1865 ; 'Poems,' 1865 ; 'Studies on the Gospels,' 1867 ; 'Shipwreck of Faith,' 1867 ; 'Plutarch,' 1873 ; 'Sermons, preached for the most part in Dublin,' 1873 ; 'Lectures on Mediæval Church History,' 1877 ; 'Brief Thoughts and Meditations on some passages in Holy Scripture,' 1884 ; 'Sermons, New and Old,' 1886.

Posthumous : 'Letters and Memorials,' ed. by M. M. F. Trench (2 vols.), 1888 ; 'Westminster and other Sermons,' 1888.

He *translated :* 'Life's a Dream, etc.,' from the Spanish of Calderon, 1856 ; and *edited :* 'Sacred Latin Poetry,' 1849 ; his mother's 'Journal' [1861] and 'Remains,' 1862 ; 'A Household Book of English Poetry,' 1868.

*TREVELYAN (*Sir* George Otto), **Bart.,** b. 1838. Born, at Rothley Temple, Leicestershire, 20 July 1838. At Harrow, April 1851 to July 1857. Matric. Trin. Coll., Camb., 1857 ; Scholar, 1859 ; B.A., 1861 ; M.A., 1864. M.P. for Tynemouth, July 1865 to Nov. 1868 ; for Hawick Burghs, 1868-86. Married Caroline Philips, 29 Sept. 1869. Civil Lord of Admiralty, Dec. 1869 to June 1870 ; Parliamentary Sec. to Admiralty, Nov. 1880 to May 1882. Chief Sec. to Lord-Lieut. of Ireland, May 1882 to Nov. 1884. P.C., June 1882. Hon. LL.D., Edinburgh, 1883. Chancellor of Duchy of Lancaster, Nov. 1884 to June 1885. Trustee of British Museum, 16 May 1885. Hon. D.C.L., Oxford, 17 June 1885. Hon. Fellow, Trin. Coll., Camb., 1885. Sec. for Scotland, Feb. to March 1886. Suc-

ceeded to Baronetcy, 1886. M.P. for Bridgeton division of Glasgow, Aug. 1887 to Jan. 1897. Sec. for Scotland, Aug. 1892 to June 1895. D.L. of Northumberland. Retired from Parliament, 30 Jan. 1897.

Works : 'Horace at the University of Athens' (anon.), 1861 ; 'The Pope and his Patron' (anon.), 1862 ; 'The Dawk Bungalow' (under pseud. : 'H. Broughton, B.C.S.'), 1863 ; 'The Competition Wallah' (from 'Macmillan's Mag.'), 1864 ; 'Cawnpore,' 1865 ; 'The Ladies in Parliament,' 1869 ; 'Speeches on Army Reform,' 1870 ; 'Life and Letters of Lord Macaulay' (2 vols.), 1876 ; 'The Early History of Charles James Fox,' 1880.

TROLLOPE (Anthony), 1815-1882. Born, in London, 1815. Educated at Harrow, 1822-25 ; at Sunbury, 1825-27 ; at Winchester, 1827-30 ; at Harrow again, 1830-33. Master in a school at Brussels for a short time. Held Post - Office appointment in London, 1834-41 ; in Ireland, 1841-59 ; in London, 1859-67. Married Rose Heseltine, 11 June 1844. Edited 'St. Paul's,' 1867-71. Visit to U.S.A., 1868 ; to Australia and America, 1871-73. Settled in London, 1873. Active literary life. Frequent contributor to periodicals. Visit to S. Africa, 1877 ; to Iceland, 1878. Removed to Hastings, Sussex. 1880 Visit to Italy, 1881 ; to Ireland, 1882. Died, 6 Dec. 1882.

Works : 'The Macdermots of Bally cloran,' 1847 ; 'The Kellys and the O'Kellys,' 1848 ; 'La Vendée,' 1850 ; 'The Warden,' 1855 ; 'Barchester Towers,' 1857 ; 'The Three Clerks,' 1858 ; 'Doctor Thorne,' 1858 ; 'The West Indies and the Spanish Main,' 1859 ; 'The Bertrams,' 1859 ; 'Castle Richmond,' 1860 ; 'Framley Parsonage,' 1861 ; 'Tales of all Countries,' 1st ser., 1861 ; 2nd ser., 1863 ; 3rd ser., 1870 ; 'Orley Farm,' 1862 ; 'North America' (2 vols.), 1862 ; 'Rachel Ray,' 1863 ; 'The Small House at Allington,' 1864 ; 'Can You Forgive Her?' (2 vols.), 1864-65 ;

'Miss Mackenzie,' 1865 ; 'Hunting Sketches' (from 'Pall Mall Gaz.'), 1865 ; 'Clergymen of the Church of England' (from 'Pall Mall Gaz.'), 1866 ; 'Travelling Sketches' (from 'Pall Mall Gaz.'), 1866 ; 'The Belton Estate,' 1866 ; 'The Claverings,' 1867 ; 'The Last Chronicle of Barset,' 1867 [1866] ; 'Nina Balatka' (anon.), 1867 ; 'Lotta Schmidt, and other stories,' 1867 ; 'Linda Tressel' (anon.), 1868 ; 'Phineas Finn,' 1869 ; 'He knew He was Right,' 1869 ; 'The Struggles of Brown, Jones, and Robinson,' 1870 ; 'The Vicar of Bullhampton,' 1870 ; 'An Editor's Tales,' 1870 ; 'Cæsar,' 1870 ; 'Sir Harry Hotspur of Humblethwaite,' 1871 [1870] ; 'Ralph the Heir,' 1871 ; 'The Golden Lion of Granpère,' 1872 ; 'The Eustace Diamonds,' 1873 [1872] ; 'Australia and New Zealand,' 1873 ; 'Phineas Redux,' 1874 ; 'Harry Heathcote of Gangoil,' 1874 ; 'Lady Anna,' 1874 ; 'The Way We Live Now,' 1875 ; 'The Prime Minister,' 1876 ; 'The American Senator,' 1877 ; 'How the "Mastiffs" went to Iceland' (priv. ptd.), 1878 ; 'Is he Popenjoy?' 1878 ; 'South Africa,' 1878 ; 'John Caldigate,' 1879 ; 'An Eye for an Eye,' 1879 ; Cousin Henry,' 1879 ; 'Thackeray,' 1879 ; 'The Duke's Children,' 1880 ; 'Life of Cicero,' 1880 ; 'Ayala's Angel,' 1881 ; 'Doctor Wortle's School,' 1881 ; 'Why Frau Frohmann raised her Prices, etc.,' 1882 [1881] ; 'Lord Palmerston,' 1882 ; 'The Fixed Period,' 1882 ; 'Kept in the Dark,' 1882 ; 'Marion Fay,' 1882. *Posthumous:* 'Mr. Scarborough's Family,' 1883 ; 'Autobiography,' ed. by H. M. Trollope (2 vols.), 1883 ; 'The Land Leaguers,' 1883 ; 'An Old Man's Love,' 1884 ; 'Thompson Hall, etc.,' 1885.

TROLLOPE (*Mrs.* **Frances**), 1780-1863. [Mother of preceding.] Born [Frances Milton], at Stapleton, near Bristol, 10 March 1780. Lived for some time in London, keeping house for her brother after her father's second marriage. Married to Thomas

Anthony Trollope, 23 May 1809. In America, Dec. 1827 to summer of 1831. Adopted literary career on her return. Contrib. to 'The Magpie,' 1832. Travelled in Belgium and Germany, 1833. Lived at Bruges, 1834-35 ; husband died there, 23 Oct. 1835. Settled at Hadley, Jan. 1836. Travelled in Germany and Austria, July 1836 to June 1837 ; returned to Hadley. Occasional visits to London. Visited Paris, 1840. Visit to Italy, 1841. Lived at Carlton Hill, Cumberland, July 1842 to April 1843. Settled in Florence, 1843. Died there, 6 Oct. 1863 ; buried in Protestant cemetery there.

Works: 'Domestic Manners of the Americans' (2 vols.), 1831 ; 'The Refugee in America,' 1832 ; 'The Abbess,' 1833 ; 'The Mother's Manual' (under initials : F. T.), 1833 ; 'Belgium and Western Germany in 1833' (2 vols.), 1834 ; 'Tremordyn Cliff,' 1835 ; 'Paris and the Parisians in 1835' (2 vols.), 1836 ; 'Life and Adventures of Jonathan Jefferson Whitlaw,' 1836 ; 'The Vicar of Wrexhill,' 1837 ; 'Vienna and the Austrians' (2 vols.), 1838 ; 'Romance of Vienna,' 1838 ; 'The Widow Barnaby,' 1839 ; 'Life and Adventures of Michael Armstrong,' 1840 ; 'One Fault,' 1840 ; 'The Widow Married,' 1840 ; 'The Young Countess,' 1840 ; 'Charles Chesterfield,' 1841 ; 'The Blue Belles of England,' 1842 ; 'A Visit to Italy,' 1842 ; 'The Ward of Thorpe-Combe,' 1842 ; 'The Barnabys in America,' 1843 ; 'Hargrave,' 1843 ; 'Jessie Phillips,' 1844 ; 'The Lauringtons,' 1844 ; 'Young Love,' 1844 ; 'The Attractive Man,' 1846 ; 'Travels and Travellers' (2 vols.), 1846 ; 'The Robertses on their Travels,' 1846 ; 'Father Eustace,' 1847 ; 'The Three Cousins,' 1847 ; 'Town and Country,' 1848 (later edn., called 'Days of the Regency,' 1857) ; 'The Lottery of Marriage,' 1849 ; 'The Old World and the New,' 1849 ; 'Petticoat Government,' 1850 ; 'Mrs. Matthews,' 1851 ; 'Second Love,' 1851 ; 'Uncle Walter,' 1852 ; 'The Young Heiress,' 1853 ; 'The Life and

Adventures of a Clever Woman,' 1854; 'Gertrude,' 1855 ; 'Fashionable Life,' 1856.

She *edited:* T. A. Trollope's 'A Summer in Brittany,' 1840 ; and 'A Summer in Western France,' 1841.

TROLLOPE (Thomas Adolphus), 1810-1892. [Son of preceding.] Born, in London, 29 April 1810. To Winchester Coll., 1820. Matric. St. Alban Hall, Oxford, 16 Oct. 1829 ; B.A. from Magdalen Hall, 1835. Visit to America with his father, 1828. Assistant Master, King Edward's School, Birmingham, 1837-38. Lived with his mother till 1 is marriage. Married (i.) Theodosia Garrow, 3 April 1848. Italian Order of St. Maurice, 1862. Wife died, 13 April 1865. Married (ii.) Frances Eleanor Ternan, Oct. 1866. Removed from Florence to Rome, 1873. Foreign correspondent to 'Standard' at Rome, 1873-86. Returned to England, and settled at Budleigh Salterton, Devonshire, 1888. Frequent contributor to periodicals. Died, at Budleigh Salterton, 11 Nov. 1892.

Works: 'A Summer in Brittany' (2 vols.), 1840 ; 'A Summer in Western France' (2 vols.), 'Impressions of a Wanderer,' 1850 ; 'The Girlhood of Catherine de Medici,' 1856 ; 'A Decade of Italian Women' (2 vols.), 1859 ; 'Tuscany in 1849 and in 1859,' 1859 ; 'Filippo Strozzi,' 1860 ; 'Paul V. the Pope and Paul the Friar,' 1861 [1860] ; 'La Beata,' 1861 ; 'Marietta,' 1862 ; 'A Lenten Journey in Umbria,' 1862 ; 'Giulio Malatesta,' 1863 ; 'Beppo the Conscript,' 1864 ; 'Lindisfarn Chase,' 1864 ; 'A History of the Commonwealth of Florence' (4 vols.), 1865 ; 'Gemma,' 1866 ; 'Artingale Castle,' 1867 ; 'The Dream Numbers,' 1868 ; 'Leonora Casaloni,' 1869 ; 'The Garstangs,' 1869 ; 'A Siren,' 1870 ; 'Durnton Abbey,' 1871 ; 'The Stilwinches of Combe Mavis,' 1872 ; 'Diamond Cut Diamond,' 1875 ; 'The Papal Conclaves,' 1876 ; 'A Peep behind the Scenes at Rome,' 1877 ; 'The Story of the Life of Pius the

Ninth' (2 vols.), 1877 ; 'A Family Party in the Piazza of St. Peter,' 1877 ; 'Sketches from French History,' 1878 ; 'The Homes and Haunts of the Italian Poets' (with F. E. Trollope), 1881 ; 'What I Remember,' vols. i., ii., 1887 ; vol. iii. ('Further Reminiscences'). 1889.

He *edited:* C. Stieler's 'Italy,' 1877.

TUPPER (Martin Farquhar), 1810-1889. Born, in London, 17 July 1810. Early education at Charterhouse School. Matric. Ch. Ch., Oxford, 21 May 1828 ; B A., 1832 ; M.A., 1835 ; D.C.L., 1847. Student of Lincoln's Inn, 18 Jan. 1832 ; called to Bar, 24 Nov. 1835. Married Isabella Devis, 26 Nov. 1835. F.R.S., 1845. Visited America, 1851 and 1876. Resided greater part of life at Albury House, near Guildford. Died there, 29 Nov. 1889.

Works: 'Poems' (anon.), 1832 ; 'Proverbial Philosophy,' 1838 ; 2nd series, 1842 ; 3rd series, 1867 : series 1-4, 1871 ; 'Geraldine,' 1838 ; 'A Modern Pyramid,' 1839 ; 'An Author's Mind,' 1841 ; 'St. Martha's' (priv. ptd.), 1841 ; 'The Crock of Gold,' 1844 ; 'Heart,' 1844 ; 'The Twins,' 1844 ; 'A Thousand Lines' (anon.), 1845 ; 'Probabilities' (anon.), 1847 ; 'Hactenus,' 1848 ; 'Surrey,' 1849 ; 'Ballads for the Times' [1850] ; 'Farley Heath,' 1850 ; 'King Alfred's Poems in English Metres,' 1851 ; 'Half a Dozen No Popery Ballads' [1851] ; 'Hymns for All Nations,' 1851 ; 'St. Martha's' (with J. Tudor), 1851 ; 'Dirge for Wellington,' 1852 ; 'Half-a-Dozen Ballads for Australian Emigrants,' 1853 ; 'A Batch of War Ballads,' 1854 ; 'A Dozen Ballads for the Times' (anon.), 1854 ; 'Lyrics of the Heart and Mind,' 1855 ; 'Paterfamilias's Diary of Everybody's Tour' (anon.), 1856 ; 'Rides and Reveries of the late Mr. Æsop Smith' (anon.), 1858 [1857] ; 'Stephen Langton,' 1858 ; 'Some Verse and Prose about National Rifle Clubs,' 1858 ; 'Alfred' (priv. ptd.), 1858 ; 'Three Hundred Sonnets,' 1860 ; 'Our Greeting to the Princess Alexandra,' 1863 ; 'Ode for the 300th Birthday of Shakespeare,' 1864 ; 'Plan of the Ritualistic Campaign' (priv. ptd.), [1865] ; 'Selections . . . Together with some Poems never before published,' 1866 ; 'Raleigh,' 1866 ; 'Tupper's Directorium,' 1868 ; 'Our Canadian Dominion,' 1868 ; 'Twenty-one Protestant Ballads' (from 'The Rock'), 1868 ; 'A Creed and Hymns,' 1870 ; 'Fifty Protestant Ballads,' 1874 ; 'Washington,' 1876 ; 'Three Five-Act Plays, and Twelve Dramatic Scenes,' 1882 ; 'Jubilate' [1886] ; 'My Life as an Author,' 1886.

He *edited :* W. G. Tupper's 'Out and Home,' 1856.

*TWAIN (Mark) [*pseud., i.e.,* Samuel Langhorne Clemens], b. 1835. Born, in Florida, Missouri, U.S.A., 30 Nov. 1835. Educated at village school at Hannibal, Mo. Apprenticed to a printer, 1848. Pilot on the Mississippi, 1858. To Nevada, as Private Sec. to his brother, the Sec. of the Territory, 1861. Also engaged in mining industry in Nevada. City editor of the Virginia 'Daily Enterprise,' 1862-65. To San Francisco, 1865. On staff of 'Morning Call,' 1865. Visit to Hawaii, 1866. Visit to Egypt and Palestine, 1867. Ed. Buffalo 'Daily Express.' 1869-71. Married Olivia Langdon, 1870. Settled in Hartford, Conn.. Oct. 1871. Lectured in England, 1872. Dramatized version of story 'The Gilded Age' (written with C. D. Warner) produced at New York, 1874. Founded publishing house in New York, 1884.

Works : 'The Celebrated Jumping Frog,' 1867 ; 'The Innocents Abroad,' 1869 ; 'The New Pilgrim's Progress,' 1870; 'Roughing It,' 1872; 'A Curious Dream, and other Sketches' [1872] ; 'Sketches, Old and New,' 1873 ; 'The Gilded Age' (with C. D. Warner), 1873 ; 'Adventures of Tom Sawyer,' 1876 ; 'Information Wanted, and other Sketches' [1876] ; 'A True Story,' 1877 ; 'The Mississippi Pilot' [1877] ; 'Punch, Brothers, Punch,' 1878 ; 'An Idle Excursion,' 1878 ;

'A Tramp Abroad,' 1880 ; 'The Prince and the Pauper,' 1881 ; 'The Stolen White Elephant,' 1882 ; 'Life on the Mississippi,' 1883 ; 'The Adventures of Huckleberry Finn,' 1884 ; 'A Yankee at the Court of King Arthur,' 1889 ; 'The American Claimant,' 1892 ; 'The £1,000,000 Bank-Note,' 1893 ; 'Pudd'nhead Wilson,' 1894 ; 'Tom Sawyer Abroad,' 1894 ; 'Personal Recollections of Joan of Arc,' 1896 ; 'Tom Sawyer, Detective,' 1897 [1896].

He has *edited :* 'Mark Twain's Library of Humour,' 1888.

TYLOR (Edward Burnett), b. 1832. Born, at Camberwell, 2 Oct. 1832. Educated at school of Soc. of Friends, Tottenham. On scientific expedition to Mexico, 1856. F.R.S., 1871. Hon. LL.D., St. Andrew's, 1873. Hon. D.C.L., Oxford, 9 June 1875. Keeper of Oxford Univ. Museum since March 1883. Reader in Anthropology, Oxford, Oct. 1883 ; Hon. M.A., by decree, 20 Nov. 1883. Gifford Lecturer, Aberdeen, 1888-89. Pres. of Anthropological Institute, 1880-81, 1891-92. Prof. of Anthropology, Oxford, 1896.

Works : 'Anahuac,' 1861 ; 'Researches into the Early History of Mankind,' 1865 ; 'Primitive Culture' (2 vols.), 1871 ; 'Anthropology,' 1881.

TYNDALE (William), 1484 [?]-1536. Born, in Gloucestershire, about 1484. Educated at Magdalen Hall, Oxford (possibly also at Cambridge). B.A., Oxford, 1512 ; M.A., 1515. Tutor in household of Sir John Welch, at Little Sodbury, 1521-23 ; in household of Humphrey Monmouth, in London, 1523-24. To Germany, 1524 ; occupied himself with his translation of New Testament into English. In consequence of this was arrested as a heretic, 1535 ; imprisoned in Vilvorde Castle ; executed there, 6 Oct. 1536.

Works : 'The New Testament translated into English,' 1525 ; 'A Treatyse of Justificacyon by Faith only,' 1528 ; 'The Obediēce of a

Christen Man,' 1528 ; 'The Parable of the Wycked Mammon,' 1528 ; 'Exposition on 1 Cor. vii.' (anon.), 1529 ; 'Translation of the Book of Moses called Genesis,' 1530 ; 'An Answere unto Sir T. More's Dialoge' [1530] ; 'The Practice of Prelates,' 1530 ; 'The prophetic Jonas' (under initials : W. T.), [1531 ?] ; 'The Exposition of the fyrste Epistle of seynt Jhon' (under initials : W. T.), 1531 ; 'The Supper of the Lorde' (anon.), 1533 ; 'The Pentateuch, newly corrected and amended,' 1534 ; 'An Exposicion upon the v., vi., vii. chapters of Matthew,' 1548 ; 'A Briefe Declaration of the Sacraments' [1550 ?].

Posthumous : 'A fruitefull Exposition . . . upon the Epistle of Saint Paul to the Romans,' 1643.

Collected Works : in 2 vols., 1572-73.

Life : by G. B. Smith [1896].

TYNDALL (John), 1820 - 1893. Born, at Leiglinbridge, near Carlow, Ireland, 21 Aug. 1820. Early education at village school. On Irish Ordnance Survey, 1839-44. Held post as engineer, 1844 - 47. Assistant Master at Queenwood Coll., Hamps., 1847. Studied in Germany, 1848-51. F.R.S., 1853. Prof. of Nat. Philos., Royal Institution, 1853 ; Resident Director, 1867 - 87. Examiner to Council of Military Education, 1855. First visit to Switzerland, with Prof. Huxley, to study glaciers, 1856. Rumford Medal, Royal Society, 1864. Hon. LL.D., Camb., 1865. Hon. LL.D., Edinburgh, 1866. Lectured in U.S.A., 1872. Hon. D.C.L., Oxford, 18 June 1873. Pres. British Association, 1874. Married Hon. Louisa Hamilton, 29 Feb. 1876. Pres. of Birmingham and Midland Institute, 1877. For some years Scientific Adviser to Board of Trade ; resigned, 1883. F.G.S. Died, at Haslemere, 4 Dec. 1893.

Works : 'The Glaciers of the Alps,' 1860 ; 'Mountaineering in 1861,' 1862 ; 'Heat considered as a Mode of Motion,' 1863 ; 'On Radiation,' 1865 ; 'Sound,' 1867 ; 'Faraday as a

Discoverer,' 1868 ; 'Natural Philosophy in Easy Lessons' *[1869] ; 'Notes of a Course of Nine Lectures on Light,' 1869 ; 'Researches on Diamagnetism,' 1870 ; 'Notes of a Course of Seven Lectures on Electrical Phenomena,' 1870 ; 'On the Scientific use of the Imagination,' 1870 ; 'Hours of Exercise in the Alps,' 1871 ; 'Fragments of Science for Unscientific People' (2 vols.), 1871 ; 'Contributions to Molecular Physics,' 1872 ; 'The Forms of Water,' 1873 ; 'Principal Forbes and his Biographers,' 1873 ; 'Six Lectures on Light,' 1873 ; 'Address delivered before the British Association,' 1874 ; 'On the Transmission of Sound by the Atmosphere,' 1874 ; 'Lessons in Electricity,' 1876 ; 'Fermentation,' 1877 ; 'The Sabbath,' 1880 ; 'Essays on the Floating Matter of the Air,' 1881 ; 'Free Molecules and Radiant Heat,' 1882 ; 'Perverted Politics' (from 'St. James's Gaz.'), 1887 ; 'Mr. Gladstone and Home Rule,' 1887 ; 'New Fragments,' 1892 [1891].

TYRWHITT (Thomas), 1730-1786. Born, in London, 1730. Educated at Eton. Matric. Queen's Coll., Oxford, 9 May 1747 ; B.A., 1750. Fellow of Merton Coll., 1755 ; M.A., 1756. Called to Bar at Middle Temple, 1755. Under-Secretary, War Dept., 1756. Clerk of House of Commons, 1762-68. Curator of British Museum, 1784. F.R.S. F.S.A. Died, 15 Aug. 1786.

Works : 'Epistle of Florio at Oxford' (anon.), 1749 ; 'Translations in Verse,' 1752 ; 'Observations and Conjectures on some Passages of Shakespeare' (anon.), 1766 ; 'Dissertatio de Babrio' (anon.), 1776.

Posthumous : 'Conjecturæ in Strabonem' [1783] ; 'Conjectura in Æschylum, Euripidem et Aristophanem,' 1822.

He *edited :* 'Proceedings and Debates in the House of Commons, 1620-21' (2 vols.), 1766 ; H. Elsynge's 'The Manner of holding Parliaments in England,' 1768 ; 'Fragmenta duo Plutarchi,' 1773 ; Chaucer's 'Canterbury Tales,' 1775-78 ; 'Rowley's

Poems,' 1777 ; 'Aristotelis De Poetica liber,' 1794.

UDALL (Nicholas), 1506-1556. Born, in Hampshire, 1506. Scholar of Corpus Christi Coll.. Oxford, June 1520 ; B.A., 30 May 1524 ; Fellow 1524; M.A., 19 June 1534. Assistant-Master, Eton, 1534. Head-Master of Westminster School. For a time Vicar of Braintree, Essex, 1537-44. Rector of Calbourne, Isle of Wight, 1552 Canon of Windsor, 1553. Died, 1556. Buried at St. Margaret's, Westminster.

Works : ' Floures for Latin Spekynge, selected and gathered out of Terence, and the same translated into Englysshe,' 1533 ; translations of Erasmus' ' Apophthegmes,' 1542, and ' Paraphrases,' 1548, etc. ; of Geminus' ' Compendiosa totius Anatomie delineatio,' 1553.

Posthumous : ' Ralph Roister-Doister.' 1566.

USSHER (James), *Archbishop of Armagh,* **1580-1656.** Born, in Dublin, 4 Jan. 1580. Early education at Dublin Free School, 1589-93. Matric. Trin. Coll., Dublin, 9 Jan. 1593 ; Scholar ; B.A., 1596 ; M.A., 1600 ; Fellow and Catechist, 1600. Ordained Deacon and Priest, 1601. Chancellor of St. Patrick's Cathedral and Vicar of Finglas, 1606. Prof. of Divinity, Trin. Coll., 1607-21 ; B.D., 1607 ; D.D., 1614. Married Phœbe Challoner, 1614. Vice-Chancellor, Trin. Coll., 1614. Chaplain in Ordinary to the King, 1620. Bishop of Meath, 1621. Privy Councillor, 1623. Archbishop of Armagh, 1624. Member of Gray's Inn, 1624. Incorporated D.D., Oxford, 24 July 1626. Removed to Oxford, 1640 ; resided there till 1645. Bishop of Carlisle 'in commendam,' 1642. At Cardiff, 1645-46. Removed to London, June 1646. Lecturer at Lincoln's Inn, 1647-55. Died, at Reigate, 21 March 1656. Buried in St. Paul's Cathedral.

Works : ' Gravissimæ Quæstionis de Christianarum Ecclesiarum . . . continua successione et statu, historia ex-

plicatio,' 1613 ; ' The Substance of . . . a Sermon before the Commons,' 1621 ; ' Discourse of the Religion anciently professed by the Irish and Scottish,' 1622 ; ' Answer to a Challenge made by a Jesuite in Ireland,' 1624 ; ' Gotteschalci, et Prædestinationæ Controversiæ ab eo motæ, historia,' 1631 ; ' Veterum epistolarum Hibernicarum Sylloge,' 1632 ; ' Immanuel,' 1638 ; ' Britannicarum Ecclesiarum Antiquitates,' 1639 ; ' Directions propounded . . . to the High Court of Parliament ' (anon.), 1641 ; ' Vox Hibernæ,' 1642 ; ' A Geographicall . . . Disquisition touching the Asia properly so called,' 1643 ; ' The Principles of Christian Religion,' 1644 ; ' The Soveraignes Power and the Subjects Duty,' 1644 ; ' Body of Divinitie,' 1645 ; ' De Romanæ Ecclesiæ Symbolo apostolico vetere,' 1647 ; ' De Macedonum et Asianorum Anno solari,' 1648 ; ' Annales Veteris et Novi Testamenti ' (2 vols.), 1650-54 ; ' De Textus Hebraici Veteris Testamenti variantibus lectionibus,' 1652 ; ' De Græca Septuaginta Interpretum versione syntagma,' 1655 ; ' The Reduction of Episcopacie unto the form of Synodical Government,' 1656.

Posthumous: ' A Method for Meditation,' 1657 ; ' The Judgement of the late Archbishop of Armagh ' (2 series), 1657-59 ; ' Eighteen Sermons,' 1659 ; ' Chronologia Sacra,' 1660 ; ' Strange and Remarkable Prophecies,' 1678 ; ' Episcopal and Presbyterian Government conjoyned,' 1679 ; ' The Protestant School,' 1681 ; ' Opuscula Duo,' 1687 ; ' Historia Dogmatica Controversiæ inter Orthodoxos et Pontificios de Scripturis et Sacris vernaculis,' 1690.

He *edited :* ' SS. Polycarpi et Ignatii Epistolæ,' 1644.

Collected Works : ed. by C. R. Elrington (17 vols.), 1847-64.

Life : by J. A. Carr, 1895.

VANBRUGH (*Sir* John), **1664-1726.** Born, in London, Jan. 1664 ; baptized, 24 Jan. Probably spent some time in Paris in youth ; afterwards served in Army. Play, 'The Relapse,' performed at Drury Lane, Dec. 1696 ; 'Æsop,' Drury Lane, Jan. 1697 ; 'The Provok'd Wife,' Lincoln's Inn Fields, May 1697 ; 'The False Friend,' Drury Lane, Jan. 1702. Practised as an architect. Built Castle Howard, Blenheim, and other important houses. Appointed Controller of Royal Works, 1702. Play, 'Squire Trelooby' (written with Congreve and Walsh), produced at Lincoln's Inn Fields, 30 March 1704 ; 'The Country House,' 1705. Built a theatre in the Haymarket. His play, 'The Confederacy,' produced there, 30 Oct. 1705 ; 'The Mistake,' 27 Dec. 1705. Clarencieux King-at-Arms, 1705-26. To Hanover, on embassy to convey Order of Garter to the Elector, May 1706. Knighted, 19 Sept. 1714. Surveyor of Gardens and Waters, 1715. Surveyor of Works, Greenwich Hospital, 1716. Member of Kit-Kat Club. Married Henrietta Maria Yarburgh, 14 Jan. 1719. Died, in London, 26 March 1726. Buried in St. Stephen's, Walbrook.

Works : 'The Relapse' (anon.), 1697 (afterwards known, in Sheridan's adaptation, as 'A Trip to Scarborough'); 'The Provok'd Wife' (anon.), 1697 ; 'Æsop,' 1697 ; 'A Short Vindication of "The Relapse" and "The Provok'd Wife"' (anon.), 1698 ; 'The Pilgrim' (adapted from Dryden ; anon.), 1700 ; 'The False Friend' (anon.), 1702 ; 'The Confederacy' (anon.), 1705 ; 'The Mistake' (anon.), 1706 ; 'The Country House' (trans. from the French of Carton D'Ancourt), 1715.

Posthumous : 'The Provok'd Husband' (completed by Cibber from Vanbrugh's 'A Journey to London'), 1728 ; 'The Cornish Squire' (trans. from Molière), 1734.

Collected Works : in 2 vols., ed. by W. C. Ward, 1893.

VAUGHAN (Henry), *the Silurist,* **1622-1695.** Born, at Skethrog-on-Usk, Brecknockshire, 1622. Privately educated at Llangattock, 1632-38. Matric. Jesus Coll., Oxford, 1638. After leaving Oxford studied medicine and took M.D. degree. Settled in practice at Brecon. Afterwards re-

moved to Skethiog. Married ; perhaps twice. Died, at Skethiog, 23 April 1695. Buried in Llansaintfraed Churchyard.

Works : 'Poems,' 1646 ; 'Silex Scintillans,' 1650 ; 'Olor Iscanus,' 1651 ; 'The Mount of Olives,' 1652 ; 'Flores Solitudinis,' 1654 ; 'Thalia Rediviva,' 1678.

He *translated :* H. Nolle's 'Hermetical Physick,' 1655 ; and *edited:* R. Vaughan's 'Discourse of Coin and Coinage,' 1675.

Collected Works : in 4 vols., ed. by A. B. Grosart, 1871.

WADE (Thomas), **1805 - 1875.** Born, 1805. Play, 'Woman's Love,' produced at Covent Garden, 17 Dec. 1828 ; 'The Phrenologists,' Covent Garden, 12 Jan. 1830 ; 'The Jew of Arragon,' Covent Garden, 20 Oct. 1830. Contrib. to 'Monthly Repository,' 'The National,' 'Illuminated Mag.,' 'People's Journal,' and other periodicals. Married Mrs. Lucy Bridgman, 1836 [?]. For a short time editor of 'Bell's Weekly Messenger' about 1840. Removed to Jersey. Edited 'Wade's London Review,' 1845-46. Died, 1875.

Works : 'Tasso and the Sisters,' 1825 ; 'Woman's Love' (anon.) 1829; 'The Phrenologists,' 1830 ; 'The Jew of Arragon,' 1830 ; 'Mundi et Cordis : de Rebus Sempiternis et Temporariis : Carmina,' 1835 ; 'The Contention of Death and Love' (anon.), 1837 ; 'Helena,' 1837 ; 'The Shadow-Seeker,' 1837 ; 'Prothanasia,' 1839 ; 'What does "Hamlet" mean ?' [1840].

WAKEFIELD (Gilbert), **1756-1801.** Born, at Nottingham, 22 Feb. 1756. Early education at private schools at Nottingham, Wilford, and Richmond. Scholar of Jesus Coll., Camb., April 1772 ; B.A., 16 Jan. 1776 ; Fellow, April 1776 to March 1779. Ordained Deacon, 22 March 1778. Curate of Stockport, Cheshire, May to Aug. 1778. Curate of St. Peter's, Liverpool, Oct. 1778 to March 1779. Married, 23 March 1779. Master at Dis-

19

senting Academy, Warrington, 1779-83. Engaged in tuition at Nottingham, 1784-90. Master in Dissenting Academy, Hackney, July 1790 to June 1791. Imprisoned at Dorchester for libel in his ' Reply to Some Parts of the Bishop of Llandaff's Address,' May 1799 to May 1801. Died, in London, 9 Sept. 1801. Buried in Richmond Church.

Works : 'Poemata, Latine partim scripta, partim reddita,' 1776 ; 'A Plain and Short Account of the Nature of Baptism,' 1781 ; 'An Essay on Inspiration,' 1781 ; 'Directions for the Student in Theology,' 1784 ; 'A Sermon preached at Richmond,'1784; 'An Enquiry into the Opinions of the Christian Writers of the first three Centuries concerning the Person of Jesus Christ' (only one vol. pubd.), 1784 ; 'Remarks on Dr. Horsley's Ordination Sermon,'1788 ; 'Four Marks of Antichrist' (anon.), 1788 ; 'An Address to the Inhabitants of Nottingham,' 1789 ; 'Remarks on the Internal Evidence of the Christian Religion,' 1789 ; 'Silva Critica ' (5 pts.), 1789-95 ; 'An Address to the . . . Bishop of St. David's,' 1790 ; 'Cursory Reflections,' 1790 ; 'An Enquiry into the Expediency . . . of Public or Social Worship,' 1791 ; 'Memoirs.' 1792 ; 'Short Strictures on Dr. Priestley's Letter,' 1792 ; 'A General Reply to the Arguments against the Enquiry into Public Worship,' 1792 ; 'Evidences of Christianity,' 1793 ; 'The Spirit of Christianity,' 1794 (3rd edn. same year) ; 'An Examination of the Age of Reason,' 1794 (2nd edn. same year) ; 'Remarks on the General Orders of the Duke of York,' 1794 ; 'A Reply to Thomas Paine's Second Part of the Age of Reason,' 1795 ; 'Observations on Pope,' 1796 ; 'A Reply to the Letter of Edmund Burke, Esq., to a Noble Lord,' 1796 ; 'In Euripidis Hecubam . . . diatribe extemporalis,' 1797 ; 'Letter to Jacob Bryant, Esq.,' 1797 ; 'Letter to William Wilberforce, Esq.,' 1797 ; 'A Reply to Some Parts of the Bishop of Llandaff's Address to the People of Great Britain,' 1798 ; 'Letter to Sir John Scott,' 1798 ; 'Defence ' (priv. ptd.), 1799 ; 'Address to the Judges . . . April 18, 1799' (priv. ptd.), 1799 ; 'Address to the Judges . . . May 30, 1799' (priv. ptd.), 1799 ; 'The First Satire of Juvenal imitated' (priv. ptd.), 1800 ; 'Noctes Carcerariæ,' 1801.

Posthumous : 'Correspondence . . . with the late Rt. Hon. C. J. Fox,' 1813.

He *translated :* First Epistle to Thessalonians, 1781 ; St. Matthew, 1782 ; 'Those parts only of the New Testament which are wrongly translated in our Common Version,' 1789 ; 'The New Testament,' 1792 ; 'Poetical Translations from the Antients,' 1795 ; 'Select Essays of Dio Chrysostom,' 1800 ; and *edited :* Gray's Poems, 1786 ; Virgil's Georgics,1788 ; Horace's Works, 1794 ; 'Tragœdium Græcarum Delectus,' 1794 ; Pope's Works (only one vol. pubd.), 1794 ; 'Works of Bion and Moschus,' 1795 ; Virgil's Works, 1796 ; Pope's Homer, 1796 ; Lucretius, 1796-97.

***WALLACE** (Alfred Russel), **b. 1823.** Born, at Usk, Monmouthshire, 8 Jan. 1823. Educated at Hertford Grammar School. Originally a land-surveyor and architect by profession, but eventually devoted himself to science. Travelled extensively, 1848-62. F.R.G.S., 1864 ; Founders' Gold Medal, 1892. Royal Medal, Royal Society, 1868 ; Darwin Medal, 1890 ; F.R.S., 1893. Gold Medal, Société de Geog. de Paris, 1870. Frequent contributor to periodicals and to journals of learned societies. Civil List Pension, 1881. Hon. LL.D., Dublin, 1882 ; Hon. D.C.L., Oxford, 1889. Gold Medal, Linnean Soc., 1892. Pres., Land Nationalization Soc., since 1881.

Works : ' Palm Trees of the Amazon,' 1853 ; 'A Narrative of Travels on the Amazon,'1853 ; 'The Scientific Aspects of the Supernatural,' 1866 ; 'The Malay Archipelago'(2 vols.),1869; 'Contributions to the Theory of Natural Selection,' 1870 ; 'On Miracles and Modern Spiritualism,' 1875 ; 'The

Geographical Distribution of Animals'
(2 vols.), 1876 ; 'Tropical Nature,'
1878 ; 'Australasia,' 1879 ; 'Island
Life, as illustrating the Laws of the
Geographical Distribution of Animals'
[1880] ; 'Land Nationalization,' 1882
(3rd edn. same year) ; 'Forty - five
Years of Registration Statistics of
Vaccination,' 1885 [1884] ; 'Bad
Times,' 1885 ; 'Darwinism,' 1889 ;
'Natural Selection and Tropical
Nature,' 1891 ; 'Australia and New
Zealand,' 1893.

WALLER (Edmund), 1605-1687.
Born, at Coleshill, Herts, 3 March
1605. Educated at Eton, and at
King's Coll., Camb. M.P. for Amer-
sham, 1621 ; for Chipping Wycombe,
1626 ; for Amersham, 1628-29, 1640 ;
for Hastings, 1661-78 ; for Saltash,
1685-87. Married (i.) Anna Banks,
15 July 1631 ; (ii.) Mary Bresse [or
Breaux ?]. Imprisoned for a year, and
fined, for high treason, 1643-44 ;
exiled, in France, 1644-53. Died, at
Beaconsfield, 21 Oct. 1687. Buried
there.

Works : Four Speeches in the
House of Commons, pubd. separately,
1641 ; 'Speech . . . 4 July, 1643,'
1643 ; 'Workes,' 1645 ; 'A Panegyrick to my Lord Protector' (under
initials : E. W.), 1655 ; 'Upon the
late Storme and Death of his Highness
ensuing the same' [1658] ; 'To the
King, upon his Majestie's Happy Return' [1660] ; 'Poem on St. James's
Park,' 1661 ; 'To my Lady Morton'
(anon.), 1661 ; 'To the Queen' [1663];
'Pompey the Great' (with others ;
anon.), 1664 ; 'Upon her Majesties
new buildings at Somerset House,'
1665 ; 'Instructions to a Painter,'
1666.
Posthumous : 'The Maids Tragedy
altered, etc.,' 1690.
Collected Works · 'Poems,' ed. by
G. T. Drury, 1893.
Life : by P. Stockdale, 1772.

WALPOLE (Horace), *Earl of Orford,* **1717-1797.** Born, in London,
24 Sept. 1717. Educated at Eton,
April 1727 to Sept. 1734. Entered
at Lincoln's Inn, 27 May 1731. To

King's Coll., Camb., March 1735.
Inspector of Imports and Exports,
1737-38 ; Usher of the Exchequer,
1738 ; Comptroller of the Pipe, 1738 ;
Clerk of the Estreats, 1738. Left
Cambridge, March 1739. Travelled
on Continent, 1739-41. M.P. for
Callington, 1741-44. Settled at Straw-
berry Hill, 1747. M.P. for Castle
Rising, 1754-57 ; for King's Lynn,
1757-68. Succeeded to Earldom of
Orford, Dec. 1791. Unmarried. Died,
in London, 2 March 1797. Buried at
Houghton.

Works : 'Lessons for the Day'
(anon.), 1742 ; 'Epilogue to Tamerlane' [1746] ; 'Ædes Walpolianæ.'
1747 ; 'Letter from Xo-Ho,' 1757
(5th edn. same year) ; 'Fugitive Pieces
in Verse and Prose,' 1758 ; 'Catalogue
of the Royal and Noble Authors of
England' (2 vols.), 1758 ; 'Observations on the Account given of the
Catalogue . . . in . . . the Critical Review,' 1759 ; 'Reflections on the
Different Ideas of the French and
English in regard to Cruelty' (anon.)
1759 ; 'A Counter-Address to the
Public' (anon.), 1764 ; 'The Castle
of Otranto' (anon.), 1765 (2nd edn.
same year) ; 'An Account of the
Giants lately discovered,' 1766 ; 'The
Mysterious Mother' (priv. ptd.),1768 ;
'Historic Doubts of the Life and
Reign of King Richard the Third,'
1768 (2nd edn. same year) ; 'Mis-
cellaneous Antiquities' (anon.), 1772 ;
'Description of the Villa . . . at
Strawberry Hill,' 1772 ; 'Letter to
the Editor of the Miscellanies of
Thomas Chatterton,' 1779 ; 'To Lady
H. Waldegrave' (anon.), [1779];
'Hieroglyphick Tales' (anon.), 1785 ;
'Essay on Modern Gardening,' 1785 ;
'The Press at Strawberry Hill to . . .
the Duke of Clarence' (anon.), [1790 ?];
'Hasty Productions,' 1791.
Posthumous : 'Letters to . . . Rev.
W. Cole and others,' 1818 ; 'Letters
to G. Montagu,' 1819 ; 'Private Cor-
respondence' (4 vols.), 1820 ; 'Me-
moirs of the Last Ten Years of the
Reign of King George II.,' ed. by
Lord Holland (2 vols.), 1822 ; 'Let-
ters to Sir H. Mann' (7 vols.), 1833-

44 ; 'Letters,' ed. by J. Wright (6 vols.), 1840 ; 'Memoirs of the Reign of King George III.,' ed. by Sir D. le Marchant (4 vols.), 1845 ; 'Letters to the Countess of Ossory' (2 vols.), 1848 ; 'Correspondence with W. Mason,' ed. by J. Mitford (2 vols.), 1851 ; 'Letters,' ed. by P. Cunningham (9 vols.), 1857-58 ; 'Journal of the Reign of King George the Third . . being a Supplement to his Memoirs,' ed. by Dr. Doran (2 vols.), 1859 ; 'Supplement to the Historic Doubts,' ed. by Dr. Hawtrey' (priv. ptd.), 1860-61.

He *edited :* P. Hentzner's 'A Journey into England,' 1757 ; G. Vertue's 'Anecdotes of Painting in England,' 1762, and 'Catalogue of Engravers,' 1763 ; Lord Herbert of Cherbury's Life, 1764 ; Count de Grammont's 'Mémoires,' 1772.

Collected Works : in 9 vols., 1798-1825.

Life : by Austin Dobson, 1890.

WALTON (Izaak), 1593-1683. Born, at Stafford, 9 Aug. 1593. Established a linen-draper's business in London [about 1620 ?]. Married (i.) Rachel Floud, 1626 ; she died, 1640. Married (ii.) Anne Ken, 1647 ; she died, 1662. Retired from business, 1643. Died, at Winchester, 15 Dec. 1683.

Works : 'Life of John Donne' (prefixed to Donne's 'Eighty Sermons'), 1640 ; 'Life of Sir Henry Wotton' (in 'Reliquiæ Wottonianæ'), 1651 ; 'The Compleat Angler,' 1653 ; 'Life of Mr. Richard Hooker,' 1665 ; 'Life of Mr. George Herbert,' 1670 ; 'Life of Dr. Sanderson,' 1678 ; 'Love and Truth' (anon.; attrib. to Walton), 1680.

Posthumous : 'Waltoniana ; inedited remains in verse and prose,' ed. by R. H. Shepherd, 1878.

Life : by T. Zouch, 1825.

WARBURTON (William), *Bishop of Gloucester*, 1698-1779. Born, at Newark, 24 Dec. 1698. At school at Newark, and at Oakham Grammar School, till 1714. Articled to an attorney, 23 April 1714, for five years. Before long gave up legal profession,

and was ordained Deacon, 1723 ; Priest, 1727. Vicar of Greaseley, 1727-28. Created M.A., Camb., April 1728. Rector of Brant-Broughton, 1728-46. Rector of Frisby, 1730-56. Chaplain to Prince of Wales, 1738. Married Gertrude Tucker, 5 Sept. 1745. Preacher to Lincoln's Inn, 1746. Prebendary of Gloucester, 1753-55. Chaplain-in-Ordinary to the King, 1754. D.D., 1754. Prebendary of Durham, 1755-57. Dean of Bristol, 1757. Bishop of Gloucester, Dec. 1759. Founded a Lectureship at Lincoln's Inn, 1768. Died, at Gloucester, 7 June 1779. Buried in the Cathedral.

Works [exclusive of separate sermons] : ' Miscellaneous Translations' (anon.), 1724 ; 'Critical and Philosophical Enquiry into the Causes of Prodigies and Miracles' (anon.), 1727 ; 'The Legal Judicature in Chancery' (anon.; with S. Burroughs), 1727 ; 'The Alliance between Church and State' (anon.), 1736 ; 'The Divine Legation of Moses' (2 vols.), 1738-41; 'A Vindication of Mr. Pope's Essay on Man,' 1740 ; 'Remarks on Several Occasional Reflections' (2 pts.), 1745-46 ; 'Two Sermons,' 1746 ; 'Apologetical Dedication to . . . Dr. H. Stebbing,' 1746 ; 'Letter from an Author to an M.P.,' 1747 ; 'Remarks upon the Principles . . . of Dr. Rutherford's Essay,' 1747 ; 'Letter to the Editor of the Letters on the Spirit of Patriotism' (anon.), 1749 ; 'Letter to Viscount Bolingbroke' (anon.), 1749 ; 'Julian,' 1750 ; 'The Principles of Natural and Revealed Religion' (3 vols.), 1753-67 ; 'A View of Lord Bolingbroke's Philosophy' (anon.), 1756 ; 'Remarks on Mr. D. Hume's Essay on the Natural History of Religion' (anon.; with R. Hurd), 1757 ; 'A Rational Account . . . of the Lord's Supper,' 1761 ; 'An Enquiry into the Nature . . . of Literary Property' (anon.), 1762 ; 'The Doctrine of Grace,' 1763.

Posthumous : 'Tracts by Warburton and a Warburtonian,' 1789 ; 'Letters . . . to one of his Friends,' 1808; 'Letters to the Rt. Hon. Charles

Yorke' (priv. ptd.), 1812 ; 'Selection from his Unpublished Papers,' ed. by F. Kilvert, 1841.

He *edited* : Pope's 'Essay on Man,' 1729 ; 'Dunciad,' 1749 ; Shakespeare's Plays, 1747 ; 'Essay on Criticism,' 1751 ; 'Works,' 1751, and 'Additions to Works,' 1776.

Collected Works: ed. by R. Hurd, new edn. (14 vols.), 1811-41. *Life:* by J. S. Watson, 1863.

WARD (Edward), 1660 [?]-1731. Born, in Oxfordshire, 1660 [?]. Settled in London, as keeper of a tavern. Prolific writer of satires. Died, in London, 1731.

Works: 'A Poet's Ramble after Riches' (anon.), 1691 ; 'The Miracles performed by Money' (anon.), 1692 ; 'Female Policy Detected' (under initials : E. W.), 1695 ; 'Ecclesia et Factio' (anon.), 1698 ; 'The Sot's Paradise' (anon.), 1698 ; 'The London Spy,' 1698-1700 ; 'A Trip to New England' (anon.), 1699 ; 'A Walk to Islington' (anon.), 1699 ; 'Modern Religion and Ancient Loyalty' (anon.), 1699 ; 'The World Bewitch'd' (anon.), 1699 ; 'The Insinuating Bawd' (anon.), 1699 ; 'A Step to Stir-Bitch Fair' (anon.), 1700; 'The Reformer' (anon.), 1700 ; 'A Frolick to Horn Fair' (anon.), 1700 ; 'The Dancing School' (anon.), 1700 ; 'The Libertine's Choice' (anon.), 1704 ; 'Helter-Skelter' (anon.), 1704; 'Honesty in Distress' (anon.), 1705 ; 'Hudibras Redivivus' (anon.; 2 pts.), 1706-07 ; 'The Wooden World Dissected' (anon.), 1707 ; 'The Humours of a Coffee House' (anon.), 1707 ; 'Female Grievances Debated' (anon.), 1707 ; 'The London Terræfilius' (anon.), 1707-08 ; 'The Modern World Disrobed,' 1708 ; 'The Forgiving Husband' (anon.), 1708 ; 'The Secret History of Clubs' (anon.), 1709 ; 'Mars stript of his Armour' (anon.), 1709; 'The Rambling Fuddle-Cups' (anon.), 1709 ; 'Marriage Dialogues' (anon.), 1709 ; 'Vulgus Britannicus' (anon.), 1710 ; 'The Tippling Philosophers' (anon.), 1710 ; 'Life and Adventures of Don Quixote;

merrily translated into Hudibrastick Verse' (2 vols.), 1711-12 ; 'History of the Grand Rebellion' (anon.), 1713; 'The Whigs Unmasked,' 1713 ; 'The Republican Procession' (anon.), 1714; 'The Field Spy' (anon.), 1714 ; 'St. Paul's Church' (anon.), 1716 ; 'Wine and Wisdom' (anon.), 1719 ; 'The Delights of the Bottle' (anon.), 1720 ; 'The Northern Cuckold' (anon.), 1721 ; 'The Wand'ring Spy' (anon.), 1722 ; 'The Dancing Devils' (anon.), 1724 ; 'The Merry Travellers' (anon.), 1726 ; 'Durgen' (anon.), 1729.

He *translated:* J. Allibond's 'Seasonable Sketch' (from the Latin), 1717 ; Secundus' 'Basia' (with E. Fenton), 1731.

*WARD (*Mrs.* Mary Augusta), b. 1851. [Niece of Matthew Arnold, *q.v.*] Born [Mary Augusta Arnold] at Hobart Town, Tasmania, 11 June 1851. Contrib. to 'Macmillan's Mag.,' and other periodicals, 1871, etc.; to 'Dict. of Christian Biog.,' 1877, etc. Married to Thomas Humphry Ward, 6 April 1872. One of founders, and Hon. Sec., of University Hall, London, opened Oct. 1890.

Works: 'Milly and Olly,' 1881 ; 'Miss Bretherton,' 1884 ; 'Robert Elsmere,' 1888 ; 'University Hall : Opening Address,' 1891 ; 'The History of David Grieve,' 1892 ; 'Marcella,' 1894 ; 'Unitarians and the Future,' 1894 ; 'The Story of Bessie Costrell,' 1895 ; 'Sir George Tressady,' 1896.

She has *translated:* Amiel's 'Journal,' 1885.

WARREN (John Byrne Leicester). *See* De Tabley.

WARREN (Samuel), 1807 - 1877. Born, in Denbighshire, 1807. Studied medicine for a short time at Edinburgh University. Student of Inner Temple, 1828 ; Special Pleader, 1831-37 ; called to Bar, 1837. Contrib. to 'Blackwood's Mag.' from Aug. 1830. Q.C., 1851. Bencher of Inner Temple, 1851. Recorder of Hull, 1852-74. Hon. D.C.L., Oxford, 9 June 1853. M.P. for Midhurst, 1856-59. Master in Lunacy, 1859-77. Died, 29 July 1877.

Works : 'Passages from the Diary of a Late Physician' (3 vols.), 1832-38 ; 'Popular and Practical Introduction to Law Studies,' 1835 ; 'The Opium Question,' 1840 (4th edn. same year) ; 'Ten Thousand a Year ' (anon.), 1841 ; 'Now and Then,' 1847 ; 'The Moral, Social and Professional Duties of Attorneys and Solicitors,' 1848 ; 'Correspondence ... relative to the trial of Courvoisier,' 1849 ; 'Letter to the Queen on a late Court Martial,' 1850 ; 'The Lily and the Bee,' 1851 ; 'The Queen, or the Pope ?' 1851 ; 'Manual of the Parliamentary Election Law of the United Kingdom,' 1852 ; 'Intellectual and Moral Development of the Present Age,' 1852 ; 'The Law and Practice of Election Committees,' 1853 ; 'Charge to the Grand Jury,' 1854 ; 'Miscellanies' (from 'Blackwood's Mag.' ; 2 vols.) 1854-55 ; 'Works ' (5 vols.), 1854-55 ; 'Labour,' 1856.

He *edited :* 'Select Extracts from Blackstone's Commentaries' (with J. W. Smith), 1837 ; 'Blackstone's Commentaries Systematically Abridged,' 1855.

WARTON (Thomas), **1728 - 1790.** Born, at Basingstoke, 1728. Matric. Trin. Coll., Oxford, 16 March 1744 ; B.A., 1747 ; M.A., 1750 ; Fellow, 1751 ; Professor of Poetry, 1756-66 ; B.D., 7 Dec. 1767. Rector of Kiddington, 1771. F.S.A., 1771. Camden Prof. of Ancient Hist., Oxford, 1785-90. Poet Laureate, 1785-90. Died, at Oxford, 21 May 1790. Buried in Trin. Coll. Chapel.

Works : 'The Pleasures of Melancholy' (anon.), 1747 ; 'Poems on Several Occasions,' 1747 ; 'The Triumph of Isis ' (anon.), 1749 ; 'A Description of . . . Winchester ' (anon.), 1750 ; 'Newmarket,' 1751 ; 'Ode for Music,' 1751 ; 'Observations on the Faerie Queene,' 1754 ; 'A Companion to the Guide, and a Guide to the Companion ' (anon.), 1760 ; 'Life . . . of Ralph Bathurst' (2 vols.),

1761 ; 'Life of Sir Thomas Pope,' 1772 ; 'The History of English Poetry ' (4 vols.), 1774-81 ; 'Poems,' 1777 ; 'Enquiry into the authenticity of the poems attributed to Thomas Rowley,' 1782 ; 'Specimen of a History of Oxfordshire ' (priv. ptd.), 1782 ; 'Verses on Sir Joshua Reynolds's Painted Window at New College ' (anon.), 1782.

He *edited :* 'The Union,' 1753 ; 'Inscriptionum Romanorum Metricarum Delectus,' 1758 ; 'The Oxford Sausage,' 1764 ; C. Kephalas' 'Anthologiæ Græcæ,' 1766 ; Theocritus' Works, 1770 ; Milton's 'Poems upon Several Occasions,' 1785.

Collected Works : 'Poetical Works,' ed. by R. Mant, with *memoir* (2 vols.), 1802.

***WATSON** (William), **b. 1858.** Born, at Burley-in-Wharfedale, Yorkshire, 2 Aug. 1858. Youth spent near Liverpool. First verses pubd. in the Liverpool 'Argus,' 1875. Civil List Pension, 1892.

Works : 'The Prince's Quest,' 1880; 'Epigrams of Art, Life, and Nature,' 1884 ; 'Wordsworth's Grave, and other poems,' 1890 ; 'Shelley's Centenary ' (priv. ptd.), 1892 ; 'Poems, 1892 ; 'Lachrymæ Musarum,' 1893 (priv. ptd., 1892) ; 'Excursions in Criticism ' [1893] ; 'The Eloping Angels,' 1893 ; 'Odes, and other poems,' 1894 ; 'The Father of the Forest,' 1895 ; 'The Purple East,' 1896 ; 'The Year of Shame,' 1896.

He has *edited :* Austin's 'English Lyrics,' 1890 ; 'Lyric Love: an anthology,' 1892.

WATTS (Isaac), **1674-1748.** Born, at Southampton, 17 July 1674. Educated at Southampton Grammar School, till 1690. At Dissenters' school in London, 1690-93. Private tutor in family of Sir John Hartopp, at Stoke Newington, 1696 - 1702. Assistant to Independent Minister at Mark Lane, 1698 ; Ordained Minister, March 1702. Severe illnesses, 1703 and 1712. Lived in house of Sir Thomas Abney, at Theobalds, 1712-48.

D.D., Edinburgh, and Aberdeen, 1728. Died, at Theobalds, 25 Nov. 1748. Buried in Bunhill Fields.

Works: 'Horæ Lyricæ,' 1706 ; 'Essay against Uncharitableness' (anon.), 1707 ; 'A Sermon,' 1707 ; 'Hymns and Spiritual Songs,' 1707 ; 'Orthodoxy and Charity United' (anon.), 1707 ; 'Guide to Prayer,' 1715; 'The Psalms of David,' 1719 ; 'Divine and Moral Songs,' 1720 ; 'The Art of Reading and Writing English,' 1721 ; 'Sermons on Various Subjects' (3 vols.), 1721-23 ; 'The Christian Doctrine of the Trinity . . . asserted,' 1722; 'Death and Heaven,' 1722 ; 'The Arian invited to the Orthodox Faith,' 1724 ; 'Three Dissertations relating to the Christian Doctrine of the Trinity,' 1724 ; 'Logick,' 1725 ; 'The Knowledge of the Heavens and Earth made easy,' 1726 ; 'Defense against the temptation to Self-Murther,' 1726 ; 'The Religious Improvement of Publick Events,' 1727 ; 'Essay towards the Encouragement of Charity Schools,' 1728 ; 'Prayers composed for the use . . . of Children,' 1728 ; 'Treatise on the Love of God,' 1729 ; 'Catechisms for Children,' 1730 ; 'Humble attempt towards the revival of Practical Religion,' 1731 ; 'The Strength and Weakness of Human Reason' (anon.), 1731 ; 'Essays towards a Proof of a Separate State of Souls,' 1732 ; 'Short View of the Whole Scripture History,' 1732 ; 'Essay on the Freedom of Will,' 1732 ; 'Philosophical Essays,' 1733 ; 'Reliquiæ Juveniles,' 1734; 'The Redeemer and the Sanctifier' (anon.), 1736 ; 'The Holiness of Times, Places and People,' 1738 ; 'The World to Come,' 1738 ; 'A New Essay on Civil Power in Things Sacred' (anon.), 1739 ; 'Essay on the Ruin and Recovery of Mankind,' 1740 ; 'Improvement of the Mind,' 1741 ; 'A Faithful Enquiry after the . . . Doctrine of the Trinity' (anon.), 1745 ; 'Glory of Christ as God-Man Unveiled' (anon.), 1746 ; 'Useful and Important Questions concerning Jesus' (anon.), 1746; 'Evangelical Discourses,' 1747 ; 'The

Rational Foundation of a Christian Church,' 1747.

Posthumous : 'Nine Sermons preached . . . 1718-19,' ed. by J. P. Smith, 1812.

Collected Works: in 6 vols., 1810-11.

Life : by T. Milner, 1834.

*WATTS-DUNTON (Walter Theodore), b. 1832. Born [Walter Theodore Watts], at St. Ives, Hunts. 1832. Educated for legal career. Became literary critic on staff of 'Examiner,' 1874 ; of 'Athenæum.' 1876. Contributor to Ward's 'English Poets,' 'Encycl. Brit.,' 'Chambers' Encycl.,' 'Nineteenth Century,' 'Mag. of Art,' etc. Assumed additional surname of Dunton, 1896.

Works : 'Jubilee Greeting at Spithead to the Men of Greater Britain,' 1897 ; 'Poems' [selected from contributions to 'Athenæum,' 'Nineteenth Century,' 'Mag. of Art,' etc.], 1897.

He has *contributed introductions* to : Borrow's 'Lavengro,' 1893 ; Edmund Gosse's 'King Eric,' 1893.

WEBSTER (*Mrs.* Augusta), 1840-1894. Born [Augusta Davies], at Poole, Dorsetshire, 30 Jan. 1840. Childhood spent at Chichester, Banff. and Penzance. Afterwards lived at Cambridge. Married to Thomas Webster, 1863. Contrib. to 'Examiner,' 1876-78. Member of London School Board, 1879-88. Frequent contributor to 'Athenæum,' and other periodicals. Died, at Kew, 5 Sept. 1894. Buried in Highgate Cemetery.

Works : 'Blanche Lisle, and other poems' (under pseud. 'Cecil Home '), 1860 ; 'Lesley's Guardians' (by 'Cecil Home '), 1864 ; 'Lilian Gray' (by 'Cecil Home '), 1864 ; 'Dramatic Studies,' 1866 ; 'A Woman Sold, and other poems,' 1867 ; 'Portraits,' 1870 ; 'The Auspicious Day,' 1872 ; 'Yu-Pe-Ya's Lute,' 1874 ; 'Parliamentary Franchise for Women Rate-payers' (from 'Examiner'), [1878] ; 'Disguises,' 1879 ; 'A Housewife's Opinions,' 1879 [1878] ; 'A Book of Rhyme,' 1881 ; 'In a Day,' 1882 ; 'Daffodil and the Croäxaxians,' 1884;

'The Sentence,' 1887 ; 'Selected Poems,' 1893.

Posthumous: 'Mother and Daughter,' ed. by W. M. Rossetti, 1895.

She *translated :* Æschylus' ' Prometheus Bound,' 1866 ; Euripides' ' Medea,' 1868.

WEBSTER (John), *fl.* **1620.** No details of life known. Said to have been clerk of St. Andrew's, Holborn, and to have belonged to the Merchant Taylors' Company. Perhaps an actor as well as dramatist.

Works [several lost] : 'The History of Sir Thomas Wyatt' (with Dekker), 1607 ; 'Westward-Hoe' (with Dekker), 1607 ; 'Northward-Hoe' (with Dekker), 1607 ; 'The White Divel,' 1612 ; ' A Monumental Columne erected to the living Memory of . . . Henry, late Prince of Wales,' 1613 ; 'The Devil's Law-Case,' 1623 : 'The Tragedy of the Dutchesse of Malfy,' 1623 ; 'The Monument of Honour,' 1624 ; 'Appius and Virginia,' 1654 ; ' A Cure for a Cuckold' (with Rowley), 1661 ; 'The Thracian Wonder' (with Rowley), 1661.

Collected Works : ed. by A. Dyce (4 vols.), 1830 ; new edn., 1857.

WEDMORE (Frederick), b. **1844.** Born, at Richmond Hill, Clifton, 9 July 1844. Educated at Weston-super-Mare ; at Lausanne ; and in Paris. To London, 1868. Married Martha Clapham, 12 Jan. 1870. Contrib. to ' Academy,' ' Fortnightly Rev.,' ' Nineteenth Century,' and other periodicals. On staff of 'Standard,' as art critic, since 1878. Visit to U.S.A., 1885 ; lectured at Harvard and Johns Hopkins Universities. Hon. Fellow Royal Soc. of Painter Etchers, 1896.

Works : ' A Snapt Gold Ring,' 1871 ; 'Two Girls,' 1873 ; 'Studies in English Art' (2 ser.), 1876-80 ; 'Pastorals of France,' 1877 ; 'The Masters of Genre Painting,' 1880 [1879] ; 'Meryon,' 1880 ; 'Four Masters of Etching,' 1883 ; 'Notes . . . on French Eighteenth Century Art' [1885] ; 'Whistler's Etchings,' 1886 ; 'Life of Honoré de Balzac,' 1890 [1889] ; 'Renunciations,' 1893 ; 'English Epi-

sodes,' 1894 ; 'Etching in England,' 1895 ; 'Fine Prints,' 1896 ; 'Orgeas and Miradou,' 1896.

He has *edited :* Michel's 'Rembrandt,' 1894 ; 'Poems of the Love and Pride of England' (with his daughter), 1897.

WELLS (Charles Jeremiah), 1800-1879. Born, 1800. Educated at a school at Edmonton. Early friendship with Keats and R. H. Horne. Lived in France, 1840-79. For a short time professor in a college at Quimper. Contrib. to ' Illuminated Mag.,' 1845 ; 'Fraser's Mag.,' 1846-47, etc. Married Emily Jane Hill. His 'Joseph and his Brethren ' reviewed by Mr. Swinburne in ' Fortnightly Rev.,' 1875. Died, at Marseilles, 17 Feb. 1879.

Works : ' Stories after Nature ' (anon.), 1822 ; 'Joseph and his Brethren ' (under pseud. : ' H. L. Howard '), 1824 [1823].

WESLEY (Charles), 1707-1788. [Younger brother of John Benjamin Wesley, *q.v.*]. Born, at Epworth, Lincs., 29 Dec. 1707. At Westminster School, 1716-26. Matric. Ch. Ch., Oxford, 13 June 1726 ; B.A., 1730 ; M.A., 1733. One of founders of ' Methodist ' Society at Oxford, 1730. Ordained Deacon and Priest, 1735. To Georgia, as Sec. to Gen. Oglethorpe, 1735. Returned to England, 1736. Active life as religious missionary in England, 1736-56. Married Sarah Gwynne, 8 April 1749. Lived in Bristol, 1749-71 ; in London, 1771-88. Died, in London, 29 March 1788. Buried in Marylebone Parish Churchyard.

Works : His publications consist almost entirely of hymns ; for the most part written with his brother John, and published anonymously, between 1744 and 1782. His 'Hymns and Sacred Poems' (2 vols.) were pubd. in 1729 ; his 'Sermons' (posthumously) in 1816 ; his ' Journal ' (2 vols.) in 1849.

Life : by J. Telford, 1886.

WESLEY (John Benjamin), 1703-1791. Born, at Epworth, Lincs., 17

June 1703. At Charterhouse School, 1714-20. Matric. Ch. Ch.. Oxford, 18 July 1720 ; B.A., 1724 ; Fellow of Lincoln Coll., 1725 ; M.A., 9 Feb. 1727. Ordained Deacon, 19 Sept. 1725 ; Priest, 22 Sept. 1728. Curate to his father at Wroote, Aug. 1727 to June 1729. Resided at Oxford, June 1729 to Oct. 1735. 'Methodist' Society founded there, 1730. To Georgia with his brother Charles and Gen. Oglethorpe, 1735. Returned to England, Feb. 1738. In Germany, June to Sept. 1738. Active missionary life, 1739-91. Married Mrs. Mary Vazeille, Feb. 1751; separated from her, 1771. Died, in London, 2 March 1791.

Works : Wesley's publications, including a large number of hymns, written with his brother Charles, and published between 1744 and 1781, number upwards of 150.

His *Collected Works* (15 vols.), ed. by T. Jackson, were pubd., 1856-62 ; the 'Poetical Works of John and Charles Wesley' (13 vols.), ed. by G. Osborn, 1868-72.

A 'Collection of Letters,' 1816, and 'Compendium of Logic,' ed. by T. Jackson, 1836, were published posthumously.

Life : by Southey, 1820 ; by J. Telford, 1886.

WHATELY (Richard), *Archbishop of Dublin,* **1787 - 1863.** Born, in London, 1 Feb. 1787. Early education at a school at Bristol. Matric. Oriel Coll., Oxford, 6 April 1805 ; B.A., 1808 ; English Essay Prize, 1810 ; Fellow of Oriel Coll., 1811-12 ; M.A., 1812. Ordained Deacon, 1814 ; Priest, 1815. Married Elizabeth Pope, 18 July 1821. Bampton Lecturer, Oxford, 1822. Rector of Halesworth, Suffolk, 1822-25. Principal of St. Alban Hall, Oxford, 1825-31. B.D. and D.D., 1825 ; Prof. of Polit. Econ., 1830-32. Archbishop of Dublin, 1831. Chancellor of Order of St. Patrick, 1831. Founded Professorship of Polit. Econ., Dublin, 1832. Bishop of Kildare, 1846. Commissioner of Nat. Education, Ireland. 1830 - 53. Died, in Dublin, 8 Oct. 1863.

Works [exclusive of separate sermons, charges, etc.] : 'Historic Doubts relative to Napoleon Buonaparte' (anon.), 1819 ; 'The Christian's Duty,' 1821 ; 'The Use and Abuse of Party Feeling in Matters of Religion,' 1822 ; 'Five Sermons,' 1823 ; 'Essays on some of the peculiarities of the Christian Religion,' 1825 ; 'Letters on the Church' (anon.), 1826 ; 'Elements of Logic,' 1826 ; 'On Confirmation' (anon.),[1827?]; 'Elements of Rhetoric,' 1828 ; 'Essays on some of the difficulties in the Writings of the Apostle Paul,' 1828 ; 'View of the Scripture Revelations concerning a Future State' (anon.), 1829 ; 'Letter to his Parishioners on the Disturbances' (anon.), 1830 ; 'The Errors of Romanism,' 1830 ; 'Introductory Lectures on Political Economy,' 1831-32 ; 'Village Conversations in Hard Times' (anon.), 1831 ; 'Essay on the Omission of Creeds . . . in the New Testament,' 1831 ; 'Thoughts on Secondary Punishments,' 1832 ; 'Education in Ireland,' 1832 ; 'Considerations on the Law of Libel' (under pseud. 'John Search'), 1833 ; 'Sermons on Various Subjects,' 1835 ; 'Easy Lessons on Christian Evidences' (anon.) 1838 ; 'Essays on Some of the Dangers to Christian Faith . . . from the teaching or conduct of its Professors,' 1839 ; 'Religion and her Name' (under pseud. 'John Search'), 1841 ; 'The Kingdom of Christ delineated,' 1841 ; 'Easy Lessons on Reasoning,' 1843 ; 'Introductory Lessons on Christian Evidences' (anon.), 1843 ; 'Thoughts on the proposed Evangelical Alliance,' 1846 ; 'On Instinct,' 1847 ; 'Four Sermons,' 1849 ; 'Introductory Lessons on the History of Religious Worship' (anon.), 1849 ; 'Introductory Lessons on the Study of the Apostle Paul's Epistles' (anon.),1849; 'Lessons on the Truth of Christianity' (anon.), 1850 ; 'Encyclopædia of Mental Science,' 1851 ; 'Lectures on the Scripture Revelations concerning Good and Evil Angels' (anon.), 1851 ; 'Lectures on the Characters of Our Lord's Apostles' (anon.), 1851 ; 'Cautions for the Times' (anon.), 1851 ; 'The Origin of

Civilization,' 1855 ; 'The Scripture
Doctrine concerning the Sacraments,'
1857 ; ' On the Present State of
Egypt,' 1858 ; •Dr. Paley's Works : a
lecture,' 1859 ; 'Introductory Lessons
on the British Constitution,' 1859 ;
'Lectures on some of the Scripture
Parables' (anon.), 1859 ; 'General
View of . . . Christianity' (from
'Encycl. Brit.'), 1860 ; 'Lectures on
Prayer' (anon.), 1860 ; 'The Parish
Pastor,' 1860 ; 'Miscellaneous Lec-
tures and Reviews,' 1861.

Posthumous: 'Judgment of Conscience and other Sermons,' 1864 ;
'Miscellaneous Remains,' 1864 (2nd
edn., with Additions, same year);
'Earlier Remains,' 1864 ; 'Romanism
the Religion of Human Nature,' 1878.

He *edited :* Archbishop King's 'Dis-
course on Predestination,' 1821 ; ' A
Selection of English Synonyms,' 1851 ;
Bp. of Llandaff's 'Remains,' 1854 ;
'Bacon's Essays,' 1856 ; Paley's 'Moral
Philosophy,' 1859 ; Paley's 'Evi-
dences,' 1859.

Life : by E. J. Whately, 1875.

WHEWELL (William), 1794-1866.
Born, in Lancaster, 24 May 1794.
Early education at Lancaster Grammar
School, and Heversham Grammar
School. Matric. Trin. Coll., Camb.,
1812 ; English Prize Poem, 1814 ;
B.A., 1816 ; Fellow, 1817 ; M.A.,
1819. Ordained Deacon, 1820 ; Priest,
1826. F.R.S., June 1820. Prof. of
Mineralogy, Camb., 1828-32 ; Prof. of
Moral Theology, 1838-55 ; B.D.,
1838 ; D.D., 1844 ; Master of Trin.
Coll., 1841-66 ; Vice-Chancellor, 1842
and 1855. Married Cordelia Marshall,
12 Oct. 1841 ; she died, 1855. He
contributed largely to the Transactions
of various Societies ; to 'Quarterly
Rev. ;' to 'Macmillan's Mag.,' etc.
Died, at Cambridge, 6 March 1866.

Works : 'Boadicea,' 1814 ; 'Elementary Treatise on Mechanics,' 1819 ;
'Treatise on Dynamics,' 1823 ; 'Architectural Notes on German Churches'
(anon.), 1830 ; 'Reply to "Observations on the plans for a New Library"'
(anon.), 1831 : 'First Principles of
Mechanics,' 1832 ; 'Introduction to

Dynamics,' 1832 ; 'Memoranda . . .
for Tide Observations' [1833] ; 'Ad-
dress' [at British Association], 1833 ;
'Analytical Statics,' 1833 ; 'As-
tronomy and General Physics con-
sidered with reference to Natural
Theology,' 1833 ; 'Remarks on Mr.
Thirlwall's Letter,' 1834 ; 'Additional
Remarks,' 1834 ; 'A Sermon' [on
John vi. 21], 1835 ; 'Newton and
Flamsteed,' 1836 ; 'Thoughts on the
Study of Mathematics,' 1836 ; 'The
Mechanical Euclid,' 1837 ; 'On the
Principles of English University
Education,' 1837 ; 'On the Founda-
tions of Morals' [1837], (2nd edn. same
year) ; 'History of the Inductive
Sciences' (3 vols.), 1837 ; ' Nugæ
Bartlovianæ' (anon. ; priv. ptd.), 1838-
40 ; 'The Doctrine of Limits,' 1838 ;
'The Philosophy of the Inductive
Sciences' (2 vols.), 1840 ; 'The
Mechanics of Engineering,' 1841 :
' Two Introductory Lectures . . . on
Moral Philosophy,' 1841 ; 'Elements
of Morality' (2 vols.) 1845 ; 'Indica-
tions of the Creator,' 1845 ; 'On a
Liberal Education' (3 pts.), 1845-52 ;
' Conic Sections,' 1846 ; 'Lectures on
Systematic Morality,' 1846 ; 'Ser-
mons,' 1847 ; 'Of Induction,' 1849 ;
'A Sermon' [on Ps. civ. 29], 1849 ;
'Inaugural Lecture' [on the Great
Exhibition], 1851 ; 'Lectures on the
History of Moral Philosophy in
England,' 1852 ; 'Of the Plurality of
Worlds' (anon.), 1853 ; 'Dialogue' on
preceding (anon.), 1854 ; 'On the
Material Aids of Education,' 1854 ;
'On the Influence of the History of
Science upon Intellectual Education,'
1855 ; 'On the Philosophy of Dis-
covery,' 1860 ; 'Six Lectures on
Political Economy,' 1863.

He *translated :* Goethe's 'Hermann
and Dorothea' (priv. ptd.), [1840?] ;
Schiller's 'The Knight of Toggenburg,'
1842 ; 'Verse Translations from the
German' (anon.), 1847 ; 'The Platonic
Dialogues,' 1859 ; and *edited :* Newton's
'Principia,' bk. i., 1846 ; Bp. Butler's
'Three Sermons on Human Nature,'
1848 ; Bishop Butler's 'Six Sermons
on Moral Subjects,' 1849 ; Bishop of
Lincoln's 'De Obligatione Conscientiæ,'

1851 ; 'Hugonis Grotii de Jure Belli et Pacis ' (with abridged translation), 1853 ; Rev. R. Jones's ' Literary Remains,' 1859 ; Isaac Barrow's ' Mathematical Works,' 1860.

Life : by Mrs. Stair Douglas, 1881.

WHITE (Gilbert), 1720-1793. Born, at Selborne, Hants, 18 July 1720. Early education at a school at Basingstoke. Matric. Oriel Coll., Oxford, 17 Dec. 1739 ; B.A., 1743 ; Fellow Oriel Coll., 1744-93 ; M.A., 1746 ; Proctor, 1752-53. Ordained Deacon, 1747 ; Priest, 1749. Curate at Swarraton, 1747-51 ; at Selborne, 1751-52 ; at Durley, 1753-55. Returned to Selborne, 1755. Vicar of Moreton-Pinkney, Northamptonshire (sinecure), 1757-93. Curate at Faringdon, 1762-84 ; at Selborne, 1784. Died, at Selborne, 26 June 1793.

Works : 'The Natural History and Antiquities of Selborne' (anon.), 1749.

Posthumous : 'A Naturalist's Calendar,' 1795 ; 'Extracts from the unpublished MSS. of Mr. White,' in the second series of E. Jesse's ' Gleanings in Natural History,' 1834.

Collected Works : in 2 vols., ed. by J. Aikin, 1802.

WHITEHEAD (WILLIAM), 1715-1785. Born, at Cambridge, Feb. 1715. Early education at Winchester School, July 1728 to Sept. 1735. Matric. Clare Hall, Camb., as Sizar, 1735 ; B.A., 1739 ; Fellow, 1742-46 ; M.A., 1743. Appointed tutor to son of Lord Jersey, 1745 ; travelled on Continent with him, June 1754 to Sept. 1756. Was an inmate of Lord Jersey's household till 1769. Play, 'The Roman Father,' produced at Drury Lane, 24 Feb. 1750 ; 'Creusa,' Drury Lane, 20 April 1754 ; 'The School for Lovers,' Drury Lane, 1762 ; 'A Trip to Scotland,' Drury Lane, 1770. Contrib. to 'The World,' 1753. Registrar of Order of Bath, 1755. Poet-Laureate, 1757. Died, in London, 14 April 1785. Buried in South Audley Street Chapel.

Works : 'On the Danger of Writing in Verse,' 1741 ; Epistle of Anne Boleyn to Henry VIII., 1743 ; 'Essay on Ridicule,' 1743 ; 'On Nobility,' 1744 ; 'Atys and Adrastus,' 1744 ; 'The Roman Father,' 1750 ; 'A Hymn to the Nymph of Bristol Spring,' 1751 ; 'Creusa,' 1754 ; 'Poems on Several Occasions,' 1754 ; 'Elegies,' 1757 ; 'Verses to the People of England,' 1758 ; 'A Charge to the Poets,' 1762 ; 'The School for Lovers,' 1762 (adapted from the French of Le Bovier de Fontenelle) ; 'A Trip to Scotland' (anon.), 1770 ; 'Plays and Poems' (2 vols.), 1774 ; 'Variety' (anon.), 1776 ; 'The Goat's Beard' (anon.), 1777.

*WHITMAN (Walt), 1819-1892.** Born, at West Hills, near Huntington, Suffolk County, New York, 31 May 1819. At school at Brooklyn, 1824-28. Lawyer's clerk in Brooklyn, 1830-32. Worked as printer in Brooklyn, 1834-37. Schoolmaster on Long Island, 1837-38. Founded and edited a weekly newspaper, 1839-40. Returned to Brooklyn, 1840 ; worked as printer till 1848. On staff of New Orleans ' Daily Crescent,' 1848. Edited Brooklyn 'Daily Eagle,' 1848-49. At Brooklyn working as housebuilder and agent, 1850-62 ; during this period contrib. to various periodicals, and published 'The Freeman.' At Washington, 1862-73. Nurse and surgeons' assistant during war, 1862-66. Held clerkships in Indian Office of Interior Dept., in Office of Solicitor to Treasury, and in Attorney-General's Office, 1865-73. Settled at Camden, New Jersey, summer of 1873. Died there, 26 March 1892. Buried at Harleigh Cemetery, Camden.

Works : 'Leaves of Grass,' 1855 ; 'Drum Taps,' 1865 ; 'Sequel to Drum Taps,' 1866 ; 'Memoranda during the War,' 1867 ; 'Democratic Vistas,' 1871 ; 'After All, not to Create only,' 1871 ; 'Passage to India,' 1871 ; 'As a Strong Bird on Pinions Free,' 1872 ; 'Two Rivulets,' 1876 ; 'Complete Works, revised to 1877' (2 vols.), 1878 ; 'Specimen Days and Collect,' 1882-83 ; 'November Boughs,' 1888 ; 'Good-bye, my Fancy,' 1891 ;

'Autobiographia,' 1892; 'Complete Prose Works,' 1892.

WHITTIER (John Greenleaf), 1807-1892. Born, at Haverhill, New England, 17 Dec. 1807. Early education at local school. Contrib. poem to 'Newbury Port Free Press,' 1826. At Haverhill Academy, 1827-28. Contrib. to 'Haverhill Gazette,' from 1828. At Boston as editor of 'American Manufacturer,' autumn 1828 to June 1829. At home at Haverhill, June 1829 to July 1830. Editor of 'Haverhill Gazette,' 1830; of 'New England Review,' 1830-31. Settled in Hartford, 1831. Sec. of Philadelphia Anti-Slavery Convention, 1833. Edited 'Pennsylvania Freeman.' Mem. for Haverhill in State Legislature, 1835-37. Contrib. to 'Democratic Rev.,' 1837-46. Removed with his family from Haverhill to Amesbury, 1840. Contrib. to 'Middlesex Standard,' 1844. Assistant-editor to 'National Era,' 1847-57. Assisted in starting 'Atlantic Monthly,' 1857. Lived retired life, entirely devoted to literature, from 1865. Died, at Hampton Falls, 7 Dec. 1892. Buried at Amesbury.

Works: 'Legends of New England,' 1831; 'Moll Pitcher,' 1832; 'Literary Remains of J. G. C. Brainard,' 1832; 'Justice and Expediency,' 1833; 'Mogg Megone,' 1836; 'Poems written during the progress of the Abolition Question,' 1837; 'Poems,' 1838; 'Lays of my Home,' 1843; 'The Stranger in Lowell,' 1845; 'Voices of Freedom,' 1846; 'The Supernaturalism of New England' (anon.), 1847; 'Leaves from Margaret Smith's Journal,' 1849; 'Poems' [collected], 1849; 'Songs of Labor,' 1850; 'Old Portraits and Modern Sketches,' 1850; 'Little Eva,' 1852; 'The Chapel of the Hermits,' 1853; 'A Sabbath Scene,' 1854; 'Literary Recreations and Miscellanies,' 1854; 'The Panorama,' 1856; 'Poetical Works' (2 vols.), 1857; 'Home Ballads and Poems,' 1860; 'In War Time,' 1864; 'Snow-Bound,' 1866; 'Prose Works' (2 vols.), 1866; 'Maud Muller,' 1867;

'National Lyrics,' 1867; 'The Tent on the Beach,' 1867; 'Among the Hills,' 1869; 'Ballads of New England,' 1870; 'Two Letters on the present aspect of the Society of Friends' (from 'Friends' Rev.'), 1870; 'Miriam,' 1871; 'The Pennsylvania Pilgrim,' 1873; 'Hazel Blossoms,' 1875; 'Complete Works,' 1876; 'Mabel Martin,' 1876; 'The Vision of Echard,' 1878; 'The River Path,' 1880; 'The King's Missive,' 1881; 'The Bay of Seven Islands,' 1883; 'Poems of Nature,' 1886; 'Saint Gregory's Guest,' 1886; 'Writings' (7 vols.), 1888-89; 'At Sundown,' 1892 (priv. ptd., 1890).

He *edited:* Harriet Martineau's 'Views of Slavery,' 1837; 'Letters from J. Q. Adams to his Constituents,' 1837; 'The North Star,' 1840; 'The Journal of John Woolman,' 1872; 'Child Life: a collection of poems,' 1873; 'Child Life in Prose,' 1874; 'Songs of Three Centuries,' 1876; 'Letters of L. M. Child,' 1883.

Life: by F. H. Underwood, 1884; 'Life and Letters,' by S. T. Pichard, 1895.

Collected Works: in 7 vols., 1888.

***WHYTE-MELVILLE (George John), 1821-1878.** Born, at Mount Melville, near St. Andrews, 1821. Educated at Eton. Entered army, 1839; Capt. in Coldstream Guards, 1846; retired, 1849. Served in Turkish army in Crimean War, 1855-56. Devoted himself to literature from 1856. Active patron of field sports. Died, from an accident in the hunting-field, in Gloucestershire, 5 Dec. 1878.

Works: 'Digby Grand,' 1853; 'Tilbury Nogo' (anon.), 1854; 'General Bounce,' 1855; 'Kate Coventry,' 1856; 'The Arab's Ride to Cairo' [1857?]; 'The Interpreter,' 1858; 'Holmby House,' 1860; 'Good for Nothing,' 1861; 'Market Harborough' (anon.), 1861; 'The Queen's Maries,' 1862; 'The Gladiators,' 1863; 'The Brookes of Bridlemere,' 1864; 'Cerise,' 1866; 'The White Rose,' 1868 [1867]; 'Bones and I,' 1868; 'M. or N.,' 1869; 'Songs and

Verses,' 1869 ; 'Contraband,' 1871 [1870] ; 'Sarchedon,' 1871 ; 'Satanella,' 1872 ; 'The True Cross,' 1873 ; 'Uncle John,' 1874 ; 'Katerfelto,' 1875 ; 'Sister Louise,' 1876 ; 'Rosine,' 1877 [1876] ; 'Roy's Wife,' 1878 ; 'Riding Recollections,' 1878. *Posthumous:* 'Black but Comely,' 1879.
He *translated :* Horace's ' Odes,' 1850.

WILKES (John), 1727-1797. Born, in Clerkenwell, 17 Oct. 1727. Early education at schools at Hertford and Thame. Afterwards at Leyden University. Returned to England, 1849. Married Miss Mead, Oct. 1749 ; separated from her soon afterwards. M.P. for Aylesbury, 1757-64. Edited (and wrote) 'The North Briton,' 1762-63. Expelled from House of Commons (for attack on the King in No. 45 of ' The North Briton '), 19 Jan. 1764. M.P. for Middlesex, 1768. Expelled from House for his part in the publication of a letter of Lord Weymouth's, 27 Jan. 1769. Re-elected M.P. for Middlesex, 16 Feb. 1769 ; re-expelled, 17 Feb. Re-elected, 16 March ; re-expelled, 17 March. Re-elected, 13 April ; unseated, 15 April. Alderman of Farringdon Without, 2 Jan. 1769. Sheriff, 1771. M.P. for Middlesex, 1774. Lord Mayor, 1774 ; Chamberlain of London, 1779-97. Died, in London, 25 Dec. 1797. Buried in South Audley Street Church.

Works : [Exclusive of separate speeches :] 'Observations on the Papers relative to the Rupture with Spain ' (anon.), 1762 ; 'The North Briton ' (2 vols.), 1763 ; 'An Essay on Woman ' (anon. ; priv. ptd.), 1763; ' Recherches sur l'origine du Despotisme Oriental,' 1763 ; 'The Present Crisis ' (anon.), 1764 ; 'Letter to the Worthy Electors of . . . Aylesbury,' 1764 ; ' Letter to a Noble Member of the Club in Albemarle Street,' 1764 ; ' Letter to . . . the Duke of Grafton ' anon.), 1767 (8th edn. same year) ; 'The History of England ' (only the Introduction ' pubd.), 1768 ; 'Ad-

dresses to the Gentlemen . . . of Middlesex,' 1769 ; 'A Letter to Sam Johnson, LL.D.' (anon.), 1770 ; 'Controversial Letters,' 1771 ; 'Speeches,' 1786.
Posthumous : 'Letters . . . to his Daughter ' (4 vols.), 1804 ; 'Correspondence,' ed. by J. Almon, 1805.
He *edited :* 'Catullus ' (priv. ptd.), 1788; 'Θεοφραστου Χαρακτηρες' Ηθικοι' (priv. ptd.), 1790 ; 'Supplement to the Miscellaneous Works of Mr. Gibbon,' 1796.
Life : by P. Fitzgerald, 1888.

WILSON (John), 1785-1854. Born, at Paisley, 18 May 1785. Studied at Glasgow Univ., 1797-1803. Matric. Magdalen Coll., Oxford, 26 May 1803; Newdigate Prize Poem, 1806 ; B.A., 1807 ; M.A., 1810. Student of Lincoln's Inn, 1806. Settled at Elleray, Windermere, 1807. Married Jane Penny, 11 May 1811 ; she died, 1837. Contrib. to ' Annual Register,' 1812. Called to Scottish Bar, 1815. In Edinburgh, 1815-17. Contrib. to ' Edinburgh Monthly Mag.,' 1817 ; to ' Edinburgh Review,' 1817. Literary editor, and contributor (under pseud. ' Christopher North ') to ' Blackwood's Mag.,' Oct. 1817 to Sept. 1852. Prof. of Moral Philosophy, Edinburgh Univ., 1820-51. Pres. of Edinburgh Philosophical Institution, 1847-54. Crown Pension, 1851. Died, in Edinburgh, 3 April 1854. Buried in Dean Cemetery, Edinburgh.

Works : 'The Isle of Palms,' 1812; ' The Magic Mirror,' 1812 ; 'The City of the Plague,' 1816 ; ' Lights and Shadows of Scottish Life ' (under pseud. ' Arthur Austin '), 1822 ; 'The Trials of Margaret Lindsay ' (anon.), 1823 ; 'The Foresters ' (anon.), 1825 ; ' Poetical and Dramatic Works ' (2 vols.), 1825 ; 'The Land of Burns ' (with R. Chambers ; 2 vols.), 1840 ; ' Blind Allan ' (anon.) [1840 ?] ; ' On the Genius and Character of Burns,' 1841 ; ' Recreations of Christopher North ' (from ' Blackwood ' ; 3 vols.), 1842 ; 'Noctes Ambrosianæ ' (from ' Blackwood ' ; anon.), 1843 ; Letter-press to ' Scotland Illustrated,' 1845 ;

'Specimens of the British Critics' (from 'Blackwood'; pubd. in Philadelphia), 1846.

Collected Works: ed. by Prof. Ferrier (12 vols.), 1855-58.

Life: by Mrs. Gordon, new edn., 1879.

WITHER (George), 1588 - 1667. Born, at Bentworth, Hants, 11 June 1588. Early education at a school at Colemore. Matric. Magdalen Coll., Oxford, 1604 [?]. Left Oxford after about three years. Imprisoned for libel, 1614. Student of Lincoln's Inn, 1615. Served as Captain in cavalry regiment under Charles I., 1639. Served in Parliamentary Army, 1642; obtained rank of Major. Governor of Farnham Castle, Oct. to Dec., 1642. J.P. for Hampshire, Surrey and Essex, 1642-58. Major-General of Forces in Surrey, 1643 [?]. Master of the Statute Office, 1655 [?]. Imprisoned for libel, March 1662 to 1665. Died, in London, 2 May 1667. Buried in the Savoy Church.

Works: 'Prince Henrie's Obsequies,' 1612; 'Epithalamia,' 1612; 'Abuses Stript and Whipt,' 1613; 'A Satyre, dedicated to His Most Excellent Majestie,' 1614; 'The Shepheards Hunting,' 1615; 'Fidelia,' 1617; 'A Preparation to the Psalter,' 1619; 'Workes,' 1620; 'Exercises upon the first Psalme,' 1620; 'The Songs of the Old Testament,' 1621; 'Wither's Motto,' 1621; 'Juvenilia,' 1622; 'Faire-Virtue,' 1622; 'The Hymnes and Songs of the Church,' 1623; 'The Scholler's Purgatory' [1625?]; 'Britain's Remembrance,' 1628; 'The Psalmes of David translated into Lyrick verse,' 1632; 'Collection of Emblemes,' 1634-35; 'Read and Wonder' (anon.; ascribed to Wither), 1641; 'Halelujah,' 1641; 'Campo-Musæ,' 1643; 'Se Defendendo' [1643]; 'Mercurius Rusticus' (anon.), 1643; 'The Speech without Doore,' 1644; 'The Two Incomparable Generalissimos,' 1644; 'Letters of Advice,' 1645 [1644]; 'Vox Pacifica,' 1645; 'The Great Assizes holden in Parnassus' (anon.), 1645; 'The

Speech without Doore defended,' 1646; 'Justiciarius Justificatus,' 1646; 'What Peace to the Wicked?' (anon.), 1646; 'Opobalsamum Anglicanum,' 1646; 'Major Wither's Disclaimer,' 1647; 'Carmen Expostulatorium,' 1647; 'Amygdala Britannica' (anon.), 1647; 'Prosopopœia Britannica,' 1648; 'Carmen Eucharisticon,' 1649; 'Respublica Anglicana,' 1650; 'The British Appeals,' 1651; 'Three Grains of Spiritual Frankincense,' 1651; 'The Dark Lantern,' 1653; 'Westrow Revived,' 1653; 'Vaticinum Casuale,' 1655; 'Rapture at the Protector's Recovery,' 1655; 'Three Private Meditations,' 1655; 'The Protector,' 1655; 'Boni Ominis Votum,' 1656; 'A Suddain Flash' (anon.), 1657; 'Salt upon Salt,' 1659; 'A Cordial Confection,' 1659; 'Epistolium Vagum-Prosa Metricum,' 1659; 'Petition and Narrative' [1659]; 'Furor Poeticus,' 1660; 'Speculum Speculativum,' 1660; 'Fides-Anglicana,' 1660; 'An Improvement of Imprisonment,' 1661; 'A Triple Paradox,' 1661; 'The Prisoner's Plea,' 1661; 'A Proclamation in the Name of the King of Kings,' 1662; 'Verses Intended to the King's Majesty,' 1662; 'Parallellogrammaton,' 1662; 'Tuba Pacifica,' 1664; 'A Memorandum to London,' 1665; 'Meditations upon the Lord's Prayer,' 1665; 'Echoes from the Sixth Trumpet' [1666]; 'Sighs for the Pitchers,' 1666; 'Vaticina Poetica,' 1666.

Posthumous: 'Divine Poems on the Ten Commandments,' ed. by his daughter, 1688.

He *translated:* Nemesius' 'The Nature of Man,' 1636.

Collected Works: 'Poems,' ed. by H. Morley, 1891.

WOLCOT (John), 1738-1819. Born, at Dodbrooke, Devonshire, 1738; baptized, 9 May. Educated at Kingsbridge Free School; at Bodmin Grammar School, and in France. For seven years assistant to his uncle, an apothecary in practice in Cornwall. M.D., Aberdeen, 1767. In Jamaica, practising **as** surgeon and physician,

1767-69. Returned to England, 1769. Ordained Deacon and Priest, 1769 ; returned to Jamaica. Vicar of Vere, Jamaica, 1772. Returned to England, Dec. 1772. Practised medicine in Truro, 1773-79. Settled in London, 1781. Prolific writer of satires, under pseudonym 'Peter Pindar.' Died, in London, 14 Jan. 1819. Buried in St. Paul's, Covent Garden.

Works : 'Persian Love Elegies,' 1773 ; [*the following all pubd. under pseud.* ' Peter Pindar :*] 'A Poetical . . . Epistle to the Reviewers,' 1778 ; 'Poems on various Subjects,' 1778 ; 'Lyric Odes to the Royal Academicians,' 1782 ; 'More Lyric Odes to the Royal Academicians,' 1783 ; 'Lyric Odes for the Year,' 1785 ; 'The Lousiad,' 1785-95 ; 'Farewell Odes,' 1786 ; 'A Poetical and Congratulatory Epistle to James Boswell,' 1786 ; 'Bozzy and Piozzi,' 1786 ; 'Ode upon Ode,' 1787 ; 'An Apologetic Postscript to "Ode upon Ode,"' 1787; 'Congratulatory Epistle to Peter Pindar,' 1787 ; 'Instructions to a Celebrated Laureat,' 1787 ; 'Brother Peter to Brother Tom,' 1788; 'Peter's Pension,' 1788 ; 'Sir Joseph Banks and the Emperor of Morocco,' 1788; 'Epistle to his pretended Cousin Peter,' 1788 ; 'The King's Ode' (anon.), 1788 ; 'Peter's Prophecy,' 1788 ; 'Lyric Odes to the Academicians,' 1789 ; 'Subjects for Painters,' 1789 ; 'A Poetical Epistle to a Falling Minister,' 1789 ; 'Expostulatory Odes,' 1789 ; 'Works' (2 vols.), 1789-92 ; ، 'A Benevolent Epistle to Sylvanus Urban,' 1790 ; 'Advice to the Future Laureat,' 1790 ; 'Letter to the Most Insolent Man alive,' 1790 ; 'Complimentary Epistle to James Bruce,' 1790 ; 'The Rights of Kings,' 1791 ; 'Odes to Mr. Paine,' 1791 ; 'The Remonstrance,' 1791 ; 'A Commiserating Epistle to G. Lowther,' 1791 ; 'More Money,' 1792; 'The Tears of St. Margaret,' 1792 ; 'Odes of Importance,' 1792 ; 'Odes to Kien Long,' 1792 ; 'A Pair of Lyric Epistles,' 1792 ; 'A Poetical . . . Epistle to the Pope,' 1793 ; 'Pathetic Odes,' 1794 ; 'Pindariana,' 1794 ; 'Celebration ; or, the Aca-

demic Procession to St. James's,' 1794 ; 'Works' (4 vols.), 1794-96 ; 'Hair-Powder,' 1795 ; 'The Convention Bill,' 1795 ; 'The Cap,' 1795 ; 'The Royal Visit to Exeter,' 1795 ; 'Liberty's Last Squeak,' 1795 ; 'The Royal Tom,' 1795 ; 'An Admirable Satire on Burke's Defence of his Pension,' 1796 ; 'One Thousand, Seven Hundred, and Ninety-six,' 1797 ; 'An Ode to the Livery of London,' 1797 ; 'Tales of the Hoy' [1798] ; 'Nil Admirari,' 1799 ; 'Lord Auckland's Triumph,'1800; 'Out at Last,'1801; 'Odes to Inns and Outs,' 1801 ; 'A Poetical Epistle to Benjamin, Count Rumford,' 1801; 'Tears and Smiles,' 1801 ; 'The Island of Innocence,' 1802 ; 'Pitt and his Statue,' 1802 ; 'The Middlesex Election,' 1802 ; 'The Horrors of Bribery,' 1802 ; 'Great Cry and Little Wool,' 1804 ; 'An Instructive Epistle to the Lord Mayor,' 1804 ; 'Tristia,' 1806 ; 'One More Peep at the Royal Academy,' 1808 ; 'The Fall of Portugal,' 1808 ; 'Works' (4 vols.),1809 ; 'Carlton House Fête,' 1811 ; 'Works' (5 vols.), 1812 ; 'An Address to be spoken at the Opening of Drury-Lane Theatre' (anon.),1813 ; 'Royalty Fog-bound,' 1814 ; 'The Regent and the King,' 1814 ; 'Midnight Dreams,' 1814 ; 'Tom Halliard,' [1815 ?].

He *edited :* Pilkington's 'Dictionary of Painters,' 1799 ; 'The Beauties of English Poetry,' 1804.

WOLFE (Charles), 1791 - 1823. Born, in Dublin, 14 Dec. 1791. At school at Bath, 1801 ; at Salisbury, 1803-05 ; at Winchester Coll., 1806-09. To Dublin Univ., 1809 ; scholar, 1812 ; B.A., 1814. Ordained, Nov. 1817. Curate of Ballyclog, Tyrone, Dec. 1817 to Jan. 1818 ; of Castle Caulfield, Donoughmore, 1818-21. Ill-health from 1821. Died, at Cove of Cork, 21 Feb. 1823.

Works : 'The Burial of Sir John Moore ; with other poems,' 1825 ; 'Remains,' ed. by J. A. Russell, with *memoir* (2 vols.), 1825.

WOLLSTONECRAFT (Mary). *See* Godwin.

WOOD (Anthony à), 1632 - 1695.
Born, at Oxford, 17 Dec. 1632. Early
education at New College School,
1641-44 ; at Thame Free School, 1644-
46. Matric. Merton Coll., Oxford, 26
May 1647 ; Postmaster, Oct. 1647 ;
Bible-clerk, 1650 ; B.A., 6 July 1652 ;
M.A., 17 Dec. 1655. Devoted him-
self to study of antiquities. Prose-
cuted for alleged libel on Earl of
Clarendon in 'Athenæ Oxonienses,'
1693 ; expelled from university.
Died, at Oxford, 29 Nov. 1695.
Buried in Merton College Chapel.

Works : 'Historia et Antiquitates
Universitatis Oxoniensis,' 1674 (English version, 1786) ; 'Athenæ Oxonienses' (2 vols.; anon.), 1691-92.
Posthumous : 'Modius Salium,'
1751 ; 'The Life and Times of Anthony Wood . . . described by himself,' ed. by A. Clark (for Oxford
Hist. Soc. ; 4 vols.), 1891-95.
He *edited :* E. Wood's 'Γνωστον του
Θεου,' 1656.
Life : T. R. Rawlinson, 1711 ; 'Life
and Times,' 1891-95 (*see above*).

WOOD (Mrs. Henry), 1814-1887.
Born [Ellen Price], at Worcester, 17
Jan. 1814 ; early life spent there.
Married Henry Wood [1830 ?]. Lived
abroad till 1860. Edited 'The Ar-
gosy' (with C. W. Wood), 1865-87.
Frequent contributor to periodicals.
Died, in London, 10 Feb. 1887.
Buried in Highgate Cemetery.

Works : 'Danesbury House,' 1860 ;
'East Lynne,' 1861 ; 'The Chan-
nings,' 1862 ; 'Mrs. Halliburton's
Troubles,' 1862 ; 'The Foggy Night
at Oxford,' 1863 [1862]; 'Verner's
Pride,' 1863 ; 'The Shadow of Ashly-
dyat,' 1863 ; 'William Allair,' 1864
[1863]; 'Lord Oakburn's Daughters,'
1864 ; 'Trevlyn Hold' (anon.), 1864 ;
'Oswald Cray,' 1864 ; 'Mildred Ar-
kell,' 1865 ; 'St. Martin's Eve,' 1866 ;
'Elster's Folly,' 1866 ; 'A Life's
Secret,' 1867 ; 'Lady Adelaide's Oath,'
1867 ; 'Orville College,' 1867 ; 'The
Red Court Farm,' 1868 ; 'Anne Hereford,' 1868 ; 'Roland Yorke,' 1869 ;
'George Canterbury's Will,' 1870 ;
'Bessy Rane,' 1870 ; 'Dene Hollow,'

1871 ; 'Within the Maze,' 1872
'The Master of Greylands,' 1873 ;
'Johnny Ludlow' (from the 'Argosy'),
1st series, 1874 ; 2nd series, 1880 ;
'Told in the Twilight,' 1875 ; 'Bessy
Wells,' 1875 ; 'Adam Grainger,' 1876;
'Our Children,' 1876 ; 'Parkwater,'
1876 ; 'Edina,' 1876 ; 'Pomeroy
Abbey,' 1878 ; 'Court Netherleigh,'
1881 ; 'About Ourselves,' 1883 ;
'Lady Grace,' 1887.
Posthumous : 'The Story of Charles
Strange,' 1888 ; 'The House of Halli-
well,' 1890 ; 'Summer Stories from
the "Argosy"' (by Mrs. Wood and
others), 1890 ; 'The Unholy Wish,'
1890 ; 'Ashley,' 1897.
Life : by C. W. Wood, 1894.

*WOODS (Mrs. Margaret Louisa),
b. 1856. Born [Margaret Louisa
Bradley], at Rugby, 1856. Educated
at home, and at a school at Leaming-
ton. Married Rev. Henry George
Woods, 1879.
Works : 'A Village Tragedy,' 1887
'Lyrics' (priv. ptd.), 1888 ; 'Lyrics
and Ballads,' 1889 ; 'Esther Vanhomrigh,' 1891 ; 'The Vagabonds,'
1894 ; 'Aëromancy, and other poems,'
1896 ; 'Songs' (priv. ptd.), 1896 ;
'Wild Justice,' 1896.

WORDSWORTH (William), 1770-
1850. Born, at Cockermouth, Cumberland, 7 April 1770. Early education at Hawkshead Grammar School,
1778-87. Matric. St. John's Coll.,
Camb., Oct. 1787 ; B.A., 1791.
Travelled on Continent, July to Oct.,
1790. Visited Paris, Nov. 1791.
Settled with his sister near Crewkerne,
Dorsetshire, autumn of 1795. First
visit from Coleridge, June 1797. Removed to Alfoxden, Nether Stowey,
Somersetshire, July 1797. Friendship
with Charles Lamb and Hazlitt begun.
In Bristol, 1798. In Germany, Sept.
1798 to July 1799. Settled at Grasmere, Dec. 1799. Visit to France,
July to Aug. 1802. Married Mary
Hutchinson, 4 Oct. 1802. Friendship
with Scott and Southey begun, 1803.
Removed to Coleorton, Leicestershire,
1806. Returned to Grasmere, 1808.
Contrib. to 'The Friend,' 1810. Re-

moved to Rydal Mount, spring of 1813. Distributor of stamps for Westmoreland, March 1813 to 1842. Visits to Continent, 1820, 1823, 1828, 1837. Hon. D.C.L., Durham, 1838. Hon. D.C.L., Oxford, 12 June 1839. Crown Pension, 1842. Poet Laureate, 1843. Died, at Rydal Mount, 23 April 1850. Buried in Grasmere Churchyard.

Works: ' An Evening Walk,' 1793 ; ' Descriptive Sketches in Verse,' 1793 ; 'Lyrical Ballads, with a few other Poems ' (2 vols.), 1798-1800 ; ' Poems' (2 vols.), 1807 ; ' On the Relations of Great Britain, Spain, and Portugal to each other,' 1809 ; ' The Excursion,' 1814 ; ' The White Doe of Rylstone,' 1815 ; ' Poems' (3 vols.), 1815-20 ; ' Thanksgiving Ode,' 1816 ; ' Letter to a Friend of Robert Burns,' 1816 ; ' Peter Bell,' 1819 ; ' The Waggoner,' 1819 ; ' The River Duddon,' 1820 ; ' The Little Maid and the Gentleman ; or, We are Seven ' (anon.), [1820?] ; ' Memorials of a Tour on the Continent,' 1822 ; ' Ecclesiastical Sketches,' 1822 ; ' Description of the Scenery of the Lakes in the North of England,' 1822 ; ' Yarrow Revisited,' 1835 ; ' Sonnets,' 1838 ; ' Poems,' 1842 ; ' Poems on the Loss and Rebuilding of St. Mary's Church,' by W. Wordsworth, J. Montgomery, and others, 1842 ; ' Ode on the Installation of Prince Albert at Cambridge ' [1847] ; ' The Prelude,' 1850.

Collected Works: ' Poetical Works,' ed. by E. Dowden (7 vols.), 1892 93 ; ' Prose Works,' ed. by W. Knight (2 vols.), 1896

Life: by C. Wordsworth, 1851 ; by E. P. Hood, 1856 ; by J. M. Sutherland, 2nd. edn., 1892.

WOTTON (*Sir* Henry), 1568-1639.

Born, at Boughton Malherbe, Kent, 30 March 1568. Early education at Winchester Coll. Matric. New Coll., Oxford, 5 June 1584. Removed to Queen's Coll. ; B.A., 8 June 1588 Travelled on Continent. 1588-95. Student of Middle Temple, 1595. Sec. to Earl of Essex, 1595-1601. In Italy, 1601-03. Knighted, 1603. M.P. for Appleby, 1614 ; for Sandwich,

1625. Served on various embassies abroad. Provost of Eton, 1624-39. Died, at Eton, Dec. 1639. Buried there.

Works: 'The Elements of Architecture,' 1604 ; ' Epistola ad Marcum Velserum Duumvirum,' 1612 ; ' Epistola de Caspare Scioppio,' 1613 ; ' Ad Regem e Scotia reducem . . . Plausus,' 1633.

Posthumous: ' Parallel between Robert, late Earl of Essex, and George, late Duke of Buckingham,' 1641 ; ' Short View of the Life and Death of George Villiers, Duke of Buckingham,' 1642 ; ' A Panegyrick of King Charles,' 1649 ; ' Reliquiæ Wottonianæ,' ed. by Izaak Walton, 1651 ; ' The State of Christendom,' 1657 ; ' Letters to Sir Edmund Baker,' 1661 ; ' Letters to the Lord Zouch,' 1685.

Collected Works: ' Poems,' ed. by A. Dyce, 1843.

WYATT (*Sir* Thomas), 1503-1542.

Born, at Allington Castle, Kent, 1503. Matric. St. John's Coll., Camb., 1515 ; B.A., 1518 ; M.A., 1520. Married Hon. Elizabeth Brooke, 1520 [?] In favour at Court of Henry VIII. Clerk of King's Jewels, Oct. 1524 to May 1531. On embassy to France, 1526. Marshal of Calais Castle, 1529-30. Commissioner of Peace for Essex, 1532. Imprisoned in Tower at time of Anne Boleyn's trial, spring of 1536 ; released soon afterwards. Knighted, 1537 [?]. Ambassador in Spain, June 1537 to June 1539. On embassy in France and Holland, Nov. 1539 to May 1540. Imprisoned in Tower on charge of high treason, 1541 ; tried and acquitted, June 1541. Grant of land from King, July 1541. High Steward of Manor of Maidstone, 1542. Died, at Sherborne, 11 Oct. 1542. Buried in Sherborne Church.

Works: Poems in the Earl of Surrey's ' Songs and Sonnets,' 1567 ; ' Poetical Works,' ed. by R. Bell, 1854 ; ed by G. Gilfillan, 1858. *Life:* by W. S. Simonds (Boston), 1889.

**WYCHERLEY (William), 1640-
1715.** Born, in London, 1640. Edu-
cated in France, 1655. Became a
Roman Catholic. Abjured Church
of Rome, and matriculated at Queen's
Coll., Oxford. Took no degree.
Student of Inner Temple, 1659. Served
in Army during war with Holland.
Play, 'Love in a Wood,' pro-
duced at Drury Lane, 1671 ; 'The
Gentleman Dancing Master.' Dorset
Gardens Theatre, Jan. 1672 ; 'The
Country Wife.' Lincoln's Inn Fields
Theatre, 1673 [?] ; 'The Plain Dealer,'
Lincoln's Inn Fields Theatre, 1674.
Married (i.) Countess of Drogheda,
1678 [?]. After her death was im-
prisoned for seven years in the Fleet
for debt. Debts paid by James II ,
who gave him a pension of £200.
Friendship with Pope begun, 1704.
Married (ii.) Miss Jackson, Nov. 1715.
Died, in London, Dec. 1715. Buried
in St. Paul's, Covent Garden.

Works : 'Love in a Wood.' 1672 ;
'The Gentleman Dancing Master,'
1673 : 'The Country Wife,' 1675 ;
'The Plain Dealer.' 1677 ; 'Epistles
to the King and Duke' (anon.), 1682 ;
'Miscellany Poems,' 1704 ; 'Works,'
1713.
Posthumous : 'Posthumous Works,'
ed. by L. Theobald, 1728.
Collected Works : 'Plays, etc.' (2
vols.), 1720.

WYCLIF (John), 1320-1384. Born,
1320[?]. Educated at Oxford. Fellow,
and afterwards Master, of Balliol
Coll. Rector of Fillingham, 1361-69 ;
Rector of Ludgershall, 1369-74. D.D.,
Oxford, 1370. Rector of Lutterworth,
1374-84. Attended conference with
Papal Legates at Bruges, 1375.
Accused of heresy, 1377 and 1378.
Forbidden to lecture at Oxford, 1381.
Again accused of heresy, 1382. En-
gaged on English translation of Bible,
from 1382. Died, at Lutterworth, 31
Dec. 1384. Buried there.

Works : Wyclif's translation of the
Bible was published complete, ed. by
J. Forshall and Sir F. Madden (4
vols.), 1850 ; 'Select English Works,'
ed. by T. Arnold (3 vols.), 1869-71 ;
'English Works hitherto unprinted,'
ed. by F. D. Matthew, 1880.
Life : by L. Sergeant, 1893.

**YATES (Edmund Hodgson), 1831-
1894.** Born, in Edinburgh, 3 July
1831. Educated at Highgate School,
1840-46. At Düsseldorf, 1846-47.
Held appointment in Post - Office,
1847-72. Contrib. to 'Court Journal,'
'Keepsake,' 'Illustrated London News,'
etc., from 1852. Married, 14 April
1853. Dramatic Critic to 'Daily News,'
1855-61. Edited 'The Comic Times,'
Aug. to Nov. 1855 ; 'The Train,' Jan.
1856 to June 1858 ; 'Temple Bar,'
1860-67 ; 'Tinsley's Mag.,' 1867.
Frequent contributor to periodicals.
Lectured in U.S.A., 1872-73. Special
correspondent to 'New York Herald,'
1873-75. Founded 'The World' (with
Grenville Murray), 1874 ; edited it till
his death. Imprisoned for libel pubd.
in 'The World,' 1884. Edited 'Time,'
1879-84 ; 'Groombridge's Mag.,' 1891.
Died, in London, 20 May 1894.

Works : 'My Haunts and their
Frequenters,' 1854 ; 'Mirth and Metre'
(with F. E. Smedley), 1855 ; 'Mr.
Thackeray, Mr. Yates, and the Garrick
Club' (priv. ptd.), 1859 ; 'After Office
Hours' [1861] ; 'For Better, For
Worse,' 1864 ; 'Broken to Harness,'
1864 ; 'Pages in Waiting' (from
'Temple Bar '), 1865 ; 'The Business
of Pleasure ' (2 vols.), 1865 ; 'Running
the Gauntlet,' 1865 ; 'Land at Last,'
1866 ; 'Kissing the Rod,' 1866 ; 'The
Forlorn Hope,' 1867 ; 'Black Sheep,'
1867 ; 'The Rock Ahead,' 1868 ;
'Wrecked in Port,' 1869 ; 'A Righted
Wrong,' 1870 ; 'Dr. Wainwright's
Patient,' 1871 ; 'Nobody's Fortune,'
1872 ; 'Castaway,' 1872 ; 'A Waiting
Race,' 1872 ; 'The Yellow Flag,'
1872 ; 'Two by Tricks,' 1874 ; 'The
Impending Sword,' 1874 ; 'A Silent
Witness,' 1875 ; 'Recollections and
Experiences ' (2 vols.), 1884. [Three
Farces ('My friend from Leatherhead,'
'A Night at Notting Hill,' 'Hit
Him !') written with N. H. Harring-
ton, printed in Lacy's Acting Edition
of Plays, vols. 29, 30, 47.]

He *edited :* 'Our Miscellany' (with R. B. Brough), 1855 ; Mrs. Mathews' 'L'fe and Correspondence of Charles Mathews,' 1860 ; Mortimer Collins's 'Thoughts in my Garden,' 1880.

*YEATS (William Butler), b. 1865. Born, at Sandymount, Dublin, 13 June 1865. Educated at school at Hammersmith, 1874-80 ; in Dublin 1880-84. Studied Art, 1883-86 ; but eventually adopted literary career. Contrib. to 'Dublin Univ. Rev.,' and other periodicals, from 1886. To London, 1888. Contrib. to 'National Observer,' 'Bookman,' etc. One of Founders of Irish Lit. Soc., and of Nat. Lit. Soc. of Dublin.

Works : 'The Wanderings of Oisin,' 1889 ; 'The Countess Kathleen,' 1892; 'The Celtic Twilight,' 1893 ; 'The Land of Heart's Desire,' 1894 ; 'Poems,' 1895 ; 'The Secret Rose,' 1897.

He has *edited :* 'Fairy and Folk Tales of the Irish Peasantry,' 1888 ; 'Stories from Carleton' [1889]; 'Irish Fairy Tales,' 1892 ; Blake's 'Poems' (with E. J. Ellis), 1893.

*YONGE (Charlotte Mary), b. 1823. Born, at Otterbourne, Hampshire, 11 Aug. 1823. First literary publication, about 1846. Edited 'Monthly Packet,' 1851-93. Has resided all her life at Otterbourne.

Works : Miss Yonge's Works number upwards of 150. A collected edition of her 'Novels and Tales' was begun in 1879. Among the best known of her separate publications are : 'The Two Guardians,' 1852 ; 'Landmarks of History' (Ancient, Middle Ages, Modern), 3 pts., 1852, 1853, 1857 ; 'The Heir of Redclyffe,' 1853 ; 'The Daisy Chain,' 1856 ; 'Hopes and Fears,' 1860 ; 'Life of J. C. Patteson,' 1874 [1873] ; 'Aunt Charlotte's Stories of English History,' 1873, 'of Greek History,' 1876, 'of Roman History,' 1877, 'of German History,' 1878 ; 'The Armourer's Prentices,' 1884 ; 'A Modern Telemachus' 1886 ; 'The Victorian Half-Century,' 1886 ; 'Under the Storm,'

1887 ; 'Our New Mistress,' 1888 ; 'Life of H.R.H. the Prince Consort,' 1890 [1889] ; 'Slaves of Sabinus.' 1890 : 'Countess Kate,' 1892 ; 'An Old Woman's Outlook on a Hampshire Village,' 1892 ; 'The Long Vacation,' 1895 ; 'The Cook and the Captive,' 1895 ; 'The Wardship of Steepcombe,' 1896 ; 'The Carbonels,' 1896 ; 'The Release,' 1896 ; 'The Pilgrimage of the Ben Beriah,' 1897.

YOUNG (Edward), 1683-1765. Born, at Upham, Hants, June 1683. At Winchester School, 1694-99. Matric. New Coll., Oxford, 3 Oct. 1702. Soon afterwards removed to Corpus Christi Coll. Law Fellowship, All Souls' Coll., 1706 ; B.C.L., 23 April 1714 ; D.C.L., 10 June 1719. Tutor to Lord Burleigh, for a short time before 1719. Play 'Busiris' produced at Drury Lane, Mar h 1719 ; 'The Brothers,' Drury Lane, 1753. Ordained, 1727 ; Chaplain to George II., April 1728; Rector of Welwyn. Herts, 1730-65. Married Lady Elizabeth Leigh, 27 May 1731. Clerk of Closet to Princess Dowager, 1761. Died, at Welwyn, 5 April 1765. Buried there.

Works : 'Epistle to . . . Lord Lansdown,' 1713 ; 'A Poem on the Lord's Day,' 1713 (2nd edn. same year) ; 'The Force of Religion,' 1714 ; 'On the Late Queen's Death,' 1714 ; 'Oratio habita in Coll. Omnium Animarum,' 1716 ; 'Paraphrase on part of the Book of Job,' 1719 ; 'Busiris,' 1719 : 'Letter to Mr. Tickell,' 1719 ; 'The Revenge,' 1721 ; 'The Universal Passion' (6 pts. : anon.), 1725-28 ; 'The Instalment,' 1726 ; 'Cynthio' (anon.), 1727 ; 'Ocean,' 1728 ; 'A Vindication of Providence,' 1728 (2nd edn. same year) ; 'An Apology for Princes,' 1729 ; 'Imperium Pelagi' (anon.), 1730 ; 'Two Epistles to Mr. Pope' (anon.), 1730 ; 'The Sea-Piece,' 1730 ; 'The Foreign Address,' 1734 ; 'Poetical Works' (2 vols.), 1741 ; 'The Complaint ; or, Night Thoughts on Life, Death, and Immortality' (anon, ; 9 pts.), 1742-46 ; 'The Consolation' (anon.), 1745 ; 'Reflections

20—2

on the Public Situation of the Kingdom,' 1745 ; 'The Brothers' (anon.), 1753 ; 'The Centaur not Fabulous' (anon.), 1755 ; 'An Argument drawn from the circumstances of Christ's Death,' 1758 ; 'Conjectures on Original Composition' (anon.), 1759 (2nd edn. same year) ; 'Resignation' (anon.), 1762 ; 'Works' (4 vols.), 1764.

Posthumous: 'The Merchant,' 1771.

Collected Works: 'Complete Works,' ed. by Dr. Doran (2 vols.), 1854.

APPENDIX

APPENDIX

A'BECKETT (Arthur William), b. 1844. [*See* p. 1.]

Add : Called to Bar at Gray's Inn, 1882. Mem. of Council, Inst. of Journalists, 1896. Editor of ' John Bull,' 1903. Captain (retired) in Militia. Metropolitan Police Magistrate.

Works : ' Comic Guide to the Royal Academy ' (with his brother Gilbert), 1863-64 ; ' The Ghost of Greystone Grange,' 1878 ; ' The Member for Wrottenburgh,' 1895 ; ' The Modern Adam,' 1899 ; ' London at the End of the Century,' 1900 ; ' John Bull Handbook,' 1903.

A'BECKETT (Gilbert Arthur), 1837-1891. [*See* p. 1.]

Add : ' Comic Guide to the Royal Academy ' (with his brother Arthur William), 1863-64.

ACTON (John Emerich Edward Dalberg), Baron Acton, 1834-1902. [*See* p. 2.]

Add : to date of birth, 10 Jan. Created K.C.V.O., 1897. Planned scheme of ' Cambridge Modern History,' of which vol. i appeared in 1902. Died, at Tegernsee, Bavaria, 19 June, 1902.

AINSWORTH (William Harrison), 1805-1882. [*See* p. 3.]

Add : Memoir, by W. E. A. Axon, 1902.

ALDRICH (Thomas Bailey), b. 1836. Born, at Portsmouth, N.H., 11 Nov. 1836. In banking house in New York, 1852-55. On staff of ' New York Evg. Mirror,' ' Willis's Home Journal,' and ' Illustrated News,' 1855-65. Contrib. to ' Putnam's Mag.' and ' Knickerbocker Mag.' Editor of ' Every Saturday,' 1865-74 ; of ' Atlantic Monthly,' 1881-90.

Works : ' The Bells ' (under initials T.B.A.), 1855 ; ' The Ballad of Babie Bell,' 1856 ; ' Daisy's Necklace,' 1857 ; ' The Course of True

Love never did run Smooth,' 1858 ; ' Pampinea,' 1861 ; ' Out of his Head,' 1862 ; ' Poems ' (2 series), 1863, 1865 ; ' The Story of a Bad Boy,' 1869 ; ' Marjorie Daw,' 1873 ; ' Cloth of Gold,' 1874 ; ' Prudence Palfry,' 1874 ; ' Flower and Thorn,' 1876 ; ' Miss Mehitabel's Son,' 1877 ; ' Rivermouth Romance,' 1877 ; ' The Queen of Sheba,' 1877 ; ' The Stillwater Tragedy,' 1880 ; ' Collected Poems,' 1882 ; ' Mercedes,' 1883 ; ' From Ponkapog to Pest,' 1883 ; ' Wyndham Towers,' 1889 ; ' The Sisters' Tragedy,' 1891 ; ' An Old Town by the Sea,' 1893 ; ' Two Bites at a Cherry,' 1894 ; ' Unguarded Gates,' 1895 ; ' Judith and Holofernes,' 1896 ; ' A Sea Turn, and other Matters,' 1902.

He has *edited :* Herrick's Poems, 1900.

ALLEN (Charles Grant Blairfindie), 1848-1899. [*See* p. 6.]

Add : Died, at Hindhead, 25 Oct. 1899.

Add to ' *Works* ' : ' The Sole Trustee ' [1886] ; ' An Army Doctor's Romance,' 1893 ; ' Historical Guides' to Florence, Paris, Cities of Belgium, 1897, to Venice, 1898 ; ' The Type-Writer Girl ' (under pseud. ' Olive Pratt Rayner '), 1897 ; ' An African Millionaire,' 1897 ; ' Tom, Unlimited ' (under pseud. ' Martin Leach Warborough '), 1897 ; ' The Evolution of the Idea of God,' 1897; ' The Incidental Bishop,' 1898 ; ' Linnet,' 1898 ; ' The European Tour,' 1899 ; ' Flashlights on Nature,' 1899 ; ' Miss Cayley's Adventures,' 1899 ; ' Rosalba ' (under pseud. ' Olive Pratt Rayner '), 1899 ; ' Twelve Tales,' 1899.

Posthumous : ' Hilda Wade ' (from ' Strand Mag.'), 1900 ; ' County and Town in England,' 1901 ; ' In Nature's Workshop,' 1901 ; ' Sir Theodore's Guest,' 1902.

He *edited* : Buckle's Works, 1885 ;
J. Runciman's 'Side Lights,' 1893 ;
White's ' Natural History of Sel-
borne,' 1900.

Memoir : by E. Clodd, 1900.

ANSTEY (F.). See‚ GUTHRIE
(Thomas Anstey).

ARCHER (William), b. 1856. [*See*
p. 8.]

Add : 'Study and Stage,' 1899 ;
'America To-day,' 1900 ; 'Poets of
the Younger Generation,' 1902.

Has *edited* : Brandes' 'Henrik
Ibsen,' 1899; and *translated* : Ibsen's
'John Gabriel Borkman,' 1897 ;
Brandes' ' William Shakespeare,'
1898 ; Brögger and Rolfsen's 'Frid-
tiof Nansen,' 1899 ; Maeterlinck's
'Interior,' 1899 ; Ibsen's ' When We
Dead Awaken,' 1900.

ARNOLD (Sir Edwin), b. 1832.
[*See* p. 8.]

Add : Order of Lion and Sun,
Persia, 1893. Married : (i) Katherine Elizabeth Biddulph, 1854 ; she
died, 1864 ; (ii) Fannie Maria Adelaide Channing ; she died, 1889 ;
(iii) Kurokawa Tama, 1897.

Add to ' *Works* ' : 'The Queen's
Justice,' 1899 ; 'The Voyage of
Ithobal,' 1901.

Has *translated* : Sa'di's 'Gulistan ;
Babs. i-iv,' 1899.

ARNOLD (Matthew), 1822-1888.
[*See* p. 9.]

Add : ' Notebooks,' ed. by Mrs.
Wodehouse, 1902.

Memoirs : by H. W. Paul (' Men
of Letters ' series), 1902 ; by G. E. B.
Saintsbury, 1902 ; by W. C. Brownell,
1902.

ASHBY-STERRY (Joseph). Born
in London.   Privately educated.
First studied painting ; contributed
drawings to ' Punch ' and other
periodicals. Eventually gave up art
for literature. On staff of 'Graphic.'

Works : ' Shuttlecock Papers,'
1873 ; ' Tiny Travels,' 1874 ; ' Bou-
doir Ballads,' 1876 ; ' A Snailway
Guide to Tunbridge Wells,' 1884 ;
' The Lazy Minstrel,' 1886 ; ' Cu-

cumber Chronicles,' 1887 ; ' Nutshell
Novels,' 1891 ; ' A Naughty Girl,'
1893 ; ' A Tale of the Thames,' 1896 ;
' The Bystander,' 1901.

ATHERTON (Gertrude Franklin).
Born [Gertrude Franklin Horn],
at San Francisco.   Educated in California and Kentucky.   Married to
G. H. Bowen Atherton.   Of recent
years has lived much in Europe.

Works : ' Hermia Suydam,' 1889 ;
' What Dreams may Come,' 1889 ;
' Los Cerritos,' 1890 ; ' A Question of
Time,' 1892 ; 'The Doomswoman,'
1892 ; ' Before the Gringo came,'
1894 ; ' A Whirl Asunder,' 1895 ;
' Patience Sparhawk,' 1897 ; ' His
Fortunate Grace,' 1897 ; ' American
Wives and English Husbands,' 1898 ;
' The Californians,' 1898 ; ' The Vali-
ant Runaways,' 1898 ; ' A Daughter
of the Vine,' 1899 ; ' Senator North,'
1900 ; ' The Conqueror,' 1902 ; ' The
Splendid Idle Forties,' 1902.

Has *edited* : 'A few of Hamilton's
Letters,' 1903.

AUSTIN (Alfred), *Poet Laureate,* **b.
1835.** [*See* p. 12.]

Add : Married Hester Mulock, 1865.
Play, ' Flodden Field,' prod. at His
Majesty's theatre, 8 June 1903.

Add to ' *Works* ' : ' The Conversion
of Winckelmann,' 1897 ; ' Victoria,'
1897 ; ' Songs of England,' 1898 ;
' Lamia's Winter Quarters,' 1898 ;
' Spring and Autumn in Ireland,'
1900 ; ' Polyphemus,' 1901 ; ' Haunts
of Ancient Peace,' 1902 ; ' A Tale of
True Love,' 1902 ; ' Flodden Field,'
1903.

AVEBURY, Baron. *See* LUBBOCK.

BAILEY (Philip James), 1816-1902.
[*See* p. 14.]

Add : Died, at Nottingham, 6 Sept.
1902.

BAIN (Alexander), 1818-1903.
Born, in Aberdeen, 11 June 1818.
Educated at Marischal Coll.   Contrib. at early age to ' Westminster
Rev.,' thereby beginning friendship with J. S. Mill.   Deputy-Prof.
of Moral Philosophy, Aberdeen,

1841-44. Prof. of Mathematics and Natural Philosophy, Andersonian Univ., Glasgow, 1845-46. Devoted much time to literature. Held post in Board of Trade, London, 1848-60. Married (i) Frances Ann Wilkinson, 1855 (she died 1892) ; (ii) Barbara Forbes, 1893. Prof. of Logic and English Lit., Aberdeen Univ., 1860-80; Lord Rector, 1881-87. Hon. LL.D., Edinburgh Univ., 1871. Founded periodical called 'Mind,' 1876, and remained proprietor till 1891. Actively interested in questions of public education. Died, in Aberdeen, 18 Sept. 1903.

Works: 'On the applications of Science to Human Health,' 1848 ; 'The Senses and the Intellect,'1855 ; 'The Emotions and the Will,' 1859 ; 'On the Study of Character,' 1861 ; 'English Grammar,' 1863 ; 'English Composition and Rhetoric,'1866 (enlarged edn., 2 vols., 1887-88) ; 'Mental and Moral Science' (2 pt.), 1868-72 ; 'Logic,' 1870 ; 'First English Grammar,' 1872 ; 'Mind and Body,' 1873 ; 'Companion to the Higher Grammar,' 1874 ; 'Education as a Science,' 1879 ; 'Rectorial Address, Aberdeen Univ.,' 1832; 'James Mill,' 1882 ; 'John Stuart Mill,' 1882 ; 'Practical Essays,' 1884 ; 'On Teaching English,' 1887 ; 'Dissertations on leading Philosophical Topics,' 1903.

He *edited:* J. Mill's 'Analysis of the Phenomena of the Human Mind,' 1869; Grote's 'Aristotle,' 1872; Grote's 'Minor Works,' 1873; Grote's 'Fragments on Ethical Subjects,' 1876 ; N. Arnott's 'Elements of Physics,' 1876 ; G. C. Robertson's 'Philosophical Remains,' 1894.

BANCROFT (George), 1800-1891. Born, at Worcester, Mass., 3 Oct. 1800. At Harvard Coll., 1813-17. Studied in Germany, 1818-21 ; Ph.D., Gottingen, 1820. Greek Tutor at Harvard, 1822-23. Kept school at Northampton, 1823-30. Began working on his 'History of the United States' while there. Contrib.

to 'North American Rev.' and 'American Quarterly,' from 1823. Married (i) Sarah H. Dwight, 1827 ; she died, 1837 ; (ii) Mrs. Elizabeth Bliss, 1838. Collector of Port of Boston, 1838-41. Secretary of Navy, 1845-46. U.S. Ambassador to Great Britain, 1846-49 ; to Prussia, 1867 ; to N. German Confederation, 1868 ; to German Empire, 1871-74. Hon. D.C.L., Oxford, 1849; Dr. Jur., Bonn, 1868. In latter years resided at Washington. Died there, 17 Jan. 1891.

Works: 'Poems,' 1823 ; 'Fourth of July Oration,' 1826 ; 'Oration delivered at Springfield,' 1836 ; 'History of the United States' (10 vols.), 1834-74; revised edns., 1876 and 1883-84 ; 'Address at Hartford,' 1840; 'Miscellanies,' 1855 ; 'Oration on the Progress of Mankind,' 1858 ; 'Memorial Address on Abraham Lincoln,' 1866 ; 'Joseph Reed,' 1867 ; 'History of the Formation of the Constitution of the U.S.A. (forming vols. x and xi of the 'History of the United States'), 1882 ; 'A Plea for the Constitution of the U.S.A.' 1886 ; 'Martin Van Buren,' 1889.

He *translated* Heeren's 'Reflections on the Politics of Ancient Greece,' 1824.

BARHAM (Richard Harris), 1788-1845. See p.17, col. i. From 'Works,' *dele* 'Look at the Clock' [1830?].

BARING-GOULD (Sabine), b. 1834. [*See* p. 17.]

Add: Married Grace Taylor, 1868.

Works: 'A Study of St. Paul,' 1897 ; 'Guavas the Tinner,' 1897; 'Bladys of the Stewponey,' 1897 ; 'Perpetua,' 1897 ; 'An Old English Home,' 1898 ; 'The Sunday Round' (4 vols.), 1898-99 ; 'Domitia,' 1898 ; 'Pabo the Priest,' 1899; 'A Book of the West,' 1899 ; 'Furze Bloom,' 1899 ; 'The Present Crisis,' 1899 ; 'The Crock of Gold,' 1899 ; 'Winefred,' 1900 ; 'A Book of Dartmoor,' 1900 ; 'In a Quiet Village,' 1900 ; 'Virgin Saints and Martyrs,' 1900 ; 'The Frobishers,' 1901 ; 'A Book of Brittany,' 1901 ; ' Royal Georgie,' 1901 ; ' Miss Quillet,' 1902 ; ' Nebo the Nailer,' 1902 ; ' A Coronatiou Souvenir,' 1902 ; ' Brittany,' 1902 ; ' Cbris of All Sorts,' 1903 ; ' A Book of North Wales,' 1903.

BARLOW (Jane). Born, at Clontarf, Co. Dublin. Educated at home. Has resided all her life in Co. Dublin.

Works : ' Bogland Studies,' 1892 ; ' Irish Idylls,' 1892 ; ' Kerrigan's Quality,' 1894 ; ' The End of Elfintown,' 1894 ; ' Maureen's Fairing,' 1895 ; ' Strangers at Lisconnel,' 1895 ; ' Mrs. Martin's Company,' 1896; ' A Creel of Irish Stories,' 1897 ; ' From the East unto the West,' 1898 ; ' From the Land of the Shamrock,' 1901 ; ' Ghost Bereft,' 1901 ; ' The Founding of Fortunes,' 1902.

Has *translated :* Homer's ' Battle of the Frogs and Mice,' 1894.

BARRIE (James Matthew), b. 1860. [*See* p. 19.]

Add : LL.D., St. Andrews. Play, ' Richard Savage ' (written with H. Marriott-Watson), produced Criterion theatre, 16 April 1891 ; ' Ibsen's Ghost,' Toole's theatre, 30 May 1891 ; ' Becky Sharp,' Terry's theatre, 3 June 1893 ; ' The Wedding Guest,' Garrick theatre, 27 Sept. 1900 ; ' Quality Street,' New York, 1901, Vaudeville, London, 17 Sept. 1902 ; ' The Admirable Crichton,' Duke of York's, 4 Nov. 1902; ' Little Mary,' Wyndham's, 24 Sept. 1903.

Add to ' Works' : ' Tommy and Grizel,' 1900 ; ' The Little White Bird,' 1902.

BAYLY (Ada Ellen). *See* LYALL (Edna), *pseud.*

BAYLY (Thomas Haynes), 1797-1839. Born at Bath, 13 Oct. 1797. Educated at Winchester High School. Began to study law, 1814, and contrib. to periodicals. At St. Mary Hall, Oxford, studying for Church, for three years ; gave up idea of Church, 1824. Devoted himself to literature. Married Helena Beecher Hayes, 11 July 1826. Became famous as song and ballad writer. Play ' Perfection' produced by Madame Vestris, 1829. This was followed by a number of plays (in all 36). Published various novels. Financial difficulties in 1831, followed by bad health. Lived in France 1833-36. Died, at Cheltenham, 22 April 1839.

Works [exclusive of a large number of separate songs and ballads] : ' Parliamentary Letters ' (anon.) [1818 ?] ; ' Rough Sketches of Bath ' (anon.), 1819 ; ' The Aylmers ' (anon.), 1827 ; ' Psychæ' (priv. ptd.), 1829 ; ' Fifty Lyrical Ballads ' (priv. ptd.), 1829 ; ' Musings and Prosings,' 1833 ; ' Kindness in Women,' 1837 ; ' Flowers of Loveliness,' 1837; ' Weeds of Witchery,' 1837.

Col'ected Works : ' Songs, Ballads and Poems, with Memoir by his widow ' (2 vols.), 1844.

BEECHING (Henry Charles), b. 1859. Born, in London, 15 May 1859. Educated at City of London School, and at Balliol Coll., Oxford ; B.A., 1883 ; M.A., 1887. Ordained Curate of Mossley Hill Church, Liverpool, 1882. Rector of Yattendon, Berks., 1885-1900. Married Mary Plow, June 1891. Oxford Sacred Prize Poem, 1896. Select Preacher, Oxford, 1896-97 ; Camb., 1903. Clark Lecturer, Trin. Coll., Camb., 1899. Chaplain to Hon. Soc. of Lincoln's Inn, 1900. Prof. of Pastoral and Liturgical Theology, King's Coll., London, 1901-03. Canon of Westminster, 1902. Hon. D.Litt., Durham, 1903. Contributor to ' Quarterly Rev.,' ' Edinburgh Rev.,' 'Cornhill Mag.,' 'National Rev.,' etc.

Works : ' Love in Idleness ' (anon., with J. W. Mackail and J. B. B. Nichols), 1883 ; ' Church and State : an Address,' 1887 ; ' Love's Looking-Glass ' (with J. W. Mackail and J. B. B. Nichols), 1891 ; ' Faith ' (sermons), 1892 ; ' Seven Sermons to Schoolboys,' 1894; ' In a Garden,'

1895 ; ' Pages from a Private Diary ' (anon.), 1898 ; ' Conferences on Men and Books ' (under pseud. ' Urbanus Sylvan '), 1900 ; ' Two Lectures introductory to the Study of Poetry,' 1901 ; ' Inns of Court Sermons,' 1901 ; ' Religio Laici,' 1902.

Has *edited* : ' A Paradise of English Poetry,' 1893 ; ' Lyra Sacra,' 1895 ; ' A Book of Christmas Verse,' 1895 ; Vaughan's Poems, 1896, etc. ; Herbert's ' Country Parson,' 1898 ; Selections from Poems of Daniel and Drayton, 1899 ; Tennyson's ' In Memoriam,' 1900 ; Milton's Poems, 1900 ; ' Lyra Apostolica,' 1901 ; Shakespeare's Sonnets, 1903.

BELLAMY (Edward), 1850-1898. Born, at Chicopee Falls, Mass., 25 March 1850. Educated at Union Coll., and in Germany. Barrister, 1871. For some time on staff of ' Springfield Union ' and ' New York Evening Post.' His work ' Looking Backward,' pubd. in 1888, aroused great discussion, and was widely translated. He died, at Chicopee Falls, 22 May 1898.

Works : ' Six to One,' 1878 ; ' Dr. Heidenhoff's Process,' 1880 ; ' Miss Ludington's Sister,' 1884 ; ' Looking Backward,' 1888 ; ' Equality,' 1897.

Posthumous : ' The Blindman's World, and other Stories,' ed. by by W. D. Howells, 1898 ; ' The Duke of Stockbridge,' 1900.

BENSON (Arthur Christopher), b. 1862. Born, at Wellington College, 24 April 1862. At Eton, 1874-81 ; matric. (as scholar) King's Coll., Camb., 1881 ; B.A., 1884 ; M.A., 1888. Assistant Master at Eton, 1885-1903. Fellow of Royal Historical Soc., Feb. 1888.

Works : Memoirs of Arthur Hamilton ' (under pseud. ' Christopher Carr '), 1886 ; ' William Laud,' 1887 ; ' Men of Might ' (with H. F. W. Tatham), 1892 ; ' Le Cahier jaune ' (priv. ptd.), 1892 ; ' Poems,' 1893 ; ' Babylonica ' (priv. ptd.), 1895 ; ' Lyrics,' 1895 ; ' Genealogy of the family of Benson ' (priv. ptd.),

1895 ; ' The Professor ' (priv. ptd.), 1895 ; ' Thomas Gray ' (priv. ptd.), 1895 ; ' Essays,' 1896 ; ' Monnow ' (priv. ptd.), 1896 ; ' Lord Vyet, and other poems,' 1896 ; 'Ode in Memory of W. E. Gladstone' (priv. ptd.), 1898 ; ' Fasti Etonenses,' 1899 ; ' Life of Archbishop Benson,' 1899 ; ' The Professor, and other poems,' 1900 ; ' Mac ' (priv. ptd.), 1900 ; ' The Schoolmaster,' 1902 ; ' Coronation Ode,' 1902 ; ' The Hill of Trouble,' 1903 ; ' Tennyson,' 1903.

Has *edited* : M. E. Benson's ' At Sundry Times and in Divers Manners,' with memoir, 1891 ; Archbishop Benson's ' Cyprian,' 1897 ; Matthew Arnold's ' Poems,' 1900 ; ' Selections from Whittier,' 1903.

BENSON (Edward Frederic), b. 1867. Born at Wellington College, 24 July 1867. Educated at Marlborough Coll., 1881-87 ; matric. (as scholar) King's Coll., Camb., 1887 ; B.A., 1890 ; Wortz Student, 1892 ; Prendergast Student, 1893 ; Craven Student, 1894. At Athens, working for British Archæological School, 1892-95 ; in Egypt, working for Hellenic Soc., 1895. Has travelled also in Italy and Algiers. First book pubd., 1893. Part editor of the ' Imperial and Colonial Mag.,' 1900, etc. Play, ' Aunt Jeannie,' prod. in U.S.A., 1902 ; in England, 1903. Contrib. to ' Spectator,' ' 19th Century,' ' Contemp. Rev.,' ' Pall Mall Mag.,' ' Harper's Mag.,' etc.

Works : ' Dodo,' 1893 ; ' Six Common Things,' 1893 ; ' Rubicon,' 1894 ; ' The Judgment Books,' 1895 ; ' Report on prospects of research in Alexandria ' (with D. G. Hogarth), 1895 ; ' Limitations,' 1896 ; ' The Babe, B.A.,' 1897 ; ' Vintage,' 1898 ; ' The Money Market,' 1898 ; ' The Capsina,' 1899 ; ' Mammon and Co.,' 1899 ; ' The Princess Sophia,' 1900 ; ' The Luck of the Vails,' 1901 ; ' Scarlet and Hyssop,' 1902 ; ' The Book of the Months,' 1903 ; ' The Valkyries,' 1903 ; ' The Mad Annual ' (with E. H. Miles), 1903.

BESANT (*Sir* **Walter**), **1836-1901.**
[*See* p. 24.]
Add : Married Mary Foster-
Barham, Oct. 1874. Died, at Hamp-
stead, 9 June 1901.
Add to '*Works*': 'A Fountain
Sealed,' 1897 ; 'The Rise of the Em-
pire,' 1897; 'The Queen's Reign,'
1897 ; 'Alfred : a Lecture,' 1898 ;
'The Changeling,' 1898 ; 'The
Orange Girl,' 1899 ; 'The Pen and
the Book,' 1899; 'South London,'
1899; 'The Fourth Generation,'
1900; 'The Lady of Lynn,' 1901 ;
'East London,' 1901 ; 'The Story
of King Alfred,' 1901.
Posthumous : 'No Other Way,'
1902; 'London in the 18th
Century,' 1902; 'A Five Years'
Tryst,' 1902 ; 'Autobiography,'
1902; 'The Strand District' (with
G. E. Mitton), 1902; 'Westminster'
(with G. E. Mitton), 1902 ; 'As We
Are and As We May Be,' 1903 ;
'Essays and Historiettes,' 1903 ;
'London in the Time of the Stuarts,'
1903.
Edited: Defoe's 'Journal of the
Plague Year,' 1900 ; G. E. Mitton's
'Chelsea' and 'Hampstead and
Marylebone,' 1902.

BIGELOW (**Poultney**), **b. 1855.**
Born, in New York, 10 Sept. 1855.
Educated abroad, and at Yale University. Travelled extensively in
youth and since. Graduated Yale,
1879. Admitted to New York Bar,
1882. Practised for few years, then
devoted himself to literature and
journalism. Has been lecturer on
Modern History at several American
universities. Mem. of Geographical
Soc. of America; of New York Historical Society ; F.R.G.S., London.
Acted as correspondent of 'Times'
during Spanish-American War,
1898. Is correspondent of 'Harper's
Weekly.' Frequent contributor to
periodicals.
Works : 'The German Emperor
and his Eastern Neighbours,' 1891 ;
'Paddles and Politics down the
Danube,' 1892 ; 'The Borderland of
Czar and Kaiser,' 1893 ; 'History

of the German Struggle for Liberty,'
1895 ; 'White Man's Africa,' 1898 ;
'The Children of the Nations,' 1901.

BINYON (**Robert Laurence**), **b.
1869.** Born, at Lancaster, 10 Aug.
1869. Educated at St. Paul's School,
and Trinity Coll., Oxford ; B.A.,
1892. Newdigate Prize Poem, 1890.
Assistant in British Museum, Dept.
of Printed Books, 1893-95 ; Dept. of
Prints and Drawings, since 1895.
Works : Contribution (with
Stephen Phillips and others) to
'Primavera' (anon.), 1890 ; 'Perse-
phone,' 1890 ; 'Lyric Poems,' 1894 ;
'Poems,' 1895 ; 'Dutch Etchers of
the 17th Century,' 1895 ; 'London
Visions,' bk. i, 1896, bk. ii, 1899 ;
'The Praise of Life,' 1896 ; 'John
Crome and J. S. Cotman,' 1897 ;
'The Supper' (priv. ptd.), 1897 ;
'Porphyrion, and other poems,'
1898 ; 'Western Flanders,' 1899 ;
'Catalogue of English Drawings in
the British Museum,' vol. i, 1898,
vol. ii, 1900, vol. iii, 1902 ; 'Thomas
Girtin,' 1900 ; 'Odes,' 1901 ; 'The
Death of Adam,' 1903.
Has *edited:* 'The Shilling Gar-
land,' 1895-98 ; 'The Artist's Li-
brary,' 1899, etc.

BIRRELL (**Augustine**), **b. 1850.**
[*See* p. 25.]
Add: Quain Prof. of Law, Univ.
Coll., London, 1896. Hon. Fellow,
Trin. Coll., Camb., Jan. 1899. M.P.
for West Fife, 1895-1900.
Add to '*Works*': 'Four Lectures
on the Law of Employers' Liability,'
1897 ; 'Sir Frank Lockwood,' 1898 ;
'Collected Essays,' 1899 ; 'Seven
Lectures on the Law and History of
Copyright in Books,' 1899 ; 'Mis-
cellanies,' 1901 ; 'William Hazlitt,'
1902 ; 'Emerson,' 1903.

BLACK (**William**), **1841-1898.**
[*See* p. 25.]
Add : Editor for short time of
'London Review' and of 'Examiner.'
Married : (i) Augusta Wenzel, 8
April 1865 ; she died, May 1866 ;
(ii) Eva Wharton Simpson, April
1874. On staff of 'Daily News,'

1870-75. Acted for some years as London correspondent of 'Leeds Mercury.' Visited U.S.A., 1876. Ill-health from 1887. Died, at Brighton, 10 Dec. 1898.
Add to 'Works': 'Wild Eelin,' 1898.
Posthumous: 'With the Eyes of Youth, and other Sketches,' 1903.
Life: by Sir T. W. Reid, 1902.

BLACKMORE (Richard Doddridge), 1825-1900. [*See* p. 27.]
Add: Died, at Teddington, 20 Jan. 1900.
Add to 'Works': 'Dariel,' 1897.

BLAKE (William), 1757-1827. [*See* p. 28.]
Add: *Life*, by A. T. Story, 1893.

BLUNT (Wilfrid Scawen), b. 1840. [*See* p. 28.]
Add: Succeeded to estate in Sussex, on brother's death, 1872.
Add to 'Works': 'Poetry of Wilfrid Blunt, selected and arranged by W. E. Henley and G. Wyndham,' 1898; 'Satan Absolved,' 1899; 'The Shame of the 19th Century,' 1901.

BODLEY (John Edward Courtenay), b. 1853. Born, 6 June 1853. After private education, matriculated at Balliol Coll., Oxford, 1873; B.A., 1877, M.A., 1879. Barrister, Inner Temple, June 1874. Private Sec. to Pres. of Local Govt. Board, 1882-85. Sec. to Royal Commission on Housing of Working Classes, 1884-85. Travelled extensively in Europe, America, and Africa, 1886-89. Since 1890 has resided in France, engaged on work dealing with France, first volumes of which appeared in 1898. Married Evelyn Frances Bell, 1891. Corresponding Mem., Institute of France, 1902.
Works: 'Roman Catholicism in America,' 1890; 'France,' vols. i, ii, 1898; 'L'Anglomaine et les traditions françaises,' 1899; 'La France' (translation by the author), 1901; 'The Coronation of Edward VII.,' 1903.

BOURDILLON (Francis William), b. 1852. Born, at Runcorn, 22 March,

1852. At Haileybury College, 1865-71; matric. as scholar, Worcester Coll., Oxford, 1871. Tutor to sons of Prince and Princess Christian, 1876-79. Then engaged for some years in tutorial work at Eastbourne. M.A., Oxford. Married Agnes Watson Smyth, 20 April 1882. Mem. of Alpine Club. Resides in Sussex.
Works: 'Among the Flowers,' 1878; 'Beachy Head,' 1885; 'Where Lilies Live,' 1889; 'Young Maids and Old China,' 1889; 'Ailes d'Alouette,' 1890, second series, 1902; 'A Lost God,' 1891; 'Sursum Corda,' 1893; 'Nephele,' 1896; 'Minuscula,' 1897; 'Through the Gateway,' 1902.
Has *translated and edited*: 'Aucassin and Nicolette,' 1887; 'Chronique Saintongeaise,' 1897.

BOYD (Andrew Kennedy Hutchinson), 1825-1899. [*See* p. 30.]
Add: Married (second wife) Janet Balfour Meldrum, 5 April 1897. Died, at Bournemouth, 1 March 1899.

BRADDON (Mary Elizabeth) [Mrs. John Maxwell], b. 1837. [*See* p. 30.]
Add to 'Works': 'Under Love's Rule,' 1897; 'High Places,' 1898; 'Rough Justice,' 1898; 'His Darling Sin,' 1899; 'The Infidel,' 1900; 'Fenton's Quest,' 1902; 'Run to Earth,' 1902; 'The Conflict,' 1903.

BRIDGES (Robert Seymour), b. 1844. [*See* p. 32.]
Add to 'Works': 'Yattendon Hymnal' (with H. E. Woolridge, 4 pts.), 1895-99; 'Poetical Works,' 1898, etc.; 'Hymns from the Yattendon Hymnal' (priv. ptd.), 1899; 'A Practical Discourse on some Principles of Hymn-Singing,' 1901.

BRONTE (Anne), 1820-1849. [*See* p. 32.]
Add: *Life*, 'The Sisters Brontë,' by Mrs. Oliphant, 1897.

BRONTE (Charlotte), 1816-1855. [*See* p. 32.]
Add: *Life*, by A. Birrell, 1887;

'The Sisters Brontë,' by Mrs. Oliphant, 1897.

BRONTË (Emily Jane), 1818-1848.
See p. 33, col. i. To date of birth, add ' 29 Dec.'
Add : Life, by A. M. F. Robinson, 1889; ' The Sisters Brontë,' by Mrs. Oliphant, 1897.

BROOKE (Stopford Augustus), b. 1832. Born, at Letterkenny, Co. Donegal, 1832. Educated at Kidderminster, at Kingstown, and at Trin. Coll., Dublin; B.A., 1856; M.A., 1858. English Verse Prize, Trin. Coll., Dublin. Ordained, 1857. Curate of St. Matthew's, Marylebone, 1857-59; Curate of Kensington Church, 1860-63; Chaplain to Princess Royal of Germany, 1863-65; Minister of St. James's Chapel, York St., 1866-75; Hon. Chaplain to Queen Victoria, 1867-74; Minister of Bedford Chapel, Bloomsbury, 1876-94. Seceded from Church of England, 1880.

Works [exclusive of single sermons] : ' Life and Letters of F. W. Robertson,' 1865 ; ' Sermons,' 1869-75 ; ' Freedom in the Church of England,' 1871 ; ' Christ in Modern Life,' 1872; ' Theology in the English Poets' (second edn. same year), 1874 ; ' Primer of English Literature,' 1876 ; ' The Fight of Faith,' 1877 ; ' Riquet of the Tuft ' (anon.), 1880 ; ' The Spirit of the Christian Life,' 1881 ; ' Notes on the Liber Studiorum of Turner,' 1885 ; ' The Unity of God and Man,' 1886 ; ' Inaugural Address to the Shelley Society' (priv. ptd.), 1886 ; ' The Early Life of Jesus,' 1888 ; ' Poems,' 1888 ; ' Dove Cottage,' 1890; ' Reasons for Secession from the Church of England,' 1891 ; ' History of Early English Literature,' 1892; ' Short Sermons,' 1892; ' The Development of Theology as Illustrated in English Poetry,' 1893; 'The Need and Use of Getting Irish Literature into the English Tongue,' 1893; ' Tennyson,' 1894;

' God and Christ,' 1894; ' Jesus and Modern Thought,' 1894; ' The Old Testament and Modern Life,' 1896 ; ' The Gospel of Joy,' 1898 ; ' The Ship of the Soul,' 1898 ; ' English Literature . . . to the Norman Conquest,' 1898; ' King Alfred,' 1901 ; ' The Poetry of Robert Browning,' 1902 ; ' The Kingship of Love,' 1903. Has *edited :* F. W. Robertson's ' Literary Remains,' 1876; ' Selected Poems of Shelley,' 1880 ; ' Christian Hymns,' 1891 ; Coleridge's ' Golden Book,' 1895 ; ' A Treasury of Irish Poetry' (with T. W. H. Rolleston), 1900.

BROOKS (Charles William Shirley), 1816-1874. Born, in London, 29 April 1816. Served his articles with view of becoming solicitor, 1832-37. Soon afterwards gave up idea of law and took to journalism. Contributed to ' Ainsworth's Mag.,' from 1842. On staff of ' Morning Chronicle,' first as parliamentary reporter, afterwards (1853) as ' special commissioner' in the East. Married Emily Margaret Walkinshaw. Play ' The Creole' prod. at Lyceum theatre, 8 April 1847; ' Anything for a Change,' Lyceum. 7 June 1848; ' The Daughter of the Stars,' Strand, 5 Aug. 1850; ' The Exposition,' Strand, 23 April 1851 ; ' Timon the Tartar' (with John Oxenford), Olympic, 26 Dec. 1861. Contrib. for some years to ' Illustrated London News' ; edited ' Literary Gazette,' 1858-59; ' Home News,' 1867-70. Contrib. to ' Punch' from 1851 ; was editor, 1870-74. Elected F.S.A., March 1872. Died, in London, 23 Feb. 1874.

Works : ' A Story with a Vengeance' (with A. B. Reach), 1852 ; ' Russians of the South,' 1854; ' Aspen Court,' 1855; ' Amusing Poetry,' 1857 ; ' The Gordian Knot,' 1858-60; ' The Silver Cord,' 1861 ; ' Sooner or Later ' (2 vols.), 1868.

Posthumous : ' The Naggletons and Miss Violet,' 1875 ; ' Wit and Humour: poems from " Punch," ' (ed. by his son), 1875.

BROUGHTON (Rhoda), b. 1840.
[*See* p. 33.]
Add to '*Works*' : 'Dear Faustina,' 1897; 'The Game and the Candle,' 1899; 'Foes in Law,' 1900; 'Lavinia,' 1902.

BROWNE (Charles Farrer). *See* WARD (Artemus), *pseud.*

BROWNING (Elizabeth Barrett), 1806-1861. [*See* p. 34.]
Add to '*Works*' : 'The Battle of Marathon' (priv. ptd.), 1820; 'Kind Words from a Sick Room' (priv. ptd.), 1891; 'Letters,' ed. by F. G. Kenyon, 1897.
Life : by L. Whiting, 1899.

BROWNING (Robert), 1812-1889. [*See* p. 35.]
Add : Life, by E. L. Cary, 1899; by A. Waugh, 1900; by G. K. Chesterton ('Men of Letters' series), 1903.

BRYCE (James), b. 1838. [*See* p. 36.]
Add : Corresp. Mem. of Institute of France, 1891 ; of Societa Romana di Storia Patria, 1885 ; of Acad. of Turin, 1896; of Acad. of Brussels, 1896; Mem. of Senate of London Univ., 1893 ; F.R.S., 1894 ; Doctor of Political Science, Buda Pest Univ., 1896 : D.C.L., Trinity Univ., Toronto, 1897; Litt.D., Cambridge, 1898. Hon. Fellow of Trinity Coll., Oxford ; and of Oriel Coll., Oxford. Pres., Alpine Club, 1899-1901.
Add to '*Works*' : 'The Flora of the Island of Arran,' 1859 ; 'Impressions of South Africa,' 1897; 'Studies in History and Jurisprudence,' 1901 ; 'The Relations of the Advanced and the Backward Races of Mankind' (Romanes lecture), 1902; 'Studies in Contemporary Biography,' 1903.

BUCHANAN (Robert Williams), 1841-1901. [*See* p. 37.]
Add : Died, at Streatham, 10 June 1901.
Add to list of *plays* produced : 'Doctor Cupid,' Vaudeville, 1889; 'A Man's Shadow,' Haymarket, 12 Sept. 1889 ; collaborated with G. R. Sims for Adelphi in 'The English Rose,' 2 Aug. 1889, 'The Trumpet Call,' 1 Aug. 1891, 'The White Rose,' 23 April 1892, 'The Lights of Home,' 30 July 1892, and 'The Black Domino,' 1 April 1893 ; 'Clarissa Harlowe,' Olympic, 6 Feb. 1890; 'Miss Tomboy,' Vaudeville, 20 March 1890; 'The Bride of Love,' Adelphi, 21 May 1890; 'Sweet Nancy,' Lyric, 12 July 1890; 'The Charlatan,' Haymarket, 18 Jan. 1894; 'A Society Butterfly' (written with H. Murray), Opera Comique, 10 May 1894.
Add to '*Works*' : 'The Devil's Case,' 1896 ; 'Effie Hetherington,' 1896 ; 'A Marriage by Capture,' 1896 ; 'The Ballad of Mary the Mother,' 1897 ; 'The Rev. Annabel Lee,' 1898; 'Father Anthony,' 1898 ; 'The New Rome,' 1899 ; 'Andromeda,' 1900 ; 'Complete Poetical Works,' 1901.
Life : by Harriet Jay, 1903.

BUCKLE (Henry Thomas), 1821-1862.
See p. 38, col. i. *Works* (*post-humous*) : *dele* 'History of Civilization in France and England, etc., 1866.'

BULLEN (Frank Thomas), b. 1857. Born, in London, 5 April 1857. At sea, 1866-83; rose to position of chief mate. Junior clerk, Meteorological Office, 1883-99. Married Amelia Grimwood, 1878.
Works : 'The Cruise of the "Cachalot,"' 1898 ; 'Idylls of the Sea,' 1899; 'The Log of a Sea Waif,' 1899; 'The Way they have in the Navy,' 1899; 'The Men of the Merchant Service,' 1900; 'The Palace of Poor Jack,' 1900; 'With Christ at Sea,' 1900; 'A Sack of Shakings,' 1901; 'The Apostles of the South-East,' 1901 ; 'Deep-Sea Plunderings,' 1901 ; 'With Christ in Sailor Town,' 1901; 'A Whaleman's Wife,' 1902 ; 'A Sailor Apostle,' 1903 ; 'Sea-Wrack,' 1903.

BURNEY (Frances), 1752-1840. [*See* p. 41.]
Add : Life, by H. A. Dobson, 1903.

BURNS (Robert), 1759-1796. [See p. 41.]
Add : Life, by J. G. Lockhart, 1828 ; by J. Currie, 1838 ; by J. S. Blackie, 1888 ; by J. C. Higgins, 1893.

BURROUGHS (John), b. 1837. Born, at Roxbury, New York, 3 April 1837. Schoolmaster, 1856-64. Married Ursula North, 13 Sept. 1857. Treasury Clerk, 1864-73. Receiver of Bank at Middletown, N.Y., 1873-84. From about 1874 has devoted himself to literature.　　　•
Works : 'Notes on Walt Whitman,' 1867 ; 'Wake-Robin,' 1871 ; 'Winter Sunshine,' 1876 ; 'Birds and Poets,' 1877 ; 'Locusts and Wild Honey,' 1879 ; 'Pepacton,' 1881 ; contrib. to 'With Others,' 1882 ; 'Fresh Fields,' 1884 ; 'Signs and Seasons,' 1886 ; 'Sharp Eyes,' 1888 ; 'Indoor Studies,' 1889 ; 'Riverly,' 1894 ; 'Writings' (collected), 1895, etc. ; 'A Year in the Fields' (selected writings), 1896 ; 'Literary Values,' 1903.

BURTON (Sir Richard Francis), 1821-1890. [See p. 42.]
Add to 'Works (posthumous)' :
'Human Sacrifice among the Sephardím,' 1897 ; 'Wanderings in Three Continents,' ed. by W. H. Wilkins, 1901.

BURY (John Bagnell), b. 1861. Born, at Monaghan, 16 Oct. 1861. Educated at Trin. Coll., Dublin ; B.A., 1882 ; Fellow, 1885 ; Prof. of Mod. Hist., 1893 ; Regius Prof. of Greek, 1898. Hon. Litt.D., Durham, 1895 ; Hon. LL.D., Edinburgh, 1898 ; Hon. LL.D., Glasgow, 1901 ; Hon. Litt.D., Oxford, 1902. Regius Prof. of Mod. Hist., Cambridge, 1902. Fellow of King's Coll., Camb., Jan. 1903. Married Jane Bury, 1885.
Works : 'History of the Later Roman Empire,' 1889 ; 'Student's History of the Roman Empire,' 1893 ; 'History of Greece,' 1900 ; 'Inaugural Lecture' (Cambridge), 1903 ; 'History of Greece for Beginners,' 1903.

Has *edited :* Euripides' 'Ιππολυτος,' 1881 ; Pindar's 'Nemean Odes,' 1890, and 'Isthmian Odes,' 1892 ; Freeman's 'History of Federal Government,' 1893 ; Gibbon's 'Decline and Fall,' 1896-1900 ; 'Foreign Statesmen,' 1896, etc. ; 'Byzantine Texts,' 1898, etc.

BUTCHER (Samuel Henry), b. 1850. [See p. 43.]
Add : Mem. of Royal Commission on University Education in Ireland, 1901.

BUTLER (Samuel), 1835-1902. [See p. 44.]
Add : Died, in London, 18 June 1902.
Add to 'Works' : 'The Evidence of the Resurrection of Jesus Christ' (anon.), 1865 ; 'On the Trapanese origin of the Odyssey,' 1893 ; 'The Authoress of the Odyssey,' 1897 ; 'Erewhon' (enlarged edition), 1901 ; 'Erewhon Revisited,' 1901.
Posthumous : 'The Way of All Flesh,' 1903.
He *translated :* Homer's 'Iliad,' 1898, and 'Odyssey,' 1900 ; and *edited :* Shakespeare's 'Sonnets,' 1899.

CABLE (George Washington), b. 1844. Born, at New Orleans, 12 Oct. 1844 ; educated there. Clerk in mercantile house, 1859-63. Served in a Confederate cavalry regiment, 1863-65. Worked in mercantile house, and on staff of 'New Orleans Picayune,' 1865-79. Married Louise S. Bartlett, 1869. Since 1879 engaged in literature. Contrib. to 'Scribner's Monthly,' 'Appleton's Journal,' 'Encyc. Brit.,' etc. Removed from New Orleans to Northampton, Mass., 1884. Founded Home-Culture Clubs in America, 1887. Hon. A.M., Yale ; Hon. D.L., Washington, and Lee Univ. Editor of 'Current Literature,' 1897.
Works : 'Old Creole Days,' 1879 ; 'The Grandissimes,' 1880 ; 'Madame Delphine,' 1881 ; 'Dr. Sevier,' 1883 ; 'The Creoles of Louisiana,' 1884 ; 'The Silent South,' 1885 ; 'Bona-

venture,' 1888; 'The Negro Question,' 1888; 'Strange True Stories of Louisiana,' 1888; 'The Busy Man's Bible,' 1891; 'John March, Southerner,' 1894; 'Strong Hearts,' 1899; 'The Cavalier,' 1901; 'Bylow Hill,' 1902.

CAINE (Thomas Henry Hall), b. 1853. [*See* p. 46.] *Add*: Play, 'The Christian,' produced at Duke of York's theatre, 1898; 'The Eternal City,' His Majesty's theatre, Oct. 1902. J.P. in Isle of Man. Member (for Ramsey) of House of Keys, 1901. Instrumental in reviving 'Household Words,' 1902. Visited U.S.A., 1898 and 1902.

CAMPBELL (Thomas), 1777-1844. [*See* p. 47.] *Add*: *Life*, by J. C. Hadden, 1899.

CAREW (Thomas), 1598?-1639? Born, about 1598. Educated at Corpus Christi Coll., Oxford. Took no degree. Was for some time secretary to Sir Dudley Carleton; accompanied him an embassy to Italy. Went to France in 1619, and was for some time at French Court. Subsequently became Gentleman of Privy Chamber to Charles I. Probably died in London, about 1639.

Works: 'Coelum Britannicum' (anon.), 1634; 'Poems,' first printed 1640; collected edition, ed. by W. C. Hazlitt, 1870; ed. by J. W. Ebsworth, 1893.

CARLETON (William), 1794-1869. *See* p. 48, col. 1. From 'Posthumous Works,' *dele*: 'Farm Ballads,' 1873; 'Farm Festivals,' 1881; 'Farm Legends,' 1882.

CARMAN (Bliss), b. 1861. Born, at Fredericton, N.B., 15 April 1861. Educated at New Brunswick Univ., B.A., 1881; at Edinburgh Univ., 1882-83; at Harvard, 1886-88. Since 1890, on editorial staff of 'New York Independent.' Frequent contributor to periodicals. Resides in New York.

Works: 'Low Tide on Grand Pré,' 1893; 'Songs from Vagabondia' (with R. Hovey), 3 series, 1894, 1896, 1900; 'St. Kavin,' 1894; 'At Michaelmas,' 1895; 'Behind the Arras,' 1895; 'A Seamark,' 1895; 'Ballads of Lost Haven,' 1897; 'The Girl in the Poster,' 1897; 'By the Aurelian Wall,' 1898; 'The Green Book of the Bards,' 1898; 'The Vengeance of Noel Brassard,' 1899; 'Ballads and Lyrics,' 1902; 'The Pipes of Pan,' 1903.

CASTLE (Egerton), b. 1858. Born, in London, 12 March 1858. Educated at Paris, Glasgow, and Cambridge Universities. Entered Inner Temple, 1882, but was not called to Bar. To Sandhurst Coll., 1881; Lieut. in 2nd W. India Regt., 1882; Lieut. Royal Engineer Militia, 1884; Capt., 1888. Married Agnes Sweetman, 18 June 1883. On staff of 'Saturday Rev.,' 1885-94. Partner in 'Liverpool Mercury' since 1890. Lectured on 'The Story of Swordsmanship,' 1891, 1903. Play, 'The Pride of Jennico,' produced in New York, 27 Dec. 1899; 'The Secret Orchard,' prod. by Mr. and Mrs. Kendal, 16 March 1901; 'The Bath Comedy,' New York, 1903. Mem. of Council of Soc. of Authors, and of Navy League.

Works: 'Schools and Masters of Fence,' 1885; 'Bibliotheca Dimicatoria,' 1891; 'Consequences,' 1891; 'La Bella,' 1892; 'English Book Plates,' 1892; 'The Light of Scarthey,' 1895; 'The Pride of Jennico' (with Agnes Castle), 1898; 'Young April,' 1899; 'The Bath Comedy' (with Agnes Castle), 1900; 'Marshfield the Observer,' 1900; 'The Secret Orchard,' 1901; 'The Star Dreamer' (with Agnes Castle), 1903; 'The Incomparable Bellairs,' 1903.

Has *translated*: R. L. Stevenson's 'Prince Otto,' into French as 'Le Roman du Prince Othon,' 1896; and *edited*: 'The Jerningham Letters,' 1896.

322   CLARKE—COURTHOPE

CLARKE (Mary Victoria Cowden), 1809-1898. [See p. 57.]
Add: Died, in Genoa, 12 Jan. 1898.
Posthumous: 'Letters to an Enthusiast,' ed. by A. V. Nettleton (Chicago), 1902.

CONGREVE (William), 1670-1729. [See p. 65.]
Add: Went to Kilkenny School, 1681.
Life: by Edmund Gosse, 1888.

CONRAD (Joseph), b. 1857. Born, in Poland, 1857. Educated at Cracow. Joined English Merchant Service; qualified as Master, and became naturalized British subject, 1884. Resides in Kent.
Works: 'Almayer's Folly,' 1895; 'An Outcast of the Islands,' 1896; 'The Nigger of the Narcissus,' 1897; 'Tales of Unrest,' 1898; 'Lord Jim,' 1900; 'The Inheritors' (with F. M. Hueffer), 1901; 'Youth,' 1902; 'Typhoon,' 1903.

CONWAY (Sir William Martin), b. 1856. Born, at Rochester, 12 April 1856. Educated at Repton, and Trin. Coll., Camb. B.A., 1879; M.A., 1882. University Extension Lecturer, 1882-85; Prof. of Fine Art, University Coll., Liverpool, 1885-88. Married Katrina Lombard, 1884. Enthusiastic explorer and climber; travelled for these purposes in Egypt, 1889; in Himalayas, 1892; through the Alps, 1894; in Spitsbergen, 1896-97; in Bolivia and Tierra del Fuego, 1898. Knighted, 1895. Chairman, Soc. of Authors, 1895, 1898-99. Slade Prof. of Fine Art, Cambridge, since 1901. Resides in London.
Works: 'The Zermatt Pocket-Book,' 1881; 'Woodcutters of the Netherlands in the 15th Century,' 1884; 'The Gallery of Art of the Royal Institution, Liverpool,' 1885; 'Artistic Development of Reynolds and Gainsborough,' 1886; 'Early Flemish Artists,' 1887; 'Climber's Guide to the Central Pennine Alps,' 1890; 'Dawn of Art

in the Ancient World,' 1891; 'Climber's Guide to the Eastern Pennine Alps,' 1891; 'The Lepontine Alps,' 1892; 'Climbing and Exploration in the Karakoram Himalayas,' 1894; 'The Alps from End to End,' 1895; 'First Crossing of Spitsbergen,' 1897; 'With Ski and Sledge over Arctic Glaciers,' 1898; 'The Bolivian Andes,' 1901; 'The Domain of Art,' 1901; 'The Rise and Fall of Smeerenburg, Spitsbergen' (priv. ptd.), 1901; 'The First Italian Renaissance,' 1902; 'Aconcagua and Tierra del Fuego,' 1902.
Has edited: 'Literary Remains of A. Dürer,' 1889; 'Conway and Coolidge's Climbers' Guides' (with W. A. B. Coolidge), 1892, etc.

CORELLI (Marie). Adopted in infancy by Charles Mackay, the song-writer. Educated mainly in France. Trained for music, and wrote an opera at fourteen. First book published, 1886. Resided for many years in London, subsequently at Stratford-on-Avon.
Works: 'A Romance of Two Worlds,' 1886; 'Vendetta,' 1886; 'Thelma,' 1887; 'Ardath,' 1889; 'My Wonderful Wife,' 1889; 'Wormwood,' 1890; 'The Soul of Lilith,' 1892; 'Barabbas,' 1893; 'The Sorrows of Satan,' 1895; 'The Mighty Atom,' 1896; 'Cameos,' 1896; 'The Murder of Delicia,' 1896; 'Ziska,' 1897; 'Jane,' 1897; 'Boy,' 1900; 'The Master Christian,' 1900; 'The Greatest Queen in the World,' 1900; 'An Open Letter to Cardinal Vaughan,' 1900; 'Patriotism or Self-Advertisement?' 1900; 'A Christmas Greeting,' 1901; 'The Passing of the Great Queen,' 1901; 'Temporal Power,' 1902; 'The Vanishing Gift: an Address,' 1902; 'The Plain Truth of the Stratford-on-Avon Controversy,' 1903.

COURTHOPE (William John), b. 1842. [See p. 66.]
Add: Married Mary Scott, Nov.

1870. Hon. LL.D., Edinburgh,
1898. Prof. of Poetry, Oxford,
1895-1901.
Add to 'Works': 'History of
English History,' vol. i, 1895, vol.
ii, 1897; vols. iii, iv, 1903; 'Liberty
and Authority in Matters of Taste,'
1896; 'The Longest Reign,' 1897.

**COURTNEY (William Leonard), b.
1850.** Born, at Poona, 5 Jan. 1850.
Educated at Somersetshire Coll.,
Bath, and at Univ. Coll., Oxford.
B.A., 1872. Fellow Merton Coll.,
1872-76. Headmaster, Somersetshire Coll., 1873-76. Married Cordelia Blanche Place, 15 July 1874.
Fellow, New Coll., Oxford, 1876.
Removed from Oxford to London,
1890. On editorial staff of 'Daily
Telegraph,' since 1890. Editor of
'Fortnightly Rev.,' since 1894.
Editor of 'Murray's Mag.,' since
1894. Hon. LL.D., St. Andrews,
1885. Play, 'Kit Marlowe,' pro-
duced at Shaftesbury theatre, 4 July
1890; 'Undine,' Liverpool, 23 Sept.
1903.
Works: 'The Metaphysics of
John Stuart Mill,' 1879; 'Studies
in Philosophy,' 1882; 'Constructive
Ethics,' 1886; 'Studies New and
Old,' 1888; 'Life of J. S. Mill,'
1889; 'Studies at Leisure,' 1892;
'Prof. H. Herkomer,' 1892; 'Kit
Marlowe,' 1893; 'The Reality of
God: two lectures,' 1893; 'The
Idea of Tragedy,' 1900; 'Undine,'
1903.
Has *edited*: Marryat's Novels,
1896, etc.; J. S. Mill 'On Liberty,'
1901.

CRAIGIE (Pearl Mary Teresa).
See HOBBES (John Oliver), *pseud.*

CRAIK (Dinah Maria), 1826-1887.
[*See* p. 68.]
Add to 'Works (posthumous)':
'The Half-Caste,' 1897.

**CRAWFORD (Francis Marion), b.
1854.** [*See* p. 69.]
Add to 'Works': 'The Novel:
what it is,' 1893; 'A Rose of Yes-
terday,' 1897; 'Corleone,' 1897;
'Ave Roma Immortalis,' 1898;

'Via Crucis,' 1899; 'In the Palace
of the King,' 1900; 'The Rulers of
the South,' 1900; 'Marietta,' 1901;
'Cecilia,' 1902; 'Man Overboard,'
1903.

CREIGHTON (Mandell), *Bishop of
London*, **1843-1901.** [*See* p. 70.]
Add: Pres. of Church Historical
Soc., 1894-1901. Dean of Chapels
Royal, 1897. Chairman, London
Church Congress, 1901. Died, at
Fulham, 14 Jan. 1901.
Add to 'Works': 'The Church
under Elizabeth,' 1896; 'The Heri-
tage of the Spirit,' 1896; 'The
Story of Some English Shires,' 1897;
'Lessons from the Cross,' 1898;
'The Idea of a National Church,'
1898; 'History of Rome,' 1899;
'The Hope of the Future: a ser-
mon,' 1899; 'The Position of the
Church of England,' 1899; 'Memoir
of Sir George Gray,' 1901.
Posthumous: 'The Church and
the Nation: charges and addresses'
(ed. by Mrs. Creighton), 1901;
'Historical Essays and Reviews'
(ed. by Mrs. Creighton), 1902;
'Thoughts on Education: speeches
and sermons' (ed. by Mrs. Creighton), 1902; 'University and other
Sermons' (ed. by Mrs. Creighton),
1903.

**CROCKETT (Samuel Rutherford),
b.1860.** Born, at Duchrae, Galloway,
24 Sept. 1860. Educated at Edin-
burgh Univ., at Heidelberg, and at
New Coll., Oxford. Minister in
Free Church of Scotland, 1886.
For some years Minister of Peni-
cuick; subsequently devoted him-
self to literature.
Works: 'Dulce Cor' (under
pseud. 'Ford Berêton'), 1886;
'The Stickit Minister,' 1893; 'The
Raiders,' 1894; 'The Lilac Sun-
bonnet,' 1894; 'Mad Sir Uchtred,'
1894; 'The Playactress,' 1894;
'Bog Myrtle and Peat,' 1895; 'The
Men of the Moss-Hags,' 1895;
'Sweetheart Travellers,' 1895;
'Cleg Kelly,' 1896; 'The Grey
Man,' 1896; 'Lad's Love,' 1897;
'Lochinvar,' 1897; 'Sir Toady

Lion,' 1897 ; 'The Standard Bearer,' 1898 ; 'The Red Axe,' 1898 ; 'The Black Douglas,' 1899 ; 'Ione March,' 1899 ; 'Kit Kennedy,' 1899 ; 'Joan of the Sword Hand,' 1900 ; 'Little Anna Mark,' 1900 ; 'The Stickit Minister's Wooing,' 1900 ; 'The Silver Skull,' 1901 ; 'Cinderella,' 1901 ; 'Love Idylls,' 1901 ; 'The Firebrand,' 1901 ; 'The Dark o' the Moon,' 1902. Has *edited* : J. Galt's Works, 1895, etc.

DARLEY (George), 1795-1846. [*See* p. 73.]

P. 73, col. i. In *Works*, for "'Nepenthe' (anon., privately printed) [1839 ?]", read : "'Nepenthe' (privately printed), 1835." *Add* : 'Selected Poems,' ed. by R. A. Streatfeild, 1903.

DARWIN (Charles Robert), 1809-1882. [*See* p. 73.] *Add* : 'More Letters,' ed. by F. Darwin, 1903. *Life* : by G. T. Bettany, 1887 ; by C. F. Holder, 1891.

DAVIDSON (John), b. 1857. [*See* p. 75.] *Add:* Married Margaret M'Arthur, 1885. His translation of Coppée's play, 'For the Crown,' produced at Lyceum theatre, London, 27 Feb. 1896. *Add to* '*Works*' : 'Godfrida,' 1898 ; 'The Last Ballad,' 1898 ; 'Self's the Man,' 1901 ; 'The Testament of a Vivisector,' 1901 ; 'The Testament of a Man Forbid,' 1901 ; 'The Testament of an Empire-Builder,' 1902 ; 'The Knight of the Maypole,' 1903.

DAVIS (Richard Harding), b. 1864. Born, at Philadelphia, 1864. Became a journalist. Reported various important events, including Spanish-American War of 1898 and S. African War of 1900-02, for New York newspapers. Married Cecil Clark, 4 April 1899. Resides in New York. *Works* : 'Soldiers of Fortune,' 1889 ; 'Gallegher,' 1891 ; 'Van Bibber and Others,' 1892 ; 'Stories

for Boys,' 1892 ; 'The West from a Car Window,' 1892 ; 'Our English Cousins,' 1894 ; 'The Rulers of the Mediterranean,' 1894 ; 'The Exiles,' 1894 ; 'The Princess Aline,' 1895 ; 'Three Gringos in Venezuela,' 1896 ; 'Cuba in War Time,' 1897 ; 'Dr. Jameson's Raiders,' 1897 ; 'A Year from a Correspondent's Note-Book,' 1898 ; 'The King's Jackal,' 1898 ; 'The Cuban and Porto-Rican Campaigns,' 1898 ; 'The Lion and the Unicorn,' 1899 ; 'Episodes in Van Bibber's Life,' 1899 ; 'With Both Armies in South Africa,' 1900 ; 'In the Fog,' 1901 ; 'Captain Macklin,' 1902 ; 'Ranson's Folly,' 1903.

DE VERE (Aubrey Thomas), 1814-1902. [*See* p. 78.] *Add :* Father's surname was De Vere Hunt ; final name dropped by royal license, 1832. Died at Curragh Chase, Co. Limerick, 20 Jan. 1902. *Add to* '*Works*' : 'Recollections,' 1897.

DICKENS (Charles), 1812-1870. *See* p. 80, col. i. From list of works *edited* by Dickens, *dele* : 'Method of Employment,' 1852. *Add :* 'Poems and Verses,' ed. by F. G. Kitton, 1903.

DISRAELI (Benjamin), 1st Earl of *Beaconsfield*, **1804-1881.** *See* p. 81, col. i. In "Works" *add :* 'The Wondrous Tale of Alroy' (including 'Ixion' and 'The Infernal Marriage '), 1833 ; 'Lord George Bentinck,' 1852.

DOBELL (Sydney Thompson), 1824-1874. Born, at Cranbrook, Kent, 5 April 1824. Parents removed to Cheltenham, 1836. Privately educated. Assisted father in wine-merchant's business, from 1836. Married Emily Fordham, 18 July 1844. Success as poet began, 1850 ; procured him many literary and artistic friends. Lived in Scotland, 1854-57. Delicate health necessitated his wintering abroad after 1862 ; near Cannes, 1862-63, in Spain, 1863-64, in Italy, 1864-66.

With these exceptions, he resided almost entirely in Gloucestershire. Died, at Barton End, 22 Aug. 1874.

Works : 'The Roman' (under pseud. 'Sydney Yendys'), 1850; 'Balder' (anon.), 1854; 'Sonnets on the War' (with Alex. Smith), 1855; 'England in Time of War,' 1856; 'The Nature of Poetry,' 1857; 'Parliamentary Reform,' 1865.

Posthumous : 'Collected Poems' (2 vols.), 1875; 'Thoughts on Art, Philosophy and Religion,' 1876; 'Life and Letters' (2 vols.), 1878.

DOBSON (Henry Austin), b. 1840. [*See* p. 82.]

Add : Married Frances Mary Beardmore, 1 Dec. 1868. Retired from Board of Trade, 1901. Hon. LL.D., Edinburgh, 1902. Civil List Pension, 1902. Contrib. to 'Encyc. Brit.,' 'Dict. of Nat. Biog.,' 'Chambers' Cyclopædia of Eng. Lit.,' etc.

Add to '*Works* ': 'Collected Poems,' 1897 (enlarged edn., 1902); 'A Paladin of Philanthropy,' 1899; 'A Whitehall Eclogue' (priv. ptd.), 1899; 'Side-Walk Studies,' 1902 (2nd edn. same year); 'Life of Richardson' ('Men of Letters' series), 1902; 'Hogarth' (enlarged edn.), 1902; 'Fanny Burney,' 1903.

Has *edited :* Goldsmith's 'Vicar of Wakefield,' 1897; Hazlitt's 'Lectures on the English Comic Writers,' 1900; Puckle's 'The Club,' 1900; Walton's 'Lives of John Donne' and 'Compleat Angler,' 1901; Goldsmith's 'Poems and Plays,' 1901; Leigh Hunt's 'Old Court Suburb,' 1902.

DODGSON (Charles Lutwige), 1832-1898. [*See* p. 83.]

Add : Born, at Daresbury, 27 Jan. 1832. At Rugby School, 1846-50. Died, at Guildford, 14 Jan. 1898.

Add to '*Works* ': 'Notes by an Oxford Chiel,' 1865-74 [comprising : 'The New Method of Evaluation as applied to π' (anon.), 1865; 'The Dynamics of a Parti-cle' (anon.), 1865; 'Facts, Fancies and Figures'

(anon.), 1866-68; 'The New Belfry of Christ Church, Oxford' (under initials D.C.L.), 1872; 'The Vision of the three T's' (anon.), 1873; 'The Blank Cheque' (anon.), 1874].

Life : 'Life and Letters,' by S. D. Collingwood, 1898.

DONNE (John), 1573-1631. *See* p. 85, col. i. *Dele :* 'Poems,' ed. by Hannah, 1843; 'Poems,' ed. by Sir John Simeon, 1858.

DONNELLY (Ignatius), 1831-1901. Born, in Philadelphia, 3 Nov 1831. Educated there. Admitted to Bar, 1853. Married Katharine McCaffray, 10 Sept. 1855. Went to Minnesota, 1857. Elected Lieut.-Gov. of Minnesota, 1859 and 1861. Mem. of Congress, 1863-69. Subsequently lived chiefly in Philadelphia, mainly engaged in journalism. Visited England, 1888. Died, at Minneapolis, 2 Jan. 1901.

Works : 'The Mourner's Vision,' 1850; 'Minnesota : an address,' 1857; 'Atlantis,' 1882; 'Ragnarok,' 1883; 'The Great Cryptogram' (2 vols.), 1888; 'Cæsar's Column' (under pseud. 'Edmund Boisgilbert '), 1889; 'Doctor Huguet,' 1891; 'The Golden Bottle,' 1892; 'Donnelliana,' ed. by E. W. Fish, with a biography, 1892; 'The Cipher in the Plays, and on the Tombstone,' 1899.

DOUDNEY (Sarah), b. 1843. [*See* p. 85.]

Add : to date of birth, 15 Jan.

Add to '*Works* ': 'Pilgrims of the Night,' 1897; 'A Cluster of Roses,' 1899; 'Lady Dye's Reparation,' 1899; 'Silent Strings,' 1900.

DOWDEN (Edward), b. 1843. [*See* p. 86.]

Add : Commissioner on Board of Nat. Education in Ireland, 1896-1901; Sec. to Council, Trin. Coll., Dublin, 1900.

Add to '*Works* ': 'The French Revolution and English Literature,' 1897; 'A History of French Literature,' 1897; 'Puritan and Anglican,' 1900.

22

Has edited : 'Select Poems of Southey,' 1895 ; 'Shakespeare's Works,' 1899, etc.

DOYLE(*Sir* **Arthur Conan**), **b. 1859.** Born, in Edinburgh, 22 May 1859. Educated at Stonyhurst Coll., 1869-75 ; in Germany, 1875-76 ; at Edinburgh Univ., 1876-81. M.D., Edinburgh, 1885. Practised medicine at Southsea, 1882-90. Married, 1885. Has travelled extensively. First novel published, 1887. Frequent contributor to periodicals. Author (with J. M. Barrie) of libretto of comic opera 'Jane Annie,' prod. at Savoy theatre, 13 May 1893. Play, 'A Story of Waterloo,' prod. by Sir Henry Irving, 1897. Senior Physician, Langman Field Hospital, S. Africa, in Boer War, Feb. to Aug. 1900. Published, in 1902, work on ' The War in S. Africa : its Cause and Conduct,' with the aim of setting the true facts before European nations. It was extensively translated and distributed, entirely as a labour of love. Knighted, 1902.

Works : 'A Study in Scarlet,' 1887 ; 'The Mystery of Cloomber,' 1889 ; 'Micah Clarke,' 1889 ; 'The Sign of Four,' 1890 ; 'The Captain of the Polestar,' 1890 ; 'The Firm of Girdlestone,' 1890 ; 'The White Company,' 1891 ; 'The Adventures of Sherlock Holmes,' 1892 ; 'The Doings of Raffles Haw,' 1892 ; 'The Great Shadow,' 1892 ; 'Jane Annie' (with J. M. Barrie), 1893 ; 'The Refugees,' 1893 ; 'Round the Red Lamp,' 1894 ; 'The Memoirs of Sherlock Holmes,' 1894 ; 'The Parasite,' 1894 ; 'The Stark Munro Letters,' 1895 ; 'The Exploits of Brigadier Gerard,' 1896 ; 'Rodney Stone,' 1896 ; 'Uncle Bernac,' 1896 ; 'The Tragedy of the Korosko,' 1898 ; 'Songs of Action,' 1898 ; 'A Duet, with an occasional Chorus,' 1899 ; 'Halves,' 1899 ; 'The Green Flag,' 1900 ; 'The Great Boer War,' 1900 (enlarged edns., 1901 and 1902) ; 'The War in South Africa : its Conduct,' 1902 ; 'The Hound of the Baskervilles,' 1902.

ELIOT (**George**) [*pseud.*, i.e. **Marian Evans**, afterwards **Cross**], **1819-1880.** [*See* p. 92.]

Add : Life, by Sir Leslie Stephen (' Men of Letters' series), 1902.

EMERSON (**Ralph Waldo**), **1803-1882.**

See p. 94, col. i. *Dele :* Edited 'Massachusetts Quarterly Review' (3 vols.), 1847-50.

FARRAR (**Frederick William**), **1831-1903.** [*See* p. 96.]

Add : Married Lucy Mary Cardew, 1860. Died, at Canterbury, 22 March 1903.

Add to '*Works*' : 'The Young Man Master of Himself,' 1896 ; 'Progress in the Reign of Queen Victoria,' 1897 ; 'The Bible : its meaning and supremacy,' 1897 ; 'The Herods,' 1897 ; 'Sin and its Conquerors,' 1897 ; 'Temperance Reform,' 1899 ; 'Texts Explained,' 1899 ; 'True Religion,' 1899 ; 'The Life of Lives,' 1900.

Posthumous : 'Three Sermons,' 1903.

FAWCETT (**Edgar**), **b. 1847.** Born, in New York, 26 May 1847. Educated at Columbia Coll. ; graduated there, 1867. Since then, engaged in literature. Frequent contributor to periodicals. Play, 'The False Friend,' produced at Union Square theatre, New York, 1880 ; 'Our First Families,' Daly's theatre, N.Y., Oct. 1880 ; 'Sixes and Sevens,' Boston Museum, 1881 ; 'Americans Abroad,' Daly's theatre, N.Y., 1883 ; 'The Earl,' Hollis Street theatre, Boston, 1886. Recently has resided in London.

Works : 'Short Poems for Short People,' 1872 ; 'Purple and Fine Linen,' 1873 ; 'Ellen Story,' 1876 ; 'Fantasy and Passion,' 1877 ; 'A Hopeless Case,' 1880 ; 'A Gentleman of Leisure,' 1881 ; 'An Ambitious Woman,' 1883 ; 'Tinkling Cymbals,' 1884 ; 'Rutherford,' 1884 ; 'The Buntling Ball' (anon.), 1884 ; 'Song and Story,' 1884 ; 'The Adventures of a Widow,'

1884; 'Social Silhouettes,' 1885;
'The New King Arthur,' 1885;
'The House at High Bridge,' 1886;
'Romance and Reverie,' 1886; 'The
Confessions of Claud,' 1886;
'Douglas Delaine,' 1887; 'Miriam
Balestier,' 1888; 'Divided Lives,'
1888; 'A Man's Will,' 1888; 'Olivia
Delaplaine,' 1888; 'Blooms and
Brambles,' 1889; 'A Demoralizing
Marriage,' 1889; 'A New York
Family,' 1891; 'An Heir to
Millions,' 1892; 'American Push,'
1893; 'Her Fair Fame,' 1894; 'A
New Nero,' 1894; 'Outrageous
Fortune,' 1894; 'The Ghost of Guy
Thyrle,' 1895; 'A Romance of Old
New York,' 1897; 'New York,'
1898; 'Voices and Visions,' 1903;
'The Vulgarians,' 1903.

FIELD (Michael).
The literary pseudonym of two
collaborators, said to be Miss
Bradley and Miss Cooper.

Works: 'Calirrhoë and Fair
Rosamund,' 1884; 'The Father's
Tragedy,' 1885; 'Brutus Ultor,'
1886; 'Canute the Great,' 1887;
'The Cup of Water,' 1889; 'Long
Ago,' 1889; 'Sight and Song,' 1892;
'Stephania,' 1892; 'A Question of
Memory,' 1893; 'Underneath the
Bough,' 1893; 'Attila, my Attila,'
1896; 'The World at Auction,'
1898; 'Anna Ruina,' 1899; 'Noon-
tide Branches' (priv. ptd.), 1899;
'The Race of Leaves,' 1901.

**FITZGERALD (Edward), 1809-
1883.** [*See* p. 100.]
Posthumous: 'Miscellanies' (ed.
by W. A. Wright), 1900; 'More
Letters of Edward Fitzgerald'
(ed. by W. A. Wright), 1901.
Life: by J. Glyde, 1900.

FLEMING (George) [*pseud.*, i.e.
Julia Constance Fletcher], b. **1858.**
Born, 1858. Has for many years
resided mainly in Italy and in
London. Engaged in literature
and drama since 1877. Play, 'Mrs.
Lessingham,' produced at Garrick
theatre, London, 1894; 'A Man
and his Wife,' Empire theatre, New

York, 1897; 'The Canary,' Prince
of Wales' theatre, London, 1899;
'The Fantasticks,' Royalty theatre,
1900; 'The Light that Failed'
(founded on Kipling's novel),
Lyric theatre, 7 Feb. 1903.

Works: 'Kismet,' 1877 (English
edition called 'A Nile Novel,' same
year); 'Mirage,' 1877; 'The Head
of Medusa,' 1880; 'Notes on a
collection of pictures by G. Costa,'
1882; 'Vestigia,' 1884; 'Andromeda,' 1885; 'The Truth about
Clement Ker,' 1889; 'For Plain
Women Only,' 1895; 'Little Stories
about Women,' 1897; 'The Fantasticks' (trans. from the French of
E. Rostand), 1900.

FLETCHER (Julia Constance).
See FLEMING (George), *pseud.*

FORMAN (Harry Buxton), b. 1842.
Born, in London, 1842. Educated
at Teignmouth. Appointed to post
in Civil Service, 1860. Married
Laura Selle, 1869. Assistant Sec.,
G.P.O. C.B., 1897.
Works: 'Our Living Poets,' 1871;
'Music and Poetry' (priv. ptd.),
1872; 'The Shelley Library,' 1886;
'The Hermit of Marlow' (priv.
ptd.), 1887; 'Shelley, "Peterloo,"
and "The Mask of Anarchy"' (priv.
ptd.), 1887; 'The Vicissitudes of
Shelley's Queen Mab' (priv. ptd.),
1887; 'Rosalind and Helen' (priv.
ptd.), 1888; 'Elizabeth Barrett
Browning and her Scarcer Books,'
1896; 'The Books of William
Morris,' 1897.
Has *edited:* Various works by
Shelley, 1876-99; Keats' 'Letters
to Fanny Brawne,' 1889; Ruskin's
'Gold,' 1891; Mrs. Browning's
'Battle of Marathon,' 1891, and
'Aurora Leigh,' 1899; Keats' 'Letters,' 1895, and Complete Works,
1900, etc.; Robert Browning's 'Men
and Women,' 1899; 'Earlier Mono-
logues,' 1900; 'Sordello,' 1902;
Matthew Arnold's 'Dramatic and
Early Poems,' 1902.

FOWLER (Ellen Thorneycroft).
Daughter of Right Hon. Sir Henry
22—2

Fowler. Novelist. Married to
Alfred Lawrence Felkin, 16 April
1903.

Works : 'Verses, Grave and Gay,'
1891 ; 'Verses, Wise or Otherwise,'
1895 ; 'Cupid's Garden,' 1897 ;
'Concerning Isabel Carnaby,' 1898 ;
'A Double Thread,' 1899 ; 'Love's
Argument,' 1900 ; 'The Farring-
dons,' 1900 ; 'Sirius,' 1901 ; 'The
Angel and the Demon,' 1901 ; 'How
to make an Angel,' 1901 ; 'Fuel of
Fire,' 1902 ; 'Place and Power,'
1903.

FOWLER (Thomas), b. 1832. [*See*
p. 102.]
Add : Vice-Chancellor, Oxford
Univ., 1899-1901 ; Hon. Fellow,
Lincoln Coll., 1901. F.S.A. Un-
married.
Add to '*Works*' : 'History of
Corpus Christi College,' 1898.
Has *edited :* Locke's 'Conduct of
the Understanding,' 1901.

FRAZER (James George), b. 1854.
Born, at Glasgow, 1854. Educated
at Glasgow Univ.; B.A., 1874.
Matric. Trin. Coll., Camb., 1874;
B.A., 1878 ; M.A., 1881. Fellow of
Trin. Coll., 1879. Called to Bar at
Middle Temple, 26 Jan. 1882. Hon.
D.C.L., Oxford; Hon. LL.D., Glas-
gow ; Hon. Litt.D., Durham.
Works : 'Totemism,' 1887 ; 'The
Golden Bough,' 1890; 'Pausanias,
and other Greek sketches,' 1900.
Has *edited :* Long's Sallust, 1884 ;
'Passages of the Bible chosen for
their literary beauty and interest,'
1895 ; and *translated :* 'Pausanias,'
1898.

FREDERIC (Harold), 1855-1898.
Born at Utica, U.S.A., 1855. For
some time edited a newspaper there;
subsequently edited 'Albany Even-
ing Journal.' European correspon-
dent of 'New York Times,' 1884-98.
Was married. Died, in London, 19
Oct. 1898.
Works : 'Seth's Brother's Wife,'
1887 ; 'In the Valley,' 1890 ; 'The
Lawton Girl,' 1890 ; 'The Young
Emperor,' 1891 ; 'The New Exodus,'

1892; 'The Return of the O'Mahony,'
1893 ; 'The Copperhead,' 1894 ;
'Illumination,' 1896; 'Mrs. Albert
Grundy,' 1896 ; 'March Hares'
(under pseud. 'George Forth'),
1896 ; 'Marsena,' 1896 ; 'Gloria
Mundi,' 1898 ; 'The Market Place,'
1898-99.

**FREEMAN (Mary Eleanor Wil-
kins).** *See* WILKINS.

**FROUDE (James Anthony), 1818-
1894.** [*See* p. 104.]
Add (Posthumous) : 'My Relations
with Carlyle,' 1903.

**FURNIVALL (Frederick James),
b. 1825.** [*See* p. 106.]
Add to '*Works*' : 'Shakspere and
Mary Fitton' (priv. ptd.), 1897.

GALE (Norman Rowland), b. 1862.
Born, at Kew, 4 March 1862. After
leaving Exeter Coll., Oxford, was
for some time engaged in scholastic
work. Subsequently adopted literary career.
Works : 'A Country Muse' (2 ser.),
1892-93 ; 'A June Romance,' 1892 ;
'Orchard Songs,' 1893 ; 'A Verdant
Country,' 1893 ; 'Cricket Songs,'
1894 ; 'On Two Strings' (with R. K.
Leather, priv. ptd.), 1894 ; 'Holly
and Mistletoe' (with E. Nesbit and
R. Le Gallienne), 1895 ; 'Songs for
Little People,' 1896 ; 'Barty's Star,'
1903.

**GARDINER (Samuel Rawson),
1829-1902.** [*See* p. 107.]
Add : Offered, but declined,
Regius Professorship of Modern
History, Oxford, 1894. Died, at
Sevenoaks, 23 Feb. 1902.
Add to '*Works*' : 'What Gun-
powder Plot was,' 1897 ; 'Oliver
Cromwell,' 1899.

GARNETT (Richard), b. 1835.
[*See* p. 108.]
Add : Retired from British Mus-
eum, 1899. Hon. Mem. American
Philosophical Soc., and of Società
Bibliografica Italiana.
Add to '*Works*' : 'History of
Italian Literature,' 1898 ; 'Life of
Edward Gibbon Wakefield,' 1898;

'Essays in Librarianship,' 1899;
'The Queen, and other poems,'
1901; 'Essays of an Ex-Librarian,'
1901; 'English Literature' (with
E. Gosse), 1903, etc.

Has *edited* : Blade's 'Enemies of
Books,' 1896; Browning's Poems,
1897; 'Library Series,' 1897-99;
Coleridge's Poems, 1898; Shelley's
'Original Poetry by Victor and
Cazire,' 1898; 'Library of Famous
Literature,' 1899; Thomas Moore's
'Anecdotes,' 1899; 'Omar Kha-
yam,' 1899; Mathilde Blind's
'Poetical Works,' 1900; Dumas'
'The Black Tulip,' 1902; E. E.
Williams 'Journal,' 1902; Nelson's
Literature Readers, 1902, etc.

GAY (John), 1685-1732. [*See*
p. 111.]

Add to '*Works*' (*posthumous*) :
'Poems on Several Occasions,'
1737.

**GILBERT (William Schwenck), b.
1836.** [*See* p. 112.]

Add : Play, 'The Fortune Hunter,'
produced at Theatre Royal, Birmingham, 27 Sept. 1897.

**GILCHRIST (Robert Murray), b.
1868.** Born, at Sheffield, 6 Jan.
1868. Educated at Sheffield Grammar School, 1875-83, and privately.
Contrib. to 'Home Chimes,' 'Temple Bar,' and other periodicals, 1884-
92; to 'Nat. Observer,' 1893. Lived
between 1893 and 1897 in remote
Peak Country, with some months
in Paris.

Works : 'Passion the Plaything,'
1890; 'Frangipanni,' 1893; 'The
Stone Dragon,' 1894; 'Hercules
and the Marionettes,' 1894; 'A
Peakland Faggot,' 1897; 'Willow-
brake,' 1898; 'The Rue Bargain,'
1898; 'Nicholas and Mary,' 1899;
'The Courtesy Dame,' 1900; 'The
Labyrinth,' 1902; 'Natives of Milton,' 1902; 'Beggar's Manor,' 1903.

GILDER (Richard Watson), b. 1844.
Born, at Bordentown, N.J., 8 Feb.
1844. Educated at school kept by
his father. Served in campaign in
Pennsylvania, 1863. Railroad work,

1864-65. Joined staff of 'Newark
Advertiser,' 1865; took share in
starting 'Newark Morning Register,'
1868; editor of 'Hours at Home,'
1869; managing editor of 'Scribner's Monthly' (afterwards 'Century Mag.'), 1870, editor-in-chief,
1881. LL.D., Dickinson Coll., 1883;
A.M., Harvard, 1890; L.H.D., Princeton, 1896. Chairman, New York
Tenement House Commission, 1894.
Resides in New York.

Works : 'The New Day,' 1876;
'The Poet and his Master,' 1878;
'Lyrics,' 1885; 'The Celestial
Passion,' 1887; 'Collected Poems,'
1887; 'Two Worlds,' 1891; 'The
Great Remembrance,' 1893; 'Five
Books of Song,' 1894; 'For the
Country,' 1897; 'In Palestine,' 1898;
'Poems and Inscriptions,' 1901.

**GISSING (George Robert), 1857-
1903.** Born, at Wakefield, 22 Nov.
1857. Educated at private schools,
and at Owen's Coll., Manchester.
Engaged for short time in tutorial
work, then adopted profession of
letters. Contributor to 'Fortnightly
Rev.,' 'National Rev.,' 'English
Illustrated Mag.,' 'Illustrated London News,' &c. Died, in France,
28 Dec. 1903.

Works : 'Workers in the Dawn,'
1880; 'The Unclassed,' 1884;
'Demos' (anon.), 1886; 'Isabel
Clarendon,' 1886; 'Thyrza,' 1887;
'A Life's Morning,' 1888; 'The
Nether World,' 1889; 'The Eman-
cipated,' 1890; 'New Grub Street,'
1891; 'Born in Exile,' 1892; 'Den-
zil Quarrier,' 1892; 'The Odd
Women,' 1893; 'In the Year of
Jubilee,' 1894; 'The Paying Guest,'
1895; 'Eve's Ransom,' 1895; 'The
Whirlpool,' 1897; 'Human Odds
and Ends,' 1898; 'The Town Travel-
ler,' 1898; 'Charles Dickens,' 1898;
'The Crown of Life,' 1899; 'Our
Friend the Charlatan,' 1901; 'By
the Ionian Sea,' 1901; 'The Private
Papers of Henry Ryecroft,' 1903.

Edited : Dickens' Works, 1900,
etc.; abridged edn. of Forster's
'Life of Dickens,' 1903.

**GLADSTONE (William Ewart),
1809-1898.** [*See* p. 113.]

Add : Died, at Hawarden, 19 May
1898; buried in Westminster Abbey,
28 May.

Add to 'Works' : 'The Eastern
Crisis,' 1897; 'Later Gleanings,'
1897.

Life : by Justin MacCarthy, 1898;
by Sir T. W. Reid, 1899; by H. W.
Paul, 1901; by J. Morley, 1903.

GOLDSMITH (Oliver), 1728-1774.
See p. 115, col. i. *Add :* Prof. of
Ancient History to Royal Academy,
Jan. 1770.

GOSSE (Edmund William), b. 1849.
[*See* p. 116.]

Add : 'Short History of Modern
English Literature,' 1898; 'Life
and Letters of John Donne,' 1899;
'Hypolympia,' 1901; 'English Lite-
rature' (with R. Garnett), 1903, etc.
Has *edited :* Fielding's Works,
1898, etc.; Hans Andersen's 'Fairy
Tales,' 1900; Penn's 'Fruits of
Solitude,' 1900; 'A Century of
French Romance,' 1901, etc.; M.
J. Cawein's 'Kentucky Poems,' 1902.

GRAND (Sarah) [*pseud.*, i.e. Mrs.
M'FALL].

Novelist. Married to Brigade-
Surgeon Lieut.-Col. M'Fall.

Works : 'Ideala' (anon.), 1888;
'A Domestic Experiment' (anon.),
1891; 'Singularly Deluded' (anon.),
1893; 'The Heavenly Twins,' 1893;
'Our Manifold Nature,' 1894; 'The
Beth Book,' 1897; 'The Modern
Man and Maid,' 1898; 'The Human
Quest,' 1900; 'Babs the Impossible,'
1901.

GRANT (James), 1822-1887. Born,
in Edinburgh, 1 Aug. 1822. Taken
to Newfoundland, where his father
had a command, in 1833. Returned
to England, 1839. Gazetted to
Army, 1840; resigned 1843, and
entered an architect's office. Soon
devoted himself entirely to novel
writing. First work published, 1845.
Married Miss Browne. Founded
Nat. Association for Vindication
of Scottish Rights, 1852. Joined

Roman Catholic Church, 1875. Died,
in London, 5 May 1887.

Works : 'The Romance of War'
(4 vols.), 1846-47; 'Adventures of
an Aide-de-Camp,' 1848; 'Memoirs
of Sir W. Kirkcaldy' (anon.), 1849;
'Memorials of Edinburgh Castle,'
1850; 'Memoirs of Sir J. Hepburn,'
1851; 'Jane Seton,' 1853; 'Both-
well,' 1854; 'Philip Rollo,' 1854;
'The Yellow Frigate,' 1855; 'The
Phantom Regiment,' 1856; 'Harry
Ogilvie,' 1856; 'Frank Hilton,'
1857; 'The Highlanders of Glen
Ora,' 1857; 'Memorials of James,
Marquis of Montrose,' 1858; 'Arthur
Blane,' 1858; 'Legends of the Black
Watch,' 1859; 'The Cavaliers of
Fortune,' 1859; 'Hollywood Hall,'
1859; 'Mary of Lorraine,' 1860;
'Jack Manly,' 1861; 'Oliver Ellis,'
1861; 'The Captain of the Guard,'
1862; 'Dick Rodney,' 1863; 'Letty
Hyde's Lovers,' 1863; 'Second to
None,' 1864; 'The Adventures of
Rob Roy,' 1864; 'The King's Own
Borderers,' 1865; 'The Constable
of France,' 1866; 'The White
Cockade,' 1867; 'First Love and
Last Love,' 1868; 'The Girl he
Married,' 1869; 'The Secret Des-
patch,' 1869; 'Lady Wedderburn's
Wish,' 1870; 'Only an Ensign,'
1871; 'Under the Red Dragon,'
1872; 'British Battles' (3 vols.),
1873-75; 'The Queen's Cadet,'
1874; 'Shall I Win her?' 1874;
'Fairer than a Fairy,' 1874; 'One
of the "Six Hundred,"' 1875;
'Morley Ashton,' 1876; 'Did she
love him?' 1876; 'History of India'
(2 vols.), 1876-77; 'Six Years Ago,'
1877; 'The Ross-shire Buffs,' 1878;
'The Lord Hermitage,' 1878; 'Vere
of "Ours,"' 1878; 'The Royal
Regiment,' 1879; 'The Duke of
Albany's Own Highlanders,' 1880;
'Old and New Edinburgh' (3 vols.),
1880-83; 'The Cameronians,' 1881;
'Derval Hampton,' 1881; 'Lady
Glendonwyn,' 1881; 'Violet Jer-
myn,' 1882; 'The Scots Brigade,'
1882; 'The Dead Tryst,' 1883; 'Miss
Cheyne,' 1883; 'Jack Challoner,'

1883 ; 'Recent British Battles,' 1884 ; 'The Master of Aberfeldie,' 1884 ; 'Colville of the Guards,' 1885 ; 'The Royal Highlanders,' 1885 ; 'History of the War in the Soudan' (6 vols.), 1885-86 ; 'The Tartans of the Clans of Scotland,' 1886 ; 'Dulcie Carlyon,' 1886 ; 'Playing with Fire,' 1887.
Posthumous : 'Love's Labour Won,' 1888 ; 'Scottish Soldiers of Fortune,' 1889.

GREEN (John Richard), 1837-1883. [*See* p. 118.]
Add to ' *Works* ' (*posthumous*) : 'Letters' (ed. by Sir L. Stephen), 1901 ; 'Oxford Studies' (ed. by Mrs. Green and Miss Norgate), 1901 ; 'Oxford Studies,' 1903 ; 'Stray Studies' (2nd ser.), 1903.

GUTHRIE (Thomas Anstey), b. 1856. Born, in Kensington, 8 Aug. 1856. Educated at King's Coll. School, and Trinity Hall, Camb. B.A. 1879. Called to Bar, 1880. Gave up law, and took to authorship under name of 'F. Anstey.' First book published, 1882. Joined staff of 'Punch,' 1887. Play, 'The Man from Blankley's,' Prince of Wales's theatre, 25 April 1901 ; 'Lyre and Lancet' (with F. K. Peile), Royalty, 1902.
Works : 'Vice Versa,' 1882 ; 'The Giant's Robe,' 1884 ; 'The Black Poodle,' 1884 ; 'The Tinted Venus,' 1885 ; 'A Fallen Idol,' 1886 ; 'The Pariah,' 1889 ; 'Voces Populi' (2 ser.), 1890, 1892 ; 'Tourmalin's Time Cheques,' 1891 ; 'The Talking Horse,' 1892 ; 'The Travelling Companions,' 1892,' 'Mr. Punch's Young Reciter,' 1892 ; 'Mr. Punch's Model Music Hall,' 1892 ; 'Mr. Punch's Pocket Ibsen,' 1893 ; 'The Man from Blankley's,' 1893 ; 'Under the Rose,' 1894 ; 'Lyre and Lancet,' 1895 ; 'The Statement of Stella Maberly' (anon.), 1896 ; 'Puppets at Large,' 1897 ; 'Baboo Jabberjee,' 1897 ; 'Paleface and Redskin,' 1898 ; 'Love among the Lions,' 1898 ; 'The Brass Bottle,' 1900 ; 'A Bayard from Bengal,' 1902 ; 'Only Toys,' 1903.

HAGGARD (Henry Rider), b. 1856. Born, at Bradenham, Norfolk, 22 June 1856. Educated at Ipswich, and privately. Sec. to Governor of Natal, 1875 ; on staff of Special Commissioner to Transvaal, 1877 ; Master of High Court of Transvaal, 1878. Lieut. and Adjutant, Pretoria House, 1879. Married Mariana Louisa Margitson, 11 Aug. 1880. Called to Bar at Lincoln's Inn, 1884. Practised at Divorce and Probate Bar till 1886. First novel published, 1884. Chairman of Committee, Soc. of Authors, 1896-98. J.P. for Norfolk and Suffolk. Chairman of Bench, Petty Sessional Division of Bungay. Has lately taken special interest in condition of rural population in England, and is an authority on agriculture. Resides in Norfolk.
Works : 'Cetewayo and his White Neighbours,' 1882 ; 'Dawn,' 1884 ; 'The Witch's Head,' 1885 ; 'King Solomon's Mines,' 1886 ; 'She,' 1887 ; 'Jess,' 1887 ; 'Alan Quatermain,' 1888 ; 'Maiwa's Revenge,' 1888 ; 'Mr. Meeson's Will,' 1888 ; 'Col. Quaritch, V.C.,' 1888 ; 'Cleopatra,' 1889 ; 'Allan's Wife,' 1889 ; 'Beatrice,' 1890 ; 'The World's Desire' (with A. Lang), 1890 ; 'Eric Brighteyes,' 1891 ; 'Nada the Lily,' 1892 ; 'Montezuma's Daughter,' 1894 ; 'The People of the Mist,' 1894 ; 'Joan Haste,' 1895 ; 'Heart of the World,' 1896 ; 'The Wizard,' 1896 ; 'Dr. Therne,' 1898 ; 'Swallow,' 1899 ; 'The Last Boer War,' 1899 ; 'A Farmer's Year,' 1899 ; 'Black Heart and White Heart,' 1900 ; 'Lysbeth,' 1901 ; 'A Winter Pilgrimage,' 1901 ; 'Rural England' (2 vols.), 1902 ; 'Pearl-Maiden,' 1903.

HAKE (Thomas Gordon), 1809-1895. Born, at Leeds, 10 March 1809. At school at Christ's Hospital. Studied medicine at Lewes, at St. George's Hospital, and at Edinburgh and Glasgow Universities. M.D., Glasgow. Afterwards travelled in Italy. Practised as a physician at Brighton, 1833-38.

Studied in Paris, 1838-39. First work published, 1839. Practised at Bury St. Edmunds, 1839-53; contributed extensively to medical periodicals. Travelled in America, and on return to England lived at Roehampton till 1872. Was physician to West London Hospital. Friendship with Rossetti began, 1869. After leaving Roehampton, travelled in Italy and Germany; then settled in London. Fracture of hip in 1891 confined him to his couch. Died, in London, 11 Jan. 1895.

Works : ' Poetic Lucubrations,' 1828 ; ' The Piromides ' (anon.), 1839 ; ' Treatise on Varicose Capillaries,' 1839 ; ' Vates ' (anon.), 1840 (incomplete) ; ' The World's Epitaph ' (anon., priv. ptd.), 1866 ; ' On Vital Force,' 1867 ; ' Madeline, with other Poems,' 1871 ; ' Parables and Tales,' 1872 ; ' New Symbols,' 1876 ; ' Legends of the Morrow,' 1879 ; ' Maiden Ecstasy,' 1880 ; 'The Serpent Play,' 1883 ; ' The Powers of the Alphabet,' 1883 ; ' The New Day,' 1890 ; ' Memoirs of Eighty Years,' 1892 ; ' Selected Poems ' (ed. by Mrs. Meynell), 1894.

HAMILTON (Eugene Lee). *See* LEE-HAMILTON.

HARDY (Thomas), b. 1840. [*See* p. 123.]
Add : ' Wessex Poems,' 1898 ; ' Poems of the Past and the Present,' 1902.

HARE (Augustus John Cuthbert), 1834-1903. [*See* p. 123.]
Add : Died, at Holmhurst, 22 Jan. 1903.
Add to ' *Works* ' : ' The Story of my Life ' (6 vols.), 1896-19C0 ; ' Shropshire,' 1898.

HARLAND (Henry), b. 1861. Born, at St. Petersburg, March 1861. Educated in New York, and at Harvard. Held post in Surrogate's Office, New York, 1883-86. Subsequently removed to London. Editor of ' The Yellow Book,' 1894-97. Married.

Works : ' As It Was Written ' (under pseud. ' Sidney Luska '), 1885 ; ' Mrs. Peixada,' 1886 ; ' The Land of Love,' 1887 ; ' The Yoke of the Thorah ' (under pseud. ' Sidney Luska '), 1887 ; ' My Uncle Florimond,' 1888 ; ' A Latin-Quarter Courtship,' 1890 ; ' Two Women or One,' 1890 ; ' Grandison Mather,' 1890 ; ' Mea Culpa,' 1891 ; ' Mademoiselle Miss,' 1893 ; ' Grey Roses,' 1895 ; ' Comedies and Errors,' 1898 ; ' The Cardinal's Snuff Box.' 1900 ; ' The Lady Paramount,' 1902.

He has *translated :* M. Serao's ' Fantasy,' 1891.

HARRIS (Joel Chandler), b. 1848. Born, at Eatonton, Georgia, 9 Dec. 1848. Educated at Oldfield. Apprenticed to printing trade as a boy ; subsequently on staff of various Georgia newspapers. Married, 1873. Joined staff of Atlanta ' Constitution,' 1876 ; editor, 1890-1901. Contributor to ' Century,' ' Atlantic Monthly,' &c. Resides at Atlanta.

Works : ' Uncle Remus,' 1880 ; ' Nights with Uncle Remus,' 1883 ; ' Mingo,' 1884 ; ' Free Joe,' 1887 ; ' On the Old Plantation,' 1889 ; ' Daddy Jake,' 1890 ; ' Balaam and his Masters,' 1891 ; ' Uncle Remus and his Friends,' 1892 ; ' A Plantation Printer,' 1992 ; ' Little Mr. Thimblefinger,' 1894 ; ' Mr. Rabbit at Home,' 1895 ; ' Sister Jane,' 1896 ; ' The Story of Aaron,' 1896 ; ' History of Georgia,' 1896 ; ' Aaron in the Wildwoods,' 1898 ; ' Tales of the Home Folks,' 1898 ; ' The Chronicles of Aunt Minervy Ann,' 1899 ; ' Plantation Pageants,' 1899 ; ' On the Wing of Occasions,' 1900 ; ' Gabriel Tolliver,' 1902 ; ' The Making of a Statesman,' 1902.

He has *transla'ed:* J. B. F. Ortoli's ' Evening Tales,' 1894 ; and written *prefaces* to : F. L. Stanton's ' Songs of the Soul,' 1894 ; J. T. Clarke's ' Songs of the South,' 1896 ; H. Weeden's ' Bandanna Ballads,' 1899 ; R. Eickemeyer's ' Down South,' 1900.

HARRISON (Frederic), b. 1831.
[*See* p. 125.]
Add : Hon. Fellow, Wadham Coll.,
Oxford, 1899. Rede Lecturer, Cam-
bridge, 1900. Vice-Pres., Royal
Historical Society.
Add to '*Works*' : 'William the
Silent,' 1897 ; 'The Millenary of
King Alfred,' 1897 ; 'Tennyson,
Ruskin, Mill, and other Literary
Estimates,' 1899 ; 'Byzantine His-
tory in the Early Middle Ages,'
1 00 ; 'George Washington and
other American Addresses,' 1901 ;
'The Writings of King Alfred,' 1901 ;
'Life of Ruskin,' 1902.
Has *edited :* Carlyle's 'Past and
Present,' 1897.

HARRISON (*Mrs.* Mary St. Leger).
See MALET (Lucas).

HARTE (Francis Bret), 1839-1902.
[*See* p. 126.]
Add : Play, 'Sue' (written with
T. E. Pemberton), prod. in New
York, Sept. 1896 ; at Garrick theatre,
London, July 1898. Died, at Cam-
berley, 5 May 1902.
Add to '*Works*' : 'Three Partners,'
1897 ; 'Some Later Verses,' 1898 ;
'Stories in Light and Shadow,' 1898 ;
'Tails of Trail and Town,' 1898 ;
'Mr. Jack Hamlin's Mediation,'
1899; 'What Happened at the Fonda,'
1899 ; 'From Sandhill to Pine,' 1900;
'Under the Redwoods,' 1901 ; 'Con-
densed Novels,' 1902 ; 'On the Old
Trail,' 1902 ; 'Sue' (with T. E.
Pemberton), 1902.
Posthumous : 'Trent's Trust, and
other stories,' 1903.
Life : by T. E. Pemberton, 1903.

**HAWKINS (Anthony Hope), b.
1863.** Born, at Clapton, 9 Feb.
1863. Educated at Marlborough
Coll., 1876-81. Matric. Balliol Coll.,
Oxford, Oct. 1881 ; B.A., 1885.
Called to Bar at Middle Temple,
Jan. 1887. Practised till 1894 ; then
adopted literary career, under name
of 'Anthony Hope.' Play, 'The
Adventure of Lady Ursula,' prod. at
Duke of York's theatre, 11 Oct.
1898; 'When a Man's in Love'

(written with E. Rose), Court
theatre, 19 Oct. 1898; 'English
Nell' (adapted, with E. Rose, from
'Simon Dale'), Prince of Wales's
theatre, 21 Aug. 1900; 'Pilkerton's
Peerage,' Garrick theatre, 28 Jan.
1902. Dramatization (by E. Rose)
of 'The Prisoner of Zenda,' prod. at
St. James's theatre, 7 Jan. 1896 ;
of 'Rupert of Hentzau,' 1 Feb. 1900.
Married Elizabeth Sheldon, 1 July
1903.
Works : 'A Man of Mark,' 1890 ;
'Father Stafford,' 1891 ; 'Mr. Witt's
Widow,' 1892 ; 'A Change of Air,'
1893 ; 'Sport Royal,' 1893 ; 'Dolly
Dialogues,' 1894 ; 'The God in the
Car,' 1894 ; 'Half a Hero,' 1894 ;
'The Indiscretion of the Duchess,'
1894 ; 'The Prisoner of Zenda,' 1894 ;
'The Chronicles of Count Antonio,'
1895 ; 'Comedies of Courtship,'
1896 ; 'The Heart of Princess Osra,'
1896 ; 'Phroso,' 1897 ; 'Rupert of
Hentzau,' 1898 ; 'Simon Dale,' 1898 ;
'The King's Mirror,' 1899 ; 'Qui-
sante,' 1900 ; 'Tristram of Blent,'
1901 ; 'The Intrusions of Peggy,'
1902.

HAWTHORNE (Julian), b. 1846.
[*See* p. 127.]
Add : Married Mary Albertina
Amelung, 15 Nov. 1870. On staff
of 'London Spectator,' 1877-81.
Literary Editor, 'New York World,'
1885. Lived in New York, 1890-94 ;
in Jamaica, 1894-97; visit to India,
1897 ; in New York, since 1898.
Add to '*Works*' : 'Love is a Spirit,'
1896 ; 'History of the United States'
(3 vols.), 1898.

**HAWTHORNE (Nathaniel), 1804-
1864.** [*See* p. 127.]
Add : Life, by Prof. Woodberry,
in 'American Men of Letters' series,
1902.

HAZLITT (William), 1778-1830.
[*See* p. 129.]
Add : 'Collected Works,' ed. by
A. K. Waller and A. Glover, 1903.
Life, by Augustine Birrell ('Men
of Letters' series), 1902.

HENLEY (William Ernest), 1849-1903.

See p. 131, col. i. To date of birth, add: 23 Aug.

Add: Play, 'Deacon Brodie' (written with R. L. Stevenson), performed at Prince of Wales's theatre, 2 July 1884; 'Admiral Guinea' (with R. L. Stevenson), Avenue, 29 Nov. 1897. Editor of 'New Review,' 1894-97. Died, at Woking, 11 July 1903.

Add to 'Works': 'English Lyrics,' 1897; 'Poems,' 1898; 'London Types' (with G. Nicholson), 1898; 'For England's Sake,' 1900; 'Hawthorn and Lavender,' 1901; 'Views and Reviews' (second series), 1902; 'A Song of Speed,' 1903.

Edited: 'The Poetry of Wilfrid Blunt,' 1898; Smollett's Works, 1899, etc.; G. W. Steevens' 'Things Seen,' 1900; Shakespeare ('Edinburgh Folio' edn.), 1901.

HEWLETT (Maurice Henry), b. 1861. Born, at Oatlands Park, Surrey, 22 Jan. 1861. Educated at London International Coll. Married Hilda Beatrice Herbert, 3 Jan. 1888. Called to Bar, 1891. Did not practise. Keeper of Land Revenue Records, 1896-1900.

Works: 'Earthwork out of Tuscany,' 1895; 'A Masque of Dead Florentines,' 1895; 'Songs and Meditations,' 1896; 'The Forest Lovers,' 1898; 'Pan and the Young Shepherd,' 1898; 'Little Novels of Italy,' 1899; 'The Life and Death of Richard Yea-and-Nay,' 1900; 'New Canterbury Tales,' 1901; 'The Queen's Quair,' 1903. Has edited: De Stendhal's 'Chartreuse of Parma,' 1902.

HICHENS (Robert Smythe), b. 1864. Born, at Speldhurst, 14 Nov. 1864. At school at Tunbridge Wells; and at Clifton Coll., 1879-80. Studied music for some years in Bristol, and subsequently at Royal College of Music, London. Studied journalism in London, 1889-90; adopted literary career, 1890. Con-

trib. to 'Globe,' 'Evening Standard,' 'Pall Mall Gaz.,' 'Pall Mall Mag.,' 'World,' 'Queen,' 'New Review,' 'Westminster Gaz.,' 'Graphic,' etc. Play, 'The Medicine Man' (written with H. D. Traill), prod. at Lyceum theatre, 6 May 1898; 'Becky Sharp' (with C. Gordon Lennox), Prince of Wales's theatre, 27 Aug. 1901.

Works: 'The Coastguard's Secret,' 1885; 'The Green Carnation,' 1894; 'An Imaginative Man,' 1895; 'The Folly of Eustace,' 1896; 'Flames,' 1897; 'The Londoners,' 1898; 'Byeways,' 1898; 'The Daughter of Babylon' (with Wilson Barrett), 1899; 'The Slave,' 1899; 'Tongues of Conscience,' 1900; 'The Prophet of Berkeley Square,' 1901; 'Felix,' 1902.

HINKSON (Mrs. Katharine Tynan). See TYNAN (Katharine).

HOBBES (John Oliver) [pseud., i.e. PEARL MARY TERESA CRAIGIE]. Born [Pearl Mary Teresa Richards], at Boston, U.S.A., 3 Nov. 1867. Educated in Paris and London. Married Reginald Walpole Craigie, Feb. 1887; obtained divorce from him, 1895. Joined Roman Catholic Church, 1892. First novel published, 1891. Contrib. to 'Times,' 'Fortnightly Rev.,' 'Anglo-Saxon Rev.,' N. American Rev.,' 'Encyc. Brit.' Play, 'The Ambassador,' prod. at St James's theatre, 2 June 1898; 'A Repentance,' St. James's, 1899; 'The Wisdom of the Wise,' St. James's, 1900; 'The Bishop's Move' (with L. N. Parker), Garrick, 1902.

Works: 'Some Emotions and a Moral,' 1891; 'The Sinner's Comedy,' 1892; 'A Study in Temptations,' 1893; 'A Bundle of Life,' 1893; 'Journeys end in Lovers' Meeting,' 1894; 'The Gods, Some Mortals, and Lord Wickenham,' 1895; 'The Herb-Moon,' 1896; 'The School for Saints,' 1897; 'The Ambassador,' 1898; 'Osbern and Ursyne,' 1900; 'Robert Orange,' 1900; 'The Serious

Wooing,' 1901; 'Love and the Soul Hunters,' 1902; 'Tales about Temperaments,' 1902; 'Imperial India,' 1903.

Has *edited*: George Sand's 'Mauprat,' 1902.

HOPE (Anthony). *See* HAWKINS (Anthony Hope).

HOPPER (Nora), b. 1871. Born, at Exeter, 2 Jan. 1871. Educated in London. Married to Wilfred Hugh Chesson, 1901.

Works: 'Ballads in Prose,' 1894; 'Under Quicken Boughs,' 1896; 'Songs of the Morning,' 1900; 'Aquamarines,' 1902.

HOUSMAN (Laurence), b. 1867. Born, 18 July 1867. Author and artist. First book published, 1894. Has illustrated a large number of books. Mystery Play, 'Bethlehem,' produced privately in London, 17 Dec. 1902.

Works: 'A Farm in Fairyland,' 1894; 'The House of Joy,' 1895; 'Arthur Boyd Houghton,' 1896; 'Green Arras,' 1896; 'All-Fellows,' 1896; 'Gods and their Makers,' 1897; 'Spikenard,' 1898; 'The Field of Clover,' 1898; 'The Little Land,' 1899; 'Rue,' 1899; 'The Story of the Seven Young Goslings,' 1899; 'An Englishwoman's Love-Letters' (anon.), 1900; 'The Tale of a Nun' (with L. Simons; priv. ptd.), 1901; 'A Modern Antæus' (anon.), 1901; 'Bethlehem,' 1902.

He has *translated:* 'Of Aucassin and Nicolette,' 1902.

HOWELLS (William Dean), b. 1837. [*See* p. 139.]

Add to '*Works*': 'The Albany Depôt,' 1897; 'Evening Dress,' 1897; 'A Likely Story,' 1897; 'Five o'clock Tea,' 1897; 'The Garotters,' 1897; 'The Landlord at Lion's Head,' 1897; 'The Unexpected Guests,' 1897; 'The Mousetrap,' 1897; 'A Previous Engagement,' 1897; 'Stories of Ohio,' 1897; 'An Open-Eyed Conspiracy,' 1898; 'The Story of a Play,' 1898;

'Ragged Lady,' 1899; 'Their Silver Wedding Journey,' 1900; 'An Indian Giver,' 1900; 'Room Forty-five, 1900; 'Literary Friends and Acquaintance,' 1900; 'Bride Roses,' 1900; 'Heroines of Fiction,' 1901; 'A Pair of Patient Lovers,' 1901; 'The Kentons,' 1902; 'Literature and Life,' 1902; 'Questionable Shapes,' 1903.

HUXLEY (Thomas Henry), 1825-1896. [*See* p. 143.]

Add: 'Scientific Memoirs' (4 vols.), 1898-1902.

Life: 'Life and Letters,' by Leonard Huxley, 1900; Memoir, by P. C. Mitchell, 1900; by E. Clodd, 1902.

JACOBS (William Wymark), b. 1863. Born, in London, 8 Sept. 1863. Educated at Kingsland, and at King's Coll., London. Held post in Civil Service, Savings Bank Dept., 1883-99. Then adopted literary career. Married Agnes Eleanor Williams, 6 Jan. 1900.

Works: 'Many Cargoes,' 1896; 'The Skipper's Wooing,' 1897; 'Sea Urchins,' 1898; 'A Master of Craft,' 1900; 'Light Freights,' 1901; 'At Sunwich Port,' 1902; 'The Lady of the Barge,' 1902; 'Odd Craft,' 1903.

JAMES (Mrs. Florence). *See* WARDEN (Florence).

JAMES (Henry), b. 1843. [*See* p. 146.]

Add to '*Works*': 'What Maisie Knew,' 1898; 'In the Cage,' 1898; 'The Two Magics,' 1898; 'The Awkward Age,' 1899; 'The Soft Side,' 1900; 'A Little Tour in France,' 1900; 'The Sacred Fount,' 1901; 'The Wings of the Dove,' 1902; 'The Better Sort,' 1903; 'The Ambassadors,' 1903, 'Life of W. W. Story,' 1903.

Has *edited*: H. Crackenthorpe's 'Last Studies,' 1897; Pierre Loti's 'Impressions,' 1898; Goldsmith's 'Vicar of Wakefield,' 1900; Balzac's 'Two Young Brides,' 1902; Flaubert's 'Madame Bovary,' 1902.

JANVIER (Thomas Allibone), b. 1849. Born, at Philadelphia, 16 July 1849. On editorial staff of Philadelphia ' Press,' ' Bulletin,' and ' Times,' 1870-81. Married Catharine Ann Drinker, 26 Sept. 1878. Travelled extensively in Colorado and Mexico, 1881-87 ; later, resided in New York ; since 1894 has lived mainly in France and in England. Mem. of Folk Lore Society. Sòci dòu Felibrige.

Works : ' Color Studies,' 1885 ; ' The Mexican Guide,' 1886 ; ' The Aztec Treasure House,' 1890 ; ' Stories of Old New Spain,' 1891 ; ' The Uncle of an Angel,' 1891 ; ' An Embassy to Provence,' 1893 ; ' In Old New York,' 1894 ; ' In the Sargasso Sea,' 1898 ; ' The Passing of Thomas,' 1900 ; ' In Great Waters,' 1901 ; ' The Christmas Kalends of Provence,' 1902 ; ' The Dutch Founding of New York,' 1903.

He has written *introductions* to : J. Isaacs' ' Maria,' 1890 ; W. Sharp's ' Flower o' the Vine,' 1892 ; F. Gras' ' The Reds of the Midi ' (translated by Mrs. Janvier), 1897.

JAPP (Alexander Hay), b. 1839. Born, at Dun, Forfarshire, 25 Dec. 1839. Educated at Montrose Acad. and Edinburgh University. Married Elizabeth Paul Falconer, 1865 ; she died 1886. Sub-editor ' Contemp. Rev.,' 1866-72. Sub-editor ' Good Words,' 1868-81. Editor ' Sunday Mag.,' 1869-79. LL.D., Glasgow, 1879. F.R.S.E. 1880.

Works : ' Memoir of Nath. Hawthorne ' (under pseud. ' H. A. Page '), 1872 ; ' Golden Lives ' (by ' H. A. Page '), 1873 ; ' Out and All About ' (by ' H. A. Page '), 1874 ; ' Noble Workers ' (by ' H. A. Page '), 1875 ; ' De Quincey's Life ' (by ' H. A. Page '), 1877 ; ' Thoreau ' (by ' H. A. Page '), 1878 ; ' Lights on the Way ' (under pseud. ' J. H. Alexander '), 1878 ; ' Wise Words and Loving Deeds ' (under pseud. ' E. Conder Gray '), 1880 ; ' Leaders of Men'(by ' H. A. Page '), 1880 ; ' Literary Bye-Hours ' (by ' H. A. Page '),

1881 ; ' Sister Edith's Probation ' (by ' E. Conder Gray '), 1881 ; ' Animal Anecdotes ' (by ' H. A. Page '), 1887 ; ' Good Men and True,' 1890 ; ' Idle Musings ' (by ' E. Conder Gray '), 1890 ; ' De Quincey Memorials,' 1891 ; ' Successful Business Men ' (with F. M. Holmes), 1892 ; ' Hours in my Garden,' 1894 ; ' The Circle of the Year,' 1894 ; ' Dramatic Pictures,' 1894 ; ' Lilith and Adam ' (under pseud. ' A. F. Scot '), 1899 ; ' Our Common Cuckoo,' 1899 ; ' Days with Industrials,' 1899 ; ' Some Heresies,' 1899 ; ' Her Part ' (under pseud. ' A. N. Mount Rose '), 1899 ; ' Offering and Sacrifice ' (by ' A. F. Scot '), 1899 ; ' Facts and Fancies from the Koran ' (by ' A. N. Mount Rose '), 1899 ; ' Darwin as an Ethical Thinker,' 1901.

He has *edited :* ' Treasure Book of Devotional Reading,' 1866, and ' Treasure Book of Consolation,' 1880 (both under pseud. ' Benjamin Orme '); ' De Quincey's Posthumous Works,' 1891, etc.

JEBB (*Sir* Richard Claverhouse), b. 1841. [*See* p. 147.]

Add : Mem. of London University Commission, 1898. Bampton Lecturer, 1899. Knighted, 1900. Mem. of Royal Commission on Irish University Education, 1901.

Add to ' *Works' :* ' Humanism in Education,' 1899 ; ' Macaulay,' 1900.

JEROME (Jerome Klapka), b. 1859. Born, at Walsall, 2 May 1859. Educated at Philological School. Held post as clerk, 1876-79. Became an actor in 1879 ; left stage in 1882. Held post as schoolmaster, 1882-85. Became a journalist, 1885. Part-editor of ' The Idler,' 1892-97 ; editor of ' To-Day,' 1893-97. Play, ' Barbara,' prod. at Globe theatre, 1886 ; ' Fennel,' Novelty theatre, 31 March 1888 ; ' Sunset,' Comedy theatre, 13 Feb. 1888 ; ' Wood Barron Farm,' Comedy theatre, 18 June 1888 ; ' New Lamps for Old,' Terry's theatre, 8 Feb. 1890 ; ' Ruth,' Oct. 1890 ; ' The Prude's Progress ' (written with Eden Phillpotts), Comedy theatre, 22 May 1895; 'The Rise of Dick Halward,' Garrick theatre, 19 Oct. 1895; 'Miss Hobbs,' Duke of York's theatre, Dec. 1899. Married Georgina Henrietta Stanley Nesza, 21 June 1888.

Works : 'On the Stage and Off,' 1885; 'Idle Thoughts of an Idle Fellow,' 1886; 'Three Men in a Boat,' 1889; 'Stage-land,' 1889; 'The Diary of a Pilgrimage,' 1891; 'Told after Supper,' 1891; 'Novel Notes,' 1893; 'John Ingerfield,' 1894; 'Sketches in Lavender,' 1897; 'Letters to Clorinda,' 1898; 'The Second Thoughts of an Idle Fellow,' 1898; 'Three Men on the Bummel,' 1900; 'The Observations of Henry,' 1901; 'Paul Kelver,' 1902; 'Tea Table Talk,' 1903.

JESSOPP (Augustus), b. 1824. Born, at Cheshunt, 20 Dec. 1824. Educated privately, and at Heidelberg, and St. John's Coll., Camb. Ordained, 1848. Curate of Papworth St. Agnes, 1848-54. Married Mary Ann Margaret Cotesworth, 15 Feb. 1848. Head Master, Helston Grammar School, 1855-59. Head Master, King Edward VI. School, Norwich, 1859-79. D.D., Oxford, 1870. Rector of Scarning, since 1879. Hon. Canon, Norwich, 1894. Hon. Fellow, St. John's Coll., Camb., 1895; of Worcester Coll., Oxford, 1895. Select Preacher, Oxford, 1896. Chaplain in Ordinary to the King, 1902.

Works : 'Norwich Schools Sermons,' 1864; 'Manual of Greek Accidence,' 1865; 'One Generation of a Norfolk House,' 1878; 'Norwich,' 1884; 'Arcady for Better for Worse,' 1887; 'The Coming of the Friars,' 1889; 'The Trials of a Country Parson,' 1890; 'Doris,' 1892; 'Pity the Poor Birds,' 1893; 'Studies by a Recluse,' 1893; 'Mr. Dandelow,' 1894; 'Random Roaming,' 1894; 'An Incident in the Career of Luke Tremain,' 1895; 'Frivola,' 1896; 'Simon Ryan,' 1896; 'John Donne,' 1897; 'The Coming and Going of Customs Ec-

clesiastical,' 1899; 'Swanton Mill,' 1900; 'Before the Great Pillage,' 1901; 'Penny History of the Church of England,' 1902.

He has *edited :* Donne's 'Essays in Divinity,' 1855; 'Letters of Henry Walpole,' 1873; A. Harris' 'Œconomy of the Fleete,' 1879; 'Visitations of the Diocese of Norwich,' 1888; T. Fuller's 'Wise Words,' 1892; Thomas of Monmouth's 'Life of St. William of Norwich,' 1896.

JOHNSON (Lionel Pigot), 1867-1902. Born, at Broadstairs, 1867. Educated at Winchester Coll., and at New Coll., Oxford. B.A., 1890. Soon after taking degree, joined Roman Catholic Church. Contrib. poems to the 'Book of the Rhymers' Club,' 1892. On staff of 'Anti-Jacobin,' 1891. Contrib. to 'Daily Chronicle,' 'Academy,' etc. Died, in London, 4 Oct. 1902.

Works : 'The Gordon Riots,' 1893; 'The Art of Thomas Hardy,' 1894; 'Bits of Old Chelsea' (with R. Le Gallienne), 1894; 'Poems,' 1895; 'Ireland, with other poems,' 1897.

JOHNSON (Samuel), 1709-1784. [*See* p. 150.] *Add :* 'The Right of the British Legislature to Tax the American Colonies indicated' (anon.), 1774.

JOHNSTON (Mary), b. 1870. Born, at Buchanan, Virginia, 21 Nov. 1870. Educated there.

Works : 'Prisoners of Hope,' 1898; 'The Old Dominion,' 1899; 'To Have and to Hold,' 1900; 'Audrey,' 1902.

JOWETT (Benjamin), 1817-1893. *See* p. 153, col. i. From 'Works,' *dele :* 'Lord Lytton, 1873.'

KIDD (Benjamin), b. 1858. Born, 9 Sept. 1858. Married Maud Emma Isabel Perry, 1887. Travelled in America, 1898; in S. Africa, 1902. Occupied on work on 'Social Evolution,' 1884-94. Contrib. to 'Encyc. Brit.,' etc , on sociological subjects.

Wor's : 'Social Evolution,' 1894; 'The Control of the Tropics,' 1898;

'Principles of Western Civilization,' 1902.

KINGSLEY (Mary Henrietta), 1862-1900. Born, in Islington, 13 Oct. 1862. Lived there and at Highgate, 1862-79; at Bexley, 1879-1886; at Cambridge, 1886-92. Parents died, 1892. Travelled in Western Africa, Aug. 1893 to Jan. 1894, and Dec. 1894 to Nov. 1895. Explored Congo region. Lectured frequently in England on W. African topics. Died, at Simon's Town, S. Africa (on her way to further travel in W. Africa), 3 June, 1900.

Works : 'Travels in West Africa,' 1897 ; 'West Africa Studies,' 1899 ; 'The Story of West Africa,' 1899.

KIPLING (Rudyard), b. 1865. [*See* p. 158.]

Add : Play founded (by 'George Fleming ') on 'The Light that Failed,' produced at Lyric theatre, 7 Feb. 1903.

Add to ' Works' : 'Schoolboy Lyrics' (priv. ptd.), 1881 ; contributions to ' Echoes by Two Writers,' 1884; contributions to 'A Quartette ' (with his parents and sister), 1885 ; 'The Light that Failed' (altered and enlarged edn.), 1891 ; verses to 'An Almanac of Twelve Sports,' 1897 ; 'White Horses' (priv. ptd.), 1897 ; 'Captains Courageous,' 1897 ; 'A Fleet in Being,' 1898 ; 'The Destroyers,' 1898 ; 'The Day's Work,' 1898 ; 'American Notes' (Boston), 1899 ; 'Stalky and Co.,' 1899 ; 'From Sea to Sea,' 1899 ; 'Kim,' 1901 ; 'Just So Stories,' 1902 ; 'Pan in Vermont,' 1902 ; 'The Science of Rebellion,' 1902 ; 'The Five Nations,' 1903.

KNIGHT (Joseph), b. 1829. Born, at Leeds, 24 May 1829. Educated there and at Bramham College. Settled in London, 1860. Contrib. to 'Lit. Gazette,' 'Sunday Times,' 'Pall Mall Mag.,' etc. Later, to 'Sat. Rev.,' 'Frazer,' 'Cornhill,' 'Fortnightly,' etc. On staff of 'Globe' since 1866, of 'Athenæum' since about 1875, of ' Daily Graphic'

since about 1890, mainly as dramatic critic. Editor of 'Notes and Queries,' since 1883. Contrib. to 'Dict. of Nat. Biog.,' etc. F.S.A., 1893.

Works : 'Life of Rossetti,' 1887 ; 'Theatrical Notes,' 1893 ; 'Life of David Garrick,' 1894 ; 'History of Victorian Stage,' contributed to 'The Stage in the Year 1900,' 1901.

LANDOR (Walter Savage), 1775-1864. [*See* p. 162.]

Add : 'Letters, and other unpublished Writings,' ed. by S. Wheeler, 1897.

LANG (Andrew), b. 1844. [*See* p. 162.]

Add to ' Works' : 'The Book of Dreams and Ghosts,' 1897 ; 'The Making of Religion,' 1898; 'The Companions of Pickle,' 1898; 'A History of Scotland from the Roman Occupation,' vol. i, 1900; 'Parson Kelly' (with A. E. W. Mason), 1900 ; 'Prince Charles Edward,' 1900 ; 'Magic and Religion,' 1901 ; 'Alfred Tennyson,' 1901 ; 'The Mystery of Mary Stewart,' 1901; 'James VI. and the Gowrie Mystery,' 1902 ; 'The Disentanglers,' 1902 ; 'Social Origins,' 1903.

Has *translated :* 'Miracles of Saint Katherine of Fierbois,' 1897 ; 'The Homeric Hymns,' 1899.

Has *edited :* 'Selections from the Poets,' 1897, etc. ; 'The Nursery Rhyme Book,' 1897 ; 'The Pink Fairy Book,' 1897 ; Dickens' Works, 1897, etc. ; 'Arabian Nights,' 1898 ; Waverley Novels, 1898, etc. ; 'The Red Book of Animal Stories,' 1899 ; 'The Grey Fairy Book,' 1900 ; 'The Violet Fairy Book,' 1901; 'The Book of Romance,' 1902.

LANIER (Sidney), 1842-1881. Born, at Macon, Georgia, 3 Feb. 1842. Educated at Oglethorpe Coll., 1857-60; Tutor there, 1860-61. Served in Confederate Army, 1861-65. Health much injured by exposure while prisoner of war in 1864. Worked as hotel-clerk, Dec. 1865 to April 1867; at same time engaged on his first book, a novel. Married Mary Day, 19 Dec. 1867. For a time schoolmaster at Prattville, Alabama, but ill-health obliged him to give this up. Lived at Macon, May 1868 to Dec. 1872; at San Antonio, Texas, Dec. 1872 to April 1873; returned to Macon. Subsequently settled in Baltimore, Dec. 1873. Obtained situation as flautist in Peabody Symphony Orchestra; besides this made his living by his pen, and lecturing in schools. Poem, 'Corn,' pubd. in 'Lippincott's Mag.,' 1875. Wrote words for Cantata for opening of Philadelphia Centennial Exposition, 1876. Lecturer on English Literature, Johns Hopkins University, 1879-81. Died, at Lynn, North Carolina, 7 Sept. 1881.

Works: 'Tiger-Lilies,' 1867; 'Florida,' 1876; 'Poems,' 1877; 'The Science of English Verse,' 1880.

Posthumous: 'The English Novel,' 1883; 'Poems' (ed. by Mrs. Lanier), 1884; 'Select Poems,' 1896; 'Letters,' 1899; 'Shakspere and his Forerunners,' 1903.

He *edited:* 'The Boy's Froissart,' 1878; 'The Boy's King Arthur,' 1880; 'The Boy's Mabinogion,' 1881; 'The Boy's Percy,' 1882.

Life: by W. M. Baskervill, 1896.

LECKY (William Edward Hartpole), 1838-1903. [*See* p. 164.]

Add: O.M., 1902. Died, 22 Oct. 1903.

Add to '*Works*': 'The Map of Life,' 1899; 'Leaders of Public Opinion in Ireland,' 1903.

LEE (Sidney), b. 1859. Born, in London, 5 Dec. 1859. Educated at City of London School, 1870-78; and at Balliol Coll., Oxford, 1878-82; B.A., 1882. Assistant-editor, Dict. of Nat. Biography, 1883-90; joint-editor with Sir L. Stephen, 1890-91; editor, 1891-1901. Clark Lecturer, Trin. Coll., Camb., 1901-02. Lecturer at Lowell Inst., Boston, U.S.A., 1903; at Johns Hopkins Univ., U.S.A., 1903; and at Princeton Univ., U.S.A., 1903. Hon. Litt.D.,

Manchester, 1900. Trustee of Shakespeare's Birthplace, Stratford-on-Avon, 1903.

Works: 'Stratford-on-Avon from the Earliest Times to the Death of Shakespeare,' 1885; 'Life of Shakespeare,' 1898 (third edn. same year); 'Life of Queen Victoria,' 1902; 'The Alleged Vandalism at Stratford-on-Avon,' 1903.

Has *edited:* Lord Berner's translation of Duke Huon of Bordeaux, 1882-87; Lord Herbert of Cherbury's 'Autobiography,' 1886; Oxford facsimile of Shakespeare First Folio, 1903.

LEE (Vernon) [*pseud.,* i.e. VIOLET PAGET], **b. 1856.** [*See* p. 164.]

Add: 'Genius Loci,' 1899; 'Penelope Brandling,'1903; 'Ariadne in Mantua,' 1903.

LEE-HAMILTON (Eugene), b. 1845. Born, in London, Jan. 1845. Educated in France and Germany; and at Oriel Coll., Oxford. Taylorian Scholar, 1864. Appointed to Diplomatic Service, 1869; at Paris, 1870-73; Lisbon, 1873-75. Serious ill-health from 1875 to 1894. Visited America, 1897. Married Annie E. Holdsworth, 1898. Resides near Florence.

Works: 'Poems and Transcripts,' 1878; 'God, Saints and Men,' 1880; 'The New Medusa,' 1882; 'Apollo and Marsyas,' 1884; 'Imaginary Sonnets,' 1888; 'The Fountain of Youth,' 1891; 'Sonnets of the Wingless Hours,' 1894; 'Forest Notes' (with his wife), 1899.

Has *translated:* Dante's 'Inferno,' 1898.

LE GALLIENNE (Richard), b. 1866. Born, in Liverpool, 20 Jan. 1866. Educated at Liverpool Coll. For some time engaged with firm of chartered accountants; then adopted profession of letters. Was for short time Sec. to Wilson Barrett. Literary critic on staff of 'Star,' 1891. Married (i) Mildred Lee, 1891; she died, 1894; (ii) Julie Norregard, 1897.

Works : 'My Ladies' Sonnets'
(priv. ptd.), 1887; 'Volumes in
Folio,' 1889; 'George Meredith,'
1890; 'The Book-Bills of Narcissus,'
1891; 'English Poems,' 1892; 'The
Religion of a Literary Man,' 1893;
'The Student and the Body-
Snatcher' (with R. K. Leather),
1890; 'Prose Fancies' (2 ser.),
1894, 1896; 'Bits of Old Chelsea'
(with L. P. Johnson), 1894; 'Holly
and Mistletoe' (with E. Nesbit and
N. Gale), 1895; 'Robert Louis
Stevenson, and other poems,' 1895;
'Retrospective Reviews,' 1896;
'The Quest of the Golden Girl,'
1893; 'If I were God,' 1897; 'The
Romance of Zion Chapel,' 1898;
'Young Lives,' 1899; 'The Wor-
shipper of the Image,' 1899; 'Rud-
yard Kipling : a criticism,' 1900;
'Travels in England,' 1900; 'The
Beautiful Lie of Rome,' 1900;
'Sleeping Beauty,' 1900; 'The
Life Romantic,' 1901; 'An Old
House,' 1903.
Has *translated :* the Rubáiyát of
Omar Khayyám, 1898; and *edited :*
A. H. Hallam's 'Poems,' 1893;
Hazlitt's 'Liber Amoris,' 1893;
Isaak Walton's 'Compleat Angler,'
1896; De Quincey's 'Opium Eater,'
1898.

**LELAND (Charles Godfrey), 1824-
1903.** [*See* p. 165.]
Add : Died, in Florence, 20 March,
1903.
Add to '*Works*' : 'Aradia,' 1899;
'The Unpublished Legends of Virgil,' 1899; 'Have you a Strong
Will?' 1899; wrote or collaborated
in a number of volumes in H. S.
Ward's 'Useful Arts' series, 1899,
etc.; 'Flaxius,' 1902; 'Kuloskap
the Master and other Algonquin
Legends,' trans. by C. G. Leland
and J. D. Price, 1903.

LILLY (William Samuel), b. 1840.
[*See* p. 169.]
Add : 'First Principles in Politics,'
1899; 'A Year of Life,' 1900; 'Renaissance Types,' 1901; 'India and
its Problems,' 1902; 'Christianity
and Modern Civilization,' 1903.

**LINTON (Mrs. Elizabeth Lynn),
1822-1898.** [*See* p. 170.]
Add : Died, in London, 14 July
1898.
Works (posthumous) : 'My Literary Life' (ed. by B. Harraden),
1899; 'The Second Youth of Theo-
dora Desanges' (ed. by G. S. Layard), 1900.
Life : by G. S. Layard, 1901.

**LOWELL (James Russell), 1819-
1891.** [*See* p. 174.]
Add : 'Early Prose Writings,'
1902.

**LUBBOCK (John), Baron Avebury,
b. 1834.** [*See* p. 174.]
Add : Created Baron Avebury,
1900. M.P. for London Univ.,
1880-1900.
Add to '*Works*' : 'Buds and
Stipules,' 1898; 'The Scenery of
England,' 1902; 'Short History of
Coins and Currency,' 1902; 'Free
Trade and British Commerce' (Cob-
den Club), 1902; 'Essays and Ad-
dresses,' 1903.

LUSKA (Sidney), *pseud.* See HAR-
LAND (Henry).

LYALL (Edna) [*pseud.,* i.e. ADA
ELLEN BAYLY), **1857-1903.** Born, at
Brighton, 1857. Educated there.
First book published, 1879. Lived
first at Lincoln, then for greater
part of her life at Eastbourne;
took active interest in philanthropic
work. Died there, 8 Feb. 1903.
Works : 'Won by Waiting,' 1879;
'Donovan,' 1882; 'We Two,' 1884;
'In the Golden Days,' 1885;
'Knight-Errant,' 1887; 'The Auto-
biography of a Slander,' 1887;
'Derrick Vaughan,' 1889; 'Their
Happiest Christmas,' 1890; 'A
Hardy Norseman,' 1890; 'Max
Hereford's Dream,' 1891; 'To
Right the Wrong,' 1894; 'Doreen,'
1894; 'How the Children Raised
the Wind,' 1893; 'The Auto-
biography of a Truth,' 1896; 'Way-
faring Men,' 1897; 'Hope the
Hermit,' 1898; 'In Spite of All,'
1901; 'The Hinderers,' 1902; 'The
Burges Letters,' 1902.

LYLY (John), 1554-1606. [*See* p. 176.]
Add: ' Collected Works' (3 vols.), ed. by R. W. Bond, 1903.

McCARTHY (Justin), b. 1830. [*See* p. 178.]
Add: M.P., N. Longford, 1892-1900. Chairman of Irish Parliamentary Party, Nov. 1890 to Jan. 1896.
Add to '*Works*' : ' The Story of Gladstone's Life,' 1898 ; ' Modern England' (2 vols.), 1899 ; ' Reminiscences.' 1899 ; ' Mononia,' 1901 ; ' The Reign of Queen Anne,' 1903 ; ' British Political Leaders,' 1903 ; ' Ireland and her Story,' 1903.

McCARTHY (Justin Huntly), b. 1860. [Son of preceding.] Born 1860. Educated at Univ. Coll. School and Univ. Coll. Occupied for many years in journalism. First book published, 1883. First play, ' The Candidate,' prod. at Criterion theatre, 2 Nov. 1884 ; followed by several others : ' The White Carnation,' ' The Highwayman,' ' The Wife of Socrates,' ' His Little Dodge,' ' If I were King.' M.P. for Athlone, 1884-85 ; for Newry, 1885-92. Married Marie Cecilia Brown (' Cissie Loftus '), 1894.
Works : ' Outline of Irish History,' 1883 ; ' Serapion,' 1883 ; ' England under Gladstone,' 1884 ; ' Camiola,' 1885 ; ' Doom,' 1886 ; ' Our Sensation Novel,' 1886 ; ' Hafiz in London,' 1886 ; ' Hours with Eminent Irishmen,' 1886 ; ' Ireland since the Union,' 1887 ; ' The Case for Home Rule,' 1887 ; ' Dolly,' 1899 ; ' Lily Lass,' 1889 ; ' Harlequinade,' 1890 ; ' The French Revolution ' (4 vols.), 1890-97 ; ' Red Diamonds,' 1893 ; ' A London Legend,' 1895 ; ' The Royal Christopher,' 1896 ; ' The Three Disgraces,' 1897 ; ' Short History of the United States,' 1898 ; ' If I were King,' 1901 ; ' Marjorie,' 1903 ; ' The Proud Prince,' 1903.
He has *translated :* ' Rubaiyat of Omar Khayyam,' 1889 ; ' Ghazels from the Divan of Hafiz,' 1893 ; ' Quatrains of Omar Khayyam,'

1898 ; and *edited :* Montaigne's ' Essays,' 1889 ; ' The Thousand and One Days,' 1893.

MACDONALD (George), b. 1824. *See* p. 179, col. i. To date of birth, *add :* 10 Dec.
Add to '*Works*' : ' Rampolli,' 1897.

MACLAREN (Ian), *pseud. See* WATSON (John).

MACLEOD (Fiona). Author ; of Highland extraction.
Works : ' Pharais,' 1894 ; ' The Mountain Lovers,' 1895 ; ' The Sin-Eater,' 1895 ; ' The Washer of the Ford,' 1896 ; ' Green Fire,' 1896 ; ' From the Hills of Dream,' 1896 ; ' The Laughter of Peterkin,' 1897 ; ' Celtic Tales ' (3 vols., partly collected from preceding), 1897 ; ' The Dominion of Dreams,' 1899 ; ' The Divine Adventure,' 1900 ; ' Celtic : a study in spiritual history,' (U.S.A.) 1901 ; ' Wind and Wave' (Tauchnitz edn.), 1902 ; ' For the Beauty of an Idea,' 1903.

MAHAFFY (John Pentland), b. 1839. [*See* p. 181.]
Add : Married Frances Mac Dougall, 12 July 1865. Hon. Mem. of Royal Acad., Berlin ; of Acad. of Sciences, Utrecht ; of Archæological Soc., Alexandria. Commissioner of Intermediate Education, Ireland, 1900. High Sheriff, Co. Monaghan, 1901-02.

MAHAN (Alfred Thayer), b. 1840. Born, at West Point, New York, 27 Sept. 1840. Appointed to U.S. Navy, 1856 ; Lieutenant, 1861 ; Lieut.-Commander, 1865 ; Commander, 1872 ; Captain, 1885. Retired, 1896. Served in Civil War, 1861-65. President of Naval War College, Newport, 1886-88 and 1892-93. Mem. of Naval Advisory Board in Spanish-American War, 1898. Delegate to Peace Conference at The Hague, 1899. Hon. D.C.L., Oxford, 1894 ; LL.D., Cambridge, 1894 ; Harvard, 1895 ; Yale, 1897 ; McGill Univ., 1900 ; Columbia Univ., 1900.

23

Works : ‘The Gulf and Inland Waters,’ 1883; ‘The Influence of Sea Power upon History,’ 1890; ‘The Influence of Sea Power upon the French Revolution and Empire,’ 1892; ‘Life of Admiral Farragut,’ 1892; ‘Life of Nelson’ (2 vols.), 1897; ‘The Interest of the United States in Sea Power,’ 1897; ‘Lessons of the War with Spain,’ 1899; ‘The Problem of Asia,’ 190J; ‘The Story of the War in South Africa,’ 1900; ‘Types of Naval Officers,’ 1902.

MALET (Lucas), *pseud.* [i.e. Mrs. **MARY ST. LEGER HARRISON**], **b. 1852.** Born [Mary St. Leger Kingsley, daughter of Charles Kingsley], at Eversley, 1852. Educated privately; at Slade School; and at Univ. Coll., London. Has travelled extensively in East and in America. Married to Rev. William Harrison ; he died, 1897.

Works : ‘Mrs. Lorimer,’ 1882; ‘Colonel Enderby’s Wife,’ 1885 ; ‘Little Peter,’ 1888; ‘A Counsel of Perfection,’ 1888; ‘The Wages of Sin,’ 1891 ; ‘The Carissima,’ 1896; ‘The Gateless Barrier,’ 1900; ‘The History of Sir Richard Calmady,’ 1901.

MALLOCK (William Hurrell), b. **1849.** [*See* p. 183.]

Add to ‘*Works*’ : ‘Aristocracy and Evolution,’ 1898; ‘The Individualist,’ 1899 ; ‘Doctrine and Doctrinal Disruption,’ 1900; ‘Religion as a Credible Doctrine,’ 1902 ; ‘The Fiscal Dispute,’ 1903.

MARTIN (Sir Theodore), b. **1816.** [*See* p. 187.]

Add : Lady Martin died 31 Oct. 1898.

Add to ‘*Works*’ : ‘Helena Faucit,’ 1900.

MARTINEAU (James), 1805-1900. [*See* p. 189.]

Add : Died, in London, 11 Jan. 1900.

ɍ *Add to* ‘*Works*’ : ‘Faith the Beginning . . . of the Spiritual Life,’ 1897.

Life : by A. W. Jackson, 1900; ‘Life and Letters,’ by J. Drummond, 1902.

MAX-MUELLER (Friedrich), 1823-1900. [*See* p. 191.]

Add : Died, at Oxford, 28 Oct. 1900.

Add to ‘*Works*’ : ‘Râmakrishna,’ 1898; ‘Auld Lang Syne’ (2 ser.), 1898-99 ; ‘The Six Systems of Indian Philosophy,’ 1899 ; ‘The Question of Right between England and the Transvaal,’ 1900.

Posthumous : ‘My Autobiography,’ 1901.

Collected Works : 1898, etc.

Life : ‘Life and Letters’ (ed. by his wife, 2 vols.), 1902.

MAXWELL (*Sir* **Herbert Eustace),** *Bart.,* **b. 1845.** Born, in Edinburgh, 8 Jan. 1845. Educated at Eton, and at Christ Church, Oxford. Married Mary Campbell, 20 Jan. 1869. Succeeded to Baronetcy, 1877. M.P. for Wigtonshire, since 1880. Jun. Lord of Treasury, 1886-92. Rhind Lecturer in Archæology, Edinburgh, 1893. Privy Councillor, 1897. Chairman, Royal Commission on Tuberculosis, 1897-98 ; represented English Govt. at Tuberculosis Conference, Berlin, 1899. F.R.S., 1898. LL.D., Glasgow, 1900. Pres., Soc. of Antiquaries of Scotland, since 1900.

Works: ‘Studies in the Topography of Galloway,’ 1887 ; ‘Passages in the Life of Sir Lucian Elphin’ (anon.), 1889 ; ‘The Art of Love,’ 1889; ‘The Letter of the Law,’ 1892 ; ‘Meridiana,’ 1892 ; ‘Life of the Rt. Hon. W. H. Smith,’ 1893 ; ‘Scottish Land Names,’ 1894 ; ‘Post-Meridiana,’ 1895; ‘A Duke of Britain,’ 1895 ; ‘Rainy Days in a Library,’ 1896 ; ‘History of Dumfries and Galloway,’ 1896 ; ‘Robert the Bruce and the Struggle for Scottish Independence,’ 1897; ‘Sixty Years a Queen,’ 1897 ; ‘Memories of the Months’ (3 series), 1897, 1900, 1903; ‘The Hon. Sir Charles Murray,’ 1898 ; ‘Salmon and Sea-Trout,’ 1898; ‘Life of Wellington,’ 1899; ‘The Chevalier of the Splendid Crest,’ 1900; ‘History of the House of Douglas,' 1902 ; ' British Soldiers in the Field,' 1902.

Has *edited* : The Sportsman's Library,' 1896, etc. ; ' The Angler's Library ' (with F. G. Aflalo), 1897, etc. ; Whyte-Melville's Works, 1898, etc. ; Sir C. A. Murray's ' Memoir of Mohammed Ali,' 1898 ; Sir J. E. E. Wilmot's ' Reminiscences of T. Assheton Smith,' 1902.

MEREDITH (George), b. 1828. [*See* p. 194.] P. 194, col. i. From ' Works,' *dele:* ' Mary Bertrand,' 1862.

Add : Educated in Germany. Studied law for a short time from 1849. Afterwards was for some years engaged in journalism, including editorship of an Eastern Counties newspaper. Special Correspondent of ' Morning Post ' during Austro-Italian War of 1866. For many years ' publisher's reader ' to Messrs. Chapman & Hall. Married Mrs. Mary Ellen Nicholls, 1849; after her death he re-married. Widower since 1885.

Add to ' *Works* ' : ' Odes in Contribution to the Song of French History,' 1898 ; ' A Reading of Life,' 1901 ; ' Short Stories,' 1902.

MERIVALE (Herman Charles), b. 1839. [*See* p. 194.]

Add : ' Bar, Stage and Platform,' 1902.

MERRIMAN (Henry), pseudonym of HUGH STOWELL SCOTT, Novelist. Died, at Melton, 19 Nov. 1903.

Works : ' Young Mistley ' (anon.), 1888 ; ' The Phantom Future,' 1888 ; ' Suspense,' 1890; ' Prisoners and Captives,' 1891 ; ' From One Generation to Another,' 1892 ; ' The Slave of the Lamp,' 1892 ; ' From Wisdom Court ' (with S. G. Tallentyre), 1893 ; ' With Edged Tools,' 1894 ; ' The Grey Lady,' 1895 ; ' Flotsam,' 1896 ; ' The Sowers,' 1896; ' The Money Spinner ' (with S. G. Tallentyre), 1896; ' In Kedar's Tents,' 1897 ; ' Roden's Corner,' 1898 ; ' The Isle of Unrest,' 1899 ; ' Dross,' 1899 ; ' The Velvet Glove,' 1901 ; ' The

Vultures,' 1902 ; ' Barlasch of the Guard,' 1903.

MEYNELL (*Mrs.* Alice Christiana). [*See* p. 195.]

Add: ' London Impressions,' 1898 ; ' The Spirit of Place,' 1899 ; ' John Ruskin,' 1900; ' Later Poems,' 1902.

Has *ed'ted:* Wordsworth's 'Poems,' 1902 ; Browning's ' Poems,' 1902.

MILLER (Joaquin), b. 1841. Born [Cincinnatus Hiner Miller, better known as ' Joaquin '], in Indiana, 10 Nov. 1841. Parents removed to Oregon, 1850. Was for a time miner in California. Returned to Oregon, 1860, and studied law. Express-Agent in Idaho, 1861. Edited ' Democratic Register,' 1863. Practised law in Cañon City, Oregon, 1863-66 ; Judge of Grant County, 1866-70. Travelled in Europe, 1870. Subsequently some years of journalism at Washington. Play, ' The Danites,' prod. in New York, 1877 ; ' '49,' 1878 ; ' The Silent Man,' 1880; ' Tally-Ho,' 1883. Since 1887 has resided in California. In Klondike, as Correspondent of ' New York Journal,' 1897-98.

Works : ' Joaquin, et al., by Cincinnatus H. Miller,' 1869 ; ' Songs of the Sierras, by Joaquin Miller,' 1871 ; ' Pacific Poems,' 1871 ; ' Songs of the Sunlands,' 1873 ; ' Life among the Modocs,' 1873 ; ' Unwritten History,' 1873 ; ' A Ship in the Desert,' 1875 ; ' The First Families of the Sierras,' 1875 ; ' The One Fair Woman,' 1876 ; ' The Baroness of New York,' 1877 ; ' The Danites in the Sierras,' 1877 ; ' Songs of Italy,' 1878 ; ' Shadows of Shasta,' 1881 ; ' Poetical Works,' 1882 ; ' Forty-nine,' 1882 ; ' Memorie and Rime,' 1884 ; ' The Destruction of Gotham,' 1886 ; ' Songs of the Mexican Seas,' 1887 ; ' My Own Story,' 1890 ; ' In Classic Shades,' 1890 ; 'The Building of the City Beautiful,' 1894 ; ' Songs of the Soul,' 1896 ; ' True Bear Stories,' 1900 ; ' Chants for the Boer,' 1902.

23—2

MILTON (John), 1608-1674. [See p. 199.]

Add: 'Nova Solyma, the Ideal City' (an anonymous romance, attributed to Milton by the editor, W. Begley), 1902.

MIVART (St. George Jackson), 1827-1900. Born, in London, 30 Nov. 1877. Educated at school at Clapham, at Harrow, and at King's Coll., London. Joined Roman Catholic Church, and went to St. Mary's Coll., Oscott, 1844. Student of Lincoln's Inn, Jan. 1846; called to Bar, 30 Jan. 1851. Devoted himself mainly to science; contrib. to 'proceedings' of scientific societies, 'Encyc. Brit.,' etc. Mem. Royal Institution, 1849; Fellow of Zoological Soc., 1858. Lecturer on Comparative Anatomy, St. Mary's Hospital, London, 1862. Fellow of Linnæan Soc., 1862; Secretary, 1874-80; Vice-Pres., 1892. F.R.S., 1869. Prof. of Biology at Roman Catholic Coll., Kensington, 1874. Degree of Ph.D. conferred by the Pope, 1876. Pres. Biological Section, British Association, 1879. M.D., Louvain, 1884; Prof. of Philosophy of Nat. History, Louvain, 1890-93. Contrib. to 'Contemporary Rev.,' 'Nineteenth Century,' 'Fortnightly Rev.,' etc. A series of articles, dealing with religious questions, in 'Nineteenth Century' led to his excommunication by Cardinal Vaughan, Jan. 1900. Died, in London, 1 April 1900.

Works: 'On the Genesis of Species,' 1871 ; 'Lessons in Elementary Anatomy,' 1873 ; 'Man and Apes,' 1873 ; 'The Common Frog,' 1874 ; 'Contemporary Evolution,' 1876 ; 'Lessons from Nature,' 1876 ; 'The Cat,' 1881 ; 'Nature and Thought,' 1882 ; 'A Philosophical Catechism,' 1884 ; 'On Truth,' 1889 ; 'The Origin of Human Reason,' 1889 ; 'Dogs, Jackals, Wolves, and Foxes,' 1890 ; 'Introduction générale à l'Etude de la Nature,' 1891 ; 'Birds,' 1892 ; 'Essays and Criticisms,' 1892 ;

'Types of Animal Life,' 1893 ; 'An Introduction to the Elements of Science,' 1894 ; 'Henry Standon' (under pseud. 'D'Arcy Drew'), 1894 (later edition, called 'Castle and Manor,' 1900) ; 'The Helpful Science,' 1895 ; 'Monograph of the Lories,' 1896 ; 'The Groundwork of Science,' 1898.

MONKHOUSE (William Cosmo), 1840-1901. Born, in London, 18 March 1840. Educated at St. Paul's School. Entered Board of Trade as Clerk, 1857 ; Assistant Sec., Financial Dept., 1893-1901. Visited S. America, 1870-71, to report on hospitals for seamen. Served on various departmental Committees. Contrib. largely to 'Dict. of Nat. Biog.,' and to various periodicals. Married (i) Laura Keymer, 1865 ; (ii) Leonora Eliza Blount, 1873. Died, in London, 20 July 1901.

Works [exclusive of descriptive text to various collections of pictures]: 'A Dream of Idleness,' 1865 ; 'A Question of Honour,' 1868 ; 'Masterpieces of English Art,' 1869 ; 'The Précis Book,' 1877 ; 'Turner' ('Great Artists' series), 1879 ; 'The Italian Pre-Raphaelites,' 1887 ; 'Corn and Poppies,' 1890 ; 'The Earlier English Water-Colour Painters,' 1890 ; 'Leigh Hunt' ('Great Writers' Series), 1893 ; 'In the National Gallery,' 1895 ; 'The Christ upon the Hill,' 1895 ; 'British Contemporary Artists,' 1899 ; 'History of Chinese Porcelain,' 1901 ; 'Life of Sir John Tenniel,' 1901.

Posthumous: 'Pasiteles the Elder,' 1901 ; 'Nonsense Rhymes,' 1902.

MOORE (George). Novelist and dramatist.

Works: 'Flowers of Passion,' 1878 ; 'Pagan Poems,' 1881 ; 'A Modern Lover,' 1883 ; 'A Mummer's Wife,' 1884 ; 'Literature at Nurse,' 1885 ; 'A Drama in Muslin,' 1886 ; 'Parnell and his Island,' 1887 ; 'Mere Accident,' 1887 ; 'Confessions of a Young Man,' 1888 ; 'Spring Days,' 1888 ; 'Miss Fletcher,' 1889 ; 'Impressions and Opinions,' 1891; 'Vain Fortune,' 1892; 'Modern Painting,' 1893; 'The Strike at Arlingford,' 1893; 'Esther Waters,' 1894; 'Celibates,' 1895; 'Evelyn Innes,' 1898; 'The Bending of the Bough,' 1900; 'Sister Teresa,' 1901; 'The Untilled Field,' 1903.

MOORE (Thomas), 1779-1852. [*See* p. 201.]
Add : Life, by J. P. Gunning, 1900.

MORIER (James Justinian), 1780 [?]-1849.
See p. 204, col. i. To 'Works,' *add :* 'The Adventures of Hajji Baba in England' (anon.), 1828.

MORISON (James Cotter), 1831-1888. Born, 20 April 1831. Educated at Highgate Grammar School; in France; and at Lincoln Coll., Oxford. After taking his degree, settled in London, occupied in journalism. Married Miss Virtue. One of founders, and part proprietor, of 'Fortnightly Review.' Contrib. to 'Athenæum,' 'and a number of periodicals. Mem. of Positivist Society. Died, in London, 26 Feb. 1888.

Works : 'The Life and Times of St. Bernard,' 1863; 'Irish Grievances,' 1868; 'Gibbon,' 1878; 'Macaulay,' 1882; 'Madame de Maintenon,' 1885; 'The Service of Man,' 1887.

MORLEY (John), b. 1833. [*See* p. 204.]
Add : Order of Merit, 1902. Hon. Fellow, All Souls' Coll., Oxford, 1903.
Add to 'Works' : 'Oliver Cromwell,' 1900; 'Life of W. E. Gladstone,' 1903.

MORRIS (Sir Lewis), b. 1833. [*See* p. 205.]
Add : Deputy Chancellor, Univ. of Wales; Vice-Pres., Univ. Coll., Aberystwyth.
Add to 'Works' : 'The Diamond Jubilee,' 1897; 'Harvest Tide,' 1901.

MORRIS (William), 1834-1896. [*See* p. 205.]
Add : Life, by J. W. Mackail, 1899.

MORRISON (Arthur), b. 1863. Born, in Kent, 1863. Educated at private schools. Held post as secretary, till 1890. Then adopted journalistic and literary career. Contrib. to 'Nat. Observer,' 'Saturday Rev.,' 'Monthly Rev.,' 'Cornhill,' 'Macmillan,' etc.

Works : 'The Shadows around us,' 1891; 'Tales of Mean Streets,' 1894; 'Martin Hewitt, Investigator,' 1894; 'Chronicles of Martin Hewitt,' 1895; 'Zig-Zags at the Zoo,' 1895; 'Adventures of Martin Hewitt,' 1896; 'A Child of the Jago,' 1896; 'The Dorrington Deed-Box,' 1897; 'To London Town,' 1899; 'Cunning Murrell,' 1900; 'The Hole in the Wall,' 1902; 'The Red Triangle,' 1903.

MURRAY (David Christie), b. 1847. [*See* p. 208.]
Add : 'My Contemporaries in Fiction,' 1897; 'This Little World,' 1897; 'A Race for Millions,' 1898; 'Tales in Prose and Verse,' 1898; 'The Cockney Columbus,' 1898; 'The Church of Humanity,' 1901; 'Despair's Last Journey,' 1901; 'His Own Ghost,' 1902.

MURRAY (George Gilbert Aimé), b. 1866. Born, at Sydney, N.S. Wales, 2 Jan. 1866. Educated at Merchant Taylors' School, and at St. John's Coll., Oxford; B.A., 1888; M.A., 1892. Hertford Scholar, 1885; Ireland Scholar, 1885; Gaisford Prizeman, 1886 and 1887; Chancellor's Latin Verse Prize, 1886; Craven Scholar, 1886; Derby Scholar, 1889. Fellow, New Coll., Oxford, 1888; Professor of Greek, Glasgow Univ., 1889-99. Hon. LL.D., Glasgow, 1900. Married Lady Mary Henrietta Howard, 1889. Play, 'Carlyon Sahib,' produced at Prince of Wales's theatre, Kennington, 19 June 1899; 'Andromache,' produced by Stage Society, Feb. 1901.

Works : ' Olympia,' 1886 ; ' Mesolonghi Capta,' 1887 ; ' Gobi or Shamo,' 1889 ; ' The Place of Greek in Education,' 1889 ; ' History of Ancient Greek Literature,' 1897 ; ' Carlyon Sahib,' 1900 ; ' Andromache,' 1900 ; contribution to ' Liberalism and the Empire,' 1900.

Has *edited :* ' Euripidis Fabulae,' 1902, etc.; and *translated* Euripides' ' Hippolytus ' and ' Bacchae,' and Aristophanes' ' The Frogs,' 1902.

MURRAY (James Augustus Henry), b. 1837. Born, at Denholm, Roxburghshire, 1837. Educated in Scotland, at London Univ., and at Balliol Coll., Oxford. Assistant Master, Hawick Grammar School, 1855-58; Master of Hawick Academy, 1858-70 ; Assistant Master, Mill Hill School, 1870-85. Married Ada Agnes Ruthven, 1867. In 1879 became editor of ' New English Dictionary ' for Philological Soc. and Oxford Univ. Press. Removed from Mill Hill to Oxford, 1885. Founded Hawick Archæological Soc., 1856. Pres., Philological Society, 1878-80 and 1882-84. Romanes Lecturer, Oxford, 1900. Hon. LL.D., Edinburgh, 1874; D.C.L., Durham, 1886 ; Ph.D., Freiburg, 1896; LL.D., Glasgow, 1901 ; D.Litt., Wales, 1902. Hon. Mem. of various foreign learned Societies.

Works [exclusive of contributions to ' Transactions ' of learned societies] : ' A Week among the Antiquities of Orkney,' 1861 ; ' The Dialect of the Southern Counties of Scotland,' 1873 ; ' New English Dictionary, vols. i, ii, 1888-93 ; vol. iii, 1897 ; vol. v, 1901 ; ' The Evolution of English Lexicography ' (Romanes Lecture), 1900.

Has *edited :* Sir D. Lyndesay's ' Minor Poems,' 1871 ; ' The Complaynt of Scotland,' 1872 ; ' The Romance and Prophecies of Thomas of Esceldoune,' 1875.

NEWBOLT (Henry John), b. 1862. Born, at Bilston, 6 June 1862. Educated at Clifton Coll., and at Corpus Christi Coll., Oxford ; B.A., 1885. Called to Bar at Lincoln's Inn, 1887 ; practised till 1899. Married Margaret Edina Duckworth, 1889. Editor of ' Monthly Rev.,' since 1900.

Works : ' Taken from the Enemy,' 1892 ; ' Mordred,' 1895 ; ' Admirals All,' 1897 ; ' The Island Race,' 1898 ; ' The Sailing of the Long-ships,' 1902.

Has *edited :* ' Stories from Froissart,' 1899 ; ' Froissart in Britain,' 1900.

NOEL (Roden Berkeley Wriothesley), 1834-1894. [*See* p. 213.]

Add : ' Collected Works,' ed. by J. A. Symonds, 1902.

NORRIS (William Edward), b. 1847. [*See* p. 214.]

Add : ' Marietta's Marriage,' 1897 ; ' The Fight for the Crown,' 1898 ; ' The Widower,' 1898 ; ' Giles Ingilby,' 1899 ; ' An Octave,' 1900 ; ' The Flower of the Flock,' 1900 ; ' His Own Father,' 1901; ' The Embarrassing Orphan,' 1901 ; ' The Credit of the County,' 1902 ; ' Lord Leonard the Luckless,' 1903.

OLIPHANT (*Mrs.* Margaret Oliphant), 1828-1897. [*See* p. 217.]

Add to ' *Works* (*posthumous*)' : ' The Lady's Walk,' 1897 ; ' Annals of a Publishing House,' 1897 ; ' That Little Cutty,' 1898 ; ' A Widow's Tale,' 1898 ; ' Autobiography and Letters ' (ed. by Mrs. Coghill), 1899; ' Queen Victoria,' 1900.

OUIDA [*pseud.*, i.e. LOUISE DE LA RAMÉE], **b. 1840.** [*See* p. 219.]

Add : ' The Silver Christ, etc.,' 1898 ; ' La Strega,' 1899 ; ' The Waters of Edera,' 1900 ; ' Critical Studies,' 1900 ; ' Street Dust,' 1901.

PAIN (Barry Eric Odell), b. 1864. Born, at Cambridge, 1864. Educated at Sedburgh School, and at Corpus Christi Coll., Camb. Married Amelia Lehmann, 1892. Contributed for some years to ' Daily Chronicle ' ; on staff of ' Black and White,' since 1894. Frequent contributor to periodicals.

Works: 'In a Canadian Canoe,' 1891 ; 'Playthings and Parodies,' 1892 ; Stories and Interludes,' 1892 ; 'Graeme and Cyril,' 1893 ; 'The Kindness of the Celestial,' 1894 ; 'The Octave of Claudius,' 1897 ; 'Wilmay,' 1898 ; 'The Romantic History of Robin Hood,' 1898 ; 'Eliza,' 1900 ; 'De Omnibus,' 1901 ; 'Nothing Serious,' 1901 ; 'Another Englishman's Love Letters,' 1901 ; 'Stories in the Dark,' 1901 ; 'The One Before,' 1902 ; 'Little Entertainments,' 1903 ; 'Eliza's Husband,' 1903.

PALGRAVE (Francis Turner), 1824-1897. [*See* p. 221.]
Add : Died, in London, 24 Oct. 1897.
Add to 'Works': 'Golden Treasury,' second series, 1897.
Life : by G. F. Palgrave, 1899.

PARKER (*Sir* **Gilbert**), **b. 1862.** Born, in Canada, 23 Nov. 1862. Educated at Trinity Coll., Toronto. Assistant-editor, 'Sydney Morning Herald,' 1886-89. Has travelled extensively in N. Canada, and in the Southern Seas. Settled in London, 1889. Married Amy E. Van Tine, 5 Dec. 1895. Play, 'The Seats of the Mighty,' His Majesty's theatre, 28 April 1897. F.R.C.S., 1898. D.C.L., Trinity Coll., Toronto, 1900. M.P. for Gravesend, since 1900. Knighted, 1902.
Works : 'The Vendetta,' 1888 ; 'No Defence,' 1889 ; 'Pierre and his People,' 1892 ; 'Round the Compass in Australia,' 1892 ; 'Mrs. Falchion,' 1893 ; 'The Trespasser,' 1893 ; 'The Translation of a Savage,' 1894 ; 'A Lover's Diary,' 1894 ; 'The Trail of the Sword,' 1895 ; 'When Valmond came to Pontiac,' 1895 ; 'An Adventurer of the North,' 1895 ; 'The Seats of the Mighty,' 1896 ; 'The Pomp of the Lavilettes,' 1897 ; 'The Battle of the Strong,' 1898 ; 'Born with a Golden Spoon,' 1899 ; 'The Lane that had no Turning,' 1900 ; 'The Right of Way,' 1901 ; 'Donovan Pasha,' 1902.

PATER (**Walter Horatio**), **1839-1894.** [*See* p. 223.]
Add : 'Collected Works,' 1900, etc.

PAUL (**Charles Kegan**), **1828-1902.** Born, at White Lackington, Somerset, 8 March 1828. Educated at Ilminster, 1836-41 ; at Eton, 1841-46 ; and at Exeter Coll., Oxford. B.A. 1849. Ordained, 1851. Curate of Great Tew, 1851-52 ; of Bloxham, 1852. 'Conduct' of Eton and Master in College, 1853-62. Married Margaret Agnes Colvile, 1856. Vicar of Sturminster Marshall, 1862-74. Adopted Positivist views and resigned living, 1874. Settled in London as "reader" to publishing firm of H. S. King ; subsequently took over management of firm and started that of Kegan Paul, Trench & Co. Edited 'New Quarterly Mag.,' 1879-80. Joined Roman Catholic Church, Aug. 1890. Died, in London, 19 July 1902.
Works : 'The Communion of Saints,' 1853 ; 'The Boundaries of the Church' (under initials 'C.K.P.'), 1861 ; 'Reading Book for Evening Schools,' 1864 ; 'William Godwin,' 1876 ; 'Biographical Sketches,' 1883 ; 'Confessio Viatoris,' 1891 ; 'Faith and Unfaith,' 1891 ; 'Maria Drummond' (by 'C.K.P.'), 1891 ; 'Miracle,' 1892 ; 'God,' 1893 ; 'St. Antony of Padua,' 1895 ; 'Celibacy,'1899 ; 'Memories,' 1899 ; 'On the Way Side,' 1899.
He *translated :* Goethe's 'Faust,' pt. I., 1873 ; F. Baur's 'Philological Introduction' (with E. A. Stone), 1876 ; Pascal's 'Thoughts,' 1885 ; J. K. Huysman's 'En Route,' 1896 ; and *edited :* Cardinal Manning's 'Temperance Speeches,' 1894.

PAYN (**James**), **1830-1898.** [*See* p. 224.]
Add : Died, in London, 25 March 1898.
Add to 'Works': 'Another's Burden,' 1897.
Posthumous : 'The Backwater of Life' (ed. by Sir L. Stephens), 1899.

PEMBERTON (Max), b. 1863.
Born, in Birmingham, 19 June
1863. Educated at Merchant
Taylors' School, and at Caius Coll.,
Camb.; B.A., 1884. Married Alice
Agnes Tussaud, 1884. Contrib. to
'Vanity Fair,' 1885; to 'St. James's
Gaz.,' 'Chambers,' and 'Standard,'
1885-87; editor of 'Chums,' 1892-
93; editor of 'Cassell's Mag.,' since
1896. Frequent contributor to
periodicals.
Works : 'The Diary of a Scoun-
drel,' 1891; 'The Iron Pirate,' 1893;
'The Sea Wolves,' 1894; 'Jewel
Mysteries I have known,' 1894;
'The Impregnable City,' 1895;
'The Little Huguenot,' 1895; 'A
Puritan's Wife,' 1896; 'A Gentle-
man's Gentleman,' 1896; 'Christine
of the Hills,' 1897; 'Queen of the
Jesters,' 1897; 'The Phantom
Army,' 1898; 'Kronstadt,' 1898;
'The Garden of Swords,' 1899;
'The Signors of the Night,' 1899;
'The Footsteps of a Throne,' 1900;
'Féo,' 1900; 'Pro Patria,' 1901;
'The Giant's Gate,' 1901; 'The
House under the Sea,' 1902; 'I
Crown thee King,' 1902; 'The Gold
Wolf,' 1903.
Has *edited :* 'Cassell's Pocket
Library,' 1895, etc.; 'The Isthmian
Library' (with B. F. Robinson),
1896, etc.

PHILLIPS (Stephen), b. 1864.
Born, at Somertown, 28 July 1864.
Educated at Stratford and Peterborough Grammar Schools. Became
an actor; was a member of F. R.
Benson's company. Afterwards
was for a short time an army tutor;
eventually adopted profession of
letters. Married May Lidyard.
Play, 'Herod,' prod. at His Majesty's
theatre, 30 Oct. 1900; 'Ulysses,'
His Majesty's, 1 Feb. 1902; 'Paolo
and Francesca,' St. James's, 6 March
1902.
Works : 'Primavera' (anon., by
Stephen Phillips, R. L. Binyon, and
others), 1890; 'Eremus,' 1894 (priv.
ptd., 1889); 'Christ in Hades,' 1896;
'Poems,' 1898; 'Paolo and Fran-

cesca,' 1900; 'Marpessa,' 1900;
'Herod,' 1901; 'Ulysses,' 1902.

PHILLPOTTS (Eden), b. 1862.
Born, at Mount Aboo, India, 4 Nov.
1862. Educated at Plymouth.
Held post in Sun Fire Insurance
Office, 1880-90. Then adopted
literary career. Married Emily
Topham, 1892. Play, 'The Prude's
Progress' (written with J. K.
Jerome), prod. at Comedy theatre,
22 May 1895. Has written several
smaller dramatic pieces.
Works : 'The End of a Life,'
1890; 'Folly and Fresh Air,' 1891;
'A Tiger's Cub,' 1892; 'Summer
Clouds,' 1893; 'In Sugar-Cane
Land,' 1893; 'Some Everyday
Folks,' 1894; 'The Prude's Pro-
gress' (with J. K. Jerome), 1895;
'A Deal with the Devil,' 1895:
'Down Dartmoor Way,' 1896; 'My
Laughing Philosopher,' 1896; 'Lying
Prophets,' 1897; 'Children of the
Mist,' 1898; 'Loup Garou,' 1899;
'The Human Boy,' 1899; 'Sons of
the Morning,' 1900; 'The Good
Red Earth,' 1901; 'Fancy Free,'
1901; 'The Striking Hours,' 1901;
'The River,' 1902; 'The Transit of
the Red Dragon,' 1903.

PINERO (Arthur Wing), b. 1855.
[*See* p. 227.]
To *list of Plays produced, add :*
'Girls and Boys,' Toole's theatre,
Oct. 1882; 'Trelawney of the
Wells,' Court, 20 Jan. 1898; 'The
Beauty Stone' (with J. Comyns
Carr, opera libretto), Savoy, 28
May 1898; 'The Gay Lord Quex,'
Globe, 8 April 1899; 'Iris,' Garrick,
21 Sept. 1901; 'Letty,' Duke of
York's, 8 Oct. 1903.
Works : For '"Plays" (11 vols.),
1891-95,' *read* '"Plays," 1891, etc.'
Add : 'R. L. Stevenson the Drama-
tist: a lecture,' 1903.

**POLLARD (Alfred William), b.
1859.** Born, in London, 14 Aug.
1859. Educated at King's Coll.
School, and at St. John's Coll.,
Oxford. B.A., 1881; M.A., 1885.
Assistant Librarian, British Museum,

since Feb. 1883. Married Alice England, 17 May 1887. Hon. Sec. Bibliographical Society, since Oct. 1893.

Works: 'Last Words of the History of the Titlepage,' 1891; 'Chaucer' (a primer), 1893; 'Early Illustrated Books,' 1893; 'Italian Book Illustration,' 1894; 'Old Picture Books,' 1902.

Has *translated*: Sallust's 'Catiline and Jugurtha,' 1882; De Laveleye's 'Political Economy,' 1884; and *edited*: Wyclif's 'Speculum Ecclesie Militantis,' 1886, and 'De Officio Regis,' 1887; Sir P. Sidney's 'Astrophel and Stella,' 1888; 'English Miracle Plays,' 1890; 'Odes from the Greek Dramatists,' 1890; Herrick's 'Hesperides,' 1891; 'Books about Books' series, 1893-94; Chaucer's 'Canterbury Tales,' 1894; 'Bibliographica,' 1895-97; 'Towneley Plays,' 1897; Chaucer's Works, 1898; 'English Bookman's Library,' 1899, etc.; 'Library of English Classics,' 1900, etc.; 'Fifteenth Century Prose and Verse,' 1903; Chaucer's 'Prologue,' 1903.

POLLOCK(*Sir* **Frederick**), *3rd Bart.*, **b. 1845.** [*See* p. 229.]

Add: Member of Royal Labour Commission, 1891-94. Hon. D.C.L., Oxford, 1901.

Add to '*Works*': 'The Etchingham Letters' (with E. Fuller-Maitland), 1899.

Has *edited*: W. K. Clifford's 'Lectures and Essays,' 1901.

QUILLER-COUCH (Arthur Thomas), **b. 1863.** [*See* p. 235.]

Add: On staff of 'Speaker' till 1899.

Add to '*Works*': 'St. Ives,' by R. L. Stevenson, completed by A. T. Quiller-Couch, 1897; 'The Ship of Stars,' 1899; 'Historical Tales from Shakespeare,' 1899; 'Old Fires and Profitable Ghosts,' 1900; 'The Laird's Luck,' 1901; 'The Westcotes,' 1902; 'The White Wolf,' 1902; 'The Adventures of Harry Revel,' 1903; 'Two Sides of the Face,' 1903.

Has *edited*: 'The Cornish Magazine,' 1898, etc.; 'The Oxford Book of English Verse,' 1900.

RALEIGH (Walter Alexander). Educated at Univ. Coll., London, and King's Coll., Camb. B.A., 1885; M.A., 1892. Prof. of Modern Lit., Univ. Coll., Liverpool, till 1900. Prof. of English Language and Literature, Glasgow, since 1900.

Works: 'The English Novel,' 1894; 'The Riddle,' 1895; 'Robert Louis Stevenson,' 1895; 'Style,' 1897; 'Milton,' 1900; 'The Study of English Literature,' 1900.

Has *edited*: Keats' Poems, 1897; Count Castiglione's 'Book of the Courtier,' 1900.

RALEIGH (*Sir* **Walter), 1552?-1618.** Born, in Devonshire, 1552? Probably at school there, and afterwards at Oriel Coll., Oxford for three years. Went to France as volunteer in Huguenot army, 1569. Remained some years in France. Distinguished himself in Irish rebellion, 1580-81. Gained much favour at Court. Knighted, 1584. Warden of Stannaries, 1585. M.P. for Devonshire, 1585-86. Sent expedition to attempt to found colony in Virginia, 1585; other expeditions, 1587-1603. Introduced potato and tobacco into England, 1586. Obtained grant of large property in Ireland, 1586; in England, 1587. Mem. of Commission for defence of country, 1588. Fitted out various privateers against Spanish fleet; in 1592 he equipped large squadron, which he intended to command, but Queen recalled him. He sailed part of way with it, and on his return was committed to the Tower, July, 1592. Released, Sept. 1592. Continual conflict with Earl of Essex at Court. Temporarily lost Queen's favour owing to intrigue with Elizabeth Throgmorton. Married her, winter of 1592. Retired from Court to Sherborne. M.P. for Michael (Cornwall), 1593. Intimate with principal men of letters in London.

Sailed to Orinoco in search of gold, Feb. 1595 ; explored, and returned same year. Held command at defeat of Spanish fleet off Cadiz, 1596. Captured Fayal, 1597. M.P. for Dorset, 1597; for Cornwall, 1601. Governor of Jersey, Sept. 1600. At accession of James I., was deprived of his offices, 1603. Accused of high treason, Nov. 1603. Sentenced to death, but reprieved ; imprisoned in Tower till March 1615. Sailed again on gold-seeking expedition to Orinoco, June 1617. Expedition was a failure. Returned to England, June, 1618. To favour Spaniards, whose forces Raleigh had attacked, King James decided to carry out former sentence of death. Executed, 29 Oct. 1618. Buried in St. Margaret's, Westminster.

Works : ' A Report of the Truth of the Fight about the Isles of Açores' (anon.), 1591 ; ' The Discoverie . . . of the Empyre of Guiana,' 1596 ; ' The History of the World' (anon.), 1614.

Posthumous : ' The Prerogative of Parliaments in England,' 1628; ' Instructions to his Son,' 1632; ' Tubus Historicus,' 1636; ' The Life and death of Mahomet' (attrib. to Raleigh), 1637; ' The Prince,' 1642; ' To-day a Man, To-morrow None,' 1644; ' The Arraignement . . . of Sir Walter Rawleigh,' 1648; ' Judicious and Select Essays,' 1650; ' The Sceptick,' 1651; ' Remains,' 1657; ' The Cabinet Council,' 1658; ' The Pilgrimage,' 1681; ' A Discourse of Sea-Ports' (attrib. to Raleigh), 1700; ' An Essay on Ways and Means' (attrib. to Raleigh), 1701; ' Three Discourses,' 1702; ' A Military Discourse,' 1734; ' The Interest of England with regard to Foreign Alliances,' 1750; ' A Discourse of Tenures' (attrib. to Raleigh), 1781.

Collected Works : in 8 vols., 1829; ' Poems' (ed. by J. Hannah), 1875.

Life : by W. Oldys, 1736; by E. Gosse, 1886 ; by W. Stebbing, 1891.

RAWLINSON (George), 1812-1902. [*See* p. 236.]
Add : Died, at Canterbury, 6 Oct. 1902. *Add to* ' *Works*': ' Memoir of Maj.-Gen. Sir H. C. Rawlinson,' 1898.

RICHARDSON (Samuel), 1689-1761. [*See* p. 239.]
Add : Life, by C. L. Thomson, 1900 ; by Austin Dobson (' Men of Letter' series), 1902.

RILEY (James Whitcomb), b. 1853. Born, at Greenfield, Indiana, 1853. Contributed verse, much of it in Western dialect, to Indiana newspapers, since 1873. On staff of ' Indianapolis Journal.' Frequent contributor to periodicals.

Works : ' The Old Swimmin'-Hole' (under pseud. ' Benjamin F. Johnson'), 1883 ; ' The Boss Girl,' 1886 ; ' Afterwhiles,' 1887 ; ' Old-Fashioned Roses,' 1888 ; ' Pipes o' Pan at Zekesbury,' 1889 ; ' Rhymes of Childhood,' 1891 ; ' An Old Sweetheart,' 1891 ; ' Neighbourly Poems,' 1891 ; ' Flying Islands of the Night,' 1892 ; ' Green Fields and Running Brooks,' 1892 ; ' Sketches in Prose,' 1892 ; ' Poems Here at Home,' 1893 ; ' Armazindy,' 1894 ; ' A Child-World,' 1896 ; ' Poems and Prose Sketches' (collected, 10 vols.), 1897 ; ' The Rubaiyat of Doc. Sifers,' 1898 ; ' Home Folks,' 1900 ; ' The Book of Joyous Children,' 1902 ; ' His Pa's Romance,' 1903.

RITCHIE (*Mrs.* Anne Isabella), b. 1837. [*See* p. 239.]
Add : Edition of Works of Thackeray, 1898, etc.

ROBERTSON (Thomas William), 1829-1871. Born, at Newark-on-Trent, 9 Jan. 1829. Coming of a theatrical family, he went early on to the stage. Was at school at Spalding and Whittlesea, 1836-43. Acted in theatrical company managed by his father, 1843-48. Play, ' A Night's Adventures,' produced at Olympic theatre, 1851 ; ' Castles in the Air,' City theatre, April 1854. Was for a year prompter at Olympic theatre, and wrote a number of farces for that house. Married (i) Elizabeth Burton, 27 Aug. 1856. Acted with her in Dublin and afterwards in England. She died, 14 Aug. 1865. Married (ii) Rosetta Feist, 17 Oct. 1867. Retired from stage about 1860; devoted himself to play-writing and contributing to periodicals. Play, ' David Garrick,' produced at Prince of Wales's theatre, April 1864; ' Society,' 11 Nov. 1865; ' Ours,' 16 Sept. 1866; ' Caste,' 6 April 1867; ' Play,' 15 Feb. 1868; ' School,' 14 Jan. 1869; ' M.P.,' 23 April 1870. A large number of plays by him were produced at other theatres (St. James's, Haymarket, Gaiety, Globe, Adelphi, and provincial theatres) between 1867 and 1871. He died, in London, 3 Feb. 1871.

Works: ' Principal Dramatic Works,' with Memoir by his Son (2 vols.), 1889. [A large number of his plays are printed in ' Lacy's Acting Edition of Plays.']

RODD (*Sir* **James Rennell**), **b. 1858.** Born, in London, 9 Nov. 1858. Educated at Haileybury Coll. 1872-76; and at Balliol Coll., Oxford. B.A., 1881. Newdigate Verse Prize, 1880. Attaché in Diplomatic Service, 1883; to Berlin, 1885; Second Sec., Athens, 1888; Rome, 1891; Paris, 1892. In charge of British Agency at Zanzibar, 1893. Married Lilias Georgina Guthrie, 27 Oct. 1894. C.M.G., 1894. Sec. of Legation, Cairo, 1894-1901. Special Envoy to King Menelik, 1897. C.B., 1897. K.C.M.G., 1899. Sec. of Embassy, Rome, since 1901.

Works: ' Raleigh ' (Newdigate prize poem), 1880 ; ' Songs in the South,' 1881; ' Poems in Many Lands,' 1883; ' Feda,' 1886; ' The Unknown Madonna,' 1888 ; ' Frederick, Crown Prince and Emperor,' 1888; ' The Violet Crown,' 1891 ; ' The Customs and Lore of Modern Greece,' 1892; ' Ballads of the Fleet,' 1897 (new edn., enlarged, 1901) ; ' Myrtle and Oak,' 1903.

Has *edited:* Sir G. Portal's ' British Mission to Uganda in 1893,' 1894.

ROSSETTI (**Christina Georgina**), **1830-1894.** [*See* p. 240.]
Add: Assisted her mother in school-teaching at Frome, 1853-54. Returned to London, 1854. Travelled abroad, 1861 and 1865. Serious illness, 1871-73. Settled in Torrington Square, London, with her mother, 1876; resided there till her death.
Life, by Mackenzie Bell, 1898.

ROSSETTI (**William Michael**), **b. 1829.** [*See* p. 241.]
Add: ' Rossetti Papers, 1862-70,' 1903.

RUSKIN (**John**), **1819-1900.** [*See* p. 242.]
Add: Died, at Coniston, 20 Jan. 1900.
Works: ' Lectures on Landscape,' 1897 ; ' Letters to F. J. Furnivall and others' (priv. ptd.), 1897.
Posthumous: ' Ruskin on Pictures: criticisms,' ed. by E. T. Cook, 1902 ; ' Letters to M.G. and H.G.' (priv. ptd.), 1903.
Life: by W. G. Collingwood, 1900; by F. Harrison (' Men of Letters' Series,) 1902.

RUSSELL (**George William Erskine**), **b. 1853.** Born, in London, 3 Feb. 1853. Educated at Harrow, 1868-72 ; matric. as Exhibitioner, Univ. Coll., Oxford, 1872 ; B.A., 1876; M.A., 1880. M.P. for Aylesbury, 1880-85, for North Bedfordshire, 1892-95. Parliamentary Sec. to Local Govt. Board, 1883-85. Under-Sec. of State for India, 1892-94; for Home Dept., 1894-95. Alderman of L.C.C., 1889-95. Hon. LL.D., St. Andrews, 1899. Contrib. to ' Spectator,' ' Speaker,' ' Nineteenth Cent.,' ' Contemp. Rev.,' ' Manchester Guardian,' ' Pilot,' ' Cornhill Mag.,' ' Quarterly Rev.'
Works: ' George Eliot: a lecture,' 1882; ' The Rt. Hon. W. E. Gladstone,' 1891 ; ' Sixty years of Empire ' (by G. W. E. Russell and

others), 1897; 'Collections and Recollections' (anon.), 1898; 'Mr. Gladstone's Religious Development,' 1899; 'For Better? For Worse?' 1902; 'An Onlooker's Note-Book' (anon.), 1902; 'The Household of Faith,' 1902; 'Henry Casey Shuttleworth,' 1902.

Has *edited :* Matthew Arnold's 'Letters,' 1895; 'Our Leader's Legacy' (compiled from writings and speeches of W. E. Gladstone), 1898.

RUSSELL (William Clark), b. 1844. [*See* p 244]

Add : 'Pictures from the Life of Nelson,' 1897; 'The Two Captains,' 1897; 'The Romance of a Midshipman,' 1898; 'The Ship's Adventure,' 1899; 'The Ship: her story,' 1899; 'The Pretty Polly,' 1900; 'Rose Island,' 1900; 'A Voyage at Anchor,' 1900; 'Overdue,' 1903.

RUSSELL (*Sir* William Howard), b. 1820. [*See* p. 244.]

Add : D.L., 1856. C.V.O., 1902.

SAINTSBURY (George Edward Bateman), b. 1845. [*See* p. 246.]

Add : 'Matthew Arnold,' 1899; 'History of Criticism and Literary Taste in Europe,' 1900, etc.; 'The Earlier Renaissance,' 1901; 'Loci Critici,' 1903.

Has *edited :* 'Periods of European Literature,' 1897, etc.; Fielding's Works, 1902, etc.; Shadwell, 1903.

SALA (George Augustus Henry), 1828-1895. [*See* p 247.]

Add to '*Works*' (*posthumous*) : 'Margaret Forster,' 1897.

SAYCE (Archibald Henry), b. 1846. [*See* p. 249.]

Add : Gifford Lecturer, Oxford, 1900-02.

Add to '*Works*': 'Murray's Handbook to Egypt,' 1896; 'Early History of the Hebrews,' 1897; 'Early Israel and the Surrounding Nations,' 1899; 'Babylonians and Assyrians,' 1900; 'The Religion of Ancient Egypt and Babylonia,' 1903. Has *edited :* 'Genesis' in 'Temple Bible,' 1901; G. Maspero's 'The Passing of the Empires,' 1900;

J. Ward's 'Pyramids and Progress,' 1900.

SCOTT (Hugh Stowell). *See* MERRIMAN (Henry Seton), *pseud.*

SCOTT (Michael), 1789-1835.

See p. 249, col. ii. To date of birth *add* '30 Oct.'; after words 'Glasgow Univ.,' *add* '1801-05'; after word 'Married,' *add* 'Margaret Boyle'; after word 'Died,' *add* 'in Glasgow, 7 Nov.'

SCOTT (*Sir* Walter), Bart., 1771-1832. [*See* p. 249.]

Add : Life, by G. E. B. Saintsbury, 1897; by W. H. Hudson, 1901.

SCOTT (William Bell), 1811-1890. Born, near Edinburgh, 12 Sept. 1811. Educated at Edinburgh High School. Married Letitia Margery Norquoy. Studied art at the Trustees Academy. Assisted his father in work of engraving. Contributed poetry to 'Tait's Edinburgh Mag.,' and other periodicals, from 1831. Removed from Edinburgh to London, 1837. Founded Government School of Design at Newcastle, 1844-64. Examiner in Art to Education Board, 1864-85. Exhibited pictures at various times in Royal Academy and other exhibitions, and did a large amount of decorative work in many places. Was connected with 'Pre-Raphaelite Brotherhood,' and intimate friend of Rossetti. Died, at Penkill Castle, Ayrshire, 22 Nov. 1890.

Works : 'Hades,' 1838; 'The Year of the World,' 1846; 'Memoir of David Scott,' 1850; 'Antiquarian Gleanings,' 1851; 'Chorea Sancti Viti,' 1851; 'Poems,' 1854; 'Half-Hour Lectures on the history of the Fine Arts,' 1861; 'Albert Durer, 1869; 'Gems of French Art,' 1871; 'Gems of Modern Belgian Art,' 1872; 'Our British Landscape Painters,' 1872; 'The British School of Sculpture,' 1872; 'Gems of Modern German Art,' 1873; 'Murillo,' 1873; 'Pictures by Italian Masters,' 1874; 'Poems,' 1875; 'William Blake,' 1878; 'The

Little Masters,' 1879; 'A Poet's Harvest Home,' 1882.

He *edited* a series of works of English poets, 1873-77.

Posthumous : 'Autobiographical Notes,' ed. by W. Minto, 1892.

SEDLEY (*Sir* Charles), Bart., **1639-1701.**

See p. 251, col. i. After word 'Married,' *add* 'Lady Catherine Savage, 23 Feb. 1657.'

SEELEY (*Sir* John Robert), **1834-1895.**

See p. 251, col. ii. From ' Works,' *dele :* ' "The Greatest of all the Plantagenets" (anon.), 1860 (new edn., called "The Life and Reign of Edward I.," 1872).'

SHAKESPEARE (William), **1564-1616.**

See p. 253, col. ii. To ' Works,' *add :* 'Passionate Pilgrim,' 1599; ' Pericles,' 1609.

Life : by Sidney Lee, 1898.

SHARP (William), b. **1855.**

See p. 254, col. i. For date of birth, read 1855.

Add to ' *Works* ' *:* 'Wives in Exile ' (English edn.), 1898; ' Silence Farm,' 1899.

Has *edited :* Selected Poems of Swinburne (Tauchnitz edn.), 1901.

SHAW (George Bernard), b. **1856.**

Born, in Dublin, 26 July, 1856. At school at Wesley Coll., Dublin. Came to London, 1876. Engaged in literary criticism for ' Pall Mall Gaz.,' artistic criticism for ' The World,' etc., 1883-88. Musical critic to ' The World,' 1888-90; dramatic critic, ' The World,' 1890-94; to ' Saturday Rev.,' 1895-98. Married Charlotte Frances Payne-Townshend, 1 June 1898. Prominent Socialist writer. Play, ' Widower's Houses,' produced by Independent theatre, 9 Dec. 1892; ' The Philanderer,' Indep. theatre, 1893; ' Arms and the Man,' Avenue theatre, 21 April 1894; ' Candida,' Indep. theatre, 1897; ' The Man of Destiny,' Croydon, 1897; ' Mrs.

Warren's Profession,' Stage Society, 5 Jan. 1902; ' The Admirable Bashville,' Imperial theatre, 8 June 1903.

Works : ' An Unsocial Socialist,' 1887; ' The Quintessence of Ibsenism,' 1891; ' Widower's Houses,' 1893; ' The Perfect Wagnerite,' 1898; ' Plays, Pleasant and Unpleasant,' 1898; ' Three Plays for Puritans,' 1901; ' The Admirable Bashville,' 1901; ' Man and Superman,' 1903.

Has *edited :* ' Fabian Essays,' 1889; Gronlund's ' Co-operative Commonwealth,' 1892; ' Fabianism and the Empire,' 1900.

SHORTER (Clement King), b. **1858.**

Born, in London, 19 July 1858. Educated at Downham Market, Norfolk. Left Civil Service to become Editor of ' Illustrated London News,' Jan. 1890. Founded ' The Sketch,' Feb. 1893; ' The Sphere,' Jan. 1900; ' The Tatler,' July 1901. Married Dora Sigerson (*q.v.*), 9 July 1896.

Works : ' Charlotte Brontë and her Circle,' 1896; ' Victorian Literature,' 1897.

Has *edited :* Goethe's ' Wilhelm Meister,' 1890; Wordsworth's ' Lyrics and Sonnets,' 1892; ' 19th Century Classics,' 1896-98; Mrs. Gaskell's ' Charlotte Brontë,' 1900.

SHORTER (Mrs. Clement). *See* SIGERSON (Dora).

SHORTHOUSE (Joseph Henry), **1834-1903.**

Add : Died, in Birmingham, 4 March 1903.

SIDGWICK (Henry), **1838-1900.** [*See* p. 257.]

Add : Died at Terling, Essex, 28 Aug. 1900.

Add to ' *Works*': 'Practical Ethics,' 1898.

Posthumous : ' Philosophy : its scope and relations ' (ed. by J. Ward), 1902.

SIDNEY (Algernon), **1622-1683.**

See p. 257, col. ii. *Add :* Life, by Miss Blackburne, 1885.

SIGERSON (Dora) [**Mrs. Clement Shorter**]. Born, in Dublin. Married to Clement Shorter (*q.v.*), 9 July 1896.

Works : 'Verses,' 1893 ; 'The Fairy Changeling,' 1898 ; 'My Lady's Slipper,' 1898 ; 'Ballads and Poems,' 1899 ; 'The Father Confessor,' 1900 ; 'The Woman who went to Hell,' 1902.

SKEAT (**Walter William**), b. **1835.** [*See* p. 258.]

Add : Married Bertha Clara Jones, 15 Nov. 1860.

Add to 'Works' : 'A Student's Pastime,' 1896 ; 'The Chaucer Canon,' 1900 ; 'Place Names of Cambridgeshire,' 1901 ; 'Notes on English Etymology,' 1901 ; 'Concise Etymological Dictionary of the English Language ; re-written and re-arranged,' 1901.

SMITH (**Goldwin**), b. **1823.** [*See* p. 260.]

Add : Married Mrs. Harriet M. Boulton, 30 Sept. 1875. Has resided in Toronto since 1875.

Add to 'Works' : 'The United Kingdom,' 1899 ; 'Shakespeare : the Man,' 1899 ; 'Commonwealth or Empire,' 1902 ; 'In the Court of History,' 1902 ; 'The Founder of Christendom,' 1903.

SOUTHEY (**Robert**), **1774-1843.** [*See* p. 263.]

Add : 'Journal of a Tour in the Netherlands,' ed. by W. R. Nicoll, 1902.

SPENCER (**Herbert**), **1820-1903.** [*See* p. 265.]

Add : Contributed to 'Westminster Rev.' on philosophic subjects, 1852-60. Died, at Brighton, 8 Dec. 1903.

Add to 'Works' : 'Principles of Biology' (revised and enlarged edn., 2 vols.), 1898-99 ; 'First Principles' (finally revised edn.), 1900 ; 'Facts and Comments,' 1902.

STANLEY (*Sir* **Henry Morton**), b. **1841.** [*See* p. 267.]

Add : M.P., North Lambeth, 1895-1900. Visited S. Africa, 1898. G.C.B., 1899.

Works : 'Through South Africa,' 1898.

STEDMAN (**Edmund Clarence**), b. **1833.** Born, at Hartford, Conn., 8 Oct. 1833. Educated at Yale. Editor of 'Norwich Tribune,' 1852-53 ; of 'Winsted Herald,' 1854-55. On staff of New York 'Tribune,' 1859-61. War Correspondent, New York 'World,' 1861-63. Member of New York Stock Exchange, 1869-1900. Has devoted much time to poetry and literary criticism. Pres., American Copyright League, 1901. Has been Lecturer on Poetry at Johns Hopkins Univ., and elsewhere. Frequent contributor to periodicals.

Works : 'Poems,' 1860 ; 'The Prince's Ball,' 1860 ; 'Alice of Monmouth,' 1864 (2nd edn. same year) ; 'The Blameless Prince,' 1869 ; 'Rip Van Winkle,' 1870 ; 'Poetical Works,' 1873 ; 'Victorian Poets,' 1876 (enlarged edn., 1887) ; 'Octavius Brooks Frothingham and the New Faith,' 1876 ; 'Hawthorne, and other poems,' 1877 ; 'Elizabeth Barrett Browning,' 1877 ; 'Lyrics and Idylls,' 1879 ; 'Edgar Allan Poe,' 1881 ; 'Poems now first collected,' 1884 ; 'Poets of America,' 1885 ; 'The Star-Bearer,' 1888 ; 'The Nature and Elements of Poetry,' 1892.

Has *edited :* Selected Poems of W. S. Landor (with T. B. Aldrich), 1874 ; 'Library of American Literature' (with E. M. Hutchinson, 11 vols.), 1888-89 ; 'Cassell's Guide to Europe,' 1891 ; Poe's Works (10 vols.), 1895 ; 'A Victorian Anthology,' 1896 ; 'An American Anthology,' 1900.

STEPHEN (*Sir* **Leslie**), b. **1832.** [*See* p. 269.]

Add : Took holy orders, but relinquished them at passing of Clerical Disabilities Act, 1870. Elected Mem. of Athenæum Club, 1877. K.C.B., 1902.

Add to 'Works' : 'Studies of a Biographer,' vols. i, ii, 1898 ; vols. iii, iv, 1902 ; 'The English Utili-

tarians,' 1900 ; 'George Eliot,'
1902 ; 'Robert Louis Stevenson :
an essay,' 1903.
Has *edited* : James Payn's 'The
Backwater of Life,' 1899 ; J. R.
Green's 'Letters,' 1901.

STERRY (Joseph Ashby).   *See*
ASHBY-STERRY (J.).

**STEVENSON (Robert Louis
Balfour), 1850-1894.** [*See* p. 269.]
Add : Studied engineering, 1868-
71. Called to Scottish Bar, 1875.
Lived at Davos, 1881-82; at
Marseilles, 1882-83; at Hyères,
1883-84; at Bournemouth, 1884-87 ;
in America, 1887-89. Plays :
'Deacon Brodie' (written with
W. E. Henley), performed at Prince
of Wales's theatre, 2 July 1884 ;
'Admiral Guinea' (with W. E.
Henley), Avenue, 29 Nov. 1897.
Add to '*Works*' : 'Moral Emblems'
(priv. ptd.), 1882 ; 'The Graver
and the Pen' (priv. ptd.), 1882 ;
'Letters to his Family and Friends,'
(ed. G. Sidney Colvin), 1899 ; 'In
the South Seas,' 1900.
Life : by G. Balfour, 1901.

STOCKTON (Francis Richard),
1834-1902. Born, in Philadelphia,
5 April 1834. Educated at Philadelphia High School. First worked
as an engraver ; but subsequently
became journalist on Philadelphia
and New York newspapers. Contributed to periodicals. Edited
'Hearth and Home,' 1870. Joined
staff of 'Scribner's Monthly,' 1872 ;
Assistant-editor of 'St. Nicholas,'
1873. Married Marian Edward
Tuttle, 1860. Died, in New York,
20 April 1902.
Works : 'Ting-a-Ling,' 1870 ;
'Roundabout Rambles,' 1872 ; 'The
Home' (with M. E. Stockton),
1872 ; 'What might have been
Expected,' 1874 ; 'Tales out of
School,' 1875 ; 'Rudder Grange,'
1879 ; 'A Jolly Fellowship,' 1880 ;
'The Floating Prince,' 1881 ;
'The Lady or the Tiger ?' 1884 ;
'The Story of Viteau,' 1884 ; 'The
Casting Away of Mrs. Lecks and

Mrs. Aleshine,' 1886 ; 'The Christ-
mas Wreck,' 1886 ; 'The Late Mrs.
Null,' 1886 ; 'The Bee-Man of Orn,'
1887 ; 'The Hundredth Man,' 1887 ;
'A Borrowed Month,' 1887 ; 'Amos
Kilbright,' 1888 ; 'The Dusantes,'
1888 ; 'The Great War Syndicate,'
1889 ; 'Personally Conducted,' 1889;
'Ardis Claverden,' 1890 ; 'The
Merry Chanter,' 1890 ; 'The Stories
of the Three Burglars,' 1890 ; 'The
Cosmic Bean,' 1891 ; 'The House
of Martha,' 1891 ; 'The Rudder
Grangers Abroad,' 1891 ; 'The
Squirrel Inn,' 1891 ; 'The Clocks of
Rondaine,' 1892 ; 'The Shadrach,'
1893 ; 'Pomona's Travels,' 1894 ;
'The Adventures of Captain Horn,'
1895 ; 'Mrs. Cliff's Yacht,' 1896 ;
'Stories of New Jersey,' 1896 ; 'A
Story-Teller's Pack,' 1897 ; 'Buc-
caneers and Pirates,' 1897 ; 'Cap-
tain Chap,' 1898 ; 'The Girl at
Cobhurst,' 1898 ; 'The Great Stone
of Sardis,' 1898 ; 'The Vizier of the
Two-Horned Alexander,' 1899 ;
'The Young Master of Hyson Hall,'
1899 ; 'The Associate Hermits,'
1899 ; 'A Bicycle of Cathay,' 1900 ;
'Afield and Afloat,' 1901 ; 'Kate
Bonnet,' 1902.
Posthumous : 'John Gaythet's Gar-
den,' 1903 ; 'The Captain's Toll-
Gate,' 1903.

STODDARD (Richard Henry), 1825-
1903. Born, at Hingham, Mass.,
2 July 1825. As a boy worked in an
iron foundry. Contributed to local
periodicals. Held post in Custom
House, 1853-70. Married Elizabeth
Drew Barstow, 1852. On staff of
New York 'World,' 1860-70. Sec.
to Gen. McClellan, 1870-73. City
Librarian, New York, 1874-75.
Joined staff of New York 'Mail and
Express,' 1880. Died, in New York,
12 May 1903.
Works : 'Footprints' (priv. ptd.),
1849 ; 'Poems,' 1852 ; 'Adventures
in Fairy-Land,' 1853 ; 'Town and
Country,' 1857 ; 'Songs of Summer,'
1857 ; 'Life of Humboldt,' 1860 ;
'The Loves and Heroines of the
Poets,' 1861 ; 'The King's Bell,'

1862; 'The Story of Little Red-Riding-Hood,' 1864; 'The Children in the Wood,' 1865; 'Abraham Lincoln,' 1865; 'The Story of Putnam the Brave,' 1870; 'The Book of the East,' 1871; 'A Century After,' 1876; 'Poets' Homes,' 1877; 'W. C. Bryant,' 1879; 'Poems' (collected), 1880; contrib. to 'With Others,' 1882; 'The Lion's Cub,' 1891; 'Under the Evening Lamp,' 1893.

He *edited*: G. Brimley's 'Essays,' 1861; Gen. Lyon's 'Political Essays,' 1861; J. G. Vassar's 'Twenty-One Years Round the World,' 1862; 'Madrigals from Old English Poets,' 1865; 'The Late English Poets,' 1865; 'Remember' (with his wife), 1869; 'Bric-à-Brac' Series (10 vols.), 1874-76; 'Treasure Trove' Series, 1875; 'Sans-Souci' Series, 1876-77; Selected Prose and Verse of Longfellow, 1882; 'Mrs. Browning's Birthday Book,' 1882; 'English Verse' (with W. J. Linton), 1883; E. A. Poe's Works, 1884; Selected Poems of Swinburne, 1884.

STUBBS (William), *Bishop of Oxford,* 1825-1901. [*See* p. 271.]
Add: Died, at Cuddesdon, 22 April 1901.
Add to 'Works' (posthumous): 'Ordination Addresses' (ed. by E. E. Holmes), 1901; 'Historical Introduction to the Rolls Series,' (ed. by A. Hassall), 1902.

SWIFT (Jonathan), 1667-1745. *See* p. 272, col. i. After 'Friendship with Esther Johnson ["Stella"] begun,' *add* 'She died, 1728.'

SWINBURNE (Algernon Charles), b. **1837.** [*See* p. 273.]
Add to 'Works': 'Rosamund, Queen of the Lombards,' 1899; 'Selected Poems' (in Tauchnitz edn., edited by William Sharp), 1901.
Has *edited*: Mrs. Browning's 'Aurora Leigh,' 1898; Herrick's 'Hesperides,' 1898.

SYMONS (Arthur), b. **1865.** Born, at Milford Haven, 28 Feb. 1865. Educated at private schools. Married Rhoda Bowser, 19 Jan.

1901. Editor of 'The Savoy,' 1896. Contrib. to 'Quarterly Rev., 'Fortnightly Rev.,' 'Monthly Rev.,' 'Saturday Rev.,' 'Athenæum.'
Works: 'Introduction to the study of Browning,' 1886; 'Days and Nights,' 1889; 'Silhouettes,' 1892; 'London Nights,' 1895; 'Amoris Victima,' 1897; 'Studies in Two Literatures,' 1897; 'Aubrey Beardsley,' 1898; 'The Symbolist Movement in Literature,' 1899; 'Images of Good and Evil,' 1899; 'Poems,' 1902; 'Plays, Acting and Music,' 1903; 'Cities,' 1903.
Has *translated*: Zola's 'L'Assommoir,' 1894; Verhaeren's 'The Dawn,' 1898; D'Annunzio's 'The Dead City,' 1900, 'Gioconda,' 1901, 'Francesca da Rimini,' 1902; and *edited*: Massinger's Plays, 1887; Leigh Hunt's 'Essays,' 1887; Day's Plays, 1888; St. Augustine's 'Confessions,' 1898; Mathilde Blind's Poems, 1900.

TAYLOR (Bayard), 1825-1878. Born, at Kennett Square, Pennsylvania, 11 Jan. 1825. Educated there and at Unionville Academy. Began to write verse at an early age. Apprenticed to a printer at West Chester, 1842. Contrib. to 'Saturday Evening Post.' Travelled in Europe, 1844-46. Letters written by him from there were pubd. in 'Tribune,' 'Sat. Evg. Post,' and 'U.S. Gaz.' Part proprietor and editor of 'Phœnixville Pioneer,' 1846-47. Appointed to post on staff of New York 'Literary World,' 1847; on staff of 'Tribune,' 1848. Edited 'Union Mag,' Jan. to Sept. 1848. Travelled in California and Mexico, 1848-50. Married (i) Mary Agnew, 24 Oct. 1850; she died, Dec. 1850. Travelled in Europe and the East, 1851-53. Engaged in lecturing, 1854-55. Travelled in Europe, 1856-58. Married (ii) Marie Hansen, 27 Oct. 1857. Built house at Kennett Square, 1859. Engaged in literature, lecturing, and extensive travel, with gradually failing health, 1859-78. Appointed

U.S. Minister to Germany, Feb. 1878. Died, in Berlin, 19 Dec. 1878.

Works: 'Ximena,' 1844; 'Views Afoot,' 1846; 'Rhymes of Travel,' 1849; 'Eldorado,' 1850; 'The American Legend,' 1850; 'A Book of Romances,' 1852; 'A Journey to Central Africa, 1854; 'The Lands of the Saracen,' 1854; 'Poems of the Orient,' 1854; 'A Visit to India, China and Japan,' 1855; 'Poems of Home and Travel,' 1855; 'Cyclopædia of Modern Travel,' 1856; 'Northern Travel,' 1857; 'Travels in Greece and Russia,' 1859; 'At Home and Abroad' (2 series), 1859, 1862; 'The Poet's Journal,' 1862; 'Hannah Thurston,' 1863; 'Poems,' 1864; 'John Godfrey's Fortunes,' 1864; 'The Story of Kennett,' 1866; 'The Picture of St. John,' 1866; 'Colorado,' 1867; 'The Golden Wedding' (priv. ptd.), 1868; 'By-Ways of Europe,' 1869; 'Joseph and his Friend,' 1870; 'The Masque of the Gods,' 1872; 'Beauty and the Beast,' 1872; 'Lars,' 1873; 'The Prophet,' 1874; 'Egypt and Iceland,' 1874; 'A School History of Germany,' 1874; 'Home Pastorals,' 1875; 'The Echo Club,' 1876; 'Boys of Other Countries,' 1876; 'Prince Deukalion,' 1878.

Posthumous: 'Studies in German Literature,' 1879; 'Critical Essays,' 1880.

He *translated*: Goethe's 'Faust,' 2 pt., 1870, 1871; and *edited*: 'Illustrated Library of Travel,' 1872-74.

Collected Works: 'Poetical Works,' 1880; 'Dramatic Works,' 1880.

Life: 'Life and Letters' (ed. by M. Hansen-Taylor and H. E. Scudder), 1884; by A. H. Smyth, 1896.

TENNYSON (Alfred), *Baron Tennyson*, **1809-1892.**
See p. 278, col. i. After '"The Falcon," St. James's,' *add* 'Dec. 1879.'

Add: *Life*, by his son Hallam, 1897; by Sir A. Lyall ('Men of Letters' series), 1902.

TENNYSON (Frederick) 1807-1898.
[*See* p. 278.]
Add: Died, in London, 26 Feb. 1898.
Add to '*Works*': 'Days and Hours,' 1854.

THACKERAY (William Makepeace), **1811-1863.**
See p. 279, col. i. For 'Separation from his wife, 1840,' *read* 'His wife lost her reason, and was placed under restraint, 1840.'
Add: Collected Works, with biographical introductions by his daughter, Mrs. Ritchie (13 vols.), 1898-99.
Life: by C. Whibley, 1903.

THOMPSON (Francis). Poet. Educated at Ushaw Coll., Durham, and Owens Coll., Manchester. First volume of poems published, 1893.
Works: 'Poems,' 1893; 'Sister Songs,' 1895; 'New Poems,' 1897.

TODHUNTER (John), b. **1839.** Born, in Dublin, 30 Dec. 1839. Educated at York School and Trin. Coll., Dublin. Vice-Chancellor's English Verse Prize, 1864, 1865, 1866. Medal for Prose Essay, Philosophical Soc., 1866. M.D., Dublin, 1867. For some years practised medicine in Dublin. Prof. of English Lit., Alexandra Coll., Dublin, 1870-74. First book published 1872. Married (i) Katherine Ball, 1870; (ii) Dora Louisa Digby, 1879. Removed to London, 1879. Play, 'In Troas,' performed, 1886; 'A Sicilian Idyll,' 5 May 1890; 'The Poison Flower,' 1891; 'The Black Cat,' Opera Comique, 8 Dec. 1894; 'A Comedy of Sighs,' Avenue, 29 March 1894.
Works: 'The Theory of the Beautiful,' 1872; 'Laurella,' 1876; 'Alcestis,' 1879; 'A Study of Shelley,' 1880; 'The True Tragedy of Rienzi,' 1881; 'Forest Songs,' 1881; 'Helena in Troas,' 1886; 'Notes on Shelley's unfinished poem

24

"The Triumph of Life"' (priv. ptd.), 1887; 'The Banshee,' 1888; 'A Sicilian Idyll,' 1890; 'The Black Cat,' 1895; 'Life of Patrick Sarsfield,' 1895; 'How Dreams come True' (priv. ptd.), 1896; 'Three Irish Bardic Tales,' 1896.

TRAILL (Henry Duff), 1842-1900. [See p. 282.] Add: Editor of 'Literature,' 1897. Died, in London, 21 Feb. 1900. Add to 'Works': 'England, Egypt, and the Sudan,' 1900.

TREVELYAN (Sir George Otto), Bart., b. **1838.** [See p. 283.] Add: In India, as Civil Servant, 1862-65. Add to 'Works': 'The American Revolution,' pt. i, 1899; pt. ii (2 vols.), 1903.

TWAIN (Mark) [pseud., i.e. **Samuel Langhorne Clemens**], b. **1835.** [See p. 286.] Add to 'Works': 'How to Tell a Story,' 1897; 'More Tramps Abroad,' 1897; 'The Man that Corrupted Hadleyburg,' 1900; 'A Double-Barrelled Detective Story,' 1902.

TYNAN (Katharine) [Mrs. H. A. Hinkson], b. **1861.** Born, in Dublin, 3 Feb. 1861. Educated at Sienna Convent, Drogheda. Lived near Dublin in youth. Married to Henry A. Hinkson, May 1893. Has resided in London since marriage. Works: 'Louise de la Vallière,' 1885; 'Shamrocks,' 1887; 'Ballads and Lyrics,' 1891; 'A Nun: her friends and her order,' 1892; 'Cuckoo Songs,' 1894; 'A Cluster of Nuts,' 1894; 'The Land of Mist and Mountain,' 1895; 'An Isle in the Water,' 1895; 'The Way of a Maid,' 1895; 'Miracle Plays,' 1895; 'Oh, what a Plague is Love!' 1896; 'A Lover's Breast Knot,' 1896; 'The Wind in the Trees,' 1898; 'The Handsome Brandons,' 1899; 'The Dear Irish Girl,' 1899; 'Led by a Dream,' 1899; 'The Land I Love Best,' 1899; 'She Walks in Beauty,' 1899; 'A Daughter of the Fields,' 1900; 'The Adventures of

Carlo,' 1900; 'Three Fair Maids,' 1901; 'A Union of Hearts,' 1901; 'Poems,' 1901; 'That Sweet Enemy,' 1901; 'A Girl of Galway,' 1902; 'The Handsome Quaker,' 1902; 'A King's Woman,' 1902; 'Love of Sisters,' 1902; 'A Red, Red Rose,' 1903. Has edited: 'Irish Love Songs,' 1892; Read's 'Cabinet of Irish Literature,' 1902, etc.

WALFORD (Mrs. Lucy Bethia), b. 1845. Born [Lucy Bethia Colquhoun], at Portobello, Edinburgh, 17 April 1845. Educated at home. Married Alfred Saunders Walford, 1869. Contrib. to 'Blackwood' and other periodicals. Works: 'The Merchant's Sermon,' 1870; 'Mr. Smith,' 1854; 'Pauline,' 1877; 'Cousins,' 1879; 'Troublesome Daughters,' 1880; 'Dick Netherby,' 1881; 'The Baby's Grandmother,' 1884; 'Nan,' 1885; 'The History of a Week,' 1886; 'Cheerful Christianity,' 1886; 'Polly Spanker's Green Feather' (anon.), 1887; 'Four Biographies,' 1888; 'Dinah's Son,' 1888; 'Her Great Idea,' 1888; 'A Stiffnecked Generation,' 1889; 'A Sage of Sixteen,' 1889; 'The Havoc of a Smile,' 1890; 'The Mischief of Monica,' 1891; 'A Pinch of Experience,' 1891; 'Twelve English Authoresses,' 1892; 'The One Good Guest,' 1892; 'For Grown-up Children,' 1892; 'The Little Elevenpence Halfpenny,' 1892; 'Bertie Boot-Boy,' 1892; 'The Matchmaker,' 1893; 'The Last Straw,' 1893; 'Money,' 1893; 'A Question of Penmanship,' 1893; 'The First Cruise of the good Ship "Bethlehem,"' 1894; 'Ploughed,' 1894; 'The Jerry Builder,' 1894; 'A Bubble,' 1895; 'Frederick,' 1895; 'Merrielands Farm,' 1895; 'Successors to the Title,' 1896; 'Iva Kildare,' 1897; 'Leddy Marget,' 1898; 'The Intruders,' 1898; 'The Archdeacon,' 1898; 'Sir Patrick,' 1899; 'The Little Legacy,' 1899; 'One of Ourselves,' 1900; 'Charlotte,' 1902; 'A Dream's Fulfilment,'

1902; 'A Woodland Choir,' 1902; 'Stay-at-Homes,' 1903.

WALLACE (Alfred Russel), b. 1823. [See p. 290.] *Add:* Married Annie Mitten, 1866. Lectured in America, 1886-87.

Add to ' Works': 'Vaccination a Delusion,' 1898; 'The Wonderful Century,' 1898; 'Studies, Scientific and Social,' 1900.

WALLACE (Lewis), b. 1827. Born, at Brookville, Indiana, 10 April 1827. Studied law and was admitted as Barrister, 1848; while a student, served as volunteer in Mexican War of 1847-48. Practised law in Indiana, 1848-61. Married Susan Arnold Elston, 6 May 1852. Served in Civil War of 1861-65; became major-general in Volunteer army. Resumed legal practice, 1865. Governor of New Mexico, 1878-81. U.S. Minister to Turkey, 1881-85. Play founded on 'Ben Hur' produced in New York, 26 Nov. 1899; in London (Drury Lane theatre), 1902.

Works: 'The Fair God,' 1873; 'Ben Hur,' 1880; 'The Boyhood of Christ,' 1888; 'Life of Gen. Benjamin Harrison,' 1888; 'The Prince of India,' 1893; 'The Wooing of Malkatoon,' 1898.

WARD (Artemus), *pseud.* [i.e. Charles Farrer Browne], 1834-1867. Born, at Waterford, Maine, 1834. As a youth, worked as compositor in printing office. First of 'Artemus Ward' series of papers pubd. in 'Cleveland Plaindealer,' 1858. Editor of New York 'Vanity Fair,' 1860. Became popular as lecturer. Lectured in England, 1866. Contrib. to 'Punch,' 1866-67. Died, at Southampton, 6 March 1867.

Works: 'Artemus Ward, his Book,' 1862; 'Artemus Ward, his Travels among the Mormons,' 1865; 'Artemus Ward, his Book of Goaks,' 1865; 'Artemus Ward among the Fenians,' 1865; 'Artemus Ward in London,' 1867.

Posthumous: 'Artemus Ward's Lecture at the Egyptian Hall,' 1869.

WARD (Mrs. Mary Augusta), b. 1851. [See p. 293.] *Add to ' Works':* 'Helbeck of Bannisdale,' 1898; 'Eleanor,' 1900; 'Lady Rose's Daughter,' 1903. Has *edited:* Works of the Brontë sisters, 1899, etc.

WARDEN (Florence) [i.e. *Mrs.* Florence Alice James], b. 1857. Born [Florence Alice Price], at Hanworth, Middlesex, 16 May 1857. Educated at Brighton and in France. Engaged in tuition, 1875-80. Went on stage, 1880; retired, 1885. Married to G. E. James, 1887.

Works: 'The House on the Marsh' (anon.), 1882; 'At the World's Mercy,' 1884; 'A Vagrant Wife,' 1885; 'A Dog with a Bad Name,' 1885; 'Doris's Fortune,' 1886; 'Scheherezade,' 1887; 'A Prince of Darkness,' 1887; 'A Woman's Face,' 1888; 'A Witch of the Hills,' 1888; 'The Fog Princes,' 1889; 'Nurse Revel's Mistake,' 1889; 'St. Cuthbert's Tower,' 1889; 'City and Suburban,' 1890; 'Pretty Miss Smith,' 1891; 'Those Westerton Girls,' 1891; 'A Shock to Society,' 1892; 'Highest References,' 1892; 'Ralph Ryder of Brent,' 1893; 'A Passage through Bohemia,' 1893; 'Grave Lady Jane,' 1893; 'A Wild Wooing,' 1893; 'A Terrible Family,' 1893; 'A Scarborough Romance,' 1894; 'My Child and I,' 1894; 'Adela's Ordeal,' 1894; 'A Perfect Fool,' 1894; 'Kitty's Engagement,' 1895; 'The Woman with the Diamonds,' 1895; 'A Spoilt Girl,' 1895; 'A Lady in Black,' 1896; 'Dr. Darch's Wife,' 1896; 'Two Lads and a Lass,' 1896; 'Our Widow,' 1896; 'Dolly the Romp,' 1897; 'The Inn by the Shore,' 1897; 'The Girls at the Grange,' 1897; 'The Mystery of Dudley Home,' 1897; 'Girls will be Girls,' 1898; 'Joan the Curate,' 1898; 'Little Miss Prim,' 1898;

24—2

'The Master-Key,' 1898; 'A Sensational Case,' 1898; 'The Bohemian Girls,' 1899; 'The Farm in the Hills,' 1899; 'The Secret of Lyndale,' 1899; 'A Very Rough Diamond,' 1899; 'The Plain Miss Cray,' 1900; 'Town Lady and Country Lass,' 1900; 'The Love that Lasts,' 1900; 'A Lowly Lover,' 1900; 'Once Too Often,' 1901; 'A Patched-up Affair,' 1901; 'The Lovely Mrs. Pemberton,' 1901; 'Morals and Millions,' 1901; 'A Fight to a Finish,' 1901; 'A House with a History,' 1901; 'A Hole and Corner Marriage,' 1902; 'Something in the City,' 1902; 'An Outsider's Year,' 1903.

WARNER (Charles Dudley), 1829-1900. Born, at Plainfield, Mass., 12 Sept. 1829. Educated at Hamilton Coll. and Pennsylvania Univ. Practised law in Chicago, 1856-60. Removed to Hartford, 1860. Edited 'Hartford Press,' 1861-67; 'Hartford Courant,' 1867-1900. On staff of 'Harper's Mag.,' 1884-98. Married Susan Lee, 1856. Died, at Hartford, 20 Oct. 1900.

Works: 'My Summer in a Garden,' 1870; 'Backlog Studies,' 1872; 'Saunterings,' 1873; 'Baddeck,' 1874; 'The Gilded Age' (with Mark Twain), 1874; 'Mummies and Moslems,' 1876 (later edns. called 'My Winter on the Nile'); 'In the Levant,' 1877; 'Being a Boy,' 1877; 'In the Wilderness,' 1878; 'Studies of Irving' (with W. C. Bryant and G. P. Putnam), 1880; 'The American Newspaper,' 1881; 'Captain John Smith,' 1881; 'Washington Irving,' 1881; 'A Roundabout Journey,' 1883; 'Their Pilgrimage,' 1886; 'On Horseback,' 1888; 'A Little Journey in the World,' 1889; 'Studies in the South and West,' 1890; 'As we were Saying,' 1891; 'Our Italy,' 1891; 'The Golden House,' 1894; 'The People for whom Shakespeare Wrote,' 1897; 'The Relation of Literature to Life,' 1897; 'That Fortune,' 1899.

He *edited:* 'The Book of Eloquence,' 1877; 'American Men of Letters' Series, 1881-1900: 'Library of the World's Best Literature,' 1896-97.

WATSON (John) [" Ian Maclaren"] b. 1850. Born, at Manningtree, Essex, 3 Nov. 1850. Educated at Stirling Grammar School; at Edinburgh Univ.; M.A., 1870; at New Coll., Edin.; and at Tübingen. Licensed by Free Church as Assistant in Barclay Church, Edinburgh, 1874; Minister of Logiealmond Free Church, 1875; Minister of Free St. Matthew's, Glasgow, 1877; Minister of Sefton Park Presbyterian Church, Liverpool, 1880. Married Jane Burne Ferguson, 1878. Lyman Beecher Lecturer, Yale Univ, 1896. Moderator of Synod of English Presbyterian Church, 1900. Hon. D.D., St. Andrews, 1886; Hon. D.D. Yale, 1897.

Works: 'Beside the Bonnie Brier Bush' (under pseud. 'Ian Maclaren'), 1894; 'The Days of Auld Lang Syne' (by 'Ian Maclaren'), 1895; 'A Doctor of the Old School' (by 'Ian Maclaren'), 1895; 'The Upper Room,' 1895; 'Order of Service for Young People,' 1895; 'The Mind of the Master,' 1896; 'The Cure of Souls,' 1896; 'Kate Carnegie' (by 'Ian Maclaren'), 1896; 'The Potter's Wheel,' 1897; 'Companions of the Sorrowful Way,' 1898; 'Afterwards' (by 'Ian Maclaren'), 1898; 'Rabbi Saunderson' (by 'Ian Maclaren') 1898; 'The Doctrines of Grace,' 1900; 'Church Folks,' 1900; 'Young Barbarians' (by 'Ian Maclaren'), 1901; 'The Life of the Master,' 1901; 'His Majesty Baby' (by 'Ian Maclaren'), 1902.

WATSON (William), b. 1858. [*See* p. 294.]

Add to 'Works': 'The Hope of the World,' 1898; 'Collected Poems,' 1899; 'Ode on the Coronation of King Edward VII.,' 1902. 'New Poems,' 1902; 'For England,' 1903.

WATTS-DUNTON (Walter Theodore), b. 1832. [*See* p. 295.]

Add to '*Works*' : 'The Coming of Love,' 1898; 'Aylwin,' 1899; 'David Gwynn's Story,' 1901 ; 'The Christmas Dream,' 1901 ; 'Christmas at the Mermaid,' 1902 ; 'The Renascence of Wonder,' 1902 ; 'Studies of Shakespeare,' 1902 ; 'Love's Second-Sight,' 1903.

Has *edited* : Borrow's 'Romany Rye,' 1900.

WEBSTER (*Mrs.* Julia Augusta), 1837-1894. Born [Julia Augusta Davies], at Poole, 30 Jan. 1837. Youth spent at Banff, at Penzance, and at Cambridge. Married Thomas Webster, Dec. 1863. Resided at Cambridge till 1870, then removed to London. Mem. (for Chelsea) of London School Board, 1879-82 ; re-elected, 1885. Died, at Kew, 5 Sept. 1894.

Works : 'Blanche Lisle' (under pseud. 'Cecil Home'), 1860; 'Lilian Grey' (by 'Cecil Home '), 1864; 'Lesley's Guardians' (by 'Cecil Home'), 1864 ; 'Dramatic Studies,' 1866 ; 'A Woman Sold,' 1867 ; 'Portraits,' 1870; 'The Auspicious Day,' 1872 ; 'Yu-Pe-Ya's Lute,' 1874 ; 'A Housewife's Opinions,' 1879 ; 'Disguises,' 1879 ; 'A Book of Rhyme,' 1881 ; 'In a Day,' 1882 ; 'Daffodil and the Croäxaxicans,' 1884 ; 'The Sentence,' 1887 ; 'Selected Poems,' 1893.

Posthumous : 'Mother and Daughter' (ed. by W. Rossetti), 1895.

She *translated :* Æschylus' 'Prometheus Bound,' 1866 ; Euripides' 'Medea,' 1870.

WEDMORE (Frederick), b. 1844. [*See* p. 296.]

Add to '*Works*' : 'On Books and Arts,' 1899 ; 'Whistler's Etchings,' 1899; 'The Collapse of the Penitent,' 1900.

WELLS (Herbert George), b. 1866· Born, at Bromley, 21 Sept. 1866. Educated at schools at Bromley and Midhurst, and at Royal Coll.

of Science. B.Sc., 1890. Married Amy Catherine Robbins.

Works : 'Text-Book of Biology,' 1893 ; 'Honours Physiography' (with R. A. Gregory), 1893 ; 'Select Conversations with an Uncle,' 1895; 'The Time Machine,' 1895 ; 'The Stolen Bacillus,' 1895 ; 'The Wonderful Visit,' 1895 ; 'The Island of Doctor Moreau,' 1896 ; 'The Wheels of Chance,' 1896 ; 'The Plattner Story,' 1897 ; 'The Invisible Man,' 1897 ; 'Certain Personal Matters,' 1868 ; 'Text-Book of Zoology' (with A. M. Davies), 1898 ; 'The War of the Worlds,' 1898 ; 'When the Sleeper Wakes,' 1899 ; 'Tales of Space and Time,' 1900 ; 'Love and Mr. Lewisham,' 1900 ; 'The First Men in the Moon,' 1901 ; 'Anticipations,' 1902 ; 'The Discovery of the Future,' 1902 ; 'The Sea Lady,' 1902 ; 'Mankind in the Making,' 1903.

WHITEING (Richard), b. 1840 Born, in London, 27 July 1840. Educated privately. Studied for some time at School of Design. Took to journalism, 1866, as contributor to 'Evening Star.' Successively on staff of 'Morning Star,' on editorial staff of Press Association, and of 'Manchester Guardian.' Married Helen Harris, 1869. Paris Correspondent of 'Manchester Guardian,' 1875; subsequently of London 'World,' and of New York 'World.' On editorial staff, 'Daily News,' 1886-99.

Works : 'Mr. Sprouts, his Opinions,' 1867 ; 'The Democracy' (under pseud. 'Whyte Thorne'), 1876 ; 'The Island,' 1888 ; 'No. 5 John Street,' 1899 ; 'The Life of Paris,' 1900; 'The Yellow Van,' 1903.

WHITMAN (Walt), 1819-1892. [*See* p. 299.]

Add : 'Calamus' (ed. by R. M. Bucke), 1897.

Life : by T. Donaldson, 1897.

WHYTE-MELVILLE (George John), 1821-1878. [*See* p. 300.]

Add : 'Collected Works,' ed. by Sir H. Maxwell, 1898, etc.

WILDE (Oscar Fingall O'Flahertie Wills), 1856-1900. Born, in Dublin, 15 Oct. 1856. At Trin. Coll., Dublin, 1873-74; Berkeley Gold Medal for Greek Essay. Matric., Magdalen Coll., Oxford, Oct. 1874; Demyship, Magd. Coll., 1874-79; B.A., 1878. Newdigate Prize Poem, 1878. Contrib. poems to 'Month,' 'Catholic Mirror,' 'Irish Monthly,' 'Kottabos,' 'Time,' etc. On leaving Oxford, became recognized leader of so-called 'Æsthetic' Movement. Lectured in U.S.A upon 'Æsthetic Philosophy,' 1882. Play, 'Vera,' produced in New York, 1882. Married Constance Lloyd, 1884; she died, 1896. Published various vols. of essays. Contrib. to 'Lippincott's Mag.,' 'Fortnightly Rev.,' 'The Chameleon,' 'Blackwood's Mag.,' 'The Spirit Lamp,' etc. Edited 'The Woman's World,' 1888-90. Play, 'The Duchess of Padua,' produced in New York, 1891; 'Lady Windermere's Fan,' St. James's theatre, London, 20 Feb. 1892; 'A Woman of No Importance,' Haymarket,' 19 April 1893; 'Salomé' (written in French), Paris, 1894; 'An Ideal Husband,' Haymarket, 3 Jan. 1895; 'The Importance of being Earnest,' 14 Feb. 1895. Sentenced to two years' imprisonment under Criminal Law Amendment Act, May 1895; released, May 1897. Subsequently lived chiefly in Paris, having assumed name of 'Sebastian Melmoth.' Died there, 30 Nov. 1900.

Works: 'Ravenna,' 1878; 'Poems,' 1881; 'The Happy Prince,' 1888; 'The Portrait of Mr. W. H.' (priv. ptd.), 1889; 'Lord Arthur Savile's Crime,' 1891; 'The Picture of Dorian Gray,' 1891; 'Intentions,' 1891; 'A House of Pomegranates,' 1891; 'Lady Windermere's Fan,' 1893; 'Salomé,' 1893; 'A Woman of No Importance,' 1894; 'The Sphinx,' 1894; 'Oscarina Epigrams' (priv. ptd.), 1895; 'The Ballad of Reading Gaol' (anon.), 1898; 'An Ideal Husband,' 1899; 'The Importance of being Earnest,' 1899.

Posthumous : 'Essays, Criticisms and Reviews' (priv. ptd.), 1901; 'Vera' (priv. ptd.), 1902.

WILKINS (Mary Eleanor), b. 1862. Born, at Randolph, Mass., 1862. Educated there. Married to Dr. C. M. Freeman, 1901.

Works : 'A Humble Romance,' 1887; 'A Faraway Melody,' 1890; 'A New England Nun,' 1891; 'Young Lucretia,' 1892; 'Jane Field,' 1892; 'The Pot of Gold,' 1892; 'Giles Corey,' 1893; 'Pembroke,' 1894; 'The Long Arm,' 1895; 'Madelon,' 1896; 'Jerome,' 1897; 'Some of our Neighbours,' 1898; 'Silence,' 1898; 'Once Upon a Time,' 1898; 'Evelina's Garden,' 1899; 'The Jamesons,' 1899; 'The Love of Parson Lord,' 1900; 'The Heart's Highway,' 1900; 'Understudies,' 1901 : 'Cinnamon Roses,' 1901; 'The Portion of Labour,' 1901; 'Six Trees,' 1903; 'The Wind in the Rosebush,' 1903.

WOODS (*Mrs.* Margaret Louisa), b. 1856. [*See* p. 304.]
Add to 'Works': 'Weeping Ferry,' 1898; 'Sons of the Sword,' 1901; 'The Princess of Hanover,' 1902.

YEATS (William Butler), b. 1865. [*See* p. 307.]
Add : Play, 'The Hour Glass,' produced by Irish National Theatre Society, Dublin, 14 March 1903.
Add to 'Works': 'The Wind among the Reeds,' 1899; 'The Shadowy Waters,' 1900; 'Cathleen ni Hoolihan,' 1903; 'Ideas of Good and Evil,' 1903; 'Where There is Nothing,' 1903; 'In the Seven Woods,' 1903.
Has *edited:* 'Beltaine : the Organ of the Irish Literary Theatre,' 1899, etc.

YONGE (Charlotte Mary), 1823-1901. *See* p. 307, col. i. For 'First literary publication, about 1846,' read : 'First publications were five works of fiction in 1841.'
Add : Died, at Otterbourne, 24 March 1901.
Add to 'Works': 'Founded on Paper,' 1898; 'John Keble's

Parishes,' 1898; 'The Patriots of Palestine,' 1899; 'The Herd Boy and his Hermit,' 1900; 'The Making of a Missionary,' 1900; 'Modern Broods,' 1900; 'Reasons why I am a Catholic and not a Roman Catholic,' 1901.

Life: by C. Coleridge, 1903.

ZANGWILL (Israel), b. 1864. Born, in London, spring of 1864. B.A., London Univ., 1883. Engaged for some time in scholastic work. Became a journalist in 1887. Editor of 'Puck' (afterwards 'Ariel'), 1890. Has lectured in Europe, America, and the East. Is an advocate of Zionism. Plays, 'Six Persons,' produced at Haymarket theatre, 1892; 'Children of the Ghetto,' Adelphi, 1899; 'The Moment of Death,' Wällack's theatre, New York, 1900; 'The Revolted Daughter,' Comedy theatre, 1901. Married Edith Ayrton, 26 Nov. 1903.

Works: 'The Premier and the Painter' (with L. Cowen, under pseud. 'J. Freeman Bell'), 1888; 'The Bachelor's Club,' 1891; 'The Big Bow Mystery,' 1892; 'The Old Maids' Club,' 1892; 'Children of the Ghetto,' 1892; 'Merely Mary Ann,' 1893; 'Ghetto Tragedies,' 1893; 'The King of Schnorrers,' 1894; 'The Master,' 1895; 'Without Prejudice,' 1896; 'Dreamers of the Ghetto,' 1898; 'They that Walk in Darkness,' 1899; 'The Mantle of Elijah,' 1900; 'The Grey Wig,' 1903; 'Blind Children,' 1903.